MASTERING

WINDOWS 2000
SERVER

MASTERING™
WINDOWS® 2000 SERVER

Mark Minasi
Christa Anderson
Brian Smith
Doug Toombs

SYBEX®

San Francisco • Paris • Düsseldorf • Soest • London

Associate Publisher: Roger Stewart
Contracts & Licensing Manager: Kristine O'Callaghan
Acquisitions & Developmental Editor: Ellen Dendy
Editors: Judy Flynn, Susan Berge, and Bonnie Bills
Project Editor: Julie Sakaue
Revision Editor: Brianne Hope Agatep
Technical Editors: Mark Kovach and Rima Regas
Book Designer: Patrick Dintino, Catalin Dulfu, and
Franz Baumhackl
Graphic Illustrators: Tony Jonick and Jerry Williams
Electronic Publishing Specialist: Kris Warrenburg
Revision Electronic Publishing Specialists:
Grey Magauran and Cyndy Johnsen
Project Team Leader: Jennifer Durning
Revision Project Team Leader: Teresa Trego
Proofreaders: Molly Glover, Jennifer Campbell,
Dave Nash, Nancy Riddiough, Camera Obscura,
Julie Connery, Sean Captain and Kathy Drasky
Indexer: Matthew Spence
Cover Designer: Archer Design
Cover Illustrator/Photographer: The Image Bank

This book is dedicated to the teachers out there, the hardworking and often under-paid people who guide their students to write their first essays, hang their first doors, take their first double integrals, or set up their first domains.

My life would be smaller were it not for the dozens of people who have willingly and graciously shared with me the formal and informal lessons of my life. I cannot pay them back, so with this and my other books I hope to "pay them forward," to share with others whatever small lessons I'm able to offer.

To all my teachers, thank you.

ACKNOWLEDGMENTS

This book was one of the greatest challenges in my experience of book writing. Windows 2000 is so completely new, different, and *larger* than earlier versions of NT that I simply could not have turned out a volume this comprehensive by myself in less than three years—and I somehow got the feeling that all of you needed it before then!

What that means is that, while no book is the work of just one person, this book relied more than most on the close working of the team of writers and editors, all of whom deserve more thanks than I can offer.

My coauthors Christa Anderson, Brian Smith, Doug Toombs, Lisa Justice, John Jensen, Todd Phillips, Darren Mar-Elia, and Tyler Regas all did a yeoman service, working with an operating system that was both unfinished—still in beta form—and complex, as Windows 2000 is without doubt the largest, most complex piece of shrink-wrap software produced to this day. I appreciate all of their efforts and I hope you enjoy their work.

I'm probably not the first person to compare managing book projects to juggling cats, but I cannot sufficiently thank those who mastered this book's flying felines. Gary Masters and Ellen Dendy got the ball rolling, and Ellen both recruited writers and helped keep them on track; as always, Gary's invaluable insights shaped the book and ensured that it was directed at the right audience. Julie Sakaue mothered the book through the editorial and production process, with the eagle eyes of Judy Flynn, Bonnie Bills, and Susan Berge scrutinizing every line to discover our many grammatical errors; many thanks to all for their patience. Due to the sheer volume of information and new material, we broke with tradition and engaged not one but *two* technical editors, who patiently tried out all of the things that we claimed worked—many thanks to Mark Kovach and Rima Regas for their painstaking checking and verifying.

There is, of course, the whole Production crew to thank as well. Without them, all we'd have is a collection of electronic files. Jennifer Durning steered the project smoothly through the Production channels, Kris Warrenburg—the creative wizard that she is—transformed the manuscripts into the handsome book before you, and the proofreaders, all *eight* of them—Jennifer Campbell, Camera Obscura, David Nash, Nancy Riddiough, Kathy Drasky, Sean Captain, Julie Connery, and Molly Glover—scrutinized the many pages to ensure that no stone was left unturned.

My assistant Brenda Davidson proofread things, arranged pictures, and generally performed mountains of the necessary scut work that goes with publishing. It was the first time that Brenda's worked with me on a book, and she hasn't quit yet—many thanks Brenda!

Once Microsoft distributed the final release of W2K, my coauthors and myself quickly and thoroughly revised the book. The editorial and production crew at Sybex, Brianne Agatep, Teresa Trego, Grey Magauran, and Cyndy Johnsen, incorporated our changes into this second edition, putting it on the shelves in record time.

Finally, we could not have done this without the assistance of Microsoft, who not only created the product but also allowed us to see it before it was finished.

CONTENTS AT A GLANCE

TABLE OF CONTENTS

INTRODUCTION

O h, no, I hear you cry, a whole new version of NT! And just when I'd figured out NT 4.... Hey, relax, you're gonna love Windows 2000. You can do all kinds of things that you couldn't do before. Remote control and administration's easier. Rolling out applications to users' machines from a central location is simpler; heck, rolling out entire PC configurations, operating system and all, is easier. You can build far larger networks than with NT 4. You can automate more processes.

It won't *all* be good news, admittedly. Yes, it's also a *new* operating system, which means that we'll probably spend as much time in the first few months discovering bugs as we will figuring out new features. And Windows 2000's hardware requirements are sufficiently onerous that you'll probably *have* to go get new hardware before you dare set up your new Windows 2000–based domains. But, as a wise old head once commented to me, "Hey, if this stuff ever gets easy, lad, we'll all have to go find jobs."

Mastering Windows 2000 Server, Second Edition, like its six predecessor editions of *Mastering Windows NT Server*, is a guide to using Windows 2000 to get your job done. I've aimed in this book to show you what Windows 2000 can and *can't* do and to show you the shortest path to getting any particular job done. My coauthors and I have tried to make this a guide that you can use on a day-to-day basis to simplify the task of managing networks. And furthermore, I intend to continue helping you out through a free new online service that I'll tell you about at the end of this introduction. Text from the advanced edition of this book was updated based on the final release of Microsoft's operating system in order to produce what you hold in your hands, *Mastering Windows 2000 Server*, Second Edition.

Having said what the book *is*, let me say one thing that it's not, or at least not intended to be—an MCSE study guide. Over the years, I have heard from literally thousands of people who've told me that they have used some of my books to successfully study for Microsoft certification exams, and I'm always happy to hear that. But if you're still standing in the bookstore trying to figure out whether or not to buy this book, then I want to stress that the goal of this book is to help you get your job done rather than to help you pass a test.

What's in This Book

To misquote Douglas Adams in *The Hitchhiker's Guide to the Galaxy*, "Windows 2000 is big…*really* big." So here's a guide to what's in this book so you'll know what to expect.

Chapter 1 is a brief introduction to the goods and bads about Windows 2000. When I say "brief," I mean it, even though the chapter is over 30 pages long: one could probably spend three times that just getting started explaining everything that Windows 2000 does. And in Chapter 2, "Getting Comfortable with Active Directory," I take you through AD in some detail, starting with some of what motivated AD—what problems was Microsoft trying to solve—followed by a look at the new tools that AD gives you, and finally finishing with some hands-on examples of how to use those new tools.

By then, I've hopefully whetted your appetite to dig in and start playing with Windows 2000, and in Chapter 3, "Installing Windows 2000 Server," my coauthor Brian Smith and I show how to get it running on your system. Brian has had the opportunity to run a huge NT enterprise, first in the NT 3.51 days and later with NT 4. He's designed and implemented large NT enterprise networks and has had a lot of time in the trenches, so he was an obvious choice when looking for coauthors. Brian wrote the lion's share of that chapter, but I contributed the piece at the end about the Remote Installation Services, a tool that lets you roll out entire Windows 2000 desktops in a ghost-like fashion.

Once you've got Windows 2000 set up, you'll need to get around in it, and you're going to soon find that you *can't find a bloody thing*…or rather it'll seem that way sometimes. Where is the blasted Network Control Panel? How do I stop a service? Why doesn't the Control Panel *do* anything any more? As the user interface has changed somewhat, you may find yourself saying quite often something like, "Where are they now?" To answer that question, I asked Lisa Justice to write Chapter 4. Lisa and I worked together years ago, and she developed the excellent coverage on user profiles in *Mastering Windows NT Server*. Lisa took it a step further, however, and shows you how to use the Microsoft Management Console to build your *own* network management tools.

After that, I take you through an introduction to and explanation of the Windows 2000 Registry in Chapter 5. Brian then returns in Chapter 6 for a chapter on handling hardware: Windows 2000's new Plug-and-Play hardware support is something of a mixed blessing, but Brian shows you how to make almost any new hardware work under Windows 2000. ("Almost" because, as was the case with NT, we Windows 2000 users are the poor stepchildren when it comes to driver availability. Even lawn mowers seem to come with Windows 98 drivers these days—but Windows 2000/NT–compatible hardware is a little more scarce.)

That new hardware support means a change in how Windows 2000 handles storage as well, as you'll learn in Chapter 7. In that chapter, Christa Anderson shows you how to connect, partition, and format drives, as well as covering Windows 2000's RAID functions. Christa was a coauthor for the first two editions of *Mastering Windows NT Server* and is now a major contributor for *Windows NT Magazine*, as well as the author of an upcoming title on Windows Terminal Server.

Lisa returns in Chapter 8 to explain the ins and outs of creating and managing user accounts. That's a *big* topic, including not only the Windows 2000 successor to profiles, but also *group policies*, the Windows 2000 successor to NT 4's system policies. That's followed by Brian covering shared folders, including how to secure those shares with both share and NTFS permissions—they're quite a bit different from NT 4's permissions—as well as coverage of Windows 2000's new Distributed File System and the File Replication Service. Chapter 9 ends with a piece by me about offline folders, a modification of the network redirector that offers greater network response, laptop synchronization support, and network fault tolerance.

John Jensen joins us in Chapter 10 to describe an all-new feature of Windows 2000: central distribution of applications. John is a long-time NT C programming Giant Brain type of a guy, and being an applications programmer gave him a few advantages in analyzing and describing the built-in software distribution tool that Windows 2000 offers. Christa returns in Chapter 11 to describe how to network printers under Windows 2000. Brian then explains, in Chapter 12, how to connect client PCs to a Windows 2000 network, whether those PCs are running DOS, Windows, or whatever.

In Chapter 13, Todd Phillips, my coauthor for the workstation companion volume to this book (*Mastering Windows 2000 Professional*), makes a cameo appearance in this book, joining Tyler Regas to show you how to connect your Macintosh to a Windows 2000 network. Christa then warms to a favorite topic of hers in Chapter 14, where she covers the built-in Terminal Services feature of Windows 2000. And if you have no idea what Terminal Services does, check out the chapter: Terminal Services makes your Windows 2000 system a multiuser computer, in many ways combining the best of the PC and the mainframe!

I needed someone to write Chapter 15, "How Running a Big Windows 2000 Network Is Different," who actually works with large Windows 2000 networks. The first person who came to mind was Darren Mar-Elia, a network manager with Charles Schwab. Schwab is one of the early implementers of Windows 2000, and so Darren was able to offer with authority some sage advice for those designing a large Windows 2000 enterprise.

And speaking of enterprises, most large ones have at least a little bit of software somewhere written by Novell, hence Chapter 16 discusses NetWare coexistence. For that chapter, I tapped Doug Toombs. Doug is another *Windows NT Magazine* contributor and a consultant (www.netarchitect.com) who's put together many an NT network for clients. His excellent coverage of NetWare connectivity with Windows 2000 is just the first of three terrific chapters he's contributed to the book.

After that, the next three chapters take up the issues surrounding TCP/IP in a network environment. Where TCP/IP was once a mildly exotic networking alternative, Windows 2000 essentially forces you to adopt TCP/IP as your primary network protocol—so you'd better be ready to implement and support it. In Chapter 17, I explain how TCP works specifically in Windows 2000 and how Windows 2000 handles the essential infrastructure issues of IP routing. Then, in Chapter 18, I show you how to design and implement an IP infrastructure with the Dynamic Host Configuration Protocol (DHCP), the Windows Internet Name Service (WINS)—and, despite what you may have heard, it's *not* dead, sadly, so be sure to read the section on WINS—and the Domain Name System (DNS). Everything about DNS is new and different under Windows 2000, so don't miss that section! The chapter also shows you how to set up the Telnet server built into every NT server, explains how to set up a free Internet mail server, and discusses Internet security a bit.

But once you get connected to the Internet, the next thing you'll probably want to do is to get a Web server up and running. Windows 2000 offers that and more, and Doug shows you how to set up the Internet Information Server version 5, including not only the Web piece but also the FTP server piece, the NNTP news server piece, and the SMTP mail server, all in Chapter 19.

In Chapter 20, Christa offers some advice and instruction on tuning and monitoring a Windows 2000–based network, and then in Chapter 21, she looks at disaster recovery—never a happy topic, but a necessary one. Finally, Doug finishes the book off with a lengthy and quite complete look at dial-up, ISDN, and Frame Relay support in Remote Access Service (RAS) in Chapter 22.

Conventions Used in This Book

As you know, when discussing any network technology, things can get quite complex quite quickly, so I've followed some conventions to make them clearer and easier to understand.

Windows 2000 versus NT

Throughout this book, you'll see me refer to Windows 2000, NT 4, and just plain NT. I don't want to confuse, so let me clarify what I mean when I use those terms.

When I say "Windows 2000" or 'NT 4," then of course I mean those particular products. But when I say "NT," I'm referring to the various versions of the NT operating system that have come out, including both NT 4 and Windows 2000. Despite the name change from NT-version-something to Windows-model-year, under the hood, NT 4 and Windows 2000 are quite similar: the underlying kernel, the piece of the operating system that manages memory, handles multitasking, and loads and unloads drivers, is largely unchanged from NT 4, with the very important exception of the new Plug-and-Play capabilities. So it seems appropriate to me to refer to either an NT 3.x–based, NT 4–based, or Windows 2000–based network as an "NT network."

Windows

Microsoft is working so hard to "brand" the name Windows that now they've attached the name to three totally different operating systems. The first of the "original" Windows—versions 1.0, 2.0, 2.1, 3.0, 3.1, 3.11, Windows for Workgroups 3.1 and 3.11, Windows 95 and 98—is an ever-evolving operating system built to extend the life of Microsoft's cash cow, MS-DOS. The second was NT, a project intended originally to extend an older operating system named OS/2. And the third is Windows CE, an OS designed for smaller diskless computers, including the of-dubious-value "AutoPC," a computer designed for your car's dashboard. (Oh, great, now I get to worry that the bozo in front of me in traffic will be distracted playing Quake; good call, Bill.) Therefore, it's getting a bit ambiguous when someone says "Windows"— so what I mean when I use the term all by itself, without a qualifier like "2000," "NT," "CE," or the like, is "Windows Classic"—Windows 3.x or its cousin, Windows 95/98. I can't wait until Microsoft sends Pella and Andersen "cease and desist" letters enjoining them from using the word *Windows* in their corporate name and product-line descriptions.

Directories

By default, Windows 2000 installs into a directory named \winnt on some drive. (See, it really *is* still NT.) You can decide at installation time to put the operating system somewhere else, but almost no one does. As a result, I've got a bit of a problem: I often need to refer to the directory that Windows 2000's installed into, and I need a phrase less cumbersome than "whatever directory you installed Windows 2000 into" or the brief and technically accurate but nonintuitive %systemroot%. So you'll see references to the \winnt directory, which you should read as "whatever directory you've installed Windows 2000 into."

Similarly, \winnt contains a directory I'll refer to now and then called system32; I'll refer to that as \winnt\system32.

Processor Names

NT was supposed to be an architecture-independent operating system when it first appeared in 1993. Microsoft had implementations for the MIPS R4000 processor (which is now likely the processor driving your palmtop Windows CE machine) and the 80386/80486/Pentium family. They later added the Digital Alpha series of processors and the PowerPC chips.

From there, however, the roll call of NT-compatible processors has dried up a bit. The MIPS and the PowerPC are no longer supported, and I've heard nothing at all about supporting Windows 2000 on any other processor architectures, sadly. But sometimes I'll still need to differentiate Windows 2000's behavior on either the Alpha or the Intel platform, so let me clarify: When I say "Intel" or "Intel chip," I am referring specifically to Intel's line of processors in the Pentium and Pentium II families. (Yes, you *could* run Windows 2000 on a 486, but I can't imagine anyone doing it.) That means that I'm talking about the original Pentium, the Pentium MMX, the Pentium Pro, the Celeron, the Pentium II, or the Xeon chip. And, I suppose, the Itanium chip, if it ever actually appears. When I say "Alpha," I'm referring to Digital's—now Compaq's—line of amazingly fast 64-bit processors. (If you can get your hands on an Alpha-based system, do it—they run Windows 2000 like the wind.)

Register to Stay Up-to-Date!

This is only the first version of this book. As Windows 2000 moves into the mainstream, people will discover problems with it, Microsoft will release fixes for problems with it, people will figure out workarounds for the problems, and we'll all figure out how to use it better. (Forty million lines of code is a *lot* of new operating system to get familiar with, even *with* top-notch coauthors!)

So I'm extending the following offer to my readers. Visit my Web site at www.minasi .com and register to receive my free Windows 2000 newsletter. Every month that I can, I'll send you a short update on tips and things that I've learned, as well as any significant errata that appear in the book—and which I'm praying don't appear.... It won't be spam—as the saying goes, "Spammers must die!"—just a short heads-up on whatever I've come across that's new (to me) and interesting about Windows 2000.

Well, okay, about the spam part: there will be *one* bit of naked marketing—when the next edition of the book comes out, I'll announce it in the newsletter.

For Help and Suggestions: *help@minasi.com*

As always, if I can help, I'm available on e-mail. Got a question the book didn't answer? Send it to me at `help@minasi.com` and I'll try to help out. I'm often traveling, sometimes for weeks at a time, and I don't pick up e-mail when I'm on the road, so if I take a week or few to respond, don't worry, I'll get back to you as soon as I can. It's easiest to help with questions which are specific but brief—please understand I sometimes open my e-mail to find over a hundred questions waiting for me!

In addition to offering help, I'd appreciate *your* help and feedback. Sybex and I have been able to get a new edition of this book out roughly annually since NT Server first appeared in 1993. I don't know everything about NT or Windows 2000—I'm not certain *anyone* does—and through the years reader suggestions and "book bug reports" have been a tremendous source of assistance in making the NT books better and better. ("Gasp! An *error*? In *my* book? No, say it isn't so!") Got a tip, something you want to share with the world? Pass it along to me, and I'll include it in the next edition and acknowledge your contribution.

And by the way, to all of you reading this book: thank you so much, and I hope you enjoy our coverage of Microsoft's ambitious new networking platform!

CHAPTER 1

Windows 2000
Server Overview

After years of talk about "Cairo" (the Microsoft code name for their "ultimate" server software) and even more years of work, Microsoft has finally shipped Windows 2000. After training us to expect roughly annual releases of new versions of NT—NT 3.1 shipped in 1993, 3.5 in 1994, 3.51 in 1995, and 4 in 1996—NT 5 finally arrived, but it was considerably later than a year after the release of NT 4. Furthermore, NT 5 arrived with a new name: Windows 2000. But the name's not all that's new.

So what took so long? Was it worth the wait? For many, the answer will be "yes." Much of NT's foundation—the internal kernel structure, how drivers are designed, how Windows 2000 multitasks—hasn't changed all that terribly much from NT 4, but network professionals really don't see that part of NT. Instead, we network types will notice that the *above-ground* structures, the tools built atop the foundation, are so different as to render Windows 2000 Server almost unrecognizable as a descendant of NT 3.*x* and 4.*x*. For comparison's sake, and to extend the structural metaphor, think of using Windows NT 3.1 Advanced Server as renting a room in someone's basement, using NT 4 as renting a 2-bedroom apartment, and using Windows 2000 Server as living in Bill Gates's new mansion on Lake Washington: more rooms than anyone can count all filled with new and wonderful electronic gadgets.

In the mansion, many of the things that you know from the basement room are unchanged—the electricity comes out of sockets in the wall, the pipes are copper or PVC, bathrooms have sinks and commodes in them—but there's so much more of it all, as well as so many new things, both useful ("Hey, cool, a garden, and automatic sprinklers for it!") and of debatable value ("What does this bidet thing do, anyway?"). That's not to say that NT's underpinnings will never change, not at all—the next (and still-unnamed) version of NT will go a step further, digging up NT's 32-bit foundation and replacing it with a 64-bit one.

The main point, however, is this: If you're an NT network administrator, be prepared for culture shock. The difference between NT 4 and Windows 2000 is at least 10 times as great as the difference between NT 3.1 and NT 4. And if you've never worked with NT in any flavor, be prepared to find Windows 2000 both delightful and frustrating—as is the case with most Microsoft software.

It would be somewhat shortsighted of me to simply say, "Here are the new features you'll find in Windows 2000," and then to just dump the features—it sort of misses the forest for the trees. So let me start off by briefly discussing the big picture and what Microsoft's trying to accomplish; then I'll move along to those new features and, finally, take a look at a few of Windows 2000's shortcomings.

Microsoft's Overall Goals for Windows 2000

The changes in Windows 2000 from NT 4 are quite significant, but they were long in coming. What was the wait all about?

Make NT an Enterprise OS

Microsoft wants your company to shut off its mainframes and do your firm's work on big servers running NT. That's why there is a version of Windows 2000 Server called Datacenter Server. Microsoft is also hoping that "enterprise" customers will exploit new Windows 2000 Server facilities such as Active Directory and Microsoft Application Server (nee MTS) and COM+ to write gobs of new and hardware-hungry distributed applications. Before they can accomplish that, however, they need to clear three hurdles: reliability, availability, and scalability.

NT Must Be More Reliable

Since their appearance in the late '70s, microcomputer-based network operating systems have been seen as fundamentally different from "big-system" OSes like IBM's MVS and OS/400, Compaq's Open VMS, and the myriad flavors of Unix. PC-based network operating systems weren't exactly seen as toys, but neither were they seen as something that one would base one's business on, if one's business was truly critical. For example, it's hard to imagine the New York Stock Exchange announcing that they'd decided to get rid of their current trading system and to replace it with a NetWare 4.1 or NT 4-based client-server system. PC-based stuff just wasn't (and largely still isn't) seen as sufficiently reliable yet to take on the big guys.

Nor is that an unfair assessment. Most of us would be a bit uncomfortable about discovering in midflight that the state-of-the-art airliner taking us across the Pacific was run by NT, or that the Social Security Administration had decided to dump their old mainframe-based software in favor of a Lotus Notes–based system running atop NT. Years ago, many firms discovered that NT servers crashed far less often if rebooted weekly; it's hard to imagine running a heart-and-lung machine on something like that.

But Microsoft wants to shed that image. They want very much to build an OS that is sufficiently industrial-strength in reliability so that one day it wouldn't be silly to suggest that AT&T's long distance network could run atop some future version of NT, Windows 2000-something. With Windows 2000, Microsoft believes that they've taken some steps in that direction.

NT Must Be More Available

A server being rebooted to change some parameters is just as down as one that is being rebooted after a Blue Screen Of Death, the symptom of a system crash that is all too familiar to NT 4 veterans. Many Windows 2000 parameters can be changed without a reboot where a change to the corresponding parameter in Windows NT 4 would require one. Unfortunately, as we will see, some of the most common parameter changes still require a reboot.

NT Must Be Able to "Scale" to Use Big Computers

Reliability's not the only big-network issue that Microsoft faces. The other one is the limit on the raw power that NT can use—to use a word that the PC industry created a few years ago, NT must be more *scalable*.

Being an "enterprise" operating system requires two different kinds of scalability which are somewhat at odds with each other: performance scalability and administrative scalability. The first asks, "If I need to do more work with NT, can I just run it on a bigger computer?" The second asks, "If I need to support more users/computers/gigabytes of hard disk/etc., can I do it without hiring more administrators?"

Performance Scalability   CPUs are simply not getting all that much faster in terms of the things they can do. To create faster or higher-capacity computers, then, computer manufacturers have been putting more and more CPUs into a box. And while NT has in theory been designed to use up to 32 processors since its first incarnation, in reality, very few people have been able to get any use out of more than 4 processors. With Windows 2000, Microsoft claims to have improved the scalability of NT—although I've not yet heard anyone say with a straight face that Windows 2000 will "run like a top" on a 32-processor system.

Besides the ability to use a larger number of CPUs, there were internal restrictions within Windows NT, such as the number of users that a SAM database would allow, that simply had to go. With Active Directory, many restrictions, including this one, have been removed.

The three versions of Server support different numbers of CPUs. Windows 2000 Server supports four processors. Windows 2000 Advanced Server supports 8 processors, and Windows 2000 Datacenter Server supports 32 processors.

NOTE Oh, and if you're looking in your Webster's for a definition of *scalability*, don't bother; it's not a real word. Microsoft made it up a few years ago. Basically, *scalable* roughly means, "As the job's demands grow, you can meet them by throwing in more hardware—processors and memory—and the system will meet the needs." It's become an issue because, while NT has theoretically supported 32 processors since its inception, much of the basic NT operating system itself can't use many processors—for example, adding a ninth processor to an eight-processor domain controller won't produce any faster logins. That's also true of NT programs; depending on whom you ask, SQL Server maxes out at four or eight processors. Beyond that, adding more processors does nothing more than run up the electric bill.

Administrative Scalability/Manageability   Large enterprises do not like to add headcount in their core business areas, much less just to administer Windows NT. Windows 2000 Server contains a number of facilities such as Intellimirror, designed to allow customers to support more users running with more complex desktop environments with fewer support personnel. Microsoft typically refers to this area as "Manageability," though I think "Administrative Scalability" better captures the flavor of the topic.

In this area, one of the most important additions to Windows 2000 is its support for both issuing and honoring digital certificates in place of userids and passwords for identification and authentication. The overall system needed to manage the life cycles of digital certificates and verify their authenticity and current validity is called Public Key Infrastructure (PKI). PKI-based security is both more secure and vastly more administratively scalable than userid+password-based security, but it is also much, much more technically complex.

Modernize NT

Three years can be an awfully long time in the computer business. The years since 1996 have seen the emergence of Universal Serial Bus, IEEE 1394, Fiber Channel, and 3-D video cards, just to name a few areas of technological growth, as well as the introduction of hundreds of new network cards, video boards, sound cards, SCSI host adapters, and so on. A new crop of network-aware PCs has appeared, PCs that understand networking right in their BIOSes and that are designed to be taken straight out of the box without anything on their hard drives, plugged into the network, and started up from the network rather than from any on-disk software. And on a more mundane note, nearly every PC sold in the past five years supports a hardware system called Plug and Play (PnP).

NT supports none of these things right out of the box. Some of these devices can be made to work, but some can't. Hardware support has always been something of an afterthought in NT, and it's amazing that Microsoft shipped NT 4 without any Plug-and-Play support, save an undocumented driver that could *sometimes* make a PnP ISA board work but that more commonly simply rendered a system unusable. NT 4's off-hand support, of PC Card laptops and its near-complete lack of support for Cardbus slots forced many an NT-centric shop to put NT Server on their servers, NT Workstation on their corporate desktops...and Windows 95 on their laptops.

One of Windows 2000's goals, then—and an essential one—is to support the new types of hardware and greatly improve the way that it works on laptops.

Make NT Easier to Support

The past 10 years have seen the rise of the graphical user interface (GUI), which brought a basically uniform "look and feel" to PC applications and made learning a PC application and PCs in general so much easier for users. We've seen programming tools go from some very simple development environments that crashed more often than they worked to today's very stable 32-bit suite of programming tools, making it possible for developers to create large and powerful 32-bit applications. Users and developers are better off—sounds good, doesn't it?

Well, it is, for them. But many of us fall into a third category: support staff. And while some things have gotten better—the graphical nature of many of NT's administrative tools helped get many new admins started on a networking career—the actual job of support hasn't gotten any easier. Consider this: Would you rather rebuild a CONFIG.SYS file to stitch back together a damaged DOS machine from memory, or would you prefer to pick through a broken Registry trying to figure out what's ailing it?

Microsoft's competition knew that support was the Achilles' heel of both Windows and NT, and so in the mid-'90s, Sun and others began extolling the importance of considering the Total Cost of Ownership (TCO) of any desktop system. It wasn't hard to make the argument that the biggest cost of putting Windows on a desktop isn't the hardware or the software—it's the staff hours required to get it up and keep it running.

With Windows 2000, Microsoft starts to reduce desktop TCO. A group of Windows 2000 improvements called Change and Configuration Management tools makes life easier for support folks and network administrators in general.

Specific New Capabilities and Features

So much for the good intentions. What about the new goodies?

Microsoft lists pages and pages of enhancements to Windows 2000—the PR people have, after all, had over three years to cook up those lists. I'm sure they're all of value to someone, but here are the things that I find most valuable in Windows 2000, arranged according to my three earlier categories—making NT more enterprise ready, modernizing NT, and improving its administrative tools/lowering TCO.

Making Windows 2000/NT More "Enterprising"

Several functions help push NT's latest incarnation to a place in the big leagues. In particular, the most significant "big network" changes to NT include:

- Active Directory
- Improved TCP/IP-based networking infrastructure
- More scalable security infrastructure options
- More powerful file sharing with the Distributed File System and the File Replication Service
- Freedom from drive letters with junction points and mountable drives
- More flexible online storage via the Removable Storage Manager

Active Directory

The crown jewel of Windows 2000, Active Directory is also the single most pervasive piece of the OS. Many of the things you'll read about in this book, many of the compelling features of Windows 2000, simply cannot function without Active Directory. Group policies, domain trees and forests, centralized deployment of applications, and the best features of the Distributed File System (to name a few) will not operate until you've got a system acting as an Active Directory server.

 NOTE The whys and wherefores of Active Directory are complex enough that they'll get a chapter all their own. In Chapter 2, you'll read about what Active Directory is trying to accomplish, how it does so, and how you can best design the Active Directory for your enterprise.

Network Infrastructure Improvements

Anyone building an NT-based network around the TCP/IP protocol needed three important infrastructure tools:

- The Windows Internet Name Service (WINS), which helped Windows 2000–and NT-based servers and workstations locate domain controllers (which handled logins and authentication in general) as well as file and print servers.

- The Dynamic Host Configuration Protocol (DHCP), which simplified and cen-tralized the once-onerous task of configuring TCP/IP on workstations.

- The Domain Name System (DNS), which did the same kind of job as WINS—it keeps track of names and addresses—but instead of helping workstations locate domain controllers and file/print servers, DNS helps programs like Web browsers and e-mail clients to find Web and mail servers. Some firms have avoided moving their networks to TCP/IP, staying instead with IPX (a protocol that owes its popularity to Novell's networking products) or NetBEUI (the main protocol for Microsoft networking prior to 1995). But with Windows 2000, pretty much everyone should be using TCP/IP, making DHCP, WINS, and DNS essential parts of any Windows 2000–based network.

WINS

Why did NT have two services—WINS and DNS—that kept track of names? This was the case because of a questionable choice that Microsoft made back in 1994. Of the two, WINS was the most troublesome and, for some networks, unfortunately the most vital. Thus, it was to many people quite excellent news when Microsoft announced that Windows 2000 would be the end of WINS.

Reports of its death, however, turned out to be greatly exaggerated. The actual story is that, if you have a network that is 100-percent Windows 2000, both on the workstation and server, then yes, you can stop using WINS. But most of us won't have that for years, so Windows 2000 still has a WINS service. Thankfully, it's greatly improved; one expert commented to me that it's ironic that Microsoft finally "fixed" WINS, just as they were about to kill it. Chapter 18 shows you how to set it up and make it work.

DNS

DNS was something of a sidelight under NT 4 as NT didn't really need DNS—DNS's main value was to assist Internet-oriented programs like Web, FTP, and POP3/SMTP mail clients in finding their corresponding servers. Under Windows 2000, however, DNS takes center stage. Without it, Active Directory won't work.

NT 4's DNS server was a pleasure to work with, although that's just my opinion: I've spoken with people who tell me that it couldn't handle high volume loads. *I* didn't have any bad experiences with it, so I can't comment. NT 4's DNS wrapped a well-designed GUI around a standard DNS implementation, making basic DNS tasks sim-pler than they would be for a Unix DNS implementation at the time. Windows 2000 takes that a step further with improved wizards. First-time DNS administrators will find that Windows 2000's DNS server almost does all the hand-holding you could need.

Additionally, Windows 2000's DNS supports dynamic updates, a process wherein adding information about new machines to a DNS database can be automated. Based on the Internet standard document RFC 2136 (the Internet's standards are described in documents called Request for Comments, or RFCs), it combines the best of NT 4's WINS and DNS servers. The DNS server also supports another Internet standard, RFC 2052, which greatly expands the kind of information that DNS servers can hold onto. For example, a pre-2052 DNS server could tell you what machines acted as mail servers for a given Internet domain, but not which machines were Web or FTP servers. 2052-compliant DNS servers can do that, and more: Active Directory now uses RFC 2052 to allow DNS to help workstations find domain controllers and other Active Directory–specific server types.

 NOTE Chapter 18 covers how Active Directory uses RFC 2052 in more detail.

DHCP

DHCP frees network administrators from having to walk around and visit every single desktop in order to configure the TCP/IP protocol. The basic idea is that a workstation broadcasts over the network, seeking an IP address (every computer on an intranet must have a unique IP address); a DHCP server hears the plea and assigns that computer its own unique IP address.

The End of Rogue DHCP Servers This is in general great, but now and then some dodo would decide to "practice" with DHCP by setting up a DHCP server on some PC. The budding new administrator's new DHCP server would then start handing out completely bogus addresses to unsuspecting workstations. Those workstations would then have IP addresses, but they'd be worthless ones, and as a result those workstations would be unable to function on the company's network.

With Windows 2000, however, not just anyone can create a DHCP server. Now, DHCP servers must be authorized in the Active Directory before they're allowed to start handing out addresses. This is a great advance, the end of what we used to call "rogue" DHCP servers.

DHCP Works with DNS to Register Clients You read before that the new DNS supports dynamic updates, a process standardized in RFC 2136 whereby the DNS server will automatically collect address information about machines on the network. This is an improvement over NT 4's DNS server because that DNS server couldn't automatically collect DNS information about machines—you, the administrator, had to type the names and IP addresses of new machines into the DNS Manager administration tool.

Windows 2000's DNS server collects its information about machines on the network with the help of those machines. When a machine starts up, one of the things it's doing while booting up—one of the reasons that booting modern PCs takes so long—is contacting the DNS server to tell the DNS server that the machine exists. In effect, each workstation and server on the network must know to *register* itself with the DNS server.

Unfortunately, as RFC 2136 is a fairly recent development in the DNS world, most existing operating systems—DOS, Windows for Workgroups, Windows 9*x*, NT 3.*x*, and 4.*x*—do not know to register themselves with a DNS server. That's where Windows 2000's DHCP server helps out. You can optionally tell the DHCP server to handle the DNS registrations for non-2136–aware workstations. This is a very useful new feature because, without it, dynamic updates wouldn't be worth much except for the rare firm that runs solely Windows 2000 on its desktops, laptops, and servers.

 NOTE You can read more about DHCP in Chapter 18.

Quality of Service

The Internet's underlying protocols, TCP/IP, have something of an egalitarian nature; when the Net's busy, it's first come, first served. But the protocols have always had a built-in capability that would theoretically allow an Internet operator to give greater priority to one user over another, to dial in a better response time for some than for others. That's called Quality of Service, or QoS. It was always there but not really implemented as it sort of ran against the way the Net was run.

The growth of corporate intranets, however, changes that story. Network operators in corporate networks aren't serving a mass public; rather, they're serving a diverse and hierarchical organization whose leaders may well want to be able to say, "We direct that this individual get more bandwidth and faster access to network resources than this other individual." That's possible if you're using expensive Cisco routers—but now you can do it if you use Windows 2000 machines as your IP routers as well.

New Security Infrastructure

As one security expert once said to me, "We knew that NT had 'made it' when hackers started targeting it." Hardly a month goes by without word of a new security hole in NT 4 and the hot fixes that are intended to plug that hole. Patch a plaster wall with Spackle enough and eventually you have to wonder if you've got a plaster wall or a Spackle wall—so Microsoft must have decided early on that one of the things that Windows 2000 couldn't live without was a new security system.

So they built *two*.

Originally, Windows 2000 was supposed to replace NT 4's authentication system, known as NTLM (for NT LAN Manager), with a system popular in the Unix world called Kerberos. Kerberos is well understood and works well in large-scale systems, assisting Microsoft in their "scalability" (there's that nonword again) goal.

Partway through the Windows 2000 development process, Microsoft decided to supplement Kerberos with a *third* security system, a public key system based on the X.509 standard. They did that mainly because a public key system is considered far more scalable than either an NTLM or Kerberos system. Several companies offer hardware readers that allow users to log in by inserting credit card–sized devices called *smart cards* into the readers.

Kerberos and public key provide as a side effect a feature that NT administrators have asked after for a long time—transitive trust relationships.

Distributed File System

NT's first and probably still most prevalent job is as a file server. And as time has gone on and versions have appeared, it's gotten better at it. Some benchmarks have rated it as fast or faster than NetWare, the guys to beat. And where NT 4's file server software was largely unable to deliver throughput faster than 90Mbps, Windows 2000 can transfer data almost 10 times faster.

Disconnecting Physical Locations from Names

But NT's file server system is hampered by the way it addresses shares on servers. A share named DATA on a server named WALLY would be accessed as \\WALLY\DATA. Although that makes sense, it's limiting. Suppose the WALLY server goes up in a puff of smoke? We install a new server, perhaps named SALLY rather than WALLY, restore the data from WALLY, and re-create the DATA share. But now it's \\SALLY\DATA rather than \\WALLY\DATA, and configurations that are hardwired to look for and expect \\WALLY\DATA will fail. In other words, if a share's physical location changes, so must its "logical" location—its name. It'd be nice to be able to give a share a name that it could keep no matter what server it happened to be on.

Windows 2000 takes NT beyond that with the Distributed File System. In combination with Active Directory, Dfs—note the lowercase in the acronym; apparently someone already owned *DFS* when Microsoft started working on the Distributed File System—allows you to give all of your shares names like *domainname**sharename* rather than *servername**sharename*. You needn't know the name of the file server that the share is on.

Fault Tolerance

You probably know that Windows 2000 offers you many ways to add reliability to your network through RAID storage and two-system computer clusters. RAID boxes aren't cheap, and clusters require a lot of hardware (two identical machines, external SCSI storage, extra network cards, and either the Advanced or Datacenter edition of

Windows 2000 Server). But there are some very inexpensive fault tolerance options for Windows 2000 networks as well; Dfs provides one.

If you have a file share that you want to be available despite network misfortune and failure, then one way to accomplish that is with a *fault tolerant Dfs share*. To create one, just create two or more file shares that contain the same information, then tell Dfs to treat them like one share. So, for example, in a domain named ROCKS, you might have a share named STUFF on a server named S1 and a share named STUFF on a server named S2. To the outside world, however, only one share would be visible as \\ROCKS\STUFF. Then, when someone tries to access \\ROCKS\STUFF, Dfs will basically flip a coin and either send her to \\S1\STUFF or \\S2\STUFF. It's not full-blown fault tolerance—if S1 goes down, nothing automatically transfers people from \\S1\STUFF to \\S2\STUFF—but it's a low-cost way to increase the chance that a given share will be available, even under network "fire."

File Replication Service

Fault tolerant Dfs requires that you maintain several network shares all containing the same information. That can be a lot of work, but then fault tolerant Dfs sounds like it could be worth it.

For example, as you'll read later, Windows 2000 makes deploying applications from a central location or a few central locations possible. So instead of having to visit hundreds of desktops to install Office 2000, you can instead put Office 2000's distribution files on a server and set up everyone's system to install Office 2000 from that server. Hmmm... hundreds of people all trying to download an application package from one file share, all at the same time, won't be very satisfactory.

It'd be better to have exactly the same application package copied to perhaps 10 other shares. You *could*, of course, create the 10 shares and copy the package to each one—but you needn't. Windows 2000 includes the File Replication Service, or FRS. FRS is a vastly improved version of an old NT feature called Directory Replication. Anyone who's ever tried to use NT 4's Directory Replication knows that it needed work—FRS is the happy result.

Junction Points and Mounted Drives

All of this helpful misdirection in file shares—the ability to disconnect file share names from their physical locations—is pretty useful. In fact, it'd be nice to be able to start doing some of that physical/logical misdirection on *local* drives—and you can.

NT's always been hampered by the fact that it can only support 26 storage volumes, A: through Z:. Tying storage volumes to letters in the alphabet was a great idea when CP/M (an early pre-PC microcompute operating system) started doing it back in 1978, but nowadays it seems more a bug than a feature.

With NT 4, you created partitions on drives and then assigned drive letters to those partitions. With Windows 2000, in contrast, you can tie any number of drive partitions to a single drive letter. The trick is this: You first create a folder (a subdirectory) in any existing NTFS drive (NTFS is a file format that—not surprisingly—only NT supports, rather than the FAT file system that DOS uses or the FAT32 file system that Windows 95/98 use). You can then associate—*mount* is the Windows 2000 term—any drive partition with that folder.

Thus, for example, suppose you've got a drive D:, which is NTFS. (If you want to follow along with this example—although you needn't in order to understand it— you'll need a drive D: formatted as NTFS and an H: drive formatted in any way, it doesn't matter.) You've got a bunch of partitions on your system and you're up to drive P:. You'd like to free up drive letter H: so you can use it to map to a home directory. Well, under NT 4, you *could* just highlight the partition currently assigned to H: and change its drive letter to Q: or some other still-unused letter.

Under Windows 2000, however, you can both free up the H: drive letter *and* keep access to the partition, *without* having to use another drive letter. First, create an empty directory on D:. (It needn't be D:; any NTFS drive will do.) Just for the sake of example, call it D:\OLDH—again, any directory name will do. Then you'd go into the Disk Manager, Windows 2000's version of the Disk Administrator. You do that by right-clicking My Computer, choosing Manage, opening up Storage in the left pane, and then opening up Disk Management inside *that*. Find the H: partition, right-click it, and choose Change Drive Letter and Path.

Where NT 4 only allowed you to associate *one* drive letter with a partition, Windows 2000 lets you associate a partition with as many drive letters as you like. Now, that won't help us much because we're trying to get *rid* of a drive letter—but the very same dialog box that allows you to add a new drive letter also lets you associate a partition with "an empty folder that supports drive paths"—in other words, with D:\OLDH. Once you've added D:\OLDH as an acceptable "name" for the partition, you can type either **DIR H:** or **DIR D:\OLDH** and you'll see the same files, because both names refer to the same directory.

But the plan was to free up H:, and we haven't done that yet. Returning to the Disk Manager, again right-click the H: partition and choose Change Drive Letter and Path. This time, you'll see that H: has two acceptable names, H: and D:\OLDH. Highlight H: and choose delete. Once you reboot (yes, you've got to reboot for this change to take effect; some things never change), H: will be free and you'll only be able to access the partition's data through D:\OLDH. And if you didn't want to do all of that with a GUI tool, there's a command-line tool named MOUNTVOL that allows you to mount and unmount drives.

NOTE You can read more about mounting disks in Chapter 7, "Managing Windows 2000 Storage."

Remote Storage

As you've already read, the Distributed File System and the File Replication Service appeared in Windows 2000. As you'll read later, Windows 2000 includes disk quotas (finally) and there's a better Backup. Clearly, storage was an issue for the Windows 2000 design team. But perhaps the most unusual new storage-related capability is Remote Storage, a program whose goal is to allow you to mix tape drive space and hard disk space as if they were one thing.

The idea with Remote Storage is this. Suppose you have a 24GB hard disk on your server; perhaps it's a nice amount of storage but not quite enough for your users' needs. Suppose also that you've got a tape backup device, a carousel device that can automatically mount any one of 16 tapes into the tape drive without the need for human intervention. Perhaps it's a DLT loader and each tape can store 20 gigabytes of data; that works out to about 320GB of tape storage and, again, 24GB of hard disk storage. Here's what Remote Storage lets you do:

It lets you lie about the amount of hard disk space you have.

You essentially advertise that you've got a volume containing 320 plus 24, or 344, gigabytes of online storage space. As people save data to that volume, Remote Storage first saves the data to the hard disk. But eventually, of course, all of that user data fills up the hard disk; at that point, Remote Storage shows off its value. Remote Storage searches the hard disk and finds which files have lain untouched for the longest time. A file could have, for example, been saved eight months ago by some user but not read or modified since. Remote Storage takes these infrequently accessed files and moves them from the hard disk onto the tape drives, freeing up hard disk space.

Ah, but what happens if someone decides to go looking for that file that was untouched for eight months? Remote Storage has been claiming that the file is ready and available at any time. If some user tries to access the file, Remote Storage finds the file on tape and puts it back on the hard disk, where the user can get to it. Yes, it's slow, but the fact is that many files are created and never reexamined, which means there's a good chance that putting the file on tape and off the hard disk will never inconvenience anyone.

I worked with mainframe systems that did things like this years ago and it was quite convenient—files untouched for six months or so would be said to be "migrated" to tape. I could "un-migrate" the tapes, and of course that would take a while, but it wasn't that much of a nuisance and it helped keep the mainframe's disks free.

NOTE You can read more about Remote Storage in Chapter 7, "Managing Windows 2000 Storage."

Modernizing NT

NT is an operating system first introduced in the '90s, so it couldn't have needed all *that* much modernizing. But it was getting awfully embarrassing not to be able to Plug and Play, so Microsoft fixed that. And while they were at it, what's a new release of Windows or NT without a bit of fiddling with the user interface?

Win2K Can Plug and Play

In what may be the feature awaited for the second-longest time (disks are no doubt the longest-awaited feature), Windows 2000 finally offers a version of NT that knows how to do Plug And Play.

That's good news, but, as when PnP first appeared in Windows 95 and ever since, sometimes the playing doesn't happen right after the plugging. Sometimes it works that way, but inserting a new board into a system often still requires a knowledge of interrupt request levels (IRQs) and other hardware characteristics, as well as a bit of CMOS spelunking. Still, it's nice to be able to finally shut up those Windows 95 guys smirking about how easy it is to add new cards to their systems.

 NOTE You can read more about this in a special chapter devoted solely to adding new hardware to a Windows 2000 system, Chapter 6.

NT Gets a User Inter-Facelift

Windows 95 introduced a brand-new, more Macintosh-like user interface to the Windows world. NT 4 followed that but didn't exactly copy the Windows 95 UI, instead improving upon it. Internet Explorer 4 brought Active Desktop, which brought a more Web-like feel to the Windows/NT desktop, although at an often unacceptable cost in performance. Perhaps Active Desktop's best innovation was the Quick Launch bar, a portion of the Taskbar that can hold any number of tiny icons representing oft-used programs: One click and the program starts. Windows 98's user interface built further upon that, and Windows 2000's desktop offers even more new features, many of which are quite useful.

For example, as time goes on, your Start-Programs menu will probably actually get *smaller*. Windows 2000 tracks how often you use programs, and if you don't use a program for a while, the program disappears off the Start-Programs menu. It doesn't disappear forever, however—instead, Windows 2000 displays a set of chevrons at the end of the menu. To see the programs (and even groups) that have disappeared because of disuse, just click the chevrons and the entire program menu returns. The Control Panel also uses this frequency-of-use information; as you no doubt know from experience with Windows 9*x* and/or NT 4, the Control Panel's Add/Remove Programs allows you to uninstall programs. That's still true with Windows 2000, but in addition to telling you what programs you can uninstall, Windows 2000 tells you how often you *use* that program. Pretty neat—if you need some more disk space and you're trying to choose which program to remove in order to *get* that space, the Control Panel even gives you useful hints about which programs you won't miss!

The "user interfacelift" isn't an unalloyed blessing, however. When I first installed beta 2 of Windows 2000, it took me about 10 minutes to find the Network Control Panel. After many years, I was used to just opening up the Control Panel, then opening the Network applet—but here, no go. Instead, I right-click on My Network Places (the name for Network Neighborhood's replacement), choose Properties, then find Local Area Connection in the resulting screen, then right-click *that*, and choose Properties again. Intuitive, no? Well, okay, intuitive NO. In any case, there's enough things that have moved around that it seemed a good idea to include a short chapter on where everything's moved to, so if you can't find the Network Control Panel, or can't figure out where to turn off a service, or are baffled about where to go to partition a hard disk, turn to Chapter 4.

Lowering TCO and Warming Administrators' Hearts

Okay, I hear you thinking, "So now Windows 2000 lets us build bigger NT networks than before—heck, maybe there's a couple of bucks in overtime to be made from larger networks—and now there's Plug and Play, great, so long as there are drivers, and by the way, many NT 4 drivers will not work under Windows 2000, so there had *better* be drivers—and now the new user interface has hidden or rearranged all of the tools that I know and lo... well, like."

So you're probably thinking, "Tell me again why I'm going to like this."

You're going to like Windows 2000 because it's got a bunch of new tools. Several tools, like the Remote Installation Services (RIS), Terminal Services, the Group Policy Editor, and the Microsoft Installer Service, will make rollouts easier; they'll simplify getting an operating system on a new computer and then simplify getting applications onto that computer. Some tools, like (again) Terminal Services, Windows 2000's new built-in telnet server, and Windows Management Instrumentation, will make remote control easier. As you'll see, it's far easier to administer Windows 2000 servers from a distance than it ever was to administer NT 4 servers remotely. And some tools, such as disk quotas, client-side caching, RUNAS, a more powerful command line, and the Internet Connection Sharing feature, are either very effective administrative tools or just plain cool.

Remote Installation Services

Those choosing to put NT not only on their servers but on their workstations as well have never had an easy time of it. Rolling out DOS or Windows 9x to hundreds of similarly equipped machines is relatively simple: Set up the operating system on one "model" computer, get it configured the way your firm needs it, and then essentially "clone" that entire configuration byte-by-byte from the model computer's hard disk to the hard disks of all of the similarly equipped computers. From there, all that needs doing is usually a bit of fiddling on each of the new workstations to customize and make each machine unique in some way. Products like Ghost and Drive Image Professional are excellent tools for getting that job done, in effect "Xeroxing" a master disk image from the central model computer to other computers.

Unfortunately, NT has never lent itself to that. Its secure nature has always required that an administrator run NT's Setup program separately on every would-be NT system, making big NT Workstation rollouts a painful process. The Ghost and Drive Image Pro folks have built some tools to try to allow administrators to use those mass-copying programs to get NT onto a computer's hard disk, but those solutions have never been sanctioned by Microsoft, putting anyone who uses them in a kind of support "Twilight Zone."

Windows 2000 solves that problem by providing a new service called the Remote Installation Services. As with Ghost-like programs, RIS directs you to first create a workstation the way that you want it configured, then a wizard (RIPRep) copies that workstation's disk image to a server—it can be any Windows 2000 server. (Unfortunately, RIS won't help you install Windows 2000 Server, just Windows 2000 Professional.) Just take a new computer out of the box, then attach it to the network, and boot it with a floppy whose image ships with Windows 2000. It asks you to identify the user who will work at that computer, and from that point on, it's a hands-off installation. RIS copies the disk image down to the new computer, runs a hardware detection to ensure that the system gets the correct drivers, the new computer reboots, and Windows 2000 Professional (for some reason, Microsoft chose to name Windows 2000 Workstation "Windows 2000 Professional") is up and running on the new system.

NOTE You can read more about RIS in Chapter 3.

Windows Terminal Server Becomes Standard

Centralized systems like mainframes were great for support people because all of the user data and configuration information resided on a small number of central locations. Solving a user's problem was then easier as most support calls could be handled from one location. Centralized systems also meant easy backup.

On the other hand, centralized systems like mainframes weren't very good at highly interactive "personal productivity" applications such as word processors or spreadsheets or more modern applications like Web browsers. The decentralized nature of desktop PCs solved that problem. Unfortunately, having computers scattered geographically around an enterprise made for a tougher support job.

How, then, to have a system that allows users to run highly interactive PC-type applications and at the same time keep all of the computing and storage in a centrally located, cheaper-to-support place?

Windows Terminal Server, that's how. WTS turns an NT machine into a kind of a mainframe. You attach dumb terminals—or PCs running programs that make them look like dumb terminals—to the Terminal Server over a network or dial-up connection, and for all intents and purposes it looks as if the user's just running a standard Windows 2000 Professional desktop. But all the user's machine is doing is providing keystrokes and mouse-clicks and receiving graphic images of the desktop. Everything else—all the data and all of the computation—is going on in the centrally located Windows 2000 servers.

Now, Windows Terminal Server first shipped late in NT 4's life, but it was a separate product. Windows 2000 lets you convert *any* Windows 2000 server into a Terminal Server with just a few mouse clicks. Additionally, users on a Windows 2000 Terminal Server have more options than did users on an NT 4 Windows Terminal Server.

 NOTE You can read more about Terminal Server in Chapter 14.

Group Policy Snap-in Replaces System Policies

One way to reduce TCO in a firm with dozens, hundreds, or thousands of Windows or NT desktops is to standardize those desktops and to control in some way what gets done on those desktops.

Windows NT 4 had a feature called *system policies* that let an administrator lock down a desktop to a certain extent. If applied in full, system policies would allow an administrator to create a user workstation that could run just a few applications—say, Word, Outlook, and Internet Explorer—and nothing else.

But system policies were difficult to work with and some of them just plain never worked. Furthermore, it was impossible to apply system policies to a group of *machines*—only groups of users. So Microsoft went back to the drawing board and redesigned the idea from the ground up. The result is the Group Policy snap-in. It creates and assigns "group" policies. The word *group* is in the name to underscore something missing from NT 4's system policies. It was simple to apply some kind of control to one user, but it was more difficult to apply policies to groups of users, which is really the only reasonable way to create and manage a control structure—it's far easier to manage a large enterprise wholesale, with groups, than to manage in a retail fashion, user by user.

 NOTE The odd part about group policies is that they don't *apply* to groups. Instead, they apply to subunits of Windows 2000 domains called *organizational units*, which you'll read about in the next chapter. You can certainly control whether a policy affects a particular individual or machine based on what group or groups they belong to, but you can't apply a policy to a group—instead, you apply policies to organizational units. (That's only basically true, as you can also apply policies to particular domains or sites, but you'll read more about that in the next chapter.)

NT 4–style system policies furthermore required building some files with the desired policy information, placing those files on a domain controller, and having to ensure that those policy files replicated properly amongst the other domain controllers. Group policies live in the Active Directory, meaning that they get replicated automatically without any necessary fussing from the administrator.

But that's not all you'll like about group policies. The list of available system policies was relatively short, and the vast majority of those policies were of no value. In contrast, there's a rich variety of group policies in the Group Policy snap-in, and many of them will solve some common administrative nightmares.

 NOTE You'll read more about group policies throughout the book, but much of the coverage appears in Chapters 8 (user accounts) and 10 (deploying applications).

Installer Service and Application Deployment

While I commented earlier that support people had gotten the short end of previous NT upgrades, that's not the case in Windows 2000. As part of their Zero Administration Windows initiative, Microsoft has built a tool into the Group Policy snap-in that allows an administrator to sit in a central location and place applications on a user's desktop without having to visit that desktop.

Previously, firms wanting to do this needed to buy and deploy the Microsoft's Systems Management Server (SMS) tool to accomplish deployment at a distance; with Windows 2000, it's built right in. But that's only the first part of the story.

We usually install programs by running the Setup program that they come with. But we never know beforehand just what the Setup program's going to do; what messes it may make on the computer. Windows 2000 has an answer for that, as well: the Installer service.

The idea with the Installer service is that you no longer run Setup programs to install applications. Instead, you feed to the Installer a file called a *Microsoft Installer* file; they're recognizable because they have the extension .MSI. But an MSI file isn't a program. Instead, it's a set of commands telling the Installer how to install an application—what Registry entries to create, where to copy files, what icons to place on the program menu, and so on. And you can examine an MSI file before installing it to find out what it's going to tell Installer to do—which means you can head off trouble at the pass.

 NOTE   You'll read more about Installer in Chapter 10.

Better Remote Control and Command Lines

One of my pet peeves with NT has always been that there are very few good remote administration tools. For example, if you want to create a file share on a remote machine, you can do it, but it's cumbersome and involves a different tool—you create a local file share from the Explorer, but you must use NT 4's Server Manager to create remote shares. Even then, Server Manager won't let you control share permissions on remote shares; for that, you've got to look to the Resource Kit and its RMTSHARE.EXE program. And that's just one example: In general, it seems as if NT 4's administrative tools are originally built to only control the local machine; any remote administration abilities either don't exist or have a distinctly "tacked on afterward" feel.

Windows Management Instrumentation

While Windows 2000 doesn't completely solve that problem, you'll find that most administrative tools work as well on remote computers as they do on the local machine. Virtually all hardware functions are now built around something called the Windows Management Instrumentation, or WMI, an eminently "remoteable" software interface. As a result, Device Manager lets you view and modify hardware settings not only for the computer you're sitting at, but any machine on the network that you can see (and on which you have administrative rights); the same is true for storage management. Where Disk Administrator let you format and partition disks, it only operated on locally attached disks—its successor, Disk Manager, lets you do any of those things locally or over the network. (Finally, we network administrators will have the respect we deserve! Just think: "Call *me* a geek, will ya? I'll just attach to your computer across the network and reformat your drive...." Just joking, just joking—we network types would *never* use our powers for Evil....)

Windows 2000 Includes a Telnet Server

Furthermore, every Windows 2000 Server ships with a telnet server. If you choose to run the telnet server on a server, you can then connect to that server with any telnet client.

Odd as it may sound, you may sometimes find yourself telnetting to your own local machine. Why? Because when you log in with a telnet session, you identify yourself with a name and password. That means that, if you're currently logged in to a machine as a user and you need to run some administrative-level command, you need to make the machine suddenly recognize you as an administrator. Telnetting is one way—but there's another as well, a new command called RUNAS that you'll meet in a bit.

Better Admin Tools: A More Powerful Command Line

That kind of leads me into my discussion of tools that aren't so much classifiable as rollout tools or as remote control tools; rather, they just fall into a category of "neat new administrative tools." Telnet offers me a segue.

Once connected, the telnet session then gives you a command-line prompt. From there, you can run any *command-line* application remotely. "But," you may be wondering, "what good is the command line? Can I create user accounts, reset passwords, and the like from the command line?" Well, according to Microsoft, one of the "must-do" items on its Windows 2000 things-to-do list was to ensure that you could do all of your administration from the command line, that in theory you would never have to use a GUI tool. I've not found that I can do *everything* from the command line, but there's a whole lot more that you can do from a command line, as you'll see throughout this book.

Unix's SU Comes to Windows 2000

I often find myself, as mentioned before, needing to change status in the machine's eyes. For example, suppose I'm at a user's workstation trying to figure out a computer problem that's plaguing her. I realize that something's set incorrectly on her workstation and I know how to fix it, but she's currently logged in, and she's only got user-level privilege, so I can't execute whatever administrative command I had in mind. What to do?

As mentioned earlier, I could telnet to the system as an administrator, but the telnet server only ships with Windows 2000 Server, not Professional. I *could* ask her to log off, and then I could log on with my administrative account. But I might not want to do that—sometimes I've got a roaming profile set up and I don't want to wait for the profile to download *and* I don't want to have to worry about deleting that profile off the user's machine. The answer? RUNAS.

The scenario described above, where someone's logged on to the system as a user and needs to briefly take on administrative powers, and perhaps doesn't want to have to wait for a logoff/logon sequence, is an old one in the Unix world. That's why most Unix implementations have a so-called Super User (SU) command. It lets you run *just one program* with a different set of credentials. In the Windows 2000 world, the command's name is RUNAS—in other words, "*run* this particular application *as* if someone else—presumably an administrator—were running it."

You must run RUNAS either from the command line or from Start/Run. RUNAS's syntax looks like this:

```
runas /user:username command
```

Username is the administrative username, and *command* is whatever command you want to run as an administrator. If the administrator's account is not in the same domain as the Windows 2000 Professional machine, then you may have to include the name of the administrator's domain as well. For example, if I wanted to modify a user account, I would do it with the Directory Services Administrator (which you'll meet in Chapter 8), a file named `dsa.msc`. If my administrative account were named Bigmark from a domain named LANGUYS, I could start up the DSA like so:

```
runas /user:languys\bigmark dsa.msc
```

Under Windows 2000, you have *two* ways of identifying an account—through the old NT 4–flavor "domain\username" approach, as I used earlier, or through a newer user-specific logon name called the *User Principal Name*. A UPN looks a lot like an e-mail address; for example, Bigmark's UPN might be `bigmark@languys.com`. I could use that formulation as well in my RUNAS command:

```
runas /user:bigmark@languys.com dsa.msc
```

You'll learn about UPNs in Chapters 2 and 8. Oh, and by the way, in case you were wondering, when you do a RUNAS, the system prompts you to enter a password; merely knowing an administrative account name isn't sufficient to become an administrator.

Disk Quotas

Let's get a drum roll on this one.... After years of waiting, it's now possible to control how much space a given user takes up on a given volume. You can only set quotas on NTFS volumes.

The disk quota system is fairly simple—you can only set quotas on entire volumes, not directories, so you could, for example, say that Joe couldn't use more than 400MB of space on E, but you *couldn't* say that he couldn't use more than 200MB in E:\DATA1 and 200MB in E:\DATA2—you can't get directory specific.

Oddly enough, you also cannot set quotas on particular user groups. Instead, you determine a good generic quota value and set that on the volume; that's the disk space limitation for each user. So, for example, suppose you set the quota to 20MB. That means that each user's personal quota is set to 20MB. You can then override that for any particular user. Sound cumbersome? It is; if you have 1,000 users from 10 different groups that access a particular volume and you want to set each user's quota based on its group membership, there's not much to do save to hand-set each user's quota amount, one at a time. But it's free, and at least it's of more value than Proquota, the profile size quota manager available under NT 4.

Backup Continues to Improve

Few things grow as rapidly as the apparent need for storage space. In the late '70s, network file servers were often built around a single shared 10MB hard disk; nowadays, it's not unusual for a desktop *workstation* to have one thousand times that much disk space.

Hard drives have gotten larger, faster, cheaper, and more reliable. But one thing that hasn't changed is the need for backup. NT's always come with a backup program, but it's always been a bit limited. It could only back up to a tape drive, so you couldn't use the NT Backup program to back up to a Jaz drive or network drive; it didn't support robotic tape changers, carousels that could automatically change the tape in a tape drive; and it was very cumbersome to use for a full server recovery.

With Windows 2000, those three objections go away. If you want to save to tape, then of course you can do that, but now you can also save to anything with a drive letter—Jaz, Superdisk, some Web-based backup system, or the like. If you use tapes but your server's disks are larger than the capacity of a single tape, you need no longer baby-sit the server waiting for the chance to swap tapes: Windows 2000 supports many tape loaders. And if you find yourself with a dead server that you need to revive quickly, you can take the most recent backup tapes from the dead server and a new computer and quickly get the contents of those tapes onto the new computer. The new computer acts in the role of the server, making disaster recovery simpler and quicker than it was under NT 4.

Client-Side Caching/Offline Files

This next aspect of Windows 2000 is not really a server function, it's a workstation (Windows 2000 Professional) function; but it'll gladden the hearts of users and administrators alike. Called either *client-side caching* or *Offline Files* by Microsoft, this function makes the network more reliable and faster and simplifies laptop/server file synchronization for mobile users.

Offline Files acts by automatically caching often-accessed network files and storing the cached copies in a folder on a local hard drive. Your desktop computer then uses those cached copies to speed up network access (or rather, they speed *apparent* network access), as subsequent accesses of a file can be handled out of the local hard disk's cached copy rather than having to go over the network. Offline Files can also use the cached copies of the files to act as a stand-in for the network when that network has failed or isn't present—such as when you're on the road.

You'll like Offline Files for several reasons. As these oft-used cached files will reside on the local hard disk, you'll immediately see what seems to be an increase in network response speed; opening up a file that appears to be on the network but is really in a local disk directory will yield apparently stunning improvements in response time, as little or no actual network activity is actually required. It also produces the side effect of reducing network traffic, as cached files needn't be retransmitted over the LAN. Having frequently used files on a local cache directory also solves the problem of "What do I do when the network's down and I need a file from a server?" If you try to access a file on a server that's not responding (or if you're not physically connected to the network), Offline Files shifts to *offline* mode. When in offline mode, Offline Files looks on your local Offline Files network cache, and if Offline Files finds a copy of that file in the cache, it delivers the file to the user just as if the server were up, running, and attached to the user's workstation.

Anyone who's ever had to get ready for a business trip knows two of the worst things about traveling with a laptop: the agony of getting on the plane only to realize that you've forgotten one or two essential files and the irritation of having to make sure that whatever files you changed while traveling get copied back to the network servers when you return. Offline Files greatly reduces the chance of the first problem because, again, often-used files tend to automatically end up in the local network cache directory. It greatly reduces the work of the second task by automating the laptop-to-server file synchronization process.

 NOTE You can read more about Offline Files in Chapter 9, "Creating and Managing Shared Folders."

Internet Connection Sharing

A very large percentage of us have some kind of connection to the Internet, whether it be a simple dial-up connection, cable modem, or DSL. A substantial portion of us have more than one PC in our house, which leads to one of the most common pieces of e-mail that I get: "How do I share my Internet connection with all of the computers in the house?" Once, the answer to that question was a fairly lengthy discussion of routers and proxy servers.

Now, however, the answer's easy: Just use Internet Connection Sharing (ICS). Anyone who's ever used Windows 9x or NT 4 to dial in to an ISP will be able to use ICS without any trouble—using it involves little more than just checking a box.

Here's how it works. You run ICS on the computer that's dialed in (or cable modemed or DSLed) to the Internet. That computer can be running either Windows 2000 Professional or Windows 2000 Server. (It can even be running the updated version of Windows 98, Win 98 Second Edition.) You check a box labeled Shared Access in your connection's properties; this activates ICS. At this point, the ICS machine acts as a DHCP server (which provides the other computers at home with their IP addresses) and as a router (which ensures that their packets get from the home LAN to the Internet and back).

 NOTE ICS is a very neat feature and will no doubt be pretty popular; you can read more about it in Chapter 17.

Bad News

It's not all wine and roses with Windows 2000, however. While it's a great improvement over NT 4, it still lacks in a number of ways.

DHCP Won't Be Fault Tolerant

The Dynamic Host Configuration Protocol (DHCP) is an essential bit of network infrastructure, and when it goes down, the network is at least partially crippled. Adding some kind of fault tolerance to DHCP made good sense and Microsoft told us it would offer it. Unfortunately, however, to implement fault tolerance on DHCP you must invest tens of thousands of dollars in hardware and software for a server cluster—a great answer for a large corporation, but impractical for the rest of us.

No Fax Server Software

NT's all-in-one small business version, BackOffice Small Business Edition, shipped with a nice, basic fax server—nothing so fancy that it would put the third-party fax server folks out of business, just a nice basic system that is to fax servers what WordPad is to word processors.

For some reason, Microsoft did not ship a fax server with Windows 2000, however. There *is* fax support, but only on a workstation-by-workstation basis. Thus, you could walk over to a server equipped with a fax modem and fax something from there, but you couldn't fax from your desktop using the server. This seems odd given that Microsoft clearly has NT-ready fax code, but perhaps the fear of Justice has stayed their hand on this matter...

Requires Powerful Hardware

Every new version of NT (or Windows, for that matter) renders entire product lines of formerly useful computers useless. For example, NT 3.1, 3.5, and 3.51 ran relatively well on 486 computers, but running NT 4 on a 486 was a quixotic venture. In the same way, Windows 2000 puts the final nail in the Pentium and the MMX coffins. Yes, you *can* run Windows 2000 on a Pentium—some of this book was written on a 266MHz MMX laptop, and some of my braver (or patient) coauthors did their testing on 133MHz and 166MHz machines—but at a noticeable loss in speed. Anyone wanting to get anything done on Windows 2000 will need at least a 350MHz Pentium II and 128MB of RAM. Domain controllers will run best with two physical hard disks. Much of the same advice goes for anyone wanting to run the Workstation version of Windows 2000, Professional; at the moment all I'm doing on my Professional workstation is editing this chapter with Word 97, and I'm using 96MB of RAM—so 96MB to 128MB minimum is definitely indicated!

Hardware/DirectX Support Is Still Spotty

One of the great frustrations about NT, whether in its 3.*x* and 4.*x* versions or in its current Windows 2000 incarnation, is its relatively thin hardware support, particularly when compared to its Windows 9*x* little brother. Windows 2000 improves upon this as it supports a wider range of hardware and because Plug and Play now makes it easier to install that hardware—but there are still many boards that plain won't work.

Furthermore, Windows 2000 claims to support the DirectX interface, the interface that most modern games are written to, but in actual fact, DirectX's performance makes the few games that I've tried on Windows 2000 unplayable. "What's that?" you say, "Games are irrelevant on servers?" Well, yes, that's probably true—but if *one* much-touted but easily tested subsystem of Windows 2000 (DirectX) doesn't work, isn't it reasonable to be concerned about the other subsystems, the ones that aren't so easy to test?

AD Is Inferior to Existing Directory Services

Directory services have been around for ages. I recall working with a competing network operating system named Banyan VINES almost 10 years ago, when Banyan introduced a directory service called StreetTalk. StreetTalk was more flexible in 1992 than Active Directory is now. For example, it's inconceivable that you cannot take two existing domains and join them into an Active Directory forest (you can read more about forests in the next chapter)—such "pruning and grafting" has been possible in Novell Directory Services (NDS) for years. Nor are Active Directory's weaknesses the fault of NT somehow; Banyan has been selling an implementation of its StreetTalk directory service for NT for at least three years, and Novell's got a version of NDS for NT as well.

Granted, Active Directory's relative weakness probably stems from the fact that it's a "version 1.0" product. But will it improve? As with all companies, Microsoft isn't primarily motivated to create good products; instead, they're motivated to sell a lot of whatever they make—and making good stuff is usually one good way to sell a lot of stuff. But that's not the only way. Sometimes the battle for market share is won by effective advertising rather than quality. And if Microsoft wins the directory services war with marketing, then there won't *be* any incentive to improve the product.

There Are Still Far Too Many Reboots

Back in 1992, I interviewed one of the higher-ups in the NT project, a fellow named Bob Muglia. Bob is a heckuva nice guy and he provided me with a lot of useful information. But I remember one comment that he made to me, a promise that we're still waiting to see fulfilled.

"NT's going to be stable," he told me. "Once you get it set up with your drivers and applications, you should never have to reboot it. If you do, then we've failed."

I've run into Bob since then on several occasions and I've never had the heart to needle him about his quote. But what he told me in 1992 made eminent sense: At minimum, an enterprise-quality operating system *doesn't need to be rebooted all the time*. And in fact, Microsoft has gone to some pains to advertise that you needn't reboot Windows 2000 as often as you did NT 4. The number of necessary reboots *has* been reduced, but it's still too much.

Having observed the positive and negative aspects, how does Windows 2000 come out in the balance? It depends on your expectations. If you wanted a vastly improved version of NT 4 with a raft of cool new doodads like Internet Connection Sharing, then you'll like Windows 2000 quite a bit. On the other hand, if you were hoping for a rock-solid, enterprise-capable network operating system that could potentially replace your existing MVS, VMS, or Unix systems, then Windows 2000 may disappoint you—

while it's good, I wouldn't feel really confident about the Dow Jones running solely on Windows 2000, nor would I be very happy about finding out that the airliner I was sitting in depended on Windows 2000. But it's definitely a positive step, a step in the direction of more power and better reliability.

The biggest part of Windows 2000, the newest and most extensive piece, is undoubtedly Active Directory. It's a whole new world, even for those already expert in NT 4—so the next chapter is an overview intended to get you started in this pivotal Windows 2000 technology.

CHAPTER 2

Getting Comfortable with Active Directory

The first thing that you probably ever heard about Microsoft's latest network operating system, Windows 2000, was that it can support larger networks than its predecessor, Windows NT Server 4, and that it accomplishes that with something called Active Directory. To read the marketing literature, you'd think that Microsoft believes that Active Directory is the single most important piece of Windows 2000.

Well, actually, they probably think that because AD probably *is* the single most important piece of Windows 2000. Unfortunately, it's also one of the most complex parts of Windows 2000, and one of the most pervasive—virtually every major feature of Windows 2000 requires Active Directory, with the possible exception of Plug and Play.

What We'll Accomplish in This Chapter

Veterans of NT 4 networks get a tired, resigned look on their faces when I talk to groups about AD. The new Active Directory name and the new user interface for AD's management tools makes most NT 4 experts feel that all of their hard-won expertise is now useless, that "everything they know is wrong." There are a bunch of new terms relevant to AD—*trees*, *forests*, *organizational units*, and so on.

If you're one of the despairing, then cheer up, I've got good news! AD is really nothing more than NT 4 domain structures with a bunch of cool improvements added. The problem is, of course, that Microsoft not only came up with a bunch of new things and gave them new names, they gave most of the old concepts new names as well. But if you're pretty up-to-speed on NT 4 networks, then you actually won't find AD terribly daunting, once someone gives you the NT-4-to-Windows-2000 decoder ring. Think of this chapter as that ring.

In this chapter, I'll explain what Microsoft's motivation was in designing this major change to its domain structure model. What kinds of problems were they trying to solve? What could justify Windows 2000 Server's increased complexity? And once we understand those problems, the next questions are how do we solve those problems with this Active Directory thing, and how well does AD solve them?

A Word on This Chapter's Structure

Before going on, however, I want to explain that the existence of Active Directory introduces a complexity to this book. Normally an author wants to explain a complex topic in a nice, sequential fashion, starting with simple elements and building to more complex ones. (And, come to think of it, normally *readers* want that, too.) I followed that approach when writing my previous books on NT 3.1, 3.5, 3.51, and 4.0. Unfortunately, Windows 2000 doesn't allow me that same start-slow-and-get-more-complex luxury, and the reason is Active Directory. You see, before you shove the first CD-ROM into the first CD drive, before you run Windows 2000's Setup for the first time, you must understand how Active Directory works because you must first *design an Active Directory structure for your enterprise.* This was true to a certain extent in earlier versions of NT—it's always a good idea to plan before doing—but most of us just started creating domains, playing around with them a bit, realizing what we'd done wrong, and then reconfiguring those domains. I suppose some folks will do the same thing with AD, just building an AD structure willy-nilly, living with it and finding out what they hate about that structure, and then blowing it all up and starting all over, but the cost of doing that would be significant. Hence this chapter.

This chapter first motivates the whole idea of Active Directory, then discusses exactly what problems AD was supposed to solve. Then I'll give you the quick-and-dirty overview of what AD offers, trying to summarize as briefly as possible what forests, trees, organizational units, and other new AD concepts mean and why you should care. Then I'll walk you through some of the practical steps, some step-by-step examples to help you understand the techniques that you'll need in order to actually build an Active Directory—which brings me to the chapter's main problem.

It seems likely that this book's audience is composed of two groups. Members of the first group are old hands at NT 4 administration; they know how to run an NT 4 network and want to build on that knowledge to make the transition to Windows 2000. (Notice I didn't say that they would transition to Windows 2000; *transition* is a verb to only marketing people and consultants.) The second group is altogether new to Microsoft networking and perhaps new to networking in general.

I decided to serve both groups by writing *two* different overviews—one for each group. I'll start off in this chapter with an explanation of the kinds of things that modern networks require and examine both how NT 4 met those requirements and how Windows 2000 meets those requirements. While it may be of interest to NT 4 veterans, it's not primarily intended to serve their needs—it's for the newbies. Following that, I've got a shorter rundown for the vets that basically answers the question, "What does Windows 2000 do for me that NT 4 didn't?" Then I'll get into the specifics of building an Active Directory.

However you read the rest of the book, though, remember: I strongly recommend that you do some real AD planning before you install your first system. Whether you're an old-timer to NT or a newcomer, you will find that you can't just start installing Windows 2000 on some systems, build a few domains, and *then* plan your Active Directory. You've really got to understand enough of AD to sit down and make a plan before you shove the first CD into the first drive. As the business management books say, "Failure to plan is a plan to fail," or something like that. (I never *was* any good at that management stuff.)

First, then, let's introduce Active Directory to the NT newbies; again, the NT 4 experts out there may choose to skip it and move straight on to "Active Directory: The Basics for NT Veterans."

Active Directory for NT Newcomers

Not that long ago, networks were small (remember when the only "networks" you cared about were CBS, NBC, and ABC?) and so were their problems. But nowadays it's not unusual to see worldwide networks connecting hundreds of thousands of PCs and users. Managing that kind of complexity brings up big problems—oops, we're supposed to call them challenges, I always forget. One of the answers to the obvious question "Why bother with Windows 2000, anyway?" is that it was designed with some of those challenges in mind. That's important because NT 4 *didn't* address many of those problems.

Security: Keeping Track of Who's Allowed to Use the Network and Who Isn't

A network's first job is to provide service—central places to store simple things like files or more complex things like databases, shared printing, or fax services. To make it possible for people to communicate in ways like e-mail, videoconferencing, or whatever technology comes up in the future. And, more recently, to make it easier for people to buy things.

Fast on the heels of that first job, however, is the second job of every network: security. Once, most computer networks were unsecured or lightly secured, but human nature has forced a change and there's no going back. Just as businesses have locks on their doors, file cabinets, and cash registers to protect their physical assets, so also do most modern firms protect their information assets. And no matter what vendor's network software you're using, computer security typically boils down to two parts: authentication and authorization. To see why, consider the following example.

Acme Industries sells pest control devices. They've got a sales manager named Wilma Wolf; Wilma wants to see how the sales of a new product, Instant Hole, is doing. Acme's got it set up so that Wilma can review sales information through her Web browser—she just surfs over to a particular location on one of the company's internal Web servers and the report appears on her screen.

Of course, Acme management wouldn't be happy about just *anybody* getting to these sales report pages, so the pages are secured. Between the time that Wilma asked for the pages and the time that she got them, two things happened:

Authentication   The Web server containing the sales reports asked her workstation, "Who's asking for this data?" The workstation replied, "Wilma." The server then said, "Prove it." So the workstation popped up a dialog box on Wilma's screen asking for her username and password. She types in her name and password, and assuming that she types them in correctly, the server then checks that name and password against a list of known users and passwords and finds that she is indeed Wilma.

Authorization   The mere fact that she's proven that she's Wilma may not be sufficient reason for the Web server to give her access to the sales pages. The Web server then looks at another list sometimes known as the Access Control List, a list of people and access levels—"Joe can look at this page but can't change it," "Sue can look at this page and can change it," "Larry can't look at this page at all." Presuming Wilma's on the "can look" list, the server sends the requested pages to her browser.

Now, the foregoing example may not seem to contain any deep insights—after all, everyone's logged into a system, tried to access something, and either been successful or rejected—but understanding how Windows 2000 Server and in particular Active Directory is new requires examining these everyday things a bit. Here's a closer look at some of the administrative mechanics of logins.

Maintain a "Directory" of Users and Other Network Objects

Every secure system has a file or files that make up a database of known user accounts. NT 4 only used a single file named SAM, short for the less-than-illuminating Security Accounts Manager. It contained a user's username (the logon name), the user's full name, password, allowed logon hours, account expiration date, description, primary group name, and profile information. Of course, the file was encrypted; copy a SAM from an existing NT 4 system and pull it up in Notepad, and you'll see only garbage.

Windows 2000 Server stores most of its user information in a file called NTDS.DIT. But NTDS.DIT is different from SAM in a few ways. First, NTDS.DIT is a modified Access database, and Windows 2000 Server actually contains a variant of Access's database engine in its machinery. (Microsoft used to call the Access database engine JET, which stood for Joint Enterprise Technology—no, the meaning isn't obvious to me either, I think they just liked the acronym—but now it's called ESE, pronounced "easy," which stands for the equally useful name Extensible System Engine.) Second, as you'll see demonstrated over and over again, NTDS.DIT stores a much wider variety of information about users than SAM ever did.

The information in NTDS.DIT and the program that manages ntds.dit are together called *the directory service*. (As a matter of fact, most folks will never say "NTDS.DIT," they'll say "directory service.") Which leads to a question: What exactly is a "directory"?

It would seem (to me, anyway) that what we've got here is a database of users and user information. So why not call it a "database"? No compelling reasons; mostly convention, but there *is* one interesting insight. According to some, databases of users tend to get *read* far more often than they get *written*. That allows a certain amount of database engine "tweaking" for higher performance. This subset of the class of databases gets a name—*directories*. I guess it makes sense, as we're used to using lists of people called "office directories" or "phone directories." I just wish the folks in power had come up with some other name; ask most PC users what a "directory" is, and they start thinking of hard disk structures. "C:\WINDOWS—isn't that a directory?"

Centralizing the Directory and *Directories*: a "Logon Server"

"Please, can't we set things up so I only need to remember *one* password?"

Consider for a moment when Windows 2000 Server will use that user information located in Active Directory. When you try to access a file share or print share, Active Directory will validate you. But there's more at work here. When fully implemented, Active Directory can save you a fair amount of administrative work in other network functions as well.

For example, suppose your network requires SQL database services. You'll then run a database product like SQL Server or Oracle on the network. But adding another server-based program to your network can introduce more administrative headaches because, like the file and print servers, a database server needs authentication and authorization support. That's because you usually don't want to just plunk some valuable database on the network and then let the world in general at it—you want to control who gets access.

So the database program needs a method for authentication and authorization. And *here's* where it gets ugly: In the past, many database programs have required their administrators to keep and maintain a list of users and passwords. The database programs required you to duplicate all that work of typing in names and passwords, to redo the work you'd already done to get your Novell, Banyan, NT, or whatever type LAN up and running. Yuk. But it gets worse. Consider what you'd have to do if you ran both NT as a network operating system *and* Novell NetWare as a network operating system: yup, you're typing in names and passwords yet again. Now add Lotus Notes for your e-mail and groupware stuff, another list of users, and hey, how about a mainframe or an AS/400? More accounts.

Let's see—with a network incorporating NT, Oracle, NetWare, and Notes, we've got each user owning *four* different user accounts. Which means each user has *four* different passwords to remember. And, every few months, four different passwords to remember to change.

This seems dumb; why can't we just type those names and passwords once into our Windows 2000 Server and then tell Oracle, NetWare, Notes to just ask the local Windows 2000 Server machine to check that I am indeed who I say I am rather than making Oracle, NetWare, and Notes duplicate all of that security stuff? Put another way, we have a centralized computer that acts as a database server, another that acts as a centralized e-mail server, another as a print server—why not have a centralized "logon" server, a centralized "authentication" server? Then our users would only have to remember (and change) one password and account name rather than four.

Centralized logons would be a great benefit, but there's a problem with it: how would Notes actually *ask* the Win2K server to authenticate? What programming commands would an Oracle database server use to ask a Microsoft "logon server" (the actual term is *domain controller*, as you'll learn later) if a particular user should be able to access a particular piece of data?

Well, if that domain controller were running NT 4, the programming interface wouldn't have been a particularly well-documented one. And third parties like Oracle, Lotus, and Novell would have been reluctant to write programs depending on that barely documented security interface because they'd be justifiably concerned that when the *next* version of NT appeared (Windows 2000 Server), then Microsoft would have changed the programming interface, leaving Lotus, Novell, and Oracle scrambling to learn and implement this new interface. And some of the more cynical among us would even suggest that Lotus and Oracle might fear that Microsoft's Exchange and SQL Server would be able to come out in Windows 2000 Server–friendly versions nearly immediately after Windows 2000 Server's release....

Instead, Microsoft opted to put an industry standard interface on its Active Directory, an interface called the Lightweight Directory Access Protocol (LDAP). Now, LDAP may initially sound like just another geeky acronym, but it's more than that— what Microsoft's done by putting an LDAP interface on Active Directory is to open up a doorway for outside developers. And here's how important it is: Yes, LDAP will make Oracle's or Lotus's job easier should they decide to integrate their products' security with NT's built-in security. But LDAP also means that it's (theoretically, at least) possible to build tools that create Active Directory structures—domains, trees, forests, organizational units, user accounts, all of the components. It means that if Windows 2000 Server gets popular but Microsoft's Active Directory control programs turn out to be hard to work with, then some clever third party can just swoop in and offer a complete replacement, built atop LDAP commands.

Which, after you spend a bit of time with the Microsoft Management Console, may not seem like a bad idea—but I'll leave you to make your own judgement about that once you meet the MMC.

Searching: Finding Things on the Network

Thus far, I've been talking about the directory service as if it only contains user accounts. But that's not true—the DS not only includes directory entries for people, it also contains directory entries describing servers and workstations. And that turns out to be essential, for a few reasons.

Finding Servers: "Client-Server Rendezvous"

Client-server computing is how work gets done nowadays. You check your e-mail with Outlook (the client), which gets that mail from the Exchange machine down the hall (the server). You're at your PC (the client) accessing files on a file server (the server). You buy a shirt at L.L. Bean's Web server (the server) from your PC using Internet Explorer (the client).

In those three cases, the copy of Outlook on your desktop had to somehow know where to find your local Exchange server, you couldn't get files from your file server until you knew which file server to look in, and you couldn't order that shirt until you'd found the address of the L.L. Bean Web server, www.llbean.com.

In every case, client-server doesn't work unless you can help the client find the server, hence the phrase "client-server rendezvous." In the Outlook case, your mail client knows where your mail server is probably because someone (perhaps you) in your networking group set it up, feeding the name of the Exchange server into some setup screen in Outlook. You may have found the correct file server for the desired files by poking around in Network Neighborhood in Windows 95/98, or in the My Network Places if your workstation is running Windows 2000 Professional, or perhaps someone told you where to find the files. You might have guessed L.L. Bean's address, saw it on a magazine ad, or used a search engine like Yahoo! or AltaVista.

Those are three examples of client-server rendezvous; many more happen in the process of daily network use. When your workstation seeks to log you in, the workstation must find a domain controller, or to put it differently, your "logon client" seeks a "logon server." Want to print something in color and wonder which networked color printers are nearby? More client-server rendezvous.

In every case, Active Directory can simplify the process. Your workstation will be able to ask Active Directory for the names of nearby domain controllers. You can search the Active Directory for keywords relevant to particular file shares and printers. And while Exchange isn't integrated with Active Directory as I write this, a future version code-named Platinum will store its user information in Active Directory and will probably insert some information into the Active Directory that will simplify finding mail servers.

Name Resolution and DNS

But merely getting the name of a particular mail, Web, print, or file server (or domain controller) isn't the whole story. From the network software's point of view, www.llbean .com isn't much help. To get you connected to the Bean Web server, the network software needs to know the *IP address* of that server, a four-number combination looking something like 208.7.129.82. That's the second part of client-server rendezvous.

In the case of a public Web site like Bean's, your computer can look up a Web server by querying a huge network of publicly available Internet servers called the Domain Name System, or DNS. The public DNS contains the names of many machines you'll need to access, but chances are good that your company's internal network doesn't advertise many of its machines' names on the Internet; rather, your internal network probably runs a set of private DNS servers.

After its inception in 1984, DNS didn't change much. But 1996 and 1998 brought two big changes referred to as RFC 2052 and RFC 2136 (you'll read about them in Chapter 18), transforming DNS into a naming system that's good not only for the worldwide Internet but also for internal intranets. Many of the pieces of DNS software

For one thing, enterprises usually want *some* level of communication between domains, and to accomplish that, the enterprises must put in place connections between domains called *trust relationships*. Unfortunately, trust relationships are a quirky and unreliable necessity of any multidomain enterprise using NT 4. With Windows 2000 Server, in contrast, the Navy need only create *one* domain and then divide it up using a new-to-NT notion called *organizational units*, usually abbreviated *OUs*.

More specifically, the Navy would solve their problem in this way:

- They'd create one domain named (for example) NAVY.

- Inside NAVY, they'd create an organizational unit named Norfolk, another called DC, and a third named San Diego. They would set up their servers and then place each server into the proper OU.

- Also inside NAVY, they'd create a user group named Norfolk Admins, and two others named San Diego Admins and DC Admins. They'd create accounts for their users and place any administrators into their proper group, depending on whether they were based in DC, San Diego, or Norfolk.

At this point, understand that the San Diego Admins (kinda sounds like a baseball team, doesn't it?) don't yet have any power: there's no magic in Windows 2000 Server that says, "Well, there's an OU named San Diego and a group named San Diego Admins, I guess that must mean I should let these Admin guys have total control over the servers in the San Diego OU." You have to create that link by *delegating control* of the San Diego OU to the user group San Diego Admins. (There's a wizard that assists in doing this, as you'll see when we walk through a delegation example later in this chapter.) We'll see that OUs are a very useful tool for building large and useful domains.

Satisfying Political Needs

"That's *my* data, so I want it on *my* servers!" As information has become the most important asset of many firms—for example, I once heard someone comment that the majority of Microsoft's assets resided in the crania of their employees—some firms have been reluctant to yield control of that information to a central IT group. Nor is that an irrational perspective: if you were the person in charge of maintaining a 5-million-person mailing list, and if that list generated one half of your firm's sales leads, then you might well want to see that data housed on a machine or machines run by people who report directly to you.

Of course, on the other side of the story there is the IT director, who wants Total Control of all servers in the building, and her reasoning is just as valid. You see, if a badly run server goes down and that failure affects the rest of the network, it's *her* head on the chopping block.

So on the one hand, the department head or VP wants to control the iron and silicon that happens to be where his data lives, and on the other hand, the IT director who's concerned with making sure that all data is safe and that everything on the network plays well with others wants to control said data and network pieces. Who wins? It depends—and that's the "politics" part.

What does Windows 2000 do to ameliorate the political problems? Well, not as much as would be nice—there is no "make the vice presidents get along well" Wizard— but Windows 2000's variety of options for domain design gives the network designers the flexibility to build whatever kind of network structure they want. Got a relatively small organization that would fit nicely into a single domain, but one VP with server ownership lust? No problem, give her an OU of her own within the domain. Got a firm with two moderately large offices separated by a few hundred miles? Under NT 4, two domains and a trust relationship would be the answer, and you could choose to do that under Windows 2000, but that's not the only answer. As Windows 2000 is extremely parsimonious with WAN bandwidth in comparison with NT 4, you might find that a single domain makes sense as it's easier to administer than two domains, but not impossible from a network bandwidth point of view. And bandwidth utilization is our next topic....

Connectivity and Replication Issues

More and more companies don't just live in one place. They've purchased another firm across the country, and what once were two separate *local* area networks are now one firm with a wide area network need. If that WAN link is fast, then there's no network design headache at all: hook the two offices up with a T1 link and you can essentially treat them as one office.

That's beneficial because each site will usually contain a domain controller—one of those servers that host the Active Directory database and which act as machines to accomplish logins. But those domain controllers must communicate with each other whenever something changes, as when a user's password changes or when an administrator creates a new user account. This is called *Active Directory replication*. The same thing happened with NT 4, as NT 4 also allowed you to put multiple domain controllers in an enterprise.

In NT 4, suppose we've got two offices connected by a slow WAN link. Suppose further that we've got a domain controller in each of these offices. They need to replicate their SAM database between domain controllers (recall that NT 4 used a user database named SAM; Windows 2000's database is called Active Directory). NT 4's domain controller updates happened every five minutes. That means that a domain controller might try to replicate changes to another domain controller every five minutes, even if they're only connected with a very slow link. All that chatter could well choke a WAN link and keep other, more important traffic from getting through.

Windows 2000 improves upon that by allowing you to tell Windows 2000 domain controllers about how well they're connected. The idea is that you describe your enterprise in terms of *sites*, which are basically just groups of servers with fast connections—

groups of servers living on the same local area network, basically. You can then define how fast (or probably, slow) the connections *between* those sites are, and Windows 2000 will then be a bit smarter about using those connections.

In particular, Windows 2000 Active Directory servers compress data before sending it over slow WAN links. Taking the time to compress data requires a certain amount of CPU power, but it's well worth it, as AD is capable of a 10:1 compression ratio!

Not only do we often face slow links, we often must live with *unreliable* links, ones that are up and down or perhaps only up for a short period of time every day. Windows 2000 lets you define not only a WAN link's speed but also the times that it is up.

NT 4's directory replications require a real-time connection called a Remote Procedure Call (RPC). RPCs are like telephone calls—the domain controller programs on each side must be up and running and actively communicating simultaneously. Inasmuch as domain controllers can be more or less busy as the day wears on, requiring this kind of shared concentration in order to get a simple directory replication accomplished is a bit demanding. It might be nicer if replications could work less like a telephone call and more like a mailing—and to a certain extent, Windows 2000 allows this, or rather points to a day in the future when it'll be possible.

It's possible for one domain controller to simply *mail* part of its replication data to another domain controller. Then, even if the receiving domain controller is not currently online, the mail message is still waiting for it, ready to be read when the receiving domain controller is again awake. Sounds good, but unfortunately, not *all* of the directory replication can happen over mail. Microsoft says that'll change in a future release, but not in Windows 2000.

Site control will make life considerably easier for those managing multilocation networks.

Scalability: Building Big Networks

Large enterprise networks found NT 4 lacking in the number of users that its SAM database could accommodate. While you could theoretically create millions of user accounts on an NT domain, it's not practical to create more than about 5,000 to perhaps 10,000 user accounts in a domain. (If you took the MCSE exam for NT Server and are looking at that number oddly, it's because they made you memorize 40,000 as the answer to the question "How many user accounts can you put on an NT domain?" In my experience, that's just not realistic, hence my 5 to 10 thousand number.)

Five thousand user accounts are more than most companies would ever need. But some large firms need to incorporate more user accounts into their enterprise, forcing them to divide their company's network up into multiple domains—and multiple domains were to be avoided at all costs under NT 4 because of the extra trouble in maintaining them.

Active Directory can accommodate many more user accounts than NT's SAM. Microsoft claims that they have stress-tested Windows 2000 domains with 1.5 million users in them, and Compaq engineers in France have successfully created and worked with 16 million user accounts on a single domain using *beta 2* of Windows 2000. While it'll be a while before we get enough real-world experience to know exactly how many users we can reasonably expect to add to Windows 2000 networks, it's clear that Windows 2000 systems will support far larger lists of users than did NT 4.

Furthermore, Active Directory allows you to build larger networks by making the process of building and maintaining multidomain networks easier. Where once an administrator of a multidomain network had to build and maintain a complex system of interdomain security relationships—the *trust relationships* I've already referred to—now Windows 2000 will let you build a system of domains called a *forest*. A forest's main strength is that once a group of domains has been built into a forest, the trusts are automatically created and maintained. There are additionally smaller multi-domain structures called trees that also feature automatic trusts; you'll read more about trees and forests later.

Simplifying Computer Names or "Unifying the Namespace"

Devices on a network mainly identify themselves by some long and unique identification number. On an intranet or the Internet, it's a unique 32-bit address called an *IP address*. Networks also commonly exploit a 48-bit address burned into each network interface card called a *MAC address*. Any Ethernet, Token Ring, ATM, or other network interface has one of these addresses, and some conventions that network manufacturers have agreed upon have ensured that no matter whom you buy a NIC from, the NIC will have a 48-bit address that no other NIC has. Some parts of NT identify PCs by their IP address (or addresses—a machine with multiple NICs will have an IP address and MAC address for each NIC), others by the PC's MAC address or addresses.

But people don't relate well to long strings of numbers—telling you that you can send me mail to mark@1100111011110110111110111001000 is technically accurate (presuming that you can find a mail client that will accept network addresses in binary) but not very helpful. It's far more preferable to be able to instead tell your mail program to send mail to help@minasi.com, which you can do. Somehow, however, your mail client must be able to look up minasi.com and from there find out where to send mail for minasi.com. In the same way, pointing your Web browser to www.microsoft.com forces the browser to convert www.microsoft.com into the particular IP address or addresses that constitute Microsoft's Web site. This process of converting from human-friendly names like minasi.com to computer-friendly addresses like 1100111011110110111110111001000 is called *name resolution*. It's something every network must do.

So why is name resolution a problem with NT? Because most of the networking world uses *one* approach to name resolution, and up through version 4, NT used a different one.

Most every firm is either on the Internet or has an internal intranet, or both. Intranets and the Internet use a form of name resolution called the Domain Name System, or DNS. DNS names are the familiar Internet names like `www.microsoft.com`. In contrast, Microsoft networking has for years used a different and incompatible naming system called NetBIOS names, which are simpler—no more than 15 characters long, no periods.

PCs resolve DNS names by consulting a group of servers around the world called, not surprisingly, DNS servers. Your company or Internet Service Provider operates one or more DNS servers and your Internet software uses these nearby DNS servers to resolve (for example) `www.minasi.com` to the Internet address 206.246.253.200.

NT-based networks using Internet software don't use DNS for much of their work. Instead, Microsoft invented its own name servers somewhat like DNS but using NetBIOS names; they called these name servers Windows Internet Name Service, or WINS, servers.

That leads to this problem: nearly every firm is on the Internet—*has* to be on the Internet—and so every firm must give DNS names to their computers. But if they're also using NT, then they need to give their systems NetBIOS names. That in and of itself is not a great burden; what *is* a burden is that these names are important to the programs that use them, and programs can typically need one of the two names and can't use the other of the two.

Let's take an example. Suppose someone wants to log onto an NT 4 domain at Acme Technologies. To accomplish that, her workstation must find a domain controller for that domain. Her workstation does that by searching for a machine with a particular NetBIOS name. Let's say that Acme does indeed have a domain controller around named LOGMEIN (its NetBIOS name) which *also* acts as a Web server with the DNS name reptiles.pictures.animalworld.com, as it hosts pages of pictures of local reptiles. Let's also suppose that for some reason ACME has no WINS servers but has a great network of DNS servers.

DNS names are of no value to the workstation looking for a logon. You could have the finest set of DNS servers in the world, but it would make no difference—without a functioning WINS server, that workstation would probably be unable to locate a domain controller to log you in. On the other hand, if someone sitting at that very same workstation sought to view the reptile pictures on `http://reptiles.pictures.animalworld.com`, she'd just fire up Internet Explorer and point it at that URL. Internet Explorer is, of course, uninterested in NetBIOS names, relying mainly on DNS names. The workstation would quickly locate the Web server and browse its pages, even as that same workstation was unable to detect that the very same server could perform logins.

Windows 2000 solves this problem by largely doing away with WINS, using DNS for all of its name resolution needs. Unfortunately, however, Windows 2000 uses DNS for all of *its* name resolution needs—older Windows 9*x* and Windows NT 4 systems still rely on WINS. So while WINS's role is diminished, it'll still be around until you've pulled the plug on the last Windows 9*x* and NT machines.

Satisfying the Lust for Power and Control

Well, okay, maybe it's not *lust*, but it's certainly *need*. Put simply, there just plain aren't enough support people around, and no shortage of users to support. In 1987, many firms retained 1 support person for every 100 users; in many companies nowadays, that ratio is more like 1 support person for every 2,000 users.

That means that where once it was once possible for a support person to physically visit every user's PC to perform support tasks, it's just not reasonable to expect any more. Support people need tools that allow them to get their support work done from a central location as much as is possible. And, while not every user is all that happy about it, one way to simplify a support person's job is to standardize each PC's desktop. In some cases, support staffs need software tools to allow them to *enforce* that standard desktop. (As you can imagine, it's a very political issue for many firms.)

In NT 4, Microsoft started helping support staffs centralize their desktop control with something called *system policies*. But system policies were lacking in a few ways. Active Directory improves upon system policies with a kind of "system policies version 2" called *group policies*.

Better security, more flexible administration options, wiser use of bandwidth, and providing godlike control to administrators: that's basically what Active Directory is trying to accomplish. But how does it accomplish that? To find out, turn to the section named "Understanding and Using Active Directory's Features." Unless, of course, you want to just keep reading—in the next section, I explain what AD means to those who are already accustomed to NT 4.

Active Directory: The Basics for NT Veterans

What does Active Directory mean for those of us who've been working with NT domains, trust relationships, and the like since 1993? Are things all that different?

How Active Directory Affects Existing One-Domain Enterprises

Well, let's first get the easy part of the answer out of the way: if your firm currently runs a single-domain NT enterprise, or even just a bunch of NT servers in a workgroup without a domain, then no, Active Directory won't change your life all that much. You'll probably choose to remain as one domain. You'll still create user accounts, albeit with a different tool than User Manager for Domains. There are still user groups, file permissions, and the like. You may have to learn a thing or two about DNS if you've never done anything with it, but even then a small network can get away with a fair amount of DNS ignorance with impunity. You *will* have to learn a lot of new management tools—as I just suggested, the User Manager for Domains is dead and is largely replaced by the Directory Services Administrator (also know as Active Directory Users and Computers)—and you'll likely have to buy new servers, as Windows 2000 requires some horsepower (350MHz Pentium II and 256MB RAM *minimum* for a domain controller), but that's about it.

That's not to say, by the way, that you should not upgrade to Windows 2000; it just means that Active Directory won't turn out to offer the biggest benefits of Windows 2000 to your enterprise. Windows 2000 *will* offer some really cool other things, however. In particular you'll probably like Plug and Play and the Change and Configuration Management (formerly known as Zero Administration Windows) tools. CCM will simplify the task of getting Windows 2000 Professional (the name for Windows 2000's version of NT Workstation) onto a computer, it'll make protecting users' data an easier task, and it'll enable you to distribute applications onto users' desktops from a central point with just a few mouse-clicks.

That's the good news. The bad news for smaller enterprises (and, well, for larger ones as well) is that while getting Plug and Play is great, the reality is that Windows 2000 runs horribly slowly on all but the most recent computer hardware, implying that you'll probably need to not only upgrade your operating system but your network's hardware as well in order to make Windows 2000 useful. And while CCM puts some wonderful centrally controlled user support tools in your hands, CCM's benefits only extend to users running Windows 2000 Professional on their desktop PC, again implying that you're going to be buying some hardware if you really want to enjoy Windows 2000's benefits.

How Active Directory Affects Multidomain Enterprises

For many NT 4 users, even the vaguest outlines of AD's capabilities sound like manna from heaven. Bigger domains and more flexible domain structures—it all sounds great.

But how much new stuff will you have to learn? Is it true that "everything that you know is wrong"? Well, some things are very different, yes. But they're rooted in what you already know.

Windows 2000 Still Has Domains

First of all, Windows 2000 still has domains, and in many ways they still look like NT 4 domains. Where NT 4 stored information about user and machine accounts in a file named SAM, Windows 2000 stores that—and much else—in a file called `NTDS.DIT`. Under NT 4, a user in a multidomain environment had to identify both herself and the name of the domain whose SAM contained her user account. That's still true under Windows 2000, but it gets a bit easier, as Windows 2000 has a database called the *global catalog* that knows every user and what domain she's from. The GC knows every user by a name called User Principal Name, or UPN. A UPN looks like an e-mail address—joeblow@acme.com. A user can then either decide to log in as "Joe from domain sales.acme.com," in which case his workstation will contact a domain controller from domain sales.acme.com, or he could log in as joe@acme.com, which would prompt his workstation to ask the GC what domain joe@acme.com belongs to. The GC would respond that he's from sales.acme.com, and the workstation would then contact a domain controller from sales.acme.com to get the information that it needs to log Joe in.

Notice another thing about domains: where NT 4 had domains with 15-character names, Windows 2000 uses DNS-style naming for domains—but more about that in a minute.

Windows 2000 Domains Can Be Bigger

You can fit about 5,000 user accounts comfortably in an NT 4 domain, forcing large enterprises to create multiple domains in order to accommodate all of their user accounts; such a domain design was called a *multimaster* model. In contrast, a Windows 2000 domain can fit 1.5 million users (or more, depending on whom you talk to) into its Active Directory database—which ought to be sufficient user accounts for even the largest companies. Windows 2000 will allow many large companies forced to use multiple domains because of the sheer size of their workforce to consolidate all of their user account domains into a single domain. Such domains can be large enough that many large enterprises can probably get away with one domain—for example, at this writing, a very large oil company is trying to implement their entire worldwide enterprise as a single Windows 2000 domain.

Many More Enterprises Can Be a Single Domain

Not only can domains be bigger, they can be wider—or at least more widely dispersed geographically.

Under NT 4, some relatively small companies decided to implement multidomain enterprises because of geography. Say a company's got an office uptown and another downtown, with 1,000 or so employees in each location and about 3,000 employees in total. Should they be one domain or many? Three hundred user accounts fit comfortably in one domain, but then there would probably have to be a domain controller in each location. Say for example that the PDC's in the uptown office and a BDC is in the downtown office. As there's a DC in each office, everyone can be logged in by a local

DC. Those two DCs must, however, be connected with some kind of full-time connection (let's suppose it's a 56K Frame Relay link), so that the PDC can inform the BDC of any changes to user accounts, passwords, and the like.

Password-changing day comes along and all 3,000 employees dutifully change their passwords. The folks in the downtown office will find changing passwords quite slow, unfortunately, because while a BDC can log a downtowner in, it can't help with password changes; logins require only reading the SAM, and a BDC can do that just fine. But changing a password requires modifying the domain's SAM, and only the PDC can do that. Password-changing traffic, then, must go over the Frame Relay link. (The downtowners have no idea that this is why password changing is so slow, by the way.) To add insult to injury, the Frame Relay link will be excessively slow on password-changing day, as the PDC will be using much of the Frame Relay's bandwidth to *tell* the BDC about these new passwords. This becomes so frustrating that the firm eventually decides to create two different domains, one for the uptown office and one for the downtown office.

Windows 2000 lets them get back together for two reasons. First, all DCs can accept changes, so a downtowner can conduct the entire password-changing ritual while talking to the local DC. But when the downtown DC updates the uptown DC about the new passwords, won't that choke the Frame Relay? No, not at all. Where NT 4 used the same chatty, bandwidth-wasting protocol to update BDCs whether they were connected with a fast or slow link, Windows 2000 detects DCs with slow connections and compresses its data before sending, and compresses it well—tests show about a 10:1 compression ratio. This firm can become one domain again.

In general, intradomain replication is far more efficient than it was under NT 4. That means that where previously under NT 4 you might have wisely chosen to implement a network in two separate cities as two domains so as to reduce replication traffic over a slow WAN link, under Windows 2000 you might just as wisely choose to build a single domain spread over a wide geographical area.

Domains Can Be Divided into Subdomains

But perhaps there's another concern—*politics*. The woman running the downtown office insists that the people who run the servers uptown not have admin control of "her" servers downtown. Now, in the NT 4 days, she could segregate her servers security-wise by just keeping them in a different domain. But there wasn't a simple way to "protect" a set of servers in domain X from some subset of domain X's domain administrators.

With Windows 2000, however, there is. The domain's architects can just create a subdomain called an organizational unit (call it downtown servers) and put the downtown servers in that OU. Next, they create a group called downtown admins or something like that and put the downtown administrators' user accounts into the downtown admins group. Finally, they tell Windows 2000 to allow only the downtown admins group to administer the downtown servers OU. This process of assigning control of an

OU's contents to a group is called *delegating* and Windows 2000 even has a wizard to assist in the process.

It's Easier to Build and Maintain Multiple-Domain Networks

If it sounds like I'm a proponent of single-domain networks, I am. The more "moving parts" (read: domains) in your network, the more things there are to break. So Windows 2000's ability to support bigger and more diverse single-domain networks is pretty cool.

If, however, after examining Windows 2000's capabilities you still choose to remain with a multidomain model, you'll find multidomain Windows 2000 networks a bit easier to manage than multidomain NT 4 networks.

If you choose to have more than one domain, Windows 2000 makes it easier to automatically build trust relationships among them by letting you create a "forest" of domains. Forests of domains can be subdivided into "trees"; the main reason you'd do that is, as you'll see, to make it easier to integrate your domain naming scheme with your DNS naming scheme.

Multiple Domains with NT 4   For example, consider the following NT 4 domain structure, pictured in Figure 2.1.

FIGURE 2.1

NT 4 domain structure

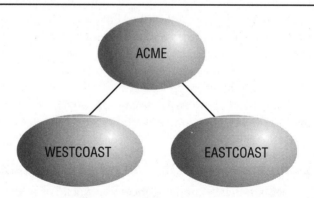

Here, Acme has decided to create three domains—ACME, which probably contains all of the *user* accounts in the entire enterprise, EASTCOAST, which probably contains all of the workstation and server accounts in their east coast office, and WESTCOAST, which probably contains all of the workstation and server accounts in their west coast office. For whatever reason, Acme's divided itself geographically, whether for political or bandwidth reasons.

In order to set this up, the Acme administrators had to do these steps:

1. Create the ACME domain and populate it with user accounts.

2. Create the EASTCOAST domain and populate it with server and workstation accounts.

3. Create the WESTCOAST domain and populate it with server and workstation accounts.

4. Build a trust relationship between EASTCOAST and ACME so that EASTCOAST trusts ACME. (In case you've forgotten what trust relationships are, they are a necessary first step when you intend to do some kind of sharing across domain lines. They're sort of like the initial treaties that former enemy countries sign so as to enable trade relations and begin selling things to one another.)

5. Build a trust relationship between WESTCOAST and ACME so that WESTCOAST trusts ACME.

6. Go to every machine in WESTCOAST, log in as a local administrator, and add ACME's Domain Users group to that machine's local Users group. Also, add ACME's Domain Admins group to that machine's local Administrators group.

7. Go to every machine in EASTCOAST, log in as a local administrator, and add ACME's Domain Users group to that machine's local Users group. Also, add ACME's Domain Admins group to that machine's local Administrators group.

Sound like fun? It's not. And the fun's not over. The Acme admins really should do a few other things as well. For one, they should sprinkle backup domain controllers from the ACME domain in both the east coast and west coast offices so that people at both offices can easily log in. Furthermore, those administrators should expect to have to monitor the two trust relationships, as they're prone to "breaking."

And remember—that example was almost the simplest multidomain example imaginable. Real-world enterprises often incorporate *hundreds* of domains.

Multiple Domains with Windows 2000   Now let's see what's involved with doing this under Windows 2000. Assuming that Acme would stay with three domains (a questionable assumption, recall, but let's use it to illustrate how much easier multi-domain enterprises are under Windows 2000), their domain structure would probably look like Figure 2.2.

FIGURE 2.2

Corresponding Windows 2000 domain structure

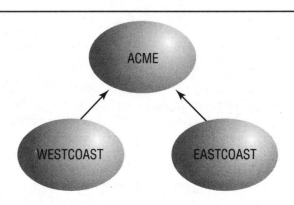

Looks similar at first glance, but a closer look shows differences. First of all, notice the names for the domains. NT 4 domain names had to be 15 characters or fewer in length, and periods in the names were a bad idea. Windows 2000 domain names are hierarchical and can be basically as long as you like. Notice also the .com suffix: Windows 2000 uses a DNS-type naming system, and for good reason—Windows 2000 *uses* DNS to keep track of domain structure. By default, one of the domain controllers in acme.com is a DNS server.

NOTE Does this mean that you must use Microsoft's DNS as your DNS server? No, it doesn't require that. You *can* run a Unix-based DNS server (or some other DNS server, for that matter), but that DNS server software will have to be pretty modern as it's got to implement some DNS features that only entered the DNS standards in the spring of 1997. More in Chapter 18.

You can extend the hierarchical naming structure as far as you like. For example, if you wanted to subdivide eastcoast.acme.com into engineering, administrative, and research divisions, you could create three more domains named engineering .eastcoast.acme.com, administrative.eastcoast.acme.com and research.eastcoast .acme.com. The hierarchical naming structure of DNS has always been DNS's strength and Windows 2000 exploits that.

Enough of the high-level stuff—how does this make life easier for administrators? Here are the steps that admins would take in order to create the three-domain system in Figure 2.2:

1. Create the acme.com domain by running a program called DCPROMO. DCPROMO is a wizard which asks questions of the admin and from there decides how to build the domain. The admin must tell DCPROMO that acme.com is a new domain, that the domain is the first domain in a new tree, and that the new tree is the first tree in a forest.

2. Once DCPROMO finishes its work—about 20 minutes of database creation—the admin creates the user accounts. If he's got an ASCII file listing the desired names, passwords, and the like, then Windows 2000 comes with a built-in VBScript program to do that automatically.

3. Next, locate a different Windows 2000 Server machine and create the eastcoast.acme.com domain, again with DCPROMO. This time, the admin tells DCPROMO that eastcoast.acme.com is a *child domain* of acme.com. Join any machines/servers to eastcoast.acme.com.

4. Do the same thing for westcoast.acme.com.

At this point, the admin is *done*. Windows 2000 automatically creates trust relationships between acme.com and eastcoast.acme.com as well as between acme.com and westcoast.acme.com. It also does all of the work necessary so that users in acme .com are recognized as users in the two child domains. Furthermore, there's an already-created group called Enterprise Administrators whose members are automatically recognized as administrators throughout the forest (that is, the three domains). Not bad, eh?

Active Directory Enables Many of Windows 2000's New Features

In addition to making domain building simpler and more flexible, Active Directory makes a bunch of Windows 2000's new features possible.

Basically, AD is a database, as you've already read. But in addition to being a database of users and machines, it's also the place that Windows 2000 stores much of its administrative information. In the following sections, I'll give you some examples.

AD Stores Zero Administration Info

Ever had to rebuild a user's workstation from scratch? How long did it take—would you measure it in minutes, hours, days, or weeks? There are commercial tools like Ghost from Symantec that can assist in that task, but Windows 2000 has a Ghost-like tool built right in called the Remote Installation Services. RIS lets you take a new computer right out the box, plug it into the network, and boot a floppy. The floppy gets the computer onto the network and locates an Active Directory server. From there, AD takes over and directs the process of getting a working disk image onto the workstation in 30 to 45 minutes, unattended. The information about where to keep those disk images and who gets which ones is stored in AD.

Anyone who's ever struggled with system policies under NT 4 knows that they're no picnic: you've got to generate a NTCONFIG.POL file, put it on a domain controller, and set up replication for NTCONFIG.POL among domain controllers. With Windows 2000, however, all of the system policy stuff—which is now called *group policies*—is stored and automatically replicated by AD.

Ever tried to "push" out an application with SMS or a similar tool? Again, no fun. But one of AD's functions is to store and decide who gets what applications.

AD Supports Directory-Enabled Networking

Windows 2000 allows you to control bandwidth within your intranet using QoS (Quality of Service) control in TCP/IP. You can, then, say that a particular person should get more bandwidth on Tuesday afternoons when she needs it for videoconferencing. And where is that information stored? In Active Directory.

AD Replaces the Browser

Over the years, Microsoft has gamely tried to support a simple way of browsing the servers on your local network. First called the Browser, then Network Neighborhood, the whole idea was that you could just open up a window and see what was available on your company's network. You'd first see the servers, and then you could drill down into a particular server to see its file and print shares.

The problem with the Browser has always been that Microsoft's networking model grew out of a peer-to-peer paradigm rather than a client-server model. Rather than letting a central server maintain a list of available servers, Microsoft's Browser depended on servers finding each other and electing one of their number to act temporarily as the keeper of the server list. It was a good try, but it never really worked that well.

The Browser still exists in Windows 2000, but it's supplemented by a central list of servers and shared resources maintained on the Active Directory. That list includes the names of servers, the shares available on the system, and the printers available on the system. As more and more Windows 2000-aware applications appear, we'll see AD act more and more as the place to go to find network services.

Understanding and Using Active Directory's Features

NT 4 domain designers had just a few tools: domains, user accounts, machine accounts, groups, and trust relationships. Windows 2000 designers, in contrast, have all of those things and also the extra tools of organizational units, trees, forests, and sites.

In this section, I'll give you an overview of Windows 2000's main enterprise-building tools:

- Domains
- User and machine groups
- Organization units
- Sites
- Trees of domains
- Forests of trees of domains
- Group policies

Domains

The typical way to explain an NT domain is to say that it is "the unit of NT security." That's true, but it's not very illuminating, so let's see what it means.

As you've read earlier in this chapter, every network with any kind of security at all needs to keep a list of information about users—the names, passwords, and other information about people authorized to use the system. In a one-server system, that list sits somewhere on the one server. But when you add a second server, the question arises: how do we tell the *second* server about the users that the *first* server knows about? There are two basic approaches: either duplicate the user list onto the second server, or enable the second server to somehow use the first server's list.

The first option initially sounds like the simpler of the two. Suppose you've got 200 users—you set up the first server, type in 200 names, and the first server now knows about the 200 users. Go to the second server, and either retype the 200 names (ugh, yuck) or just copy the file containing the list of the 200 users to the second server (better, but still not perfect). There are two problems with this. First, not every network operating system lets you copy the file that contains the list of users—in particular, NT 4 did not. You typed names into a file named SAM on one server and you could not just copy that SAM to another server. Assuming you can get past the first problem, a second problem soon appears: password-changing day. Users may not realize that their user accounts appear on two different servers and so they may not know that when they want to change their passwords they must do it in *two* places. And of course things get more complex when you add the third, fourth, and five-hundredth server.

Windows 2000 still uses a SAM. SAM is the name of the file that Windows 2000 machines—servers and workstations—use to store *locally built* and maintained accounts. If you wanted to, you could implement dozens of Windows 2000 servers, *not* create a domain, and only use their local SAMs. I have no idea why you'd want to do that— you'd have to retype usernames and worry about how you'd keep user passwords in sync across all of the servers—but you could choose to do that if you liked.

The better answer for any type of network is not to attempt to maintain dozens or hundreds or thousands of separate parallel user account lists, but rather to build just one list and share it somehow. NT 4 solved the problem with a networked SAM, a single machine with a central SAM.

Windows 2000 still does something very like that, although technically the net-worked file isn't a SAM, it's called NTDS.DIT or, more commonly, the Active Directory.

A relatively small number of machines hold a copy of the NTDS.DIT database file. Other machines needing authentication refer to the NTDS.DIT holders. Through a process called *multimaster replication*, the NTDS.DIT holders ensure that they all have a consistent set of data in their NTDS.DIT.

But "machine that holds a centralized NTDS.DIT" is a bit cumbersome, so let's define a few terms to make this all easier to refer to. Any one of the machines holding a copy of NTDS.DIT is called a *domain controller*, *Active Directory server*, or, sometimes, *logon server*. The group of machines that refer to a set of domain controllers for authentication is col-lectively called a *domain*. So presume that you join Acme, which for the moment we'll say is a one-domain company. Someone "builds your user account," which means that they add a record to the user database describing you and giving you a password. When you try to log onto your workstation, the workstation wants to know who you are so that it can figure out whether or not to let you log on; you respond by telling it your name, password, and the fact that you're from domain acme.com. The workstation then locates an Active Directory server for acme.com and verifies your identity.

As with NT 4, Windows 2000 locates user accounts in a particular domain: *locate* here means "place a record in the Active Directory database." You wouldn't say that a particular user lives in a particular forest or tree—you'd refer to a given user account as being in a domain. NT machines and Windows 2000 machines also have accounts (called machine accounts, not surprisingly) that live in a particular domain. In the last paragraph I said that the group of machines that refer to a set of domain controllers for authentication is called a domain—the machines in that group all have machine accounts in that domain. As you read earlier, Microsoft says that you can put up to 1.5 million user accounts on a domain.

 NOTE That's not a hard limit, however. Some people have experimented with 16 million accounts and have reported good results.

Let's stop and summarize how NT 4 and Windows 2000 store user information:

- Both NT 4 and Windows 2000 will let you create local user accounts, accounts only recognized on the one system upon which they reside. The file that these accounts are stored in is called SAM in both cases.
- NT 4 offered a centralized SAM which would sit on a machine called a domain controller.
- In contrast, when Windows 2000 centralizes a list of users, it doesn't use SAM, it uses a differently structured database file called NTDS.DIT. Just as with NT 4, any Windows 2000 server with a copy of the central user list on it is called a domain controller.

That's basically how domains are structured; now let's look at a great time-saver for managing access to things in a domain—groups.

User (and Now Machine) Groups

Much of a network engineer's job involves using the built-in security features of a network OS to enforce company policy. For example, there might be files on the network that only the managers of the Manufacturing division should see. If people were all trustworthy, then you could just mark a file "Manufacturing managers only, please" and leave it at that. But sadly, they aren't, so Windows 2000, like virtually all network OSes around today, includes the notion of file *permissions*, meaning that you can attach a list to any file or group of files, a list that describes who may access those files and what level of access they should enjoy. So you can protect that Manufacturing-only file by applying permissions to it which restrict its access to Manufacturing managers only.

But how to apply those permissions to just the Manufacturing managers? Well, of course you *could* figure out which of the user accounts belong to those managers, then you could grant access to each of those accounts one at a time. That'd be a lot of work, however, and furthermore, it would *remain* a lot of work, as you'd have to shuffle permissions around every time someone joined or left the ranks of the Manufacturing managers.

A far better answer, and one that Windows 2000 enables, is to create a special kind of account, which is neither a user account nor a machine account, called a *group*. You'd create a group named Manufacturing Managers—any name will do, actually. Then you can choose particular user accounts to add to that group. Finally, you'd modify the file permissions by granting access rights not to a particular user account or accounts, but instead to the group. Anyone in the group would essentially inherit file access by virtue of being a member of the group.

In other words, if Jane, Sue, and Tom are all promoted to Manufacturing manager and you were then directed to give them access to the 10 shares that Manufacturing managers have exclusive access to, then without groups, you'd have to visit each one of those shares, adding the three names to each one. In contrast, with groups, then you would have already visited those shares a long time ago and just told the shares that anyone in the group Manufacturing managers had access to those shares. Having done that in the past, *now* all you have to do is to just add Jane, Sue, and Tom to the Manufacturing managers group, and they instantly get access to the 10 shares.

Both Users and Machines Can Exist in Groups

NT 4 didn't let you put machine accounts into a group, and that was unfortunate, as it would have often been convenient to create groups of machines upon which to apply system policies. Windows 2000 fixes this, and you can now have groups that contain machines, users, or a combination of those two. You cannot, however, apply policies to groups, oddly enough—you apply them to organizational units, covered a bit later, and yes, you can put machines into OUs.

Groups Can Exist inside Groups inside Groups inside Groups...

Sometimes it's convenient to put a group inside a group. For example, every server has a group built into it called Administrators. Anyone in the group is, as you'd guess, treated by that server as an administrator, someone with the power to perform any task on that server. But what if I had a group in the enterprise that I wanted to be able to act as administrators on *every* machine? Well, I *could* walk over to every single machine in the company and add each of those enterprise-wide administrators' names to the local Administrators group of each machine. Yuk. No fun.

It's a bit easier to create a group on some computer somewhere called BigDogs or something like that and make all of the enterprise-wide administrators' user accounts a member of BigDogs. Then I can visit each machine in the company and just add the BigDogs group to each of those machines' Administrators group. Sure, it's still a lot of work, but this way I only have to add *one* thing—the BigDogs group—to each Administrators group, instead of having to add a whole bunch of user accounts to each Administrators group. And if someone gets fired or hired, I need only delete/add a user account to BigDogs, and it'll automatically be recognized as a former or present BigDog.

So putting groups inside groups was something of a convenience for administrators. But Microsoft didn't want to have to worry about what might happen if you put group A inside group B, then put group B inside group C, and then accidentally put group C inside group A; that could be confusing for NT to decode. As a result, Microsoft simplified the groups-inside-groups abilities of NT. In general, they figured that there would be groups like Administrators, which really only describes a specific machine; being a member of Administrators for machine X doesn't mean that you have any power at all on machine Y—you'd have to be a member of machine Y's Administrators group for that. As these groups were really only relevant to their local machines, they were called local groups.

In contrast, groups like BigDogs get created on some machine, but they're not really connected to that machine closely. BigDogs was interesting because it could be placed into the local Administrators group of some other machine. Such groups could, one supposes, be called traveling or export groups, but Microsoft called them *global* groups.

To ensure that you couldn't put a group inside a group, which was inside another group, and so on—the more exact way to say that would be "to ensure that you couldn't *nest* groups in more than one level"—Microsoft designed NT to allow you to put global groups into local groups. As a global could not go into a global, and as a local couldn't go into anything, you could not nest groups beyond one group inside another group. The net effect was one level of nesting—a global goes into a local and that's that.

Windows 2000 extends the notion of groups by increasing the number of group types from two to four and allowing more nesting levels. The old local group has been replaced by two types of local groups: *machine local* groups and *domain local* groups. Global groups work largely as they did before, although they're a bit more flexible. And an entirely new type of group, a *universal* group, lets you do just about anything that you want with it, albeit at a price in performance and compatibility with NT 4. Let's take a look, then, at Windows 2000's four kinds of groups:

- Machine local groups
- Domain local groups
- Domain global groups
- Universal groups

Machine Local Groups   Machine local groups do pretty much what they did before. Every machine has a prebuilt group called Administrators, one named Users, another named Backup Operators that defines a person powerful enough to run the backups but not powerful enough to get into the kind of mischief that a full-fledged administrator could. If you're a member of the Users group, you can log onto that machine and perform basic functions. If you're a member of the Administrators group, you can do anything. There are other groups as well; you can see a machine's machine local groups by right-clicking My Computer, then choosing Manage. An MMC window will appear. In its left-hand panel, open System Tools. Within that, open Local Users and Groups. Within *that*, open Groups. You'll see something like Figure 2.3.

FIGURE 2.3

Machine local groups
for Windows 2000
machine

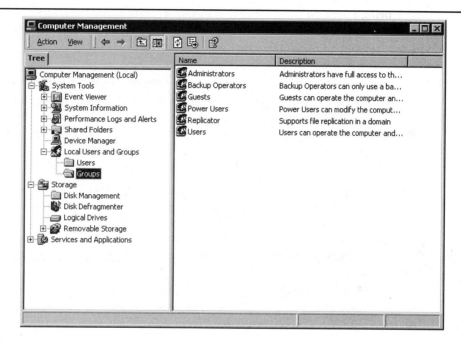

Machine local groups can include global groups, as always. They can also contain:

- Universal, global, or domain local groups from their home domain
- Universal or global groups from any trusted Windows 2000 domain
- Global groups from any trusted NT 4 domain

Domain Local Groups   NT 4 keeps its list of user accounts and groups in a file called SAM, as you've read before. Windows 2000 machines still have SAMs, but only workstations (Windows 2000 Professional) and member servers actually *use* their SAMs.

 NOTE   They won't use them *much*, however. In an NT 4–based network with an NT 4 domain, it never made much sense to create a bunch of user accounts on the local SAM as user accounts built on the domain SAM were more flexible. That's still true for Windows 2000 networks: you'll almost always want to use accounts built in a domain's Active Directory rather than on a local SAM.

Domain controllers, in contrast, don't use SAMs; they keep all of their account information in NTDS.DIT—the Active Directory, recall. But DCs can find use for local groups as well—an Administrators group, Backup Operators group, and so on—and so Active Directory has local groups as well. As they're not implemented in SAMs, however, I guess Microsoft felt that they needed a new name, leading to *domain local groups*.

You don't use the My Computer/Manage sequence to see domain local groups. Instead, you run the MMC snap-in called Active Directory Users and Computers. You'll either find it on the Administrative Tools program menu, or just click Start/Run and fill in **dsa.msc** and press Enter.

 TIP The *dsa* in dsa.msc stands for Directory Services Administrator, its name in Windows 2000 prior to beta 3. You'll still hear people refer to the program as "the DSA," probably because saying "Active Directory Users and Computers" takes *way* too long to say, and ADUC just really doesn't cut it as an acronym.

You'll see your domain name with a plus sign next to it; open it and you'll see several folders. Open up the Users folder and it'll look something like Figure 2.4.

FIGURE 2.4

Groups in an Active Directory folder

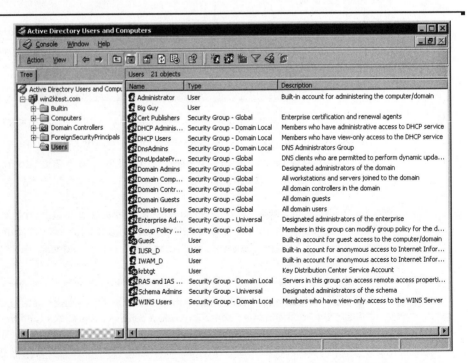

You see all three kinds of groups here—domain locals, globals, and universals. You'd use a domain local group as you'd use a machine local group; they're just on domain controllers. You can put the following things in domain local groups, in addition of course to user accounts:

- Universal, global, and other domain local groups, provided they are from the same domain
- Universal or global groups from any domain in the same forest

Global Groups   I didn't mention it earlier, but NT 4 experts already knew that global groups were a bit more "special" than NT 4 local groups because you could create a global group only on a domain controller. That's still true in Windows 2000; global groups can be created only on a DC. You use global groups as before—a place to collect a bunch of user accounts that you will then place inside some local group. Besides user accounts, the only thing that you can put in a global group is another global group from the same domain.

Universal Groups   If the artificial division between groups that mainly receive other groups and user accounts (local groups) and groups that mainly exist to be placed in other groups (global groups) seems a bit contrived, well, perhaps it is. Why not just have a type of group that can contain other groups (as with a local group) and that can also "travel" to other groups (as with a global)? Windows 2000 has just such a group, called a *universal* group. A universal group can contain *any* global or universal group from *any* domain in the forest.

NOTE   Despite the "universal" name, a universal group *cannot* contain anything from a domain outside of the forest. Forests don't share any security information unless you explicitly create a trust relationship between their domains. And there's no way to make two forests trust each other—you can only make two domains trust each other. So I suppose there *is* a way to make two forests trust each other: just go to each domain in each forest and make that domain trust every domain in every other forest, one domain at a time…. No, on second thought, I don't think so.

The logical question, then, is "Okay, why don't we use universal groups whenever we need groups?" Two reasons: first, you can't create a universal group until all of your domain controllers are Windows 2000 machines (NT 4 machines can be backup domain controllers in a Windows 2000 domain), and second, universal groups have a significant effect on the size—and therefore the responsiveness—of something called the *global catalog*.

Mixed versus Native Mode and Universal Groups   For compatibility's sake, Windows 2000 domains can include NT 4 domain controllers as backup domain controllers. But as NT 4 domain controllers don't have the same abilities as Windows 2000 machines, a Windows 2000 domain that includes NT 4 domain controllers must forgo some of its capabilities. One of those capabilities is the notion of heavily nested groups. As universal groups are the most "nest-able" of Windows 2000 group types, a Windows 2000 domain can't support universal groups until all of its domain controllers are Windows 2000 machines; the last NT 4 domain controller must be shut off.

When first installed, Windows 2000 domains assume that there's at least one NT 4 domain controller around. For safety's sake, then, all new Windows 2000 domains start up in Mixed mode and will not create universal groups.

Once all of your domain controllers are Windows 2000 machines, you can shift your domain to Native mode, which will allow universal groups. You can view your domain's mode by clicking Start/Programs/Administrative Tools/Active Directory Domains and Trusts, or Start/Run and domain.msc. You'll see a list of domains in your forest; right-click the new domain and choose Properties and you'll see something like the Figure 2.5.

FIGURE 2.5

Currently in Mixed mode, can shift to Native mode

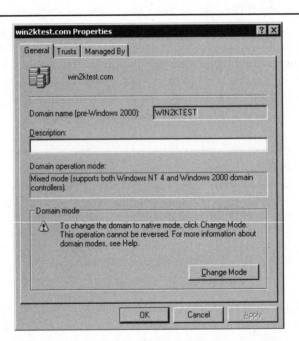

If you click the button to change your domain to Native mode, it'll ask you if you're sure. Once you do and then close domain.msc, you'll see the dialog box in Figure 2.6.

FIGURE 2.6

Finishing up the mode switch

Once all of the DCs in the domain have gotten the message that they should switch over, and after you reboot all of those DCs, your domain will be in Native mode.

 TIP If you're sure that you're never going to incorporate any NT 4 domain controllers, install the first Windows 2000 domain controller in your new Windows 2000 domain and shift it over to Native mode immediately. That way, you don't have to run around rebooting domain controllers and any domain controllers installed after you've shifted to Native mode will automatically be in Native mode.

The Global Catalog and Universal Groups   One reason that you sometimes wouldn't use universal groups is because of their effect on something called the *global catalog*. But what's a global catalog?

As I've hinted so far and as you'll read a bit later, Windows 2000 helps you build big multidomain networks by allowing you to create a multidomain structure called a *tree* or a larger structure called a *forest*. Without stealing the later tree-and-forest section's thunder, let me motivate the global catalog discussion by saying that one of the benefits of having a tree/forest of domains is that anyone from any domain can log onto any workstation from any other domain in the tree/forest. This is great in theory but in practice constitutes a major performance hassle. Suppose we had a forest with 50 domains: every time you wanted to log on to a workstation, that workstation would have no idea which of the 50 domains to query to authenticate your logon. So it would have to search one domain after the other ("hey, do you know a guy named Ralph023?"), and the result could be *extremely* slow logons.

The global catalog solves that problem. It's an abbreviated version of *every domain in the forest*. Clearly this could get to be pretty big, but the global catalog remains manageable in size because it only contains a small subset of information from the Active Directory: what users each domain includes and what domain they're from is one of those pieces of information. (There's another value here as well, but I'll cover it later when I discuss forests and trees.)

Another piece of information stored in the GC is the name of each global group in each domain in the forest. That wouldn't constitute too much space and wouldn't make the global catalog grow too much. But universal groups are a completely different story: the global catalog not only knows all of their names, it also knows what users are members of each universal group! As a result, heavy use of universal groups could considerably slow down network logons—so it's a good idea to use universals sparingly.

In case you're wondering, there is not, as far as I know, any tool that lets you directly browse or examine the global catalog—although some search operations use it.

Group Size Is Limited to 5,000 Members

Groups can also contain groups, as you'll see later in this chapter, and that turns out to be useful. For some reason, groups cannot contain more than 5,000 members, meaning that if you need a group with more than 5,000 members, you'll have to create a number of groups, each with under 5,000 members, and then place *those* groups into a single "super" group, then apply whatever permissions you want to that "super" group. Yes, it's a pain, but it's probably one of those things they've left undone so we'll have a reason to buy NT 6.

Thus far, we've seen domains, which are a way of defining a collection of users and machines which share the same security rules, and groups, which make managing access to servers easier. Next, let's see how to subdivide a domain, with organizational units.

Organizational Units (OUs)

Sometimes a domain is too large an area to cede control of. For example, suppose you've got to hire some people to act as backup operators, and suppose that your domain is spread out geographically. You might not want someone who can get to your system from a St. Louis machine to be able to waltz into the San Francisco office and log into one of those machines. You'd like such people to have backup operator power, but not over the entire network—just over a subset of the network.

Or perhaps you need a staff of people who can reset passwords, or manage printers, or adjust permissions on a set of servers. But you don't want those folks to have those powers over the entire domain. That could be true for either geographic reasons (St. Louis and San Francisco) or organizational reasons (e.g., the marketing department might want their own password-changer person).

The answer in each case is to subdivide the domain into organizational units, or OUs.

Organizational Units Are Folders

OUs look like folders when viewed with Windows 2000's administrative tools. When you create a user account in a Windows 2000 domain, you can choose to either create the account right in the domain or create it inside one of the folder-like things that you'll see in that domain. When you first create a Windows 2000 domain, you'll automatically get a folder named Users and another named Computers. While it may *seem* that user accounts should go into the Users folder and machine accounts should go in the Computers folder, that's not the case at all. (That'd be too obvious.) Instead, the only real reason for the Users and Computers folders—which are essentially organizational units, even though Microsoft doesn't call them that—is so that Windows 2000 has a place to put any user accounts and machine accounts from an upgraded NT 4 domain. The folders are also useful because, if you use some third-party tool to create user accounts and the tool was built for NT 4, then Windows 2000 will sense that and put any user accounts the tool creates into the Users folder.

What You Can Do with OUs

OUs have three main uses. You can:

- create sets of users with different account policies so, for example, you can give them more or less stringent password requirements.

- give control of a set of user and/or machine accounts to a set of users, allowing you to, for example, define a set of people who can reset passwords in a particular department without having to make them administrators of greater power than might be desirable and furthermore restricting the range of people whose passwords they can change to a small set of users.

- control and lock down user desktops through the use of *group policy objects*, control tools like NT 4's system policies; despite their name, however, group policies aren't applied to user groups—they apply to organizational units, domains, or sites.

Using OUs for Special Account Policies   Under NT 4, you could set account policies—things like how often users must change their passwords, whether or not to lock out users who've entered too many incorrect passwords, and how long "too many" is, to offer just a few examples—but you could only set them on a domainwide basis. In contrast, suppose you've got a group of enterprise-wide administrators, people with accounts that could do a great deal of damage if compromised. You might want to make those folks change their passwords pretty frequently, perhaps as often as every other week. But under NT 4, you'd have to force *all* domain users to change their passwords every other week if you wanted to force the enterprise administrators to change their passwords every other week: there wasn't a way to offer different rules for different groups of people. With Windows 2000, in contrast, you need only create an OU named Eadmins or something like that, and another OU called Everyone Else. Then create the admins' user accounts in Eadmins and everyone else's in, well, Everyone Else. You can also move accounts around, so if someone's status changes between admin and non-admin, just a click and drag or two will make the change.

Using OUs to Create Sub-Administrators   Or suppose the Graphics department has a bunch of expensive printers shared on the network. They don't want the regular IS people controlling the printers for some reason; they want their local techies to serve as the printer admins. In that case, you could create an OU called graphics printers or the like and put the fancy printers into that OU. Then you can give control of that OU and, in the process, of the printers in the OU to a particular user account or perhaps a group containing the names of the admins that Graphics likes.

 NOTE   The process of giving a user or group of users control of an OU is called *delegating control* of that OU. Right-click the OU and you can run the Delegation Wizard to make that adjustment.

If the International Trade and Arbitrage department's VP insists on a separate set of administrators for her servers, OUs can meet her needs. Again, just create a separate OU for her servers, a group for her admins, and delegate control of the OU to the group.

You'll see an example of delegation later in this chapter.

Multiple Domains versus OUs: When Each Makes Sense

Notice in each case cited here that you could *also* accomplish those same ends with multiple domains. International Trade could be their own domain with their own administrators and trust relationships to the rest of the firm. Ditto Graphics. In the first case, all of the administrators could be lumped into a domain off by themselves, and indeed that's been done many times with NT 4—and could still be done for Windows 2000.

When, then, should you use one domain divided into OUs, and when should you have different domains? There are a few reasons:

Replication problems due to poor bandwidth   Probably the best reason. All domain controllers in a domain really need to be online to each other all of the time. If one office is in Timbuktu and the other's in McMurdo Base and they don't really share much save for very limited WAN support, make them separate domains.

Politics   Same as it ever was.

We just found it this way, honest!   Your firm buys another firm and you've got to blend the two organizations. There are probably third-party tools around that will help assimilate the new domain into your existing domain, but that'll be a big undertaking and maybe you don't have the time to do that just at the moment. In that case, you're living in a multidomain world for a while.

I know I've said it already, but let me weigh in again with my opinion about multiple domains, or rather, why I'd avoid them. First of all, NT 4 multiple domain enterprises were a major pain, as trusts tended to break. Supposedly this won't happen under Windows 2000 and thus far I haven't seen it, but in general, the fewer "moving parts" in my enterprise, the better. Additionally, NT has had its growing pains over the years about security. What if the next "NT security hole" appears in Windows 2000 trusts?

And then there's the issue of bugs in general: I'd prefer to work with the parts of Windows 2000 that have been tested most thoroughly. For example, my personal experience with multiple processor machines running NT is that they're more fragile and a bit more crash-prone. I can't prove it, but my guess is that, if Microsoft's got 200 people on campus testing Windows 2000, the majority of them have a single-processor machine on their desks. Isn't it logical to assume then that NT has been better tested on single-processor machines than multiprocessor machines? For the same reason, ask yourself: of all of the people beta-testing Windows 2000 (or Windows 2000 Service Pack 1 or Windows 2000 Service Pack 2 or whatever), do you think most of them tested it in a single-domain or multidomain environment? My guess is the former— which would imply that it's the better way to go for reliability. Understand, however, that these are just guesses on my part.

OUs versus Groups

So far, I've described two kinds of things that hold other things—that is, I've described something called a *group*, which can contain users and/or machines, and I've described something *else* called an organizational unit, which *also* can contain users and/or machines.

So... what's the difference? Well, in an oversimplified sense, you put the things that you want to control into an OU. Then you grant that control to a group. If you wanted to, for example, create a sub-group of an enterprise like a department and then designate a group of people who could act as administrators to that department, then the department would be an OU and the desired administrators would be a group. You'd then delegate authority for the OU to the group. But here's some more detail.

A user account can only be in one OU, but it can be a *member* of as many groups as you like. A user account or machine account exists in only one domain in a general sense, but the account may also live in an OU *inside* that domain, much as you or I can live inside some city in a state, but we each live in only one city. In contrast, no matter which city you live in, you can be a member of as many associations—groups—that you like.

You can use groups to assign permissions—you can, for example, deny access to a file to anyone in a given group. Windows 2000 won't let you do any permission work with OUs; you can't deny access to a printer or a file share to an entire OU.

In contrast, you can use OUs to designate a collection of users who must change their passwords more frequently or less frequently than other users. You can't do that with a group. You can apply a group policy (for example, roll out an application) to a particular OU, not to a group.

OUs let you define *logical* divisions in a domain. But knowing about the *physical* subdivisions is important as well: I might not want to transfer that half-gigabyte file to server DISTRIBUTE01 if I knew that it's only connected to the rest of the domain with a 56K link. That's where sites come in handy.

Sites

As you read earlier in this chapter, one of NT 4's weaknesses was the fact that domain controllers replicate data amongst themselves in a very "chatty," bandwidth-intensive way. That's not a problem for domain controllers on the same LAN, as there's typically bandwidth to burn on a LAN, but WAN links are nothing to toss away lightly.

Windows 2000 improves upon that with the notion of *sites*. In addition to knowing about machines and users in an enterprise, AD also keeps track of the geographic aspects of an enterprise. Each LAN-connected area is called a *site*. Windows 2000 uses the insights that you give it about your physical layout to figure out where the WAN links—the slower and more expensive part of your network—are. It then does two very helpful things: first, it compresses the replication traffic (again, by a factor of *10*, quite impressive!), and second, it uses route costing information that you supply to figure out how best to route the replication traffic at lowest cost.

By the way, if you've got experience with Exchange, then all of this will sound somewhat familiar, and it should—Exchange first pioneered the idea of sites several years ago.

At this point, you've met domains, groups, organizational units, and sites. Next, let's meet two ways of organizing *collections* of domains: trees and forests.

Trees of Domains

Real-world experience with NT from version 3.1 through 4.0 showed that people needing multiple-domain enterprises tended to build *hierarchies* of domains, what computer people call "tree structures" despite the fact that computer trees tend to have their roots up top in the air and their "leaves" at bottom. Microsoft designed Windows 2000 to use DNS as a naming system, and DNS is hierarchical in nature anyway, so Windows 2000 exploits this happy coincidence and encourages you to build multidomain enterprises as hierarchies.

 NOTE Hierarchies of names are sometimes alternatively called *namespaces*. Thus, if Acme is divided into acme.com, westcoast.acme.com, and eastcoast.acme.com, then you might hear the Acme managers refer to the "Acme namespace" or perhaps "Acme's Active Directory namespace." All *namespace* means here is "the system that we use to choose names that make some kind of sense."

The first Windows 2000 domain that you create is called the *root* of the tree. Suppose, following the earlier example, that the root's name is acme.com. Domains below it are referred to as *child domains*, as you've read. You can decide to divide your organization geographically—for example, eastcoast.acme.com and westcoast.acme .com—or organizationally, as perhaps manufacturing.acme.com, finance.acme.com, and sales.acme.com. You can then create another level if you choose—perhaps sales .ecoast.acme.com, manufacturing.ecoast.acme.com, finance.acme.com and sales .wcoast.acme.com, manufacturing.wcoast.acme.com and finance.wcoast.acme.com (six domains!)—and another and another, to create as complex a system as you want. Windows 2000 helps you by creating trust relationships between each domain and its child domains. For example, merely creating wcoast.acme.com automatically creates a two-way trust relationship between wcoast.acme.com and acme.com. This two-way trust means that acme.com administrators may choose to extend file and print permissions to finance.acme.com users and vice versa.

Additionally, under Windows 2000, trust relationships are *transitive*. Creating finance.wcoast.acme.com creates a two-way trust relationship between finance.wcoast .acme.com and wcoast.acme.com, but it doesn't stop there: because wcoast.acme.com and acme.com *also* have a two-way trust, finance.wcoast.acme.com ends up with an automatic trust relationship with acme.com. (If that doesn't sound interesting, then you didn't work with NT 4 and earlier versions, which required you to hand-build every single trust relationship.)

Forests of Domains

Domain trees, then, offer the benefits of automatic trust relationships, a very good thing. But there's just one minor problem with that—all of the domain names must fit into a nice hierarchy.

Forest Basics

Suppose in contrast that your enterprise divides into acme.com and apex.com, two former rivals that have merged. Suppose further you've decided to go with a multiple-domain enterprise and want to keep some of your firm as acme.com and some as apex.com.

It looks like two things are true, then: first, you're probably going to have two domains, and second, those two domains won't fit into a tree.

 NOTE "Probably", by the way, because even though all of this Active Directory naming *looks* like a DNS structure, and even uses DNS servers to keep track of all of the names, those machine names need not be the actual presented-to-the-Internet DNS names, as you'll see in the later chapter on DNS. That means that if you don't mind doing a fair amount of work, then you can build a single domain with an Active Directory name like ourfirm.com but set up that domain's DNS names so that the outside world sees some of the machines as having names ending in acme.com and others ending with apex.com.

You can choose to blend these two Windows 2000 domains into a structure, but it can't be a tree because of their dissimilar names. Instead, you can choose to create a *forest*. A forest is just a group of trees, as you see in Figure 2.7.

Here, you see a forest built from the acme.com and apex.com trees. Windows 2000 requires that one domain be the forest root domain; in this case, I've drawn acme.com as the forest root. The decision about which domain is the root is simple—the first one created is the root.

FIGURE 2.7

*Example Active
Directory forest*

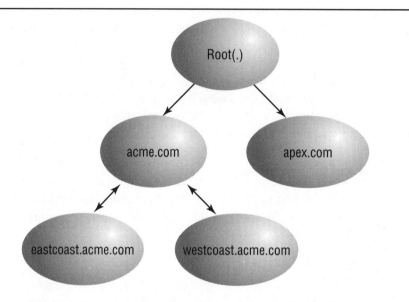

Other than different naming hierarchies, the trees in the forest act like one tree in terms of their trust relationships—Windows 2000 builds transitive trusts automatically.

The Bad News

This sounds great, and of course it's a terrific improvement over NT 4. But hidden in this potentially rich notion of many domains joined into a tree and, as you'll read in the next section, many trees joined into a forest is a dirty little secret.

 WARNING   You cannot join already-existing domains into a tree. Nor can you join already-existing trees into a forest. The only way to add a domain to a tree, or a tree to a forest, is to build it from scratch onto an existing tree or forest.

Attaching existing domains to existing trees or forests is called *pruning and grafting* and it can't be done, at least not with the tools supplied by Windows 2000. Thus, for example, if Exxon buys Mobil, and Exxon already has a domain named exxon.com and Mobil's got a domain named mobil.com, it's not possible to join them together in a tree with the supplied Windows 2000 tools.

With domains, groups, organizational units, sites, trees, and forests covered, we're almost done with our overview of Active Directory tools. But I saved the best for last—"best," that is, if you hanker for power and control—and so let's finish up this section with an explanation of group policies.

Group Policy Overview

I've talked so far in mildly vague terms about how you can accomplish different kinds of control in an Active Directory. The specific tool for exerting much of that control is group policies, the successor to NT 4's system policies. Here's an overview of what they do and how they work.

Differences in System Policy and Group Policy Implementation

With NT 4's system policies, you could control a wide variety of things—you could give a user a particular Start/Programs menu, give him a particular look to a desktop, restrict the user from running many programs, and the like. All of these restrictions would be collected into a single file called NTCONFIG.POL, which you'd then place on each of the domain controller's NETLOGON shares. You can't have more than one NT 4 policy file.

In contrast, with Windows 2000 there is no tangible and separate file for policies. Instead, Windows 2000 stores the policy information in the Active Directory. You put this information into the AD in the form of *group policy objects*, or GPOs. You can put as many or as few particular policies into a given GPO as you like. For example, suppose you wanted to accomplish three things with policies:

- You want everyone to be able to change the system time on their workstations. (By default, normal users can't modify the time on their Windows 2000 workstations.)
- You want everyone's My Documents folder to be stored on the network rather than (as is default) on the local hard disk so that everyone's documents can be centrally backed up.
- You want to deploy Word 2000 to everyone from a central server.

I've simplified this by saying that I want these things to happen to *everyone*; you'll see later how to restrict these policies to a smaller set of users. In any case, the point I was trying to make about GPOs is this: you could create a single GPO and include all three of these policies in it, then apply that one GPO to everyone. Or you could create three separate GPOs, put only one policy in each, and then apply each of the three policies to everyone, or any in-between option—one GPO with two of the policies and another with the remaining policy, with both GPOs applied to everyone, would once more produce the same effect.

Well then, it's reasonable to ask, why *would* you create multiple GPOs or separate GPOs? The fewer the GPOs, the faster the logins. Every time a user goes to log in, the

Active Directory must scan all of its GPOs to see which of those GPOs applies to that user. On the other hand, you might create different GPOs if you wanted to apply different policies to different people—if you wanted the folks in one OU to be able to change their workstation times but wanted a different OU's My Documents folder on the network, then you'd create one GPO that allowed users to change their workstation time and apply that GPO to the first OU, and you'd create a different GPO moving My Documents to the network and then you'd apply that to the second OU.

Group Policies Apply to Sites, Domains, and OUs—Not Groups (Mostly)

Why did I use OUs in my previous example rather than groups? Because oddly enough, *group* policy objects don't apply to groups—they can apply either to sites (which would let you exert control over all machines in a particular site), domains, or OUs. You can't directly say, "Everyone in the ACCOUNTANTS group gets QuickBooks 2002 deployed to their desktop." Now, if ACCOUNTANTS were an OU rather than a group, then you *could* deploy QuickBooks 2002 to all of the accountants. (As I write this, there isn't a QuickBooks 2002, but I'm guessing that by 2002 Intuit will have a Windows 2000–compliant version of their bookkeeping software.)

Is it *completely* impossible to apply a policy to a group, then? Well, not exactly....

Policy Filtering and Group Policies

What I said in the preceding section wasn't completely true—you *could* deploy an application to a group. But how you do it is a bit sneaky.

As you've read, Windows 2000 lets you apply policies to sites, domains, and/or organizational units. Microsoft even has an acronym for those three—SDOU. But you can use someone's group membership to influence whether or not he gets the effect of a particular policy.

I've already said that GPOs are not files, but they share one thing with files—they have permissions associated with them. And you can apply permissions to groups. One of the permissions associated with GPOs is Apply Group Policy; if this permission isn't granted, then the policy doesn't apply.

To apply a policy to just the ACCOUNTANTS group, then, we'd apply a policy to the entire domain, but then we'd set permissions for the Domain Users group so that Apply Group Policy was not allowed, and then we'd add a separate permission for just the Accountants group, allowing them to apply the group policy.

Policy filtering is a bit troublesome for two reasons. First, it can greatly complicate trying to figure out what someone else did when setting up policies: if you were to walk into an already-configured enterprise without any documentation and try to figure out what policies are supposed to do for that enterprise, you'd have your work cut out for you. As a matter of fact, there's an acronym relevant to that: RSOP, which stands for Resultant Set Of Policy. To see what it means, consider the following question. I've got a new user, Bob, in a given organizational unit, which is in a particular domain, and Bob's machine is in a particular site. That means that the site may have policies that apply to Bob, the domain may have policies that apply to Bob, and the OU may have policies that apply to Bob. And don't forget that OUs can live inside OUs, so there might be an entire hierarchy of OUs that Bob lives in—each of *those* OUs could have policies attached to them. And on top of it all, policy filtering may affect whether or not all of those policies apply to Bob. The question is, which policies apply to Bob? It's not an easy question—you've got to thread through which policies apply, the order in which they apply—a later policy generally overrides an earlier policy, although it can be configured differently—and then policy filtering's got to be taken into account. Determining the set of policies that actually affect Bob—his RSOP—is a difficult computational task, and you'll see a class of applications called *RSOP modelers* whose job is to do that very thing.

The second concern about policy filtering is that it slows down the process of applying GPOs to a user when logging in, which slows down the login process.

Group Policies Only Apply to Windows 2000 Machines

While group policies are great, they're similar to so many of Windows 2000's best-sounding features—they only work on Windows 2000 machines. If your users are still running Windows 95 or 98, you can only use system policies to control their desktops; if they're running NT 4, you'll have to use NT system policies to control their desktops.

Group Policies Undo Themselves When Removed

One of the troublesome things about NT 4's system policies is that once a system policy is applied to a user account or a machine, the policy remains in place even if it is removed from the domain controllers. So, for example, if for some reason you'd created a system policy to set everyone's background color to green, then the Registry of every computer that logs on from that point on will be changed to set the background to green. If enough users screamed about this and you removed the policy, their screens would remain green. They could certainly *change* the color themselves, but it'd be nice if the policy had undone itself on the way out. With Windows 2000, that happens: remove a policy and its effects are reversed. This can be quite powerful: for example, if you've used a group policy to deploy an application and then remove the policy, the application uninstalls itself!

You Needn't Log On to Get a Group Policy

NT 4 only applied system policies at start-up (for machine policies) and logon (for user policies). In contrast, Windows 2000 applies group policies every 90 minutes or so for workstations and member servers and every five minutes for domain controllers.

What You Can Do with Group Policies

You can do basically anything with group policies that you could do with system policies, and lots more. Here are a few examples:

Deploy software   You can gather all of the files necessary to install a piece of software into a *package*, put that package on a server somewhere, and then use group policies to point a user's desktop at that package. The user sees that the application is available, and again, you accomplish all that from a central location rather than having to visit every desktop. The first time the user tries to start the application, it installs without any intervention from the user.

Set user rights   You may know from NT 3.*x* and 4.*x* that NT had the notion of "rights," the ability to do a particular function. One such example is the one I've already used about a standard user not being able to change his or her workstation's time and date. Under NT 4, you had to visit a machine to modify user rights; now it's controllable via a GPO, meaning again that you needn't wear out any shoe leather to change a distant machine's rights.

Restrict the applications that users can run   You can control a user's desktop to the point where that user could only run a few applications—perhaps Outlook, Word, and Internet Explorer, for example.

Control settings on Windows 2000 systems   The easiest way to control disk space quotas is with group policies. Many Windows 2000 systems are most easily controlled with policies; with some systems, policies are the *only* method to enable and control those systems.

Set logon, logoff, start-up, and shutdown scripts   Where NT 4 only supported logon scripts, Windows 2000 allows any or all of these four events to trigger a script, and you use GPOs to control which scripts run.

Simplify and restrict programs   You can use GPOs to remove many of the features from Internet Explorer, Windows Explorer, and other programs using GPOs.

General desktop restriction   You can remove most or all of the items on a user's Start button, keep her from adding printers, disallow her from logging off or modifying her desktop configuration at all. With all of the policies turned on, you can really lock down a user's desktop. (Too much locking down may lead to unlocking the automatic rifles, however, so be careful.)

That's the overview of what Active Directory is supposed to do; now let's play around with it a bit.

Logons Under Active Directory

All of the machinery that Active Directory includes enables Windows 2000 to be a bit smarter about logons than NT 4 was. Here's a brief look at how AD uses sites and DNS to log on machines and users.

When you start your Windows 2000 desktop machine up, it must log onto your Windows 2000 domain—machines log on as well as people, or at least machines running Windows 2000 or NT must log on—Windows 9x systems don't.

The hard part about logons is in finding a domain controller. Once your system's found a DC, then transacting all of the Kerberos back-and-forth stuff about checking your password and user ID (or your machine's password and user ID) is very simple. The problem is finding a machine to *present* these credentials to.

In its most basic form, a machine finds a domain controller by asking DNS, "I'm a member of the win2ktest.com domain. Do you know of any machines in that domain which are registered as servers using port 389?" "Port 389" is Internet-ese for "LDAP server," and machines communicate with domain controllers using LDAP. Therefore, asking for an LDAP server is the same as asking for a domain controller.

But actually DNS servers under Windows 2000 are even smarter than that, as they not only have a list of LDAP servers for a given domain, they also have a list of sites for that domain *and* a list of LDAP servers broken down by site. Thus, a machine can say to DNS, "Give me the name of a domain controller in the downtown site and the win2ktest.com domain." Now, not every site may *have* a domain controller. In that case, DNS just hands the system the address of any old domain controller.

Once the client machine has a DC's address, it opens communications with the DC. Part of the DC's job, however, is to make sure that the client is talking with a close-by DC if at all possible. That's necessary because a laptop may have been installed at the Nome site but has been carried to the Miami site. The laptop queries DNS for a Nome DC, and DNS gives the laptop the address of a Nome DC. When the laptop starts logging in via the Nome DC, however, the Nome DC notices that the laptop has an IP address (which the laptop got from a local DHCP server in Miami) that indicates that it's in Miami. The Nome DC then looks that address up in the Active Directory and deduces that the laptop is currently in Miami. The DC then queries DNS for the name of a DC in Miami, or at least close to Miami, and then tells the laptop to instead log on with that closer machine rather than communicating all of the way up to Nome.

Summarized, then, Windows 2000 systems find domain controllers by first using their knowledge of their site locations and domain names to query DNS for the names of nearby domain controllers. The machines then contact the nearby domain controllers and ask them to log them on. The DC that agrees to log them on first checks that it is the closest DC available, and if it is *not*, then it redirects the machine to a closer DC.

You can find out which server logged you on by opening up a command prompt and typing **SET**. One of the pieces of information that you'll get is a line starting with "LOGONSERVER=;" to the right of the equals sign is the name of the DC that logged you on.

Building an Active Directory: Some Hands-On Experience

While I'm trying more to pass along an overall understanding of Active Directory than I am trying to explain the click-by-click stuff in this chapter, it's probably a good idea to provide an example at this point. Let's build a small tree of domains to get a feel for what the Active Directory process looks like. In this tree, I'll create two domains: one called win2ktest.com and another, child domain called div2.win2ktest.com. As I'll want an account that can act as an administrator across the whole tree, I'll also create a user named bigguy with those powers.

If you want to do something like this, you'll need two machines because, under Windows 2000, a single machine can only be a domain controller for one domain; two domains, therefore, would require two machines—more, in fact, if you wanted to start adding replica DCs or member servers.

Building the First Domain

One of the really nice things about Windows 2000 is that Microsoft separated the process of installing Windows 2000 from the process of creating a domain controller. You can do a fairly vanilla installation of Windows 2000 Server (or have an equipment supplier preinstall Windows 2000 Server, as companies like Dell do) without having to worry about two of NT 4's biggest pains—that you needed to designate a machine as a domain controller during Setup, and that you couldn't install a backup domain controller unless your computer was connected live on the LAN to the domain's PDC. So you can start this process from pretty much any machine running Windows 2000 Server. But before you do, consider four caveats: memory, DNS, NTFS, and disks.

Before You Start

The memory part is easy. As far as I can see, any Windows 2000 domain controller uses *at least* 136MB of memory. You don't *need* to have 136MB of actual RAM in a machine before using it as a Windows 2000 domain controller, but if you *don't* have at least that much, be prepared for nearly constant disk activity as Windows 2000 pages pieces of itself on and off disk. It's a matter of taste, but I found all of that disk chattering extremely annoying and so I upgraded my machines to 256MB of RAM—thank heavens memory's finally dropped in price!

The second caveat is about DNS. As I've said, I'm going to build this example around a domain called win2ktest.com. I'm able to do that because I've registered that domain name with the Internet authorities. If *you* try to create a domain named win2ktest.com on a machine connected live to the Internet, then you'll get an error message, as the DNS code on your test machine will go out to the InterNIC (the folks who maintain most of the worldwide DNS root servers) and be told that no, you may *not* establish a domain named win2ktest.com as someone else has already done that. You can do two things to avoid this problem: first, you can try this out on a network *not* connected to the Internet, a network whose DNS servers do not communicate with the InterNIC's servers, and second, you can just make up some other name like aaaaabbbbbcccc.com and use that instead of win2ktest.com.

The third consideration is relatively easy. Active Directory servers *need* an NTFS partition, so before trying to make a server a domain controller, be sure that it's got at least one NTFS partition.

Finally, you'll get better performance out of your Active Directory servers if you can put at least two physical hard disks in the servers. It wouldn't hurt for one of those to be SCSI either. You'll see exactly why a bit later.

Of course, none of this is a problem if all you're going to do is just read the text and follow along with the screen shots.

Running DCPROMO

To convert a Windows 2000 server to a domain controller—it must be a server, you can't make a Professional machine a DC—click Start/Run and then type in **DCPROMO**. That starts the Active Directory Installation Wizard, as you see in Figure 2.8.

You use this not only to convert member servers into domain controllers, but the reverse as well, to "demote" a domain controller to a member server. The wizard asks a series of questions and then, based on the answers to those questions, sets up a new tree, forest, or domain or creates a replica domain controller in an existing domain. Click Next and you'll see a screen like Figure 2.9.

The way that you create a new domain is simple: set up a machine as the first domain controller for that domain. Building a domain's first domain controller and creating a new domain are exactly the same thing. But you wouldn't have just one domain controller for most domains. For one thing, each site within a multisite domain will usually have at least one DC, to enable logins. Another reason you'd have multiple DCs on a single domain—whether single or multiple site—is to handle many login requests. As you know, login requests don't space themselves out nicely throughout the day. Instead, most login requests happen all around the same time, first thing in the morning. The more DCs, the more logins your domain can handle. The second, third, fourth, and so on domain controllers in a domain were called *backup* domain controllers under NT prior to Windows 2000, but Windows 2000 calls them *replica* domain controllers.

FIGURE 2.8

Starting DCPROMO

FIGURE 2.9

Choosing whether or not to create a new domain

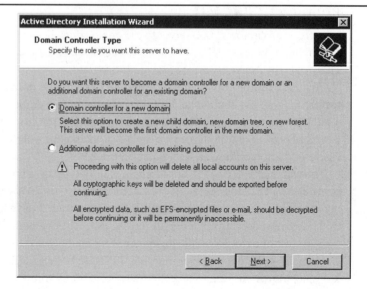

TIP So would it be a good idea to make all of your Windows 2000 servers into domain controllers, to speed logons? No. Making a server a DC takes up memory and CPU power. Additionally, too many DCs means extra LAN chatter as they keep each other updated on changes to the Active Directory. The warning at the bottom of the screen is trying to say that non-DCs have a SAM with local accounts, and DCs instead have an NTDS.DLT. DCPROMO deletes a computer's SAM contents when the computer becomes a DC.

The first question that DCPROMO asks, then, is whether to create a whole new domain or a replica DC in an existing domain. We're creating a new domain, so I select that and click Next. That leads to the screen in Figure 2.10.

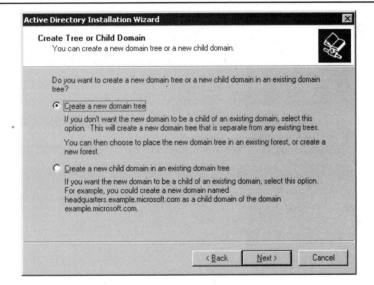

This is the first domain in a new tree, so I choose that and click Next. The screen then looks like Figure 2.11.

Recall that Windows 2000 lets you build domains into trees and trees into forests, so logically the Active Directory Installation Wizard must know where to put this new tree—in an altogether new forest or in an existing forest? Again, this is a new forest, and I select that and choose Next, leading to a screen like Figure 2.12.

Sometimes these wizards are a bit chatty; here's an example. Just type in the name of the new domain, which in this case is win2ktest.com. Clicking Next leads to the screen in Figure 2.13.

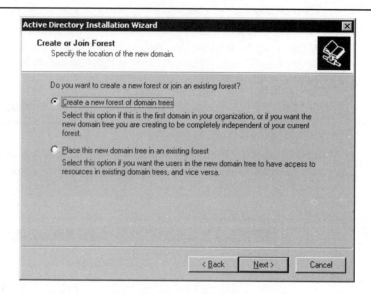

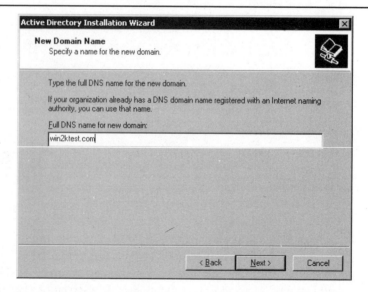

Unless your network is 100-percent Windows 2000, both servers and workstations, then your network contains machines running network software written in the NT 3.*x* and 4.*x* days, when domain names could be no more than 15 characters long and could not have a hierarchy of any kind. Those older systems—and you know, I tend to want to call them "legacy" systems, as that's been the *chic* term for old software for about 10 years now, but it seems that the current Microsoft term is "downlevel" systems—wouldn't understand a domain named win2ktest.com, and so they need a more familiar name. For that reason, Windows 2000 domains have two names—their DNS-like name (e.g., win2ktest.com) and an old-style domain name (which can be anything that you want, but win2ktest seems like a good choice). As network names under NT 3.*x* and 4.*x* were chosen to accommodate an old network programming interface called NetBIOS, this old-style domain name is also called a NetBIOS name. The wizard will by default offer the text to the left of the leftmost period, so it here offers the NetBIOS name WIN2KTEST, which is fine. I click Next and the screen in Figure 2.14 appears.

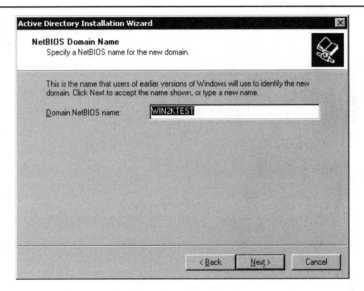

FIGURE 2.13

Legacy domain name

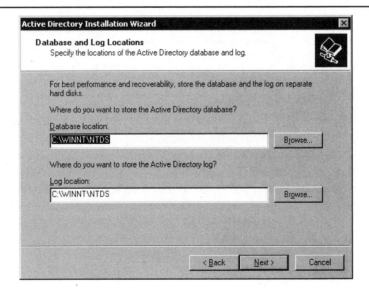

FIGURE 2.14

Placing system files

Windows 2000 stores the Active Directory database in two parts, as is often the case for databases—the database itself and a transaction log. Two things to bear in mind here are that the actual Active Directory database file should be on an NTFS volume for better performance and that it's a good idea to put the transaction log on a different physical hard disk than the Active Directory database. (You see them on the same drive in the screen shot because the machine I was doing this on had only one physical hard disk.) Putting the transaction log on a different physical drive means that the system can update both the AD database and the log simultaneously, and believe me, in a production environment, you'll see a significant difference in performance by using a two-drive system rather than a one-drive system. But we're not finished with drives yet; click Next and you'll see why, in Figure 2.15.

FIGURE 2.15

*Placing the SYSVOL
volume*

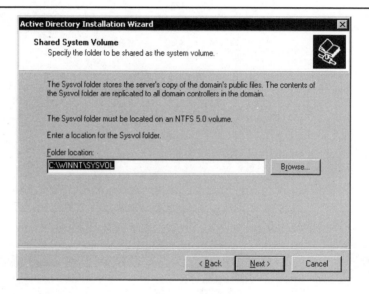

Remember the caution earlier on that you need at least one NTFS drive on an Active Directory server? This is where you'll use it. Anyone who's ever set up an NT 4 domain controller will soon realize how cool this is. You see, NT 4 stored a lot of important user configuration and control information in a directory named NETLOGON on the primary domain controller—system policy files, default profiles, and login scripts. But *backup* domain controllers needed the NETLOGON information as well, so network administrators had to somehow ensure that all of the files from the PDC's NETLOGON would somehow get copied to the BDC's NETLOGONs. With Windows 2000, however, that's not a problem: all of that data goes into a directory called the Sysvol directory, which is *automatically* replicated to other domain controllers. It's an excellent labor saver and a hidden "plus" for Windows 2000! I click Next, and it's time to start worrying about DNS, as you see in Figure 2.16.

Here, DCPROMO has tried to find and contact the DNS server for win2ktest.com. Some trouble occurred along the way, leading to this warning message. This message means one of two things:

- **DCPROMO didn't get a response from any of the DNS servers for win2ktest.com.** In the particular case of win2ktest.com, I registered it with the InterNIC, as I mentioned earlier. (You can read more about how that works in Chapters 17 and 18.) In order to register a domain with the InterNIC, you've got to tell that organization the IP addresses of two machines which will serve as DNS servers for the domain. I told it that the primary DNS server would be on this *particular* machine, and as I'm still in the process of setting it up, there's not a DNS server running—hence this error message. By the way, I could have averted this message by first setting up the DNS server service and the win2ktest.com DNS domain on this machine before running DCPROMO. You'll see how to set up a DNS server in Chapter 18. By the way, you'll also get this message even if you're not connected to the Internet—DCPROMO needs to find the address of the DNS server for your new domain, whether it's from a bunch of private DNS servers or from the worldwide DNS system of servers.

- **DCPROMO *got* a response from the DNS servers for win2ktest.com, but found that they didn't accept dynamic updates.** Suppose I'd already set up a machine as the DNS server, but the machine was an NT 4 server. The DNS service that shipped with NT 4 didn't include support for RFC 2136, probably because NT 4 shipped *before* RFC 2136 was released. RFC 2136 supports the idea of *dynamic updates*, which are very important to the way that Windows 2000 maintains information about domains and other Windows 2000 services.

Why are dynamic updates so important? Well, DNS is just a database of address information. The vast majority of records in the world's DNS databases are just simple A records, entries that relate machine names to IP addresses, as in "the machine named bass.fishing-geeks.com is located at 209.111.75.13." So when people add new machines to the Internet (or a corporate intranet), A records for those machines must somehow be entered into some DNS server. Throughout most of the time that we've had DNS in the Internet, those entries have been "static" in the sense that someone had to sit down at a computer and type them in, oftentimes to a simple ASCII file; it was also static in that many DNS server implementations required that you turn them on and then off in order to get them to reread those ASCII files and incorporate the new records. But Active Directory wants to be able to add new data to its domains' DNS databases on a regular basis, without the need to restart DNS all the time. That's where dynamic updates come in—RFC 2136 specifies a protocol for adding, modifying, and deleting DNS records on-the-fly. Active Directory relies upon this heavily and so *must* have RFC 2136–compliant DNS servers for its domains. As a result, once DCPROMO finds a domain's DNS server, the first thing that DCPROMO does is to ask it, "Do you accept dynamic updates?" If it doesn't, then DCPROMO can't go any further.

I expected this error message, so I click OK and the next screen, shown in Figure 2.17, appears.

FIGURE 2.17

Permission to set up a DNS server

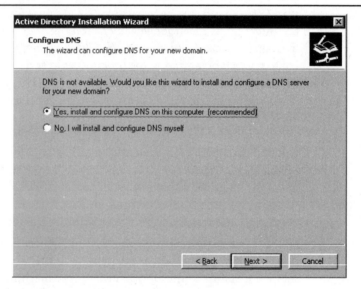

If Windows 2000 stumbles in its attempt to find a DNS server for your new domain, it'll offer to automatically set up DNS for the domain. If, on the other hand, it *finds* the DNS server but the DNS server can't take dynamic updates, *then* you'll get a different error message to the effect that DCPROMO can't go on—you simply cannot set up a domain under Windows 2000 unless you can get DNS to play along, which is why it's so important to make sure that your DNS infrastructure is ready for Windows 2000—a topic we'll take up in the section "Get the DNS Infrastructure Ready" later in this chapter. Click Next and one more warning appears, as you see in Figure 2.18.

This message only appeared starting in later betas of Windows 2000. Apparently, as the message indicates, in order to allow NT 4 RAS servers to authenticate dial-in users, Windows 2000 has to loosen up its security structure a bit—not a very appetizing prospect given the raft of security problems that have plagued its NT 4 predecessor. Make this judgement call yourself, but it looks as if it might be a good idea to think about upgrading your NT 4 RAS servers if possible. Click Next, and you'll get a screen like Figure 2.19.

FIGURE 2.18

Choose whether or not RAS will be in the network.

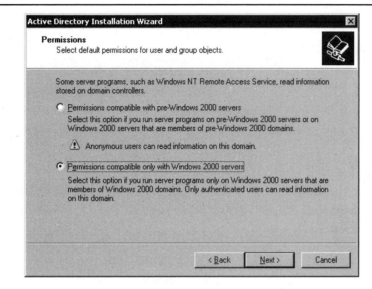

FIGURE 2.19

Directory Services repair password

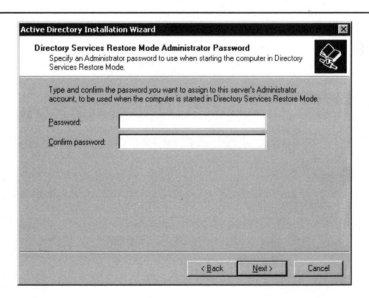

One of Windows 2000's at-boot-time options is to rebuild a damaged Active Directory database to restore it to an earlier version that is internally consistent, but which has probably lost a lot of information. You don't want just anyone doing that—a malicious individual telling Windows 2000 to rebuild its database is basically telling it to *destroy* its database—so Windows 2000 asks for a password that it'll use to challenge anyone trying to rebuild the AD database. Fill that in and click Next, and you'll see the screen in Figure 2.20.

FIGURE 2.20

Confirming your choices

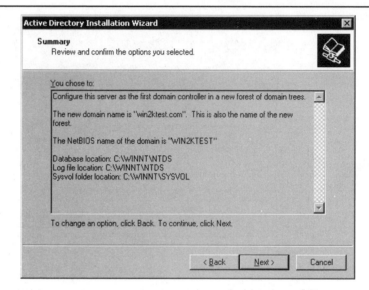

Read this last screen carefully, and if you did anything that you didn't like, back up and make the changes before clicking Finish! The reason is simple: once the Active Directory setup process starts, you'll see a screen like Figure 2.21.

FIGURE 2.21

Starting up the AD creation process

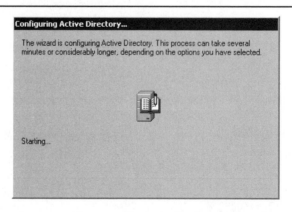

You'll be seeing *that* screen for a goodly time, at least 20–30 minutes in my experience. You can speed that up a bit with two SCSI hard disks, as mentioned before, but it takes a while. The reason to be double-sure before clicking Finish is that, if you realize after the AD creation process is underway that you want to go back and redo something, then you have to *first* sit through the entire AD creation process, *then* you get to reboot the server—never a quick process with Windows 2000—and *then* you get to run the Active Directory Installation Wizard again to break down the domain, *then* you get to reboot again, and finally you run the Active Directory Installation Wizard a *third* time, getting all the settings right this time, and of course, once that's done, it's another 20–30 minutes waiting and a reboot. Total elapsed time between "Oops, I clicked Finish and didn't mean it" and "Ah, now it's finally fixed" can be on the order of an hour and a half—plenty of time to kick yourself. Anyway, once the directory's ready, the wizard ends with a screen like the one in Figure 2.22.

FIGURE 2.22

Final DCPROMO report

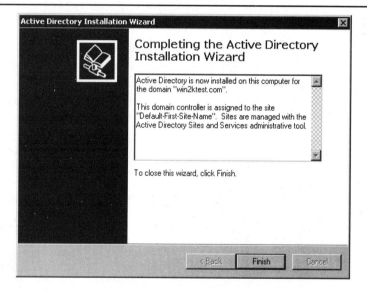

Once it's done, you'll have to reboot this new domain controller.

Shifting My Domain to Native Mode

Windows 2000 domains have two possible modes, Mixed and Native. When first created, domains are in Mixed mode, which means that they can accept NT 4 domain controllers as one of their own. That's theoretically terrific, but in actuality you'll find that much of Windows 2000 doesn't work until you move your domain from Mixed mode to Native mode. You'll do that with just a few steps.

Once the new domain controller has rebooted, you log on as Administrator with whatever password you assigned to that account. Click Start/Programs/Administrative Tools and choose Active Directory Domains and Trusts. You'll see an icon labeled with the name of your new domain; right-click it and choose Properties and you'll see a button labeled Change Mode, just like the screen that you saw back in Figure 2.5. Click the button and accept the confirmation. Again, reboot.

Creating a Forest-Wide Administrator

Now that I've got win2ktest.com out of the way, I next want to create its first child domain, div2.win2ktest.com. But before I do, I need to create an administrative account that will be recognized as an administrator throughout this domain forest that I'm creating. Creating user accounts is covered later in Chapter 8, but here's a quick cheat sheet on creating a forest-wide admin.

Once that first domain controller for win2ktest.com is up and running, I log in as its local administrator as that's the only extant account at the moment. As win2ktest.com was the first domain created in the tree, it's a little bit special and is called the *forest root*—special because any other trees or domains that you create after this first domain sit below that first domain.

Running Active Directory Users and Computers

Anyway, once logged into the win2ktest.com domain controller, I click Start/Programs/Administrative Tools. The first time you do this, you'll notice that you've got three new tools: Active Directory Sites and Services, Active Directory Domains and Trusts, and Active Directory Users and Computers. As you can guess, you create user accounts with Active Directory Users and Computers, the DSA. This application is also the tool you use to modify user accounts. When started, its first screen looks like Figure 2.23.

FIGURE 2.23

Opening DSA screen

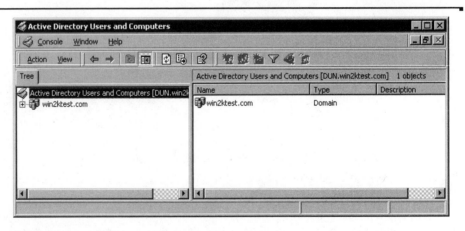

This is showing you the current domain, win2ktest.com. Click on the plus sign to open it up and you see a screen like Figure 2.24.

Now you see five things that look like folders—Builtin, Users, Computers, ForeignSecurityPincipals and Domain Controllers. While it'll be no surprise when I tell you that the folder labeled Users contains user accounts, I want to stress that its not necessary to use that folder—the folder is just created to provide a default place to keep user accounts. If for some reason you wanted to create all new user accounts in the folder labeled Computers, nothing would stop you and you could make everything work just fine. If you knew at this point that your domain would be subdivided into an OU called hatfields and another called mccoys, then you could create those OUs right now and create each new user account in either the hatfields OU or the mccoys OU.

FIGURE 2.24

Default domain contents

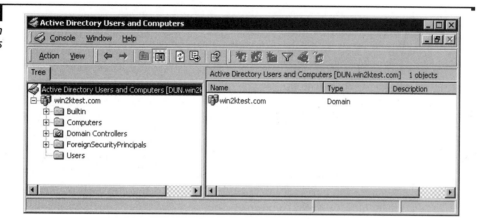

Creating a New User Account   I'm going to be unoriginal here, however, and just create a user account in the Users folder. To do that, I just right-click the Users folder. The context menu will offer a submenu labeled New, and one of the options will be User...; I choose that and get a screen like Figure 2.25.

FIGURE 2.25

Creating the new user account

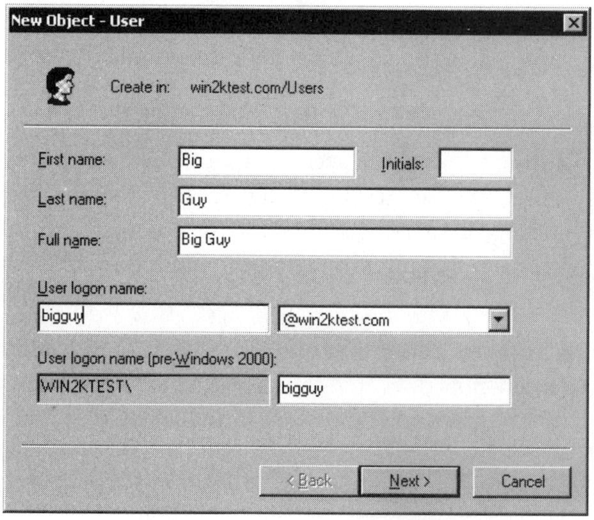

Much of this is self-explanatory, but let's go through this screen. First you fill in a first and last name as well as a full name. These three characteristics are largely just labels of very little use save for displays and searching. The fifth field, User Logon Name, is the "magic" name, the one that this user will use to log on. Note that you can add an @ suffix to the name and a domain name, giving you a logon name that looks like an e-mail name. Now, there's some complexity in that name that's not immediately apparent, so let me digress a bit about logon names.

User Principal Names (UPNs) or Logon Names   If you worked with NT 4, then you'll recall that it was possible to have an enterprise built of many different domains that trusted each other, where *trusted* in this context means "allowed each other to share security information and logins." Thus, if I had a user account named Mark that was built in a domain named ORION but wanted to log onto a machine which was a member of a different domain named AQUILA, then the AQUILA machine would in general refuse to log me in unless the AQUILA domain *trusted* the ORION domain. I'd then log into the machine from AQUILA by telling it three things: my username, password, and domain. If I'd merely tried to log in as Mark from AQUILA, the login would have been refused, as no AQUILA domain controller would have a Mark account—only the ORION ones would. By saying that I was "Mark from ORION," I told the AQUILA machine how to find a domain controller that could vouch for me—I was telling it, "Go find one of the ORION domain controllers, they can verify that I'm me."

In a multidomain Windows 2000 world, you can still do that. If I already had div2.win2ktest.com built and I wanted to log onto a div2.win2ktest.com machine with a Mark account from win2ktest.com rather than div2.win2ktest.com—two different domains, recall—then I could sit down at a div2.win2ktest.com machine and, as before, say "I'm Mark from win2ktest.com," and so the div2.win2ktest.com machine would know to go find a win2ktest.com machine to verify my login. But Windows 2000 offers *another* way to identify myself at login as well—I can use a User Principal Name (UPN), a term for a name looking like *name@domainname*. (Personally, I'd just call it a universal login name or the like, but who knows, maybe Microsoft liked UPN as an acronym better than ULN.)

Getting back to this account that we're creating, you see that by default Windows 2000 suggests that BigGuy's UPN should be bigguy@win2ktest.com. Presuming that I agree and create his account with that UPN, he can then sit down at any machine in the forest and log in with just bigguy@win2ktest.com, and a password, without having to fill in a domain name.

UPN Suffixes and the Global Catalog   At this point, you may be thinking, "Big deal—how does that save any typing?" Whether you type in that you're someone@somedomain and a password, or whether you alternatively type in that you're "someone" from "somedomain" with a given password, what's the difference? What's the big deal?

Well, now, *that's* the interesting part.

You see, you can basically specify any domain name that you like after the name. If I wanted to, I could give bigguy's UPN the suffix @microsoft.com, even though I clearly don't own the microsoft.com domain name. The latter part of a user's UPN need not have *anything to do with the user's domain.* You could have domains acme.com, apex.com, and greatstuff.com, with user accounts scattered throughout the three domains, but could then give everyone UPNs like *somename*@acme.com.

This raises two questions. First, why would you do this, and second, how does it work? The answer to the first question is that obviously Microsoft intended the name to be your e-mail name, like joe.blow@acme.com. As one Microsoft person explained to me, "You might change jobs in the organization, so you might have accounts in different domains over time, but it's likely that your e-mail account name won't change. It's convenient, then, to be able to offer the user a consistent logon name even if his or her underlying domain changes."

That seems reasonable. But how the heck would it work? If I call myself mark@microsoft.com, how does the machine that I'm trying to log onto know to go look on a win2ktest.com domain controller for my account rather than flailing around looking in vain for a microsoft.com domain controller? The answer is an Active Directory service mentioned a few times before in this chapter called the global catalog (GC). The GC service runs on one or more domain controllers, and among other things, it keeps an index relating people's UPNs—their logon names—to the names of their actual domains. Thus, if I created an account for myself with UPN mark@microsoft.com and tried to log on to a win2ktest.com machine, that machine would quickly pop over to a local GC server (which, by the way, the machine finds by looking it up in DNS—that's one of the many examples of Active Directory services that systems use DNS to find) and ask the GC server, "Where does mark@microsoft.com *really* live?" The GC server would reply, "In win2ktest.com," and so my workstation would then contact a domain controller in win2ktest.com (finding a DC for win2ktest.com in DNS) and log me in. Before moving on, however, see the sidebar "How Do I Add a UPN Suffix?"

How Do I Add a UPN Suffix?

In the example about UPN suffixes and the global catalog, I suggested that I could give myself a UPN of mark@microsoft.com. But a bit of clicking around the DSA doesn't yield any obvious ways to give myself the microsoft.com suffix. How to get the DSA to let me use another suffix?

1. Click Start/Programs/Administrative Tools/Active Directory Domains and Trusts.

Continued

CONTINUED

2. In the left-hand pane, there's a list of the domains in your enterprise. Above that list is a line Active Directory Domains and Trusts; right-click that and choose Properties. You'll see a dialog box like the following figure.

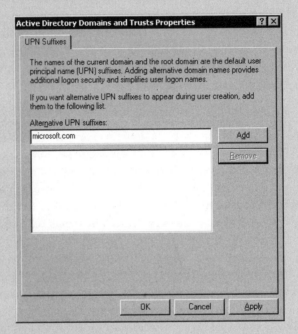

3. Fill in the suffix that you'd like, such as microsoft.com or whatever. Click Add.

4. Click OK.

5. Close Active Directory Domains and Trusts.

Finishing Up the User Account   Anyway, back to creating bigguy, notice that Windows 2000 simultaneously creates a downlevel username. This is the name that bigguy would be recognized as if he tried to log onto an NT 4 or earlier server. Simply sticking with bigguy for a downlevel name seems fine, so I click Next and the screen changes to Figure 2.26.

A straightforward screen; click Next and I'm asked to confirm the account information and click Finish. Opening up the Users folder, I can see that bigguy is now created, as you see in Figure 2.27.

Notice the groups that Windows 2000 automatically creates when you build a domain controller. The one we're interested in is the group named Enterprise Admins; anyone in that group is recognized as an administrator all around the forest. Adding bigguy to that group is simple. First, I open up the Enterprise Admins group by either double-clicking it or by right-clicking it and choosing Properties, and I see something like Figure 2.28.

FIGURE 2.26

Setting a password

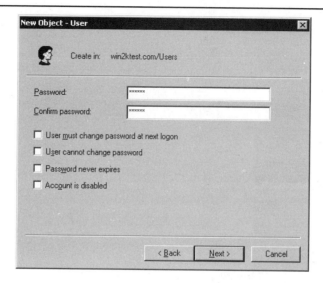

FIGURE 2.27

Contents of the Users *folder after creating* bigguy

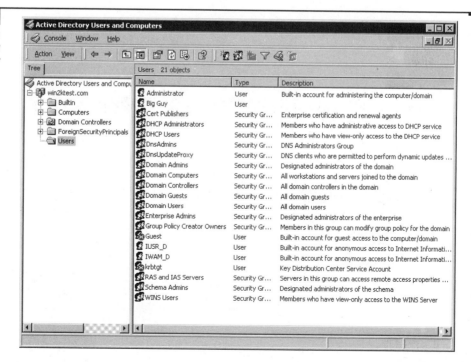

FIGURE 2.28

Enterprise Admins folder properties

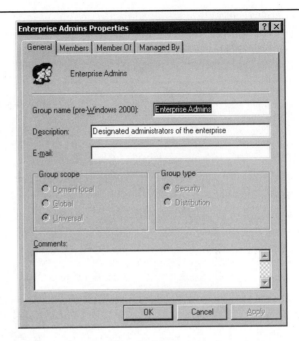

Clicking the property page tab labeled Members shows the list of members of Enterprise Admins, as you see in Figure 2.29.

FIGURE 2.29

Members of Enterprise Admins

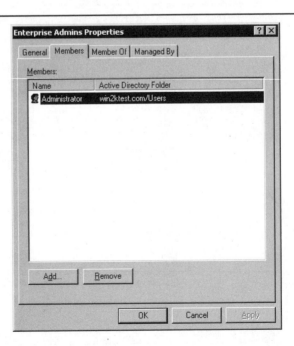

Notice that the local administrator account for the win2ktest.com domain controller is an Enterprise Admin. Windows 2000 causes that to happen automatically. Recall that win2ktest.com is the root domain and there's got to be at least one forest-wide administrator. By clicking the Add button, I get a dialog box like Figure 2.30.

I just highlight the bigguy account, click Add and OK, and bigguy's a forest-wide administrator.

 TIP By the way, even now Bigguy isn't a complete Superman in this domain. There is a group that the Enterprise Administrators aren't a part of—the Schema Administrators. This group can, as its name suggests, make changes to the forest's schema, which includes changing what the global catalog stores. By default, the only member of the Schema Administrators group is the default Administrator account on the PDC of the domain which is the forest root. Also, machines in the domain would not allow Bigguy to sit down and administer them—they would not recognize him as an administrator. To fix that, put Bigguy in another group, Domain Admins. So to make Bigguy *truly* a Big Guy, add him to Schema Administrators and Domain Admins. Or put Enterprise Administrators inside Schema Administrators.

FIGURE 2.30

Adding bigguy to Enterprise Admins

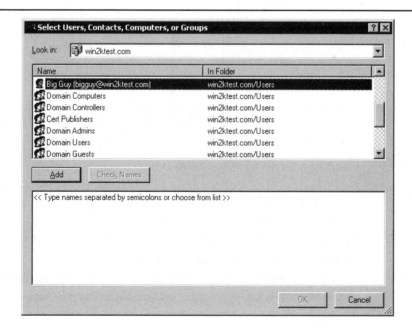

Building Subdomain Control with an Organizational Unit

You've read earlier that one of Windows 2000's strengths is that it can let you grant partial or complete administrative powers to a group of users, meaning that it would be possible for a one-domain network to subdivide itself into Uptown and Downtown, Marketing and Engineering and Management, or whatever. Let's look at a simple example of how to do that.

Let's suppose that there are five people in Marketing: Adam, Betty, Chip, Debbie, and Elaine. They want to designate one of their own, Elaine, to be able reset passwords. They need this because "I forgot my password, can you reset it for me?" is probably the number one thing that Marketing calls the central IS support folks for. The central IS folks are happy to have someone local to Marketing take the problem off their hands, freeing them up to fight other fires.

Here's the process:

1. Create an organizational unit called Marketing. (You can call it anything that you like, of course, but Marketing is easier to remember later.)

2. Move Adam's, Betty's, Chip's, Debbie's, and Elaine's already-existing user accounts into the Marketing OU.

3. Create a group called MktPswAdm, which will be the people who can reset passwords for people in the Marketing OU. (Again, you can actually give it any name that you like.)

4. Make Elaine a member of the MktPswAdm group.

5. Delegate password reset control for the Marketing OU to the MktPswAdm group.

If you want to follow this along as an exercise, get ready by creating accounts for Adam, Betty, Chip, Debbie, and Elaine as you did for BigGuy, except don't make them administrators.

Creating a New Organizational Unit   Creating a new OU is simple. Just open up the DSA (recall, the Directory Service Administrator, also labeled Active Directory Users and Computers), right-click the domain's icon in the left-hand pane, and choose New/Organizational Unit. A dialog box will prompt you for a name of the new organizational unit. Fill in the name and click OK and you're done.

Moving User Accounts into an OU   Next, to move Adam, Betty, Chip, Debbie, and Elaine to the Marketing OU, open up the DSA, open up your domain (mine's win2ktest.com, yours might have another name), and then open up the Users folder. (If you created the five accounts somewhere other than Users, then look there.)

Choose all five user accounts by clicking Adam, then holding down the Control key and left-clicking the other four accounts. Then right-click on one of the five accounts and you'll get a context menu that includes an option Move: select Move and you'll get a dialog box asking you where to move the "object." It'll originally show you your domain name with a plus sign next to it, just click the plus sign and the domain will open up to show the OUs in your domain. Choose Marketing and click OK and all five accounts will move to the Marketing OU. In the DSA, you can open the Marketing OU and you will see that all five accounts are now in that OU.

Creating a MktPswAdm Group   Next, to create a group for the folks who can reset Marketing passwords. Again, work in the DSA. Click Action/New/Group. (You can also right-click the Marketing OU and choose New/Group.) You'll see a dialog box like Figure 2.31.

FIGURE 2.31

*Creating a new
Domain Local group*

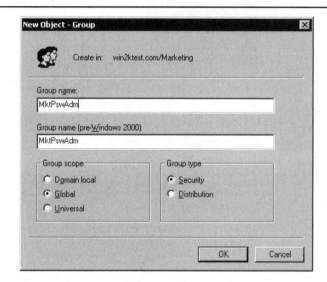

You see that the dialog box gives you the option to create any one of the three types of groups in an Active Directory. A global group will serve our purposes well, although in this particular case—the case of a group in a given domain getting control of an OU in that same domain—then either a domain local, global, or universal group would suffice. I've called the group MktPswAdm. Click OK and it's done.

Next, put Elaine in the MktPswAdm group. Right-click the icon for MtkPswAdm and choose Properties, as you did earlier when creating BigGuy. Click the Members tab, then the Add button, then Elaine's account, then Add, then OK, and you'll see that Elaine is now a member of MktPswAdm. Click OK to clear the dialog box.

Delegating the Marketing OU's Password Reset Control to MktPswAdm

Now let's put them together. In the DSA again, locate the Marketing OU and right-click it. Choose Delegation and the first screen of the Delegation of Control Wizard will appear, as you see in Figure 2.32.

FIGURE 2.32

Opening screen of the Delegation of Control Wizard

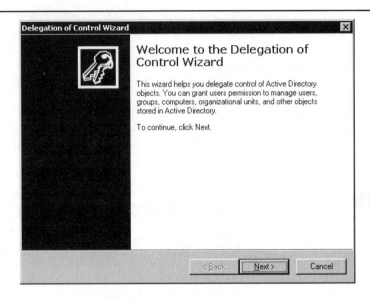

The wizard is a simplified way to delegate, and it'll work fine for our first example. Click Next and you'll see Figure 2.33.

FIGURE 2.33

Before selecting a group

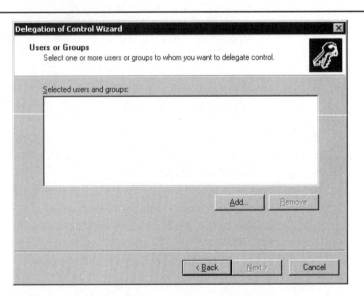

Next, you've got to tell it that you're about to delegate some power to a particular group, so you've got to identify the group. Click Add and choose the MktPswAdm group. Note that when the DSA shows you user accounts in the Add function, it ignores OUs and just lists all accounts and groups in the domain. This is quite handy as it makes finding a particular account much simpler. After choosing MktPswAdm and clicking OK to dismiss the Add dialog box, the screen looks like Figure 2.34.

FIGURE 2.34

MtkPswAdm selected

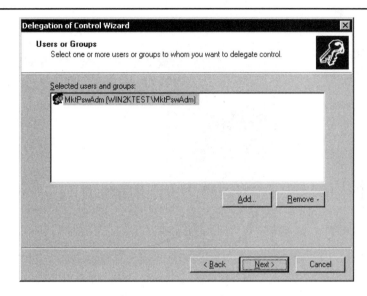

Now click Next, and you'll get a menu of possible things to delegate, as you see in Figure 2.35.

FIGURE 2.35

Options for delegation

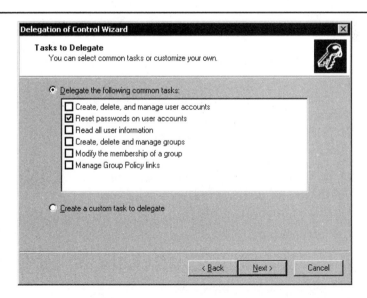

Once we do a bit of exploring here, you'll see that there are many, many functions that can be delegated. Rather than force you to wade through a long list of things that you'll never care about, however, Microsoft picked the top six things that you'd be most likely to want to delegate, one of which is the "reset passwords" ability. I've checked that in the figure; press Next and the final screen in the wizard appears, as you see in Figure 2.36.

FIGURE 2.36

Confirming your choices

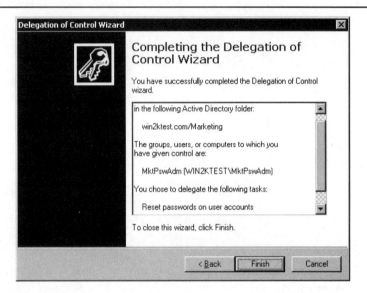

Click Finish, and it's done.

Remember, delegation lets you designate a set of users who have some kind of control over a set of users and/or computers. You accomplish that by putting the controlling users into a group, the things that you want them to control into an OU, and then delegate control of the OU to the group.

 TIP   Or, to put it in a bit more eccentric fashion, think of it this way: the victims go into an *OU*, the oppressors into a *group*.

Advanced Delegation

While that's a nice—and useful—example, it only hints at the power of delegation. You actually needn't use the wizard to delegate, it just makes things simpler for a range of common applications. Here's how to more directly manipulate delegation.

First, open up the DSA and click View/Advanced Features. New things will pop up on the screen, as in Figure 2.37.

Right-click Marketing and choose Properties. You'll get a property sheet with a tab labeled Permissions. Click it, and you'll see something like Figure 2.38.

FIGURE 2.37

DSA with View
Advanced Features
enabled

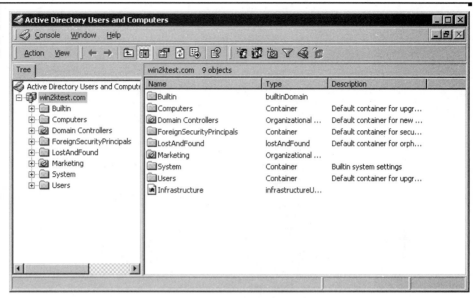

FIGURE 2.38

Security tab on
Marketing OU

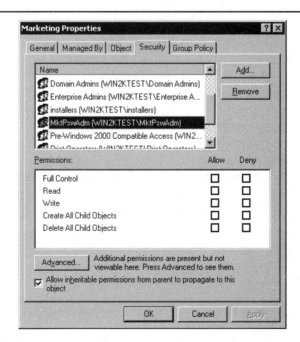

Here, I've scrolled down a bit to see what the dialog box tells us about the MktPswAdm group. It appears that the group can't do anything—until you click the Advanced button, which results in a screen like Figure 2.39.

FIGURE 2.39

Advanced security set-tings for Marketing OU

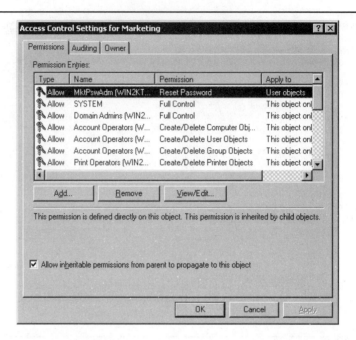

Again scrolling down to highlight MktPswAdm, there's not much said here—Reset Password control of user objects. "Reset Password" is one specific set of administrative powers, but there are many other specific sets of admin power that you can build to suit your need. To dive further into the delegation structure of an organizational unit and see those specific abilities, click View/Edit, and you'll see something like Figure 2.40.

As you can see from the figure, there are a *lot* of powers that you can grant to a particular group in controlling a particular OU!

Where might you make use of this? Well, you gave MktPswAdm the ability to change passwords, but you didn't take it away from the groups who originally had it—the domain admins, enterprise admins and the like can still reset passwords. That's not a bad idea, but if you really ever *do* come across a "feuding departments" scenario, wherein Marketing wants to be sure that they're the *only* people who can administer accounts, then you'd first delegate the Marketing OU to some group, and then you'd go in with the Security tab and rip out all of the other administrators.

Creating a Second Domain

But suppose we're not happy with just one domain; that OU stuff just wasn't enough for the boss. Resigned to politics, I'm ready now to create the second domain, div.win2ktest.com. Recall that one machine can only be a domain controller in one domain, so I need a second machine to act as DC for div.win2ktest.com before I can create that domain. As before, I need a machine running some variation of Windows 2000 Server and I start DCPROMO on it.

FIGURE 2.40

Specific MktPswAdm abilities

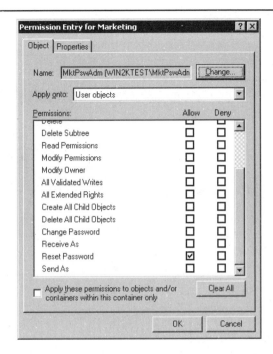

DCPROMO starts out as before. I tell it that I'm creating a new domain but not a new tree: the new domain will be a child domain to the existing win2ktest.com domain. But I can't create a child domain under win2ktest.com without win2ktest.com's permission—which is where bigguy will become useful. Once I tell DCPROMO that I'm creating a child domain, I get a screen like Figure 2.41.

FIGURE 2.41

Establishing credentials for creating a child domain

Active Directory Installation Wizard

Network Credentials
Provide a network user name and password.

Type the user name, password, and user domain of the network account you wish to use for this operation.

User name: bigguy
Password: ******
Domain: win2ktest.com

< Back   Next >   Cancel

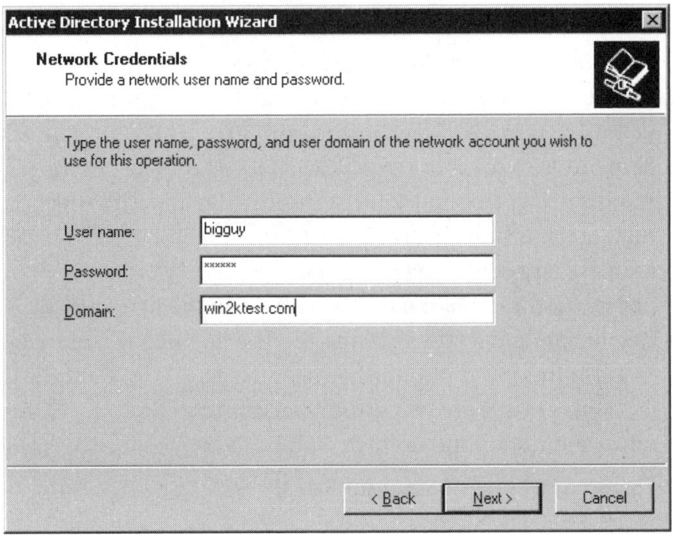

Here, I've filled in bigguy's login information. DCPROMO pauses a bit to authenticate the bigguy account. Once I've filled that in, I click Next and the screen in Figure 2.42 appears.

FIGURE 2.42

Naming the child domain

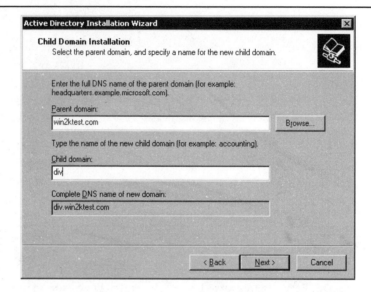

DCPROMO now needs to know which domain to add a child to, and what to call the child. I fill in that the parent's name is win2ktest.com, or I could have just pressed the Browse button and chosen from the domains in the forest. The child domain will be named div.win2ktest.com, but DCPROMO just wants you to type in **div** for the child name and it then assembles it and the parent domain into the complete name div.win2ktest.com for the child domain.

I then progress through DCPROMO much as with the first domain, so I'll spare you the screens—but notice Figure 2.43.

The win2ktest.com domain got the downlevel name (or NT 4 or NetBIOS name, take your pick, they all mean the same thing) of win2ktest. But how to name the child domains with the more complex names—just take out the periods and take the leftmost 15 characters? Do some kind of truncated name with tildes on the end, in the same way that long filenames get converted to 8.3 names? Well, you can actually give your domains any downlevel name that you like, but the default ones are just the leftmost portion of the domain name, as you see in the figure. As *div* is the leftmost portion of the domain name, the domain gets the downlevel name div by default.

From this point on, I just answer DCPROMO's questions as I did for the first domain, so I'll spare you those screens. Another 20 to 30 minutes of Active Directory setup and the second domain is done.

FIGURE 2.43

*Downlevel name for
child domain*

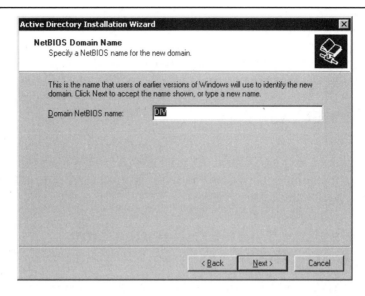

Before leaving here, let me make a few points about using DCPROMO to build
domains. First, as you've already read, get DNS ready before starting. Second,
DCPROMO's kind of rigid about the order in which you create domains. The first
domain that you create in a forest is the forest root domain, and there's no changing that. Third, you've got to add domains by creating them—you can't create a
domain green.com and another yellow.com separately and then decide later to
merge them into a forest—instead, you've got to first create green.com as the first
domain in a forest and then create yellow.com as the first domain in a new tree but
in an existing forest.

Planning Your Active Directory Structure

The idea of this chapter has been to give you an overall idea of how AD's pieces work.
I strongly suggest that you peruse the rest of this book before starting in on building
your AD structure, as AD *permeates* Windows 2000. But here are few hints on how to
get started on designing your AD structure.

Examine Your WAN Topology

Domain controllers in a domain must replicate amongst themselves in order to keep
domain information consistent across the domain. DCs need not be connected
exactly 24/7—you *could* just dial connections between branch offices and the home

office every day or so and then try to force replication to occur, although it's not simple and may lead to problems down the road—but on the whole you'll find that domains work best if they have constant end-to-end connection. If you have an area that's poorly or sporadically served by your WAN connections, perhaps it's best to make it a separate domain.

Lay Out Your Sites

Once you know where the WAN connections are, list the sites that you'll have, name them, and figure out which machines go in what sites. Also document the nature of their connections—speed and cost—to assist Windows 2000 in using the intersite bandwidth wisely.

Figure Out Which Existing Domains to Merge and Merge Them

You'll probably want to reduce the number of domains in your enterprise. One way to do that would be to merge old resource domains into an old master domain. The idea here would be that you first upgrade the master domain to Windows 2000, then merge the old NT 4 resource domains into that master domain as organizational units.

Ah, but there's just one problem there: Microsoft doesn't give you a tool to do that merging. You get to do it by hand, so here's the simplest way. First, recall from NT 4 that a resource domain in theory has very few user accounts, just a lot of machine accounts. The strategy then will be to first convert both the master domains and the resource domains to Windows 2000. Next, you'd create OUs for each of the old resource domains. Finally, you'd use a program in the Windows 2000 Resource Kit, NETDOM, to move the machines in the old resource domains to the new OUs in the master domain.

To use NETDOM, you'll need a user account in the old resource domain that has administrative powers, a user account in the master domain, again with administrative powers, the name of the master domain—the one that you want to move the machine's account to—as well as the name of the organizational unit in the master domain that you want the machine's account in. The NETDOM command then looks like this:

```
netdom move machine_name /d:destination_domain_name
➡/uo:current_domain_admin_account_name /po:password_for_current_domain
➡/ud:new_domain_admin_account_name
➡/pd:password_for_new_domain /ou:OU_name /reboot
```

Thus, for example, suppose you were moving a machine named lemon.fruit.com from a domain named fruit.com to a domain named citrusfruits.com. Suppose also that you have an administrative account in the old domain, fruits.com, named fruit-boss with password rind and an administrative account in citrusfruits.com named Vit-aminC with password ascorbic. Let's say also that lemon is going into an OU called yellowfruits in the citrusfruits.com account. You could sit down to any command prompt and type the following command, which would move lemon.fruit.com to the citrusfruits.com domain in the yellowfruits OU:

```
Netdom move lemon.fruit.com /d:citrusfruits.com
➥/uo:fruit\fruitboss /po:rind /ud:citrusfruits\vitaminc
➥/pd:ascorbic /ou:yellowfruits /reboot
```

The "reboot" option remotely reboots lemon, as that's necessary for the changes to take effect. Alternatively, you could buy a "domain consolidation tool" from Fastlane Systems or Mission Critical Software. They cost from $6/user to $20/user—which can be a fair amount of money to pay for a program you'll only use one time—but it may be worth it in your enterprise.

What Needs an OU and What Needs a Domain?

As you read earlier, you can divide up enterprises either by breaking them up into multiple domains or by creating a single domain and using organizational units to parcel out administrative control, or you can do any combination of those.

This is largely a political question, but you can get a head start by looking at the perceived needs of the organization. Is administration centralized or decentralized? Do the company's divisions work together closely, or is there not very much collaboration? And be sure to get corporate sign-off on these matters from the executive suite or be prepared to deal with the bruised egos later.

From a technical point of view, there's really only one reason to use more than one domain: replication traffic. If you have two large domains connected only by a slow WAN link, then you may find that it makes sense to keep them as separate domains. But think carefully about it—Windows 2000 is very efficient at using WAN links for domain replication traffic.

Choose an OU Structure for Delegation, *Then* for Group Policies

I haven't discussed group policies all that much in this chapter—they'll get more coverage later in Chapters 8 and 10 and other places—but one thing worth noting about group policies is that they're a tool for controlling users and computers.

As you read earlier, group policies don't really apply to groups, they apply to OUs. That would seem to mean that you should organize groups of people that you want to control into OUs so that it's easy to create and apply group policies to them.

On the other hand, recall that the great strength of organizational units under Windows 2000 is that you can create groups of users which you can give varying degrees of control ("delegate") over those OUs. In the end, you'll find that delegation can affect system performance more than group policies, so when you're chopping up your domains into OUs, choose OUs that make sense from a delegation point of view. Does Manufacturing want their own local administrators? Put the Manufacturing users into an OU. Does Publicity want to control their own printers? Then put their printers into an OU. In any case, you probably won't find much conflict between an OU structure that's group policy–centric over an OU structure that's delegation-centric: after all, any group that wants to share an administrator probably also wants that administrator to have control over it through group policies.

Use Just One Domain if Possible

Sorry for the repetition, but let me say one more time: minimize the number of domains. In fact, minimize them to just *one* domain, if possible. Windows 2000 domains can be truly huge, able to contain between 1.5 million and 20 million objects (depending on whom you talk to), large enough for almost any enterprise. And Windows 2000's site-awareness allows it to make good use of your low-speed, expensive wide area network bandwidth.

Develop Names for Your Domains/Trees

Windows 2000 allows a wider variety of domain names than NT 4 allowed, but sometimes you can have too much of a good thing, too *many* options. If you're going multidomain, how will the domains fit together? Do you divide geographically, by division, by function? Where are the lines of control in the organization now?

Get the DNS Infrastructure Ready

The chances are very good that if your firm currently uses non-NT DNS servers (probably Unix boxes of some kind), then suggesting that the company move to Windows 2000–based DNS servers won't exactly be met with cheers and applause. (And if the company currently uses *Linux* servers for DNS, then don't even suggest moving to Windows 2000 DNS servers if you value your life.)

But Windows 2000 depends on having at least one DNS server to use to keep track of much of its organizational unit, domain, tree, and forest information, so you've got to do *something* to accommodate those needs. There are several alternatives.

You're Already Using NT 4–Based DNS Servers

No sweat. Just upgrade those puppies to Windows 2000 and all will be well.

You're Using Relatively Current Non-NT DNS Servers

Most people use a Unix or Unix-derivative machine running a program called Bind to act as their DNS server. Windows 2000 can work perfectly well in an environment where a Unix-based Bind server acts as its DNS server, so long as it's a version of Bind that supports SRV records (RFC 2052) and dynamic updates (RFC 2136) and permits machine names with underscores.

In that case, you need not configure a Windows 2000 system as a DNS server.

You've Got Older Non-NT DNS Servers

If you're running an older version of Bind or some other non-NT DNS server, then that DNS server cannot serve a Windows 2000 domain. Consider upgrading it to a more recent version with RFC 2052 and 2136 as well as underscore support.

You've Got Older Non-NT DNS Servers and You Can't Upgrade

"Put up a new version of Bind? Over my dead body!" the Unix guys down the hall say. What to do then? Several possibilities:

- **Create a child portion of your current DNS names and delegate the control of those names to a Windows 2000 system.** For example, if you've already got several hundred Unix, Windows, and NT machines in an Internet domain named acme.com and the DNS server for acme.com is an ancient Bind implementation, then you can always tell the old Bind server that there's a new subdomain (a "zone" in DNS-ese) called win2k.acme.com (which would contain machines with names like bluebell.win2k.acme.com, rover.win2k.acme.com, or metrion.acme.com) that will have its own name server. Of course, that name server will be one of your new Windows 2000 servers. Windows 2000 doesn't insist upon having RFC 2052, 2136, and underscore support for all of the company's machines—just the Windows 2000 machines.

- **Let a Windows 2000 server act as a DNS server for the Windows 2000 domain, but do not connect that DNS server to the Internet.** There's not a reason in the world why you can't run a solipsistic little network of your own, with DNS servers that don't relate to any other DNS servers. You need only have your machines refer to two DNS servers—the internal one that isn't connected to the outside world, which keeps track of the Windows 2000 domain information, and the enterprise's other DNS servers, the ones that *do* connect to the outside world. If you do this, however, don't give your internal not-connected-to-anything-else domain a name shared by a machine on the *real* Internet; if you do, then no one on your network will be able to access any machines on that real-world domain. For example, let's just say that you build a not-connected-to-anything-else

DNS server for your domain and you decide that it'd just be a hoot to call your domain microsoft.com. When you try to actually get to Microsoft's Web site and point your browser to www.microsoft.com, the browser will consult DNS for the IP address of www.microsoft.com. The outside DNS servers—the Bind machines that don't support the newfangled stuff—will know exactly where the real www.microsoft.com is. But your Windows 2000 machines will *first* pass their DNS inquiries to their local Windows 2000 DNS server. *That* server will gleefully respond that www.microsoft.com either doesn't exist or is just the name of someone's Web server down the hall.

- **Armed insurrection, seizure and shutdown of the Unix DNS servers followed by a Windows 2000 takeover.** Not suggested, as those Unix guys probably know about more Windows 2000 security holes than *you* know about Unix security holes. Making them angry is therefore probably unwise, so avoid this strategy until after Microsoft makes Windows 2000 truly secure. (Don't hold your breath.)

Use the Power of Inheritance

The notion of things existing inside things runs throughout Windows 2000: organizational units can exist inside other OUs, and of course all OUs ultimately exist inside domains, domains exist inside trees, and trees exist inside forests.

When you set a permission or some other security policy on an object (*object* here meaning an OU, domain, forest, or tree), then anything created thereafter inside that object takes on that security policy. This is called *inheritance*. So, for example, if you wanted every user account in a forest to have to change its password every 10 days, it's far easier to set that rule up at the top of the forest before creating other domains, trees, OUs, and the like, because in general, from that point on, any new trees, domains, or OUs created in the forest will have the 10-day-password-change rule. (I said "in general" because it's possible to block inheritance; it's possible for an administrator to configure an object to ignore effects from higher-level objects.)

Overall AD Design Advice

There's lots to consider in building your AD and only you know what your organization needs and wants—I can't pass along a standard one-size-fits-all design for an AD. But overall, remember these things:

- Use sites to control bandwidth and replication.
- Use organizational units to create islands of users and/or computers which you can then delegate administrative control over.

- Use domains to solve replication problems and possible political problems.
- Use forests to create completely separate network systems. If, for example, your enterprise had a subsidiary that wasn't completely trusted (in the human sense, not the NT sense) and you were worried that the automatic trust relationships (in the NT sense) created by common membership in a forest might lead to unwanted security links, then make them separate forests. The value of separate forests is that there is no security relationship at all between two forests unless you explicitly create the relationship using NT trust relationships.

While this chapter wasn't intended to cover everything about Active Directory, it was intended to get you started, to set the stage so that the following chapters make more sense. In order to help you think about the design of your Active Directory from the beginning, however, I needed to put the cart just a bit ahead of the horse, and I'll atone for that starting with the next chapter, where you'll see how to set up Windows 2000.

CHAPTER 3

Installing Windows 2000 Server

FEATURING:

Ever since the early days of Windows 3.1, the Windows line of operating systems has become increasingly complex and cumbersome, while the installation procedures themselves have become easier and more intuitive. Windows 2000 continues in this tradition. Plug and Play becomes a functioning reality, making hardware configuration much easier and more foolproof. Domain controllers and member servers all come from the same installation seed. Unattended installs are more capable, including a remote installation option. In short, installing Windows 2000 is *usually* a straightforward affair. Anyone with a half-decent collection of hardware components and the "click Next to continue" capabilities of a 7 iron can probably install Windows 2000 Server and get it to boot up on the first try, almost every time.

The hard part comes when you want not only a stable, reliable installation, but also a *repeatable process*. This repeatable process will allow one-stop shopping for all of your installation needs and give you that clean and efficient install every time. However, to produce those perfect results time and time again, the planning and preparation phase of the install becomes even more important. Failure to properly plan out an install will most certainly result in a reinstall.

Throughout this chapter, I'll cover key fundamental planning steps, help you prepare your system for Windows 2000, run through an install, and finally, troubleshoot the mess we got ourselves into.

Planning and Preparation

First of all, what is all this hubbub about planning? Well, anyone who has done a significant amount of NT installs has had to format and start over at least once. Usually this is due to a lack of planning. In my case, it is usually that I partitioned wrong, built a member server when it should have been a domain controller, or some other simple lack of foresight. Windows 2000 does do us a favor in a few areas. For starters, with Windows NT, you had to decide early in the installation process whether you wanted a member server or domain controller. Once you made your choice, you were stuck with it. With Windows 2000, this isn't an issue. Every initial install begins with a server. That's it, plain and simple. Once you are up and running with a stable server, you can promote it to a domain controller.

 NOTE Actually, the domain controller as we have been used to it has changed significantly. The Active Directory becomes the driving force with a whole new set of concerns that could completely throw off the balance of an install. With Windows 2000, we can just throw this factor out and deal with it later. Look for this in the preceding chapter, "Getting Comfortable with Active Directory."

Next comes Plug and Play. Yes, NT 4 gave you some quasi plug-and-play functionality, but it was spotty at best and only applied to *ISA* Plug and Play, which is fairly unusual, rather than the more common PCI-based PnP boards. Windows 2000 takes another step in that direction. Plug and Play is *supposed* to make your life easier in the hardware preparation department. Sometimes, however, even the most modern Plug and Play–based system will trip over its drivers, and hybrid PnP/legacy systems can be a bit of trouble to install. For good or ill, however, you probably won't run into too many systems with a combination of Plug and Play and non-PnP boards, as you'll find that Windows 2000's demands on hardware are so great that you'll probably only be installing Windows 2000 on relatively new hardware—which is likely to be entirely Plug and Play. Windows 2000 also has a Remote Installation Services option, which can serve as a central, Ghost-like source for distributing Windows 2000 across your network.

These enhancements, improvements, and new features increase the possibility of a smooth installation process but still define why it's best to plan ahead of time. Planning doesn't just save you from making mistakes. It can make your installation a lot more than just installing Windows 2000. With proper planning, you can utilize Windows 2000's features and enhancements to save time for each install and build an entire installation process for use throughout your enterprise.

System Requirements

Once again, Microsoft has upped the ante on system requirements. No longer can we get by with a 486 Intel *processor*. A Pentium is in order, running at 166MHz or higher, although the truth of the matter is that you really should have at least a Pentium II–class processor: a Celeron, a Xeon, or a Pentium II or III. The so-called "front-side bus" on the processor should be a minimum of 100MHz, which means that your system should be a 350MHz or faster system. The one exception: the 366MHz processor is *not* a 100MHz front-side bus, it's only a 66MHz and so should be avoided.

However, while processing dictates how fast your computer will do the job, *memory* decides *if* your computer can do the job. Where NT 4 let you get by with 16MB of RAM, Windows 2000 Server will not let you install with anything less than 64MB on an Intel box. When deciding how much memory you will need, try to consider what your server will be doing. Simple file and print sharing is not as resource intensive on a server as running applications like Exchange, SQL Server, Web services, and so on. Anytime you put the server side of a client/server application on your system, it means that your server is performing processing that would have otherwise been done by the workstation. This directly influences your memory and processor requirements. For example, a system that is merely serving a few print queues and shared directories can get by with the bare minimums. On the other hand, tack on Web hosting, mail servicing, and user logon validation for several thousand users and you may need memory well up into the triple digits, and a processor that could fry eggs. I'd put a *minimum* of 128MB of RAM on a Windows 2000 server (96MB for a Windows 2000 Professional workstation).

More memory means more places for the memory hardware to fail, however, and that's why you need ECC (Error Correcting Code) memory. You may recall something called *parity*, a set of circuits attached to memory systems of PCs in the '80s whose job was to monitor the memory and detect data loss in a PC's RAM. Such data loss could be caused by a bad memory chip (which you can ward off by testing your RAM with a good RAM tester program like CheckIt or QAPlus before deploying the server), but random events also cause data loss; static electricity, power surges, and (believe it or not) infrequent extremely low-level radioactivity from the memory chips *themselves* can damage memory data. (Don't worry, you won't get cancer or mutations from your memory chips. Many, many everyday things in our world are mildly radioactive: the bricks cladding your house and indeed most kinds of ceramic produce an extremely small amount of radioactivity. Memory chips produce a radioactive particle once in a great while, and when they do, that particle may happen to cross paths with a location in memory—and when *that* happens, the memory may be flipped from a 0 to a 1 or vice versa!)

In any case, parity was kind of frustrating in that it could detect that *something* was wrong, but it didn't know *what* was wrong. PCs with parity memory were usually designed to simply shut down the PC when a memory error was detected using the parity method (which the error message would usually incorrectly call "a parity error" rather a "memory error"—after all, if parity detected the memory error, then parity was working fine!), and shutting down an entire system just because parity discovered one damaged bit is a trifle extreme.

In contrast, most modern Pentium II–based systems (which, again, include the Xeon and Celeron) can go a step further and implement ECC. ECC's cool because it not only *detects* memory errors, it *corrects* them automatically. So when that stray alpha particle or (more likely) power glitch scrambles a bit, ECC finds that problem and fixes it without ever bothering you.

Now you may be wondering, "How much would such a wonderful feature cost?" Well, back in the old days, I worked on minicomputer systems with ECC that cost thousands of dollars. But most Pentium II–based systems can do it for about $20 per 128MB of RAM. Here's the trick: most PC memories these days are implemented as Synchronous Dynamic Random Access Memory, or SDRAM, packages. SDRAMs come in a 64-bit version or a 72-bit version. When I last priced 128MB SDRAMs, the difference in price between a 64-bit and 72-bit SDRAM was $20 on a $200 SDRAM, a fairly cheap "insurance policy" in my opinion.

You may have to go into your system's setup BIOS in order to turn on the ECC feature. Not all systems activate ECC by default.

Hard disk space requirements for Windows 2000 Server have been upped to 850MB plus an additional 100MB for each 64MB of system RAM. Of course, this will vary depending on your optionally installed components and future intentions for the server. I would recommend 1GB as the bare minimum and up to 2GB for servers that have numerous server components installed.

A *bootable CD-ROM drive*, although not required, is always highly recommended. A time always comes when your server crashes and you need a reinstall fast. Rather than scrambling for boot disks to get you connected to your installation source on the network, you simply pop the CD in and off you go.

All of your hardware requirements can be further summed up by referencing the *Hardware Compatibility List (HCL)*. Every piece of hardware in your system should be on the list. Anything not on the list could generate problems from application failures to system crashes and probably won't even install at all. Why? Most likely, if your hardware is not on the list, you will have a hard time locating a driver. Should you happen to have an OEM driver that came with the hardware, you are risking system instability because Microsoft hasn't tested or guaranteed it to work. Why do you care? Because if you get on the phone to Microsoft and give them the requisite $200 in order to get them to help you with a problem, and *then* you tell them that you've got hardware that's not on the HCL, the Microsoft support person gets to say, "Golly, I'm sorry, your stuff isn't on the HCL, that's the problem," and hang up. Result: a free two hundred bucks for Bill and no solution for you. If you trust the manufacturer of the hardware who provided the driver to have fully tested it with all aspects of Windows 2000, fine. Be cautious, though. The best recommendation is that if you are buying new hardware, consult the list first. You can find the HCL on your Windows 2000 CD or on the Web at www.microsoft.com/hwtest/hcl/.

Preparing the Hardware

Once you have your hardware, it is highly advisable that you get it working and compatible first. Throughout the process, Setup will examine, activate, reexamine, configure, poke, and prod at every piece of hardware in your system that it can find. This is where the Plug-and-Play intricacies come in. If everything in your system is true Plug and Play, this process should go off without a hitch. Mix in a few older devices that don't fit this bill and you could get some serious problems, including complete setup failure.

In this section, we'll do whatever we can to avoid these problems before we even launch Setup. To resolve these same issues after the installation is complete, see Chapter 6, "Installing Hardware in Windows 2000."

Preparing the BIOS

Most machines have highly configurable BIOSes, which can really play an important role in how Windows 2000 operates. For the pre-Setup phase, you can look for obvious settings that may interfere with your installation. Your boot device order may need customizing to allow you to boot to the CD. This, I find, is one of the most convenient ways to do an install. But then again, if you weren't expecting the CD to be bootable, you could inadvertently keep rebooting into the initial install phase from the CD over and over again, thinking you were getting the hard drive. Nothing major, but it has happened to the best of us.

The most important parts of the BIOS you'll prepare are Plug-and-Play configuration and interrupt reservations. Because most systems capable of running Windows 2000 are fairly modern by default, this step gets a little bit easier. The problem comes when you try to add older, non-Plug-and-Play components into your Plug-and-Play system. For example, you may have a non-Plug-and-Play device that is an old ISA network adapter, hard-coded for interrupt 10. When your Plug-and-Play devices come online, you may have one that prefers to initialize on interrupt 10, not knowing that your ISA card will soon request the same. As soon as the driver initializes the ISA card...conflict.

The best thing to do is to configure interrupt 10 under your Plug-and-Play BIOS settings to be reserved for a non-Plug-and-Play card. This tells any Plug-and-Play device to leave that interrupt alone. But now we have the problem of determining *what* those interrupts are *before* we start the install. Your non-Plug-and-Play device may have a configuration disk that programs it for specific settings. There may be jumpers on the hardware. Most troublesome, there may be no obvious clue as to what it is set for. In this case, a DOS-level hardware analyzer may be required to identify those resources being used.

Once you have identified and recorded all required hardware information, return to your BIOS configuration. You may have a Plug-and-Play configuration screen that lets you define whether certain interrupts are available for general use—including being allocated by Plug-and-Play boards—or if they should be reserved for ISA boards. Since non-Plug-and-Play boards are generally not BIOS aware, they will continue to use the IRQ that has been reserved, but note that when your Plug-and-Play boards initialize, they will be denied the resource usage as defined by the BIOS.

In most cases, the procedure of reserving resources through the BIOS will allow all hardware to work in harmony. If not, you may find it necessary to remove all nonessential, non-Plug-and-Play devices from your system before you begin. Then, once you have a successful install, add your hardware.

 NOTE See Chapter 6, "Installing Hardware in Windows 2000," for more details.

Partitioning

In my opinion, planning the partitioning scheme seems to be one of the most over-looked portions of the installation process. Although Windows 2000 gives you some more advanced features for managing your partitions after the install, what you decide on prior to the install will most likely stick with you throughout the life of your server.

Knowing what type of server you are building plays a tremendously big part in the planning process. Let's go back to our simple member server that serves out several shared directories and a few print queues. You may find it more convenient in the long run to keep your data on one partition and the system on another. Keeping that in mind, you may want to size your system partition based on your minimum requirements, 400MB, plus some breathing room, let's say a few hundred MB, plus some extra room to grow as your business needs grow. Planning this extra room is a delicate balance between how much you anticipate adding to the server side for run-ning applications and how much additional data space your users may require. With storage space as cheap as it is today, I wouldn't create a system partition any less than 1 gigabyte.

If you are intending to use the Remote Installation Services, then be sure to set aside a *big* partition solely for its use. RIS cannot store system images on either the boot par-tition (the partition that the system boots from, usually C:) *or* the system partition (the one containing \WINNT).

With the introduction of dynamic volume attachments, you will find your parti-tions more easily expandable in the future. This will help eliminate the problem of having too small a system partition. Simply mount a new partition to any directory on your NTFS 5 partition, and you're back in business.

File Systems

Choosing file systems for your partitions is usually a bit more straightforward. You have your standard choices of FAT, FAT32, and NTFS. NTFS offers obvious advantages over FAT and FAT32, which will play an extremely large part in your file system deci-sions. However, there are times when the FAT formats are still required. Mostly, this comes into play when you are keeping a machine in a dual-boot format with DOS, Windows 3.*x*, Windows 95, or Windows 98 and want those operating systems to be able to access data on those partitions. There may also be times when you want your system partition in one of the FAT formats. Corrupt or missing files on the system partition can be difficult and time-consuming to repair if you are dealing with NTFS. FAT, on the other hand, allows you to boot with a simple boot disk and either replace whatever files happen to be damaged or back up essential data files before rebuilding.

WARNING   You used to have a safe feeling when you made your system partition NTFS—that no one could simply sit down at the console, pop in a DOS boot disk, reboot your server, and have full access to your data. NTFS was not readable from a DOS boot disk, and the NTFS file system itself was just too big to fit on a single disk. Well, those safe feelings can now be tucked into the same category as the feelings you get when sitting in your car at a stoplight in downtown Washington, DC with your wallet lying casually on the passenger seat and your windows rolled down. Anyone can download the necessary drivers to boot up a simple DOS disk with NTFS access. My point here: NTFS is more secure than FAT, but NTFS only provides the same level of protection as locking your car door and rolling up the windows. If someone wants your data and has access to your server, they can get it. Physically securing the server is the only way to truly protect your data.

That said, I've always been partial to creating a C: formatted as FAT that's 2GB in size. I then put the system installation files (\I386) on there and the system as well. That way, it can be easily worked on by just booting from a DOS floppy. But wait, doesn't Windows 2000 have a built-in "safe boot" mode that works even with an NTFS C: drive? Sure, but the system still can't get you to a C: prompt unless a lot of the system's functioning right, which kind of defeats the purpose of providing an "emergency" command prompt. I'm more comfortable knowing that I can get to my boot and system drive—C:—with just DOS in the event of a disaster. I then format the rest of the drives as NTFS and put applications and data on those drives.

When choosing NTFS for Windows 2000, there are still considerations to be made. Windows 2000 has new features added to NTFS that are not available in NT 4, pre-Service Pack 4. Those features unique to NTFS 5 are:

- Encryption
- Dynamic volume extensions
- Disk quota capabilities
- Distributed link tracking
- Volume mount points
- Indexing

These new file system features make NTFS 5 volumes unavailable locally to NT 4, pre-Service Pack 4. If you were confident enough to upgrade NT 4 servers to Service Pack 4 or higher, you will be in the clear.

NOTE   For all the details on file system considerations, refer to Chapter 7, which covers Windows 2000 storage issues.

NOTE Keep in mind that all of these file system incompatibilities I have been talking about are only relevant in cases of dual-boot systems. For example, boot into Windows 98 and you won't see your NTFS partitions. However, once data is shared out to the network, any Windows 2000–capable client will have access to the share. For full client considerations on these extended NTFS options, see Chapter 12.

Knowing what type of file systems you will want for your finished product is essential prior to installation, but just in case there is any question, go with the lowest common denominator, which is FAT. You can always convert up to NTFS later, but you can't convert NTFS back to FAT.

Server Name

This seems like a no-brainer, but it's a good idea to plan your naming convention. There are two ways that most people make living with server names difficult. The first is underestimating the importance of server names. The second is overdoing it when it comes to a standard convention.

By underestimating naming conventions, you end up with server names like GEORGE, ELROY, JUDY, and ASTRO on your network. This is fine for a small office LAN that will never grow too far beyond your ability to remember these names. When you start getting more than those few servers, it gets difficult to remember who is what.

Sometimes people overdo standard conventions by defining so many formats, items, and indexes into the name that it becomes just as confusing. Some of the things people put in a name is the server's geographical location, building location, room number, role, and an index. For example, a server in Annapolis residing in the Commerce Center building that is an Exchange server might be named ANNCCBEXC01. This information is fine, but keep it to useful information that resembles the important features in your network. Do your network or users really care what building the server is in? What about the city? What if you add another Exchange server in the courthouse? That would be named ANNCRTEXC01. Perhaps a better method here would be to put the EXC first. Simplicity is key. You may want to define your network into systems and that's it. If you had two Exchange systems, one for the Commerce Department and one for the Treasury Department, you may want COMMAIL01 and TREMAIL01. This may allow a better grouping of servers.

The bottom line here is to really think about it. Get the customers and the people who will manage the network involved. Get a consensus on what is important and what is not important. Although you can easily change the name of the server later, you can't easily change the hundreds or thousands of users' workstations that connect to them.

WARNING And *never* name the machine and the user the same! Several errors crop up when you're logged on to a machine named X using a user account that's also named X.

Network Connection and Options

Not knowing your network configuration ahead of time isn't usually going to be a show stopper. Knowing it can save you time though.

Protocols

You will most likely be using either TCP/IP or NetBEUI. Find this out ahead of time. By default, Windows 2000 installs only TCP/IP. TCP/IP has some configuration concerns that will make a tremendous difference in your ability to connect to the network later. If you use TCP/IP, do you have a DHCP server on the network? If you don't have a DHCP server, you will need static information. The most critical elements are your IP address, subnet mask, and some sort of name resolution, whether WINS, DNS, or a HOSTS or LMHOSTS file. Without those components, you will not get anywhere with TCP/IP. If the servers you need to contact are on another subnet, you will need to define your default gateway.

 NOTE See Chapter 17 for more details on what your IP address, subnet mask, and name resolution settings are and how they work.

If you are using NetBEUI on your network, you don't have the same concerns with configuring the protocol. NetBEUI is a simple, straightforward protocol designed for small LANs and has extremely low configuration requirements. It does, however, have another concern. NetBEUI does not route. This means that your routers between subnets of your network will not pass the NetBEUI protocol. You are as good as stranded. If you use bridging between subnets, you're back in business. Find out how your network is configured before you try to rely on NetBEUI.

 TIP Resistance is futile. Just use TCP/IP.

Domain Membership

Almost every server will be a member of a domain rather than a workgroup. Windows 2000 makes this decision easier. In NT 3.*x* and 4.*x*, you had the choice of making your server a member of a workgroup, a member of a domain, a primary domain controller, or a backup domain controller. This was a critical decision during the install. You could switch a server from a workgroup to domain and back very easily, but you could not change roles between a member server and domain controller. You also could not change the domain you controlled. Once you had a domain controller in one domain, you couldn't then make it a controller of another domain. You don't need to make that decision to install Windows 2000. You'll only have the choice of joining a workgroup or domain.

If you're joining a domain, you will need to have a computer account created in the domain. A computer account is almost identical to a user account, and like a user account, it resides in the accounts database held with the domain controllers. If the server is a member of a domain, it can assign rights and permissions to users belonging to its member domain or any of its trusted domains. This is important to your users. They should log on once to the network and never have to be asked for a password again. If the server resides in a workgroup, then the ability to give rights to domain users is out of the question, causing multiple login points.

Whether you're a member of a workgroup or a domain, you can promote the server to a domain controller later by running the Active Directory Installation. This feature sounds like a nice, simple advantage, but it has a bigger impact than is obvious. In an NT 4 environment, you have to define a standard installation for member servers and one for domain controllers. Let's say you want to automate the installs for NT servers across the network. Defining which domain you want a server to control can get tricky. Do you build a different installation setup for each domain? Do you force someone to sit at the console during the installation to answer this question? With Windows 2000, you can build one installation for all servers by putting them in a workgroup and change the membership later.

Networking Components

These are the additional services to be installed, like Internet Information Server and DNS Server. This is where I like to say things like "Ooh...Quality of Service Admission Control Protocol...sounds neat, gimme that." That's exactly what we shouldn't say. Don't overdo it here. Every option selected installs another service or utility that will consume more resources on your server.

Also be aware of the affect certain services may have on the rest of your network. Some services will require clients to be connected explicitly to a given server. On the other hand, some, like DHCP Server, act on a broadcast level and can affect clients just by being present. In addition, most services, just by being present, have an adverse affect on available system resources. Hard disk space is consumed for additional files, memory is taken up by loading more programs, and processor cycles are consumed by running excessive services that really don't have anything to do with what your server is intended to do. Unless you will specifically be using the service on this particular server, don't install these additional components.

Server Licensing

Licensing options remain the same in Windows 2000. You are given per-seat or per-server licensing modes:

- Per-seat licensing requires that every client on the network that accesses your server has its own license. This is the easiest method of adding up your licensing because you only account for how many clients you have; you don't need to worry about either concurrent connections from those clients into a single server or to how many servers each client holds a connection.

- Per-server licensing differs in that each client-to-server connection requires a license. If a client connects to 25 different servers, that client will take up 1 license on each server, totaling 25 licenses. You may know this as a "concurrent use license." It's simpler because it's easy to track—once that 26th person tries to attach, he's just denied the connection—but it's usually more expensive because you've then got to buy a bunch of licenses for *each* server.

Microsoft licensing has always been complex; here's a quick bit of advice about which way to go.

Per-seat is usually the cheapest licensing method if you have more than one server. Under per-seat licensing, you buy a Client Access License, or CAL, for every *computer* that will attach to your enterprise's servers. Again, that's *computer*, not person. So if Joe Manager reads his Exchange mail from the computer on his desktop sometimes, reads it on the road with his laptop sometimes, and once in a while comes in through the firewall from home, then you need to buy *three licenses for Joe Manager*. Surprised? Most people are. On the one hand, it means that if three people share a computer, then those folks only need one CAL. On the other hand, nowadays everyone's got one *or more* computers, so CALs start to add up. By the way, CALs list for around $40, although you can buy them in bulk more cheaply and large organizations usually have some kind of an unlimited-client deal. But you don't want to run afoul of the software watchdogs, so if you go with per-seat licensing, then be darn sure that you've got every computer covered! (And, sadly, that may mean that you've got to disallow employees from checking their e-mail or using other corporate resources from their home, unless they're using a company-issued laptop.)

Per-server licensing is simpler. You tell a server that you've purchased some number of CALs. The server's Licensing Service (a built-in part of Windows 2000) then keeps track of how many people are connected to the server at any moment. If you've got X licenses and the $X+1$st person tries to attach to the server, that person is denied access.

This sounds simple, but the problem is that you've got to buy a CAL for each connection for each server. For example, suppose you've got 4 servers, 25 employees, and

40 workstation PCs—there are more PCs than employees because of laptops and "general access" PCs. Suppose your goal is that all 25 employees can access any and all servers at any time.

Under per-server licensing, you'd have to buy 25 CALs for *each* server, or 100 CALs total.

Under per-seat licensing, you'd license each of the machines—all 40 of them—with a CAL. That one CAL would enable someone sitting at a machine to access any and all of the servers, no matter how many domains your system contains. Thus, in this case, 40 CALs would do the trick. In general, you'll find that per-seat is the cheaper way to go, but again, be careful about remembering to license all of the laptops and (possibly) home PCs.

Most likely, especially in larger environments, the licensing has already been worked out ahead of time. Prior to starting your first install, make sure that your licensing is best suited not just for your network, but also for the way your clients use the network.

Installation Type

Finally, you need to decide whether or not you will be upgrading an existing operating system or performing a clean install. In most cases, this decision is a no-brainer; however, with each type also comes some unique advantages and disadvantages, which will affect your decision.

For the decision phase, let's start with a machine that is currently an NT 4 server that you want to upgrade to Windows 2000. Before you jump straight into an upgrade, you should think about how a Windows 2000 clean install will compare. Maybe your partitioning scheme currently has your system partition maxed out. Perhaps your NT 4 installation has left you with some residual problem that has just never gone away. Even if you're reinstalling the same operating system, there are performance benefits to running a clean install every so often anyway. The Registry has a unique ability to grow, and grow, and grow, without ever cleaning itself up.

If you have ever installed a disk defragmenting utility, you also know how fragmented a well-used system can become. When it comes to fragmentation, one of the heaviest hit files happens to be the system pagefile, which takes enough of a toll on system resources as it is. All of this clutter and excessive work being placed on your system just so it can manage itself consumes excessive amounts of otherwise free cycles left to serve your users. Backing up your data and system information, and even wiping your partitions, could yield a cleaner, more efficient, and even more stable server following the install.

This, however, is where too many people go overboard. When doing a clean install, many people want to revisit server options, service configurations, and even naming conventions. Although this is the best time for the system administrator to reinvent the wheel, it puts an unnecessary burden on your users. The more integrated your systems become, the more effect one slight configuration change will have on another.

You must take careful note of all services, configurations, shares, and other settings that are defined within your system. A full system backup and a rollback plan are invaluable. If you are rebuilding an NT 4 primary domain controller, you will want to promote a backup to primary before you do anything. This will ensure that all of your account and security information is secured on another system. Finally, be ready to test every function of the server from the client's point of view when you are done. This will give you the necessary lead time to resolve any problems before your users discover them.

If you've decided on a clean install, there isn't much more you need to do. If you're running an upgrade, there are still a few considerations. The last thing you want to do is upgrade a cluttered system and carry over any issues that belong to the clutter. Many people sit in front of the server so much that they install their mail client, office suite, and other programs and utilities that are not related to what the server is supposed to be doing. These should all be uninstalled before running an upgrade. Look at your services on the server. Any third-party services, such as antivirus, web publishing, disk defragmenting, or other types of software, should also be removed prior to beginning an upgrade. By doing so, there is much less to get in the way of your install.

Which way is the best? That depends on your needs and those of your users, but let me finish this section with a bit of advice that you'll probably find unpleasant. When you look at the time involved in rebuilding user accounts, shares, services, permissions, and who-knows-what else, you'd think that upgrades are the way to go. But in my experience upgrading from NT 3.1 to 3.5 (I lost my printer shares), 3.5 to 3.51 (some domain controllers simply refused to work), and 3.51 to 4 (a number of miscellaneous problems), I must admit that I'd be *very* wary of simply upgrading a machine, particularly a domain controller, to Windows 2000. If there's any way at all to do a clean install of Windows 2000 on your former NT 4 servers, I strongly recommend it. I should stress that this isn't a fear based on any actual NT-4-to-Windows-2000 problems that I've experienced, just general experience with upgrades.

Setting Up and Installing

Now that we have analyzed the life out of planning for an install, we should be ready to go. The actual installation is broken into three stages. The first is the preinstallation setup wizard. This process defines those options that configure *how* to do the install. The second stage is the text-based setup, which simply defines where to install. Finally, the graphical-based setup stage, also called a setup wizard, customizes everything from installed protocols and services to computer name and domain membership to the system time and date. After this final stage is complete, your server should be ready for final cleanup.

Preinstallation: Phase 1

The first thing you need to do is, of course, connect to your install source. Preferably, you would connect directly to your CD or a network copy of the CD. However, certain circumstances may make this impossible, such as, for example, a system with no operating system, no CD drive, and no DOS-based network drivers to connect you to your install source. In these cases, you'll need the dreaded boot disks. Once you have connected to your source, you need to be in the directory that corresponds to your processor—i386 for Intels. With boot disks, you simply boot the system to the first disk.

Windows 2000 Setup Boot Disks

Boot disks are no longer created using the WINNT command-line parameters. Disk images are stored on your Windows 2000 CD's bootdisk directory with a simple batch file and utility that allows you to create them. Another change is that boot disks no longer come in sets of three; instead, they come in sets of four. (As we all know, bigger software is always better, right?) Here's how you create the disks:

1. Prepare four blank 1.44MB floppy disks.
2. Change to your CD's bootdisk directory.
3. Execute **makeboot.exe:**.
4. Follow all prompts to create the four disks.

From MS-DOS, Windows 3.1, or Windows for Workgroups 3.11, you will need to start your setup in the DOS-based mode found with WINNT.EXE.

From a Windows 9x system, or earlier versions of NT, you'll launch the installation from the WINNT32.EXE. This GUI version of the setup executable gives you that user-friendly, yes-or-no click method of initiating the install. For this example, I'm using the drive letter F: as the CD source on an Intel-based system. To follow along, select Start/Run and enter the following:

```
F:\i386\WINNT32.EXE
```

If you have a system that can be upgraded to Windows 2000 Server, you will immediately reach the prompt to decide whether to run a clean install or an upgrade. If you do not have an upgrade-capable machine, you will be informed that an upgrade is not available, and the upgrade option will be grayed out.

NOTE Only Windows NT servers can be upgraded to Windows 2000 Server. Windows 9*x* and Windows NT workstations can be upgraded to Windows 2000 Professional.

Following the licensing agreement, you may continue to the Special Options screen. The special options let you define language options, advanced options, and accessibility options:

- Language options give the choice of installing multiple languages by holding the Control key down while selecting or deselecting languages with the left mouse button. You can also select your default language, which Setup uses to define all default date, time, currency, number, character set, and keyboard layouts.

- Advanced options customize the way the installation actually happens (see Figure 3.1):

  - Location of Windows 2000 Files refers to the place from which you will be installing Windows 2000. I'm installing from an Intel system from F:\I386. This entry is filled in based on where you launch the install. However, if you would like to redirect Setup to another location, enter that location here.

  - Windows Installation Folder indicates the directory under which Windows 2000 will be installed. This defaults to \WINNT, but it can be changed to another directory if desired. If dual-booting with other installations of NT or Windows 2000, you may need to specify a unique directory name. Do not include the drive letter designation.

  - Copy All Setup Files creates a complete setup source on one of your local hard drives under the directory \win_nt.~ls. Under this directory, you will find the i386 source we are so familiar with.

 NOTE Most systems won't need the Copy All Setup Files option selected. Windows 2000 will do a pretty good job of loading the right drivers to reconnect you to your source after the reboot. However, if you fail to find your source for the text-based setup, this option will get you back on track.

  - I Want to Choose the Installation Partition During Setup allows you to define which partition you will be installing Windows 2000 in. If selected, you will get a prompt following the reboot to choose your partition.

- Accessibility options available for Setup include the Narrator and Magnifier. By selecting these options now, the tools will be available during the next installation phase.

FIGURE 3.1

Advanced Options

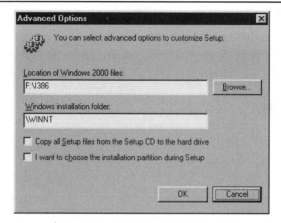

At this point, the installation files will be copied to your hard disk, the system will be prepared for the text-based portion of Setup, and you will be prompted for a reboot.

Anatomy of a Machine Ready for Setup Phase 2

Ever wonder what makes a system continue along its setup path after a reboot? Or have you ever started into the second phase of the setup, had all sorts of problems, and wanted to start from scratch? It will help to know exactly what causes the second phase to start upon reboot so you can easily remove it later. These components are going to be present on your system after completion of the preinstallation phase of the setup:

- On the boot partition, a directory named win_nt.~bt has been created.
- All critical Windows 2000 boot files, including enough drivers to access the network or CD source, have been copied to the win_nt.~bt directory.
- In the win_nt.~bt directory, a file named winnt.sif contains the information you provided from the first phase of the setup.
- The Windows 2000 boot files have been copied to the boot partition if not already present. The system is now Windows 2000 bootable.
- The boot.ini is configured to default to the win_nt.~bt\bootsect.dat after 5 seconds.

Text-Based Setup: Phase 2

The text-based portion of Windows 2000 Setup is very similar to previous versions of Windows NT, only less cluttered. We get our welcome screen, make a few selections on where we want to do our install, and then we sit back and watch the Setup program copy a whole bunch of files. It's a really simple click-next-to-continue process, but there are some gotchas hiding in the deeps.

As soon as your machine boots into the text-based portion of Setup, you may notice a prompt at the bottom of the screen that tells you to press F6 if you need to install additional SCSI or RAID drivers. If you don't want these additional drivers, just wait a few seconds and it will go away. In the real world, you don't use that F6 selection a whole lot anyway, so it is more convenient to just wait a few seconds rather than to keep having to say, "No, I don't want additional drivers." It's kind of like the press F1-tab-F10 or some other machine-specific command to enter the BIOS setup. How would you like to have to press Escape to bypass the BIOS setup utility every single time you reboot your machine? To make a long story short, this F6 prompt comes up quickly. If your system has a SCSI or RAID controller that you know isn't going to initialize without an OEM-provided driver, you'll need to pay attention and hit F6.

The install starts off with a Welcome to Setup screen. You have the choice to set up Windows 2000, repair an existing Windows 2000 installation, or quit. The Press F3 to Quit option will live with you throughout this phase of the setup. If at any time during this phase you decide that you want to abort your setup attempt, this will be your escape route. Upon this exit, your system will be rebooted, but be aware that your boot.ini file has not been changed. Subsequent reboots will still by default cause your machine to restart the setup after 5 seconds at the boot menu. To get rid of this permanently, edit your boot.ini to reflect the default equal to your other operating system boot path of choice. My machine looked like the following:

```
[Boot Loader]
Timeout=5
Default=C:\$WIN_NT$.~BT\BOOTSECT.DAT
[Operating Systems]
multi(0)disk(0)rdisk(0)partition(2)\WINNT="Microsoft Windows 2000 Server"
➥/fastdetect
C:\="Microsoft Windows 98"
C:\$WIN_NT$.~BT\BOOTSECT.DAT="Microsoft Windows 2000 Server Setup"
```

To restore my machine to its original boot preferences, I changed the Default line back to my Windows 2000 Server boot selection and deleted the entire Windows 2000 Server Setup option. Consequently, my boot.ini looked like this:

```
[Boot Loader]
Timeout=5
Default=multi(0)disk(0)rdisk(0)partition(2)\WINNT
```

```
[Operating Systems]
multi(0)disk(0)rdisk(0)partition(2)\WINNT="Microsoft Windows 2000 Server"
➥/fastdetect
C:\="Microsoft Windows 98"
```

To continue along with the setup, press Enter, and you'll arrive at the Disk Partitioning and Installation Location Selection screen. Be careful here. There are two things to do. The most obvious is the selection of the partition in which you want Windows 2000 installed. Highlight the partition where you would like Windows 2000 installed, and press Enter.

Let's take this a step farther. Beneath this screen is a very handy disk partitioning utility. From here, you can completely redo your partitioning scheme. You can delete existing partitions, create new partitions out of unpartitioned space, and format partitions in either the NTFS or FAT format file systems.

 NOTE You can find more information on disk partitioning in Chapter 7.

Before we begin partitioning our drives, let's go back to the planning session we had earlier. Let's say our ideal goal is to have a 1GB Windows 98 C: partition (on which we will leave our current operating system), a 2GB system partition on drive D:, and a 4GB data partition on drive E:. Just to give us all the necessary scenarios to describe how the setup phase partitions drives, we'll assume we have a current partition scheme of a 1GB C: with Windows 98, a 1GB D:, a 2GB E:, and a 3GB F: partition. To go from a 1-1-2-3 gigabyte partition scheme to a 1-2-4 gigabyte partition scheme, we are forced to delete almost all partitions, since we cannot reorder partitions. In other words, we cannot massage our existing second partition of 1GB into a 2GB partition without giving it more room first.

Let's start by deleting the 1GB D: partition. Use the arrows to highlight the D: partition, and press D to delete. A confirmation screen will appear asking you to now either press L to continue the partition deletion or Escape to abort.

 WARNING Always take this opportunity to second-guess yourself. Once you press L to confirm the deletion of the partition, your partition and everything that was on it is gone. Ask yourself what data was on the D: drive. Make sure you can afford to lose it all. Do you have a backup of the data? If it contains a previous NT or Windows 2000 installation, do you have a backup of the security and accounts databases? If rebuilding a domain controller, have you promoted someone else to PDC? Do you have a recent Emergency Repair Disk available? If you are 100-percent confident that you don't need anything on the partition, press L.

When you come back to the main Disk Partitioning screen, you'll see that the second partition of 1GB is now marked as unpartitioned space. Of course, it does no good to repartition this space now because the most you'll get is 1GB again. That would defeat the purpose of the exercise. You need 2GB. So move on down the list to what was the 2GB E: partition and delete it in the same fashion. When you return to the main screen again, after confirming the deletion of the 2GB partition, you'll find that the adjacent, unpartitioned spaces have turned into a single block of unpartitioned space equaling 3GB. Just to keep it simple, we now have our 1GB C:, a 3GB unpartitioned space from our combined, deleted 1GB and 2GB partitions, and a remaining 3GB partition.

At this point, we'll go ahead and create our new 2GB D: partition. Highlight the 3GB free space and press C for create. You'll move into a new screen where you're shown the total available space within which you can create a partition and are asked how large of a partition you want to make. By default, the maximum available space is filled in...3GB. We want to drop that down to 2GB. Press Enter and presto! We have a 2GB new (unformatted) partition, followed by our remaining 1GB that we left out and the 3GB data partition.

After we delete our 3GB partition, it will melt into the adjacent 1GB partition, forming a 4GB unpartitioned space. We can create the new 4GB space and we're set...with partitioning anyway.

Now we still have to format our partition before we can use it. To format a partition, highlight the space listed as New (Unformatted) and press Enter to select the partition as your Windows 2000 installation directory. Really, you're not selecting a partition to format, you're just selecting a partition in which to install Windows 2000. If Setup finds that your chosen installation partition is not formatted, you'll get an additional screen to do just that. You are shown options to format FAT or NTFS. Once again, go back to our planning phase of the setup. We should already know what format we want. Once the format is complete, we continue onward with the installation.

 TIP If you want to simply partition and format drives without continuing to do an installation, you can always choose to go backward after the format and select another partition to format or install to, or you can simply exit the installation program.

Setup will now examine your disks. This examination is not an intensive look into the reliability of your disk. It merely runs a CHKDSK-like utility to verify a clean file and directory structure. After the examination, Setup will copy all Windows 2000 files to your chosen install location. Finally, the system will ready itself for the graphical setup phase and reboot.

Changes in the Windows 2000 Text-Based Setup

You may notice some things missing from this phase of the Windows 2000 setup compared to the setup for previous versions of Windows NT. You no longer get the options to define the following:

- Basic PC type
- Video system
- Keyboard
- Country layout for keyboard (defined in phase 1)
- Mouse

Perhaps these deletions from the text-based setup can be attributed to the better hardware detection found with Plug and Play. With these changes, or reductions to the text-based setup, you will find this stage much quicker and easier than it was in NT.

Graphical-Based Setup: Phase 3

As soon as you boot into the graphical-based setup phase of the install, Windows 2000 will run a Plug-and-Play detection phase to configure all of your hardware. (This will take a while—it's often the most lengthy part of Setup—so now's a good time to go grab a Pepsi, check the voice mail, or run 5 miles.) Surprisingly enough, Windows 2000 did a better job on my particular system than Windows 98 ever did. How could that be? It's simple, really. The Plug-and-Play detection phase tries to attach the correct driver to each device in your system, so a driver must be present for each device. If no driver is available, you'll get an "unknown device" message or a generic device driver will be installed.

Since Windows 2000 has a more recent compilation of drivers, you can expect that some newer hardware will show up for Windows 2000 that otherwise wouldn't in Windows 98. More than anything, this should stress the importance of the Hardware Compatibility List (HCL). Once again, it doesn't hurt to double-check the HCL. Look at www.microsoft.com/hwtest/hcl/ for any recent updates or additions to the list. Some devices that were once thought unsupported may be found. If your device isn't on the HCL, it won't have a driver immediately available. You will be able to install a device driver later, however, if one becomes available.

TIP If you have a device that isn't supported on the HCL or doesn't have a prepackaged device driver on the CD, you can use the /copysource or /copydir switch to copy an additional directory to be used during the setup. This can be used to make your device drivers available for detection. Look for more details in "Performing Unattended Installs" later in this chapter.

Once the Plug-and-Play detection phase is finished, the first dialog we come to is the Regional Configuration screen. This stop defines settings such as number, currency, time, date, and keyboard locale formats.

Next is the Name and Organization dialog. The name and organization listed here show who the product is registered to; it isn't used for anything related to the computer name or other means of defining the server on the network.

The next dialog configures your licensing options, which are the same as previous versions of NT. There is per-seat licensing and per-server licensing. Enter this information in accordance with how you purchased Windows 2000.

Next comes the computer name and administrator password definition. The computer name has already been thought out. The administrator password, especially for a clean install, is extremely important. For a clean install, this is going to be your only way to log on. Don't forget this. And please don't leave it blank unless this is just a machine you're playing around with. The default Administrator account is both powerful and dangerous because, by default, it can't be locked out. That means that someone can potentially crack your system by running a program that tries to log on with the default Administrator account by trying every word in the dictionary or every combination of numbers, letters, and characters. Make their work harder by putting a long and complex—numbers, letters, and characters—password on your default Administrator account.

The Components Selection dialog defines the additional server components that are bundled with Windows 2000, including:

- Certificate Services
- Internet Information Server
- Management and Monitoring Tools
- Connection Manager Component
- Directory Services Tools
- Network Monitor Tools
- SNMP
- Message Queuing Services
- MS Indexing Services
- MS Script Debugger

- Networking Services
- COM Internet Services Proxy
- Domain Name System
- Dynamic Host Configuration Protocol
- Internet Authentication Services
- QOS Admission Control Service
- Simple TCP/IP Services
- Site Server LDAP Services
- Windows Internet Name Service
- Other Network File and Print Services
- File Services for Macintosh
- Print Services for Macintosh
- Print Services for Unix
- Remote Installation Services
- Remote Storage
- Terminal Services
- Terminal Server Licensing

Individually select each component that will be used on your server, and click Details to view subcomponents (see Figure 3.2). A white box with a check mark means the entire component, including all subcomponents, will be installed. A white box with no check mark means that none of the components or subcomponents will be installed. A gray check box with a check mark means that only some of the subcomponents of the main component will be installed.

If a modem was detected, a modem configuration screen will be next. This is where you define your calling options—in particular, your area code and what number to dial to get an outside line. These options are included in the setup so that you (hopefully) won't have to configure each dial-up session in the future to dial a 1 for long distance, a 9 for an outside line, and so on. This little part was not included in the setup phase of previous versions of Windows NT.

The standard date, time, and time zone configuration gives you a last chance to set your system clock. Setting the correct time zone is important, especially in networks that span multiple time zones. Many utilities automatically take into account the time zone and adjust the displayed time accordingly. A server configured with the wrong time zone, even if the time is correct, would display the wrong time.

FIGURE 3.2

Windows Components

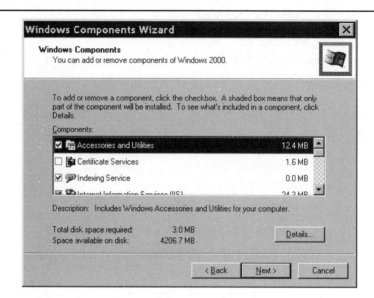

 WARNING Windows NT and Windows 2000 services have become extremely sensitive to time synchronization. Certain services rely on expiration dates, which could be greatly affected if one server has an incorrect time or date setting. Users can even be denied access to network resources if the time is off by a certain amount. Under Windows 2000, you need not synchronize time on all servers anymore because that's done automatically. But that means that the primary domain controller—the first domain controller you install—*must* have accurate time, as every other system looks to that machine for the proper time. Windows 2000 Server now has a built-in Time Service that can be used to synchronize the time. Alternatively, spend about 100 bucks and get a desktop clock from Arcron Zeit that gets its time from radio signals from the U.S. atomic clock in Colorado, then connects to a server with an RS-232 port to deliver the correct time to your server whenever you want; I'd just schedule the server to read the time from the clock twice a day. They're available from many sources, but I got mine at www.thegoodies.com.

The network settings give you two choices: typical and custom. The typical settings assume that you will want the Client for Microsoft Networks, TCP/IP using DHCP addressing, and File and Print Sharing.

By choosing custom settings, you can add, remove, or customize protocols, clients, and services. If you want to assign static IP information, highlight TCP/IP and click Configure. By clicking the Add button, you will be given a choice of Client, Protocol, or Service. This is also reminiscent of a Windows 9x machine. You can add more clients, like Client for Novell Networks, more protocols, like NetBEUI, or more services.

NOTE The terminology for network settings has changed in Windows 2000. For NT-based systems, there is the Server service, which is responsible for passing information out to the network, and the Workstation service, which is responsible for accessing other servers and your local system. Windows 2000 has adopted the Windows 9x terminology. Instead of having a Workstation service per se, you have a Client service. It means the same thing, but it more explicitly defines the Workstation service as a client, which corresponds to Client for Microsoft and Client for Novell. The Server service is now broken into two standard services: File Sharing for Microsoft Networks and Print Sharing for Microsoft Networks.

At the WORKGROUP/DOMAIN selection page, you can join either a workgroup or domain by selecting the appropriate radio button and typing the workgroup or domain name in the corresponding box. If you join a domain, you must have an account created for your machine name. You can do this two ways.

The first way is to select the Create Computer Account button. After clicking OK to join the domain, you will be asked to enter an administrative account name and password. This account must be one with either Administrator or Account Operator rights. If you're using an account from the domain you are joining, enter the account name and password. If you're using an account from a trusted domain of the one you are joining, type the full domain and account name in the *DOMAIN\USERNAME* format. This will inform the validating domain controller of the location of your account. The account creation will be initiated from the server you are installing.

The second method is to not select Create Computer Account and have one created ahead of time. You may want to employ this method if the person running the install doesn't have the appropriate rights and doesn't want to hunt down an administrator when this step comes up. In this scenario, go to Server Manager for the domain on which you want to add the server and select Computer/Add to Domain, or go to Active Directory Users and Computers and select New/Computer. Select NT Workstation or Server and type the name of the computer. During the installation of the server, leave the Create Computer Account option unselected, enter the correct domain name, and you should be set.

Because of security concerns, though, the computer account you create will change its password immediately upon a successful joining of the domain. This means that if you for some reason redo a clean install of a machine that already has a computer account, you can't have your new install assume that account. You must either delete and re-create the account with the same name or build the new server with a different name.

Computer Accounts

Computer accounts are just like user accounts except they are "hidden" accounts. They do not appear in the User Manager window with your users. If you have enabled auditing of successful account management on the domain, you will see an Account Manager security event #624 logged on the PDC. A 624 event is a "create user account" event. Let's say we create a computer account for a new server named CADDY in the LAB domain. Under the details of the security event, the account name that was created will show as CADDY$. This CADDY$ account will be used for all communication between the server and the domain, such as validating user passwords. Once the new server and the PDC "shake hands," the server will initiate a password change for the CADDY$ account. Every 7 days thereafter, the server will again initiate a password change. The same procedure of account and password maintenance is used between domains for trust relationships.

So why is changing a password such a big deal? Well, the server is going to assign permissions to its resources based on domain user accounts. The server isn't going to blindly trust that anyone who claims to be from the LAB domain is a valid user; it wants to make certain that she is in fact a LAB user from the real LAB domain. By having this unique account with a highly secured password, the server can do just that. If the server asks the LAB domain to validate a user but the LAB domain doesn't recognize the correct CADDY$ account and password, authentication fails. This makes it nearly impossible to transport a server out of its domain and gain access to its data.

We're just about done with the install. The Setup Wizard finishes copying the files, configures the system, and performs a final cleanup. The boot.ini will now be changed to reflect the new Windows 2000 install as the default boot option. There is, however, one more step that can optionally be done here. If you need to run another program, perhaps a setup program for some utility or application, then you can tell Setup to run it automatically, using the WINNT32.EXE command-line parameter /cmd:command. (Of course, using this command-line parameter means that you needed to add that /cmd option when you *started* running Setup, so if you've been doing Setup while following along, this advice is a bit late.) This could be used to run a batch file or utility to perform such tasks as transferring user data, installing programs, or other means of further automating your installs. (This is covered in more detail later in this chapter in the section on unattended installs.) The system will now reboot into a full-fledged Windows 2000 operating system.

Post-Installation Procedures

After the installation is complete, there are still a few more steps to perform to finalize the server and prep it for production:

- On the first reboot, the Server Configuration Wizard will pop up automatically. It will identify the last few steps that must be completed to configure your server based on the additional network components you installed. It will also ask you some questions about your existing network to help you determine if you want to install an Active Directory.

 NOTE See Chapter 2 for more information about Active Directory and when and how to launch the Active Directory Installation Wizard.

- Check your device manager for undetected or nonfunctioning hardware components. If you removed any hardware prior to the install due to conflicts, add them back in now. Before we are truly done with the install, every piece of hardware should work properly.

 NOTE See Chapter 6 to learn how to manage hardware from within Windows 2000.

- You'll want to finalize your disk partitions. In many clean install scenarios, you may have unpartitioned space left on your hard drive. Refer to Chapter 7 and take care of these partitions now.
- For most new installations using TCP/IP, a DHCP address will be in effect. This may not be a standard practice for production servers. If necessary, acquire and configure the appropriate static TCP/IP information.
- In many larger network environments, certain services, utilities, tools, or other programs are loaded on all servers. For example, some sites may utilize enterprise management tools that require the usage of an agent that runs on the server to collect and pass information up to a management console. Most likely, some sort of backup software will need to be installed also. Find out what additional software is needed and install it now.

TIP You always want to completely configure a server and install all of its additional components *before* it goes into production. By production, we mean the point at which the first user connects to the server. Since many additional services, configurations, and software components will require a reboot, you'll want this out of the way up front to avoid further disruptions of your users' work.

- Run through the Control Panel applets to set all server configurations the way they should be for the long haul. Especially noteworthy is the System Control Panel settings for the pagefile and maximum Registry size.

 NOTE Check Chapter 20 for information about Control Panel applets.

- At this point, you may get the urge to walk away. Well, hold on just a minute. Too many times, people make some last minute changes, like the Control Panel settings, and leave it at that. Even though you were never told to reboot the system—your changes were instantly accepted—there may be some unexpected side effects the next time you reboot. Just in case, give it another reboot now, before your users begin counting on the server being available.

- If the system is a dual-boot machine, which is usually not the case on a server, boot into all operating systems to make sure the system integrity is intact and all data is available from all required operating systems.

- Once the system itself is complete, create an Emergency Repair Disk. And as an extra safeguard, you may also want to run a full backup.

- Finally, a step we rarely perform is documenting the server. Ask yourself if anyone else could take care of the server should you decide to take a week off for a golf vacation. If there are any special things you have to do, like restart a service every day, it should be documented. This is a step you *must* take before you can consider your operating system "installed." See Chapter 21, which covers preparing for and recovering from server failures, for more details.

At this point, you should have a production-ready server and a method for creating this same server time and time again. It seems like, in addition to actually installing Windows 2000 Server, there is a lot of extra work required, but it is well worth the trouble.

Performing Unattended Installs

Got 50 servers to install? Getting a little tired of shoving CD-ROMs into drives and baby-sitting the setup process, answering the same dumb questions over and over again? Then you need to learn about unattended installs!

An unattended install is simply a method of providing the answers for the setup questions before they are asked in order to automate the installation process. There is no other difference in the install itself. But why do we need to automate? Usually, automation is most beneficial in large networks where Windows 2000 machines will frequently be built. By automating these installs, numerous hours can be spared that would otherwise be spent sitting at the console. Another benefit of unattended installs is that they can be run by non–Windows 2000 experts and produce the same wonderful results every time. This could help in those environments where the only on-site server operator is not an experienced administrator. Rather than spend hours walking them through an install to your specifications, you can merely give them a single command line and be done with it.

We have two ways of reducing the time spent at the console. First is the command-line parameters attached to the WINNT.EXE or WINNT32.EXE. These parameters define how the first preinstallation phase will copy files and prepare your system for setup. The second is an *answer file* that Setup uses to answer questions about server components and options in the graphical-based setup phase.

Command-Line Automation

The command-line parameters tell the Setup program where your source installation files are, where you want to install Windows 2000 Server, where your answer file is located, and other information needed to prepare for the setup. A command-line parameter can also be used to copy an additional folder to your setup source so that those files will be available during the installation. This is handy when you have OEM drivers for the hardware you want to install during the setup rather than waiting until afterward.

Before you start using command-line parameters, it is important to *really* understand them. They can have a very profound impact on the installation process, so let's go over them:

/checkupgradeonly   Whenever Windows 2000 Setup begins, it checks to see if an upgrade is possible. Setup will not attempt to actually run the install.

/cmd:command   This option will launch the given command line before the setup process has completed, which will allow you to perform some additional customization or launch other programs.

/cmdcons   If you have a failed installation on your system, this option will add a Recovery Console item to your boot.ini operating system selection menu.

/copydir:folder   When you're doing automated installs for a large number of machines, this may be one of the most useful options in your arsenal. How many times have you been stopped in the middle of an installation because your network card drivers are, well, on the network? You resort to copying files to a floppy, spend 10 minutes trying to find one, format it, copy files, and hike them back to your server. What a bother. The copydir option can really help you out here. It will copy the specified folder to your installation directory during setup—while you're still connected to your network.

/copysource:folder   Similar to the copydir option, the copysource option copies a specified folder to your installation directory. The major difference between the two is that the copysource directory is deleted after setup is complete.

/debug[level][:filename]   You can tell Setup to log debugging information to a given file based on the following criteria. Level 0 logs severe errors only, 1 adds regular errors, 2 includes warnings, 3 adds all informational messages, and 4 incorporates detailed information about the setup for complete debugging purposes.

/m:folder   This option can be dangerous. When the setup process begins to copy files, the /m option tells it to look in the specified folder first. If that folder contains files to be used in setup, those files be will used. If the files are not present, they will be retrieved from the regular installation source. This can be helpful if a hotfix or alternative version of a file that you choose to utilize for every install (rather than the default version on the CD) is available. Instead of running your install and then running an update or replacing files, you can use /m and perform these tasks in one swift step.

/makelocalsource   Have you ever had problems reconnecting to your installation source after you've rebooted and started the setup? This could be due to things like Setup not recognizing your CD-ROM or network card. This option tells Setup to copy the entire source to your hard drive so that you can guarantee it will be available later.

/noreboot   There may be times when you want to launch the first stage of Setup, get your machine ready for the installation, but not reboot quite yet. This option will bypass the screen at the end of the first setup wizard and return you to your existing operating system without a reboot. When you do reboot, though, Setup will continue.

/s:sourcepath   This seems like a redundant switch. You've already found your source path if you've gotten as far as launching the setup. Setup even knows where it's coming from. This parameter does help identify where your source is—the i386 directory—but it also does something better. You can specify multiple source paths and have Setup copy files from each simultaneously. This can really save you time if you have a slow CD and a slow network. Be careful, though; the first source path identified must be available or Setup will fail.

/syspart:drive   Another very powerful option here when you're considering mass deployments is the syspart parameter. This will start your setup to the specified drive and mark that drive as active. Once Setup is complete, you can physically take that hard drive out of the system, place it in a new system, and boot right into Setup. You must use the /tempdrive parameter with syspart.

/tempdrive:drive   Setup will use the specified tempdrive to place temporary setup files. If you have space concerns with drives or merely a preference on where you want temporary files to go, use this parameter.

/unattend   The unattend option will do an automated, no-input-required upgrade of your previous operating system. All configurations and settings of the old operating system will be used for the upgrade.

/unattend[num]:answer_file   This launches one of the most powerful features of unattended installations—the answer file. The answer file is a text file containing any or all answers to be used throughout the entire setup process. We'll talk about building the answer file in the next section. If your current operating system is Windows 2000, you can also specify a time delay for the reboot, determined by [num].

/udf:id[,udf_file]   One of the problems with automated installations is that you can't fully automate an install unless you provide a name for the server, and all servers—all machines for that matter—on your network *must* have a unique name. This requires that you either enter the name during the setup or use an answer file on all machines, giving them the same name. Neither of those are viable options. The /udf parameter allows you to specify unique information about each installation based on the file specified in the UDF file— uniqueness database file. Here's how it works. In the UDF file, there is a listing of names and a section matching each name with computer-specific information. Usually the computer-specific information will be just the computer name, but anything you put in this file will override the same entry in the answer file. Take a look at a sample UDF file named unattend.udf:

```
;SetupMgrTag
[UniqueIds]
    BS01=UserData
    BS02=UserData
    BS03=UserData
    BS04=UserData
    BS05=UserData
```

```
[BS01:UserData]
    ComputerName=BS01
[BS02:UserData]
    ComputerName=BS02
[BS03:UserData]
    ComputerName=BS03
[BS04:UserData]
    ComputerName=BS04
[BS05:UserData]
    ComputerName=BS05
```

I have five specified, unique computers defined—BS01 through BS05. If I'm sitting down to install a Windows 2000 machine for BS03, I would send the /udf:BS03,unattend.udf parameter. The Setup program will look in the UDF file and have any entries under the BS03 section override those in the standard answer file. So if the ComputerName entry in the answer file is BSxx, Setup will substitute BS03 in its place for my installation.

Those are all of the possible command-line parameters that you can feed the WINNT32 program. To better see how they work, let's try a few samples of running WINNT32 from the CD located in F:.

We are installing to a server that is very specific about using OEM drivers for the network card. If we start the setup and reboot, the default drivers with Windows 2000 won't get us back online. We'll use the /copysource option to copy down our drivers from the network folder of Z:\NIC\OEM. Just to be on the safe side, we also want to use a /makelocalsource option so we have all files available for use. We'll launch the following command:

```
F:\I386\WINNT32 /copysource:z:\nic\oem /makelocalsource
```

During the first phase of Setup, the entire z:\nic\oem directory will be copied to the hard drive to be used during the installation. Once completed, the directory will be removed to free up our space again. We will also get a complete copy of the i386 directory copied to our local installation source. Between the two, we should have no problems with the installation not being able to find files.

Now, we want to launch a setup using an answer file named C:\w2k\setup\unattend.txt and a uniqueness database file named c:\w2k\setup\unattend.udf. To keep parity with the earlier scenario, we'll install this machine with the BS03 ID. In this case, we run this command:

```
F:\I386\WINNT32 /unattend:c:\w2k\setup\unattend.txt
➥/udf:BS03,c:\w2k\setup\unattend.udf
```

Answer Files

We've talked about how to launch Setup using answer files; now let's look into them to see what they are and how to create them. For starters, an answer file is like a typical INI file, around since the early days of Windows. There are sections of the file that are broken up into groups; they're identified by their headers and surrounded by square brackets, like [HEADER1]. Within each section are different settings and the corresponding values to be used during the setup, formatted as ITEM=VALUE. Here is an answer file that I created, designed to provide every single answer for the setup:

```
;SetupMgrTag
[Unattended]
    UnattendMode=ProvideDefault
    OemPreinstall=Yes
[GuiUnattended]
    AdminPassword=Caddy^Green
    TimeZone=35
[UserData]
    FullName=BS
    OrgName=BSI
    ComputerName=BS01
[Display]
    BitsPerPel=16
    Xresolution=800
    YResolution=600
    Vrefresh=72
[LicenseFilePrintData]
    AutoMode=PerServer
    AutoUsers=5
[TapiLocation]
    CountryCode=1
    Dialing=Tone
    AreaCode=410
[RegionalSettings]
    LanguageGroup=1
    Language=00000409
[MassStorageDrivers]
[OEMBootFiles]
[OEM_Ads]
[SetupMgr]
    DistFolder=c:\nt5dist
    DistShare=nt5dist
```

```
[GuiRunOnce]
     Command0=\\setupserver\winnt\welcome.bat
[Identification]
     JoinDomain=BS
     CreateComputerAccountInDomain=Yes
     DomainAdmin=bs\brian
     DomainAdminPassword=lemmein
[Networking]
     InstallDefaultComponents=No
[NetAdapters]
     Adapter1=params.Adapter1
[params.Adapter1]
     INFID=*
[NetClients]
     MS_MSClient=params.MS_MSClient
[params.MS_MSClient]
     RPCSupportForBanyan=No
[NetServices]
     MS_SERVER=params.MS_SERVER
[params.MS_SERVER]
[NetProtocols]
     MS_TCPIP=params.MS_TCPIP
     MS_NetBEUI=params.MS_NetBEUI
[params.MS_TCPIP]
     DNS=Yes
     UseDomainNameDevolution=No
     EnableLMHosts=Yes
     AdapterSections=params.MS_TCPIP.Adapter1
[params.MS_TCPIP.Adapter1]
     SpecificTo=Adapter1
     DHCP=Yes
     WINS=No
     NetBIOSOptions=0
[params.MS_NetBEUI]
```

The first section is [Unattended]. The Unattended mode defines how you want the answers in the answer file fed to the Setup program. Here, I've chosen "provide defaults," which will fill in the answers I've selected but allow the person running the setup to override my answers with his own.

NOTE   See the next section, "The Setup Manager Wizard," for complete information on all unattended mode options.

The [GUIUnattended] section contains answers for some basic questions asked during the graphical-based setup. Look at the AdminPassword setting. This password is going to be used as the local machine's Administrator account password. It is not encrypted. If you are going to be using an answer file to build servers, you may want to make sure that your answer file itself is secured.

[UserData] contains user-specific or installation-specific information, such as name and organization entries and computer name. Remember, any of these values are overridden with the use of the UDF.

[GUIRunOnce] contains the various command lines you want to execute once setup is complete and the new server boots up. I've chosen to have the server run a welcome batch file from a single location on the network. In this batch file on the network, I'll put in some customization routines to finalize my production-ready server. The RunOnce commands—and I'm sorry to put it this way—run once. After the commands in RunOnce execute, they will never be called again.

The [Identification] section tells Setup where to have this new server report, whether to a workgroup or domain. In my example, I've elected to put the server in the BS domain. As mentioned earlier, each Windows 2000 machine in a domain needs a computer account. I'm going to have Setup create this account for me on-the-fly by having the CreateComputerAccountInDomain entry set to YES. The next step in creating a computer account is of course having enough permissions to create the account. You must be an Account Operator or Administrator on the domain to do this honor. The DomainAdmin specifies the account I'm going to be using, and Domain-AdminPassword, the corresponding password.

 WARNING   Again, and I hate to harp, but this password is *not* encrypted. This one, however, is a little more dangerous than the local Administrator password. The local Administrator password can be changed after the install and it would only affect the one machine. The DomainAdmin account and password have administrative rights to the entire domain. If this account and password are jeopardized, the entire domain are jeopardized.

TIP Notice my entry for DomainAdmin–bs\brian. The bs\ portion tells the target domain that the brian account is coming from the bs domain. Granted, since I'm joining the bs domain, the validating server will assume that I'm coming from the bs domain. However, if I wanted to use an account from a trusted domain, I could use a fully specified domainname/username to avoid confusion.

The [Networking] section allows you to use either default components or custom components. Default components include File and Print Sharing (your basic server service or ability to share files on the network), Client for Microsoft Networks (your basic workstation service or ability to connect to other resources on the network), and a dynamically assigned TCP/IP address for your TCP/IP protocol. In my installation, I chose not to use the default settings.

The next set of sections works a little differently. You'll see that one section has a value that points to yet another section—for example, the [NetClients] MS_MSClient= params.MS_MSClient. This is telling Setup to, first of all, install the MS_MSClient (this is Client for Microsoft Networks, by the way). Next, it tells Setup that the parameters to be used for MS_MSClient are found in the params.MS_MSClient section. Look a little farther down in the answer file and, lo and behold, a [params.MS_MSClient] section.

As you can see, the answer file contains a lot of information. It's actually quite easy to create an answer file, but using the right sections, items, and answers can be difficult.

The Setup Manager Wizard

The easiest way to create answer files and launch automating installs is by using the Windows 2000 Setup Manager Wizard, which is found in the Windows 2000 Resource Kit Deployment Tools. This wizard walks you through all of the questions you will need answered during a setup and builds your answer file for you.

Building the Answer File

Upon launching the Setup Manager Wizard, you will be asked whether you want to:

- Build a new answer file.
- Build an answer file based on your current computer's configuration.
- Modify an existing answer file.

The easiest way to duplicate an install is to build the absolutely perfect Windows 2000 system and run the Setup Manager from that machine using the option to duplicate the current configuration. No muss, no fuss. Select that option and out comes an answer file that will provide all of the options you have already installed. Using the New Answer File option, you can specify any options for the setup that you want, but you can also leave some unanswered for the user to input. This lets you create completely unattended installations or just partially unattended installations.

In the Installation Product screen, you have options of Windows 2000 Server, Windows 2000 Professional, Remote Installation Services, or a Sysprep Install. Select the type of operating system installation you want to automate and the wizard will immediately begin walking you through all relevant setup options to build an answer file.

As shown in Figure 3.3, the User Interaction Level screen defines how the setup is to proceed in regards to the level of input required from the user.

You have the following options:

Provide Defaults   You fill in the default answers and the user only has to accept those defaults or make changes where deemed necessary.

Fully Automated   You fill in all answers and the user just sits back and watches. This option is of course the most automated and will be extremely useful when building multiple servers that have the exact same load. There won't, however, be too many cases where this will be 100-percent effective for servers. The most you could expect is to build baseline servers with the automation and configure your additional software and components later. Most likely, this option will be primarily used for building Windows 2000 Professional desktops.

Hide Pages   The user will only get a chance to interact with Setup where you did not provide information. All pages where you did provide information are skipped. This could be a useful alternative to those scenarios where a fully automated install just doesn't quite make sense. You'll still need someone to provide some data, but you can automate entries that will be standard.

Read Only   This option is similar to the Hide Pages option with the exception that the install will still show all pages but will not allow the user to change the defaults that you provide.

GUI Attended   This option will only automate the second phase, or the text-based portion, of the setup. The third graphical phase of Setup will be like a normal install, asking the user to manually enter all information. This option could be handy in circumstances where you merely want to save yourself some time at the console. You should have fairly standard partitioning schemes for this option to work consistently, but you have added flexibility when it comes to customizing server hardware and components during the install.

Once you've selected the type of install, the next series of questions will be almost identical to the questions you encounter during the actual setup process. For each question covered during the normal, manual installation, there will be a similar question in the Setup Manager Wizard. In addition, you will get the chance to define SCSI devices that were typically done via the F6 command during Setup, as well as the option to define an additional Hardware Abstraction Layer—HAL—if your particular server requires one to recognize the system. You'll see many questions that have an option to not specify an answer at all. This will allow the user to fill in the appropriate information.

WARNING   Be careful when automating setup options. If you consider the planning phases of a setup to be important, double that importance for automated installs. The choices you make for an automated install will be the ones you live with not only once, but for as many times as you use the answer file. Really think things through here.

WARNING   Remember the security risks when creating the answer file. You'll be asked to specify the Administrator password for each machine that uses the answer file. This is helpful for skipping the need to enter that information, but as discussed earlier, the output answer file does not encrypt this password even though the wizard only displays asterisks in the password box as you type.

Building a Distribution Folder

Now that your answer file is complete, the Setup Manager Wizard needs to know how you plan on using it. You can either use the file in conjunction with the installation source on the Windows 2000 Server CD or build a *distribution folder* (see Figure 3.4).

A distribution folder is a single source that contains the installation source files, the unattended answer files, batch files to kick off the setup with answer files, OEM drivers, and other custom files that you choose to include. This could be most helpful in large networks where you want to be able to create your unattended installation with the least amount of future maintenance as possible. How? Well, instead of installing from a CD (where the path would be F:\I386), getting your OEM drivers from Z:\OEM (in which case Z: is mapped to \\SETUPSERVER\WINNT), and using an answer file from a floppy disk, you can have one location to remember, one source, one batch file, and most importantly, only one set of data to maintain. If connecting to a single source for installations is a concern due to network issues like a slow WAN connection, a CD source may still be your best bet. We're going to walk through the creation of a distribution folder, but remember to focus on the advantages of a distribution folder—a single source.

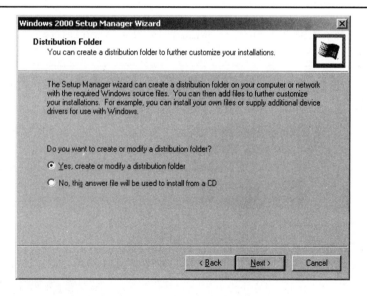

FIGURE 3.4

Creating a distribution folder

The first thing you need to do is come up with a name for your distribution folder and a location, as shown in Figure 3.5. I've chosen to place the folder in my c:\w2k\dist folder and have it shared as w2kdist.

FIGURE 3.5

Modifying a distribution folder

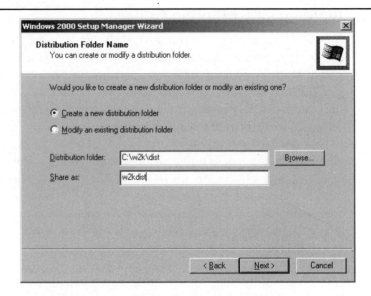

You can also select an existing distribution folder to modify. This will allow you to change your answer files in the folder, incorporate new OEM drivers, and so on.

Two dialogs will present opportunities for you to incorporate additional mass storage drivers (Figure 3.6) or Hardware Abstraction Layers.

FIGURE 3.6

Creating additional mass storage drivers

Mass storage drivers are used in the event your hardware requires an OEM driver that otherwise has no support from the default Windows 2000 installation source. To install additional drivers, select the Browse button and browse through your computer's drives and network connections to point to the driver's file location. You can repeat this process to add as many additional drivers as you like.

The Command to Run option, shown in Figure 3.7, will launch the specified commands at the end of the setup but before the system has rebooted and logged back on.

To add a command, type it into the Command to Run box and click Add. Again, repeat this process to get as many commands into the command list as you like. To remove one, select the item in the list and click Remove. The types of commands you might want to consider here could be simple copy statements to customize your server. For example, you may want to copy a shortcut to your Administrative Tools folder to your desktop. You can also use the Move Up and Move Down buttons to optimize the order of the commands as desired.

OEM branding is a nice way to customize what your screen will look like while the GUI portion of Setup is running (Figure 3.8). The background must be 640x480 with 16 colors in order to look right. The logo will be placed in the upper right-hand corner of the screen during setup.

FIGURE 3.7

Commands to run at the end of setup

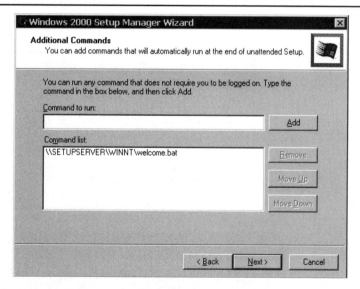

For both entries, either type out the path to your bitmap or select the Browse button to search for it. One thing to note here is that once you find the files, they will be copied to your distribution folder. So even though I have selected a file that is local to my machine, it won't tell all installations to look for the files in that exact directory. Instead, the files will be referenced from the distribution folder share.

FIGURE 3.8

*The OEM Brand-
ing screen*

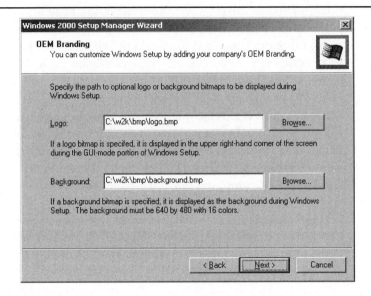

Here comes a really neat part of distribution folders—the additional files or folders
selection (Figure 3.9).

FIGURE 3.9

*Copying additional
files or folders*

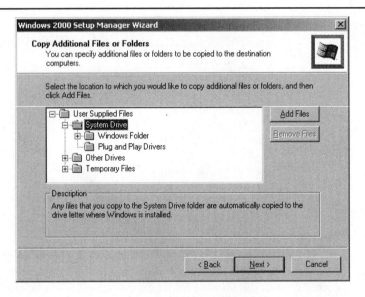

You can add as many files or folders as you like into several different locations, and
they will be added to your distribution folder. These folders are defined as follows:

System Drive The system drive folder is our installation location for Windows 2000. Select the plus sign next to the System Drive folder and you'll see

additional folders named Windows Folder and Plug and Play Drivers. Click the plus sign under Windows Folder and you'll see the SYSTEM32 directory. Anything you put into these folders will be copied down to the installing computer's corresponding location and will stay there after the install.

Other Drives   You can also add files or folders to specific drives. Expand your Other Drives folder to get a list of hard drives to copy files to. Again, these files and folders will stay after the setup is complete.

Temporary Files   There could be times when you just want files, like maybe the Command to Run batch file routines, to be available for the setup but gone afterward. Add those here. Keep in mind, though, once Setup is done, these files or folders will be deleted.

So let's figure out what our goal is, where we need to put the file or folder to accomplish it, and of course, how to get it there. Let's say we have a new Plug-and-Play device—an ATI video card—that won't have the latest and greatest drivers available on the Windows 2000 CD. In this case, the Plug and Play Drivers folder under the System Drive selection would be our target. Expand System Drive, then select the Plug and Play Drivers folder. Click Add Files, then browse for the directory that contains the drivers. Mine is a folder named ATI (see Figure 3.10). Once you select the folder, you'll see it under the Plug and Play Drivers folder.

FIGURE 3.10

The Plug and Play Drivers *folder expanded*

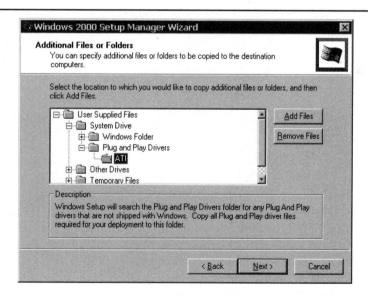

If you want to install a set of batch files and commands that you use on your servers to the D partition, you'd add those to the Other Drives/D folder. Repeat this process as many times as necessary to put all files and folders into your distribution folder.

We're almost done. Now you need to select a name and location for the answer file, as shown in Figure 3.11. Make sure you put it into a location where it is readily accessible to those using it, like the distribution folder.

This falls into that category of remembering why we're using distribution folders. If I'm building my distribution folder on c:\w2k\dist, I don't want to put my answer file in c:\.

 WARNING Now here is a *big* problem. We'll call it an inadvertent feature of the Setup Manager distribution folder creation process. I have chosen to place my answer file in the C:\w2k\dist folder. Guess what else happens in this folder? The installation source files, or the CD's i386 directory, gets copied in here next. In that directory on the CD is a sample unattend.txt file. My unattend.txt file is going to be overwritten as soon as the CD source file copy takes place. You should name your answer file something else, like myanswerfile.txt. This will prevent it from being overwritten.

FIGURE 3.11

Naming the answer file

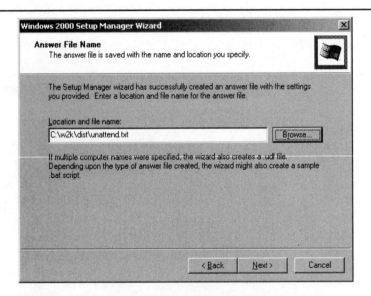

Next, choose the location from which you want to copy the files to build your installation source. You can use the CD or some other source, as shown in Figure 3.12. If you've already customized your installation source on a network share with updated driver files, you might want to use that source.

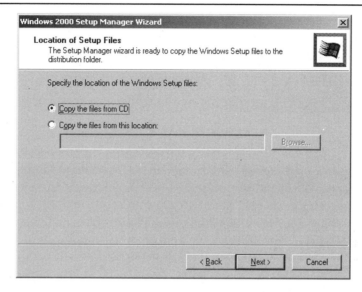

After the files have been copied down from your specified source, you are given confirmation that the Setup Manager Wizard has completed successfully and are told where the answer file, sample batch file, and if applicable, the uniqueness database file has been created (Figure 3.13).

TIP It might be a good idea to take a look at these files now, just to make sure they have been created the way you thought they would. This is where I found out that my unattend.txt file was overwritten with the default file that came on the CD.

For a better look at your distribution folder, open Explorer. Figure 3.14 shows my distribution folder.

At the root of the distribution folder, c:\w2k\dist, you can tell by the icon of a folder with the hand underneath that it is shared to the network already. All files required for the installation are mirrored from the CD source to the distribution folder root. This includes all files under the c:\W2k\dist folder and the directories COMPDATA, LANG, SYSTEM32, UNIPROC, WIN9XMIG, WIN9XUPG, and WINNTUPG. You can also see an OEM folder. This contains all of those additional files and folders that I added to the setup. In the root of OEM are copies of my specified command lines and my OEM branding bitmaps. Look back at Figure 3.9 to correlate where those files and folders were actually placed. The folders below OEM are $$, which corresponds to Windows Folder and has the SYSTEM32 subdirectory, and $1, which is my System Drive folder with a Drivers subdirectory beneath it, containing my specified Plug-and-Play drivers (my ATI file was placed here). Finally, I have a C and D subdirectory, where anything placed under Other Drives goes.

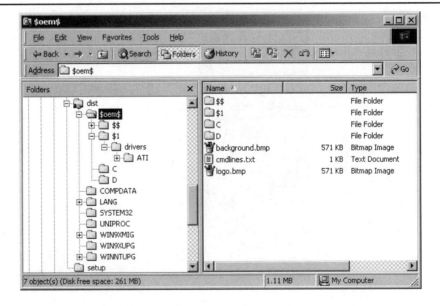

Setup Wizard Output Components

Whether you used a distribution folder or not, the Setup Manager Wizard creates two or three files:

Unattend.txt   This file is the actual answer file. It contains all of your answers from the Setup Wizard in an INI file format.

Unattend.udf   The UDF is the uniqueness database file. This file will only be created if you specified multiple computer names to be used with the unattended installation. When launching the unattended install, you will need to use unattend.bat.

Unattend.bat   This batch file includes a sample command line required to launch the unattended install that you have just created. Several environment variables are set within the batch file:

- AnswerFile is set to the location where you saved Unattend.txt.
- UdfFile is set to the location of your uniqueness database file.
- ComputerName is fed to Unattend.bat by a parameter that you must specify. This parameter must match one of the computer names that you specified during the setup wizard because the install will try to match this parameter to one contained in the UDF file.
- SetupFiles points to the distribution folder's UNC name. This parameter is fed to Setup as the source file location. Before you try to use the Unattend.bat, you may want to look at how this variable is being set. Although the share name created with a distribution folder defaults to nt5dist, it is highly unlikely that your server is also named nt5dist. Check and modify this path if necessary.

Launching an Unattended Install

All you need to do now is actually use your answer file. To launch the unattended install, simply connect to your distribution folder or go to the location of the files we created and launch Unattend.bat with a parameter containing your appropriate server name. If, instead of defining multiple computer names to be used with your answer file, you left the entry blank, selected uniquely generated names, or specified only a single name, the UdfFile and ComputerName variables will be left out of the install. In these cases, simply launching Unattend.bat will work just fine.

Alternatively, you could launch the setup and answer file manually, using the command-line parameter /unattend:filename. So, for example, if you had a CD in drive F: and an unattended installation script named unattend.txt in C:\, you could start the unattended install with the following command:

```
F:\i386\winnt[32] /s:f:\i386 /unattend:c:\unattend.txt
```

Using SYSDIFF

The SYSDIFF utility is an install automation of another sort. Typical automation generally deals with walking through an installation *process*. I say "process" because the typical installation of an application like, let's say, Microsoft Project not only copies its files to a specific application folder on your hard drive, but to your Windows directory, probably the system and system32 directory, and makes all sorts of Registry changes. This prevents you from simply copying the source files to your machine and launching the program. The installation must perform all of these little tasks or the program doesn't work, leaving you with two options: run the install manually or feed the installation program the answers automatically. Sometimes, this can be inconvenient.

This is where SYSDIFF comes in. SYSDIFF is really simple. SYSDIFF allows you to take a snapshot of your computer. This snapshot is like a picture of everything on your system. Every file, every Registry setting, everything. Next, you install whatever program you want, make whatever changes you want, and take another snapshot. SYSDIFF then calculates the difference between the two snapshots. Everything from files copied, changed, and replaced to Registry changes gets recorded. This difference file can now be used on other systems to make the same changes.

Creating the SYSDIFF Package

Before you create the package, you need a baseline system. The more complicated your pre-snapshot system is, the harder it will to be to get a difference file that can be accurately used on multiple target machines. If you plan to use SYSDIFF for repetitive clean installs, start the same way you would typically start.

The first step is the preinstall snapshot. To take this snapshot, run SYSDIFF /snap snap_file. Snap_file is the filename of the snapshot file that you will be creating. Next, install your application and run SYSDIFF /diff snap_file diff_file. This will compare your current system with your snap_file and produce your difference file. A key point to remember here is that you cannot run a difference file unless your snapshot file was created on the same installation of Windows 2000. In other words, you can't take your first snapshot on a machine, reinstall Windows 2000, install your applications, and then take your difference snapshot.

Applying the Difference File

Once your difference file is ready, you can either apply it to new target machines or build an installation source in your distribution folder that was created using the Setup Manager Wizard.

To apply the difference file to a target machine, run SYSDIFF /apply diff_file. A major caveat here is that the system root directory must be the same on the target machine as it was on the source machine. This includes the drive letter and folder name. I hate to harp on it, but refer back to "Planning and Preparation" earlier in this chapter. I can't stress strongly enough that even the smallest details will come back to haunt you if you don't plan properly.

Now we'll do a walk-through of a SYSDIFF package creation and application to a new machine. We'll assume that I have a typical Windows 2000 Server installation for my network. The first thing I need is my before snapshot. I'll run the following command:

```
SYSDIFF /snap c:\snapshot.1
```

Now I have a picture of my server. The next step is to install the new program, utility, service, or whatever it is I need to do. I run the application setup program, let it do its own thing, and reboot the server if necessary. To conclude the difference file creation process, I need to let SYSDIFF find out everything on my server that has changed since I took my first snapshot. So I run the following command:

```
SYSDIFF /diff c:\snapshot.1 c:\diff.1
```

I've taken my c:\snapshot.1 file, used the /diff option to calculate the difference, and sent the resulting differences to the C:\diff.1 file. That's it—I now have a difference file that will effectively reproduce the installation process that I went through between the two SYSDIFF commands. All I have to do now on any new server installations where I would have otherwise wanted to run the application setup is to merely apply the difference file I created. What I'll do is copy the difference file to \\SETUPSERVER\WINNT\diff.1. Now I know it will be available to any new Windows 2000 installation. From my new server, I'll run the following command:

```
SYSDIFF /apply \\SETUPSERVER\WINNT\diff.1
```

All changes that were recorded into the difference file will be applied to my new server. Just to be on the safe side, I'm going to do a reboot to make sure all new Registry entries are read, DLLs are loaded, and my obsessive-compulsive attitude toward server reboots is satisfied. Once the server is rebooted, it should look like I ran the setup as I normally would.

Troubleshooting an Installation

Windows 2000 produces a relatively smooth installation. Plug and Play helps in many ways by eliminating the need to know and preconfigure all of your hardware prior to launching an install. There will be a few instances where you will have problems though.

We discussed failed hardware components earlier. If your system locks up during the hardware detection and configuration phase, you have something that does not play nicely in the sandbox. Sometimes it will be obvious which component is the culprit. Sometimes it won't be so easy. Start with the obvious methods of troubleshooting—the debug setup parameter discussed in "Command-Line Automation" earlier in this chapter. This will definitely help identify where the install goes wrong. The next step is to either resolve or work around the problem.

If you have hardware conflicts causing problems with your install, you have a couple of options. First, you could configure the hardware and BIOS, as was discussed earlier in "Preparing the Hardware," to get along with the other hardware. Maybe the troublesome hardware is a sound card that refuses to accept the detection phase. Rather than spend x amount of time trying to get it to work, pull it out of the system. Get your Windows 2000 system running first. Then add the component later.

Let's say you completely blow an install at some point. You want to start over from scratch, but you don't want to format your partition and lose potential data. There are three things on your hard drive related to the install that you will want to clean up before starting over:

- The `$win_nt$.~ls` directory if you copied all files to the system

- The `$win_nt$.~bt` directory

- A line in your `boot.ini` pointing to `$win_nt$.~bt\bootsect.dat`

Removing these entries will make your system completely forget that an install was ever happening, allowing you to start over at square one. Be careful when modifying the `boot.ini`. If you're reverting to an old operating system, make sure your `boot.ini` default is put back to the way it was. Leaving an entry pointing simply to C:\ will let your DOS or Windows 9x operating system's files boot the system. Here's a sample `boot.ini` file for a dual-boot Windows 2000 and Windows 98 machine:

```
[boot loader]
timeout=30
default=C:\
[operating systems]
multi(0)disk(0)rdisk(0)partition(2)\WINNT="Microsoft Windows 2000 Server"
C:\="Microsoft Windows 98"
```

The [boot loader] section defines how your boot menu will act. This example shows a time-out of 30 seconds, at which point the default operating system on C:\ will be booted. Once the boot process continues to the C:\, it will require the standard boot files of that operating system. In Windows 98's case, that is the `MSDOS.SYS` and `IO.SYS`. The [operating systems] section defines the selection menu and where the operating system corresponding to each choice resides. Here, Windows 98 resides in C:\, and Windows 2000 resides on `multi(0)disk(0)rdisk(0)partition(2)\WINNT`. This translates into the \WINNT directory of the disk and partition defined by the address of `multi(0)disk(0)rdisk(0)partition(2)`.

NOTE See Chapter 7, "Managing Windows 2000 Storage," for complete details on how logical drives are defined in Windows 2000.

 NOTE If you want to get rid of the Windows 2000 boot menu altogether and return to your single boot up into Windows 9*x*, you must delete the boot.ini, NTDETECT, and NTLDR from your boot partition. After they are gone, you will need to re-SYS your boot partition to make it fully DOS- or Windows 9*x*–bootable again. The best way to make sure this will work is to first boot into your DOS or Windows 9*x* operating system, format a bootable floppy, and copy SYS.COM to the floppy. Delete the Windows 2000 boot files listed above, reboot your system to the floppy, and run a SYS C: command.

The Recovery Console

Windows 2000 has a nifty new Recovery Console that can go miles farther than the old methods of fixing broken installations. Take this scenario—one that I've dealt with numerous times. An important system file gets corrupted, umm...deleted. You know how it goes, "Let's see, NTFS.SYS, I never use NTFS.SYS, let's just delete it to make more space." The next time you reboot, the system won't come up. Go figure. Now you need to copy a new NTFS.SYS to your hard disk. You make a bootable floppy, put NTFS.SYS on it, reboot to the floppy, and find out that your system partition is NTFS. We all know that you can't boot to a DOS floppy and access an NTFS partition. Enter the Recovery Console.

What is the Recovery Console? It is a scaled-down cross between a DOS command-line environment, certain Windows 2000 setup functions, and partition-correcting utilities, all with the capability to access NTFS partitions.

The first thing you need to do is get into the Recovery Console. There are two ways to do this. First, you can launch the WINNT32 setup program with the /cmdcons parameter. A brief setup routine and file-copying session will take place to create your console. Once completed, your boot.ini will reflect a new operating system selection, Microsoft Windows 2000 Command Console. Simply boot your machine and then select that menu item. Of course, this method would only work if one had the foresight to install the console before the system broke down. If you haven't created it ahead of time, don't worry, you can get there from the normal setup routine.

Launch setup like you normally would—from the CD, the boot floppies, whatever you prefer. At the Welcome to Setup screen, select the repair option. From there, you will get the option to repair your installation using either the emergency repair process or the Recovery Console, and off you go.

Once you enter the console, you get a selection of all Windows 2000 installations on the system. Enter the number of the installation you want to work on and press Enter.

 NOTE When entering the console from Setup, you go straight into the console. When entering the console from your boot menu, you'll need to press F6 at the "Press F6…" prompt to install SCSI drivers. This will let you access your SCSI hard drives or CD-ROMs that require a driver.

The next step is validation. One of the major differences between the FAT and NTFS file systems is security. Even though you can see the NTFS partitions now, you still need to have access to the file system. The console will ask you to enter the Administrator password. After you enter the password, you are dropped at a command prompt in the systemroot directory of the installation you chose. Simple!

Well now what? You're at this command prompt. What do you do with a command-prompt-only version of Windows 2000? Start off with a HELP command, which shows you a list of all available commands. You can do things like copy files, change directories, format drives, and other typical DOS-like file operations. To resolve the current problem, you would just copy your NTFS.SYS from your floppy to your Windows 2000 installation folder and you should be back in business. In addition, there are some other commands that can help you get back into Windows 2000:

DISKPART This command will launch a disk partitioning utility almost identical to the utility we used during the text-based phase of setup.

FIXBOOT This command will make a new boot sector on your drive of choice and make that partition your new boot partition. If you happened to destroy your boot sector information and can't boot at all, this may be your best bet.

FIXMBR The FIXMBR command will repair the master boot record on the selected drive.

DISABLE If you are having problems with a device that is not letting Windows 2000 boot completely—let's say you accidentally changed a device's startup parameter or installed a new service that keeps killing your system—the DISABLE command will let you prevent that service or device from starting.

ENABLE This is just the opposite of DISABLE. Let's say you disabled an important boot device; reenabling it may be the easiest solution.

LISTSVC Both the DISABLE and ENABLE commands require that you tell it *which* service or device to alter. This command will give you a list of all devices and services.

SYSTEMROOT   This command gives you a quick return path back to your systemroot directory without having to fight those long pesky CD commands. It also helps you when you forget which drive and directory your chosen Windows 2000 installation resides in.

LOGON   The logon command takes you back to your first prompt of the Recovery Console so you can choose another installation to repair.

HELP   In case you can't remember the command, this is a nice little reminder.

Now that you know what the Recovery Console does, let's run through a couple of examples. We'll take the first example from our scenario earlier, a known missing or corrupt NTFS.SYS. Once we've logged in to the Recovery Console for our Windows 2000 installation and copied a fresh NTFS.SYS to our A: drive, we need to copy it to our systemroot directory. We should already be in the systemroot directory, but just to be sure, we type **SYSTEMROOT**. Now, we type **COPY A:\NTFS.SYS**. Easy huh?

Here's another problem. We have recently installed a new service named Billy-BobY2KChecker. It is set to start automatically during boot up, but as soon as it does, blue screen! Into our Recovery Console we go. At the prompt, type **LISTSVC**. We should see amongst our many devices and services BillyBobY2KChecker service set to automatic. Now, we type **DISABLE BillyBobY2KChecker**. Next time we reboot into Windows 2000, we should get in just fine and should probably uninstall the problem software.

The Recovery Console is a handy utility that can get you out of a lot of trouble. Once you have installed Windows 2000, it might not be a bad idea to run the WINNT32.EXE with the /cmdcons parameter. This won't actually launch setup, just configure the console. You will always have the console available in your boot menu, although it won't be set as default.

Installing Windows 2000 on Workstations with Remote Installation Services

Well, by now, you've probably tried shoving the CD-ROM into some computer's drive and installed Windows 2000. You may well have had some luck at it and found that after a bit of twiddling, you could make it work quite well. "Cool," you might have thought, "Installing Windows 2000 will be a snap."

But then, you probably realized that you'd have to do it for *several hundred machines*. Let's see now, doing the exact same set of twiddling several hundred times would take…well, more patience and time than many of us have. It would be nice to be able to spend a fair amount of time on just one computer, getting it just right, and then to "xerox" that configuration onto dozens or hundreds of other computers.

And for years, many of us did just that. Back when I worked in training labs teaching Windows 3 running atop DOS 5, it was a simple matter to just boot up a workstation with a floppy containing the Novell client software, format the workstation's C: drive, and then XCOPY an entire drive image from a Novell shared volume onto the workstation. The whole process was completely automated once I got it started and took no more than about 20 minutes.

Later on, with the advent of bigger operating systems like Windows 95, drive copier programs like Ghost and Drive Image Pro came out. These drive copiers didn't care what files were on a computer; they'd just copy a physical hard disk or partitions from that hard disk to a network folder for you. Then you could set up a new computer to look just like the prototypic computer by booting the new computer from floppy and then pulling down the Ghost or Ghost-like (would that be "Ghostly"?) image.

That worked fine for Windows, but not for NT, as NT's secure and so each computer with NT installed on it has long and machine-specific strings of numbers embedded in it, numbers called Security IDs or SIDs. Cloning one machine's NT image onto thousands of machines would lead to thousands of machines with identical SIDs. While that might not *sound* terrible, it could have some very bizarre side effects.

For example, suppose you start up a new PC with a cloned copy of NT Workstation/ Windows 2000 Professional on it, logging in the first time as the default administrator. The first order of business is then to create a local user account for yourself. But inside NT, that account would get an SID. As this is the first account created besides the built-in Administrator and Guest accounts, that account's SID will be the first available in the range of SIDs on this machine.

Now imagine that Janice down the hall, who has a machine containing the exact same cloned image on her system, also logs onto her new machine as its default administrator and creates herself an account. It'll have a different name than your account— but that won't matter. NT doesn't really care what your name is; it cares what your SID is. And what value SID does Janice have? Well, as it's the first created account, you guessed it—her account now has the same SID as yours.

What does that mean? Well, suppose you made your local account an Administrator account. That means that when she's logged on to her own machine with her own account, she can use Windows 2000's remote control tools to do administrator-like things to your system over the network. That's not a good thing, unless you and Janice are really good buddies.

As a result, disk cloning vendors have come up with "SID scrambler" programs. You copy the cloned image onto a new machine and then run the SID scrambler. It creates a unique set of SIDs on the newly cloned machine and all should be well. Microsoft, however, says that the SID scramblers from the two big players, Symantec's Ghost and PowerQuest's Drive Image Pro, won't do the whole job. I honestly don't know if this true or if it's just Microsoft...well...being Microsoft. In any case, now

Microsoft's got a method for rolling out a single workstation image to dozens, hundreds, or thousands of machines while simultaneously ensuring that each machine has unique SIDs. It's a service called the Remote Installation Services, or RIS. In this section, you'll learn how to set it up and how to get those images out to all of those PCs hungering for an operating system.

RIS Overview

RIS lets you designate a server or a set of servers as *RIS servers*. A RIS server contains the files necessary to install Windows 2000 *Professional*—yes, sadly, RIS only helps you distribute the workstation software, not server software, onto a computer from across the network. RIS can deliver an operating system to a waiting PC in one of three formats:

Simple I386-based installation   In this simplest form, RIS is just a place to store the Windows 2000 Professional installation files. How's it different than just putting I386 onto a directory on any old file server and then sharing that directory? Not very much except in one way: you can go to the PC that you intend to put Windows 2000 Professional on and boot it with just one floppy and you'll be off and running, no messing around with the DOS Client for Networks or the like. Of course, once this installation starts up, you've got to sit at the computer and answer all of Setup's questions, baby-sitting the computer while Setup runs.

Scripted I386 install   This installation is like the preceding situation, with the added benefit of unattended installation. You just go out to the target PC, boot the floppy, and away it goes. These first two options are called *CD image format* images.

Complete system image with minimal setup interaction   This option is really the more interesting. In this situation, you build an entire prototypical machine, complete with applications, then use RIS to create an image of that machine on a RIS server. You then boot the target PC with a RIS-built floppy again, and RIS transfers the entire disk image, complete with operating system and applications, to the target PC. It's not entirely hands-off, however, as it needs a bit of machine-specific customization: you need to punch in a unique machine name, for example. This kind of image is called a *RIPRep image format* image.

RIS Limitations

Before getting too excited about RIS—it's nice, but the Ghost guys needn't worry about being put out of business—let's look at what it *can't* do.

RIS Delivers Only Windows 2000 Professional Images

You can't use RIS to deliver Server images, NT 4, Windows 9*x*, Linux...only Windows 2000 Professional images. Microsoft says they're working to make it more generic and I hope they accomplish that, but for now, it's only a Windows 2000 Professional deployment tool.

RIS Clients Must Have Particular PCI Network Cards, Laptops Need Not Apply

I'll cover this later, but you can only get a RIS system image onto a computer that knows how to ask for one, and the only way that a system knows how to ask is if you boot that system with a floppy generated by the Remote Boot Floppy Generator, a program supplied with RIS. The problem is that the resulting floppy just contains drivers for 25 PCI-based network cards. As it only supports PCI cards, laptops—which in general use PC Card or Cardbus network cards—can't be helped by RIS. So you're back to Ghosting for the mobile users, which is kind of silly; at least in my experience, I end up reinstalling operating systems on laptops far more frequently than on desktops.

RIS Can Only Image the C: Drive

When you build a prototypic computer whose image you will then propagate all over the enterprise, you'd better build a computer with just one hard disk partition C:. RIS will merely copy the C: drive and whatever's on it.

RIS Has a Fairly Sparse Administrative UI

While RIS doesn't require a *lot* of administration, there are few tasks that you'll do frequently, and RIS doesn't provide a very good way to do them. For example, if you had a RIS server that contained many system images, but you didn't want every user to see every possible image (which is very likely—odds are that you'd have one image for the accounting folks, another for the programmers, and so on), then the only way to restrict the choice of images that a user sees is through NTFS permissions rather than via some simple administrative interface.

Steps to Making RIS Work

The first time you set up a RIS server, it can seem a bit complicated if you're not ready for it, as RIS is a bit different from other Windows 2000 services. What I'm referring to is that to install most Windows 2000 network services, like IIS or WINS, you just install them on a server, reboot the server, and you're done. Setting up RIS on a server, however, requires fiddling a bit with Active Directory.

TIP Before you can use RIS, you must have a Windows 2000–based domain running with an Active Directory domain controller. You also need a functioning DNS server integrated with the Windows 2000 domain—that is, a DNS server that supports RFC 2052 SRV records and RFC 2136 dynamic updates, as described in Chapter 2.

To get a RIS server working, follow these steps:

1. Set up a Windows 2000 server and make it a member of a Windows 2000 domain. The server must have a fairly large drive available, and that drive can't be the boot drive or the drive containing the operating system.

2. Authorize the soon-to-be-RIS server in the Active Directory as a Dynamic Host Configuration Protocol (DHCP) server, even though it's *not* a DHCP server.

3. Add the Remote Installation Services service to the server and reboot it.

4. Run RISETUP, the Remote Installation Setup Wizard, to prepare the large drive for receiving RIS images and to put an initial image on the drive—it's just a simple copy of I386.

5. At that point the RIS server is ready. You can add new images to it with a wizard called RIPRep.

We'll examine each of these steps in the following pages.

Getting Ready for RIS

RIS's job is to let you take a PC with an empty hard disk, attach the PC to your enterprise network, put a RIS-created floppy disk into the PC's A: drive, and boot the PC. The small program on the floppy disk is just smart enough to get an IP address for the PC, then locate an Active Directory domain controller, and ask the Active Directory domain controller where to find a RIS server. Once the PC finds the RIS server, it can then start the process of pulling down a particular system image so that the PC becomes useful.

Necessary Infrastructure

But Windows 2000 needs some infrastructure to make all of this work right. The PC gets an IP address from a DHCP server—so you'll need at least one DHCP server running in your enterprise to make RIS work. (In case you've never worked with an IP-based NT network before, DHCP's job is to automatically assign unique network addresses to each server and workstation on the network. TCP/IP *requires* that every machine have a unique IP address or the network software just doesn't work.) Once it has an IP address, the PC finds an Active Directory server by looking it up in DNS—so you'll need a DNS server. And the PC can't query an Active Directory domain controller for the location of a RIS server unless you've got an Active Directory domain controller—so you'll need an

Active Directory–based domain (as opposed to a bunch of Windows 2000 servers in a domain built out of NT 4 domain controllers). Of course, if you're running an Active Directory–based domain, then you've *got* to have DNS running, so the simplified list of things you'll need before RIS will work is an Active Directory–based domain and at least one DHCP server.

A Drive for SIS

Furthermore, the RIS server needs a partition to store the RIS images. For some reason, RIS will not store images on the boot partition—which is usually drive C:—or the system partition, which is the drive that contains \WINNT and the other NT system files. I found this kind of frustrating the first time I went to set up RIS, as the server that I intended to put RIS on had only two drive letters and Windows 2000 installed on the D: drive. C: was the boot, D: the system, and so RIS wouldn't install. I reinstalled Windows 2000 on the C: drive, freeing up D:, and RIS worked fine. You can have other things on RIS's drive, like files of other types, you just can't have the system files on the drive. Remember that, while RIS will make an image of whatever file system is on the original workstation, it must be placed onto an NTFS partition on the server.

While it's not entirely clear to me why RIS is allergic to system files, there's a very good reason why it wants a drive pretty much to itself. Imagine a RIS server that contained 20 system images—how much space would that need? Well, Windows 2000 Professional itself takes up about 450MB on a hard disk, so let's be generous and say that the applications added to the image only total 50MB, leading to a 500MB image; it's just easier to calculate this way. Ten half-gigabyte images totals five gigabytes. But now let's look more closely at those 10 images. The vast majority of the files in the images are identical: for example, each image contains a file named DRIVERS.CAB that's nearly 50MB in size, and the file is exactly the same for each of the 10 images. That's a terrible waste of space—500MB to store 10 identical copies of a 50MB file!

RIS solves that problem with a service called the Single Instance Store, or SIS. SIS is a service that runs in the background and searches a particular drive letter—for some reason, it's only built to attach itself to a single drive letter rather than system-wide—looking for duplicate files. It then frees up space by deleting the duplicate files, putting in their place a directory entry that makes it appear as if the duplicate is still in place. In actuality, however, the duplicate is no more than a sort of pointer to the complete copy of the file. Clearly a trick like this will require a bit of magic, and that magic comes from a combination of SIS and Windows 2000's version of NTFS—that dedicated-to-RIS drive must be an NTFS volume.

It's a shame that SIS only loads as part of RIS; I could easily imagine many cases wherein recovering space from duplicate files could be beneficial, such as in the case of a server containing hundreds of users' home directories—there's likely to be *plenty* of duplication there.

Authorizing RIS in Active Directory

Microsoft figured—probably rightly—that you wouldn't want just *anybody* putting a RIS server on the network. So before you can get the RIS service working on a server, that server must be authorized in the Active Directory. For some reason, however, you don't authorize it as a RIS server; you authorize it as a DHCP server.

To do that, find a DHCP server and log onto it with an account with administrative powers. Click Start/Programs/Administrative Tools/DHCP. Click Action on the menu bar, and you'll see the option Manage Authorized Servers, which is shown in Figure 3.15.

FIGURE 3.15

DHCP Action menu

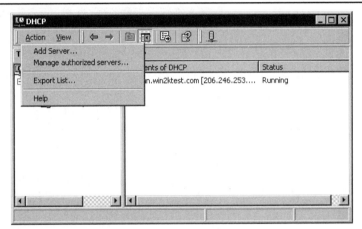

Choose Manage Authorized Servers and you'll see the list of currently authorized DHCP servers like the one in Figure 3.16.

FIGURE 3.16

List of current authorized servers

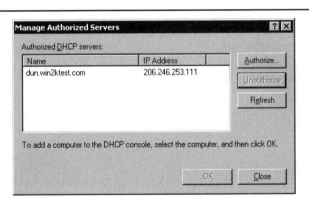

Click Authorize and you'll get a dialog box like the one in Figure 3.17, letting you punch in the IP address of the server that you're going to make into a RIS server.

FIGURE 3.17

Entering IP address of new RIS server

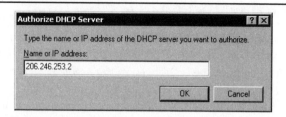

Click OK, and it'll confirm your choice, as Figure 3.18 shows.

FIGURE 3.18

Confirming the new server

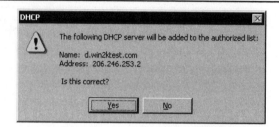

NOTE If you *don't* know the IP address of the soon-to-be RIS server, go over to that server and log in to it. Then open up a command prompt (Start/Programs/Command Prompt), type **ipconfig**, and press Enter. It will report the IP address; if you have several IP addresses, take the one in the section labeled Ethernet Adapter Local Area Connection rather than PPP Adapter.

Now that Active Directory's ready for RIS, let's get RIS ready.

Installing RIS

Next, you'll put the RIS service on the server:

1. Log on to the server that you want to add RIS to using an Administrator account and open up the Control Panel (Start/Settings/Control Panel).

2. Start the Add/Remove Programs applet.

3. Choose the Add/Remove Windows Components icon.

4. A wizard screen labeled Welcome to the Windows Components Wizard will appear; click Next and it will show you the optional server components, as you see in Figure 3.19.

FIGURE 3.19

*Windows Compo-
nents screen*

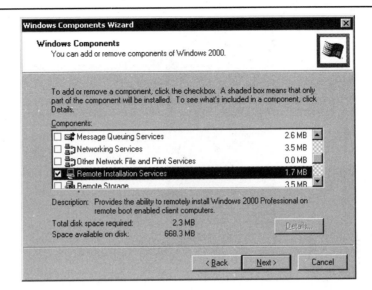

5. Scroll down and check the box labeled Remote Installation Services. Then click Next and Finish.

6. You'll be prompted to reboot, so reboot the server.

Running RISETUP

When installing most Windows 2000 services, you just choose the option in Windows Components, wait for the Control Panel to pull the new service off I386, reboot the computer, and it's up and running. RIS is a bit more work than that, however, as RIS must claim its drive and set up SIS. For good measure, RIS also creates a first image. That first image is the simplest one possible—it's just a copy of the I386 directory from the Windows 2000 Professional CD-ROM.

Log on to the would-be RIS server with an administrative account and run RISETUP (either from a command prompt or click Start/Run, fill in **risetup**, and press Enter) and the Remote Installation Services Setup Wizard starts. The initial screen is shown in Figure 3.20.

Click Next and the wizard will quickly scan your drives looking for a likely place to keep RIS's files. In my case, it found drive F:. It wants to create a directory named RemoteInstall, as you can see in Figure 3.21.

FIGURE 3.20

RISetup initial screen

FIGURE 3.21

Suggested location for RIS images

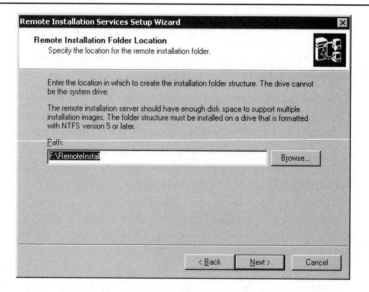

After you click Next, RISetup will ask you if you want the server to respond to requests from PCs for operating systems, as shown in Figure 3.22. Inasmuch as you don't have any useful images on the RIS server at the moment, tell the server not to respond to those requests.

FIGURE 3.22

Telling RIS to ignore requests until we're done configuring it

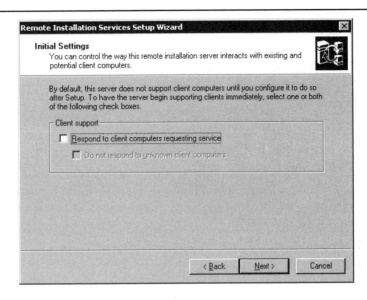

Click Next and, as you can see in Figure 3.23, RIS will ask where to find a Windows 2000 Professional CD-ROM.

FIGURE 3.23

Looking for a fresh copy of Windows 2000 Professional

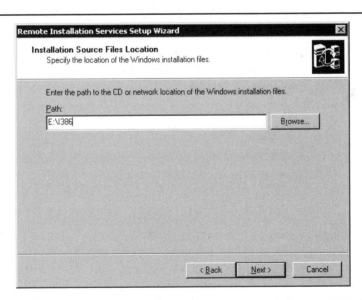

Now's a good time to pop the Windows 2000 Professional disc into your CD-ROM drive—more than likely you've *currently* got the Windows 2000 *Server* disc in there from when you installed RIS. RISetup usually isn't bright enough to know that the files are in I386, so it'll typically just suggest the drive letter of your CD-ROM. For example, if your CD-ROM drive is G:, it'll suggest that the Windows 2000 Professional files are at G: rather than G:\I386, so you'll probably have to help it out and tell it where to find the files. Alternatively, if you have Windows 2000 Professional's I386 directory on one of your hard disks, you can point RISetup there. Click Next and you'll get the screen you see in Figure 3.24.

FIGURE 3.24

*Folder name for the
simple* I386 *option*

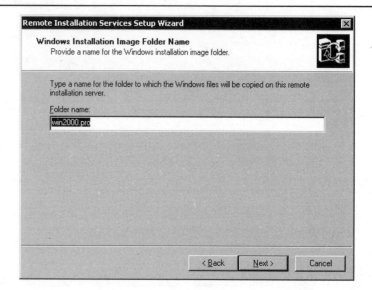

Recall that a RIS server can have many images on it. Each image gets a folder within the \RemoteInstall folder. This first, simple I386 image needs a name too, and RISetup suggests just win2000.pro, which is probably fine for our needs. Click Next to continue and you'll see a screen in which you can describe the image, as shown in Figure 3.25.

When someone plugs a new machine into the network and boots from the RIS-prepared boot floppy, she may be offered a number of choices of OS images to download. (After all, one of the things that RIS is supposed to offer is the ability to keep a bunch of images around for different uses.) This screen lets you add some descriptive text. Click Next and you'll get a summary "this-is-your-last-chance" screen like the one in Figure 3.26.

FIGURE 3.25

*Describing the
simple image*

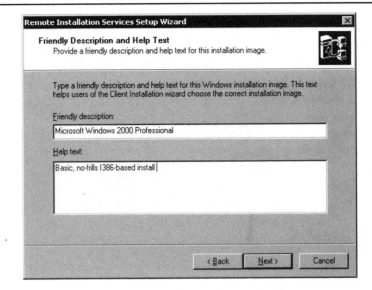

FIGURE 3.26

*Checking on
the settings*

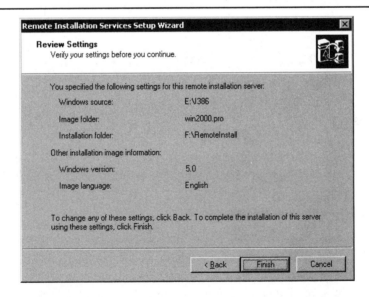

Click Finish and go away for a while. A screen like Figure 3.27 will appear.

FIGURE 3.27

*Progress indica-
tion screen*

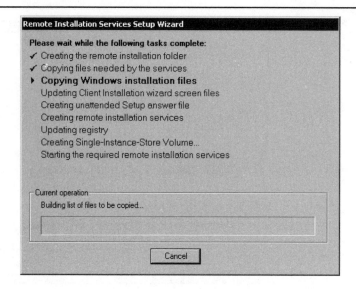

As you see from the screen, RISetup's got a lot to do. It copies the I386 files over to its local folder, starts SIS, and does other housekeeping. Expect it to take 10 minutes or so at least.

Enabling RIS for Clients

Amazingly, after RISetup does its work, the RIS server does not reboot! But it's time to put the RIS server to work, or at least to respond to requests for I386 installs. Make sure you are logged in as a domain administrator at the RIS server, then click Start/Run, fill in **DSA.MSC**, and press Enter. If the RIS server happens to be a domain controller, then it's even easier—just click Start/Programs/Administrative Tools/Active Directory Users And Computers. (Notice that you've got to start the DSA from Start/Run because for some reason Setup *installs* the Active Directory tools on all servers, but only puts entries for those tools on the Start/Programs menus of domain controllers.)

In the left-hand pane of the window, you'll see an icon depicting a number of computers, intended to represent your domain. Open it (double-click or click the plus sign) and it'll open to a number of folders, including one named Computers. It's likely that your RIS server is there. Right-click the RIS computer's icon and choose Properties. You'll then see a property page.

My RIS server is named D (it came after A, B, and C…and yes, some days I'm just not as creative as I would like to be), and there are several property tabs, one labeled Remote Install. Click on that and you'll see a page like the one in Figure 3.28.

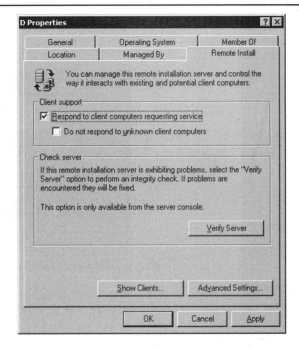

There's not much in the way of an administrative and management interface for RIS, just this page and a few tabs on the Advanced screen, which you'll see a bit later.

On this screen, there's not all that much to do except to turn it on. Check Respond to Client Computers Requesting Service, and it's ready to go!

Installing Windows 2000 Professional on a Workstation from the RIS Server

It's working; let's give it a try. The RIS server is up on the network and the Active Directory knows about it. Suppose I have a computer that I want to put Windows 2000 Professional on (call it the target computer); these are the steps.

The target computer gets the attention of the RIS server through something called the Preboot eXECution, or PXE, protocol, pronounced "pixie." (Is that acronym a reach, or what?) Some computer vendors sell PCs with PXE in the BIOS. To connect a PXE-equipped PC to a RIS server, you don't even need a floppy disk; you just plug it into the network, turn it on, and you'll eventually get a prompt like "boot from the network y/n?" If you let it boot from the network, it'll first seek out a DHCP server, then find an Active Directory server with DNS, and kick off RIS—all the code for doing that is in the PC's BIOS ROM.

Those of us less fortunate, however, are not let out of the fun. Microsoft includes a utility with RIS that will generate bootable floppy disks that replace the PXE BIOS for the PXE-deaf among us. It's called RBFG.EXE, and you'll find it on any RIS server in the \RemoteInstall\Admin\I386 directory. Run it and you'll see a screen like Figure 3.29.

FIGURE 3.29

Remote Boot Disk Generator dialog box

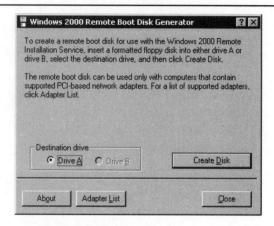

Running it is pretty simple—just put a floppy into A: and press the Create Disk button. A great improvement over its older cousin, the Network Client Administrator, the Remote Boot Disk Generator doesn't require that you provide it with blank floppies. That's the good news.

The *bad* news is that this will only work if your computer has PCI expansion slots and one of the 25 supported PCI network cards. Fifteen years' experience with network software has made me conservative enough that almost all of my NICs are made by 3Com—not because I think 3Com makes a better card, but because I don't want to have to search after drivers—and so RBFG supports all of my machines. But that might not be the case for all of your systems.

Actually, let me take that back. Not all of my systems will work with an RBFG floppy—my laptops won't. Laptops don't have PCI slots in them (unless they're in some kind of docking station), so if your laptop connects to a network with a PC Card or CardBus slot (as 99.9 percent of them do), then you won't be able to use RIS to get Professional on your system, sadly.

But what about the fact that new network cards appear all of the time? It's not unreasonable at all to suggest that a year after Windows 2000's release you might find yourself trying to install Professional on a system with a brand-spanking-new network card that RBFG simply doesn't know how to handle. How do you introduce RBFG to a new set of drivers?

Unfortunately, you can't. Microsoft has said that they'll update RBFG.EXE regularly and perhaps distribute it over the Web, and it could be that they will—but we'll see.

In any case, if you generate a PXE boot disk, stick it into the target machine and boot the machine.

You'll see a screen with something like the following text:

```
Windows 2000 Remote Installation Boot Floppy
© Copyright 1999 Lanworks Technologies Co. a subsidiary of 3Com
Corporation
All rights reserved.

3Com 3C90XB / 3C90XC EtherLink PC
Node: 00105AE2859F
DHCP...
TFTP............. . .
Press F12 for network service boot
```

Press F12, and a text screen appears that says:

```
Welcome to the Client Installation wizard. This wizard helps you quickly
and easily set up a new operating system on your computer. You can also
use this wizard to keep your computer up-to-date and to troubleshoot
computer hardware problems.
In the wizard, you are asked to use a valid user name, password, and
domain name to log on to the network. If you do not have this
information, contact your network administrator before continuing.
Press Enter to continue
```

You are looking here at some client software downloaded from the RIS server called the Client Install Wizard. Look back to the first screen and notice the TFTP with all the periods after it—that was the Trivial File Transfer Protocol transferring a very simple text-based operating system to your computer.

What's kind of interesting about this is that the introductory screen, and all of the other text screens that you'll see from the Client Install Wizard, are built on a slightly modified version of HTML. You can see the "source code" for that first screen by looking on the RIS server in \RemoteInstall\OSChooser\English directory and examining the file named welcome.osc. It looks like the following:

```
<OSCML>
<META KEY=ENTER HREF="LOGIN">
<META KEY=F3 ACTION="REBOOT">
<META KEY=ESC HREF="LOGIN">
<META KEY=F1 HREF="LOGIN">
<TITLE>  Client Installation Wizard Welcome</TITLE>
<FOOTER>  [ENTER] continue </FOOTER>
<BODY left=5 right=75>
<BR>
<BR>
<BR>
Welcome to the Client Installation wizard. This wizard
```

```
helps you quickly and easily set up a new operating system
on your computer. You can also use this wizard to keep your
computer up-to-date and to troubleshoot computer hardware
problems.
<BR>
<BR>
In the wizard, you are asked to use a valid user name,
password, and domain name to log on to the network. If you
do not have this information, contact your network
administrator before continuing.
</BODY>
</OSCML>
```

If you've got any familiarity with HTML, then understanding this is simple—things surrounded by angle brackets <> are *tags*, commands to the computer. They're often in pairs like right and left parentheses—<oscml> starts the "program," </oscml> ends it. That forward slash (/) indicates that it's the end of a command—for example, <TITLE>Client Installation Wizard</TITLE> indicates that there's a command, <TITLE> (which, as you can guess, puts a title in the screen), then there's the text that's supposed to go into the title, and then </TITLE>, which says, "That's the end of the title text." Again, they're like left and right parentheses. The <META KEY> commands tell the wizard what to do when you press particular keys. <META KEY=ENTER HREF="LOGIN"> means, "When the user presses the Enter key, run the program login.osc." <META KEY=F3 ACTION="REBOOT"> means that if the user presses the F3 key, then just reboot the system.

My intent here isn't to document the entire programming language—Microsoft hasn't completely documented it yet, to my knowledge—but to point out that you could *easily* change the generic welcome text to something customized to your particular company.

Anyway, once you press Enter, you're prompted for a username, password, and domain. The account that you log in with must have the ability to create new computer accounts. You'll next be advised that the process will delete any data on the existing hard disk:

```
The following settings will be applied to this computer installation.
Verify these settings before continuing.
Computer account: ADMINMARK1
Global Unique ID: 00000000000000000000000105AE2859F
Server supporting this computer: D
To begin Setup, press Enter. If you are using the Remote
Installation Services boot floppy, remove the floppy diskette from the drive
and press Enter to continue.
```

Here, the RIS client software has chosen a name for the computer, ADMINMARK1, that it constructed by taking my login name—ADMINMARK was the account I used at the time—and adding a number to it. The Global Unique ID, or GUID (pronounced "gwid") is just an ID number that RIS assigned to that computer. PXE-capable machines all have a GUID built right into them, but machines using RIS boot floppies get a GUID constructed for them consisting of 20 hex zeros followed by their NIC's MAC address. Finally, the Client Install Wizard tells you the name of the RIS server that it's getting its image from. Once you press Enter to confirm, pop the floppy out of the A: drive and walk away for a half hour or so. When you return, Windows 2000 Professional will be installed completely hands-off on the machine.

RIS sets the system up like so:

- The new machine joins the RIS server's domain.

- RIS repartitions the machine's hard disk into just one large partition and formats that partition as NTFS, no matter how the drive was previously partitioned.

- The new Windows 2000 Professional system has all of the settings you'd find in a typical install.

Want to change any of that? Then you'll need to create some system images.

Creating a System Image with RIPRep

Even doing a no-frills installation on a new system with RIS is pretty nice. But it would be nicer to provide not only a vanilla operating system but perhaps a few settings and certainly an application or two—now, *that* would make the Ghost guys sweat! (But not sweat all *that* much, as you'll see. Ghost is still better than RIS. But Ghost costs money, and RIS comes free with Windows 2000.) You can do such a thing, creating what's called a *RIPRep image format* image. Here's how you do it:

1. Set up a prototypical Windows 2000 Professional system as you'd like it. Make sure that all of the code and data are on drive C:—no other drives will be copied by RIS.

2. Run the RIS preparation wizard, RIPRep, which strips the SIDs off the prototypical machine.

3. Once the image is on the RIS server, it's available to new systems for installation.

For my example, I've installed Office 2000 onto a Windows 2000 Professional workstation To create the RIPRep image, I log onto that prototypical machine with a domain administrator account. I then open up My Network Places and navigate over to my RIS server, the machine named D. RIS creates a share called REMINST on every RIS server. I open REMINST, then I open up the folder inside labeled Admin, and then I open the folder inside that labeled I386. Inside is a file named `riprep.exe`. I double-click on it and see the opening screen, as shown in Figure 3.30.

FIGURE 3.30

Opening screen of RIPRep

Click Next to see the screen shown in Figure 3.31.

FIGURE 3.31

Choosing the destination RIS server

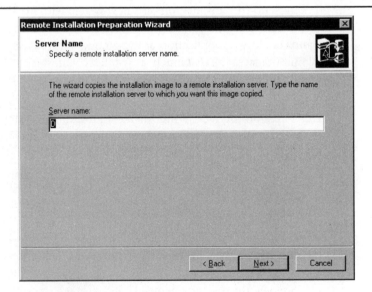

You can send the resulting image to any RIS server; I'll choose the one I've been working with, the server named D, and click Next, which leads to the screen in Figure 3.32.

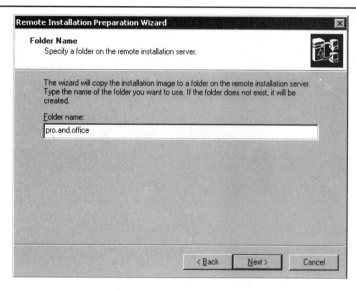

As with the CD image that RISetup insisted upon, this new image will need a folder name. Once I name the folder and click Next, a screen in which I add a description appears, as shown in Figure 3.33.

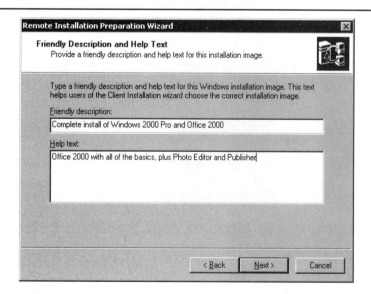

Finally, in the next two screens (Figures 3.34 and 3.35), I confirm that I want RIPRep to actually do the work.

FIGURE 3.34

Confirming my choices

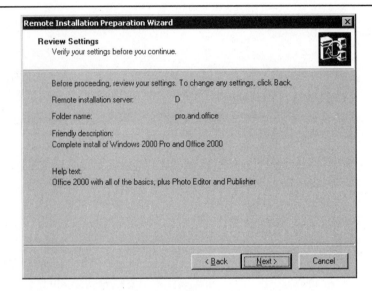

FIGURE 3.35

RIPRep finishes with informational messages

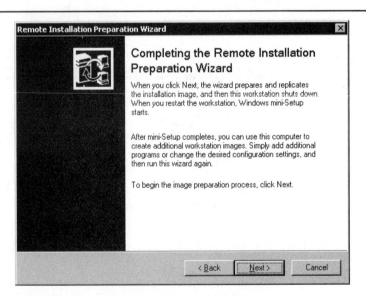

Reconfiguring the Prototype

After transferring the system image to the RIS server, you're directed to reboot the prototype. You'll then see something odd—it looks as if the prototype is running Windows 2000 Setup all over again! In order to make the prototype's image usable to

RIS, RIPRep scrubs all of the user-specific settings and SIDs off the machine. Once you reboot, your system runs a kind of "mini-setup" to restore that information. Once the system reboots, you'll be prompted to do the following:

- Agree to the license agreement.
- Choose a keyboard and localization.
- Fill in a username and organization.
- Specify a computer name and password for the default Administrator account.
- Pick a time zone.
- Decide whether to do typical or custom network settings.
- Join either a workgroup or domain.

The mini-setup doesn't take nearly as long as Setup did, however, as it's not necessary to run Plug and Play.

Delivering a RIPRep Image to a Target PC

Now how do you deliver that operating-system-with-applications image to a target PC? In exactly the same way that you got the first one onto a target PC. Either press F12 when the PXE ROM tells you to or boot from an RBFG-generated floppy.

NOTE You do not need to build a separate RBFG-generated floppy for each system. You can build just one and carry it with you, using it to start as many different RIS image transfers as you'd like.

Now that you've got more than one image on your server, the Client Installation Wizard will offer you one more screen. After you log in, it'll list the available images and their descriptions, allowing you to choose one. Then, as before, it'll remind you that it's about to destroy any data on the hard disk and, from there, all you need do is to pop that RBFG floppy out of the floppy drive, walk away, and come back in a half hour—the entire install is hands-off.

WARNING Well, "hands-off" according to the Microsoft documentation. I find with beta 3 that the Setup Wizard runs hands-off for a while, but then it requires me to click Next at the Localization screen.

WARNING Once again, don't take the "this will zap the hard disk" warning lightly. If (for example) your RIPRep image is based on a system with a 1500MB C: drive formatted as FAT32, then RIS will repartition and reformat the C: drive of the target PC to 1500MB and FAT32 no matter how the drive was partitioned on the target PC before. RIS will leave any remaining space unpartitioned.

Enabling Users to Start RIS Transfers

The idea, then, with RIS is this: Joe comes into your office and tells you that his computer's hosed and would you reinstall his operating systems and applications when you get a chance? You reply that you've got an even better idea and hand him an RBFG floppy. You tell him to boot it, press F12 when prompted, then log into the Client Installation Wizard and choose the Standard Productivity Desktop option, an image that you've built with all of the company's standard desktop software—Office, the PalmPilot HotSync software, and Lotus Organizer.

Now, if Joe goes back and tries this, he'll see an error message like this:

The user Joe currently logged on to this computer does not have the permissions needed to create a computer account or modify the computer account NEWPC (NEWPC$) within the domain apex.com.

This error may also indicate that the server D supporting this client cannot contact the directory service to perform the operation.

Restart this computer and try again. If the problem persists, contact your network administrator for assistance.

What's going on here is that, in the process of installing the RIS image on Joe's machine, RIS must also create a *machine account*—remember, in Windows 2000 domains, machines have accounts just as people do—and not just any old user can create machine accounts. By the way, he's also got to be able to delete machine accounts, as there's probably already a machine account floating around that has the same name as the one he's about to create, as well as a few other machine permissions.

You *could* make him a member of the Account Operators group for just a day so that he could do the install, but that's an awful lot of power to give a user just so he can kick off a RIS image transfer. So instead, let's create an altogether new group called Installers, which will have the power to create and delete machine accounts but nothing else. Now, creating the Installers group will be a bit of a lengthy procedure, but you'll only have to do it once. Once you've got the Installers group defined, you can then just simply add any user to that group before giving him an RBFG floppy to reinstall his system. (And for safety's sake, you can remove him the next day, after he's got his system back up and running.)

Creating the Installers Group

You'll find creating the Installers group easiest while sitting at a domain controller:

1. Log in using an account with domain administrator rights and then start the Directory Service Administrator DSA.MSC by clicking Start/Programs/Administrative Tools/Active Directory Users and Computers. In the left-hand pane, you'll see an icon representing your domain with a plus sign next to it; click the plus sign to expand the domain.

2. Next, create the Installers group. Right-click on the Users folder and choose New/Group.

3. That raises a dialog box called Create New Object-(Group). In the field Name of New Group, fill in **Installers**. This will create a global group named Installers, which is what we want, so click OK and the dialog will close.

4. Back in the DSA's menu, click View/Advanced Features. That will show the Security tab on the property page, which will be essential to give Installers the permissions that it needs.

5. Next, we're going to give some domain-wide permissions to the Installers group, so right-click the domain's icon and choose Properties. You'll get a dialog box named *Domain Name* Properties.

6. Click the Security tab in the property page. Installers doesn't currently have any permissions, so we'll need to add a record for them. Click the Add button and you'll now see a dialog named Select Users, Computers or Groups.

7. Click the Installers group, click Add, and then click OK to dismiss the dialog box.

8. Back in the *Domain Name* property page, find Installers in the Name list box and click it, then click the Advanced button.

9. You'll see a dialog box labeled Access Control Settings for *Domain Name*. Again, locate Installers—this part of the operating system isn't intended for regular old users, so the UI's a bit convoluted here—to indicate the Installers record that you created. It'll currently have some very basic permission like Read or the like. Click the View/Edit button.

10. Now you'll see a dialog named Permission Entry for *Domain Name*. Scroll down in the list box labeled Permissions to find the Create Computer Objects permission. You'll see two columns of check boxes, one labeled Allow and the other Deny. Check the Allow box and do the same for the next permission, Delete Computer Objects. In the list box labeled Apply To, choose This Object and All Child Objects. What you're doing here is giving Installers the right to create and destroy new objects in the directory, but *only* computer objects—machine accounts. Click OK to clear the Permission Entry for *Domain Name* dialog box.

11. That permission made the folders accept the new machine objects. But once created, Installers have no control over the machine accounts themselves, so we'll add another permission record to give Installers complete control over machine accounts. From the Access Control Settings for *Domain Name* dialog box, click Add, choose Installers, and click OK. The Permission Entry for *Domain Name* dialog box then appears.

12. Click the Apply Onto drop-down list box and choose Computer Objects. Check the Allow box next to the Full Control permission. Click OK and Windows 2000 will return you to the Access Control Settings for *Domain Name* dialog box.

13. Scroll down in the Permission Entries list box and you'll see that there is now a new entry for Installers, a "create/delete" permission—that's what you just created—as well as a "full control" record for "machine objects."

14. Click OK to dismiss the Access Control Settings For dialog box.

15. Click OK to dismiss the *Domain Name* property page.

Now that that's done, you can put Joe into the Installers group:

1. Open the Users folder and locate the Installers group.

2. Right-click Installers and choose Properties.

3. Click the Members tab.

4. Click the Add button.

5. Find Joe's account, click Joe, click OK, and then click OK again.

Finally done. Yes, that was a bit of work, and you'd kind of wonder why Microsoft didn't just build the group for us. I sure don't know.

Restricting RIS Image Choices

Once you turn Joe loose with that floppy, you just might not want him accidentally loading the wrong image. He might just decide that he'd *love* to download the Programmer's Workstation image, complete with the C++ and Java compilers, interactive debuggers, and the like—none of which he has any use for. You can, as it turns out, keep him from seeing all of the images on the RIS server. But you'd never guess how you do it.

The RIS server has a set of directories that exist in \RemoteInstall\Setup\English\ Images\. If you've got a simple I386 installation called win2000.pro, then its image is in \RemoteInstall\Setup\English\Images\Win2000.Pro. Each RIS image, then, has a directory inside \RemoteInstall\Setup\English\Images\; remember that.

Each image contains a folder named I386, which contains yet *another* folder named Templates. *That* folder contains a file named with the extension .SIF. It's an answer file that RIS uses to be able to do the installation without any user intervention. So, for example, if you have an image called Programmers, there's an SIF file in `\RemoteInstall\ Setup\English\Images\I386\Templates`.

The way that you keep Joe out of the Programmers image is to set the NTFS permissions on the SIF file so that he's denied Read access. Once RIS sees that he's not supposed to see the file, the Programmers image won't even be offered to him.

Putting It All Together

Before you can say that you have truly mastered installing Windows 2000, you will need to apply all the bits and pieces of the install to your network. Exactly what are you tasked with? Building a single server? Probably a manual install will suffice. Building a Windows 2000 Server rollout for a large enterprise? You might consider building an unattended install using a distribution folder. Use the option to include additional folders under the distribution folder so that all of your OEM drivers are included. You may also want to include all additional server components in your distribution folder, like our network management agent. Finally, use the /cmd parameter to launch an installation batch file, or even a SYSDIFF to have those last components installed. Just to cover all components, let's do a high-level walk-through of a best-case installation scenario:

- The actual installation is going to use a fully automated answer file that we've built with the Setup Manager Wizard.

- We'll specify multiple computer names and use a uniqueness database file with our answer file, or we'll have a randomly generated computer name. This way, we don't need to worry about duplicate names on the network.

- In the Setup Manager Wizard, we'll tell Setup to have the Administrator account automatically log on once the installation is done. This will help kick off the next step, without requiring us to come back to log on.

- We'll incorporate the GUIRunOnce command of `\\setupserver\winnt\welcome.bat` in our answer file. That will run after Setup has completed and Windows 2000 boots up into normal operational mode for the first time.

- `\\setupserver\winnt\welcome.bat` will contain, amongst other things, a SYSDIFF /apply `\\setupserver\winnt\diff.1` command that will apply all new applications that are not bundled with the regular Windows 2000 setup routine.

- `\\setupserver\winnt\welcome.bat` could also contain a SHUTDOWN command from the Resource Kit to reboot the server.

Our end result should be that we kicked off an unattended installation, came back later, and sat down at a server that was 99 percent production ready. The last 1 percent will be left to our post-installation procedures, like assigning a static IP address, documenting our server, and performing a follow-up reboot.

Ideally, your installation itself should be considered a deliverable product—a single-point-and-click process that completely builds a server that is ready for production. True, the odds of an enterprise-wide Windows 2000 rollout being that simple are really slim. However, the amount of time you spend putting an installation package together up front will be saved for each server that uses it later on. Let's say it takes you a solid, uninterrupted 40-hour week to build this installation source, an average of 4 hours per manual install, but only 1 hour per automated install. Compare the time commitments between building an automated installation source and using automated installs with running all manual installs when dealing with only 15 server installations:

$$40 \text{ hrs} + (15 \times 1 \text{ hr}) = 55 \text{ total hrs}$$

$$15 \times 4 \text{ hrs} = 60 \text{ hrs}$$

Remember, even though an automated install may still take several hours to complete, we only need to be at the server for a very small portion of that time. Using similar estimates, the time difference in a network where you are installing 100 servers would be 140 hours to 400 hours. Like I said before, anyone can install Windows 2000. Making that installation a repeatable process that works for an entire enterprise while reducing the amount of time and cost required for such a rollout is the tricky part. Look beyond the actual installation, plan it out ahead of time, and treat your installation as more than just installing Windows 2000.

CHAPTER **4**

The Windows 2000 Server UI and MMC

When I first installed Windows 2000, it looked to me a lot like Windows NT 4. So they added a couple of snazzy new icons on the desktop—big deal. "This'll be a snap," I thought. "What's all the fuss?" But then I opened the Control Panel. Don't bother looking for the Network applet, because it's not there. And it's not the only thing missing. The Services Control Panel? Gone. The Administrative Tools group is still there, but most of our old friends, like Server Manager and User Manager for Domains, have been eaten by this ever-present thing called the Microsoft Management Console (MMC).

Where is everything? What's an old administrator to do? If you've already been fooling around with the Windows 2000 betas, then you know the answers to these questions and you can safely skip this chapter. If you are completely new to Windows 2000, this chapter will help you find those tools in their new homes. Plus we'll take a peek into the MMC framework and get you started customizing MMC tools to fit your administrative needs.

Where Are They Now?

When NT 4 was released, NT 3.51 administrators were comforted by the fact that most of the administrative tools were the same. We didn't have to relearn those everyday tasks. To add network services and protocols, you went to the Network Control Panel; for user and group configuration, you went to User Manager and User Manager for Domains. To administer servers and shares and services remotely, we had Server Manager. So it is very disconcerting to see, upon loading Windows 2000 Server, that the three most commonly used tools seem to have disappeared. Microsoft has decided the Control Panel will now be for user options and simple configuration changes, so several items have been moved out of the Control Panel and integrated into new administrative tools. In this section, we'll take a look at some of the most glaring interface changes that an NT 4 administrator must face, and I'll show you the new procedures for those common tasks. I won't bore you with too many details; rather, I just want to get you pointed in the right direction. Specifically, I'll answer these questions:

- Where'd they put the Network Control Panel?
- What happened to the User Manager and User Manager for Domains?
- No more Server Manager?
- Where is the Disk Administrator?
- What happened to the device management tools in the Control Panel (SCSI, Tape Device, etc)? Where do install I a new device now?
- Where is the Services Control Panel ?
- What is this Network and Dial-Up Connections tool?
- Did they do away with NT Diagnostics?

This quick reference should help you weather the interface changes gracefully and have you navigating Win2K like a pro in no time at all.

Where'd They Put the Network Control Panel?

Under NT 4, to configure almost any network-related information, you only had to open the Network applet in the Control Panel. There you could change the machine name and workgroup name, join a domain, and add/remove adapters, protocols, and network services like DHCP, WINS, or DNS. Win2K takes a different approach. These functions have been dispersed into several different tools.

Changing a Machine Name or Workgroup/Domain

To change a machine's name or a workgroup name or to join a domain, open System Properties by choosing Start/Settings/Control Panel/System (or just right-click My Computer on the Desktop and choose Properties). Select the Network Identification tab, shown in Figure 4.1. The rules that apply for joining a workgroup or domain in NT 4 also apply to Windows 2000; you must be logged on as a local administrator, and if you wish to join the computer to a domain, you must also have a valid user-name and password to create the machine account. Also, please note that if the machine is a domain controller, you will not be able to change the identification information here.

FIGURE 4.1

The Network Identification tab in the System Control Panel

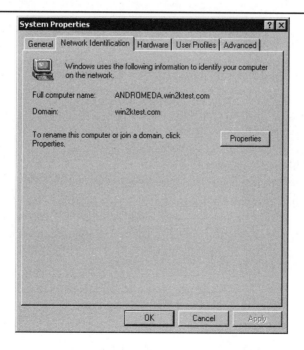

Click the Properties button to bring up the Identification Changes dialog box, shown in Figure 4.2. From here, you can change the machine name and workgroup or domain affiliation. Click the More button if you wish to change the DNS suffix (domain name) or the NetBIOS name for the computer as well.

FIGURE 4.2

*The Identification
Changes dialog box*

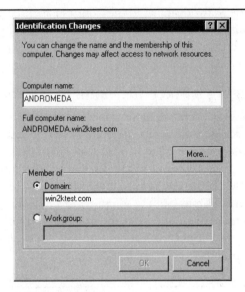

Adjusting Network Protocols

Under Windows 2000, you use Network and Dial-Up Connections to install protocols. Click the Start button and choose Settings, then Network and Dial-Up Connections (or right-click My Network Places on the Desktop and select Properties). As shown in Figure 4.3, each connection will display an icon. For instance, if the server has a modem and two network cards, you'll see an icon for each network adapter (they are labeled Local Area Connection by default, but you can rename them), one for each dial-up networking connection, plus the Make New Connection icon. The dial-up networking connections don't represent different modems, but rather what we used to call Address Book entries in NT 4. You can see the type of connection and status on the left in the window when you highlight the icon. It's a good idea to rename the Local Area Connection icons to something meaningful, especially if the machine has multiple networking devices.

FIGURE 4.3

The Network and
Dial-Up Connections
window

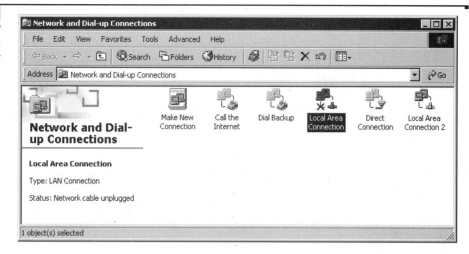

To add a protocol, select the Local Area Connection icon for the device which will use the protocol, then right-click it and choose Properties. Figure 4.4 shows the property page. Now this is beginning to look familiar. Click the Configure button to display the device information, or click Install to add a client, protocol, or service to this device.

FIGURE 4.4

The Local Area
Connection properties

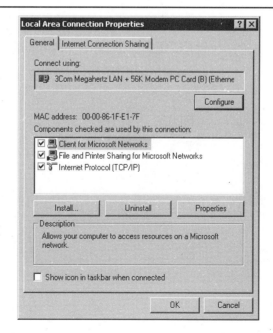

Figure 4.5 shows the dialog box where you select a network component to install. Choose to add a protocol, and you'll be shown a list (Figure 4.6). If you add a protocol, it becomes available to every connection. Likewise, if you remove a protocol as opposed to just unchecking the box (shown back in Figure 4.4) that indicates the device driver is to use that protocol, it is removed for all connections. Also, you can't add or remove all of the same network components here as you could in NT 4's Network Control Panel, but you can add and remove the Microsoft and NetWare redirector and server components.

FIGURE 4.5

The Select Network Component Type dialog box

FIGURE 4.6

The Select Network Protocol dialog box

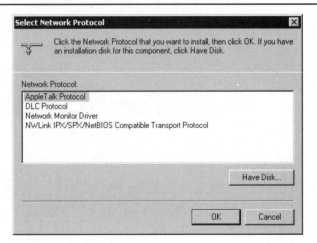

Adjusting and Adding/Subtracting Network Services

To load, unload, or configure Microsoft File and Print Services or the Gateway (and Client) Services for NetWare, use the property page for the correct connection in the Network and Dial-Up Connections window, as described in the preceding section. By the way, the Workstation service is now called the Client for Microsoft Networks, and the Server service is called File and Printer Sharing for Microsoft Networks. Presumably this provides consistency with Windows 95 and Windows 98. However, they are still called the Server and Workstation services if you want to stop, pause, or restart them.

Services like DNS, WINS, and DHCP are added using Add/Remove Programs. Open Control Panel/Add Remove Programs/Add or Remove Windows Components. This kicks off the Windows Components Wizard. After the initial screen, select Networking Services and choose Details. Figure 4.7 shows some of the networking services components that can now be loaded.

FIGURE 4.7

The Networking Services dialog box in the Windows Components Wizard

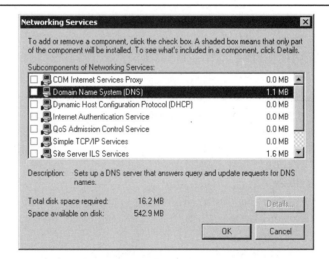

If you still happen to be using the Web Content view instead of the classic view for your folders, there is also a helpful link (called Add Network Components) in Network and Dial-Up Connections, visible on the left-hand side of the window. This link opens the Windows Optional Networking Components Wizard. Although Web Content for folders is generally annoying, and I'll show you how to turn it off later in the chapter, this link is worth mentioning because it saves you a few mouse-clicks (or touch pad taps, as the case may be). As you see in Figure 4.8, this wizard offers a subset of the components from the Windows Components Wizard, namely management tools like SNMP and Network Monitor, Other Network File and Print Services (Print Services for Unix, Services for Macintosh), plus the full list of networking services shown in Figure 4.7.

FIGURE 4.8

Optional networking components

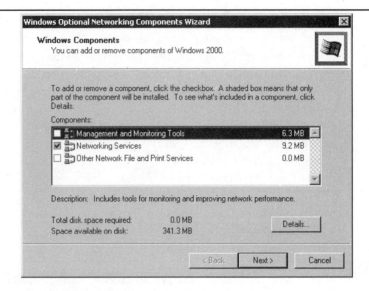

Configuring and Installing/Removing Network Adapters

How do you add a network adapter under Win2K? Hopefully, you won't have to. Plug and Play takes away most of your hardware woes. But once in a while you might need to add an adapter manually. For instance, at one point I wanted to load the Microsoft loopback adapter on my laptop to run some tests. In case you don't already know, the loopback adapter is a software-based *virtual adapter* that allows you to load network protocols and services without having an actual network card installed. The problem is, it's not Plug-and-Play compliant, as you would deduce—how do you autodetect a virtual adapter? The trick to remember here is that an adapter (even the Microsoft loopback adapter) is considered hardware. So you'll need to invoke the Add/Remove Hardware Wizard.

To add an adapter, follow these steps:

1. Choose Start/Settings/Control Panel and then Add/Remove Hardware. You can also open the System applet, go to the Hardware tab, and click the Hardware Wizard button (see Figure 4.9).

2. From the Welcome screen, choose Next, then select Add/Troubleshoot a Device in the next window, as shown in Figure 4.10. The annoying thing is that the wizard now searches for new Plug-and-Play hardware. It would be nice to have an option to skip the detection attempt.

FIGURE 4.9

Access the Hardware Wizard by clicking its button in the System property page.

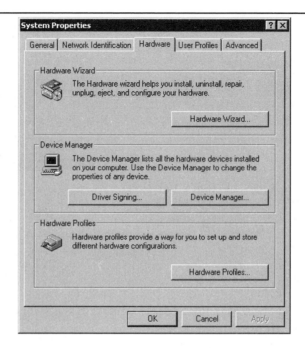

FIGURE 4.10

Choosing a hardware task

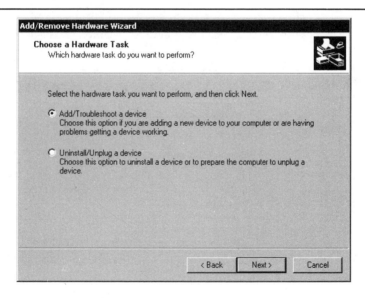

3. Next, the wizard presents a list of devices installed on your system. Select Add a New Device and click Next (see Figure 4.11).

FIGURE 4.11

Adding a new device

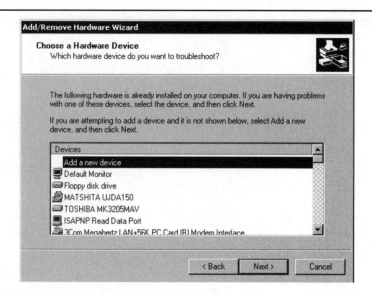

4. The wizard now asks you whether to search for new hardware (again!) or choose it from a list. Actually, if you choose to search for new hardware, Win2K searches for hardware that is not Plug-and-Play compatible. If you choose to select your device from a list, the wizard will display a list of device types, as shown in Figure 4.12. Scroll through the list and choose the device type you wish to install, such as a network adapter, and click Next.

FIGURE 4.12

Choosing the type of hardware you want to install

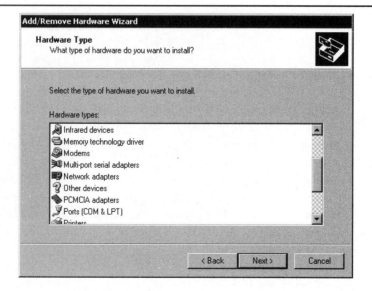

5. Next, select your adapter from a list of known devices (see Figure 4.13) or choose Have Disk if it's not on the list and you have the driver from the manufacturer. Click Next. If you've selected from a list of known devices, just confirm the choices you've made and finish the wizard. If you've chosen Have Disk, point the wizard to the driver files (on a disk, floppy, or other location). From that point, the installation procedure depends on the device. Depending on the device, you may or may not be prompted for device settings.

FIGURE 4.13

Selecting the adapter to install

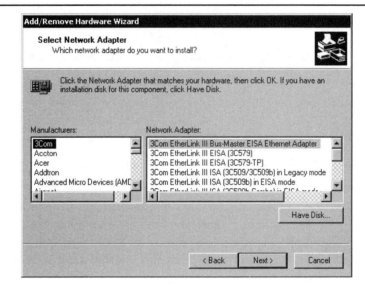

What Happened to User Manager and User Manager for Domains?

We'll discuss user and group management more thoroughly in Chapter 8, but for now, just remember that where NT 4 created both local user accounts and domain accounts with slightly different versions of the User Manager, Windows 2000 stores local user and domain accounts in very different places and with somewhat different tools. *Local* user accounts (on stand-alone and non–domain controller systems) are created using the Computer Management tool, and *domain* accounts, or any accounts on a domain controller for that matter, are created with Active Directory Users and Computers (by the way, what an awkward name for an admin tool). These Win2K tools can be used to add and modify user accounts; assign home directories, login scripts, and profiles; create and manage groups; and reset a user's password. However, you may recall that the NT 4 User Manager tools are also used to set account password and lockout policies, assign user rights, and even create trust relationships. Except for trust relationships, these functions are now administered using Group Policy or the Local Security Policy tool.

Controlling Account Password and Lockout Policies

To set account password and lockout policies for the local machine, use the Local Security Policy tool. However, if your system is part of an Active Directory domain, you'll set the domain-wide password and lockout policy using the Domain Security Policy tool. Details about setting local and group policies are included in Chapter 8, but here's a quick rundown, from the domain perspective. Log on to a domain controller as a domain administrator and follow these steps:

1. Start the program named Domain Security Policy in the Administrative Tools group.

2. In the left pane, open Account Policies (shown in Figure 4.14). From this point on, setting account and lockout policies for the domain is very similar to using the Local Security Policy tool to set policy for a stand-alone server. Expand Password Policy or Account Lockout Policy and double-click the policy items that appear in the right pane. You'll see check boxes to turn on the policy (Define This Policy Setting) and, depending on the policy, parameters to set, like Minimum Password Age or Account Lockout Count.

3. Once you've defined your setting, click OK and you'll see the changed setting displayed in the right pane of the window. Simply close the tool and the change is saved. There is no menu item to apply or save changes.

Audit policy, user rights, and some other miscellaneous security options that were previously only available by editing the Registry (or using some Resource Kit tool) are found in the Local Policies component under Security Options.

FIGURE 4.14

Setting the machine's password policy

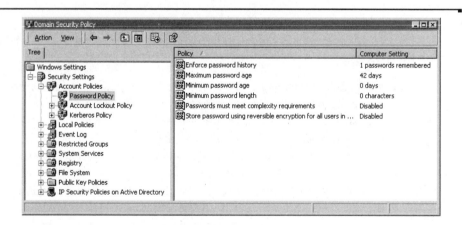

Building Trust Relationships

In Windows 2000, you shouldn't have to create trust relationships at all; trust is implicitly built when new domains are created in an existing forest. See Chapter 2 for an explanation of Active Directory domains, forests, and trees. Only when you wish to set up access to resources in other preexisting forests will you need to create trust relationships. This is done using Active Directory Domains and Trusts. Go to Administrative Tools/Active Directory Domains and Trusts. Right-click the icon representing your domain. Choose Properties and you'll see a property sheet with a tab labeled Trusts. From that point, it's just like establishing a trust relationship in NT 4. You can add a trusted domain or add domains that trust your domain.

No More Server Manager?

There is no more Server Manager tool in Windows 2000. Okay, it's still there, like the File Manager from NT 3.51 persisted in NT 4. It's not included in the Administrative Tools group anymore, but you can open it by clicking Start/Run, then filling in **srvmgr.exe**. And Server Manager is still useful for administering NT machines in a domain. But the problem with the Server Manager tool lies in the fact that it attempts to cover two different areas of remote administration: those functions that are machine specific, such as shares and services, and those functions that relate to domain administration, such as promoting backup domain controllers. Win2K attempts to clear up the confusion by separating types of functions into separate components (although not necessarily into separate tools).

 TIP   You'll find that Windows 2000 comes with a number of tools that Microsoft didn't put in Start/Programs. Many of those tools have been implemented as MMC snap-ins (see "A Microsoft Management Console Primer" later in this chapter for more information on MMC), and a great way to locate them is to search for *.msc files with Start/Search/For Files or Folders.

The functions of Server Manager that are machine related (such as shares and services) have moved to the Computer Management tool. Those related to domain management have moved to Active Directory Users and Computers and, to a lesser extent, Active Directory Sites and Services.

Shares, Services, and Alerts

To create and manage file shares on your local machine or on a remote machine, open Computer Management in the Administrative Tools group. If you want to create a share remotely, highlight Computer Management, choose Connect to Another Computer from the Action menu, then select the remote machine from the list. Expand System Tools to Shared Folders, and then open Shares, as shown in Figure 4.15. From the Action menu, or by right-clicking in the details pane (on the right), you have the option to create a new file share. This kicks off the Create Shared Folder Wizard. This new wizard allows you to select the directory to share by browsing; you can even create a new folder, which is a big improvement over the remote sharing in Server Manager, where you had to magically remember the full path of the directory you wanted to share. Once you've supplied the necessary info like the local path, share name, and description, click Next and choose one of the basic share permissions, or set custom permissions. Click Finish to create the share. Now, right-click the new share and choose Properties to change the description or share permissions and to set NTFS security on the directory. The Shared Folders tool also allows you to view user sessions and open files as Server Manager did, with the option to disconnect the session or the file if necessary.

To configure alerts for particular events on specific servers, there is now a special tool in Computer Management\System Tools called Performance Logs and Alerts. Now you can configure alerts without opening the Performance Monitor. The application doesn't have to be running in the foreground anymore to do performance logging or generate alerts. Plus, now you can configure Win2K to respond to alert events by creating log events, by sending a network message, or by running a command file. These are Big Improvements.

 NOTE See Chapter 20, "Tuning and Monitoring Your Win2K Network," for specifics on configuring performance alerts.

FIGURE 4.15

Viewing shared folders

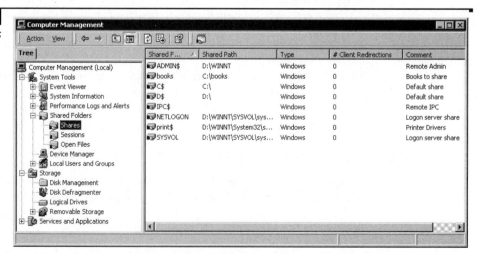

Domain Management Functions

To create a new machine account in a domain, open Active Directory Users and Computers, then select the domain and container where you want to add the machine account. There is already a Computers container for computer accounts, but you don't really have to use it. Select the Computers container (for example), and choose New/Computer from the Action menu. Supply the computer name in the dialog box that appears. If you are creating an account for an NT machine, be sure and check the box to allow pre–Windows 2000 computers to use the account. Now click OK to create the new machine account. See Chapter 2, "Getting Comfortable with Active Directory," for a complete overview of Active Directory.

Promote/Demote a Domain Controller

Windows 2000 doesn't require a primary domain controller (PDC) as NT 4 did. In Win2K, they are called *replica domain controllers* and all DCs are more or less equal, although there is a PDC emulator to accommodate certain requirements of legacy clients. So we really don't promote and demote domain controllers in the NT 4 sense of the words. However, a stand-alone machine or a member server may become a domain controller (without reinstalling!), and a domain controller can become a stand-alone machine or a member server (also without reinstalling). You will still have to reboot the machine after running DCPROMO to complete the transformation, though.

To create a new domain controller account, go to Active Directory Sites and Services in the Administrative Tools group. Open the Sites folder and choose the site where you want to create the new domain controller. Right-click Servers and choose New/Server. When prompted, supply the name of the new domain controller.

It's also possible to create the domain controller account during the process of converting a non–domain controller into a domain controller, if you have the appropriate local and domain administrative rights. Run DCPROMO.EXE from the Start/Run menu on the machine to be promoted and a wizard kicks in that lets you join the machine to a domain, create a new domain, or become a domain controller in an existing domain.

Control Services on a Remote Machine

To view and configure services on a remote machine as you did in Server Manager, go to the Computer Management tool. From the Action menu, choose Connect to Another Computer and select the remote machine from a list, or just type in the machine name. Once you are connected to the remote machine, expand Services and Applications to reveal the Services node. Highlight Services and you'll see in the right pane a list of services on the remote machine. You can now stop, start, and even restart services using your ever-useful right-click function, or you can use the Action menu. You can even use those cute tape recorder–like icons on the toolbar. The Properties option leads you to the equivalent of the old (NT 4) Configure button with more information and configuration options, such as a Recovery tab and a Dependencies tab.

NOTE The Services tool in the Administrative Tools group also replaces the Services Control Panel; see "Where Is the Services Control Panel?" for more details.

Where Is the Disk Administrator?

The Disk Administrator is now called Disk Management, and it can be found in the Storage component of Computer Management (see Figure 4.16).

Disk Management deserves a separate discussion (see Chapter 7), but let's just say that all the old functions are still there, more or less intact, plus the tool is now "remoteable." In other words, you can create and remove partitions on remote Win2K machines, with the proper administrative credentials, of course. But if you're in a rush and need to partition and/or format a drive, then open Computer Management (Start/Programs/Administrative Tools), then open the folder labeled Storage, and then open the folder inside *that* labeled Disk Management. From there, partitioning, volume naming, and formatting are all GUI driven.

FIGURE 4.16

The Disk Management tool

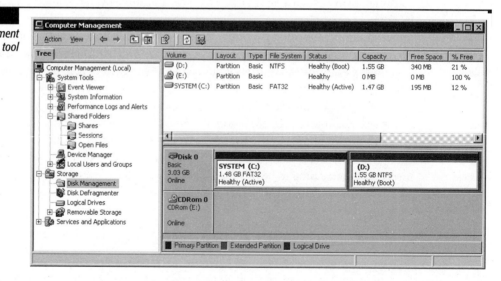

What Happened to the Device Management Tools in the Control Panel?

Some of the applets in the Control Panel, like Mouse, Display, and Sounds and Multimedia, still exist, but Win2K now takes the attitude that the Control Panel is for user-level options and not for advanced configuration. So you can still adjust your display and mouse settings, but the SCSI and Tape Device applets are gone away (see Figure 4.17

for a typical view of the new Control Panel applets). The Devices applet is also no more, replaced by the long-awaited and much more useful Win2K version of Device Manager (accessible through the Hardware tab of the System Control Panel or the System Tools component of the Computer Management tool). Actually, the Win2K Device Manager is much more useful than its Windows 9*x* predecessors because it is remoteable. That's right, now you can view devices and update drivers on your servers from the comfort and luxury of your own cubicle, assuming that you've got administrative privileges on the remote machine.

To view existing devices and drivers on a local or remote machine, go to the Computer Management tool in the Administrative Tools group. For a remote machine, highlight the root of the console (Computer Management) and choose Connect to Another Computer from the Action menu. Then go to the System Tools component and open Device Manager. From here, right-click the machine name at the top (or any device type on the list) to scan for hardware changes. For anything that is not detected, however, go to Add/Remove Hardware in the Control Panel on the local machine. This wizard allows you to manually add and configure a device.

If you haven't noticed already, it will be a relief to learn that the System Control Panel persists, although with a noticeable face-lift; virtual memory settings and environmental variables as well as startup and recovery options are configured using the Advanced tab (see Figure 4.18).

FIGURE 4.17

A typical view of the Control Panel

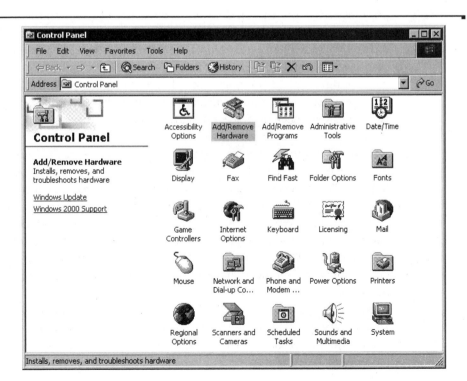

FIGURE 4.18

*The System Control
Panel's Advanced tab*

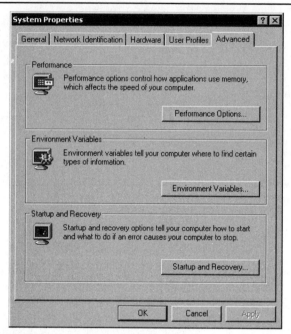

Where Is the Services Control Panel?

The functions of the Services Control Panel are now managed and configured using the Services tool. This is accessible as a stand-alone administrative tool but also takes the form of a snap-in or an extension, where it can be used remotely in the Computer Management tool. Choose Start/Programs/Administrative Tools/Computer Management, or right-click My Computer and choose Manage. Expand Services and Applications, then Services, as shown in Figure 4.19. Here you see a list of services on the computer. Right-click them to stop, start, pause, or resume. Also, when you do, notice there is a restart option; with one button, you can stop and then start a service.

Win2K has improved on the old Services Control Panel significantly; you can now see a brief description of the service (so you don't accidentally disable something important) and its current status, start-up value, and security context all in one view. At least, you could if the descriptions weren't as long as postdoctorate theses.

To configure a Win2K service, highlight a service and double-click it, or right-click and choose Properties, and you'll see the new, improved configuration options for Win2K services. Figure 4.20 shows the General tab, which allows you to change the description and even the display name of the service. You can change the description of a service to something meaningful, such as "Do not stop this service under any circumstances." You can also change the status or the start-up value here. To change the security context (to have the service log on as a particular user) or to change the password of the user account the service uses, select the Log On tab.

FIGURE 4.19

Services in Computer Management

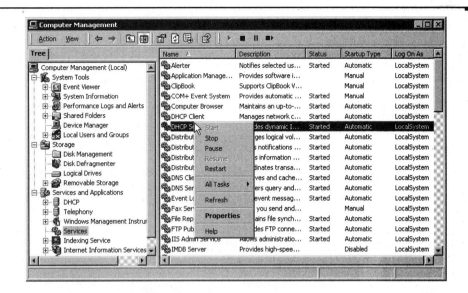

FIGURE 4.20

The property page of a service

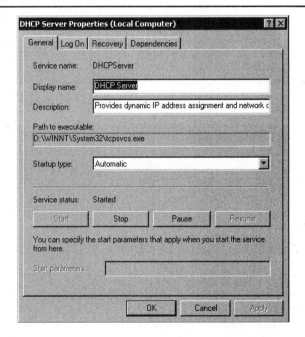

The Recovery tab, shown in Figure 4.21, displays a new set of options, including what to do if the service fails. In addition to choosing the response (from Take No Action all the way to Reboot the Computer) that will occur on the first, second, and subsequent attempts, you can provide the details. There is also a Dependencies tab to tell you what services depend on this one and what services this one depends on, which is good to know *before* you stop the service. In NT 4 you had no way of knowing about dependencies (other than from experience or a separate Resource Kit application) until you tried to stop the service.

NOTE It's a small thing, but when you right-click a service, you'll notice that in addition to Stop, Start, Pause, and Continue, there's a new option, Restart. This is deceptively cool—you see, choosing Restart causes Windows 2000 to stop a service and then start it again in just one click, a great time-saver compared to NT 4, where you had to first stop the service, then wait for the service to stop, and then start it again.

FIGURE 4.21

Options in the Service Properties Recovery tab

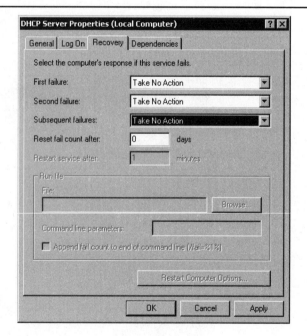

What Is This Network and Dial-Up Connections Tool?

The Network and Dial-Up Connections tool brings together the functions of Dial-Up Networking and NT 4's Network Control Panel. The idea here is that a connection is a connection, whether it's a serial cable to another computer on your desk, a dial-up connection to the Internet, or a network connection using an Ethernet card that provides access to the corporate network in your office.

Each connection represented in this tool contains the necessary device and protocol-specific information for its purposes. In other words, each connection's properties and configuration information is specific to the connection type and instance. For example, a Dial-Up Connection is much like an Address Book entry in NT 4 Dial-Up Networking; it knows which device (modem), phone number, and authentication protocol to use, and there are network protocols and services specified for it. A Local Area Connection entry is really not so different, containing information about the device to use (the network card type and hardware address), as well as network protocols and services to be used.

Figure 4.4 (a few pages back) shows the properties of a sample Local Area Connection. Microsoft has just simplified the Network Control Panel options here by removing the Network Identification and Services configuration options. Different types of connections are all grouped together in this tool. So you may see several different dial-up connection entries (the dial-up icon includes a telephone), just as you saw multiple Address Book entries in Dial-Up Networking under NT 4, but you'll also see different Local Area Connection icons if you have multiple network cards (the connection in the network icon appears to be a BNC T-connector). If your server contains another type of networking device, such as an X.25 card or ISDN device, it will have an icon as well.

Where Did They Put NT Diagnostics?

WINMSD is gone. Well, the tool as we knew it is gone, replaced by a tool called System Information, which can be found in the Computer Management console under System Tools. Like many other tools we knew under NT 4, WINMSD has been replaced by a snap-in to the MMC. However, if you enter **WINMSD** in the Start/Run dialog box, the System Information tool opens by itself in a console, as shown in Figure 4.22. So if you really want to, you can put a shortcut to WINMSD in your Administrative Tools folder and feel right at home. The System Information tool is a huge improvement over WINMSD.EXE and an invaluable resource for system information.

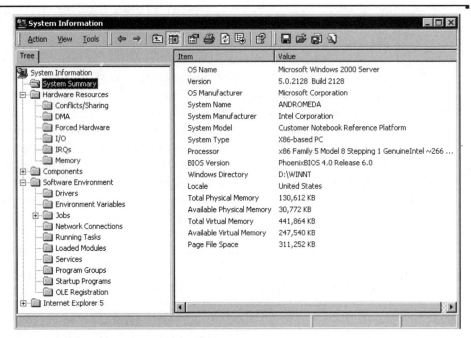

FIGURE 4.22

The System Information tool

Fixing Windows 2000's GUI

If you're an administrator, then you may find Windows 2000's slightly new desktop a bit annoying. Personally, I find the Web content that appears on the left-hand side of every window to be just a waste of space. Additionally, whenever I want to go do some maintenance in the `Program Files` or `System` directories, I've got to click past patronizing user-proofing screens that essentially say, "Hey, look, buddy, you're probably too stupid to mess with these files, are you *sure* you want to see this directory?" I need to see the hidden and system files, and in general, Details view is best for maintenance operations. Additionally, I've never found the address bar or standard buttons of much value in administrative tasks; they just rob me of screen space.

The first thing that I must do, then, when faced with a new system is to get it into "administrator-friendly" mode. To save you time, here are the steps:

1. Open My Computer.

2. From its menu bar, choose Tools/Folder Options.

3. In the General tab, under Web View choose Use Windows Classic Folders.

4. Click the View tab.

5. Check the box labeled Display the Full Path in the Title Bar.

6. Click the radio button labeled Show Hidden Files and Folders.

7. Uncheck the box labeled Hide File Extensions for Known File Types.

8. Uncheck the box labeled Hide Protected Operating System Files (Recommended) and click Yes when it asks you to confirm your choice.

9. Click OK.

10. Back in the main My Computer folder, click View/Details.

11. Right-click any blank space to the right of the menu bar and uncheck Standard Buttons.

12. Right-click any blank space to the right of the menu bar and uncheck Address Bar.

13. Hold down the Shift key and then click the close icon on the My Computer window—the icon in the upper right-hand corner that looks like an *X*. Hold down the Shift key so that the user interface will remember these settings.

Now that you've "saved" these settings with Shift+close, you'll reopen My Computer and apply those settings to all folders:

1. Click Tools/Folder Options.

2. Click the View tab.

3. Click the button toward the top of the page labeled Like Current Folder.

4. Click Yes to confirm the message.

5. Click OK to close Folder Options.

6. Close My Computer.

From now on, you'll be ready to get work done instead of appreciating the lovely "Web content"!

A Microsoft Management Console Primer

Let's face it, NT 4 admins. Our old familiar administrative tools—like the User Manager and User Manager for Domains, Server Manager, Event Viewer, and even Disk Administrator—have been assimilated into these things called Microsoft Management Console (MMC) tools.

I've discussed the shocking absence of Network Control Panel and how to deal with it. I've explained how to add a protocol or service. If only that were enough. To master Win2K's graphical changes, you must fully understand the Microsoft Management Console. In this section, I'll explain how MMC is not evil just because it has assimilated our friends, discuss key MMC terms you should know, briefly look at the Computer Management console, and finally, introduce you to creating your own MMC-based administrative tools.

What Is This MMC Thing?

In NT 4, administrators had to master multiple administration tools. A whole set of built-in tools, plus independent third-party tools, made administration sort of a mess. Although many admin tools functioned remotely, you had to install some of them separately (unless your desktop happened to be an NT server), and with third-party tools, you often had to jump through hoops to get them to work remotely, if at all. Even worse, with menus, buttons, toolbars, wizards, tabs, HTML, Java (you get the picture), just learning how to navigate new software was a chore. Also, there was no simplified version of User Manager for Domains that could be given to account operators and no way to hide menu items in administrative tools for those without full administrator rights.

So we complained. "As administrators, we need to be able to administer our networks from the comfort and luxury of our cubicles. And we don't want to waste time exploring all the windows, wizards, and tabs in every new tool. And we need more flexible tools," we said. Behold, Microsoft has heard our cries, and their response was the Microsoft Management Console.

MMC is a framework for management applications, offering a unified interface for Microsoft and third-party management tools. MMC doesn't replace management applications; it integrates them into one single interface. There are no inherent management functions in MMC at all. It uses component tools called snap-ins, which do all the work. MMC provides a user interface; it doesn't change how the snap-ins function.

Why Is MMC Good and Not Evil?

MMC offers the following benefits:

- You only have to learn one interface to drive a whole mess of tools.

- Third-party (ISV) tools will probably use MMC snap-ins. At best, Microsoft is encouraging software vendors to do so.

- You can build your own consoles, which is practical and fun. Admins can even create shortcuts on the console to non-MMC tools like executables, URLs, wizards, and scripts.

- By customizing MMC consoles, admins can delegate tasks to underlings without giving them access to all functions and without confusing them with a big scary tool.

- Help in MMC is context sensitive; it displays help subjects for only the appropriate components. Okay, that's not really new, but it's still cool (the Action menu is also context sensitive, but nobody uses menus anymore; everybody just right-clicks instead).

MMC Terms to Know

This section defines important terms you'll need to know when working with MMC.

A *console*, in MMC-speak, is one or more administrative tools in an MMC framework. The prebuilt admin tools, like Active Directory Users and Computers, are console files. You can also make your own consoles without any programming tools—you needn't be a C or Visual Basic programmer, as I'll discuss a bit later. The saved console file is a *Microsoft saved console (MSC)* file and it carries the .MSC extension.

 NOTE It's important to distinguish between Microsoft Management Console and console tools. MMC provides a framework to create customized console-based tools. MMC.EXE is a program that presents administrators (and others creating console tools) with a blank console to work with. It might help to think of a new instance of MMC.EXE as providing the raw material for a tool. In that case, Microsoft Management Console provides the rules and guidelines for building the tool, and the new console you create is the finished product.

Snap-ins are what we call administrative tools that can be added to the console. For example, the DHCP admin tool is a snap-in, and so is the Disk Defragmenter. Snap-ins can be made by Microsoft or by other software vendors. (You *do* need programming skills to make these, in other words.) A snap-in can contain components called nodes, or containers, or even leaves, in some cases. Although you can load multiple snap-ins in a single console, most of the prebuilt administrative tools contain only a single snap-in (including the Computer Management tool).

An *extension* is basically a snap-in that can't live by itself on the console but depends on a stand-alone snap-in. It adds some functionality to a snap-in. Some snap-ins work both ways. For example, the Event Viewer is a stand-alone snap-in, but it's implemented as an extension to the Computer Management snap-in. The key point is that extensions are optional. You can choose not to load them. For example, Local Users and Groups is an extension to the Computer Management snap-in. If you remove the extension from the COMPMGMT.MSC file used by your support folk, or simply don't include it in a custom console that uses the snap-in, those who use the tool won't have the option to create or manage users and groups with the tool. They won't even see it. (Please note that this will not prevent them from creating users and groups by other means, if they have the correct administrative privileges.)

Admins can create new MSC files by customizing an existing MSC file or by creating one from a blank console. The MMC.EXE plus the defined snap-ins create the tool interface. Also, it's possible to open multiple tools simultaneously, but each console runs one instance of MMC. Open an MSC file and look in Task Manager while it's running—you only see the `MMC.EXE` process running, not the MSC file, just as you see `WINWORD.EXE` running in Task Manager, but not the Word document's name.

By default, prebuilt console tools open in *User mode*. Changes cannot be made to the console design. You can't add or remove snap-ins, for example. To create or customize a console, use *Author mode*. When a user is running a tool and not configuring it, it should be running in one of the *User modes*. The tool will actually look different in User mode than it does in Author mode.

Figure 4.23 shows a sample console tool, with the parts of the interface labeled. This console is running in Author mode to show all the parts of the MMC interface. This is a custom console, but to open any existing tool in Author mode, invoke it from the Start/Run dialog box with the /a switch.

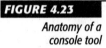

FIGURE 4.23

Anatomy of a console tool

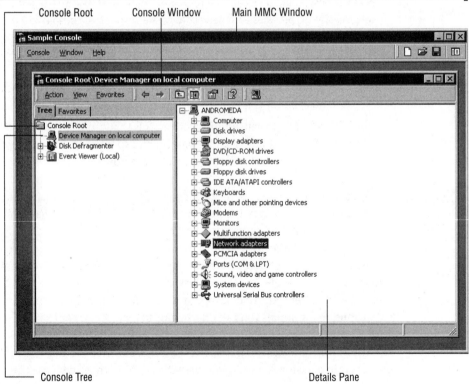

In Figure 4.23, the Main MMC window is present because the tool is open in Author mode. In User mode, the Main MMC window, with menus and buttons, is hidden and you only see the Console window. The Console menu in the Main window is basically a File menu, but it's also used to add and remove snap-ins and set console options. The Console window Action menu is context sensitive and will reflect the options of the selected snap-in tool or component. The hierarchical list of items shown by default in the left pane is called the *console tree* (hence the "tree" label on the tab), and at the top is the *console root*. The Favorites tab displays any created links to places in the console tool. The right pane is called the *details pane*. Snap-ins appear as nodes on the console tree. The contents of the details pane change depending on the item selected on the console tree.

The Computer Management Console

The Computer Management console is *the* main tool for administering a single server, local or remote. If you only have one server on your network and you only want to use one admin tool, Computer Management fits the bill. To open the Computer Management console, select the tool from the Administrative Tools folder or right-click My Computer and choose Manage. You can also right-click the machine's icon in Active Directory Users and Computers and choose Manage.

There are three nodes in the Computer Management console tree: System Tools, Storage, and Services and Applications (see Figure 4.24). Notice that the focus is on the local machine by default; to connect to other computers on the network, highlight the Computer Management icon at the root of the tree and choose Connect to Another Computer from the Action menu.

FIGURE 4.24

The Computer Management console tree

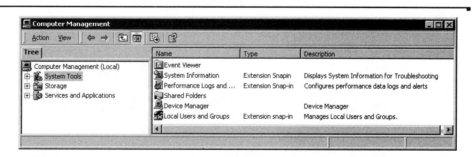

Expand the nodes in the Computer Management console tree to reveal the configuration tools and objects, as shown in Figure 4.25. Most of the core functions are under System Tools. Some functions even work remotely on NT 4 machines (you can view a remote machine's Event Logs, for example), but new features require the remote machine to be a Win2K box.

FIGURE 4.25

*The expanded
Computer
Management
console tree*

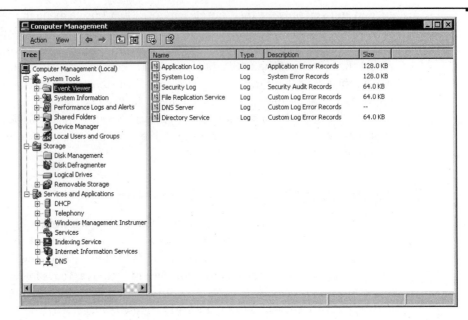

In the System Tools node, you can complete the following tasks:

- View events and manage the Event Logs. Basically the Event Viewer tool turned into an MMC snap-in. Notice that some services, such as DNS and Directory Service (Active Directory software) now have their own logs.

- View system information. The export option in these consoles is great for generating reports and documenting your server configuration. System Information provides details about hardware resources, system components configuration information, and software components (see Figure 4.26).

- Set up performance logs and alerts without opening Performance Monitor (see Chapter 20 for specifics on configuring performance alerts.).

- Manage shared folders. View, create, and manage shares; view sessions and open files; and disconnect sessions. This replaces those functions in the Control Panel's Server applet for local management and the remote shares management feature in Server Manager.

- Manage devices. The long-awaited Device Manager is fully remoteable and a great place to track down information about your hardware, update drivers, and troubleshoot resource conflicts.

- Create and manage local users and groups (Chapter 8 is all about creating and managing users and groups).

FIGURE 4.26

Viewing system information

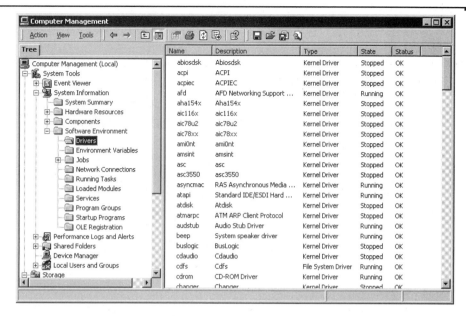

The Storage node (shown back in Figure 4.25) includes options for managing removable storage (a new feature), along with the new Disk Defragmenter tool and the Disk Management tool, which is the equivalent of the Disk Administrator in NT 4. There is also a component to view logical drives, including network drive mappings, and their properties. This is useful if you want to quickly view free space or set NTFS security at the root of a partition, for example. Too bad you can't browse directories like you can in Explorer. Oh well, I guess we don't need *another* desktop shell program, do we?

The Services and Applications node (also shown in Figure 4.25) includes telephony settings, services configuration, Windows Management Instrumentation (WMI), indexing, and IIS management stuff, the last of which is also available in the Administrative Tools group by itself (the tool is called Internet Services Manager, while the extension in Computer Management is called Internet Information Services). The Services tool replaces the Services Control Panel and the remote service management feature of Server Manager. Expect the components available in the Services and Applications node to change depending on what services are installed. For instance, if the server is a DHCP server or is running DNS, these management components will appear under Services and Applications—otherwise, you won't see them.

Other MMC Tools

If you're like me, you don't want to click here and click there and basically get carpal tunnel syndrome just to open something from the Administrative Tools group. If you prefer to use Start/Run to invoke your tools, it's nice to know their filenames. Table 4.1

outlines some of the core MMC-based tools files to save your hand and your sanity. Keep in mind that some tools, like DNS and DHCP, might not be present on the system if the corresponding service is not installed. Also, you need to include the program extension in the Start/Run box. Just entering **DSA**, for example, doesn't work. You'll need to enter **DSA.MSC**.

TABLE 4.1: MAIN MMC-BASED FILES

MSC File	Common Name
MSINFO32.MSC*	System Information
COMPMGMT.MSC	Computer Management
DCPOL.MSC	Domain Controller Securtiy Policy
DEVMGMT.MSC	Device Manager
DFRG.MSC	Disk Defragmenter
DFSGUI.MSC	Distributed File System
DISKMGMT.MSC	Disk Management
DOMPOL.MCS	Domain Security Policy
DOMAIN.MSC	Active Directory Domains and Trusts
DSA.MSC	Active Directory Users and Computers
DSSITE.MSC	Active Directory Sites and Services
EVENTVWR.MSC	Event Viewer
FAXSERV.MSC	Fax Service Management
FSMGMT.MSC	Shared Folders
GPEDIT.MSC	Group Policy
LUSRMGR.MSC	Local User Manager
NTMSMGR.MSC	Removable Storage Manager
PERFMON.MSC	Performance Monitor
RRASMGMT.MSC	Routing and Remote Access
SECPOL.MCS	Local Security Policy
SERVICES.MSC	Services Configuration
TAPIMGMT.MSC	Telephony
COMEXP.MSC*	Component Services
DHCPMGMT.MSC	DHCP
DNSMGMT.MSC	DNS
IIS.MSC*	Internet Information Services

Another caveat: most of these tools are found in the /winnt/system32 directory and are therefore in the default search path. A couple, however, are found in other directories that are not included in the default search path. The tool to manage Internet Information Services (IIS.MSC) is a good example; it's found in /winnt/system32/inetsrv. These errant tools are marked with an asterisk (*) in Table 4.1. The quickest way to find them is to use the Search option on the Start button. Once you locate them, there are a bunch of options. You can copy the tool to /winnt/system32 or just put a shortcut right on the desktop if you don't mind the clutter. The other alternative is to change the search path to include these directories. It's a bit more of a pain; you'll need to open the System applet in Control Panel, then go to the Advanced tab and choose the Environmental Variables button. Edit the system variable called Path. Oh, yes, and then reboot. Is it worth it? Many don't think so. One strategy I like to use combines these approaches. I copy all the tools I want to a separate directory, then add *that* directory to my search path. That way I don't have to edit the path variable multiple times. I just edit it once to add my tools directory, then copy tools into the directory to make them quickly accessible from the Run routine. You may think this is a lot of trouble to use a couple of tools, but just wait until you install a bunch of third-party tools on your server. They all use their own installation directories. Although Microsoft is reportedly requiring new third-party admin tools to go in the /winnt/system32 directory, they've caved in on requirements before, so it's best to be prepared.

Creating Microsoft Management Consoles

If the existing MMC tools don't fit your needs exactly, you can create a customized tool with your most frequently used components. Creating your own admin tool is easy using the MMC framework and snap-ins provided by Microsoft and third-party software vendors. Yes, keep in mind that your next version of a backup program or virus scanner or who knows what could be managed by a vendor-supplied MMC snap-in.

Although it's actually quite simple to create a customized MMC tool, there are so many options for customizing that I can't tell the full story here. Nevertheless, no discussion of the new Win2K interface would be complete without an example or two of authoring administration tools.

Building a Simple Microsoft Saved Console

To configure your own custom admin tool, open a blank MMC in Author mode by opening Start/Run and typing **mmc.exe**. This will open up an untitled console (Console1) and display a generic console root, shown in Figure 4.27. You can now open existing MSC files (just as you open DOC files in Word or XLS files in Excel) by choosing Open from the Console menu. These files will automatically open in Author mode if you open them in a blank console. If you wish to open and fiddle with existing MSC files, most (but not all) of them are in the WINNT/SYSTEM32 directory. Just be sure to leave the original MSC files intact; you might need them again. In the example that follows, you'll be creating a tool from scratch, starting with a blank console and loading snap-ins.

FIGURE 4.27

A generic console root

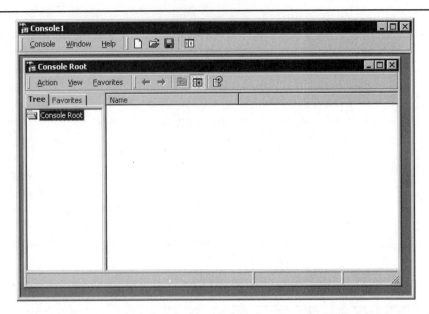

Suppose you need a tool for hardware management and troubleshooting. To create it, follow these steps:

1. Start by renaming the console root Hardware Tools; right-click the console root and choose Rename (you can actually do this step later if you prefer).

2. Now you're ready to add snap-ins. Choose Add/Remove Snap-in from the Console menu in the Main window. As you can see in Figure 4.28, you must choose where to add the snap-in. Right now, it's only possible to add snap-ins to the console root (now called Hardware Tools), but you can also group related tools by first adding folders to the console root.

3. To add folders to the console root, choose the Add button to open the Add Standalone Snap-In dialog box (see Figure 4.29). You'll now see both dialog boxes, sort of cascaded. Items chosen from the list in the Add Standalone Snap-In dialog box will appear in the list of snap-ins in the parent dialog box. Scroll through the list until you see a folder called Folder. Choose Add and the folder appears in your list of snap-ins in the Add/Remove Snap-In dialog box. Choose Add again and you'll see two. Close the Add Standalone Snap-In dialog box to return to Add/Remove Snap-In, then click OK to close it.

4. Back at the console in progress, right-click the folders to rename them. Figure 4.30 shows a Hardware Tools console with three folders, renamed to Disk Tools, Other Tools, and Web Sites.

FIGURE 4.28

Choosing where to add
snap-ins

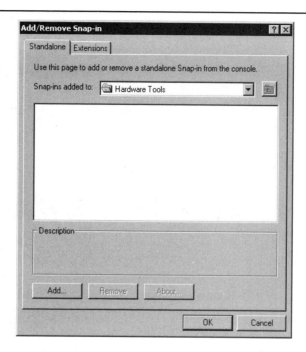

FIGURE 4.28

Choosing where to add
snap-ins

FIGURE 4.29

The Add Standalone
Snap-In dialog box

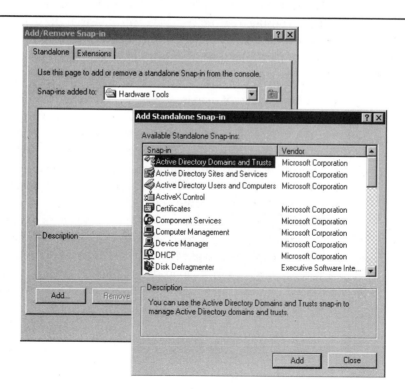

FIGURE 4.30

Customizing the console

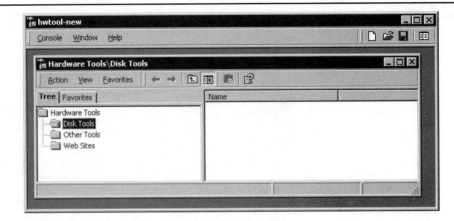

5. The Web Sites folder will contain snap-ins which are actually hyperlinks to hardware vendor and support sites. To add links to the Web Sites container, open the Add/Remove Snap-In dialog again (choose Add/Remove Snap-In from the Console menu), select the Web Sites folder as the container, choose Add, then scroll through the list until you find Link to Web Address. Click the Add button, and from this point, it's just like creating a new Internet shortcut; fill in the URL and give the shortcut a friendly name. Choose OK to close the Add/Remove Snap-In page and return to the console. When you select the link in the console tree, the Web page will appear in the details pane. You can actually surf the Web from the console, although you'll technically need links to get off that particular site.

To add tools to the other folders, go through the same process and choose the appropriate tools from the list of snap-ins available. Presumably, third-party software vendors will provide tools as snap-ins, so this list will expand and vary with the configuration and software installed. Some tools will prompt you to select a computer to manage. Others, such as the Event Viewer snap-in, also present the option to choose the machine when you start the tool from the command line, as shown in Figure 4.31. To change the focus of the tool when you kick it off, enter **tool.msc /computer=*computername*** in the Start/Run box or at a command prompt.

While adding the stand-alone snap-ins, be sure to check out the available extensions for them. It's interesting to note that the Computer Management snap-in components are all implemented as extensions (see Figure 4.32), although most also exist as independent snap-ins. You can load the Computer Management snap-in and deselect the extensions that aren't needed for your custom tool. All available extensions are added by default.

Selecting a computer
for the snap-in to
manage

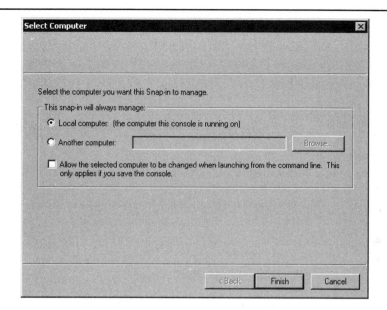

Select or deselect
extensions

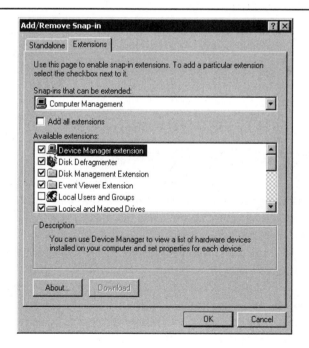

In Figure 4.33, you can see what your final tool could look like, a customized Hardware Tools console. This one consists of a Disk Tools folder (with Defragmenter and Disk Management), a folder called Other Tools that includes the Device Manager and System Information, and a Web Sites folder that can be filled with helpful hardware support–related links.

FIGURE 4.33

*A custom Hardware
Tools console*

To save the custom console, open Save from the Console menu, name the file and specify a path to save it in, then click Save. Now the MSC file is ready to use.

Designing Tools with Taskpad Views

It's possible to design simple views of an MMC tool for newbie administrators, foregoing their need to learn the different tools and navigate the console tree nodes. You might also wish to present a limited set of tasks and hide others that are normally available in a regular MMC tool view. Taskpad views fill this need and allow you to create a tool that looks like the one shown in Figure 4.34. This tool presents a limited set of tasks instead of the entire console tree structure. Now novice administrators can perform delegated tasks without drilling down through the tree, expanding and collapsing, hoping to find the right tool, then looking for the choice on the Action menu. Instead, they can just click the icon and go right to the task.

Taskpad views are HTML-based pages that can include links to console menu commands, wizards, scripts, other executables, even URLs. At least one snap-in is required to create a taskpad view, although you can create links to tasks that are unrelated to the snap-in, such as scripts. To include menu command and property page tasks, however, the corresponding snap-in must be loaded beforehand.

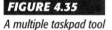

Before designing a console with taskpad views, or any type of console for that matter, put your thinking cap on and visualize the tool you need. What tasks will the tool include? Which snap-ins will be required? You'll need to be somewhat familiar with the available snap-ins and their functions. Will your tool include only one taskpad view with a bunch of tasks in a single window? Or do you need a tool with several tabs, each containing a set of related tasks? Figure 4.34 shows a tool with only one taskpad view; tasks are all together in one window, and the console tree is hidden from the user. Figure 4.35 illustrates a multiple taskpad tool, perhaps for a more experienced support person who needs to perform several different types of tasks and doesn't want to load a different tool for each one.

FIGURE 4.35
A multiple taskpad tool

There are a couple of possible strategies for creating taskpad views. One is to just assemble a specific set of tasks into one or more taskpad views. For example, when the tool is opened, you might see a single taskpad view called Routine Admin Tasks with links labeled Create New User or Create New Share. If you to click the link called Create New User, the dialog box or wizard to create new users appears. In a tool like this, you might want to hide the console tree to prevent users from navigating around and present only the taskpad view.

Another technique is to create taskpad views for particular items in the tree, for example a taskpad for Users and Groups, another for Shared Folders, and a third for the Event Viewer. Again, you might choose to hide the actual console tree and normal views for this tool. In that case, you should create a main taskpad with links to the other taskpads located at different branches of the tree. So imagine a taskpad view called Main Taskpad which contains links called Open Services and Manage IIS. Click the former and another taskpad appears with a list of services and links to stop, start, or restart a service. Use the Forward and Back buttons on the toolbar (like we do in Explorer) to return to the Main Taskpad view.

Alternately, you might choose to present these taskpad views in addition to the normal views without hiding the console tree. In this case, the taskpad will enhance the functionality of the console tool by presenting a set of simple task options (for people who don't like playing Marco Polo in admin tools) without imposing any limitations on what the user can see or access.

Whichever approach you choose, keep in mind that taskpad views are meant to simplify and facilitate the use of a console. They can even limit, to some extent, the administrative options that are presented. However, you should not consider them a foolproof way to limit admin types from performing certain tasks. Even if they can't get around the limitations of the custom console, which is by no means certain, they may have access to other tools that are not restricted. The best way to limit another admin's power is to use all of the other built-in security options that are available in appropriate combinations: security group memberships, rights, group policies, and delegation of control are some of the more reliable tools for this purpose. Don't rely on a customized, locked-down console tool instead.

In this section, I'll show you how to create a Main Taskpad view for the Computer Management snap-in and how to create tasks. Then I'll demonstrate how to set up taskpad views for particular items in the console tree, with links from the main taskpad. Finally, I'll reveal how to customize the interface to hide the console tree and present a simplified interface to the user.

Creating Taskpad Views

Once you've decided which tasks your user or admin person will perform with this tool and identified the necessary snap-ins, you are ready to create the console. In this example, you'll create a view and a select set of tasks from the Computer Management snap-in to keep things simple. This tool will be for gathering information; we'll use the Event Logs, System Information, and Device Manager functions. Open a blank console as described earlier (Start/Run and enter **mmc.exe**) and load the required snap-ins. You can also use an existing custom console that contains the necessary snap-ins as long as you open it in Author mode.

To follow along with this example, load the Computer Management snap-in in your blank MMC console; it encompasses all the tasks for this tool. It's also possible to add the three snap-ins separately (Event Logs, System Information, and Device Manager), but the Computer Management snap-in has a special capability that will facilitate remote information gathering, as you'll see in a moment.

To create a taskpad view at the top of the Computer Management node, follow these steps:

1. Select the Computer Management node in the console tree, right-click it (or pull down the Action menu), and choose New Taskpad View.

2. A New Taskpad View Creation Wizard appears. Click Next to continue.

3. Next, select the style of the taskpad view (shown in Figure 4.36). Choose whether to display the actual items that would normally appear in the details pane (such as a list of users or a list of services), and if so, whether you want a vertical list (to accommodate lots of columns) or a horizontal list (for longer lists). In this case, we're just going to create a view of links and don't want to see the details pane information, so choose No List. If you were to choose a list type, however, you would use the List Size option box to determine how much of the window pane can be taken up by the list. I'll demonstrate a taskpad view with a list in a moment. Now, select the style you want for your task descriptions. If you needed a longer explanation to appear alongside the link, you would choose Text. However, we want a description that just pops up when you hover over the link, thus leaving more room for task links, so choose InfoTip. All of the tasks created later will use this style. Choose Next to continue.

FIGURE 4.36

Configure the style of the taskpad.

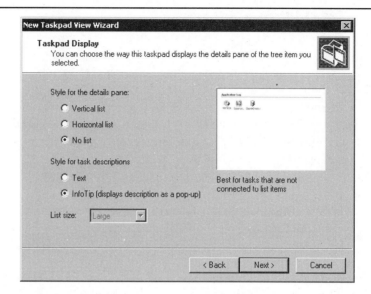

4. In the next screen (Figure 4.37), you must decide whether to apply the view to the selected tree item only or to any other tree item of the same type. If you choose the latter, you have the option to change the default details pane display for those items to the taskpad view (although the normal view will still exist). However, let's choose to apply the view only to the selected tree item. This taskpad view will only display when the Computer Management root node is selected. Choose Next.

FIGURE 4.37

Select a taskpad target.

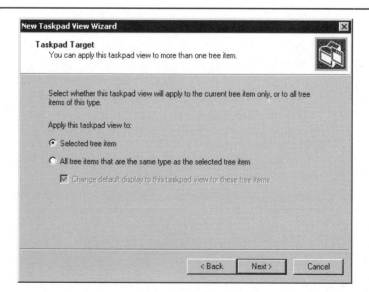

5. Now, supply a name for your taskpad (mine is called Main Taskpad) and a description if you wish. The description you supply will appear under the title in the details pane. That's it! In the final screen of the wizard, you have the option to kick off the New Task Wizard and start creating tasks (uncheck the box beside Start New Task Wizard to avoid creating a new task for now). Click Finish to close the wizard and create the new taskpad view.

Figure 4.38 shows the new taskpad before any tasks are created. Notice the squared-off tabs that allow you to move between the taskpad view and the normal view of the details pane. In a moment, I'll show you how to hide the console tree on the left and remove the normal view tab to achieve the look and feel of the console shown in Figure 4.34.

A console with a taskpad view

If you want to create another taskpad view, like the one in Figure 4.35, just choose New Taskpad View again from the Action menu. Or choose Delete Taskpad View to delete a selected one. If you want to make changes to a taskpad, select Edit Taskpad View from the Action menu (you may have to click the taskpad's tab first—blast those pesky context-sensitive menu commands!). In the taskpad view property page, shown in Figure 4.39, you can go back and change the style of the view and add, remove, or modify tasks.

FIGURE 4.39

*The taskpad
property page*

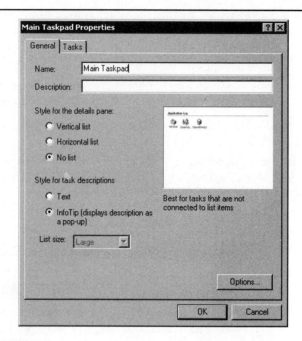

Creating a Task

To create tasks for the new taskpad, select the Start New Task Wizard check box in the last screen of the Taskpad View Creation Wizard, or choose Edit Taskpad View from the Action menu. Move to the Tasks tab and click New to start the same wizard. The following steps illustrate how to create a task which uses the Connect to Another Computer command (in the Computer Management Snap-in):

1. In the New Task Wizard, click Next to begin creating a new task. The wizard asks whether the task will be a menu command (from the context or Action menu in the console), a shell command, or a navigation command, which points to a link in the Favorites tab (see Figure 4.40). Although shortcut menu commands are limited to the functions of a loaded snap-in, a shell command could be an executable (like a wizard), a shell script or other type of script, even a URL. In any of these cases, the shell command task actually kicks off the command called, so in that sense, it's just a taskpad's version of a shortcut to something outside of the tool itself. For example, you can create a shell command task and point it to the Calculator (CALC.EXE) if you want (that way, it's handy for those binary-to-decimal conversions). Click the radio button beside the desired type of task. We'll create a menu command in this example, but if you choose to create a shell command at another time, you'll need to specify the path to the command and any command-line parameters (also called arguments), the "start in"

directory, and whether the command should run in a normal window, minimized, or maximized. Figure 4.41 shows the dialog box where you create a shell command task.

FIGURE 4.40

Creating a new task

FIGURE 4.41

Creating a shell command task

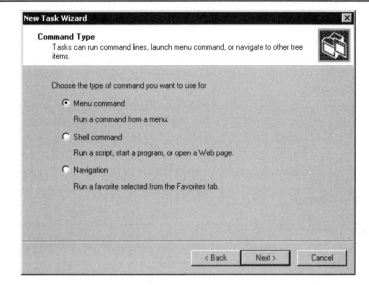

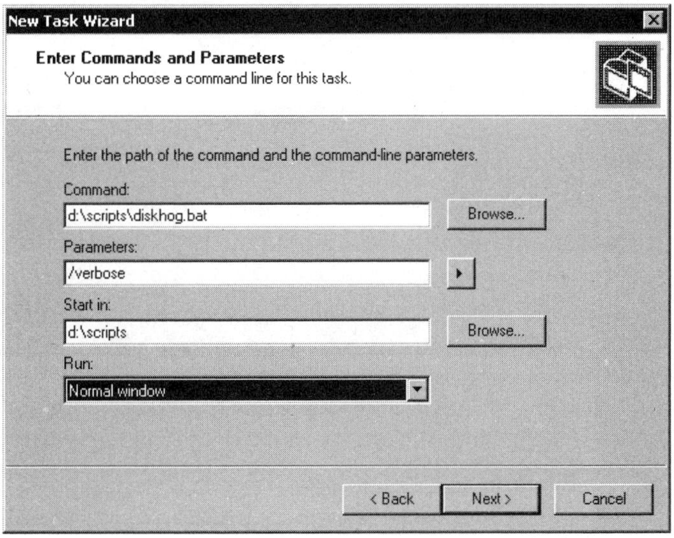

NOTE In contrast to shell command tasks, which refer to commands outside the tool, navigation command tasks are shortcuts to places within the console. For instance, if you want a shortcut to the Disk Defragmenter, find it in the tool, then add it to the tool's favorites (just choose Add to Favorites from the Favorites menu). Then, when you create your task, just choose the shortcut to Disk Defragmenter from the list of existing favorites. Once the shortcut is created, clicking on the task icon whisks you down to the Disk Defragmenter tool.

2. After choosing to create a menu command, select a source for the command in the next screen (see Figure 4.42) and choose a command from those available on the right. You can choose whether the source of the command will be an item in the details pane or a specific item in the console tree. In this case, we are creating the latter, a tree item task. Now you'll see the Computer Management node in the left pane and Connect to Another Computer is among the available commands on the right. Highlight Connect to Another Computer and click Next.

FIGURE 4.42

Select a menu command.

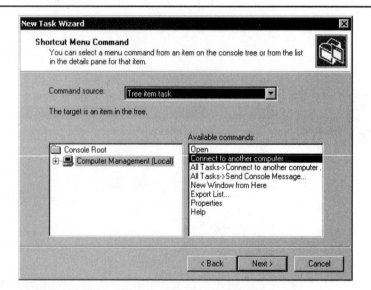

3. Give the task a name and a description. The description you supply will either appear alongside the task icon or will pop up when you hover over it, depending on the style choice you made for the taskpad. Click Next.

4. In the next screen (shown in Figure 4.43), choose a task symbol. Unfortunately the selection of symbols is pretty limited. However, some tasks have recommended symbols; the wizard may highlight one for you but will of course leave the final choice up to you. Click Next.

FIGURE 4.43

Choose an icon for the task.

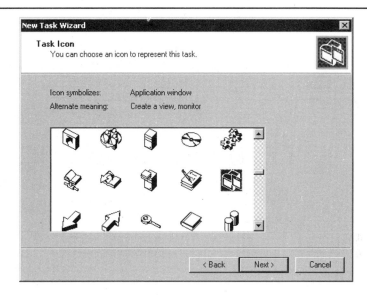

5. The wizard confirms your task creation (see Figure 4.44), displaying a list of created tasks and giving you the option to run the wizard again to create another task. Click Finish, then click OK to close the Taskpad property page. The new task will appear in the taskpad as a link. Just click once on the link to run it.

FIGURE 4.44

Completing the New Task Wizard

6. Just for practice, run the New Task Wizard again, creating a new menu command based on another tree item. Scroll through the Computer Management tree and locate Shares under Shared Folders. The task you're looking for is New File Share. Create a task to create a new share on the computer. Now your taskpad should look like the one shown in Figure 4.45. Using the tasks you've created, you can now connect to remote machines and create shares on them.

FIGURE 4.45

A taskpad with tasks

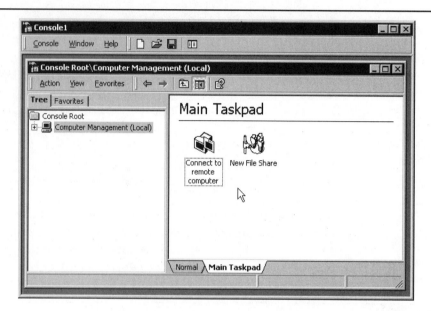

Steps 1 through 5 illustrate how to create a task to connect to another computer, which is important if the tool is to function remotely. This is why the Computer Management snap-in was used instead of the individual component snap-ins. When adding individual component snap-ins like the Event Viewer, you must choose to have it always manage the local machine or a particular remote machine.

TIP When you load a snap-in, there is an option to specify the machine to be managed when the tool is started from the command line, but this requires that you close and reopen the tool to administer a different machine; that's just too much trouble. With the Connect to Another Computer task that's built in to the Computer Management snap-in, you can easily change the focus for any task created without closing and reopening the console.

Some Notes about Taskpads and Tasks

When you were creating the taskpad in our example, you had the choice in Step 4 to apply the view to the selected tree item only or to any other tree item of the same type.

When a taskpad view is applied to the selected tree item, it will only be visible when you navigate to the node in the console tree or use a link such as a Favorite to get there. When a taskpad view applies to other tree items and is set to display by default instead of the normal details pane view, the taskpad would theoretically contain mostly generic menu commands, like Open or Properties, so that as you navigate to a certain part of the tree, you see a consistent taskpad view and set of link commands in the details pane on the right. Unfortunately, Microsoft is still working out the kinks in this area, because taskpad views created in this way don't seem to display except at the node where they are created, and the documentation is pretty silent about it.

When you're choosing a menu command source, if your command source is the list in the details pane, your choices are limited to menu commands available at that level. However, you can still create tree item tasks that point to any item on the tree. Menu item command tasks are not limited by the item to which the taskpad is linked. So why would you want to create tasks that are limited to the commands in the details pane at all? Well, this capability is useful if you need to apply the same tasks to different items in the list. You see, with tasks that use the command list in the details pane, you first choose the item from a horizontal list in the taskpad, for example, then you choose the task link. The command applies to the selected item. As an example, let's create a taskpad view for the Services node and create tasks to stop, start, and resume the selected service in the taskpad:

1. First, create the new taskpad for services configuration. Go to the Services node in the console tree (it's under Computer Management\Services and Applications\Services) and choose New Taskpad View from the Action menu. The wizard will open. Click Next to continue.

2. Select display options for the taskpad. For Services, there will be a long list, so a vertical list is appropriate, although selecting a horizontal list will allocate more room to display the columns. I also recommend leaving the task description style on InfoTip, as this will allow more room for task links. Click Next.

3. Choose to apply the taskpad view to the selected tree item. These commands will be specific to the Services node. Choose Next.

4. Give the taskpad a name (I just called mine Services) and a description, which will appear under the name in the details pane. Click Finish to create the taskpad and start the New Task Wizard (if you left the box checked, it's selected by default).

5. To create a task, click Next in the New Task Wizard. Choose to create a menu command and click Next.

6. This time, in the Shortcut Menu Command page, you'll choose your command from the list in the details pane for Services. As you can see in Figure 4.46, these are also the commands that are available in the context menu when you select a

service and right-click it. Select Restart (it doesn't really matter which service is selected on the source side at this point) and click Next.

FIGURE 4.46

*Creating a service con-
figuration task*

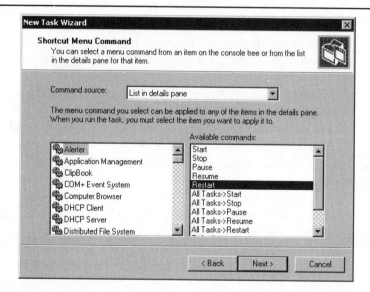

7. Supply a name for the task and a short description. I changed the description for the Restart task because the default description, which appears when you hover your cursor over the symbol in the taskpad, was incorrectly service and machine specific (another small kink). Click Next.

8. Choose an icon from the list, click Next, click Finish in the confirmation page, and you're done.

9. Repeat Steps 5 through 8 as necessary to create tasks for Start, Stop, Pause, Resume and Properties.

Now the Services taskpad should appear with the list of services displayed in a list. The tasks you've created appear alongside (or under) the details pane. To restart a given service, select it from the list and click Restart. Figure 4.47 shows the final Services taskpad with several service-related tasks, although you might not want to include the Properties task if you don't want the user of the tool to change the configuration of the services.

FIGURE 4.47

The Services taskpad

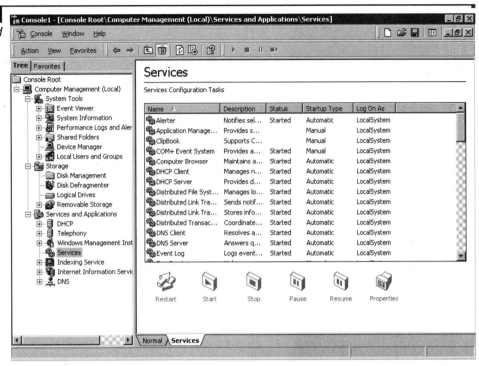

Customizing the Console Interface

You can give the customized tool a simplified look and feel by hiding the console tree and those navigation tabs that allow users to move between the normal view and the taskpad views.

Ya know, that reminds me, if we hide the console tree and the navigation tabs, lock the tool down, and prevent the user of the tool from navigating the console tree, they have no way of getting to the Services taskpad we created in our earlier example. They'll be stuck at the Main taskpad. So before we customize the console interface, we need a task in the Main taskpad which acts as a link to the Services taskpad. There are two ways to accomplish this, and both seem to work equally well.

The first way to create a link to another taskpad is to navigate to the node while the console tree is visible in Author mode and add that location to the list of Favorites. Then, create a navigation task in the Main taskpad and select the Services Favorite as the destination. The Favorites link must exist, however, before you can create a navigation task for it.

If you don't want to use the Favorites method, create a menu item task in the Main taskpad and select as the source a tree item task. Navigate down the tree to Services and select the command Open (shown in Figure 4.48). This will create a task to open the Services node where the taskpad will display by default.

FIGURE 4.48

Creating a task to
open a console
taskpad view

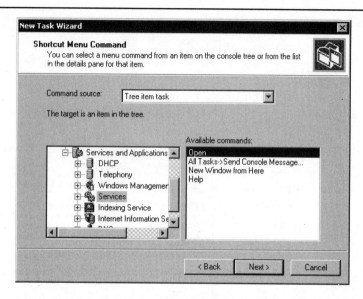

Now, to customize the console interface, choose Customize from the View menu in the Console window. A set of view options is shown in Figure 4.49. Items are shown when the boxes are checked and hidden when they are cleared. While clearing the Console Tree check box does hide the Tree tab in the console pane on the left, it doesn't hide the pane itself; you'll still see the Favorites tab. If that's not agreeable to you, use the Show/Hide Console Tree button on the toolbar. It actually hides the entire tree side of the Console window.

FIGURE 4.49

Customizing the view
of a console

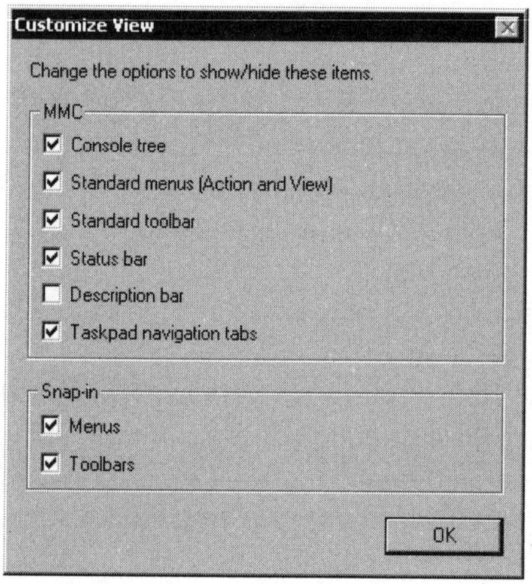

Hide the Action and View menus by clearing the Standard Menus check box. Removing the Action menu prevents the user from selecting an item from a horizontal or vertical list in a taskpad and pulling down the Action menu to see a complete set of task options, but he can still use the context menu by right-clicking if you don't disable it (see the next section for instructions on disabling the context menu). If you clear the check box labeled Standard Toolbar, the toolbar with the forward and back buttons (as well as the "up one level" and "show/hide console" buttons) disappears. You need those buttons if the tool has to navigate the tree. Consider our earlier example of a Main taskpad with a link to the Services taskpad. If the Standard toolbar is removed, you cannot return to the Main taskpad from the Services taskpad without a link in the Services taskpad. If the console tool is only running wizards or scripts, however, removing the navigation buttons won't be a problem. To really simplify the window, clear both the Status Bar and the Description Bar check boxes (the status bar is displayed by default, but the description bar is not). Clear the Taskpad Navigation Tabs check box to remove the Normal tab from the bottom of the details pane, and users will only be able to view the taskpads you've created.

Each snap-in can have its own menu items and toolbar buttons. To hide these for all snap-ins in the tool, clear the two check boxes in the Snap-In section of the dialog box. You can't pick and choose which toolbars and buttons to hide; you either hide them for all snap-ins or reveal them for all snap-ins.

Packaging Up the Tool for Users

When the tool is ready to be published, choose Options from the Console menu of the Main window and change the tool's name (from Console1 to something descriptive), as shown in Figure 4.50. The new name will now appear in the title bar. You might also want to assign a different icon than the generic MMC icon. Finally, assign a default mode to the MSC file. Choose Author mode, and it will always open with the main MMC window and main menu/toolbar, allowing changes to be made to the tool. Otherwise, only the Console window is available. If you aren't sure what I mean by the terms *Main MMC window* and *Console window*, glance back at Figure 4.23 "Anatomy of a console tool." Use one of the three User modes to prevent changes, like adding and removing snap-ins. The three different User modes represent varying degrees of restrictions, such as whether the user can open multiple windows. Limited access-single window is the most restrictive.

FIGURE 4.50

*The Console Options
dialog box*

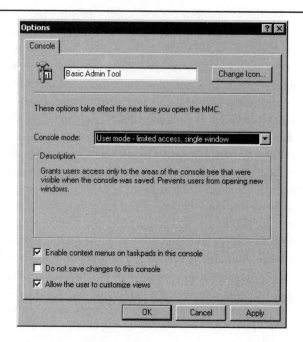

Notice the three configuration check boxes at the bottom of Figure 4.50. To disable all context menus on all taskpads in the console, uncheck the box that says Enable Context Menus on Taskpads in This Console. If you created that Services taskpad and left out a Properties task, for example, the user could still right-click a service in the list and choose Properties, unless the context menus are disabled (see the preceding section for instructions on removing the Action menu, which also shows a full set of possible tasks when an item is selected). Check Do Not Save Changes to This Console to prevent users from saving any changes to the console. Users can customize views by default. To prevent this, uncheck the box that says Allow the User to Customize Views. Choose OK, then save the console as an MSC file if you haven't already.

Figure 4.51 shows our basic Admin Tool running in User mode with limited access and a single window. The console tree and taskpad navigation tabs, as well as the Action and View menus, are hidden. This tool does reveal the Standard toolbar, however, since it's necessary to be able to go forward and back in the tool. Too bad you can't hide some buttons and not others. The buttons to show the console tree and to go up a level are also available.

FIGURE 4.51

The final product

Distributing the Tool

When the tool is finished, just distribute it as you would a normal file; e-mail it to someone, put it on the network file server in a shared folder, or use Active Directory services to publish it. Appropriate administrative permissions for the tasks and access to the snap-ins, either on the local machine or on the network, are required to use the tool.

Unfortunately, these custom tools will only run on other Win2K machines, unless Microsoft has plans to distribute a compatible version of MMC for Windows 9*x* and NT 4 clients.

Editing a Custom Console Tool

Making changes to the console is easy, even when the tool opens in User mode by default. The tool can be opened in Author mode using one of several methods. If you open it using Start/Run and enter the filename with the /a switch, the MSC file will open in Author mode. Right-clicking on the file's icon and choosing Author is another method. Also, you can open a blank console using Start/Run and entering **mmc.exe** and then choose open from the Console menu to pull up any MSC file in Author mode. But how can you keep others from making changes to the tool using these tricks? Chapter 8 explains how to restrict access to Author mode, and even particular snap-ins, using group policies.

In this chapter, you learned how to gracefully weather the user interface changes that come with administering Windows 2000 Server. You should now feel confident configuring network software without the Network Control Panel, among other things. We also explored the Microsoft Management Console and learned a few of its inner secrets. Now you are ready to unleash the real power of MMC, by using its authoring features to create consoles that fit the needs of your MIS/IT department.

CHAPTER 5

Understanding the Registry Database

Anyone who works with Windows 2000, whether as a user or as an administrator, makes a fair number of adjustments to it, from the small ones, such as changing a background color, to larger ones, like changing a network IP address. Similarly, when you use an application, you inevitably end up configuring it as well, directing it where to save files, how the application should start up, whether to automatically run macros, and the like. And, of course, when you reboot Windows 2000 or whenever you start up an application, you expect your configurations to still be in effect—the things that you tell an operating system or application to do should survive a reboot. But where are these customizations stored?

Over the years, different operating systems have answered that question in different ways. Windows 2 and 2.1 actually stored a lot of their configuration information inside their own program files, which unbelievably meant that every time you made a change like installing a new video card, the Windows Setup program would build an entirely new copy of Windows with that driver's information embedded in the Windows program itself! Not every configuration change in Windows 2.x required a rebuild of the operating system, thankfully, as Windows 2.x and then 3.x used ASCII text files with names like WIN.INI, SYSTEM.INI, CONTROL.INI, and so on to store configuration information. INI files weren't a bad thing overall—their ASCII nature made changing them simple, a task for Notepad or an easy-to-write BASIC program—but the growing complexity of Windows in both its 9x and Windows NT incarnations created a need to be able to store more complex configuration information.

Microsoft's answer to that increased need arrived with the first version of NT, Windows NT 3.1, in the summer of 1993. The answer was a group of files with the collective name of the *Registry*. (Microsoft always capitalizes it—the Registry—so I will, too, but it always seems a bit overdone, don't you think?) The Registry is terrific in that it's one big database that contains all of the Windows 2000 configuration information. Everything's there, from color settings to users' passwords. (In case you're wondering, you can't directly access the part with the passwords.) Even better, the Registry uses a fault-tolerant approach to writing data to ensure that the Registry remains intact even if there's a power failure in the middle of a Registry update.

So you've just *got* to like Windows 2000's Registry. Except, of course, for the *annoying* parts about the Registry, including its cryptic organization and excessively complex structure. But read on and see what you think.

What Is the Registry?

The Registry is a hierarchical database of settings that describe your user account, the hardware of the server machine, and your applications. Anytime you make some change with the Control Panel or some other MMC snap-in, the effect of that change is usually stored in the Registry. (I say "usually" because some information is stored in the Active Directory, which is separate from the Registry.)

If you can make changes to your system and they're then stored in the Registry, you might ask, "Who cares? What's the value of the Registry?" Well, consider how much time you spend configuring a new workstation or server. If that machine died for some reason, you'd want to set another machine up to replace the now-dead one—do you really want to spend all that time reconfiguring the replacement machine to look like the original? No, of course not. You would much prefer to be able to just put Windows 2000 on the new machine and then restore all of the preferences and settings in one fell swoop, and you can do that, *if* you've got a backup of the old machine's Registry. Then all you need do is to put Windows 2000 on the replacement machine and then restore the old machine's Registry to the new machine. That, then, is the Registry's first value: when backed up, it preserves much of a machine's "state."

 NOTE Of course, another way to preserve the state of a Windows 2000 Professional machine is to store its image on a Remote Installation Services (RIS) server, as described in Chapter 3. Unfortunately, however, you can't use RIS to store the state of a member server or domain controller.

Preserving user settings is nice, but it's not the Registry's sole value. In addition to storing the settings that *you've* made in the Registry, Windows 2000 saves many settings that you never see, such as dynamic settings that Windows 2000 makes to itself every time it boots—for example, whenever Windows 2000 boots, it creates a census of the hardware attached to it and stores that census in the Registry. The Registry also contains internal adjustments that Windows 2000's designers preset with the intention that you would never touch them—and *that's* where the fun begins, at least for us noodlers.

Ninety-nine point nine percent of Windows 2000's settings are of no interest whatsoever. But a few are quite powerful and largely undocumented or documented solely by obscure Knowledge Base articles. The occult nature of these Registry settings has predictably become the source of countless "tips and tricks" about how to tune up NT's and Windows 2000's performance or how to solve some knotty problem. Perhaps the most remarkable of these appeared a few years ago when NT internals expert Mark Rossinovich discovered that the only real difference between NT Workstation 3.51 and NT Server 3.51 was *a few Registry settings*! Twiddling the Registry, then, is often of value to Windows 2000 troubleshooters.

The tough part about working with the Registry for NT/Windows 2000 is in grasping the programs and terminology used in editing the Registry. You're just supposed to *understand* sentences like these:

> When you receive upon logon the message 'A domain controller for your domain could not be contacted…' then you may need to increase Netlogon's timeout value.

> To increase the amount of time Netlogon waits before timing out during an interactive logon using a Domain User account, the following registry setting can be used… In the subkey HKEY_LOCAL_MACHINE\SYSTEM\CurrentControlSet\ Services\Netlogon\Parameters, create a new value ExpectedDialupDelay of type REG_DWORD and fill in a value between 0 and 600, representing the new Netlogon delay.†

Sentences like these are a major reason for this chapter. You will come across phrases like that in Microsoft literature, magazine articles, and even parts of this book. Much of that information contains useful advice that will make you a better network administrator if you understand how to carry it out—in fact, these snippets are incredibly useful if you've got a busy network and people are having trouble logging in. My goal for this chapter, then, is to give you a feel for the Registry, how to edit it, and when to leave it alone.

Registry Terminology

What did that stuff with all the backslashes mean? To get an insight, let's look at the Registry. You can see it by running the program REGEDT32.EXE (it's in the \Winnt\ SYSTEM32 directory); just click Start/Run and fill in **REGEDT32.EXE**. There is another Registry Editor as well named REGEDIT.EXE—there are two because NT originally had REGEDT32, and then Windows 95 shipped with a different editor for *its* Registry named REGEDIT. We still have both editors because REGEDT32 has a few features that REGEDIT doesn't, and vice versa. (Oddly enough, this state of affairs has existed since mid-1996; you'd think that by the time Windows 2000 shipped, Microsoft would have just merged all of the best of both editors into a single one, but they haven't.)

Run REGEDT32 and click on the HKEY_LOCAL_MACHINE window. You'll see a screen like the one in Figure 5.1.

FIGURE 5.1

Registry Editor screen

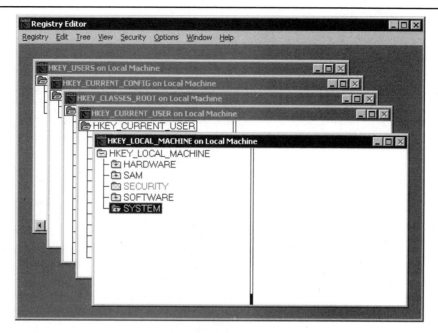

The terms to know in order to understand the Registry are *subtree, key, value, data type*, and *hive*.

WARNING It's easy to accidentally blast important data with the Registry Editor, so it might be a good idea at this point to put the Editor in *read-only* mode by clicking on Options, then on Read Only Mode. You can always reverse the read-only state whenever necessary in the same way. It is truly simple to render a server completely unusable with a few unthinking Registry edits, so be careful, please.

Subtrees

Windows 2000's Registry is spread out physically as it is saved in several separate files (called *hives*), as you'll learn later, and the Registry is also spread out *logically* into separate parts called *subtrees*.

The main reason for this is that the Registry stores all information about a computer and its users by dividing them up into five subtrees, as shown in Table 5.1.

TABLE 5.1: THE FIVE SUBTREES OF THE REGISTRY

Subtree	Description
HKEY_LOCAL_MACHINE	Contains information about the hardware currently installed in the machine and the settings for systems running on the machine. You do most of your work in this and the next subtree.
HKEY_CURRENT_USER	Contains the user profile for the person currently logged on to the Windows 2000 Server machine. Contains user preferences and settings for desktop applications running on this machine.
HKEY_USERS	Contains a pointer to the HKEY_CURRENT_USER subtree and also to a profile called the DEFAULT profile. The DEFAULT profile describes how the machine behaves when no one's logged on. For example, if instead of a blue background you wanted a machine to display a green background when no one was logged on, or if you wanted to display a particular wallpaper when no one was logged on (which I've found quite useful for keeping clear in my mind which machine was which when using a keyboard switch or just a table full of identical-looking machines), then you'd modify that DEFAULT profile.
HKEY_CLASSES_ROOT	Holds the file associations, information that tells the system, "Whenever the user double-clicks a file with the extension .BMP in Windows Explorer, start up PBRUSH.EXE to view this file." It also contains the OLE registration database, the old REG.DAT from Windows 3.x. This is actually a redundant subtree as all its information is found in the HKEY_LOCAL_MACHINE subtree. It also gets placed in the HKEY_CURRENT_USER\SOFTWARE\CLASSES key.
HKEY_CURRENT_CONFIG	Contains configuration information for the particular hardware configuration you booted up with.

In general, you'll do most of your work in the first two subtrees. Some Registry entries are specific to a machine (HKEY_LOCAL_MACHINE, HKEY_CLASSES_ROOT, HKEY _CURRENT_CONFIG), and some are specific to a user (HKEY_USERS, HKEY_CURRENT_USER, as well as other Registry files that are in the \WINNT\DOCUMENTS AND SETTINGS\USER ID directories). That's important, and it's a great strength of the Registry's structure. The entries relevant to a particular machine should, of course, physically reside on that machine. But what about the settings relevant to a user: the background colors you like, the programs you want to see in your Start menu, the sounds you want on the system? These shouldn't be tied to any one computer; they should be able to move around the network with that user. Indeed, they can. Windows 2000 supports the idea that "roving users" can have their personal settings follow them around the network via *roaming profiles*, which you will learn more about in Chapter 8.

Registry Keys

In Figure 5.1, you saw the Registry Editor display five cascaded windows, one for each subtree. HKEY_LOCAL_MACHINE was on top; you can see the other four subtrees' windows too. HKEY_CURRENT_USER's window has a right and left pane to it. The pane on the left looks kind of like a screen from the Explorer or the old Windows 3.1 File Manager.

In the File Manager, those folders represented subdirectories. Here, however, they separate information into sections, kind of in the same way old Windows INI files had sections whose names were surrounded by square brackets, names like [386enh], [network], [boot], and the like. Referring back to the HKEY_LOCAL_MACHINE picture shown in Figure 5.1, let's compare this to an old Windows 3.*x*–style INI file. If this were an INI file, the name of its sections would be [hardware], [sam], [security], [software], and [system]. Each of those folders or sections are actually called *keys* in the Registry.

But here's where the analogy to INI files fails: You can have keys within keys, called *subkeys* (and sub-subkeys, and sub-sub-subkeys, and so on). Let's open the SYSTEM key. It contains subkeys named ControlSet001, ControlSet002, CurrentControlSet, Select, and Setup, and CurrentControlSet is further sub-keyed into Control and Services.

 NOTE If you use REGEDIT, it will show you where you are in the Registry at the bottom of the window. That's one of the things it does that REGEDT32 doesn't.

Notice, by the way, the key called CurrentControlSet. It's very important. Almost every time you modify your system's configuration, you do it with a subkey within the CurrentControlSet subkey.

Key-Naming Conventions

The tree of keys gets pretty big as you drill down through the many layers. Current-ControlSet, for example, has dozens of subkeys, each of which can have subkeys. Identifying a given subkey is important, so Microsoft has adopted a naming convention that looks just like the one used for directory trees. CurrentControlSet's fully specified name would be, then, HKEY_LOCAL_MACHINE\SYSTEM\CurrentControlSet. In this book, however, I'll just call it CurrentControlSet to keep key names from getting too long to fit on a single line.

Value Entries, Names, Values, and Data Types

If I drill down through CurrentControlSet, I find subkey Services, and within Services, there are many subkeys. In Figure 5.2, you can see some of the subkeys of CurrentControlSet\Services.

FIGURE 5.2

The subkeys of
CurrentControl-
Set\Services

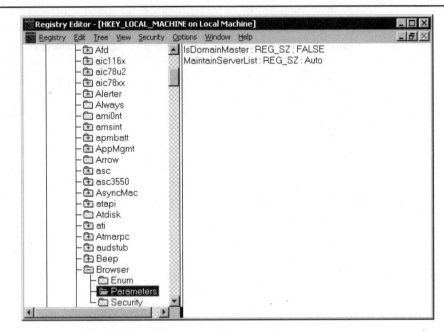

One of those keys, Browser, contains subkeys named Enum, Linkage, Parameters, and Security. Once we get to Parameters, however, you can see that it's the end of the line—no subkeys from there. Just to quickly review Registry navigation, the key that we're looking at now is in HKEY_LOCAL_MACHINE\SYSTEM\CurrentControlSet\ Services\Browser\Parameters.

In the right-hand pane, you see two lines:

```
IsDomainMaster : REG_SZ : False
MaintainServerList : REG_SZ : Auto
```

This is how the Registry says what would be, in the old INI-type files, something like this:

```
IsDomainMaster=False
MaintainServerList=Auto
```

Each line like IsDomainMaster:REG_SZ:False is called a *value entry*. The three parts are called *name*, *data type*, and *value*, respectively. In this example, IsDomainMaster is the *name*, REG_SZ is the *data type*, and False is the *value*.

Microsoft notes that each value entry cannot exceed about 1MB in size. It's hard to imagine one that size, but it's worth mentioning.

What is that REG_SZ stuff? It's an identifier to the Registry of what *kind* of data to expect: numbers, messages, yes/no values, and the like. Microsoft defines five data types in the Registry Editor (although others could be defined later), as shown in Table 5.2.

TABLE 5.2: DATA TYPES AS DEFINED BY THE REGISTRY EDITOR

Data Type	Description
REG_BINARY	Raw binary data. Data of this type usually doesn't make sense when you look at it with the Registry Editor. Binary data shows up in hardware setup information. If there is an alternative way to enter this data other than via the Registry Editor—and I'll discuss that in a page or two—then do it that way. Editing binary data can get you in trouble if you don't know what you're doing. The data is usually represented in hex for simplicity's sake.
REG_DWORD	Another binary data type, but it is 4 bytes long.
REG_EXPAND_SZ	A character string of variable size, it's often information understandable by humans, like path statements or messages. It is "expandable" in that it may contain information that will change at runtime, like %username%—a system batch variable that will be of different sizes for different people's names.
REG_MULTI_SZ	Another string type, but it allows you to enter a number of parameters in this one value entry. The parameters are separated by binary zeroes (nulls).
REG_SZ	A simple string.

Those who first met a Registry with Windows 95 will notice a few differences here. Windows 95 has six subtrees, but only three data types—*string*, which encompasses REG_SZ, REG_MULTI_SZ, and REG_EXPAND_SZ; *dword*, which is the same as REG_DWORD; and *binary*, which is identical to REG_BINARY.

And if you're wondering how on earth you'll figure out what data type to assign to a new Registry value, don't worry about it; if you read somewhere to use a particular new value entry, you'll be told what data type to use. Failing that, I usually just guess REG_SZ if it's textual in nature, REG_DWORD if it's numeric.

Working with the Registry: An Example

Now, I know you want to get in there and try it out despite the warnings, so here's an innocuous example. Remember, it's only innocuous if you *follow* the example to the letter; otherwise, it will soon be time to get out your installation disks.

That's not just boilerplate. Don't get mad at *me* if you blow up your server because you didn't pay attention. Actually, you *may* be able to avoid a reinstallation if the thing that you modified was in the CurrentControlSet key; Windows 2000 knows that you often mess around in there, and so it keeps a spare. In that case, you can reboot the server and, when the boot menu arrives, prompting "Please select the operating system to start:," press F8 for the Windows 2000 Advanced Options menu. One of the options you'll get will be Last Known Good Configuration. That *doesn't* restore the entire Registry; it just restores the control set. Fortunately, the current control set is a *lot* of the Registry. It doesn't include user-specific settings, however, like "What color should the screen be?" Thus, if you were to set all of your screen colors to black, rendering the screen black on black (and therefore less than readable), rebooting and choosing Last Known Good Configuration wouldn't help you.

In any case, let's try something out, something relatively harmless. Let's change the name of the company that you gave Windows 2000 when you installed it. Recently my firm changed names from TechTeach International to MR&D. Suppose I'd already installed a bunch of Windows 2000 machines and filled in TechTeach International when prompted for an organization. Suppose also that I want to change that so the Help/About dialog boxes say that I'm Mark Minasi of MR&D, but I don't feel like reinstalling. Fortunately, the Registry Editor lets me change company names without reinstalling:

1. Open the Registry Editor. From the Start menu, choose Run.

2. In the command line, type **REGEDT32** and press Enter.

3. Click Window and choose HKEY_Local_Machine. Maximize that window and you'll see a screen somewhat like the one in Figure 5.3.

4. We're going to modify the value entry in HKEY_LOCAL_MACHINE\Software\ Microsoft\Windows NT\CurrentVersion. Double-click the Software key, then double-click the Microsoft key, then double-click the Windows NT key, and finally, double-click the CurrentVersion key. You'll see a screen like the one in Figure 5.4.

FIGURE 5.3

*Registry Editor-
HKEY_LOCAL_
MACHINE on Local
Machine dialog box*

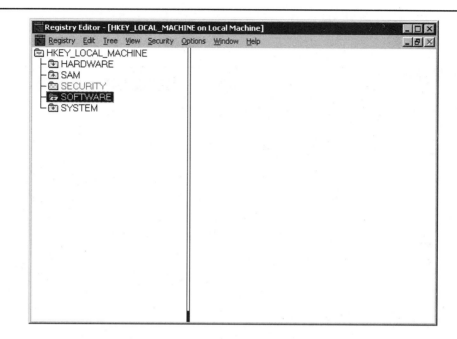

FIGURE 5.4

*CurrentVersion-
Registered-
Organization*

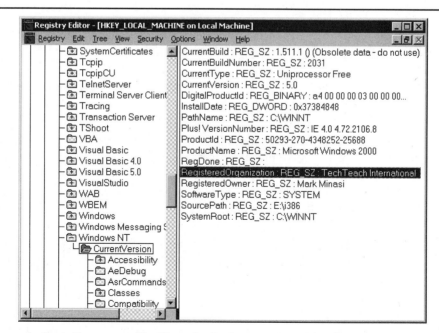

In the left pane, you'll still see the Registry structure. On the right, you'll see the value entry `RegisteredOrganization`.

5. Double-click on `RegisteredOrganization`, and a screen like the one in Figure 5.5 appears.

FIGURE 5.5

*The String Editor
dialog box*

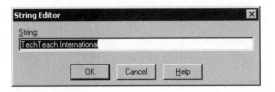

6. Highlight the old value and replace it with **MR&D**. Click OK, and close up the Registry Editor.

Now click Help/About for any program—even the Registry Editor will do—and you'll see that your organization is now MR&D.

WARNING Click all you like, you will not find a Save button or an Undo button. When you edit the Registry, it's immediate and it's forever. So, once again, be *careful* when you mess with the Registry.

How Do You Find Registry Keys?

How did I know to go to HKEY_LOCAL_MACHINE\Software\Microsoft\Windows NT\ CurrentVersion in order to change my organization name? I found it by poking around the Registry.

If you have the Windows 2000 Resource Kit from Microsoft—and if you don't, then *get it!*—you'll find 150 pages detailing each and every key. (That, by the way, is why there isn't a complete key guide in this book. First of all, there wasn't anything that I could add to what's in the Resource Kit; second, Microsoft has already published the Kit; and third, 150 pages directly lifted from someone else's publication is a pretty serious copyright violation. I don't think it's possible to paraphrase 150 pages of reference material.) Additionally, the Registry keys are documented in an online help file. Unfortunately, some keys aren't documented anywhere except in bits and pieces on Microsoft TechNet or the like, and I'll mention *those* in this book.

In my opinion, the Registry Editor has a glaring weakness: no effective search routine. Suppose you knew that there was something called `RegisteredOrganization` but you had no idea where it lives in the Registry? You'd be out of luck. Regedit32 includes a View/Find Key, but it only searches the names of *keys*, not value entries. In contrast, the newer REGEDIT.EXE *can* search keys, values, and names. I could then search for "RegisteredOrganization". I'll contrast REGEDT32 and REGEDIT later on in this chapter.

Even More Cautions about Editing the Registry

If you're just learning about the Registry, you're probably eager to wade right in and modify a value entry. Before you do, however, let me just talk a bit about using caution when you manipulate the Registry. (I know I've mentioned it before, but it's important, so I'm mentioning it again.)

The vast majority of Registry items correspond to some setting in the Control Panel, Active Directory Users and Computers, or some other MMC snap-in. For example, you just saw where we could change the RegisteredOrganization directly via the Registry Editor. I only picked that example, however, because it was fairly illustrative and simple to understand. In general, *don't use the Registry Editor to modify a value that can be modified in some other way.*

For example, suppose I choose to set a background color on my screen to medium gray. That color is represented as a triplet of numbers: 128 128 128. How did I know what those color values meant? Because they're the same as Windows 3.*x* color values. Color values in Windows are expressed as number triplets. Each number is an integer from 0 to 255. If I input a value greater than 255, the Registry Editor would neither know nor care that I was punching in an illegal color value. Now, in the case of colors, that probably wouldn't crash the system. In the case of *other* items, however, the system could easily be rendered unusable. For example, I'm running Windows 2000 Server on a system with just a single 486 processor, so the Registry reflects that, noting in one of the Hardware keys that Windows 2000 is running a "uniprocessor" mode. Altering that to a multiprocessor mode wouldn't be a very good idea.

Why, then, am I bothering to tell you about the Registry Editor? Three reasons.

First, there are settings—important ones—that can only be altered via the Registry Editor, so there's no getting around the fact that a Windows 2000 expert has to be proficient in the Editor.

Second, you can use the Registry Editor to change system value entries on *remote* computers. To use a very simple example: I'm at location A and I want to change the background color on the server at location B, and to do that I have to physically travel to location B in order to run the Control Panel on the Windows 2000 machine at that location. Instead of doing that, however, I can just start up the Registry Editor, choose Registry/Select Computer, and edit the Registry of the remote computer. (This assumes that you are running Windows 2000 Server and you have the security access to change the Registry of the remote computer—that is, you're a member of the Administrators group on that computer.)

Third, a program comes with the Resource Kit called `REGINI.EXE` that allows you to write scripts to modify Registries. Such a tool is quite powerful; in theory, you could write a REGINI script to completely reconfigure a Windows 2000 setup. Again, however, before you start messing with that program, *please* be sure that you have become proficient with the Registry. I've explained the various kinds of mischief that you can cause working by hand with the Registry Editor. Imagine what kinds of *automated* disasters you could start at 450MHz with a bad REGINI script!

By the way, there's another way to automate Registry changes, through REGEDIT. You can create an ASCII text file with the desired Registry changes, then use an undocumented /s (for "silent") switch to introduce the changes.

The file has a particular format. The first line must be "Windows Registry Editor Version 5.00," followed by a blank line. Then you enter a line with the full name of the Registry key that contains the value that you want to modify, surrounded by square brackets. Then type a line for each value that you want to modify, with the name of the value, an equal sign, and the desired value. Strings should be surrounded by quotes, and numbers—as in the DWORD type—should be prefixed by DWORD:; for example, consider the following file:

```
Windows Registry Editor Version 5.00

[HKEY_LOCAL_MACHINE\SOFTWARE\Microsoft\Windows NT\CurrentVersion]
"RegisteredOrganization"="MR&D"
"NumberOfLicenses"=dword:00000003\
```

The first line identifies the file as a set of Registry changes. That first line is probably to keep someone from accidentally feeding some random file to REGEDIT, causing untold havoc from just an ill-thought-out mouse click. Then there's a blank line and then the description in square brackets. The line afterward sets the RegisteredOrganization, as described earlier, and the final entry is just an imaginary setting that I created just to show how to do a number. If I put those five lines—it's *five*, remember the blank line—into a file and called it `mystuff.reg`, I could make REGEDIT modify the Registry with it like so:

```
Regedit /s mystuff.reg
```

And by the way, here's a useful tip: if you use REGEDIT's "export" function (Registry/Export Registry File), the resultant exported file is ASCII and in the proper format for using /S to apply the values to another computer.

Where the Registry Lives: Hives

The Registry is mostly contained in a set of files called the *hives*. ("Mostly" because some of it is built automatically every time you boot up your system. For example, Windows 2000 doesn't know what devices are on a SCSI chain until you boot.) Hives are binary files, so there's no way to look at them without a special editor of some kind, like the Registry Editor. Hives are, however, an easy way to load or back up a sizable part of the Registry.

Most, although not all, of the Registry is stored in hive files. They're not hidden, system, or read-only, but are always open, so you're kind of limited in what you can do with them.

A Look at the Hive Files

The machine-specific hive files are in the \WINNT\SYSTEM32\CONFIG directory. The user-specific hive files are in the \WINNT\DOCUMENTS AND SETTINGS\USER ID directories. You can see the hive files that correspond to parts of the subtree listed in Table 5.3.

TABLE 5.3: HIVE FILES

Subtree/Key	Filename
HKEY_LOCAL_MACHINE\SAM	SAM (primary) and SAM.LOG (backup)
HKEY_LOCAL_MACHINE\SECURITY	SECURITY (primary) and SECURITY.LOG (backup)
HKEY_LOCAL_MACHINE\SOFTWARE	SOFTWARE (primary) and SOFTWARE.LOG (backup)
HKEY_LOCAL_MACHINE\SYSTEM	SYSTEM (primary) and SYSTEM.ALT (backup)
HKEY_USERS\DEFAULT	DEFAULT (primary) and DEFAULT.LOG (backup)
HKEY_USERS\Security ID	NTUSER.DAT
HKEY_CURRENT_USER	NTUSER.DAT
HKEY_CLASSES_ROOT	(Created from current control set at boot time)

Table 5.3 needs a few notes to clarify it. First, about the HKEY_CLASSES_ROOT subtree: It is copied from HKEY_KEY_LOCAL_MACHINE\SOFTWARE\Classes at boot time. The file exists for use by 16-bit Windows applications. While you're logged on to Windows 2000, however, the two keys are linked; if you make a change to one, the change is reflected in the other.

The user profiles now live in \Documents and Settings*username*, where each user gets a directory named *username*. For example, I've got a user account named mark, so there's a directory named \Documents and Settings\mark on my computer. If I look in it, I find the files ntuser.dat and ntuser.dat.log.

To summarize, then, the core of the Registry is the four *S*s and DEFAULT:

- SAM
- SECURITY
- SYSTEM
- SOFTWARE

SAM contains the user database; SECURITY complements SAM by containing information such as whether a server is a member server or a domain controller, what the name of its domain is, and the like. SYSTEM contains configuration information like "what drivers and system programs does this computer use, which should be loaded on bootup, and how are their parameters set?" SOFTWARE tends to contain more overall configuration information about the larger software modules in the system, configuration information that does *not* vary from user to user. And then every user has an NTUSER.DAT with her specific application preferences in it.

One question remains about the hive files, however. Why do all the files have a paired file with the extension .LOG? Read on.

Fault Tolerance in the Registry

Notice that every hive file has another file with the same name but the extension .LOG. That's really useful because Windows 2000 Server, and Windows 2000 workstations for that matter, uses it to protect the Registry during updates.

Whenever a hive file is to be changed, the change is first written into its LOG file. The LOG file isn't actually a backup file; it's more a journal of changes to the primary file. Once the description of the change to the hive file is complete, the journal file is written to disk. When I say "written to disk," I *mean* written to disk. Often, a disk write ends up hanging around in the disk cache for a while, but this write is "flushed" to disk. Then the system makes the changes to the hive file based on the information in the journal file. If the system crashes during the hive write operation, there is enough information in the journal file to "roll back" the hive to its previous position.

The exception to this procedure comes with the SYSTEM hive. The SYSTEM hive is really important because it contains the CurrentControlSet. For that reason, the backup file for SYSTEM, SYSTEM.ALT, is a complete backup of SYSTEM. If one file is damaged, the system can use the other to boot.

Notice that HKEY_LOCAL_MACHINE\HARDWARE does not have a hive. That's because the key is rebuilt each time you boot so Windows 2000 can adapt itself to changes in computer hardware. The Plug and Play Manager, which runs at boot time, gathers the information that Windows 2000 needs to create HKEY_LOCAL_MACHINE\HARDWARE.

Confused about where all the keys come from? You'll find a recap in Table 5.4. It's similar to Table 5.3, but it's more specific about how the keys are built at boot time.

TABLE 5.4: CONSTRUCTION OF KEYS AT BOOT TIME

Key	How It's Constructed at Boot Time
HKEY_LOCAL_MACHINE:	Plug and Play Manager
HARDWARE	SAM hive file
SAM	SECURITY hive file
SECURITY	SOFTWARE hive file
SOFTWARE	SYSTEM hive file
SYSTEM	
HKEY_CLASSES_ROOT	SYSTEM hive file, Classes subkey
HKEY_USERS_DEFAULT	DEFAULT hive file
HKEY_USERS\Sxxx	Particular user's NTUSER.DAT file
HKEY_CURRENT_USER	Particular user's NTUSER.DAT file

Remote Registry Modification

You can modify another computer's Registry, perhaps to repair it or to do some simple kind of remote maintenance, by loading that computer's hive. You do that with the Registry Editor by using the Load Hive or Unload Hive command.

You can only load or unload the hives for HKEY_USERS and HKEY_LOCAL_MACHINE. The Load Hive option only appears if you've selected one of those two subtrees. Unload Hive is only available if you've selected a subkey of one of those two subtrees.

Why, specifically, would you load a hive or a remote Registry?

First of all, you might load a hive in order to get to a user's profile. Suppose a user has set up all of the colors as black on black and made understanding the screen impossible. You could load the hive that corresponds to that user, modify it, and then unload it.

Second, you can use the remote feature to view basically *anything* on a remote system. Suppose you want to do something as simple as changing screen colors. You'd do that on a local system by running the Control Panel, but the Control Panel won't work for remote systems. Answer: Load the Registry remotely.

You could load and save hive files to a floppy disk, walk the floppy over to a malfunctioning machine, and load the hive onto the machine's hard disk, potentially repairing a system problem. This wasn't possible if you used NTFS on the boot disk of an NT 4 system unless you had multiple copies of NT 4—there wasn't an easy way to get to a system with an NTFS boot drive. Under Windows 2000, however, you can go to the advanced boot options and boot to a command prompt even if the system's damaged.

There is yet another way to control Registries remotely, through something called system policies, which are covered in the next chapter.

Backing Up and Restoring a Registry

By now, it should be pretty clear that the Registry is an important piece of information and that it should be protected. It protects itself pretty well with its LOG files, but how can you back it up?

Unfortunately, the fact that Registry hive files are always open makes it tough to back up the Registry since most backup utilities are stymied by open files. The NTBackup program that comes with Windows 2000 works well, but it only backs up to tape. Nevertheless, if you use NTBackup—and it's pretty good, particularly for its price—then you should tell it to back up your Registry every night.

NT 4 had a terrific tool named RDISK that would back up your entire Registry with just a few keystrokes, but that's nowhere to be found in Windows 2000. The replacement for RDISK can be found in the Backup program, which offers to create an Emergency Repair Disk, just as RDISK did, through these steps:

1. Start Backup (Start/Programs/Accessories/System Tools/Backup).

2. Click the Backup tab.

3. Make sure all directories and files are unchecked.

4. Look under My Computer's list of drives; the last option will be System State; check that.

5. Next to the list box labeled Backup Media or File Name, fill in a filename or click Browse and choose a filename; this is where the Registry backup will go.

6. Click the Start Backup button.

7. In the resultant dialog box, click the Advanced button.

8. Uncheck Automatically Backup System Protected Files with the System State.

9. Click OK to dismiss the dialog box.

10. Click Start Backup. Backup will then save the Registry. You can restore the Registry with Backup as well.

What if you want to only back up a portion of the Registry? The Windows 2000 Resource Kit includes a program called REG.EXE that lets you back up the Registry from the command line and while the system is running—but only *one subtree at a time*. It looks like REG SAVE HKLM*subtreename destination*, where *destination* is the place that you want the backup to go, and the subtree names are, of course, SECURITY, SAM, SYSTEM, and SOFTWARE in the case of HKEY_LOCAL_MACHINE. Note also the abbreviation: REG accepts HKLM in place of HKEY_LOCAL_MACHINE, HKCU in place of

HKEY_CURRENT_USER, HKCR in place of HKEY_CLASSES_ROOT, and HKCC in place of HKEY_CURRENT_CONFIGURATION.

A complete Registry backup to a directory named C:\RB would, then, require several lines:

Reg save HKCR c:\rb\hkcr
Reg save HKCC\Software c:\rb\hkccsoft
Reg save hkcc\system c:\rb\hkccsys, and so on.

You'd restore the Registry with REG as well.

REGEDIT versus REGEDT32

Since Windows NT 4 arrived, we've had a choice of Registry editors. NT 3.*x* always shipped with REGEDT32, but Windows 95 included REGEDIT and Microsoft decided to offer it for NT 4 (and Windows 2000, of course) as well. Are there good reasons to use one or the other?

REGEDT32 has a couple of features that REGEDIT lacks. For one thing, you can set the size of the display font that REGEDT32 uses. That may not sound exciting, but I get a lot of use out of it when teaching classes. It seems like more and more Microsoft administration tools use *really* tiny fonts, making online demonstrations difficult in a room holding more than about 20 people. REGEDT32's greater strength, however, is its ability to set security on Registry keys. As with everything else in Windows 2000, each key in the Registry has a *security descriptor* or *Access Control List (ACL)*, a description of who is and who isn't allowed to modify that key. Sometimes Microsoft will discover a "hole" in Windows 2000 security caused by some incorrect security setting, and you must use REGEDT32 to seal that security hole—REGEDIT can't do the trick here.

For most other work, I use REGEDIT. First of all, I like the fact that the status bar at the bottom of its window always tells me the complete path to my current position in the Registry. The ability to search for any string is convenient as well. For example, one time I'd gotten my system so confused that it kept asking for a particular program every time I booted up. Clearly the command to start this program was somewhere in the Registry—but where? A quick search solved the problem, showing me where in the Registry the problem lay, making it easy for me to undo the problem. Perhaps the best capability, however, is in REGEDIT's built-in Registry modification language. As mentioned earlier in this chapter, it's a convenient way to record favorite software settings in an ASCII file and then play them back onto a new system whenever you want.

No one *wants* to play around in the Registry, but in real life, most network administrators will find a bit of Registry spelunking to be the only answer to many problems. Knowing how the Registry is organized and what tools are available to modify it will prove valuable to all Windows 2000 fixers.

CHAPTER 6

Installing Hardware in Windows 2000

FEATURING:

Hardware management in Windows 2000, like many other tasks, has become much easier. With Plug-and-Play technology a working reality in Windows 2000, the Windows NT line of products takes a major stride towards seamless integration between hardware and software. Windows 2000 is by default a hardware hog. The operating system itself is big. It needs a lot of memory, a really fast processor, and a lot of disk space to make it all work. Put these together and you've forced yourself to get a fairly modern machine. With a fairly modern machine, you have fairly modern components. Modern components are generally going to be Plug and Play. If all components are Plug and Play, you may never find much of a need for this chapter. (Don't go away just yet though.)

Another big step towards simplicity of hardware management in Windows 2000 comes with the variety of hardware wizards. I know what you're thinking, and I hate wizards as well. They take the skill requirements out of our profession and make it so anyone can do our job, right? Well, get over it. Sorry, I'm just kidding—kind of. Wizards do reduce the skill requirements, but they make your job easier. They make managing hardware easier. There is nothing wrong with that. Besides, wouldn't you rather spend your time doing something better?

So hardware management is easy. That's fine, but there are some serious pitfalls along the way. What if you don't have all Plug-and-Play devices? What if the wizard doesn't work? This is where the truly skilled stick out above the "click-next-to-continue" masters. There are a lot of details to know concerning hardware components. Anything from IRQ settings to device drivers can cause device failure or system failure. In this chapter, we will discuss the common properties of hardware so that we can build a foundation for managing hardware. Next, we will go through real-world, practical hardware management issues. How do you add a device? How do you remove a device? How do you fix a device that is not working properly? Finally, we will walk through all of the hardware management components in Windows 2000 Server to apply our practical hardware foundation to the job at hand.

Hardware Resources: The Basics

There are several basic fundamentals of hardware that define how a device works with your system:

- I/O addresses
- DMA channels
- IRQ levels
- ROM addresses

The reason that you care about these hardware resources is that you can run out of them—in particular, it's fairly easy to run out of IRQs or to have *conflicts* in IRQs, I/O addresses, or the other resources. These conflicts can make new hardware fail to work, leading you to think (incorrectly) that your new hardware is no good.

Someone may have told you that you needn't worry about these conflict issues anymore because of Plug and Play. If only it were true. Plug and Play doesn't always work, and when it doesn't, it can be a very difficult beast to tame. Learn these basic concepts, and you will have some solid ground to stand on.

I/O Addresses

I/O addresses can be defined very easily. First, what is the I/O? I/O is short for input/ output, of course. Every component on your computer deals with either input or output. Take for example a user typing an A on the computer. A keyboard is an input device. It takes information from some outside agent, like you, and inputs it into the computer. The CPU processes the data into something, like a digital representation of the letter A, and sends it to the appropriate output device—in this case, most likely the display adapter, which in turn sends it to the monitor. Now there's the problem of the CPU finding the display adapter and the keyboard. The CPU needs to map an address for each piece of hardware. This address is a hexadecimal number defining each hardware location just like a mailbox in front of your house. As each device is defined in the computer, it registers its address. From that point on, the CPU needs only to send or retrieve information from the right address. Let's go back to our example. The CPU receives a stream of data from some I/O address number 64. This stream of data will come in the form of electrical pulses that were generated by the keyboard to specifically define an A. First, the CPU must recognize who sent this information. It came from address 64, which corresponds to the keyboard. The operating system and application have told the CPU what to do with data from the keyboard: send it to the screen. The screen can be reached via the display adapter, which resides at I/O address 3B0. The CPU generates the information for the display adapter, and ships it off.

Alternative Number Systems

It's never fun, but anyone talking about hardware addresses soon runs up against having to talk in hex and perhaps binary. If you're not familiar with these alternative methods of representing numbers—or if you maybe just need a short refresher—then this box is for you.

Hexadecimal numbers are used very frequently, not only in hardware applications, but in many software applications. It is very important to understand how this numbering scheme works. Before we jump into hexadecimal, let's go over the whole "numbering system" thing.

Continued

CONTINUED

Decimal

Decimal numbering is what we are used to. Decimal numbering is also referred to as base 10. The *dec-* in *decimal* means 10; each place increases by a multiple of 10. From right to left, we have the 1s place, the 10s place, the 100s place, the 1000s place, etc.

Take a sample number: 175. First, figure out what each digit represents. Working down from the 100s place, we have:

$100 \times 1 = 100$

$10 \times 7 = 70$

$1 \times 5 = 5$

Now, add each digit together. $100 + 70 + 5 = 175$. Simple!

Let's go the other way. This takes some imagination. We naturally speak in base 10, but try to forget what those numbers put together mean. We do this by working down from the highest, or leftmost, digit. Start with the 1000s place just for kicks. The point here is to make sure that you start with a 0 on the left. If you start too low, then you end up with something ridiculous like 17 10s, and no 100s. So here we go:

How many 1000s are there in 175? **0**

How many 100s? **1**

Okay, we've now taken 100 out; we're left with 75.

How many 10s? **7**

We're down to $175 - 100 - 70 = 5$.

How many 1s in 5? **5**

Line those digits up in a row and you have **175**.

Binary

Before we go into hexadecimal, let's talk binary, or base 2. Binary is equally as important as, if not more important than, hexadecimal in hardware terms. Hardware talks in electrical pulses. Either on or off. On is represented by a 1, and off by a 0. Base 2 increases each digit by a power of 2, rather than by a power of 10. In this system, our digits increase from right to left with a 1s column, 2s, 4s, 8s, 16s, etc.

So let's jump right into drawing out 175 in binary. First you need to get to the column that is too big for 175. Start at the smallest placeholder and work your way up until you

Continued

reach a place that no longer fits: 1-2-4-8-16-32-64-128-256. Okay, obviously 256 is too big for 175.

How many 256s in 175? **0**

How many 128s in 175? **1**

175 − 128 = 47

How many 64s in 47? **0**

How many 32s in 47? **1**

47 − 32 = 15

How many 16s in 15? **0**

How many 8s in 15? **1**

15 − 8 = 7

How many 4s in 7? **1**

7 − 4 = 3

How many 2s in 3? **1**

3 − 2 = 1

How many 1s in 1? **1**

Put it together and you have **10101111**.

Let's work it back the other way. We'll draw out our places values from top to bottom, starting with 128, and put their corresponding binary digits next to them. Multiply them together to get the actual value for each digit.

128 × 1 = 128

64 × 0 = 0

32 × 1 = 32

16 × 0 = 0

8 × 1 = 8

4 × 1 = 4

2 × 1 = 2

Continued

$1 \times 1 = 1$

$128 + 32 + 8 + 4 + 2 + 1 = 175$

This still sounds like a long way to put it together. Just wait, it gets necessary.

Hexadecimal

In *hexadecimal, hex-* means 6, and *dec-* means 10. Therefore, *hexadec* means 16. The numbers in our numerical representation increase by powers of 16. Here's where it gets interesting. With base 10, just by nature of each digit increasing by a power of 10, we had to come up with 10 different symbols to represent each value: 0, 1, 2, 3, 4, 5, 6, 7, 8, and 9. With base 2, we only need 2 symbols. Conveniently enough, we use 0 and 1. Now we have a problem. With base 16, we need 16 different numerical symbols. Obviously we can't put a double-digit number in a single-digit place. How confusing would that be? We need more symbols beyond 9. So we improvise. 0, 1, 2, 3, 4, 5, 6, 7, 8, 9, A, B, C, D, E, and F. A = 10; B = 11; C = 12; D = 13; E = 14; and F = 15. (If it is base 16, why don't we need a symbol for 16? The 0 counts as a digit, so we only need 15 more.) Our digit places now go like this, right to left: the 1s place, the 16s place, the 256s place, the 4096s place, etc. Just keep multiplying by 16.

I'm sure you can see that 175 is going to go very quickly in hexadecimal. Again, start big. There are no 4096s in 175. There are no 256s either, so we'll start there:

How many 256s in 175? **0**

How many 16s in 175? **10**, or as we will call it, **A**

We just took 10 16s out of 175, or 160.

$175 - 160 = 15$.

How many 1s in 15? **15**, or **F**

Put them together and you have **AF**.

Work it back the other way. AF translates as follows:

$16 \times A$ *or* $16 \times 10 = 160$

$1 \times F$ *or* $1 \times 15 = 15$

Add them together and you have 175.

So that's it. From now on, when you see that the I/O address for COM1 is 3F8, you will say $3 \times 256 = $ **768**. $F \times 16 = $ **240**. $8 \times 1 = $ **8**. $768 + 240 + 8 = $ **1016**. COM1 is at address 1016. Or you can save some time by using the Windows calculator in scientific mode. To convert 3F8 to decimal, put your calculator in hexadecimal mode, enter **3F8**, and click the decimal button. Voila! 1016. But what fun is that anyway?

DMA Channels

I/O channels provide a means for the CPU to talk to all hardware components. In a similar fashion, there are memory addresses, which the CPU uses to talk to different areas of memory. Memory is the lifeblood of the computer. A CPU can only process one thing at a time.

Take a simple command like 3 + 5. There are three different major components in the command. First is the 3. Next is the operator, "plus." Then comes the second argument, 5. Actually, there is a whole lot more to 3 + 5 than three simple steps. Think binary—like a computer. We want to add 011 (3) and 101 (5). First the processor receives the 011. Let's stick it in a register. (This register is an area in our memory banks by the way.) Now take the 101 and stick it in behind it. The addition part is where it gets tricky. How does the processor take a series of electrical pulses of 011, off-on-on, and 101, on-off-on, and somehow add them up to get 8? A portion of the processor is actually dedicated to this function. The processor will take the series of data stored in the registers and send it to the "addition" department. This is a lot of steps: Read number. Store number. Read second number. Store second number. Read operator. Determine function to run numbers through. Addition? Subtraction? Addition it is. The addition process itself takes several tiny commands to actually determine the answer. To make things worse, it hasn't even begun to determine how to make that answer show up on a screen in the form of the figure 8.

As you can see, the processor is going to get very busy when you start throwing complex commands at it. This is where DMA channels come into play. Why does the processor need to run interference on every single simple command that may be requested? Take data transfer from a file on a hard disk into memory. If every bit of that data has to go through the processor, it can get really ugly. The processor will have to read a chunk of data from the hard disk, and write it to memory. Read a chunk; write a chunk. Read a chunk; write a chunk. With a DMA channel, you get the ability to send the data straight from the hard drive to the memory.

You're most likely to run across DMA usage in sound cards and in ECP ports, the more modern, high-speed, bidirectional version of parallel ports.

Interrupt Request Levels—IRQs

Most hardware components in a computer work at different speeds. Compare a Pentium III processor running at 450MHz with a circa 1983 daisy wheel printer plugged into the same machine. I know, this is quite an extreme comparison, but let's go with it. The CPU wants to print "The quick brown fox jumps over the lazy dog." Unfortunately, the CPU can't flood the printer with the whole sentence all at once, so it first says, "Print a T." Obviously, our 450MHz CPU is going to be ready to move on to the next character before the printer will. So the CPU asks the printer if it's done. No response. "Done now?" Nothing. This can continue for an apparent eternity to our

450MHz processor. Even 1 second of wait time translates into 450 million ticks of time to the processor. Now, to the single-tasking operating system, one that can only do one job at a time, this waste of time is irrelevant. After all, it has nothing else to do but wait. But to a multitasking system like Windows 2000, this is a tremendous amount of wasted cycles that could be better spent doing other jobs. This is where interrupts come in. Instead of asking if the printer is done, the CPU tells the printer to just say when it's done, and do so on line 7. Now the CPU gets to work on other things and completely forget about the printer. So our CPU is happily working away when line 7 lights up. It's the printer, ready for more. Take an "h."

IRQ Cascading

Now computers have a nice little system for letting every component that operates at a different speed do its own job at its own rate, but without causing the CPU to spend half its time idling. Well, not necessarily every component. Modern systems have 15 interrupt request levels. This lets 15 different components in your system interrupt the processor. Older systems had only eight IRQs, because their interrupt handling circuitry was built around the Intel 8259 chip, which could only handle eight interrupts. Later (post-1984) systems needed more IRQs, so PC designers added another 8259.

But those designers didn't want to change the "newer" motherboards too radically, so they looked for a way to shoehorn those extra eight IRQs into the PC design. But to do that, they needed to make that second 8259 a second-class citizen, putting it in line for the CPU's attention *behind* the first 8259. The *first* 8259 communicates directly with the CPU whenever it gets an interrupt—that is, whenever something activates IRQ0 through IRQ7. When one of the second 8259's IRQs—IRQ8 through IRQ15—activates, then the second 8259 doesn't tell the CPU; rather, it tells the first 8259. You can see how this works in Figure 6.1.

Thus, when something activates one of the IRQs between IRQ8 and IRQ15, the second 8259 responds by activating IRQ2 on the first 8259, which then responds by informing the CPU that there's been an interrupt. There are two implications of this dual-8259 architecture.

First, we *did* gain eight more IRQs with the second 8259, but we also lost one, as IRQ2 is now dedicated to paying attention. Second, the line on the PC expansion slots that once served IRQ2 is now irrelevant, as IRQ2 is no longer available to expansion boards. IBM—the premier hardware vendor of the time—decided to just reallocate that line to IRQ9. Despite the fact that this happened fifteen years ago, a lot of software and board documentation is still labeled poorly, and sometimes you'll see references to IRQ2 that *really* mean IRQ9. This whole process of having one 8259 (for IRQs 0 through 7) act as a kind of go-between for another 8259 (for IRQs 8 through 15) is called *IRQ cascading*.

 TIP Get used to hearing things like "there are 16 of something," but seeing that the highest number is 15. The zero counts too.

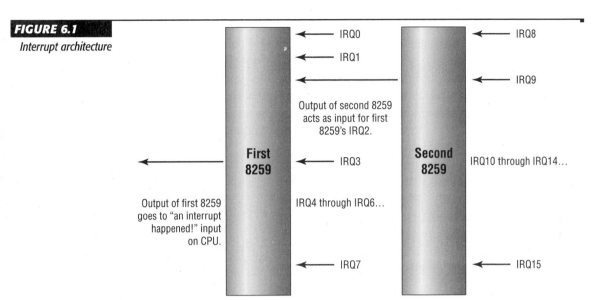

FIGURE 6.1

Interrupt architecture

IRQ Priority

The 16 IRQs in the system are answered in order of priority. If, per some chance, all 16 light up at the same time, the CPU will answer IRQ0 first, then 1, then 2, and so on. Remember our cascading of IRQs 8 through 15 to IRQ2? Well, they fit in at IRQ2's priority. In other words, IRQ priority follows in order of 0, 1, 2 (8, 9, 10, 11, 12, 13, 14, 15,) 3, 4, 5, 6, and finally 7. For those that really like to tweak their systems to the max, you can order your devices on IRQs based on this priority. If you have a network card, and a sound card in your server, you may want to put the sound card at the lowest priority, or highest IRQ level, and the network adapter at a higher priority, or lower IRQ level. Although the sound card in a server probably won't get in the way of your network card very much, this could help the hardware in your system respond in a more appropriate manner. The common IRQs are given in Table 6.1.

TABLE 6.1: COMMON IRQS

IRQ	Device	Description
0	Timer	You can't change this.
1	Keyboard	You can't change this.
2	IRQ9 cascade	You can't change this.
3	COM2 or COM4	Can only be one or the other COM port.
4	COM1 or COM3	Can only be one or the other COM port.

TABLE 6.1 CONTINUED: COMMON IRQS

IRQ	Device	Description
5		Usually free.
6	Floppy disk controller	
7	LPT1	
8	Clock	You can't change this.
9		Usually free; but due to its link to IRQ2, may be mis-labeled as "IRQ2."
10		
11		
12	Mouse port	This is usually the built-in mouse port.
13	Coprocessor	The coprocessor interrupt is still used on processors with the coprocessor built into the processor chip. You can't change this.
14	Primary EIDE adapter	You *could* change this and the next IRQ if your system allows you to disable the EIDE adapters built onto the motherboard, but be sure that whatever host adapter you boot from uses IRQ14, or some software may give you trouble.
15	Secondary EIDE adapter	

Look through Table 6.1. At the top of the priority list is the timer. This is the system timer, which serves as the pacemaker of the entire system. Obviously, when this device says tick, the rest of the system needs to know fairly quickly. Next is the keyboard. You will pretty much want the system to respond right away to your key presses. IRQ2 comes next, which sends us to 8 through 15. Then there's the clock, which should also stay right on top of things and not lag behind when everything else gets busy. In some applications, time inconsistencies can produce very unfavorable results.

 NOTE When looking at priority for IRQs, keep in mind that differences between priorities may mean only a few milliseconds, if that.

Next is IRQ9, the cascading IRQ, which is sometimes available for use with an add-on card. IRQs 10 and 11 are available at the higher end of the priority list so that you can still give things like your network adapter or SCSI hard disk controllers a good response. The farther down the priority list you go, or the higher up the IRQ-level list, the less important the device, down to the lonely old printer on LPT1.

ROM Addresses

Some hardware devices contain their own code, or ROM. This code is used for hardware to hold prepackaged routines and instruction sets. For example, a video card may have its own set of code defined to draw a circle on your monitor, which is more efficient than letting your processor stumble around trying to do something it knows little about.

The system will need a way to find, or address, that code, which is where *ROM addresses* come into play. A block of memory is set aside as the address for the device's ROM. So whenever the system needs to access the ROM, it can call up its defined memory address and cruise right along.

Watch out for ROM address conflicts. Many older devices that use ROM addresses do not allow them to be changed. Much like with some old IRQ hoarding devices, this is the case because too much software was written specifically for a certain configuration that can't be retrofitted for today's use. Most new devices, however, will let you change these addresses.

Practical Hardware Tutorial

Once you understand the nuts and bolts in hardware, it comes time to work with it. In this section, we will go over how to add new hardware, how to troubleshoot existing hardware that is malfunctioning, how to adjust hardware settings, how to remove hardware, how to configure multiple hardware profiles, and how to update device drivers.

Adding New Hardware to a System

You've bought a new hardware component. Whether a modem, a video card, a keyboard, or a monitor, you will follow the same approach to getting it integrated into your system.

Is It Supported?

Before you even begin, you want to verify that the hardware is compatible with Windows 2000 and that you have a suitable driver. Start with the Hardware Compatibility List (HCL). The HCL can be found on the Windows 2000 Server CD, under the \SUPPORT directory, as HCL.TXT. The HCL can also be found on the Web at http://www.microsoft.com/hwtest/hcl/.

So what is the significance of the HCL? Every item on the HCL has passed compatibility testing with Windows 2000. It is sort of like your guarantee from Microsoft that the hardware will work with the operating system. Granted, there is still a possibility that something will cause problems later down the road, but if you ever want help from Microsoft, you'll need sponsorship from the HCL. In fact, the Troubleshooter

Wizard won't even continue if your hardware isn't on the list. Don't lose hope though. The list is a living list, constantly being updated by Microsoft. Brand new hardware may eventually show up there after the compatibility testers get their shot at it.

Locate a Driver

Beyond the mere fact of being "on the list," your hardware needs a driver. Most supported hardware will have a driver included in the Windows 2000 Server CD. If the hardware is too new to have a driver on the CD, it probably came with a driver. Look in the documentation or browse the media that came with the hardware to find the driver.

I recently bought an ATI XPERT 98 Video Card. There were a few things on the box that identified it as a potentially "compatible" card. Microsoft has a logo system that identifies hardware as being compatible with certain operating systems. At the time I bought the card, Windows 2000 wasn't mainstream, so a logo for that particular operating system wasn't stamped on the box. Instead, there were logos that said, "Designed for Microsoft Windows 95" and "Designed for Microsoft Windows 98." This told me, for one, that the recent initiatives such as Plug and Play would have been followed. (I expect that a "Designed for Microsoft Windows 2000" logo is going to become more prevalent in the near future with new add-on cards.)

The next thing to do is to look in the existing Microsoft driver files, included on the Windows 2000 CD. Start through the Add Hardware Wizard, and choose to add a new device. Tell the wizard that you want to select your hardware from a list, rather than try to detect one, and you will be given a list of all included drivers, broken into category. In my case, a video card falls under the Display Adapter category. By selecting the ATI Technologies manufacturer, I got a list of all ATI cards that have drivers included with Windows 2000. Well, there was no XPERT 98 listed anywhere. However, video cards are a little different in that each card is driven by a particular graphics chip, or engine as they are sometimes called. This XPERT 98 said that it was powered by the RAGE PRO PCI chip. Sure enough, under my ATI manufacturer list was the RAGE PRO PCI listing. So I took a chance that the XPERT 98 using the RAGE PRO PCI chip would work. Much to my delight, and my checkbook's, it did.

The next option for locating a driver is the Internet. Most every manufacturer has a section on their Web site from which you can download drivers for any of their supported operating systems. In my case, the Web site address for ATI Technologies was posted right there on the box. From the Web site, surf your way down through something like support, or drivers. Each Web site will be different, but should be easily navigable. ("Should" is the operative word here; there is no guarantee that your manufacturer will make anything easy on you.) By following the downloading, licensing, and installation instructions from the manufacturer, you should be able to make the driver available to Windows 2000.

Verify Hardware Configuration

Windows 2000 has a neat feature within the Device Manager that lets you view your system resources and what components are plugged into them. In other words, instead of seeing a list of devices, drilling down into the properties of each, and determining what IRQs they use in order to find a free IRQ, you can simply select View Resources by Type and get a list of all occupied IRQs and their corresponding devices. This is an extremely helpful feature. From a single glance, you can see if IRQ10 is available or occupied. You can see this list of information for IRQs, DMAs, I/O addresses, or memory addresses.

Of course, if your system is entirely Plug and Play, this listing of information will not really be needed. You would merely plug your new device in and the Plug and Play Configuration Manager would take care of the rest. If this device is an older ISA card though, you may better spend your time looking into your current hardware configuration for a minute or two now, as opposed to spending an hour or two playing trial-and-error hardware configuration while watching your system lock up every time you try to boot.

The best advice here is to check all IRQs, I/O addresses, and other pertinent hardware information. Get a hard copy, and keep it handy. Every time you go to add new hardware, check your list first.

 TIP In the Device Manager, you can generate a printed report. Once in Device Manager, select View/Print. You can either print a system summary of all components, a report on each component, or a report on just the component selected.

Install the Hardware

Now for the actual hardware installation process. We will take two different approaches—one for Plug-and-Play devices, the other for non-Plug-and-Play devices.

Plug and Play   Plug-and-Play devices, by definition, will be detected by your Plug-and-Play operating system, given the appropriate resources, and be activated with no, or minimal, input required. Theoretically, it should be this simple:

- Shut down the server.
- Physically install the hardware.
- Boot the server.
- Watch Windows 2000 recognize the new hardware, and install a driver for it.

You could always be presented with the problem that a driver isn't included in the Windows 2000 device list. This will happen if the device is newer than the compilation of drivers included with the Windows 2000 source CD. In such a case, you should use the drivers that came with the device, or go to the manufacturer's Web site for the appropriate files. Given these files, though, the procedure will be a breeze.

Once again there is a catch: What if you have a non-Plug-and-Play network card in the last ISA slot that is coded to use IRQ10? Now you install a brand new Plug-and-Play sound card in a PCI slot that for some reason prefers IRQ10 and has no clue that the ISA card will request the same. By installing this Plug-and-Play card, you have an IRQ conflict looming on the horizon. The card that used to work just fine now has to give way to the Plug-and-Play card. What to do? In Chapter 3, we talked about preparing the BIOS for Windows 2000. Your best, and by far safest, bet is to identify your non-Plug-and-Play board's resources before you even start your installation or hardware detection phase. Once identified, enter your Plug-and-Play BIOS configuration and reserve those resources for non-Plug-and-Play devices. This is how an installation of the Plug-and-Play ATI video card worked on my system:

1. I shut down the system, performing no prep work whatsoever other than preliminary research and determining that the device would be supported.

2. I popped open the case, bolted the new video card into an available PCI slot, and closed the case.

3. I plugged the monitor cable into the new video card.

4. I powered on the system and began booting into Windows 2000.

5. After logging on to the system, the dialog box shown in Figure 6.2 popped up, indicating that new hardware was detected in the form of a VGA-compatible video controller.

FIGURE 6.2

Found new VGA

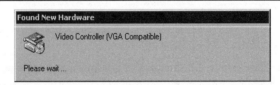

6. Several seconds later, the system began searching for a driver for this new hardware (see Figure 6.3).

FIGURE 6.3

Searching for a driver

7. After searching through the devices, the system at last recognized the device as an ATI RAGE PRO PCI video card.

8. After initializing the new video card, the system detected the monitor that was attached to it and configured it into that card.

No conflicts were reported, the Plug-and-Play detection and configuration phase found a driver that was packed with Windows 2000, the driver worked, the device initialized properly, and my display worked without a problem. We'll call this the best-case scenario.

But there are a couple of different scenarios in which this process would go, well, not so smooth. First, you could have a device without a driver. In that case, you will be faced with either finding a driver or delaying the install until you can find one.

Or you could have a conflict with another card in the system, causing this new device to fail, the other device to fail, or, more commonly, both devices to fail. This will be evident by the fact that the device doesn't work or another device has stopped working, or in a last-ditch effort, errors will appear in the Device Manager window. Now you won't always be told that there is an error in the Device Manager. This is why it becomes a good practice to go to the Device Manager after completing any device installation. Even though the installation itself went smoothly, and even if the device is working, you can't guarantee that the server is good to go for the long haul. Check it out. For a better description of what you're looking at, see the "Device Manager" section a little later.

Non-Plug-and-Play Devices   There will be occasions where ISA, EISA, and even PCI devices simply will not be detected during the Plug-and-Play detection phase. Most of the time, Windows 2000 will actually see a new device in the system. It could be reported as a totally unknown device, or it could be categorized as an unknown device of a certain type. In these situations, you have two different fundamental approaches to getting the hardware into the system.

The first method is to install the device in Windows 2000 before you actually plug the device into the system. In other words, prepare the operating system by installing the driver and telling the operating system exactly what to expect the next time it boots. Once you complete the software installation of the driver, you will be told to shut down the system and install the hardware. After it's plugged in, a reboot should bring the system up with the new device installed and working like it was there all along.

The other method is to physically install the device before telling Windows 2000 anything about it. Windows 2000 may detect and configure the device perfectly the first time around, in which case you do nothing. If the device fails detection at any level, you will have to intervene and tell Windows 2000 what the device is.

Removing Hardware

There really isn't much to removing hardware. There shouldn't be any problems with a device that isn't there, should there? Well, there is one possible error. If you remove a device without telling Windows 2000 that it is going to be removed first, it could have a problem trying to attach a driver to a device that it expects to be there. When removing devices from a Windows 2000 machine, remove the device—not the physical piece of hardware, but the listing of the device in Device Manager—from the operating system first. Once that is gone, shut down the system, physically unplug the device, and then boot the system.

Windows 2000 Hardware Management

Now that the basics about hardware are out of the way, it's time to apply them to Windows 2000 management. In this section, we will discuss the components that manage hardware, how they work, what they do, and of course, how to get to them. The different components of Windows 2000 hardware management are:

- Device Manager
- Driver signing
- Add/Remove Hardware Wizard
- Found Hardware Wizard
- Hardware profiles
- Troubleshooter

Device Manager

The Device Manager in Windows 2000 is nearly identical to the device manager found in Windows NT 4 or Windows 9x. It is a view of all hardware components in your system, how they are configured, what drivers are controlling them, and what resources they are occupying. It is also a tool for installing, removing, configuring, and troubleshooting hardware.

View Modes

There are four different ways to view hardware within the Device Manager: View Devices by Type, View Devices by Connection, View Resources by Type, and View Resources by Connection. The two options View Resources by Type and View Resources by Connection are new to Windows 2000. Previous versions of Device Manager were able to tell you what IRQs, I/O addresses, and other resources certain devices were using, but if you wanted to find out which device used IRQ10, you had to go into each device until you found it. Finally, there's a better way. Instead of viewing all of the devices or device categories in your main tree view, with the details of those devices beneath them, you can select a View Resources By view mode that shows a listing of resources at the first level and the devices attached to those resources under each. Compare the view modes View Devices by Type (Figure 6.4) and View Resources by Type (Figure 6.5).

FIGURE 6.4

View Devices by Type

FIGURE 6.5

View Resources by Type

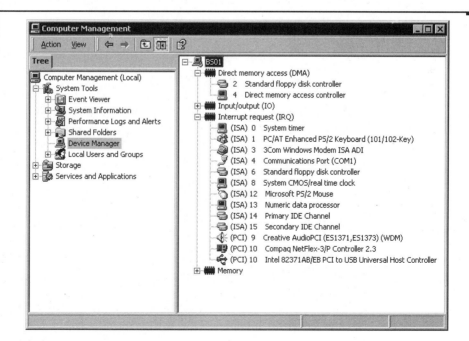

In Device Manager, you also get two different sorting methods: By Type and By Connection. The By Type mode sorts hardware based on what category of hardware the device is. All monitors go under Monitors, all modems under Modems, etc. (see Figure 6.6).

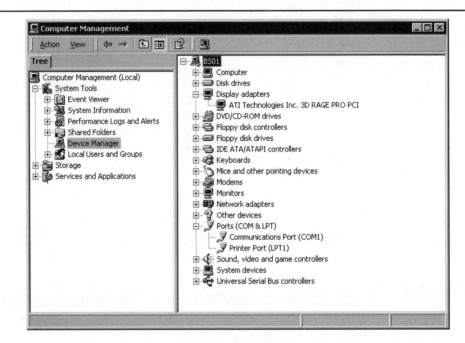

The By Connection view mode organizes your devices according to how they are physically plugged into the system. All devices on the PCI bus are shown below the PCI bus device. Since the monitor is plugged into the video adapter, you will find the listing for the monitor beneath its video adapter within the Device Manager (see Figure 6.7).

FIGURE 6.7

View Devices by
Connection

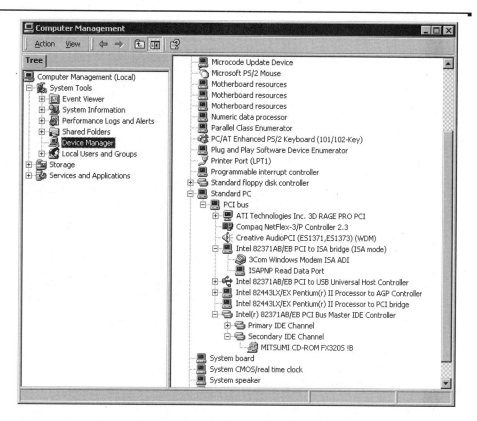

Device Properties

From within each device, you can view the detailed properties of that device by either selecting the Action menu properties, right-clicking the device and selecting Properties, or simply double-clicking the device.

General   Once within the device properties, the General tab, shown in Figure 6.8, will provide some key information.

Particularly important is the Device Status window. In here, you will see whether or not the device is working, and if it isn't, a general description of why. The Troubleshooter button will launch the Troubleshooter Wizard to walk through correcting problems with a device (see the "Troubleshooter" section later in this chapter).

FIGURE 6.8

Device properties,
General tab

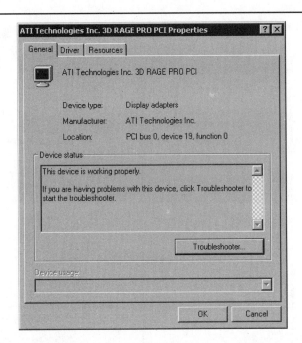

Also on this page is the Device Usage selection. Within this drop-down selection-box, you determine when the device will be used. If your machine uses multiple hardware profiles, as is usually the case with laptop/docking station machines, you will be given the options "Use this device (enable)," "Do not use this device in the current hardware profile (disable)," and "Do not use this device in any hardware profile (disable)." By not using a device in a hardware profile, you are telling Windows 2000 that in certain boot-up hardware configurations, the device either will not be installed, or is expected not to be used (see the "Hardware Profiles" section, also in this chapter).

Driver   The next device properties page is the Driver tab. Important information on the driver provider, date, and version are displayed on this page (see Figure 6.9).

These driver details may come in handy when working with vendors to trouble-shoot faulty devices. The Driver Details button will bring up another page showing all files associated with a particular driver. If you suspect file corruption is the cause of your hardware woes, this is a simple method to find out which files you may need to replace.

Oddly, the Uninstall button is located under the Driver page; this button will completely remove the device from your system.

FIGURE 6.9

Driver details

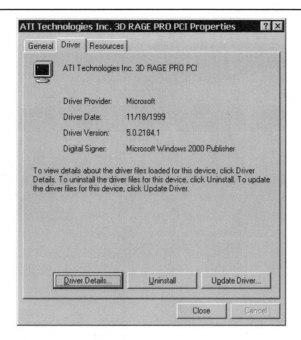

The Update Driver button launches the Upgrade Device Driver Wizard, which follows a series of prompts similar to those that you would go through once a new device has been detected in your system. Typically, this wizard will only be run after you have received a new device driver from the manufacturer or Microsoft that contains important upgrades to the device driver features and capabilities or bug fixes. In most cases, after launching the wizard, you will want to select "Search for a suitable driver for my device," as shown in Figure 6.10.

From there, you can select multiple sources in which to search for new drivers, as shown in Figure 6.11. The floppy and CD-ROM drive options will, of course, search those areas for drivers for your new device. Specify a Location will allow you to point to a folder on your hard drive or a network drive that contains the driver files. Microsoft Windows Update will connect to Microsoft's Web site to look for the driver. To select this last option, you will need to be connected to the Internet, or have an available connection to the Internet for the wizard to use.

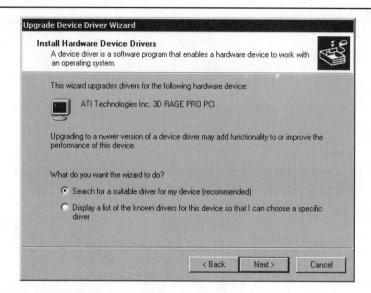

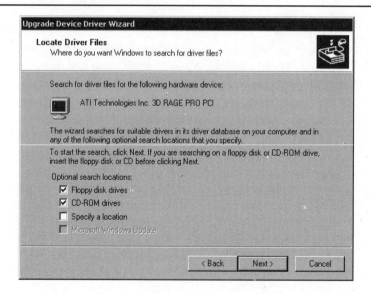

Resources The Resources page holds the good stuff that concerns how your hardware is physically configured. All of the device's IRQ settings, ROM addresses, I/O addresses, and more are displayed in the Resources tab, as shown in Figure 6.12.

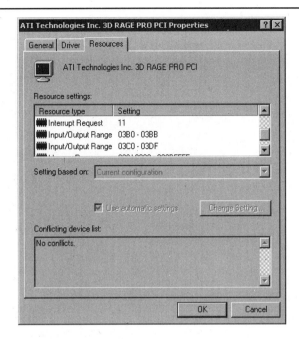

FIGURE 6.12

Device resources

If any resources are causing conflicts, you will see a list of those conflicts and the devices that they conflict with in the Conflicting Device List area.

Some devices will also have configurable resources. By clearing the Use Automatic Settings check box, you will be allowed to change the Settings Based On options to select different prepackaged resource configurations, or, in some cases, you will be able to manually change individual resource settings by double-clicking the resource in question. If the Use Automatic Settings check box is grayed out, the device cannot be assigned new resources manually.

Other Tabs   Some devices will have more tabs present across the top of the device properties page. These other tabs could be labeled Properties, Settings, Advanced, or some other name. Under these pages will be hardware specific configuration settings. For example, Figure 6.13 shows how the CD-ROM has special settings that control how the hardware works within Windows 2000.

Check your devices to see which ones contain these extra pages. These settings could really come in handy to customize the performance and feel of your hardware in Windows 2000.

FIGURE 6.13

CD-ROM properties

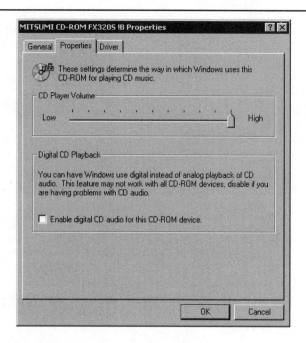

Device Manager Actions

Back in our Device Manager main window, there are some more actions that we can have the Device Manager carry out for us.

The Scan for Hardware Changes action works kind of like a refresh. Any changes, additions, or removals of hardware that has happened behind the Device Manager's back will be detected at this time, and the Device Manager window will be updated to reflect those changes. Any changes detected will launch the Found New Hardware Wizard, which will walk you through the installation of the Plug-and-Play device.

 NOTE The Scan for Hardware Changes action will not work with non-Plug-and-Play hardware. To install new non-Plug-and-Play devices, use the Add Hardware Wizard.

You can also disable hardware directly from the Device Manager Action menu. Let's say you have an incompatible or faulty piece of hardware in the system that is integrated into the motherboard and you don't want Windows 2000 to keep trying to install it every time you boot the machine. Select the device in the Device Manager window, select the Action menu, and select Disable. This action will mark the device with a red X through the device icon, and will inform Windows 2000 to leave the device alone.

Finally, you can uninstall devices by selecting the Action/Uninstall command. This will remove device drivers and information from Windows 2000, letting you physically unplug a device following a system shut down.

Driver Signing

A new option to Windows 2000, driver signing lets you control how Windows 2000 secures your device drivers. All drivers on the Windows 2000 CD come digitally signed. This is a verification that the driver is an authentic, Microsoft-approved driver. When updating certain software or devices in your system, the program may attempt to overwrite your existing driver, which could cause side effects that you won't be prepared for. To find the driver-signing configuration screen, you'll need to start in the System Control Panel and select the Hardware tab. From there, click the Driver Signing button. With driver signing, you get three levels of security to control how Windows 2000 notifies you about attempted changes in driver files (see Figure 6.14).

The Ignore option will not perform any signature verification and will allow any device driver file to be overwritten. The Warn option will notify you if an attempt has been made to overwrite a driver file that does not contain a signature. The Block option is the most secure option; it will not allow any driver that has not been signed to be installed.

NOTE We're talking about a security feature that prevents an unwanted ability to change your device drivers. If your system partition is NTFS, then chances are, you'll need to be an administrator just to even see the folder and files where your drivers are kept. This driver-signing security is more of a feature to either keep you from accidentally overwriting drivers while performing some other installation, or to keep unruly system administrators from overstepping their bounds.

Add/Remove Hardware Wizard

The Add/Remove Hardware Wizard is obviously the tool you will use whenever you add or remove hardware, but it is also used to help troubleshoot hardware or prepare the system to unplug or eject hardware like PCMCIA devices in laptops.

To launch the Add/Remove Hardware Wizard, open the System Control Panel and select the Hardware tab. Click the Hardware Wizard button, and select either to add or troubleshoot a device, or to uninstall or unplug a device. By selecting the add-or-troubleshoot option, the wizard starts off with a Plug-and-Play detection phase. If new hardware is found, the Found New Hardware Wizard will appear. If no devices are found, you will be shown a list of all hardware currently installed in your system, and be given an additional option labeled Add a New Device (shown in Figure 6.15).

FIGURE 6.15

The Add/Remove Hardware Wizard with the Add a New Device option

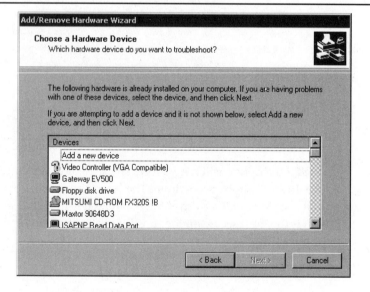

From this screen, you can either add a new device that wasn't detected through the Plug-and-Play detection or select an existing device to troubleshoot. If you select an existing device to troubleshoot, the Troubleshooter will start (see the "Troubleshooter" section later in this chapter).

If you choose to add a new device, you can either have the wizard search for new hardware or you can enter the hardware information into the system manually. This sounds redundant to have the wizard search for hardware—it just ran a Plug-and-Play detection phase two clicks ago. This detection phase, however, is a little bit different. This detection is similar to the way Windows NT 4 searches for hardware. The hardware wizard will go through all known hardware device types, and try to get a response. Once the hardware responds, it should be identified and a driver should be attached. Of course, "should" is the operative word here. Some devices are more easily identified than others. If this process fails, or doesn't get it quite right, you may need to go the manual road.

To manually identify your hardware, you will first select the category of hardware that your device falls under. The next dialog box will contain a list of known manufacturers for the selected category, and, once selected, a list of supported devices for a manufacturer (see Figure 6.16).

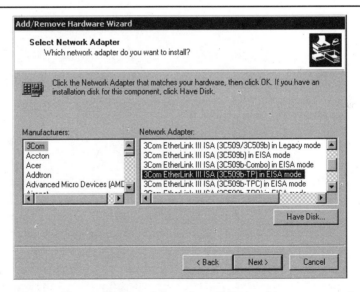

FIGURE 6.16

Select the device driver

After completing the installation of the selected device drivers, your system will most likely require a reboot. Since this won't be purebred Plug-and-Play hardware that you have just manually set up, it may need the driver to initialize the device upon a reboot, rather than on the fly.

Found New Hardware Wizard

The Found New Hardware Wizard shows up whenever Windows 2000 detects new Plug-and-Play hardware in your system. The first thing that happens is that the wizard tries to attach an appropriate device to the new hardware. This process is identical to the process that was used in the Upgrade Device Driver Wizard earlier. Either display a list of known devices, or search your specified locations for a suitable driver. Once the driver has been found and loaded, you are set to go.

But what if there is no device? A completely unsupported piece of hardware. I've got this system with a built-in video adapter that absolutely has no driver available for Windows 2000. Surprisingly, the Found New Hardware Wizard actually does detect a VGA-compatible display adapter, but that's about all. After searching high and low, I finally resigned to accept the choices given to me in Figure 6.17.

FIGURE 16.17

Failed driver files search

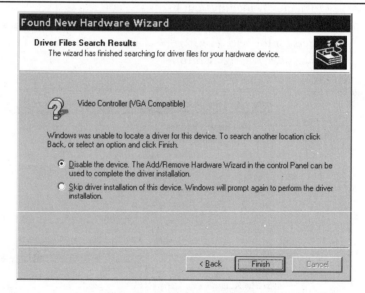

If no driver is available, Windows 2000 can't use the hardware. The device can either be disabled, or the installation can be skipped. If disabled, the device will be shown with a red X over its listing in the Device Manager (see Figure 6.18).

If at a later date, you obtain a driver for the device, you can launch the Add New Hardware Wizard to reinstall the device. If you elect to skip the installation, you should physically remove the hardware, or else the Found New Hardware Wizard will only go through the same process again the next time you reboot.

FIGURE 6.18

Disabled Hardware

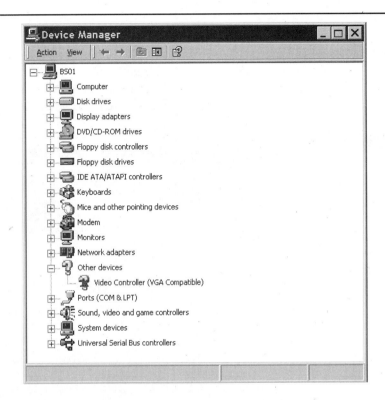

Hardware Profiles

Hardware profiles are used to allow your system to boot cleanly with various hardware configurations. Most commonly, this feature will be used on laptops with docking stations. In some cases, you will boot up just the laptop. In other cases, you will boot up while plugged into the docking station with additional hardware components such as a hard drive and a network card. Upon booting the system, you will get an additional menu from which you can select which hardware profile to use. By using properly defined hardware profiles, you can avoid extraneous errors and Plug-and-Play detection phases.

To configure multiple hardware profiles, you will need to start off once again in the System Control Panel and select the Hardware tab. To create multiple profiles, you'll begin by copying the first profile. Notice that you can't select to create a *new* profile. A new profile would imply a complete return to square one of the hardware detection phase. That would create a lot of unnecessary work. Instead, you just copy your current, working hardware configuration into a new profile and fine-tune it. Once you have more than one profile named in the Hardware Profile screen, you can configure your various components for usage in those profiles. To do this, go into the properties of a device from the Device Manager, then set the Device Usage to determine which profiles will use the selected component. You can either enable or disable the device for all profiles or disable the device for the current profile. It seems strange, but you cannot enable a device for just the current profile. If you want the device available for only your current profile, you will need to boot into the other profiles and select the option to disable the device in just that current profile (see Figure 6.19).

FIGURE 6.19

Hardware profiles

For each profile, you can also tell Windows 2000 if the profile is used for a portable computer or if it is docked or undocked. If Windows 2000 can determine the docking state on its own, you won't be able to change this setting.

Troubleshooter

The Windows 2000 Hardware Troubleshooter is a self-guided, point-and-click, question-and-answer help file. If you run the troubleshooter from the Device Manger properties of a faulty device, the troubleshooter will start off at exactly the proper place. If there's a resource conflict, it will start right at the point of how to deal with resource conflicts. If there's a driver failure, it will, of course, start right at how to deal with driver failures. The troubleshooter can also deal with many common problems related to specific devices. It will ask questions about the nature of your problem, what does work and what doesn't work, and will eventually narrow your problem down to the source. If you are having a problem that is hardware related, but isn't necessarily manifesting itself in the form of a warning or failure on any device, you want to start at the device that is related to the problem. From within the device properties, a Troubleshoot button will start you off with a series of very general questions to get you started (see Figure 6.20).

FIGURE 6.20

*The Hardware
Troubleshooter
main menu*

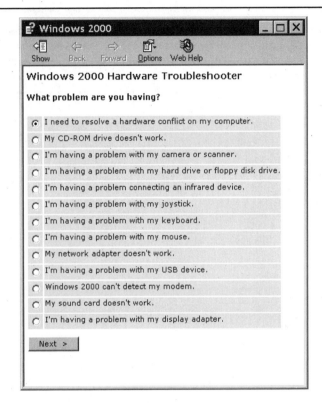

 TIP In some cases, you will want to start at the very top of the troubleshooter. To get to the root level of the troubleshooter, select Start/Help. In the left-hand column, double-click the Troubleshooting and Other Resources book, followed by the Troubleshooting book, Troubleshooting Overview, and finally, the Troubleshooters help option. A table on the right will show various troubleshooters, from which you can select the Hardware Troubleshooter. Another way to get into the troubleshooter is to select a properly working device in the Device Manager, like the network adapter. Go under the Properties tab and select Troubleshooter. Some devices will start you at a device-specific troubleshooter, so you may need to try a different one.

After running through the troubleshooter questions, you could either be presented with the solution to your problem or be given a reference to a Microsoft Knowledge Base article that provides more information on the suspected problem.

 WARNING   The troubleshooter may ask if your hardware is listed on the Hardware Compatibility List. If you answer "No," your troubleshooting session will be terminated very abruptly. (Actually, your answer for no is given as, "No, my device isn't on the HCL. I'll contact the manufacturer for further assistance.")

CHAPTER 7

Managing Windows 2000 Storage

FEATURING:

Whether your Win2K server is a print server, an e-mail server, a Web server, or whatever kind of server you can think of, it's still in many ways a file server. No matter what kind of resources a server's providing to the network, the server has to store a lot of files to support those resources.

A lot of files means a lot of storage, and a lot of storage means maintaining it. In this chapter, I'll talk about the tools Win2K includes to help you maintain your disks and other storage media. At one time, this mostly meant the Disk Administrator. We're going to start with the Tool Formerly Known As the Disk Administrator (now called the Disk Management tool), but there's a lot more to it than that: encryption, new disk formats, and disk quotas.

Using the Disk Management Tool

Server disks must be faster, more reliable, and larger than their workstation-based cousins. How do you achieve those goals of speed, reliability, and size? Well, there's always the simple answer: spend more money for a drive with more of those three characteristics. But the past few years have yielded another solution: a group of mediocre drives can band together and, acting in concert, can provide speed, capacity, and high fault tolerance. This solution is called *Redundant Array of Independent Disks (RAID)*. Until relatively recently, putting a RAID on your server required buying an expensive hardware-based RAID system (the drives are inexpensive, but the entire RAID subsystem isn't, unfortunately). However, Win2K changes that with the Disk Management tool. With it, you can take a bunch of hard disks and "roll your own" RAID system. This doesn't make hardware-based RAID obsolete by any means, since hardware RAID is more flexible than software. Software RAID just offers a less-expensive option for those who want this kind of data protection.

The Disk Management tool offers a lot of options. This section explains what your organization and protection options are and how you can use the Disk Management tool to best arrange your data for your particular situation.

Although you'll set up the initial disk partitioning when you install Win2K Server, you can use the Disk Management tool (in the Computer Management section of the MMC; Computer Management is in the Administrative Tools program group) to edit the logical divisions of your disk after you've installed Win2K.

The Disk Management tool is not just a warmed-over version of the Disk Administrator from NT 4. Whereas the Disk Administrator required you to reboot after any change to the partition system, or possibly if you breathed too hard on the hard disk, here you can create and delete volumes without rebooting. You can mount partitions to paths on other NTFS volumes instead of just assigning drive letters to new volumes. You can format volumes while creating them rather than having to format them from the command prompt or from Explorer as you've had to do in the past. All in all, it's a good tool and a *great* improvement over previous iterations of the Disk Administrator. With the Disk Management tool, you can do the following:

- Create and delete partitions on a hard disk and make logical drives.
- Get status information concerning these items:
  - The disk partition sizes
  - The amount of free space left on a disk for making partitions
  - Volume labels, their drive-letter assignment, file system type, and size
- Alter drive letter and file mounting assignments.
- Enlarge disk volumes.
- Create, delete, and repair mirror sets.
- Format any volume.
- Create and delete stripe sets and regenerate missing or failed members of stripe sets with parity.

Don't recognize some of these terms? Hang on, they're defined in the next section.

Disk Management Terminology

Before we get into the discussion of how you can use the Disk Management tool to arrange and protect your data, you need to know some of the terms that we'll be tossing around. These terms will be explained further in due course, but this section introduces them.

SLED

An acronym for *single large expensive drive*, SLED is a way of arranging your data on one very large, very (hopefully) reliable drive. SLED is a popular method of arranging data for two reasons:

- It's simple. You only have to buy one disk and store your data on it.
- Dedicated RAID hardware has been expensive in the past. Even though it's not as expensive as it used to be, it still reflects an added cost.

Trouble is, if that one very large and very reliable drive fails, then your data goes with it. That's where RAID comes in.

RAID

"Apply a shot of RAID, and all those nasty data problems will be gone!" No, it's not really a household product. RAID, which stands for Redundant Array of Independent Disks, is a method of protecting your data by combining hard disks in such a way that your data redundancy and therefore data security is increased, in the sense that if you lose a disk you can still read your data. There are six kinds of RAID implementation, each of which works in a different way and has different applications. Win2K Server supports levels 0, 1, and 5, also known as striping without parity, disk mirroring, and striping with parity, respectively. We'll talk about exactly what those levels are later in this chapter.

NOTE Strictly speaking, RAID isn't always redundant. RAID level 0 (disk striping without parity) isn't fault tolerant because it contains no redundant data to help you re-create lost data.

Basic Disks versus Dynamic Disks

Win2K supports two kinds of disk storage: dynamic and basic. Basic storage is the kind of storage that NT has typically supported, allowing for primary and extended disk partitions and logical drives. If you're upgrading NT 4 to Win2K, then the basic disks may still include the mirror sets, volume sets, and stripe sets that you created under the previous version of the operating system.

Basic disks have their limits. For compatibility reasons, they conform to the four-partition limit imposed by the structure of the disk partition table (a 64-byte file in the first sector of any disk; the partition table lists the physical locations of any logical partitions on the disk but can only describe four partitions because each description takes up 16 bytes). Basic disks also don't support new fault-tolerant volumes. If you want to use Win2K's RAID, you'll need to upgrade the basic disks to dynamic disks. Dynamic disks let you create, extend, and delete fault-tolerant and multidisk volumes on-the-fly, not requiring the reboots that the fault-tolerance driver in NT 4 did.

There's a catch to dynamic disks: lack of compatibility. They're incomprehensible—in fact, invisible—to any locally installed operating system other than Win2K. Additionally, although you can revert a dynamic disk to a basic disk, you can only do this so long as the dynamic disk doesn't have any volumes on it. In other words, if you upgrade a basic disk that already has data on it to a dynamic disk, you'll have to delete the volumes in which that data is stored (and thus delete the data) before you can revert the disk to basic. In fact, that's worth a warning.

WARNING If you're running a dual-boot system with NT and Win2K, do *not* convert the disk with the system partitions on it to dynamic. If you do, you'll have to delete and restore the data to run NT again, and you won't be able to run NT to save any Registry settings first.

In short, if you want to create new fault-tolerant volumes or multidisk volumes, you'll need to upgrade your disks to dynamic. If you need local compatibility with other operating systems, then you'll need to stick with basic disks. If you've only got one disk in the server and don't plan to add more, you might as well leave it basic and save yourself the 4MB of space that the dynamic metadata would use.

Free Space versus Unallocated Space

The definition of *free space* seems obvious. "Free space on a disk is just space that's free, right?" It's not. Free space does not refer to unused areas within established drives. Rather, *free space* is an extended partition that doesn't yet have any logical drives in it, or the space within that partition not yet divided into a logical drive. (Hang on—I'll get to what extended partitions and logical drives are in a minute.) By default, the bar on top of an area of free space is bright green.

This definition of free space is different from the one used in NT 4 and previous versions, wherein free space was space on a disk that was not part of a volume. Disk space formerly called free space is now called *unallocated space*. It's not committed to be part of any volume or partition. Both basic and dynamic disks may have unallocated space; its color-coding is black.

Physical Disks versus Logical Partitions

Getting the difference between physical disks and logical drives or partitions clear is worthwhile. A *physical disk* is that contraption of plastic and metal that you inserted in your server's case or have stacked up next to it. The Disk Management tool identifies physical drives by numbers (Disk 0, 1, 2...; CD 0, 1, 2...) which you cannot change.

 NOTE If you have multiple disks in your computer, they're numbered by their status on the drive controller. For example, in a SCSI chain, the disk with SCSI ID 0 will be Disk 0, the drive with the next SCSI ID will be Disk 1, and so on. The SCSI ID and the disk number are not directly related and will not necessarily match—the only correspondence lies in the disk's priority in the system.

You cannot change the size of a physical disk. The size given to it when it was low-level formatted (something you almost certainly don't have to worry about if you're installing Win2K on the disk; you can't low-level format an EIDE drive and don't need to low-level format a SCSI drive—it's done before you buy it) is the size the drive will remain.

NOTE By the way, if you're putting a number of physical hard disks on a PC, the PC may only recognize two of those drives when it boots up. Don't worry about that; what you're seeing is a limitation of the DOS-based BIOS on the SCSI host adapter. Once you've booted Win2K, it will be able to see however many drives you've attached to your system. Similarly, if you've got an older BIOS on your computer, the Win2K installation program may tell you that you've only got 1GB on your hard disk, even if you have a larger disk. The installation program is misinformed because it's still relying on your PC's BIOS, which can't see more than 1GB. Once Win2K is up and running, however, it will see all of your hard disk. Computers with an up-to-date BIOS (something you should have for Y2K compliance anyway) generally won't have this problem.

In contrast to a physical disk, a *partition* or volume is a logical construct: a logical drive, primary partition, or anything else in the Disk Administrator that is assigned a drive letter or mounted to a path on an NTFS volume. You can change drive letter assignments and adjust the sizes of logical partitions, as they have no physical presence. A logical partition can be part or all of a physical disk or even (in the case of volume sets, mirror sets, and stripe sets) extend across more than one physical disk.

 NOTE You can format a partition smaller than 4GB (4096MB) with any file system that Win2K supports; FAT, FAT32, or NTFS. For volumes larger than 4GB, you'll be limited to FAT32 or NTFS.

Mounted Drives

In the Disk Administrator you used with previous versions of NT, you had to identify each logical disk volume by a drive letter. This method is simple and has the advantage of making a really short way of leaping to that partition. The disadvantage, of course, is that so long as Win2K insists on using the Roman alphabet, you're limited to a total of 26 letters for all local drives and mapped network connections. To get around this problem, Win2K supports mounting volumes to empty folders on NTFS volumes.

The basic idea of mounting a partition to a folder is that you're redirecting to the partition all read and write requests sent to that folder. Mount a new partition to X:\Mount Volume Here and every file I/O request you send to X:\Mount Volume Here will be rerouted to the new partition, even though the *real* drive X: is on a different physical disk entirely. You can mount a volume to as many paths as you like. The only restrictions are that the folders must be empty at the time of mounting and not mapped to any other volumes, and they must be on NTFS volumes on the local computer. NTFS 5 is the only file format that Win2K supports that can use the reparse points that redirect path information.

The mounted volumes show up as subfolders in the path you mounted them from, but as you can see in Figure 7.1, the mounted volumes show up as drives instead of folders.

FIGURE 7.1

Mounted volumes within a folder

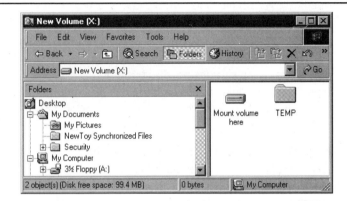

Why bother with mounting volumes to NTFS paths? Three reasons. First, it means that you're in no danger of running out of drive letters for local and network partitions.

Second, you can use this technique to effectively enlarge a volume on a basic disk, which you cannot do otherwise. For example, say that drive X: is running short of room. It's on a basic volume, so you can't make drive X: any bigger. Instead, you add a new disk and create a 2GB volume on that disk, then map the new 2GB volume to an empty folder on drive X:. Drive X: is now effectively 2GB larger.

Third, you can use this technique to create a fault-tolerant area on a non-fault-tolerant volume. That 2GB volume you created can be a stripe set with parity or a mirror set, even if the disk that drive X: is on is a basic disk and therefore does not support fault-tolerant volumes. For example, you could create a new folder on drive X: called Home Directories, then map a RAID volume to that folder. Whenever someone saves a file to any subfolder of X:\Home Directories, it's going to the RAID volume even if the rest of drive X: is *not* fault tolerant.

Volume mappings are transparent to the user base, incidentally. Just as a user doesn't have to care whether drive G: is on the computer she's working on or on a file server, the same user doesn't have to care whether the folder she's saving to is located on the same physical disk as the rest of drive X: or on another disk altogether. You can also mount a drive to multiple paths or both mount it and assign it a drive letter.

Experiment with mounting drives to NTFS paths. They're a really cool addition to Win2K's storage management capabilities.

Partitions

A *partition* is a portion of a hard disk set up to act like a separate physical hard disk, rather like splitting a single physical hard disk into several logical drives. There's two kinds of partitions: primary and extended.

Primary Partitions   A *primary partition* is a portion of a physical hard disk that the operating system (such as Win2K) marks as bootable. Under DOS, you can only have one primary partition. Under Win2K, NT, or Windows 9x, you can have multiple partitions on a drive; one partition at a time is marked "active," meaning you can boot from it. You can't break primary partitions into subpartitions, and you can create only up to four partitions per disk because that's all there's room for in the partition table. You might partition your hard disk so one primary partition is running Win2K and another is running OS/2. In the Disk Management tool, a primary partition has a dark blue stripe across the top and gets a drive letter.

Extended Partitions   Four logical divisions on the disk aren't enough? You can create an *extended partition* from unallocated space on a physical disk. Once you do, you'll see a new area of free space on the drive, with a dark green border. The dark green border identifies the extended partition's area. You can only have one extended partition on a physical disk, but you can supplement it with up to three primary partitions.

You can't put any data into an extended partition or assign it a drive letter—it's just free space. To make it able to hold data, you'll need to break that extended partition into one or more logical drives.

Logical Drive

A *logical drive* is a logical division of an extended partition that behaves like an entity unto itself. You can divide an extended partition into as many logical drives as you like, so long as you make each partition the minimum size required (this will be shown in the wizard helping you to create the partition).

Logical drives are indicated in the Disk Manager display with a royal-blue stripe. Because they're part of an extended partition, they'll have a green border that encompasses all drives in the partition and any free space left in it after you create the drives.

Basic disks support partitions and logical drives. If you want more flexibility, upgrade disks to dynamic and use the volume types described in the next section.

Volume

A *volume* is a logical division of the unallocated space on a hard disk. It works like a logical drive or primary partition except for one major difference: whereas logical drives and primary partitions must be confined to a single disk and can't be made larger, volumes may exist either on one disk or on more, and you can add more unallocated space to them. This makes volumes much more flexible—and potentially more space efficient—than partitions or drives. As you can see in Figure 7.2, it's much easier to figure out how to fit 30MB of data into a 35MB volume set than it is to fit it into one 20MB logical drive and one 15MB logical drive.

Win2K supports two kinds of volume sets: simple volumes, which start out only taking up space on one disk, and spanned volumes, which start out taking up space on multiple disks. You can extend either kind of volume; if you extend a simple volume onto another disk, then it becomes a spanned volume. You cannot make the volume set smaller unless you delete it and create a new one.

FIGURE 7.2

How a volume set works

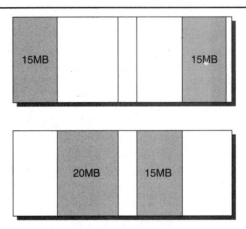

In this figure, 65MB of free space is available, but no more than 20MB of this space is contiguous. To get the most efficient use of this space, you could combine it in a volume set so all of the data is considered in one large chunk. Once this free space has been made into a volume set, you could store a 65MB chunk of data in it, even though the largest contiguous space is only 20MB in size.

NOTE   You can only extend NTFS-formatted volumes.

Volume sets do not protect your data; they only let you use available drive space more efficiently. If something happens to one of the hard disks used in a volume set, that volume set is dead, even if the other hard disks are fine. Because the more hard disks you have, the more likely it is that one will fail at any given time, be sure to back up volume sets regularly.

In the Disk Management tool, simple volumes have a mustard-yellow stripe; spanned volumes have a purple stripe.

Mirror Set

Mirror sets are the simplest form of Win2K data redundancy, writing two copies of all data onto volumes on two separate disks so that if one disk fails, the data is still available. If anything happens to the disk storing your original data, you still have an identical copy on the other half of the mirror set.

Collectively, the two volumes are called a *mirror set*. They have a couple of advantages:

- You can mirror an existing simple volume set, making it fault tolerant.
- You only need two physical disks to create a mirror set instead of the minimum of three that RAID 5 volumes require.

Disk mirroring is simpler to use in Win2K than it was in NT 4. You can create mirrored volumes on-the-fly and don't have to regenerate data to recover it if one of the disks supporting the mirror crashes. The data will remain available—it just won't be fault tolerant until you mirror it again.

If you've ever heard or read anything about disk mirroring, you've probably also heard the term *disk duplexing*. Disk duplexing is much the same as disk mirroring, except that duplexing generally refers to mirroring information on two separate disks—each with its own disk controller—so that the data is not vulnerable to controller failures. When Win2K Server talks about disk mirroring, it is referring to both duplexing and mirroring, as Figure 7.3 demonstrates.

FIGURE 7.3

Disk mirroring versus disk duplexing

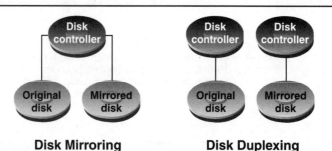

Disk Mirroring   **Disk Duplexing**

Mirror sets secure data well, but they're not very space efficient because every piece of data that you record has an identical twin on the other half of the mirror set. You need exactly twice as much storage space as you have data. The Disk Management tool displays mirror sets with a dark-red stripe across the top.

Stripe Set

Volume sets are useful because they allow you to combine many differently sized areas of unused disk space into a single volume. However, they don't offer any performance benefits. To use space on multiple disks and decrease read and write times, consider using disk striping without parity, also known as RAID level 0.

When you create a stripe set from free space on your disks, each member of the stripe set is divided into stripes of equal size. Then, when you write data to the stripe set, the data is distributed over the stripes. A file could have its beginning recorded onto stripe 1 of member 1, more data recorded onto stripe 2 of member 2, and the rest on stripe 3 of member 3, for example. If you're saving data to a stripe set, a file is never stored on only one member disk, even if there is room on that disk for the entire file. Conceptually, striping looks something like Figure 7.4.

If you take free space on your disks and combine it into one stripe set with its own drive letter, the seek-and-write time to that drive will be improved since the system can read and write to more than one disk at a time. To do striping without parity information included, you need at least 2, but not more than 32, disks.

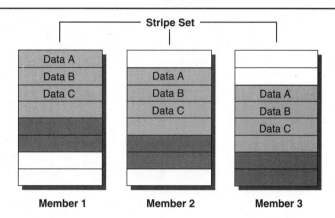

FIGURE 7.4

Stripe set without parity

Different data files are represented here with different shades of gray. As you can see, an entire data file is never all put onto one member of the striped set. This improves read time since, if Data A is called for, the disk controllers on all three members of the set can read the data. With a SLED data arrangement, only one of the members could read the data.

Disk striping has a speed advantage over volume sets, but consider this:

- You cannot extend a stripe set like you can a volume or extend it over more disks once it's created. The size that you make the stripe set is the size it will stay.

- You cannot mirror a stripe set, although you *can* mirror a simple volume. There is simply no way to make a stripe set fault tolerant other than backing it up.

In other words, stripe sets are not always the way to go. If you're looking for performance, use nonparity stripe sets. If you're looking for flexibility, expandability, or fault tolerance, use simple or spanned volume sets.

RAID 5 Volume

For data protection, or to decrease your disks' read time, you can select areas of unallocated space on your disks and combine them into a *RAID 5 volume*, also known as a *stripe set with parity*. RAID 5 volumes are the most cost-effective form of RAID that Win2K supports.

How Disk Striping with Parity Works   Every time you write data to disk, the data is written across all the striped disks in the array, just as it is with regular disk striping (RAID level 0). Parity information for your data is also written to disk, always on a separate disk from the one where the data it corresponds to is written. That way, if anything happens to one of the disks in the array, the data on that disk can be reconstructed from the parity information on the other disks.

Level 5 RAID differs from level 4, which also uses parity information to protect data, in that the parity information in level 5 RAID is distributed across all the disks in the array. In level 4, a specific disk is dedicated to parity information. This makes level 5 RAID faster than 4, as it can perform more than one write operation at a time. This is shown in Figure 7.5.

FIGURE 7.5

Disk striping with parity information

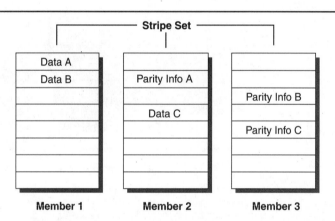

As you can see, no single member of the stripe set keeps all the original data or all the parity information. Instead, the data and parity information are distributed throughout the stripe set so, if one member disk fails, the information can be reconstructed from the other members of the strip set.

If you think about it, writing parity information every time you save a document could turn into a big waste of space and time. Take, for example, the document I'm creating for this book. If I've protected my data with level 5 RAID and parity information is stored to disk every time this file is saved, does that mean that there is parity information for every incarnation of this document from the time I began writing? If so, how can all the parity information and data fit on the disks?

The answer is, of course, that it doesn't, and this is what produces the performance degradation that's unavoidable in striped disk writes. Every time a document is saved to disk, its parity information must be updated to reflect its current status; otherwise, you would have to keep backup parity information for every version of the document that you ever saved.

Updating the Parity Information   There are two ways to update the parity information. First, since the parity information is the XOR (exclusive OR) of the data, the system could recalculate the XOR each time data is written to disk. This would require accessing each disk in the stripe set, however, because the data is distributed across the disks in the array, and that takes time.

What is an *XOR?* On a *very* simplistic level, the XOR, or *exclusive OR arithmetic,* is a function that takes two 1-bit inputs and produces a single-bit output. The result is 1 if the two inputs are different or 0 if the two inputs are the same. More specifically:

$$0 \text{ XOR } 0 = 0 \qquad 1 \text{ XOR } 0 = 1 \qquad 0 \text{ XOR } 1 = 1 \qquad 1 \text{ XOR } 1 = 0$$

When you're XORing two numbers with more than one bit, just match the bits up and XOR them individually. For example, 1101010 XOR 0101000 equals 1000010. The result you get from this function is the parity information, from which the original data can be recalculated.

A more efficient way of recalculating the parity information, and the one that Win2K Server uses, is to read the old data to be overwritten and XOR it with the new data to determine the differences. This process produces a *bit mask* that has a 1 in the position of every bit that has been changed. This bit mask can then be XORed with the old parity information to see where *its* differences lie, and from this the new parity information can be calculated. This seems convoluted, but this second process only requires two reads and two XOR computations rather than one of each for every drive in the array.

Installing a New Physical Disk

When you first add a new hard disk to your computer, Win2K will not recognize the new disk even if it shows up at boot time (SCSI or IDE). You must add support for the new drive, either manually or by following the Write Signature and Upgrade Disk Wizard. The wizard will start up automatically when you open the Disk Management folder in the Computer Management tool and have new physical disks attached.

There are two steps to setting up a new hard disk: writing a disk signature and choosing whether the disk should be basic or dynamic. Win2K writes disk signatures automatically when it detects the disks or as part of the Write Signature and Upgrade Disk Wizard.

To add a new disk, follow the wizard. It's not really much of a wizard anymore (in early betas of Win2K, it was longer, asking you to specify disks that you wanted to sign instead of just writing the signature automatically). All you're doing is picking disks to upgrade to dynamic, something you should consider before doing. Win2K will write a signature to the disks automatically when it detects a new disk and upgrade any that you choose.

Using Basic Disk Features

Basic disks, recall, are the default in Win2K. A basic disk is a normal disk, available from any operating system and using primary and extended partitions to divide up physical disk space into logical units. You'll need to stick with basic disks if you want to make disks available to operating systems other than Win2K. This will keep you from using RAID, but then again, even before Win2K introduced dynamic disks you couldn't access mirrored or other RAID volumes from any operating system other than NT anyway. On basic disks, you can create primary partitions, extended partitions, and logical drives.

Using Primary Partitions to Store Operating Systems

As noted earlier, you can boot the computer from a primary partition. When you install Win2K, the Setup program will automatically create a primary partition to put Win2K on. If you want to create more bootable partitions, or just another partition to store data that's separate from your system partition, then right-click on any area of unallocated space on the hard disk and choose Create Partition from the menu to start the Create Partition Wizard. Click through the welcome screen, then choose the type of partition you want to create (see Figure 7.6).

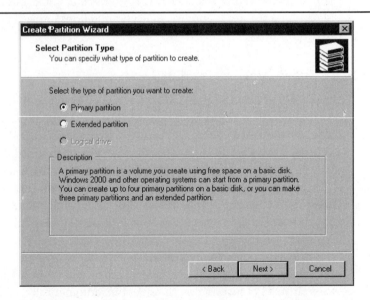

FIGURE 7.6

You can create primary partitions from unallocated space.

In the next screen of the wizard, specify the size of the primary partition. It can be anywhere from the minimum specified in the wizard to the full size of the unallocated space. Make sure that you make the partition as big as it will ever need to be, because you can't extend primary partitions. Even if you make the disk a dynamic disk, you won't be able to extend the partition space—only volumes created on dynamic disks from the beginning may be extended.

In the next screen of the wizard (see Figure 7.7), you have three options: choose a drive letter for the new primary partition, mount it to an empty folder on an NTFS volume, or do neither.

 NOTE At some point, you'll have to assign the partition a drive letter or path if you want to use it. You can't save data to an area of disk that isn't named or format it with Explorer—there's no way to get its attention, so to speak.

FIGURE 7.7

Pick an identifier for the partition.

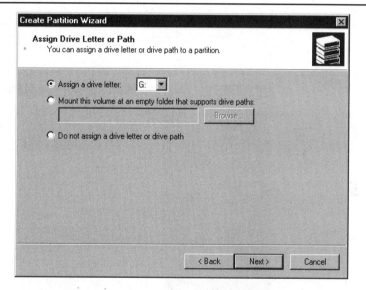

Next, you'll be prompted to choose a format for the disk (see Figure 7.8). Win2K supports NTFS (the default file format), FAT, and FAT32. You'll only have the option to compress the volume if you format with NTFS. Quick formats, which just wipe the disk without checking it for errors, are available with any format type.

You don't actually have to format the partition now—you can format a volume at any time by right-clicking it and choosing Format from the pop-up menu—but you'll have to format it before you use it.

When you've finished, you'll see a finish screen like the one in Figure 7.9. Review your choices to make sure you've got the new partition set up the way you want it and click Finish.

FIGURE 7.8

Choose a disk format.

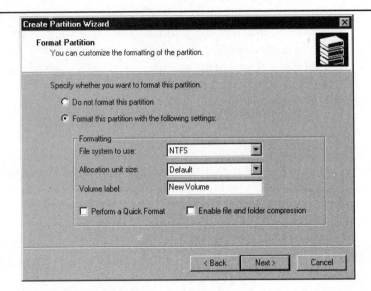

FIGURE 7.9

Review your choices before finishing the logical drive.

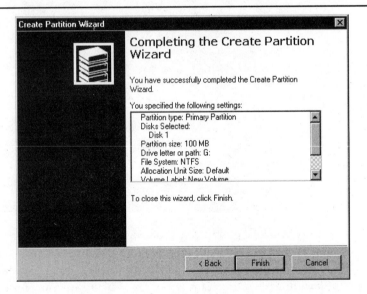

The Disk Management tool will set up your new partition. When it's done, you'll see a new volume with a dark blue stripe, and you'll be able to watch the progress of the disk format if you chose to format the partition.

Using Logical Drives to Organize Information

Even if you rely on the SLED model for your data storage, you may want to divide that single large physical drive into smaller logical ones. You could, for example, keep all the accounting information on logical drive C, the engineering information on logical drive D, the personnel information on logical drive E, and so on. As discussed earlier, you can also mount logical drives to NTFS volumes on other local disks to effectively enlarge the other volumes. Although you can also do all this with primary partitions, logical drives have an advantage: no four-division limit per disk.

To create a logical drive, you must first take unallocated space and convert it to an extended partition. Creating an extended partition is much like creating a primary partition, except for the different partition type that you'll choose in the first page of the wizard and the fact that you won't be asked to format or label the new partition. The new extended partition will be labeled Free Space and have a green border around it.

Once you've created the extended partition, you're ready to create a logical drive. To do so, right-click on free space in the extended partition and choose Create Logical Drive from the pop-up menu. This will start the Create Partition Wizard that you've seen before. Click through the first screen, and you'll see the one shown in Figure 7.10.

FIGURE 7.10

Choose to create a logical drive.

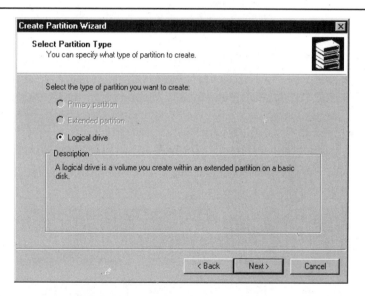

Notice that you only have one option here; you can't create partitions within an extended partition. Click Next to open the next page of the wizard and choose the size of the drive you want to create (see Figure 7.11).

In the next screen of the wizard, you can once again choose to either mount the drive or assign it a drive letter. Format the drive with the file system you want, and you'll arrive at the finish screen showing you the options you picked. Click Finish, and the logical drive will appear in the extended partition.

The details differ slightly depending on the type of volume, but that's the process in a nutshell.

FIGURE 7.11

Specify the size of the new logical drive.

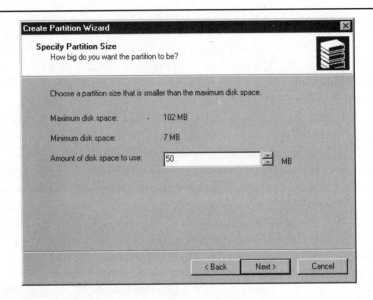

Formatting and Labeling a Logical Volume

Notice that formatting the volume while it's being created is an option (a nice change from NT 4), but not required. If you don't format a volume while creating it, you'll need to do so before you can use the disk. You may also want to reformat an already formatted volume to quickly delete all data.

To format a volume from the Disk Manager, right-click it and choose Format from the pop-up menu that appears. You'll open the dialog box shown in Figure 7.12.

FIGURE 7.12

Format and label a new volume.

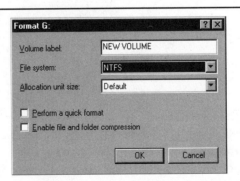

Type in any name you like, then choose the disk format you want to use: NTFS, FAT32, or FAT. Click OK, and Win2K will format the selected volume. Of course, any data already on the disk will be irrevocably deleted in the course of the format, so if you're reformatting, be sure that you've already saved any data on the volume that you want to keep.

NOTE If you open Windows Explorer and try to access the new drive letter before you format it, you'll get a message telling you that the disk is not formatted and asking if you want to format it now. Say OK, and the Format dialog box will open. Oddly enough, if you start the format in this manner, the default file format is FAT, not NTFS.

Deleting a Dynamic Disk Volume

To delete any volume, just find it in the Disk Management tool, right-click it, and choose Delete (*Volume Type*) from the pop-up menu.

What if you're using data on the disk? If you're using any data, or even if you have Explorer open to display the contents of a disk volume, the Disk Management tool will fuss at you when you attempt to delete the volume. You *can* force the deletion of the drive even if it's being used, but generally speaking, it's a lot smarter to find out who's using the drive and let them save their data elsewhere before deleting the volume.

Deleting a Basic Disk Volume

To delete any basic disk volume, right-click it and choose the Delete Partition or Delete Logical Drive option (whichever applies). A dialog box will pop up and warn you that any information in the volume that you're deleting will be lost and ask if you're sure you want to continue. (Surprisingly, the default option is Yes, which strikes me as a bit dangerous.) Click Yes to delete the volume.

The deleted basic disk volume will revert to whatever it was before you created the volume. Primary partitions and extended partitions revert to unallocated space on the drive; logical drives revert to free space.

Converting a Basic Disk to a Dynamic Disk

Even after you partition it, you can convert a basic disk to a dynamic disk so that any new volumes you create can span multiple physical disks. Before you start converting, however, there's a few things you should consider.

Not All Disks Are Upgradeable   These instructions will not work on every disk. If you don't see an option to upgrade a basic disk, there may be a reason:

- Only fixed-disk drives may be dynamic disks. Removable disk drives such as Jaz drives and CD-Rs can only be basic disks.

- If the disk has a sector size larger than 512 bytes, then you won't be able to upgrade it. Notice that that's the *sector* size, not the *cluster* size. I'll get into the difference more in the later section on formatting, but for the moment just understand that (a) this is a problem you're unlikely to encounter, and (b) you can't change the sector size of your disks with a Win2K format. Cluster size, yes, sector size, no.

What's Happening to My System and Boot Partitions? Before upgrading, consider what effect the change will have on existing system data—both for Win2K and for any other operating systems on the computer:

- You will *not* be able to install Win2K onto a volume on a dynamic disk unless the volume was upgraded from a basic disk. That is, the volume must have existed on the physical disk before you upgraded it to dynamic. You can't install Win2K onto a volume that you created after the disk became dynamic. The installation program needs the partition information of a basic disk and can't interpret partition information of a dynamic disk.

- You can (usually) upgrade the disk with the system partition on it, but the upgrade will not take effect until you restart the computer. (Actually, this is true for any disk that has files open during the upgrade, not just the system partition.) This is one of the few times that you'll need to restart the computer for a change in the Disk Management tool to take effect.

- You can't upgrade a basic disk with a system partition if that disk has NT 4 RAID volumes on it.

- You will not be able to access the dynamic disks from any locally installed operating system other than Win2K. That is, you'll be able to get to them from across the network, but in a dual-boot computer, the other operating systems will not be able to see the dynamic disks. That, by the way, includes *booting* from those dynamic disks, so don't convert the disk with other operating systems on it.

Keep in Mind What You've Got You may not *want* to upgrade a basic disk to dynamic. Seriously. You'll need to do it to get the full benefits of Win2K's multidisk volumes and software RAID support, but upgrading can be hard to reverse and a pain to resolve if you can't. Keep the following in mind:

- If you upgraded NT 4 to Win2K, the basic disk may have RAID volumes (stripe sets or mirroring) on it. To continue using these multiple-disk volumes as fault-tolerant volumes, you must upgrade each disk in the RAID volume to dynamic.

- You cannot extend the volumes on the converted disk if the volumes were originally created on a basic disk. Only volumes originally created on a dynamic disk may be extended to other disks or made larger with unallocated space on the same disk.

- Although you always have the option of converting dynamic disks back to basic disks, you must delete any volumes on the disk first.

Upgrading the Basic Disk Now that you're thoroughly intimidated, let's go through the process of doing the conversion:

1. In the Disk Management tool, right-click the gray area on the left side of the physical disk you want to convert (see Figure 7.13).

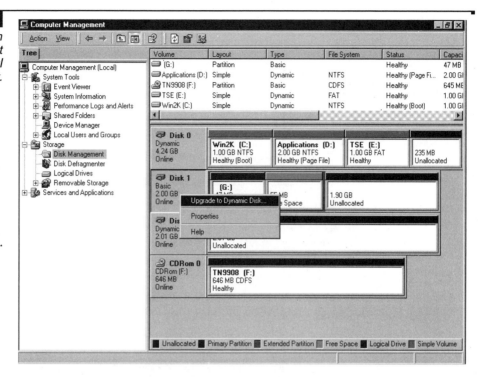

2. From the pop-up menu that appears, choose Upgrade to Dynamic Disk to open the dialog box in Figure 7.14. All basic disks on the computer that are available to be converted (recall, this includes only fixed-disk drives) will be listed and identified by number.

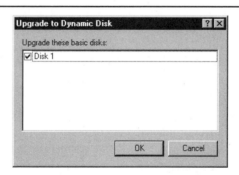

3. Click OK, and the Disk Management tool will then display a list of the disks it's going to convert. This dialog box is much like the preceding one except for a Details button. Click this button, and you'll see a list of the logical drives on the physical disks (see Figure 7.15).

FIGURE 7.15

The Disk Management tool will show you what logical drives are on the disk to be converted.

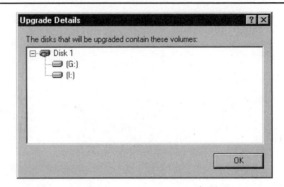

4. Exit the Details box and return to the Disks to Upgrade box by clicking OK. If you're still sure you want to upgrade, click the Upgrade button. You'll see a message like the one in Figure 7.16, warning you that previous versions of Windows will no longer be able to boot from this disk. Click Yes, and you'll get *another* message warning you that all mounted file paths will be dismounted. (If you regret upgrading a disk to dynamic, it's not going to be Microsoft's fault.) Click OK to get through this message box.

FIGURE 7.16

Be sure not to convert any basic disks that other versions of Windows will need to access.

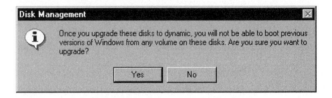

Once you've clicked OK, and the hard disk will grind away for a couple of minutes. When the operation is completed, any partitions or logical drives that had previously been on the disk will now be simple volumes.

What if the Upgrade Doesn't Take? If you upgraded a disk with open files (say, the disk with the system partition on it), you'll need to reboot to complete the upgrade. If the upgrade didn't work, then there's two scenarios that are most likely. If the disk has I/O errors, then Win2K will be unable to read it to update. Similarly, if you disconnect or replace every other dynamic disk while the computer is rebooting, then the upgrade won't work. The problem is that the Disk Management tool stores information about all dynamic disks on the other dynamic disks so that all disks can recognize each other. If it can't find any previously established dynamic disks when rebooting, then it can't upgrade the disk that isn't quite upgraded yet.

Understanding Dynamic Disks

You'll need to use dynamic disks if you want to use Win2K's software RAID protection. Read on for more information about how to create and delete RAID volumes and use them to make your Win2K system fault tolerant.

Creating a Dynamic Disk Volume

Creating a dynamic disk volume is much like creating a volume on a basic disk, but you'll have some more options depending on the number of dynamic disks you have available. The basic process goes like this:.

1. In the Disk Management tool, right-click unallocated space on any dynamic disk to open the context menu. Choose Create Volume.

2. You'll open the Create Volume Wizard. Click past the opening screen to the one shown in Figure 7.17. Pick a type of volume to create.

 NOTE   Not all volume types will always be available. If you have only a single dynamic disk with unallocated space, you'll only be able to create a simple volume. Two dynamic disks with unallocated space will permit you to create a stripe set, spanned volume, or mirror set. To create a stripe set with parity, at least three dynamic disks with unallocated space must be present.

FIGURE 7.17

Choose a type of dynamic volume to create.

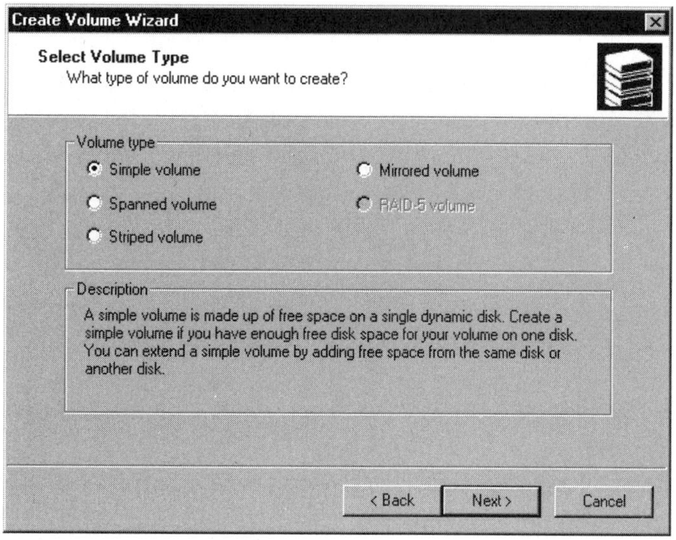

Create Volume Wizard

Select Volume Type
What type of volume do you want to create?

Volume type
- ⦿ Simple volume
- ○ Spanned volume
- ○ Striped volume
- ○ Mirrored volume
- ○ RAID-5 volume

Description
A simple volume is made up of free space on a single dynamic disk. Create a simple volume if you have enough free disk space for your volume on one disk. You can extend a simple volume by adding free space from the same disk or another disk.

< Back | Next > | Cancel

3. In the next screen, choose the disk or disks that you want the volume to be on. The currently selected disk will be in the list on the right-hand side (see Figure 7.18) and the available disks will be on the left-hand side. Select a disk and click the Add or Remove buttons to pick the disks you want the volume set to be on.

FIGURE 7.18

Choose the disks that should support the volume.

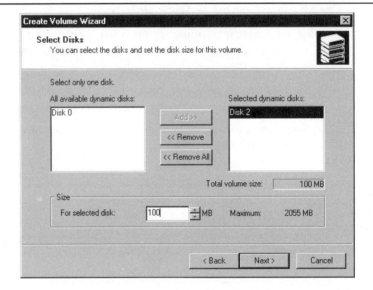

4. In the same screen of the wizard, pick the size you want the volume to be. By default, the new volume will be as large as possible, based on the amount of unallocated space available on the disks you've chosen. You can make it smaller than this size, down to 1MB, but you obviously can't make the volume bigger.

5. In the next screen of the wizard (see Figure 7.19), choose a drive letter or map the new volume to a path on an NTFS volume. Although you don't have to do either at this time, you will need to call the new volume *something* before you can use it.

6. Click to open the next screen of the wizard and choose a disk format for the new volume: NTFS, FAT32, or FAT. Again, as you can see in Figure 7.20, you don't have to format the volume while creating it, but you will need to format it before you can use it.

NOTE You can always perform a quick format on a volume (just wiping the volume and not checking for bad clusters), but file and folder compression—and other features such as disk quotas and file encryption—are only available for NTFS volumes.

FIGURE 7.19

Choose a drive letter
or mount the volume
to a drive path.

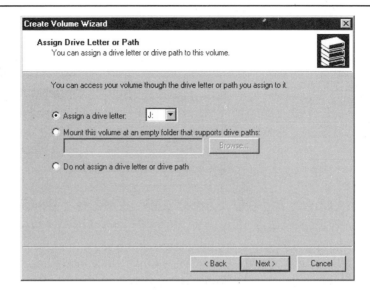

FIGURE 7.20

Format the new
volume.

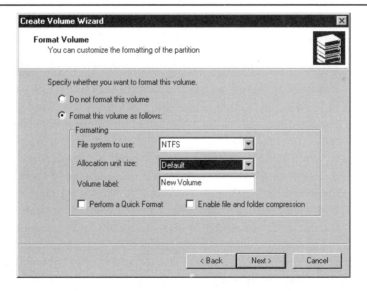

The final screen of the wizard displays the choices you've made so that you can go back and change them if need be. Otherwise, click Finish, and the new volume will be immediately accessible—no rebooting required.

Deleting a Dynamic Disk Volume

Deleting a dynamic disk volume is straightforward: right-click the volume to delete and pick Delete Volume from the context menu. You'll see a message like the one in

Figure 7.21, warning you that you're about to delete any data on that volume. Click Yes to continue deleting the volume, and it's instantly gone—no rebooting or further warnings required.

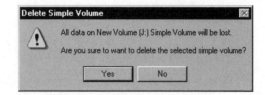

Converting a Dynamic Disk to a Basic Disk

If you mistakenly upgrade a basic disk to dynamic, all is not lost. You can reverse the process. The only catch is that you can't revert volumes on a dynamic disk to basic disk volumes, so the disk must be empty and unpartitioned for the conversion to work. If you've got volumes on the disk, then the Revert to Basic Disk option in the disk's context menu will be grayed out.

Assuming that the disk is empty, however, the process is simple. Right-click the gray area of the physical disk (all the way to the left in the Disk Management tool's display) and choose Revert to Basic Disk from the context menu. That's it.

Oops! Recovering from Temporary Disk Failures

If you accidentally switch off an externally mounted drive, or if the drive comes loose in the box, any volume sets or nonparity stripe sets that depended on that disk will be temporarily dead—reasonable, because for all practical purposes, one of its disks has failed. The missing disk will either not show up in the Disk Administrator at all (if you rebooted with the disk off) or will show up with a Missing note on it (see Figure 7.22).

However, all is not lost. If it's a simple matter of a loose cable or an accidentally flipped power switch, just reconnect the cable or switch the drive back on. After you've done so, right-click on the Disk Management tool's icon in the left-hand pane with the rest of the Computer Management tools and choose Rescan Disks. You'll see an informational dialog box telling you that the Disk Management tool is rescanning. When it's done, right-click the failed volume and choose Reactivate from the context menu. Win2K will caution you to run CHKDSK on the volume. Click OK, and your disk will appear as it was before and the volume set will again have a drive letter and be operational.

Well, maybe. This will *not* work unless you're restoring the drive that originally had part of the spanned volume or stripe set on it. If a disk is well and truly dead and you had to replace it, then you will not be able to recover the data in the volume set or nonparity stripe set.

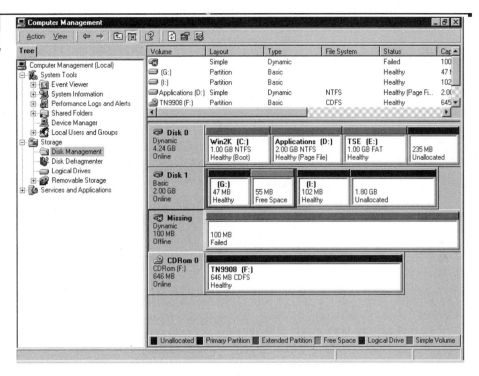

FIGURE 7.22

A dead drive in the Disk Management tool

Creating a Volume Set

I explained how to build any dynamic disk volume in the earlier section, "Creating a Dynamic Disk Volume." The only volume-set-specific parts to remember are these:

- Simple volume sets will only use space on one dynamic physical disk.
- Spanned volume sets may use space on from 2 to 32 dynamic physical disks.

Other than that, the process of creating a simple or spanned volume is now blessedly simple: pick the disks to place the volume on, pick a size for the volume, assign the volume a drive letter or mount it to a path, format it, and you're done.

Enlarging a Volume Set

If it turns out that your NTFS-formatted volume set is smaller than you need it to be, it's not necessary to delete it and re-create it from scratch. Instead, you can *extend* it by adding areas of free space to its volume.

NOTE You cannot make a volume set *smaller*. To do that, you must delete the volume set and create it again.

To extend an existing simple or spanned volume set, follow these steps:

1. Right-click the simple or spanned volume set you want to expand and choose Extend Volume from the context menu. You'll start up the Extend Volume Wizard.

2. Click through the initial page of the wizard to display the screen shown in Figure 7.23. From here, choose the disk or disks onto which you want to extend the volume set. Only dynamic disks with unallocated space will be available.

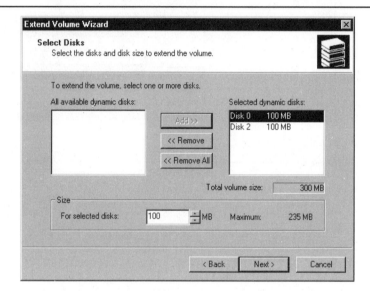

3. In this same screen, choose the amount of unallocated disk space you want to add from the new disk. The Disk Management tool will display both the amount of space that you're adding and the total size of the newly extended volume.

4. The final screen of the wizard will show the choices you've made. Review them and either click Back to make changes or Finish to extend the volume set.

The volume set is now the larger size that you specified, and all the area in it will have the same drive letter. The unallocated space that you added is automatically formatted to the same file system as the rest of the volume set—NTFS.

There are a few catches to extending volume sets:

- You can only extend NTFS volumes, so you'll need to reformat or convert FAT or FAT32 volumes to NTFS before you can extend them.

- Although converting a basic disk to dynamic makes any partitions on the disk become simple volumes, you cannot extend *those* simple volumes. Only volumes originally created on a dynamic disk are extensible. (Any volumes you create on that disk after it's converted to dynamic are extensible, however.)

- Again, you cannot use this procedure to make a volume set smaller. To do that, you need to delete the volume set and create a new one.

- You cannot combine two volume sets, nor can you add a logical drive to a volume set.

Creating a Stripe Set

Creating a stripe set without parity is just like creating any other dynamic disk volume: make sure that you've got at least two dynamic disks with unallocated space available, right-click an area of unallocated space, and choose Create Volume to start the wizard. In the first screen that includes any data, make sure that you've selected the Striped Volume type as shown in Figure 7.24.

FIGURE 7.24

Choose striped volumes to decrease disk access times.

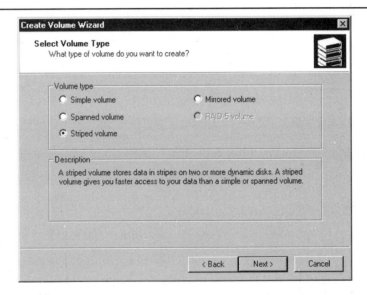

From here, the volume creation process is the same for all dynamic volumes, as described in the earlier section, "Creating a Dynamic Disk Volume." Just keep in mind the following:

- Stripe sets must include at least 2 and no more than 32 physical disks.

- Each stripe will be the same size. That is, if the largest area of unallocated space on Disk 0 is 50MB, then the largest stripe set you can create on three disks is 150MB, even if Disk 1 and Disk 2 each have, say, 200MB of unallocated space.

- Stripe sets do not include any parity information, so the volume size the wizard lists is an actual reflection of the amount of data you can store on the striped volume.

If anything happens to any member disk of your nonparity stripe set, all the data in the set is lost. It doesn't hurt the other disks in the stripe set, but it means that the data in the stripe set itself is unavailable.

Deleting a Stripe Set

If you make a stripe set too small or too big, there's no way to resize it. You'll need to delete the stripe set and start over. Just right-click it and choose Delete Volume from the context menu. As always, you'll be prompted to confirm that you want to delete the volume, and when you do, the stripe set will disappear.

Establishing a Mirror Set

To create a mirror set, you can either start from unallocated space on a dynamic disk or mirror an existing simple volume.

 NOTE   You cannot mirror a volume on a basic disk. The only mirrors that Win2K supports on basic disks are those resulting from upgrading NT to Win2K.

To create a mirror set from unallocated space, right-click an area and choose Create Volume from the context menu. Go through the wizard as described in the earlier section, "Creating a Dynamic Disk Volume," noting the following:

- You'll need two dynamic disks with unallocated space on them.
- Both halves of the mirror set will be the same size. You cannot mirror a large volume with a smaller one.
- A mirror set can use any disk format: NTFS, FAT32, or FAT.

To mirror an existing simple volume, right-click the volume and choose Add Mirror from the context menu. You'll open a dialog box like the one in Figure 7.25, asking you to select the disk that you want to create the mirror on. Click the disk so that it's highlighted—this won't work otherwise.

 NOTE   Only dynamic disks with areas of unallocated space big enough to mirror the selected volume will be listed. If no area of unallocated space is big enough, then you won't have the option of mirroring the volume.

Click the Add Mirror button, and the Disk Management tool will create in the unallocated space a partition that's the same size as the simple volume being mirrored. The partition will be formatted to match the file system on the original volume, and the redundant data will be regenerated. (Depending on the size of the volume you're mirroring, this may take a while. It's not a fast process on large volumes.)

FIGURE 7.25

Choose a dynamic disk to hold the mirrored data.

The new partition will have the same drive letter or mounted path as the one you mirrored and will be available immediately—no reboot required.

Getting Rid of a Mirror Set

If you don't want to maintain redundant information anymore, then the mirror set is history. *How* you get rid of it depends heavily on what you're trying to do:

- If you don't want any of the information in the mirror set anymore, then *delete* the mirror set.
- If you only want to keep half the data in the mirror set (either the original volume or the redundant half), then *remove* the mirror set.
- If you want to keep all the data—original and redundant—but don't want to mirror it anymore, then *break* the mirror set.

You don't have to delete, remove, *or* break a mirror set if half of it fails—it just won't be fault tolerant until you replace the failed disk and establish a mirror again.

Deleting a Mirror Set   To destroy all data in a mirror set, right-click the mirrored volume (normally displayed with a dark-red stripe) and choose Delete Volume from the context menu. The Disk Management tool will ask you if you're sure; click Yes to continue deleting the mirror.

This will delete both halves of the mirror set—and destroy the original data—so only do this if you've backed up. (Strictly speaking, you shouldn't mess around with your data unless you've backed up anyway, but this time you'll *definitely* delete it.)

Removing a Mirror Set   If one of the disks dies, the data on the still-functioning disk will still be accessible, but it won't be protected anymore (see Figure 7.26).

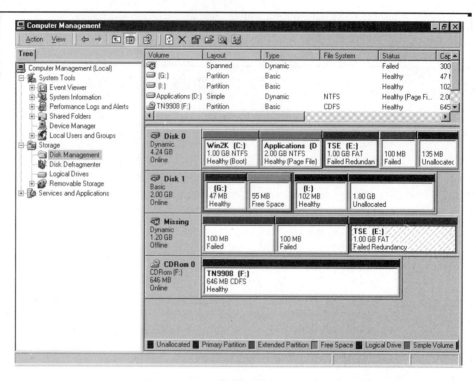

To protect it again, you'll need to remirror the volume. However, you can't *remirror* a mirrored volume, and even if half of it's dead, the mirror itself is still valid. To start protecting the data again, you'll need to get rid of the original mirror.

To delete one half of the redundant data and stop mirroring, remove the mirror set. Right-click the mirror set and choose Remove Mirror from the context menu. You'll see a dialog box like the one in Figure 7.27.

FIGURE 7.27

Pick a half of the mirror set to remove.

Be sure to pick the half with the data that you *don't* want to keep. When you click Remove Mirror, the Disk Management tool will ask if you're sure. Click Yes to continue. The partition you selected will be deleted. The mirrored partition that you *didn't* select will become a simple volume. Its data will not be affected.

Breaking a Mirror Set   If both halves of the disk are still working, but you don't want to mirror the data anymore, then you can break the mirror set and thus make the two volumes act again like simple volumes.

To break the mirror set, right-click a mirror set that's still functioning (if the mirrored volume has failed, then you'll have to remove the mirror, not break it) and choose Break Mirror from the context menu. You'll see a message asking if you're sure and warning you that your data will no longer be fault tolerant. Click Yes to continue.

NOTE   If an application is referencing data stored in the mirror set—even if its contents are just displayed in Explorer—you'll see an error message telling you that the volume is in use. Stop using the mirror set before breaking it if you want to copy the data currently being viewed to both halves of the mirrored volume.

The two halves of the mirrored volume will now become simple volumes. One half will retain the drive letter that had belonged to the mirrored volume, and the other will have the next available drive letter.

Mirroring Considerations

As you're deciding whether or not to protect your data by mirroring it, keep these things in mind:

- Mirroring to drives run from the same drive controller does not protect your data from drive controller failure. If any kind of controller failure occurs, you won't be able to get to the backup copy of your data unless you are mirroring to a disk run from a separate controller.

- For higher disk-read performance and greater fault tolerance, use a separate disk controller for each half of a mirror set.

- Disk mirroring effectively cuts your available disk space in half. Don't forget that as you figure out how much drive space you've got on the server.

- Disk mirroring has a low initial cost, since you must purchase only one extra drive to achieve fault tolerance, but a higher long-term cost due to the amount of room your redundant information takes up.

- Disk mirroring will slow down writes, as the data must be written in two places every time, but will speed up reads, as the I/O controller has two places to read information from. For multiuser environments (like the network you're using Win2K Server for), it gets the best performance of all the fault-tolerant RAID levels.

- You cannot extend a mirrored volume. The size it is when mirrored is the size it will stay.

Establishing RAID 5 Volumes

To create a RAID 5 volume on a computer, follow these steps:

1. Right-click any area of unallocated space on any dynamic physical disk. From the pop-up menu that appears, choose Create Volume.

2. Click through the opening screen of the wizard. On the first real screen, select RAID-5 Volume as shown in Figure 7.28.

FIGURE 7.28

Choose RAID 5 to establish a stripe set with parity.

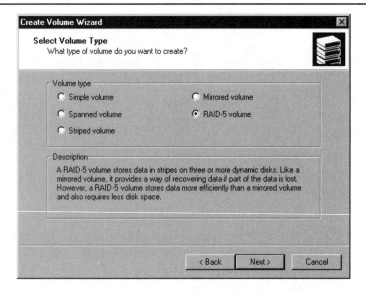

3. In the next screen (see Figure 7.29), choose at least three disks that you want to be involved in the stripe set. The disk you started with (the one with the area of unallocated space) will be in the right-hand column of disks to use; the other dynamic disks with unallocated space will be on the left-hand side. In the figure, I've selected three disks to use. To add a disk to the stripe set, select it in the list of all available dynamic disks and click the Add button. To remove a disk from the stripe set, select it in the list of selected dynamic disks and click the Remove button.

4. In this same dialog box, pick the size of the stripe set. In the Size box, the Disk Management tool will display the maximum size of the stripes based on the unallocated space on the chosen drives. You can go smaller than this amount, but not bigger. The value in Total Volume Size will reflect the total amount of room available for *data*, not the total space in the stripe set. Since 1/*n* of the space in a RAID 5 volume (where *n* is the number of disks in the set) is used for parity information, the more disks you have, the larger percentage of room for data you'll get.

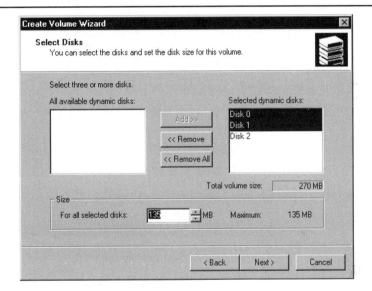

FIGURE 7.29

Select the disks to be in the stripe set and the size of the set.

NOTE   The amount of unallocated space on each physical disk will determine the size of the stripe set. Each section of the stripe set must be the same size, so if one disk has only 50MB unallocated space on it, then the entire stripe set can be no more than 150MB, even if the other disks have 500MB of unallocated space each. That said, not all the unallocated space must be contiguous. If a disk has one chunk of unallocated space that's 50MB and another that's 100MB, then the disk can contribute to the RAID 5 150MB Volume.

5. Choose to assign a drive letter or mount the volume to an NTFS path (see Figure 7.30).

6. Choose whether or not to format the new volume right away and the disk format you want to use (see Figure 7.31).

7. Review your choices, backing up to change any of them or clicking Finish to create the RAID 5 volume.

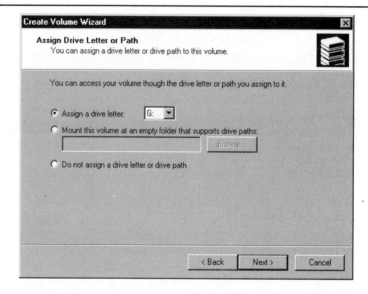

FIGURE 7.30

Assign the volume a drive letter or path.

FIGURE 7.31

Pick a format for the volume.

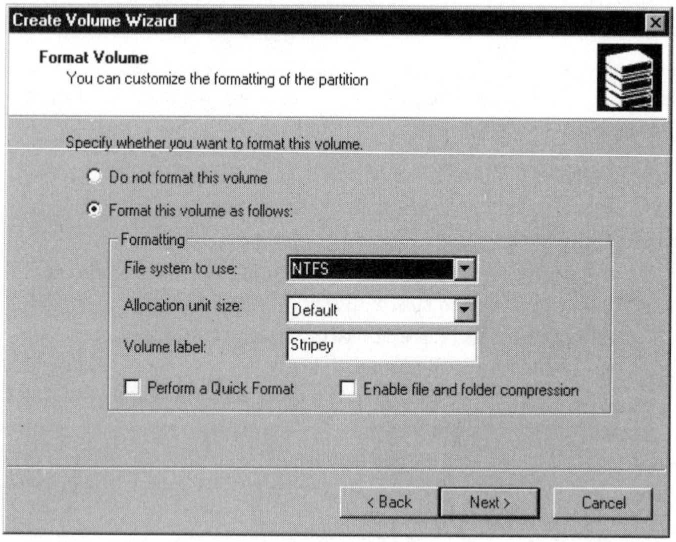

Win2K will grind away for a few minutes, setting up the new stripe set. When it's done, the RAID 5 volume will be immediately ready to use.

Retrieving Data from a Failed Stripe Set

If an unrecoverable error to part of a striped set with parity occurs, you'll still be able to read and write to the volume, but the volume will be marked Failed in the Disk Management tool (see Figure 7.32). This is a warning: lose one more disk, and the data will be inaccessible and unrecoverable.

To make the volume fault tolerant again, replace the failed disk, rescan the disks, and reactivate the disk. If this doesn't make the volume healthy again, then right-click on the stripe set and choose Reactivate Volume. The computer will chug away for a couple of minutes, rebuilding the missing data with the parity information on the remaining disks, and the stripe set will be back in one piece. You don't have to reboot.

FIGURE 7.32

You can still read and write to failed RAID 5 volumes, but they're no longer fault tolerant.

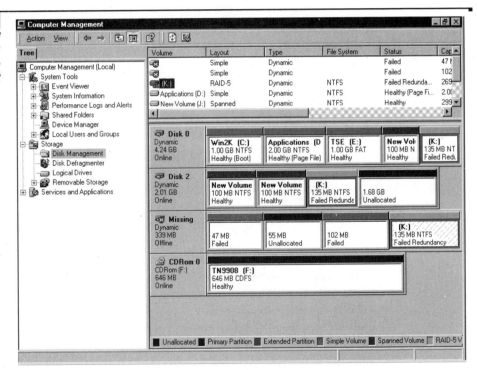

Deleting a Stripe Set

Deleting a stripe set is quite simple. Right-click on the volume and choose Delete Volume from the context menu. You'll see the usual warning message telling you that you're about to delete the volume and lose data; click through it, and the stripe set will again be unallocated space. Don't forget that deleting a stripe set destroys the data in it—even the parity information.

Things to Remember about Disk Striping with Parity

Keep these things in mind when it comes to disk striping with parity:

- Striping with parity has a greater initial hardware cost than disk mirroring does (it requires a minimum of three disks rather than two). Nevertheless, it allows you to get more use out of your disk space.

- You cannot make a stripe set bigger (even if more unallocated space becomes available) or extend it to another physical disk.

- Although you can access the information in a stripe set even after one of the members has failed, you should regenerate the set as quickly as possible. Win2K Server striping cannot cope with more than one error in the set, so you're sunk if anything happens to the unregenerated stripe set.

- Striping with parity places greater demands on your system than disk mirroring, so add more memory to the server if you plan to use disk striping.

- If you have fewer than three dynamic disks on your server with unallocated space, you cannot make stripe sets with parity.

Hardware or Software RAID?

You've seen here that you can install a bunch of drives on your computer and arrange them into RAID sets and mirror sets. That all sounds good from a fault-tolerance point of view since the probability that you'll actually lose any of your data is considerably reduced. Consider what you'll do when drive damage does occur, though.

You've got a mission-critical system up and running and one of the four drives in a stripe set with parity goes to its maker. Your next move is to bring the server down, replace the bad drive with a new good one, and then reintegrate that new one into the stripe set in order to recover the data.

Sounds good, until you really think about it. First of all, you've got to bring down this mission-critical server while you take out the old drive, install a new drive, and put the stripe set back together. We're not talking about a two-minute fix here. In contrast, you could buy a *hardware* RAID system, a box containing several drives that act as one and that look to the Win2K system as just one drive. An external RAID box costs a bit more, but a hardware-based RAID system can rebuild itself faster than can Win2K software. And best of all, most hardware-based RAID systems allow you to "hot-swap" the bad drive—that is, to replace the bad drive without bringing down the server. So if your application is *truly* mission critical, think about investing in RAID hardware. Of course, if you can't afford it, Win2K's solution is a heck of a lot better than nothing.

Performing Disk Maintenance

The job doesn't end with setting up disk volumes on the physical disks. To keep those volumes working well, you'll need to perform some routine maintenance on them.

Background: Disk Geometry and File Formats

Before getting into disk formats, disk defragmenting, and CHKDSK, let's take a quick look at the relationship between Win2K and hard disks and how this relationship makes all these tasks necessary.

A hard drive is actually not one but several disks called *platters*. Each platter is divided two ways: pie-shaped wedges and concentric circles. The pieces defined by the intersection of these divisions are called *sectors* and are the physical units of storage on a hard disk. Each sector on a disk is normally 512 bytes in size.

Win2K doesn't know a sector from a hole in the ground. To let its file storage component store and retrieve data on the disk, Win2K must impose some kind of logical structure over the physical structure of the disk. That logical structure is called a *disk format*, and it groups sectors together in logical units called *clusters*. The number of sectors in a cluster varies, depending on the size of the disk partition (all other things being equal, larger disks typically have more sectors per cluster) and the disk format you're talking about. All clusters have at least one sector in any file system that Win2K supports.

A cluster is the smallest organizational unit that the file system can recognize, which means that you can only store one file per cluster. If a file is too big to fit into a single cluster, then it will be spread over multiple clusters, as close together as possible. If a file is smaller than the cluster size, it will still fit into a single cluster and any unused space in that cluster goes to waste. Larger clusters reduce the likelihood that files will get fragmented, but smaller clusters generally use file space more efficiently.

Sound irrelevant? Trust me: you'll need this background on clusters and sectors when it comes to performing basic disk maintenance.

Formatting Disks

Win2K is the first generation of NT sensible enough to let you format volumes while creating them with the Disk Management tool. However, you can still format volumes from Explorer or from the command prompt, as you needed to do in NT 4.

Disk Formats Supported in Win2K

Win2K supports three disk formats: the old FAT format that includes long filename support, the FAT32 file format introduced with Windows 95 OSR 2, and an updated version of the NTFS format that's been around since NT 3.1.

FAT and FAT32   FAT is the granddaddy of Microsoft file systems, the one that all Microsoft operating systems support. It uses a simple catalog called the *file allocation table* to note which cluster or clusters a file is stored in. If a file's stored in more than one cluster, then the cluster includes a pointer to the next cluster used for that file until the final cluster includes an End of File marker.

FAT and FAT32 have a great deal in common: a simple set of attributes that note creation and access dates and the settings of the hidden, archive, system, and read-only bits. The main difference between FAT and FAT32 lies in their relative cluster sizes. FAT is actually FAT16, which means that it uses a 16-bit addressing scheme that allows it to address up to 2 to the 16th power (65,536) clusters. To address very large volumes that include a lot of sectors, therefore, FAT must organize those sectors into very large clusters and can't format a volume larger than 4GB.

FAT32, in contrast, has 32-bit addresses, which means that it can name up to 2 to the 32nd power (4,294,967,296) clusters. Because of this, FAT32 can use much smaller clusters even on large volumes; on volumes up to 8GB, it uses 4KB clusters. Other than this difference, however, it's the same as FAT.

The main reasons FAT and FAT32 are included with Win2K is for backward compatibility with other operating systems. Most often, the advanced features of NTFS will make it your first choice for a server file system.

NTFS   NTFS is the filing system especially designed for use with Win2K and NT Server:

- NTFS is designed for system security (that is, setting file permissions); FAT and FAT32 are not. (You can, however, restrict access to *shared* directories even when using FAT.) To learn how file permissions work, see Chapter 9.

- Only NTFS volumes support Win2K file encryption, disk quotas, volume mounting, and data compression. Only volumes formatted with NTFS may be extended.

- NTFS keeps a log of activities in order to be able to restore the disk after a power failure or other interruption. It won't replace *data* on the NTFS drives, but if it's interrupted in the middle of a write procedure, it will restore the volume structure. This prevents the disk's volume from becoming corrupted.

Win2K uses a later version of NTFS than NT 4 does. Not only that, if you install Win2K onto a machine with NT 4 already installed, Win2K will automatically upgrade the NTFS volumes to NTFS 5, rendering those volumes unreadable by NT 4.

The good news is that NT 4 can read and write to the latter version of NTFS if you install Service Pack 4 or later. To set up a dual-boot system, install NT 4, install SP4, then install Win2K. That way, when NTFS volumes exist, you'll never have a time when you can't read the NTFS volumes from NT 4.

Naming Conventions for Long Filenames

All disk formats in Win2K support long filenames. Even FAT uses the extensions that make this possible. Filenames in Win2K can be up to 256 characters long with the extension, including spaces and separating periods. You can use any upper- or lower-case character in a long or short filename except the following, which have special significance to Win2K:

```
? " / \ < > * | :
```

Even though NTFS supports long filenames, it maintains its compatibility with DOS by automatically generating a conventional FAT filename for every file. The process doesn't work in reverse, however, so don't save a file with a long filename when working with an application that doesn't support long filenames, or else you'll only have the abbreviated name to work with. If you do, the application that doesn't like long names will save the file to the short name and erase all memory of the long filename. The data won't be erased, however; only the descriptive filename is affected.

When converting a long filename to the short format, Win2K does the following:

- Removes spaces.
- Removes periods, all except the last one that is followed by a character—this period is assumed to herald the beginning of the file extension.
- Removes any characters not allowed in DOS names and converts them to underscores.
- Converts the name to six characters, with a tilde (~) and a number attached to the end.
- Truncates the extension to three characters.

Given how long filenames convert to 8.3 conventions, you may want to keep that in mind when using long filenames so that your filenames make sense in both versions. For example, you could name a file PRSNLLET-Personal letters file.DOC, so that the shortened name would be PRSNLL~1.DOC.

You can't format a floppy to NTFS format. There's a good reason for this: the NTFS file structure is complex so that finding data on large disks is fast and easy, but it takes up more room than a floppy disk can supply. Floppy disks don't need NTFS.

However, you can create files with long names on a floppy since the Win2K version of FAT supports 256-character filenames. Win2K keeps two names for floppy files, the long name that you originally assigned and a truncated 8.3 name. DOS sees the shorter 8.3 name, however, making it possible for you to work with files that have long names under Win2K but short names under DOS.

Which File System?   Which file system should you use? Table 7.1 gives you an at-a-glance comparison of NTFS and the FAT file systems.

TABLE 7.1:   COMPARING NTFS AND FAT IN WIN2K

	NTFS	FAT32	FAT
Filename length	256 characters	256 characters	256 characters under Windows 9x, NT, Win2K; 8.3 under DOS
File attributes	Extended	Limited	Limited
Associated operating system	Win2K and Windows NT	Win2K, Win98, Win95 OSR2	DOS
Organization	Tree structure	Centrally located menu	Centrally located menu
Software RAID support?	Yes	Yes	Yes
Accessible when you boot the computer from a DOS floppy?	No	No	Yes
Maximum volume size supported	1024GB	32GB (and will not format volumes smaller than 512MB)	4GB
Cluster size on a 1GB volume	2KB	4KB	32KB

When *shouldn't* you use NTFS? The only times NTFS won't work for you is when you need to support other operating systems on the same computer as Win2K. FAT is widely supported by other operating systems, so you should use it on any volume that you'll need to have accessible to other operating systems on the same computer. (You'll also need to put those volumes on a basic disk, recall.) The exception to this is Windows 95 OSR 2 or Windows 98. FAT32 is more space efficient than FAT, so you should use FAT32 on any volumes that need to be locally accessible to both Win2K and Windows 9x. FAT32 volumes are *not* readable by NT 4 without the FAT32 support available for purchase from www.sysinternals.com, so if you need to keep data for NT 4, Windows 9x, and Win2K, you should use FAT.

Leave a FAT Partition?

In *Mastering Windows NT Server 4*, I recommended that you format the system partition with FAT. If you did this, then you could copy the installation files from the CD to the system partition. That way, if you needed to reinstall, you could reinstall from the hard disk after booting from a floppy instead of using the slower CD.

The only trouble with keeping all system files and said installation files on a FAT-formatted partition is that doing so is enormously wasteful of disk space. Like many of the rest of us, Win2K/NT has gotten fatter as it's gotten older. The \I386 folder on the Win2K CD is 327MB. The NTFS-formatted Win2K system directory on one Win2K server—*not* including the \I386 folder—is about 850MB. (For comparison, the FAT-formatted system partition on an installation of Windows NT 4, Terminal Server Edition I've got is 427MB, not including any installation files.) To be pretty sure I wouldn't run out of room, I'd need a system partition at least 2GB in size. You can format a 2GB partition with FAT—barely. That's the largest amount of disk space that FAT can "see" under Win2K. But doing so is horribly wasteful. As discussed earlier in this chapter, the FAT file system is wasteful of space on large partitions because it organizes the disk into very large clusters. 2GB might not be enough to store all the system files.

Thankfully for the bloat problem, a new tool in Win2K called the Recovery Console makes formatting the system drive with FAT no longer necessary. I'll go into the Recovery Console in detail in Chapter 21, but the short version is that it's an NTFS-compatible command-line recovery tool that you can use to get at your system directory and make repairs. You can get to this tool from the Win2K Setup program, so as long as you have the original CD or the Setup boot floppies, you can get to the Recovery Console and fix things.

FAT system partition or no, it's still a good idea to copy the installation files to the hard disk. That way, you've always got an easily accessible copy of them when you need them to install a new driver or service.

Using the Formatting Tools

Formatting a volume outside of the Disk Management tool is simple. If you access an unformatted volume (one you created but didn't format) from Explorer, you'll see a message telling you that the disk (volume, really, but it says "disk") isn't formatted and asking if you want to format the volume now. Click Yes to format the disk, and you'll open the Format dialog box in Figure 7.33.

FIGURE 7.33

*Choose a file system
for the new volume.*

In the Format dialog box, choose the file system that you want to use on the partition: FAT (the default, for some reason), FAT32, or NTFS. If you format with NTFS, you can even change the cluster size—but don't do that. The default works fine for most uses. For best security, make all of your partitions NTFS, which is locally accessible to Win2K and to NT with Service Pack 4 or later installed and accessible to any operating system across the network. The only exception to this is if you happen to be running a dual-boot machine, in which case you'll need to use a file system that both operating systems can understand. The Recovery Console (discussed in Chapter 21) makes it no longer necessary to format the system partition with FAT for recovery purposes.

Formatting with Win2K is a little different from formatting in NT. First, fault-tolerant volumes can use any format that Win2K supports, not just NTFS. (That said, you'd be smart to use NTFS anyway. NTFS's transaction logging, which makes the disk essentially invulnerable to volume corruption that can render a disk inaccessible, is a good idea for any fault-tolerant volume. FAT32 and FAT don't support Win2K disk compression, either, and they're more inefficient in their use of disk space than NTFS is.) Second, you can use the Quick Format option to format the volume on any new volume, even fault-tolerant volumes, which you could not do with NT 4.

Click the Start button to begin the format. A dialog box will appear and ask you to confirm the format; click OK and the format operation will begin. A dialog box will show you the process of the format. Be warned: although the dialog box has a Cancel button, canceling the format won't necessarily restore the partition to its original condition.

If you're addicted to the command prompt, you can still use it to format disks. To do so, open the Command Prompt located in the Accessories folder and type the following:

```
format driveletter: /fs:filesystem
```

Driveletter is, of course, the drive letter of the logical drive, and *filesystem* is FAT, FAT32, or NTFS. For example, to format a newly created drive E: as NTFS, you would type **format e: /fs:ntfs**. You must specify a file format—there's no default.

Converting FAT to NTFS

If you have FAT or FAT32 volumes on your disk that you'd like to be NTFS, you don't have to back up their data, reformat the disks, and then start over. Instead, you can use the CONVERT command-prompt utility. Its format is simple:

```
convert driveletter: /fs:ntfs
```

So, for example, to convert drive P: to NTFS, you'd type **convert p: /fs:ntfs**. You'd see output like the following:

```
The type of the file system is FAT32.
Determining disk space required for filesystem conversion
Total disk space:              51200 KB.
Free space on volume:          50395 KB.
Space required for conversion:  2303 KB.
Converting file system
Conversion complete
```

Notice that you must have a certain amount of free space (in this case, *free space* means unused space in the partition) on the volume to convert it. That's a place to store data while the clusters are being reorganized. If you don't have enough free space, then you can't convert the volume. Thus, it's a good idea to convert volumes before they get too full.

You cannot convert to any file system other than NTFS, and you cannot reverse the process. You also can't convert the current drive, which means that you cannot convert the system drive to NTFS without rebooting. The conversion will happen during the reboot process.

Defragmenting Disks

One of the simpler ways you can improve disk performance is to regularly defragment disks that need it, thus putting all the parts of each file into the same place on the disk for easier retrieval.

Defragmenting? Recall that each cluster can hold only one file at most, and that if a file is too big to fit into a single cluster, then the remaining file data will go in the next available cluster, and the next, and the next, until the file is completely stored. Each cluster that the file's stored in contains a pointer to the next cluster where that file's data is contained until you get to the last cluster containing data for that file. When you open a file stored on disk, the file system driver looks in the file catalog at the top of the disk and finds the clusters that the file is stored in. It then pulls the data from those clusters and reads it into memory.

How Disks Get Fragmented and Why You Care

When a disk is new, the available clusters are all next to each other, so it doesn't matter much if a file is distributed among several clusters. As you use a disk, however, this is likely to change. Create and delete files, though, and clusters get freed up unevenly. And the file system driver doesn't look for a run of clusters big enough to store all a file's data in one place; it just stores data in the first clusters available. If clusters 1–3, 10, and 15–100 are available, File A needing 5 clusters will go into clusters 1–3, 10, 15, and 16, not into clusters 15–20. When a file is spread among several noncontiguous clusters, it's said to be *fragmented*.

 NOTE Because large FAT volumes use much bigger clusters than large NTFS volumes, NTFS volumes are more likely to be fragmented. This isn't an argument in favor of using FAT–those larger clusters also imply more wasted disk space, and you don't get the other benefits of NTFS–but an observation about how clusters work.

Data is stored in the cluster it's originally put in—if a more convenient cluster becomes available, then the data isn't moved. Even if clusters 4–9 become free when a file is deleted, File A will keep using the same clusters it started with.

This isn't terrible. You'll still get all the data from the file, even if the file is fragmented. However, it will take a little longer to open fragmented files, and in case of serious disk errors, it's harder to recover badly fragmented files than ones stored in contiguous clusters. A very fragmented system disk can actually cause Win2K to crash. Therefore, it's a good idea to keep your disks defragmented.

Using the Defragmenting Tool

Win2K comes with a defragmenting tool. To defragment a volume or see whether it needs to be defragmented, right-click the volume in Explorer and open the volume's property sheet. Turn to the Tools tab that's shown in Figure 7.34.

Click the Defragment Now button to open the screen shown in Figure 7.35.

Notice that only local volumes are listed. You can't defragment volumes across the network.

First, see whether the disk needs to be defragmented at all. Highlight the volume in the list and click the Analyze button. The defragmenter will chug away for a minute (it's pretty fast—a 2GB volume took only a few seconds to analyze) and then display its recommendation (see Figure 7.36).

FIGURE 7.34

The Tools tab contains all disk maintenance tools.

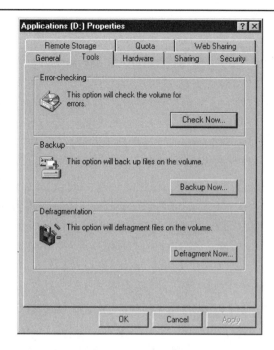

FIGURE 7.35

The Disk Defragmenter shows all logical volumes on the computer.

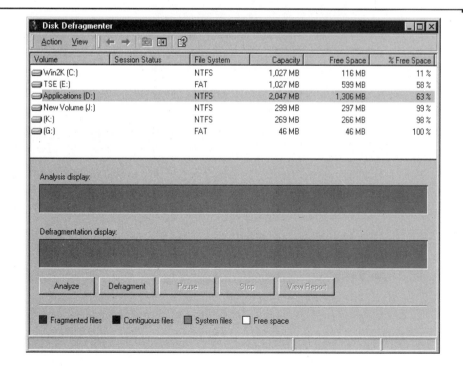

FIGURE 7.36

Analyze disks before defragmenting them.

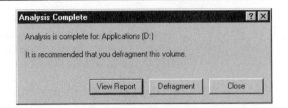

If you want to see more information about how fragmented your disk is, click the View Report button to open the dialog box shown in Figure 7.37.

FIGURE 7.37

View the report to see how badly the disk is fragmented.

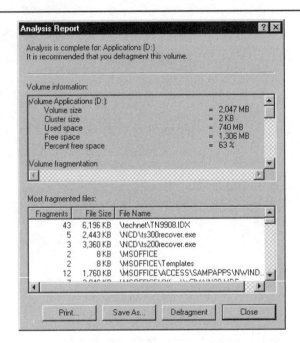

What are you looking at here? The top part of this dialog box displays six types of information:

- Basic volume statistics
- Volume fragmentation
- File fragmentation
- Pagefile fragmentation
- Folder fragmentation
- Directory table fragmentation

Most of the information about the volume should be pretty simple to figure out: the volume size is the size of the partition, the cluster size is the size of each logical storage unit on the drive (in this case, 2KB, or 4 sectors), and the rest of the section describes how much space on the disk is currently used, how much is free, and what the percentage of free space is.

The Volume Fragmentation section below the Volume Information section is a little more relevant to the question of how much file reads are delayed, describing the status of the files themselves. The total fragmentation describes how fragmented the entire disk is; the file fragmentation how fragmented the used parts of the disk are (that is, the proportion of files that are fragmented), and the free space fragmentation describes how fragmented the unused space on the disk is. Free space fragmentation matters when it comes to creating new files—the more fragmented the unused space, the more likely it is that new files will be fragmented too.

File Fragmentation gives you file-level fragmentation information. This area lists the total number of files on disk, the average size of a file, the total fragments, and the average number of fragments per file. Ideally, the value for fragments per file should be as close to 1.00 as possible, as that number indicates that all files are contiguous. In this example, the ratio is 2.09, which indicates that files are, on average, fragmented into two pieces. The Most Fragmented Files window at the bottom of this dialog box gives you more specifics about which files are most fragmented, but you don't need to worry about this except if you're interested in comparing the "before" and "after" results.

 TIP If you *are* interested in comparing the "before" and "after" readings, click the Save As button to save the entire fragmentation report as a text file.

The rest of the information shows fragmentation for specific parts of the disk volume structure so you can see just how fragmented the pagefile and directory structure are.

That's the current status of your volume. To fix it, close any files (including application files) using the fragmented volume, then click the Defragment button. The tool will start reorganizing the files on the disk to put them into contiguous clusters. Defragmenting the disk will *not* free up space on the disk, but it will group all free space together to allow it to be used more efficiently.

 NOTE You can defragment a volume with open files, but it will take much less time if you close all files first. This makes it difficult to defragment the system volume.

By the way—defragment your disks before they get too full. The Disk Defragmenter requires 15 percent of free volume space to store data that it's rearranging. If the volume is too full, you'll need to remove files or extend the volume before you can defragment it.

Using Chkdsk

File data is stored in clusters. If a file is stored in more than one cluster, then each cluster the file's stored in contains a pointer to the next cluster holding file data. If those pointers are lost, you can't pull up the entire file from disk.

NTFS's transaction logging prevents this from happening. Each NTFS volume maintains a *transaction log* of all proposed changes to the volume structure, checking off—*committing*—each change as it's completed and only then. When you restart the system, NTFS inspects the transaction log and rolls the state of the disk back to the last committed change. Basically, it's similar to the Last Known Good option that you can choose on startup to restore your server to its status at the last successful boot, except that transaction logging and rollback is automatic. Notice that transaction logging works only for *system* data, not for user data. If the disk failed in the middle of a write action, then the data that was supposed to be written to disk is lost. However, the volume structure of the disk will be all right. Any data already written to disk will be recoverable.

FAT and FAT32 do not have transaction logging. If the disk fails—perhaps due to a kicked power cord—before a write action is completed and you restart the disk, there's no record of the last valid disk structure. You may need to run chkdsk to check the pointers used in the file allocation table. This isn't to say that there's never any need to run chkdsk on an NTFS volume—NTFS protects the integrity of file system data, or *metadata*, not user data. You can use the command-line version of the tool to edit the size of the transaction log or to check the disk for bad sectors (sectors to which the file system shouldn't write because they're damaged and might not read properly). Read on to learn more about what chkdsk is doing and how to use the graphical and command-line versions.

What Is Chkdsk Doing?

Let's take a look at how chkdsk works on an NTFS volume. When you run chkdsk, you're telling the tool to make three passes over the specified drive to examine the structure of the metadata on the disk—again, that's the data describing how user data is organized on the disk. Metadata tells the file system what files are stored in which clusters, how many clusters are free and where they are, and what clusters contain bad sectors. In addition, it provides pointers to files.

During chkdsk's first pass over the selected drive, it scans each file's record in the Master File Table (MFT). It examines each file's record for consistency and lists all the file records in use and which clusters those file records are stored in. It then compares this record with the drive bitmap stored in the MFT. Any discrepancies between the two are noted in chkdsk's output.

During the second pass, chkdsk checks the drive's directory structure. It makes sure that each index record in the MFT corresponds to an actual directory on the drive and that each file's record in the MFT corresponds to a file stored somewhere in the volume. Chkdsk also makes sure that all time and date stamps for all files and directories are up-to-date. Finally, it makes sure that no files with an MFT entry but no existence in any directory are present on the volume. If the MFT entry is complete, the file can usually be restored to the directory where it should be kept.

The third pass of chkdsk is for checking the integrity of the security descriptors for each file and directory object on the NTFS volume. During this pass, chkdsk makes sure that all security settings are consistent. It does not check the security settings to make sure that they're appropriate to a particular folder or even to make sure that the group or user account named exists. The security pass of chkdsk simply makes sure that, assuming all security information is correct, the security settings for the files and directory objects in the volume will work.

The final and optional pass of chkdsk tests the sectors in the volume reserved for user data (the metadata sectors are always checked) to see whether all of them can be read from and written to correctly. If chkdsk finds a bad sector, then it marks the placement of this sector in the volume report. If the sector was part of a cluster that was being used, chkdsk will regenerate and move the data to a new cluster that contains only good sectors if the volume is fault tolerant or fill the bad sector with a string that means "no data should be stored here." As you can see, the data in the bad sector won't be recovered unless there's some redundant data to copy it from, but at least the file system won't store more data in the cluster containing the bad sector.

How long does this process take? Depends on the size of the volume, the depth of the check, and what else the computer is doing during the check. Chkdsk is extremely CPU and disk intensive, and if it must contend with other processes for CPU time, then the check will necessarily take longer. The best rule of thumb is that, if you can avoid it, you shouldn't run the disk checker on a computer that it actively trying to do something else. In any case, you can't run chkdsk on a volume that currently has files open. If you attempt to do so, chkdsk will tell you that it can't get exclusive control of the volume and ask if you want to schedule the check for the next time the computer restarts.

There are two forms of chkdsk in Win2K: the graphical tool and the command-line utility. The graphical tool is simpler, but the command-line utility has many more options and is more flexible.

 NOTE The version of chkdsk that came with NT 4 is not compatible with Win2K because the file structure is different. To check NTFS volumes under Win2K, you'll need to use the version of chkdsk that comes with the OS.

Running Chkdsk from Explorer

The simplest way to run chkdsk is from Explorer, as this tool doesn't demand that you know the command syntax and just uses the default options. To use the tool, select a drive in Explorer and open its property sheet. Turn to the Tools tab, then click the Check Now button to open the dialog box in Figure 7.38.

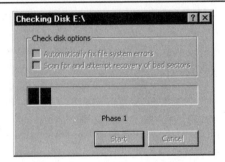

There are two options available from the graphical version of chkdsk. If you tell chkdsk to attempt to fix file system errors, then it will try to resolve any orphaned files—files that have entries in the file system catalog but don't appear in a directory on the volume. If you check the box that tells chkdsk to scan for and attempt recovery of bad sectors, you're telling it to make the optional fourth pass of checking each sector on the disk instead of just the ones containing metadata. As you'll recall from the description of just what chkdsk is doing, data in bad sectors will not always be recoverable—only if the volume is fault tolerant and chkdsk can get the data's redundancy information elsewhere is the data recoverable.

To begin checking the selected volume, click the Start button. The computer will begin grinding away using the options you supplied. (If you don't check either box, chkdsk runs in read-only mode. Since the graphical tool doesn't display a report, read-only mode doesn't help you much.) The dialog box will display each phase of the disk check and display a status bar showing how far along each pass is until it's completed.

When the disk check is done, a message will appear telling you that the disk has been checked. No report of bad sectors or other information will appear. You can check another disk by exiting the current drive's property sheet and selecting another drive from Explorer.

Running Chkdsk from the Command Prompt

You have little control over how chkdsk works when you run it from Explorer. If you'd like more control, you'll need to use the command prompt. The command-line options can be a little tricky to use, but they're faster and more flexible than the GUI once you get accustomed to them.

Without any arguments, chkdsk runs in read-only mode on the current drive. You'll see command-line output showing the progress of each pass over the volume, and then you'll get a report like the following, showing you how the total disk space is used:

```
2096450 KB total disk space.
1011256 KB in 9214 files.
   2248 KB in 539 indexes.
      0 KB in bad sectors.
  31116 KB in use by the system.
   4096 KB occupied by the log file.
1051830 KB available on disk.

   2048 bytes in each allocation unit.
1048225 total allocation units on disk.
 525915 allocation units available on disk.
```

You should recognize the terminology used from the previous discussions of how NTFS organizes files on disk. The indexes are in fact directories on the disk. The log file is the transaction log used to record changes to the volume metadata so that any incomplete changes can be rolled back. The allocation units are clusters.

So—you've got a disk report, but that report doesn't allow you to do anything. To control the process, you'll need to plug in one or more of the switches explained in Table 7.2.

TABLE 7.2: COMMAND-LINE SWITCHES FOR CHKDSK

Switch	What It Does
/f	Tells chkdsk to attempt to fix file system errors, such as orphaned files. The help file for this switch says that it fixes errors on the disk, but that's not really accurate. It fixes inconsistencies in the file system catalog.
/v	Has different results depending on whether you use the switch on FAT volumes or on NTFS. On FAT volumes, this switch lists the full path of every file on the volume. On NTFS volumes, it runs chkdsk in verbose mode, reporting any cleanup messages relevant to fixing file system errors or missing security descriptors.
/r	Checks every sector on the disk to make sure it can be written to and read from. Any bad sectors are marked as bad.
/x	Forces the volume to dismount first if dismounting is necessary to run chkdsk (that is, if there are open handles to the chosen volume). Choosing this option will dismount all volumes.

Continued ▐▶

TABLE 7.2 CONTINUED: COMMAND-LINE SWITCHES FOR CHKDSK	
/i	Tells chkdsk not to check the indices on NTFS volumes. In other words, chkdsk will skip the second pass of the disk checking operation. Although selecting this option can save you quite a bit of time on volumes with a lot of directories, it's not a good idea to use this switch unless you must since any inconsistencies in the directory structure will go unnoticed.
/c	Tells chkdsk not to check for cycles on the NTFS volume. Cycles are a rare kind of disk error wherein a subdirectory becomes a subdirectory of itself, creating an infinite loop. You can probably turn this switch on safely since cycles are rare, but it won't save you much time.
/l[:size]	On NTFS volumes, specifies a new size for the transaction log. The default size is 4096KB, and for most purposes that's just fine.
Volume	Specifies the mount point, volume name, or (if followed by a colon) the drive letter of the logical volume to be checked.
filename	On FAT volumes, tells chkdsk to evaluate the specified filename to report on how fragmented it is. This option does not work on NTFS volumes.

The order of the switches is as follows:

```
chkdsk [volume[[path]filename]]] [/f] [/v] [/r] [/x] [/i]
➡[/c] [/l[:size]]
```

Using Encrypted NTFS

One of the new features of Win2K is its support for native public key encryption, allowing you to secure your documents and folders so that only you—or the people you give the key to—can view the documents. It's a handy way of keeping even shared documents private or of protecting files on a machine that can be easily stolen, such as a laptop. Encryption doesn't conceal the fact that the documents exist. Rather, when you attempt to open an encrypted file, Win2K checks to see whether you have a key to that file. If you don't, then you're forbidden access to the file. This denial is not application dependent—for example, a Word document won't be accessible in Word *or* WordPad. The user without the public key can't open the file object at all.

 NOTE The process of checking for an encryption key is pretty compute intensive, so it's probably best not to encrypt files stored on a terminal server or other CPU-bound server.

Encryption is only supported on NTFS 5 volumes—it's an attribute, like compression or the archive bit—giving you one more reason to use NTFS.

How Win2K Encryption Works

When you encrypt data, you're generating a request for a new security certificate identifying you to Win2K as who you say you are. A *cryptographic service provider (CSP)* generates two 56-bit keys: a public key, used for encrypting data for you, and a private key, used for decrypting that data. The two keys are unrelated—knowing a public key does not give you the ability to guess the private key.

The CSP passes the public key to the certificate authority, which uses it to create a public key for you. The certificate and public key are stored in the `Personal/Certificates` folder located in the Certificates add-in to the MMC (see Figure 7.39).

FIGURE 7.39

Personal encryption certificate

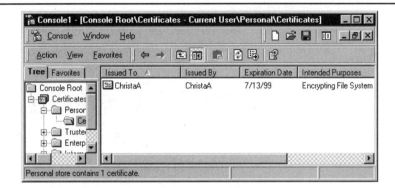

Issued To	Issued By	Expiration Date	Intended Purposes
ChristaA	ChristaA	7/13/99	Encrypting File System

NOTE Don't worry about the certificate expiration date of 7/13/99, which would seem to imply that I can no longer use this certificate to prove my identity and decrypt files. Ignoring the hype about Y2K and the need to use 4-digit dates whenever possible to avoid confusion, Microsoft only used two-digit numbers in the MMC to show when certificates would expire. If you open the certificate and look at the details tab, you'll see that the certificate expires on July 13, *2099*.

Win2K users can encrypt data across the network, but the certificate will always be originally on the Win2K machine where the data is stored. The private key is stored in the Registry of the computer where the data is stored.

Only Win2K users and clients will be able to encrypt data. Even though NT and Windows 9*x* users can read and open files on NTFS 5 volumes—and even though encryption standards apply to them, too—the NT and Windows 9*x* users don't have the tools they'd need to encrypt the data unless they're running a Win2K session.

This information isn't required when it comes to encrypting or decrypting your own data, but it could come in useful when it comes to recovering someone else's encrypted data or protecting laptop encryptions. We'll do the simple part first, then return to the question of why you need to protect certificates and how you can do it.

Encrypting Files

To encrypt a file or folder from Explorer, right-click the file or folder (you cannot encrypt entire volumes) and open its property sheet. On the General tab, there's an Advanced button.

 TIP If there isn't an Advanced button, make sure that you're looking at an NTFS volume, not a FAT or FAT32 one.

Click that button to open the Advanced Attributes dialog box shown in Figure 7.40.

FIGURE 7.40

Encryption is an advanced NTFS attribute.

You can either compress or encrypt file data, not both. Check the option you want and click OK. If the folder containing the file is not encrypted, you'll be warned of this and prompted to encrypt both the folder and the file. Normally, it's a good idea to let Win2K encrypt the folder as well. If you leave the folder unencrypted, changes to the file that make it appear to be a new file will leave the file unencrypted. All new files created within a folder inherit the folder's encryption attributes.

Copying and Moving Encrypted Files

New files in a directory inherit the encryption attributes of that directory: if the directory is encrypted, the file will be encrypted as well. If the directory is not encrypted, the file won't be encrypted. What about files *copied* to a directory? This is where it can get a little tricky:

- If you copy or move an unencrypted file to an encrypted NTFS folder, that file will become encrypted.
- If you copy or move an encrypted file to an unencrypted NTFS folder, the file will remain encrypted.
- If you move an encrypted file to a compressed folder, the file will gain the compression attribute but lose the encryption attribute (files and directories cannot be both encrypted and compressed).
- If you copy or move an encrypted file to a FAT or FAT32 folder, that file will no longer be encrypted (since encryption is an NTFS attribute).

The encryption attribute is now set. If anyone but you, even someone with administrator privileges, attempts to open the file or run the encrypted executable, they'll be denied access. There's no obvious visual cues (such as blue text) telling you that certain files or folders are encrypted, but if you look in the left-hand pane of the Win2K Explorer window when an encrypted file is displayed, you'll see the listing.

You can also encrypt files from the command prompt with the CIPHER command. To encrypt a single folder in the current directory, type **cipher /e** *foldername,* where *foldername* is the name of the folder you want to encrypt. To decrypt the same folder, replace the /e switch with /d, like this: **cipher /d** *foldername.* The command will report back to you whether the operation succeeded or not. You can't encrypt or decrypt a folder's contents if they're in use (or even displayed in an Explorer window), so be sure that no one's looking at files that you're attempting to manipulate.

NOTE Again, you can't encrypt compressed data or vice versa. If you attempt to encrypt a compressed file or folder with CIPHER, you'll get an "Access Denied" error. Uncompress the file or folder and try again to encrypt it, and the operation should work.

Normally, CIPHER will only encrypt the files in the immediate folder you specify, not the subfolders. It will also only encrypt parent folders if told to, leaving the files' parent directories unencrypted. To keep from accidentally decrypting a file (by apparently making it new in a decrypted folder), encrypt the folder as well by typing **cipher /e /s:*foldername* /a**. This will encrypt all files within the specified folder and all subfolders to that folder.

Enforcing Encryption

Encrypted files don't have any obvious differences alerting people to their off-limits status, and the contents of an encrypted folder are displayed like any other shared or locally available data. The only way you can tell that you've attempted to open an encrypted file is that you won't be able to do so.

Sadly, the error messages you get when attempting to access files that someone else has encrypted represent a help desk call waiting to happen. Whether accessing the encrypted file locally or from the network, from Win2K or from an earlier operating system, you'll see an error message like the one in Figure 7.41.

What about administrators? If someone with administrator privileges opens the file's property sheet and edits the encryption attribute, they'll be unable to apply the change—they'll be denied access. What happens if an administrator takes ownership of the file? File ownership doesn't actually matter to encryption. Even if you (as the administrator) take ownership of an encrypted file, you won't be able to read it.

Protecting Encryption Keys

Microsoft positioned Win2K's encryption services especially for laptop users who wanted to keep their data secure even if their laptop was stolen. However, there's one major hole in this security plan. If someone *does* steal a laptop and can log in with Administrator rights, they can edit the certificate settings in a way that allows them to decrypt the data.

NOTE Of course, if you don't password-protect your laptop, then decrypting your files is as easy as logging on as you.

To avoid this problem, Microsoft recommends exporting each user's certificate and saving it to disk, then deleting the certificate on the computer. To do so, follow these steps:

1. In the MMC, add the Certificates snap-in.

2. In the `Personal` folder, open the `Certificates` folder. The per-user certificates on the computer will be displayed in the right-hand pane.

3. Right-click the certificate that you want to export as a file and choose Export from the All Tasks menu. This will start the Export Certificate Wizard, which asks whether you'd like to export the private key along with the certificate. You'll need the private key to decrypt data.

4. In the next screen, choose the export options, including the file type, the strength of encryption you want to use, and what you want to do with the local key if the export works. (Personally, I'd delete it manually once I was sure that the export had worked rather than letting Win2K delete it for me.)

5. If you chose to export the private key, you'll need to supply a password to import the key again. Choose this password carefully, as it's protecting your encryption.

6. Choose a filename for the key by either typing a path or browsing for it. You can save the file on any volume, not just NTFS.

7. The final screen of the wizard will display your choices. Review them carefully, then click Finish to export the keys. If the export operation worked, Win2K will pop up a quick message box to tell you so.

Save the certificate on a floppy disk or, better yet, a safe network location where it can get backed up, then delete it from the computer. You'll be able to open encrypted files, but the certificate will no longer be on the machine.

To import the certificate to another computer or replace it on the same one, open the same `Personal` folder, right-click the `Certificates` folder, and choose Import from the All Tasks menu. This will start the Import Certificate Wizard:

1. Browse for the file you saved.

2. If the certificate you're importing includes the private key, you'll need to supply the password assigned when the key was exported. Type it in and choose the degree of control you want over the private key.

3. Specify where the new key should go. For user keys, the `Personal` folder should be fine.

4. Review the importing options, then click Finish to import the key. Win2K will tell you if the importing action succeeded.

Decrypting Files

Decrypting encrypted files is a simple matter if you're the person who encrypted the file in the first place. When you open it, the file is automatically decrypted—the action is completely transparent to the user.

That decryption is temporary, however—as soon as you close the file, it's encrypted again. If you want other people to be able to use the file, then you'll need to decrypt it. To decrypt a file or folder from Explorer, open its property sheet and click the Advanced button on the General tab. Uncheck the box next to Encrypt Contents to Secure Data. The file is now open to anyone who has access to it.

Enough of That! Managing Disk Quotas

Most administrators found NT incomplete in one way or another, and one of the perennial complaints was NT's lack of quota management tools. Without quota management, it's hard to control the amount of disk space people on the network use; even in these days of cheap and plentiful storage there comes a limit to the amount of time and money you want to put into storing every single e-mail message John Doe saves.

Several NT-compatible quota management applications exist, but adding quota management to NT has historically not been cheap. To help those who need a basic form of quota management, Win2K now includes simple quota management tools. Win2K's tools don't include all the functionality some third-party products do, but they're not bad at all and have the usual advantage: you've already paid for them.

Background: How Quota Management Works

The process of quota management is straightforward: the quota manager keeps an eye on writes to the disk of protected lettered volumes based on criteria set by the network administrator. If the protected volume reaches or exceeds a certain level, then a message is sent to the person writing to the volume warning them that the volume is near quota, or the quota manager prevents the user from writing to the volume altogether, or both. The mechanics of how all this works varies from product to product, but the basic effect is the same: users can't write to volumes that are at or exceed their preset quota.

Win2K's quota management is based on user identity and the folder the user is storing information in, so you can control not only how much space a person uses but *where* they're using it.

Setting Up User Quotas

By default, Win2K quotas are turned off. To start working with quota management, open Explorer and right-click the volume you want to protect. This can be any NTFS 5 volume with a drive letter, whether local or a drive letter mapped from another server. Turn to the Quota tab shown in Figure 7.42.

 NOTE You cannot set quotas on a folder within a volume; you can only set them on the entire volume.

FIGURE 7.42

*Disk quotas are dis-
abled by default.*

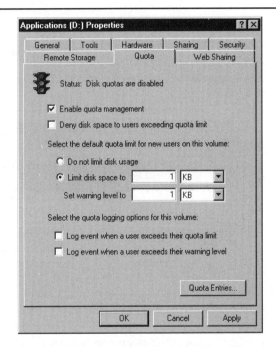

The first order of business is to enable quotas. To turn on disk quotas and make the management options available, check that box. You can set up all the options before clicking OK or Apply to enable quotas. Choose Apply to keep the property sheet open.

Next, choose whether to enforce quotas by denying disk space to anyone violating a quota. If you don't check this box (it's not checked by default), then people violating their disk space quotas will still be able to write to the volume.

WARNING Never enforce a quota on a system partition and deny disk space to those exceeding it. When booting, Win2K writes data to the disk. If you enforce quotas, then the system may not be able to boot. Actually, there's really no reason to put quotas on the system partition if it's separate from the data partition.

Third, set a default quota limit. Notice that the default value is 1KB, which means that unless you're in a particularly draconian mood, you're going to want to change the default to something a bit more reasonable. You might, for example, limit each user's quota on the volume containing home directories to 10MB.

Finally, set the logging options, sending events to the System log in the Event Viewer tool when users exceed their quotas or reach the warning level. Users will be identified by name in the System event log, so you know who is running out of assigned disk space.

You've now done the basic job of setting up quota management on the volume. Next, you'll need to create quotas for each person who'll be using that volume. To do so, click the Quota Entries button to open the screen in Figure 7.43.

FIGURE 7.43

*Add quota entries
to the list.*

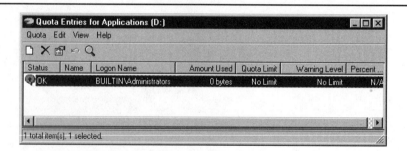

When you start, the only entry will be the default one for the local server's administrator. To add a new entry, choose New Quota Entry from the Quota menu. You'll see the dialog box in Figure 7.44.

You can choose accounts from either the local user account database or the one for the domain. When you've selected the names for which you want to create entries, click the Add button to display the names in the lower half of the window. Once the names are displayed, you can click OK to move to the next stage of creating the entry.

 TIP Because quotas are enforced on a per-user basis, you can't create quota entries on a per-group basis. However, you can create quota entries for multiple users by Ctrl+clicking the names. All users will start with the same settings.

FIGURE 7.44

All user accounts on the domain or the local server will be listed.

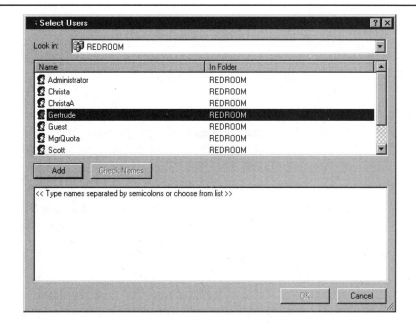

In the window shown in Figure 7.45, choose whether to enforce quotas for the new entries, and (if so) how much disk space in the volume they get. The amounts shown in this window will be the default you set on the Quota tab.

FIGURE 7.45

Specify the amount of disk space allocated to the new quota entry.

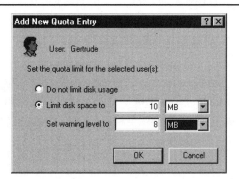

In this same box, specify the level at which the users will be warned that they're about to run out of disk space. The warning level, obviously, should be less than the quota limit. Win2K will fuss at you if the warning level is more than the quota and make you edit the value so that the warning level is less than or equal to the quota.

Click OK, and you'll return to the list of quota entries. The new entries will be listed and take effect immediately. If a user attempts to write to the volume and is over quota, she will get a write error. The exact nature of the error message will depend on what application users are using when they attempt to write to the volume, but the basic idea will be the same: they're denied access to the volume because it's now write-protected. To write to the volume, they'll need to delete some of their files to get below quota or have someone else take ownership of their files.

 NOTE Some quota management software allows users a "grace write" when they're over quota, permitting them to save the file they're working on before locking them out. Win2K's quota management does not.

If you want to use the same quota limits on more than one NTFS 5 volume, you can export the quotas and import them on the new volume. To export a quota, select it in the list in the Quota Entries management tool and choose Export from the Quota menu. The extension for the export files is not displayed. Choose a name for the file and save it. To import the quota settings, open the Quota Entries management tool for that volume and choose Import. Browse for the file, and you can import the quotas.

Quotas may not work as expected on volumes that you originally formatted with FAT or FAT32 and then converted to NTFS. Any files that users created on the FAT volumes will appear to the quota manager to belong to the Administrator, not to the person who created them, since the FAT file systems don't distinguish file ownership like NTFS volumes do. Therefore, the files that people created on the FAT volume before it was converted to NTFS won't be charged to their quotas, but to the Administrator.

Managing Quota Entries

Some time after you implement quotas in your network, people will start running up against them. If you open the Quota Entries folder, you'll see three possible statuses for quotas. Quotas may be within acceptable limits, at warning levels, or over quota (if you haven't prevented users from writing to volumes for which they're over quota).

Win2K doesn't include any messaging tied up to quota limits, so you'll need to keep an eye on this yourself. You can sort the entries in the list by clicking the columns, so if you need to find all the people (for example) who have crossed the warning threshold for quotas, you'd click the Status column. Sadly, there's no mechanism from here to send people messages; you'll need to rely on e-mail or some other messaging technique.

Archiving Data with Remote Storage

Thus far in this chapter, I've discussed the data that's on your hard disk(s). Win2K makes it possible for you to have an entire other set of user data that's not on hard disk, but on tape, archived there to save you room on the hard disk. Win2K's Remote Storage feature makes it possible for you to conserve room on relatively expensive hard disk media by automatically moving rarely used files to relatively cheap tape media when disk space starts getting rare. Although setting up and managing the Remote Storage service isn't for sissies, it can help you keep disk space for current data instead of tying it up with files people haven't touched for months or years.

In simple terms, the service works like this: The Remote Storage Service (RSS) monitors the amount of free space on logical volumes that you've told it to keep an eye on. During setup, you have also directed RSS as to which files (according to their size and last accessed date) may be archived. When the amount of free space on those logical volumes dips below the level you've specified, RSS copies the file data to the remote storage media set, leaving on the logical volume a "placeholder" file that's a link to the real file on the remote media. Thereafter, when a user tries to open that file, RSS goes and pulls the file for the user, displaying a dialog box that lets the user know that the file was on the remote media (and thus implying that the user should be a little patient—it takes longer to read a file from tape than from disk).

 TIP Because it does take longer to read files from tape than from disk, try to arrange your rules so that only rarely used files are eligible for archiving. *Never* set up rules that would allow any system files to be archived.

RSS is not a walk in the park to set up. Why bother? Potentially, RSS can offer all of the following advantages:

- Supplementing hard disk space with tape space, to expand storage capabilities at a lower cost
- Transparent access to archived data, without having to find and restore the backups that the archives are stored on
- Automation of the archiving system, so that once you make up a set of archiving rules, you can let the service take care of things
- The ability to share one set of remote storage among multiple logical drives

How Archiving Works

From a conceptual point of view, there are two parts to the remote storage service. The upper level of *local storage* consists of Win2K NTFS volumes of the computer running RSS. Note that this means that only local NTFS volumes—not network-accessible drives or local drives formatted with FAT or FAT32—may be managed with this service. You can manage RSS remotely, but you can't run it remotely. Disk volumes that come under the purview of RSS are called *managed volumes*.

The second level of *secondary storage* is a tape library or tape drive connected to the computer running RSS. This level of the hierarchy stores the data that has been copied from local storage to an online library or additional storage device and may consist of a group of one or more managed volumes, a single optical compact disk library, or a single tape library. All drives in the remote storage media should be on the same SCSI chain if you're using SCSI.

 NOTE RSS supports all SCSI class 4mm, 8mm, and DLT tape libraries on the Win2K Hardware Compatibility List. Microsoft does not recommend that you use RSS with Exabyte 8200 libraries, and the QIC format is not supported. As with any new operating system, do check to make sure that drivers are available for the tape drives *before* you buy the drive for use with RSS.

From a software perspective, two Win2K services support RSS: Removable Storage Services and Remote Storage. When you set up Win2K to use RSS, tools for managing both these services are in the Remote Storage tool in the `Administrative Tools` folder.

The Removable Storage services are in charge of managing the hardware supporting the archiving process and have the following jobs:

- Creating media pools and setting security and other configuration settings for those pools
- Keeping track of which media are available (online) and which are not (offline)
- Mounting and dismounting the media as the network administrator requests
- Displaying the state of readiness for media in the media pools
- Inventorying media for faster retrieval of data

The Remote Storage Service is the service that actually manages how the archiving process works, using the guidelines you set. Using this tool, you can:

- Identify and configure remote storage devices (such as tape drives) and media (such as tapes)
- Set security and configuration options for all remote storage functions or for particular parts of the remote storage service

- Configure volume management settings for the volumes in RSS

- View information about current and logged RSS activity

- Keep track of RSS events with an Event Viewer dedicated to this service

Those are the pieces. RSS is the main player when it comes to data archiving, using Removable Storage to copy data to the media, as shown in Figure 7.46.

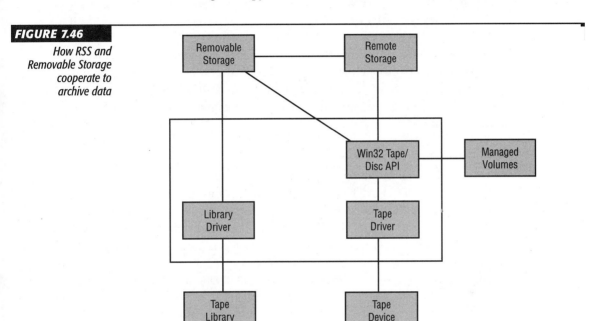

FIGURE 7.46

How RSS and Removable Storage cooperate to archive data

Getting Started

Remote management is not something you can just try out—you need to prepare ahead of time. Before you begin, make sure you've done all the following:

- Checked your hardware against the Hardware Compatibility List

- Made sure that the tape drive or library is up and running

- Installed RSS

- Created media pools as needed to support the archiving

- Configured user permissions to let people use the removable storage volumes

Let's take a more detailed look at what this prep work entails.

Compatibility Check: Choosing Hardware

Checking your archiving hardware against the HCL is harder than it looks. The contents of the HCL on the Microsoft Web site do not specify which tape devices are compatible with RSS and which are not, but according to TechNet and the RSS online help, not all tape devices are compatible with RSS. In other words, the tape device you use for backing up may not work with RSS. You can tell whether it does or not by setting up RSS— one of the first steps of the setup process is finding the RSS-compatible hardware. If Setup finds no hardware that works with RSS, then Setup will fail.

Once you've established that the hardware is RSS compatible, get it set up and working properly by installing it with the New Hardware Wizard that should start up the first time you boot Win2K after installing the archiving device. If Win2K doesn't identify the new hardware and start installing it, then make sure the device is connected properly.

Installing the Software

Either before or after installing a compatible tape drive, install Remote Storage Services from the Add/Remove Programs applet in the Control Panel. Remote Storage should be checked in the box on the screen listing all the available Win2K components. Finish the wizard, let Setup copy all the files it needs from the i386 folder on the Win2K installation CD, and you're set. When RSS is installed, the Remote Storage tool will be in the Administrative Tools folder.

The first time you use RSS, you'll need to install it. Double-click its icon in the Remote Storage tool to run the Setup wizard, which will walk you through the following steps:

1. First, Setup will make sure that you have the right privilege set to run Setup (you need administrative rights) and look for a supported device to use with RSS.

2. Indicate whether you want to use RSS with all volumes or only user-specified volumes. It's a good idea to only manage the volumes with user data on them so you don't accidentally archive system files when space on the system partition runs low. If you chose the latter, pick the local NTFS volumes that you want to manage.

3. Specify the file criteria that RSS should use to manage the selected volumes, setting a percentage of free space that the service should maintain on the selected volumes and choosing wildcards and file types to show which files should be included and excluded from the archiving process. Also pick a minimum file size to archive, since larger files are more likely to take up room.

4. Select the media type to use with RSS. Be sure to pick the right option, since you cannot change your mind about this option.

5. Configure a schedule for managing volumes. According to the intervals you set in this schedule, RSS will run a job on the managed volumes, evaluate the amount of free space on the volumes, and then (on any volumes running short of free space) archive the files that meet the management criteria you set.

NOTE The space on disk is not actually cleared when RSS copies the archived files to the remote storage media. Only when you need disk space are the archived files deleted from the hard disk.

6. Review your choices, and either click Back to edit them or Finish to apply those choices to your RSS setup.

Configuring Remote Storage Properties

Once RSS is installed, you can set up your media pools from the Remote Storage tool. Once the media pools are set up, configure them with the settings you want. In most cases, the default settings are fine. Do check the settings on the Security tab (see Figure 7.47) to make sure that users and administrators have the proper settings they need to either access or manage the remote storage media.

FIGURE 7.47

Configure security settings for remote media

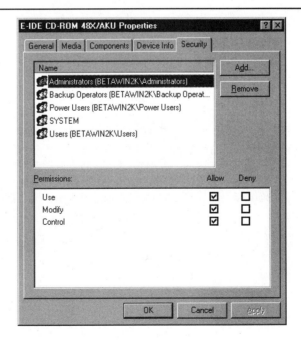

By default, local administrators and the System account may use, modify, and control remote media; power users and users may use it, and backup operators may use and modify remote media. You can add any groups or users on the machine or in trusted domains by clicking the Add button and choosing names from the list of available account names.

Management Tasks

Once you've set up Remote Storage, you're still not done. You may need to do any or all of the following management tasks that determine which files are archived and how aggressively:

- Manage local disk volumes
- Add a volume for management
- Discontinue managing a volume
- Set the desired free space for a volume
- Specify basic file-selection criteria
- Add a file rule
- Change or delete a file rule
- Change priority of file rules
- Set the runaway recall limit
- Change the file-copy schedule
- Set advanced schedule options
- Copy files to remote storage
- Validate files
- Create free space immediately

Win2K's storage management includes many features new to the operating system—features that many network administrators have clamored for for years. In this chapter, you've seen how the new Disk Management tool works, learned about the options available when it comes to choosing a disk format, and learned how to use some of the new advanced features of NTFS: disk quotas, encryption, and file compression. Using these tools, you should be better able than ever to protect and manage your data files.

CHAPTER <u>8</u>

Managing and Creating User Accounts

By now you've learned the basics of Active Directory, how to install and configure major components of Win2K Server, the ins and outs of the new user interface and MMC, as well as the care and feeding of the Registry. Now let's tackle something at the heart of an administrator's job: creating and managing users and groups. This chapter will take you through the steps to create users and help you to understand the new group structure in Active Directory. Then I'll take on managing the users' work environments and explain Group Policy in plain, simple English. Along the way, you'll also learn how to deploy both user profiles and system policies to manage your legacy clients in a Win2K Server environment.

Use Computer Management for Local Accounts

The bulk of the chapter assumes an Active Directory context. By this point, you have already read about domains, forests, and trees and know the benefits of using Active Directory on your network. In many cases, particularly if you have NT 4 workstations or Win2K systems as clients, it is desirable to create a domain, even if you only have one server, in order to take advantage of all the additional features of Active Directory. However, it is possible that a small organization might want to keep life very simple, or even (brace yourself here) that the company's primary network OS is not Win2K/NT. For example, in a network that is Unix or NetWare based, there may be a need to set up a special-purpose NT server without all that AD stuff. In that case, if your Win2K machine is not a domain controller and you aren't using Active Directory, create your user accounts using the Computer Management tool (COMPMGMT.MSC). Users and groups created with COMPMGMT.MSC are local accounts, which is to say they exist and are valid on that local machine only. However, COMPMGMT.MSC is a remote-able tool, so you can use it to create and manage local users and groups on remote member servers in a domain or on remote stand-alone servers. Just choose Connect to Another Computer from the Action menu to do this.

 TIP The Action menu is the menu that you see (instead of the File menu) at the top left in the Microsoft Management Console tools. See Chapter 4 for an overview of MMC and console anatomy.

 TIP If the machine you are working on is a domain controller, you have to use Active Directory Users and Computer (DSA.MSC) to create accounts. On a domain controller, the Local Users and Groups node is disabled in COMPMGMT.MSC, and there is an *X* in a red circle over the function to indicate that it's deactivated.

Creating user accounts on a non–Active Directory server in Win2K is pretty much the same as creating local accounts on a non–domain controller in NT 4 except that you use the Computer Management tool instead of User Manager. In COMPMGMT.MSC, open System Tools, then Local Users and Groups, as shown in Figure 8.1. Notice the users and groups that are created by default when you install Win2K. On a stand-alone server, with no particular network services like IIS, Terminal Services, DHCP, or DNS installed, the only built-in accounts are Administrator and Guest. The Guest account is disabled by default as a security precaution. This account, on a stand-alone server or in an AD context, is used primarily to blow a huge hole in the security of a system by allowing unauthenticated access. That's right, unauthenticated access. No password is required for the Guest account. You can use it without any knowledge of a username or password, which is why it's disabled by default. It's a good thing that Guest is a very poor account as far as powers and abilities are concerned. The Administrator account, of course, has powers and abilities well beyond those of mortal users. It cannot be deleted or disabled, even if you set stringent account lockout policies (which lock the account after a certain number of bad logon attempts). The Administrator account is not ordinarily subject to this policy and therefore cannot be locked out, even after a million bad logon attempts, which could be more than enough to crack a weak password.

FIGURE 8.1

Computer Management Local Users and Groups

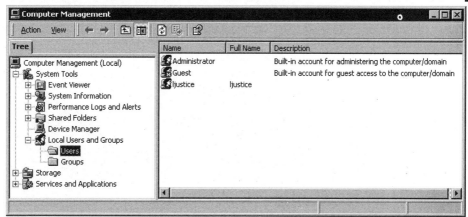

NOTE One common, and highly recommended, security practice is to rename both the Guest and Administrator accounts. This hinders a would-be intruder from taking advantage of the well-known usernames when attempting to log on.

The standard local groups that are built into a stand-alone server are Administrators, Backup Operators, Guests, Power Users, Replicator, and Users. Additional built-in groups are created on a domain controller system, as you'll see in a moment. These built-in groups have a predefined set of rights and permissions. To empower users with those rights and permissions, just make them members of the appropriate group. For a rundown of the built-in groups and their rights, see Table 8.2 later in this chapter.

To create a new user account on a non–domain controller Win2K system, open the Users folder under Local Users and Groups, then choose New User from the Action menu, or right-click Users in Local Users and Groups and choose New User. Fill in the fields for User Name, Password, and Confirm Password (the others are optional) as shown in Figure 8.2 and choose Create. To change account properties, to assign group memberships, a login script, and a home folder, or to grant dial-in permission to the user, right-click the user account and choose Properties. To set a user's password, high-light the account and right-click, then choose Set Password. All of these options and more will be discussed a bit later when we're creating AD accounts.

FIGURE 8.2

Creating a local user

  NOTE The local accounts you create on a stand-alone server, member server, or worksta-tion are stored in the SAM (Security Accounts Manager) database, just as they are in NT 4. The SAM is still located in \winnt\system32\config.

That's it! If you want to set account policies such as lockout restrictions or audit-ing, use the Local Security Policy tool (SECPOL.MSC) or the Group Policy snap-in (GPEDIT.MSC). The process is very similar to configuring Group Policy with the Active Directory tools except that, since the machine is not a domain controller, changes will apply to the local policy for the machine (I'll show you how to use the

Group Policy snap-in to set account lockout and password policy for the domain later in the chapter). The policies created will be local policies, which will live in the local machine's Registry database. Not surprisingly, the scope of policy settings is more limited for local polices than for group policies in an Active Directory environment. I'll also discuss group policies, and how they differ from local policies, later in this chapter.

Use Active Directory Users and Computers for Domain Accounts

In Win2K, Active Directory Users and Computers (DSA.MSC) is the primary administrative tool for managing user accounts, security groups, organizational units, and policies in a single domain or in multiple domains. As a Microsoft Management Console (MMC) application, the tool can be run on any Win2K machine, although it's only installed on Win2K servers (and it only appears in the Start menu programs on domain controllers) by default. To run DSA.MSC on a Win2K non–domain controller system, you can publish the application using Active Directory, and it can then be installed on Win2K Server or Professional desktops using Add/Remove Programs. There is a prepackaged set of admin tools called the Admin Pack (found in winnt\system32\ADMINPAK.MSI) that can be published using Group Policy, which installs the three Active Directory tools on a machine. See Chapter 10 for more information on publishing software in the Active Directory. DSA.MSC is also useful for managing computer accounts, organizational units, resources like printers and shared folders, and even domain controllers. However, the focus in this chapter is on creating and managing users and groups, including management of users' environments and group policies.

 TIP Computer accounts in Windows 2000 are now more like user accounts in that they can be included in groups and organizational units.

Where Do User and Group Accounts Live?

As in NT 4, local user accounts on a stand-alone server, member server, or Win2K Professional workstation are stored in a Security Accounts Manager (SAM) database, usually located in C:\winnt\system32\config, but it depends on where you created your WINNT (system root) directory.

For Active Directory, the file is called NTDS.DIT, and it's found in %systemroot%\NTDS by default, but you can specify a path in the DCPROMO routine. As you learned in Chapter 2, the NTDS.DIT database stores a lot more information than the SAM does. It also stores information about servers and workstations, resources, published applications, and security policies. NTDS.DIT and the software that runs it are generally referred to together as the *directory service*, or the Active Directory. This data structure is replicated throughout the domain to all replica domain controllers for fault tolerance and load balancing. It's actually a modified Access database based on the Lightweight Directory Access Protocol (LDAP) specified in RFC 1777. Unfortunately, you can't open it in Access or otherwise view or edit it directly. It can, however, be queried and modified using the Active Directory Services Interface (ADSI). As I'll discuss later, the Resource Kit for Win2K includes several VBScript files created for just that purpose (at least, it did include these tools as I was writing this).

Security Identifiers

User accounts, when first created, are automatically assigned a *security identifier* (SID). A SID is a unique number that identifies an account. SIDs have been used since NT began; the system doesn't really know you by your name, but rather by your SID. User IDs are just there for the human interface. SIDs are never reused; when an account is deleted, its SID is deleted with it. SIDs look like this:

> S-1-5-21-D1-D2-D3-RID

S-1-5 is just a standard prefix (actually, the 1 is a version number, which hasn't changed since NT 3.1, and the 5 means that the SID was assigned by NT); 21 is also an NT prefix; and D1, D2, and D3 are just 32-bit numbers that are specific to a domain. Once you create a domain, D1 through D3 are set, and all SIDs in that domain henceforth have the same three values. The *RID* stands for relative identifier. The RID is the unique part of any given SID. Each new account always has a unique RID number, even if the username and other information is the same as an old account. This way, the new account will not have any of the rights and permissions of the old account, and security is preserved.

Quick Tour of User and Group-Related Functions in *DSA.MSC*

Active Directory Users and Computers provides the network administrator with the means to perform the following tasks:

- Create, modify, and delete user accounts
- Assign logon scripts to user accounts
- Manage groups and group memberships
- Create and manage group policies

Open DSA.MSC by running it from the Start menu, or choose Start/Programs/Administrative Tools/Active Directory Users and Computers.

By default, `DSA.MSC` will seek out the Operations Master DC and send any change or create requests directly to that machine. If the Operations Master is offline or cannot be contacted, you can connect to another DC which will make the changes you request and synch up with the Operations Master at a later time. Just be aware that the DC honoring your request cannot guard against conflicts—namely, it cannot verify the uniqueness of a new account ID—until the Operations Master can be contacted. You will see a message to that effect if you create a user ID while the Operations Master is unavailable. In `DSA.MSC`, you will see the name of the contacted domain controller at the top of the console tree and your domain name right under the console root, as shown in Figure 8.3.

FIGURE 8.3

AD Users and Computers console

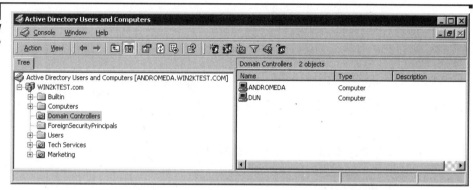

In the left pane, you see listed a set of containers and organizational units that were created automatically with the domain: `Builtin`, `Computers`, `Domain Controllers`, `ForeignSecurityPrincipals`, and `Users` (`Tech Services` and `Marketing` are organizational units created by an administrator). As with all the console applications, click an object in the console tree (on the left) to see its contents and information in the details pane (on the right). Notice also that the description bar for the details pane tells you how many objects there are in the container. The description bar, like the status bar and the toolbars, can be hidden if you want a more simplified view. Just choose Customize View from the Action menu and uncheck the Description Bar check box.

The `Users` and `Computers` containers are the default places to put user, group, and computer accounts when a machine is upgraded from NT 4. They gotta go somewhere. But you don't have to put new ones there, and you can move them to OUs as needed. As you'll quickly discover, you can put a user account in any OU, even directly in the "domain" container. When I first created a few user and group and machine accounts, I just created them in the domain root, then moved them to OUs as they were set up.

`Builtin` is the container for those special built-in local groups—such as Administrators, Account Operators, Guests, and Users—that exist on every Win2K Server machine, including domain controllers. More on this in a bit.

`Domain Controllers` is the default OU for new Windows 2000 domain controllers. This is where the accounts are located when you first create a DC. Like the accounts in the `Computers` container, DC accounts can be moved to other OUs.

`ForeignSecurityPrincipals` is a default container for object from external, trusted domains. In this chapter, we'll be working only with users and groups from this domain.

To create something new, select the container object where you want to locate it, then select New from the Action menu or right-click to select New from the Properties context menu. As shown in Figure 8.4, you can choose to create a shared folder, a user account, a printer, an OU, a group account, a contact, or a computer account. Any of these choices kicks off a corresponding wizard to create the object. In each case, to fill in all the details, go back and edit the properties of the object after creating it (right-click the object and choose Properties).

FIGURE 8.4

Creating a new object

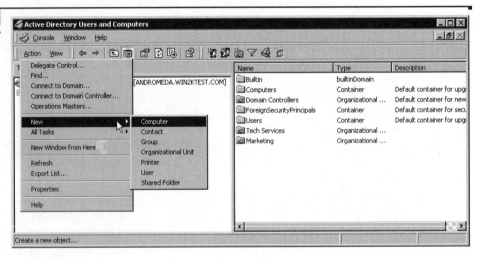

 NOTE Because they aren't really OUs, but instead mere "containers," you can't create an OU inside the `Users` or `Computers` containers, and you can only create users, computers, and groups inside the `Builtin` container.

Right-clicking an object brings up its context menu. The choices displayed change with the object you right-click. Right-click on a user account and you have the option to disable it or reset the password, for example; right-clicking on a computer account reveals options like Move and Manage (Manage opens up `COMPMGMT.MSC` connected to the selected computer).

This chapter is really not about managing machine accounts or printers or shared folders, so we'll leave those discussions for another chapter. However, contacts and OUs do relate to user and group management, so we'll take a look at those new items in a moment.

Prebuilt Accounts: Administrator and Guest

If you have just created a new domain, you'll notice that two accounts called Administrator and Guest are built already. The Administrator account is, as you've guessed, an account with complete power over a machine or a domain, depending on the context. You can't delete the Administrator account but you can rename it.

You assigned the password for the Administrator account when you installed Win2K and then again when you ran DCPROMO.EXE to create a new domain. The first was a local Administrator account and password, but once you created a domain, the new Administrator account and password for the domain replaced it. Don't lose that password, as there's no way to get it back! (Well, you can always rebuild from scratch, but it's no fun.)

The other account is the Guest account. *Guest* means "anyone that Win2K doesn't recognize." By default, this account is disabled, and it should *stay* that way. If you've ever worked with a different network, like a Unix or NetWare network, you're probably familiar with the idea of a guest account—*but Win2K works differently, so pay attention!* You can get access to most other operating systems by logging on with the username Guest and a blank password. That Guest account is usually pretty restricted in the things it can do. That's true with Win2K as well, although the Everyone group also includes guests.

Here's the part that *isn't* like other operating systems. Suppose someone tries to access a shared printer or folder on a Win2K server or domain that has the Guest account enabled. She logs on to her local machine as melanie_wilson with the password happy. Even without an account on the server or domain, Melanie can still work on her local machine. Windows 95/98 machines don't care who you are, having no local accounts at all. On an NT 4 or Win2K workstation, she would have to log on to an account on the local machine. However, none of these operating systems require you to log on to a server or domain in order to get access to the local workstation. Suppose that this domain or server doesn't even *have* a melanie_wilson account. Now she's working at a computer and tries to access a domain resource. Guess what? She gets in.

Even though an explicit domain login requires that you use a username of Guest, you needn't explicitly log on to a domain to use guest privileges. If your network is attached to my network and your Guest account is enabled, I can browse through your network and attach to any resources that the Guest account can access. I needn't log on as Guest; the mere fact that there *is* an enabled Guest account pretty much says to Win2K, "Leave the back door open, okay?" So be careful when enabling the Guest account.

Creating a New User Account

Before I discuss the ins and outs of all the user settings like account properties, UPN names, profile information, and so forth, let's just go through the steps to create a new user account with the wizard. Then I'll go back and discuss all the settings for the newly created account.

To create a user account, in DSA.MSC select the Users container (or any other container/OU where you want the account to be located), then select New/User from the Action menu (shown in Figure 8.4 a few pages back). A wizard appears with a dialog box shown in Figure 8.5. Fill in the First Name, Initials, Last Name, and Full Name fields as shown in the figure (Intitials and Last Name are optional fields). Next, fill in the user logon name (jblomberg) and choose the Universal Principal Name (UPN) suffix to be appended to the username at logon time. The UPN suffix is typically the DNS name of the domain, and unless you've set up alternate suffixes, you won't be able to choose any but the default domain name (WIN2KTEST.COM, in this case). UPN names are modeled after e-mail names, thus the @ symbol. The UPN suffix is a pointer to the domain containing the user account, so it's important when a user is logging on in a multiple-domain environment. We'll talk about UPN names in a moment. For logging on to an NT 4 or Windows 95/98 machine, there is also a down-level logon name, which uses the old-style DOMAINNAME\username syntax from previous versions of NT.

FIGURE 8.5

Creating a new user

Usernames in Win2K must follow these rules:

- The name must be unique to the machine for local accounts (or unique to the domain in the case of domain accounts). However, a domain user account name may be the same as a local account name on a non–domain controller which is a member of the domain, a fact which causes much confusion because they are completely separate entities.

- The username cannot be the same as a group name on the local machine for a local account (or the same as a group name on the domain in the case of domain accounts).

- The username may be up to 20 characters, upper- or lowercase or a combination.

- To avoid confusion with special syntax characters, usernames may not include any of the following:

  " / \ [ ] : ; | = , + * ? < >

- The name may include spaces and periods, but may not consist entirely of spaces or periods. Avoid spaces, however, since these names would have to be enclosed in quotes for any scripting or command-line situations.

Once you've filled in all the username information, choose Next. In the following screen, shown in Figure 8.6, set a password for the user account and confirm it. Set the password and account options summarized in Table 8.1, then choose Next. None of the account options are selected by default, so it's a good idea to go ahead and select User Must Change Password at Next Logon.

FIGURE 8.6

Setting password and account options

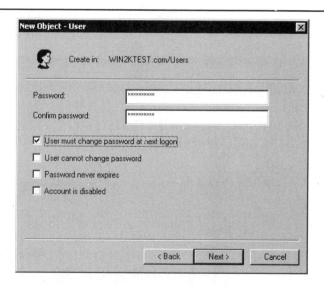

TABLE 8.1: PASSWORD AND ACCOUNT OPTIONS FOR CREATING A NEW USER ACCOUNT

Option	Description
User Must Change Password at Next Logon	Forces a user to change their password the next time they log on; afterward the box will be unchecked.

Continued

TABLE 8.1 CONTINUED: PASSWORD AND ACCOUNT OPTIONS FOR CREATING A NEW USER ACCOUNT

Option	Description
User Cannot Change Password	If checked, prevents the user from changing the account's password. This is useful for shared accounts and accounts that run services like Exchange.
Password Never Expires	If checked, the user account ignores the password expiration policy, and the password for the account never expires. This is useful for accounts that run services and accounts for which you want a permanent password (such as the Guest account).
Account Is Disabled	If checked, the account is disabled and no one can log on to it until it is enabled (it is not, however, removed from the database). This is useful for accounts that are used as templates and for new user accounts that you create well in advance, such as new hires that will not begin work for several weeks.

The final screen of this Create New Object Wizard, shown in Figure 8.7, simply confirms all the information you've supplied, including the container/OU where the account will live, the full name, the logon name, and the password or account options selected. Choose Finish and your user account is created.

FIGURE 8.7

Confirming new user information

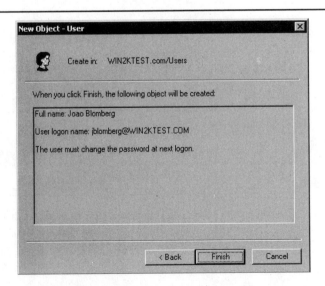

User Account Properties

Now let's go back and look at the properties of the account we just created. Right-click the user account object and you'll see several options in the context menu, shown in Figure 8.8. From here you can quickly copy the account, manage the user's group memberships, disable or enable the account, reset the user's password, move the account to a different container or OU, open the user's home page or send him mail (these last two require that the home page URL and e-mail address be specified in the account information). You can also choose to delete or rename the user account from this menu.

FIGURE 8.8

User's context menu

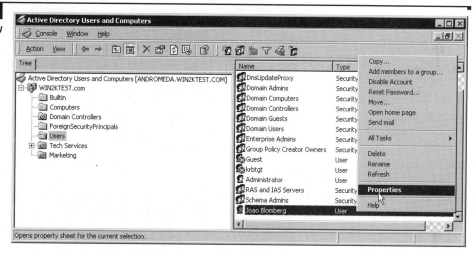

 WARNING Each user and group account is assigned a unique identifier, called a SID, when it is created. Deleting a user or group account deletes the unique identifier. Even if you re-create an account with the same name, the new account will not have the rights or permissions of the old account.

Choose Properties from the context menu to bring up the full user account information. In the General tab, shown in Figure 8.9, you can add a description of the user account, put in the name of the office where the user works, and add telephone numbers, an e-mail address, even Web page addresses.

The Address tab in Figure 8.10 shows fields for a user's mailing address. The Telephones tab (Figure 8.11) offers a place for home, pager, mobile phone, fax, and IP phone numbers, as well as a place to enter comments.

FIGURE 8.9

General user properties

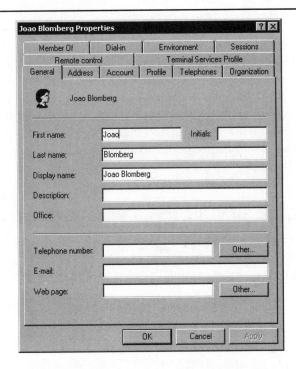

FIGURE 8.10

User Properties Address tab

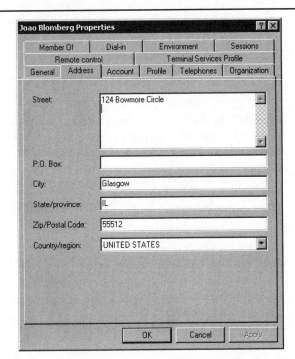

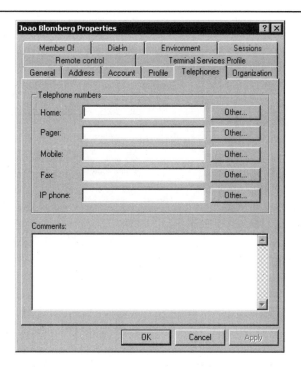

In Figure 8.12 you see the Organization tab, where you can enter information about someone's actual job title and her position in the pecking order of the organization.

So four of the tabs in the user account properties are about contact information, not what we old-time NT admins would call account properties. You know, you could enter almost all of this stuff in the Exchange mailbox properties, so I know you are wondering, like I did, "What's the deal, are they integrated now? Will Exchange actually use Active Directory to create mailboxes?" At this writing, Exchange and Win2K Active Directory are not actually integrated, so you still have to create Exchange mailboxes and fill out the related contact information in parallel (if you choose to do so). However, the next version of Exchange (code-named Platinum), which is in beta at this time, is supposed to integrate with Active Directory and eliminate the need for parallel user accounts and mailboxes. We shall see.

We'll leave the Dial-In tab to Chapter 22, which covers Remote Access Service. The next few sections will deal with managing account settings, profile information, and group memberships.

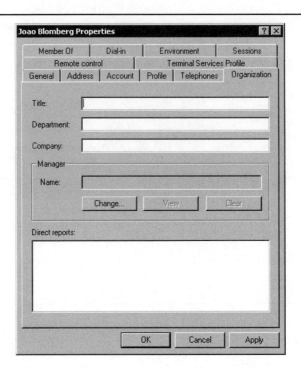

FIGURE 8.12

*User Properties
Organization tab*

 NOTE If Terminal Services are installed on your Win2K box, there will be several additional User Properties tabs to configure. See Chapter 14 for more information.

Account Settings

If you need to modify the user's login name or UPN suffix, go to the Account tab (Figure 8.13). This is also the place to specify permissible logon hours, account options, and all that stuff. By default, users are allowed to log on any day of the week at any time of the day (24/7), but you can choose the Logon Hours button to set particular hours and days that are permitted (see Figure 8.14).

 NOTE By default, a user will not be logged off automatically when logon hours expire, but there is a setting to accomplish this. The setting is called Automatically Log Off Users When Logon Hours Expire, and it's found in the Group Policy snap-in, under `Computer Configuration\Windows Settings\Security Settings\Local Policies\ Security Options`. This parameter can also be set using the Domain Security Policy tool or the Local Security Policy tool (depending on the context). In either case, look for the setting under `Local Policies\Security Options`.

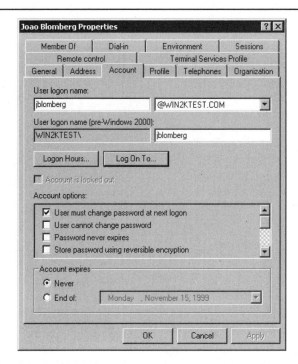

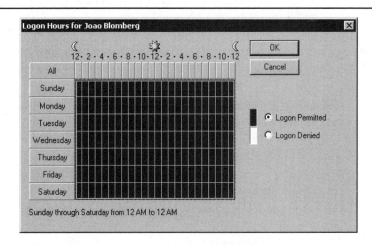

By default, users can log on to the domain from any workstation, but logon workstations may still be specified by NetBIOS name (see Figure 8.15). However, you must still be using NetBIOS on your network in order for this to be enforced.

FIGURE 8.15

Permitted logon work-
stations

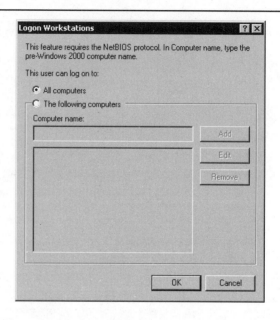

Looking back at the Account tab (Figure 8.13), you see the Account Is Locked Out check box. If the account is locked as a result of bad logon attempts (configurable using one of the various Policy tools, as I'll explain later), the box will show up as checked and available. If you wish to manually unlock the account, just uncheck the box. At the bottom of the Account tab you see the account expiration setting. By default, an account never expires, but if you enable the option, the default interval is six weeks. Notice also that there are more account options than were offered in NT 4 (scroll down in the Account Options box to see all the options). Several of these, like User Must Change Password at Next Logon, are familiar to NT 4 administrators and fairly self-explanatory to others. Several options are new and more obscure. The Store Password Reversible Encryption option is used for Windows 95/98 clients. That's not really new; it was just not an exposed option in NT 4. The smart card option is new and to be used if you opt for a public key infrastructure such as X.509. Select the Do Not Require Kerberos Preauthentication option if the account will use an implementation of the Kerberos protocol other than the one supplied with Win2K. Not all versions of the Kerberos protocol use this feature, but Windows 2000 does. Select the Use DES Encryption Types for This Account option if you need the Data Encryption Standard (DES). DES supports multiple levels of encryption, including MPPE Standard (40-bit), MPPE Standard (56-bit), MPPE Strong (128-bit), IPSec DES (40-bit), IPSec 56-bit DES, and IPSec Triple DES (3DES).

Notice that the user's password cannot be reset from the Account tab. To reset the user's password, close the account property sheet and right-click the username in the details pane of DSA.MSC. Choose the option to reset the password and you will be able to type in and confirm a new password, as shown in Figure 8.16. There is also a convenient check box to have the user change their password at next logon.

FIGURE 8.16

Resetting a user's password

What's in a UPN Name?

I'd like to take a moment to explain how the user naming convention has changed in Win2K. Notice in Figure 8.13 that there are two types of user logon names. The Win2K name is jblomberg@WIN2KTEST.COM, and the pre–Windows 2000 logon name is WIN2KTEST\jblomberg. In NT 3 and 4, usernames followed the convention *MACHINAME\username*, or *DOMAINNAME\username* if the user account was in a domain (although most users weren't aware of this fact). Usernames in Win2K are based on an Internet standard (RFC 822), *Standard for the Format of ARPA Internet Text Messages*, which in English means that Win2K usernames follow common e-mail naming conventions. Each user account has a Universal Principal Name consisting of a prefix, which is the username, and a suffix, which is the domain name. The prefix and suffix are joined by the @ sign. The UPN suffix indicates where to look for the user account at logon and is by default the DNS domain name. However, you'll notice that you just can't change the UPN suffix arbitrarily in a user's account record. It must be a UPN suffix specified for the domain in Active Directory Domains and Trusts. The tool allows you to specify alternate UPN suffixes for the domain. Only then can you change the UPN suffix from the default to one of the alternate UPN suffixes.

That said, the alternate UPN suffix you set up in Active Directory Domains and Trusts doesn't have to be an actual domain name. You can make it any domain name you want. For instance, during the research phase of this book, I watched a humorous demonstration of Mark Minasi logging on to the win2ktest.com domain as mark@microsoft.com. The idea here is to tell the machine in which domain to look for your account. For example, Joao's account may be located in the win2kgeeks.com domain, but he works for a company called Green Onion Resources, which consists of the win2kgeeks.com domain and four other domains. So his default UPN name might be jblomberg@win2kgeeks.com, but if Green Onion doesn't want to advertise their various Win2K domains to the world, or confuse their employees, they can designate green-onion.com as an "alternate" UPN suffix for win2kgeeks.com. So Joao can log on as jblomberg@green-onion.com and have that on his business cards as an e-mail address.

Also, a person might change jobs within an organization and his user account may be moved to a new domain, but it's not necessary to change his e-mail address each time, and it's very inconvenient to change logon names just because you got a promotion. So UPN names allow the account to be located easily and make the account's location transparent to the user. All they have to know is "I'm jblomberg@green-onion.com." They don't need to be bothered with "well, your user account has to moved to the win2kgeeks .com domain, so you'll have to log on from now on as…oh yes, and your e-mail address is changing so tell all your friends and business contacts…."

Profile Information

The Profile tab, shown in Figure 8.17, is the place to specify a user's profile path, a logon script, and a home folder. Mostly, these options are for *downlevel clients* (a condescending new term for any pre-Win2K clients) because these same settings and many more can be specified with Group Policy settings. However, Group Policy only works on Win2K systems, and it may be a while before companies begin to standardize on Win2K Professional desktops. Until then, you'll want to use these options. I'll be discussing user profiles and login scripts in more detail in the sections to come, but the following paragraphs will give you the main ideas about these features.

A user's desktop settings, from Start menu content right down to a color scheme and mouse orientation, can be stored in a network location so that the user can log on from any system on the network and see the same desktop. You can specify a shared network location for that purpose. This is also useful if you want to force a user (or group of users) to keep the same settings all the time. Such a thing is called a *roaming profile* if it's not forced on a user and if they can make changes. If the user is compelled to load that profile and can't log on without it, it's called a *mandatory profile* (or a *shared mandatory profile*, if more than one user is shackled to it). Win2K group policies allow you to configure folder redirection and other desktop settings, eliminating much of the need for NT 4–style roaming and mandatory profiles, so this feature is most useful for NT 4 clients. For many more details, refer to "Working with NT 4 User Profiles" later in this chapter.

A *logon* or *login script* is one that runs at logon time to configure a user's environment and assign network resources, such as mapped drives and printers. Though the art of the login script is well known in other network operating systems, such as NetWare, login scripts in Microsoft networks have not always been emphasized. Many Microsoft networks were small in the beginning, and users could "browse" for network resources. Login scripts are, however, filling a more important role for Windows environments; networks are larger now, and administration of resources and users is becoming increasingly more complex. See "Zen and the Art of Login Scripts" later in this chapter for more details, but for now, you should know that Win2K has a default path where the login script will be stored (in the SYSVOL, which is by default in the \WINNT directory, but it's configurable). That's why you only need to specify the script's name in the dialog box. However, it is possible that the login script could be stored in a subdirectory of SYSVOL, for example in SYSVOL\Sales\saleslogin.bat. In that case, you would need to specify the relative path from the SYSVOL root, such as Sales\saleslogin.bat.

FIGURE 8.17

User profile properties

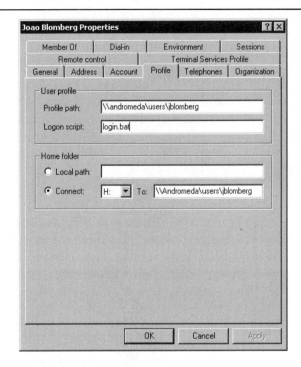

A *home folder*, also known as a *home directory*, is a folder assigned to the user for their private use. Although applications may have their own default folder for saving and opening files, the home folder will be the default working folder for a user at the command prompt. It is possible to specify a local path for a user's home folder, but it's only useful if the user will be logging on locally to the machine. For users logging on from the network, you need to choose the Connect option and specify a network path following the UNC convention *machinename**servername**directoryname*. You can also use a variable as a folder name, %username%, to indicate that the home folder name is the same as the user ID.

When you specify a home folder path for the user, if the network share already exists and you have permission to write to it, Win2K will create the user's home folder automatically. This saves admins a lot of time. If you need a step-by-step procedure to create and assign home folders, see Chapter 9, which covers creating and managing shared folders.

In any discussion about home folders, questions about how to limit disk space consumption are bound to arise. In NT 4 there was no built-in mechanism to set or enforce disk quotas at all. One strategy was to set up a separate partition for user directories, confining the problem to that partition (kind of like growing horseradish). The hapless admin might then run routine "diskhog" scripts and ask, beg, or publicly humiliate users into cleaning up their home folders. Others threatened to start deleting files at random if users didn't comply. But the best option was to purchase a third-party disk quota tool. Now Win2K comes with a simple quota management system; you simply enable it for a volume and then set thresholds for warnings and so forth. Read about it in Chapter 7.

Group Memberships

To specify group memberships for a user account, open the Member Of tab in the account property sheet. As you see in Figure 8.18, by default a new user is a member of the group Domain Users. The Active Directory Folder column on the right indicates the container or OU path for the group. To add a user to another group, choose Add and select from a list of available groups (Figure 8.19). Highlight the group name and double-click it or click the Add button to add it to the bottom pane. If scrolling through the list is too tedious for you, just type in the group names, separated by semicolons. Then use the Check Names button to confirm that the names you typed are valid group names. Choose OK and you're back at the Member Of tab with the new groups showing in the window. Choose OK again and you're done. To remove users from groups, use the Remove button in the Member Of tab. See the section "Working with Security Groups" for the skinny on group memberships.

FIGURE 8.18

*Setting group
memberships*

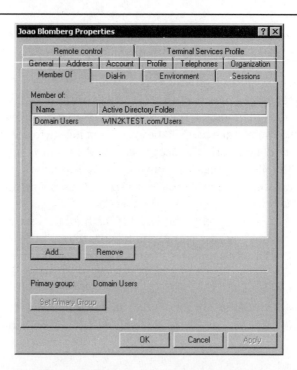

FIGURE 8.19

Selecting users and groups

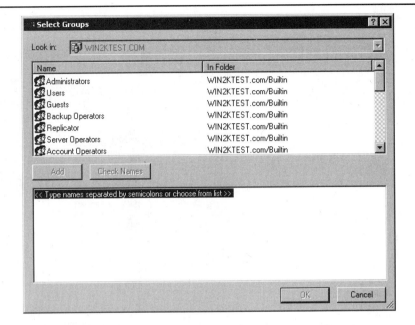

Managing Accounts

In the previous sections, I discussed how to make changes to a single user account. Now let's talk about how to make changes to several (or many) accounts at once. While we're on the subject, I'll cover a couple of other multiple-account issues, like how to create a bunch of users at a time.

In DSA.MSC you can select multiple accounts in the details pane by holding down the Shift key while you work the down arrow, or you can hit the Ctrl key as you click each of the accounts, then right-click to see the context menu while those accounts are selected. As you see in Figure 8.20, you can chose to move them all to another container or OU, add them to a group (to remove members of a group, you'll need to go to the property sheet of the group itself), disable accounts, or enable accounts. You can also send them all mail, assuming you have specified e-mail addresses for the accounts.

TIP   Remember, changes to a user's account, such as group memberships, will not take effect until the next time the user logs on.

FIGURE 8.20

*Selecting multiple
users in* DSA.MSC

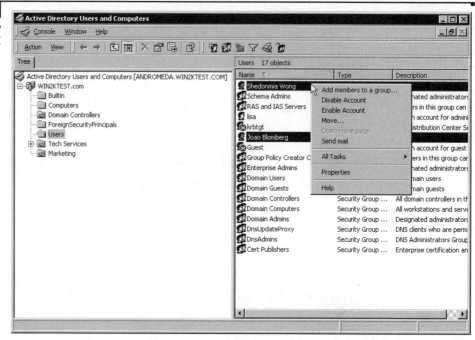

You can also create an account template and copy it to create users with like set-tings. Properties that are copied include account settings (such as Password Never Expires), group memberships, account expiration date (if supplied), and the UPN suffix. The profile information (home directory, user profile path, and logon script) is also copied, and if you used the %username% variable to set up the template user's home folder, it will be created automatically for new users when the account is copied.

Okay, those are nice options, but where is the Select Members by Group option from our old friend the User Manager for Domains (USRMGR.EXE)? You could use that tool to select all the members of a given group at once instead of scrolling through a list and selecting the users one-by-one. Come to think of it, you could manage a wider set of account properties with USRMGR.EXE, like logon hours and home directo-ries, and even make them all change their passwords at next logon. There doesn't seem to be a way to do these things with DSA.MSC. I actually did stumble across a Properties on Multiple Objects dialog box by selecting several accounts and pressing Alt+Enter, but it didn't work. It only set the properties of the first account selected.

So how do I make changes to several users at once, and how will I create, say, 50 or 500 users at a time?

It seems like the answer to these questions is more complicated than it has to be, unless Microsoft is hiding something from us. The Active Directory can be queried and modified using the Active Directory Services Interface (ADSI). So if you master ADSI and learn about Active Directory class objects and attributes and so forth, and if you know some VBScript or JScript, some Java or VB or C, or even some C++, you could create your 50 users at a time, presumably. Or even better, some bright, shining third-party vendor will figure it out for us and slap a user-friendly interface on it. We only have to wait for it to appear.

NOTE The beta 3 version of the Resource Kit included several VB scripts that ran in conjunction with the Windows Scripting Host. These scripts, with names like CREA-TEUSERS.VBS and USERGROUP.VBS, allowed you to use the command line or an input file to create, modify, and delete user and group accounts. Once you got the hang of the naming conventions for AD objects, these scripts were extremely useful. Unfortunately, they were not included in the RC2 Support Tools. Let's hope they reappear in the actual release of the Win2K Resource Kit.

Understanding Groups

Assigning users to groups makes it easier to grant them both rights to perform tasks and permissions to access resources like printers and network folders. To assist you in this endeavor, there are several built-in groups with built-in rights that you should be familiar with. You'll also want to create your own user groups and assign them certain rights and permissions. The members of the groups you create may in turn be granted the ability to administer other groups and objects, even whole organizational units. To top it all off, groups in Win2K can now contain computers and contacts as well as users and other groups. They can also be used as e-mail distribution lists. So it's important to understand the different types of groups that exist now in Win2K and how to work with them to delegate control, grant access to necessary resources, and configure rights. This is the subject of the next few sections.

Creating Groups

To create a new group in Active Directory Users and Computers, navigate to the container where you want the group to live. Groups can be created at the root of the domain, in a built-in container like Users, or in an OU. While you have the container highlighted, choose New and then Group from the Action menu (Figure 8.21). Supply the name of the group (Engineering) and the downlevel name if it will be different, then choose the group scope and group type, shown in Figure 8.22. By default, the group scope is Global and the type is Security. For an explanation of group types and group scope, see the following sections. Choose OK to create the group in the selected container.

FIGURE 8.21

Creating a new group

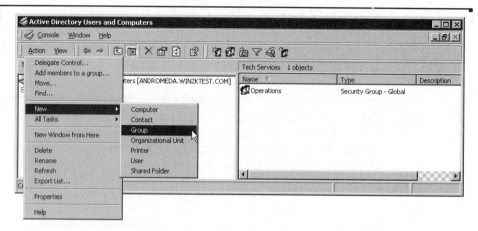

Now let's fill in the rest of the group information and add users to the new group. Find and double-click the group you just created to open the Group property sheet. In the General tab shown in Figure 8.23, fill in a description if you wish and an e-mail address if a distribution list exists for the group.

FIGURE 8.22

New Group Information

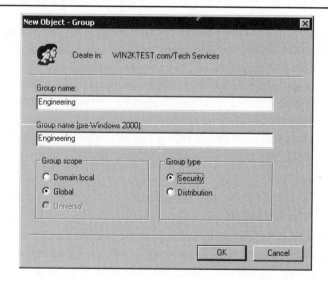

FIGURE 8.23

*Group Properties
General tab*

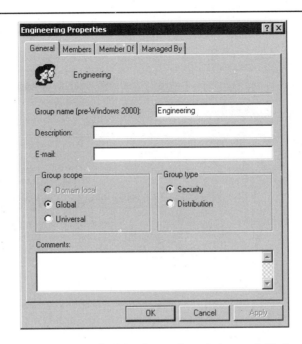

To populate the group, go to the Members tab and choose Add. As you see in Figure 8.24, Win2K allows users, other groups, and even computers to belong to groups, although there are rules for group nesting, as you'll read in the next few sections. Group members can also come from different OUs. Highlight the users or groups and choose Add, or type in the names, separated by semicolons, then choose Check Names to verify the typed-in names (it's not necessary to check the names if you selected them from the list). Choose OK to finalize your additions and return to the property pages. To view or modify the local and universal groups Engineering belongs to, for example, open the Member Of tab (Figure 8.25). The Managed By tab is for optional contact information and does not necessarily reflect any direct delegation of control.

Another way to add members to a group is to right-click the user account and choose Add Members to a Group. If you want to add several selected users to the same group at once, hold down the Ctrl key while you select several users, then right-click and choose Add Members to a Group. You'll also find a button on the toolbar to add one or more selected objects to a group. As I mentioned earlier, there is unfortunately no option to select all of the members of a group, which would allow other account properties to be managed as well.

One final how-to note: It will probably be necessary to move a group from one container to another at some point, since having groups in OUs facilitates delegation. To do this, right-click the group icon in the details pane of the console and choose

Move. Navigate to the container that will be the new home for the group (Figure 8.26), select it, and choose OK.

FIGURE 8.24

Adding users to a group

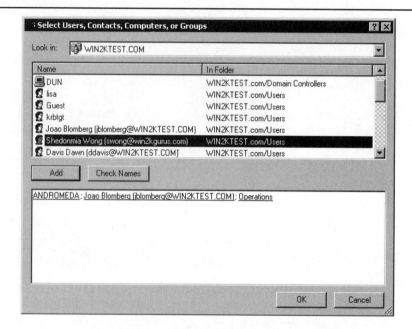

FIGURE 8.25

Nested groups

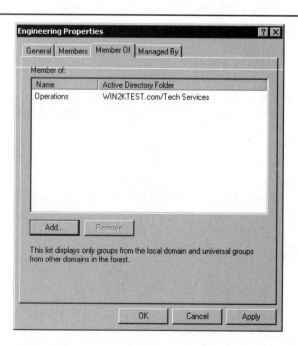

FIGURE 8.26

Moving a group to another container

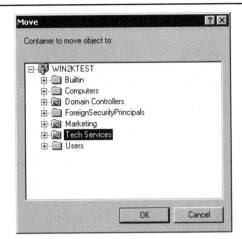

Group Types: Security Groups versus Distribution Groups

When creating group accounts in Win2K, you have the option to classify a group as a *security group* or as a *distribution group*. Security groups are not really new; they are equivalent to user groups as we knew them in all versions of Windows NT. They are only being called security groups now in order to distinguish them from distribution groups, which are sort of "non-security groups" and are new to Win2K.

Security Groups Overview

Security groups are groups used to assign rights and permissions. Like user accounts, security groups are assigned SIDS. When you view or edit an object's Access Control List (ACL), for example, the group names that appear on the list are security groups (sometimes they show up as SIDS if the friendly names are slow to resolve). These user and group SID entries on the ACL are matched up with a user's credentials to permit or deny access to the object.

There are three major types of security groups, local, global, and universal, although you might prefer to think of them as four different groups: local, domain local, global, and universal.

Local groups are the kind of groups you find on a stand-alone server, a server that is a member of a domain, or a Win2K Professional workstation. Local groups are local to the machine. That is, they exist and are valid only on that workstation or non–domain controller server.

Domain local group is the special name for a local group that happens to be on a domain controller. Domain controllers have a common active directory that is replicated between them, so a domain local group on one replica DC will also exist on its sibling DC. As you'll see when we start getting into the details, they are different than other local groups.

Global, universal, and of course, domain locals live on the domain controllers in the Active Directory. Global groups are still pretty much like they were in NT 4; they are used to grant access rights and permissions across machine (and domain) boundaries.

Universal groups are new to Win2K and can also serve the function of global groups, granting rights and object permissions throughout domains and between domains. They are more useful than globals or locals because they are infinitely more flexible with regard to nesting, but you can really only use them when your domain has gone "native," which requires that all NT 4 domain controllers be upgraded to Win2K.

Distribution Groups and Contacts

In NT 4, every group was a security group and could be used for controlling access to resources and granting rights. A distribution group is simply a non-security group. Distribution groups don't have SIDs and don't appear on ACLs. So what are they for? If you've worked with Exchange or a similar product, you are familiar with distribution lists. These are groups of recipient addresses. It's easier to send mail to ACME Managers, for example, than to individually select each manager's name from a list.

Assuming that you have entered mail addresses for your users, your security groups in the Active Directory are also unofficial distribution lists. Just right-click a group name in DSA.MSC and you'll see the option to send mail to the group members, just as you see the option to send mail to a user account when you right-click it. This will kick off your default mail handling program, and the system will try to send mail using the e-mail address supplied in the account information. So, if you have a set of people working in the finance department and you place all those people in a security group called Finance, you can not only assign permissions for resources to the Finance group, but you can also send mail to the members of the Finance security group, assuming you have filled in the e-mail information for each member.

The interesting part about these distribution groups is Win2K's close integration with the next version of Exchange, currently in beta and code-named Platinum. If you have administered Exchange and NT together, you know that it's a pain to maintain two lists, one for security and one for communication purposes. The next version of Exchange is supposed to integrate Exchange with Active Directory so you won't have to keep separate mailboxes and user accounts.

 NOTE If you are upgrading to Win2K or setting up a new Win2K server on a network with Exchange, you should make sure that there are no preexisting groups with the same name as the display name of an Exchange distribution list. Rename either the distribution list display name or the NT group name to avoid conflicts.

Distribution lists are not always the same as security groups, though. For instance, say your company is a communications provider and has a distribution list called Outage Alert. This distribution list is used to notify certain people in the case of a major outage that will affect service to your customers. The members of this list might include people from operations, customer relations, even the chief executive officer. Plus, the distribution list could include external e-mail addresses of key business partners (also known as *contacts*). These people will not have a security group in common, and it's silly to have to create a separate security group just because you need a distribution list. Since Microsoft is so determined to integrate Active Directory and Exchange, you can classify a group in the Active Directory as a distribution group, a group with no security privileges. No security identifiers are created for a distribution group, so the membership is not included in a user's credentials at logon time. You can't grant permission to use a printer to a distribution list since it doesn't appear in the ACL. The group is strictly for e-mail. Presumably, this will allow us to manage a good part of Exchange mailboxes and distribution lists without using a separate Exchange administration tool.

 NOTE You can change a security group to a distribution group and back again, but not if you're still running in Mixed mode. As with everything else that's truly useful in Win2K, you have to be running in Native mode.

Similarly, contacts are objects that store information about people, including e-mail, telephone, and related information. Contacts can be members of security or distribution groups, but they are not accounts, so there is no security identifier (SID) for a contact and no user rights or permissions can be assigned to them.

Group Scope: Locals, Globals, and Universals

Where are they recognized and what can they contain? These are the main issues surrounding local, global, and universal groups. Since they are used to grant rights and permissions, we need to know where that group membership means something, or where it is accepted (kind of like American Express). Since we want to nest groups to simplify the granting of rights and permissions, we need to know the rules and recommendations for nesting as well.

Regular local groups are the only type of group that exists on stand-alone servers and Win2K Professional systems. A stand-alone server or Professional workstation, which is not a member of a domain, is like an island nation with no knowledge of the outside world. It only recognizes its own local groups and users. Local groups are the only ones that can be granted permission to access resources, and membership is limited to local users. When the machine joins the domain, however, that island nation becomes a member of a greater governing body, like a federation of island nations. This "member server" or "member workstation" keeps its local users and groups, but will now accept non-local members from the "federation" into its local group memberships. Global groups and "federation" (domain) accounts now can be referenced on object permissions lists (Access Control Lists, or ACLs) as well.

Domain local groups, living on Active Directory domain controllers, exist in a different context than the local groups on workstations, stand-alones, or member servers. These machines are, by definition, aware of their home domain and any other domains in the AD forest. Domain local groups can therefore contain members from any domain in the forest. They can contain users, globals from your domain or a trusted one, and universals. Although domain local groups are more flexible in their membership, they are only valid in their home domain since they are only used on ACLs in the same domain. Other domains have their own domain local groups. If the domain local group were valid in another domain, it wouldn't be "local" anymore, would it? Moreover, domain local groups don't replicate to the global catalog, although membership information replicates between domain controllers in the same domain. Membership of domain local groups should be relatively small and use nesting.

 NOTE The global catalog is a domain controller that also keeps a database of basic information on all objects in the home domain, as well as information on objects in other domains in the forest. The first DC in a domain is by default a global catalog server, but others can be designated. The global catalog facilitates logins and supplies directory information on objects in other domains.

Win2K global groups are like NT 4 global groups. Global groups can only contain members from the same domain. Now in Win2K, you can put other global groups in them, but only in Native mode. You can't put a local group or a universal group into a global group, just user accounts and global groups from the same domain. Global group membership is exactly the reverse of membership in domain local groups; membership in global groups is limited, but its acceptance is wide. Global groups can be used on any ACL in the forest, even in other forests if you establish an old-fashioned-style trust relationship. Think of global groups as containers for users and groups that need to be accepted on other machines and other domains. Global group information is also replicated between sibling domain controllers, but the global catalog only contains group names, not members.

Universal groups are new to Win2K and can be created on any domain controller. They can contain members from any domain in your forest and can be used on an object's ACL within the forest. Membership in universal groups is infinitely flexible, and membership is universally accepted within the forest (remember from Chapter 2 that all domains in the forest benefit from transitive trust relationships). So why don't we just use universal groups for everything and not even worry about local or global groups anymore? There are two reasons. First, universal groups can only be used in Native mode. Native mode is only possible after you have upgraded all NT 4 domain controllers; they will not be able to handle this universal group thing. Second, if you use only universal groups, your global catalog will become bloated and replication issues could occur. You see, universal group names and membership are both replicated to the other global catalog servers (typically, there will be one for each site), while global group names appear in the global catalog, but its members don't. With multiple domains, the global catalog contains replicated information for every domain in the forest, and the size (and replication time) will increase exponentially if universal groups contain a large number of objects. Therefore, universal group membership should be fairly static. Avoid adding users directly, and only nest other groups. On the other hand, if you only have one domain for your entire organization, your global catalog servers don't have to replicate information from other domains, which cuts down on replication overhead immensely. In that case, universal groups can be used exclusively. In fact, you probably want to do away with global groups completely in a single-domain setting and just use universal groups instead.

 TIP Groups can only contain 5,000 members each. So if you have a group that you want to have 15,000 members, you have to break it up into, say, three smaller groups and put those smaller groups into a group together.

Global and universal groups can span domains, even forests. Domains and machines in different forests do not trust each other automatically and therefore do not exchange group information, but this can be accomplished with old-fashioned manually created trust relationships, as you handled multiple domain matters in NT 4.

So there you have it—the skinny on local, global, and universal groups. It's really not so hard once you know and understand the rules of thumb, which are as follows:

- Use local groups to grant local privileges and access to local resources. Put other groups into local groups and keep membership small.

- Use global groups to collect users and other same-domain global groups who will need the same privileges or access to the same resources. Put these global groups into local groups that have the desired privileges and access permissions.

- Use universal groups any way you like once you've done away with all NT 4 domain controllers, but for replication reasons, it's best to nest global groups (as opposed to user accounts) inside universal groups.

- Even though you can, don't nest groups too deeply or you'll see a performance hit.

Oh, yes, and I think it would be helpful to summarize the new nesting rules in Win2K.

Local groups (on a Win2K Professional workstation or a member server) can contain:

- Domain locals, globals, universals from the home domain
- Globals and universals from trusted Win2K domains
- Globals from trusted Windows NT 4 domains

Domain local groups (on a domain controller) can contain:

- User accounts from any domain in the forest
- Universals and globals from any forest domain
- Locals from the same domain only

Global groups can contain:

- Users from the same domain
- Other global groups from the same domain

Universal groups can contain:

- User accounts from any domain in the forest
- Other universal groups
- Global groups from any domain in the forest

Working with Security Groups

Alright, enough talk about global, local, and universal groups. You need some examples of how this works. However, let me first emphasize how important it is to think about your group structures ahead of time. Once you've "pre-nested" your larger membership groups (like the local and universal groups) and granted access to the local groups when you set up your resources, you'll only have to fiddle with global and universal group memberships from then on. This will save time and simplify the task of granting object permissions.

Some good basic nesting examples can be drawn from the nesting patterns that are set up automatically within a domain. One is the nesting of administrator groups. The Administrator account on a Win2K machine draws its powers from membership in the local Administrators group. Take Administrator out of the Administrators group and the account has no special powers or abilities (I don't recommend it). The Active Directory automatically creates the Domain Admins global group, although it doesn't assign broad admin rights to the group as you might think. When a Win2K machine joins a domain (or becomes a domain controller), the global group Domain Admins and the universal group Enterprise Admins are automatically placed in the membership of the local Administrators group. Figure 8.27 shows the membership of the domain local group Administrators for the WIN2KTEST.COM domain. The net effect of this nesting is that a member of the Domain Admins or Enterprise Admins group is a local administrator on every member machine in the domain. You can override this default behavior by removing Domain Admins or Enterprise Admins from the local Administrators group on a machine, but again, I don't recommend it unless there is a special reason to do so. You can replace the Domain Admins or Enterprise Admins group membership in the local Administrators groups with more specific Admin-type global groups, like F&A Admins or CS Admins, but having no global or universal groups at all in the local Administrators group limits control to local Administrator accounts and unnecessarily complicates remote administration tasks.

Another example of group nesting is the membership of the local Users group. On a domain member or domain controller, Users automatically includes Domain Users. When you create a new user account in a domain, the new user is automatically assigned to the Domain Users group. It's sort of an "All Users in the Domain" group. The net effect is that a user account in a domain is automatically granted local user privileges on every domain member machine by default. The user account goes into the global group Domain Users and the global group Domain Users goes into the local group Users, which is granted local rights and permissions on a system.

You should also know, just for the record, about a couple of other nestings. Domain Guests is automatically a member of the local group Guests on all domain member machines, and Enterprise Admins (a universal group) is a member of the local Administrators group.

FIGURE 8.27

Members of the Administrators domain local group

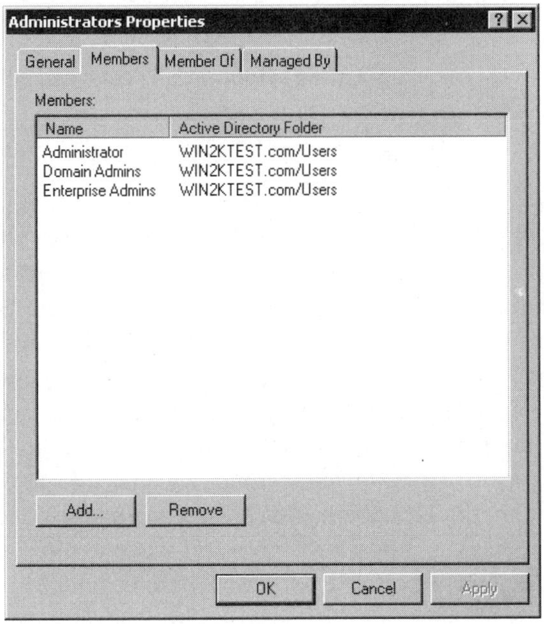

Now let's look at the fictional case of Green Onion Resources (GOR), a national IT consulting and integration firm. Green Onion uses Win2K's Active Directory with both Win2K and NT 4 domain controllers. GOR has grouped the company's IT resources into domains by regional offices—for example, GOR South domain, GOR West domain, and GOR East domain. Finance and Accounting (F&A) people are similarly grouped into global groups by region, as are other functional units of GOR. So there are global groups called F&A South, F&A West, and F&A East. Keeping the Finance people in different global groups in different domains allows finer control of region-specific resources and administration. But there are some central resources that must be accessible to all F&A people at GOR. Those resources are located in the Central Finance share on the Win2K server called GOR_ALPHA1. Now, administrators (or their delegates) have set up a local group called F&A Central on GOR_ALPHA1 and put each global group (F&A South, F&A West, and F&A East) into the local group called F&A Central. The local group F&A Central has access to the shared resource Central Finance. The following diagram illustrates the GOR strategy for F&A Central access:

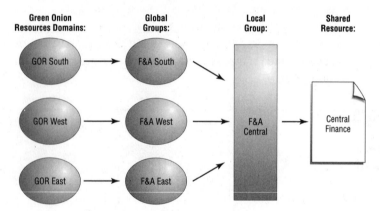

This will work and is definitely the way to go in Mixed mode. When someone is hired or leaves one of the F&A departments, admins have only to add or remove the user account from the global group to grant or deny access. This will also grant access to the region-specific resources that the global groups can already get to. But when Green Onion Resources upgrades all existing NT 4 domain controllers, they go into Native mode and the fun begins. Now they can keep the granularity of having global groups by functional unit and region but also group these different F&A regional groups into a new universal group called GOR F&A. GOR enterprise admins put the three groups, F&A South, F&A West, and F&A East, into the universal group GOR F&A. They can now use the universal group to directly permit access to F&A organization-wide resources, like the central finance folder, instead of using the three global groups, although it's still considered good form to put the universal group into a local group and grant access to the local group. The following diagram illustrates the adjustment once GOR switches to Native mode.

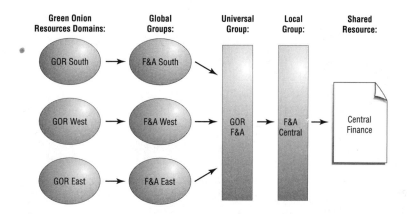

Why should we keep nesting global and universal groups into local groups even after Native mode? You can certainly just put a bunch of accounts into the GOR F&A universal group instead. If you have a single domain for your organization and never plan to have more, this strategy is perfectly acceptable. With multiple domains, however, remember that the global catalog must replicate the names and members of all universal groups throughout the forest, so having all 600 or so bean counter accounts from the different domains in one universal group becomes a replication (read "performance") issue.

You can also grant access to the shared resource directly to the universal group and bypass the local group nesting altogether. Current thinking holds that it's easier to just set up access on the resource once, then modify it by manipulating the membership of the group that has access. This was especially true under NT 4, when managing permissions on remote shares was a bit cumbersome, but Active Directory management is likely to change all that. Granting access directly to the universal group would seem to be in keeping with that principal, though, if you plan to keep your universal group membership down and limit it to other groups. The problem here is that domains and their global groups might come and go, especially in Win2K, since an entire domain can be wiped out without reinstalling the operating system. If ACL entries refer to global or universal groups that are no longer recognized as the result of a defunct domain or a broken trust relationship, ACL will report an entry as "Account Unknown" and the Forces of Darkness will increase and multiply and chaos will reign...well, maybe not. But it's messy. If you always grant access to a local group, the machine will always recognize it. Then you can just grant or deny access to a resource by manipulating the membership of that local group.

Built-In Domain Local Groups

You might have noticed in our earlier tour of DSA.MSC that all the built-in user accounts, like Guest and Administrator, are placed by default in the Users container. There are also predefined global groups in the Users container. But some groups are listed under the Builtin container. As you see in Figure 8.28, the groups in the Builtin container are labeled Builtin Local, and the ones in the Users container (Figure 8.29) are Domain Local, Global, or Universal. What's the difference? Well, for one thing, remember from Chapter 2 and our earlier discussion that local groups are specific to the machine, while global groups can be accepted throughout the domain or in a trusted domain. Built-in local groups have predetermined rights and permissions for the purposes of administration. Membership in these (or any) groups grants the user all the powers and abilities granted to the group. This is a way to quickly assign well-defined administrative roles instead of having to create them from scratch. For example, Server Operators have an inherent set of rights that allow them to create file shares and manage services. Backup Operators have the right to back up files and directories, even if they don't have permission to read or modify them. Table 8.2 lists the built-in domain local groups and their special abilities. Built-in local groups are common to all Win2K systems of the same ilk (server/DC/workstation) and provide convenient container groups for granting local administrative authority. Note that you can't delete these groups. You can, however, create other users and groups in the container, although they won't have any special rights unless you assign them.

FIGURE 8.28

DSA.MSC Builtin
container

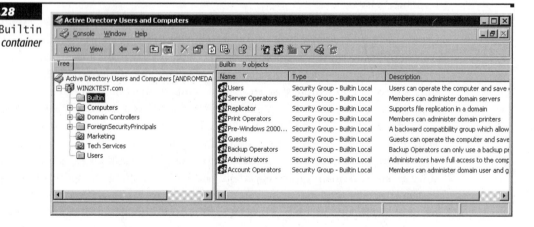

FIGURE 8.29

DSA.MSC Users container

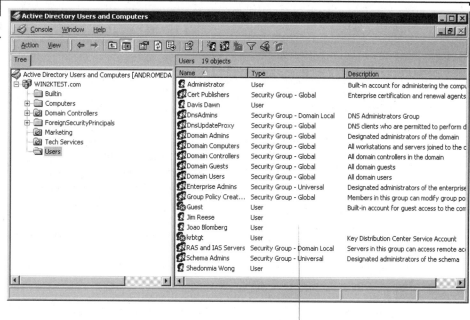

 TIP In general, rights grant the ability to do something, often something admin related or otherwise restricted, while permissions give us the ability to access resources like files and printers as well as Active Directory objects such as group policies.

TABLE 8.2: BUILT-IN GROUPS AND THEIR RIGHTS

User Rights	Members Can Also
Group: Administrators	
Log on locally	Create and manage user accounts
Access this computer from the network	Create and manage global groups
Take ownership of files	Assign user rights
Manage auditing and security log	Manage auditing and security policy
Change the system time	Lock the server console
Shut down the system	Unlock the console
Force shutdown from a remote system	Format the server's hard disk
Back up files and directories	Create common program groups
Restore files and directories	Keep a local profile
Add and remove device drivers	Share and stop sharing directories
Increase the priority of a process	Share and stop sharing printers

Continued ▶

TABLE 8.2 CONTINUED: BUILT-IN GROUPS AND THEIR RIGHTS

User Rights	Members Can Also
Group: Server Operators	
Log on locally	Lock the server
Change the system time	Override server's lock
Shut down the system	Format the server's hard disk
Force shutdown from a remote system	Create common groups
Back up files and directories	Keep a local profile
Restore files and directories	Share and stop sharing directories
	Share and stop sharing printers
Group: Account Operators	
Log on locally	Create and manage user accounts, global groups, and local groups[1]
Shut down the system	Keep a local profile
Group: Print Operators	
Log on locally	Keep a local profile
Shut down the system	Share and stop sharing printers
Group: Backup Operators	
Log on locally	Keep a local profile
Shut down the system	
Back up files and directories	
Restore files and directories	
Group: Everyone	
Access this computer from the network	Lock the server[2]
Group: Users	
(None)	Create and manage local groups[3]
Group: Guests	
(None)	(None)
Group: Replicator	
(None)	(None)

1. They cannot, however, modify Administrator accounts, the Domain Admins global group, or the local group's Administrators, Server Operators, Account Operators, Print Operators, and Backup Operators.
2. In order to actually do this, the member of the group must have the right to log on locally at the server.
3. In order to actually do this, the user must either have the right to log on locally at the server or have access to DSA.MSC tool.

Administrators   Administrators have almost every built-in right, so members are basically all-powerful with regard to administration of the system.

Backup Operators   Members of Backup Operators have the right to back up and restore files whether or not they have permission to access those files otherwise.

Server Operators   The Server Operators local group has all of the rights needed to manage the domain's servers. Members can create, manage, and delete printer shares at servers; create, manage, and delete network shares at servers; back up and restore files on servers; format a server's fixed disk; lock and unlock servers; unlock files; and change the system time. In addition, Server Operators can log on to the network from the domain's servers as well as shut down the servers.

Account Operators   Members of the Account Operators local group are allowed to create user accounts and groups for the domain and to modify or delete most of the domain's user accounts and groups.

A member of Account Operators cannot modify or delete the following groups: Administrators, Domain Admins, Account Operators, Backup Operators, Print Operators, and Server Operators. Likewise, members of this group cannot modify or delete user accounts of administrators. They cannot administer the security policies, but they can add computers to a domain, log on at servers, and shut down servers.

Print Operators   Members of this group can create, manage, and delete printer shares for a Win2K server. Additionally, they can log on at and shut down servers.

Power Users   This group exists on non–domain controllers and Win2K Professional systems. Members can create user accounts and local groups and can manage the membership of Users, Power Users, and Guests as well as administer other users and groups that they have created.

Users   Users can run applications (but not install them). They also can shut down and lock the workstation. If a user has the right to log on locally to a workstation, they also have the right to create local groups and manage those groups they have created.

Guests   Guests can log on and run applications. They can also shut down the system, but otherwise their abilities are even more limited than Users. For instance, they cannot keep a local profile.

Replicator   This group is strictly for directory replication. A user account is used to run the Replicator service, and it should be the only member of the group.

In the Users container, other predefined domain local groups and global groups may be created as part of the configuration of a certain service. They might serve to allow users access to certain services (like DHCP Users and WINS Users) or to provide a group container for administrators of the service, as in the case of DHCP Administrators and DNS Admins. These and other predefined global groups may also have special rights and/or permissions for particular things, but they don't have the broad rights and permissions of Administrators, Server Operators, or another built-in local group.

 NOTE   Some predefined groups, like Domain Computers and Domain Controllers, are designated for machine accounts, although you can add a user account to Domain Computers if it gives you a thrill.

Win2K has several built-in global groups, among them Domain Admins, Domain Users, and Domain Guests. These will only appear on domain controllers. In fact, it's possible to create global groups *only* on domain controllers. Although you might use an administration tool while sitting at a non-domain controller to create the global groups, they exist only on domain controllers. Table 8.3 describes the most important built-in global groups.

TABLE 8.3: BUILT-IN GLOBAL GROUPS

Group	What It Does
Domain Admins	By placing a user account into this global group, you provide administrative-level abilities to that user. Members of Domain Admins can administer the home domain, the workstations of the domain, and any other trusted domains that have added this domain's Domain Admins global group to their own Administrators local group. By default, the built-in Domain Admins global group is a member of both the domain's Administrators local group and the Administrators local groups for every NT or Win2K workstation in the domain. The built-in Administrator user account for the domain is automatically a member of the Domain Admins global group.
Domain Users	Members of the Domain Users global group have normal user access to, and abilities for, both the domain itself and any NT/Win2K workstation in the domain. This group contains all domain user accounts and is by default a member of every local Users group on every NT/Win2K workstation in the domain.
Domain Guests	This group allows guest accounts to access resources across domain boundaries if they've been permitted to do so by the domain administrators.

Special Built-In Groups

In addition to the built-in local and global groups, several special groups that are not listed in DSA.MSC (or Computer Management Users and Groups for that matter) will appear on Access Control Lists for resources and objects, including the following:

INTERACTIVE   Anyone using the computer locally.

NETWORK   All users connected over the network to a computer.

SYSTEM   The operating system.

CREATOR OWNER   The creator and/or owner of subdirectories, files, and print jobs.

AUTHENTICATED USERS   Any user that has been authenticated to the system. Used as a more secure alternative to Everyone.

ANONYMOUS LOGON   A user that has logged on anonymously, such as an anonymous FTP user.

BATCH   An account that has logged on as a batch job.

SERVICE   An account that has logged on as a service.

DIALUP   Users who are accessing the system via Dial-Up Networking.

Incidentally, the INTERACTIVE and NETWORK groups together form the Everyone local group.

User Rights

User access to network resources—files, directories, devices—in Win2K is controlled in two ways: by assigning to a user *rights* that grant or deny access to certain objects (for example, the ability to log on to a server) and by assigning to objects *permissions* that specify who is allowed to use objects and under what conditions (for example, granting Read access for a directory to a particular user).

Consider the groups Users and Administrators. What makes administrators different from users? Well, administrators can log on right at the server; users can't. Administrators can create users and back up files; users can't. Administrators are different from users in that they have rights that users don't have. You control who gets which rights in Win2K by using Group Policy. Rights generally authorize a user to perform certain system tasks. For example, the average user can't just sit down at a Win2K server and log on right at the server. The question "can I log on locally at a server?" is an example of a right. "Can I back up data and restore data?" "Can I modify printer options on a shared printer?" These are also user rights. User rights can be assigned separately to a single user, but for reasons of security organization, it is better to put the user into a group and define which rights are granted to the group.

Permissions, on the other hand, apply to specific objects such as files, directories, and printers. "Can I make changes to files in the OPERATIONS directory on the BIGMA-CHINE server?" is an example of a permission. Permissions regulate which users can have access to the object and in what fashion.

As a rule, user rights take precedence over object permissions. For example, let's look at a user who is a member of the built-in Backup Operators group. By virtue of membership in that group, the user has the right to back up the server. This requires the ability to see and read all directories and files on the servers, including those whose creators and owners have specifically denied Read permission to members of the Backup Operators group; thus the right to perform backups overrides the permissions set on the files and directories. But don't worry about your privacy; the Backup Operators group's rights are only valid in conjunction with a backup routine; they can't just open files on the server and read the contents, for example.

Win2K's built-in groups have certain rights already assigned to them; you can also create new groups and assign a custom set of user rights to those groups. As I've said before, security management is much easier when all user rights are assigned through groups instead of to individual users.

To view or modify the local rights assignment for a user or group, open the Local Security Policy tool from the Administrative Tools group on a non–domain controller, or use the Domain Controller Security Policy tool for a domain controller. Open Local Policies\User Rights Assignment. A listing of rights and the users or groups that have been granted them will display in the details pane on the right, as shown in Figure 8.30.

To add or remove a right to a user or group, double-click the right displayed in the details pane, or right-click the selected right and choose Security. In Figure 8.31 you see the Security information for the right to change the system time. To remove a right from a group, highlight the name of the group and choose Remove. To add a group or user to the list, choose Add and, in Select users of Groups dialog box, type in a name or choose Browse to select a name. Table 8.4 lists user rights with descriptions.

FIGURE 8.30

Local user rights policy

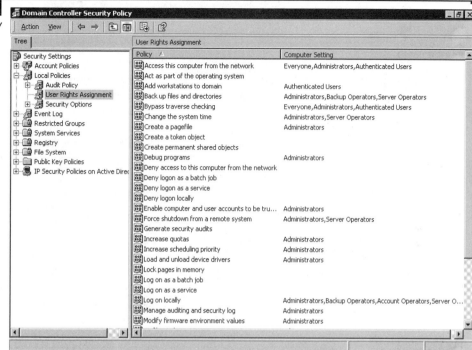

FIGURE 8.31

Local security policy setting for a user right

TABLE 8.4: LOCAL USER RIGHTS

User Right	Description
Access this computer from the network	Connect over the network to a computer.
Act as part of the operating system	Act as a trusted part of the operating system; some subsystems have this privilege granted to them.
Add workstations to domain	Make machines domain members.
Back up files and directories	Back up files and directories. As mentioned earlier, this right supersedes file and directory permissions.
Bypass traverse checking	Traverse a directory tree even if the user has no other rights to access that directory.
Change the system time	Set the time for the internal clock of a computer.
Create a pagefile	Create a pagefile.
Create a token object	Create access tokens. Only the Local Security Authority should have this privilege.
Create permanent shared objects	Create special permanent objects.
Debug programs	Debug applications.
Deny access to this computer from the network	Opposite of the Access this computer from the network right; specifically revokes the right to users/groups that would normally have it.
Deny logon as a batch job	Revokes the right to log on as a batch job.
Deny logon as a service	Revokes the right to log on as a service.
Deny logon locally	Revokes the right to log on locally.
Enable computer and user accounts to be trusted for delegation	Designate accounts which can be delegated.
Force shutdown from a remote system	Force a computer to shut down from a remote system.
Generate security audits	Generate audit log entries.
Increase quotas	Increase object quotas (each object has a quota assigned to it).
Increase scheduling priority	Boost the scheduling priority of a process.
Load and unload device drivers	Add or remove drivers from the system.
Lock pages in memory	Lock pages in memory to prevent them from being paged out into backing store (such as PAGEFILE.SYS).
Log on as a batch job	Log on to the system as a batch queue facility.
Log on as a service	Perform security services (the user that performs replication logs on as a service).

Continued ▐▶

TABLE 8.4 CONTINUED: LOCAL USER RIGHTS

User Right	Description
Log on locally	Log on locally at the server computer itself.
Manage auditing and security log	Specify what types of events and resource access are to be audited. Also allows viewing and clearing the security log.
Modify firmware environment values	Modify system environment variables (not user environment variables).
Profile single process	Use Win2K profiling capabilities to observe a process.
Profile system performance	Use Win2K profiling capabilities to observe the system.
Remove computer from docking station	Remove a laptop computer from its docking station.
Replace a process level token	Modify a process's access token.
Restore files and directories	Restore files and directories. This right supersedes file and directory permissions.
Shut down the system	Shut down Windows 2000.
Synchronize directory service data	Update Active Directory information.
Take ownership of files or other objects	Take ownership of files, directories, and other objects that are owned by other users.

Many rights, such as the one to debug programs and the one to profile a single process, are useful only to programmers who are writing applications to run on Win2K, and most are not granted to a group or user.

In general, I find that the only user right that I ever end up granting is the right to change the system time; regular users need that ability in order for their login scripts to successfully synchronize time with the time server, although members of the Power Users group already have it. Also, many third-party applications, like backup programs and virus scanning engines, require an Administrator-level user account that can "log on as a service."

How Do Organizational Units Fit in Here?

Organizational units (OUs) are logical containers in a domain. They can contain users, groups, computers, and other OUs, but only from their home domain. You can't put global groups or computers from another domain into your domain's OU, for example.

The usefulness of OUs is strictly for administration. Administrators can create and apply group policies to an OU, and they can delegate control of OUs as well. The idea is to have a subdivision of a domain but still share common security information and resources. Grouping users, groups, and resources into organizational units allows you to apply policies in a more granular fashion and also to decide who manages what and to what extent. So whatever anyone says about how to group your OUs, keep in mind that the tool must fit your hand; your organization may be unique, so your approach to OUs may be as well.

Rather than creating OUs for locations (that's what sites are for), departments, and so on, think about how your organization will be administered. Design your OUs with delegation in mind. Keep it simple for your own sake. Thousands of nested OUs just make more work for you. Also, OUs are unrelated to the process of locating resources on your network, so you needn't group them with a browse list in mind, either.

What's the difference between an OU and a container? An OU is a container, but not just a container like the Users container in DSA.MSC. You can delegate control of a container (you can delegate control of anything), but you can't apply Group Policy to one.

How are OUs different than groups? A user can be a member of many groups but can only be in one OU at a time. Like groups, an OU can contain other OUs. Group names appear on ACLs, so you can grant or deny access to groups. OUs do not appear on ACLs, so you can't give everyone in the Finance OU access to a printer, for example. On the other hand, you can't assign everyone in a security group a designated set of desktop applications, but you can publish or assign the company accounting package to the entire Accounting OU.

Zen and the Art of Login Scripts

Login scripts are an ancient revered method for configuring a user's working environment and assigning network resources. Before we had Network Neighborhood, in a time before Microsoft networks came into prominence, network clients were relatively unenlightened about the network around them. Login scripts were written in the common language of the client and ran from the server on the client at the time of logon. These scripts would create local drive mappings to the servers, redirect local ports to assign printers, synchronize the system clock with a central designated time server, and perform other honorable related tasks. One could say, Grasshopper, that login scripts reached their peak in the Age of NetWare, when the color red blanketed the networking world. In the Age of NT 4, networking clients become more aware of the network around them. In small isolated networks, the Art was all but abandoned, but login scripts still flourished in large complex environments, prized for their eternal usefulness. During this time, the Art became more sophisticated. While login scripts are now used to perform increasingly complex tasks, the essential Art, the True Art, has remained unchanged.

Today Win2K offers us the ability to use not only login scripts but also logout scripts, start-up scripts, and shutdown scripts. You're no longer confined to a limited set of shell commands, either. Organizations now use a myriad of scripting and even programming languages to accomplish eye-popping configuration feats compared to those of 10 years ago. There is no way to do justice to everything that's out there in the few pages allotted here, but I will discuss your options in a scripting language, take a look at an example login script, and tell you how to assign one in Win2K.

Scripting Languages

A wide variety of scripting environments and languages are available today, including DOS/NT/Win2K shell commands, Windows Scripting Host (WSH), KiXtart, XLNT, Perl, VBScript, JScript, even Python. You can literally use any language that is useful to you and that your client machine understands. Login scripts are only limited by a couple of things: developers and clients. A script developer (that includes you) must know how to use the chosen tool. It's no good to try writing a login script program in C if you can't even figure out how to make it say "Good Morning." The vast majority of us aren't programmers, so we must use simpler tools, like shell scripts or special login script languages like KiXtart or XLNT. The client must understand the language of the script as well, so if you want to use Perl, for example, you need a Perl interpreter installed on each client system.

Win2K/NT/Windows 9x shell commands are an obvious choice for login scripts. No special client software is required. If you have pre-NT clients, your command set is rather limited, but the NT 4 command-line language is actually fairly robust in comparison to the earlier set of commands. Plus, all of the NT 4 scripts I've tried on Win2K systems still work, so there is a great deal of backward compatibility built in to the Win2K shell language. In my humble opinion, however, NT/Win2K shell scripting is still less flexible or intuitive than any of the various Unix shell languages. Remember that Windows software (even Win2K and NT) was not designed primarily for command-line geeks, but for people with mice (the electronic kind). However, Microsoft is showing some improvements in the command-line arena, so let's encourage them.

KiXtart 95 was designed by Ruud van Velsen at Microsoft Benelux. It is a freeware login script processor which also serves as an enhanced batch language. KiXtart is extremely flexible and easy to use. A version was released in the NT 4 Resource Kit, but you will want to download the latest version from `kixtart.to/script/`. There is also an online manual at this site. Again, I am assuming that most of your clients will not be Win2K Professional systems yet, although the KiXtart scripts I use run perfectly well on Win2K machines.

Perl (Practical Extraction and Reporting Language) was initially developed for system administrators as a tool to run reports. It has become much, much more. Platform independent like Java, but without the memory overhead of the Java virtual machine, Perl has already proven its usefulness to Unix administrators and developers and is quickly becoming one of the more popular scripting languages in the Windows world as well. You will have to install a Perl interpreter and modules on your clients, although this process is relatively painless. Alternately, there is a utility called Perl2Exe that converts Perl scripts to executables. If you don't mind the overhead of running a program that's around 700K (script, interpreter, and any modules) across the network whenever users log on, download it from www.demobuilder.com. The latest version of Perl for Windows 95/98/NT, ActivePerl, is available from www.activestate.com/ActivePerl/. ActivePerl includes Perlscript, an ActiveX scripting engine like VBScript or JScript. There is also a wealth of information on Perl in bookstores and at www.perl.com.

The Windows Scripting Host (WSH) is an environment for running Visual Basic Scripting Edition (VBScript) and JavaScript natively on Windows 95/98, NT, or Win2K. The Scripting Host (and a Script Debugger) are included with Win2K, and WSH is an installation option for Windows 98, but you'll need to download WSH for 95 or NT from msdn.microsoft.com/scripting/windowshost. The site is also a good source of information, and there is a link to wsh.glazier.co.nz/, a site that focuses on using WSH for login scripts. You'll find examples of WSH login scripts there.

There are numerous other scripting environments, like C shell, PythonWin, XLNT, and the MKS Toolkit by Mortice Kern Systems, Inc. (MKS is a toolkit which includes Korn shell, Vi editor, AWK, and more, for you Unix-heads). These are available for either evaluation or as freeware from www.microsoft.com/NTServer/nts/exec/vendors/freeshare/develope.asp. Yes, Microsoft has a third-party software download area. Really!

Assigning the Login Script

Specify a login script in the user account profile information in DSA.MSC, or assign scripts using Group Policy. Either way, the scripts and any other necessary files need to be in the SYSVOL share, found in \winnt\SYSVOL\sysvol. Pre-Win2K clients look for a share called NETLOGON for the script. Win2K machines create a NETLOGON share in \winnt\SYSVOL\sysvol\domainname\scripts for backward compatibility. If you have Win2K Professional machines as clients, Group Policy can be used to assign a login script. Scripts assigned to Win2K machines using Group Policy run asynchronously in hidden windows, so the user shell may actually start before logon script processing is complete. Scripts assigned in account properties run synchronously in visible windows by default. In that case, the user shell does not start until the script is done.

Example Login Script

The following sample scripts serve to illustrate the types of things you can do in a login script. This is an abbreviated version of an actual login script; as they used to say on that old TV show, "The names have been changed to protect the innocent." In this configuration, login.bat, the designated login script, calls the main script (login.scr), which uses KiXtart 95 scripting language to map drives according to group memberships. At the end of login.scr, a script called setmail.bat is called to check for a user's Exchange mail profile and to create one if it doesn't already exist. The setmail script is not included here, but I show the call command in the main routine as an example of using login scripts to ease configuration tasks other than mapping network drives.

The KiXtart script (`login.scr`) uses semicolons for comments, which I have supplied to explain to anyone who reads the script what the commands are doing. `Login.bat` uses native shell scripting, so comment lines are preceded by the command REM.

Since this is a sample login script and not a textbook example of shell scripting or KiXtart scripting, I've included numerous comments instead of a line-by-line explanation, and instead of the usual commented-out statements in the script, to let you know what's going on.

All of the executables used in the scripts are kept in NETLOGON for simplicity's sake (we have NT 4 workstations and a few straggling Windows 95 clients).

Example 8.1: *Login.bat* (Designated Login Script)

First, turn off the command echo:

```
@echo off
```

Since NT and 95/98 call login scripts differently, let's check the %OS% variable to see if it's set to Windows_NT and, if it isn't, skip to the subroutine for Windows 95/98 clients:

```
@if not "%OS%"=="Windows_NT" GOTO 950S
```

NT machines can run the script with a UNC path. The KIX32 executable takes as its argument the name of the script:

```
:NTOS
\\SERVER1\NETLOGON\kix32.exe \\SERVER1\netlogon\LOGIN.scr
GOTO EOF
```

Windows 95/98 machines temporarily map the Z: drive to NETLOGON during the logon sequence. They cannot run the script using a UNC path. The path statement is not for KIX32.EXE, but rather for other executables called later:

```
:950S

path=z:\
z:\kix32.exe z:\Login.scr
GOTO EOF


:EOF
EXIT
```

Example 8.2: *Login.scr* (KiXtart Login Script Called by *Login.bat*)

```
:STAGE1
```

Statements preceded by a question mark (?) cause the text that follows on the same line to be displayed on the console screen, much like ECHO does in the native shell language:

```
? "NXT login script now processing..."


? "Querying your System Information..."
```

We need to check again for 95/98 versus NT machines because variables are set differently for each. @INWIN is a KiXtart variable used for this purpose. Again, the script processing skips to the appropriate subroutine, SETVARNT or SETVAR95, depending on the OS. Win2K boxes will process as NT machines and Windows 98 systems will process like Windows 95 machines:

```
IF @INWIN = 1
    GOTO SETVARNT
ELSE
    GOTO SETVAR95
ENDIF
```

These commands set variables on 95/98 clients using SHELL and WINSET.EXE. SHELL is a KiXtart routine to call a native shell command, and WINSET.EXE is actually an executable from the Windows 95 CD which sets environmental variables. @USERID and the other words preceded by @ are variables that KiXtart understands. Thus, we are using KiXtart variable values to set actual system environmental variables:

```
:SETVAR95
SHELL "winset.exe USERNAME=@USERID"
SHELL "winset.exe ADDRESS=@ADDRESS"
SHELL "winset.exe COMPUTER=@WKSTA"
SHELL "winset.exe DOMAIN=@DOMAIN"
SHELL "winset.exe COMMENT=@COMMENT"
SHELL "winset.exe FULLNAME=@FULLNAME"
SHELL "winset.exe HOMEDIR=@HOMEDIR"
SHELL "winset.exe HOMESHR=@HOMESHR"
SHELL "winset.exe LSERVER=@LSERVER"
SHELL "winset.exe PRIV=@PRIV"
GOTO STAGE2
```

On NT and Win2K boxes, the commands below set variables without "shelling out" to the native command environment. The SET command sets user variables, while SETM defines system variables:

```
:SETVARNT
;set variables on NT clients using set command
SET USERNAME="@USERID"
SETM ADDRESS="@ADDRESS"
SETM COMPUTER="@WKSTA"
SETM DOMAIN="@DOMAIN"
SET COMMENT="@COMMENT"
SET FULLNAME="@FULLNAME"
SET HOMEDIR="@HOMEDIR"
SET HOMESHR="@HOMESHR"
SET LSERVER="@LSERVER"
SET PRIV="@PRIV"
```

KiXtart includes a special executable to query for group memberships. I put it in the NETLOGON share for convenience:

```
:STAGE2
? "Querying your group memberships..."
;SHELL "\\server1\netlogon\kixgrp.exe /s"
```

Time synchronization is an important function in many login scripts. The SERVER1 listed here is a designated time server that synchronizes regularly with a reliable external time source:

```
? "Synchronizing your system's clock"
;synchronize with time server
SETTIME \\server1
```

Next, we check to see if the time synchronization was successful. If it wasn't, a message box pops up to get the user's attention:

```
IF @error = 0
   ? "System clock synchronized"
ELSE
   MESSAGEBOX ("Cannot synchronize the system clock.
   Please inform your administrator.","XYZ Login Script", 0)
ENDIF
?
```

The following commands will use group membership to map network drives. Just in case, we'll delete any preexisting drive mappings first. Again, if there are errors deleting previous drive mappings, a message box will get the user's attention:

```
? "Now mapping network drives..."
?
;delete any previous drive mappings and check for errors
USE "*" /DELETE
IF @error = 0
   ?"Previous mappings deleted..."
ELSE
   MESSAGEBOX ("Cannot delete previous drive mappings.
   Please inform your administrator.",
   "XYZ Login Script", 0)
ENDIF


;MAP Drives by Group Membership

;Map Domain F & A to M: drive
IF INGROUP ("Domain F & A") = 1
   use M: "\\server1\F&A Control"
   ? "F & A Drive Mapped"
ENDIF


;Map Domain Sales to S: drive
IF INGROUP ("Domain Sales") = 1
   use S: \\server1\Sales
   ? "Sales Drive Mapped"
ENDIF


;Map Domain Tech Services to T: drive
IF INGROUP ("Domain Tech Services") = 1
   use T: \\server1\TechSvcs
   ? "Tech Services Drive Mapped"
ENDIF
```

```
;Map common drives for Domain Users
IF INGROUP ("Domain Users") = 1
    use G: \\server1\apps
    use P: \\server1\public
    use N: \\server1\infosys
    use H: @HOMESHR
    ? "Global Drives and Home Directories Mapped"
ENDIF
```

Finally, the script will call the `setmail.bat` script for NT boxes only. It only runs this for NT boxes because some of the executables used in the script don't work reliably on the few remaining 95 machines on our network. SETMAIL.BAT checks the system for the existence of an Exchange mail profile for the user and, if one does not exist, automatically creates one:

```
IF @INWIN = 1
    ? "Checking for your Mail Profile..."
    shell setmail.bat
ENDIF

? "Login Script Complete"
EXIT
```

Working with Group Policies

An administrator's work is never done. Users are constantly fiddling with their settings, it's hard to maintain "standard builds," and rolling out new applications is a big headache, in large networks or small. It's a pain to package up applications, remote management systems like SMS are unnecessarily complex, and Admin privileges are needed to install many applications on NT or Win2K machines. What a marketing opportunity!

When it comes to configuration management, there are a lot of buzzwords flying around these days: system policies, Group Policy, Change and Configuration Management (CCM), Intellimirror. What do these words mean to an everyday admin who just wants to maintain some continuity in desktop configurations?

CCM and Intellimirror are marketing monikers for a group of Win2K desktop management features, including roaming profiles and folder redirection, offline folders, software distribution, and desktop configuration control (I mean management). Despite the fancy terms, many of these features, including folder redirection, software distribution, and remote desktop configuration, are easily implemented with group policies.

What kinds of things can you do with group policies? Here's a brief list:

- Publish or assign software packages to users or machines.
- Assign start-up, shutdown, logon, and logoff scripts.
- Define password, lockout, and audit policy for the domain.
- Standardize a whole bunch of other security settings for remote machines, settings which were previously only configurable by editing the Registry or using a third-party security configuration tool. Some features, like the ability to enforce group memberships and services configuration, are completely new.
- Define and enforce settings for Internet Explorer.
- Define and enforce restrictions on users' desktops.
- Redirect certain folders in a users' profiles (like Start Menu or Desktop) to be stored in a central location.
- Configure and standardize settings for new features like offline folders, disk quotas, even Group Policy itself.

Many of these new features are discussed in sections of their own throughout this book. Software distribution will be discussed in Chapter 10, "Software Installation." Chapter 9, "Creating and Managing Shared Folders," will touch on offline folders. User profiles will be discussed later in this chapter. Folder redirection is really a lightweight approach to user profiles ("Profiles Lite"), allowing you to use a subset of the full roaming profile features, so we'll talk about that later in this chapter as well. The key point here is that Group Policy provides a single point of administration, allowing administrators to easily install software and apply standardized settings to multiple users and computers throughout an organization.

Before Win2K, a much smaller subset of these things, mostly just desktop restriction and a few security settings, were accomplished using system policies. Group policies have improved on system policies in a couple of major ways. For one thing, system policies write permanent changes to the Registry when they are applied. This phenomenon is commonly called *tattooing*. Remove the policy, and the settings remain. You actually have to "reverse the policy" (by applying a policy with opposite settings) or change the settings manually. Group policies, on the other hand, write their information only to certain parts of the Registry, so they are able to clean up after themselves when the policy is removed. System policies are applied only once: at logon for user settings, at start-up for computer settings. Group policies are also applied this way, but they are reapplied at specific intervals. Finally, group policies do a lot more than just modify Registry settings. The bad news is that they only work on Win2K Server or Professional machines, and they require Active Directory, although it is possible to apply a more limited set of "local policies" without AD.

WARNING You can only use group policies to control Windows 2000 Server and Windows 2000 Professional machines. If your users run Windows 95/98 or Windows NT Workstation 4 on their desktops, you'll have to use the same old tools as before—Windows 9*x* profiles and system policies and Windows NT 4 profiles and group policies. Yes, you read that right—you could potentially have to worry about one set of policies for the Windows machines, another for the NT 4 machines, and a set of group policies for the Windows 2000 machines. In the same way, you might have a set of profiles for Windows 9*x* users, another for the NT 4 users, and a third set for the Windows 2000 users. If it's any consolation, you can store all of these things on a Windows 2000 server—it's not like you've got to keep an old NT 4 server around to hold the NT profiles.

Group policies are stored partially in the Active Directory and partially in the SYSVOL share, so you don't have to worry about replicating them around. The File Replication Service (FRS), a grown-up version of NT 4's rather lame Directory Replication Service, automatically replicates the Active Directory and SYSVOL contents among domain controllers.

In the sections that follow, you will learn how group policies work and how to create and modify group policies. You will become familiar with the different nodes and settings in the Group Policy snap-in and look at a few examples of deploying group policies in your organization. Finally, we'll discuss some of the dos and don'ts of Group Policy.

Group Policy Concepts

First, let's discuss some important concepts, terms, and rules you need to know to master Group Policy. As I explain the functionality of Group Policy, I will mention several settings without showing you how to turn them on in the Group Policy snap-in. Just focus on the concepts for now, and later on in this section, we'll take a full tour of the Group Policy snap-in. At that time, I'll point out the all settings (such as No Override and Block Inheritance) that are discussed in this section.

Administrators configure and deploy Group Policy by building *group policy objects* (*GPOs*). GPOs are containers for groups of settings (*policies*) that can be applied to users and machines throughout a network. Policy objects are created using the Group Policy snap-in, usually invoked with the Group Policy tab in DSA.MSC or DSSITE.MSC. The same GPO could specify a set of applications to be installed on all users' desktops, implement a fascist policy of disk quotas and restrictions on the Explorer shell, and define domain-wide password and account lockout policies. It is possible to create one all-encompassing GPO or several different GPOs, one for each type of function.

There are two major nodes in the Group Policy snap-in, User Configuration and Computer Configuration. User configuration policies apply to user-specific settings, like application configuration or folder redirection, while computer configuration policies manage machine-specific settings like disk quotas, auditing, and Event Log management. However, there is a good bit of overlap. It's not unusual to find the same policy available in both the User Configuration and Computer Configuration nodes. Be prepared for a certain amount of head-scratching while you search for the policy you want to activate and decide whether to use the user-based policy or the computer policy. Keep in mind that you may create a policy that uses both types of settings, or you may create separate user and computer configuration policy objects.

Contrary to their name, group policies aren't group-oriented at all. Maybe they are called group policies because a bunch of different configuration management tools are *grouped* together in one snap-in (maybe "assorted policies" just didn't have the same ring to it). In any case, you cannot apply them directly to groups or users, but only to sites, domains, and OUs (which Microsoft abbreviates with the term *SDOU*). This act of assigning GPOs to a site, domain, or OU is called *linking*. GPOs can also be linked to local policy on a particular Win2K machine, as you'll see in a moment. The GPO-to-SDOU relationship may be many to one (many policies applied to one OU, for example) or one to many (one policy linked to several different OUs). Once linked to a site, domain, or organizational unit, user policies are applied at login time, while computer policies are applied at system start-up. Both are also periodically refreshed, with a few important exceptions.

NOTE Group policies aren't just Registry changes. Several policies are applied with Client Side Extension (CSE) DLLs. Some examples are disk quota policy, folder redirection, and software installation. In fact, there is a CSE DLL that processes the Registry changes, USERENV.DLL.

NOTE When I said GPOs were stored in the AD, that wasn't exactly correct. Group policy objects are stored in two parts, a Group Policy Container (GPC), and a policy folder structure in the SYSVOL. The container part is stored in the Active Directory and contains property information, version info, status, and a list of components. The folder structure path is WINNT\SYSVOL\sysvol\Domainname\Policies*GUID*\ where *GUID* is a Global Unique Identifier for the GPO. This folder contains administrative templates (ADM files), security settings, info on available applications, and script filenames with command lines.

NOTE Group policy objects are rooted in the Active Directory of a domain; you can't copy them to other domains, but you can link them across domain boundaries, although it's not recommended.

Policies Are "All or Nothing"

Each group policy object contains many possible settings for many functions; usually you'll configure only a few of them. The others will be left "inactive," sort of like putting REM in front of a command in a script or using a semicolon at the beginning of a line in an INF file. Win2K still has to read the whole policy, but it only acts on the options you've enabled. However, once you've configured a set of policies and told AD that "this GPO is linked to the win2ktest.com domain," for example, the individual settings or types of settings cannot be selectively applied. All user configuration settings will be applied to all users on Win2K systems in the linked domain. All computer configuration settings will be applied to all Win2K machines in the domain. Remember that neither will be applied to NT 4 or 95/98 clients.

Now, let's say you've created a GPO that deploys a set of standard desktop applications like Word, Excel, and Outlook, and you threw in a bunch of shell restrictions to prevent users from changing their configurations. If you don't want your IT support group users to be subject to those ridiculously stringent shell restrictions (although they may need them most of all!), you can do a couple of things. You can create a separate GPO for those policies and link it to a lower-level container, like an OU that contains all the regular users. But that OU will be the only one that gets the Office applications. You can alternately set permissions on the GPO which prevent the policy from being applied to the IT support group (this is called filtering). However, if you use filtering to solve this problem, none of the settings in the GPO will apply to the IT support group at all. Group policy application is all or nothing, so sometimes you really need separate policies for separate functions. The best way to approach this might be to create a GPO for standard software deployment and a GPO for shell restrictions. Both could be applied at the domain level, but shell restrictions can be filtered for the IT support group. The point is, it's not possible to create one monolithic policy and then specify who gets what settings, and you wouldn't want to do that anyway. At least, you wouldn't want to troubleshoot it.

Policies Are Inherited and Cumulative

Group Policy settings are cumulative and inherited from parent Active Directory containers. For example, win2test.com domain has several different GPOs. There is a domain-level policy that sets password restrictions, account lockout, and standard security settings. Each OU also has a policy to deploy and maintain standard desktop applications as well as folder redirection settings and desktop restrictions. Users and computers who are in both the domain and the OU receive settings both from the domain-level policy and from the OU-level policy. So some blanket policies can be applied to the entire domain, while others can be hashed out according to OUs.

Group Policy Application Order

This inheritance and accumulation is all nice and simple as long as the policies they receive from the domain are changing different settings from those specified in the OU policy. But what if they are the same? What if they both change the same setting and the domain policy says one thing while the OU policy says something else?

Policies are applied in the following order: local policy, sites, domains, organizational units, then OUs inside of OUs. If the domain policy says, "You must be logged in before you can shut down the machine," and OU policy says, "Allow shutdown before logon," the OU policy is applied last and therefore takes precedence. If one policy says, "Lock it down," and the next one says, "Not configured," the setting remains locked down. If one policy says, "Not configured," and the next one says, "Lock it down," it's locked down as well. If one policy says, "Leave it on," and the next one says, "Turn it off," it's turned off. If one policy says, "Turn it off," and another, closer one says, "Turn it on," then a third one says, "Turn it off," guess what? It ends up turned off. However, for the preservation of your sanity, it is desirable to avoid these little disagreements between policies.

No Override and Block Inheritance

Just as filtering can be used to counter the blanket application of policies, Block Inheritance is a special setting on a policy to prevent higher-level policies from trickling down. When it's turned on, the settings of higher policies won't be applied to lower containers at all. For example, if you create a GPO for a specific OU, like Accounting, and set up all the necessary settings for the Accounting OU, and then you want to prevent the win2ktest domain GPOs from affecting the Accounting OU, turn on Block Inheritance. The only policies applied will be the Accounting OU policies.

There is also a counter to the Block Inheritance counter. (Isn't this becoming like a *Batman* episode? "Robin, they've blocked our transmission. It's time for the block-anti-block Bat-transmitter!") When No Override is turned on for a policy, settings in subsequent policies are prevented from reversing the ones in the No Override–enabled policy. For example, if domain admins have a set of highly disputed settings turned on at the domain level, and those renegade accounting admins set up their own OU with its own policies and turn on Block Inheritance, the Accounting OU effectively escapes the disputed settings...but only until the domain admins get wise and turn on No Override. Then the domain admins win and the Accounting OU people have to live with the same restrictions as everyone else. No Override beats Block Inheritance (just like paper covers rock).

Like all secret weapons, No Override and Block Inheritance are best used sparingly. Otherwise, in a troubleshooting situation it becomes rather complicated to determine what policies are applied where. This could be detrimental to the mental health of a network administrator.

Refresh Intervals for Group Policy

Policies are reapplied every 90 minutes, with a 30-minute "randomization" to keep the domain controller from getting hit by dozens or even hundreds of computers at once. They are refreshed on DCs every 5 minutes, but there's a policy to configure all of this, as you'll see in the section coming up, "Group Policy Policies." (So, if I set a policy for the refresh interval on Blanket Vanilla Policy Policy, would that be referred to as Blanket Vanilla Policy Policy Policy?) Exceptions to the refresh interval include folder redirection and software installation. These are only applied at logon or system start-up time; otherwise, you might end up uninstalling an application while someone is trying to use it. Or a user might be working in a folder that is being redirected to a new network location. That would be bad.

Local Policies and Group Policy Objects

When you use Active Directory Users and Computers or Active Directory Sites and Services to create and link group policies, you are working with group policy *objects* to specify a collection of settings to be applied at user logon or machine boot time. The information in the GPO says things like "change this, change that, install this, disable that." But administrators also need to be able to view the actual settings for these policies sometimes. In NT 4, the System Policy Editor could also be used to view and edit those Registry entries for the local machine (instead of creating or editing a policy, you chose to open the Registry). As such, it served as a more user-friendly Registry editing tool than REGEDIT.EXE or REGEDT32.EXE. Similarly, the Group Policy snap-in provides the ability to view local policy settings on a machine.

If you open the Group Policy tool provided with Win2K (GPEDIT.MSC), it automatically focuses on the local machine, as shown in Figure 8.32. Administrators can use the tool as they would use the Local Security Policy tool to configure account settings (like minimum password length and number of bad login attempts before locking the account) and set up auditing. With the exceptions of software installation and folder redirection, all of the settings from Group Policy are also available for local policy configuration.

FIGURE 8.32

Group Policy snap-in

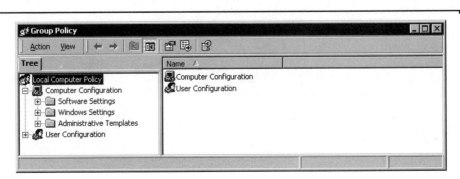

NOTE The local group policy folder structure is equivalent to that of other GPOs and is found in `\winnt\system32\GroupPolicy`.

To focus on another computer's local policy, you must have Administrator rights on that machine. You can select a computer while adding the Group Policy snap-in to a custom management console, as shown in Figure 8.33. If you know the name of the computer, just fill it in, or choose the Browse button. The snap-in can focus on a local machine or on a group policy object; the Browse button allows you to locate and find group policy objects linked to sites, domains, OUs, or computers (Figure 8.34). Additionally, if you select the option to allow focus to change when opening the snap-in from the command line, it's possible to select the policy object as an argument when you start the console. GPEDIT.MSC, the Group Policy console that ships with Win2K, has this option turned on. The syntax to open GPEDIT.MSC and look at the local policy on a remote machine is as follows:

```
GPEDIT.MSC /gpcomputer: machinename
```

So you could type, for example:

GPEDIT.MSC /gpcomputer: dun

Or you could type:

GPEDIT.MSC /gpcomputer: dun.win2ktest.com

Be sure to include a space between /gpcomputer: and the machine name, though.

FIGURE 8.33

Adding the Group Policy snap-in

FIGURE 8.34

Selecting a group policy object

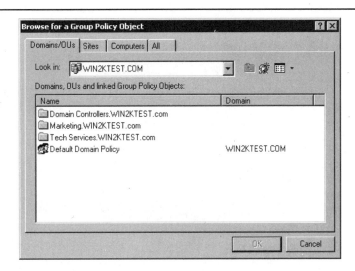

There is one important limitation when using GPEDIT.MSC to modify policy on a remote machine. The security settings extension to the Group Policy snap-in will not work when the tool is focused on a remote machine. That's worth saying again. You cannot open GPEDIT.MSC with the switch /gpcomputer: *computername* and modify the security settings on a remote machine. Apparently, Microsoft considers it a security vulnerability to allow it. Another example of software telling us what's best for us?

NOTE If you are using group policies, local policy is always processed before site, domain, or OU group policies.

Creating Group Policies

Now that you understand the major concepts surrounding group policies and know the difference between local policies and group policy objects, let's go through the steps of creating and editing a group policy object. In this section, I'll show you all the settings we discussed in the preceding "theory" section.

To open the Group Policy snap-in in DSA.MSC, right-click your domain name at the root of the console and choose Properties from the context menu. Move to the Group Policy tab, shown in Figure 8.35, to see what GPOs have been linked at the domain level. If you haven't already created other policies, you'll only see the default domain policy listed. Notice the Block Policy Inheritance check box at the bottom left of the Group Policy tab. It prevents any group policy settings at a higher level from trickling down to this one. Remember the order that policies are applied: first is the site level, then the domain level, then policies for OUs.

FIGURE 8.35

Group Policy tab

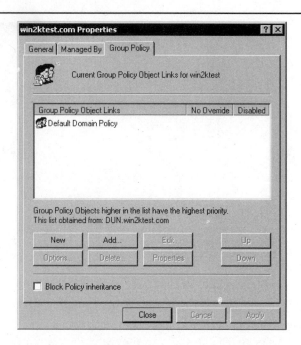

 NOTE To view the group policy objects that are linked to a container (site, domain, or organizational unit), right-click the object in the console (DSA.MSC for domains and OUs, DSSITE.MSC for sites) and choose Properties from the context menu. Then navigate to the Group Policy tab. From that point, the interface to configure policies is the same regardless of the container it's linked with.

To turn on No Override, highlight the policy and choose Options, then select the No Override check box (see Figure 8.36). When this setting is on, other policies applied down the line are prevented from defeating the settings of this one, even with Block Inheritance. Note that Block Inheritance is turned on at the link level (site, domain, or OU), while No Override is turned on per policy. Check the Disabled box to turn off the policy so that it won't be processed or applied at this level. Disabling the policy doesn't disable the object itself. For example, the same policy, disabled at the domain level, could theoretically be applied at the site or OU level. If either option (No Override or Disabled) is turned on, there will be a check in the corresponding column of the Group Policy tab. Both options may be activated using the context menu for the policy. Just right-click a selected policy to view the context menu.

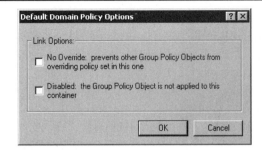

Back in the win2ktest.com property sheet, choose New to create a new GPO. Win2K will create a policy called New Group Policy Object and then allow you to rename it. If you miss that opportunity and end up with a policy called New Group Policy Object, just highlight the policy, right-click, and choose Rename from the context menu. Choose Properties to view and modify your new group policy object's properties. The General tab shown in Figure 8.37 shows creation and revision information as well as options to disable the user or computer configuration portion of the policy. Depending on how you subdivide your domain into OUs, you may choose to create some policies with only computer settings and others with only user-specific settings. In that case, if the unused portion of the GPO is disabled altogether, policy application and updates are faster. If, however, your cold medicine has caused a momentary lapse of reason and there are important settings in the node you disable, those settings will be removed from the client machine. So Win2K will ask you to confirm that move, just to be sure.

The Links tab gives you the opportunity to search for sites, domains, or OUs that use this GPO, if there are any. Because searching for other links takes a few moments and some resources, no linked containers will be displayed until you perform the search. Click the Find Now button to start the search.

The Security properties tab reveals the default permissions on the GPO (see Figure 8.38). Highlight a name at the top to view the permissions in the lower section. Notice that Domain Admins and Enterprise Admins have Read and Write permissions as well as Delete and Create All Child Objects, while Authenticated Users only has Read and Apply Group Policy. Read and Write are required to change a policy, while Read and Apply are required to be a recipient of the policy.

FIGURE 8.38

*Group policy
permissions list*

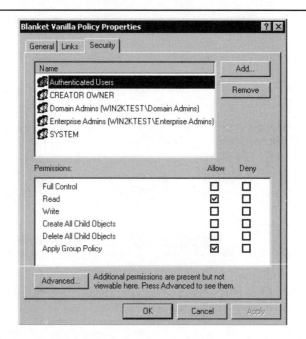

NOTE Don't think that Domain Admins and Enterprise Admins are not subject to a group policy's settings just because they are not granted Apply Group Policy permission by default. A user will have all the permissions of all their groups, so as members of Authenticated Users, members of Domain Admins and Enterprise Admins will also be granted Apply Group Policy permissions.

Back in the Group Policy tab of our win2ktest.com domain property page, if you highlight the new GPO that you have just created and choose the Up or Down buttons, you can move the policy up or down in the window. This is an important tidbit to know: if there are multiple GPOs linked to one container, as you see in Figure 8.39, they will be applied from the bottom up, so the one at the top is applied last. Therefore, GPOs higher in the list have a higher priority. If there are conflicting settings, the higher policy wins.

FIGURE 8.39

Increasing the priority of group policy objects

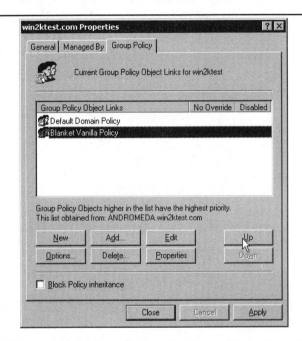

To delete a GPO, or to just remove it from the list, highlight the policy and choose Delete. Win2K will present you with the option to delete it altogether (Figure 8.40) or to remove it from the list while preserving the policy to be linked to another container at another time.

FIGURE 8.40

Removing a group policy object

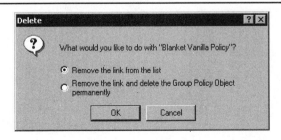

Choose the Add button on the Group Policy tab to link an existing group policy object to the desired container. As you see in Figure 8.41, you can look for GPOs that are linked to other domains/OUs or other sites, or you can just ask for a list of all GPOs. It took me a minute to grasp this simple operation: click the container name (like the OU for Marketing.win2ktest.com) to view the policies linked to it. Then highlight the policy and choose OK to add it to the list back on the Group Policy tab.

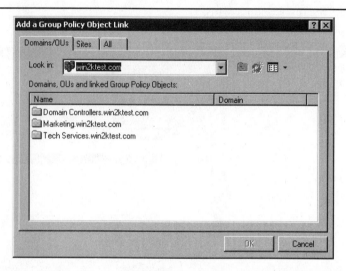

Now let's view and modify our new policy. Back in the Group Policy tab, highlight the policy and choose Edit. This will open the Group Policy snap-in in a separate window, and you'll see the policy object name at the root of the namespace, in this case Blanket Vanilla Policy [DUN.win2ktest.com] Policy. This indicates to us what policy is being viewed and edited. Figure 8.42 shows the policy expanded in the console tree to show the major nodes of the group policy object.

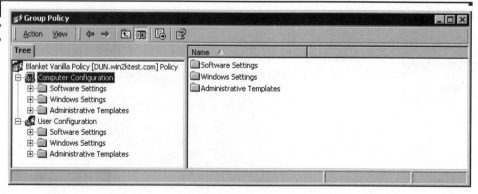

There are two major types of settings, as I mentioned earlier. Computer configuration settings are applied to machines at start-up and at designated refresh intervals. User configuration settings are applied to the users' working environments at logon and at designated refresh intervals.

We'll explore the various policies according to subject matter later, but prepare yourself for the fact that policies are not all configured in a uniform way as far as the interface is concerned. You'll need a few examples to see what I mean:

- To specify software packages under `Software Settings\Software Installation`, open the folder and choose New/Package from the Action menu. An Open dialog box asks for the location of the package. Once it's been located and selected, you configure the package properties.

- To set the interval that users can wait before changing passwords, go to `Computer Configuration\Windows Settings\Security Settings\Account Policies\ Password Policy`, then double-click Maximum Password Age in the details pane on the right, enable the setting by clicking the box that says Define This Policy Setting, and supply a time interval value.

- To set a policy that restricts group memberships, go to Restricted Groups under Security Settings in `Computer Configuration\Windows Settings` and choose Add Group from the Action menu. A dialog box asks you to enter a group or browse for it. Once the group is added to the list in the details pane on the right, double-click the group name to open a dialog box and supply the names of the users that must be or are allowed to be in the group. You can also define group memberships for the group itself.

- To set up folder redirection, go to `User Configuration\Windows Settings\ Folder Redirection` and choose a folder (for example, `Start Menu`). The details pane on the right will be blank. Right-click on white space in the details pane (or pull down the Action menu) and choose Properties. The property page appears and you can now specify a location for the Start menu and configure redirection settings.

The point of this wild ride through the Group Policy snap-in interface is not to disorient you, but rather to illustrate the fact that the Group Policy snap-in contains several different nodes to accomplish various tasks, and procedures to specify settings will vary with the node and the task. There is no one way to configure a setting, although many do follow the pattern of the second example. So, when in doubt, right-click or look at the Action menu. It's a strategy to live by.

Once you've configured your Group Policy settings, simply close the Group Policy window. There is no Save or Save Changes option. Changes are written to the GPO when you choose OK or Apply on a particular setting, although the user or computer will not actually see the change until the policy is refreshed.

Filtering Group Policy

Now that you've grasped the basics of Group Policy theory and have created a policy, let's look more closely at filtering group policies for security groups. Let's go back to the Security tab in the property pages for a group policy object: open DSA.MSC (or

DSSITE.MSC, depending on where the link is). Right-click the container linked to your GPO (in our example, the domain) and choose Properties. Select the Group Policy tab and highlight the policy you wish to filter. Choose the Properties button and go to the Security tab (shown again in Figure 8.43). Now you see the Access Control List (ACL) for the policy object. As I pointed out before, Domain Admins and Enterprise Admins have Read and Modify permissions, while Authenticated Users has Read and Apply Group Policy. It may happen that you create a policy to restrict desktops and you don't wish to apply it to a certain group of people. The group Authenticated Users includes everyone but guests, so by default, the policy will apply to everyone but guests, so even Domain Admins and Enterprise Admins will receive the policy settings. To prevent Domain Admins and Enterprise Admins from also receiving this policy, you must check the box in the Deny column next to Apply Group Policy (Figure 8.44). A member of both groups will only need the Deny setting for one of the two groups, but you'll need to check the Deny box for both groups if the members of Domain Admins and Enterprise Admins are not the same people. To "excuse" others from receiving the policy, put them all in a security group and add that group to the list. It is not enough to "not check" the granted box for Read and Apply Group Policy; the users in your special security group are also members of Authenticated Users, so you actually need to choose the Deny option for them as well. Deny takes precedence over Allow.

FIGURE 8.43

*Group policy
Security tab*

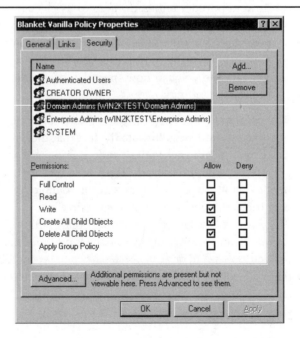

FIGURE 8.44

*Denying Apply Group
Policy permission*

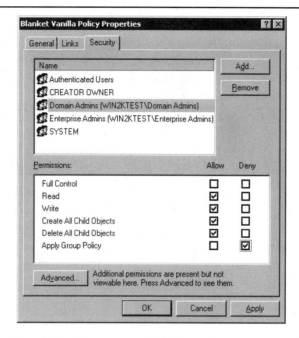

If you wish to filter policy for a certain Win2K machine (or group of machines), follow the same strategy. Add the computer accounts to a security group, add that group to the ACL for the policy object, then deny the group Read and Apply Group Policy permissions.

There is an alternative to adding a security group to the ACL and denying them Read and Apply permissions. One could also remove Authenticated Users from the ACL altogether, preventing anyone from receiving the group policy. Then you would simply add entries to the ACL for any security groups you *do* want to receive the policy. Be sure to allow them both Read and Apply Group Policy, though. Figure 8.45 shows the permissions list for Blanket Vanilla Policy in which Authenticated Users has been removed and the Engineering group has been added. This is a useful strategy if you don't want the policy to apply to all users and computers in the linked container by default.

By the way, there is nothing to prevent you from adding individual users to the permissions list for a group policy object. It's simply not considered good form.

NOTE Although members of Domain Admins and Enterprise Admins by default do not have Apply permissions, administrators are also members of Authenticated Users, and Authenticated Users does have Apply permission. Because admin types are also members of Authenticated Users, policies will apply to them as well, unless they are denied the permission Apply Group Policy.

FIGURE 8.45

*Group Policy
ACL without
Authenticated Users*

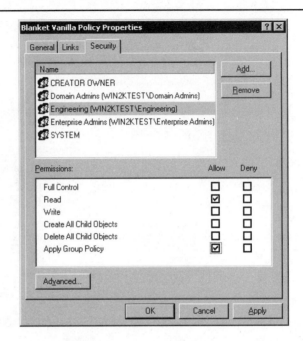

Delegating Group Policy Administration

The ability to delegate the creation and configuration of group policies to administrative personnel (or others, for that matter) is extremely useful, especially in a large organization. In this section I'll explain how to allow persons who are not members of Domain Admins or Enterprise Admins to create and manage policies for designated sites, domains, or organizational units.

Group policy objects, by default, can be created by a member of the Administrators group for the domain or by members of the global group called Group Policy Creator Owners. However, while members of Administrators have full control of all group policy objects, members of Group Policy Creator Owners can only modify policies they have created unless they have been specifically granted permission to modify a policy. So, if you put a designated group policy administrator into the security group Group Policy Creator Owners (that's almost as awkward as Active Directory Users and Computers), they can create new policy objects and modify them.

It's one thing to create a group policy; linking that GPO to a site, domain, or organizational unit is another matter. Administrators have this power by default, but a special permission called Manage Policy Links must be granted on the ACL of the site, domain, or organizational unit before anyone else can create policy links to it. Also, there doesn't seem to be a way to create a group policy without linking it to something, at least initially. So if you want to use the Group Policy Creator Owners security group, you need to go ahead and set permissions on a container object to allow them to manage policy links. You'll need to use the Delegation of Control Wizard to accomplish this.

To allow members of Group Policy Creator Owners to create links to a particular OU, for example, right-click the OU in DSA.MSC. Choose the option Delegate Control from the context menu. Choose Next in the initial screen to go to the part where you choose to add the users and groups to whom you will delegate control. Choose Add and select Group Policy Creator Owners from the list. Choose Add again, then OK to return to the Users or Groups window, as shown in Figure 8.46. The GP Creator Owners will appear in the Selected Users and Groups box. Choose Next, then select Manage Group Policy Links from the predefined common tasks to delegate (see Figure 8.47). Choose Next, then confirm your choices in the last screen by clicking the Finish button. Members of Group Policy Creator Owners can now create new GPOs linked to that OU. They can also modify policies that they have created, but if there are other policies on the OU, members of Group Policy Creator Owners can't edit them by default. You'll have to grant the group Read and Write permission on the policy object's ACL.

FIGURE 8.46

Delegation of Control Wizard's Users or Groups window

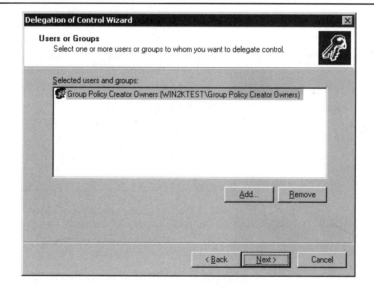

FIGURE 8.47

*Delegating
management of
group policy links*

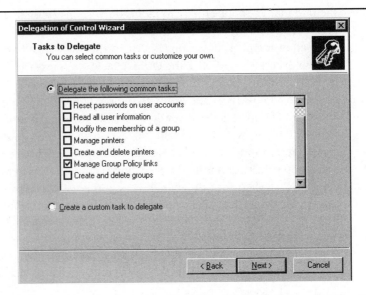

Designating a regular user or junior admin as a member of Group Policy Creator Owners and giving them the ability to manage group policy links, even if it's just at the OU level, is a real exercise in faith and quite taxing for us control freaks (I mean "letting-go challenged" people). If you want finer control when delegating group policy administration tasks, set up a custom MMC console. You may even limit administration to a certain GPO by loading the GP snap-in focused on that GPO. Enable only the extensions you want your delegate to use. It's further possible to configure a policy to permit the use of certain Group Policy snap-in extensions and prevent the use of others, just in case the delegate stumbles on to Author mode by accident. See the section "Group Policy Policies" later in this chapter for specifics.

 TIP See Chapter 4 for a discussion on customizing Microsoft Management consoles.

That was a lot of information, so let's review:

- To create a GPO you must either be a member of the Administrators group (and this includes nesting, so membership in Domain Admins is acceptable, for example) or be a member of Group Policy Creator Owners. If you insist on the McGyver approach, however, you at least need access to a domain controller, Read/Write permissions on SYSVOL, and Modify permission on the directory container.

- To edit a policy, a user must (a) have full Administrator privileges, or (b) be creator owner of the GPO, or (c) have Read and Write on the ACL of the GPO.

User and Computer Configuration Settings

Now that you've learned all about creating and linking and delegating administration of Group Policy, we'll explore some of the policy settings themselves in the next few sections. Since you can use various types of policies to configure a range of settings, we can't cover every single setting in the pages allotted to this chapter (otherwise it could be a book all by itself!). Rather, think of this section as an overview of the things that group policies can accomplish to make your life easier as an administrator. To follow along, open the Group Policy snap-in for a GPO by navigating to the Group Policy tab in the container's property pages, then highlight an existing policy and click the Edit button.

As you see in Figure 8.48, there are two main nodes to the Group Policy snap-in: User Configuration and Computer Configuration. Both nodes have the following subnodes: Software Settings, Windows Settings, and Administrative Templates. The difference between the two is this: policies set for User Configuration will apply to the user's settings, and those set for Computer Configuration will apply to the machine configuration. For example, if Registry settings are involved, as is the case with Administrative Templates, the changes will be written to HKEY_CURRENT_USER (HKCU) for User Configuration stuff and to HKEY_LOCAL_MACHINE (HKLM) for Computer Configuration settings. Otherwise, the differences aren't so obvious, and there is some overlap in the settings, just as HKCU contains some of the same entries as HKLM. You may wish to create separate policies for machines and users, just to keep things straight, but be on the lookout for any conflicts. If a value set in the computer settings is also specified in the user policy settings, the User Configuration settings will take precedence by default.

FIGURE 8.48

Group Policy nodes and subnodes

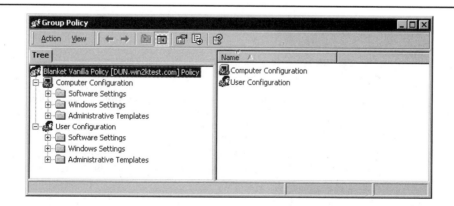

For both User Configuration and Computer Configuration, Software Settings\ Software Installation can be used to publish, assign, update, and even remove applications from a user's desktop. See Chapter 10, "Software Installation," for the full story on using group policies to set up application packages.

Specify Scripts with Group Policy

You can specify logon and logoff scripts, as well as scripts to run at system start-up and shutdown, using Windows Settings in the User Configuration node or the Computer Configuration node, respectively. Expand Windows Settings to reveal Scripts, then select the script type (start-up, shutdown, logon, or logoff) in the details pane on the right; Figure 8.49 shows the scripts available in User Configuration. From here, double-click on the script type (such as Logon) or highlight it and choose Properties from the Action menu. Add scripts to the list using the Add button (Figure 8.50). Supply a script name and parameters when prompted. To edit the script name and parameters (not the script itself), choose Edit. If more than one script is specified, use the Up or Down button to indicate the order in which the scripts should run.

FIGURE 8.49

*Group Policy
start-up scripts*

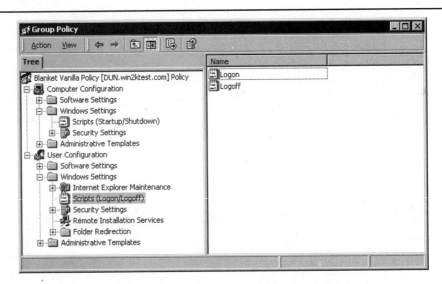

The scripts you create and assign should be copied to the following path in the SYSVOL directory: \winnt\SYSVOL\SysVol*domainname*\Policies\{GUID}\Machine\ Scripts\Startup or Shutdown (or User\Scripts\Logon or Logoff, depending on whether you are assigning scripts to the Computer Configuration or to the User Configuration node). The Global Unique Identifier (GUID) for the group policy object is a long string that looks like {FA08AF41-38AB-11D3-BD1FC9B6902FA00B}. If you wish to see the scripts stored in the GPO and possibly open them for editing, use the Show Files button at the bottom of the property page. This will open the folder in Explorer.

FIGURE 8.50

Adding a script to Group Policy

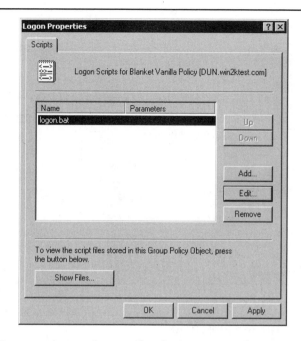

As you may know, you may also specify a login script in the property page of the user account in DSA.MSC. Microsoft calls these *legacy logon scripts* and encourages us to assign scripts with Group Policy for Win2K clients. Of course, Windows 95/98/NT clients don't use group policies, so you'll still assign their logon scripts in the account properties. Other than that, the only real advantage to using the group policy scripts is that they run asynchronously in a hidden window. So if several scripts are assigned, or if the scripts are complex, the user doesn't have to wait for them to end. Legacy logon scripts run in a window on the desktop. On the other hand, you might not want the scripts to run hidden (some scripts stop and supply information or wait for user input). In that case, there are several policy settings to define how group policy scripts behave. These are located in the Administrative Templates node under System\Logon/Logoff for User Configuration and under System\Logon for Computer Configuration. There you'll find settings to specify whether to run a script synchronously or asynchronously and whether it should be visible or invisible. Legacy logon scripts can be run hidden like group policy scripts by using the setting shown in Figure 8.51. The Computer Configuration settings also include a maximum wait time for group policy scripts, which is 600 seconds by default. This changes the time-out period, which is the maximum allotted time for the script to complete.

FIGURE 8.51

*Policy to run legacy
scripts hidden*

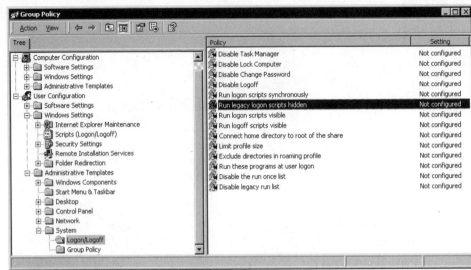

Folder Redirection

One of the more useful things you can do with User Configuration settings in Group
Policy is tell a user's Application Data, Desktop, Start Menu, or My Documents folder
to follow her around from computer to computer. These folders are important elements in a user's working environment. Application Data stores application-specific
user information (Internet Explorer uses it, for example), while Desktop may contain
important folders and shortcuts that need to be just one click away for the user. Start
Menu contains program groups and shortcuts to programs, while My Documents is the
default place to save and retrieve files, sort of like a local home directory. Using user
profiles in NT 4 and now Win2K, you can preconfigure these folders' contents and
assign network locations. With the System Policy Editor for 95/98 or NT, it was also
possible to specify a location for these folders. But unlike the Default User profiles
behavior, redirected folders live in one designated place all the time. They are not
copied to each machine the user logs on to, causing "profile build-up." Instead of
using the folder in the user's local profile, she will be *redirected* to the location specified in the group policy. Group policy folder redirection replaces and enhances those
functions offered previously in system policies, with additional options to manage
the redirected folder behavior.

There are several good reasons to use folder redirection. For one thing, it's convenient for users who log on to different machines. Also, if you specify a network location for some or all of these folders, they can be backed up regularly and protected by

the IT department. If roaming profiles are still in use, setting up folder redirection speeds up synchronization of the server profile with the local profile at logon and logoff, since the redirected folders need not be updated. Redirecting the Desktop and Start Menu folders to a centralized, shared location facilitates standardization of users' working environments and helps with remote support issues, since help desk personnel will know that all machines are configured in the same way. Best of all, you can mix and match. It's possible to specify a shared location for the Desktop and Start Menu folders while allowing each user to have his own My Documents and Application Data folders. Let's take a look.

To set a network location for the Start Menu folder in Group Policy, go to User Configuration\Windows Settings\Folder Redirection\Start Menu, right-click the highlighted Start Menu folder, and choose Properties from the context menu. The property page will reveal that no policy is specified by default for Start Menu redirection. Choose Basic from the drop-down box to specify a single location for the Start Menu folder, to be shared by all the users, or choose Advanced to set locations based on security group membership. If a single location for a shared Start Menu folder is desired, just fill in the target location with a network path or browse for it. For different locations, first choose a security group and then specify a network path. Figure 8.52 demonstrates redirecting the Start Menu folder for all members of Win2KTEST\Engineering to the Central share on the server Andromeda. In our example, all of Engineering will use the same Start Menu folder, but in either case, it's possible to set up individually redirected folders by appending %username% to the path. This creates a subfolder named after the user. Next, click the Settings tab to configure the redirection settings.

For the sake of completeness, the redirection settings for My Documents are shown in Figure 8.53. The redirection settings for all the other folders are the same except that My Documents has the My Pictures subfolder, so there are a couple of extra items to configure.

The options you see in Figure 8.53 show default selections. The user will have exclusive access to the folder, so uncheck this box if everyone is sharing a folder. The contents of the corresponding folder will be copied to the new location by default. Even after the policy is removed, the folder will remain redirected unless you say to "un-redirect" it. One notable exception is the Start Menu folder. We can pretty much assume that a redirected Start Menu folder is a shared Start Menu folder (otherwise, why bother?), and making it private or copying over it would generally be a bad thing, so both the option to grant exclusive rights and the option to move the contents of a user's Start Menu folder to the new location are grayed out in the Settings tab.

FIGURE 8.52

Policy to redirect the user's Start Menu *folder*

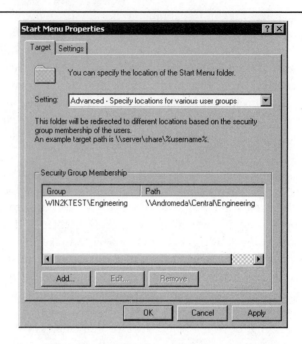

FIGURE 8.53

Policy to redirect the My Documents *folder*

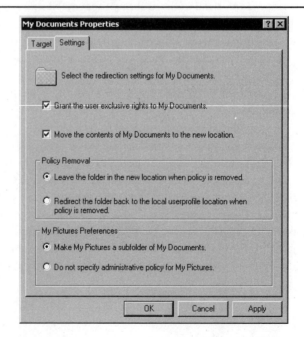

Security Settings

Security Settings, along with Administrative Templates, makes up a large part of Group Policy. The default security settings for Win2K security are purposely open to keep down administrative headaches and to ensure that users and applications work as intended. As security increases, users and applications have more restrictions and support time goes up. In other words, security is inversely proportionate to convenience. As you start locking down systems, something is bound to stop working. Hey, regular users can't even install applications on a Win2K system by default. When you start enforcing passwords that are 8 characters or more, contain both letters and numbers, can't use any part of a user's name, and cannot be reused until 15 other passwords have been used, things get complicated for the everyday Joe. As important as security is, Microsoft judged (wisely, I believe) that functionality had to come first. For organizations that want to increase security, there are tools and guidelines. There is one problem with this approach. A big problem.

If you've ever "hardened" an NT server according to established military or other high-security guidelines, you know that you have to set particular permissions on particular folders, you must change the default permissions on certain Registry keys, and you must change or create other Registry entries as well. All in all, it takes a few hours of work on a single server, even for an efficient admin. What if you have 50 servers and 500 Professional workstations? Some things can be scripted, but others can't. Try as they might, there is no Microsoft or third-party tool that does everything automatically for all machines.

Here's where Group Policy comes to the rescue. Assuming you are going to standardize throughout the organization somewhat, you only have to change those sticky Registry permissions and settings once, using Group Policy. You only have to set the NTFS permissions once. They can even be set up in one policy and copied to another. Whether you need a lot of security or just a little more than the default, chances are you'll want to make at least some standardized changes, and the Security Settings node will certainly make your life easier. The bulk of Security Settings is found under `Computer Configuration\Windows Settings\Security Settings`, although public key policies are also found in the User Configuration node in the same path. The following summarizes the major categories of settings under Security Settings:

Account Policies   Specify password restrictions, lockout policies, and Kerberos policy.

Local Policies   Configure auditing and assign user rights and miscellaneous security settings.

Event Log   Centralize configuration options for the Event Log.

Restricted Groups   Enforce and control group memberships for certain groups, such as the Administrators group.

System Services   Standardize services configurations and protect against changes.

Registry   Create security templates for Registry key permissions to control who can change what keys and to control Read access to parts of the Registry.

File System   Create security templates for permissions on files and folders to ensure that files and directories have and keep the permissions you want.

Public Key Policies   Manage settings for organizations using a public key infrastructure.

Importing Security Templates

A full discussion of all these security settings is certainly beyond the scope of this chapter, but you should be aware that security settings templates are available and installed with Win2K Server to ease the burden of wading through and researching all of the settings. It's also safer to configure settings offline and then apply them than it is to play with a live working group policy. These templates take the form of INF files and are found in `\WINNT\Security\templates`. There are several to choose from, from basic workstations or servers to secure, highly secure, and dedicated domain controller configurations. When applied directly or via Group Policy, these templates incrementally modify the default settings. You can view and modify them using the Security Templates snap-in, shown in Figure 8.54. As you see in the figure, these settings are the same as those found in Group Policy Security Settings with the exception of Public Key Policies and IP Security Policies, which cannot be configured with templates. The values for the settings in each template are preconfigured to meet the necessary level of security. These templates, or new ones you create, can then be applied directly to a Win2K machine's local policy by using a command-line program called `SECEDIT.EXE`, or they can be imported into Group Policy.

Every fresh installation of Win2K gets a standard set of local computer policies with default security settings, so it's a good idea to export your existing settings to a file by using the Group Policy snap-in focused on the local machine (`GPEDIT.MSC` will open that way by default) before making any drastic changes. Security settings for upgraded systems do not have their local policy changed in case the configuration has been customized. For upgraded Win2K servers, Microsoft suggests we first apply the Basic configuration template and then apply an appropriate security settings template with all the settings specified explicitly.

To import a security template into Group Policy, go to `Computer Configuration\ Windows Settings\Security Settings` and right-click Security Settings. Choose Import Policy from the context menu, then select your policy from the list of templates. Group Policy automatically looks for the template in `\WINNT\security\ templates`, but you can tell it to look someplace else if necessary. The INF file will be imported to modify the settings in the selected group policy object.

FIGURE 8.54

*Security Templates
snap-in*

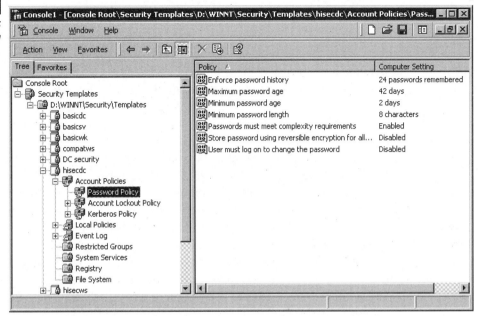

In the spirit of this template idea, the different subcomponents of Security Settings (like Account Policies or Local Policies) also support a copy-and-paste function, which appears in the context and Action menus when the subcomponent is selected. An admin person can actually copy that part of the template information to the Clipboard and apply it to another policy.

Administrative Templates

Administrative Templates is the part of Group Policy that is most like System Policies in NT. The settings available here are based on template files (ADM files, like those used in NT and Windows 95/98 System Policies). These settings specify Registry entry changes to adjust various aspects of a user's environment or a machine configuration, including those famous options to restrict a user's desktop to the point where they can only run a limited set of programs and nothing else.

The user changes specified in Administrative Templates are written to HKEY_CURRENT_User\Software\Policies and computer changes are written to HKEY_LOCAL_Machine\Software\Policies. The two ADM files that Win2K uses are system.adm and inetres.adm, found in \WINNT\inf. Capabilities of Administrative Templates can also be extended with custom ADM files.

 NOTE When you load an Administrative Template, the ADM files are copied to \SYSVOL\Domainname\Policies\GUID\Adm.

What's the difference between User Configuration and Computer Configuration with regard to Administrative Templates? Good question. Depending on the nature of the configuration settings, some live in the user part of the Registry (HKCU), while others live in the machine part (HKLM). Other settings exist in both, which makes things really confusing. Settings for Task Scheduler, for example, are exactly the same in both places. So, other than asking yourself, "Which node has the setting I want?" the difference is whether the policy should apply to the machine, regardless of who logs on, or whether the policy should apply to the users and follow them from machine to machine.

What can you do with Administrative Templates settings? Among its primary functions is "keep users from changing X" or "disable or hide option Y." But mostly it's just a large collection of configuration options loosely organized together to ease our administrative burden and help us achieve the power and control of our networks and users that we crave and feel we truly deserve. An attempt to catalog each subnode and all of its policy settings would be a boring and futile exercise in the Microsoft style of documentation and is best left to those who write the Resource Kits. Besides, many of these policies should not be discussed in a vacuum and are best approached in the context of the particular application or service they configure. However, this section would be lacking if it did not include at least a few pointers on individual policies. So here are a few highly opinionated comments on some of the settings you'll find in Administrative Templates. For a few more suggestions on how to lock down a user's desktop, see the system policies section later in this chapter. You'll find the same options (and more) in Group Policy as you did in the System Policy Editor.

Windows Components

For every setting in Internet Explorer, there seems to be policy to disable it. Considering that much time at work is spent surfing the Web, it's a particularly cruel and clever thing to impose such control over IE settings. Unfortunately, many companies use Navigator instead of Internet Explorer.

While you might want to implement those cool Windows Explorer restrictions to the Map Network Drive and Disconnect Network Drive options or remove particular drives in My Computer, this will only work with inexperienced users. Anyone who can access a command line can circumvent these restrictions, so be sure and check out the method (mentioned later) to restrict the programs that can run from Explorer. A more useful setting is the one to "not track shell shortcuts during roaming." This tells Explorer to resolve shortcuts in roaming profiles to local paths instead of tracking the source and attempting to open a program or file on a remote computer (this caused me much gnashing of teeth and pulling of hair before I figured out how to stop it). The same principal applies to the Start menu and Taskbar and Desktop options. Experienced users will not be prevented from running unblessed programs just because Run is removed from the Start menu. But the settings may be useful to guard against inexperienced users' tendency to fiddle with things randomly. Plus, there is something to be said for a simplified and consistent Start menu and Desktop throughout an organization. I personally love the options to hide "Computers Near Me" or "Entire Network" in My Network Places; with these hidden, users are not tempted to poke around on different servers to see what they can access.

Control Panel Settings

The Control Panel node includes several options to disable or remove all or part of the Add/Remove Programs applet. Disabling Add/Remove Programs will not prevent users from running setup routines in other ways.

The Display policies prevent users from changing Display settings like screen resolution, screen savers, and background wallpaper—in other words, customizing the display. While it is desirable to prevent a user from changing the display to settings incompatible with hardware, it's not really necessary since Win2K does include safeguards against that eventuality. Unless the machine is in a library or school or someplace where a standardized desktop appearance is necessary, I see no point in preventing access to these settings. Unless you work someplace where everyone has to wear a blue or black suit every day, and the desktops are subject to the same dress code, there are better ways to reassure ourselves of our superiority as network administrators.

The policies that prevent users from adding or deleting printers are useful if your users are in the habit of doing that, and then calling to say, "Why can't I print?" Also, it is helpful to specify an Active Directory path for printers to assist with searches.

System Settings

Use the Century Interpretation for Year 2000 entry to set programs to interpret two-digit date references consistently and correctly. This parameter, when enabled, defaults to 2029, so a reference to 01/06/29 is interpreted as 2029, while 01/16/30 is interpreted as 1930.

Disabling Registry editing tools prevents users from running REGEDT32.EXE and REGEDIT.EXE, which is not a bad idea, although regular users only have Read access to the vast majority of the Registry anyway.

The famous setting Run Only Allowed Windows Applications is found in the System node under User Configuration (not Computer Configuration). If you enable the policy, you must add a list of allowed applications, or users will be able to run nothing at all. Figure 8.55 shows the policy enabled with a sample list of allowed applications. Use of this policy is often combined with the policy to hide My Network Places and Internet Explorer from the Desktop, remove Run from the Start menu, and apply other restrictions found in the Windows Explorer policies node.

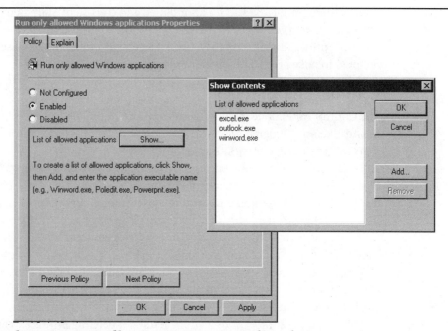

FIGURE 8.55

*Policy to run only
allowed applications*

Using Group Policy to Set Password and Account Lockout Policy

In NT 4, any account policies set in User Manager for Domains applied to domain account and password functions, while the audited events, such as restarts, failed logon attempts, and security policy changes, were those occurring on domain controllers. Group policies are much more powerful. If you choose to create a policy at the domain level, the settings will apply to all domain member machines—servers, workstations, and domain controllers included. It is possible, however, for OU policies to override local policy settings such as auditing and user rights.

One big note about password, account lockout, and Kerberos group policies: they are applied at the domain level only. Domain controllers will receive their settings from domain-level account policies and ignore the settings in policies linked to OUs. In fact, you'll see an error in the Event Log if an OU-level policy contains these settings. So unfortunately, you still can't make administrator types change their passwords more often than everyone else does (not without a big stick, anyway). Different Local Policy settings can be applied to OUs, however, so audit policy can be stricter on "high-security" OUs and more lax on others.

Password Policy includes the following options:

Enforce Password History   Enable this option and supply a number of new passwords that must be unique before a given password can be used again.

Maximum Password Age   This option sets the time period in which a password can be used before the system requires the user to pick a new one.

Minimum Password Age   The value set here is the time that a password has to be used before the user is allowed to change it again.

Minimum Password Length   This option defines the smallest number of characters that a user's password can contain. Eight characters is a good length for passwords.

Passwords Must Meet the Complexity Requirements of Installed Password Filter   Password filters define requirements like the number of characters allowed, whether letters and numbers must be used, whether any part of the username is permitted, and so forth.

Store Passwords Using Reversible Encryption   Windows 95/98 clients and Macintosh clients need to authenticate with a lower-level encryption.

User Must Log On to Change Password   This option prevents unauthenticated users from changing an account password through brute force attacks. Also prevents a user from changing his password after it's expired.

Account Lockout Policy, once enabled, prevents anyone from logging on to the account after a certain number of failed attempts:

Account Lockout Threshold   This value defines how many times the user can attempt to log on before the account will be locked out.

Reset Account Lockout Counter After   This setting defines the time in which the count of bad logon attempts will start over. For example, suppose you have a reset count of two minutes and three logon attempts. If you mistype twice, by waiting two minutes after the second attempt, you'll have three tries again.

Account Lockout Duration   This setting determines the interval that the account will be locked out. After the time period expires, the user account will no longer be locked out and the user can try to log on again.

Using Group Policy to Manage MMC

Delegation is a great feature of Win2K, and the Microsoft Management Console is a big part of that. Many Win2K administrators will want to create consoles to accomplish particular tasks and distribute them to the responsible parties. Group Policy offers options to control MMC so that others can't make changes to existing MMC tools or access snap-ins and extensions that are off-limits, not the least of which are the Group Policy snap-ins and extensions.

You see, in NT 4, users could either run the Server Manager tool or they couldn't. If they could run the tool, they might only be able to create machine accounts (if they were members of Account Operators) and not promote domain controllers. That didn't keep users from seeing the option in the menu or from attempting operations that were not permitted in their security context. With Win2K, not only can you design a tool that only includes the snap-ins and extensions that you want your admin types to use, but you can also explicitly forbid any changing of the tool (by preventing Author mode). What's more, you can completely forbid access to a particular snap-in, regardless of the tool employed by the user. Please note that this does not actually set a user's security level (that's what security groups and rights are for), but it can effectively limit access to certain administrative tools. Cool, eh?

The Microsoft Management Console policies are found under Administrative Templates in the User Configuration node (see Figure 8.56). The main policies shown in this figure are to restrict Author mode (which prevents the user from creating console files and from adding or removing snap-ins) and to restrict users to an explicit list of permitted snap-ins. These two policies are not exactly mutually exclusive, as you might think, nor does enabling the first eliminate the need for the second.

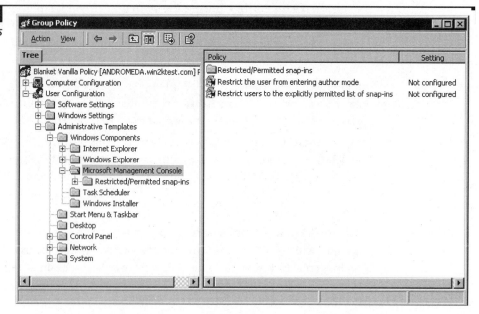

FIGURE 8.56

MMC group policies

If a user is not permitted to enter Author mode, he is unable to do the following:

- Run MMC.EXE from the Start menu or a command prompt; it opens, by definition, in Author mode with a blank console window.

- Open any console with the /a (Author mode) switch.

- Open any console that is configured to always open in Author mode.

All of the prebuilt administrative consoles that are included in Administrative Tools are User mode tools, so they can be used when the restriction is activated.

However, if you create a console and distribute it but forget to set it to open in User mode, the user will not be able to access the tool with this policy in effect.

If the policy to restrict users to only the expressly permitted list of snap-ins is enabled, users will not be able to add or remove restricted snap-ins or extensions to console files when in Author mode (they will not even appear in the list of available snap-ins). More importantly, if a console file already contains a restricted snap-in or extension, when the tool is run by a user who is subject to this policy, the restricted snap-in or extension will not appear in the console. For example, if you don't have access to the Group Policy tab for Active Directory tools (set this policy in the Group Policy node under `Restricted/Permitted Snap-Ins`), you won't even see the tab in Active Directory Users and Computers (or AD Sites and Services) when you open the properties of the site, domain, or OU.

If you do choose to restrict users to only the expressly permitted list of snap-ins, be sure to filter the policy for exempt admin types. Also, you need to go to the `Restricted/Permitted Snap-Ins` folder and enable those that you want to be available. Otherwise, *no snap-ins will be available* to nonexempt users regardless of their power and status on the network. This could be very bad, so think carefully before you disable access to the Group Policy snap-in, or you might not be able to reverse the damage.

Even if you don't enable the policy to restrict snap-in and extension use, you can still deny access to certain snap-ins. You see, if the policy Restrict Users to the Explicitly Permitted List of Snap-Ins is configured, enabling a certain snap-in means that it *can* be used. But if you leave the policy turned off, enabling a certain snap-in means that it *cannot* be used.

Figure 8.57 shows the snap-ins that can be permitted or restricted. There is a separate list of extension snap-ins that can be restricted/permitted (Figure 8.58). Extensions are implemented as dependent modules of snap-ins, but sometimes they do the same things as full-blown snap-ins. For example, the Event Viewer is a snap-in and can exist by itself in a console, as it does in the Event Viewer administrative tool, but it is also implemented as an extension in the Computer Management tool. So you'll need to know whether the thing you want to restrict is a full snap-in or an extension. See Chapter 4 for additional information on MMC consoles and snap-ins.

FIGURE 8.57

Permitted or restricted MMC snap-ins

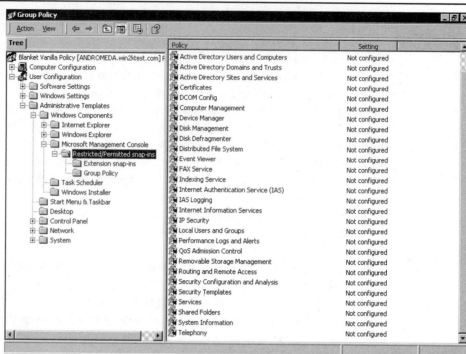

FIGURE 8.58

Permitted or restricted MMC extensions

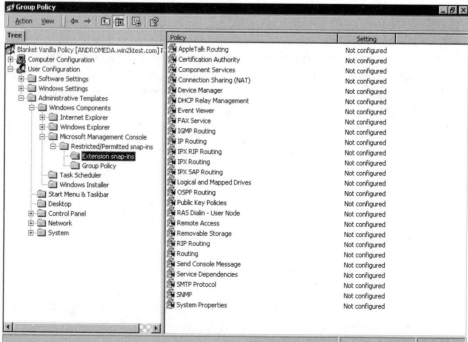

There is a separate folder for the Group Policy snap-in and related extensions (Figure 8.59). These allow you to restrict or permit access to the individual parts of Group Policy so that delegated admin types can assign software to be installed, for example, without having access to the Security Settings node. *Be careful when restricting access to the GP snap-ins.* This policy should be filtered for trusted, responsible (and polite) administrators.

A final note about MMC policies: If the user doesn't have all of the necessary components installed on her machine, the MSC file won't work properly and may not even run. There is a very useful policy called Download Missing COM Components which directs the system to search for those missing components in the Active Directory and download them if they are found. For some reason, this policy is found in `User Configuration\Administrative Templates\System` and in the corresponding path of Computer Configuration.

FIGURE 8.59

Group Policy snap-in restrictions

Managing Group Policies

In the preceding section, we touched on using Group Policy settings to restrict access to certain MMC snap-ins and extensions, including the Group Policy snap-ins. Let's finish up our discussion of group policies with an exploration of the other Group Policy configuration options that are actually included as group policies ("group policy policies"). Then I'll close with a few select observations and suggestions for configuring and managing group policies in your organization.

Group Policy Policies

Policies to control Group Policy are found in `Administrative Templates` of both the User Configuration and Computer Configuration nodes (`Administrative Templates\System\Group Policy`). Figures 8.60 and 8.61 show the User Configuration and

Computer Configuration options for Group Policy. The following information summarizes the most important configuration options.

FIGURE 8.60

User configuration settings for Group Policy

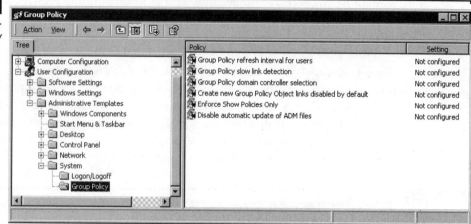

FIGURE 8.61

Computer configuration settings for Group Policy

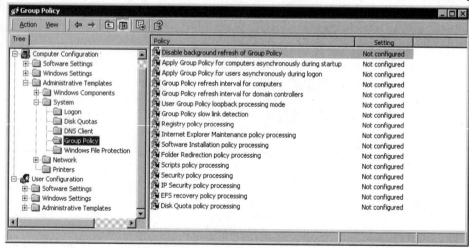

Group Policy Refresh Intervals for Users/Computers/Domain controllers These separate policies determine how often GPOs are refreshed in the background while users and computers are working. These parameters permit changes to the default background refresh intervals and permit tweaking the offset time.

Disable Background Refresh If you enable this setting, policies will only be refreshed at system start-up and user login. This might be useful for performance reasons, since having 1,500 computers refreshing policies every 90 minutes could cause congestion on an Ethernet.

Apply Group Policy for Users/Computers Synchronously during Start-up Enable this setting to prevent users from logging on until all group policies have been applied. Otherwise, policies apply in the background and a user will able to log on while policy settings are still changing.

Policy processing options These policies, with names like Registry Policy Processing and Folder Redirection Policy Processing, are available to customize the behavior of the different GPO components. Each policy (see Figure 8.62 for an example) presents at least two of the following three options:

Allow Processing across a Slow Network Connection For slow connections, some policies can be turned off to enhance performance (you can define what a "slow link" is by using the Group Policy Slow Link Detection setting). Security settings and Registry policy processing will always apply, however, and cannot be turned off.

Do Not Apply during Periodic Background Processing Specify which components will be refreshed periodically. Software installation and folder redirection policies will never be refreshed while a user is logged on, so the option is not available for them.

Process Even if the Group Policy Objects Have Not Changed To conserve network and system resources, GPOs are, by default, not refreshed if there have been no changes. To increase security, however, and guard against a user changing a policy setting, enable the policy to ensure that all settings are reapplied at each refresh interval. Please note that enabling this policy may cause noticeable performance degradation.

FIGURE 8.62

Disk quota policy processing options

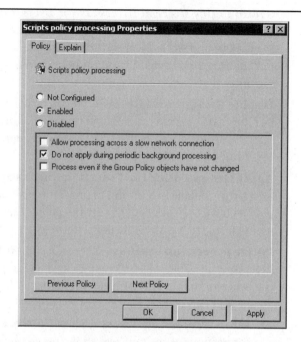

User Group Policy Loopback Processing Mode   By default, user policies are processed after computer configuration policies, and user policies will take precedence if there are conflicts. Also by default, users receive their policy regardless of the machine they use to log on. Sometimes this is not appropriate and policies need to be applied according to the computer's policy objects instead. For example, if I log on to a server to do administration, it's not appropriate for my office productivity applications to start installing themselves. Another example of when you would want computer policies to override user policies is if you want to apply more stringent policies for machines that are exposed to the anonymous public, such as machines in libraries, university computer labs, or kiosks in shopping malls or tourist attractions. There are two different modes to control this behavior (see Figure 8.63): Merge mode and Replace mode.

Merge Mode   Process user policies first, then computer policies. Computer policies will therefore override conflicting user policies.

Replace Mode   Disregard user policies and processes only computer policies.

FIGURE 8.63

*User Group Policy
Loopback Processing
Mode policy*

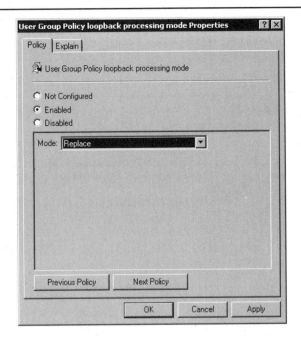

Group Policy over Slow Links

Group Policy still works over slow links such as dial-up connections. Even better, policy is applied whether a user logs on using Dial-Up Networking or whether they log on with cached credentials and then initiate a connection. However, application of Group Policy over slow links can pose performance issues, so Win2K includes policy settings to define a slow link and to define how policies are applied over a detected slow link.

The default definition of a slow link, as far as group policies are concerned, is anything under 500 kilobits per second. The system performs a test using the Ping utility to determine the speed of the connection. If the Ping response time is under 2000 milliseconds, the connection is fast. You can change the definition of a slow link, however. This policy setting, called Group Policy Slow Link Detection, is available in both the User Configuration and Computer Configuration, under Administrative Templates\System\ Group Policy (see Figure 8.64 for the property page of the policy). To change the default parameter, enter a number in Kbps, or enter 0 to disable slow link detection altogether. If you disable slow link detection, all policies will be applied regardless of the connection speed.

FIGURE 8.64

FIGURE 8.64

*Group Policy Slow
Link Detection
properties*

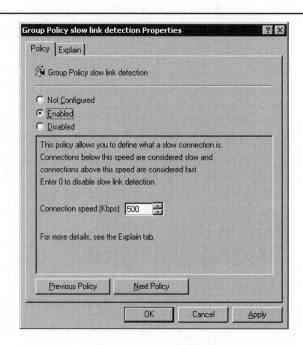

As I mentioned in the preceding section, policy processing settings for individual policy components (these have names like Folder Redirection Policy Processing and are found in the same path as the slow link detection setting, under `Computer Configuration\Administrative Templates\System\Group Policy`) allow you to specify whether a portion of the policy object will be processed over a slow link connection. Again, this is not an option for Registry-based policies or for security settings; they will always be processed, even over slow links. The other modules will not be applied over slow links by default.

To have logon scripts run over slow links, for example, open the policy called Scripts Policy Processing. Enable the policy, as in Figure 8.65, and check the box beside Allow Processing across a Slow Network Connection. Choose OK and the policy is set. Repeat as necessary for the other policy processing entries.

FIGURE 8.65

Policy processing
options

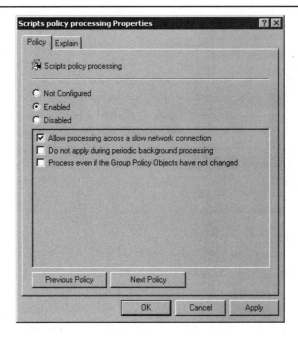

A Few Final Thoughts on Group Policy

In the last few sections, I have discussed the concepts of group policies, including local policies. We have created a sample group policy and seen how to turn on the various settings, like No Override and Block Inheritance. We've looked at filtering policies for security groups and delegating policy administration to others. We have explored many of the actual policy settings, including administrative templates for desktop control, security settings, folder redirection, MMC management, even Group Policy policies. But before you close this chapter and begin to configure group policies on your network, there are two more big issues that you want to be very aware of. One is that group policies affect network and system performance. The other is that group policies are difficult to troubleshoot if something goes wrong.

The performance issue is pretty simple: the more policies to apply, the longer the logon time. Each time a user logs on (or a computer is restarted), each of the GPOs associated with the user's or computer's containers (SDOUs) is read and applied. This can slow down logons considerably, and users may start calling the help desk to ask, "What's wrong with the network?" Therefore, you should keep the number of policies to a minimum. Another thing that can bog down a machine or a network is the background refresh rate. Refresh policies too often and you'll see a hit because the machine is always busy asking for policy changes. Think about disabling the background refreshes altogether unless you're worried about users changing their settings to escape policies. If the background refresh is disabled, user and computer policies are only reapplied at logon and start-up, respectively. The worst thing you could do for performance is have a bunch of different policies in effect and tell Group Policy to reapply at each refresh interval even if there are no changes. Another way to streamline GPO processing is to avoid assigning GPOs from different domains. Just because you can do it doesn't mean it's a good idea.

The problem with troubleshooting policies stems from an inability to view the cumulative policy settings that are actually in effect for a user or machine. This capability to display actual policy settings, currently referred to as the Resultant Set of Policy (RSOP), is necessary for managing and troubleshooting policies. Without it, you have to look at the properties of each site/domain/OU to see what policies are linked to what containers. Then you must view the ACLs to see if there's any filtering and check out the disabled, Block Inheritance, and No Override options. Finally, you need to view the settings of the policies in question before you can get to the bottom of things. You'll need to take notes. So until Microsoft comes out with an RSOP tool, promised soon after the release of Win2K, here are a few suggestions to help minimize troubleshooting time:

- Keep your policy strategy simple. Group users and computers together in OUs if possible, and apply policy at the highest level possible. Avoid having multiple GPOs with conflicting policies that apply to the same recipients. Minimize the use of No Override and Block Inheritance.

- Document your group policies heavily, both individual settings and framework. You may want to visually depict your policy structure and put it on the wall like your network topology diagrams. That way, when a problem arises, you can consult the documentation to see what's going on before you go fishing.

- Finally, test group policies before deployment! This is absolutely essential to save your help desk and ensure that applications and system services continue to run properly.

Working with NT 4 User Profiles

User profiles are still around in Windows 2000, and they work about the same way as they did in NT 4 despite some restructuring of the profiles directories themselves. But group policies (and particularly, Folder Redirection policies, which you read about in the preceding section) take care of many of the things we previously used user profiles (and system policies) for. In fact, I have not yet found a compelling reason to use roaming or mandatory profiles on Win2K machines at all. Unfortunately, Group Policy does not work on NT 4 or Windows 9x clients, so we'll still have to rely on user profile configuration and system policies for them. While more and more organizations are standardizing on NT 4 workstations, it will probably take a year or two for organizations to begin migrating desktops to Win2K Professional. Until then, we're stuck with our old tools of NT 4 user profiles and system policies. Accordingly, this section and the next focus on desktop configuration management for legacy clients (NT 4 and 95/98). This section addresses using NT 4 (Workstation) profiles in a Win2K Server environment, while the next deals with system policies for NT (and 95/98) clients.

A user profile is a set of configuration settings that make up a user's Desktop, including color scheme, screen saver, shortcuts, and program groups. These settings may be configured by a user who wishes to personalize her Desktop, by a system administrator responsible for configuring Desktops, or by a combination of the two. In other words, a user may create shortcuts and select a screen saver, while an administrator may configure special program groups for the user's Desktop. However, the two are not mutually exclusive. By default, every user on an NT 4 machine (except members of the Guests group) keeps a local profile directory that NT names after the user ID. Guests are not allowed to keep local profiles.

User profiles can be implemented in several different ways, according to the needs of your organization. In situations where a network-based solution is not feasible or not desirable, there are still several options to keep in mind:

Local profiles   Users keep only local profiles and create and configure these profiles themselves.

Preconfigure the default user profile   Users keep only local profiles, but an administrator preconfigures the default user profile to set up a customized template for new local users.

Preconfigured local profiles   Users keep only local profiles, but an administrator preconfigures all or part of the local user profiles.

Network-based solutions include the following:

Roaming profiles   Add a user profile path to the user's account information to automatically create and maintain a copy of the user profile in a network location (the user can configure her own profile).

Preconfigured roaming profiles   Add a user profile path to the user's account information and copy a preconfigured profile to the network location specified (the user can make changes to her profile).

Network default user profiles   Create a default user profile and copy it to the NETLOGON share of the authenticating domain controller(s). This will hand out default profiles to all new users (users can make changes to their profiles). This option can be used in conjunction with roaming or local profiles.

Mandatory profiles   Add a user profile path to the user account, copy a preconfigured profile to that path, and use special filename and directory name extensions to specify that this is a mandatory profile. The user must use the profile and cannot make any changes. A mandatory profile can be shared by a group of users.

Anatomy of an NT 4 User Profile

A local user profile is created automatically by the system the first time a user logs on to an NT machine. This profile directory is located in %SYSTEMROOT%\PROFILES. Figure 8.66 shows the contents of the \PROFILES directory. This directory contains a profile for every user who logs on to the NT machine (in this case, user Lisa and the user Administrator), as well as a directory called \All Users and one called \Default User. The \All Users directory stores common program groups (programs available to all users on a specific machine) and shortcuts that will appear on every user's Desktop on that machine. For example, Administrative Tools is stored in the \All Users folder, so the programs listed in this group will be made available to anyone logging on to the machine. The Default User folder exists because NT uses it as a template for creating individual profiles for new users. Figure 8.67 shows the contents of an individual user profile directory, C:\WINNT\PROFILES\LISA.

FIGURE 8.66

Profiles directory

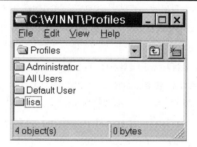

FIGURE 8.67

Individual profile directory

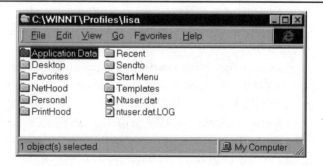

Each user's profile contains several folders with links to various Desktop items plus the NTUSER.DAT file, which contains configuration settings from the Registry. NTUSER.DAT.LOG is a transaction log file that exists to protect *NTUSER.DAT* while changes are being flushed to disk. There is no NTUSER.DAT.LOG for the Default User profile directory because it is a template. The other folders store information on the contents of the user's Desktop and Start menu items, including shortcuts and program groups. Remember that a user's profile also includes the common program groups and shortcuts indicated in the All Users folder. Table 8.5 describes the various folders in a user profile.

TABLE 8.5: FOLDERS IN AN NT 4 USER PROFILE	
Folder	**Explanation**
Application Data	A place for applications to store user-specific information.
Desktop	Any file, folder, or shortcut in this folder will appear directly on the user's Desktop.
Favorites	Shortcuts to favorite Web sites and bookmarks can be stored here.
NetHood *	Shortcuts placed here will appear in Network Neighborhood.
Personal	Sort of a mini home directory; many applications save things here by default.
PrintHood *	Shortcuts placed here will appear in the Printers folder.
Recent *	NT automatically puts shortcuts to recently used files here. Linked to Documents in the Start menu.
SendTo	Place shortcuts to apps, printers, and folders here to quickly copy an item to a predefined place, to open a file within a specific application (such as Notepad), or even to print a file.
Start Menu	Contains personal program groups and shortcuts to program items.
Templates *	Contains shortcuts to templates created by applications such as PowerPoint and Word.

* These folders are hidden by default.

In addition to the folders, a user profile includes numerous user-definable settings for Windows NT Explorer (View All Files, Display Full Path in the Title Bar, and Show Large Icons), the Taskbar (Auto Hide, Show Small Icons in Start Menu, and Show Clock), Control Panel (command prompt, mouse, and display preferences), and Accessories (Calculator, Clock, and Notepad). Network Printer, Drive Connections, and Windows NT Help bookmarks are also saved in the user profile. Virtually any application written for Windows NT can remember user-specific settings. These settings, not directly linked to Desktop items, are contained in the NTUSER.DAT file. NTUSER.DAT is the Registry part of a user profile. It corresponds to the HKEY_CURRENT_USER subtree in the Registry Editor (REGEDT32.EXE), shown in Figure 8.68.

FIGURE 8.68

The HKEY_
CURRENT_USER
Subtree

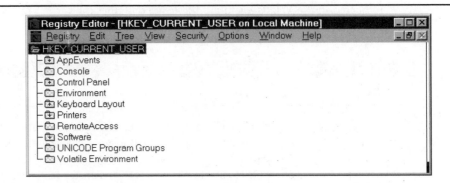

Configuring Your Own NT 4 User Profile

Before you configure user profiles on your network, you will need to master techniques for configuring your own profile. You can then use these skills to configure profiles for other users.

The NTUSER.DAT file for the user currently logged on may be edited using a Registry editing tool such as REGEDT32.EXE or REGEDIT.EXE, although these tools are not particularly intuitive (an understatement if I have ever heard one). The System Policy Editor (POLEDIT.EXE, covered in the upcoming section on system policies) that comes with Windows NT Server and Win2K Server is more user-friendly and can be used to directly edit a number of selected settings in the local Registry.

The System Policy Editor is a "selective" Registry Editor and is easier to use, as it does not require any knowledge of Registry syntax or structure. While this application offers several options that are not available in the graphical interface, very little would be of interest to normal users setting up their own profiles, even assuming that they have access to the application (it's not included with NT Workstation). Even though the System Policy Editor can be used to edit the machine's local Registry, as shown in Figure 8.69, most of the Local User options focus on restricting a user's Desktop. Joe User probably would not do that to himself. However, this little piece of information will come in handy when *you* want to restrict other users' Desktops.

Actually, the best way to configure the NTUSER.DAT part of your profile is simply to configure your Desktop. By using the applets in the graphical interface to change your color scheme, map network drives, and connect to printers, you are making changes to NTUSER.DAT. Use a Registry Editor only when you want to make a change that is not offered in the Control Panel. For example, under NT 3.51, the only way to change the icon title font, size, and style was in the Registry, under HKEY_CURRENT_USER\CONTROL PANEL\DESKTOP. In NT 4, however, these and other formerly unavailable options can be adjusted using the Appearance tab in Control Panel/Display.

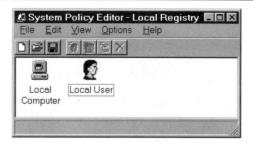

 WARNING As I've warned you before, you're just asking for trouble if you start playing with your machine's Registry for no good reason. Don't edit the Registry if you can make the changes using the Control Panel.

To configure the Taskbar, program items, and shortcuts in your profile folder, right-click the Taskbar and choose Properties. The Taskbar Options tab (Figure 8.70) allows you to adjust a couple of things in the Taskbar. Toggle the check boxes to see how your display will change. The Start Menu Programs tab (Figure 8.71) allows you to add and remove shortcuts and folders from the Start menu. The Add and Remove buttons are the easiest way to go, but Advanced gives you more flexibility. The Advanced button takes you directly to your Start Menu folder in NT Explorer (Figure 8.72). Add a folder to create a program group and add a program. Folders and shortcuts may be added in NT Explorer or by double-clicking My Computer on your Desktop. Either way, changes to the folders in your profile directory show up right away on your Desktop.

 TIP You can create shortcuts and drag them right onto your Start menu button to create a shortcut at the top of the Start menu. The shortcuts to the command prompt and to PowerPoint Viewer shown in Figure 8.72 were created in this way. You can also create a folder in this location with shortcuts to several program items. Microsoft calls these *custom program groups*.

FIGURE 8.70

*Specifying Taskbar
options in the Taskbar
property sheet*

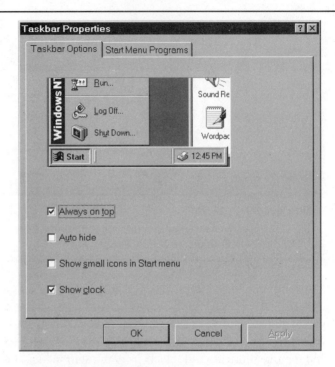

FIGURE 8.71

*Customizing the Start
menu in the Taskbar
property sheet*

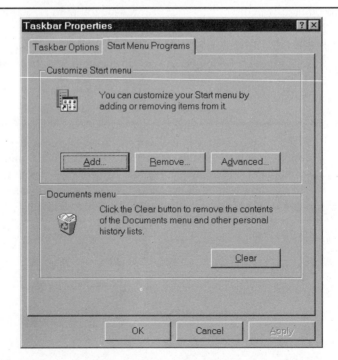

FIGURE 8.72

The Start Menu *folder in NT Explorer*

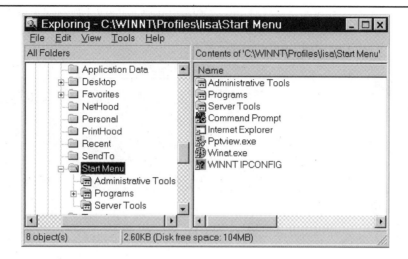

TIP Add a few shortcuts to the SendTo folder in your profile. If SendTo contains short-cuts to your home directory, word processing or spreadsheet applications, and printers, you can right-click a file to copy it to your home directory, open it in Word, or even print it!

Birth of an NT 4 Profile

The next step in mastering user profiles is to understand how NT creates a user profile and how a user obtains one. In short, when a user (we'll call him Sneezy) logs on for the first time (and therefore does not yet have a local profile), a new profile folder is created for him. The Default User profile information is copied to that new directory. This information, along with the shortcuts and program items found in the All Users folder, is then loaded to create Sneezy's Desktop. The new profile now exists in a folder named after the user in the same path as the Default User profile directory, %SYSTEMROOT%\PROFILES\SNEEZY. After NT creates the local profile, any user-specific changes made by Sneezy, such as Desktop color schemes, shortcuts, persistent network connections, or personal program groups, will be saved to Sneezy's profile. (For information about ownership and permissions, see Chapter 9.)

NOTE Only users who are members of the local Administrators group may make changes to the All Users folder.

By the way, if that profile is created on an NTFS partition, Sneezy will be the *owner* of the profile because he created it. Permissions will be set to allow him to modify his own profile. SYSTEM and Administrators will also have full access to the profile. Figure 8.73 shows permissions of the profile created for the user SNEEZY on the NT Workstation \\SWEETIE.

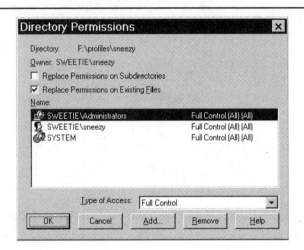

Roaming Profile Basics in NT 4

A network administrator might choose to specify a path on the network to store a user profile. A profile is a *roaming profile* (rather than a local profile) when the user account information indicates a profile path, even if that path is local. In the simplest of scenarios, the administrator has simply created a share on the server, set appropriate permissions on the share (and directories), and indicated in Computer Management Users and Groups or Active Directory Users and Computers that a copy of the user's profile should be stored there. NT will keep a local copy on Sneezy's workstation, but now the profile will follow Sneezy around. When he has to go downstairs and log on to the domain from Grumpy's NT workstation, NT will download the copy of his profile from the server. Sneezy also has made a "backup" of his local profile and stored it in a network location in case of disaster.

To specify a roaming profile path for a user, complete these two easy steps:

1. Create a shared directory. I like to create a share and name it profiles or PRO-FILES$ (to hide it from the browse list). Set share level permissions to Change or Full Control to allow all users storing profiles to alter their profiles. You do not have to create profile directories for the users. The NT 4 system will create the profile directory for the user and set appropriate permissions.

2. Open Active Directory Users and Computers, navigate to the user account in question, open its property page, go to the Profile tab, and fill in the path for the user profile directory as shown in Figure 8.74. The figure shows the user's roaming profile located in \\ANDROMEDA\profiles\ddavis. Profiles is the name of the share, not the directory name, so if you created a hidden share for the profiles, as mentioned in step 1, you'll need to use profiles$ instead. Use %USERNAME% in place of the username if you are specifying roaming profiles for more than one user account. You may also specify the user profile path as the user's home directory, as shown in Figure 8.75.

FIGURE 8.74

The Profile Path field in the user account property page

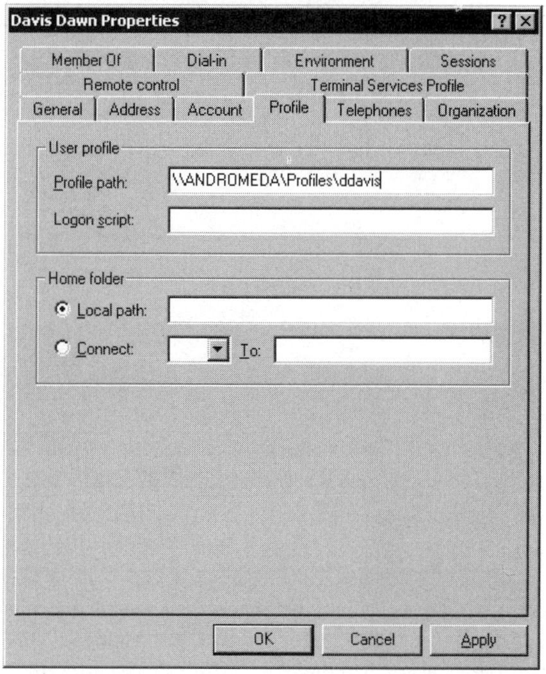

The next time Sneezy logs on, the NT workstation will see that there is a network path specified for the profile. Now, if you have been following our story, you'll know that Sneezy already has a local profile stored on his NT workstation. This appears to pose a problem, however—there is no profile on the server yet, and one does exist on the local machine. So, the workstation simply loads the local profile and creates a directory on the server to store the roaming profile. When Sneezy logs off, NTW will copy the local profile directory to the network path. In other words, NTW used the preexisting local profile to create the roaming profile directory on the server. From now on, whenever Sneezy logs on, NTW will check to make sure that the profiles still match (using a time stamp) and will load the most recent version. NTW will save any changes Sneezy makes to both profiles: the local copy and, when Sneezy logs off,

Sneezy's profile directory on the server. Okay, why all this rigmarole about saving the user profile to the local path and to the server? By default, NT will always keep a local profile folder to ensure that the user can access his profile if the network profile is unavailable. This is also useful with slow network connections.

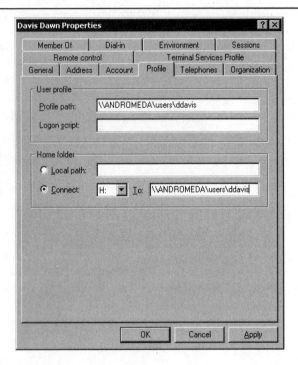

NOTE If the profile directory on the server is unavailable for some reason when Sneezy logs on (because the server is down, for instance), NTW will simply let him know this and load the local copy. In that case, NTW will not attempt to copy changes to the server when Sneezy logs off. The next time Sneezy logs on, NT will display another dialog box saying, "Your local profile is more recent than your server profile." Sneezy can then choose which profile to load. In case you are wondering, this scenario for Win2K profiles can be managed with group policies.

What if newcomer Dopey also has a roaming profile path specified in the Active Directory and he logs on his NT machine for the first time? Like Sneezy, Dopey doesn't have a profile directory on the server at all. Unlike Sneezy, he has no local profile on the workstation. In this case, NT will use the information in Default User on the local machine to create a local profile and will also create a profile directory in the network path. Just as with Sneezy, when Dopey logs off, NT will copy his local profile, including any changes, into the newly created directory.

Table 8.6 illustrates the order for loading a user profile, given the two scenarios we've discussed.

TABLE 8.6: LOADING A USER PROFILE WHEN THE ROAMING PROFILE IS NOT YET CREATED

Situation	What NT Does
A local profile exists.	NT loads the local profile and creates a roaming profile directory on the server. Changes to the local profile are updated automatically. When the user logs off, the contents of the local profile directory are copied to the server profile directory.
No local profile exists.	NT uses a Default User profile to create a local profile. The local profile is updated dynamically. A roaming profile directory is created on the server. When the user logs off, NT copies the contents of the local profile directory to the server.

 NOTE While it is possible to specify a roaming profile for a local account on an NT workstation in DSA.MSC, it's not really useful unless you are preconfiguring mandatory profiles for the local machine. And it's not really a roaming profile at all in this case because it cannot be loaded when the user logs on elsewhere. Also, do not expect consistent roaming profile behavior if the user is logging on locally and has a roaming profile path specified on the local machine.

Preconfiguring NT 4 User Profiles

Whether you want to create a preconfigured roaming profile or preconfigure the Default User profile, the principles are the same. It is a good strategy to create a bogus account to which you log on to configure the profile. This way you won't have to change your own profile and go through the hassle of cleaning it up. Use the Taskbar, Explorer, and the Control Panel applets to configure the Desktop, program items, and Start menu to your satisfaction, then log off. Log back on to that machine using an account that is a member of the local Administrators group.

Now you can copy the contents of the newly created profile over the existing contents of the Default User profile on the local machine. You can also copy that profile folder to a server location to implement a preconfigured roaming profile. You can even change the name and assign appropriate permissions during the process if you use the System applet to perform the copy rather than Explorer or another file management utility. Although a copy from Explorer would work in some scenarios, you would still have to set the directory permissions separately. Also, in certain other procedures regarding user profiles, NT needs to know that we are dealing with *profiles* here, not just files and directories. Get into the habit of using the System applet when dealing with user profiles.

Figure 8.76 shows the User Profiles tab in the System applet. Select the profile you have configured (Sneezy, in my case) and choose Copy To. Specify the path for the copy as shown in Figure 8.77, and remember to change the Permitted to Use information or only the bogus user (Sneezy) will be able to load the profile.

FIGURE 8.76

The User Profiles tab in the System applet

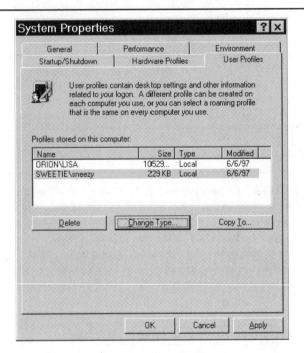

FIGURE 8.77

Copy the profile over Default User

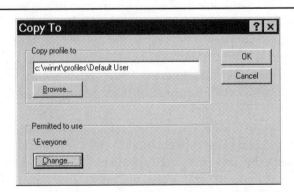

How Do I Create and Copy a Preconfigured User Profile?

That's a good question. Fortunately, it's as easy as this:

1. On an NT workstation, create a new user account using User Manager. For this example, I'll call the new user account Sneezy. Sneezy doesn't need any particular user rights or group memberships.

2. Log off and log back on to the workstation as Sneezy. NT will create a user profile for Sneezy using the default.

3. Customize Sneezy's Desktop. Create any Desktop shortcuts and put those short-cuts into the Start menu. Set up persistent network connections. Using Windows NT Explorer or by right-clicking the Taskbar and choosing Properties, you can add new program groups or shortcuts to the Start menu folders. By default, any user can change his profile.

4. When the profile is exactly the way you want it, log off. The system will now save the changes in the user's profile directory (\\%SYSTEMROOT%\PROFILES\SNEEZY). Actually, they are flushed to disk as you make changes to the profile.

5. Log back on to the workstation as a local administrator. Right-click My Computer and choose Properties to get the System applet (also accessed through Control Panel/System). Choose the User Profiles tab. You should see at least a user profile for your administrator account and for Sneezy; if no one else has ever logged on to the workstation, that's all you will see.

6. Use the mouse to highlight the template profile, then choose Copy To. Browse to the location of the directory or type in the path. This may be a local path or a net-work path. NT will create the profile directory where you specify as long as you have permissions to write to that path. Be sure to give the Everyone group (or the appropriate users or groups) permission to use the profile; Sneezy is the only user that has access right now. Choose OK to start the copy process. Figures 8.76 and 8.77 show the dialog boxes you will be using in this step.

7. Log off. You're done!

The Path's the Thing

This procedure can be used for several functions, depending on the path you specify. On the local level, you may copy the customized profile to C:\WINNT\PROFILES\ DEFAULT USER to preconfigure profiles for all new users on the NT workstation who do not already have a roaming profile stored on a server. It's also possible to copy the customized profile to other NT workstations if you have administrative rights on them. Take advantage of the fact that the system root directory on all of the worksta-tions is shared as ADMIN$. Use the path \\*MACHINENAME*\ADMIN$\PROFILES\DEFAULT USER to preconfigure the Default User profile on other NT workstations.

You can easily overwrite existing user profiles by typing in **%SYSTEMROOT%\PROFILES\ USERNAME**, or the appropriate UNC path, but again, don't forget to set permissions. You also need permission to overwrite the user's existing profile.

Set up preconfigured roaming profiles by copying the profile to the same UNC path you specified in the user account properties. In other words, copy the profile to the path *MACHINENAME*\PROFILES\SNEEZY and also use that path as the user profile path for the user.

Preconfigured local profiles may be set up this way, but you must specify a path in the user's local account information. Do not try to put the directory into the %SYS-TEMROOT%\PROFILES directory: NT has no way of linking that profile with the new user, so the machine will just create a new directory (for example, SNEEZY001).

Interestingly enough, you can copy the profile to the NETLOGON share on a domain controller to set up a domainwide Default User profile. You see, if a user is logging on to a domain, the machine first checks in the NETLOGON share (Win2K provides a NETLOGON share in \WINNT\SYSVOL\sysvol*domainname*\SCRIPTS to support Windows 95/98 and NT clients) of the authenticating domain controller to see if there is a Default User directory there. Only if no Default User directory is found in the NETLOGON directory does the machine use the local Default User information. If a DEFAULT USER directory exists in this network path (where login scripts and system policies are also stored), all new domain users with NT workstations will use this as the domainwide Default User template instead of using the local Default User directory. Specify the path as *MACHINENAME*\SYSVOL*domainname*\SCRIPTS\DEFAULT USER. Alternatively, you can save the profile directly to the NETLOGON share (*MACHINENAME*\NETLOGON\DEFAULT USER) if you are in the Administrator group (by default, the Everyone group has Read permission only to the share, while the Administrator group has Full Control per-mission). Be sure to name the directory Default User and grant permission to Every-one (or another appropriate group) to use the profile.

In any of the scenarios described above, users can still modify their own profiles once they are created. A variation of this procedure is used to set up mandatory pro-files; it will be discussed later.

Editing the *NTUSER.DAT* Hive File in NT 4

You can change many user profile settings by editing the contents of the folders or by configuring the Desktop. However, if you want to place restrictions on the preconfig-ured Default User or roaming profile to protect the system from inexperienced users, you will need to edit the hive file (NTUSER.DAT) of the template profile. To do this, you will need a Registry-editing tool.

WARNING As always, *do not edit the Registry unless you really know what you're doing.* Editing the Registry can have disastrous consequences: you could ruin your system configuration and have to reinstall your whole operating system. Be careful!

 NOTE Unfortunately, you cannot log on as a user named Default User and make changes directly to the Default User profile. If you try it, NT will get really confused. If you create a user DEFAULT USER and set the profile path in User Manager as %SYSTEMROOT%\PROFILES\DEFAULT USER, of course NT will use the Default User directory to create the profile. NT will also create a DEFAULT USER.000 profile directory for the user, and any changes you make to the profile while logged on as DEFAULT USER will not be saved to the Default User directory. In fact, they won't be saved to DEFAULT USER.000, either. You might even find that changes the user makes do not even apply on the Desktop!

Using *REGEDT32.EXE*

To edit user profiles using REGEDT32.EXE, open HKEY_USERS, as shown in Figure 8.78. Usually HKEY_USERS only contains two keys: .DEFAULT and the SID of the user currently logged on. The key .DEFAULT is not the Default User hive file, as you might think. That is located in %SYSTEMROOT%\PROFILES\DEFAULT USER\NTUSER.DAT. The hive file represented in Figure 8.78 is loaded from C:\WINNT\SYSTEM32\CONFIG\.DEFAULT and is known as the *system default profile*. Microsoft describes it as the profile in effect when nobody is logged on. This seems to be a dangling chromosome from NT 3.51 profiles, when each profile was its own hive file.

FIGURE 8.78

HKEY_USERS *subkey*

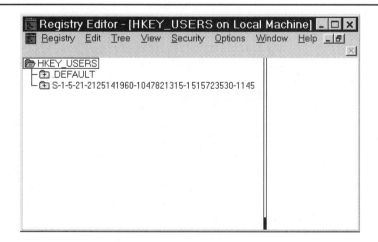

The system default and Default User profiles are independent of each other. That is, changing the color scheme in the Registry for the .DEFAULT hive will not affect the Default User profile hive in %SYSTEMROOT\PROFILES. Otherwise, when I set the system default (.DEFAULT) profile to use some neat (I mean practical and informative) bitmap wallpaper, any user who logged on without an already established profile would also get stuck with my wallpaper.

NOTE Have you ever wanted to change that default Windows bitmap you see on the screen when nobody is logged on? Well, that bitmap is the wallpaper for the SYSTEM profile (also known as the system default profile). Since SYSTEM is a user (or at least an entity) under NT, it makes sense that SYSTEM should have a profile, right? The SYSTEM default profile is the profile in effect when no one is logged on (you see the Ctrl+Alt+Del login dialog box). Simply use a Registry Editor such as REGEDT32.EXE or REGEDIT.EXE to specify different wallpaper. The entry is found in HKEY_USERS\.DEFAULT\CONTROL PANEL\DESKTOP. Edit the value entry for Wallpaper, specifying the full path of the bitmap that tickles your fancy as the value of the string. You will be editing the hive file %SYSTEM-ROOT%\SYSTEM32\CONFIG\DEFAULT. Screensavers in effect when no one is logged on can be specified in the same way. By the way, this works for Win2K systems as well.

You can use REGEDT32 to edit a user profile other than the system default and the profile that is actively loaded. Load the hive file using the Load Hive option from the Registry menu (Figure 8.79). This may be the NTUSER.DAT file from the Default User profile directory or any NTUSER.DAT file; you can browse for it (Figure 8.80). NT will prompt you for a temporary key name (Figure 8.81) and will then load the hive into the Registry Editor, as shown in Figure 8.82. Make changes to the Registry settings of the Default User profile. To finish up, select the loaded hive and choose Unload Hive from the Registry menu to save changes and clear the hive from the Registry Editor.

FIGURE 8.79

Loading hive in REGEDIT.EXE

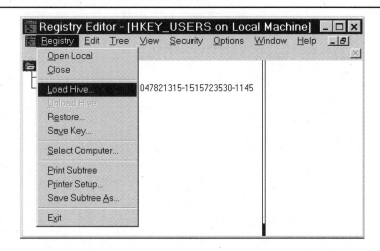

FIGURE 8.80

*Browsing to find
the hive file*

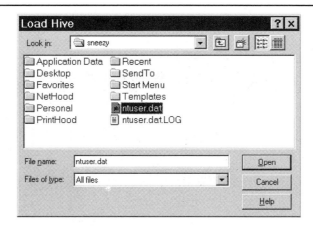

FIGURE 8.81

*Assigning a temporary
key name*

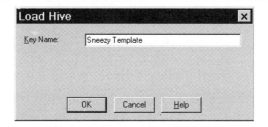

FIGURE 8.82

Hive is loaded.

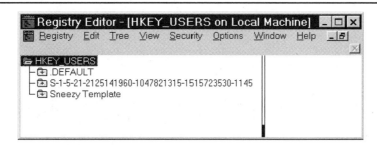

So which changes do you make once the hive is loaded? Ahh, that is the real question. You might configure all profiles to wait for login scripts to execute before starting the user's shell. That way, any drive mappings or environmental variables specified in the login script will take precedence over those in the user's profile. This entry is called RunLogonScriptSync (run login scripts synchronously) and is found in HKEY_USERS*KEYNAME*\\SOFTWARE\\MICROSOFT\\WINDOWS NT\\CURRENTVERSION\\WINLOGON (Figure 8.83). Although I could suggest a couple of other Registry entries to modify, the fact is that REGEDT32.EXE and REGEDIT.EXE are not all that user-friendly. Without spending copious amounts of our time reading Registry documentation (which is not always helpful) and experimenting, we do not know what is possible. We need a GUI Registry Editor. At this point, the System Policy Editor steps back onto the scene.

FIGURE 8.83

The RunLogon-ScriptSync *entry*

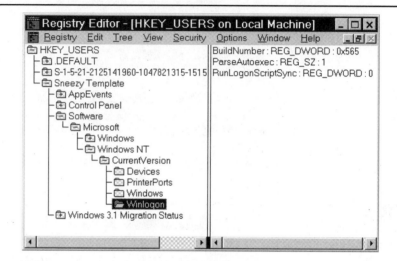

NT 4 System Policy Editor to the Rescue

Instead of trying to hack everything out in REGEDT32.EXE, you can use the System Policy Editor to place restrictions directly on the profile. (I know we haven't covered the System Policy Editor yet, but we will soon; forgive me for jumping the gun, but this won't take long.) Run the System Policy Editor (POLEDIT.EXE) while logged on as the template user SNEEZY. In this scenario, you will be using the Policy Editor as a user-friendly Registry Editor, instead of as a tool to impose system policies on your network. Choose File/Open Registry/Local User, as shown in Figures 8.84 and 8.85. Now you can actually read about your options in English (Figure 8.86). Apply your restrictions. You'll notice that you can take away the Run, Find, and Settings in the Start menu, as well as many other potentially dangerous "built-in" options on the Desktop. You'd better be careful, though: changes will apply immediately to the open profile you are configuring, so you might want to make that the last thing you do when configuring the profile. Also, don't touch Local Computer or you will be making changes to your other local hive files (like the System hive). These restrictions are written to the Registry. You can now go back and view them by looking under HKEY_CURRENT_USER\SOFTWARE\MICROSOFT\WINDOWS\CURRENTVERSION\POLICIES\EXPLORER (Figure 8.87). When you finish, close POLEDIT.EXE, log off, log back on as an administrator, and follow the steps outlined earlier to copy the profile, restrictions and all, to the Default User or Roaming Profile path.

FIGURE 8.84

Open local Registry

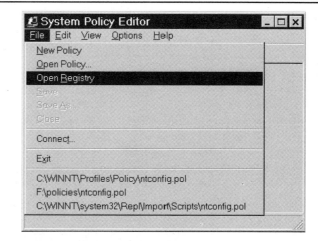

FIGURE 8.85

Local User/Local Registry

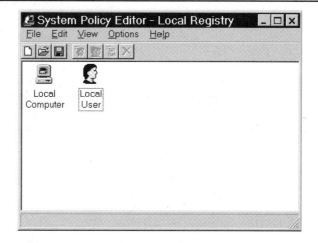

If you are configuring a domainwide default profile, log on to the domain as a new user; you will get the preconfigured default profile and any restrictions you built in. This will be a good opportunity to inspect your work and look for any loopholes or problems. Remember to create your own profile or an administrator profile before doing this stuff or it will apply to you as well.

FIGURE 8.86

Local User properties in POLEDIT.EXE

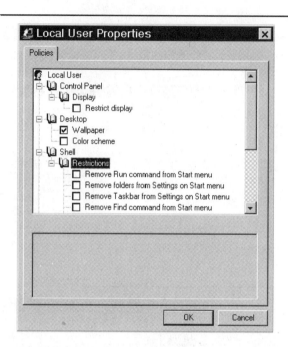

FIGURE 8.87

REGEDIT32 policies subkey

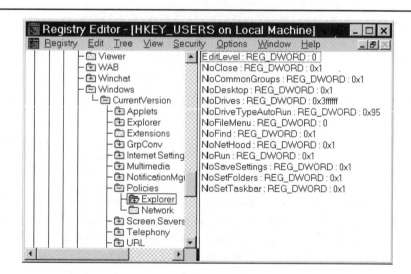

A Note about System Policy Editor's Day Job   Another way to apply restrictions is the more traditional method of using System Policy Editor, as you're going to learn in a few pages. Use POLEDIT.EXE to create a new policy, placing restrictions on DEFAULT USER and/or specific groups, users, or computers. Save that policy as NTCONFIG.POL, placing it in the NETLOGON share on your PDC emulator. What is the difference between the two methods? In the first scenario, restrictions are "built in" to the Default User profile. Unless you specify a mandatory profile, and depending on how you restricted Default User, users may be able to change their Desktop and Registry settings once they get their own profile. A savvy user could theoretically edit the Registry directly (unless you disabled Registry-editing tools for the Default User profile) and remove your restrictions. However, if NTCONFIG.POL exists in the NETLOGON share, NT will find the policy and reapply it every time a user logs on. Also, if NTCONFIG.POL specifies restrictions to be placed only on Default User, these would apply only the first time a user logs on and gets a new profile template.

The Bad News about NT 4 Preconfigured Default Profiles

The problem with a "powerless, preconfigured" Default User profile becomes apparent when a new administrator or some such person logs on for the first time. Your new administrator's profile will be created from this template and she will be the irritated but unintentional recipient of a highly restricted desktop (oops). In this case, you would need to keep a stash of unrestricted profiles in reserve somewhere (preconfigure them or make a copy of an untouched Default User profile). Users who should not get these powerless, preconfigured profiles must have unrestricted profiles specifically assigned to them. Furthermore, these profiles will have to exist in the network path specified in User Manager or User Manager for Domains before the user ever logs on. If she has already logged on and received the altered Default User profile, you have to delete her profile from the local machine and from the server to remedy the situation. In other words, the user will need to start over with a new profile and will lose any changes made to customize her Desktop.

Problems with Preconfigured and Roaming Profiles

As you create profiles for users, or simply allow them to have roaming profiles, keep in mind that a user profile includes settings on screen placement, window sizes, and color schemes. The display adapters and monitors on the workstations should be taken into consideration. If Sneezy has a 21-inch monitor with the latest and greatest AGP card and sets up his Desktop accordingly, he may have an unpleasant surprise when he logs on to Grumpy's machine equipped with lesser video capabilities (no wonder he's grumpy). When preconfiguring a profile for a user, sit at a computer that has the same video capabilities as the user's primary workstation. If you are configuring a Default User profile or one that will be used by multiple users, those workstations must have the same video capabilities. Alternatively, use the lowest common denominators to ensure that the settings will work on all platforms.

A Special Note about Shortcuts   Video problems are not all of it. If you are installing applications on the Desktop, always use default installation directories so that shortcuts created will resolve more smoothly. Also, keep in mind that NT shortcuts will first attempt to resolve using the *link tracking* method, which is the *absolute* path for the shortcut. Failing that, the shortcut will try to resolve with the *search method*, which means it will search the local drive. In other words, if you created a shortcut to Notepad on \\WOMBAT, saved the profile as a roaming profile, then sat down and logged on at \\POLECAT, the shortcut would first try to resolve to \\WOMBAT\WINNT\SYSTEM32\NOTEPAD.EXE. If the user cannot connect to \\WOMBAT, the system will supposedly search for the program in %Systemroot%\SYSTEM32\ NOTEPAD.EXE. But if \\WOMBAT exists, the user is prompted for a username and password to access \\WOMBAT\C$, the hidden drive share that's reserved for remote administration. This leaves users scratching their heads, saying, "What did I do?" or worse, calling the help desk to ask, "What did you do?" To prevent this problem, when creating shortcuts, use expandable variables (like %WINDIR%, %SYSTEMROOT%) whenever possible. Luckily, shortcuts work just fine when they point to a shared directory on the server, as long as they are created properly and permissions are appropriate.

Also, take into consideration that when users on your network regularly move from one NT machine to another, every machine they use will store a copy of their local profile. These will eventually add up and take up a chunk of disk space. Local profiles may be deleted periodically by an administrator, using the Delete option in the User Profiles tab of the System applet. You may also use System Policy Editor to delete cached copies of roaming profiles when the user logs off, as shown in Figure 8.88. This is a machine-specific setting, so the easiest way to implement it is with an NTCONFIG.POL file in the NETLOGON share. However, you can edit the workstations' Registries remotely. You will need to add an entry to HKEY_LOCAL_MACHINE\SOFTWARE\MICROSOFT\WINDOWS NT\ CURRENTVERSION\WINLOGON. The name of the value entry should be DeleteRoamingCache, with a datatype REG_DWORD and a value of 1 (it should read, DeleteRoamingCache:REG _DWORD:1).

Finally, accessing roaming profiles across a WAN link is not recommended. Whenever possible, load profiles from a server locally. Besides eating up network bandwidth (when the profile is sucked off the server at login and copied back to the server at logoff), time-out intervals for slow connections will cause numerous problems in synchronizing the local and server copies of the profiles.

NOTE   DELPROF.EXE, a command-line utility included in the NT Workstation and NT Server Resource Kits, allows administrators to delete user profiles on a local or remote computer running any version of Windows NT through 4.0 but not Windows 95/98. Of particular interest is its ability to delete profiles that have been inactive *x* number of days.

FIGURE 8.88

Delete roaming cache

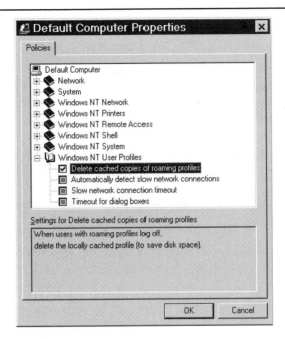

"Cached" Profiles: A Tip

It doesn't precisely fit in here, but talk of mandatory profiles reminded me of a peculiar behavior of NT, one that may bedevil you if you're extremely security conscious.

Suppose I've given you an NT 4 workstation named \\PC027, but I've not created a local account for you. Instead, I've given you a domain account on the SONGBIRDS domain and told you to log in from that. Thus, every morning you sit down at your workstation and tell your machine that you want to log in from a SONGBIRDS account, not a PC027 account—you want your workstation's Local Security Authority not to look in your workstation's SAM but instead to use NETLOGON to communicate with one of the domain controllers in SONGBIRDS and then to ask one of those controllers to look up your user account in the domain SAM.

Sounds good—but what about those times when you get that dratted "No domain controller found" error message? If your workstation's NETLOGON can't find a domain controller, it seems that there's no way for your local LSA to establish your credentials. That seems to mean also that if there's no domain controller around, you can't get on your workstation, doesn't it?

Or does it?

The first time this happened to me, I was somewhat taken aback to see that my NT workstation logged me in *anyway*, using "cached credentials." The idea is that, if you got in all right *yesterday*, we'll give you the benefit of the doubt *today*, even if the local LSA *can't* find a domain controller. Cool, eh? Well, yes, it might be cool for many, but the more security conscious among us might be quite unhappy about the idea that if a network administrator modifies or deletes your account on Tuesday, by Wednesday your workstation might not know about it.

Fortunately, there's a Registry setting that you can use to make a workstation require a domain logon. Just go to HKEY_LOCAL_MACHINE\Software\Microsoft\Windows NT\ CurrentVersion\Winlogon and create a value entry called CachedLogonsCount of type REG_DWORD and set its value to 0. Make this change on every NT workstation that you want to require strict logins. And if making all of those Registry changes sounds like a lot of work, stay tuned—a little later I'll show you how to use a tool called *system policies*, a neat way to let you remotely (and automatically) control Registries.

Mandatory Profiles in NT 4

So far in this discussion, all of the types of user profiles allowed users to make changes to customize their own profile (assuming you did not set up System Policy Editor to discard changed settings at logoff). Another option for controlling user profiles is to assign a *mandatory profile* to the user or to a group of users.

A mandatory profile is a read-only profile that the user must use. Mandatory profiles are a tad more work since the profile must exist ahead of time, and it must exist in the path you point to or the user cannot log on. Remember, with roaming profiles, we could just let NT copy the profile to the network path unless we wanted Sneezy to use a profile we created for him.

Mandatory profiles are a type of roaming profile in that you must specify a profile path in the user's account information. To create a mandatory profile directory, name it with the extension .MAN (for example, \\ALDEBARAN\PROFILES\SNEEZY.MAN). This tells NT that the profile is mandatory and that the user will not be able to log on if the profile is unavailable. In that case, the user will see a dialog box that says:

Unable to log you on because your mandatory profile is not available.

Please contact your administrator.

Also, rename the NTUSER.DAT file to NTUSER.MAN so that the user cannot save changes to the profile. Once the local profile is created on the workstation, the locally created copy of the profile will also be read-only. This does not set permissions on the profile per se, so it works on FAT or NTFS. Nor does changing the name to NTUSER.MAN set the read-only attribute on the file. It's just a special extension for the profile that tells NT not to save changes at logoff (changes will apply while the user is logged on but will be lost when the user logs off). This feature is useful if you want to assign one profile to a group of users and you do not want these users to be able to save changes. In other words, everybody shares a copy of the same profile, and it is protected against users' "personal touches."

NOTE Strangely enough, if the mandatory directory does exist in the specified path, but permissions on the directory do not grant at least read access to the user, that user will be able to log on using a default profile. The user encounters the following message (this is actually a problem in the USERENV.DLL and is corrected in Service Pack 3): "You do not have permission to access your central profile located at *SERVERNAME**SHARENAME*\\ *USERNAME*.MAN. The operating system is attempting to log you on with your local profile."

The following are your options for setting up mandatory profiles:

Use a read-only profile   Simply rename the file NTUSER.DAT to *NTUSER*.*MAN* before you assign the profile to the user or users. Keep in mind that when a user first logs on, NT does not know that this user's profile is a mandatory profile since the directory name is *USERNAME*, not *USERNAME*.MAN. If the profile is unavailable, the system will load a local or default profile. However, once the system loads the mandatory profile from the profile path, the System applet on the workstation shows the profile as mandatory. The user or users will not be able to save changes to the Desktop. At this point, if the network profile becomes unavailable, the system will load the local profile, but because NT now considers it a mandatory profile, changes will not be saved. Incidentally, renaming the NTUSER.DAT file to NTUSER.MAN can be done as an afterthought as well. In other words, if a user formally has a local and configurable profile, you can go to the C:\WINNT\PROFILES\USERNAME directory and rename the hive file. It will be read-only from that point on.

Force the user to load a particular profile   If you specify the directory path on the server as DIRECTORYNAME.MAN but do not rename the hive file to NTUSER.MAN, the operating system will not see it as a mandatory profile. If the hive file is not named NTUSER.MAN, the workstation will classify it merely as a roaming profile. At login, however, the user will not be able to log on if the profile directory does not exist in the specified path. Users can make changes to their Desktops, however, since it's not a real mandatory profile to NT.

Create a read-only profile that must be used   Specify the directory name as DIRECTORYNAME.MAN and rename the NTUSER.DAT file to *NTUSER*.*MAN*. This is ideal if you want to force users to load a profile off the network and you want to prevent them from making any changes.

How Do I Configure a Mandatory Profile for NT 4 Clients?

Mandatory profiles are created in much the same way preconfigured profiles are created. Mandatory profiles can be assigned to individual users or to groups. In the example below, I'll show you how to create a shared mandatory profile and assign it to everyone in a particular group (Research Users).

1. Create a user, log on as that user, and set up the Desktop.
2. Apply any restrictions you want at that time using the System Policy Editor as described earlier. Log off.
3. Log back on to the machine as an administrator.
4. Use the System applet (you can find it under Control Panel/System/User Profiles) to select the profile and copy it to a shared directory on the network, naming it SOMETHING.MAN. Remember to set permissions to allow your user (or a group) at least Read and Execute access to the profile and its contents. As you can see in the following Copy To dialog box, I named the directory RESEARCHUSERS.MAN and assigned permissions to the group Research Users.

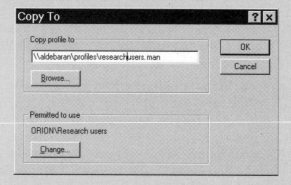

5. Use Explorer or your favorite file management tool to rename the copied NTUSER.DAT file to NTUSER.MAN.
6. In the property sheet for the user account, fill in the profile directory path, pointing to your mandatory profile directory.
7. You are now ready to have users log on and receive their mandatory profiles.

Continued

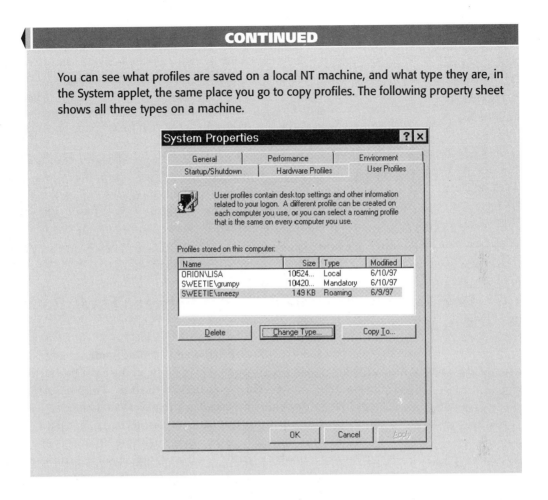

CONTINUED

You can see what profiles are saved on a local NT machine, and what type they are, in the System applet, the same place you go to copy profiles. The following property sheet shows all three types on a machine.

Setting Up a Group Template Profile for NT 4 Clients

As you can see, it's relatively easy to assign "shared" profiles to users and groups. However, any time two or more users are pulling their profiles from the same profile directory, it should be a mandatory profile. Otherwise, changes made by each user to the group profile directory on the server will be saved. Happy and Grumpy will have to deal with Sneezy's eggplant color scheme or Ninja Turtles icons.

How much more trouble is it to preconfigure and assign profiles based on, say, group membership, which will then be under the control of the individual user? This would not be a mandatory profile but just a point of departure for the user. Actually, it's a lot more trouble. Sure, you can make profile templates for groups, but how do you assign them and still let users customize the Desktop according to their own preferences or needs?

Assigning User-Configurable Profiles to Groups

If you use the standard preconfigured user profile procedure, follow these steps.

First, make group template profiles by creating three security groups (CLEAVERS, ADAMS, and CLAMPETTS). Then create three bogus group member accounts, naming them, for instance, Clampetts template, Adams template, and Cleavers template (you were getting pretty tired of the Seven Dwarfs stuff, weren't you?). Log on and off as each bogus user, and then configure the group profiles.

Before you add Ward or June user to the Cleavers group, open the System applet and copy the Cleavers group template profile to a shared profile directory, renaming it after the new user you are about to create. Then create the user, specifying his profile path as *MACHINENAME**PROFILESHARENAME**USERNAME*, where *PROFILESHARENAME* is the directory where you copied the profile. This is not overly complicated, but you will have to remember to copy a new profile to the shared directory and assign the profile to that specific user each time you create a new account.

How Does an NT 4 Client Choose between Local, Roaming, and Mandatory Profiles?

In all of this discussion about locally cached profiles, roaming profiles stored on a server, and mandatory profiles, it's important to understand the order in which NT looks for a profile and how the system chooses among the three. Plus, there are a couple of considerations that have not been explained yet. To make this simple, let's view the scenarios from two perspectives: a user that has never before logged on to that NT workstation (Morticia) and a user that has logged on to the machine already (Gomez).

Morticia logs on to her newly assigned NT 4 workstation. Assume that there is no profile path specified for Morticia in her account information. She will only have a local profile. NT must create a profile for her from a Default User directory. If Morticia is logging on to a Win2K domain, the operating system will first look in the NETLOGON share for a Default User profile (it has to look there anyway for the login script; why not just kill two birds with one stone?). No Default User directory in the NETLOGON share? Oh well, the system will just have to use the Default User info from the local machine.

If there is a profile path specified for her account, however, the system will look in that path for the profile directory. If the profile exists, NT will load it and use it to make a local copy. This may be a roaming or a mandatory profile. If no profile exists in the path and the path was indicated as mandatory—\\SERVERNAME\SHARENAME\USERNAME.MAN, for example—the user will not be allowed to log on at all! If there is no profile in the specified path and a roaming profile is specified (\\SERVERNAME\SHARENAME\USERNAME), NT will make one. Again, for a Win2K domain login, the system first checks in NETLOGON. If no Default User directory is found there, the system creates Morticia's profile from the local Default User directory.

So far, so good. Now let's tackle Gomez, who has been using his NT 4 workstation for a few weeks already. If no profile is specified in his account information, nothing changes for Gomez. He continues to use his locally stored profile.

If by chance you decided to implement roaming profiles one evening or weekend and Gomez comes in the next morning and logs on, NT has to check a few things. First, if a profile path exists in the account info, NT must first check to see if Gomez has changed his roaming profile type back to local. Aha! You see, Gomez might get tired of waiting for his roaming profile to load off the server and may decide to tell his workstation not to bother, to just use the local copy all the time. He does this by opening the System applet and the User Profiles tab, selecting his own profile, and choosing Change Type. Gomez then sees the dialog box shown in Figure 8.89. Gomez could not do this if the profile was mandatory, and of course, you cannot change a local profile to a roaming profile unless you are changing it *back* to a roaming profile.

Changing a user profile from roaming to local

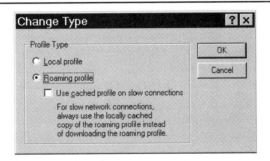

Any user may change an unrestricted roaming profile back to local and may also choose the option to automatically "use cached profile on slow connections." If Gomez checks that box, he's saying to NT, "If there is a slow network connection, just go ahead and load my local copy and don't bother me." What qualifies as a slow connection? That depends on an interval set in the Registry, called SlowLinkTimeout. The default interval is 2 seconds. Generally, if the 2-second interval is exceeded, Gomez will see a dialog box stating that a slow network connection has been detected and asking whether to load the local or the roaming profile. By default, Gomez has 30 seconds to choose (that value is determined by a Registry entry called ProfileDlgTimeout), after which time the system will load the local profile. But if Gomez chooses to "use cached profile on slow connections," NT will automatically load the local profile without asking Gomez. Hmmm.

The Registry entries affecting detection of slow network connections are found in HKEY_LOCAL_MACHINE\SOFTWARE\MICROSOFT\WINDOWS NT\CURRENTVERSION\WINLOGON. All of the following values may be set using the System Policy Editor:

SlowLinkDetectEnabled Has a data type of REG_DWORD and possible values of 0 (disabled) or 1 (enabled). Slow link detection is enabled by default and the system is told to be aware of slow network connections.

SlowLinkTimeOut   Has a datatype of REG_DWORD and a default value of 2000 (2 seconds expressed in milliseconds). Possible values are 0–120,000 (up to 2 minutes). When this threshold is exceeded and SlowLinkDetectEnabled is set to 1, users can log in by using a local profile instead of the roaming profile.

ProfileDlgTimeOut   Has a datatype of REG_DWORD and a default value of 30 (expressed in seconds). This value determines how long a user has to choose between a local or server-based profile when the value of SlowLinkTimeOut is exceeded.

Assuming that there is not a slow network connection and assuming Gomez has not changed his roaming profile back to a local profile (he hasn't had a chance yet, right?), the system will check to see whether (1) the profile is mandatory or (2) the profile on the server is more current.

If (1) or (2) is true, the system will load the server copy. If neither is true, then Gomez gets a pesky dialog box. You see, if (2) is not true, then the profile on the server is not more current than the local copy. This implies that there was a problem in synchronizing the profiles the last time Gomez logged off. So NT will announce that the local profile is more recent than the network profile and will ask if Gomez wants to load the local instead.

Whew! That was a bit complex, so maybe the following flow charts will help. Figures 8.90 and 8.91 describe Morticia (new user to the workstation, local profile and roaming profile), and Figure 8.92 follows Gomez (an existing user with locally stored profile). Finally, I've thrown in Figure 8.93 to show how a user's profile is saved at logoff.

FIGURE 8.90

How a new user gets a local profile

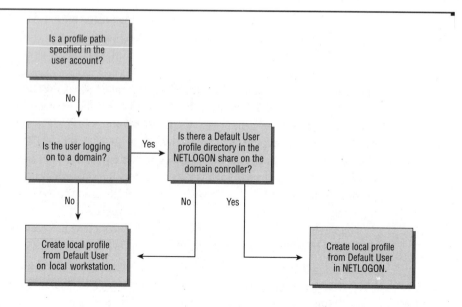

FIGURE 8.91

How a new user gets a roaming profile

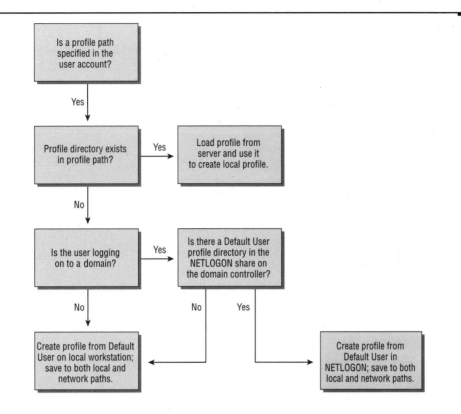

FIGURE 8.92

How a user with a local profile gets a roaming profile

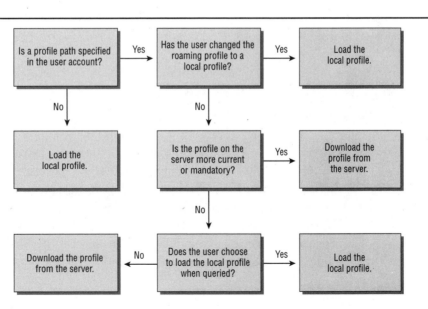

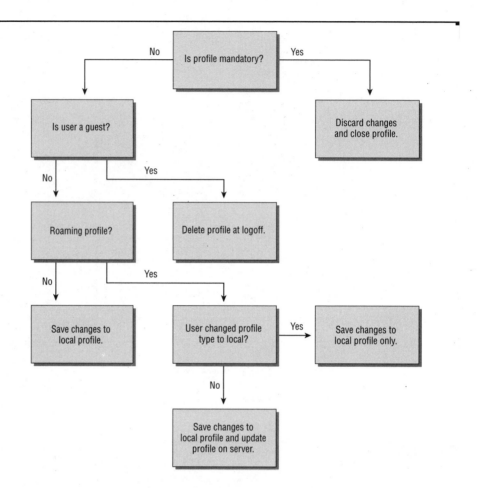

FIGURE 8.93

How user profiles are saved at logoff

Which Type of NT 4 Profile Is Right for My Network?

Now that you are an NT profile guru, you'll need to decide what kind of profiles to implement on your network. Even if you do nothing, you are still making a choice to let users just keep local profiles. For that reason, the following paragraphs summarize the pros and cons of the different types of profiles:

Local profiles only   Local profiles may be the best choice in a mixed client environment or where users don't need to roam. Windows 95/98 profiles are not interchangeable with NT Workstation profiles, though the Desktop is similar, so users moving from one client OS to another need either local profiles only or two roaming profiles. (Do you feel a migraine coming on?) This option has the lowest administrative overhead and offers the fewest options for pre-configuring profiles and controlling Desktops. However, you can still use System Policy Editor to configure Desktops and impose restrictive policies without implementing roaming profiles.

Roaming profiles   A roaming profile has two major benefits: mobility and fault tolerance. Not only can users move from desktop to desktop and have their preferred settings follow them, they also have a "backup" of their profile stored on the server. If you have to reinstall the workstation, the user doesn't necessarily have to reconfigure the Desktop. Plus, you can let NT create the profile for you as long as there are no special settings to hand out to users. This is also the option to use if you want profiles to be centrally located and controlled. The downside is that roaming profiles may follow you to another machine but may not work flawlessly once they are downloaded. Shortcuts to applications that exist only on the user's "home workstation" and different video adapters and monitors are only two of the possible problems users may encounter. Also, roaming profiles shooting across your Ethernet every time a user logs on or off will generate more traffic and slow down user logons. If it's a consideration at 10Mbps, consider the problems if you have an ISDN connection at 64Kbps. Finally, remember that NT will store a local copy of the profile for every user that logs on to a given NT machine. If users roam and roam and roam, they leave copies behind, taking up hard drive space as well as presenting a security issue (my Desktop may have a few items on it I don't want to leave behind). To address this problem, set up the machines to delete cached copies of roaming profiles.

Mandatory profiles   Mandatory profiles, because they are also roaming profiles, have the benefit of being mobile and fault tolerant. They can also be centrally located and controlled, like roaming profiles. Plus, mandatory profiles are the only way you can force a user to load a particular profile. Because it is read-only, users can share a profile; you keep fewer profiles stored on the server instead of one for every single user. While mandatory profiles offer more control than roaming profiles, they also require more setup on your part. You must manually create a mandatory profile and place it in a network path; NT can't create a mandatory profile for you. Finally, if a user attempts to log on and the mandatory profile is unavailable, NT will not allow the user to log on. This prevents a malicious user from logging on with the Default User profile and running amok, but it can also be seen as a drawback if you are preventing a legitimate user from logging on, thus causing loss of productivity in the organization.

Network Default User profile   One of the best things about a domain-wide Default User profile is that it may be implemented in conjunction with roaming profiles. This offers a great way to preconfigure all new user profiles, and although it does not help you hand out special program groups to, say, the accounting department, it can be used as a point of departure. You can use the System Policy Editor to hand out custom Start menu items to group members. However, if you place heinous restrictions on the Default User profile in the NETLOGON share, you'll have to create a special roaming profile and assign it to folks who shouldn't get the restrictions (like new MIS employees).

Implementing NT 4 User Profiles: An Example

Let's see what we've learned by looking at a sample situation and determining the best way to use profiles.

Suppose you manage several computer labs at a university, and each lab has 35–100 NT 4 workstations. Up to 10,000 students at the university, who all have accounts on the university-wide system, visit various labs using various machines. A few students cause problems in the network. Some of these students are malicious, while some are just inexperienced.

If you stand by and do nothing, users will leave profiles behind when they log off. You'll have to periodically delete profiles. If you allow users to have access to all possible tools on the Desktop, administrative overhead increases as you troubleshoot problems and reinstall the OS on the workstations.

Solution #1: Preconfigure a Domainwide Default User Profile   You may have to create more than one if user accounts are in multiple domains. Restrict profiles as necessary, assign roaming profiles, and delete cached copies of roaming profiles using System Policy Editor or the Resource Kit utility, DELPROF.EXE.

This is a good solution, but it poses one big problem. Even if users have restrictions placed on the profile, with roaming profiles for every user, the network servers will hold thousands of copies of the very same profile. Not only that, but savvy users may be able to change their own Registry settings and break free of restrictions.

Actually, there is a very simple solution to the profile detritus problem. Rather than going to the trouble of setting up a policy to delete cached copies of roaming profiles, editing the Registry of every machine, or running DELPROF.EXE at regular intervals, you can make every user a guest at the local machines in the lab. Although this approach has several other implications that might make it unfeasible for your situation, it would take care of profile buildup. Members of the Guests group are not allowed to keep local profiles unless they are also members of the Users group.

Solution #2: Create a Shared Mandatory Profile   A better solution is to create a restricted profile directory, name it USERS.MAN, rename the hive file to NTUSER.MAN, and assign this as a shared mandatory profile to all users. You'll also need to delete cached copies of roaming profiles. This way, even if a user manages to edit the Registry settings to take off the restrictions, changes will be discarded at logoff. You also save space on the network servers.

There is one possible problem with this solution: if many students try to download the mandatory profile at exactly the same time, they may experience sharing violations (NT 4 Service Pack 2 fixed this problem).

Distributing NT 4 User Profiles

You may also want to keep several copies of the mandatory profile (for example, one in each lab) for load balancing. There is a way to distribute user profiles across domain controllers using the undocumented environment variable %LOGONSERVER%: create a share of the same name on each domain controller, put the mandatory profiles into each of the shared directories, then indicate the profile path in account properties as something like \\%LOGONSERVER%\PROFILES\USERS.MAN. To prevent major profile synchronization problems, don't use this variable with regular roaming profiles, use it only with mandatory profiles.

What if you don't want to store profiles on the domain controllers, or what if not every lab has one? If the students logged on at the same lab every time, there wouldn't be any problem. You could just point to the local server for that lab in the user account's information. Unfortunately, you can't count on each student using the same lab every time.

You can tell the workstation where to look for the profile by creating a new environmental variable on each of the NT workstations. The new environmental variable will be %SERVERNAME% and will point to the local lab server keeping the mandatory profile.

How Do I Make NT 4 Users Load Profiles from Local Servers?

Use the System applet Environment tab to set a system variable pointing to the local server, as shown in the following System property sheet. Fill in the information as shown. In this case, the local lab server will be LAB01FSUNC. (Do not include % signs or \\ as part of the variable.) Choose the Set button and OK. Although the new variable

Continued ▌▶

CONTINUED

will be set, you will need to restart NT before these settings take effect since NT reads the system variables at start-up.

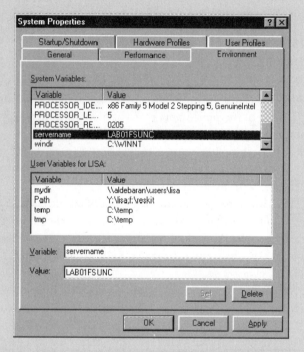

Once you have defined the %SERVERNAME% variable on each of the NT workstations (REGINI.EXE, a Resource Kit utility, can be pretty handy for that type of thing), created a share of the same name on each server, and copied the mandatory profiles to those shared directories, you may indicate the profile path in the user's account properties as \\%SERVERNAME%\PROFILES\USERS.MAN.

Windows NT 3.51, NT 4, and Windows 95/98 Profiles

As you can see, there's a lot that can be done with NT 4 user profiles in an NT/Win2K Server environment. However, in case you are not yet managing a network of just NT 4 clients, let's round out our discussion with a quick rundown of the differences between NT 3.51, NT 4, and Windows 95/98 user profiles. The important thing to keep in mind is that Windows 95/98, NT 3.51, and NT 4 profiles are not cross-platform profiles. In other words, a user who requires a roaming profile and customarily sits at several types of clients would need a Windows 95/98 profile and an NT profile for each version.

NT 3.51 Profiles

In NT 3.51, each user profile is a single hive file (found in %SYSTEMROOT%\SYSTEM32\ CONFIG), and profiles are stored with the rest of the Registry hive files (see Figure 8.94). Instead of a bunch of folders and a hive file, everything is included in the one file, for example, LISA000.

FIGURE 8.94

NT 3.51 user profile

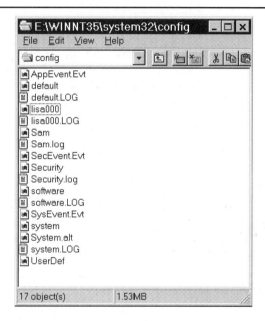

NT 3.51 supports per-user profiles (equivalent to roaming profiles) and mandatory profiles. The profile path for an NT 3.51 personal profile would be specified as \\SERVERNAME\SHARENAME\USERNAME.USR in the User Manager for Domains and, for a mandatory profile, \\SERVERNAME\SHARENAME\FILENAME.MAN.

Because there was no System Policy Editor under NT 3.51, options for restricting profiles were limited. NT 3.51 did provide a tool called User Profile Editor (UPEDIT.EXE), shown in Figure 8.95, which allowed you to log on as your bogus user, configure the Desktop, and save a configured profile with a skimpy set of restrictions to the current user or system default. This was also the tool used to save the profile to a specified path when implementing per-user or mandatory profiles.

NT 4 profiles use the Windows 95/98 profile structure, so NT 3.51 profiles will be converted to NT 4 profiles when upgrading from 3.51 to NT 4. NT 3.51 per-user profiles were simply files, whereas NT 4 profiles are entire directories, so NT 3.51 profiles formerly named USERNAME.USR, for example, will be converted to a directory called *USERNAME.PDS*. Likewise, mandatory profiles named USER.MAN will be converted to a directory called *USER.PDM*. If a user is in a mixed environment, she will have a separate profile for each version, and they will not be synchronized (changes made to one won't show up in the other) if changes are made after the initial migration.

Windows 95/98 Profiles

In Windows 95/98, individual profiles are not created by default but must be enabled in Control Panel/Passwords. If roaming profiles are enabled on the Windows 95/98 machine, they will be stored automatically in the user's home directory and will then operate in the same way as the NT Workstation profiles. You need not specify a profile path for the user in Active Directory Users and Computers.

Individual mandatory profiles can be used in Windows 95/98, but shared mandatory profiles cannot. For this reason, the administrator must create a profile for each user and copy it to that user's home directory.

The structure of a Windows 95/98 user profile contains differences from an NT user profile. Instead of an NTUSER.DAT file, Windows 95/98 has a USER.DAT file. Instead of

NTUSER.DAT.LOG, the log file that stores changes to the NTUSER.DAT file, Windows 95/98 uses a file called USER.DAO. These two files are not exact equivalents. Windows 95/98 uses USER.DAO as a "backup," writing a copy of USER.DAT to USER.DAO every time the user logs off. NT 4 uses NTUSER.DAT.LOG as a transaction log file to protect the hive file while it is being updated. To create a read-only mandatory profile, rename the 95/98 USER.DAT file to USER.MAN. NT 4 and Windows 95/98 use basically the same folder structure, except that the Application Data folder does not exist in Windows 95/98.

Additional differences in Windows 95/98 profiles include the following:

- Not all Desktop items will roam, only LNK (shortcuts) and PIF (program information) files.

- Common program groups aren't supported in Windows 95/98.

- Windows 95/98 can't use a centrally stored Default User profile.

System Policies for Legacy Clients

Although Win2K's Group Policy doesn't work for NT clients, there are two tools built in to NT 4 that make it a bit easier to support and control hundreds of workstations from a single point. The first is *user profiles*, which you read about in the preceding sections. The other tool is *system policies*.

So what's a system policy and why do you care? That's the topic of the next few dozen pages, but first let's look at the overview. System policies are essentially *central control of users' Registries*.

Why Would You Want to Control Registries?

As you know, virtually *everything* that has anything to do with controlling an NT 4 client machine (and a Win2K or Windows 95/98 machine, for that matter) is in the Registry. But I'll bet you didn't know all of the things that you can control with the Registry; certainly some of these surprised *me*. Here are a few examples:

- The contents of the folders that a user sees when she clicks the Start button

- Which icons and controls appear on the Desktop

- Whether or not a user can directly access the drives on her computer

- Which programs she can use on her computer

The basic idea is this: you can use Registry entries to lock down a Windows NT workstation or Windows 95/98 Desktop, thereby offering users a consistent and simplified user interface and making the support task simpler. Cool!

Using System Policies with Legacy Clients

Well, cool except for the fact that to change these important Registry entries on a bunch of machines, it seems like you'd have to walk around the building, sit down at each computer, and run REGEDT32 or REGEDIT to modify its Registry. Don't worry: there's an answer to that. There's an automatic feature built right in to Windows NT and Windows 95/98 machines that can make remote Registry modification much easier. Whenever a user logs on to a domain from a Windows NT or Windows 95/98 machine, the machine looks on the domain controller for a file called a *system policy* file. The system policy file basically consists of a bunch of instructions, like "Make sure that HKEY_LOCAL_ MACHINE\System\CurrentControlSet\Services\Browser\Parameters has a key named MaintainServerList, and be sure to set it to No." This system policy can centrally control *any* Registry entry except for those of type REG_MULTI_SZ, and this isn't a big restriction, as there aren't that many REG_MULTI_SZ entries.

Central Registry control through system policies is a neat feature, but there are a few problems with it:

- First, a user must be logging on to a domain or the user's system will not even look for the system policy file.

- Second, you can't have one common system policy file for both the Windows NT and Windows 95/98 machines; you have to build one set of policies for Windows NT desktops and another for Windows 95/98 desktops.

- Third, because these system policies are just changes to the Registry and because different Registry entries get read at different times, it can be a little confusing to try to figure out whether a system policy actually took effect—it may take an extra reboot to see the change in action.

The system policy files are created for Windows NT and Windows 95/98 with programs named System Policy Editor. I say "programs" because there is a version for Windows NT and a version for Windows 95/98. Actually, Windows 2000 includes one as well. All of the System Policy Editors are actually user-configurable Registry Editors. But unlike REGEDT32 and REGEDIT, they do not show all of the Registry: you essentially "program" them to work with the small subset of Registry entries that you care about, using files called *templates*. Fortunately, you don't usually need to do any of that "programming" as Microsoft includes some prebuilt templates that will serve most people's needs.

 NOTE For networks that have a mix of Win2K and NT machines, Win2K machines can read and apply system policies created with the NT System Policy Editor using NT 4 templates. However, this is not enabled by default to prevent system policies from conflicting with group policies.

Using the Registry to Restrict a Desktop: A Basic Example

But before I get into the specifics of system policies, let's try out one of those Registry changes that I mentioned.

A lot of the Registry changes that we'll find useful for central control of desktops are Registry entries that restrict the user shell program EXPLORER.EXE. EXPLORER.EXE— what's that? Well, you probably know that all of the programs that you run on a PC are just specially designed files with the extension .EXE or, on some older programs, .COM. (There are no NT programs that use .COM, but there are some old DOS programs that do.) You probably also know that the Registry just contains program-specific settings; for example, the Word for Windows section of the Registry contains settings that are only obeyed by Word—put a Registry parameter intended for the Computer Browser service into the Word section, and it'll be ignored.

If I asked you what Windows program you ran most often, you might tell me Word, your Web browser, or perhaps your e-mail program. But there's a Windows program that you use much more—the *shell program* EXPLORER.EXE. Explorer is the program that puts the Desktop on your screen; it starts automatically when you log on to a Windows NT computer. Explorer is the program that knows, when you double-click an icon, to go out and start the program associated with that icon. Explorer puts the Start button on the Desktop and controls what possible actions you can take when you push Start. It's also the program that displays the time in the system tray area of the Taskbar.

So, again, what's the value of controlling Explorer? Well, as you'll see, Explorer is normally the program that you use to start *other* programs: Word, Internet Explorer, Solitaire, or whatever. Being able to control which programs a user can run adds up to some real power.

One of the things that Explorer shows you is the Network Neighborhood folder. Let's see how to modify Explorer's Registry settings to make Network Neighborhood disappear.

The Network Neighborhood icon that appears on Windows 95/98 and Windows NT Desktops can be more trouble than it's worth. As you know, NetHood (as it's known internally to NT) is the user interface for the network browser, which allows someone to view the servers and shares on a network. It's nice, but in many cases it's also super-fluous, as the network's administrators probably create premapped drives for users. Network Neighborhood can, then, end up being an invitation to waste time browsing the local network. You can keep NetHood from appearing on a Desktop by adding an entry in the Registry to USER\Software\Microsoft\Windows\CurrentVersion\Policies\ Explorer, where *USER* is the user-specific part of a Registry. The new value (the entry is almost certainly not there by default) is NoNetHood, of type REG_DWORD. Set it to 1, and the next time that user logs on, she won't see the Network Neighborhood icon. You can demonstrate it on your own account (I'll show you how to undo it, don't worry) like so:

1. Open up REGEDIT.

2. Open up HKEY_CURRENT_USER\Software\Microsoft\Windows\CurrentVersion\ Policies\Explorer.

3. With the cursor on the Explorer folder, right-click and choose New/DWORD Value. The screen will look the one shown in Figure 8.96.

4. Click Edit/Rename, change New Value #1 to NoNetHood, double-click NoNetHood, and then change the value from 0 to 1.

5. Exit REGEDIT.

6. Log off and log back on using the same username.

You'll see that the Network Neighborhood icon isn't present any more.

FIGURE 8.96

Setting a new value in Registry Editor

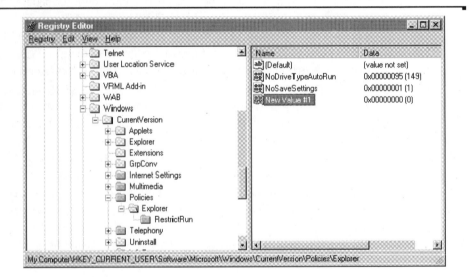

 NOTE To make NetHood appear again, return to REGEDIT and change the 1 value to 0, exit REGEDIT, and again log off and log back on.

Following the steps above imposed the restriction on *your* account. But suppose several people share a particular NT machine; can you modify how the machine treats them? Sure; it's just a bit more work.

By default, REGEDT32 and REGEDIT only load the Registry for the user who's currently logged on and the Registry for the System default user, the settings that are in effect when no one's logged in. (For example, if you set the Desktop background color to red for the "default" user, the screen background will be red when no one's logged in at the computer.) But if you've got a number of people who use a given computer, that computer will retain Registry settings for those people; you just need to grab those settings in order to modify them.

Unfortunately, you can't tell REGEDIT to load the Registry settings for another user. However, you *can* tell REGEDT32 to load another user's Registry settings. I sometimes use a user account called TESTUSER on my machine; as a result, there are Registry settings for TESTUSER, and I'll demonstrate how to load them.

 NOTE You'll need to be working on a computer with an account named TESTUSER in order to follow along. TESTUSER must have logged on to and off of this computer at least once for TESTUSER's Registry entries to be sitting on the computer.

To load the Registry settings for TESTUSER, follow these steps:

1. Run REGEDT32; again, REGEDIT won't work here.

2. Open the HKEY_USERS subtree and click the HKEY_USERS key.

3. Click Registry/Load Hive, and you'll get a dialog box labeled Load Hive, which looks like a normal File/Open dialog box.

4. Navigate over to whichever directory and drive hold your operating system. In my case, it's E:\WINNT, but it'll be different for you. Within that directory is a directory named PROFILES. You'll see a dialog box like the one shown in Figure 8.97.

FIGURE 8.97

Viewing user profiles using the Load Hive dialog box

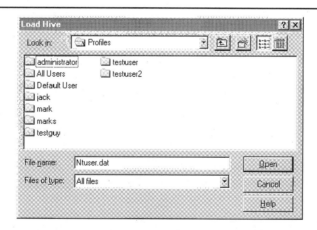

There's a directory for every person who's ever logged on to this computer—Administrator, jack, mark, marks, testguy, and TESTUSER—as well as a couple of extra directories labeled All Users and Default User.

5. Open up the TESTUSER folder; you'll see the dialog shown in Figure 8.98.

6. Select the file NTUSER.DAT because it contains the user-specific Registry entries for this user. Click Open. REGEDT32 then needs to know what to call this new hive, as shown in Figure 8.99.

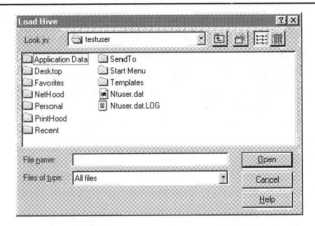

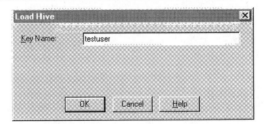

7. Name it **TESTUSER**. Click OK and REGEDT32 will look like Figure 8.100.

8. Now you can edit the Registry entries for TESTUSER just as I did for my own entries—just navigate down to HKEY_USERS\TESTUSER\Software\ Microsoft\Windows\CurrentVersion\Policies\Explorer and add NoNetHood as before.

9. Once you're done modifying TESTUSER's settings, click the TESTUSER key and choose Registry/Unload Hive.

The next time TESTUSER logs on, he won't see a Network Neighborhood folder.

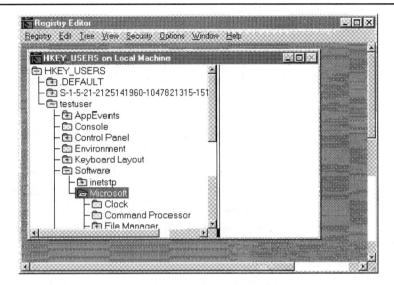

Desktop Control Policy Entries for NT 4 or 95/98 Clients

There are about two dozen settings like NoNetHood that you can use to restrict the NT (or 95/98) Desktop located in various places in the Registry. I'll discuss them according to their location. But before going any further, read this important warning and note.

WARNING My experiments show that many of these Registry entries have no effect whatsoever unless you're running Service Pack 2 or later on your NT Workstation machine.

NOTE If you have worked with Windows 95/98 system policies, read this section carefully because NT includes some *extra* policies that Windows 95/98 doesn't have.

Explorer Policies

The first bunch is located near NoNetHood, in a user's HKEY_CURRENT_USER\Software\ Microsoft\Windows\CurrentVersion\Policies\Explorer. Each entry is of type REG_DWORD. You activate these settings with a value of 1 and deactivate them with a value of 0 unless otherwise stated:

NoClose Removes the Shut Down option from the Start button if set to 1. The user can still shut down using the Security Dialog (Ctrl+Alt+Del).

NoCommonGroups Removes the common groups from the Start/Programs menu if set to 1. Recall that "common groups" are the program icons that everyone who logs on to this computer sees. If you've never noticed them before, click Start/Programs, and you'll see one or more lines separating some of the program groups; the bottom bunch shows the common groups. If you don't want particular users seeing those common groups, use this Registry entry.

NoFileMenu Removes the File menu from NT Explorer. Removing it largely "de-fangs" NT Explorer, as it's one less tool a user can employ to create, move, copy, or delete files.

NoTrayContextMenu Removes the little pop-up menu (the official term is the *context menu*) that you get when you right-click the Taskbar.

NoViewContextMenu Removes *all* the pop-up (oops, I mean *context*) menus that appear in the Explorer user interface. This keeps menus from appearing if you right-click the Desktop, My Computer, the Taskbar, or any other object on the Desktop.

NoNetConnectDisconnect Removes the option to connect and disconnect to/from network resources using Network Neighborhood and My Computer. You might not have even known that you can do this, but if you right-click My Computer or Network Neighborhood, two of the options you'll get on the context menu (hey, that "context menu" stuff kind of slips off the tongue after a while, doesn't it?) will raise dialog boxes to control network connections; forget that possibility and you're leaving a hole in your Desktop.

DisableLinkTracking Prevents shortcuts (LNK files) from attempting to resolve with the tracking method instead of the search method. Links that resolve with tracking remember if they originally referred to programs on other machines, whether you want them to or not. If you disable link tracking, shortcuts will search for the target and resolve to a local path if one exists.

ApprovedShellEx If set to 1, tells the shell to show items on the Desktop or in program menus only if they have recognized file extensions, like .EXE, .LNK, .TXT, or the like. As far as I can see, it's of no use; after all, if you put an object in one of those places that *doesn't* have an extension that NT recognizes, you can't do anything with it anyway.

NoDesktop Removes everything from the Desktop when set to 1. You don't see Internet Explorer, Briefcase, or any user-supplied icons. This can be very useful if you're just going to pare a user's options down to just a couple of applications. So far as I know, it's the only way to get rid of the My Computer folder, which is pretty useless anyway when you've removed all the drives from it (see the NoDrives setting, covered a bit later).

NoFind If enabled (set to 1), removes the Find option from the Start menu.

NoNetHood   Described earlier. There are two related settings that you might find useful if you *are* using the Network Neighborhood: NoEntireNetwork and NoWorkgroupContents, both of which are in a different Registry key, HKEY_LOCAL _USER\Software\Microsoft\Windows\CurrentVersion\Policies\Network. NoEntireNetwork removes the Entire Network entry from the Network Neighborhood, and NoWorkgroupContents hides machines, not just the Entire Network entry. To see the machines in your workgroup, you'd actually have to click Entire Network, then Microsoft Windows Network, then your workgroup's name. It's not clear to me why this is useful, but it's available.

NoRun   Removes the Run option from the Start menu.

NoSaveSettings   In theory, ignores any user changes to the Desktop—colors, icons, open windows, and the like—and on Windows 95/98 machines, it works fine. Unfortunately, under NT it doesn't work at all, and a call to Microsoft support got an official acknowledgment of that fact. Maybe Service Pack 23?

NoSetFolders   Has a name that doesn't offer much of a clue about what it does. If set to 1, the Settings folder (the one that normally contains the Control Panel and the Printers folder) does not appear on the Start menu.

NoSetTaskbar   Removes the ability to set options for the Taskbar if set to 1. That's the dialog box that lets you set AutoHide and the like for the Taskbar.

NoStartMenuSubFolders   Associated with custom program folders. You'll read in a page or two how you can control exactly what the user sees when she clicks Start/Programs. But if you *do* use a custom program folder, then you must set NoStartMenuSubFolders to 1 or NT will not only display your nice handcrafted program folders, it'll *also* show the standard ones, which you probably didn't want to happen if you created your own program folders.

NoDrives   Allows you to hide one or more drives from the My Computer folder. How it works is a bit esoteric, so don't worry if you have to read this a couple of times. The REG_DWORD value is a 32-bit number that isn't just 0 or 1. Rather, it uses the rightmost 26 bits of the 32-bit number (see, I told you it was esoteric) to describe whether or not to show a given drive. The rightmost bit in the number controls whether or not you see drive A:. Set it to 0 and you see A:, set it to 1 and you don't. The next bit to the left controls B: in the same way:

- Suppose you wanted to only hide the C: drive. The C: drive is the third drive, so you'd set the third bit over from the right to 1 and the others to 0. The correct value for NoDrives would then be 00000000000000000000000000000100 in binary, which is 4 in decimal. (Use the Calculator if you hate converting between binary and decimal.)

- Another example: Suppose you wanted to hide the floppy drives from My Computer. They're drives A: and B:, first and second, so set only the two rightmost bits to 1, a value of 00000000000000000000000000000011, or in decimal, 3.

- In most cases, you'll want to hide *all* drives, so the value for NoDrives should be 00000011111111111111111111 to hide all 26 drive letters. That's 03FFFFFF in hex or 67,108,863 in decimal. This removes all drives *from My Computer and the Explorer*—not the old Windows 3.*x* File Manager, which still ships with NT as WINFILE.EXE.

Now that you know how you can set Explorer policies to lock down what a user sees when running Explorer, let's look at how you can set them to restrict the programs the user runs.

Restricting What Programs a User Can Run with Explorer Policies

RestrictRun is another mildly complex Registry setting, but it's incredibly powerful. You can use it to say to the Windows interface, "Do not run any programs unless they are on the following list." For example, you could say, "The only programs that this user can run are Word and Internet Explorer." RestrictRun is another 1 or 0 Registry setting. A value of 0 says, "Don't restrict which programs this user can run," and 1 says, "Only allow this user to run the programs listed in HKEY_CURRENT_USER\Software\Microsoft\ WINDOWS\CurrentVersion\Policies\Explorer\RestrictRun." *That* key is just a list of applications that can run, and it consists of as many value entries as you like, all of type REG_SZ, and one application to a value. The name of the first entry must be, simply, 1 and again should contain the filename of the acceptable program. The second would be named 2, and so on. It's probably easiest to see an example, as in Figure 8.101. In that example, I've allowed this user to run (respectively) the Calculator, Internet Explorer, Word, and Command Prompt.

I've said RestrictRun is a powerful way to control what runs on a Desktop, but it's not perfect.

As you read a few pages back, one of the main reasons to control Explorer, the Windows user interface, is so you can control which programs run on a given computer. Whether you start a program by clicking an icon on the Desktop, by clicking Start/Programs, or by opening up My Computer and clicking an icon from one of the drives, the program is launched by Explorer. Suppose you use RestrictRun to tell Explorer, "Allow user Max to run only WINWORD.EXE, EXCEL.EXE, CMD.EXE (the command prompt), and IEXPLORE.EXE (Internet Explorer). Reject attempts to run any other programs." Suppose then that Max decides that he wants to run FreeCell. He opens up My Computer and looks around for FREECELL.EXE, the actual FreeCell program. He double-clicks it and gets a message, "This operation has been canceled because of restrictions in effect on this computer. Please contact your system administrator." Same message when he tries to run FreeCell from Start/Programs/Accessories/Games/FreeCell. If he tries to run it from the NT Explorer, he won't even get started: the NT Explorer isn't on the approved list, so it won't run either. Is Max FreeCell-less?

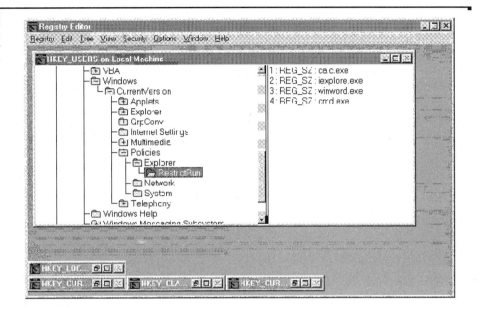

No, and that's one of the weaknesses of the policies approach. It only controls the behavior of the Explorer. Max *could* open up a command prompt, type **freecell**, and FreeCell would start up! Why? Because Explorer didn't start FreeCell; CMD.EXE, the command prompt, did. In most cases, the launching pad for applications is Explorer; but in this case, CMD.EXE started FreeCell. So to really lock down a Desktop—to control absolutely what applications get run on a given computer—you'd need restrictions on CMD.EXE. Unfortunately, that's not an option. As a result, it's probably not a good idea to include CMD.EXE on the "approved" programs list if you intend to restrict what programs can run on a user's Desktop.

Are there any other program loopholes? Other ways to launch programs? Yes, unfortunately: someone who knows what she's doing can write a three-line Word macro that will launch a program from inside Word, and again, there are no ways to restrict what programs launch from inside Word. I'm sure other programs have macro languages as powerful.

How about browsing the hard disks? Any way to do that on a locked-down Desktop? Believe it or not, Internet Explorer is a lockdown hole big enough to drive a truck through. Go to the URL line, type **C:**, and you'll get a complete view of your C: drive, complete with icons for your viewing and clicking pleasure. You won't be able to run any restricted EXEs from IE, but you can certainly view, copy, and delete files. So, in the final analysis, be aware that RestrictRun is a *nice* feature, but not an airtight one.

Keeping People from Getting to the Display Applet in the Control Panel

In HKEY_CURRENT_USER\Software\Microsoft\Windows\CurrentVersion\Policies\System, there's a setting, NoDispCPL, that will keep Windows NT from allowing a user to access the Display part of the Control Panel. When set to 1, this setting keeps a user from changing the screen by either right-clicking the Desktop or opening the Control Panel.

This could be particularly useful in a classroom setting, where you don't want users wasting time playing with colors and background bitmaps.

Keeping People from Using the Registry Editing Tools

After restricting the Explorer, you don't want people using the Registry Editors to undo your work. You can do that by adding an entry in HKEY_CURRENT_USER\Software\Microsoft\Windows\CurrentVersion\Policies\System for a particular user. The entry's name is DisableRegistryTools and, if set to 1, it will keep the user from running either REGEDIT or REGEDT32. Be aware though, that it will *not* keep that user from running POLEDIT, the System Policy Editor that we'll work with in a few pages. POLEDIT can modify the Registry, so either keep it off the approved list of programs (assuming you're using RestrictRun) or just make sure that it's not anywhere that a user can easily get to.

Getting Rid of the "Welcome" Tips

I know this is a matter of taste, but I find that welcome screen with the helpful tip *really* annoying. Yes, you can check the box that says, "Don't show me these any more," but I create and use a lot of accounts for testing purposes and so I'm forever clicking the darn box. Instead, however, you can use a Registry entry, which we'll control over the network, to keep the silly box from appearing in the first place. In HKEY_CURRENT_USER\Software\Microsoft\Windows\CurrentVersion\Explorer\Tips, just create a key named Show of type REG_DWORD and set it to 0. Set it to 1 and the dumb tips appear.

On the other hand, you might want to be *sure* that people read the tips. You might do that because you can redefine the tips, as they live in the Registry in HKEY_LOCAL_MACHINE\Software\Microsoft\Windows\CurrentVersion\Explorer\Tips. There is a value entry for each tip; they're all of type REG_SZ, and the value entry names are just numbers: 1, 2, and so on. You *could* use the central Registry control that we're leading up to in order to essentially "download" a bunch of tips to everyone's machine. They'd see those tips whenever they logged on to their system.

Controlling the Start Programs Folders

Part of creating a custom Desktop for a user includes controlling the programs that he can run. Once you've gone to all the trouble of keeping him from running all but a few programs, you'll have to give him a way to *get* to those few programs.

Most of the items that you see on the Start menu are just folders that various Registry entries point to. Look in any user's Software\Microsoft\Windows\CurrentVersion\ Explorer\User Shell Folders and you'll see the values AppData, Desktop, Favorites, Fonts, NetHood, Personal, PrintHood, Programs, Recent, SendTo, Start Menu, Startup, and Templates. They contain the locations of directories that contain user-specific information. For instance, Startup contains the location of a folder that contains short-cuts to the programs that you want that user to automatically run when he logs in.

Where the Menus Come From

The folder that we're most interested in at the moment is Programs. How can a disk directory correspond to menu items? Take a look at Figure 8.102, a full screen shot of a Windows NT 4 Desktop with some menus and sub-menus opened.

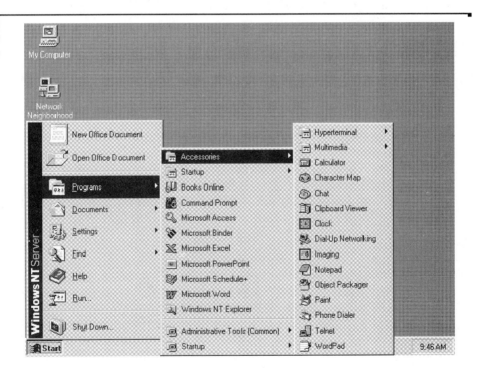

Note that the Programs menu has four submenus: Accessories, Start-up, Administrative Tools (Common), and another Start-up. You can tell from the folder-and-PC icons for the Administrative Tools (Common) and lower Startup folders that they are common folders. In a fully controlled Desktop, they probably wouldn't appear, as you'd use the NoCommonGroups Registry entry to keep them out of the picture anyway, so let's just focus on the Programs menu without the common folders. In addition to the Accessories and upper Start-up submenus, there are icons for Books Online, Command Prompt, Microsoft Access, Microsoft Binder, Microsoft Excel, Microsoft PowerPoint, Microsoft Schedule+, Microsoft Word, and Windows NT Explorer. I've also opened the Accessories submenu, which contains a number of items and two of what might be called "sub-submenus," Hyperterminal and Multimedia.

To look under the hood and see how this is actually accomplished, I go to the Profiles directory of my Windows NT installation. I'm currently logged on as MarkS, and I've installed NT in a directory called \TORUSMM; so if I look in \TORUSMM\PROFILES\ MARKS, I will see a number of folders, and one of them will be named Start Menu. Looking in that, I find a folder named Programs, which has shortcuts for each icon that appears on the menu. There is also a folder named Accessories in the Programs folder, and opening that shows me, again, shortcuts corresponding to each icon in the Accessories menu. In Figure 8.103, you see the open Programs and Accessories folders. The top one shows the shortcuts that appear when user MarkS clicks Start and Programs, the bottom one when that user clicks Start/Programs/Accessories.

FIGURE 8.103

Two open applications directories

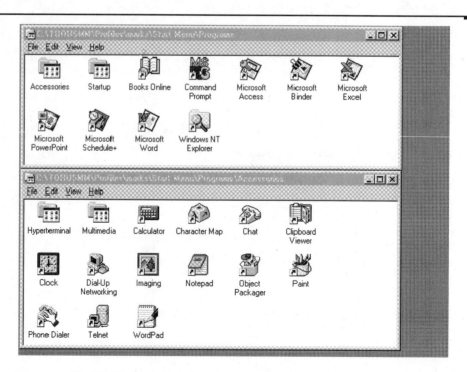

How can all of this help *you*? Well, again, suppose you've got a set of approved applications that you want to restrict users to. Just create a folder on the network that contains shortcuts to those applications. Then modify each user's Registry so that `Software\Microsoft\Windows\CurrentVersion\Explorer\User Shell Folders\ Programs` points to the UNC of that folder. When the user logs in, his only program icons will then be the ones that you've placed in this centrally located folder.

A Sample Custom Programs Folder

You can try this out by creating a "throwaway" user account and giving it a very limited menu of programs. I'm going to tell you to place all of the relevant files on the local system so you don't even need a network to try this out: even a copy of Windows NT Workstation would work fine. I'll assume for the example that you've installed NT in the default location, `C:\WINNT`:

1. Create a folder named `PROGS` on the root of C:, `C:\PROGS`.

2. In `C:\PROGS`, create shortcuts for Internet Explorer, the Calculator, and Notepad. (You can do this either by right-clicking in the folder, choosing New/Shortcut, and following the wizard or by just locating `IEXPLORE.EXE`, `CALC.EXE`, and `NOTEPAD.EXE` and dragging them into the `C:\PROGS` folder. The shell will automatically create shortcuts rather than copy the files.)

3. Create a bogus user account; BOGUS would be a perfectly good name.

4. Log on and off once as BOGUS so that NT will create a directory for the BOGUS user account in the `Profiles` directory. Log back on with an account with administrator level of privilege.

5. Start up REGEDT32 and load the Registry for user BOGUS. Put the cursor on the top of `HKEY _USERS`, click Registry/Load Hive, navigate to `C:\ WINNT\Profiles\ Bogus`, select the file `NTUSER.DAT`, and give it a name when prompted—again, bogus works just fine.

6. In `BOGUS`, open `Software\Microsoft\Windows\CurrentVersion\Explorer\User Shell Folders` and look at the current contents of the Programs entry. It's probably currently `C:\WINNT\Profiles\Bogus\Start Menu\Programs`; change it to `C:\PROGS`.

7. While you're there, go to `Bogus\Software\Microsoft\Windows\CurrentVersion\ Policies\Explorer` and add a new value, `NoStartMenuSubFolders`; type **REG _DWORD**, and set it to 1. In the same key, add `NoCommonGroups`, again **REG_DWORD**, set to 1.

8. Click the top of the `Bogus` tree and unload it with Registry/Unload Hive.

9. Confirm that you do want to unload the hive. Exit REGEDT32.

10. Log on as BOGUS. Click Start/Programs. See the difference? On my computer, when I click Start/Programs, my screen looks like Figure 8.104.

FIGURE 8.104

Limiting the
Programs *folder*

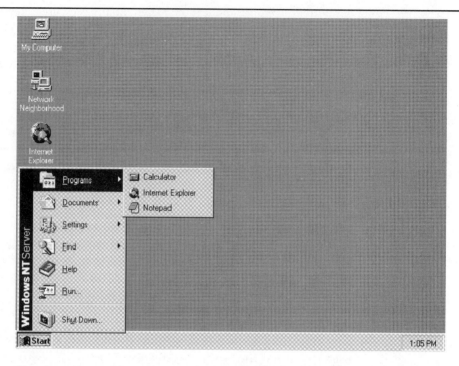

If you're interested, let's take this a bit further and *really* lock down this Desktop. In addition to the NoCommonGroups and NoStartMenuSubFolders settings, add NoDesktop, NoFind, NoRun, NoSetFolders, NoTrayContextMenu, and NoViewContextMenu (remember that they all go in Software\Microsoft\Windows\CurrentVersion\Policies\ Explorer) and set them all to 1. The result is a *very* simplified Desktop, perfect for someone who just needs to run a few programs and doesn't want to be bothered with the other NT 4 and Windows 95/98 Desktop clutter.

Again, this simple example was pretty labor intensive, and I'll show you very soon how to network this kind of control. But there's an important point to be made here: Eventually I'll have to network the folder that I called PROGS so that I can deliver the same set of program icons to everyone. But NT shortcuts refer to particular locations, so how can one set of program shortcuts serve an entire network? For example, my Calculator icon has embedded in it the fact that the Calculator program's full path is C:\TORUSMM\SYSTEM32\CALC.EXE, as that's where I've got the Calculator on my system. If I networked the PROGS folder and distributed it to a user whose Calculator wasn't in C:\TORUSMM\SYSTEM32, she wouldn't be able to access the Calculator. How, then, do you create a set of common program folders that are networkable?

One way is to network the apps; point the shortcuts not to drive letters like C:\TORUSMM\SYSTEM32 but to UNCs like \\APPSERVER\ENGINEERING\. This won't work for complex applications like Office 95, as Office 95 *must* install some files to the local hard disk before running. (Office 97 and 2000 are better behaved but still pose some problems.) The other possible approach is to standardize the locations of applications on each workstation's hard disk. If one machine loads Word in C:\MSOFFICE, make sure that they *all* do. It's a bit of a pain, but it's necessary to make networked program groups work—and it's useful for networked user profiles, as well.

NOTE   Remember, if you intend to distribute program menu folders to multiple users, you *must* be sure that all of the users have the applications that are in those folders in the same directories: if Word is in C:\MSOFFICE\WINWORD on one computer, make sure it's in C:\MSOFFICE\WINWORD in *all* of those users' computers. Otherwise, Word will show up as an option on the program menu, but clicking it won't do anything.

You can also control what a user sees in the *common* program folders, if you allow those folders; there is a key in HKEY_LOCAL_MACHINE that lets you designate a location for common folders. Look in any of the "machine" icons in the System Policy Editor.

Distributing Registry Changes to NT 4 Clients with *NTCONFIG.POL*

Just that little demonstration of controlling a program menu illustrated how powerful a few Registry changes can be—imagine if you were to take what we did a step further and use RestrictRun to let that computer run only Internet Explorer, Calculator, and Notepad. Then, not only would the user see only those three, but they would be the only things that would run. I'm simplifying the matter a trifle, of course, if you recall the discussion of all the loopholes in the user interface. But with a few more changes, you could pretty quickly bolt down a user's Desktop. (As I mentioned a page or two back, in addition to RestrictRun, I'd use NoDesktop, NoFind, NoRun, NoSetFolders, NoTrayContextMenu, and NoViewContextMenu.)

This sounds like a lot of work, and indeed it would be if you had to go out to every user's machine and hand-edit his Registry. So, as I mentioned in the beginning of this section, NT has this cool built-in way to order changes to Registries automatically over the network. (It'll allow you to control Windows 95/98 Registries as well, with a little extra work, as you'll see.)

The trick is this: When an NT workstation (or a Windows 95/98 computer, for that matter) logs on to an NT domain, the networking client software is designed to look on the primary domain controller's NETLOGON share—the place where you normally keep login batch scripts—for the system policy file that I mentioned earlier. More specifically, the system policy file is a binary file called either NTCONFIG.POL (the file that NT machines look for) or CONFIG.POL (the file that Windows 95/98 machines look for).

NOTE NT and Windows 95/98 clients look for the system policy file in the NETLOGON share of their PDC. Win2K doesn't really have PDCs anymore, but it does create the NETLOGON share for 95/98 and NT clients. There is also a PDC emulator feature. By default, the first domain controller created will be the PDC emulator. So NT and 95/98 clients look in the NETLOGON share of the Win2K server that is the PDC emulator for the system policy file.

It's logical at this point to wonder why there are different files for NT policies versus Windows 95/98 policies. It's because Windows 95/98 stores character data using ASCII (the American Standard Code for Information Interchange, a 35-year-old, English-centric method for storing characters), while NT, surprisingly, does *not* use ASCII; rather, it uses a more flexible character set called Unicode. NT's use of Unicode is one reason that it works so well in international environments. Microsoft's decision to *not* use Unicode in Windows 95/98 was unfortunate, but it's one of the dozens of reasons to use NT instead. (One Microsoft person—an *NT* developer, mind you, not a 95/98 developer—wryly commented to me that it was a sad example of what he called "MESE thinking." MESE is pronounced "meezie," and he explained that it stood for "Make 'Em Speak English.")

Bottom line is this: you'll have to build all your policies twice, once for the Windows 95/98 machines and once for the Windows NT machines. And when I say the files use ASCII or Unicode, I don't mean that these are simple text files—they're not—but that the portion of the file that *is* text is either stored as ASCII or Unicode. The other reason you end up with two different policy files is that Windows NT and Windows 95/98 Registry entries are *similar* but not identical—Windows 95/98 has some Registry entries that Windows NT doesn't, and vice versa.

Again, the POL file is largely binary, neither ASCII nor Unicode, so you can't just create one with Notepad. You've got to use a particular tool called the System Policy Editor to create a POL file.

These POL files essentially contain commands that your system uses to modify its Registry. So, before going any further, let me summarize some specifics of how the POL files work:

- The files must be created by one of the System Policy Editors.
- POL files will affect only the behavior of Windows 95/98, Windows NT 4, or NT Server 4 machines. They won't work with NT 3.*x* or Windows 3.*x* machines. They can be processed on Win2K machines, but the option is turned off by default.
- They must reside on the NETLOGON share of the PDC emulator domain controller.
- This is a "pull" technology in the sense that the PDC emulator never forces the POL files, or their effects, on the workstations. Rather, a workstation *requests* a file as a side effect to a domain logon, which brings me to the next point.

- This approach works *only* if you're doing a domain logon. You have to specifically configure a Windows 95/98 workstation to do a domain logon (Control Panel/Networking/Client for Microsoft Networks/Properties), and in the same way you've got to be logging on to a domain account from an NT machine for the NT system policies to take effect.

- These changes are Registry changes, so they won't always take effect until after the user's rebooted.

NOTE   To find out which Win2K Server in a domain is the PDC emulator, open up Active Directory Users and Computers, highlight the domain name, and choose Operations Masters from the Action menu. Go to the PDC tab to see which domain controller is the PDC emulator.

NOTE   The NETLOGON share on Win2K machines is found in \WINNT\SYSVOL\sysvol\ domainname\SCRIPTS.

Using *NTCONFIG.POL* to Modify an NT 4 User's Registry

The first example I gave of a Registry change was to eliminate the Network Neighborhood from TESTUSER's Desktop. Let's do that again, but this time let's do it with the System Policy Editor.

Before, I walked over to the computer that I usually use, fired up a Registry Editor, and directly edited HKEY_CURRENT_USER\Software\Microsoft\Windows\CurrentVersion\ Policies\Explorer, logged off, and then logged back on. *Now*, I'm going to use the System Policy Editor (the NT version, as my desktop operating system is NT) to create a CONFIG.POL with instructions to remove Network Neighborhood, and I'll save that CONFIG.POL on my domain's PDC emulator. If you want to follow along, you'll need a user account named TESTUSER.

First, I'll need the NT System Policy Editor. A System Policy Editor program is included with Win2K Server, although it's not exposed to the Desktop. You'll have to open Start/Run and type in **POLEDIT.EXE** to open it. Also, the Windows 2000 Administrative Tools package (ADMINPAK.MSI) includes the System Policy Editor for installation on Win2K Professional machines. The NT System Policy Editor that shipped with NT 4 Server appears in Start/Administrative Tools (Common) on that platform. If you're using NT Workstation, you'll get the System Policy Editor with the other administration tools in the \CLIENTS\SRVTOOLS directory from the NT Server

CD-ROM. Start up System Policy Editor, and you'll see a blank screen. Select File/New Policy, and you'll see something like Figure 8.105.

There's an icon of a PC and an icon of a gray-colored guy. Why the two icons? Well, recall that Registry entries tend to be either machine specific, like the things in HKEY_LOCAL_MACHINE (SAM, SECURITY, SYSTEM, SOFTWARE), or user specific, like the things in the \WINNT\PROFILES directory (NTUSER.DAT.LOG). You modify machine Registry entries through PC icons, and you modify user-specific Registry entries through user icons.

 WARNING The icons that appear automatically, the Default Computer and Default User icons, are *extremely powerful* and *extremely dangerous*.

FIGURE 8.105

Creating policies in Systems Policy Editor

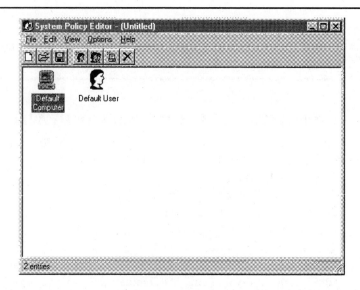

Any policies that you impose through Default Computer or Default User apply to every machine or every person, even domain controllers and administrators. Do something like hide the Desktop of the Default User and set Default User to a very restricted set of program folders, and *no one* will be able to undo that from an NT workstation; it's very possible that poorly set policies on Default User or Computer would make you have to rebuild your entire domain.

WARNING   Any changes that you make to Default User will automatically be copied to *all specific user policies*. (Ditto machines.) This makes it extremely difficult to create a diverse set of policies, as the dumb Default User keeps overwriting what you've done. My advice: don't do anything with Default User or Computer unless you've got a really good reason.

In fact, you can delete Default User and Default Computer, and I usually do. If you ever want them back, just re-create a user named Default User or a machine named Default Computer.

So, because I want to affect only *my* Desktop, I'll tell System Policy Editor to create a policy for just user TESTUSER. I know that I'm modifying a user icon rather than a machine icon because I know that the entry that I want to modify is in the user part of the Registry rather than the machine part.

Choose Edit/Add User, and you'll see a dialog box allowing you to either type in a username (like ORION\TESTUSER in my case, as that's the name of my master domain) or to browse a list of users. I browse over to my ORION domain, where TESTUSER lives, and choose TESTUSER. My screen now looks like the one shown in Figure 8.106.

FIGURE 8.106

Adding a new user

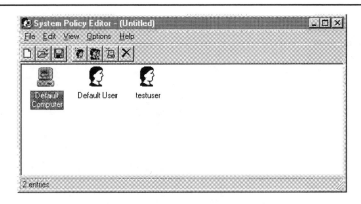

Now double-click TESTUSER, and you'll see a dialog box, as shown in Figure 8.107.

Hey, *this* looks quite a bit different from the Registry editing tools! System Policy Editor is organized completely differently than REGEDT32 and REGEDIT are. As I mentioned earlier, System Policy Editor doesn't contain all of the thousands of Registry entries, just a small subset that it has been directed to offer you. (I will explain later how you can control which Registry entries show up.) Open up the Shell book (click the plus sign), and you'll see another book, labeled Restrictions; open that up and you'll see a screen like Figure 8.108.

FIGURE 8.107

The User Properties
dialog box

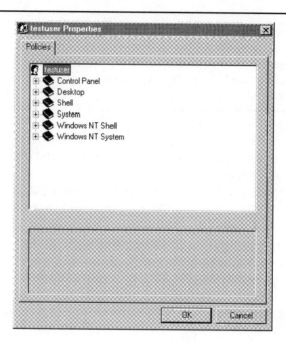

FIGURE 8.108

User Properties
Restrictions

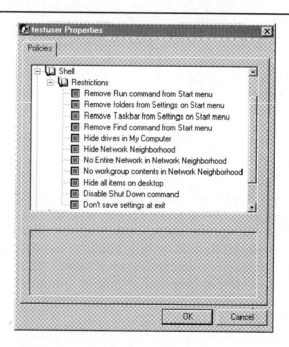

See the entry labeled Hide Network Neighborhood? Click it, and it'll show up as a checked box. A checked box means "Set the value to 1." Click it again, and you'll see that it is now a cleared box. A cleared box means "Set the value to 0." Click it again, and it becomes gray, as it originally was. A gray box means "There's no system policy about this, so leave it alone." Finally, click it yet again, and it will appear checked: recall that we want the value of NoNetHood to be 1 so that the Network Neighborhood will not appear. Then click OK to clear the TESTUSER Properties dialog.

Next, tell System Policy Editor to save the policy file so that it'll take effect. Click File/Save As and navigate over to the NETLOGON share of your domain's PDC emulator. Save it as file NTCONFIG.POL.

Next, I log off and log on to the domain using the TESTUSER account. (Again, TESTUSER must log on to an *NT* machine to see the effect of the policy change; there's no Windows 95/98 policy file, and so if I logged on to the domain with a Windows 95/98 computer as TESTUSER, I'd still see the Network Neighborhood.) The result: no Network Neighborhood. How did checking Hide Network Neighborhood cause a change in the Policies key of the Registry? Through template files, which I'll explain later. But first, let's see how to undo a policy.

Undoing the NT 4 System Policy

Now suppose I want to restore the Network Neighborhood to TESTUSER, or better, what if TESTUSER tries to *take* it back? Can he just edit his Registry to restore Net-Hood? Actually, TESTUSER can't change the NoNetHood entry; by default, regular old user accounts only have Read permission on entries in the HKEY_CURRENT_USERS\ Software\Microsoft\Windows\CurrentVersion\Policies key. But suppose he *could* change his Registry. Would that let him get NetHood back? No. The next time he logged on, his system would read NTCONFIG.POL, see the order to remove NetHood, and he'd be back where he started.

Suppose, however, that while he can't modify his own local Registry, he talks some administrator into erasing NTCONFIG.POL. Then what happens? As it turns out, nothing. In the same way, what if an administrator decides to change the Hide Network Neighborhood policy from checked to gray—what happens? Again, nothing; our user still doesn't have a Network Neighborhood.

The sequence of events for central Registry control goes like this: assume there's an NTCONFIG.POL on the PDC and the file has a no-NetHood policy in it. Over on TESTUSER's desk, TESTUSER turns on his computer. The computer powers up and reads its local Registry, the part relevant to the machine only. The PC doesn't know who's going to log on to it. Next, TESTUSER logs on to the domain using his account. When TESTUSER's workstation PC contacts the PDC emulator, the NTCONFIG.POL file essentially tells TESTUSER's workstation, "Change the value of HKEY_CURRENT_USERS\ Software\Microsoft\Windows\CurrentVersion\Policies\Explorer's NoNetHood to 1 and then log this TESTUSER guy in." The local user-specific Registry information for TESTUSER gets changed accordingly, and so as Explorer starts up, it leaves out NetHood.

Now suppose someone erases NTCONFIG.POL in the NETLOGON share. TESTUSER logs off and then back on. Will that get NetHood back?

No. Remember that the NoNetHood=1 setting is in his *local Registry on the workstation's hard disk*. He must either modify that Registry (which he can't do, as he has only Read access to the Policies key) or ask an administrator to use a system policy to return the Network Neighborhood to his Desktop.

So TESTUSER comes to you, his friendly administrator, and asks that NetHood be returned to him. How do you do it? Start up the System Policy Editor, load the policy file, and open up TESTUSER back to the Shell/Restrictions screen.

Recall that the check box had not two, but three states: checked, which meant "Force TESTUSER not to have NetHood"; unchecked, which meant "Force TESTUSER to *have* NetHood"; and gray, which meant "Do not modify this part of TESTUSER's Registry." If you were to simply say, "We don't care anymore what users do with their NetHoods" and gray the box, where would that leave TESTUSER? He still wouldn't have a Network Neighborhood, as gray means "Don't change anything," and the current state of his Registry says to not show NetHood. To restore NetHood would require a three-step process:

1. First, clear the box. Don't check it or leave it gray.

2. Then ask TESTUSER to log on. He should now have NetHood back.

3. The current system policies now *force* TESTUSER to have NetHood, but you want the policy to be silent. Once TESTUSER's logged off, go back and edit NTCON-FIG.POL to make the box gray.

NetHood is now restored.

NOTE It's not intuitive (until someone explains it), but it's important to understand the preceding steps. Remember, to release people from a policy, it's not sufficient to simply gray the policy's box. You must first reenable whatever the policy disabled, *then* gray the box.

Changing a Policy about a Machine

In most cases, you'll use the System Policy Editor and the POL files to control user settings. But what about machine settings? Let's look at a couple that are built in: the logon legal notice caption and whether or not to update the "access time" information in the file system. You can set your systems up so that they will display a legal notice banner when someone tries to log on to them, a message along the lines of "You'll be prosecuted if you try to hack this computer." To turn this on, find the two Registry entries in HKLM\System\CurrentControlSet\Software\Microsoft\Windows NT\CurrentVersion\Winlogon; one is called LegalNoticeCaption and the other is LegalNoticeText. The caption is the text that goes on the title bar of the warning dialog box, and the text is the text inside the dialog box. Anyway, open up a machine icon in the System Policy Editor, open up the Windows NT System book, and open up the Logon book, and you'll see a dialog like the one shown in Figure 8.109.

This option isn't enabled by default, so I checked it to allow you to see the caption and text fields. You can put any text that you like into the fields; if you want to try it out, check the box and type in the text of your choice.

The other possible change effected in System Policy Editor is whether or not to update a field in NTFS called Access Time. Not only does NTFS keep track of when you created a file, it also remembers when you last modified it and when you last accessed it. That's useful, but constantly recording when a file was last looked at can slow the computer down a bit. So there's a Registry entry that says, "Don't bother keeping track of when the file was last accessed."

Anyway, while neither the legal caption setting nor the "Don't keep track of the last access time" setting is earth-shattering, they're good, simple examples of when you make a change in NTCONFIG.POL versus when the change takes effect.

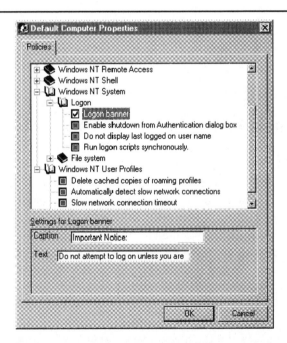

Suppose you make this policy change for some specific machine, say a machine named PPRO200, the name of one of my NT machines. When does the change take effect? Well, unlike group policies, the system policy file only gets read when a user logs in. Suppose I log in at PPRO200. In the process of logging me on to the domain,

PPRO200 reads `NTCONFIG.POL` and receives the commands to incorporate the legal caption and not to record access times. The relevant questions here are:

- When will I first see the legal notice?
- When will the system stop logging access times?

The legal notice change is a modification to a Registry entry for Winlogon, the program that runs whenever you press Ctrl+Alt+Del to log on to a system. How often, then, does Winlogon check its Registry for changes? Every time someone logs on. As a result, you'll see the legal notice caption the next time you log on to that machine.

The access-time information is part of the Registry entries for NTFS, however. When do *they* get examined by NTFS? Only at system boot time. You could log on 50 times and not see the "Don't keep track of access times" change take place. Reason: You must reboot the computer for these changes to take effect. Moral of the story: System policies can drive you crazy because when you make a bunch of changes (like the two I just made), you see some of them take effect almost immediately and some may take a day or two. That is, you may not have the occasion to reboot for that long, and so you won't see your changes until then. So before you start tearing your hair out, stop and analyze the matter: What change *did* the System Policy Editor make to the Registry? Should I reboot before the change will take effect? And, here's one of my favorite dumb things to do when playing with system policies—did you remember to *save* the updated `NTCONFIG.POL`?

Which Domain to Save the Policy To?

Let's consider the following question. I log in as MarkA, my administrative account, which is a member of a domain named ORION. But my workstation, PPRO200, is a member of domain TAURUS. Now, I want to save a policy that affects my *machine*, which again is a member of domain TAURUS, not me. So the $64,000 question is, should I create (or modify) the `NTCONFIG.POL` on the ORION PDC emulator or the one on the TAURUS PDC emulator?

My analysis says to put it on the user's domain, not the machine's domain. Examining the power-up and logon sequences with a network monitor, I see that the machine upon power-up certainly communicates with a domain controller so that the NT machine can essentially "log on to" its domain, but it never looks for `NTCONFIG.POL`. It's only when a user logs in that `NTCONFIG.POL` gets read. Therefore, oddly enough, even though your machines may be members of one domain and your user accounts are members of another domain, *all* policies, user and machine, should go on the PDC emulator of the user's domain.

Group-Based System Policies

You may have noticed that the System Policy Editor not only allows you to create policies for particular users, you can also create policies for particular domain-wide groups.

Unfortunately, system policies based on security groups won't apply to NT 4 clients in a Win2K Server environment. Enhanced security settings prevent the system from querying the Active Directory for groups, which leaves us with only Default User, Default Computer, and individual user and machine-level policies. It's also possible to set policies for a specific "template" user, then copy those settings to other individual users. Copy settings to the Clipboard by selecting the icon for the configured user, then choosing Edit/Copy. Select one or more other user icons (careful, don't choose Default User!) and choose Paste. Confirm that you want to copy the settings, and each of the selected users will now have the identical settings of your "template" user. Cold comfort if you have hundreds of users, though. Plus, what a pain to change one setting! And how do you know if they get out of synch? Way to go, Microsoft.

Using Templates to Create New Policies

Let's return to a question I posed a few pages back: Why does clicking Remove Network Neighborhood from Desktop cause a change in HKEY_CURRENT_USERS\Software\Microsoft\Windows\CurrentVersion\Policies\Explorer? Because of *policy templates*. Rather than simply presenting a somewhat raw and sometimes cryptic set of Registry entries, the System Policy Editor uses a simple kind of programming language that allows its user to see a somewhat more friendly, explanatory interface. The files containing the programming commands are called *templates*.

Introducing the Template Language

The templates that System Policy uses are ADM files, and they use a special programming lingo to tell Poledit what policy choices to present to humans and to create the POL file. As I said, templates are intended to make the System Policy Editor look friendlier, but *friendly* isn't the word I'd use for the programming language itself. Here's the code that you'd use to tell the System Policy Editor to produce a check box for Remove Network Neighborhood from Desktop; it will create an entry in HKEY_CURRENT_USERS\Software\Microsoft\Windows\CurrentVersion\Policies\Explorer. System Policy Editor will call the entry NoNetHood and will set it to either 0 or 1:

```
CLASS USER
CATEGORY "Shell"
  CATEGORY "Restrictions"
    KEYNAME Software\Microsoft\Windows\CurrentVersion\Policies\Explorer
      POLICY "Hide Network Neighborhood"
        VALUENAME "NoNetHood"
      END POLICY
  END CATEGORY      ; End of Restrictions category
END CATEGORY      ; End of Shell category
```

See, I *told* you it was ugly. Put these lines into an ASCII file and load them into the System Policy Editor (I'll show you how in a moment), and you'll see *just* the NetHood adjustment, as shown in Figure 8.110.

NOTE Win2K uses a later version of ADM files (version 3 and above) for Group Policy administrative templates. Although NT 4–style ADM files are supported for system policies processing in Win2K, you cannot use version 3 ADM syntax on NT or Windows 95/98 machines. You can't load the `inetres.adm` or `system.adm` files (the Group Policy snap-in administrative templates files) to the System Policy Editor, for example.

Here's how the template program works. First, recall that policies are either relevant to a machine or relevant to a user; the first line, CLASS USER, defines which it is—the alternative is CLASS MACHINE. The next two commands are CATEGORY; they define the books that you see. As you can have books inside books, each CATEGORY command is paired with an END CATEGORY command. Anything that appears on a line after a semi-colon is ignored—it's a comment for *your* use, not the System Policy Editor's—and so I've added comments to clarify which END CATEGORY goes with which CATEGORY command. Note that CATEGORY really doesn't have anything to do with which Registry entries you're modifying; it's just there to allow you to define the user interface. As you've probably guessed, the labels in quotes after the CATEGORY command ("Shell" and "Restrictions", in the two examples you see here) are the labels that should appear in the System Policy Editor.

FIGURE 8.110

Changing user properties in System Policy Editor

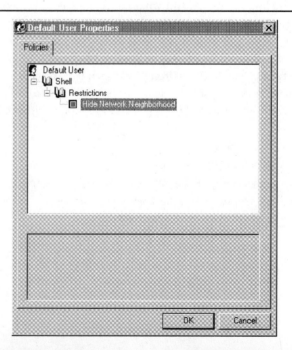

The next four lines, KEYNAME, POLICY, VALUENAME, and END POLICY, all go together. KEYNAME and VALUENAME together define the actual Registry entry to work with. KEYNAME, as you'd guess, defines the particular Registry key that we're working with. VALUENAME is the name of the particular Registry entry. The POL-ICY/END POLICY pair just does some more System Policy Editor user-interface stuff, defining the Hide Network Neighborhood label.

Creating and Using a New Template

If you want to try this out, then do the following steps:

1. Using Notepad, create a file with the nine lines shown earlier.

2. Save the file in your \WINNT\INF directory as TEST.ADM. Check that Notepad hasn't helpfully named it TEST.ADM.TXT; I sometimes have to open up My Computer and rename the file myself.

3. Start System Policy Editor.

4. Click Options/Policy Template, and you'll probably see a dialog box like Figure 8.111.

FIGURE 8.111

Adding a policy template

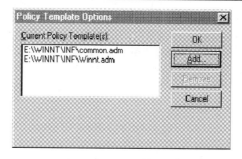

5. For all files listed in Current Policy Template(s), click the template file and then click Remove.

6. Once you've cleared out all of the existing template files, click Add and choose TEST.ADM. (System Policy Editor template files use the extension .ADM.)

7. Click OK.

8. Click File/New Policy and open Default User.

You'll see the System Policy Editor showing just the Network Neighborhood policy, as in the screen shot a couple of pages back. To restore your System Policy Editor back to where it was, close the policy (File/Close), open the Templates dialog box (Options/Policy Template), and add WINNT.ADM and COMMON.ADM back; again, you'll find them in \WINNT\INF.

The Existing Template Files

You probably noticed that there are three ADM files: WINNT.ADM, WINDOWS.ADM, and COMMON.ADM. Why three files? Because you'll probably want to create POL files for both NT Desktops and Windows 95/98 Desktops, but the Windows NT and Windows 95/98 Registries aren't exactly the same. Microsoft thought about what Registry entries an administrator would find useful to control as policies, and so they built these three templates to save you the trouble of having to build a template. Both the Windows NT and Windows 95/98 System Policy Editors use the same format for their templates, however, so you can load COMMON.ADM into either System Policy Editor.

COMMON.ADM contains the Registry entries that are common to both Windows NT and Windows 95/98. WINNT.ADM contains Registry entries that don't exist in Windows 95/98, and WINDOWS.ADM contains Registry entries that exist in Windows 95/98 but not in Windows NT. Remember, however, that you *cannot* use the NT System Policy Editor to create a policy file that Windows 95/98 machines can understand or respond to. So, then, to summarize how you'd use the System Policy Editors and the templates to control Registries on machines in a domain:

- Windows NT computers will respond to a file that is named NTCONFIG.POL. So will Win2K, if system policy processing is enabled.

- Windows 95/98 computers will respond to a file called CONFIG.POL.

- You must create NTCONFIG.POL using either the Win2K version or the NT version of System Policy Editor. Load the WINNT.ADM and COMMON.ADM templates, as well as any templates you've defined, to help you create an NTCONFIG.POL. NTCONFIG.POL must be stored on the NETLOGON share on the PDC emulator of your users' domain.

- You must create CONFIG.POL using the Windows 95/98 version of the System Policy Editor from a Windows 95/98 machine. You can install the tool from the Windows 95 or 98 CD-ROM; you'll find it in ADMIN\APPTOOLS\POLEDIT. (Not all Windows 95 and 98 CDs contain this file, but most do. If yours doesn't have it, you'll definitely find it in the Windows 95 or Windows 98 Resource Kit.) Load the WINDOWS.ADM and COMMON.ADM templates, as well as any templates you've defined, to help you create a CONFIG.POL. CONFIG.POL must also be stored on the NETLOGON share on the PDC emulator of your users' domain. Windows 95/98 will ignore policies unless the user explicitly logs on to the domain.

- And remember that policy files get read when *users* log in, not when machines start up, so put the policy files into the NETLOGON share of the *users'* domain's PDC emulator.

Programming More Complex Entries

Thus far, we've seen REG_DWORD entries whose values are only 0 or 1. But how do you set up the System Policy Editor to offer you one of several options? You may have read that you can prevent your machine from participating in browser elections, and thereby reduce network chatter, by introducing a setting to all of your NT Workstation machines: Just modify the entry MaintainServerList in HKLM\System\CurrentControlSet\ Services\Browser\Parameters, setting it to No. The result is that when your domain is holding network elections to determine who will be the master browser, the work– stations won't take part in the election, lessening the number of candidates and thus reducing network chatter. (Again, don't worry so much about the details; I'm just using this as an example.)

Setting up a MaintainServerList policy will be a bit more complex than the poli- cies we've looked at so far, so we'll have to delve further into the template program- ming language. I can't document every possible command in the template language here, but if you need to do something fancy with System Policy Editor, look to the existing ADM files for examples. As far as I know, the only time that Microsoft has documented this was in the Windows 95 Resource Kit; I can't find it in any of the other Resource Kits.

In addition to No, MaintainServerList can also accept values of Auto or Yes. Auto, the default value for workstations, means "I'm willing to be the master browser if neces- sary." Yes means "Not only am I willing to be a browser, but I'd like my machine to be a preferred candidate to be a browser." Yes gives a small edge to that machine during the election. As you've probably guessed, MaintainServerList is of type REG_SZ. Previously, I set up a check box with System Policy Editor, which System Policy Editor translates into (1) use REG_DWORD and (2) if checked, store a value of 1, and if unchecked, store a value of 0. MaintainServerList is a bit different—first, it uses REG_SZ values, and sec- ond, it should respond to only a few particular values (Yes, No, and Auto). How do you get System Policy Editor to offer only three options?

If you want System Policy Editor to offer anything but the most basic check boxes, you've got to create what it calls a *part*. A part allows you to define in some detail what kinds of values a user can give to a System Policy Editor item. Here's how you'd set up MaintainServerList:

```
CLASS MACHINE
CATEGORY "Browser Elections"
  KEYNAME System\CurrentControlSet\Services\Browser\Parameters
  POLICY "Can this machine act as the master browser?"
    PART "Possible options:" DROPDOWNLIST REQUIRED
      VALUENAME "MaintainServerList"
      ITEMLIST
        NAME "Do not ever act as a browser" VALUE NO
        NAME "Request Preference in Being Selected" VALUE YES
```

```
           NAME "Willing to be a browser if necessary" VALUE AUTO
        END ITEMLIST
     END PART
  END POLICY
END CATEGORY
```

Much of this looks familiar: the CLASS, CATEGORY, KEYNAME, POLICY, and VALUENAME commands. But notice that between POLICY and VALUENAME comes PART. PART defines the user-interface component that the System Policy Editor should use to offer options to a user: CHECKBOX for a simple check box, NUMERIC for a single value that should be a number, EDITTEXT for a single value that should be textual information, COMBOBOX for a single value with suggested possible values, or DROPDOWNLIST for a single value with only a few possible legal values. The REQUIRED keyword means "Don't accept this policy unless the user picks a value, and don't take null or blank as an option."

Once you've chosen DROPDOWNLIST, you must specify the list of possible legal values; that's what the ITEMLIST/END ITEMLIST group does. Each NAME line lets you specify labels that the user will see, like "Do not ever act as a browser," along with the corresponding value to store in the Registry. Create a template like that, and the System Policy Editor will look like the one shown in Figure 8.112.

FIGURE 8.112

Using parts to offer a limited number of values

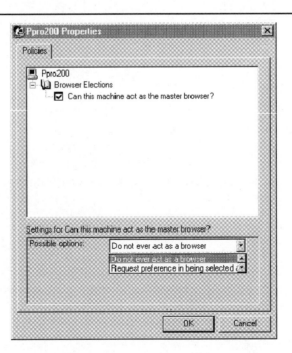

What if those labels need to correspond to numeric values? Suppose the possible legal values of MaintainServerList were −1, 0, and 1 rather than No, Yes, and Auto.

How would you tell System Policy Editor to save those values? With just one extra parameter on VALUE, VALUE NUMERIC. The ITEMLIST would then look like this:

```
ITEMLIST
   NAME "Do not ever act as a browser" VALUE NUMERIC -1
   NAME "Request Preference in Being Selected" VALUE NUMERIC 0
   NAME "Willing to be a browser if necessary" VALUE NUMERIC 1
END ITEMLIST
```

Allowing Numeric Inputs   Sometimes you'll need to create a policy that affects a numeric Registry entry that ranges from some minimum to some maximum. Use a NUMERIC part for that; they look like this:

```
PART label NUMERIC DEFAULT value MIN value MAX value SPIN value REQUIRED
```

Here, DEFAULT, MIN, and MAX specify the default value, the minimum allowable value, and the maximum allowable value. REQUIRED again means that the user must specify a value or the System Policy Editor should not store the policy. SPIN tells System Policy Editor what increments to use for the numeric spinner; you can use the default value of 1, or you can disable the spinner with a value of 0.

Due to a bug in the System Policy Editor, it can't handle an integer larger than 32767. If that number looks odd, it shouldn't: it's the largest integer (well, okay, the largest *signed* integer, an integer that can take either a positive or negative value) that can fit into 16 bits. Unfortunately, most Registry numeric values have *32* bits to play with, so whoever programmed the System Policy Editor to only handle 16 bits was seriously derelict in his or her job. The bottom line is that, if you want to create a policy with a numeric value, it'll work best if you keep the value under 32767. So if you want to do the above example, change 172800 to 32767 and it'll work. Once you do that, the System Policy Editor looks like Figure 8.113.

Sometimes you'll just want your users to punch in a numeric value and you don't want to show them the spinners; in that case, add the parameter SPIN 0, which makes the spinners disappear. Alternatively, you may want to keep the spinners but have them increment by, say, 100 with each click; you can do that with the parameter SPIN 100. That would modify the PART statement above to look like this:

```
PART "Time interval in seconds:" NUMERIC MIN
➥60 MAX 32767 DEFAULT 600 SPIN 100
```

Allowing Free-Form Text Input   We've seen check boxes, text input restricted to a few options, and numeric input, but how can you create a policy that allows the user to type in any old text that she likes? For example, you've probably noticed that if you click Help/About on any screen, you get the name and organization name that someone typed in when he or she installed NT on the computer. Can you change that: can you force the organization name to be consistent across all computers? Sure. It's in a Registry key HKLM\Software\Microsoft\Windows NT\CurrentVersion, with entry name RegisteredOrganization. It's a REG_SZ, and you can type in any old thing; there is no maximum length that I know of save for the practical one of length. So let's build a policy that makes sure that every PC in the company uses Acme Technologies as the organization name.

FIGURE 8.113

Using parts to allow numeric inputs

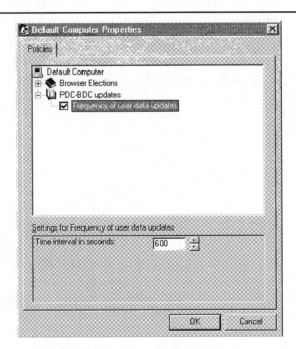

The part type we'll need is a simple one, EDITTEXT. It can have the REQUIRED and DEFAULT parameters, as well as a MAXLEN parameter. So, for example, if we wanted to set the maximum length of the RegisteredOrganization to 80 characters, we'd build a template like the following:

```
CLASS MACHINE
CATEGORY "General Information"
  KEYNAME "Software\Microsoft\Windows NT\CurrentVersion"
  POLICY "Setup info"
    PART "Organization name:" EDITTEXT MAXLEN 80
      VALUENAME "RegisteredOrganization"
    END PART
  END POLICY
END CATEGORY
```

Straightforward by now, but notice that I had to use quotes in the KEYNAME line; that's because there was a space in the key's name. You can see what it looks like in Figure 8.114.

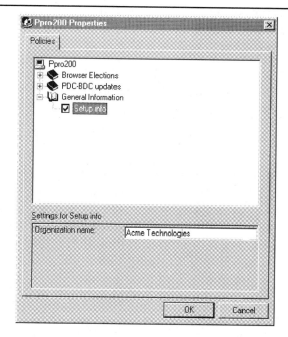

FIGURE 8.114

Using parts to allow free-form text input

I hope you've learned three things here: First, you can create a wide array of templates to allow you to control the Registry entries of systems all throughout your network. Second, the language is a bit obtuse, but not impossible to master. Third, you'll have to be ready to do a fair amount of experimentation, as the System Policy Editor and templates are a bit buggy. But before you get *too* heady a rush at the prospect of controlling everything from your desktop, recall that system policies *cannot* modify any Registry entries of type REG_MULTI_SZ.

Another Example: Assigning Mapped Drives with NT System Policies

Here's another great application of system policies, and it illustrates how you can start from a Registry entry and use system policies to propagate user configurations.

Suppose you want a given user upon logon to see a drive V: connected to \\BIGSERVE\COOLDATA—how would you accomplish this? Of course, you can use logon batch scripts to assign this drive; just add this line to the logon batch script:

```
Net use v: \\bigserve\cooldata
```

But a little poking around in the Registry shows that once you've mapped a drive, it appears in your user profile. Under HKEY_CURRENT_USER, you'll find a key called Network, which contains a key for each drive letter. The keys are named *F* for the mapped F: drive, *V* for the mapped V: drive, and so on. Thus, if I'd mapped my V: drive to \\bigserve\

cooldata, I'd find (after logging off and then on) a key HKEY_CURRENT_USER\Network\V. It contains these value entries:

ConnectionType A numeric value equal to 1

ProviderName A string equal to "Microsoft Windows Network"

ProviderType A hex value 20000

RemotePath A string containing the UNC (\\bigserve\cooldata)

UserName Another string with my name (ORION\MarkM)

 NOTE A bit of experimentation shows that UserName works just as well with a blank value. That's probably because, when the user tries to use the V: drive and NT's security system asks, "Who are you?" the user's workstation simply replies with the user's name. One could imagine a case when you'd want to attach under another name, but not often.

Let's see how to make this a policy. The first question is, does this go in USER or MACHINE? Simple—we found the Registry entry in HKEY_CURRENT_USER, so it's CLASS USER. We'll have a key Network\V, as that's the name of the key with the drive mapping information.

This template item will have five value entries in it, four of which we don't want to have to fill in—ConnectionType, ProviderName, ProviderType, and UserName—as we already know what values they're supposed to take. Rather than hard-wiring RemotePath to \\bigserve\cooldata, let's allow an administrator to tailor this to her needs. So it would be neat if we could build a template that essentially says, "If you enter a UNC for the V: drive, I'll automatically also fill in these four other value entries." You can, with a thing called *ActionListOn*. It's best explained in the template itself, which follows:

```
CLASS USER
Category "Map Drive V:"
     Policy "Map drives"
     KeyName "Network\V"
          ActionListon
                VALUENAME ConnectionType      VALUE NUMERIC 1
                VALUENAME ProviderName         VALUE
                ➥"Microsoft Windows Network"
                VALUENAME ProviderType         VALUE NUMERIC 131072
                VALUENAME UserName             VALUE ""
          End ActionListon
     Part "Drive V:" EditText
          VALUENAME RemotePath
```

```
        End Part
      Part "Enter the UNC path." TEXT END PART
      END Policy
  End Category
```

The one thing here that may be a bit odd-looking is the numeric value 131072; where did that come from? Again, recall that the original value for `ProviderType` was 20000, but that was a hex value, and policies want decimal. A few mouse-clicks in Calculator convert 20000 hex to 131072 decimal.

Notice how the `ActionListOn` part works. Between `ActionListOn` and End `ActionListOn`, I just specify some value entries and their desired values. When the associated part—the `EditText` part—is used, the items in the `ActionListOn` group just "wake up."

Locking Down an NT 4 Desktop

Let me just wrap up this section on locking down a Desktop with Registry entries and system policies with a set of policies that you can use today to greatly simplify both the user interface that your users see and your support task.

Open up the System Policy Editor using the standard `WINNT.ADM` and `COMMON.ADM` templates; you don't need to build any custom templates. Then enact the following policies, all of which are user policies rather than machine policies.

In Shell/Restrictions   Remove Run command from Start menu, remove folders from Settings on Start menu, remove Taskbar from Settings on Start menu, remove Find command from Start menu, hide drives in My Computer, hide Network Neighborhood, and hide all items on Desktop.

System/Restrictions   Run only allowed Windows applications (and name them, of course).

Windows NT Shell/Custom Folders   Create a folder, as you learned earlier in this section, containing shortcuts to the programs that you want the users to be able to access.

Windows NT Shell/Restrictions   Remove File menu from Explorer (if you've allowed Explorer in the first place), remove common program groups from Start menu, disable context menus for the Taskbar, and disable Explorer's default context menu.

Windows NT System   It's just personal taste, but I disable the Show Welcome Tips at Logon setting.

Remember that you've got to come up with a completely standard set of locations for program files across the enterprise or your users won't be able to get to their applications. And a final piece of advice: Make these policies specific to a group, not to Default User, or you'll have a domain that you can't do any administration from!

CHAPTER **9**

Creating and Managing Shared Folders

FEATURING:

Windows 2000 throws a plethora of services and features at your network. At the root of all of these services are your file and folder sharing capabilities. File sharing is not only one of the primary functions of your server, but the primary reason why your users access the server. In this chapter, we will discuss what file sharing really is, and why this very simple aspect of Windows 2000 Server is so important. We will also cover permissions from top to bottom. Next, we will talk about one of the new—or should I say *enhanced*—features of Windows 2000 Server, the Distributed File System. Finally, we'll extend our file-sharing capabilities right to the Web browsers, and make our files available for offline use.

Basics of File Sharing

The core component of any server is its ability to share files. In fact, the Server service in all of the Windows NT and now Windows 2000 lines handles the server's ability to share file and print resources. But what exactly does that mean, and why is it so important? By default, just because you have a server running doesn't mean it has anything available for your users. Before they can actually get to resources on the server, you must share out your resources. Let's say you have a folder on your local D: drive named APPS with three applications in subfolders, as shown in Figure 9.1.

When you share this folder out to the network under the name of Applications, you allow your clients to *map* a new drive letter on their machines to your D:\APPS folder. By mapping a drive, you are kind of placing a virtual pointer directly to where you connected. If you map your client's M: drive to the Applications share of the server, their M:\ will look identical to the server's D:\APPS. (Don't worry, I'll slow down and explain how to create this share later, and I'll explain how to connect to it in Chapter 12.) See how a client connection of M:\ being mapped to the server's APPS share—Figure 9.2—looks identical to the real D:\APPS from Figure 9.1?

That's really all there is to it. Sharing resources means that you will allow your users to access those resources from the network. No real processing goes into it as far as the server is concerned; it just hands out files and folders as they are.

FIGURE 9.1

Subfolders in
D:\APPS

FIGURE 9.2

M:\ mapped to
D:\APPS

Creating Shared Folders

Before you can create a shared folder, you must have appropriate rights to do so. This requires that you are either an administrator or a server operator. There are also several ways you can create shares: you can use the Explorer interface when sitting at the server, or use the Computer Management console from the server, or do it remotely.

Creating Shares from Explorer

If you're sitting at the server, the Explorer interface provides a very simple and direct means for creating and managing all properties of a share. Let's go back to the D:\APPS folder that you want to make available to the network under the name of Applications.

 NOTE Don't forget that not all clients can handle names longer than eight characters. This applies to shares as well. If you have old DOS LanManager clients, they won't be able to interpret names such as Applications. For this chapter, I am assuming a Windows 98 user base, so long file and share names won't be a problem.

In Explorer, right-click the APPS folder and select the Sharing menu option. This will bring up the properties dialog box for the folder APPS, already set to the Sharing properties page. To share the folder, click the Share This Folder radio button, as shown in Figure 9.3.

FIGURE 9.3

Properties for the Applications share

APPS Properties

General | Web Sharing | Sharing | Security

You can share this folder among other users on your network. To enable sharing for this folder, click Share this folder.

○ Do not share this folder
◉ Share this folder

Share name: Applications

Comment:

User limit: ◉ Maximum allowed
○ Allow [   ] Users

To set permissions for how users access this folder over the network, click Permissions. [Permissions]

To configure settings for Offline access to this shared folder, click Caching. [Caching]

[New Share]

[OK] [Cancel] [Apply]

NOTE Incidentally, if you want to stop sharing this folder later through the Explorer interface, go back into the properties as we just did and select the button to not share this folder.

The Share Name option is the most critical entry. The share name is how your users will reference this share. For our purposes, we are sharing this folder as Applications. The Comment field is used to provide more descriptive information about this share. This information will be visible to the users when they browse the My Network Places for available shares, as shown in the Explorer window in Figure 9.4.

FIGURE 9.4

Browsing network shares

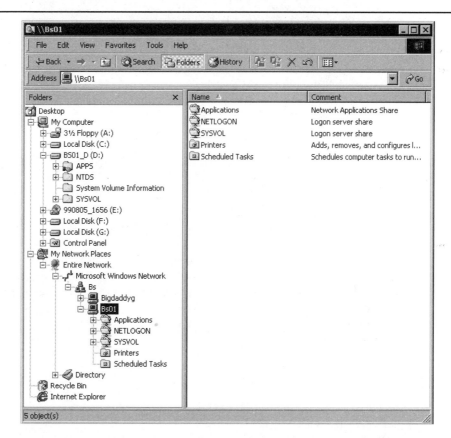

The next step is securing your share. Using the Permissions button, you can define your share permissions. I'll discuss this in more detail later in this chapter.

Another new feature you can enable here lies behind the Caching button. Caching allows offline file and folder access for your users. Once again, this will be covered a bit later, in the section on Offline Files.

Once you select OK, your share is enabled and ready for immediate use by your users.

Setting User Limits

You can also configure how many users can connect to a share simultaneously (in the User Limit area of the Sharing properties page). Let's say that the applications under your share are each licensed for 100 concurrent users. Even though you may have 200 users on your network, you can configure your server share to maintain a user limit of only 100 users at a time. As users connect to the share, they build up to the user limit. As users log off, or disconnect from the share, the number drops. This type of licensing enforcement can be very handy in reducing your licensing costs.

Be careful on your licensing. Not all applications have a concurrent license mode, as compared to a client license mode. (Unfortunately, as Microsoft has abandoned concurrent licensing, more and more other firms have stopped offering this very useful licensing option.) In such cases, the manufacturer doesn't care how many users are accessing the application at any give time, they just care about how many people have installed the application altogether. This user-limit option will not protect you in these cases.

Another thing to keep in mind is that this user-connection concurrency limit is based on the entire share. It cannot be defined further to each folder within a share. If Application 1 under the Applications share has a concurrency limit of 100, while Application 2 and Application 3 are unlimited, you don't want to inadvertently limit those other applications.

Finally, you need to consider how your users connect to the share to use these applications before you limit them based on concurrency. If your users all connect to the share upon logging in, but don't disconnect until logging off, your concurrency limit may be used up based on who shows up for work first. If connections are made only when actually using the application, the user limit will work quite nicely. Otherwise, you will have 100 people using up your concurrency limit, while maybe only a small percentage of them are actually using the application.

Remotely Creating Shares with the Computer Management Console

Within your Administrative Tools program group, you have the Computer Management console. With this tool you can, among other things, create and manage shares locally or remotely. In contrast, within the Explorer interface, if you right-click a folder that is not local to your machine, you won't see the Sharing menu option. If you are going to be creating a share using the Computer Management console from your local machine, you're set. If you want to manage a share on a remote server, you have to first connect to that server. Right-click the Computer Management (Local) icon, and select Connect to Another Computer. From there, you can type in the name of the server you want to manage, or browse the network for the computer you want.

To begin with the share management, you need to drop down to `Computer Management\System Tools\Shared Folders\Shares`, as shown in Figure 9.5.

FIGURE 9.5

Computer management, shares

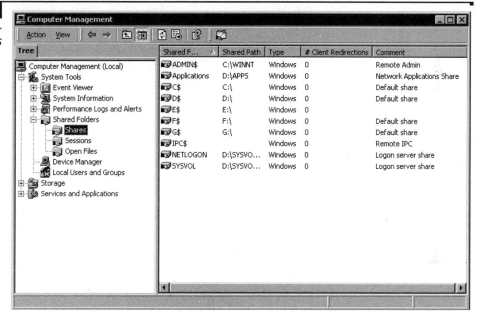

You can now either hit the Action button or right-click in the Shares window, then select New File Share. A new wizard-like dialog box, shown in Figure 9.6, greets us with spaces to enter all essential components of a share. First, select the folder that you want to share out. You can browse through the given drives and folders, or you can create a new folder on the fly by simply typing out the full drive and folder name in the Folder to Share box. Again, we want to share the D:\APPS folder. Enter the name you want this share to be given, along with a brief description, and select Next.

From here, we jump straight to defining our share permissions. In this next dialog box, you are given four options for defining permissions: "All users have full control" allows everyone to exploit the maximum amount of access as allowed by the file and directory access permissions. "Administrators have full control; others have read-only access" ensures that your users cannot modify or delete anything within the share, but still gives your administrators the appropriate rights to manage the data. "Administrators have full control; other users have no access" seems like an odd choice. Why would you share something out to the network, and not allow anyone except administrators in? Of course, you could want a share that is used by administrators only to access certain network management resources, but more importantly, this option is a good way to keep security under control. When creating a share, you don't have to start with a wide-open door. Why not start off with a closed door and open it up per your specifications later? Well, the logic behind this argument seems moot when looking at the next option—"Customize share and folder permissions"— but it really isn't. The customize option lets you define permissions based on specific users or groups that you desire. However, if you don't know which users and groups belong just yet, don't sweat it. Select the "Administrators have full control" option as shown in Figure 9.7; other users will have no access for now, and you can open the door when you finish collecting the information you need.

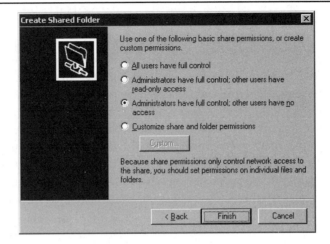

Managing Permissions

Now that you've shared out your resources to the world, it's time to protect them *from* the world. There are numerous ways to secure your server and its resources, but the two most efficient are *share permissions* and *file and directory permissions*. These permissions let you control who accesses your data and what they can do with it.

Share Permissions

Each share that you create has permissions assigned to it. These are different from file and directory permissions, but can greatly affect file and directory permissions. Consider that the share permissions are like the write-protect tab on a floppy disk. Even if, technically, you have the ability to do whatever you want to the files on the floppy, as long as that tab is in place, you can't change anything. Share permissions work in a similar manner. They are the first set of permissions you come through. Let's say that you grant users full control over files and folders, but the most they have at the actual share connection they are coming through are read permissions. Once they map their drive to the share, any reference through that drive is limited to those share-level permissions.

Here's another way to think of it. Forget what the user sees; think of what the server sees. Share-level permissions are the first-level filter for incoming requests. The server accepts connections to a share called DATA. At the share, permissions are defined so that users can only read, but can't write or delete anything. When a user connected to the DATA share sends a write request through that share connection, it will be denied simply based on those share permissions. If they send a read request, it will be accepted through the share and passed on to the next-level filter—the directory and file permissions.

To put this into practical terms, share permissions will override file and directory permissions—*if* the share permissions are more restrictive. This also means that you need to define share permissions so that they are not any more restrictive than the least restricted files and folders within the share. If all folders under the share DATA will only require that users read but not write to them, then we can assign read-only permissions to the share. If even one out of a million files under the DATA share will require that write permissions be assigned, it takes priority, and we must allow write permissions to the share. In most cases, unless absolutely positive, you should create shares with everyone having full-control access to the share. This will simplify management of the share, and let you control access via file and directory permissions.

NOTE   There are cases every once in a while where you will choose one of the FAT file systems for your logical drives. FAT has no file and directory permission capabilities, leaving your data very insecure. However, you can alleviate some of these pains through share permissions. Even on FAT partitions, you can share out folders and assign whatever level of share permissions you like. Unfortunately, this still doesn't prevent an intruder from accessing data directly at the console. Physical security of the server is your only surefire protection.

Defining Share Permissions

To define share permissions, we will work through the Computer Management console. Select the share you want to secure by right-clicking the share name and selecting Properties. You can get to the same place from Explorer by right-clicking the locally shared folder, selecting Sharing, and then clicking the Share Permissions tab, shown in Figure 9.8.

NOTE   The properties dialog box you see now is different than you may be used to. You will notice that there is the familiar Security tab and a new Share Permissions tab. The Security tab takes you straight to the folder permissions.

FIGURE 9.8

*The Share
Permissions tab*

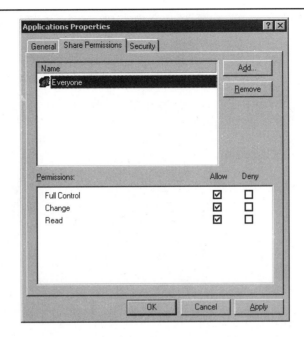

You are shown a Name box that lists users and groups assigned to the share; when a user or group is selected, the permissions for that user or group to access the share are revealed. You can assign different levels of permission for different users and groups. At the share level, we have the following types of permission:

Permission	Level of Access
Full Control	The assigned group can perform any and all functions on all files and folders through the share.
Change	The assigned group can read and execute, as well as change and delete, files and folders through the share.
Read	The assigned group can read and execute files and folders, but has no ability to modify or delete anything through the share.

Our example in Figure 9.8 shows full-control access for everyone. If we want to restrict share permissions to give "everyone" read-only rights and administrators full control, we will need to reduce everyone's rights to read only, and add a new set of rights for administrators. While sitting on the Everyone selection, clear the check boxes for Change and Full Control. Now you need to add full control for administrators. Select the Add button, then find the Administrators group and press Add. You will come back to the Share Permissions tab with the Administrators group added to the display. Select the Full Control check box, and as you can see in Figure 9.9, everything else is checked automatically.

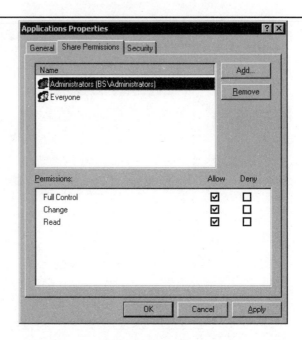

FIGURE 9.9

Share permissions, full control for administrators

Again, keep in mind that share-level permissions are just your first filter. Whatever level of permissions you get at the share level will be the highest level of permissions you can get for files and directories. If you get read-only rights to the share, but full-control rights to the file, the share will not let you do anything other than read.

File and Directory Permissions

The old days of Microsoft networking utilized share-level permissions only. Once connected to a share with a given set of permissions, you had those permissions for everything under the share. If you had a thousand users who all wanted private access to their data, you would have to create a thousand shares with specific permissions on each share. Then, with the introduction of Windows NT to the Microsoft networking platform, you could create one share for all users, and customize access via file and directory permissions—permissions that could be assigned directly to the files and folders. With this new feature came an unending ability to customize the security of your data.

You may hear a lot about how NTFS, in conjunction with file and directory permissions, can help you protect the server itself from an intruder. Theoretically, this is true. Assuming that you do not know an administrator username and password, if you sit down at the server, you cannot gain access to the server's data. The idea is that NTFS will not let you boot to anything less than the NT operating system and view files. This feature lets us relax a bit about the physical security of the server. We know that no one can log into the server, and that our partitions are NTFS. Pop a DOS boot disk in, reboot the server, and you can't see a thing on the hard drive.

Well, it was only a matter of time. Someone *did* come up with a utility that allows us to gain access to NTFS partitions via a simple boot disk. Back to square one—if you want to secure your server completely, lock it up in a secured room.

Permission Types

Before we assign permissions to our files and folders, we need to have a good understanding of what those permissions mean, and how they work. Now, there are two different levels of permissions. One is the higher-level conventional permissions, and the other is the lower-level sub-permissions that make up the higher-level permissions. For example, the permission "write" is actually made up of four different components. We could always accept write for, well, *write*, or we could break it down a little further to customize the way we want our users to access data. For convenience purposes, there is a nice way of thinking about these different levels of permissions. The lower-level sub-permissions work at the *atomic* level. They are the smallest possible bits of permissions. At the higher level, we have groupings of atomic permissions. We'll call those groupings of atomic groupings *molecular* permissions. Look at Table 9.1 to see how groups of atomic permissions in the left-hand column make up molecular permissions.

TABLE 9.1: ATOMIC AND MOLECULAR PERMISSIONS

Atomic	Write	Read	List Folder Contents	Read and Execute	Modify	Full Control
Traverse Folder/Execute File			x	x	x	x
List Folder/Read Data		x	x	x	x	x
Read Attributes		x	x	x	x	x
Read Extended Attributes		x	x	x	x	x
Create Files/Write Data	x				x	x
Create Folders/Append Data	x				x	x
Write Attributes	x				x	x
Write Extended Attributes	x				x	x
Delete Subfolders and Files						x
Delete					x	x
Read Permissions	x	x	x	x	x	x
Change Permissions						
Take Ownership						x

These rules of molecular makeup apply to both file and directory permissions, with the exception of List Folder Contents (these permissions only apply to folders). In the atomic world, there are several instances where one atomic permission applies to both folders and files, but with slightly different meanings. In each of these cases, it seems like the atomic permissions should have been two completely different items. Yet somehow they are together. I suppose there wouldn't be times when you would ever want one atomic permission and not the other, but they are close enough in meaning that it shouldn't cause any problems. Now, let's try and understand these permissions at both the atomic and molecular level.

Atomic Permissions

We'll start at the atomic level. These permissions are the building blocks of the permissions that we normally speak of, like Read, Modify, and Full Control. You will probably never see these permissions, much less refer to them on their own.

Traverse Folder/Execute File   Traversing folders applies to folders only. There are times when you execute files that call other files in other folders. Let's say you execute a file in the APP1 folder, to which you have read-only permissions. Sure, read permissions will let you do whatever you need to actually execute the file. But what if that program file tries to call another file in a subfolder, three levels deep beneath APP1, if the folders one and two levels beneath APP1 have no access? Typically, when you try to pass through—traverse—a folder with no access, you will get an "access denied." Traverse checking will allow you to pass through those permissions to get to your target.

The Execute File atomic permission applies to files only, and if the file is an .exe, .com, or other executable file, it lets you actually execute that file.

List Folder/Read Data   List Folder permissions allow you to view file and folder names within a folder. Read Data permissions allow you to view the contents of a file. This atomic right is the core component of Read.

Think of the separation between these two atomic permissions. Is there really much of a difference? Yes, but probably not for long. Remember the days when we called everything files and directories? Now the file and *folder* terminology has become mainstream. Just when we start really getting used to it, another term is coming into play: *objects*. Everything on your machine is an object—both files and folders. This atomic permission could almost be rephrased to *read object*. Regardless of whether this permission applies to a file or folder, this right lets you examine the contents of an object.

Read Attributes   Basic attributes are file properties such as Read-Only, Hidden, System, and Archive. This atomic-level permission allows you to see these attributes.

Read Extended Attributes   Certain programs include other attributes for their file types. For example, if you have Microsoft Word installed on your system, and you view the file attributes of a .doc file, all sorts of attributes will show up, like Author,

Subject, Title, etc. These are called *extended attributes*, and they vary from program to program. This atomic permission lets you view these attributes.

Create Files/Write Data   The Create Files atomic permissions allow you to put new files within a folder. Write Data allows you to overwrite existing data within a file. This atomic permission will not allow you to add data to an existing file.

Create Folders/Append Data   Create Folders allows you to create folders within folders. Append Data allows you to add data to the end of an existing file, but not change data within the file.

Write Attributes   This permission allows you to change the basic attributes of a file.

Write Extended Attributes   This permission allows you to change the extended attributes of a file.

Delete Subfolders and Files   This atomic permission is strange. Listen to this: With this permission, you can delete subfolders and files, even if *you don't have Delete permissions on that subfolder or file*. Now how could this possibly be? If you were to read ahead to the next atomic permission—Delete—you would see that that permission lets you delete a file or folder. What's the difference? Think of it this way: If we are sitting at a file or folder, Delete lets us delete it. But let's say I'm sitting at a folder and want to delete its *contents*. This atomic permission gives me that right. There is a very vague difference between the two. One lets us delete a specific object, the other lets us delete the *contents* of an object. If we are given the right to delete the contents of a folder, we don't want to lose that right just because one object within that folder does not want to give us permissions. Hey, it's my folder, I can do with it what I want.

Delete   Plain and simple this time, Delete lets you delete an object. Or is it plain and simple? If you have only the atomic permission to delete a folder, and not its big brother atomic permission to delete subfolders and files, and one file within that folder has no access, can you delete the folder? No. You can't delete the folder until it is empty, which means that you need to delete that file. You can't delete that file without having either Delete rights to that file, or Delete Subfolders and Files rights to the file's parent folder.

Read Permissions   The Read Permissions atomic permission lets you view all NTFS permissions associated with a file or folder, but you can't change anything.

Change Permissions   This atomic permission lets you change the permissions assigned to a file or folder.

Take Ownership   We'll talk about what ownership is and what it does in more detail later, but this atomic permission allows you take ownership of a file. Once you are the owner, you have an inherent right to change permissions. By default, administrators can always take ownership of a file or folder.

Molecular Permissions

A full understanding of what atomic permissions do and of Table 9.1, which shows the atomic makeup of molecular permissions, provides exceptional insight into what these molecular permissions are and how they work. This section will try and put the atomic makeup of permissions in better perspective, but flip back and forth to the table while you read about these permissions. This information will form a very solid foundation to help you manage permissions later.

Read   Read permissions are your most basic rights. They allow you to view the contents, permissions, and attributes associated with an object. If that object is a file, you can view the file, which happens to include the ability to launch the file, should it be an executable program file. If the object in question is a folder, Read permissions let you view the contents of the folder.

Now here is a tricky part of folder read. Let's say that you have a folder to which you have been assigned Read permissions. That folder contains a subfolder, to which you have been denied all access, including read access. Logic would say that you could not even see that subfolder at all. Well, the subfolder, before you even get into its own attributes, is *part of* the original folder. Because you can read the contents of the first folder, you can see that the subfolder exists. If you try to change to that subfolder, then—and only then—will you get an "access denied."

Write   Write permissions, as simple as they sound, have a catch. For starters, Write permissions on a folder let you create a new file or subfolder within that folder. What about Write permissions on a file? Does this mean you can change a file? Think about what happens when you *change* a file. To change a file, you must usually be able to open the file, or read the file. To change a file, Read permissions must accompany your Write permissions. There is a loophole though: if you can simply append data to a file, without needing to open the file, Write permissions will work.

Read and Execute   Read and Execute permissions are identical to Read, but give you the added atomic privilege of traversing a folder.

Modify   Simply put, Modify permissions are the combination of Read and Execute and Write, but give you the added luxury of Delete. Even when you could change a file, you never really could delete the file. You'll notice that when you select permissions for files and folders, if you select Modify, then Read, Read and Execute, and Write are automatically checked for you.

Full Control   Full Control is a combination of all previously mentioned permissions, with the abilities to change permissions and take ownership of objects thrown in. Full Control also allows you to delete subfolders and files, even when the subfolders and files don't specifically allow you to delete them.

List Folder Contents   List Folder Contents permissions apply similar permissions as Read and Execute, but they only apply to folders. List Folder Contents allows you to view the contents of folders. More important, List Folder Contents is only *inherited* by folders, and is only shown when looking into the security properties of a folder. It will allow you to see that files exist in a folder—similar to Read—but will not apply Read permissions to those files. In comparison, if you applied Read and Execute permissions to a folder, you would be given the same capabilities to view folders and their contents, but would also propagate Read and Execute rights to files within those folders.

Assigning File and Directory Permissions

Once you understand what different permissions mean, assigning them to files and folders is a piece of cake. We'll start off in Explorer. Find the file or folder you want to assign rights to, right-click it, select Properties, and then select the Security tab. Take a look at Figure 9.10.

FIGURE 9.10

*The Security
properties tab*

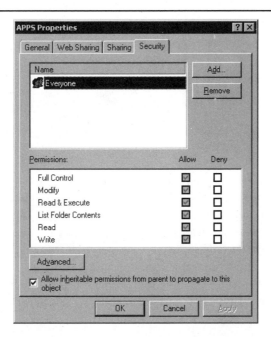

The top window shows the different groups or users to whom permissions are assigned, and the bottom window shows the permissions assigned to the selected user or group. I'm starting off in my APPS folder. Ideally, since this is for applications, I want all users to have Read and Execute permissions and not have the ability to change, add, or delete anything. I want to get rid of that Everyone entry, because it opens a door to my data that is extremely dangerous. I also want to keep administrators in full control, so they can still maintain the data. So I'll start off by adding Administrators and giving them full control. Press the Add button, and a list of users and groups is displayed like the one shown in Figure 9.11.

FIGURE 9.11

Select users

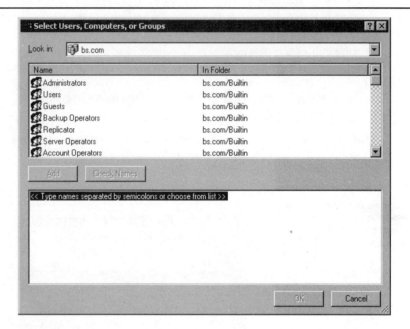

We'll try and do both groups at the same time. Select the Administrators group and press Add. Likewise, select the Users group and press Add. (If you don't want to spend the time searching for the group or user, you can type it in the Name box, press Add, and then press Check Names. That would cross-check your manually typed entry with the actual list of names to find a match.) Once we have added Administrators and Users, our dialog box should look like the one shown in Figure 9.12.

Click OK, and we see the two newly added groups, along with our Everyone group in the upper box—as shown in Figure 9.13.

Just to finish cleaning things up, go ahead and select the Everyone group and click Remove. Hmm. when I tried to do that, I got the error message shown in Figure 9.14.

FIGURE 9.12

*Add Administrators
and Users*

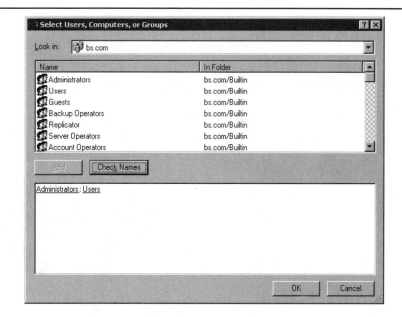

FIGURE 9.13

*The new groups in the
Security tab*

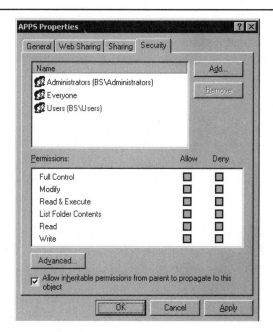

FIGURE 9.14

*Error removing the
Everyone group*

What happened is that the inheritance check box in the lower portion of the Security tab says to use the parent folder's permissions. The parent's permissions give Everyone full control. Obviously, we want to get rid of that inheritance. Uncheck the inheritance box and the question in Figure 9.15 appears.

FIGURE 9.15

*Preventing inherited
permissions*

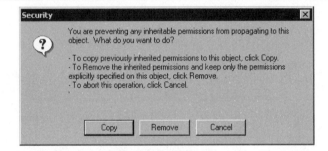

When unchecking this box, we are changing the Everyone group from having permissions based on its parent folder's permissions to having its own permissions. At this point, Everyone has no permissions of its own, so we have to start off brand new. What we are being asked is if we want to start off with the inherited permissions as a baseline (Copy), if we want to start from scratch (Remove), or if we want to cancel and forget anything happened. The Copy command will turn off the inheritance, but leave the inherited permissions intact so we have something to work with. This will be helpful if we want to customize the parent's permissions and not reinvent the wheel. But right now we don't care at all about the Everyone group, so let's choose Remove. This will take the Everyone permissions received from the parent and throw them away. Fine.

We are now down to just our Administrators and Users groups. All we have to do is assign the correct permissions. For administrators, we wanted full control. Highlight the Administrators group, and check the Full Control box in the Allow column. The Security tab should now look like Figure 9.16.

FIGURE 9.16

New permissions

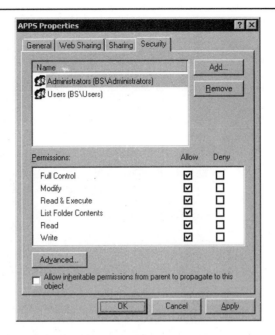

Now repeat this process for Users. Highlight Users and check Read and Execute.

NOTE You need to be careful when selecting some permission levels. Selecting Read and Execute includes all of the rights of Read, so Read is automatically checked. If, on the other hand, you want to clear Read and Execute, unchecking the Read and Execute box won't automatically uncheck Read.

You could press OK here and let the permissions take hold, but let's look into the advanced properties first by pressing the Advanced button. Some of the information shown here is the same as what we saw in the Security properties page, just reworded a bit (see Figure 9.17).

The Permission Entries box shows your selected groups and users, with a description of their rights that you have assigned. Nothing different there. The "Allow inheritable permissions from parent to propagate to this object" check box is the same. But here we get a new check box, "Reset permissions on all child objects and enable propagation of inheritable permissions." Now there's a mouthful. In part, this is the same as the Windows NT version of applying permissions to all files and subfolders, but Windows 2000 doesn't do it quite the same way. The second part of that statement—*enable propagation of inheritable permissions*—says that it will give all subfolders these permissions by turning on each one's "Allow inheritable permissions from parent to propagate to this object" check box.

FIGURE 19.17

Advanced access control properties

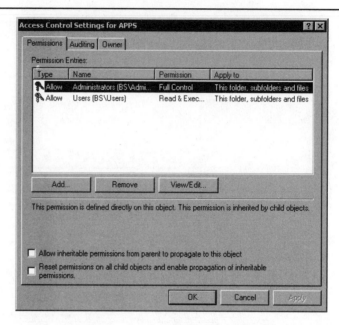

The next feature of the Access Control Settings dialog box is the ability to tailor your extended permissions. Select Users, then press the View/Edit button. You'll get the options shown in Figure 9.18.

FIGURE 9.18

Advanced permissions

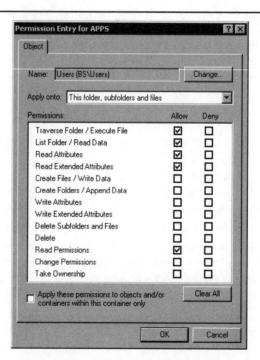

These permissions break down Read and Execute into smaller parts. If you want your users to have all the benefits of Read and Execute, but don't want to allow them to view permissions, you could simply clear the Read Permissions box. From there, you also have more specific means of propagating these custom permissions. The Apply Onto drop-down box lets you assign advanced permissions to any combination of the current folder, the current folder's subfolders, and the files. In order to use the Apply Onto selection, though, you must check "Apply these permissions to objects and/or containers within this container only."

Conflicting Permissions

You can assign permissions to files, and you can assign permissions to directories. Just as share permissions can conflict with file and directory permissions, file permissions can conflict with directory permissions. In share-level conflicts, the share wins; in file and directory permission conflicts—the file wins. If you assign read-only rights to a directory, but change rights to a file within that directory, you will still be able to change the file.

Of course, there *must* be an exception to every rule, and here it is: deletions. Let's say a directory says that you do have rights to delete files, but the file itself says that you can *not* delete it. In this case, the directory wins, and you will be able to delete the file. How can this be? Imagine the file with read-only permissions. You open the file and try to save it—the *file itself* is being changed. But if you delete a file, are you *really* changing the file? Not really. All you are changing is the directory structure. You are removing the entry within the directory for that specific file, but aren't doing anything to the file itself. Similarly, you can still rename a file, even though you have no permissions on the file.

Multiple Permissions

Now for another problem. We have given our Administrators group full control over a file, and everyone else has read permissions only. Here is where permissions once again come into conflict. Everyone is everyone. Even Administrators are part of Everyone. Hmmm. How does this work? Well, in the case of multiple permissions, the *least restrictive* permissions will prevail. Let's say we have an administrator named Bob. Bob is part of the Everyone group, which has read-only rights. Bob is also part of the Administrators group, which has full control. In this case, Bob will get full control because it is least restrictive.

Deny Permissions

Because of the way groups can overlap and allow a user more permissions than are apparent, it can become quite difficult to secure data the way we want to. Think of a corporate bonus-award spreadsheet file that you are trying to protect. You want everyone to see the file, but you only want the managers to be able to actually change the file. It makes sense: grant EMPLOYEES read-only rights and MANAGERS full control.

Let's imagine that somewhere along the line, some low-level supervisor falls into both groups. If you leave the permissions as we just described, this supervisor is going to get the best of both worlds—full control. For this reason, you decide that you don't want anyone in EMPLOYEES to have full control. Now what?

Easy enough, Windows 2000 gives us the ability to deny permissions. What you need to do is find out which permissions you specifically do *not* want EMPLOYEES to have, and instead of checking those permissions in the Allow column, check them in the Deny column. Figure 9.19 shows how you would make sure that EMPLOYEES have read-only rights.

FIGURE 9.19

Deny permissions

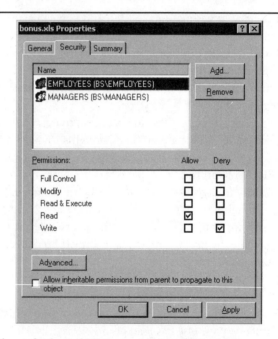

Notice how we've only denied Write permissions? Wouldn't we want to deny Full Control and Modify permissions as well? Not really. Whenever you select Full Control, everything else is automatically selected because Full Control *includes* all permissions. What this means is that if you select to deny Full Control, you deny Write, Read, Read and Execute, and Modify. If you deny Modify, you deny Read and Execute, Read, and Write. If you deny Read and Execute, you also deny plain old Read. Back to our example, we want to allow Read and deny Write. We don't care so much about Read and Execute for this type of file, and in either column, Modify or Full Control overrides the other column's Read or Write.

Ownership

Through the course of assigning and revoking permissions, you are bound to run into the problem where no one, including the administrators, can access a file. And you can't change the file's permissions because you need certain permissions in order to assign permissions. This could be a really sticky situation. Fortunately, ownership can help you out.

There is an attribute of every object called an *owner*. The owner is completely separate from permissions. There will always be *some* owner for *every* object. Yeah, that's great, but how does that help me? Well, the owner of an object has a special privilege—the ability to assign permissions. So if I'm the owner of a file, but don't have access to the file, I can take advantage of my ownership to reassign permissions to myself. Neat-o.

Well, how do I get to be the owner anyway? For starters, whoever creates an object is the default owner. Should that person be a regular user, he is the owner. If there is no apparent creator of the object, which is the case for many system files and folders, ownership is set to the domain's Administrators group.

Here is another problem: The file that you are trying to get to but have no permissions for was created by a user and therefore is owned by that user. So you don't have permissions, and you're not the owner, which means that you can't reassign the permissions. Aha. There is a right that is assigned to Administrators that allows them to take ownership of objects. With this right, you can go into that restricted object, seize ownership, and then use that new ownership to reassign permissions.

Let's walk through this whole scenario: I have a share called USERS. Under USERS is a folder named `Brian`, to which I have installed Full Control permissions for Brian only. While logged on as Administrator, I try to access the `Brian` folder and receive an "access denied" message. The time has come for me to check out what Brian has been up to. I right-click the `Brian` folder and select Properties, then select the Security tab. I receive the dialog box shown in Figure 9.20.

FIGURE 9.20

Permissions for the
`Brian` *folder*

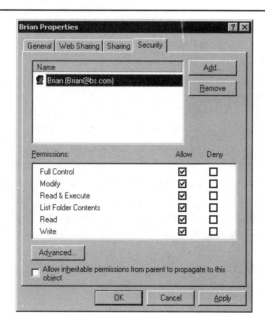

We can see that Brian has full control, but no one else is in the access list at all. But wait a minute, if I'm not in the access list, how am I even seeing these permissions? I select the Advanced button, and then select the Owner tab. A dialog box like Figure 9.21 appears, showing my ownership.

FIGURE 9.21

Current owner

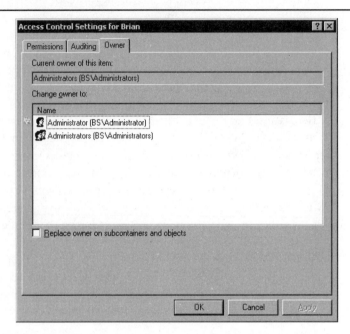

That's right, I was the one who originally created the folder `Brian`, so I'm the owner. As the owner, I can reassign permissions. That does it, I'm adding Administrators to the access list with full control. I cancel out of the advanced properties dialog box and return to the permissions screen. I select Add, find the Administrators group, and then grant them full control. My permissions now look like Figure 9.22.

Now, back to Explorer, I click on the `Brian` folder and I'm in, only to find a folder that Brian created, named `secret`. I click on that folder—access denied. Easy enough, I'll just go in and do the same thing. I right-click `secret`, select Properties, and then select Security. This time, I get a different message, as shown in Figure 9.23.

I don't have permissions, but I can take ownership. Why is it different this time? Well, last time I was the owner, therefore I could still view and change permissions. This time I'm not the owner, so I have no inherent rights to even see the permissions. This becomes obvious when I see the Security properties tab shown in Figure 9.24.

I am looking at the Security properties tab, but I can't see who has what permissions. I also can't add or change permissions. In fact, everything in this dialog box is grayed out, except for the Advanced button. Well, let's hit it. Under the advanced properties, I see a similar sight—the advanced permissions options are grayed out entirely. So I select the Owner tab (see Figure 9.25).

FIGURE 9.22

New permissions

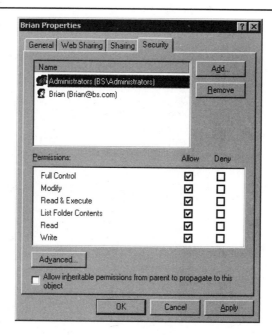

FIGURE 9.23

No permissions

I can't tell who the owner is, but it is safe to say that it isn't me. From here, I want to take ownership. Under the Change Owner To box, you will see the different users or groups that you belong to who have rights to take ownership. As you can see, I can select either Administrator or Administrators. Do I want to use the individual Administrator account or the Administrators group? In this case, I won't want every administrator on the network to be able to view Brian's secret folder, so I'll just select Administrator. If I simply select Administrator, and hit OK, I'll be given rights to the folder, but will probably run into the same roadblock with subfolders and files. To get it all over with in one shot, I select "Replace owner on subcontainer and objects." A translation of this into old Windows NT terms would be "Replace owner on subdirectories and files." I hit OK, and return to the permissions dialog box. I'm still grayed out, so I'll hit OK again to close out and implement the changes.

FIGURE 9.24

Permissions when not
the owner

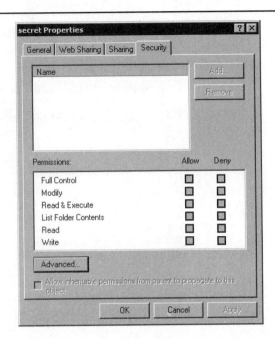

FIGURE 9.25

Unknown owner

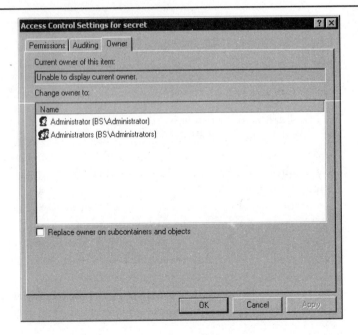

Now I'm the owner. I try to change into the `secret` folder again—access denied! Being the owner, I don't yet have rights to the objects, but I now have rights to change permissions. I right-click the `secret` folder, select Properties, and then select Security. Aha (see Figure 9.26)!

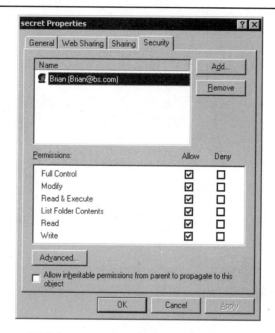

As shown in Figure 9.26, I can now see that Brian has full control. What I need to do next is add the Administrator account with full control. I select Add, and enter the Administrator account. Again, before I close out, I want to make sure that I get this for all subcontainers and objects, so I select Advanced, then check "Reset permissions on all child objects and enable propagation of inheritable permissions," as shown in Figure 9.27.

This will pass my new permissions down throughout the entire `secret` directory structure. When I return to the Explorer window now, I finally have full control.

FIGURE 9.27

Enabling propagation

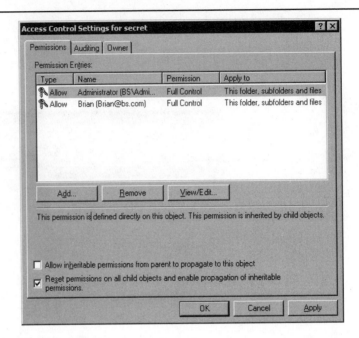

Hidden Shares

As we've seen before, once we share a folder out to the network, it becomes visible to the user community. But what if we don't necessarily want everyone to see the share? For example, I have created an installation source share on my server so that whenever I go to a user's workstation, I can install whatever applications I need to without having to bring CDs. It's really just a convenience for me, but at the same time, I don't want the users clicking away through the shares, installing every program they can get their hands on. Sure, I could limit the share to allow permissions only to me, but that is kind of a pain too. I don't want to log off the user and log on as myself every time I do an install, especially if user profiles are being used. This is where creating hidden shares can help. I want the share to be there and available, but just not as easily visible. Although not a completely secure solution, it is a deterrent to the overly browse-active.

To create a hidden share, proceed as normal in sharing a folder, except place a dollar sign at the end of the name. That's it. Now, whenever the server registers its information to the browse list with its available resources, it simply will not register that hidden share.

The share that I am creating will be called INSTALL$, which will be shared from `D:\Install`. I create the share as normal, making sure to call it INSTALL$ instead of INSTALL (see Figure 9.28).

FIGURE 9.28

*Creating a
hidden share*

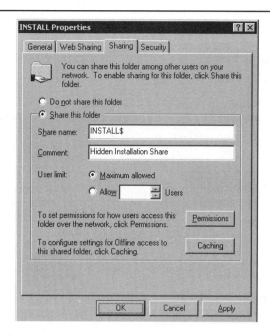

Now, from my client workstations, I will not see the INSTALL$ share listed in the browse list, but can still map a drive to the INSTALL$ drive connection if I manually type the share name like I've done in Figure 9.29.

FIGURE 9.29

*Mapping to a
hidden share*

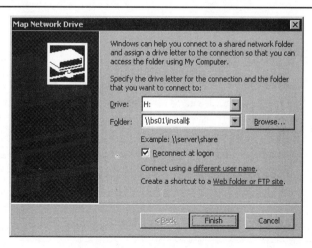

Although the hidden share will not show from your Explorer browse list, the share is visible through the Computer Management console. This helps keep you from forgetting which hidden shares you have created.

Common Shares

In Windows 2000, you may find that several common shares have already been created for you. Most of these shares, you will find, are hidden shares (see Figure 9.30).

FIGURE 9.30

Common hidden shares

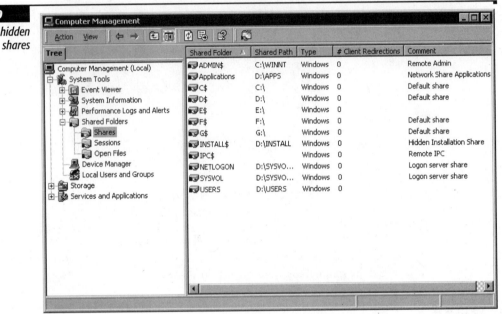

C$, D$, etc.

All drives, including CD-ROM drives, are given a hidden share to the root of the drive. This share is what is called an *administrative share*. You cannot change the permissions or properties of these shares; however, you can stop sharing them altogether. These shares come in handy for server administrators who do a lot of remote management of the server. Mapping a drive to the C$ share will be the equivalent of being at C:\ on the server.

 NOTE Only administrators or backup operators can map to administrative shares.

ADMIN$

ADMIN$, like its C$, D$, and other drive share counterparts, is an administrative share. This share maps directly to your system root, or where your Windows 2000 operating system resides. I installed my Windows 2000 operating system to D:\Winnt, so that's where my ADMIN$ maps to.

Why is this necessary? Let's say I manage 50 servers, and I want to copy an updated .ini file to all servers to have them configured differently. (Of course, I have already tested the configuration change thoroughly. The last thing you want to do remotely is change the configuration of an operating system without knowing exactly what is going to happen when you reboot or otherwise initiate the change.)

The problem is that about half of my servers are new Windows 2000 servers with the system installed into C:\Winnt. The other half are a mixed bag of old upgraded servers and random installs performed by different admins, so my system root can be anything from D:\Winnt to C:\Windows2k to who knows what. Thus the ADMIN$ share. I have my one common connection point that I can connect to across the board, with no guesswork required.

PRINT$

Whenever you create a shared printer, the system places the drivers in this share. See the chapter on printing services (Chapter 11) for more information.

IPC$

The IPC$ share is probably one of the most widely used shares in interserver communications. We know how you can map a drive letter to a share on a server, and use that drive to access files and folders. What about other resources? How do you read the event logs of another computer? You don't actually map a drive, you use *named pipes*. A named pipe is a piece of memory that handles a communication channel between two processes, whether local or remote. Here's a good check. At a DOS prompt, type a **net use** statement to view your network connections. Leave the DOS window open, and go launch an Event Viewer connected to some remote machine. Now, leave your Event Viewer open on that machine, switch back to your DOS window, and do your **net use** command again. You will now see a connection to the server's IPC$ share like the one shown in Figure 9.31.

FIGURE 9.31

IPC$ connection

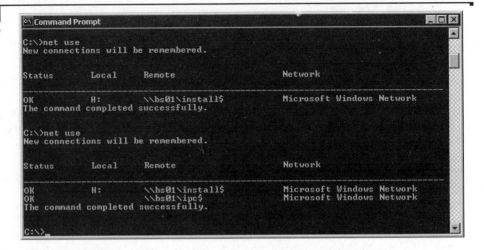

```
Command Prompt                                                        _ □ X

C:\>net use
New connections will be remembered.

Status      Local      Remote                   Network

OK          H:         \\bs01\install$          Microsoft Windows Network
The command completed successfully.

C:\>net use
New connections will be remembered.

Status      Local      Remote                   Network

OK          H:         \\bs01\install$          Microsoft Windows Network
OK                     \\bs01\ipc$              Microsoft Windows Network
The command completed successfully.

C:\>_
```

REPL$

Whenever the replication service is used, a REPL$ share is created on the export server. The export server sends a replication pulse to import servers. The individual import servers connect back to the export server to get a replicated set of the data. This REPL$ share is where your import computers will connect. This share is a critical element of replication, so it is best to leave it alone.

NETLOGON

The NETLOGON share is used in conjunction with processing logon requests from users. Once users successfully log on, they are given profile and script information that they are required to run. This script is usually going to be a batch file. For example, I have a common batch file that I want all of my users to run every time they log on. This allows me to have all clients run a standard set of commands, like copying updated network information, mapping standard network drives, etc. These batch files, scripts, and profiles go in the NETLOGON share.

Connecting to Shares via the Command Line

Now that you've got these shares, how do people use them? Assuming that I've got a share called APPS on a server called BS01, how would someone attached to the network get to that share? There are several ways to use the GUI to get to shares:

- Right-click My Network Places and choose Map Network Drive, then follow the wizard that starts.

- Browse the network from My Network Places.
- Look for a share in the Active Directory.

All of those techniques are convenient, but they require a fair amount of network "superstructure"—they only work well if the network's working well. But sometimes you need to attach to a share when things aren't working so well—in fact, sometimes you need to attach to a share specifically *because* things aren't working so well, and the share contains some tools to help you get it working right. That's where the command line comes in handy.

Introducing *net use*

The command I'm talking about is `net use`. In its basic form, it looks like this:

```
net use driveletter \\servername\sharename
```

For example, to attach to the share APPS on the server named BS01, and then to be able to refer to that share as drive V: on my system, I'd open up a command prompt and type this:

```
net use v: \\bs01\apps
```

If I didn't want to worry about figuring out which drive letters are free, I'd just use an asterisk instead of a drive letter, as in the following:

```
net use * \\bs01\apps
```

`net use` will then just choose the first available letter.

Using a Different Account with *net use*

Sometimes you're logged onto one account and need to connect to a share, but you've only got permissions to access that share from another account. In such a case, you can tell `net use` to try to connect you with the share while using that different account with the `/user:` option. With this option, `net use` looks like

```
net use driveletter \\servername\sharename password
    /user:domainname\username
```

So, for example, if I were logged onto a domain named CANISMAJOR—note we're talking older NetBIOS-type domain names here (`net use` seems not to understand the newer DNS-type names)—under an account named Joe, and wanted to access a share named DATA on a server named RUCHBAH on a domain named CASSIOPEIA, then I might have a problem, particularly if the CASSIOPEIA domain doesn't have a trust relationship with CANISMAJOR. But perhaps I have an account named Mark on the CASSIOPEIA domain, with password "halibut." I could then type this:

```
net use * \\ruchbah\data halibut /user:Cassiopeia\mark
```

You needn't type the password, in case you're concerned that someone might be watching. Leave it off, and `net use` will prompt you.

"A Set of Credentials Conflicts…"

Sometimes when you're trying to attach to a share, you'll get an error message that says something like, "A set of credentials conflicts with an existing set of credentials on that share." What's happening there is this: You've already tried to access this share and failed for some reason—perhaps you mistyped a password. The server that the share is on has, then, constructed some security information about you that says that you're a deadbeat, and it doesn't want to hear anything else about you. So you've got to get the server to forget about you so that you can start all over. You can do that with the /d option. Suppose you've already tried to access the \\BS01\APPS share and apparently failed. It might be that you *are* actually connected to the share, but with no permissions. (I know it doesn't make sense, but it happens.) You can find out what shares you're connected to by typing just **net use** all by itself. Chances are, you'll see that \\BS01\APPS is on the list. You've got to disconnect from that BS01 server so that you can start over. To do that, type

```
net use \\bs01\apps /d
```

But then do another **net use** to make sure that you've got all of those connections cleaned up; you may find that you have *multiple* attachments to a particular server. *Then* your `net use` will work.

net use-ing over a WAN

I work from several different locations connected with Frame Relay WAN links. My Network Places isn't always so good about being able to convert server names into IP addresses, so `net use \\bs01…` might just return an error to the effect that the computer couldn't *find* \\BS01. Even if it *does* work, name resolution—converting a name like BS01 to a network address—takes time.

If you know the IP address of the server that you're trying to contact, then you can use the IP address in lieu of the server's name. For example, if I know that BS01's IP address is 134.81.12.4, I could type

```
net use \\134.81.12.4\apps
```

Know the `net use` command; you'll find it useful.

The Distributed File System

In the world of Windows NT, we had a nice little service called Directory Replication. This service allowed us to place files and folders in one place, and have them replicated to other servers. Why would we want to do this? For starters, let's assume that we simply cannot just connect all of our users to the same server. This could be the case due to several reasons. Maybe our servers are distributed over a wide area network that is connected by rather slow connections. Maybe there are just more users hitting this particular set of files than is practically efficient for one server to manage. Typically, Directory Replication is used for logon scripts. Whenever a user logs on to the network, one domain controller handles user validation, then hands that user a script, or batch file, as defined in their user account properties. Remember, any domain controller can validate a user of its domain, regardless of where it is physically located. What you don't want to happen is to have 20 different domain controllers giving a user a different logon script every time they log on. Similarly, you don't want to have to edit a login script once for each domain controller you have. This is where replication comes in. By replicating a set of files automatically, you have only one maintenance point for making changes. Edit the file on the primary export server, and it will get copied out to the import servers when the next replication interval takes place.

With Windows 2000, there is no more Directory Replication as we remember it. Instead, we have the Distributed File System, or Dfs. Dfs has the same capabilities of Directory Replication—you can have a set of data replicate from one primary server to child servers. But we also get some new things, like fault tolerance, load balancing, and an ability to simplify client connections, that make Dfs a real treat to your network.

Understanding a Dfs Tree

Dfs is a logical, hierarchical file system that combines resources from all across a site into a single namespace. In other words, you can take all of your resources, from all over your network, and from numerous different servers, and combine them into one logical view for your users—or better put, into one logical share on your network. Let's say you had the following set of shared resources across the network:

UNC Path	Resource Description
\\BS01\APPS	All generic applications
\\BS02\APPS	The same applications as \\BS01\APPS
\\BS99\SALES	The corporate sales data
\\BS20\USERS	All user directories
\\BS20\FINANCE	The corporate financing data
\\BS21\APP2	Miscellaneous applications

This could become a real pain for users, who have to remember where to go to connect to their various resources. There are five different servers housing resources. This also means that if a client needed to access APPS, SALES, USERS, and FINANCE all at the same time, they would be required to make four different connections. Well, four doesn't sound too bad, but I have been in large networks where there were literally no more available drive letters left on clients to map another share; every single letter from A: to Z: was mapped to something. You also have to remember which clients connect to \\BS01\APPS, and which connect to \\BS02\APPS. Again, not a big deal in this particular example, but if you had 50 servers containing the same set of APPS, this could become a nightmare to keep track of.

 NOTE As you can probably see, Dfs is going to be most beneficial in large enterprises, and probably not worth the effort in small office networks.

Let's put this into a Dfs. For starters, you would put all APPS under a single Dfs link as replicas. This will allow you to keep both \\BS01\APPS and \\BS02\APPS in sync, and it will let you forget about maintaining multiple configurations on clients—they will all connect to the root. For our purposes here, we'll let BS01 be the root. Another thing you may want to do is put all resources into the same namespace for clients, thereby allowing them to make one connection and see everything they need. Let's call this new namespace CORP. I'll show you how to do all of this later, but our end result will look like Figure 9.32.

FIGURE 9.32

Dfs root view

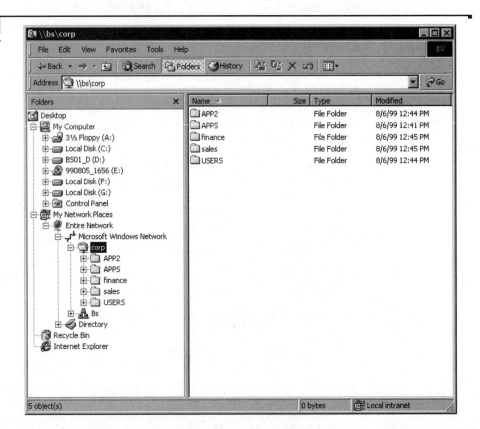

All resources, no matter where they reside, show up under the domain's CORP Dfs root volume. What you can't see, and this is by design, is that there are two different servers' shares hiding under the APPS folder. The clients don't care which server and share they connect to, they just get one.

Dfs Terminology

The next thing to understand is the terminology. Just like with the Active Directory, a whole new set of concepts and terms comes into play.

You start with a *root*. This translates roughly into the share that will be visible to the network. In our example, CORP was our root. You can have many roots in your site, but each server can house only one root. A root is shared out to the network, and actually operates like any other share. You can have additional files and folders within the shared folder.

Under a root, you have a *Dfs link*. The link is another share on the network that is placed under the root. I guess the term *link* is part of our never-ending terminology shift. In this case, it seems to be shifting to more of an Internet nomenclature. The link within the Dfs hierarchy is like a hyperlink on a Web page that automatically directs you to a new location. You don't need to know where. Once you find your home page (the Dfs root) you can place hyperlinks to any other Web site you want (your Dfs links). These newly placed links will now work like any other folder underneath the root.

A *replica* can refer to a root or a link. If you have two identical shares on the network, usually on separate servers, you can group them together within the same link, as *Dfs replica members*. You can also replicate an entire root as a *root replica member*. Once replicas are configured, the File Replication Service manages keeping the contents of roots in sync.

Creating a Dfs Root

To get to the Dfs manager, select Start/Programs/Administrative Tools/Distributed File System. Now, the first thing you need to do is create the root. Right-click the Distributed File System in the left-hand pane, and select New Dfs Root Volume. Of course, a wizard greets you. Select Next at the welcome screen, and you are then asked which kind of root you want to create (see Figure 9.33).

Your choices for the root type are domain Dfs root and standalone Dfs root. A domain root will publish itself in the Active Directory, while a standalone root will not. This fundamental difference is the source of all other differences. Most important, a domain root must be hosted on a domain controller, so that there is an Active Directory to post to. By using the Active Directory, a full topology structure of roots, trees, branches, and leaves is allowed. This lets domain roots have a virtually unlimited hierarchy depth in comparison to standalone roots, which allow only single-level hierarchies. In fact, the only limitation to how deep you can create child nodes for domain roots is based on the Windows 2000 limitation of a 260-character file path name. I would surmise that this would be an adequate depth for most Dfs topologies. By being published in the Active Directory, domain roots can also have replica roots. Since the roots require the Active Directory to be replicas at this level, standalone roots cannot be or have replicas. Since my server, BS01, is already a domain controller, I'll choose a domain root.

FIGURE 9.33

Select Dfs root type

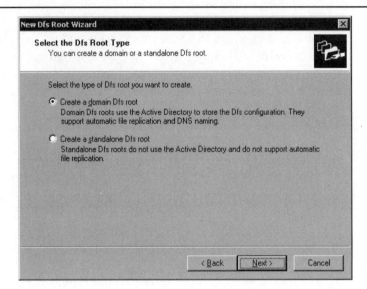

The next step is choosing a domain that will host the Dfs, as shown in Figure 9.34. If you were to select a standalone Dfs, you would not get this option.

FIGURE 9.34

Select a domain to host Dfs

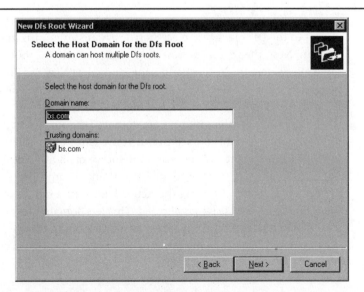

The purpose behind selecting a domain to host the root is to publish the Dfs into the Active Directory. This clues us into yet another *big* advantage of using fault-tolerant roots. Jump forward in your mind, if you will, to what this may look like to the clients later on. If you publish this root called CORP into the Active Directory on the domain BS.COM, you will later see this shared out to the world under the name of BS.COM\CORP, as well as BS01.BS.COM\CORP. If you were using a standalone root, you would only be able to see this as BS01.BS.COM\CORP. How does this help? This is one less thing you have to configure at the workstation level. Simply point all of your clients to BS.COM, and they never need to worry about which server houses which resources.

After you select which domain will host the root, you select the server that will host the root, as shown in Figure 9.35. This is where the actual resource will reside.

FIGURE 9.35

Select a server to host Dfs

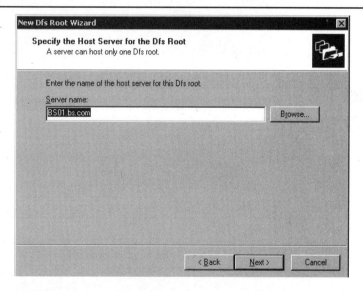

Now you define the actual share for the root. Remember, this can be a regular share. You can select an existing share on your host server to be the root of your Dfs, or you can create a new one on the fly (see Figure 9.36).

I've decided to make a new share called CORP. This is going to be my CORP-orate resource Dfs root. I don't already have one, so I've chosen to create a new share. If the path for the share does not exist, it will be created automatically, so don't worry about Alt+Tabbing back and forth just to get your folder set up ahead of time. Finally, you select a name for the Dfs root (see Figure 9.37).

FIGURE 9.36

*Select a share for the
Dfs root*

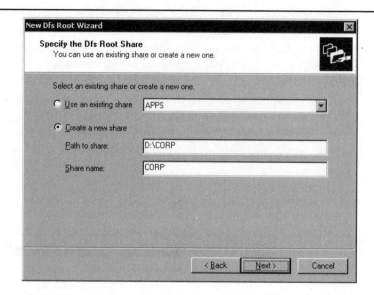

FIGURE 9.37

*Provide a Dfs
root name*

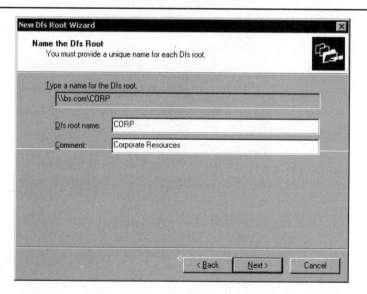

The name for each root must be unique for the domain. Unlike shares, whose names could be the same as long as they were on different servers, there can only be one CORP Dfs root per domain. This is a side effect of having the Dfs root accessible from the domain instead of the server. I would say a very acceptable side effect. Also, notice in Figure 9.37 how the path appears as \\bs.com\CORP, not \\bs01.bs.com\CORP or even \\bs01\CORP.

Finally, you are shown a confirmation dialog box with all of your selections, and the root is created. When we return to the Dfs manager console, we see the new root listed as \\bs.com\CORP, as shown in Figure 9.38.

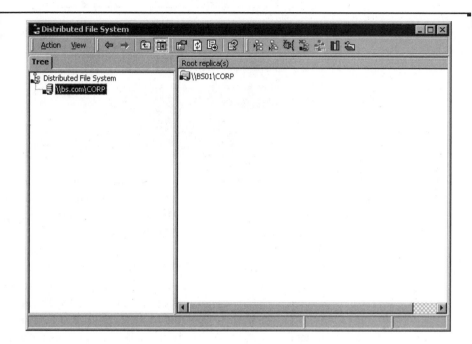

Adding Links to a Dfs Root

Once we have our root, we need to add our Dfs links. Let's start with APPS. First, you want to select your new root in the left-hand pane of the console. You will notice that in the left-hand panel, our root is \\bs.com\CORP, indicative of its membership with the domain, whereas the right-hand panel shows that the share, or the physical location of the resource, is \\BS01\CORP. Right-click the root—that would be \\bs.com\CORP—and select New Dfs Link. This is where you add another network resource to your Dfs. We're going to start with the \\BS01\APPS share (see Figure 9.39).

Pay attention to the terminology in this dialog box: "When a user opens \\BS\ CORP\"—link name blank—"Send the user to this shared folder"—blank. To fill in the blanks in our example, we want to say, "When a user opens \\BS\CORP**APPS**, send the user to this shared folder: **\\BS01\APPS**." The first blank—Link Name—doesn't have to exist already. Simply type it in. The second blank—"Send the user to this shared folder"—is the name of an existing share on the network. You can enter the UNC for the share, or browse your network for the share that you want to point users to. Sorry, but you can't create a share on the fly here, it must exist ahead of time.

FIGURE 9.39

Add the Dfs link

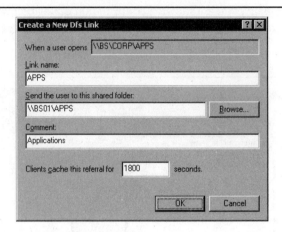

The "Clients cache this referral for [blank] seconds" value tells the client how long to wait before they check back with the hosting server to update share information. When a client connects to \\BS\CORP\APPS, they are told by the hosting server, which happens to be \\BS01, to connect to \\BS01\APPS, *but* check back with me in 1800 seconds. At that time, the client will call back the Dfs host to see if everything is okay. If you take a link offline—applicable when you have replica links, or if you simply redirect a link to a different share, the client will be told this information at that time, and will be directed back to the appropriate share accordingly. Think about this value carefully. The shorter the interval, the higher the network traffic. The longer the interval, the longer it takes a client to check back for an update. Let's say you have defined an interval of 3600 seconds, or one hour. A client connects to \\BS\CORP\APPS at 10:00 exactly, and is redirected to \\BS02\APPS. They won't check back until 11:00. At 10:10, you find out that you need to take the server down. You want to take BS02 offline, and redirect all clients to a replica member of APPS on BS01. (We'll cover replicas in a minute.) So you configure your replica set to have BS02 offline. If you take BS02 down now, your client who connected at 10:00 could lose data. The best thing to do is wait until all clients have reported back so they can see that BS02 is offline, and redirect to BS01. This means that you may have to wait the longest possible interval before shutting down your server—an hour. If your interval was 10 minutes, then you could guarantee that within 10 minutes, BS01 would be free from any client connections.

Going back to the network resources given earlier, we will repeat the above process to create all child nodes—except for \\BS02\APPS—using the information below:

When a User References	Send the User To
\\BS\CORP\APPS	\\BS01\APPS
	\\BS02\APPS
\\BS\CORP\SALES	\\BS99\SALES
\\BS\CORP\USERS	\\BS20\USERS
\\BS\CORP\FINANCE	\\BS20\FINANCE
\\BS\CORP\APP2	\\BS21\APP2

When we're done, the Dfs console will look like Figure 9.40.

FIGURE 9.40

The new child nodes in the Dfs console

Configuring Dfs Replicas

Now we want to make a replica link of APPS. Remember how we had \\BS01\APPS and \\BS02\APPS? We want to combine those into one logical resource: \\BS\CORP\APPS. Right-click on the APPS link, and select New Replica. What you get is a condensed version of the dialog box that created the Dfs link in the first place (see Figure 9.41).

FIGURE 9.41

*Add a new Dfs
replica member*

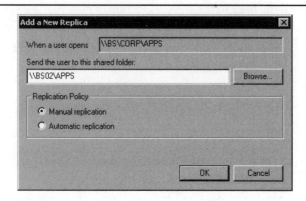

Enter the path for the next share that is to be available as part of this resource, and check whether you want automatic or manual replication configured. (We'll go over replication in a minute.)

Select OK, and you will see in your console that your child node now shows two shares in the right-hand panel—one for \\BS01\APPS, and one for \\BS02\APPS (see Figure 9.42).

FIGURE 9.42

Replica members

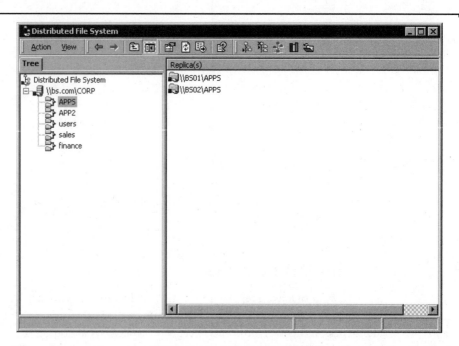

From now on, when our clients connect to \\BS\CORP\APPS, they will be directed to either \\BS01\APPS or \\BS02\APPS. We can add up to 128 different members to any given replica set.

To remove a replica member, right-click the member and select Remove Replica. If I want to take \\BS02\APPS out of the replica set, leaving only \\BS01\APPS, I could remove it from the Dfs just like that. When removing a replica member, however, nothing on the replica member's server is altered in any way. \\BS02\APPS will still be shared, and all data will still be available within that share. The only thing that is affected is the Dfs topology.

Dfs Replication

Replication itself is very simple. Right-click the child node with multiple members, and select Replication Policy. The dialog box shown in Figure 9.43 will be presented.

FIGURE 9.43

The Replication Policy dialog box

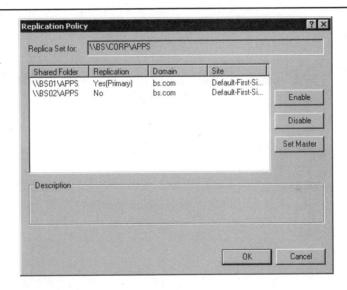

Each member within the replication set is shown, along with its replication properties. In Figure 9.43, \\BS01\APPS is configured to replicate, and is set as the primary system for replication. In other terminology, the export server. All other members of the replication set will have their data synchronized by the primary system. Members can be replica child nodes, but cannot actually be replication partners. To change the replication configuration of each member, highlight the member in the Replication Policy dialog box, and select either Enable or Disable. Similarly, if you want to change which server is to act as the primary, or export, server for replicated data, highlight the member, and select Set Master.

Managing Dfs

After you have configured your Dfs, there are a few certain steps you must go through to properly manage the roots, links, and clients connected to it.

Taking Replica Members Offline/Online

When you have multiple members belonging to a replica set, you may find occasions to take one offline. This could be because you need to perform maintenance on a server. You don't want to just take a server down and have users lose their connections. You also don't want to go through the process of dropping a member from the replica set and adding it again later once your maintenance is done. Instead, right-click the member share and select Take Replica Member Offline/Online. This will toggle a member's status. When offline, a yellow warning icon will appear over the member, as shown in Figure 9.44.

FIGURE 9.44

An offline member

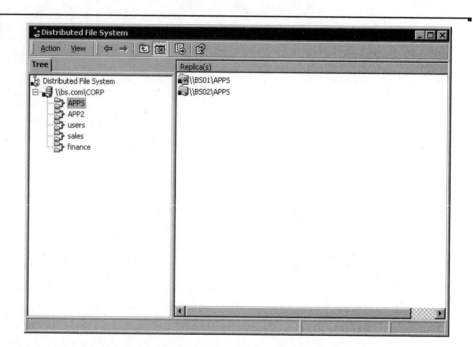

Checking Node Status

Periodically, you should verify the status of each link within the Dfs topology. To check the status of a link, right-click the share in question and select Check Status. A green check mark indicates that the node is working properly. A red icon with an X through it indicates a problem (see Figure 9.45).

FIGURE 9.45

A failed node

A failed node indicates that there is a problem accessing the shared folder to which the child node refers. Try checking out the share directly to make sure it is still available to the network. More severely, the entire server that hosts the child node could be down.

Deleting Child Nodes

In Figure 9.45 above, the SALES node has failed. (It really failed because I stopped sharing SALES on the server where the resource actually resided.) Now I want to completely remove SALES from my Dfs. Right-click the child node in the left-hand pane and select Remove Dfs Link. This will remove the SALES folder from the CORP hierarchy, but will not touch the actual SALES share or any of its data on the remote server. Users will still be able to connect to \\BS99\SALES. If I wanted to finish this job, I could stop sharing and delete SALES from BS99.

Connecting and Disconnecting from Roots

Within the Dfs management console, you can connect to any Dfs root on your network to manage. Right-click the Distributed File System line in the top of the left-hand pane, and select Display an Existing Dfs Root. From there, you can browse your network for roots or type in the location of the root. For my CORP root hosted on BS01, I could type in \\BS\CORP. To remove a Dfs root from the console, right-click the root and select Remove Display of Dfs Root.

Web Sharing

Web sharing is another new feature of Windows 2000. It allows you share folders directly for use via HTTP requests coming from Web browsers.

 NOTE You must be running Internet Information Services for this option to be available. If your server doesn't support Web access at the *server* level, it won't matter whether your shares are "web enabled" or not. Your users won't be able to get to those shares through their Web browsers anyway.

Configuring Web sharing is extremely simple. Within your Windows Explorer, right-click the folder you want to share out to the Web and select Sharing. At the top of the folder properties dialog box that appears, you'll notice a Web Sharing tab (see Figure 9.46). Selecting that tab allows you to configure how this folder will be shared out to the Web. I'm going to enable Web sharing for my Marketing folder.

FIGURE 9.46

Web Sharing folder properties

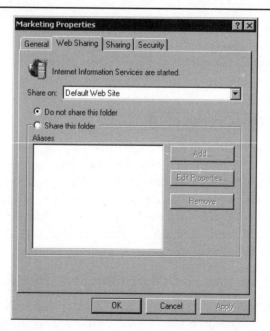

At the top of the Web Sharing tab is a Share On drop-down box. In that box are the different Web sites that have been created via the Internet Services Manager. Select the Web site that you want to add this folder into. Most of the time, the default Web site will be just fine, and this is where I am choosing to place my Marketing folder.

The next step is to select the radio button for Share This Folder. Once selected, a dialog box will pop up to configure the Web alias for this folder, as shown in Figure 9.47.

FIGURE 9.47

The Edit Alias dialog box

The alias is what Web clients will refer to in order to access this resource. Choose which permissions you would like Web clients to have for the data in this share. You can select any combination of Read, Write, Script Source Access (which allows clients to execute scripts through this share), and Directory Browsing (which allows clients to see folder lists without being required to enter a valid filename to view). Choose the application permissions level from None, Scripts, and Execute. Once completed, you will be returned to your Web Sharing tab and will have the new alias shown as a configured alias (see Figure 9.48).

You can add more aliases for this folder by selecting the Add button, or remove unwanted aliases by selecting the alias and clicking the Remove button. You can also revisit alias properties by selecting the alias and clicking Edit Properties.

Once you press OK, the alias will be registered to your selected server's Web site and ready for browsing. Go to your Web browser and enter the URL for this alias. On my machine, that would be http://bs01.bs.com/marketing/. Since I enabled directory browsing for my alias, I can see the files and folders within that folder, and I see the Web page shown in Figure 9.49.

WARNING I tried to combine a few of these features into one step by enabling my CORP share—which is my Dfs root—as a Web folder. When I look at \\BS\CORP within the regular Explorer, I can see the full Dfs. But if I try to look at my own D:\CORP folder, I can see all the directories corresponding to my child nodes, but since they are not *real* resources on my machine—rather redirections to other shares somewhere else—the server gives me an "access denied" message. When I enable Web sharing for the CORP share on my server, and try to access http://bs01.bs.com/corp—access denied, of course.

FIGURE 9.48

The configured
Web alias

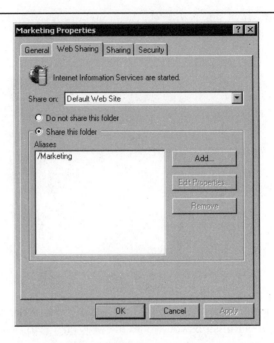

FIGURE 9.49

Browsing the
Web folder

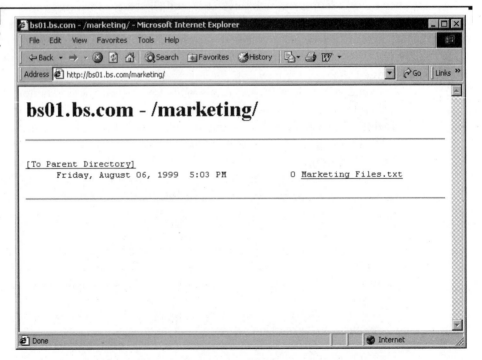

Using Offline Files/Client-Side Caching

As you've seen, Windows 2000's file server functionality has grown to include Dfs as well as Web folders, while retaining the old NT file server capabilities. But it doesn't stop there: not only does Windows 2000 improve the *server* side of file servers, it also jazzes up the *client* side.

Introducing Offline Files

While many of Windows 2000 Server's new capabilities will largely appeal to network administrators, Win2K's Offline Files, or Client-Side Caching (Microsoft uses both names interchangeably), feature will appeal to almost anyone who uses a network. Offline Files provides three main advantages: it makes the network appear faster to its users, smooths out network "hiccups," and makes the now-difficult task of keeping laptop files and server files in sync simple and transparent.

How Offline Files Works

Offline Files acts by automatically caching often-accessed network files, storing the cached copies in a folder on a local hard drive, a folder not surprisingly called `Offline Files`. Offline Files then uses those cached copies to speed up network access (or apparent network access), as subsequent accessing of a file can be handled out of the local hard disk's cached copy rather than over the network. Offline Files can also use the cached copies of the files to act as a stand-in for the network when the network has failed or isn't present—such as when you're on the road.

Offline Files is a write-through caching mechanism; when you write a file out, it always goes to the network, and it is also cached to your local hard disk. And when you want to access a file that Offline Files has cached, then as you've already read, Offline Files would *prefer* to give you the cached (and faster) copy, but first Offline Files checks that the file hasn't changed at the server by examining the file date, time, and size both on the server and in the cache; if they're the same, then Offline Files can give you the file out of the cache without any worries; otherwise, Offline Files fetches the network copy, so you've got the most up-to-date copy.

As a network file could easily be modified by someone else when you're not using it, there's a pretty good chance that the network copy of a file would often be different from the cached copy. But if *that*'s the case, then what good is Offline Files? After all, if the file changes on the network a lot, then you'll just end up having to retrieve it from the network instead of enjoying the speed of getting it from cache. Offline Files increases the chances that it's got the most up-to-date copies of your cached files by doing background synchronizations in a number of user-definable ways. This synchronization is largely invisible to the user, who simply utilizes My Network Places or a UNC to access network files, as has been the case with earlier versions of NT and NT client software.

 NOTE Offline Files only works on Windows 2000 machines; you can't get this benefit if you've got Windows 9*x* or NT 3.*x* or 4.*x* on your Desktop. If you *are* using a Win2K Desktop, however, Offline Files will be useful even if you're accessing a server running pre-Windows 2000 software, like NT 3.*x* or 4.*x*.

You'll like Offline Files for several reasons. As these oft-used cached files will reside on the local hard disk in the Offline Files folder, you'll immediately see what seems to be an increase in network response speed: opening up a file that appears to be on the network but which is really in a local disk folder will yield apparently stunning improvements in response time, as little or no actual network activity is required. It also produces the side effect of reducing network traffic, as cached files needn't be retransmitted over the LAN. Having frequently used files on a local cache folder also solves the problem of "What do I do when the network's down, and I need a file from a server?" If you try to access a file on a server that's not responding (or if you're not physically connected to the network), Offline Files shifts to "offline" mode. When in offline mode, Offline Files looks on your local Offline Files network cache and, if Offline Files finds a copy of that file in the cache, it delivers the file to you just as if the server were up, running, and attached to the user's workstation. And anyone who's ever had to get ready for a business trip knows two of the worst things about traveling with a laptop: the agony of getting on the plane, only to realize that you've forgotten one or two essential files, and the irritation of having to remember when you return to make sure that whatever files you changed while traveling get copied back to the network servers. Offline Files greatly reduces the chance of the first of those problems because, again, often-used files tend to automatically end up in the local network cache folder. It greatly reduces the work of the second task by automating the laptop-to-server file synchronization process.

Enabling Offline Files on Your Desktop—the Basics

When you first install Windows 2000, Offline Files does not work by default. You must turn it on in one of two ways: either by telling Offline Files to keep track of a particular file, or by going to Folder Options—it's available in the Control Panel, or in the Tools menu of any folder window. Then just check the box labeled Enable Offline Files.

Once activated, Offline Files will often *automatically* cache a file just as a side effect of you using the file. (I'll get to why it *often* rather than *always* does it in a bit.) You can, however, tell Offline Files to *ensure* that a particular file or an entire folder on the network is always in the Offline Files folder (recall, the name for the Offline Files cache) in just two steps: First, find the desired file (or folder) in My Network Places. Second, right-click the file. My Network Places will then display the file's context menu with the usual items—Open, Rename, Delete, and the like—but some files' context menus will include the option Make Available Offline, as you can see in Figure 9.50.

"Pinning" a file so that it is always in the Offline Files folder

Forcing Offline Files to keep a copy of a particular file in the `Offline Files` folder (that is, forcing Offline Files to keep a copy of a file on the PC's local hard disk) is called *pinning* that file or folder. The first time that you pin a file, Offline Files will start up a configuration wizard, called the Offline Files Wizard, that asks a few questions, then sets up Offline Files to run based on your answers. And while it *sounds* like a great idea, be careful about making entire folders available offline, as that has the effect of copying the entire folder and all of its contents to your local hard disk. That can take some time when it's first set up, and of course it can be a bit chagrining when if fills up your hard disk. (Subsequent synchronizations may be quite quick, as you'll read later.)

If you choose Tools/Folder Options, you'll see the property page shown in Figure 9.51.

In the Offline Files Settings page, the first check box tells a Windows 2000 machine to enable its Offline Files capability. The second tells Offline Files to compare every file in the `Offline Files` folder with the file's "actual" values out on the network servers, forcing Offline Files to synchronize its local file copies with the file originals every time you log off. (That's only one of *several* options you have for controlling offline file synchronization, and you'll read more about those options later.) The next check box controls how Offline Files tells the user that one or more servers are not currently available, leading Offline Files to place that server or servers into offline mode. If you'd like, you can tell Offline Files to remind you every so often that one or more servers are in offline mode with a ToolTip-like balloon such as you see in Figure 9.52.

FIGURE 9.51

Options for Offline Files

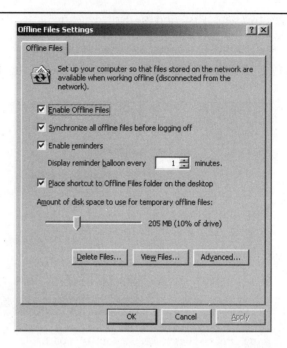

FIGURE 9.52

Offline Files reminding you that you're offline

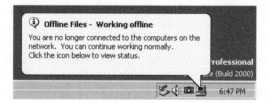

If you know that one of your servers is about to go offline, or if you're a mobile user about to go on a trip, then you will often need to know whether or not a particular file is already in your PC's cache, its Offline Files folder. You can see which files are in the local Offline Files folder, as well as their status, in a few ways: In the Offline Files Settings page, click the View Files button. Alternatively, in a check box on the same page, you can direct Windows 2000 to place a shortcut to your Offline Files folder right on your Desktop.

While the whole idea of network file caching is attractive, there's a built-in limitation to how many files can be cached on a user's local hard drive. There are often tens of gigabytes worth of files out on the network, and under a gigabyte of free space available on most workstations. It is entirely possible that you could, in a short period of time, examine more files on the network than would fit on your hard disk. Clearly, if left to itself, Offline Files could use up all of your free disk space, but you can control how much free space Offline Files is allowed to fill up in the Offline Files Settings page.

However, you can only control how much space Offline Files allocates to the automatically cached files, and when that space is exhausted—by default, it's 10 percent of your disk's space—then Offline Files just drops the file that hasn't been used in the longest time to make room for more automatically cached files. In contrast, you can pin as many files as you like, forcing Offline Files to cache *them*—but you of course could run out of disk space doing that. If that happens, Offline Files just pops up a dialog box directing you to either unpin some files or to free up some disk space.

Getting and Keeping Things in the Offline Files Folder

Once you've turned Windows 2000's Offline Files feature on, how do you use it? In a given day, you may access many files on a network—which ones get copied into the Offline Files folder?

It's easier to conceptualize how Offline Files caches files if you understand that files get into the Offline Files folder in one of two ways: either you *direct* Offline Files to cache a file by pinning it (recall that you do that by choosing Make Available Offline from a file's context menu) or Offline Files decides by itself to cache some files without you having to ask it to. Offline Files calls these automatically cached files "temporary offline files."

Situations in Which Files Won't Cache

You can't always cache network files, however. Sometimes you'll look at a network file's context menu and the Make Available Offline option doesn't appear; when that happens, Offline Files won't cache the file either by pinning or by making it a temporary offline file. One of three things causes this caching prohibition: First, if the file is on a non-SMB server, such as a NetWare server, then you don't get the option to cache the file. Offline Files can only cache files on SMB servers, which means that it can cache files from NT 3.*x* and 4.0 servers and workstations as well as Windows 9*x* machines running File and Printer Sharing services. (Of course, it can also cache files from Windows 2000 servers and workstations.) Second, if you have disabled Offline Files by unchecking Enable Offline Files in Folder Options, the option won't appear. Third, you will not get the option to pin a file if the shared folder that the file resides in has been declared non-cacheable by a network administrator. A network admin may declare a share non-cacheable in the share's property page at that share's server. They just right-click the shared folder and choose Sharing, then click the Caching button. A dialog box like the one shown in Figure 9.53 will appear.

If the network administrator unchecks the option "Allow caching of files in this shared folder," then no one will be able to cache files in that folder.

FIGURE 9.53

Adjusting cache settings for a shared folder

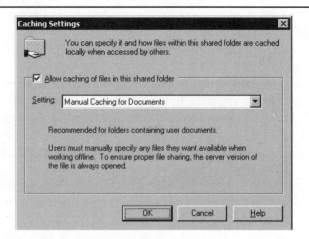

Manual and Automatic Caching

Assuming that you're working at your workstation and trying to access a network file that *can* be cached, pinning that file will prompt Offline Files to immediately copy the network copy of the file to your local `Offline Files` folder; a dialog box appears showing you the progress of that copy.

Other files get cached in the `Offline Files` folder if the files are in a network share on a Windows 2000 machine and if that share has been designated for *automatic* caching. Using the Caching Settings dialog box, an administrator can designate a share as Manual Caching for Documents—the default setting—or as either Automatic Caching for Documents or Automatic Caching for Programs. Either of the latter two server caching settings will cause automatic caching. When you open any file from a share configured for automatic caching, then that share's server tells your workstation, "While you're at it, cache this file." Your workstation then makes a local copy in the `Offline Files` folder, noting that the copy is a temporary offline file. The only difference between caching for documents or for programs is that Offline Files will run an `.exe` in a cached-for-programs folder without checking to see if it's up to date—without synchronizing that file first. It's a bit quicker that way, though of course it could cause trouble if you modified that `.exe` frequently.

How Offline Files Manages Cache Space

Offline Files allocates space for pinned files a bit differently than it does for temporary Offline Files. Recall that the Offline Files Settings page includes a slider that you can use to control how much of your hard disk space to allow Offline Files to use. A second look shows that this amount only applies to the *temporary* Offline Files. The space taken by the files that you *pin* into the cache does not count against the space allocated in the Offline Files Settings page. As I said earlier, if the `Offline Files` folder is full and Offline Files automatically caches a new temporary offline file, it must drop one or more older files from the Offline Files folder to keep the size of the temporary offline files below the maximum allowed amount given in Offline Files Settings.

And don't bother looking on your hard disk for the Offline Files folder—it's actually a series of folders inside \Winnt\Csc hidden not with the Hidden attribute, but the System attribute. You can find it, but first you've got to go to the Winnt folder, then choose Tools/Folder Options, then go to the View tab and uncheck "Hide protected operating system files (recommended)" and confirm the choice. You'll then be able to browse through \Winnt\Csc. What you *won't* find there are useful filenames—all cached files are tagged with long numerical names rather than their actual names.

Offline Files in Action: Before the Trip

Now that you've got Offline Files set up, let's put it to work. It's useful to both mobile and fixed-location users, but its benefits are most dramatic for those mobile users, so here's a step-by-step look at how someone might use Offline Files to make life on the road easier.

Putting the Files in Cache

A user named Jim is about to go on a trip. He connects his laptop into his company's corporate network and opens a share named Shareac on a server named Coral. Jim's network administrator has set up the Shareac share as an "automatic caching for documents" share. Shareac contains two files that Jim needs, file1.txt and file2.txt. Jim right-clicks those files and chooses Make Available Offline. Over the course of the day, he also accesses file3.txt and file4.txt, although he does not pin them.

Ensuring They're in the Cache

Before shutting down the laptop prior to getting on the road, Jim wants to double-check that copies of file1.txt and file2.txt are on his laptop's hard disk. He opens his Offline Files folder and sees a screen something like the one in Figure 9.54.

FIGURE 9.54

Jim's Offline Files *folder contents after accessing the Coral server*

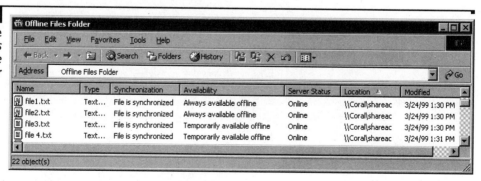

Note that under the Availability column, `file1.txt` and `file2.txt` are designated as Always Available Offline, meaning that they've been pinned; note also the little blue modification to the files' icons indicating that they are pinned. Note also that `file3.txt` and `file4.txt` are in the `Offline Files` folder, even though Jim didn't pin them—Offline Files automatically cached them. You can tell this because under the Availability column head, these files are noted as being Temporarily Available Offline. They could end up pushed out of the Offline Files cache without warning, were Jim to reattach to his corporate network and start accessing other cacheable files.

Note also that the server status of Online means that Jim's still attached to the corporate network and that Coral is online. Actually, his laptop will consider Coral online until the laptop notices that Coral is not responding to attempted communication. Jim can view his `Offline Files` folder either via a shortcut on the Desktop (assuming he has configured his system to show one), or he can navigate to the Offline Files Settings page and click the View Files button.

Getting the Most Recent Version of the File

If Jim has even more files to synchronize, perhaps entire folders, then he can employ Mobile Sync, available by choosing Start/Programs/Accessories/Synchronize. When started, its screen looks like Figure 9.55.

Mobile Sync lists all of the folders that contain pinned files that Offline Files knows of. Jim can then check the folders he's interested in synchronizing and click the Synchronize button. Clicking Properties just displays the contents of the `Offline Files` folder, and the Setup button allows Jim to configure synchronization when he's *not* traveling (see the later section "Controlling Synchronization for Non-Mobile Users").

FIGURE 9.55

Choosing shares to synchronize with Offline Files

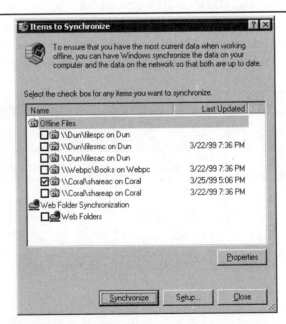

Working and Making Changes on the Road

On the plane to a client site, Jim starts up his laptop and opens My Network Places. His Desktop looks the same as it did back at the office, except now his system tray contains a small icon depicting a PC. Moving a mouse over the PC icon gets the message "Offline Files—the network is not available." Right-clicking that file offers a context menu that includes Status, which will simply report again that the network is not available; Synchronize, which obviously won't accomplish much until he's reconnected to the network; View Files, which opens up the `Offline Files` folder; and Settings, which brings up the Offline Files Settings page.

Accessing "Network" Files on the Road

Despite the fact that Jim is not attached to any network, My Network Places shows a "networked folder" icon for Coralshareac on Coral. If he opens up that folder, he'll see `file1.txt`, `file2.txt`, `file3.txt`, and `file4.txt`, just as if he were connected to the corporate network. He could open a command window and type `net view \\CORAL` to get a list of shares available on Coral, including Shareac. He could alternatively find `file1.txt` in the `Offline Files` folder.

Jim sees a problem with `file1.txt` and edits the file and saves it, and Offline Files allows Windows 2000 Professional to make it seem as if he's attached live on the corporate network. He also makes a few changes to `file2.txt`. After a meeting, he creates a completely new file, `file5.txt`, and saves it in the Shareac volume, again as if he were connected to the company network.

Warning: Sometimes Offline Files Don't Work

Oh, by the way, this all sounds good, but sometimes it has gone haywire on me. In the typical traveling scenario, I've got a laptop and a file server and I pin some files or perhaps a complete share or folder on the file server. Whenever you pin an entire folder, you've got to wait a minute or two while Offline Files goes out and copies all of the files from the pinned folder to your local hard drive. In the case where my laptop is a member of a different domain than the file server, I've seen Offline Files *look* like everything syncs up fine when I pin the folder. But when I disconnect from the network and try to *access* the files, I've gotten error messages like "The network name is not available." I've also had situations wherein I originally logged in under a particular username and then had to enter a different username in order to access some share. When I then pinned that share, again Offline Files looked as if it were copying every single file. When on the road, however, Offline Files refused to let me view or work with the file, claiming that it didn't exist at all. My advice follows in the warning.

WARNING If you are going to depend on Offline Files, make sure that your laptop, file server, and user account are all in the same domain. If that's *not* the case, be absolutely sure while you're still in the office to disconnect the network cable after synchronizing your pinned files and double-check that you can access those files. Offline Files is great, but don't trust it until you can be really sure of it!

Back in the Office: Syncing Up

After Jim returns from his trip, he plugs his laptop into his company's network and powers up the computer. He has updated `file1.txt` and `file2.txt` and created a completely new file, `file5.txt`, and he wants all three of these new or modified files written to the network servers.

As his laptop's operating system loads, it senses that it's back on the corporate network and tries to update the three files on Coral's share. `file1.txt` and the new `file5.txt` are no problem—the version of `file1.txt` is the same as it was before Jim left, so Offline Files overwrites the server copy with Jim's updated copy. `file5.txt` didn't exist before, so there's no conflict and Offline Files writes it to the server share. But unknown to Jim, someone *else* modified `file2.txt` while he was on the road. This presents a conflict to Offline Files, a conflict that it can't resolve by itself, so it prompts Jim for guidance (see Figure 9.56).

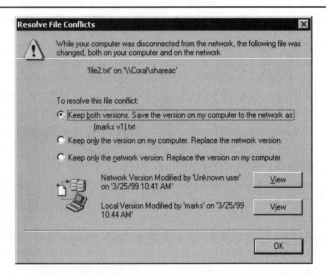

Jim uses the View buttons to examine both versions and decides that his update has more recent information, so he clicks the "Keep only the version on my computer"

button and then clicks OK. At this point, the files on his laptop and the ones on the network servers are synchronized.

Applying Offline Files to the Office: When Servers Fail

But suppose you're not a traveling user. What does Offline Files offer you? Greater network reliability and speed. By caching commonly used documents, Offline Files offers you a safety net in the event that the network fails.

Bulletproofing Word with Offline Files

Suppose you're working on a Microsoft Word document. You keep the .doc file on a server rather than your local hard disk so that you can work on it from any workstation and because it'll be automatically backed up every night. But Word's frequent background saves and Autorecover writes mean that your workstation must often communicate with the server where the document resides. A network failure or even a short hiccup in network or server response can cause problems that can lead to Word losing your document. With Offline Files, Word has a much softer landing. Once the server becomes unresponsive, Offline Files automatically shifts all of that server's folders to offline mode. Your first clue that there's a network problem, other than the initial delay from an unresponsive network, is that the Offline Files PC icon has appeared in your system tray, and a balloon message tells you that the server you were working with is now offline. You can continue to work with and save the file, but of course it'll really save to the Offline Files folder, at least until you reconnect to the server and synchronize. Additionally, you'll see this kind of network fault-tolerant behavior on *any* cached file, whether a pinned file or a temporary offline file. As you saw before, Offline Files will cache any file that you access on an automatically cached share, or any file that you pin in a manually cached share. This suggests that you should consider either pinning all of the Word files that you use from a server or set the server shares' caching settings to Automatic Caching for Documents.

Resuming Normal Operation

When the server is available again, Offline Files will sense that and modify its icon as shown in Figure 9.57.

Click the Offline Files icon, and you'll see a dialog box offering to reestablish connection to the server, as you see in Figure 9.58.

FIGURE 9.58

*Reestablishing network
connection with
Offline Files*

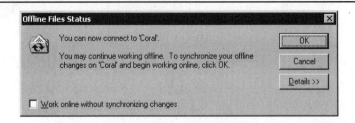

Click OK and you'll get a warning to close whatever files you are working on, as Windows 2000 will have to close any open files before it can synchronize them.

Controlling Synchronization for Non-Mobile Users

In addition to its fault-tolerant-like benefits, Offline Files's other great strength for non-mobile users is that it can improve a user's network experience by reducing the time between when a user requests a file on the network and when the user gets that file. There's no magic in that quick response, of course: Offline Files gets those files to the user so quickly because the files are already sitting on the user's hard disk in the `Offline Files` folder. But that's really only half the story. Sure, it's nice to get your files quickly—but are they the *right* files? The answer is yes, but there's a lot of underlying machinery insuring that.

Before offering the locally cached file copy as correct, Offline Files does a quick synchronization with the original network file. That synchronization need not be an entire copy; instead, it is a simple consistency check. For example, try pinning a large 100+MB file to your `Offline Files` folder. The initial synchronization will be a simple file copy, and it'll take a good long time. But then right-click the large file and do a synchronization, and you'll see that synchronization finish in seconds. This is true even for large files; for example, in one test, a 4MB JPEG file on a network server was pinned to a workstation's `Offline Files` folder, then the JPEG file was modified by another workstation, reducing its size by 30 percent. Synchronizing the first workstation to the JPEG file's new size took less than 5 seconds.

So you might find when accessing a file via the `Offline Files` folder that there is a short delay while your workstation synchronizes with the offline file's original copy. That might be acceptable, but Offline Files improves further upon that performance by periodically re-synchronizing its offline files *before* you need them.

In addition to the synchronizations that occur when you reconnect after being offline, when actually accessing the file, or after choosing Synchronize on a pinned file's context menu, you can also configure your Windows 2000 workstation to synchronize at logon and/or logoff, when the workstation is idle, or at particular times of day. You configure these synchronizations either by starting Mobile Sync via Start/Programs/Accessories/Synchronize and then clicking the Setup button, or by opening a folder and choosing Tools/Synchronize and then clicking the Setup button on the resulting page. You get a properties page like the one shown in Figure 9.59.

FIGURE 9.59

Initial synchronization configuration screen

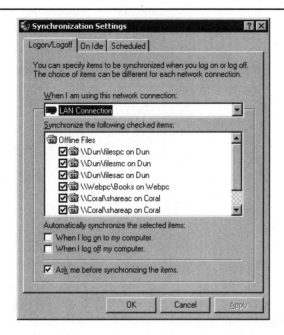

There are three tabs on this properties page: Logon/Logoff, On Idle, and Scheduled. The first two have a single-selection drop-down list box labeled "When I am using this network connection" that allows you to specify whether you want this synchronization done over a LAN or WAN connection.

In the first tab, you can instruct Offline Files to synchronize at logon or logoff or both. And if you think that synchronizing might be a lengthy process and would like to be able to skip it, you can select "Ask me before synchronizing the items," and Offline Files will display the Mobile Sync screen, letting you choose which—if any—folders to synchronize.

The second tab allows Offline Files to essentially synchronize in the background, waiting until your computer sits idle (see Figure 9.60).

FIGURE 9.60

*Controlling fore-
ground/background
synchronization*

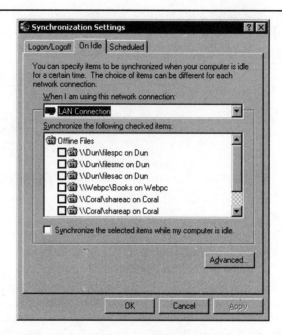

As with the Logon/Logoff tab, you can specify which folders to synchronize. The Advanced button lets you control how long your workstation should be idle before synchronizing, and how often to synchronize if the computer is idle for long periods of time.

The final tab, Scheduled, lets you set up synchronizations for particular times of day. You can tell it to synchronize every *n* days, every day, or every weekday.

Cleaning Out Offline Files

Sometimes Offline Files won't go away, however. Say you once connected to a server named MANGO and pinned a couple of files. You'll never see MANGO again and the files aren't important any longer, but the system keeps wanting to synchronize with MANGO and you get an error message every time you log on or log off. What to do?

Simple. Go to the Offline Files folder and unpin all of the files (or perhaps folders) in MANGO. Alternatively, you should be able to do that in My Network Places. Unpin everything related to MANGO, reboot, and you *should* hear no more about MANGO. Sometimes, however, it just stays around forever. In that case, zap *all* of the cached files. (Be sure to synchronize the folders that are still relevant first!)

You might want to flush out all offline files for a number of reasons. You might be about to give a laptop or desktop to someone and don't want them poking around inside your Offline Files folder or \Winnt\Csc. Or maybe you've just gone a bit pin-crazy and have so much stuff cached that you don't have any hard disk space left. In that case, unpin what you can first. But finish the job by choosing Start/Programs/

Accessories/System Tools/Disk Cleanup. You'll notice that one of the things that Disk Cleanup will do is to wipe out your offline files.

WARNING Again, make sure there's nothing cached that you want to synchronize with the file server before doing this; if you've made changes and haven't synchronized, cleaning out the Offline Files folder will lose your changes!

You'll probably first notice Offline Files when you see how much easier it makes keeping laptop files and network files in lockstep. But you may soon notice that your in-house network is a bit snappier, and that the occasional network failure doesn't keep you from getting work done. And if *that* isn't a killer app, what is?

CHAPTER **10**

Software Installation

One of the most common problems a network administrator faces almost daily is software installation and distribution. Isn't it heartwarming when your boss comes into your office and tells you, "We just bought a site license to XYZ Application. Can you install it on all 400 of our computers by the end of next week? Thanks!" Doesn't her confidence in you just make you proud?

Trust me—if it does, then it's likely that you haven't done this before.

At the firm where I work, we've tried everything from Microsoft's SMS to third-party solutions to home-grown solutions to alleviate this problem. Some work okay—most don't. Well, I suspect that a network administrator must have snuck onto the Windows 2000 development team because Software Installation (SI) is one of the most significant time-saving (and therefore money-saving) features in Windows 2000.

What Microsoft has done is integrate software installation into the operating system—and with that, allow it to be centrally controlled, distributed, and managed. You can automatically install an application company-wide or restrict it to a specific list of locations or a group of individuals. When you are done with it, or when you discover the licensing doesn't allow you to roll it out to the entire company, then you can forcibly remove it from all computers in one fell swoop. All of this is integrated into the operating system and Active Directory.

To help implement SI, Microsoft made some changes to the Winlogon service, OLE automation (COM), and the shell. Aside from that, these are the components of SI:

- Software Installation in Group Policy

- The Windows Installer Service

- The Add/Remove Programs in the Control Panel

You use Software Installation within group policy objects (GPOs) to control and manage the applications you are distributing, called *packages*. Everything else is used to install or remove the packages based on what you set up in Group Policy. There are two ways you can distribute a package to a user or to computers: *publishing* or *assigning*. When you publish a package, you're making it available to users or computers and it is at their option that it gets installed. To install it, the user simply goes to the Add/Remove Programs icon in the Control Panel. You cannot publish a package to computers. When you assign a package to users or computers (you *can* assign packages to computers), you are basically stating that they must have this package and that it will be installed for the users the next time they log in (sort of, but more on that later) and for the computers the next time they boot up.

These GPOs are stored in the Group Policy Container, which is a Directory service object—yet another benefit of Active Directory. The Group Policy Container also stores the class store. The class store is where all programs and APIs are stored for the publication and assignment of packages.

NOTE "But where do you get packages from?" I hear you cry. Microsoft is pushing software vendors hard to offer their new software releases in MSI (Microsoft Installer) format. If you see a file on a vendor's distribution CD with the extension .MSI, then that vendor has created a ready-for-Windows-2000 package. Alternatively, as you'll read later in this chapter, you can build your own packages with third-party products, including one that comes free with Windows 2000—VERITAS's WinInstall.

Publishing a Package to Users

Let's start off with an example that fixes a headache that's plagued Windows NT administrators for years: Windows 2000 and NT 4 only install domain administration tools on the servers. Most administrators are not always sitting at a server when they need these tools. So, as they gained experience, they would copy the tools with any extra DLLs to a network share and create shortcuts that ran the tools from the network share. This worked fine under NT 4. However, under Windows 2000, the administration tools are all COM objects, and as COM objects, they must be registered before they can be used. On Windows 2000 domain controllers, Microsoft includes adminpak.msi, which allows you to publish the administrator tools however you want.

 NOTE As suggested earlier, MSI is a new file type that is the data file for the Windows Installer—the service that performs all of the work for SI. MSI stands for Microsoft Software Installer. A package can be just the MSI or it can include other files as well.

Here are the steps to publish the package:

1. Copy adminpak.msi to a network share.
2. Create a GPO called AdminPak (you can call it anything you like).
3. Filter the GPO so that only enterprise admins and domain admins can install the package.
4. Add the package to the GPO.

Step One: Copy *adminpak.msi* to a Network Share

This first step is easy. I created another subdirectory called C:\Packages and shared it as packages. Within C:\Packages, I created yet another subdirectory and called it AdminTools. Then I copied adminpak.msi from C:\winnt\system32 to my new AdminTools subdirectory. Figure 10.1 shows what I did.

FIGURE 10.1

Copying `adminpak.msi` *to a network share*

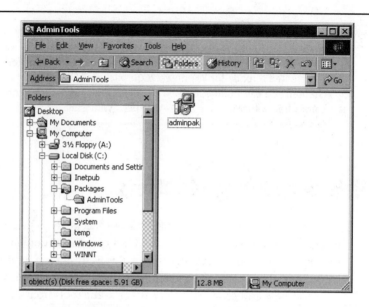

Step Two: Create a GPO

Next, start up the DSA (also known as Active Directory Users and Groups), and then right-click the domain name and choose Properties. Click the Group Policy tab, then the New button, type **AdminPak**, and hit Enter (see Figure 10.2).

FIGURE 10.2

Naming the GPO that deploys AdminPak

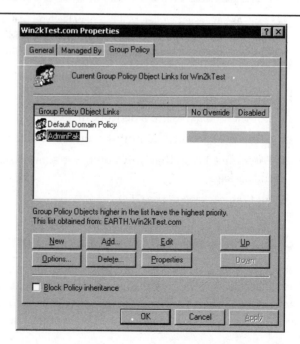

Step Three: Filter the GPO

The default behavior for Windows 2000 is to apply GPOs to all users in an organization, but with filtering, you have complete control. It's a good habit to get into because you can choose the users and computers to which a GPO applies. I'll cover filtering later in this chapter.

To apply a filter, click the Properties button, then the Security tab. Make sure the Apply Group Policy permission is unchecked for all groups but Domain Admins and Enterprise Admins. Then click OK. When you first create a GPO, it does not apply to administrators. For this example, we want it to apply as Figure 10.3 shows.

FIGURE 10.3

This GPO applies to Domain Admins.

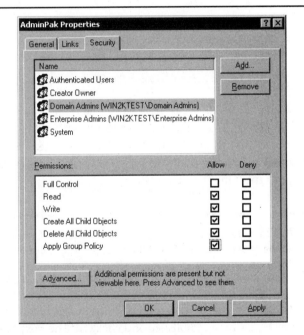

Step Four: Add the Package to the GPO

Next, click the Edit button. This will launch the Group Policy snap-in with your new group policy open and ready to be edited. At this point, you must make a decision. When you add a package to a group policy, you can assign or publish the package to users, or you can assign it to computers. Packages are added to the GPO under `Software Settings\Software Installation` in either `Computer Configuration` or `User Configuration`, as Figure 10.4 shows.

FIGURE 10.4

Add packages to a GPO in Software Installation.

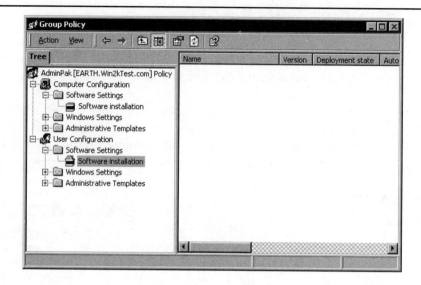

We'll add the adminpak.msi to User Configuration\Software Settings\Software Installation. To do that, right-click on User Configuration\Software Settings\ Software Installation and choose New/Package. Now find the adminpak.msi on your network. Mine is located on \\EARTH\Packages\AdminTools\adminpak.msi, so I'll just type it in. Then click OK.

NOTE Be sure to use the full UNC path name. If you don't, the Windows Installer will not be able to find and install the package and all installations will fail. Luckily, the Group Policy snap-in warns you if you don't use a network path.

At this point, we are prompted for the package deployment method, as shown in Figure 10.5. Choose Published and click OK. The next time you create your own package, don't worry too much about getting the deployment method right. It can be changed later by right-clicking the package and selecting Assign.

We now have the adminpak.msi ready for installation by any domain or enterprise administrator. To test the package, go to a Windows 2000 Professional workstation that is a part of your domain and log in as a domain or enterprise administrator. Go to the Control Panel and click Add/Remove Programs and then Add New Programs. You should see a screen like the one in Figure 10.6.

FIGURE 10.5

Specifying that the package will be published

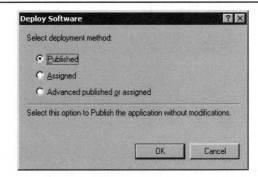

FIGURE 10.6

From Add/Remove Programs, you can install published packages.

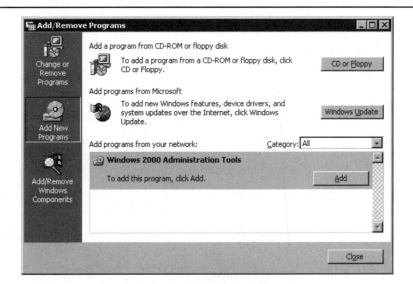

As you can see, all you need to do to add Windows 2000 Administration Tools is click the Add button. After you've installed the package, it then shows up under Add New Programs as Installed and Change or Remove Programs.

NOTE You can repair any published application by clicking Add/Remove Programs in the Control Panel, then clicking Change or Remove Programs, and then clicking the Support Information link. A dialog will be displayed with some basic support contact information and a Repair button to reinstall the package.

Filtering Group Policy

In the first example, we touched on what filtering group policies does for us in Software Installation. Simply put, thanks to filtering, we can place a GPO anywhere in our domain organization and use security to control who will get the software packages the GPO contains. No matter what the reason, be it licensing, security, or politics, you can control who gets a package. You can decide that one user gets the package or a thousand users get it, one computer or a thousand computers—it doesn't matter where in the organizational structure the user or computer falls.

Filtering is completely controlled by using the Security tab on the GPO's properties dialog box that you see in Figure 10.7. Any user, computer, or security group (or any security group the user or computer is a member of) in the Name list will get the package if the Allow check box for the Apply Group Policy permission is checked, unless, of course, the Deny check box next to Apply Group Policy is checked for the user, computer, or security group (or any security group the user or computer is a member of). Authenticated Users refers to any validated domain user on the network.

FIGURE 10.7

Set up filtering from the Security tab on the GPO's properties dialog.

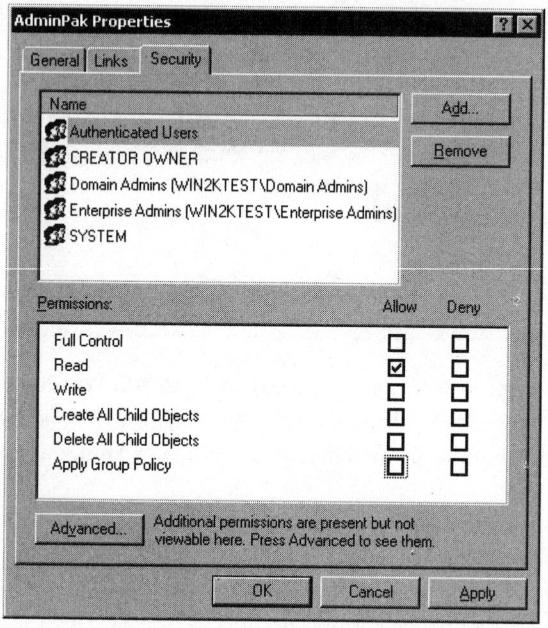

Don't expect the Security tab for the GPO to grant rights to users so they can use the features or information of an application. It won't. You can set the AdminPak GPO to apply to any domain user and any domain user would be able to install it—and that's it.

So, what happens if a GPO that had applied to a user or computer no longer applies? Let's say we have a user called LittleMutt who was in the Domain Admins group. When we set up our AdminPak GPO, it applied to all members of the Domain Admins group, including LittleMutt, and LittleMutt installed the package. Well, later we discover that LittleMutt is too young and inexperienced for the far-reaching power granted by being a member of the Domain Admins group, so we remove him from the group. Now the AdminPak GPO no longer applies to him, so what happens to the package he already installed? Does it get removed? The default behavior is that it doesn't—unless you have the Uninstall This Application When It Falls Out of the Scope of Management check box checked.

You can check this option by right-clicking the package once you are editing your GPO. Click on the Deployment tab and you'll see a dialog like the one shown in Figure 10.8.

FIGURE 10.8

The Deployment options tell Windows 2000 what to do when a GPO no longer applies to users or computers.

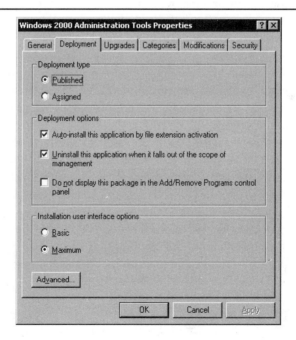

Using Organizational Units

You can also use organizational units (OUs) to control package distribution within Active Directory. Your OUs will sometimes follow your company's organizational structure, which makes the use of OUs very natural for package distribution for two reasons. The first reason is that you can use OUs for beta-testing both the application and the rollout of the application. The second is, of course, politics.

Whenever you roll out a new application, you probably assign a group of users and computers to be your beta testers. The users and computers in this group will usually change based on the application, but it is useful to have, let's say, a Beta Testers OU. You can add any users or computers you like to that OU and then create the GPO that will control the new application's package. You would create the GPO with the correct security and security group membership in place and test the rollout and the application. You could then add the GPO to other Beta Testers OUs within other sites of your company to test the remote install of the new package. When you are ready to roll the package out to the rest of the company, simply add the GPO to any other OU or to the domain and remove it from the Beta Testers OUs. This leaves the GPO and package completely unchanged and eliminates the need for any last-minute changes. Last-minute changes are frequent causes of problems with package distributions or implementations.

In addition, if you are rolling out a new version of an application currently in use, you can isolate the new version to the members of your Beta Testers OU while all other users continue to use the prior version. This is a powerful technique to aid you during upgrades.

With politics, the reasons are different but the methods and results are the same. The GPO that controls your package is added to the OUs that want the package. You can still have one security group to help manage which users or computers get the package within the OUs that are supposed to get it.

As with GPO filtering, when a user or computer no longer belongs to an OU, then any package that was installed because of membership in the OU will be uninstalled if you've checked the check box Uninstall This Application When This GPO No Longer Applies to Users or Computers on the package's properties dialog.

Assigning a Package to Users or Computers

Assigning a package to a user or a computer is the coolest thing about this Software Installation stuff. As with publishing an application, the current user doesn't need administrator privileges on the computer and the package will still get installed. However, if the package is assigned to a user, it gets installed when the user logs in. If the package is assigned to a computer, it gets installed when the computer boots up and no one needs to be logged in. If the user tries to delete the application, the package will be reinstalled or repaired. When you assign a package to a GPO, the package is *advertised* to every user and computer that GPO applies to.

The interesting thing about assigning a package is that it gets only partially installed at login or boot. An install program for an application typically does only a few relatively simple things: copy files to the computer, associate file types to the application, register any COM objects, and set up Start menu shortcuts. Well, at login or boot time, the Winlogon process only performs *part* of the installation of your package; it takes care of the shortcuts, file associations, and COM registration. To the user, this makes it appear that the software is installed. Consider Microsoft Excel, for instance. Excel is on the menu, and if any file with the .XLS extension is opened, Excel will launch. In addition, the icon for all XLS files is changed to the Excel icon. The user can't see that COM objects are registered, but we know that they are there. We can see them by running REGEDIT and looking in the HKEY_CLASSES_ROOT for the Excel.Application key, followed by several others. The installation is finished when the user clicks the application shortcut in the Start menu or opens any file associated with the application.

There are a couple of cool things about this. First, only those applications used by the user, or even the parts used by the user, will get completely installed. This saves time and disk space. Second, when the user logs into another computer, assigned packages follow her and appear to be already installed. Perhaps the user is on another computer temporarily because she has gotten a new computer. If all of her applications have been assigned, they will get installed as she uses them.

To demonstrate how a package is assigned, we'll use Microsoft Office 2000 Premium. Distributing a package by assignment is very much like publishing one. Here are steps to assign the package:

1. Run the administrative setup.

2. Create a group policy object called Office 2000 (you can call it anything you like).

3. Add the package to the GPO.

4. Customize the package properties.

Step One: Running the Administrative Setup

Start by installing a network-accessible copy of Office 2000 on some file server. You can run the administrative setup by clicking Start/Run, typing **d:\setup /a d:\data1.msi**, and clicking OK. You are then asked for your CD key and the location to which you want to install Office 2000. After a couple of minutes, the install is done and we're ready to begin.

NOTE Be sure to enter your CD Key. If you don't, your users may be prompted for one when the product is installed when they click on the Start menu.

The first thing I'm going to do is set up a Beta Testers group within my Corporate HQ OU and move the LittleMutt user to that group, as shown in Figure 10.9. Your OUs may be different, but I ended up with what is in Figure 10.9. Remember that we removed LittleMutt from any administrators groups, so he is a regular user without any administrator privileges on the domain and he doesn't need them on our test workstation either.

FIGURE 10.9

This is the Beta Testers OU.

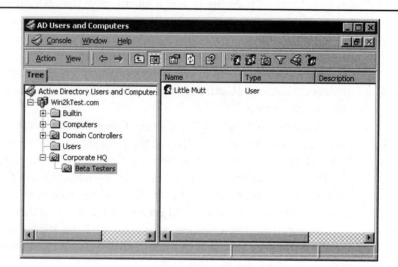

Step Two: Create a Group Policy Object

Next, start up the DSA, right-click the Beta Testers OU, and choose Properties. Click the Group Policy tab, then the New button, type **Office 2000**, and hit Enter (see Figure 10.10).

Now press the Properties button and click the Security tab. By default, the GPO is created so that it applies to Authenticated Users (as you can see in Figure 10.11), which means to any user or computer that is in our OU. This is perfect for our example, so we'll leave it as it stands. Click OK to close the dialog.

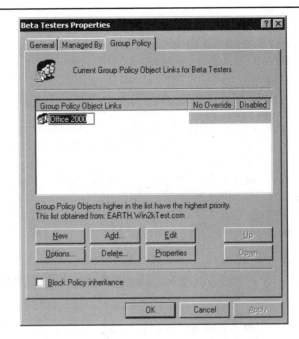

FIGURE 10.10

Creating an Office 2000 GPO

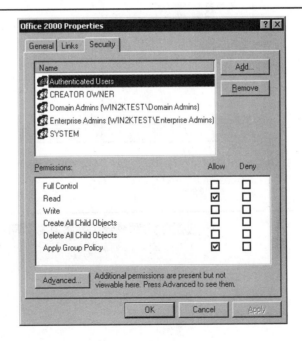

FIGURE 10.11

This GPO applies to all authenticated users.

In the real world, it's at this point that you'd probably want to set up your own filtering because you wouldn't want all users (that's what the Authenticated Users group means) to get Office 2000. You can do this by clicking the Add button and selecting the security group you want the GPO to apply to.

Step Three: Add the Package to the GPO

The next step is to click the Edit button. This will launch the Group Policy snap-in with the Office 2000 GPO open. We want to add the package to User Configuration\ Software Settings\Software Installation, as Figure 10.12 shows. Right-click Software Installation (or right-click in the empty right window pane) and choose New/ Package. My Office 2000 is located on \\EARTH\Packages\O2KPremium\data1.msi, so I'll just type it in. Then click OK. Be sure to use a network path or the package installation won't work.

FIGURE 10.12

The Software installation for the Office 2000 GPO

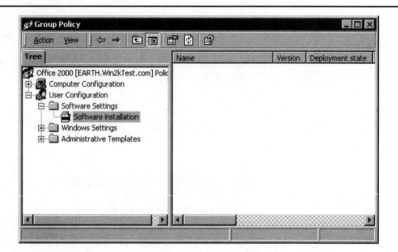

At this point, we're prompted for the package deployment method, shown in Figure 10.13. Choose Assigned and click OK.

FIGURE 10.13

Deploying Office 2000 via assignment

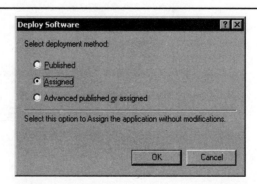

Step Four: Customize the Package Properties

Next, double-click on the package; this will bring up the properties dialog. The first thing we want to do is make sure the Uninstall This Application When It Falls Out of the Scope of Management check box is checked. Also, set Installation User Interface Options to Basic to minimize the dialogs that the users will see. Figure 10.14 shows the Deployment tab for the package as I've set it up.

FIGURE 10.14

Select Uninstall This Application When It Falls Out of the Scope of Management.

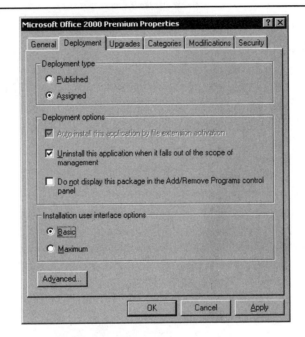

Now click OK and we are ready to test our deployment. To test the deployment, we need to log on as user in our Beta Tester OU. That is good ol' LittleMutt, so go to a Windows 2000 workstation that is part of your domain and log on as LittleMutt. Now, in addition to the standard messages in the logon dialog, toward the end you will see "Applying software installation settings." It is at this point that the Winlogon process is performing the first half of the installation. It's doing things like associating file types, registering COM objects, and setting up Start menu shortcuts.

These associations, registered COM objects, and shortcuts are exactly what you and I are used to. They are advertised components and features of an application. By "advertised," I mean that they are available and ready to be used but not completely installed and copied to the local hard drive. Remember when I said that some changes were made to the Winlogon server, OLE Automation, and the shell? Well, we know how Winlogon changed; now comes an explanation of how OLE Automation and the shell changed. The first time an advertised COM object is used, the modified shell will install the feature via the Windows Installer Server, and the same thing happens the first time an advertised shortcut is used.

Since you are now logged on as LittleMutt, you should see the Office 2000 short-cuts on the Start menu. Click the Excel shortcut and you'll see a Windows Installer dialog like the one shown in Figure 10.15. This is the rest of the installation taking place, where the application is actually being copied to the computer.

FIGURE 10.15

Windows Installer is beginning the Excel install.

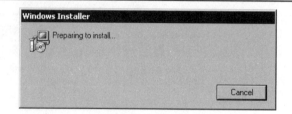

Removing a Package

The process for removing packages is very easy and very powerful. It is the same regardless of whether the package is published or assigned. Bring up the Group Policy snap-in to edit the GPO that contains the package you wish to remove. Next, right-click the package and choose All Tasks/Remove. You will then see a dialog like the one shown in Figure 10.16. Now we have two choices.

FIGURE 10.16

Deciding how Windows 2000 is to handle the already installed copies of the package

If we select the first option, we can immediately remove our package from the users or computers to which it is published or assigned. What *immediately* really means is that the package will be removed the next time the user logs in (if the package is published or assigned to the user) or the next time the computer boots (if the package is assigned to the computer). While this may not be immediate in the literal sense, it will uninstall your package from wherever SI previously installed it, so make sure this is what you want to do before you click OK. The next time the user logs on, he will get the message "Windows Installer removing managed software *name of package*," where *name of package* is the name of the package you just removed.

If, on the other hand, we select the second option, any existing installations of our package will remain where they are and no new installs will take place. One word of caution: Once you select the second option and remove the package, the existing installations of your application are orphaned and you no longer control them. In other words, if you decide later that they should be removed, your only choice is to go to every workstation that has the application and manually remove it yourself.

Redeploying a Package

With software distribution, it is often useful to have the ability to force the package to be reinstalled everywhere. Maybe you've added modifications to a package. For this and other reasons, Microsoft included a feature that gives you that ability. Within the Group Policy snap-in, right-click the package you wish to redeploy, then choose All/Tasks/ Redeploy Application and you'll get the dialog like the one shown in Figure 10.17.

FIGURE 10.17

The redeploy warning

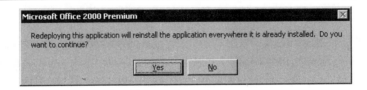

Be sure this is what you really want to do since your package will get reinstalled for all users and computers—even if it means 10 thousand users or computers.

Creating Your Own MSI

In the not so distant future, applications will come with an MSI that we can deploy via Software Installation. But what do we do for now? Well, Microsoft's answer is to include the VERITAS Software Console and WinINSTALL Discover. The VERITAS Software Console allows you to view and edit an MSI and WinINSTALL Discover helps you to create one. Now don't confuse WinINSTALL Discover with the WinInstall service. They are very different—just named alike. WinInstall installs packages via an MSI. WinINSTALL Discover allows you to create an MSI from an application that was installed using an old-style install or setup program.

The big picture on how you create your own MSI is this: You take a *Before snapshot* of a computer, install the new application, then take an *After snapshot* of the computer; then the two snapshots are compared and the differences are output to the MSI. The steps are as follows:

1. Create a clean computer.

2. Take the Before snapshot.

3. Install the application and reboot.

4. Test the application.

5. Take the After snapshot and compare.

6. Make any customizations.

7. Test the application installed by the new MSI.

Step One: Create a Clean Computer

A clean computer is one that has only the operating system and its operating system service packs installed. If you install any other software on the computer prior to creating the Before snapshot, you run the risk of making the new application dependent upon the other software being installed first. The reason for this is simple. WinINSTALL Discover only notices the differences between the Before and After snapshots. It won't care that the new application didn't install a DLL or make a needed Registry entry because the DLL or Registry entry was already there.

Here's an example that will help me explain my point. Windows 2000, with the latest and greatest service packs installed, has version 1.0 of the ABC.DLL. You then install some other software that, unknown to you, upgrades the ABC.DLL to version 1.1. Then you take the Before snapshot. Now your new application also needs version 1.1 of the ABC.DLL. However, when you run the setup for your new application, it probably will not copy the ABC.DLL again because it sees that it is already there. Even if it did, WinINSTALL Discover will see no difference between the Before and After version of the ABC.DLL. The bottom line is that your new application will not work when installed with the MSI unless the other software is installed first. The same thing goes for Registry entries. The goal of this whole procedure is to find out everything your new application needs and include it in the MSI.

By the way, having a clean computer also means you shouldn't install VERITAS Software Console and WinINSTALL Discover. You wouldn't want your new application to require VERITAS Software Console or WinINSTALL Discover for it to work, would you?

Step Two: Take the Before Snapshot

Go to your clean computer and log on as a user with administrator privileges on that computer. This is, of course, so that you can install the new application. Now run WinINSTALL Discover. It's best to run it from the Start/Run menu and to run it from the network without mapping a drive to a network share. My command was \\Earth\ C$\Program Files\VERITAS Software\Wininstall\DiscoZ.exe, but of course, yours will be different.

The first dialog that comes up gives you a brief explanation of what WinINSTALL Discover is about to do. Click the Next button and the next dialog asks for your new application name, the location and name of the MSI, and whether the application is a 16- or 32-bit application. For this example, I installed the Windows 2000 Resource Kit, so I answered the questions as Figure 10.18 shows.

FIGURE 10.18

Defining your new application

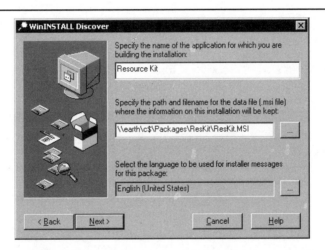

Next you're asked for a drive to store temporary work files. Now this can be a local drive or a network drive, but it's best if you use a local drive. Don't worry, the temporary work files won't show up in your MSI.

The next dialog asks which drives to scan. These are the drives WinINSTALL Discover will use to take the Before snapshot. It is important to be careful to select any drive that might change as a result of installing your new application. You wouldn't, though, want to select network drives, CD-ROM drive, and so on. Figure 10.19 shows what I selected.

FIGURE 10.19

*Telling WinINSTALL
Discover which drives
to watch for changes
(which drives to scan)*

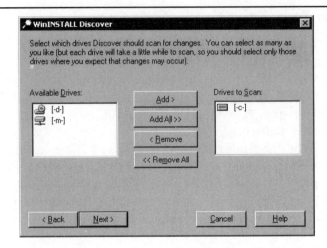

After you click Next, you are asked what files to exclude from the scan, as shown in Figure 10.20. I kept the defaults, but you can, of course, change them to exclude any other files you need excluded. This is where the temporary work files that are a part of WinINSTALL Discover's Before snapshot process are excluded from the scan.

FIGURE 10.20

*You can select which
files to exclude from
scanning.*

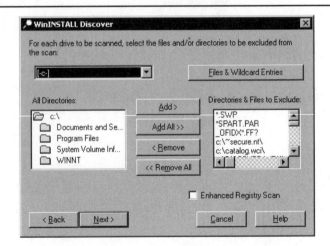

After you click Next, the process begins. It will take a few minutes as each drive you selected, and the Registry, is scanned.

Step Three: Install the Application and Reboot

This part sounds pretty simple and it is. You simply need to install your new application exactly as you want the MSI to install it. You should reboot the computer since many application setup programs install the last couple of files they need during the next reboot. This is often because the setup program needs to replace a file that is currently in use. So to be safe, we reboot.

Step Four: Test the Application

Now you need to configure and test the application to ensure that it is working as you want and expect it to. The only thing you need to keep in mind is that any change you make will probably end up in the MSI.

Step Five: Take the After Snapshot and Compare

Again, you need to log on as a user with administrator privileges on what was the clean computer. Then run WinINSTALL Discover again to take the After snapshot. It's a good idea to run it from the Start/Run menu and to run it from the network without mapping a drive to a network share. My command was \\Earth\C$\Program Files\ VERITAS Software\Wininstall\DiscoZ.exe, although, again, yours will be different.

The first dialog you'll see will look like Figure 10.21. Now WinINSTALL Discover knows that it has taken the Before snapshot on this computer already, so it asks whether you want to take the After snapshot or abandon the Before snapshot so you can start the process over.

When you're creating your own MSI, it is quite likely that you will need to do the entire "Before snapshot–install the application–After snapshot" process a couple of times. Keep in mind that if you do, your computer is no longer clean and you should get it back to a clean state before starting over. Yes, that may mean reinstalling Windows 2000.

Luckily for us, WinINSTALL Discover remembers all of the long path names we typed in so we don't have to type them in again. Make sure Perform the 'After' Snapshot Now is selected, as it is in Figure 10.21, and click Next.

FIGURE 10.21

Beginning the After snapshot

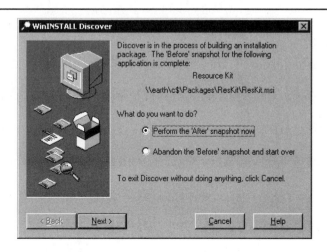

Now as soon as you click Next, WinINSTALL Discover is off and running, taking the After snapshot. This will take about as long as taking the Before snapshot. As it takes the After snapshot, it compares the snapshot to the Before snapshot and writes any differences it finds to your new MSI. When it's done, you may see a dialog like Figure 10.22.

FIGURE 10.22

The new MSI has been generated.

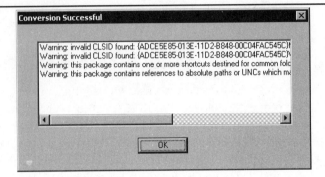

This dialog means that WinINSTALL Discover was successful but here are the peculiarities it found. You'll typically get warnings at this point, and you should look through them to see if any throw red flags for you. Other than that, it means you need to test the application when it is installed by your new MSI.

Step Six: Make Any Customizations

What you want to do now is take a look at the MSI you just made and possibly modify it. You can do so by using the VERITAS Software Console. From the Start menu on the server that has your new MSI, choose Program Files/VERITAS Software/VERITAS Software Console. Then choose File/Open and select your new MSI. Once you've opened your MSI, you should see a window that looks somewhat like Figure 10.23.

The General information contains the basics, but the really useful information is under the other titles. If you click Files in the lower-left section of the window, you should see something like Figure 10.24. These are all of the files in your MSI. This is how you can find out what files are being installed by the package—whether it's your new MSI or an MSI provided by an off-the-shelf commercial application.

FIGURE 10.23

The opening window
with the MSI opened

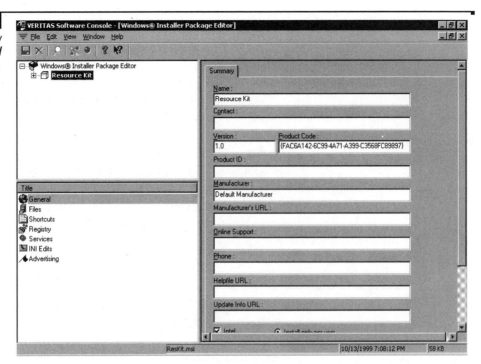

FIGURE 10.24

The files in the MSI

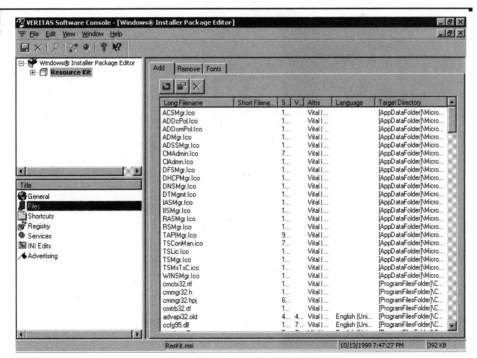

Why is this useful? What would we want to change here? If an application requires these files, we probably shouldn't remove any. Well, each application we install on a workstation (or server, for that matter) has its own set of required files. And of those files, at least some are shared by other applications. It is the shared files, typically DLLs, that cause us trouble.

For instance, say we have an application called Abc that requires a DLL called `shared.dll` version 2. Also, let's say we have another application, Def, which also requires `shared.dll`, but this time it needs version 1. Because we install application Abc and then Def, we end up with version 1 of `shared.dll` and application Abc ends up not working. By using VERITAS Software Console to edit your MSIs, you potentially can do something about the problem.

Scroll down the file list, find a file called `comdlg32.ocx`, and double-click it (Figure 10.25). You know the shared file problem? Well `comdlg32.ocx` is one of the most widely shared ActiveX controls around. It seems that every application nowadays installs its own version of it.

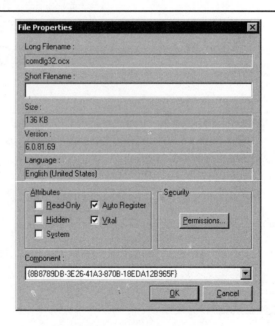

At the bottom of the dialog is a drop-down list called Component. This is the part of the application that needs this DLL—write the number down or print the screen and then click OK to close the properties dialog. Now in the tree in the upper left portion of the console window, double-click Resource Kit. The tree will open up and display another line labeled Resource Kit; double-click that one as well.

 NOTE An MSI is the install database of an application. So the first level in the tree is the name of the application. Within the application there are features, the second level of the tree. Within features are components, the last level of the tree.

Now scroll down and click the component you took note of earlier. Click the General title and you will see, as shown in Figure 10.26, where all of the files for this component will be installed.

This is the install location of comdlg32.ocx. You can change it here if you like. If you click the File title, you can also delete the file from the MSI, skipping its installation altogether.

FIGURE 10.26

The install location of comdlg32.ocx

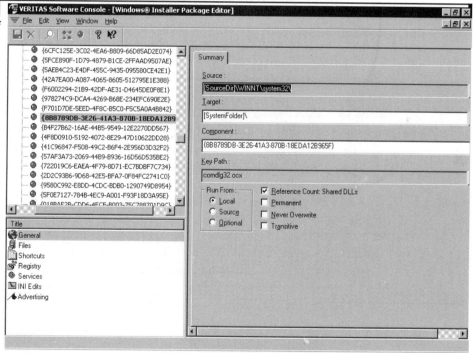

Step Seven: Test the Application Installed by the New MSI

Now this is the moment of truth. You need to use the new MSI to install the new application on several different computers and to test all of its features. This is how you determine if this entire process worked. You need to test all of the new application's features to see if any part of the installation was missed.

You can install and test the application on a clean computer, but you need to install and test it on one that is not clean as well. This is so you can find out if the new application will conflict with other applications, and it is by far the most important and time-consuming part of the process.

Distributing the Easy Way: Using ZAP Files

What if you can't or don't want to create your own MSI? Maybe you don't have the time or maybe the installation is complex or unique enough that you don't want to risk breaking it. Well, instead of creating MSIs, you can use ZAP files.

ZAP files give us a way to publish an application's installation program through the Windows 2000 SI feature. That saves a lot of time up front. Since we are publishing the package, we can still control which users are allowed to install it. Notice that I didn't mention computers. Remember, we cannot publish packages to computers; we must *assign* packages to computers. ZAP files can only be published to users.

When you use a ZAP file to publish a package to users, the user can use Add/Remove Programs in the Control Panel to install the application. Once it's installed, you can use Add/Remove Programs to reinstall or remove the application as if it were an MSI installation. What you don't get is the ability to have applications repaired automatically, nor do you get the ability to upgrade the application automatically through SI.

ZAP files do borrow a function from the process for assigning a package. In the ZAP file, you can associate a file extension with the package installation so that, when a user double-clicks a file with that extension, the package installation is launched. Now this is not what we think of as normal file association because the file type is not really associated with the installation program. Windows 2000 simply knows that if the file is not associated with any program, it shouldn't run the installation program.

These are the steps to publish an application via a ZAP file:

1. Create a ZAP file.

2. Share the ZAP file and installation files.

3. Add a package to a GPO.

Step One: Create a ZAP File

A ZAP file is nothing more than a text file with a .ZAP extension. The example I am using here is listed below, and as you can see, it has the format of an INI file:

```
[application]
FriendlyName = "WinZip Version 7.0"
SetupCommand = \\Earth\Packages\WinZip\WinZip70.EXE
DisplayVersion = 7.0
[ext]
ZIP =
```

The first line in the "application" section is FriendlyName and is simply the name that you and I will see for a package description in the GPO editor and that the users will see when they install the package. The next line is SetupCommand. This is the actual installation program that will be run when the user selects the application in Add/Remove Programs or when the user double-clicks a file with the right extension (.ZIP in this example). DisplayVersion is exactly what it sounds like and is displayed with the package in the GPO editor.

The next section is "ext" and it needs to contain any file extension you want associated with the installation. In our example here, ZIP = is all we need to tell Windows 2000 to run what we've defined for the SetupCommand if no program is associated with the file extension.

Step Two: Share the ZAP File and Installation Files

We've been doing this all along with SI. I created a directory called WinZip in the Packages share on Earth, so the full path of my installation program is \\Earth\ Packages\WinZip\WinZip70.exe. My ZAP file was placed right next to it, and its full path is \\Earth\Packages\WinZip\WinZip.zap.

Step Three: Add a Package to a GPO

You can either create a new GPO or add a new package to an existing GPO. To create a new GPO, first start up the DSA and then right-click the OU you want to contain the GPO (I used Beta Testers again), then choose Properties. Click the Group Policy tab, then the New button, and give your GPO a name. Once you have the GPO created, just click it and hit the Edit button to start the GPO editor.

Now we must add the package to User Configuration/Software Settings/Software Installation. Right-click Software Installation (or right-click in the empty right window pane) and choose New/Package. My ZAP file's full path is \\Earth\Packages\

WinZip\WinZip.zap. As Figure 10.27 shows, be sure to change the file type to ZAP files. Then click Open.

FIGURE 10.27

Selecting a ZAP file for the package

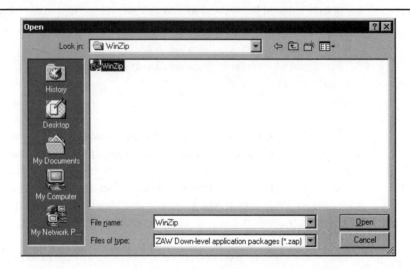

At this point, we are prompted for the package deployment method shown in Figure 10.28. Notice that we cannot choose Assigned. Choose Publish and click OK.

FIGURE 10.28

Publishing a ZAP file

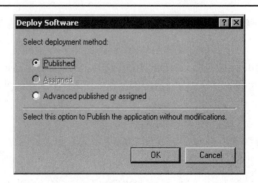

Once that is done, so are we—other than testing of course. The users that the GPO applies to can install the package at any time. The next time those users log in, they will be able to double-click a ZIP file and install WinZip.

Checking Out Those Off-the-Shelf Applications

You can use the VERITAS Software Console for more than just editing your own MSI. You can use it to edit the MSIs that comes with any off-the-shelf application. "Why in the world would I want to do that?" you ask. Thanks for the lead-in; I'm glad you asked. The answer is pretty simple: you want to find out what the installation is doing and where it's doing it.

Installation programs copy DLLs to all parts of your hard disk, make Registry entries, and register COM objects. Nothing stops them from overwriting another application's DLLs, Registry entries, or COM objects. Nothing but you, that is. With the VERITAS Software Console, you can now take a look at any install (provided it's an MSI) and see what it is doing. If you browse an application's MSI and find that it is overwriting a DLL that is critical to another application, or to the operating system, you have the chance to do something about it early on. At the very least you now know what applications to test. If you want to take a more proactive course of action, you can change the location to which the DLL is copied to a place that only the new application can get to it. Another option is to remove the file completely from the MSI. The same choices are available to you if you find Registry entries being made that overwrite another application's.

If you do decide to edit the MSI, you should keep in mind that doing so is a tricky business. For instance, some software publishers will support you grudgingly, if at all, if you have modified their MSI. On the technical side, your required thoroughness increases dramatically. Also, be warned that today's applications use COM quite a bit. What this means to us is that if we change the location to which a DLL is copied and that DLL is a COM object, then one of two events could occur. The first is that the COM object won't work and the new application will fail, and maybe others. The second is that the new application works fine, while other applications may or may not fail because they are still using the new COM object. Keep in mind that COM objects are not retrieved by their full path on the hard disk. They are retrieved by the location specified in the Registry. Simply put, applications will be able to find a COM object (and its DLL) no matter where you put it on the hard disk as long as the COM object is properly registered.

Customizing Packages

So far, I've only talked about how you can deploy an application using an MSI. Unless you edit it using VERITAS Software Console, you are deploying the application unmodified. We have another option available to us called *modifications*.

Modifications are files similar to MSIs in that they describe how an application is to be installed. While MSIs define the official way an application is to be installed (according to the software publisher), modifications describe how it will be installed differently from what is in the MSI—kind of like saying, "Yes, but this is how I really want to do it this time." Modifications have an .MST extension (because they were originally called *transforms*). Modifications provide a safe way to customize the installation of an application.

 NOTE MST is a new file type for the modification files. These files give you a way to customize the application installation without actually editing the MSIs.

You can make an MST by using a tool provided by the software publisher. For instance, to create one for Microsoft Office 2000, you need the Custom Installation Wizard found in the Office 2000 Resource Kit (which you can download from Microsoft). Once you have an MST, using it is quite easy—but you only have one chance to use it.

 NOTE MSIs can only be applied when first adding a package to a GPO. You must choose Advanced Published or Assigned in the Deploy Software dialog.

Creating an MST

The first thing you need to do is to download and install the Custom Installation Wizard if you don't already have it. To download the wizard, go to www.microsoft.com/office/ork/2000/appndx/toolbox.htm and download the ORKTools.exe. Once you've extracted and installed the Office Resource Kit Tools, you can start the Custom Installation Wizard by selecting Start/Programs/Microsoft Office Tools/Microsoft Office 200 Resource Kit Tools/Custom Installation Tools.

The first dialog of the wizard is the welcome screen giving a short description of the wizard's features. Click Next and you'll come to the dialog shown in Figure 10.29. Here we'll use the same MSI we've been using for Office 2000, \\EARTH\Packages\ 02KPremium\data1.msi. In the dialog, the wizard is assuring us that nothing will happen to our MSI. Keep in mind that the purpose of the MST is to customize the MSI without changing it.

Click Next and you'll see the dialog in Figure 10.30. Here we either create a new MST or open an old one. For this example, we want to create a new one, so make sure Do Not Open an Existing MST File is selected, then click Next.

FIGURE 10.29

Opening the MSI that
you'll be customizing

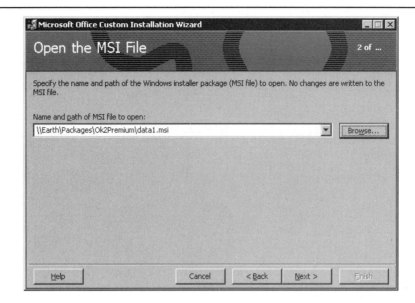

FIGURE 10.30

Opening an existing or
new MST

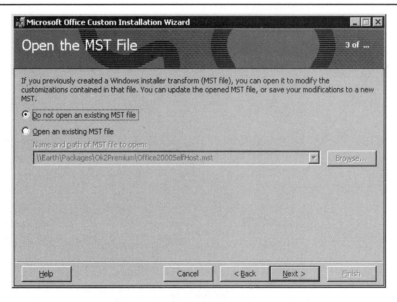

At the dialog in Figure 10.31, we are only asked for the new MST's path and file-name. There's really not much to this step since we don't have to worry about where the MST is actually stored at this point. In order to use the MST with an MSI in a package, the MST must be located in the same directory (which also must be network accessible). Click Next.

FIGURE 10.31

Naming the new MST

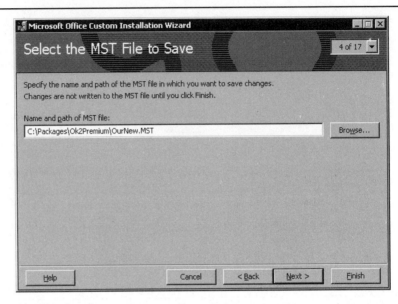

The dialog in Figure 10.32 begins our customizations. First, you can change where Office 2000 will be installed. Second, you can change your company name. While you may not want to change the location of Office 2000, you probably will want to fill in your company name. Once you've done that, click Next.

FIGURE 10.32

The Office install path

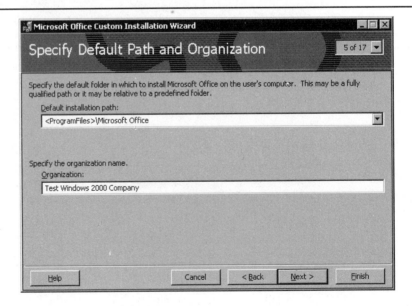

The Remove Previous Versions dialog in Figure 10.33 is where you decide if you want earlier versions removed during the Office 2000 installation or whether you want to leave it up to the user. The Default Setup Behavior option leaves it up to the user—but only to a point. If any earlier versions of Office are found, the user is asked if she wants *all* previous versions removed. She won't be able to leave the old version of Excel and remove the old version of Word. She can only leave them both or remove them both. The second option is where you decide now to remove old versions. If you select this option, the user will not have a choice and the old versions will simply be removed.

Figure 10.34 shows you how you can select which features of Office to install and, if installed, the location from which they will be run. Your choices are Run from My Computer, Run from Network, and Installed on First Use. If you select the first choice, the program files will be installed locally. For the second, the program files will be used from the network. And for the third, files will be installed locally the first time the user tries to use the program.

FIGURE 10.33

Removing previous versions

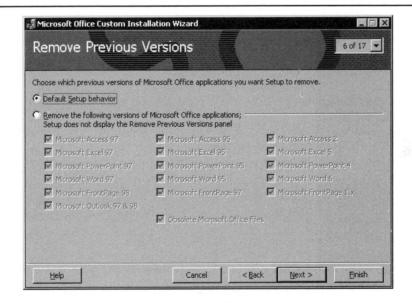

FIGURE 10.34

*Setting feature
installation options*

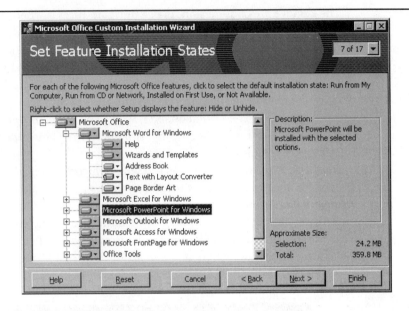

That said, keep in mind that the MSI and the MST you are building can be run interactively. When you run them interactively, all of the options in the preceding paragraph are available. If you distribute everything in a package, then the standard behavior of SI will take precedence and program files will be installed the first time they are used. By the way, some of the little disk pull downs are gray because they have more installable features beneath them. The white ones are the end of the line. Click Next to move on to the next screen.

Now for you Office gurus out there, there is the dialog shown in Figure 10.35. It allows you to get really fancy with your installs of Office. It does this by utilizing yet another part of the Office Resource Kit, the Office Profile Wizard (also downloadable from Microsoft's site). With the Profile Wizard, you can customize the behavior and look and feel of Word and Excel at install time—things like toolbars, dictionaries, templates, and the default save format. The standard options are good enough for our example, so click Next.

The Add Files to the Installation dialog in Figure 10.36 means exactly what is says. You can use it to install your own dictionaries, templates, and the like, or even your own programs, with the Office install. This makes for a much cleaner install of the "company standard." No longer do you have to install Office and then figure out how you get the company standard dictionary installed as well. Click Next.

FIGURE 10.35

You can customize the application settings using an OPS file from the Profile Wizard.

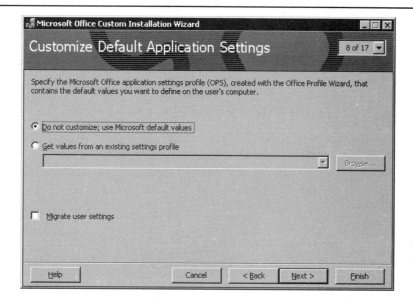

FIGURE 10.36

Adding your own files to the installation

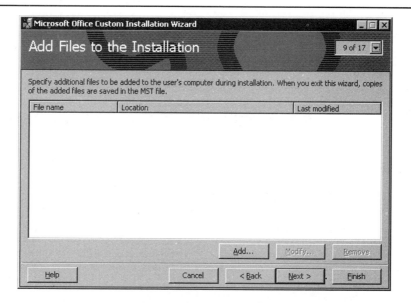

The Add Registry Entries dialog in Figure 10.37 does for the Registry what the preceding dialog does for files. You can make your own Registry entries a part of the Office install. Click Next.

FIGURE 10.37

*Adding your own
Registry modifications
to the installation*

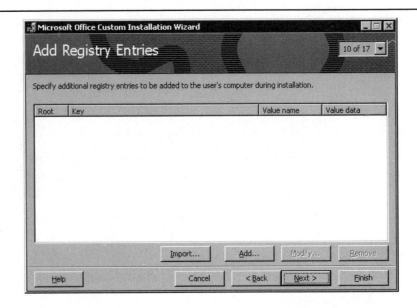

The dialog in Figure 10.38 allows you to control where Office shows up on the Start menu. You can also add new items to the menu for your own programs that you added to the install. Click Next.

FIGURE 10.38

*Changing where Office
shows up on the
Start menu*

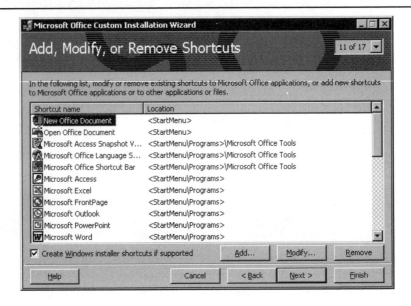

The Identify Additional Servers dialog in Figure 10.39 lets you set up multiple sources for the installation files. These are the servers and shares from which the Windows Installer will pull files when it needs to. They are used when you first install Office from the network onto a computer and when you've selected Installed on First Run. Click Next.

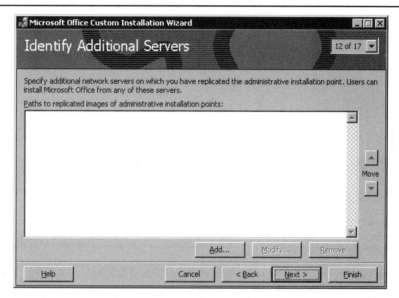

In Figure 10.40, we see yet another way you can add your own stuff to the installation. Here you can specify additional programs to be run after the Office install is complete. Any programs you add are run one after the other, in the sequence you specify. When one ends, the next will be launched. If one hangs, then the trailing programs won't be run. Click Next.

In the dialog in Figure 10.41, you can customize the default Outlook profile. Keep in mind that Outlook stores the user's profile in the system part of the Registry. If the user does not have the required rights to make changes to that part of the Registry, she will not be able to change her Outlook profile. Click Next.

The dialog in Figure 10.42 lets you define how you want to install Internet Explorer 5, which is required for some features of Office. If you're installing Office on a Windows 2000 computer, it should already have Internet Explorer 5 installed. Click Next.

FIGURE 10.40

Adding your own
programs to the
installation

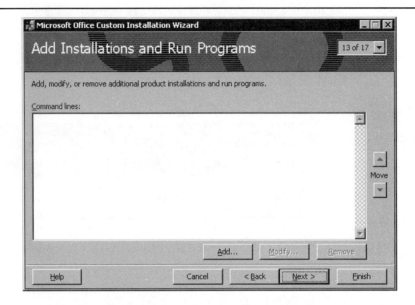

FIGURE 10.41

Customizing Outlook

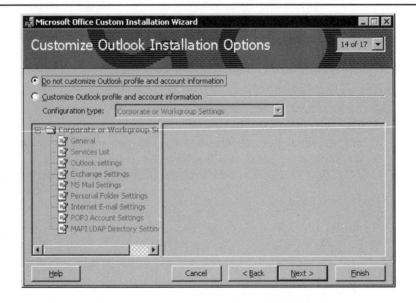

FIGURE 10.42

Setting up the installa-
tion of Internet
Explorer 5

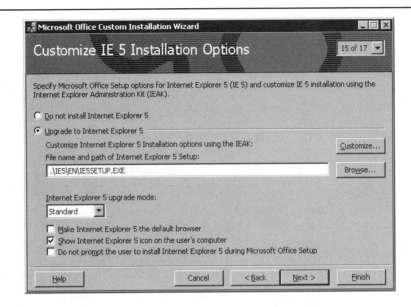

Many of the choices you made throughout this process are stored as properties of
the setup. These are shown in the dialog in Figure 10.43, where you also can change
anything you like. You can't remove any of the standard properties, but you can add,
change, or remove your own. Click Next and you are asked to save your changes.
Click Finish to do so.

FIGURE 10.43

Changing the installa-
tion properties

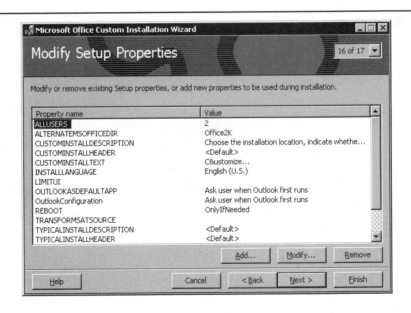

The dialog in Figure 10.44 wraps up the MST creation. You are also given a command line you can use to test the Office install with your new MST.

FIGURE 10.44

Completed creation of the MST

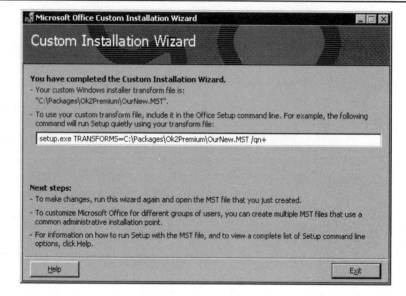

Using an MST

To create a package with an MSI and an MST, you start off like you would normally start off to add a package—by editing your GPO in the Group Policy snap-in , right-clicking User Configuration\Software Settings\Software Settings, and choosing New/Package. Then select your MSI (a ZAP file cannot be used). Once the MSI is selected, you will see the Deploy Software dialog, shown in Figure 10.45.

FIGURE 10.45

Select Advanced Published or Assigned.

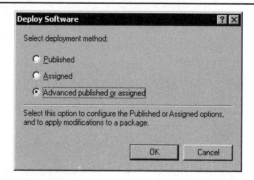

In the Deploy Software dialog, select Advanced Published or Assigned and then click OK. If you choose either Published or Assigned, you won't be able to add modifications to your package. Your only option will be to delete the package (not the MSI) and start over.

Now click the Deployment tab shown in Figure 10.46. Here you can select your deployment method, either Published or Assigned. You may also want to check Uninstall This Application When This GPO No Longer Applies to Users or Computers. To minimize interaction with the user, select Basic under Installation User Interface Options.

Next, click the Modifications tab and click the Add button. Select your MST and click OK.

NOTE Be sure your MST is in the same directory as your MSI. If not, your package will not work properly.

Once you've selected your MST, you should see something like Figure 10.47. At this point, you can add other MSTs if you like and control the order in which they are applied.

Microsoft Office 2000 Premium Properties ? X

General | Deployment | Upgrades | Categories | Modifications | Security |

Deployment type
- ○ Published
- ● Assigned

Deployment options
- ☑ Auto-install this application by file extension activation
- ☑ Uninstall this application when this GPO no longer applies to users or computers
- ☐ Do not display this package in the Add/Remove Programs control panel

Installation user interface options
- ● Basic
- ○ Maximum

Advanced...

OK | Cancel | Apply

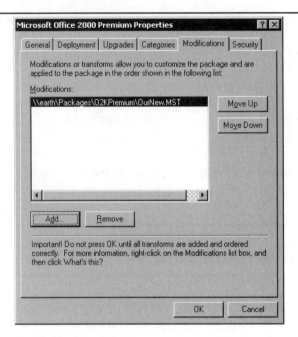

FIGURE 10.47

*All modifications for
the Office 2000
package*

Now click on OK and you can begin testing your package.

Upgrading Applications

So you've been on Windows 2000 for some time now, and you've deployed all of your applications via packages with MSIs. Then you get a new version of an application—now what? Well, the answer is, of course, to upgrade the application with another MSI.

Upgrading an application is very easy and not much different from distributing any other application. Very simply, you start with any package that is based on an MSI. Now this is the package that *is* the upgrade. For my example, I'm using Office 2000. So to begin, start with the GPO in the Group Policy snap-in, right-click the package, and select Properties. Then click the Upgrades tab and you'll see something like Figure 10.48.

Now click the Add button to see a dialog like Figure 10.49. You can upgrade an application in your current GPO, or you can select another GPO and any package within it. There is one exception: you cannot upgrade a package that is based on a ZAP file. To continue our example, select A Specific GPO, then click Browse.

FIGURE 10.48

Starting with an empty Upgrades tab

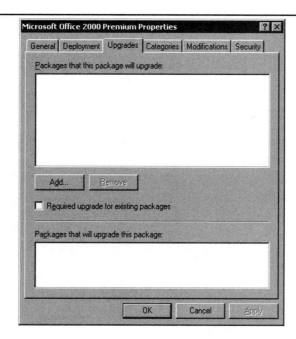

FIGURE 10.49

The Add Upgrade Package dialog

NOTE You cannot upgrade a package that is based on a ZAP file. Packages must be installed via an MSI for them to be upgradable.

At the Browse for a Group Policy Object dialog shown in Figure 10.50, click the All tab. You can browse any way you like, but I find using the All tab easier. However, if I had thousands of GPOs, I'm sure I'd think differently.

FIGURE 10.50

Browsing for all GPOs in the domain

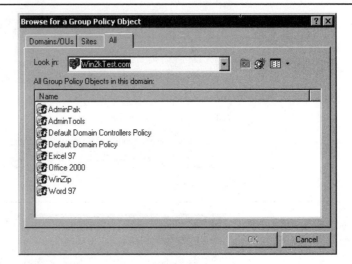

The package I want to upgrade with Office 2000 is Word 97, so select it and click the OK button. Now we're back at the Add Upgrade Package dialog, only this time, we see all the packages in the GPO, as in Figure 10.51. In this example, there is only Microsoft Word 97, so select it. Now there is a decision to make: what should be done with the old application? The first choice is to uninstall it before installing the new application; the second choice is to leave the old application alone and install the new application on top of it. Select Uninstall the Existing Package, Then Install the Upgrade Package; then click OK.

Now the GPO properties dialog shows that Office 2000 is replacing Microsoft Word 97, as shown in Figure 10.52. Click the Required Upgrade for Existing Packages option. Once we click OK, any user who is managed by the Word 97 GPO will have Word 97 uninstalled the next time they log in. The icon for Word will remain on the Start menu until selected. Then, Office 2000 will be installed.

I hope you can see how extremely useful Software Installation can be. This is not just a cool new feature that we would like to use and that would give us more capabilities. This is a feature that actually saves us time, and headaches, in our day-to-day lives. It gets most of its power from its tight integration with Windows 2000's Active Directory and the heavy reliance on security and group policy objects. Unfortunately, because of that integration, to get the most from Software Installation, Windows 2000 must be installed on your users' computers, not just your servers.

FIGURE 10.51

Selecting Microsoft Word 97

FIGURE 10.52

Office 2000 is replacing Microsoft Word 97.

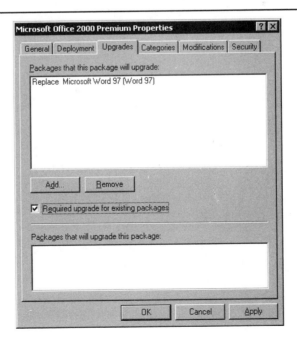

Also, this is the first implementation of this feature integrated into the operation system. As more and more software publishers begin using MSIs and MSTs to install their products, our jobs will become...well, maybe not easier, but at least more consistent. In future versions of Windows 2000, Microsoft will likely improve the process even more, giving us even more useful features—features we haven't even thought of yet.

CHAPTER **11**

Configuring and Troubleshooting Network Print Services

FEATURING:

"Paperless office" my sore head. Even after years of interoffice e-mail and online documents, in many offices it's not official until you hold the printed evidence in your hand. Printing isn't sexy, but it's an inescapable—and vital—part of life in the networked office.

It's simply not practical—or necessary—to provide everyone in the office with a personal printer. Instead, you connect a printer to a print server and share the printer from there so that dozens or hundreds of people can use one printer. Of course, once dozens or hundreds of people are dependent on a single piece of equipment, that piece of equipment becomes pretty crucial. It needs to be up and running, dependable, and accessible to those who need it but off-limits to those who don't.

Hence this chapter. In the following pages, I'll talk about how to use Windows 2000 Server to complete the following tasks:

- Create a new local printer or connect to one already set up on the network or Internet.
- Configure printer settings to help people find and troubleshoot print jobs.
- Secure the printer so that only those people who should be using it have access to it.
- Speed up printing by making multiple printers look like one.
- Connect to a printer from a variety of different platforms.
- Troubleshoot the printing problems that will inevitably occur.

In the course of this chapter, I'll use the Microsoft terminology for referring to printers and printing functions. If you're not familiar with this vocabulary, read on before jumping in.

Print Services Terminology

Contrary to what you might have believed, a *printer* is, in fact, not that putty-colored box that you put paper into and printed documents come out of. In the Microsoft world, a printer is a logical device that's an intermediary between user applications and the *print device* (the thing that actually does the printing). All configuration settings apply to printers, not to print devices. The ratio of printers to print devices is not necessarily 1:1. You can have one printer and one print device, two printers for a single print device, or one printer and several print devices. I'll talk about *why* you might want to do any of these in the course of this chapter.

When you send documents to a printer, they become part of the printer's *queue*, the group of documents waiting to be printed. Although in other operating systems, such as OS/2, the queue has been important as a primary interface between the application and printing devices, in Windows 2000 (and all forms of Windows NT), the printer plays this role.

Most often, the printer is accessible to the network via its connection to a *print server*, the computer on which printer drivers are stored. Most of this chapter will operate under the assumption that your network's printers are connected to a print server running Windows 2000. A *network-interface printer* is a printer directly connected to the network via a built-in network card.

> **NOTE** Even if the rest of your network is running Win2K, your print server doesn't have to be—and vice versa. A print server can run Windows for Workgroups, Windows 9x, any version of NT Workstation or Server, LAN Manager, or (if you install MS-Net) Windows 3.x or DOS. The options available to you will depend on the operating system; if your print server runs an operating system other than Win2K, then some of the information in this chapter may not apply to you.

Getting Acquainted with the Windows 2000 Printing Interface

As with much of Win2K, the first step in learning how to administer printers is to find out where all the printer management tools *are*. I won't get into the details of how to use these tools just yet, but when you're looking for the right tool for the job, this sidebar should help you find it.

To set up the printer for using forms, to configure printer ports, to add or update printer drivers, or to set spooling or error management options, you'll need to configure the printer server, not the printer or print device. Printer server properties are available from the Properties option in the File menu of the Printers window. The Printers window is accessible from the Control Panel, or from the Settings section of the Start menu.

Individual printer properties, such as the printer's description, sharing options, port used, spooling options, and device settings, are set from printer-specific property sheets. You can get to them either by right-clicking a printer's icon in the Printers menu or by choosing Properties from the File menu of a particular printer's queue window. Editing one printer's property sheet has no effect on any other printer.

The Win2K Printing Model

The process of printing is a bit more complex than it (hopefully) looks from the outside. The Win2K model uses several components to render application data for graphical output, get the data to a printer, and then help the printer manage multiple print jobs. Some of the following information on *how* Win2K printing works is background, but it's also helpful when it comes to troubleshooting, so wade through it if you can.

The main chunks of Win2K printing are the Graphics Device Interface (GDI), the printer driver, and the print spooler.

The Graphics Device Interface

The Graphics Device Interface (GDI) is the portion of Win2K that begins the process of producing visual output, whether that output is to the screen or to the printer. Without the GDI, WYSIWYG output would be impossible. To produce screen output, the GDI calls the video driver; to produce printed output, the GDI calls the printer driver, providing information about the print device needed and the type of data used.

The Printer Driver

Printer drivers are the software that enable the operating system to communicate with a printer. They're not compatible across operating systems, so although any Win32 operating system can print to a Win2K Server print server without first installing a local printer driver—they'll just download it from the print server—you'll have to make sure the drivers are available for the clients that will be using the printer. That means that even though you've attached the printer to a Win2K computer, you'll need to install the Windows 98 printer drivers if any network client computers are running Windows 98.

Win2K printer drivers are composed of three sub-drivers that work together as a unit:

- Printer graphics driver
- Printer interface driver
- Characterization data file

The printer graphics driver renders the GDI commands into Device Driver Interface (DDI) commands that can be sent to the printer.

You need some means of interacting with and configuring the printer, and the role of the printer interface driver is to provide that means. The printer interface driver is your intermediary to the characterization data file, providing the information you see in a printer's property sheet.

The characterization data file provides information about the make and model of a specific type of print device, including what it can do: print on both sides of a piece of paper, print at various resolutions, and accept certain paper sizes.

The Print Spooler

The print spooler (SPOOLSS.DLL, in *%systemroot%*\system32) is a collection of dynamic link libraries (DLLs) and device drivers that receive, process, schedule, and distribute print jobs. It's implemented with the spooler service, which is required for printing, and is composed of the following components:

- Print router
- Local print provider
- Remote print provider
- Print processors
- Print monitor

The Print Router

When a Win2K client computer connects to a Win2K print server, communication takes place in the form of remote procedure calls from the client's print router (WINSPOOL.DRV) to the server's print router (SPOOLSS.DLL). At this point the server's print router passes the print request to the appropriate print provider: the local print provider if it's a local job and either the Windows or NetWare print provider if sent over the network.

The Print Provider

To find the right print provider, the print router polls the Windows print provider. This provider then finds the connection that recognizes the printer name and sends a remote procedure call to the print router on the print server. That local print provider then writes the contents of the print job to a spool file (which will have the extension .SPL) and tracks administration information for that print job.

 TIP By default, all spool files are stored in the *%systemroot%*\system32\spool\printers directory. If you like (perhaps if you've installed a faster hard drive), you can change that location by adjusting the value of the print server settings on the Advanced tab. To get there, open the Printers Control Panel and choose Server Properties from the File menu. Move to the Advanced tab, and you'll see the spooler settings, including the location of the spool file.

Win2K normally deletes spool files after the print job they apply to is completed because they only exist to keep the print job from getting lost in case of a power failure to the print server. If you want to keep track of such data as the amount of disk space required by spool files and what printer traffic is like, you can enable spooler event logging.

The Print Processor

A print processor works with the printer driver to de-spool spool files during playback, making any necessary changes to the spool file based on its data type.

Er—*data type?*

The data type for a print job tells the print spooler whether and how to modify the print job to print properly. This is necessary because methods of print job creation aren't standardized; for example, a Win2K client won't create a job the same way a Unix client does. Therefore, a variety of print server services exist to receive print jobs and prepare them for printing. Some of these print services assign no data type (in which case Win2K uses the default data type in the Print Processor dialog box), and some assign a data type.

The spool file can accept data from the print provider in one of two forms: Enhanced Metafile (EMF) or RAW. EMF spool files are device-independent files used to reduce the amount of time spent processing a print job—all GDI calls needed to produce the print job are included in the file. Once the EMF file is rendered, you can continue using the application from which you were printing. All the rest of the print processing will take place in the background. Unlike EMF spool files, which still require some rendering once it's determined which printer they'll be spooled to, RAW spool files are fully rendered when created. Modern NT-based operating systems such as Win2K and NT 4 use RAW spool files for local print jobs, for encapsulated PostScript print jobs, or when otherwise specified by the user. Windows 9*x* uses EMF files for local printing but sends RAW data to a networked print server. Windows NT 4 uses EMF files for both local and networked printing, and NT 3.*x* uses RAW whether printing locally or to a network printer.

 NOTE All else being equal, EMF spool files are normally smaller than RAW spool files because they're generic instructions for rendering, not complete renderings.

WinPrint, the Win2K/NT print processor, understands four versions of EMF data files (1.003–1.008), three kinds of RAW data files, and TEXT files, which have the characteristics shown in Table 11.1.

TABLE 11.1: WHICH DATA TYPE DO I NEED?		
Data Type	**Description**	**Supported By**
EMF	Tells WinPrint that the job was created in Windows and is already partially rendered. WinPrint works with the GDI and printer driver to complete the rendering, then returns the job to the local print provider. Returns control to the application quicker than the RAW data type does.	NT and Win2K print clients
RAW	Tells WinPrint not to modify the print job at all, but to return it to the local print provider.	All printer clients
RAW [FF Auto]	Tells WinPrint to check for a form-feed command at the end of the print job. If one isn't there, WinPrint adds it and then returns the job to the local print provider.	All printer clients
RAW [FF Appended]	WinPrint adds a form-feed command to the print job and then returns the job to the local print provider.	All printer clients
TEXT	Tells WinPrint that the print job is ASCII text to be printed as hard copy and as is. WinPrint uses the GDI and the printer driver to produce this output, then sends the new job to the local print provider.	All printer clients

The default data type is RAW, supported by all Windows clients. To select a different data type, open a printer's property sheet and turn to the Advanced tab. Click the Print Processor button to display a list of possible print processor types. Select a different data type from the list and click OK. The new data type will be used for all print jobs.

That said, you won't likely need to change the data type Win2K is using, and unless you're working in an all–NT/Win2K environment, it's not a good idea. Windows 9x clients use a version of EMF to print locally but must use the RAW data type when printing to a print server. If you specify EMF for the default data type, Windows 9x clients won't be able to print via the print server. Their jobs will be sent to the printer and you won't see any errors, but the print jobs will never get to the queue. Unless your network only has Win2K- or NT-based print clients and won't ever have Windows 9x clients, stick with the RAW data type.

The EMF data type returns control to the printing application quicker than RAW does, but don't worry. Win2K applications that support EMF will use it without referring to the default data type specified for the printer, so making RAW the default data type won't affect your clients that can use EMF.

The Print Monitor

The print monitor is the final link in the chain getting the print job from the client application to the print device. It's actually two monitors: a language monitor and a port monitor.

The *language monitor*, created when you install a printer driver if a language monitor is associated with the driver, comes into play only if the print device is bidirectional. A bidirectional print device can send meaningful messages about print job status to the computer. In this case, the language monitor sets up the communication with the printer and then passes control to the port monitor. The language monitor supplied with Win2K uses the Printer Job Language. If a manufacturer created a printer that spoke a different language, it would need to create another language monitor, as the computer and print device must speak the same language for the communication to work.

The *port monitor's* job is to transmit the print job either to the print device or to another server. It controls the flow of information to the I/O port to which the print device is connected (a serial, parallel, network, or SCSI port). The local port monitor supplied with Win2K (LOCALMON.DLL) controls parallel and serial ports; if you want to connect a print device to a SCSI port or network port, you must use a port monitor supplied by the vendor. Regardless of type, however, port monitors interface with ports, not printers, and are in fact unaware of the type of print device to which they're connected. The print job was already configured by the print processor.

By default, only the locally required print monitor (LOCALMON.DLL) is installed. To use another monitor, you'll have to create a new port in the printer configuration settings.

The Printing Process

Those are the parts of the printing process. Here's how they fit together when printing from a Win2K client:

1. The user chooses to print from an application, causing the application to call the GDI. The GDI, in its turn, calls the printer driver associated with the target print device. Using the document information from the application and the printer information from the printer driver, the GDI renders the print job.

2. The print job is next passed to the spooler. The client side of the spooler makes a remote procedure call to the server side, which then calls the print router component of the server.

3. The print router passes the job to the local print provider, which spools the job to disk.

4. The local print provider polls the print processors, passing the print job to the one that recognizes the selected printer. Based on the data type (EMF or RAW) used in the spool file, any necessary changes are made to the spool file in order to make it printable on the selected print device.

5. If desired, the separator page processor adds a separator page to the print job.

6. The print job is de-spooled to the print monitor. If the printer device is bidirectional, then the language monitor sets up communications. If not, or once the language monitor is done, the job is passed to the port monitor, which handles the task of getting the print job to the port the print device is connected to.

7. The print job arrives at the print device and prints.

That's how Win2K sees printing. Good stuff to know when it comes time to troubleshoot printing problems. For the rest of the chapter, however, we'll concentrate on how *you* see printing.

Setting Up a Printer Connection

The day hasn't yet come when you can always plug a printer into a Win2K server and expect the server to find it without your help. Until it does, if you want to use a printer from Win2K, you'll need to either create the printer locally or connect to a printer on the network. You will need to set up support for a local printer if any of the following conditions apply:

- You're installing support for a printer connected directly to one of the parallel or USB ports of the local machine.
- You're installing support for a network-interface printer.
- You're defining a printer that sends information to a file (as opposed to a print device).
- You're making a second printer for a print device.

I'll describe first how to set up a new printer and then how to connect to a printer already installed on the network.

Installing a Printer on a Print Server

If you're coming to Win2K from NT 3.5*x*, then you're used to setting up a new printer from the Print Manager. The Print Manager, however, went out with NT 4—all functions of the Print Manager are now part of the Printers window, available either from its shortcut in the Control Panel or from the Settings folder off the Start menu. There's an Add Printer Wizard in the Printers folder that you must run to set up a printer on the local computer.

Unlike NT 4, the Win2K Add Printer Wizard prompts you for all options before installing the printer drivers. To create a new printer connected to the local machine, follow these steps:

1. Open the Printers menu and click the Add Printer icon you'll see there. Click Next in the opening screen of the Add Printer Wizard (the opening window isn't important; it tells you only that you're using the Add Printer Wizard in case you hadn't figured that out) to get to the screen shown in Figure 11.1. For this example, choose the default option, Local printer, and click Next.

FIGURE 11.1

Specify first whether the printer is connected to the local computer or on the network.

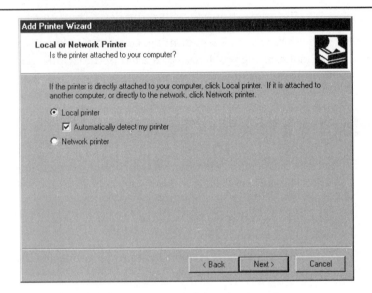

2. If you're using a Plug-and-Play printer, you can tell Win2K to detect it by clicking the checkbox visible in Figure 11.1. If not, or if you're creating a printer to send output to a file, you will have to tell the Add Printer wizard which port the printer is connected to. Indicate the port the printer is connected to (see Figure 11.2). Most times, the one you want should be fairly obvious—just make sure you've selected the port the printer is plugged into. If you don't see the port you need listed, perhaps if you're setting up support for a network interface printer, then click the Create a New Port radio button and choose Standard TCP/IP Port from the drop-down list. To create a printer that stores print information in a file, choose the FILE option near the bottom of the list. A printer connected to a terminal server client will use one of the TS ports near the bottom of the list. Click Next.

FIGURE 11.2

Choose the printer's
port from the list.

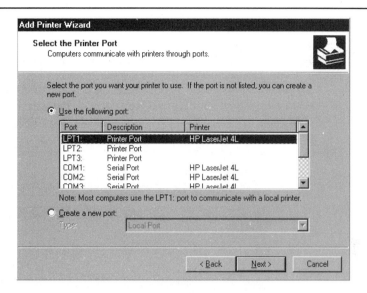

3. Next, you'll choose the driver needed for your particular printer. From the list presented, choose the printer's manufacturer from the left and the printer model from the right. By default, Win2K will use its own printer driver. If you've got a newer one from the manufacturer or from the manufacturer's Web site, click the Have Disk button and provide the path to the driver. If the Win2K server is connected to the Internet, you can alternatively click the Windows Update button to automatically download a newer driver from the Microsoft Web site, if one is available. Click Next.

 TIP If the driver you need is already installed on the system, perhaps for a different printer that you already created, Win2K will ask if you want to use the existing driver or replace it with the new one. Generally speaking, newer is better.

4. After you've chosen a driver to use, the Add Printer Wizard asks you to name the printer using, by default, the printer's model name (see Figure 11.3). The name cannot contain a comma, backward slashes, or an exclamation point, but it has few other restrictions. The name you choose can be quite long—up to 220 characters—but I don't recommend making the name any longer than is strictly necessary to be descriptive. Click Next to move on.

TIP Keep printer names short. First, if you're ever connecting to or managing the printer from the command line, do you really want to have to type "This is the printer by the coffee machine; it's got a single paper tray and faces west" when prompted for the name of the printer? Even identifying the printer in the Printers dialog box is harder if all the printers have overly long names, because the names get cut off in the display. Second, some applications can't work with a name longer than 31 characters. If you can't fully identify a printer without creating a long name, you can always add a location and printer description, as I'll describe in a moment.

FIGURE 11.3

Choose a local name for the printer.

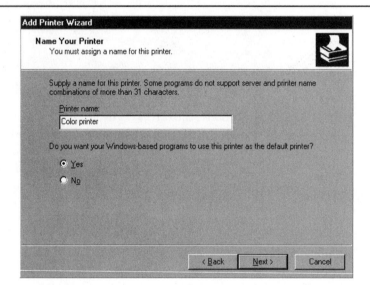

5. Next, if you're sharing the printer, choose a share name for it. If the name you've given the printer has more than one word or a forward slash, the wizard will delete the spaces and combine the words until it has a single word up to eight characters long (see Figure 11.4). The reason for this is backward compatibility: DOS clients won't be able to connect to printers with names more than eight characters long or with spaces.

   If you don't have DOS clients to worry about, you can make a new name for the printer. Once again, the name may be up to 220 characters long and include spaces, but it can't contain commas, backward slashes, or exclamation points.

By default, the Add Printer Wizard will make a DOS-compatible name for the printer.

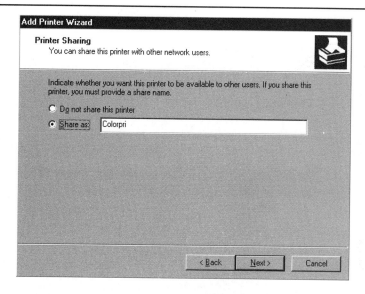

6. In the next stage of the installation, you'll have a chance to describe the printer and location (see Figure 11.5). The usefulness of these descriptions varies. All clients (DOS, NT, Windows 9*x*) will display the information you enter into the Comment text box, but they won't be able to display what you enter into the Location box. Win2K clients will be able to display both. Therefore, unless your network is composed entirely of Win2K servers and clients, all important information should go into the Comment box. Click Next to move to the next screen.

Only Win2K clients will be able to see all the descriptive information you enter here.

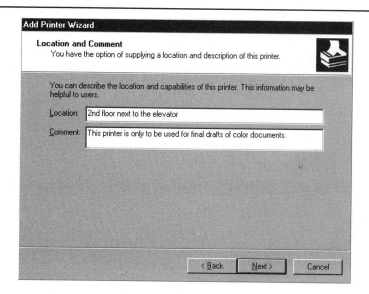

7. The next screen asks whether you'll want to print a test page when you're done. Choose the Yes or No radio button and click Next.

8. The final screen in the information-gathering part of the Add Printer Wizard (see Figure 11.6) shows the options that you entered at each stage so you can go back and change options if necessary. Review your choices and click the Finish button if you want to keep the settings.

FIGURE 11.6

Review your choices before committing yourself with the Finish button.

9. The Add Printer Wizard will prompt you for the location of the setup files. Put the Win2K installation CD in the CD-ROM drive, or provide the path to the installation files if you copied them to disk. Win2K will copy the drivers needed and, if you told it to do so, print the test page.

At this point, you've got one printer for one print device. If you'd like to create a second printer—perhaps to configure a different set of permissions for it—you can do so in the same way you created the first printer. Follow the procedure I just described, making sure you do two things:

- Give the new printer a different local name and share name.

- Choose the exact same settings (port, printer manufacturer and model, etc.) you chose for the first printer.

Sending documents to the new printer will cause them to print on the same print device. The only difference will lie in the configuration options you set for the new printer.

Preparing for Web Printing

One of Win2K's new features is its support for Web-based printing, allowing users to print or manage documents from their Web browser. This takes a little more preparation than standard network printing, but it can be handy for providing Win2K clients with remote access to your printers without providing access to your LAN. I'll show you how this works in the section "Getting the Printer to the Clients," but for now, keep in mind that instead of providing the server name, clients connecting to the printer for Web support will give the printer's URL.

In case it's not obvious, for a print server to support Web-based requests, the print server must also be a Web server. For a Win2K Server print server, this means that you'll need to install the Internet Information Services (IIS) on the print server and run the service. (Win2K Professional print servers will use the Personal Web Server.)

Once you've got IIS installed, open the Internet Services Manager in the Administrative Tools program group. All the Web servers in the domain will be listed below the Internet Information Services folder. Find the Web print server in this list. Within its Default Web Site folder, look for the Printers folder. At this point, your management console should look something like the one in Figure 11.7.

FIGURE 11.7

Find the Printers folder for your Web printer.

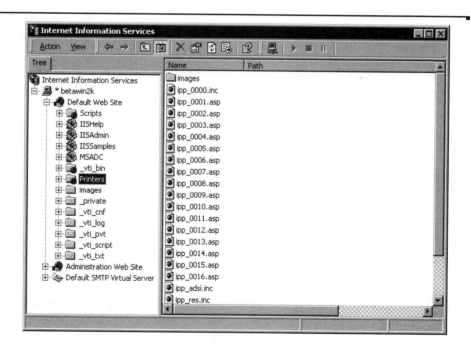

Now, right-click the Printers folder and choose Properties from the context menu that appears. You'll see a tabbed property sheet like the one in Figure 11.8.

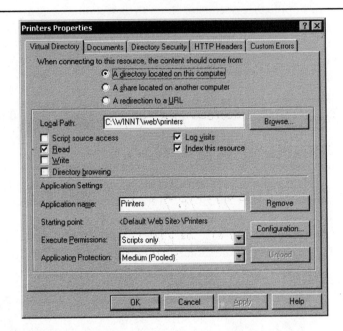

FIGURE 11.8

The property sheet for the Printers *folder*

On the Virtual Directory tab shown here, make sure the entry points to the right information for printing. Secure access to the printer from the Directory Security tab (see Figure 11.9).

User authentication is set from the Authentication Methods dialog box (see Figure 11.10), accessible from the Directory Security tab when you click the Edit button for Anonymous Access and Authentication Control. Web folders may be set up for anonymous access, using the terminal server account, with the privileges assigned to that account. Edit this account to use any domain account by clicking the Edit button and browsing for a new account to use (see Figure 11.11).

Alternatively, you can require that anyone connecting to the printer via the Web get authenticated on the network first. Set up the Printers virtual folder for basic authentication if you want people to be able to manage printers from any browser. Win2K will fuss at you for choosing this option because it sends passwords in clear (unencrypted) text, but if you choose Kerberos (Integrated Windows authentication) or challenge/response (Digest authentication) for greater security, you'll limit yourself to managing printers from Internet Explorer 4 or later. By default, authentication will be based on the domain that the Web printer is part of; to choose a different domain, click the Edit button and browse for the domain you want to use. If the box in the Browse dialog box is blank, the local domain will be used for authentication.

FIGURE 11.9

Printer Security settings

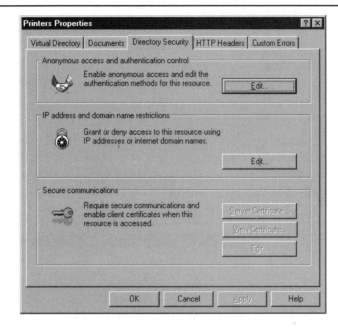

FIGURE 11.10

Choose an authentica-tion method for Web print management.

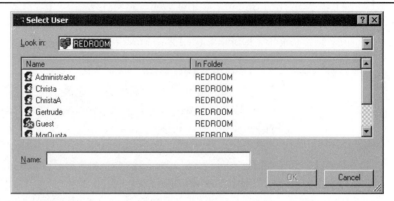

FIGURE 11.11

You can choose a different account for people accessing the Printers *folder.*

Another method you can use to restrict access to a Web printer is to permit only members of a particular domain or only those with a specific IP address. To do so, go back to the Directory Security tab and click the Edit button for IP Address and Domain Name Restrictions. You'll see a dialog box like the one in Figure 11.12.

FIGURE 11.12

A list of permitted or forbidden domains and networks

When you first open this dialog box, no one will be specifically denied or granted access. (Note that you can use this dialog box to either explicitly permit or deny access.) To add an entry to the list, first click the appropriate radio button to indicate whether you're adding a "denied" entry (the Denied Access radio button) or a "permitted" entry (the Granted Access radio button). When you've made your choice, click the Add button to open the dialog box in Figure 11.13.

TIP Be sure to pick the right radio button (Granted Access or Denied Access) before you define the IP address to which you're permitting or denying access. Otherwise, you'll have to re-create the entry.

Choose the domain name, IP address, or network to which you want to permit or deny access to the Web printer.

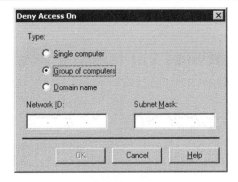

To permit or deny a single IP address, use the Single Computer option. Of course, if that single computer is getting its IP address from a Dynamic Host Configuration Protocol (DHCP) server, this option won't always apply to the same computer. A more effective method of restricting printer access is to define access for a group of computers, using the network IP address and the subnet mask (when you click each option, the boxes to fill in change accordingly). You *can* also permit or deny access to the computer based on domain membership, but this is an expensive operation. If you identify a domain by name, the name must be resolved on both ends of the connection before the Web server can identify the domain, and this will slow down print jobs considerably.

Once you've identified the computer(s) for which you want to permit or deny access to the Web printers folder, they'll appear in the list in the IP Access and Domain Name Restrictions dialog box, as shown in Figure 11.14. Permitted addresses will have a key icon; denied addresses will have a lock icon.

List of networks permitted access to the `Printers` folder on the Web server

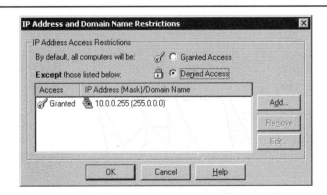

How fast *is* Web printing? The protocol used in Web printing depends on whether the printer is available on the LAN or on a WAN. Web printing uses the Internet Printing Protocol (IPP), encapsulated within the Hypertext Transfer Protocol (HTTP) used for browsing the Web. Printers on the local LAN will use the faster remote procedure calls (RPCs) to send jobs to the printer, just as they do for traditional print jobs.

Using Client-Side Printers in a Terminal Server Environment

When the Terminal Services Edition of Windows NT was first released, the display protocol—the protocol downloading application output to the client machines and uploading keystrokes and mouse clicks to the server—had some holes in it. Remote and local sessions didn't share a Clipboard, so you couldn't cut and paste between applications running on the client and those running on the server. Remote control of sessions wasn't supported. Session clients couldn't use their locally connected printers without sharing them from the network and then connecting to them from the terminal server session.

Win2K filled some of these holes, including the problem of getting local access to client-side ports. Using the new desktop client, clients can access their local printer from a terminal server session without sharing the printer with the network. The only catch is that it's not quite as simple as that for all clients.

 TIP Win2K supports redirected client-side printers connected to COM and LPT ports, not those connected to USB ports. To redirect a USB printer, you'll need to use NCD's Thin-Path Plus! add-on to terminal services, available for free download from NCD's Web site at www.ncd.com.

Win32 (Windows 9*x*, NT, and Win2K) desktop client print requests sent to local printers will be automatically redirected to the local printer so long as you've previously installed the driver needed for the printer on the terminal server. You'll have to manually configure Windows terminals and Win16 clients to use locally attached printers.

Automatically Redirecting Printers

Other than making sure the driver is installed on the terminal server, you don't have to do anything to set up an automatically redirected printer. When a person with a client-side printer logs onto a terminal server and initiates a session, a fake print job owned by the Administrator is sent to the printer. This isn't a real print job, just a notice to the printer that it's being redirected for use with the terminal server session—you'll probably never notice it if you don't deliberately look at the status box for the printer during the second or two required for the redirection to take place. If you look in the Printers folder for the terminal server session, you'll see the redirected printer there, identified by its name, the name of the computer it's connected to, and the number of the terminal server session. For example, the printer HPLaser that's connected to the computer MONSTER, using Session ID4, will be identified in the Printers folder as HPLaser\MONSTER\Session 4. No one else on the network will see this printer unless you've shared it with the network.

If the printer *doesn't* automatically redirect, check the System event log on the terminal server to find out why. One possible problem is that you forgot to install the printer driver on the terminal server. Another is that the printer isn't properly installed on the client or is plugged into a USB port. As you'll recall, Win2K's terminal services cannot redirect client-side printers connected to USB ports. You'll need NCD's ThinPath Plus! to redirect USB printers.

Manually Redirecting Printers

Win16 clients and those using Windows-based terminals will need to manually redirect printers. As of this writing, this isn't possible with a WBT since the RDP client for WBTs hasn't yet been updated to version 5 (version 4 does not support redirection of client-side printers). However, the Windows CE RDP client should be updated soon so you can upgrade your WBT printer clients.

 NOTE You cannot manually redirect a printer connected to a USB port.

To manually redirect a printer for a terminal services client, follow these steps:

1. Get the name or IP address of the client device. (If your Window's terminals don't use names—not all do—you'll need to use the terminal's IP address.) Start a terminal session from that client machine.

2. Start the process of manually adding a locally connected printer to the terminal server.

3. In the part of the wizard where you're choosing the port the printer is connected to, scroll down in the list until you see the name or IP address of the client computer with the printer attached, like this:

   Ts002 CLIENTPC LPT1

4. Choose that port to attach the printer to, and install the printer normally.

When a client disconnects or logs off a session, the printer queue is deleted and any incomplete or waiting print jobs are deleted. Once you have manually redirected a printer for a terminal session, that redirection will take place automatically thereafter, and the print queue will be automatically created from the information stored on the client.

Preventing Printers from Being Redirected

But what if you don't want clients to use their local printers during terminal server sessions? You may not, especially if the client is connecting to a printer across a dial-up connection. Sending a print job from terminal server to client-side printer may be acceptable at LAN speeds but unwise over a 56Kbps modem connection. Or, you may want people to use a networked printer for their terminal server sessions for auditing purposes. Whatever the reason, you want to disable printer redirection.

To prevent printer redirection on a per-user basis, open the user's account profile in the Active Directory or in the Local Users and Groups section of the MMC. Open the user's property sheet and turn to the Environment tab. On that tab is a section called Client Devices, underneath which are three checkboxes that control whether that person has access to client-side drives and client-side printers and whether that client should automatically print to the client-side default printer. By default, all three boxes are checked, enabling all client-side printers and drives. To keep the client's printer from being redirected to the terminal session, deselect the box that says Connect Client Printers at Logon. To permit the user to redirect client-side printers but to keep the default printer from changing to the client-side default, deselect the box that says Default to Main Client Printer.

If you don't want *anyone* connecting to the terminal server via a given display protocol to use their local printers, you can do this as well. Open the Terminal Services Configuration tool that's in the Administrative tools section of the terminal server. Click the Connections folder in the left-hand pane so that the installed display protocols (only RDP, unless you have MetaFrame installed) appear in the right. Open the property sheet for RDP and turn to the Client Settings tab.

There are two sections on this tab. The Connection section on the top is a duplicate of the Client Devices section of the per-user Environment properties discussed above. By default, the per-user settings control, but if you want to apply the settings discussed above not just to individual users but to everyone using the display protocol, you can deselect the option that says Use Connection Settings from User Settings and edit the entries accordingly. The section at the bottom of the Client Devices tab controls which client-side resources are disabled. Disable client-side printing as follows:

- To prevent users from redirecting any client-side printers, deselect Windows printer mapping.
- To prevent terminal users from redirecting client-side printers attached to parallel ports, disable LPT port mapping.
- To prevent terminal users from redirecting client-side printers attached to serial ports, disable COM port mapping.

Mass Printer Migrations

What if you're moving printers from one server to another? You might think that you'd have to re-create each printer and configure its settings on the new printer, but luckily for those with many printers, there's an easy way to move the printer settings to the new server.

1. Open the `Services` folder in the Services and Applications section of the Computer Management tool, and stop the Print Spooler service, which sends print jobs to the printer.

2. From the print server, open REGEDT32, the native Win2K Registry Editor. (This won't work with REGEDIT—you'll be using some REGEDT32-only functionality.)

 TIP If you're editing a remote print server, first map a drive to the remote server so you can easily save files.

3. In HKLM\SYSTEM\CurrentControlSet\Control\Print, there's a key called `Printers`. If you open this key, you'll see a folder for each local (not networked) printer already created on the print server.

 NOTE Network printers will show the name of their server and have two commas in front of their key's name, like this: `, , SERVER1,HP5`.

4. Select the `Printers` key and choose Save Key from the Registry menu, saving the key as text.

5. Run REGEDT32 from the new printer server and highlight that `Printers` key. Choose Restore from the Registry menu and select the file to which you saved the other `Printers` key.

6. Restart the Print Spooler service on the new print server.

You've now replaced the present contents of the `Printers` key with all the Registry settings for the printers installed on the other print server. The only thing you have to do now is make sure the drivers you need are installed on the new server.

Configuring Printer Settings

The printer connection is set up, but that's generally not the end of the story. You haven't yet added support for separator pages used to help dozens of printer users from picking up each other's documents, and you haven't configured messaging so the right people get printer messages. And what about setting up printer priorities so that Win2K will print user documents on the right printer, without user intervention?

 NOTE The options described in this section apply to both network and locally connected printers.

To configure a printer's settings, right-click its icon in the printer's property sheet and choose Properties from the pop-up menu that appears (see Figure 11.15).

FIGURE 11.15

Use this dialog box to fine-tune a printer's settings.

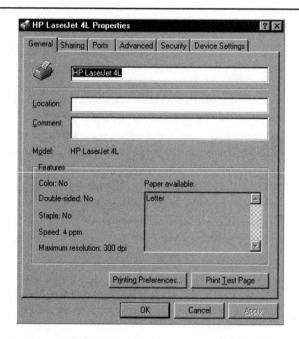

Most of the basic configuration options, such as name changes and sharing, are pretty self-explanatory once you look at the screen. I'll go over the more complex options, but if you're trying to figure out where an option is configured, refer to Table 11.2 for a quick guide to what's where.

TABLE 11.2: PRINTER OPTIONS AND LOCATIONS

Option to Change	Location	Reason to Edit
Add more client drivers	Additional Drivers dialog box, available from the Sharing tab	Load drivers for printer clients so they can be automatically downloaded to the client (available for 32-bit Windows only).
Add more ports	Ports tab	Restore ports that you've deleted or add support for direct network connections to the printer.
Change port time-outs	Ports tab when you click the Configure Port button	Increase port time-out settings to make ports wait longer to receive printer data. Helps if the print job isn't getting to the printer quickly enough.
Edit printer settings	Device Settings tab	Edit the printer settings, including the amount of memory installed, fonts installed on the printer, page protection, and the like.
Edit user or group permissions to the printer	Security tab	Edit the list of users or groups with access to the printer or change the permissions they have.
Set the hours printer will accept print jobs	Advanced tab	Edit to shut off a printer after certain hours, perhaps when the workday is over.
Identify local printer name	General tab	Use for printer identification.
Identify network printer name	Sharing tab	Use for printer identification.
Set the page order	Layout tab of Printing Preferences dialog box, available from the Printing Preferences button on the General tab or the Printing Defaults button on the Advanced tab	Toggle between printing pages in normal or reverse order.

Continued ▮▶

TABLE 11.2 CONTINUED: PRINTER OPTIONS AND LOCATIONS

Option to Change	Location	Reason to Edit
Set paper orientation	Layout tab of Printing Preferences dialog box, available from the Printing Preferences button on the General tab or the Printing Defaults button on the Advanced tab	Toggle between portrait and landscape orientation of printer output.
Identify the paper source	Paper/Quality tab of Printing Preferences dialog box, available from the Printing Preferences button on the General tab or the Printing Defaults button on the Advanced tab	Choose a different paper tray to print from, perhaps for higher-quality paper or printing from transparencies.
Set the print processor	Advanced tab	Toggle between default print formats (EMF, TEXT, or RAW).
Set the printer spooling	Advanced tab	Toggle between using printer spooling and sending documents directly to the printer.
Edit separator pages	Advanced tab	Specify a new separator page for print jobs.

Creating Multiple-Personality Printers

Sometimes, it's not easy to choose a single set of options for a particular print device. Disparate groups of people are using the printer, and the same permission sets don't really work for all groups. In a situation like this, one easy way to manage access to a print device is to create multiple printers for a single print device. Multiple printers means support for multiple device settings, including:

- Printer names and comments
- Hours the printer is available
- Kind of access to the printer users and groups have
- Default paper tray used

And there are others. Any options that you configure from a printer's property sheet you can fine-tune by creating a second printer for a single print device. Once you've edited the new printer's settings, you can assign printer access to the appropriate people. There's no upper limit on the number of printers you can make for a single print device, although the more printers you make, the more complicated your printer management will be. You can't manage all the printers for a single print device from a single console even though it's only one print device and it's connected to the print server.

The process of adding a second (or third, or fourth, etc.) printer is nearly identical to that of adding the first one. Start the Add Printer Wizard from the Printers folder and follow the instructions as prompted. Just make sure that you choose a new name for the printer and choose the same printer driver the original printer uses.

At this point, you can configure each printer as you see fit, as described in the following sections.

 WARNING Not all options set in a printer's property sheet are printer specific. Port time-outs, for example, apply to any parallel port on the print server. One printer's time-outs will apply to *all* printers.

Defining Port Settings

Port settings control how the print server sends print jobs to its ports. You can't do too much to configure ports other than define which port a printer sends print jobs to and, in the case of parallel ports, how long the printer is willing to wait for an expected print job before reporting an error condition. Unless I say otherwise, you'll be controlling most port settings from the Ports tab (see Figure 11.16).

Assigning a Printer to a New Port

If you move a print device from one port to another, you'll need to edit the device's port settings. Open the printer property sheet, turn to the Ports tab, and check the box next to the correct port. Notice that you can select multiple ports only if printer pooling is enabled.

Not sure what all those ports are? TS ports are printer ports of terminal server sessions. LPT ports are parallel (8-bit) ports. COM ports are serial (1-bit) ports. Finally, any port prefaced with a server name indicates a network connection. The terminal server session ports show the ports attached to currently connected terminal server clients and can be used to manually redirect ports, as described in "Manually Redirecting Printers."

FIGURE 11.16

The Ports tab for a
printer

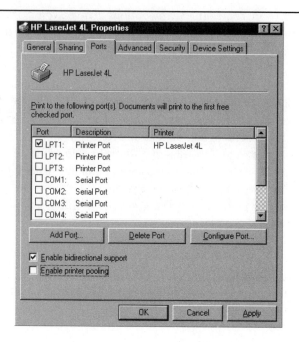

Creating a Printer Pool

As I mentioned in the beginning of this chapter, the ratio of printers to print devices isn't always 1:1. You've already seen how you can create multiple printers for a single print device. I'm talking here about how to make a single printer support multiple print devices.

Why would you want to do this? It's mostly a matter of efficiency. Even with the fast printers (I'm talking about the actual piece of hardware now), busy offices may have more print jobs coming through than one printer can handle. To keep things running smoother and reduce delays, you can distribute print jobs among multiple printers, as shown in Figure 11.17. Print clients will all send their print jobs to the same printer, but the jobs will go to the printer that's least busy at any given time. This is called *printer pooling*.

To set up a printer pool, turn to the Ports tab for the printer. Make sure the box enabling printer pooling is checked, then select all the ports to which printers in the printer pool are attached. These ports can be local ports, ports connected to terminal server clients, or network ports.

There are a couple catches to printer pooling. First, the printers in the pool must be identical to each other—same make, model, and amount of installed memory. Second, I highly recommend putting the pooled printers in the same physical location.

It's not going to endear you to your user base if they have to wander from place to place looking for their print jobs.

FIGURE 11.17

Use printer pooling to reduce printing delays.

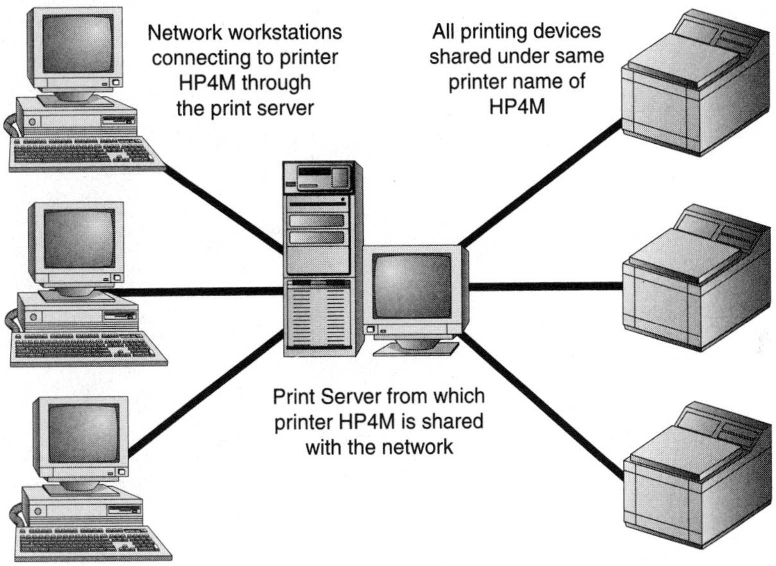

Network workstations connecting to printer HP4M through the print server

All printing devices shared under same printer name of HP4M

Print Server from which printer HP4M is shared with the network

TIP Consider using separator pages in printer pools since users will not necessarily know which printer their job went to.

Sending Documents Directly to the Printer

As I explained in the description of the Win2K printing model at the beginning of this chapter, Win2K normally creates a spool file that's sent to the printer for printing rather than sending documents directly to the printer port. Spooling documents means the application you're printing from is only tied up for the time it takes to create the spool file, not to print the entire document. This is called *printing in the background*.

If you can't use print spooling for some reason—perhaps if the print server's hard disk is so full that it can't create the spool file—then you can send documents directly to the printer port, without creating a spool file or using print server resources. Turn to the Advanced tab of the printer's property sheet and select Print Directly to the Printer, as shown in Figure 11.18.

FIGURE 11.18

Disabling print spooling

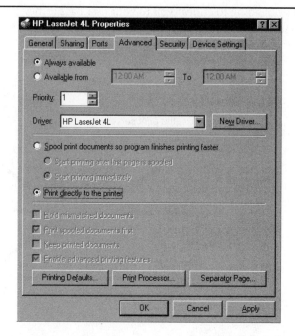

This is not something you'll often want to do. Spool files allow you to print large and complex documents without running out of printer memory. They also allow users to regain control of their applications quicker. Only disable print spooling if you can't print otherwise.

Using Separator Pages

When a lot of people are using the same printer, keeping print jobs organized can get complicated. To help you minimize the number of people who wander off with each other's print jobs, Win2K supports separator pages. These extra pages are printed at the beginning of documents to identify the person doing the printing, the time, the job number, or whatever other information is defined in the page. (I'll explain how you can tell what information a page will print, and how you can create your own custom separator pages, in a minute.)

 TIP Like other printer options, separator pages are assigned to printers, not to print devices, so you can use a different separator page for each printer.

Choosing a Separator Page

By default, printers don't use separator pages. To use one of the default separator pages provided with Win2K, move to the Advanced tab of a printer's property sheet and click the Separator Page button. You'll see a dialog box like the one in Figure 11.19.

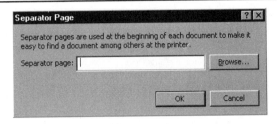

Type the name of the separator page or click the Browse button to open the %*systemroot*%\system32 folder (where the pages are stored) and find the one you want. Table 11.3 describes the four separator pages that come with Win2K.

TABLE 11.3: DEFAULT SEPARATOR PAGES

Page Name	Description	Compatibility
SYSPRINT.SEP	Prints a blank page before print jobs	PostScript
PCL.SEP	Switches a dual-language printer to PCL mode	PCL
PSCRIPT.SEP	Switches a dual-language printer to PostScript mode	PostScript
SYSPRTJ.SEP	Prints a blank page before print jobs sent to a PostScript Printer	PostScript

There's one catch to choosing a separator page: the page must be available locally. Although you can choose a SEP file stored in a network-accessible folder, a separator page that's in a networked location will not print. The system won't fuss at you either when you choose the SEP file or when you send a print job to a printer, but print jobs will have no separator page.

Creating a New Separator Page

Given that the separator pages that come with Win2K are mostly necessary in specific instances, you'll probably want to create your own separator pages if you use them at all. Separator page files are just text files, so you can create the file in Notepad.

On the first line of the new file, type a single character—any character will do— and press Enter. This character will now be the escape character that alerts Win2K that you're performing a function, not entering text, so make it one that you won't need for anything else. Dollar signs ($) and pound signs (#) are both good escape characters, but the only rule is that you can't use the character as text.

Once you've picked an escape code, customize the separator page with any of the variables shown in Table 11.4. Be sure to include the escape character before each function, as I've shown in this table with a dollar sign.

TABLE 11.4: SEPARATOR PAGE FUNCTIONS

Variable	Function
BS	Prints text in block characters created with pound signs (#) until you insert a $U. Be warned—printing text like this takes up a lot of room. You probably don't want to use this option.
$D	Prints the date the job was printed, using the format defined on the Date tab of the Regional Options applet in the Control Panel.
$E	Equivalent to the Page Break function in Word; all further functions will be executed on a new page. If you get an extra blank separator page when you print, remove this function from the SEP file.
$F*pathname**filename*	Prints the contents of the specified file to the separator page, starting on a blank line. As separator pages are strictly text-only, only the text will be printed—no formatting.
$H*nn*	Sets a printer-specific control sequence, where *nn* is a hex ASCII code that goes directly to the printer. Look in your printer manual for any codes that you might set this way and for instructions on how and when to use them.
$I	Prints the job number. Each print job has a job number associated with it.
$L*xxx*	Prints all the characters following (represented here with *xxx*) until it comes to another escape code. Use this function to print any customized text you like.
$N	Prints the login name of the person who submitted the print job.
$*n*	Skips *n* lines (where *n* is a number from 0 to 9). Skipping 0 lines just moves printing to the next line, so you could use that function to define where line breaks should occur.
$T	Prints the time the job was printed, using the format defined on the Time tab of the Regional Options applet in the Control Panel.
$U	Turns off block character printing.
$W*nn*	Sets the line width, where *nn* is a number of characters. Any characters in excess of this line width are truncated. The default (which you don't have to define) is 80 characters.

For example, the following .SEP file

```
$
$N
$0
$D
$L This is a separator page. Only use these pages to organize
$L print jobs because they're otherwise a waste of paper.
$1
$T
```

produces this output:

> Christa
>
> 5/6/99 This is a separator page. Only use these pages to organize print jobs because they're otherwise a waste of paper.

> 3:49:11 PM

Notice that there are only line breaks if you specifically include them. Without the $n codes, all output will be on a single line.

When you're done, save the separator page file with a SEP extension to the %systemroot%\system32 folder if you want to store it with other separator pages. Otherwise, you can store the page anywhere locally available to the print server. To use the new page, just load it as you would one of the defaults.

 WARNING When saving the SEP file in Notepad, be sure to choose All Files in the Save as Type drop-down list. Otherwise, you'll save the file as FILENAME.SEP.TXT and you won't be able to load it as a separator file.

Setting Printer Priorities

You can set printer priorities to give one person's print jobs higher priority than those of others. This can be handy if you're sharing a printer from your Windows 2000 workstation and want to make sure your print jobs have first crack at the printer, or if the print jobs that one group of people create are more important than those most other people are creating. Regardless of priority, all print jobs are scheduled, but the jobs sent to the higher-priority printer will be spooled first to the print device.

Set printer priorities from the Advanced tab of the printer's property sheet (see Figure 11.20). The default value is 1; higher numbers (up to 99) have higher priority.

FIGURE 11.20

Raise printer priorities if you want jobs sent to a certain printer to be processed first.

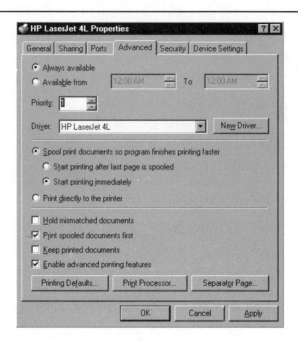

You can only set one priority on a single printer—you can't set one priority for one group, a second for a particular user, and a third for yet another group. Instead, you'll need to create one printer for each set of priorities you want to assign.

Adjusting Print Server Settings

To edit server-wide printer settings, open the `Printers` folder, make sure that no installed printers are highlighted, and choose File/Server Properties. You'll see a dialog box like the one in Figure 11.21.

 TIP To make sure you're editing server-wide settings, highlight the Add Printer icon in the `Printers` folder before choosing Server Properties from the File menu.

Choosing Form Settings

Win2K spaces its print jobs based on forms, which define a template for where text should appear. Win2K comes with a long list of predefined forms (see Figure 11.22) you can choose from, but it also allows you to define your own form settings for customized needs such as printing to company letterhead.

FIGURE 11.21

Edit server properties to change settings that apply to all printers.

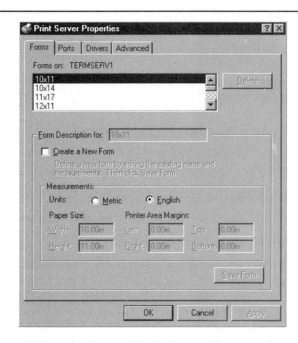

FIGURE 11.22

Server-wide form settings

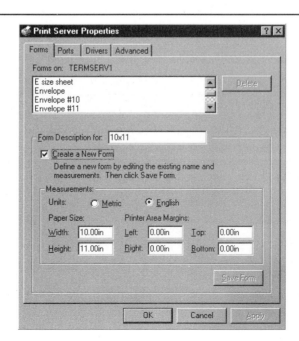

Win2K is set up to print on blank 8.5 × 11 paper (the standard size). To choose a new form, find it in the list. To create a new form, edit the settings in the dialog box, choose a new name for the form, and then click the Save Form button.

 NOTE You must choose a new name for the form. You can't overwrite or delete the forms provided with Win2K.

Configuring Server Port Settings

Although the following settings can be configured from any printer's property sheet, I think it's less confusing to edit them in the server properties. That way, you're reminded that the settings you make here apply not just to a single server but to all affected servers.

Adding and Deleting Ports

Most people won't need to add or delete ports, but here's how you do it if you need to.

1. Open the print server's property sheet and turn to the Ports tab. You'll see a list of the currently installed ports.

2. Click the Add Port button to open the Printer Ports dialog box.

3. Click the New Port button and provide a name for the port in the text box that appears, then click OK.

4. Back in the Printer Ports box, click Close to return to the Ports tab.

The new port should appear in the list of installed ports.

 NOTE Add COM ports if you've got a multiport serial adapter and will support more than four serial printing connections. Add network ports if you're supporting a printer connected directly to the network.

This will add a new port listing to HKLM\Software\Microsoft\Windows NT\ CurrentVersion\Ports—no reboot required.

To delete a port, just select it in the list and click the Delete Port button. You'll be prompted to confirm that you really want to delete the port. When you do so, the port listing will immediately disappear from the Registry.

Oops! I Deleted a Port I Was Using!

It is easy to replace accidentally deleted parallel ports. Click the Add Port button and choose to add a local port. Give the port the appropriate name (such as LPT1) and you're done.

It is *not* so easy to replace an accidentally deleted serial port. In that case, you'll need to add the port, then edit the Registry to define it as a serial port. Add the port as described earlier, then open REGEDT32 and move to HKLM\Software\Microsoft\ Windows NT\Current Version\Ports. Find the value for the port you deleted, then double-click it to edit its value to **9600,n,8,1**. Unless you deleted every COM port, you'll have other COM port values there for reference.

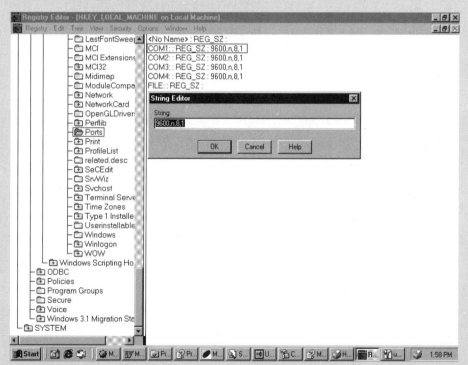

Parallel, file, terminal client, and network connections have no values in the Registry—just entries.

Editing Port Time-Outs

A print device connected to a parallel port (identified as LPTx) will wait a certain interval from the time it expects to receive a print job to the time it gets it. If the print device doesn't get the job within that time, it will notify the person sending the print job that there's an error. Technically speaking, it's not the printer that's complaining, but the parallel port.

You can adjust the interval of time that a parallel port will wait before complaining that it hasn't yet received an expected print job. Turn to any printer's Ports tab, select a port, and click the Configure Port button. You'll see a dialog box like the one in Figure 11.23.

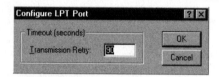

The normal time-out period is 90 seconds. Raise or lower this value by typing in a new number. The lower the value, the more sensitive the port will be to delays. Higher values may make the printer more forgiving of transmission delays, but if you do have a real problem printing, it will take longer for you to discover this.

Adding or Updating the Printer Driver

One of the cool things about using Win32 clients for network printing is that you don't have to install local driver support anymore. This really speeds up the client installation process and makes it easier to update drivers since you no longer have to run from workstation to workstation with the new disk.

For this to work, however, you *do* need to install support for those clients on the server end so that the client can access them as necessary. Drivers are added on a server-wide basis—if you have more than one printer of the same type connected to your print server, you'll update all drivers at once, not just the ones that printer is using.

To add a driver:

1. Turn to the Drivers tab of the printer server's property sheet. You should see a list of installed drivers that looks like the one in Figure 11.24.

2. Click the Add button on this screen to start the Add Printer Driver Wizard. Click through the opening screen to the point where you can choose the manufacturer and printer model you're adding support for.

FIGURE 11.24

Drivers previously installed on the server

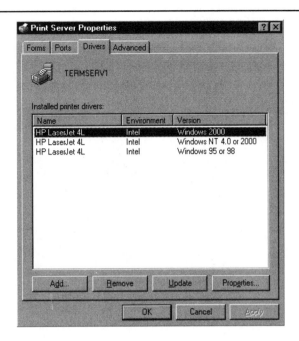

 TIP The list of available printer drivers includes only those that come on the Win2K installation CD. If you've got an updated driver, click the Have Disk button and provide the path to the driver file.

3. From the list that appears (see Figure 11.25), choose all the Win32 clients that will be connecting to this printer from the network. Win2K supports drivers for the following operating systems and platforms:

- Alpha (NT versions 3.1–4)
- Intel (Win2K, NT versions 3.1–4, Windows 9*x*)
- PowerPC (NT versions 3.51 and 4)
- MIPS (NT versions 3.1–4)

 NOTE Remember, the fact that DOS and Windows 3.*x* drivers aren't listed doesn't mean that you can't print from those clients. It just means that those drivers are not included with Win2K, and the clients will need to have them locally available.

FIGURE 11.25

Choose the clients that you'll need to support.

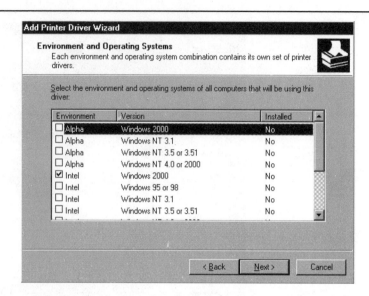

FIGURE 11.25

Choose the clients that you'll need to support.

4. When you click Next, you'll see the wizard's final screen, telling you what driver support you have added.

Updating a driver is simpler:

1. From the Drivers tab of the server's property sheet, highlight the driver you want to update and click the Update button. Win2K will ask you whether you're sure you want to update the driver.

2. You'll be prompted for the location of the driver files—either the installation CD or a floppy or network connection.

That's it—the driver's updated.

 TIP Not sure where to get driver updates? Forget any floppy disks that came with your hardware—those drivers are apt to be very out-of-date. Instead, go to the printer manufacturer's Web site and look for a Downloads section. The most recent drivers should be available there.

Keeping Track of Your Printing

Win2K offers some messaging and logging capabilities that you can use to monitor the printing process or refer to for troubleshooting when something's not going right. To configure these capabilities, turn to the Advanced tab of the server's property sheet (see Figure 11.26).

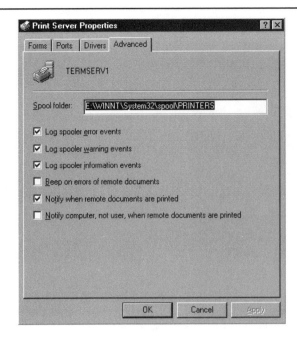

Most of these options are fairly self-explanatory. The spooler error, warning, and information events go into the logs visible from the Event Viewer. They don't record every print job sent to the printer (thank goodness, or you'd end up with a huge event log), only spool events.

Messaging is configured from the same tab. By default, the person originating a print job gets a message when the print job is completed or if there's a problem with it. You can disable messaging here, send the error message to the *computer* originating the job, or set up the print server to beep when there's a printing error. Most of the time, the default options will work fine.

Managing Printer Availability

I suppose it would be nice if someone could actually *use* this printer you've set up so carefully. Read on to learn how to connect a variety of clients to the printer, as well as how to tweak the printer's browse settings.

Getting the Printer to the Clients

The method you use to connect a client workstation to a networked printer depends on the operating system the client is using. DOS clients have to connect from the command line and need locally installed drivers, 16-bit Windows clients can connect from the graphical interface and need their own drivers, and 32-bit Windows clients connect from Network Neighborhood or My Network Places and don't even need locally installed printer drivers.

NOTE As you may recall, 16-bit Windows is not an operating system, it's a graphical operating environment for DOS. All DOS workstations must have locally installed printer drivers. You may need to install the driver more than once or install it to application directories to make sure the applications see the printer. You'll also need to manually update drivers should new versions become available (unlikely as that is).

Connecting from DOS

To set up LPT1 from DOS, type **net use lpt1:*server**printername*** at the command prompt, where *server* is the name of the Win2K print server and *printername* is the name of the printer. If you want to reconnect to this printer every time you log on to the network, add the /persistent:yes switch to the end of the command. Just typing **/persistent** won't do anything, but if you leave off the switch altogether, the connection will default to the persistency settings previously defined.

TIP Not sure of the name of the print server or the printer? Type **net view** at the command prompt to see a list of all servers. Type **net view *servername*** to see a list of all resources shared from that server.

For example, suppose you're setting up network printer support for a DOS workstation that does not have a locally connected printer. Some older DOS applications don't give you a chance to select an output port—it's their way or the highway. Therefore, you'd like to automatically redirect *any* output sent to LPT1 to be intercepted by the network-accessible printer HP5 attached to the Win2K server BIGSERVER. You want to remake this connection every time you log on to the network so that you don't have to worry about printer support.

The command to fulfill this set of conditions would look like this:

```
net use lpt1 \\bigserver\hp5 /persistent:yes
```

Connecting from Windows 3.x or Windows for Workgroups

To connect to a shared printer from network-enabled Windows or from Windows for Workgroups, select the Printers icon in the Control Panel. You should see a dialog box that shows the printer connections you already have, like the one in Figure 11.27.

FIGURE 11.27

A list of installed printers for Windows for
Workgroups

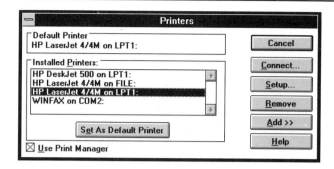

What you do from here depends on whether you're just reconnecting to a previously established network connection, creating a new network connection to a
printer you can support, or starting at the beginning by installing local support for
the printer.

Connecting to an Available Printer To connect to any of these previously connected printers, you'd just click the Connect button to open the dialog box shown in
Figure 11.28. Click OK, and you're done.

FIGURE 11.28

Connecting a Windows
for Workgroups client
to a previously
installed network
printer

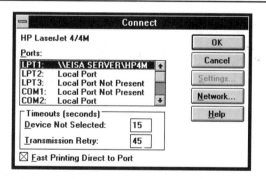

Creating a New Network Connection If you're connecting to a new printer, then
instead of clicking Connect, choose the Network button to open the dialog box
shown in Figure 11.29. Find the print server and printer you want and click OK.

Installing a Printer Driver for Win16 Operating Systems If you haven't already
installed support for the printer, you've got a couple steps ahead of you. Rather than
clicking the Connect or Network button, click Add to see a list of installed printers
and available printer types (see Figure 11.30).

FIGURE 11.29

Creating a new connection to a networked printer

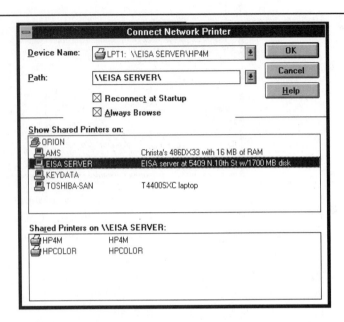

FIGURE 11.30

A list of available printer types

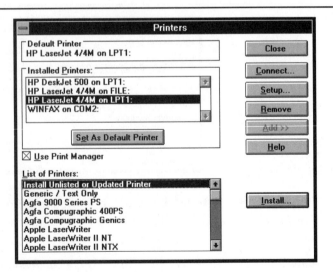

Find the printer you want from the list and click the Install button. The system will prompt you for the location of the printer drivers. Browse for the drivers or insert the requested disk. Once you've installed the correct driver, you can create the network connection to the printer and connect to it.

Connecting from Windows 95 or NT Clients

The first time I connected to an NT printer from an NT Workstation back in 1993 (NTW predated Windows 95, you may recall), I thought that I must have missed a step—it was too easy. You don't have to install local driver support at all; just connect to the printer. 32-bit Windows clients don't use locally stored drivers but instead reference the ones you've installed on the server to support them. This not only saves you a step in the process of installing printer support, it makes it much easier to update printer drivers. When there's a new driver out, you don't have to run around to each client with a floppy disk or set up some kind of remote installation script—you just install it to the server, and when the clients connect, they'll use it automatically.

To install a printer from Windows *9x* or Windows NT, open the `Printers` folder, accessible as a shortcut from the Control Panel, and start the Add Printer Wizard. Click the Next button to open the dialog box shown in Figure 11.31.

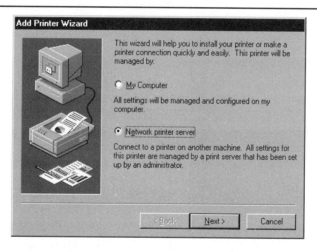

FIGURE 11.31

Specify that the printer is connected remotely, not locally.

Be sure to say that the printer will be managed by a printer server, not locally. Click Next and choose the printer you want from the list, as shown in Figure 11.32. Click Finish and the printer is locally available.

TIP If you want to connect to multiple printers, you must do so one printer at a time.

You can also connect to network-accessible printers from the NT and Windows *9x* Network Neighborhood. Open Network Neighborhood and double-click the appropriate print server. As shown in Figure 11.33, Network Neighborhood will then display all resources shared from that server, including printers.

FIGURE 11.32

FIGURE 11.32

Choose a printer from the list of servers and printers.

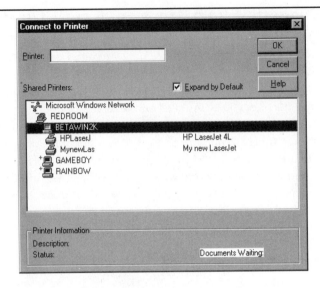

FIGURE 11.33

Installing printer support from Network Neighborhood

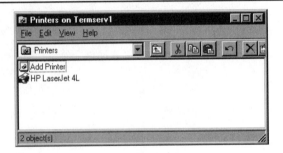

From here, you can right-click the appropriate printer and either capture the printer port (redirecting all output sent to, say, LPT1 to the network printer) or install support for the printer to make it accessible with UNC nomenclature.

Connecting from Win2K

The Add Printer Wizard in Win2K looks a little different from the one in Windows NT or Windows 9x, but the basic effect is much the same:

1. Start the Add Printer Wizard and click through the obligatory Welcome to the Add Printer Wizard opening screen. When asked whether you want to create a local or network connection to a printer, choose the network option, as shown in Figure 11.34.

FIGURE 11.34

When connecting to a
network printer, be
sure to specify the
network connection.

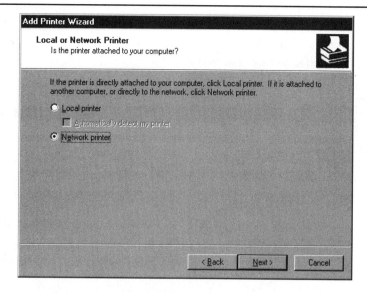

2. Next, indicate the printer's location. What happens here depends on whether your network is using NT 4 domains or the Win2K Active Directory.

If you're connecting from a Win2K computer that's part of an NT 4 domain, then, as you can see in Figure 11.35, Win2K supports connecting to printers either in terms of the printer's name or by an intranet/Internet address, such as `printer.redroom.com`. If you aren't sure of the printer's name, you can leave that space blank and browse for the print server. The browse function doesn't work for printers with their own name or URL; you must enter a valid name for the printer if you choose that option.

 TIP You don't need to enter the name of the server to which the printer is connected, just the printer name.

3. If you choose to browse for a printer, you'll see a browse list like the one in Figure 11.36, showing the printers on the network and the servers they're connected to. As you can see, any location information or comments attached to a printer will show up when you select a printer, so you can easily find the one you want.

If you're connecting from a Win2K computer using the Win2K directory structure, you have another option: searching the Active Directory for the printer you want. Check the box that says Find a Printer in the Directory and click Next, and instead of browsing as described above, you'll open a dialog box from which you can browse for printers by a collection of different criteria and in different parts of the Active Directory (users, computers, domain controllers, and so forth). You can also search for printers based on their name or on other criteria, such as what features they support.

FIGURE 11.35

Type the name of the printer's server or its URL.

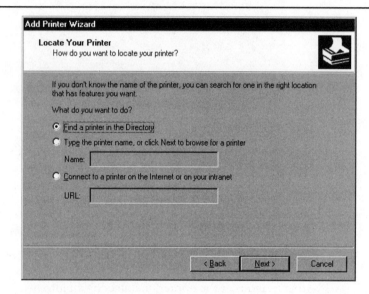

FIGURE 11.36

Scan the list of available printers and choose the one you want to connect to.

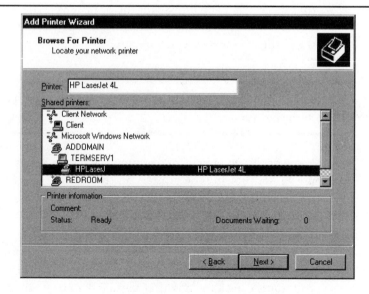

Three tabs in the dialog box for finding printers in the Active Directory include all the search options. From the Printers tab, you can search for printers by name, location, or model number of the printer. From the Features tab, you can look for printers that have certain capabilities, such as double-sided printing, color printing, and stapling. On this same tab, you can specify minimum requirements in pages per minute printed and in the paper sizes the printer supports. The Advanced tab contains the same settings on the Printers and Features tab, only in more detail, allowing you to find printers even if you're not sure of their names and letting you choose from a more defined feature set. Choose the options you want to search for and an area of searching in the In box, and click the Find button.

4. Once you've chosen the printer, the wizard will ask if you want to set up the printer as the preassigned printer for all applications (Figure 11.37). If you've already got a preassigned printer, the default option is No; if this is the first printer connection you're setting up, the default is Yes.

FIGURE 11.37

Specify whether the new printer should be the one all applications choose to print to.

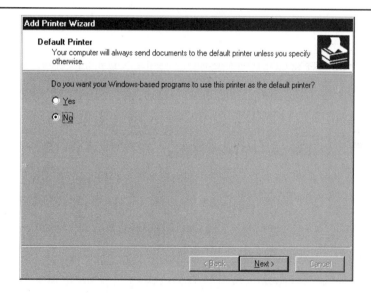

NOTE The default printer will have a check mark next to its icon in the Printers folder.

5. Finally, the Add Printer Wizard will show you the options you've chosen so far, letting you either click Finish to install support or Back to change an option. If you've already got the drivers installed, that's it—you can use the new printer immediately. Otherwise, you'll have to copy the new drivers from the CD or your installation directory.

The printer should appear in the Printers dialog box. Its icon will look like that of a locally connected printer, with the addition of a network connection attached to it.

Securing the Printer

Just because you've networked a printer doesn't mean you want everyone with a domain account to be able to use it. Maybe you'd like to reserve the color printer for people who need to use the more expensive ink, or you want to keep people from printing their resumes after hours. Perhaps it's something as simple as wanting to make sure people connect to the right printer so you're not plagued with people complaining that their job didn't print when they've actually sent five copies to the wrong printer.

 TIP Printer security doesn't always give you the degree of granularity you need to give everyone the permissions they need and no more. Consider setting up multiple printers for each print device, setting different permissions for each, and only giving people access to the printer tuned for their needs.

Setting Available Hours

By default, a printer will always accept print jobs. You can determine the hours during which a printer will send jobs to the print device. If a print job is sent to a printer after hours, the job will be queued but not printed until the printer is again available.

To edit a printer's hours of availability, turn to the Advanced tab of its property sheet (see Figure 11.38) and set new times. All that this does is tell Win2K to hold print jobs in the spooler until the printer is again available, so the new settings won't affect any jobs that have already been sent to the printer.

If you want a print device to be always available to some users and only available during certain hours to others, you'll need to create multiple printers for the single print device. Once you've done so, you can configure the printing hours separately for each printer, with the results as shown in Figure 11.39.

FIGURE 11.38

Define times for the printer to be available.

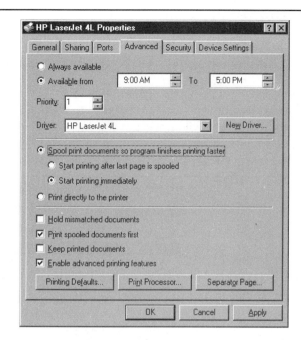

FIGURE 11.39

Restricting printer hours for a specific group of users

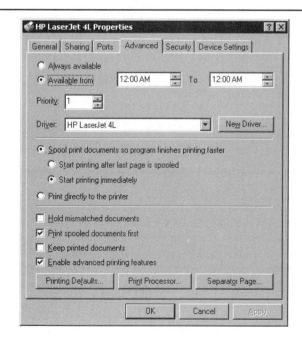

Setting Printer Permissions

Those familiar with the NT/Win2K argot will remember that you secure a Win2K network by defining user rights for what people can *do* on the network and setting permissions for the resources that people can *use*. Printer security is controlled with permissions on a per-group or per-user basis.

To set or edit the permissions assigned to a printer, log on with an account that has Administrator permissions, open the printer's property sheet, and turn to the Security tab. You'll see a dialog box like the one in Figure 11.40.

FIGURE 11.40

Default printer permissions

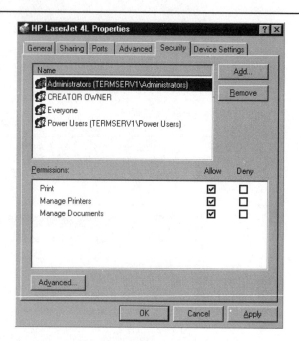

TIP If you turn to a printer's Security tab and see a list of Security IDs (SIDs) instead of user or group names and the cursor changes to an hourglass when over the dialog box, don't panic. The print server is retrieving the names from the domain controller and will show the user and group names after a few seconds. If this doesn't happen—if the SIDs never resolve to user and group names—then there's something wrong with either the domain controller or the connection between the two servers.

From here, you can edit the basic permission sets of the groups for whom some kind of printer access has been defined, denying or granting explicit access in three areas: printing (the ability to send print jobs to the printer), managing print jobs (the ability to control whether a print job is printed or the order in which it's printed relative to other jobs), or managing the printer.

 NOTE Table 11.5 includes a complete list of all permissions and how they apply to printers.

Not sure how to interpret the check boxes? If a permission is checked, then it's explicitly enabled or disabled, depending on which box is checked. If a permission is clear on both sides, then it's implicitly enabled. Shaded permission boxes imply that a permission is granted or denied through inheritance. You can explicitly enable or disable the permission by checking the appropriate box.

Fine-Tuning Printer Access

The first page only shows the default groups and the basic permissions they've been assigned. For more control over the permission process, click the Advanced button to open the dialog box seen in Figure 11.41.

FIGURE 11.41

Setting advanced printer permissions

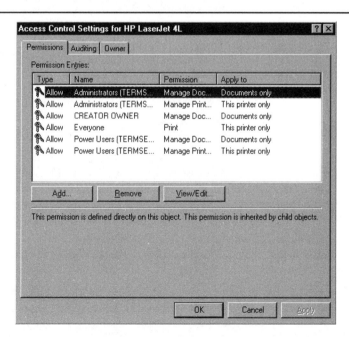

From here, you can see the state of the defined permissions. A key icon symbolizes a granted permission; a padlock symbolizes a denied one. (When you first open this dialog box, you should only see keys—no permissions are explicitly denied by default.) The comment below the list of users and groups notes whether the highlighted permission applies to the basic membership of that group only or to subgroups within that group.

You can adjust these permissions either by adding new users or groups to the list (getting them from the domain controller) or by editing the permissions of the groups already there.

To define permissions for a new user or group, click the Add button. The print server will retrieve a list of users and groups from the domain (or server; you can pick either from the list) displayed in the Look In box. Choose a user or group from the list and click it. You'll open a dialog box like the one in Figure 11.42. The permissions listed here have the characteristics outlined in Table 11.5.

 TIP If the user or group you want isn't displayed in the list, type it into the box. If you've already created an account for this user or group, you'll be able to edit its permissions.

FIGURE 11.42

Defining the permissions of a new user

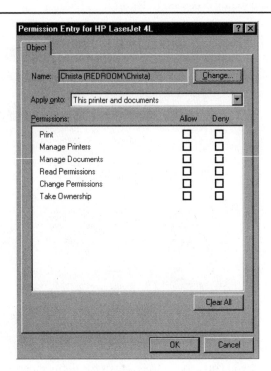

TABLE 11.5: PRINTER PERMISSIONS AND THEIR IMPLICATIONS

Access Type	Effect	Tied To...
Print	User can send jobs to the printer.	Read permissions
Manage Printers	User can change printer properties and permissions.	Print, read permissions, change permissions, and take ownership of the printer
Manage Documents	User can control document-specific settings and pause, resume, restart, and delete spooled print jobs.	Read permissions, change permissions, and take ownership of the printer
Read Permissions	User can see the permissions all users and groups have for that printer.	NA
Change Permissions	User can change the permissions all users and groups have for that printer.	Read permissions (although this won't be checked)
Take Ownership	User can take ownership of the printer.	Any permissions assigned to Creator/Owner of the printer

You can customize user permissions by explicitly permitting some actions and denying others. For example, permission to manage printers normally implies permission to change permissions for that printer. However, you can get around this by allowing printer management while denying the ability to change permissions. This doesn't always work—you can't permit people to print yet deny them the ability to read permissions—but it's worth experimenting to see whether you can get the degree of granularity you want in access permissions.

 NOTE Printer permissions can apply to the printer only, to documents only, or to both the printer and the documents printed on it.

When making your changes, remember how permissions work in Win2K:

- If a person or group is a member of more than one group, the least restrictive set of permissions applies. For example, if Sue is a member of Everyone, who can print documents but may not manage them, but also a member of Power Users, who can manage documents, then Sue can manage documents.

- The only exception to this rule is when an option is explicitly denied. A denied access overrides any other permissions a person may have as a member of another group.

Changing permissions for an existing user or group works in much the same way: select a name, click the View/Edit button, and you'll see the same set of options to explicitly grant or deny permissions.

 TIP If you want to cancel all permission changes for a user or group and start over, click the Cancel button. If you want to remove every granted or denied permission associated with a user or group, click Clear All.

Auditing Printer Access   Curious to know who's doing what to the printers under your care? Turn to the Auditing tab (accessible from the Advanced button of the Security section of a printer's properties) to set up auditing to list events in the event log.

Setting Up Printer Auditing

Win2K does not audit by default. For auditing to work properly, you'll have to first turn on auditing. This is a bit more of a pain than it was in NT 4, but once you get comfortable with the Microsoft Management Console, it'll get easier.

The Group Policy snap-in is an extension of the Computer Management snap-in, and you'll need to make sure you've got it in your management tools.

To enable auditing, run the Microsoft Management Console and add the Group Policy add-in under Computer Management. Under `Computer Configuration\Windows Settings\ Security Settings\Local Policies`, you'll find the `Audit Policy` folder. Enable the logging types you're interested in.

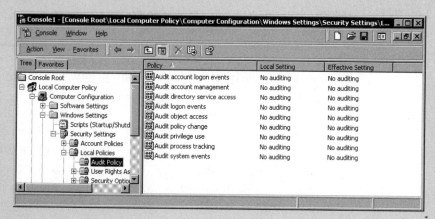

By default, Win2K doesn't log printer use or security events, so the list on the Auditing tab of a printer's property sheet will be empty when you originally turn to it. To add events to audit, click the Add button to move to the dialog box shown in Figure 11.43.

FIGURE 11.43

Choose a group or user to audit.

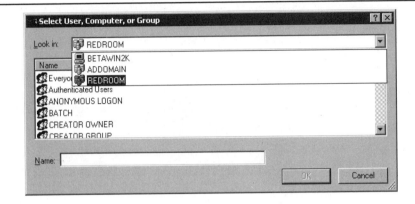

As when setting printer permissions, you'll first choose a group or user to audit from the list, then you'll choose events to audit. After you've chosen a group or user to audit and clicked OK, you'll move to a dialog box like the one in Figure 11.44.

FIGURE 11.44

Choose the events to audit.

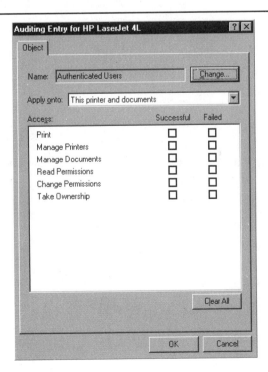

The dependencies shown here work the same way as the ones described in Table 11.5. The main difference is that here you're monitoring the attempts to *do* these things, not granting or denying permission to do them. Also, the Successful and Failed columns aren't mutually exclusive like the Allow and Deny ones are—you can monitor both failed and successful attempts to take ownership of a printer, for example. When you've finished tweaking the auditing options, click OK to return to the main auditing tab, which will now look something like the one shown in Figure 11.45. Entries for these audits will now appear in the Security portion of the event log.

FIGURE 11.45

A list of users and events to audit

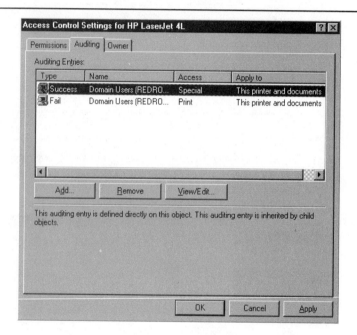

Assigning an Owner to a Printer Administrators can give the printer to a new owner from the Owner tab of the Access Control Settings dialog box accessible from the advanced security options. The options are the person who made the printer in the first place and an administrator of the domain, as you can see from Figure 11.46.

FIGURE 11.46

*A list of possible own-
ers for the printer*

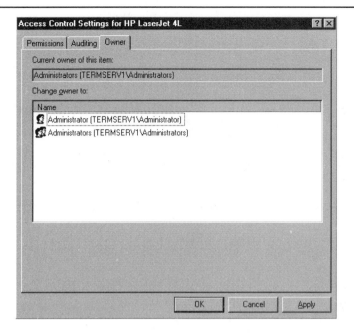

Hiding Shared Printers

The best way to secure any network resource is to conceal the fact that the resource even exists. Printers are no exception to this rule. To keep a shared printer (or any other shared resource, for that matter) out of the browse list, put a dollar sign at the end of its name, like this: PRINTER$. The printer name will not show up in the browse list, but a user who knows that the printer exists and which server it's connected to will be able to connect to it with NET USE, like this:

```
Net use \\servername\printername
```

Setting Printer Publishing Options

The Group Policy settings in the Microsoft Management Console include some policies you can tweak to configure how the printer appears in the Active Directory or in the domain (see Figure 11.47). To get to these settings, open the Group Policy snap-in and move to the Administrative Templates section of the Computer Configuration settings. As you can see from Table 11.6, some of these settings apply only to Win2K clients, but others apply to any client.

FIGURE 11.47

Administrative template printer browsing settings

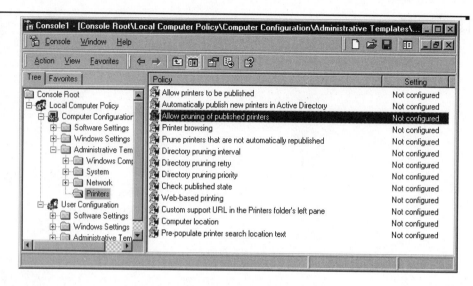

TABLE 11.6: PRINTER PUBLICATION POLICIES

Policy	Description	Default Value (When Non-Configured)
Allow printers to be published	Toggles to allow printers to be published. If a printer isn't published, clients can't find it in the Active Directory. When configured, overrides Automatically Publish New Printers in Active Directory policy.	On (permits publishing)
Allow pruning of published printers	Controls whether the pruning service may remove printers that it can't find when browsing for them. If you enable this option, you can tune it with the pruning interval, retry, and priority policies.	On (will prune)

Continued ▶

TABLE 11.6 CONTINUED: PRINTER PUBLICATION POLICIES

Policy	Description	Default Value (When Non-Configured)
Downlevel Printer Pruning	Controls the circumstances under which a printer connected to a downlevel print server (that is, one running an operating system other than Win2K) will be removed from the browse list. Choosing to prune only if the server is found means the printer will only be removed from the browse list if it's confirmed that the printer is gone. Choosing to prune whenever the printer is not found means the printer can be removed even if it's not confirmed that the printer is gone because the browse service can't find the print server. By default, missing printers will not be pruned. Printers connected to Win2K print servers are not affected by this setting because they're automatically published by default.	Never
Automatically publish new printers in the Active Directory	Controls whether printers are published automatically or whether you have to publish them. If Allow Printers to Be Published policy is set, this policy is ignored.	On (will publish)
Directory Pruning Interval	Determines the interval at which printers that haven't announced themselves recently are removed from the directory of published printers. The pruner reads this value every hour, so changes will not take effect immediately.	8 hours
Directory Pruning Retry	Determines how many times the pruning thread will attempt to contact a print server before giving up and deleting that printer's entry from the Active Directory.	2 tries

Continued ▶

TABLE 11.6 CONTINUED: PRINTER PUBLICATION POLICIES

Policy	Description	Default Value (When Non-Configured)
Directory Pruning Priority	Tunes the priority of the pruning thread, responsible for deleting outdated printer entries in the Active Directory. The higher the priority of the pruner thread (or any thread), the more often it will get CPU cycles and thus the more often the Active Directory will be updated—but the fewer CPU cycles the other threads will get. You can set this value to Lowest, Below Normal, Normal, Above Normal, or Highest.	Normal
Check published state	Verifies that published printers are indeed in the Active Directory. You can set this value to Never (the default) or at varying intervals ranging from 30 minutes to 1 day.	Never
Printer browsing	Controls whether the print subsystem can add printers to the browse list. In a Win2K domain that uses the Active Directory, the print subsystem does not announce printers to the master browsers in the domain. If you disable printer browsing, you prevent the print subsystem from announcing the printers even in an NT 4 domain.	Off in domains using the Active Directory; on in NT 4 domains dependent on browsing to pub-lish resources.

Continued ▶

TABLE 11.6 CONTINUED: PRINTER PUBLICATION POLICIES		
Policy	**Description**	**Default Value (When Non-Configured)**
Prune printers that are not automatically republished	Controls the circumstances under which a printer connected to a computer running an operating system other than Win2K or a printer published outside its own domain may be pruned. Choosing Never means that the printer will never be pruned. Choosing Only When the Print Server Is Found means that the printer will be pruned if the print server is found but the printer isn't available. Choosing Only When the Printer Isn't Found prunes printers that are not automatically republished. This setting applies only to printers published from Active Directory Users and Computers, not from the Printers section of the Control Panel.	
Web-based Printing	When disabled, won't accept print requests sent via HTTP, or publish printers to the Web.	Off
Custom Support URL in the Printer Window's Left Pane	Ordinarily, the left window of the Printers folder displays the Microsoft URL and (if available) the URL for the printer's maker. If you enable this policy and type in a URL, you can point people to a different location—perhaps a customized troubleshooting guide on the company Web site.	Off
Computer location	Identifies the location of the printer server.	Used to help people figure out not only where a printer is, but where the printer server it's connected to is
Pre-populate printer search location text	Enables location tracking (based on the subnet of the printer server and the client) and a browse feature.	On

When you first install Win2K, none of these settings will be configured, so they'll be effectively disabled. You'll need to activate the ones you want to enable. Right-click on a policy and choose Properties from the pop-up list that appears. You'll see a dialog box that looks like the one in Figure 11.48.

Click the check box to check or clear the box. If you need more information about what a policy actually does if enabled, turn to the Explain tab. Once you've chosen to actively clear or check a box, the policy's entry will change from Not Configured to Enabled or Disabled.

 TIP You can run through the list of policies with the Previous Policy and Next Policy buttons without exiting and reentering the policy Properties box. The only catch is that if you cancel out of one policy change, you'll cancel *every* policy change you made while the window was open.

FIGURE 11.48

Configuring print server policies

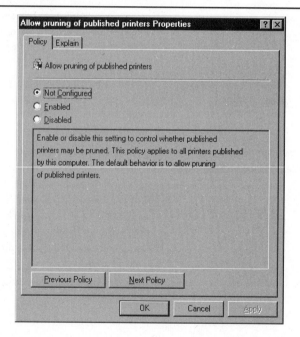

Managing Print Jobs

Managing print jobs is pretty straightforward. If you double-click a printer's entry in the Printers folder, you'll see all print jobs currently waiting to be printed and the following information (see Figure 11.49):

- The filename of the document being printed
- The job's status (printing, spooling, paused)
- Who sent the job to the printer
- How many pages are in the job and how many remain to be printed
- The file size of the print job
- The time and date the user submitted the job

When you select a job in the list, you can use the tools in the Document menu to pause a job, resume a paused job, restart a print job from the beginning, or delete a print job. The only catch is that you have to do all this while the job is still spooling to the print device. You can't control the parts of the job that have already spooled to the physical printer's memory from this console.

FIGURE 11.49

A job waiting to be spooled to a printer

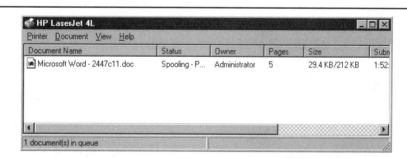

If you pause a print job, you can edit its priority or printing times in the middle of printing. From the Document menu, choose Properties to open the dialog box in Figure 11.50.

From here, you can view many properties inherited from the printer and passed to the job, and you can raise or lower the job's priority. The higher a job's priority, the higher its place in line, so you can use this feature to manipulate the order in which jobs print even if one job got to the printer before another did. This can be very useful on those occasions when the person printing the 200-page manual sends their job before the person creating a cover sheet for the FedEx package that has to be ready by 3:30.

FIGURE 11.50

*Properties of a
print job*

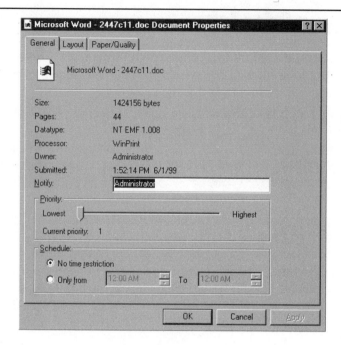

Troubleshooting Printer Problems

Printing under Win2K is usually pretty trouble-free, but every once in a while you may run into problems. The remainder of this chapter describes some of the more common printing problems and tells you how to solve them.

Basic Troubleshooting: Identifying the Situation

First, try to figure out *where* the problem lies. Is it the printer? The application? The network? If you can tell where the problem lies, you'll simplify the troubleshooting process.

TIP The printing problem that frustrates me most is paper jams. Getting that last shred of jammed paper out of the printer can drive you to madness. To minimize paper jams, store paper somewhere with low humidity (curled paper jams easier), don't overfill the paper tray, and keep paper neat before it goes in the tray.

Printer troubles can happen due to any combination of three different causes:

- Hardware errors
- Software errors
- User errors

 TIP One basic part of printer troubleshooting is to make sure the person is connected to the right printer and knows which print device is associated with that printer. Some troubleshooting jobs end with the task of finding the printer with five unclaimed print jobs on top of it.

No One Can Print

If no one can print, check the print device and network connection. Check the easy stuff first: Is the printer on and online? Does the cartridge have ink? Is the printer server up and running? Did the printer *ever* work, or is this its maiden voyage? If it never worked, make sure you've got the right driver installed, or try downloading a newer one from the manufacturer's Web site.

From the console, check the port settings. Is the printer sending data to the port the print device is connected to?

Also, see if you can print from the print server. There could be a network problem preventing people from reaching the print server.

Make sure there's enough space on the print server's hard disk to store spool files. If the print server can't create spool files, it can't print from a spool.

Make sure the printer is set up to use the proper print processor.

Some People Can't Print

What do those people have in common? Are they all in a single subnet? In the same user group? Using the same application? Printing to the same printer? Find the element they have in common, and that's probably the element that's causing the printing problem.

One Person Can't Print

If only one person can't print, try to narrow down the source of the problem. Can the person print from another application? Can the person print from another computer? If this person can't print at all, see if someone else can print from their computer. If so, check the permissions attached to the person who can't print. They may be denied access to the printer altogether.

TIP If only one person is having printing problems, try rebooting the computer and retrying the print job. Some applications (such as Netscape Navigator 4.51) have a problem if they crash in the middle of creating a print file—they won't accept another one because they think the previous job is still being created. Sometimes, this problem will prevent *any* application from printing from that computer. In such a case, the only thing to do is reboot and try again. Logging off and on again won't do it.

Using Online Resources

If you get completely stuck, try the links included in the left-hand pane of the `Printers` folder. (Note that these links will be visible only if you've got Web content enabled. If you disabled Web content to clean up the desktop, you can re-enable it for this folder only by opening Tools/Folder Options and, on the General tab of the Folder Options dialog box, choosing Enable Web Content on My Desktop.)

The More Info link leads to a printer page on the Microsoft Web site at `www .microsoft.com`, the manufacturer's link leads to their printing page (if they have one), and the Microsoft Support link leads to the printing home page in the Microsoft support area of their Web site. (I'd provide the link, but given how often Microsoft rearranges their Web site, by the time you read this it wouldn't be accurate.) If your print server has an Internet connection, you can connect directly from the `Printers` folder, but if not, you can still plug the URLs into a browser to see if the online resources can help you with your question.

 TIP Considering how often Microsoft reorganizes their Web site, you might be better off using the URL policy I described earlier to link to a custom home page with a troubleshooting guide and perhaps the latest drivers. Nothing is more frustrating than being desperate enough to try the Web tool but then discovering the link is dead.

Unglamorous as printing is, it's an essential service for just about any organization. In the previous pages I've talked about how to set up printers for local use or for your network, how to get those printers to the people who need them, and how to keep those printers from those who haven't any reason to be using them. After reading this chapter, you should feel ready to do your part to help keep those recycling bins full.

CHAPTER 12

Connecting Clients to Windows 2000 Server

You've built your server, created your users, and shared your resources. Now you need to get your clients to that server. In this chapter, I'll show you how to set up various workstations with networking components, how to log on to the network, how to connect to shared resources, and, when applicable, how to find and connect to the Windows 2000 Active Directory.

Throughout this chapter, I'm going to use the various operating systems to connect to the same server, on the same domain, and with the same user account.

- My username is bsmith.
- My resource server name is BS01.
- My computer name is BS99.
- My domain is BS.
- My full domain name is BS.COM.

Connecting Windows 95 and Windows 98 Workstations

Connecting a Windows 95 or Windows 98 workstation to the network *can* be an easy thing to accomplish. We have Plug and Play on our side, which (usually) takes the guesswork out of installing the network card, and networking is an inherent capability of our workstation. In other words, the installation and configuration of all networking components does not require us to do much more work or know much more than would be required to simply install the client itself. In contrast, the older Windows 3.*x* clients had a whole slew of manual configurations and additional files to modify: `protocol.ini`, `autoexec.bat`, `config.sys`, `system.ini`, etc. Those older Windows platforms just weren't network ready. Theoretically, installing your networking components in Windows 95/98 *and* making them talk to the server are as easy as point, click, and go—as long as you know where to point and click. The coverage in this section applies to both Windows 95 and Windows 98, as their networking components work nearly identically.

Configuring the Workstation

To start off, I'll assume that your workstation is fully up and running with Windows 95/98 and has no networking components installed. We start in the Network Control

Panel (select Start/Settings/Control Panel, then open up the Network applet). You should see an empty network configuration dialog box like the one shown in Figure 12.1.

FIGURE 12.1

The Configuration tab of the Network Control Panel for Windows 98

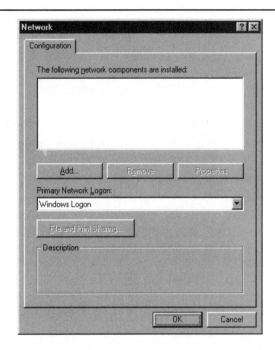

You need to have at least one type of networking *client*, at least one *protocol*, and at least one network *adapter*. Additionally, you can add a *service*, such as file and print sharing. Since you presumably have none of these, you'll press the Add button. You are now asked which type of networking component you wish to add (see Figure 12.2).

FIGURE 12.2

The Select Network Component Type dialog box

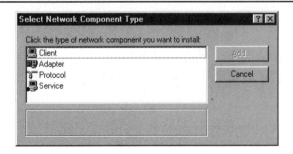

We'll start off by adding an adapter. From the list of component types, select Adapter, then press Add once again to open up the dialog box shown in Figure 12.3.

FIGURE 12.3

The Select Network Adapters dialog box

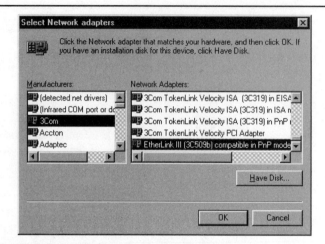

In the Select Network Adapters dialog box, you'll see a list of adapter manufacturers on the left and corresponding adapters on the right. Choose your adapter and press OK. After a quick file copy or two, you'll find yourself back at the Network Control Panel applet. Here's the neat thing: an adapter is useless without both a client to bind to and a protocol to talk with. Windows knows this and installs a set of defaults to make your life easier. In Windows 95, you usually get the Client for Microsoft Networks as your client, and IPX/SPX and NetBEUI as your default protocols. In Windows 98, as you can see in Figure 12.4, you get the Client for Microsoft Networks, but the only protocol listed is TCP/IP.

For convenience' sake, TCP/IP is configured to use DHCP automatically. If you need to change this to reflect the configuration of your particular environment, you can choose the protocol in the Network Control Panel, then select Properties. Likewise, you can configure your network adapter particulars to suit your needs.

FIGURE 12.4

A full complement of networking components is installed by default.

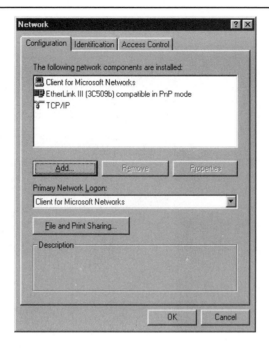

Attaching to the Network

As shown in Figure 12.4, in addition to the Configuration tab, you'll find two additional tabs in the Network Control Panel. Pay particular attention to the Identification tab, which is shown in Figure 12.5.

As you can see, the computer name for me is BS99. The computer name must be unique, just like in Windows NT and Windows 2000 machines. The workgroup is BS.

NOTE BS? My domain is BS. Why is my workgroup BS? The workgroup is where your computer belongs. When you open up your Network Neighborhood, this is where you start. By putting your machine into the same workgroup as your domain, your domain resources will be more readily available to your workstation with less browsing required. Also, if your Windows 95/98 workstation is running a service, such as file and print sharing, it registers itself into the browse list of this workgroup.

FIGURE 12.5

The Network Control Panel's Identification tab

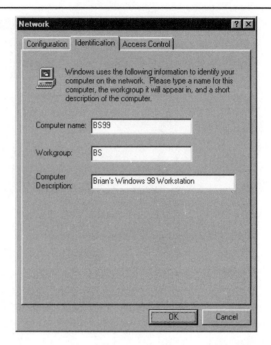

Now we'll talk about our domain. Unlike a Windows NT or Windows 2000 machine, and more like a Windows for Workgroups machine, a Windows 95/98 machine does not have to *belong* to a specific domain in order to log into the domain. This lets us be in one workgroup, but still log into any domain. Back in the Configuration tab of the Network Control Panel, you can specify the properties of your Client for Microsoft Networks by either double-clicking the client, or selecting it once and pressing Properties. You'll see the dialog box shown in Figure 12.6.

By placing a check in the Log On to Windows NT Domain box, you're telling your workstation that you are going to want to be validated with an official domain user account before you get into the operating system. In the Windows NT Domain box, enter the domain where your user account resides .

NOTE Here, you are only specifying that Windows 95/98 require you to log into a domain. Again, Windows 95/98—unlike its Windows NT and Windows 2000 counterparts—is not secure and will not require you to log in to access the workstation. When prompted to log in, you can simply press Cancel, and you're in—to the workstation, but not the domain.

FIGURE 12.6

Client for Microsoft Networks Properties

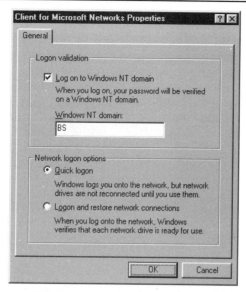

From this point on, you'll get a handy logon-request dialog box every time you boot up your workstation. Changing passwords is a snap too. If your password expires, you'll get a handy little message, along with a separate dialog box in which to change it.

Accessing Network Resources

Now that we're in, we need to find and connect to the resources that drew us to the network in the first place. We're going to find our resources by double-clicking the Network Neighborhood icon on the Desktop (my Network Neighborhood is shown in Figure 12.7).

FIGURE 12.7

Network Neighborhood

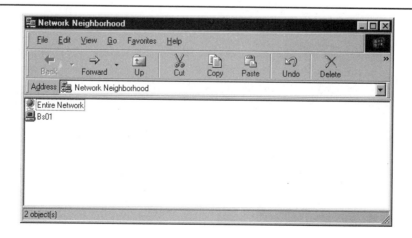

What you are looking at in your Network Neighborhood is your browse list for your workgroup—or domain, if the name is the same. In my domain, BS, BS01 is the only server registering into the browse list. Double-clicking the server reveals a list of shared resources on that server, shown in Figure 12.8.

FIGURE 12.8

BS01 shared resources

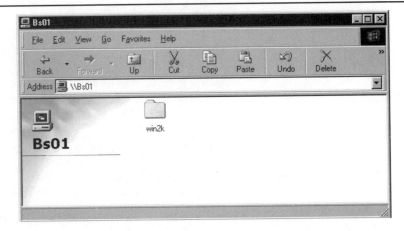

In Figure 12.8, you can see that my only share is win2k. (If you've shared any printers, printer shares will also be visible here.) You can browse deeper into the files and folders of a shared folder, or map a drive directly to the share by right-clicking the share and choosing Map Network Drive. To attach to a printer, you can choose Start/Settings/Printers; from there, choose Add Printer, and select your resource as we did earlier.

Accessing the Active Directory

There's another neat feature for Windows 95 and 98 clients. On the Windows 2000 CD, under the clients directory, is a Win9x directory. In that directory, you will find a single executable, which installs the Directory Service Client for Windows. This Directory Service Client allows your Windows 9x client to see the new Active Directory in Windows 2000. The installation is a simple click-next-to-continue and reboot process. No configuration issues, no selections to make.

Now that we have this Active Directory client installed, exactly what is it that we have? There is no utility that brings up the Active Directory, and there is no new program installed. Most importantly, what we do have are new options and capabilities under the Find menu within the Windows Explorer. A previously unavailable choice in the Find menu is Printers. Another new option is integrated with a new version of the Windows Address Book; it lets you find People published in the Active Directory. (The Windows Address Book is updated during the Active Directory client installations.) Obviously, this little client installation doesn't give you a direct tap into the heart of the Active Directory, but it does give you the essential functionality required to make your Active Directory published resources available to your Windows 9x clients.

Connecting Windows NT Workstations

Windows NT workstations, even more so than Windows 95/98 clients, come networking ready. All of the essential components of networking are inherent to and already included in the basic installation of Windows NT. If you've installed Windows NT, chances are you've already installed all the networking components required to get you going. Just to be on the safe side, we'll walk through the key requirements. This section, like the previous one, will assume that you have a fully functioning operating system, cover the configuration of networking components, and finally, show you how to connect to Windows 2000 resources.

Configuring the Workstation

Windows NT will have almost all of your networking components installed by default—the Workstation service, the Server service, and a dial-up adapter or network adapter if you have either a modem or network card present in your machine. However, you will probably want to revisit all of these options just to make sure you are set up for your particular network. To do this, you need to open the Network Control Panel. Obviously, the foundation of networking lies with a network adapter. So select the Adapters tab. To install your network card, click Add; you will be shown a list of supported network cards, as shown in Figure 12.9.

Selecting a network adapter

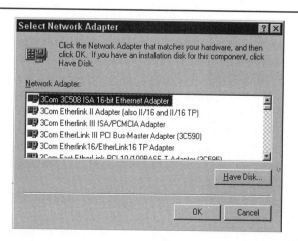

Scroll down to find your network adapter, or select Have Disk to locate a driver or an unlisted—but supported—network adapter. The next step is selecting protocols.

This selection is entirely dependent upon your specific network. To install additional protocols, select the Protocols tab, then select Add. You will be shown a list of supported protocols to select from. To configure an installed protocol, if required (as is the case with TCP/IP), highlight the protocol and select Properties. The TCP/IP properties page is shown in Figure 12.10.

FIGURE 12.10

TCP/IP properties

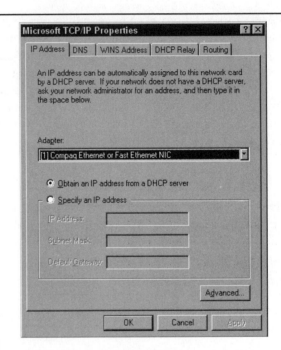

In the real world, you will have a static IP address for 99 percent of your servers 99 percent of the time. For workstations, however, the reduced administration requirements of DHCP will almost always prevail. With that said, we will continue using DHCP with our clients. If you select the "Obtain an IP address from a DHCP server" radio button, TCP/IP will be assigned a DHCP address. By selecting this option, the DHCP server can supply any or all values to your TCP/IP configuration, and not just the actual IP address. Your local network configuration will have everything to do with how these settings are assigned. Keep in mind, though, that any entries within the TCP/IP properties pages—such as DNS servers, WINS servers, default gateways, or domain names—will override any setting that the DHCP server gives you.

Another section of note in the NT Network Control Panel is the Services tab. Services here are referred to differently than we have become used to in Windows 9*x* and Windows 2000. In Windows NT, terms like *Client for Microsoft Networks* and *File and Print Sharing* are replaced by the terms *Workstation* and *Server*. Take a look at Figure 12.11.

FIGURE 12.11

Network services

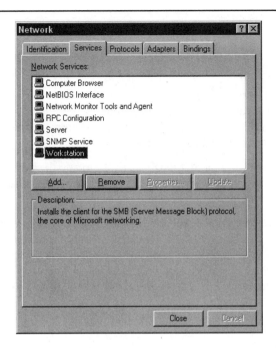

The Workstation service is our basic network client. This is the one that gives us the ability to use the network. The Server service allows us to share our resources. These basic components require little to no configuration for the workstation to operate effectively as a network client.

In the Network Control Panel's Identification tab, you will see your computer name and domain or workgroup membership configuration. Unlike a Windows 9x or 3.x client, a Windows NT machine—whether it is a Windows NT workstation or Windows NT server—must have a computer account created in the domain it wishes to belong to. Because the computer account is nearly identical to a user account, you must have Account Operator or Administrator privileges to join a domain. On the other hand, to join a workgroup, you do not need to hold any special domain privileges. Of course, to change these settings in either case, you will need Administrator rights on the local workstation or server.

Well, it sounds like a real pain—joining a domain—so why bother? If a Windows NT workstation or server is only in a workgroup, domain users cannot be assigned permissions to any resource on the workstation or server, nor can they log on with that account. This creates a nightmare situation when you want to log on to a machine and still be able to access resources on a domain. To make a long story short, you will want to join the domain.

Logging into Windows NT Machines after Joining a Domain

When a Windows NT workstation or Windows NT server joins a domain, users from that domain can—if assigned the appropriate permissions—log on directly to that machine. They will not have to have separate accounts on the local machine and domain to access resources in both places.

It doesn't end there, though. Users from any domain that is trusted by the domain in which the machine belongs can be assigned permissions to and, if allowed, log on directly to the local machine.

Um, let's clarify that a bit. My machine, BS99, belongs to the BS domain. The BS domain trusts the MANAGEMENT domain. I can add users and global groups from both the BS and MANAGEMENT domains into my BS99 local groups and assign permissions for my resources to those users—including the right to log on to BS99. If there is another domain out there, SALES, that is not trusted by BS, users cannot log on to BS99 with their SALES accounts.

To join a domain, select the Change button from the Identification tab. You will be shown your current domain and workgroup membership, along with your current computer name. You can change either your computer name or your workgroup/domain membership option. As soon as you begin changing one, the other becomes grayed out, so if you want to change both, you'll have to come back after changing the first. My computer name, BS99, is fine, but I want to join the BS domain (see Figure 12.12).

In the Identification Changes dialog box, select the Domain radio button to type your domain choice in the corresponding text box. Before pressing OK, you need to have a computer account for your machine. If one has already been created, either from Server Manager for Domains or within the Active Directory Users and Computers management console, you should be set to go. If not, check the Create a Computer Account in the Domain check box. Once checked, you can fill in a username and password to be used to actually create the computer account. This username and password, as I mentioned earlier, must have either Account Operator or Administrator rights on the domain you are joining. I always like to be on the safe side and enter the full domain qualified name. Instead of simply typing `Administrator`, I type `BS\Administrator`— this ensures that I use Administrator from the BS domain.

FIGURE 12.12

Changing domain

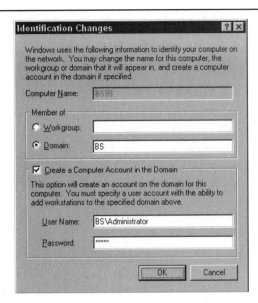

After you've completed the domain membership change, you will be prompted to reboot the server for the changes to take effect. After you reboot, your logon dialog box will allow you to enter the username and password for the domain that you just joined.

Why Reboot?

If all you did was change your domain and workgroup membership, you don't really have to reboot to let the changes take effect. What the reboot does is allow all services to register with the new domain membership. Without the reboot, you will still be part of the domain and will still be able to use the new domain membership.

This is helpful to know if your workstation or server ever loses its "trust relationship" with its domain. This happens when the NT machine account password gets out of sync between the machine and the domain. To correct this, you need to remove the machine from the domain—join a workgroup—delete the machine account from the domain, and finally, rejoin the domain, creating a new computer account as you go. You could be forced to reboot twice, or simply ignore the reboot suggestion and do it all in one shot. If the machine in question is a workstation, you shouldn't run into problems, but on production servers, I would recommend rebooting every chance you get.

After you have configured all of your adapters, services, and protocols, you will probably find a request to reboot upon closing the Network Control Panel. Do so, and you should be ready to connect to your Windows 2000 server.

Accessing Network Resources

In Windows NT, when you come to the Logon Information screen, you will notice that you can't manually enter a domain name in the Domain selection box. Instead, you are given a predefined list of domains from which to choose. This list goes back to our conversation about Windows NT machines joining a domain. We can log on with accounts from our own local machine—like my BS99, which will not have domain access—accounts from our own domain that we are a member of, and accounts from any domain that our domain trusts.

 TIP Why the option of logging in with accounts from a trusted domain? Let's say I am in a network that has a Windows NT master domain model. To make it simple, I have the ACCOUNTS domain, where all accounts reside, and the RESOURCE domain, where all resources reside. When I add a Windows NT workstation to the network, where should I add it? Many people think that it belongs in ACCOUNTS, so that I can log in with my user account from that domain. But that's not really the best place. I put the workstation in the RESOURCE domain instead. When I log into my machine, my domain choices will be my own machine (of course), the RESOURCE domain, which has no accounts, and finally, the ACCOUNTS domain. Placing NT workstations and member servers in the RESOURCE domain instead of the ACCOUNTS domain will keep your network more organized.

To connect to a network resource with a Windows NT client, you can simply right-click the Network Neighborhood and choose Map Network Drive. A dialog box will appear, similar to the one shown in Figure 12.13.

This dialog box works just like it does with any other client, except we have that additional feature of *Connect As*. The Connect As option allows you to connect to a network share with a different set of credentials or another user account. Simply type the username in the Connect As box, or as I have shown, type in the full *domain\username* to let the target machine know exactly which domain the username belongs to. One thing to keep in mind when using this option is that Windows NT can only map to a given server with one set of credentials. If I have already connected to a server, I can't specify a different username for a new connection, even if connecting to a different share.

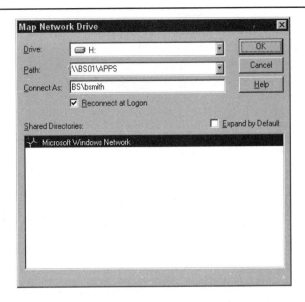

FIGURE 12.13

Mapping a drive

There are times, though, that you may get the error message that your credentials conflict, indicating that you are already connected to a server under a different username but don't have any drive connections to that server. What you need to do is go to a DOS prompt and type a **NET USE** statement. Chances are, you will see a connection to that machine's IPC$ share without a drive letter specified. This happens when you do things like open Server Manager for Domains or Event Viewer to a machine. You don't realize that you have connected to that server already, but you have. First, make sure all programs using that connection are closed, then drop the connection by typing **NET USE *server**share* /d**. For example, if I had opened Event Viewer to BS01 and saw a NET USE connection to \\BS01\IPC$, I would type NET USE \\BS01\IPC$ /d.

If you don't specify a user to connect as, Windows NT will use the credentials of the logged-on user to establish the network connection. Press OK, and you'll either be connected, or, if you used a different set of user credentials, be prompted for a password. That's all there is to it.

Connecting Windows for Workgroups Workstations

Before creating a Windows for Workgroups to Windows 2000 Server relationship, you need to be aware of basic limitation . The Active Directory—and all the benefits that come with it—is not available. You are pretty much limited to basic network share access. I know that in today's world, you probably won't find many occasions to connect Windows for Workgroups computers to the network, but when that occasion does arise, it might not hurt to be prepared. It's probably safe to say that we have all gotten too used to the Windows 9x, Windows NT, and Windows 2000 Desktop interface to be efficient when sitting in front of an old Windows for Workgroups machine. Everything is in a different place. That Program Manager just sits on top of our desktop. There's no Start menu! How embarrassing would it be to sit down at a workstation—you being the senior server administrator—and not have the slightest clue how to connect to your servers? Well, relax. In this section, we'll walk through configuring the basic networking components of Windows for Workgroups, and we'll touch back on how to connect to network shares.

It is very common—even on a machine with a network adapter present—to have a Windows for Workgroups machine that is completely ignorant of your network. In the Program Manager window, you'll find a Network program group, which contains a Network Setup icon. Launching that icon will present a dialog box like the one shown in Figure 12.14.

FIGURE 12.14

The Network Setup dialog box

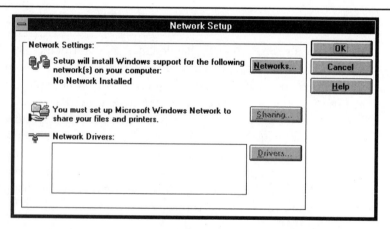

The dialog box in Figure 12.14 shows no configured networking support. To add this support, select the Networks button to install what we would call in Windows 9x or 2000 terminology your Client for Microsoft Networks (see Figure 12.15). In the Networks dialog box, select the Install Microsoft Windows Network button.

The next step is installing our adapter. Go back to the Network Setup dialog box and select the Drivers button; the resulting dialog box will contain both network adapters and protocols. Press the Add Protocol button, and you will see a list of all supported network adapters (see Figure 12.16). You can find your adapter in the list, or, if you're brave, you can press the Detect button to have the setup program attempt to detect it for you.

FIGURE 12.15

Selecting networks

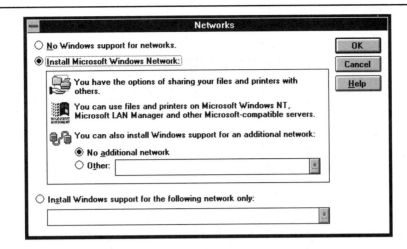

I say you have to be "brave" to use the Detect button because the Windows for Workgroups programming predates Plug and Play by quite some time. The risk of system lockup during this detection phase is substantial. Nevertheless, on my old 486 with a 3Com EtherLink III ISA network adapter, the setup program was able to detect my adapter.

FIGURE 12.16

Selecting an adapter

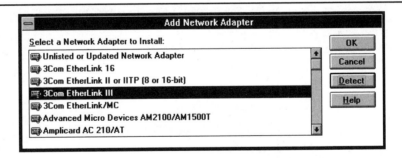

After selecting your adapter, you'll be returned back to the Network Drivers dialog box. You will see, as shown in Figure 12.17, that a set of default protocols has been automatically installed as well.

If the default protocols, NetBEUI and IPX/SPX, don't meet your needs, you can remove whichever protocol your don't want by highlighting it and pressing Remove. You can then add new protocols by clicking the Add Protocol button. In the event that multiple protocols are used, you can easily select a primary protocol by highlighting the protocol of choice and pressing the Set as Default Protocol button. Likewise, if a protocol such as TCP/IP needs configuring, you can highlight the protocol and press the Setup button.

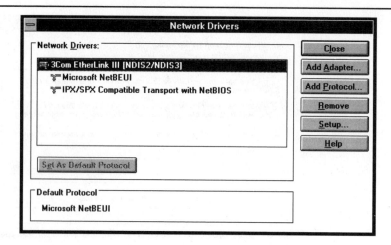

FIGURE 12.17

*Installed networking
components*

Once you have added and configured all required protocols—and have done your suggested reboot—you should be almost set to go networking. To finish things off, you need to configure your workgroup and logon settings. Now that you've set up a network, there is a new applet in your Control Panel, the Network applet. Launching that will present a screen like the one shown in Figure 12.18.

FIGURE 12.18

*The Network applet in
Windows for
Workgroups*

In this screen, you can configure your computer name and workgroup. These settings determine how your system will register itself on the network and how it will receive browse lists. Finally, you need to configure who you log into the network as—and where you log in. Pressing the Startup button will present you with the screen shown in Figure 12.19.

FIGURE 12.19

Startup options

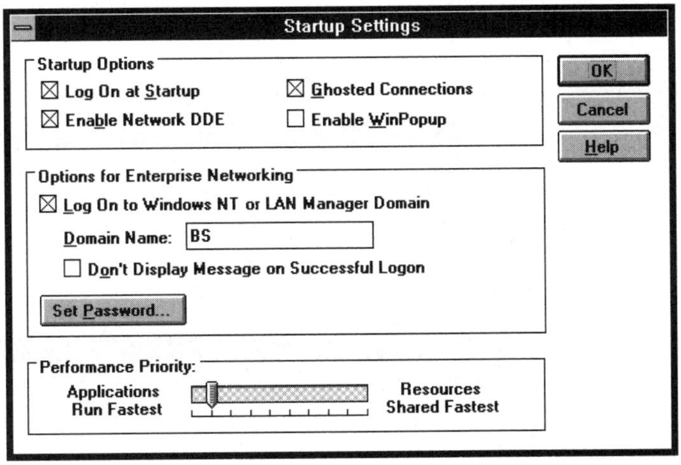

Startup Settings

┌─ Startup Options ─────────────────────────────┐
☒ Log On at Startup   ☒ Ghosted Connections
☒ Enable Network DDE   ☐ Enable WinPopup

OK
Cancel
Help

┌─ Options for Enterprise Networking ────────────┐
☒ Log On to Windows NT or LAN Manager Domain

Domain Name: BS

☐ Don't Display Message on Successful Logon

Set Password...

┌─ Performance Priority: ────────────────────────┐
Applications   Resources
Run Fastest   Shared Fastest

Some key parameters in this window are Log On at Startup, which tells Windows for Workgroups to present you with a logon dialog box before the Program Manager loads your desktop, and Log On to Windows NT or LAN Manager Domain. The latter option allows you to specify which domain you want to be authenticated in.

NOTE Windows for Workgroups will require the NetBIOS name of the domain—BS, in my case—and will not be able to use the fully qualified BS.COM.

Attaching to the Network

Now that your Windows for Workgroups client is configured, you need to log on to the domain and connect to your resources. Logging on with Windows for Workgroups is a little different and a bit more simplistic than it is with its bigger brothers Windows 9*x*, NT, and 2000. The desktop—Program Manager in this case—is not tied in to any user-specific information like the Windows Explorer is. Every user that logs into a Windows for Workgroups machine—and those that do not log in at all—receives the same program groups, desktop, and program settings. User profiles simply do not exist. What does this mean to Windows for Workgroups? You can log on and off from within the Program Manager or the Network program group, or (if you checked the Log On at Startup button) you can restart Windows to get the same old familiar logon box with fields for username, password, and domain.

After you log in, you can go to the File Manager and find a new set of commands in your menu bar: Connect To and Disconnect Network Drive. Pressing these will bring up a dialog box like the one shown in Figure 12.20. In it, you can browse the network for available shares or type in a share name. Once connected, the drive will show up in your File Manager window, and you can go to work.

FIGURE 12.20

The Connect Network
Drive dialog box

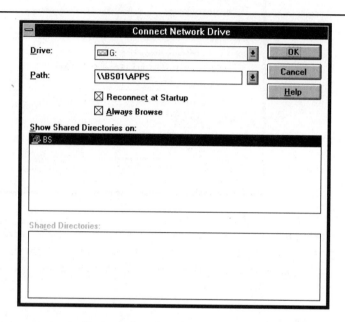

> **NOTE** Sorry, but you can't view or access Active Directory information with a Windows for Workgroups client.

One of the limitations of Windows for Workgroups clients is that they can't run commands via full UNC names. If I have a share on my server named \\BS01\INSTALL that contains a batch file named SETUP.BAT, I can't simply run a new command line of \\BS01\INSTALL\SETUP.BAT. Instead, I have to map a drive—I'll call it Z:—to \\BS01\INSTALL, then launch Z:\SETUP.BAT.

Connecting DOS Workstations

Now we enter into the realm of the forgotten GUI-less operating system: DOS. You may recall that in the days of Windows NT 3.*x* and 4.0 we had two convenient, or at least semi-convenient, tools at our disposal. The first was the MSCLIENT, a built-in DOS client. The second was the Network Client Administrator utility, which allowed us to make DOS-based, network-bootable floppy diskettes that helped us connect to our installation source. Needless to say, both of those little tools are gone with Windows 2000. Why? Well, there are a couple of reasons. Probably in the forefront of Microsoft's mind is the simple little fact that DOS is no longer a "supported" operating system. By not "supported," I mean that if you decide to burn up a handful of extra money to call up the Microsoft support folks and tell them that you are having problems connecting your DOS workstations to a Windows 2000 server, then you will find that the satisfaction of burning extra money is all you get. Another reason for the lack of DOS tools on the Windows 2000 Server CD is that there are new and improved installation methods. You used to not be able to pop in a CD, reboot your machine, and have the CD fire up an install. Instead, you had to boot to a DOS diskette with CD or network drivers and then connect to your install source. You also now have more capable installation methods: You don't need to wipe a machine clean before trying to do an install. You can instead put faith in an upgrade—that is, when you are upgrading from one *supported* operating system to Windows 2000 Server. In short, the inclusion of DOS tools on the CD is merely for the purposes of launching an install. That's it. They aren't there so you can run around the office and set up all the workstations as DOS-only machines. With that being said, you still have options in this department of install. You can boot to the CD, you can create setup boot floppies, you can launch the install from an existing operating system, etc.

 NOTE See Chapter 3 for more details on connecting to and launching the setup program.

Now comes our other problem: connecting to our installation source covers only half of our need to have DOS on hand, and doesn't do anything for the real issue we face. The real issue is connecting clients to Windows 2000 servers. Again, Windows 2000 Server doesn't come with a handy utility to create your DOS installation or even your DOS network driver installation, so if you absolutely *must* have a prepackaged DOS installation, you are going to need to get your hands on an NT 4.0 Server CD. To summarize a DOS installation ready for networking, you have at least three components:

- A config.sys that loads a driver for your network card
- An autoexec.bat or config.sys that loads a program to handle networking functions
- A command-line utility that executes network commands, like NET.EXE

What we are going to focus on is the third component, the NET.EXE program.

NOTE Actually, I have found that a lot of people don't realize that NET is a self-standing utility. They type NET USE and NET VIEW and all sorts of NET commands all day, but fail to see how it really works. NET simply calls up your network program, while the next parameter, like USE, is the function you want to perform. Next, depending upon the function called, are parameters to tell the function where or on what to perform that function. Understand that NET is a simple command-line utility, and everything else is a little less confusing.

In DOS, we will focus on three major functions of the NET command. First and foremost is LOGON. This actually logs you on to your domain. For me, to log on with my user credentials as identified in the beginning of this chapter, I type NET LOGON BSMITH /DOMAIN:BS. What I am doing is logging on as BSMITH, in the domain BS. Be careful though: the domain entry is the downlevel domain name, not the new, fully qualified domain name of BS.COM—DOS doesn't recognize those type of domain names.

The next function is VIEW. The NET VIEW statement is more important for DOS clients than for any other. This is because DOS has no browser to show you a nice, neat list of resources across your network. Instead, you have to manually find them with NET VIEW commands. You have two ways to focus you VIEW. First is at the domain. For me, typing NET VIEW /DOMAIN:BS will provide a list of servers that are registered on the BS domain. From that list, you can focus your VIEW at each individual server for a list of shared resources. If I want to see all shares on my server—BS01—I would type NET VIEW \\BS01.

Now we've found our target share, which is APPS under BS01, and we need to connect to it. You can't really make much use of programs and printers via a NET interface, so you need an actual drive letter or printer port connection. Enter USE. If I want to map the G: drive to the above listed server and share, I type NET USE G: \\BS01\APPS. This must be in the UNC format of *servername**share*. Similarly, if I want to map my LPT1 printer port to a printer shared from BS01 as CANON, I would type NET USE LPT1: \\BS01\CANON.

There are also some other NET functions worth mentioning. NET LOGOFF logs you off the domain you logged into. NET TIME \\BS01 synchronizes my computer clock with that on the server BS01. NET PASSWORD /DOMAIN:BS BSMITH old new changes my BSMITH account password on the BS domain from old to new.

That's really all there is to it. Sure, you may only deal with DOS workstations about once for every thousand workstations you visit, but there is still some good foundation knowledge hiding inside that little black box known as the DOS prompt. I hate to say it, but all those fancy little buttons and browse lists just combine the different functions of the native NET.EXE command into a simple user-friendly environment. Make certain that you know how to connect to your network with a DOS workstation—it will always be your lowest common denominator and can come in handy when you're stuck. Besides, would you rather have a command prompt, or a wizard?

CHAPTER 13

Connecting Macintoshes to Windows 2000

A large network is likely to contain more than just Windows computers. If your network includes Macintosh computers, this chapter will give you the necessary information to connect them to your Windows 2000 servers for file and print services.

Though many people mistakenly think that MacOS-based computers are really only good for graphics and publishing, they remain real computers, just like Windows-based systems but with a different way of looking at things. Because of this, it is not uncommon to find Macs in many network environments, and often for graphics and publishing. Regardless of what the Macs are actually used for, however, they are often served by Windows NT–based servers running File and Print Services for Macintosh. Unfortunately, getting Macintosh support in Windows NT 4 was akin to pulling teeth. The good news is that the Windows 2000 Server Services for Macintosh (SFM) is vastly improved and integrated into the operating system much better, easing administrative woes.

That's not where it stops, though. There are two other possibilities to consider, AppleShare IP and MacOS X Server, both of which are capable of supporting Windows-based workstations for file and printer sharing. AppleShare IP 5.x and above (currently to version 6.2) has built-in support for the SMB networking protocol, the native language of Windows. MacOS X Server can have SMB support added through a utility from the Unix world called Samba.

Though it is often a good thing to have diversity in environments, as it drives innovation and lowers prices, here it helps little. We now have a number of potential solutions to various cross-platform problems, and the more choices we have, the more confusing it can become. And while some networks may be purely Apple-centric, which greatly eases administration, many network designers understandably recognized the power of Windows NT 4 Server for large storage server solutions. To raise the bar, Windows 2000 makes these tasks much easier, but there are still concerns for security in a mixed environment.

This chapter explains the options available in Windows 2000 for supporting Macintosh clients; it also covers other solutions from the Macintosh side of the equation.

Getting Started

Before you jump right in and install SFM, you should take a look at your existing network and its hardware and make sure everything is set up so that SFM works properly. Among the things you should consider when connecting your Macs to a Windows 2000 network is the physical hardware required.

10Base-T, 100Base-T, or 1000Base-T?

Today it is nearly a foregone conclusion that some form of Ethernet will be used in the LAN network environment. The question remains, "How fast will we go?" For you, this will be an easy decision because you can make the same choice for all of your platforms. Gone are the days of slow and incompatible LocalTalk networking. Ethernet has made major inroads into the Macintosh platform for many years now. Part of the equation depends on the type of Macintosh equipment you have (see the next section for an overview).

 TIP Your best tool in a Macintosh arsenal is GURU from Newer Technologies, makers of RAM upgrades. This free utility lists every known Apple Macintosh and MacOS clone system in existence. It not only covers what Newer Technologies RAM will upgrade your 7200/120, but every other technical note worth knowing about the various models. There's also an unmistakable dash of nonsense thrown in to make you laugh in between reading about maximum throughput numbers for the serial bus on the Performa 5250 and figuring out how many VRAM slots there are in a 7300/200. Pick up your copy at www.newertech.com.

As for deciding which type of Ethernet to support, this depends almost entirely on two things: what you're already wired for and what your Macs support natively. As you'll see in the next section, most Power Macs come with built-in Ethernet, which can be good and bad.

Knowing the Macintosh

Understanding the systems that you work with day in and day out is crucial. If something goes down, you need to know either what to do to fix it or where to find the information that will help you. Here's some helpful information about the Macintosh that will give you an edge.

Pre–Power Mac/68k Series

The venerable 68k series of Macs come in many configurations and various form factors. If your company still has these types of Macintosh in use, you may still be using LocalTalk. If you are, stop. Migrate to Ethernet. All of your legacy Mac hardware can be integrated into your Ethernet network for less than $130 per computer. Granted, the connection to the network will still only be as fast as the serial port on the Mac can handle, but 57,600 isn't too bad, considering that most operations involve small amounts of data and documents.

First-Generation Power Mac

The first generation of Power Macs is made up of transition systems that were meant to make the move from 68k CISC to PowerPC RISC as seamless as possible. It worked. There were very few problems associated with the complete migration to the new CPU architecture, despite the fact that all 68k operations are performed in *emulation*. The majority of these systems, based on the then-powerful PowerPC 601, came with either built-in 10Base-T Ethernet ports (RJ-45) or an AAUI-15 port, which can use an Ethernet transceiver for adaptation to Ethernet (around $30 a unit). These systems all have NuBus slots. 10/100 cards from Asante are around $300 for the few models that do not have built-in Ethernet.

Second- and Third-Generation Power Mac

Though the first-generation systems were bulletproof, the second- and third-generation computers proved that Apple could continue to develop powerful and stable machines. This was also the age of the Power Mac Performa. Almost all non-Performa systems shipped with built-in Ethernet configured in the same way as first-generation machines. This collection also spawned the best-selling Power Macs of all time, the 8500 and 9500 (the iMac has sold over 2 million units as of this writing, making *it* the new sales leader).

 TIP A new market for CPU replacement has emerged that allows you to upgrade even a lowly 6100/60 to a new G3. How? Simple, really. The companies that sell these cards employ the little-used PDS (Processor Direct Slot) to connect a card with the necessary circuitry. Later Power Macs mount the factory CPU on a daughter card for easier upgradability. So, don't throw out those old Macs! Prices for the upgrades range from $250 for 250MHz and $900 for a 466MHz. Check out www.maccpu.com for the latest information. They oughta know, they sell them!

Fourth-Generation and G3 Power Macs

Apple continued its strong lead by releasing some updates to their most popular machines. These were the 7300, 8600, and 9600. Stocked with powerful 604e CPUs, PCI slots, the ability to hold 1GB of RAM, and very easy-to-open cases, they sold well. The jig was up, though, as Apple caused sales on the latest Power Macs to go somewhat limp. Apple had already announced the successor to the 60x line, the G3 (known internally at Motorola as the PowerPC 740; G3 is an Apple name for the CPU). People decided that it was easier to wait a few more months and get a much more powerful computer.

The first G3 Power Macs came in a desktop case and a mini tower case that looked identical to two earlier Mac favorites, the 7300/200 and 9600/350. In fact, other than a slightly faster bus and a G3 CPU inside, they were no different, with one serious exception: they were limited to 384MB of RAM. For serious users and companies that rely on the latest, this was potentially disastrous, especially to video and sound professionals who typically have up to 1GB of RAM installed. Subsequent models, however, have proven to be better suited to their common purpose. The first-generation G3s made were for the next wave.

 NOTE All fourth-generation Power Macs and first-generation G3 Power Macs have built-in Ethernet.

G4 Power Macs

Late-breaking news! By the time we were preparing this chapter for publication, Apple announced the general release of the next-generation G4 systems. Billed as a desktop SuperComputer, these systems truly have the ability to perform over 1 *billion* gigaflops per clock tick with a theoretical limit of four! A G4 500 is purported to be able to outrun, by three times mind you, a Pentium III 600. Neato. This type of speed and raw instruction parsing power was previously only available to those who could pony up the several hundred thousand dollars it took to buy a real supercomputer. You can now buy one for $1,599. Monitor sold separately.

The G4s are mostly architecturally identical to the G3s in relation to RAM (1GB max.) and drive (1TB max. in the box) space. The PCI slot arrangement has been modified a bit. There is now a real AGP 2x slot for the video card on board. The remaining slots are the same as on the previous model: one dedicated video slot and three 64-bit PCI slots for additional expansion. These new systems also have built-in 10/100 Ethernet support and an option for a 1000Base-T card to be installed.

You also may have heard that the new Power Macs do not have floppy drives. This is true. Apple decided that it would be better to leave out the cost of a floppy drive ($80 for a Mac because they have auto-eject, unlike manual PC floppy drives that run around $20) and put that money elsewhere. There are also no traditional Macintosh expansion ports to speak of. Instead, there are USB and FireWire (also called IEEE 1394) ports, which are hot-pluggable and much, much faster. Support for USB is growing quickly, thanks to the iMac, but FireWire support is still fledgling, despite efforts on Sony's part to change that.

The iMac and B&W G3 Power Mac

So phenomenal is the success of the iMac that it is often overlooked by systems administrators as a toy, and they'd be wrong. The first iMac came with a measly 233MHz G3, 4GB HDD, 32MB of RAM, 15-inch monitor, and 10/100 Ethernet. It also revived a slipping USB market. Today, and for exactly the same price as when it was introduced ($1,299), you get a powerful 333MHz G3, 64MB of RAM, an 8GB HDD, 15-inch monitor, and

10/100 Ethernet. They are solid performers and already have the hardware to integrate into a network.

 TIP The iMac was designed in part to act as a network computer (NC). Using a feature afforded by MacOS X Server, an iMac can be booted up over the network without requiring a local system folder. The iMac's system resides on the server and is sent to the iMac when it requests a boot session. A single MacOS X Server can use its Netboot capabilities to provide bootable systems for 50 iMacs at the same time, but more on that later.

 WARNING The iMac does not ship with a floppy drive, nor is one available at extra cost. Though it is uncommon for anyone to actually use the little plastic guys anymore, it's a safe bet that when you drop an iMac on their desk, they'll immediately require one. If you need to provide workstation storage, consider a low-cost SCSI Zip drive for around $100.

It wasn't long after the iMac devoured old sales records that the oddly monikered B&W G3 arrived. Emblazoned with a huge crystal-white Apple and sporting a door that can open as wide as a two-car garage, the B&W Power Mac G3 arrived to rave reviews. The system can handle 1GB of RAM and a terabyte of storage space all inside the roomy case. The large door on the right side can be opened without interrupting system operation.

 NOTE The B&W G3 Power Mac is so named for its translucent blue outer case and white trim. Apple has chosen not to provide version or model identifiers to their shipping systems, preferring to upgrade the internals regularly in relative obscurity.

In the last month, Apple has announced new iMac models, straying somewhat from the one-model ethic well established since the iMac's introduction. There are now three to choose from: The basic model, which sells for $999, is Apple's first foray into the sub-$1k market. This model comes in only one color, has a 350MHz G3 CPU, 64MB of RAM, a 6GB hard disk drive, a 24x CD-ROM, a 56k modem, and a 10/100 Ethernet port. The new iMac models, the DV (for digital video) and DV Special Edition, come in all of the previous colors including a new, very attractive slate gray. The iMac DV has a 400MHz G3 CPU, 10GB hard disk drive, 4x DVD-ROM, and two 400Mbps FireWire (IEEE 1394) ports. The iMac DV Special Edition adds another 64MB of RAM and bumps the HDD to 13GB. They are priced $1299 and $1499, respectively.

One of the more attractive aspects of the new DV systems is their built-in video capabilities. Apple even goes so far as to provide the software required to perform video editing. Simply plug your digital camera into one of the supplied FireWire ports, and you're good to go (most middle and high-end video cameras have been shipping with IEEE 1394 support for the last few years). Needless to say, this is a very inexpensive way to add video-editing capabilities to your company's toolbox.

Network Adapters

Ethernet provides the most cost-effective, universal, and sturdy network media format for Windows 2000 servers and yields the best transmission speeds. As you read earlier, most Power Macs come with Ethernet capabilities built in. Some, like the 7300, 8600, and 9600, offer an RJ-45 and AAUI, while most provide an AAUI-15 port which requires a transceiver (roughly $25–$30 per unit, less in bulk). There is no loss of performance when using an AAUI interface transceiver; however, the built-in Ethernet in most of these older Power Macs is limited to 10Base-T, so an upgrade is necessary for all other speeds.

TIP All Power Mac systems from the fourth generation to today use PCI, exactly the same as in PCs. Adapters are also available for the NuBus interface (for older Macintosh systems using the 680x0 processor and first- and second-generation Power Macs). Network adapters for Macs include Ethernet, Token Ring, Fiber Distributed Data Interface (FDDI), and fiber optic. The Ethernet adapters can be either standard 10Mbps coax or unshielded twisted pair (UTP), 100Mbps cards using Category 5 UTP cable, or the newly standardized 802.3z, also known as Gigabit Ethernet. Apple will put a brand-new Gigabit Ethernet card into your brand-new B&W G3 Power Mac if you ask for it. It's a measly $200 option and it replaces the 10/100 card that is standard issue for the B&W G3s. Hyperspeed on the cheap!

Cabling

Though you are most likely boringly familiar with cabling, we feel it is important to mention that Macs use exactly the same cable for the job as a PC would. Macs can also be added to any topology you might require or that already exists.

Physical Topologies

As touched on earlier, Macs can participate on every physical topology that Windows 2000 can—nothing new there. It's also fair to say that Ethernet has dominated the networking world with its lower cost of implementation and its fast, reliable performance.

Today, even 100Base-T implementations of Ethernet are quite affordable and offer even better performance. Perhaps the best part of using Ethernet is that you probably already have the necessary equipment in your Windows 2000 server. If you have the proper adapter card, Macs can use coax cable to attach to older 10Base-2 or 10Base-5 networks, although this is increasingly uncommon. Twisted pair (commonly referred to as UTP; the *U* stands for unshielded) is the versatile media of choice these days. Considering how cheap a single Ethernet installation is (approximately $30–$40 per seat), it's well worth the investment to upgrade if you're still using LocalTalk, even though it is very unlikely you are. Add to this the fact that almost all Macintosh computers have a built-in Ethernet port, and making the decision is quite easy.

 NOTE The first Power Mac was introduced in March of 1994. Since the Mac's introduction in 1984, there have been well over 60 million Macintosh computers sold. Roughly 60 percent of these computers have built-in Ethernet capabilities, including the very first Power Mac, the 6100/60.

Topologies available for Ethernet include the star and bus or possibly a combination of the two, depending on your needs, physical location, and reliability requirements. Bus topologies typically use either 10Base-2 or 10Base-5 coax cable to connect the nodes together and can reach over fairly long distances (185 meters for 10Base-2 and 500 meters for 10Base-5). Star topologies allow for up to four hubs between any two nodes, for a total length of about 100 meters.

File and Print Server Considerations

Windows 2000 Server can provide file and print servers for Macintosh computers, but it does not include a client service that would allow it to connect to a Macintosh computer to retrieve files. To accomplish that task, you would need to purchase one of the NetBIOS network packages for the Macintosh computer. The most common use for the File and Print Servers for Macintosh is to provide greater storage capacities and a common drop point for both Windows and Macintosh clients.

 NOTE Thursby Software makes DAVE, a NetBIOS client for the MacOS. DAVE allows the Mac to look like a Windows client to the rest of the network. A demonstration copy is available at www.thursby.com.

Back in the days of yore, disk partitions for the Macintosh operating system were limited to a maximum size of 2GB. But with System 7.5, the capacity rose to 16GB, and today with OS 8, it has risen to 2 terabytes. With the earlier operating systems for the Macintosh, it was very important to find a server solution with greater capacity for file storage. At that time, Windows NT Server gave Macintosh users a solution for a network server with much greater storage capacities. If you are setting up the File Server for Macintosh for Macs that are not using more recent versions of the MacOS, bear in mind that they will be limited in the size of volume they can see. If you support Macs that are pre–System 7.5, they are not able to see more than 2GB in a single volume. (And if you're still supporting pre–System 7.5 Macs, shame on you! Apple has made System 7.5.5 freely available for download at `www.apple.com`.) You must limit the size of the Macintosh-accessible share to 2GB for these clients, or upgrade. When you install the File Server for Macintosh, it will automatically create one shared folder to contain the Microsoft User Authentication Modules (UAMs). Unlike Windows NT 4, Windows 2000 doesn't require that you create the Macintosh-accessible volume to contain your shared files at the time of install. Instead, when you share a folder, you make the decision to provide access to Windows clients, Macintosh clients, or both. You will also be able to limit the size of the shared folder to comply with the needs of the particular Macintosh operating system version.

It's also easy to set up printing from a Macintosh to a Windows 2000 server. The Print Server for Macintosh can make any physically attached print device available on the network for Macintosh clients. It can also attach to, and even capture, AppleTalk printers on the network. When you choose to capture the AppleTalk printer, only the Windows 2000 server can send jobs to the printer.

One of the old complaints on Macintosh networks involves the use of different revisions of print drivers. Every time a Macintosh client sent a job to an AppleTalk printer, it had to load its driver on the printer first. If several Macintosh clients were doing this with different versions of the driver, it could result in a "printer war," where the printer was spending all of its time changing drivers and not actually printing. The fix was to capture the printer so it would only accept incoming jobs from the print server. Fortunately, this is no longer the case. LaserWriter 8 software is much more capable and intelligent. We'll get into the details later on.

Gathering Information for the SFM Installation

When planning for the installation of the SFM, make the effort to gather some basic information first. This will help to make the install process as painless as possible. Create a table that includes the information you'll need to configure the servers. For instance, you should document the following:

- The type and name of adapters in the server
- The IP address range that the Macs fall inside of

Continued ▮▶

CONTINUED

- The network number for AppleTalk, if applicable
- Any zone names that may have been applied inside the Mac network
- Whether the server will be seeding the network. *Seeding* is an AppleTalk term that describes the process of generating initial network information such as zone names and network numbers

Installing the Servers for Macintosh

With Windows 2000 Server, the SFM is separated into File Server for Macintosh and Print Server for Macintosh. You can opt to support both services or install only the service your clients require. When either service is installed, the AppleTalk protocol will automatically be installed, even if your Macintosh clients are using TCP/IP.

To begin the installation process in Windows 2000 Server, follow these steps:

1. Open Control Panel and double-click Add/Remove Programs. When the dialog opens, select the Add/Remove Windows Components button.

2. Click Add/Remove Windows Components to bring up the list of available components (see Figure 13.1).

FIGURE 13.1

The Windows Components Wizard showing the Other Network File and Print Services option

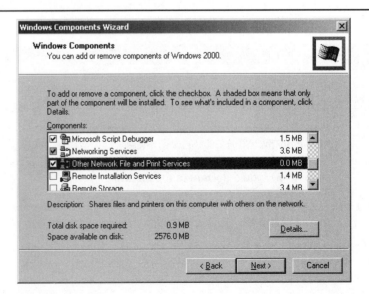

3. Select Other Network File and Print Services and click the Details button to show the subcomponents.

4. Select File Services for Macintosh if you want to allow Macintosh users to access the server for files. Select Print Server for Macintosh if you wish to enable Macintosh users to print to a shared printer controlled by the Windows 2000 server. Check the boxes beside the services you want to install, then click Next to install the components.

TIP You will achieve better performance on your Windows 2000 server by selecting only the services you really need to install. This is true of any optional components, because every service requires system resources to run. This means that, if your Macintosh clients only need access to a laser printer controlled by the Windows 2000 server, you should only install the Print Server for Macintosh.

Once you have successfully installed the SFM, you can do some basic configuration to customize the appearance of your server on the network. One way to do this is to define a custom logon message that the Macintosh clients will see when they log on to the Windows 2000 server. To set a new message, or to edit an existing message, follow these steps:

1. Choose Start/Programs/Administrative Tools/Computer Management.

2. Expand System Tools and then right-click Shared Folders.

3. Select Configure File Server for Macintosh from the context menu.

4. On the Configuration tab of the property sheet, type your message in the Logon Message text box (see Figure 13.2).

5. Click OK when you are satisfied with your changes.

The Configuration tab can also be used to define the total number of user sessions that will be allowed at one time. You can set the name of the server as it will appear to Macintosh clients, although it will default to the NetBIOS name of your server.

WARNING Most users—Mac, Windows, or otherwise—despise logon messages. If you must include one, make it short and sweet. If not, skip it.

FIGURE 13.2

The Configuration tab of the property sheet for the File Server for Macintosh

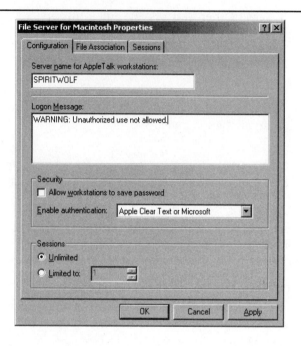

Creating Macintosh Shares

Once the File Server for Macintosh is installed, you'll be able to create shared folders that will be accessible to your Macintosh clients. Windows 2000 Server gives you the ability to create and manage shared folders with the Computer Management snap-in (COMPMGMT.MSC) of the Microsoft Management Console (MMC).

NOTE Administrators familiar with serving Macs on Windows NT 4 will find the changes made to Macintosh administration both much easier and frustratingly mislocated. All systems administration functions have been moved to the MMC, as you read in Chapter 4.

Before you begin sharing volumes, let's go over some ground rules:

- You cannot share the same folder twice as two different Macintosh volumes. We've grown used to being able to do this in the Windows NT world, but it isn't allowed for Macintosh volumes.

- You cannot create a Macintosh volume inside of a share as another Macintosh volume. This means that if the first path listed here is shared as a Macintosh volume, you cannot have the second path as a separate Macintosh volume. The third path, however, is acceptable as long as it remains a separate path:

    Good D:\Mac

Bad   `D:\Mac\Programs\Graphics`

Good `D:\MacOS\Other\Directory`

- Third, there are some limits on the number and naming of Macintosh volumes for the File Server for Macintosh. An underlying AppleTalk protocol buffer determines the number of volume names. The volume names can be up to 27 characters in length. If you will have multiple Macintosh volumes, you should balance the need to have clear names with the limits of the buffer space. To determine the number of volume names that can be displayed, use the following formula:

N * (M+2) <= 4624

N is the number of volume names, and *M* is the average length of the names in characters (bytes). Any names that exceed this limit will not be viewable to the Macintosh clients.

 NOTE You cannot create a Macintosh volume name with more than 27 characters with the Computer Management tool in Windows 2000 Server. If you need to create a volume with a longer name, use the `MACFILE.EXE` command from the command prompt.

To create a Macintosh-accessible share, follow these steps:

1. Choose Start/Programs/Administrative Tools/Computer Management.

2. Expand the entry for System Tools, then expand `Shared Folders` (see Figure 13.3).

3. Right-click `Shares` and select New File Share. This will launch the Create Shared Folder Wizard (see Figure 13.4).

4. Select the folder to share by either typing the full path to the folder in the Folder to Share text box or browsing for it by clicking the Browse button to the right of the field. If the folder does not already exist, the wizard will create it for you if you type the information in the Folder Name text box.

5. In this dialog, you can set the name of the shared folder as your users will see it while browsing, and you can apply a comment to the share.

6. In the same dialog, check the box next to each operating system that will be supported for this shared folder. Options include Microsoft Windows, Novell NetWare, and Apple Macintosh clients. Click the Next button when you've checked the options you need.

7. Click Next. You may be prompted to confirm that you want to share the folder if it is located on a file system other than NTFS. If you confirm it, the permissions dialog opens (see Figure 13.5).

FIGURE 13.3

The Computer
Management screen
showing the Shared
Folders *group*

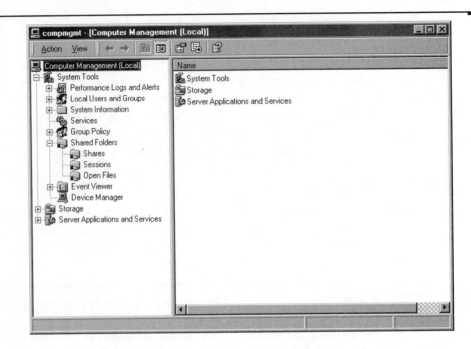

FIGURE 13.4

The Create Shared
Folder Wizard

WARNING You can create a Macintosh-accessible folder on either NTFS or the CD-ROM file system (CDFS). You cannot create Macintosh volumes on either FAT or FAT32. If your computer's drive is formatted with FAT or FAT32, you'll be able to install the Print Server for Macintosh but not the File Server for Macintosh.

FIGURE 13.5
The permissions dialog

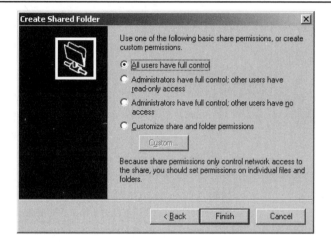

8. Select the appropriate level of permissions for your users and then click Next.

9. The Completing the Create Shared Folder Wizard dialog opens, summarizing the options you've selected. Click Finish when you're satisfied, and the wizard will create the shared folder for you. You will be asked if you would like to create more shares and given Yes and No options.

These steps will make your new share available to your Macintosh clients. In addition, you can set the permissions for the shared folder to restrict access or leave it set to its defaults to allow general access for all users.

The permissions applied to a Macintosh shared folder are different in Windows 2000 than they were in Windows NT 4. NT 4 used the standard Macintosh permissions of See Files, See Folders, and Make Changes. The File and Print Services for Macintosh in NT 4 would also apply any NTFS permissions, even though the Macintosh clients could not see them. In Windows 2000, you set permissions on the shared folder or at the NTFS level just as you would for a normal Windows share. Figure 13.6 shows the shared folder permissions for a Macintosh share.

FIGURE 13.6

The shared folder permissions dialog for a Macintosh-accessible share

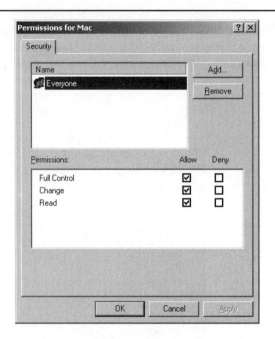

The shared folder permissions are the same as they are in earlier versions of Windows NT, but the interface for assigning them is quite different. The available permissions are as follows:

Full Control   Allows a user to do anything in the share. The user can read, write, execute, delete, change permissions, and take ownership.

Change   Allows a user to modify files and folders within the share. A user with Change permission can read, write, execute, and delete files and folders within the share.

Read   Allows the user to read and execute. The user with Read permission can view any file or folder in the share and run programs found there.

No Access   Denies any access to a user. The No Access permission always overrides all other permissions.

NOTE   Notice that the interface (shown in Figure 13.6) no longer includes a specific option to assign No Access permission. To accomplish the equivalent of No Access, simply uncheck each permission that is listed in the dialog. By not giving any permission, you are essentially assigning No Access without the possible unexpected results, such as the administrator or even the operating system not having access.

To assign permissions to a Macintosh share, use Explorer or My Computer to browse for the local path of the shared folder and right-click the folder. Choose Sharing from the context menu and click the Permissions button. If you set the permissions through the Computer Management tool, you are actually setting NTFS permissions on the folder and files instead of setting shared folder permissions. This works as well if not better because you can define different permissions at any level of the hierarchy, not just at the root folder of the share.

Sharing Printers

One of the reasons most people install the services for Macintosh is to allow their Macintosh clients to access a shared printer on a Windows 2000 server. There are two basic types of printer that you can share this way: an AppleTalk print device on the network or a locally connected print device.

Macs can create print jobs in PostScript format and can have special code sent directly to the printer via a specially developed driver, but the default output format is QuickDraw, the Mac's native display engine. This allows you to provide a wide range of printer choices to both Windows-based machines and Macintosh clients.

 WARNING   There is another less-used technology that has moved out of favor with Apple that is called QuickDraw GX. This was supposed to be Apple's next-generation graphics engine and was available as an add-on component for some time, but management problems and efforts to integrate Display PostScript, a technology familiar to Unix users, caused a premature death for the powerful technology. Apple has now wholly embraced SGI's OpenGL as its next graphics engine.

If your Macintosh clients require printing output to be in PostScript, it is not a problem, even if the printer receiving the job is not a PostScript printer. The Print Server for Macintosh provides PostScript emulation for print jobs submitted from a Macintosh client. This means that any print job sent to a Windows 2000 server from a Macintosh will be automatically converted from PostScript to a form suitable for the print device.

 NOTE   It is important to remember that the key to good printing is a good driver. It is the driver that provides the printer with the information that correctly renders the print job. Check with the printer's vendor to see if there is a compatible MacOS driver or one optimized for network printing to an NT server providing Mac print services. They are out there.

LaserPrep Wars?

One of the old issues with printing to a network from Macintosh clients was something Mac users called *LaserPrep Wars*. A LaserPrep file is a configuration file that describes how a laser printer should handle a print job. This file comes with the PostScript driver and is specific to any version of the Chooser. What happens in a LaserPrep War is that one Macintosh client sends version 6 of the LaserPrep file and PostScript driver to the printer, then another client sends version 7 of the LaserPrep file and PostScript driver. For each version that it receives, the print device must go through a reset to change modes. The real problem with this is that things can reach a point where virtually all the print device is busy doing is switching modes.

If you maintain an older Macintosh network and have these multiple driver versions blues, then SFM solves the time issue by sending the LaserPrep file along with every job that is sent to the printer. This takes a little extra effort on the part of the server, but it actually results in faster performance because the print device doesn't go through the work of making the file resident in its own memory.

Another way to smooth this process is by capturing the printer. If the Windows 2000 server captures the printer, then no one else can submit jobs to it to interfere with the settings. Using SFM can actually prevent LaserPrep Wars from ever occurring.

Of course, Apple has been aware of the problem and long since fixed it. The solution is called LaserWriter 8 (LW8), and it is Apple's PostScript engine for the MacOS. A Macintosh doesn't even need to have a printer installed to use LW8. The current version is 8.6.1 and it is freely available on Apple's software updates Web site (asu.info.apple.com). If you would like to print to LaserWriter printers from your Windows NT computers, you can also download the Windows driver.

Assuming that you have installed the Print Server for Macintosh, sharing an AppleTalk print device is easy. The process is the same as redirecting a local port to a network print device. That sounds easy, doesn't it? The idea here is that you are creating a print queue for a network interface print device that communicates with the AppleTalk protocol.

To install and share an AppleTalk printer, follow these steps:

1. Open the Printers window and double-click Add Printer to start the Add Printer Wizard. (You may also go to Start/Settings/Printers and choose Add Printer if you have modified the proper settings in the Taskbar property sheet.)

2. The first choice to make is whether your printer is installed locally or on the network. Choose Local and click Next. Note that the Automatically Detect and Install My Plug and Play Printer option is checked by default.

3. Next, you must choose the local port to which the print device is connected (see Figure 13.7). Click the Create a New Port radio button and select AppleTalk Printing Devices from the Type drop-down list. Click Next. Windows 2000 will attempt to locate all of the AppleTalk print devices on the local network.

NOTE For some interesting reason, your Macintosh clients will still be able to access file shares for Macs even if the AppleTalk service is not running. This is because Macs use TCP/IP like all other computers. Not having AppleTalk running, however, will cause you not to be able to set up an AppleTalk printer for sharing. Double-check that your AppleTalk service is in operation before beginning. The Mac clients will still be able to access TCP/IP-based printers, however.

FIGURE 13.7

The Select the Printer Port dialog showing the AppleTalk Printing Devices setting

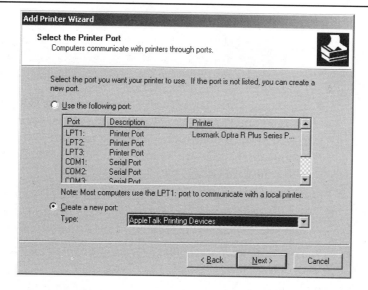

4. Select the AppleTalk printer that you want to install and click OK. When prompted to capture the port, select Yes.

5. The next dialog requests that you select the manufacturer and model of the print device. Choose the manufacturer from the list on the left, and then select the correct model on the right. Click Next.

6. Enter a name for the printer (see Figure 13.8). This name is only used locally on your computer; it won't display in the Active Directory or the browse list. If you already have one or more printers installed on your system, you must decide whether this printer will be used as the default printer by your Windows applications. When you have completed all settings, click Next.

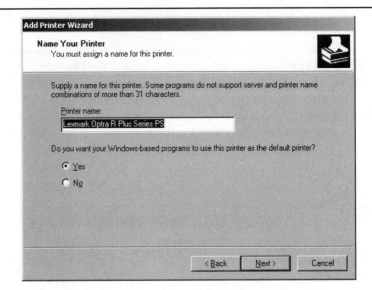

7. The next decision is whether to share the printer. Click the radio button next to Share As and then enter a name for the shared printer. This name will be displayed in the browse list and may be published to the Active Directory. Be sure to use a name that can be viewed from all network clients that will need to access this printer.

8. Click Next to open the Location and Comment dialog (see Figure 13.9). Enter a meaningful description of the location of the printer and provide a comment that gives the users any additional information they might need. Click Next.

9. The Print Test Page dialog gives you the opportunity to test the printer installation by sending a test job. Click Next.

10. The final step is to confirm all selected options (see Figure 13.10). When you click Finish, the wizard will install the drivers and finalize all settings for the printer. It is a good idea to review these settings carefully before clicking Finish.

FIGURE 13.9

The Location and Comment dialog gathers information that can be published to the Active Directory.

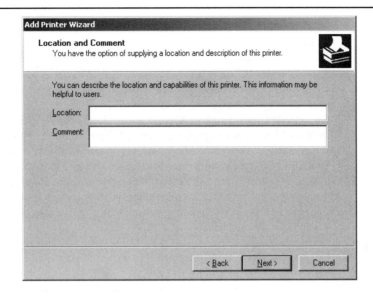

FIGURE 13.10

The final dialog of the Add Printer Wizard gives you an opportunity to verify all options before creating the printer.

NOTE To complete this procedure, you need to actually have an AppleTalk print device located somewhere on your local network. When a printer is shared in this way, your Macintosh clients will be sending their jobs to the printer using the AppleTalk protocol. AppleTalk over TCP/IP is nearly as fast as TCP/IP itself, so you should not be concerned about any perceptible performance degradation as a result of using this manner of printer sharing. You may, however, use an AppleShare IP server to act as a print server for both Mac and Windows clients, as AppleShare IP allows printing over TCP/IP for both operating systems. There is another possible way to share a printer installed on a Windows 2000 server. It requires that you connect at least one of your Macs as a NetBIOS network client, attach it to the shared printer as a Windows client, and then share it again as an AppleTalk printer. Once this is done, the other Macs can print to the NetBIOS print gateway and pass through to the Windows 2000 printer. This is more complicated, but it will work if needed. This also provides TCP/IP printing for both Mac and Windows clients, but it's more difficult to configure and maintain.

TIP For more on AppleShare IP and other mixed-platform networking solutions, see "Network Alternatives" later in this chapter.

The Print Server for Macintosh makes any printer that is installed locally on the Windows 2000 server available to your Macintosh clients. Once the printer has been installed on the server, the Print Server for Macintosh will begin advertising the printer to AppleTalk clients on the network. To install a printer to be used by your Macintosh clients, follow these steps:

1. Open the Printers window by selecting Start/Settings/Printers.

2. Double-click the Add Printer icon to start the Add Printer Wizard.

3. The first choice to make is whether your printer is installed locally or on the network. Choose Local and click Next. Note that the Automatically Detect and Install My Plug and Play Printer option is checked by default.

4. Next, you must choose the local port to which the print device is connected. Typically, the print device will be attached to your first parallel port, LPT1. Once you have selected the correct port, click Next.

5. In the next dialog, you will select the manufacturer and model of your print device. This will ensure that you're installing the correct driver. If you have a third-party driver to install, select Have Disk and browse for the location of the drivers.

6. Enter a name for the printer. This name is only used locally on your computer; it won't display in the Active Directory or the browse list. If you already have one or more printers installed on your system, you must decide whether this printer will be used as the default printer by your Windows applications. When you have completed all settings, click Next.

7. The next decision is whether to share the printer. Click the radio button next to Yes and then enter a name for the shared printer. This name will be displayed in the browse list and may be published to the Active Directory. Be sure to use a name that can be viewed from all network clients that will need to access this printer.

8. Click Next to open the Location and Comment dialog. Enter a meaningful description of the location of the printer and provide a comment that gives the users any additional information they might need. Click Next.

9. The Print Test Page dialog gives you the opportunity to test the printer installation by sending a test job. Click Next.

10. The final step is to confirm all selected options. When you click Finish, the wizard will install the drivers and finalize all settings for the printer. It is a good idea to review these settings carefully before clicking Finish.

After you have added a new printer to be used by the Print Server for Macintosh, it's a good idea to restart the service. This allows the print spooler to correctly recognize the new printer. In Windows 2000, this function has moved from the Control Panel's Services applet to the Computer Management console in Administrative Tools. To stop and restart the print spooler, use these steps:

1. Open Computer Management from the Administrative Tools group on the Start menu. (You may alternately right-click My Computer and select the Manage item.)

2. Open the Services and Applications item and click Services to open the list of services available on the computer (see Figure 13.11).

3. Scroll down through the list until you find the Print Spooler service. Click once on this service to highlight it and then click the Restart Service button.

4. When prompted to also stop and restart the Print Server for Macintosh, click OK. Figure 13.12 shows the prompt you will receive to restart the Print Server for Macintosh.

5. After the services have restarted successfully, close the Computer Management console application.

FIGURE 13.11

Windows 2000 Server includes the option to stop and restart services with a single click.

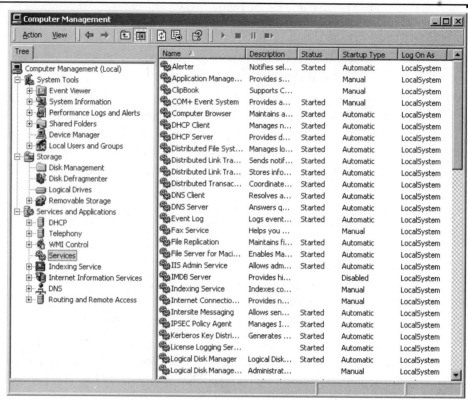

FIGURE 13.12

Restarting the print spooler automatically restarts the Print Server for Macintosh.

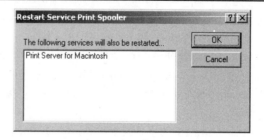

TIP This technique is also used fairly often when troubleshooting the printing architecture on Windows 2000. Should documents get stuck in the print queue at any time on Windows 2000 or earlier versions of Windows NT, try restarting the print spooler to reset the spool. Many people will actually try rebooting the server or flushing the queue in this scenario, when all they really need to do is restart the spooler service.

Accessing Server Resources

Once the SFM is installed on the Windows 2000 server, you will be able to begin using the resources from your Macintosh clients. This section discusses the usage from the Macintosh side of the equation.

Macintosh clients will typically use the Chooser to make network connections for printing or for files. To access the network, the Chooser requires that AppleShare be installed and running. Most Macintosh systems will attempt to make the initial connection through TCP/IP if it is installed, but they still require that the AppleTalk protocol be installed as support for the AppleShare functionality.

There are, however, some things to be aware of. In the latest version of the MacOS, 8.5 with an update to 8.6, the Chooser is bolstered by the Network Browser, an eminently more useful network tool. Users can browse and select network resources using the Open/Save dialog box format of the Network Browser interface. The older Chooser Control Panel was somewhat cumbersome to use. This change is welcome. The most current version of the Chooser is 7.6.2, and AppleShare is up to 3.8.3, which gives Mac networking full compatibility with all MacOS-accepted protocols.

 NOTE The folks at Apple have not been resting on their laurels. By the time you read this, they will have shipped their newest version of the venerable OS, MacOS 9. SRP'd at $99, this is a hefty upgrade, but worth it. There are many fixes and a slew of new additions that make this update a worthy buy.

The primary driving force behind all these networking capabilities is Open Transport (OT), the technology that replaced the aging and incomplete MacTCP. OT has many capabilities, one of the most powerful being the ability to change networking configurations on the fly, not requiring a restart as in Windows, NT or otherwise. A quick visit to the TCP/IP Control Panel will reveal an easy-to-use interface (to change to Advanced or Administrator views, go to Edit/User Mode and make your choice). You also have the option to restrict access to the Control Panel via a password. The Advanced and

Administrator views are identical except that in the Administrator view you can lock each individual group of items (by, of course, clicking the little lock icon to toggle it on or off as desired) to restrict option access inside the Control Panel itself.

I'll first show you how to access a Windows 2000 server for files and programs, and then, later in the section, I'll show you how to connect to a shared printer.

Accessing Shared Folders

A Windows 2000 server can make a wonderful file server for Macintosh clients. Many networks can benefit from the use of this configuration to store large multimedia files or simply to share the files for both Windows and Macintosh clients. Once you have set up the shared folders on your Windows 2000 server as discussed in the earlier sections of this chapter, you will be able to use those folders for Macintosh files and programs.

When you want to get to the shared Macintosh-accessible volume from a Macintosh client that is pre-MacOS 8.5, follow these steps:

1. From the Apple menu, select Chooser.

2. Once Chooser opens, select AppleShare (see Figure 13.13). You'll have the choice to either select the server name from the list or, if the name does not appear, click the Server IP Address button to enter the IP address of the Windows 2000 server.

FIGURE 13.13

The Chooser window showing the available connection options

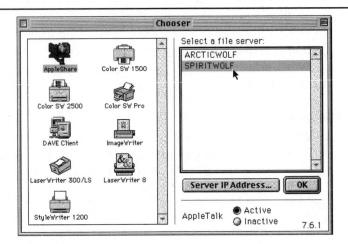

3. You'll receive a prompt to choose your authentication method (see Figure 13.14). Apple Standard UAMs will transmit the user authentication in clear text when contacting the Windows 2000 server. Microsoft Authentication will use an encrypted logon to the server. Click OK to begin logon.

4. Enter your username and password and then click OK. If your logon is authenticated, you will receive a list of Macintosh-accessible shared folders on the Windows 2000 server, as shown in Figure 13.15.

5. Click the shared folder you want to connect to. You can place a check mark beside the share name if you want the share to be connected at boot time. Click OK to continue.

FIGURE 13.14

Chooser presenting a choice of authentication modes

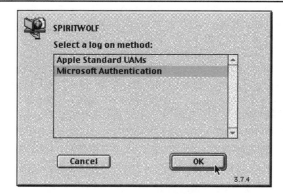

FIGURE 13.15

Chooser displaying a list of available shares on the Windows 2000 server

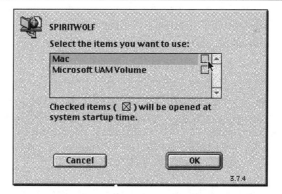

 TIP You can mount several volumes at once from a single server. Simply hold the Shift key and select each volume you would like to mount immediately. If you only select one and there are more available, you will have to go back into the Chooser or Network Browser to mount the remaining volumes.

This will connect you to the shared folder. Any files that have been saved to the folder by Windows clients will appear as text documents with a PC label at the top of the icon. MacOS 8.x includes a conversion utility that will automatically change the files to a format that the Macintosh can read. The files can be worked with directly from the shared folder or copied down to the Macintosh.

WARNING If Macintosh clients save files to the folder, the files will have the normal icons stored within their resource fork. Use caution when working with the files on the Windows 2000 server because Windows operating systems don't use the concept of multiple forks of data within a file. NTFS provides the ability to store two data forks for a single filename, but Windows 2000 doesn't use this method of storage for itself. Fortunately, if you do move a Macintosh file in Windows 2000, a prompt will appear asking if you would like to strip the resource fork or not. Click No and be happy. There is also, oddly, an option named Forkize that allows a Windows 2000 workstation or server to add a resource fork to a file destined for use on a Mac, alleviating the need for pesky and unreliable filename extensions.

When you want to mount the shared volumes from a Macintosh client that is running MacOS 8.5, follow these steps:

1. From the Apple menu, select the Network Browser item.

2. Once Network Browser opens, select the name of the server you wish to connect to. Note that there are small, blue arrows to the immediate left of the name. Click the arrow.

TIP For the Macintosh uninitiated: The little blue arrows work similarly to the plus/minus signs in a Windows tree view hierarchy. Click the arrow and the contents of the item next to it will appear below. Additional blue arrows will appear as needed.

3. A dialog will appear and you'll receive a prompt asking to authenticate yourself. Enter your logon information and click OK to begin logon.

4. If your logon is authenticated, a list of shared folders on the Windows 2000 server will appear in the familiar Macintosh list view.

5. Double-click the shared folder you want to connect to and its icon will appear on your desktop. If there are additional authentications required, enter the information for each one and click OK.

Accessing Shared Printers

Connecting to shared AppleTalk printers on a Windows 2000 server is much like connecting to a shared folder from the Macintosh. To connect to a shared printer with a pre-MacOS 8.5 system, follow these steps:

1. From the Apple menu, open the Chooser.

2. In the Chooser window (see Figure 13.16), select the appropriate printer type in the left pane. If you are printing to a PostScript printer other than an Apple printer, you can use the LaserWriter 8 type to connect. Once you have selected the printer type, Chooser will display the available printers on the network.

3. Select the printer you want to connect to and click the Create button.

 NOTE The first time you install a printer using these steps, the button text in Chooser will read Create. After that first install, the text will read Setup.

4. The Setup screen lets you choose a specific PostScript Printer Description (PPD) file, configure the settings for the printer, and retrieve printer information. When you are satisfied with the options, click the OK button.

FIGURE 13.16

The Chooser showing the Setup option for a shared printer

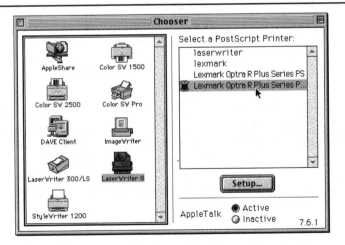

After the last step, the printer will be created on your desktop and set as the default printer. If you have more than one printer installed, you'll need to open the print configuration panel in every open application to set the correct printer selection after installing the new printer.

When you want to access network printers from a Macintosh client that is running MacOS 8.5, follow these steps:

1. From the Apple menu, select the Network Browser item.

2. Once Network Browser opens, select the name of the printer you wish to connect to.

3. Once you are connected to the printer, its icon, which you can use to drop documents onto, will appear on your desktop.

 NOTE Any Macintosh user connecting to a shared printer on a Windows 2000 server will be affected by printer permissions just as Windows clients are. The Mac user won't see any indication in his printer window as to what permissions have been assigned to him. If Macintosh users have not been given permission to use the shared printer, they will not be able to connect to it at all.

Implementing Security

User security is an issue with Macintosh clients just like it is with any other platform. The normal user authentication provided by AppleShare networking is to require a username and password. These credentials are transmitted in clear text, making it easy for someone skilled in the ways of cracking to compromise your network's security. Microsoft has taken steps to provide encrypted user-authentication capabilities for Macintosh clients.

 NOTE The reality is that crackers, popularly and incorrectly known as hackers, are few and far between, at least any that can compromise a MacOS Web server or a well-designed Windows security model. Most self-styled "hAcKeRz" are really 15 year olds with not much else to do and a yen for Nintendo. Don't take this to mean that you can leave your sensitive data lying about anywhere, but don't go overboard when designing your security model either.

There are three basic modes of authentication when a user at a Macintosh computer tries to log on to a Windows 2000 server:

Guest   This option lets the users log on using the Guest account on the Windows 2000 server. This option not only has no security involved, it fails to provide any kind of audit trail to track what the users are doing on the server while connected. The Guest account is normally disabled in Windows 2000.

Authenticated User   This option requires the user to log on using a valid user account. It does provide the ability to track users through the use of auditing, but it uses the standard Apple UAM that transmits the credentials as clear text.

Microsoft Authentication   This final option requires the presence of the correct version of the Microsoft UAM for your installed version of AppleShare. Microsoft authentication will encrypt all user credentials prior to transmitting them to the server.

The heart of Windows 2000's security features for the File Server for Macintosh is the User Authentication Module (UAM). The UAM allows a Mac user to participate in standard Windows 2000 user-level security and encrypts the credentials before transmitting them to the server. The encrypted form of the credentials is stored on the Windows 2000 server. When the Macintosh user logs on to the Windows 2000 server, the credentials are encrypted and sent to the server. The Windows 2000 server then compares the credentials sent by the client to the credentials stored on the server.

 WARNING   The UAM data can also be intercepted. Windows 2000 Server comes with 40-bit encryption capabilities to satisfy United States export laws regarding, that's right, munitions. If you prove you are located in the U.S. or Canada and agree to a restrictive EULA (End User License Agreement), you may download an updater that will bring Windows 2000 to 128-bit encryption. 40-bit encryption can be beat inside of a week on a single Pentium 133, so don't feel that safe.

The standard authentication is fine for most environments, even though it uses clear text when transmitting the password. But if your environment requires additional security, you should require your users to install the Microsoft UAM for Windows 2000.

 NOTE   If you have used the Macintosh services in Windows NT Server and then upgraded to Windows 2000 Server, you will need to install the new UAM on your Macintosh clients.

In past versions of Windows NT Server, the installation procedure for the Microsoft UAM was to simply copy the UAM folder for the version of AppleShare that you're using to your System folder on a Macintosh computer. This wasn't too difficult, but it did require you to know exactly which version of AppleShare was supported on your computer. Choosing the wrong version meant either a hang or a fatal error any time you tried to use the authentication.

Windows 2000 Server has introduced an even easier method for installing the UAM. Macintosh users will connect to the Microsoft UAM shared folder on the Windows 2000 server and double-click the Microsoft UAM Installer. This runs a native Macintosh program to select the appropriate version of the Microsoft UAM and then automatically copy the needed files to the System folder on the client. Users will also find a document in this share that describes the need for the Microsoft UAM and how to install it.

The Microsoft UAM runs a small program on the Macintosh client when a user tries to log on. The program provides spaces for the user to enter a name and password as well as a Windows 2000 domain to log on to. Once this has been filled in, the credentials are encrypted and transmitted.

To effectively use this security for your Macintosh clients, you must configure the properties for the File Server for Macintosh to allow Microsoft encryption. You can choose between multiple security schemes to decide whether you will accept standard Apple security, Microsoft security, or both. To configure the File Server for Macintosh, follow these steps:

1. Open Computer Management from the Administrative Tools group on the Start menu.

2. Click the plus sign beside System Tools to expand it.

3. Right-click Shared Folders in either the left or the right pane of the console, and select Configure File Server for Macintosh from the context menu.

4. In the resulting dialog, select the Security drop-down list box and then choose the appropriate method of logon. Click OK to save the changes.

Enabling the Microsoft encrypted logons will let your users connect to the Windows 2000 server with encrypted credentials instead of the standard clear text. You may actually find that the standard authentication is fine for most resources and that the Microsoft encrypted logons are more trouble than they're worth. But if you require security in your network environment, this will provide an adequate level of authentication for most purposes.

Setting Advanced Options

Occasionally it may be necessary to change some of the Registry settings for the SFM instead of using the graphical management tools provided by Windows 2000 Server. Normally, you would change all of these settings by using the Computer Management tool in the Administrative Tools group. These Registry settings are found in two basic locations: the adapter key(s) and the AppleTalk parameters key.

The values in Table 13.1 are found in this location:

```
HKLM\System\CurrentControlSet\Services\AppleTalk\Parameters
```

TABLE 13.1: THE REGISTRY SETTINGS IN THE APPLETALK PARAMETERS KEY

Value	Description
`DefaultPort Data type:REG_SZ`	This value determines the default port to which the AppleTalk protocol will be bound. If you aren't routing AppleTalk, only the Macs located on the local network will be able to access the server. The default value set at the time the SFM is installed is the first Ethernet adapter found on the server.
`DesiredZone Data type:REG_SZ`	This value sets the zone in which the SFM will participate. If no data is present in this value, SFM will use the default zone for the network.
`EnableRouter Data type:REG_DWORD`	This value determines whether the Windows 2000 server should act as an AppleTalk router for all of its installed network interfaces. Do not enable this setting unless you have more than one network adapter in the server and wish to use it as a router.

The settings listed in Table 13.2 have to do with the network adapter and will be present in multiple keys if there are multiple adapters present. The settings are found in the following location:

```
HKLM\System\CurrentControlSet\Services\AppleTalk\Parameters\
    Adapters\<network adapter name>
```

TABLE 13.2: THE REGISTRY SETTINGS IN THE ADAPTER KEY

Value	Description
`AarpRetries Data type:REG_DWORD`	This hexadecimal value determines how many times the Apple Address Resolution Protocol (AARP) will attempt to resolve a network address. The default is 0xA.
`DdpCheckSums Data type:REG_DWORD`	This value tells Windows 2000 to use the checksums in the DDP layer of the AppleTalk protocol. The default is 0x0 (false).
`DefaultZone Data type:REG_SZ`	This value contains the name of the default zone. This setting is only used if the Windows 2000 server is being used to seed the network.

Continued ▶

TABLE 13.2 CONTINUED: THE REGISTRY SETTINGS IN THE ADAPTER KEY	
Value	**Description**
`NetworkRangeLowerEnd Data type:REG_DWORD`	This value defines the lower end of the network number range and is only used if the server is being used to seed the network. The range of acceptable values is 0x1 to 0xFEFF.
`NetworkRangeUpperEnd Data type:REG_DWORD`	The same as the preceding value, but this value sets the upper bound of the network numbers available on the network. Acceptable ranges include 0x1 to 0xFEFF.
`PortName Data type:REG_SZ`	This value assigns a name in the form *adaptername@computername* to the adapter using AppleTalk so that it may be easily identified on the network.
`SeedingNetwork Data type:REG_DWORD`	This values determines whether the adapter will be seeding the network. If the value is 0x1 (true), AppleTalk will read the other seed information, and, if it's correct, AppleTalk will seed the network to set the default values for the Macintosh clients.
`ZoneList Data type:REG_MULTI_SZ`	If the adapter will be used to seed the network, this value defines the available zone names for the network.

As always, when editing the Registry, use extreme caution. Whenever possible, adjust these settings through the graphical user interface or the command prompt.

Supporting Applications across Platforms

Many of the applications your users will be using on Macintosh computers have Windows-based counterparts. This was one of the reasons for installing the SFM that I discussed at the beginning of this chapter. Fortunately, most of these applications are well documented and the necessary file extension information has already been entered into the SFM on Windows 2000.

Both the Windows and Macintosh platforms use some kind of file extension information to associate a document with the program that created it. If you stop and consider that these two platforms are really quite different, you'll begin to appreciate the convenience of this common approach.

With this association in place, a Macintosh user can create a Word document on his Mac and save it to the shared folder on a Windows 2000 server using the SFM. When a Windows user views the same document through a Windows share for the same server folder, she will see the icon associated with Word on her computer. She can then open the file natively in Word 97, make changes, and save them back to the network folder. When the Mac user comes along, he will find the document just as he left it, but with the changes added.

If by some chance you have an application for both platforms that is not already defined in Windows 2000 Server, you can add or modify the file extension associations. To add new file associations for the SFM, follow these steps:

1. Open Computer Management from the Administrative Tools group.

2. Expand System Tools and right-click Shared Folders.

3. Select Configure File Server for Macintosh from the context menu.

4. Click the File Association tab of the properties dialog.

5. In Files with MS-DOS Extension, enter an extension or select one by clicking the arrow. If the extension is already associated with a file type and creator, it will automatically be selected under Creator.

6. Under Creator, select a creator program and file type that you want to associate with this file extension.

7. To complete the operation, click Associate. Click OK to apply the change and close the window.

These associations affect the icons that users of each platform will see when they access the Macintosh share. When you've added a new file extension association, it will only affect files that are created after the association is made. Files that were created before the association will have the icon given to them by the creating application.

Network Alternatives

Windows 2000 is not the only player in the game. Apple's very own AppleShare IP has received many enhancements over the past two years, including the ability to serve Windows clients *natively*. That's right, AppleShare IP (ASIP) speaks SMB fluently and treats both Mac and Windows clients equally with one exception: Windows clients are limited to printing over TCP/IP only. This, however, is not often a real limitation in the modern network as most printers are capable of being accessed over TCP/IP.

AppleShare IP 6

ASIP 6 was the first version of ASIP to offer Windows connectivity. The previous version came bundled with an AppleTalk for Windows client that allowed ASIP to see the Windows machine as a Mac on the network. This was not particularly stable or reliable. So, what does this mean to you? Easy—a Mac can be loaded with ASIP to provide your entire network with TCP/IP printer access, regardless of platform.

ASIP's more multiplatform-friendly nature makes it a great alternative to complex (and rightly so!) Windows servers. There are some caveats to this convenience. One of the reasons ASIP is so easy to administer is its simplicity. ASIP combines a file, print, mail, FTP, and Web server in one package. Apple customers demand power made simple, so ASIP was designed to fit this need. As a result, some possibly powerful security features are not present.

 WARNING Even though an ASIP server can be added to a Windows workgroup, it cannot be added to a domain. ASIP does not have the functionality it would need to participate as a domain member. It does, however, work wonderfully as a workgroup server in mixed company.

This is not to say that an ASIP Web server is not secure. In fact, it's one of the most difficult to crack. It's quite the bear to break into a Mac Web server as evidenced by the Crack-A-Mac challenge (www.crackamac.com). The site successfully withstood constant attack by would-be crackers for three months before one particularly creative individual was able to exploit a chink in SiteEdit for Macintosh. The hacker was able to gain access to the server through another product and view all files on the drive and retrieve the passwords file. After gaining access to the SiteEdit password file, the hacker was able to use SiteEdit to modify the home page.

The fault lay in the combination of software and not in a particular security hole presented directly by a particular server product. Once this hole, which apparently was very difficult to find (the cracker maintained secrecy and did not make the hole available to the public), was patched, the Mac became secure again. The challenge has since been closed as there is no interest in a server-cracking challenge that cannot be won.

 NOTE For some perspective, the prize that was offered was an Apple PowerBook 3400/240, now two years old and much slower than the PowerBook G3/350 available today. That's a long time for a server that is constantly barraged with solicited attacks to only be illegally accessed once.

That's Not a Mac?

For much greater security in the Mac world, one would need the services of Apple's latest arrival, MacOS X Server. Essentially OpenStep, Apple cofounder Steve Jobs's operating system based on the MACH kernel, MacOS X Server gives the familiar Mac face a real tweaking with the MacOS-compatible Unix variant. Running on the well-known Unix-like MACH 2.5 kernel, it is capable of running slightly modified Unix software, POSIX software, and the MacOS (in an emulation environment called the Yellow Box, of course), and it even includes a command line, a first for any version of the Macintosh system software.

 NOTE Familiar with the iMac? Who isn't, right? Well, MacOS X Server can use its Netboot capabilities to provide bootable systems for up to 50 iMacs from one server. Plug the iMac into the server via Ethernet, remove the HDD from the iMac, set up Netboot services on the server, and turn on the iMac. The iMac will boot directly from the server with only a cursory glance to see if there's a HDD. Each iMac has its own boot configuration and never has to store anything locally. The network computer lives!

Despite its attractive exterior, the server is a powerful and secure engine with all the benefits of Unix and few of the interface complexities, making it quite attractive to Mac networks that were serving via Windows NT. The one major drawback? No built-in Windows serving capabilities. There is, however, a version of Samba available for MacOS X Server, and the source is available if you're familiar with modifying code for recompilation.

Its benefits? Most Windows NT/2000 administrators have at least a passing familiarity with Unix in some form or another. MacOS X Server is a powerful and inexpensive Mac-savvy server that has the ability to work hand-in-hand with Windows on a network with a little tweaking. It also has security possibilities far above and beyond ASIP.

So, What Are You Saying?

Since you're wondering why all the Mac server talk, it's simple. Windows 2000, which has a strong foundation in Windows NT, is not the perfect solution for all problems. Any admin will agree that there are other solutions that are worth investigating. In the case of the Mac, if they do populate a portion of your network, they should be given every consideration. Most people who use Macs in an office setting would experience drastically reduced work performance if forced to supplant their old Mac for a Windows machine.

For this it is important to remember the Mac. If they were added to or originally populated the network before your arrival, it's because someone felt it important or felt that progress could be made if some employees were offered an alternative. Give these users and the company an opportunity to use the Mac technology and leverage the available technologies that make solid use of the Mac in a network environment, even a mission-critical environment.

NOTE There is a project at UCLA called Appleseed that combines eight G3/400 Power Macs together via 100Base-T Ethernet and special software to create a parallel-processing supercomputer that can beat the pants off of a Cray T3E-900. Running ZDNet's PIC test-bench series, an Appleseed four-CPU arrangement was able to finish the test in 421 nanoseconds compared to the Cray's 481. Total cost for Appleseed? Eight Macs, 2.30GB RAM, 48GB disk cost $22,461. Total cost for the Cray? Let's just say that eight years ago, one Cray cost $20 million. They're still not cheap.

Just keep in mind that in the end, regardless of what we prefer or what we think will work better, it's the best solution that is most important. Windows 2000 provides all needs and more for a cross-platform network, but it can use a hand in a few departments. That's where MacOS X Server or AppleShare IP can come in. They're easy to work with and require very little maintenance. A friend of mine has a Power Mac 7100/80 that runs MacOS 8.1 and ASIP 6.1 and serves as a file server for his in-home network. It's been running, with five exceptions for restarts and one power outage, for eight months non-stop (this is a "consumer" machine!). Keep that in mind the next time someone tries to offer you the benefits of Windows over the Mac.

CHAPTER 14

Supporting Clients with Windows Terminal Services

Multiuser Windows, server-based computing, thin client computing—whatever you call it, it's part of Windows 2000's server line.

Multiuser Windows has been around for quite a while. Citrix created MultiWin, the set of extensions to Windows NT that allows it to run multiple user sessions from the same machine. The first MultiWin product was multiuser NT 3.51, Citrix's WinFrame. Starting in July 1998, Microsoft began shipping its Terminal Server Edition of NT 4 (TSE).

So the support for terminal services in Win2K isn't new. What *is* new about the multiuser support in Win2K is that this is the first time that support for server-based computing has been an intrinsic part of a base Windows operating system. Terminal Services is now something you can turn on or off as needed, making it just one more handy tool in the operating system. And it *is* handy.

Setting up Terminal Services is not always easy. There's a fair amount of tweaking to be done once you get past the basic fact of running applications from the terminal server. If you're serious about administering a terminal server, I *highly* recommend that you make the Terminal Services section of the Microsoft Knowledge Base your favorite pleasure reading, because this is new territory to Microsoft and they're still working the bugs out. But don't stress too much about it, because it's really not hard to get Terminal Services up and running.

 TIP Keeping up with new Knowledge Base articles can be a big job. To help you, *Windows NT Magazine* publishes a free biweekly Terminal Services newsletter that includes Terminal Services news and a summary of the new Knowledge Base articles related to Terminal Services. To subscribe to the newsletter, go to the *Windows NT Magazine* Web site at www.winntmag.com.

Why Care About Terminal Services?

Why care about server-based computing at all? Three reasons: you can use lower-end hardware and thus break that upgrade cycle, you can more easily keep people from misconfiguring their computers, and you can install applications in a central location rather than on each client PC. Finally, Terminal Services allows you to manipulate the server from another console, which can be handy.

Less Processing Power Required on the Client

First, about those ever-more-powerful computers… Does it take a 450MHz Pentium II with 64MB of RAM installed to check e-mail, do accounting, and poke around on the

Web a bit? Of course it doesn't, but, as of mid-1999, that's what you get if you go shopping for a new system. Not that these computers are too expensive in absolute terms; I'm wryly amused by the fact that every time I buy a new computer, I pay less for a system more powerful than the last one I bought. But although they're not too expensive in absolute terms, the new computers aren't always worth it because what you're doing doesn't demand all that much from your hardware. Ironically, you're often more likely to need a powerful computer at home than at work, as game hardware requirements are so high. It takes more computing power to play a few swift rounds of Diablo than it does to write a report. (Fighting demons is hard work.)

The trouble is, sometimes you do need those more powerful computers if you're planning to keep up with existing software technology. True—you don't need the world's fastest computer to do word processing. You may, however, need a computer faster than the one you've got if you're going to keep up with the latest and greatest word processing package that everyone's using. If you want to be able to read all those charts and graphs, you can't always do it when the word processor you're using is six years old, even if it still suits your in-house needs. Keeping up with those new hardware requirements can get expensive and time consuming. Making old software work on new hardware can be at least as much of a headache, as you discover that although that old 486 is still as fast as you need, it won't run Win2K Professional.

Using Terminal Services allows you to put that 450MHz to work for many people, not just one.

Simplifying the User Interface

Then there's the myriad of options available on operating systems nowadays. I'm not sure why Microsoft keeps talking about how using a computer gets easier and easier. Speaking as the favorite source of free tech support for my parents (and some of my friends and *their* parents), I, for one, am not buying this idea. Experienced users may find it easier to customize their interface, but those who are less experienced find all sorts of pitfalls when it comes to using their computers: so many options that they get confused, and too many ways to break something. Most people use the computer as a tool to get their jobs done, not as an end in itself.

Thin client computing, in combination with group policies, can make the interface more task oriented for users. This is particularly true with Windows-based terminals, which are little more than a monitor, a box, and a keyboard and mouse. There's nothing local to break and no way to break it. Set up user rights and system policies thoughtfully, and users can't configure the Win2K terminal environment either.

Centralized Deployment of Applications

One great benefit to Terminal Services is how it simplifies application deployment. You don't need to install applications locally, don't need to develop unattended installation scripts that will install an application suite, don't need to worry about bandwidth or locally available resources when pushing applications to the desktop. Install it once, and everyone who should have access to the application will. If the application runs on the terminal server, it'll run for the terminal client—end of story.

Well, not *quite* the end of the story. Some applications work better in a single-user environment than in a terminal server environment. I'll talk more about how you need to install applications in a multiuser environment to make them work properly. And in case you thought that installing applications on a terminal server meant that you could support many users with a single license, think again—you'll still need to pay for application licensing for each user or computer connecting to the applications published on the terminal server. However, the basic fact remains true: set an application up once on the terminal server, and it's available to everyone who has access to the terminal server.

Remote Server Administration

Terminal services aren't just convenient for your user base; they're convenient for you, too. I've really gotten to like the convenience of popping onto my server from my desktop—without moving. If you don't use terminal services for anything else, consider using them as a remote access tool so that you can edit server settings from anywhere on the network, even across the Internet.

That's why I care about server-based computing. But why Windows 2000? Mostly, it's a matter of cost and features. If you want to make a Win2K Desktop available to clients who wouldn't ordinarily be able to have it, and you want to do it in the most cost-effective manner possible, you'll use Win2K. You'll need to have Win32 clients, you'll need to run TCP/IP on your network, and you won't get some of the cool features that add-ons like MetaFrame can get you. But Windows 2000 Server is an excellent tool for providing basic terminal services.

The Ultimate Solution for Zero Administration Networking ... *Not*

Every once in a while, someone asks me whether server-based computing is going to replace fat client computing. My answer to that is always an unqualified No.

Why won't terminal services replace fat PCs? Two main reasons:

- Demanding applications or users
- Not all applications work well in multiuser environments

Similar as these explanations are, they're not quite the same thing.

Demanding Clients

First, Terminal Services is not built to provide a full-scale 450MHz screamer to all clients. The point of Terminal Services, after all, is that much of the power of that 450MHz screamer is going to waste when only one person is using it. If it *isn't* going to waste for a person or a particular application, then that person or application is not a good candidate for a terminal server environment. Terminal Services is not suitable for really power-hungry applications or heavy usage. It's best for those people on your network who need light and occasional access to a PC. For those who do serious calculations or graphics work—or anything else that requires a lot of CPU power—you're better off with powerful PCs.

 TIP Often, the best terminal server environment is a hybrid environment. Load power-hungry applications locally and lighter applications on the terminal server.

Uncooperative Applications

Second, not all applications run equally well in a terminal server environment. As I've mentioned and will mention again when I talk about application tweaking, some applications are too demanding to cooperate well with others, or aren't served well by RDP. Additionally, not all *types* of applications work well.

Terminal Services works best for Win32 applications. The reason for this has to do with how Win2K itself runs Win32 and Win16 applications. Win2K is itself a 32-bit application, and it can't run Win16 applications on its own. Instead, it creates a Virtual DOS Machine (VDM), which is a 32-bit application, and runs the Win16 application within the context of that VDM. The practical upshot of this, combined with the fact that translating 16-bit calls to the operating system into 32-bit calls takes some overhead, means that Win16 applications perform less well in this environment than Win32 applications. They'll work—a good thing, since you may not have a choice about running them if that's what you're using—but they'll use more memory than Win32 apps.

 TIP You can see the list of executable images, which map to processes, from the Terminal Services Manager tool in the Administrative Tools program group.

DOS applications present another kind of problem. Actually, they present two other kinds of problems. First, DOS applications were written for a single-user, single-tasking environment. To be as responsive as possible, DOS applications constantly poll the keyboard buffer, looking for input that's meant for them. This means that a DOS application in the foreground, even when not doing anything, is using up an astounding amount of CPU time. This is acceptable in a single-user environment, but won't work when that CPU time has to be shared with a dozen people.

 NOTE Turn to the "Session Time-outs" section later in this chapter to see how to reduce the amount of time DOS—and Windows—applications spend checking for input. In Chapter 20, I'll talk more about how to use the System Monitor to detect application-caused stresses on the system.

Second, DOS applications with a GUI don't use Windows graphics rendering instructions, but bitmaps. Bitmaps take much longer to download to the client than GDI rendering instructions, so session responsiveness will suffer. Bitmap-displaying applications are jerky at best in a terminal server environment, and more often are completely unusable.

You *can* run DOS and Win16 applications in a terminal server environment. They just won't cooperate with other applications as well as Win32 applications will. DOS applications in particular probably won't look as good as they would running locally.

Thus, Terminal Services is best for people who run Win32 applications and don't require a powerful computer devoted to their needs. Those who don't fit this profile will continue to need personal computers.

What's Missing in Windows 2000 Terminal Services?

Win2K isn't the be-all and end-all of thin client computing. On the plus side, the shared Clipboard included in Win2K is vital to any kind of session transparency, if you truly want users to not care whether their applications are running locally or on the terminal server. Session shadowing gives you an invaluable troubleshooting tool for seeing what terminal users are doing and helping them resolve problems while you sit at your desk. And it's handy to be able to use a locally connected printer without having to go through the rigmarole of sharing the printer with the network and then connecting to the share from the terminal server session. However, there are also some features that would be nice to have in Win2K terminal services that are presently only available in third-party products, among them:

Support for Non-Windows Clients Strictly speaking, Terminal Services in Win2K does not even support all Windows clients—it works only with Win32 operating systems and Windows for Workgroups. If you have Windows 3.*x* or DOS clients, or some brand of Unix (including Linux) or Macintosh clients that you'd like to run Windows applications in a native Win2K environment, you'll need Citrix's MetaFrame.

Although Linux, Unix, and Java versions of RDP (the display protocol used by Win2K terminal services) exist, they're very new and kludgy at this writing. For best performance with non-Windows applications in a terminal server environment, at least as of the beginning of 2000, I'd recommend using ICA, which means using MetaFrame.

Multiprotocol Support Terminal Services uses the Remote Display Protocol (RDP) to pass user input and terminal output between client and server. RDP is dependent on TCP/IP, which means that both the client and the server must be running it. This isn't all that big a deal, because the Win32 clients that Terminal Services supports all come with TCP/IP. The ubiquity of the Internet makes TCP/IP the transport protocol of choice on most networks anyway, but Terminal Services does lock you into one protocol. The ICA protocol used with Citrix's MetaFrame, in contrast, supports IPX/SPX and NetBEUI.

Seamless Client Sessions The window displaying a terminal server session or Desktop is the same size as the local window—ask for a 1024 × 768 window, and you've got one. The only catch to this is that the frames for the session window and the Taskbar on the bottom of the screen mean that you must scroll around to see the entire session window, or else run in full-screen mode, with no same-screen access to your locally running applications. Microsoft did this on purpose, but I think it's a mistake, and prefer Citrix's tactic of shaving the window slightly so that it's actually a little smaller than the listed resolution. Personally, I miss a few pixels less than I mind having to scroll back and forth to see everything on my Desktop. (You can use the Ctrl+Alt+Break sequence to toggle between a Win2K terminal server full-screen session and the local Desktop, however.)

Server Farming With Win2K, you can create client connections that supply only applications, but the user must know which server is running the application and make an explicit connection to it. With MetaFrame 1.8, you can create general client connections to a set of servers running a certain application, without the client having to know or care which server is providing the application. Server farming automatically downloads the links to the applications to the client desktop via the Program Neighborhood, instead of making clients pull the applications to themselves. (Not all ICA clients currently support the Program Neighborhood, but Citrix is working on updating all their clients and by the beginning of 2000 should have Program Neighborhood capabilities for most or all of them.)

Load Balancing Load balancing is not unique to multiuser Windows; it's the ability of multiple servers to work in tandem so that the least-busy server processes client requests. Windows 2000 Server does not support load balancing. Win2K *Advanced* Server and Win2K DataCenter do, but only for user logons, not for running applications. To get application load balancing, you'll need a third-party product such as

NCD's ThinPath Load Balancing Services, or, if you're using MetaFrame, Citrix's Load Balancing Services (separate from MetaFrame).

Sound   I don't find much use for sound in an office environment, but there are those who do. The RDP display protocol that Win2K supports does not transport audio output at this time. If you want sound, you need either MetaFrame or NCD's ThinPath Plus! installed on the terminal server. (Incidentally, ThinPath Plus! is free for download from NCD's Web site at ncd.com.) That said, the sound you're going to get isn't all that great no matter what product you're using. Network protocols—even the streaming ones like TCP/IP—don't do sound well, and your ear won't be as forgiving as your eye is.

High-End Video Support   This limitation isn't restricted to Win2K's terminal services. As of this writing, *no* display protocols support color depth greater than 256 colors. For high-quality video in a thin client environment, you'll need direct video support like that found in the MaxSpeed MaxStations. MaxStations eliminate the limitations of display protocols by skipping them altogether. Instead, they use a piece of Category 5 UTP and Citrix's Direct ICA protocol (part of MetaFrame) to provide a direct video feed to the client from the server. Three of the four wires of the cable download output to the client, while the fourth uploads keyboard and mouse input to the server. As of this writing, the MaxStation's direct video support is only 256 colors, too, but the video display is much quicker than what you can get with a display protocol, making it possible to run even games in a thin client environment. MaxSpeed expects to release their Win2K-only direct video driver in 1999, so by the time you're reading this book, the next generation of direct video should be out and you'll be able to get direct video to a MaxStation without buying MetaFrame. The new MaxStations are supposed to support color depths of 64,000 colors at 800 × 600, or even 24-bit color at 640 × 480. 1024 × 768 resolutions will display up to 256 colors. (We'll see how that goes. At iForum 1999, I was talking with a MaxSpeed representative about this, and he admitted, "This is a little more complicated than we'd originally thought.")

All that said, Win2K Terminal Services is a perfectly serviceable tool for implementing terminal services in your network. And Win2K has one *great* advantage over third-party products: if you've bought Windows 2000 Server, you've already paid for it. MetaFrame is not cheap and even *it* doesn't come with all the bells and whistles you might want.

The Terminal Server Processing Model

Thin client networking refers to any network in which the lion's share of all application processing takes place on a server, instead of a client. The term refers to a network by definition, so it leaves out stand-alone small computing devices such as personal data assistants (PDAs) or handheld PCs, although you can add thin client support to some of these devices. What makes thin client networking and computing "thin" is not the size of the operating system nor the complexity of the apps run on the client, but how processing is distributed. In a thin client network, all processing takes place on the server. All video output is rendered on the client.

You may have heard thin client networking described as a return to the mainframe paradigm. (This has been less politely phrased as, "You just reinvented the mainframe, stupid!") This comparison is partly apt and partly misleading. It's true that applications are stored and run on a central server, with only output shown at the client. However, the applications being run in the thin client environment are different from those run in a mainframe environment; mainframes didn't support word processing or slideshow packages, and the video demands on the Windows client are necessarily greater than they were with a text-based green-screen terminal. Yet the degree of control that thin client networking offers is mainframe-like, and I've heard one person happily describe thin client networking and the command it gave him over his user base as, "a return to the good old mainframe days."

Why the move from centralized computing to personal computers and back again? Business applications drove the development of PCs—the new applications simply couldn't work in a mainframe environment. Not all mainframes were scrapped, by any means, but the newer application designs were too hardware-intensive to work well in a shared computing environment. But those applications came back to a centralized model when it became clear that the mainframe model had some things to offer that a PC-based LAN did not. Grouping of computing resources to make sure none are wasted. Centralized distribution of applications. Clients that don't have to be running the latest and greatest operating system with the latest and greatest hardware to support it. Client machines that don't require power protection, because they're not running any applications locally.

Thin client networking is not for everyone or for every situation. However, it's got some good things to recommend it.

Anatomy of a Thin Client Session

There are three parts to a thin client networking session:

- The *terminal server*, running a multiuser operating system
- The *display protocol*, which is a data link layer protocol that creates a virtual channel between server and client through which user input and graphical output can flow
- The client, which can be running any kind of operating system

The Terminal Server

In Win2K, Terminal Services is one of the optional components that you can choose to install during Setup, like Transaction Services or Internet Information Services. If you've enabled Terminal Services, when Win2K boots up and loads the core operating system, the terminal service begins listening for client connection requests at a TCP port. At the same time, a special client session for the console (that is, the interface available from the terminal server itself) is created, along with two dormant client connections. So that client connections may load quickly, the first two connections will use those dormant sessions. The console session is assigned session ID 0. Additional sessions are numbered in order, with the caveat that even when a client session is closed (logged off, not disconnected, so the session no longer exists on the terminal server) its session ID is not reused.

Every session has the parts shown in Table 14.1.

TABLE 14.1 PROCESSES COMMON TO TERMINAL SERVICES SESSIONS

Component	Function
Win32 Subsystem	Win32 subsystem required for running Win32 applications (including the Win2K GUI).
User Authentication Module	Logon process responsible for capturing username and password information and passing it to the security subsystem for authentication.
Executable Environment for Applications	All Win32 user applications and virtual DOS machines run in the context of the user shell.

The other processes in the session will depend on the applications that the user is running. The really crucial points to be learned from this are that every session has its own copy of the Win32 subsystem (so it has a unique Desktop and unique instances of the processes that support the Desktop) and its own copy of the Winlogon application that authenticates user identity. Note that session processes are not spawned by the Terminal Server process, but are created by the Session Manager.

About those other files: Win2K does not have to run a separate copy of each application used in each session. When you start up an application, you're loading certain data into memory. For example, if you run MyApp 99, you'll load files A–E into memory to provide basic functionality. However, if you start a second instance of MyApp, is it really necessary to load all those files into memory again? You could do this, but as more and more sessions started up on the terminal server the duplicated DLLs would cause the server to quickly run out of memory. But if you let all instances of

MyApp use the same copies of A–E, then if one instance needs to write on part of that information, all other instances will be affected. To get around the wasted-space/data-corruption dilemma, Win2K uses *copy-on-write* data sharing. Data is available on a read-only basis to as many applications that need it and are able to reference it. Let an application *write* to that data, however, and the memory manager will copy the edited data to a new location for that application's exclusive use.

Single-user operating systems also have to deal with multiple instances of applications (for example, if you're running two copies of Word), and they preserve memory with the same copy-on-write mechanism. Copy-on-write and other memory management functions work the same way in a multiuser environment as they do in a single-user environment. The main difference in memory management lies in how the kernel memory space is accessed. Because the kernel memory space is visible to every process active on the system, it's visible to all *sessions*. Thus, in multiuser Windows, a new address range located in the kernel 2GB and called SessionSpace maps all running processes to a session ID. Each time a remote user connects to Win2K, a new session ID is generated. All the processes created to run within that session are associated with that session ID. This keeps Win2K from becoming confused as to which process in which session asked for what data.

The Remote Desktop Protocol

You can run all the sessions you like on the terminal server, but that won't do you any good unless you can view the session output from a remote computer and upload your input to the terminal server for processing. The mechanism that allows you to do both is called the *display protocol*.

A display protocol downloads instructions for rendering graphical images from the terminal server to the client, and uploads keyboard and mouse input from the client to the server. Win2K natively supports the Remote Desktop Protocol (RDP) version 5, and with Citrix's MetaFrame add-on to Terminal Services, it supports the Independent Computing Architecture (ICA) protocol. RDP is based on the T.120 protocol originally developed for Net Meeting, and as such has some theoretical capabilities that aren't realized in the release product. The way it's implemented now, RDP is a point-to-point connection that runs with TCP/IP to display the Windows 2000 Server Desktop to the Desktop of a client running any Win32 operating system (including Windows CE) or Windows for Workgroups 3.11.

 NOTE   Yes, you can run multiple sessions from a single client, and even multiple sessions for a single user. However, each session is still a point-to-point connection.

RDP in Win2K has some features that were not supported in Windows Terminal Server Edition. The Clipboard now works between local and remote applications, so you can copy text from the copy of Microsoft Word running on the terminal server to your local instance of Notepad. When running a terminal server session from a PC, you can now print to a locally connected printer. (With TSE, you had to share the printer from your local PC and then connect to it from the terminal session like a net-work share, or else use a third-party product that supported local printing.) Bitmap caching is improved in the new operating system to speed up screen redraws on the client end. And Win2K supports session shadowing, which allows you to take control of someone else's terminal session and either see what they're doing or manipulate the Desktop for them, all from another terminal session. RDP still only runs with TCP/IP, and it still only supports Win32 clients, but it works quite well for what it does.

The Client Session

So we've got a terminal server running sessions, and a display protocol to pass information to and from the sessions. All we're missing now is someone to *use* the sessions.

A client session starts when a client computer logs into the terminal server (see Figure 14.1). During this session, client input in the form of mouse clicks and keystrokes is uploaded to the server via the virtual channel. The commands to render bitmaps showing the interface are downloaded to the client via the same virtual channel.

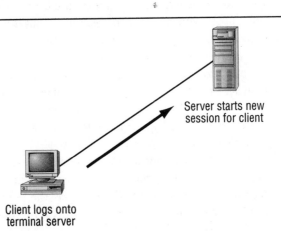

Server starts new
session for client

Client logs onto
terminal server

Session 0—the console session—does not use the same keyboard and video drivers that client sessions use. Whereas Session 0 uses the NT video and keyboard drivers, the client sessions use drivers based in the Remote Desktop Protocol.

Once the graphics rendering instructions are downloaded to the client, the client-side CPU and RAM create the images for display. The processing demands placed on the client are reduced by two factors. First, the display protocol only supports up to 256 colors, so the demands on the video card won't be all that great.

Second, RDP has a feature called *client-side caching* that allows the client to "remember" images that have already been downloaded during the session. With caching, only the changed parts of the screen are downloaded to the client during each refresh. For example, if the icon for Microsoft Word has already been downloaded to the client, there's no need for it to be downloaded again as the image of the Desktop is updated. Data is stored in the cache for a limited amount of time and then eventually discarded using the Least Recently Used (LRU) algorithm. When the cache gets full, the data that has been unused the longest is discarded in favor of new data.

 NOTE In Win2K, the image on the screen is updated about 20 times per second when the session is active. If the person logged into the session stops sending mouse clicks and keystrokes to the server, then the terminal server notes the inactivity and reduces the refresh rate to 10 times per second until client activity picks up again.

During the course of the session, the user can work on the terminal server as though he or she were physically at the terminal server, using the client machine's keyboard and mouse. As the client runs applications, loads data into memory, accesses shared resources on the network (see Figure 14.2), and generally uses the operating system, the applications use the CPU time and memory of the server. The only restrictions on the client are those defined by security settings and those inherent to the display protocol used. Clients can only run the applications on the server to which they're given access (you can control this with security policies).

FIGURE 14.2

The client is not limited to accessing the terminal server, but can use shared resources within the domain.

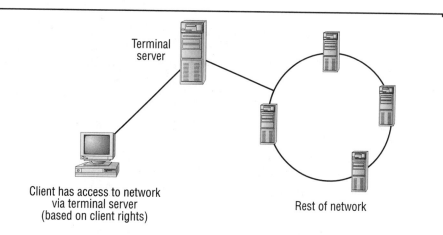

Terminal server

Client has access to network via terminal server (based on client rights)

Rest of network

The terminal session keeps per-session processes from corrupting each other or viewing each other's data. However, although the sessions are allowed to ignore each other, they still have to coexist. That is, a session is separate from any other sessions already running or that begin while that session is in progress (see Figure 14.3). However, all sessions use the same resources—CPU time, memory, operating system functions—so the operating system must divide the use of these resources among all of them.

Each session has a high-priority thread reserved for keyboard and mouse input and display output. Because all session threads have the same priority, the scheduler processes user input in round-robin format, with each session's input thread having a certain amount of time to process data before control of the CPU passes to another user thread. Thus, the more active sessions that are in place, the more competition there is for CPU time.

The number of sessions that a terminal server can run depends on how many sessions the hardware can support and how many licenses are available. When a session ends, the virtual channel to the client machine is closed and the resources allocated to that session are released.

FIGURE 14.3

Sessions are separate, but tap into the same resource pool.

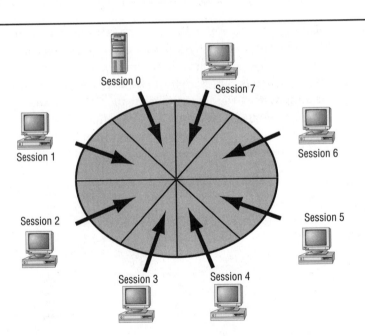

Note that in addition to each client session, there's also a session for the server's use. All locally run services and executables run within the context of this server session.

TIP If a terminal server client disconnects from an active session without logging off, that session remains active on the Terminal Services server. Active sessions get CPU time even if they don't have data to process. Thus, although it's handy to terminate a session and find yourself back in exactly the same place, if a session will be unused for a while, it's a good idea to end it altogether and log back on later.

Server and Client Requirements

The computing model for thin client networking means that the horsepower is typically concentrated on the server end, not the client. Because the server will be supporting one or two dozen people—maybe more, if the client usage load is light—this is not the time to skimp on power.

Server Hardware

The notion of using a bigger server so that you can skimp on client-side hardware isn't new. That's all a file server is: a computer running a big, fast hard disk so that you don't have to buy big, fast hard disks for everyone in the office. Terminal servers are designed on a similar principle: if most of the processing takes place in a single location, you can concentrate the hardware resources needed to support that processing in a single location and worry less about power on the client end.

For the purposes of running an efficient terminal server, the bare minimum required to run Win2K won't cut it. It was technically possible to run a TSE session from a terminal server with a Pentium 133 and 32MB of RAM—I've done it. So long as only one person is connected to the terminal server, such a configuration would work fine. Run a few more sessions from that computer, however, and performance will slow to a crawl. Given that the base operating demands of Win2K are much greater than those of NT 4, this is even truer today. In fact, if you're upgrading to Win2K from TSE, you'll definitely need to beef up your servers even if nothing else has changed. The much heavier demands of the operating system will impact the performance of client sessions.

Instead of working from those bare minimums, load up the server's CPU, RAM, and adapter cards. Get a fast processor, or a multiprocessor-capable machine so you can add more processors. (Typically, you can support about 12–15 users per CPU and get acceptable performance, a few more if usage is light, and a few less if usage is heavy.) Windows 2000 Server supports up to four processors, and you'll likely end up needing that kind of support if you're providing terminal services to a lot of people. Install lots of memory, basing your estimates on the applications that people use and the memory demands of the files they open. (PowerPoint presentations will stress the system more than, say, text-based e-mail.) Most people I've seen are using from 512MB to 1GB of RAM in their terminal servers. Use a PCI network card instead of an ISA so that you get data on and off the network as quickly as possible without stressing the CPU. Because of the copy-on-write memory management that lets you get reuse processes loaded in memory, it's better to have a few very powerful terminal servers than many less powerful terminal servers, but you'll need to make sure that those few powerful ones are up to the task. The resource you're most likely to run out of first is memory.

 TIP This recommendation of a few powerful servers over many less powerful ones applies to thin client networking within a LAN. If your network extends over several remote sites, consider putting at least one terminal server at each site so that clients can access the terminal server locally, rather than over the slow WAN link.

One thing you needn't worry too much about is video support. Because display protocols only support a maximum of 256 colors, that's all you'll need on the server end. And even if the server's video card can only display 16 colors, the client display is dependent on client capabilities, not server capabilities, so client computers will display 256 colors even if the server doesn't.

 NOTE For more information about how to use the performance monitoring tools to determine what kind of hardware you'll need on the terminal server, turn to Chapter 20.

If you're looking for specific guidelines on how much memory and CPU power you're going to need to power your terminal server, I'm afraid that there aren't any universal rules other than Think Big (as in, lots of it) and Think Expandable. Use the System Monitor and other performance monitoring tools to get an idea as to how your applications and usage patterns will stress your system, and plan accordingly.

The specifics of how much hardware you need on the server end depends heavily on the stress you're planning to put on the terminal server. The degree of stress, in turn, is a function of the applications that will run on the terminal server, the number of people who will be using those applications, and how intensely those people are going to be using them.

Client Hardware

When connecting to a terminal server, you'll use a PC with a Win32 operating system loaded, a Windows-based terminal (WBT), or a handheld PC using Windows CE.

Windows-Based Terminals

In its narrowest definition, a Windows-based terminal (WBT) is a network-dependent thin client device that supports the RDP protocol. Some WBTs also support ICA, the display protocol used to connect to Citrix versions of multiuser Windows.

A WBT includes a CPU, some amount of memory, network and video support, and input devices: a keyboard (or equivalent) and mouse (or equivalent). The case is sealed, and a monitor is not included. The operating system (Windows CE, NT Embedded, Linus, or a proprietary operating system) is stored in local memory. As no applications are processed on the client side, a WBT doesn't need much memory or CPU power. That said, a WBT's "thin" profile would put many older PCs to shame. A typical WBT might have a 200MHz CPU and 32MB of memory installed; as recently as when Windows 95 hit the market, a reasonably well-equipped PC had 8MB of RAM and a 486DX CPU. WBTs are thin, but they're not going to replace Kate Moss on the modeling circuit.

Not all WBTs fit perfectly into this definition. Some devices sold as WBTs actually have some characteristics more like those of network computers (NCs), including the ability to run some applications locally. One example of such a computer is Netier's Netxpress SL2000 WBT, which has a locally installed operating system (NT Workstation), and a locally stored browser, and a locally stored media player for faster performance. In September 1999, Microsoft created a new class of Windows-based terminals called "Windows-based terminals Professional" that are configured like the Netier devices but use NT Embedded instead of NT Workstation. Windows-based terminals based on Windows CE are "Standard" Windows-based terminals. WBTs are identified not by their operating system but by their class.

 NOTE Some Linux-based terminals that are capable of displaying Windows sessions also support RDP, but, as of this writing, you're not likely to use them in a Win2K-only environment with no MetaFrame installed. The Linux RDP client is not as fast as the native Windows ones, and, in general, although Linux Windows terminals are apt to have a lower list price than Windows-based terminals, they're more of a pain to administer and don't perform as well in an RDP-only environment.

PC Clients

At this point, more people are using PCs than WBTs for terminal server client machines. This is due to a couple of factors. First, unless they're starting afresh, they've already got the PCs. Even though WBTs are a little less expensive than low-end PCs—not much, though—they're still an added cost. Second, because not all applications work well in a terminal server environment, it's often best to run some applications from the terminal server and some locally. Unless you're buying new hardware and don't anticipate any need to run applications locally, you're more likely to have to work with PCs.

To work with Win2K's Terminal Services, the PCs must be running a Win32 OS, have support for the RDP display protocol installed, and have a live network connection using TCP/IP and a valid IP address.

Handheld PCs

Handheld PCs (H/PCs) aren't all that common yet, but they're likely to become so. They're a handy substitute for a laptop, being inexpensive, lightweight, and thrifty with their power, so that you can actually use them during the entire flight instead of having to give up two hours after takeoff. Normally, they run WinCE and, thus, only WinCE-compatible applications such as Pocket Office. By downloading and installing the Terminal Services client for Handheld PCs, you can run Windows-based applications when connected to Win2K Terminal Services over wired, wireless LAN, or dial-up connections.

A handheld PC looks a little like a laptop's younger sibling. The Hewlett-Packard Jornada 820 I have, for example, is about $8 \times 10 \times 1$ inches and weighs about 2.5 pounds. It has a total of 16MB of RAM: 8MB for running applications—all it needs since the applications are designed for running in a low-memory environment—and 8MB for data storage. A handheld PC does not have any drives—hard disk, floppy disk, or CD. It has an internal modem, but no network card, so to get network support you'll need a PC-Card network card designed to work with WinCE. The keyboard is 76 percent the size of a normal 101-key keyboard, but with a little practice, even those with huge hands (yes, we tried this in the name of science) can type at normal speed.

Unlike laptops, a handheld PC isn't really in a position to replace a desktop PC. Instead, it's normally used in cooperation with a desktop machine with which it's partnered. Among other things, the desktop partner can install applications on the H/PC while the two are connected via the network or with the synchronizing cable that comes with the H/PC.

A handheld PC that runs WinCE can support an RDP client available for download from the Microsoft Web site. (Because Microsoft rearranges their Web site regularly, there's no use providing a link to the RDP client, but if you look in the Downloads section of the WinCE area on www.microsoft.com, you should be able to find it.)

Installing (or Removing) Support for Terminal Services

Terminal Services is one more service that you can run under Win2K. As such, you can turn this capability on and off by installing or uninstalling the service. Installing Terminal Services enables the multiuser capabilities of Win2K and adds some administration tools to the Administrative Tools group, while uninstalling the services makes Win2K single-user again and removes the tools. You must reboot after installing or removing support for Terminal Services.

To add Terminal Services to a Win2K server:

1. Open the Add/Remove Programs applet in the Control Panel.

2. Choose Add/Remove Windows Components.

3. From the list available, check the box next to Terminal Services (see Figure 14.4). You do not need to install Terminal Services Licensing to run terminal sessions, although you'll need to install the licensing tool on *some* Win2K server in the network to keep track of terminal license use.

FIGURE 14.4

Check the box next to Terminal Services to enable Win2K's multi-user capabilities.

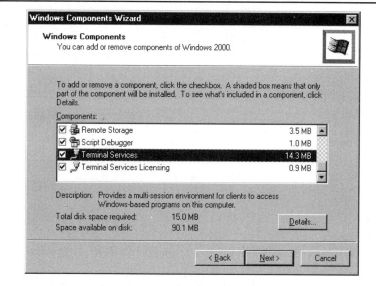

4. If you click the Details button to display the screen shown in Figure 14.5, you'll see that you can install either the client creation files or the files needed to supply Terminal Services. Check the options you need (both are selected by default) and click OK.

5. Click Next to move to the Terminal Services Setup screen. As you can see in Figure 14.6, you have two choices for setting up Terminal Services. Remote administration mode allows you to make up to two connections to the Win2K server for administrative purposes only—that is, you can't use these connections to serve applications, and the server will be set up to give equal time to all processes instead of favoring those in the foreground. This is the default option. Application server mode is the mode of Terminal Services we'll talk about in the course of this chapter, and the one you'll need to choose to permit users to run applications from the terminal server. Choose the option you want and click Next.

FIGURE 14.5

You can install either the client files or the Terminal Services capabilities, or both.

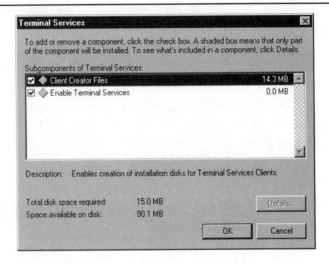

FIGURE 14.6

Win2K allows you to install Terminal Services either for administrative purposes or for supporting client application needs.

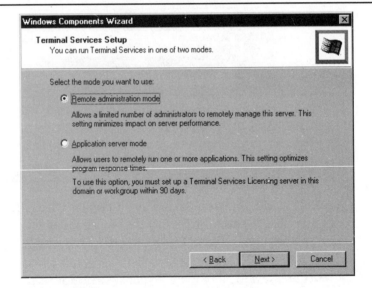

6. Choose the security context you want to use for terminal services. Choosing Win2K mode locks down the terminal server more securely by making some of the system folders read-only to users. Doing so will prevent some applications from running under Wind2K terminal services. If you change your mind later about the types of permission you want to grant, then you can do so from the Terminal Services Configuration tool—without reinstalling the service.

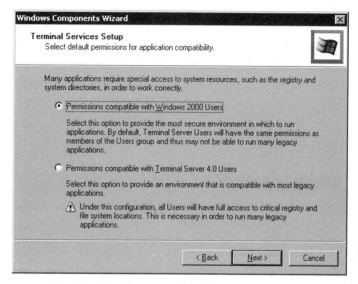

7. Win2K will copy the files from the installation CD (or, if you didn't insert it, will prompt you for the path to the files). When it's done, you'll be prompted to restart the computer to make the changes take effect.

When you restart the server, the Terminal Services tools will be added to the Administrative Tools folder. These tools will be available whether you installed Terminal Services in remote administration mode or in application server mode.

To remove Terminal Services from a Win2K server:

1. Open the Add/Remove Programs applet in the Control Panel.

2. Choose Add/Remove Windows Components.

3. From the list available, check the box next to Terminal Services.

4. Click Next, and wait for Win2K to check for the existence of all the files it needs to run the services that you still have loaded (it will do this even if you loaded those services earlier).

Restart the machine when prompted. The Terminal Services tools will be removed from the Administrative Tools program group.

Creating a New Terminal Server Client

The procedure for connecting a client to the terminal server varies slightly depending on whether you're talking about PC clients, handheld PCs, or WBTs.

PC-Based RDP Clients

To connect a PC-based client to Terminal Services, you have to run a short installation program on the PC to install client support for RDP. This process is quite simple and (wonder of wonders in the Windows world) does not require that you reboot the computer afterwards to use the client. The only catch is that you have to *get* those installation files to the client.

You can either create installation disks with the Terminal Services Client Creator or share the client files on the network and run the Setup program from the client.

Creating Setup Disks

From the terminal server, run the Terminal Services Client Creator found in the Administrative Tools (Common) program group on the terminal server. You'll see a dialog box like the one shown in Figure 14.7.

FIGURE 14.7

Creating an RDP client disk

Notice that each client type requires a different number of disks: the Win16 client requires 4, and the Win32 client requires 2. Notice also that only Intel clients are supported for Win2K terminal services; although beta versions of Win2K included support for Alpha Win32 clients, this support is no longer included, even for NT4 clients running on Alphas. The client creator doesn't format the disks by default, but I choose to format mine on general principles (after making sure that nothing important was on the disks, of course). I'm unlikely to remember that anything else important is on a disk labeled "RDP Client for Windows NT (Intel)."

You can't create a disk to any location other than a floppy drive. To make the client setup network-accessible, your best bet is to share the directories where the client files are stored.

Distributing via Network Share

Creating clients disks is clumsy. For those clients who have a direct network connection to the terminal server, it's easier to install the files over the network. In the net folder are two folders: Win16 for Windows for Workgroups clients and Win32 for x86-based Windows 9x and NT clients. To install the files follow these steps:

1. From the terminal server, share the folder: %*systemroot*%\system32\clients\tsclient\net. There are three folders within the net folder: Win16 (for Windows for Workgroups clients), Win32 (for *x*86-based Windows 9*x* and NT clients), and Win32a (for NT Alpha clients).

 TIP If you're having your users install their own client files, it's important to make sure that they install the right files for their operating system. To avoid user misunderstandings about which installation files to use, you could share each client installation set individually. If you *really* want to eliminate the possibility that someone will install the wrong files, set user- or group-specific permissions on the shares so that only those who need access to each client type have access. This level of control is probably overkill for most people, but it's worth noting.

---

2. From each client Desktop, locate and connect to the share, tunneling to the Disk 1 folder within the appropriate directory and running Setup.exe from there.

Installing and Configuring the PC Client

However you choose to get the Setup program to the PC clients, the process of installing it is the same, and much like installing any Microsoft application. Supply your name and the name of your company, agree to the EULA requirements, and choose a destination directory for the files if you don't like the default location of a new folder in the Program Files directory.

Start the copying process, and that's the end of it. A few seconds later, you'll see a message box stating that the client was successfully installed. Click OK, and you're ready to use the client. It will be in the Terminal Services Client program group on the client.

 TIP You can set up the Terminal Services client to run from the terminal server's console, and it's a good idea to do so. You can't remotely control user sessions from the console, but only from within another session. If you're working on the console, you can shadow a session only by starting a terminal server session—even one on the same terminal server. For more on how to remotely control user sessions, turn to the later section "Taking Control of User Sessions."

Creating, Deleting, and Modifying Connections

The simplest way to connect to a terminal server is to run the Terminal Services Client found in the Terminal Services Client program group. When you do, you'll see a dialog box like the one in Figure 14.8, showing all available terminal servers on the network.

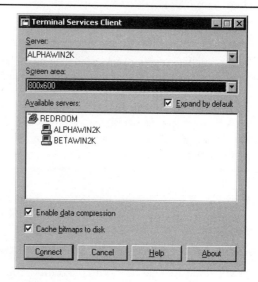

To connect to a server, select its icon in the list and choose the resolution you want the client session to use. If the server you want isn't listed, try typing its IP address in the Server box at the top of the dialog box.

 NOTE A lower resolution doesn't give you a lower resolution full-screen client session, it gives you a smaller window. For example, if your client computer's local resolution is 1024 × 768 and you choose a terminal server session resolution of 800 × 600, the session window will be smaller than your Desktop but will have the same resolution as the Desktop, instead of looking as it would if you changed your display settings to make the display 800 × 600.

Once you click the Connect button, the client will find the selected terminal server and begin a session. If you included logon information in the settings, they'll be logged on; if not, they'll see the usual Win2K logon screen. Clients should supply their domain username and password, and they'll be logged in.

TIP If the client gets an error message saying that the terminal server is busy, try again later, check the client TCP/IP settings and make sure that it's got a valid IP address and subnet. If it doesn't, the client will get the "too busy" message.

The Terminal Services Client is easy to use, but the default options aren't always what's needed. To set up client custom settings, skip the Terminal Services Client and choose the Client Connection Manager from the same program group. From here, you can create new connections with personalized settings, save those connection settings for future reference, edit the settings later, and delete session settings if you no longer want to use them.

Creating a New Connection   To create a customized connection, choose New Connection from the File menu and complete the following steps as they're presented:

1. Choose a name for the new connection and a server to connect to. If your network includes a WINS or DNS server, you can use the name of the server. If not, then supply the terminal server's IP address. (The RDP client, recall, requires TCP/IP). If you don't know what terminal servers are available, click the Browse button to display a list of available terminal servers in the domain, as follows.

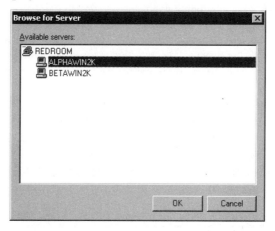

2. If you want to automatically log on to the server when starting the connection, check the box and fill in the appropriate account name, password, and domain or workgroup.

3. Choose the session display settings: session display resolution, whether the session should run in a window or take up the entire screen. You can only choose a resolution less than or equal to the client window size. That is, if your client computer's display is set for 1024 × 768, the session resolution can be no greater than 1024 × 768.

TIP For a completely seamless feel to your terminal services session, run the Desktop in full-screen mode so that only the remote session is displayed. You can switch back and forth between the session Desktop and the local Desktop by pressing Ctrl+Alt+Break.

4. Indicate whether you'd like to use data compression and bitmap caching to improve performance. Data compression is really only important over a slow network (such as a dial-up connection), but I'd use bitmap caching, because that will store a copy of bitmaps locally so that RDP will only have to update them if there are changes.

5. Specify whether you want the session to display an application or the entire Desktop. If you choose the Desktop, you'll be able to run any application accessible to your user account. Running a single application means that only that application will be displayed, and that if you exit the application, the session will end. You must know the name and path of the application to connect to—there's no Browse function.

NOTE Although it might seem logical to name the application location by its Unicode name, this isn't how it works. Instead, you must enter the path as it appears from the terminal server's perspective; e.g., C:\msoffice\office\winword.exe. This may seem odd, but it's because you're connecting to the application locally, not via the network.

6. Specify how the session will be displayed. You can add the connection to the Terminal Services Client program group (or to another program group that you specify, if, for example, you'd like users to be unaware that they're running the application from the terminal server) so that you can use it without running the Client Connection Manager. You can also edit the connection's icon, perhaps to that of the application that the session will open.

TIP Use the Search tool in 32-bit Windows to find icons, which have an .ico extension.

When you've entered all this information, you'll see a Finish screen. The client connection settings will be ready to use immediately. You can make as many connection settings as you need, to different terminal servers or different applications or at different resolutions. Just keep in mind that each separate session running on the terminal server, whether it's an application or a full Desktop, uses resources on the terminal server and gets a timeslice of the CPU cycles.

Reusing Connections on Other Computers   You can also transfer connection settings to another client computer without typing them in again. First, save the connection to a file. Highlight it in the Client Connection Manager and choose Export from the File menu. Choose a name for the file and click Save. If password information was part of the connection settings, you'll be asked whether you want to save the password along with the rest of the configuration information for that connection. If you do, then click Yes—just don't forget that doing so means that anyone logging onto the terminal server with that connection will use the identity of the person the connection was originally created for. The exported connection will be saved with a .cns extension and will be quite small—around a kilobyte.

To start using that connection, open the Client Connection Manager at the client computer that you want to have access to the terminal server. Choose Import from the File menu, move to the location of the saved connection, and select it.

Editing and Deleting Connection Information   Not all session settings are engraved in stone after you've created the connection. To edit a connection, highlight it in the Client Connection Manager and choose Properties from the File menu (see Figures 14.9–14.11).

FIGURE 14.9

The General tab is for editing the name of the server, its description, and any automatic logon information.

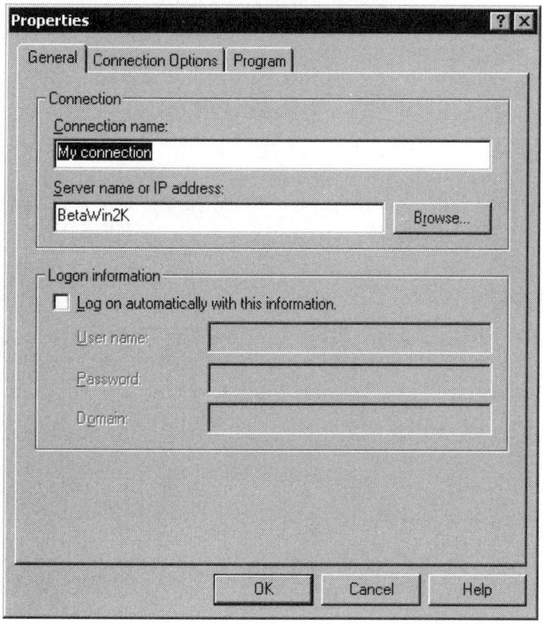

FIGURE 14.10

The Connection Options tab covers session display settings, including the size of the window and the speed of the connection between server and client.

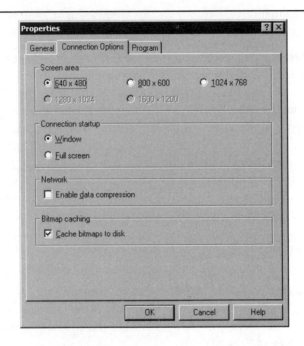

FIGURE 14.11

In the Program tab, choose a new application to run in the terminal server session, or change the icon or program group associated with the session settings.

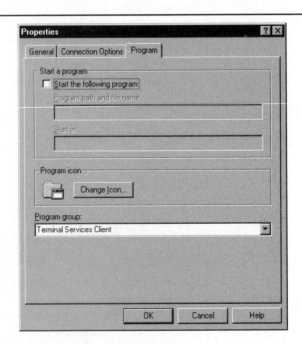

Finally, to delete a session from the Connection Manager, just highlight it and press the Delete key.

Client Catch-22s

By and large, using a connection to the terminal server is largely idiot-proof once you've got everything set up. However, there are a couple of things that your users should be aware of before they use one of their terminal server connections. One applies to all PC users (but not to Windows terminals), and one applies only to Win16 clients.

Normal Keyboard Shortcuts Don't Work If you're accustomed to using keyboard shortcuts to navigate between applications on your Desktop, you may wonder how to make the shortcuts work in your terminal server session. The simple answer is that you can't—those shortcuts are picked up by the local buffer for use on the local console. Instead, you'll need to substitute keyboard shortcuts as shown in Table 14.2.

TABLE 14.2: KEYBOARD SHORTCUTS IN TERMINAL SERVICES CLIENT SESSIONS

Function	Locally Used Combination	Session-Specific Combination
Brings up application selector and moves selection to the right	Alt+Tab	Alt+PgUp
Brings up application selector and moves selection to the left	Alt+Shift+Tab	Alt+PgDn
Swaps between running applications	Alt+Esc	Alt+Insert
Opens the Start menu	Ctrl+Esc	Alt+Home
Right-clicks the active application's icon button in the upper left of the application window	Alt+Spacebar	Alt+Del
Brings up the Windows NT Security window	Ctrl+Alt+Del	Ctrl+Alt+Esc

The copy, cut, and paste commands will work as usual in both local and remote sessions. The commands will apply to whichever session is in the foreground. If you copy in one session and then move the other session to the foreground to paste, the text will be pasted in the second session.

Connecting with the Win16 Client Windows for Workgroups clients must save their domain password in their password list when logging on (there's a checkbox in the logon screen that allows them to do this). Otherwise, they'll get an unhelpful error message: "Error code: 0x906 SL_ERR_SECCTXTINITFAILED (0x906) SL: InitSecurity-Context call failed." All this means is that the domain controller can't find the password. This does not apply if your network is organized as a workgroup, only if it's using domain security.

Setting Up and Connecting a Windows-Based Terminal

Setting up a WBT for the first time is pretty simple. It's largely a matter of plugging everything in (power supply, monitor, network connection, mouse, and keyboard) and supplying the information the WBT needs to interact with the terminal server. For this example, I'll set up an NCD ThinStar 300, a Windows CE–based WBT, on a LAN. Although some WBTs have different options from others, the basic setup information required is the same on all CE-based WBTs.

Setting Up the Terminal

Once everything is plugged in and you've powered on the unit, the Setup Wizard walks you through the following steps:

1. First off you're faced with the end-user license agreement, which states that use of the unit with Terminal Services is predicated upon your having a valid Terminal Services user license and that you must follow the licensing for any applications run from the terminal server. You must click Accept to continue with the wizard.

2. Indicate whether the WBT is connecting to the terminal server via a LAN (the default) or dial-up connection.

3. Choose the display protocol that should be used to make connections. You have the option of the Microsoft Terminal Server Client (the default, which I'll use here) or the Citrix ICA client, which you'd choose if connecting to a terminal server running WinFrame or MetaFrame. Most modern Windows terminals also offer some kind of terminal emulation support, but you will not use this to connect to a Windows terminal server.

4. The Setup wizard will attempt to locate a DHCP server on your network. If it can't find one, the wizard will tell you so. You'll have the option of telling the wizard to use the IP information supplied by DHCP or supplying a static IP address.

 TIP If you have a DHCP server and the wizard doesn't detect it, make sure that the DHCP service on the server is up and running properly and that the server is connected to the network. If it is, then restart the wizard to see whether it finds the DHCP server. Don't just tell the wizard to use DHCP information if it's not able to find it, or you may run into problems in getting an IP address assigned to the terminal. No IP address, no connection to the terminal server.

5. If you choose to supply a static IP address, you'll be prompted for it, the subnet mask, and (if applicable) the default gateway. The IP address, recall, is the iden-

tifier for the network node, while the subnet mask identifies the network segment that the node is on. The default gateway is only necessary if the network is subnetted and the WBT will need to connect to another subnet.

6. Next, you'll be prompted to supply the servers used for name resolution: WINS, DNS, or both. You'll need to know the IP addresses of the servers, as there is no Browse function. If you're using one or the other name resolution service, be sure to check the box that enables that service. Otherwise, the connection won't work, and you'll have to edit it to use the IP address instead of the NetBIOS name. To establish support for WINS, you'll need to reenter the unit's network setup.

7. Choose a video resolution. The default option is Best Available Using DDC. DDC, which stands for Display Data Channel, is a VESA standard for communication between a monitor and a video card. If it supports DDC, a monitor can inform the video card about its capabilities, including maximum color depth and resolution.

 WARNING Only choose DDC if you're using the terminal with a new monitor that you're positive supports DDC. There's no Test option for DDC as there is for other video resolutions, and if your monitor doesn't support DDC, you won't be able to read the display when you reboot. The terminal will have some option for starting the unit in video safe mode, displaying only 640 × 480 (in the case of the ThinStar, you do it by pressing Ctrl+F5 when restarting the system), but it's a pain nevertheless. I strongly recommend that you explicitly choose the resolution and refresh rate that you want and use the Test button to make sure that it's supported, rather than use DDC.

When you click the Finish button in the final screen, you'll be prompted to restart the terminal to make the settings take effect. After restarting the system, you'll begin the second half of the terminal setup: the connection.

 TIP To manually restart a WBT, turn the unit off and back on again. There's no Reset button. If you're one of those people (like myself) who normally leaves PCs on, don't worry. Turning off a WBT is equivalent in seriousness to turning off a printer.

Creating a New Connection

To create a new connection, follow these steps:

1. Choose a name for the new connection, and the name of the terminal server that you're connecting to. If using a dial-up connection instead of a LAN, be

sure to check the Low-Speed Connection box so that RDP will compress the data a little further.

2. To configure the terminal for automatic logon to the terminal server session, fill in the name and password and domain of the person using the terminal. If you leave this section blank, you'll have to explicitly log in each time you connect to the terminal server. For tighter security, leave it blank; if it doesn't matter whether someone can log onto the terminal server, you can set it up for automatic login.

3. Choose whether you want the terminal server session to display a Desktop or run a single application. Once again, there's no Browse function, so you need to know the name and path (from the server's perspective) of any application you choose. If you don't provide correct path information, the connection will fail.

At this point, the connection is set up and you're ready to go. The NCD ThinStar Connection Manager displays a list of the available connections. To use one, select it and click the Connect button. You'll see a logon screen (assuming that you didn't set up the connection for an automatic login). Type your name and password, and you're in.

 TIP If you have a WBT set up to work with Windows Terminal Server and are wondering how you're going to update it to work with the server you updated to Win2K, relax. When you make a preset connection, the terminal will connect to the Win2K terminal session without a hitch, with no help from you. The terminal manufacturer should supply the flash update that you can use to upgrade the terminal from RDP4 (used by NT Terminal Server Edition) to RDP 5 (used by Win2K and required for the advanced features of terminal services in Win2K).

Setting Up a Handheld PC

To use a handheld PC to connect to a terminal server, you must install the RDP client on the H/PC and then create a session on the client.

First, you must get the RDP client. Go to the Microsoft Web site and navigate to the Downloads section of the WinCE section. You'll have to go through some screens where you agree that you understand that having the RDP client installed does not imply that you're licensed to access a terminal server. (There's also a link to a place where you can buy more licenses if you need to.) Download the 1MB client setup program (hpcrdp.exe) to the desktop partner of the handheld PC.

 NOTE As of this writing, the client is located at http://www.microsoft.com/windowsce/products/download/term-serv.asp, but it may have moved by the time you read this.

To install the RDP client on the handheld PC, follow these steps.

1. Turn on the handheld PC and connect it to the desktop partner. Make sure that they're connected.

2. Run `hpcrdp.exe` to start the installation wizard.

3. Click Yes to agree to the EULA.

4. Choose an installation folder for the client on the desktop partner. The default location is a subfolder of the `Windows CE Services` folder, which you'll have installed in the course of partnering the desktop machine and the handheld PC.

5. The installation program will start copying the files to the handheld PC. This may take a few minutes if you're using the sync cable instead of a network connection—a sync cable is a serial connection.

6. Once the files have been copied, click Finish on the desktop side to end the Setup program.

To set up a connection, go to the handheld PC and look in Start/Programs/Terminal Server Client. There are two options here: the Client Connection Wizard and the Terminal Server Client.

To use the default connection settings, click the Terminal Server Client and type in the name or IP address of the terminal server you want to connect to. Click the Connect button, and the client will search for that terminal server. You'll need to log on as if you were logging onto the server or domain.

For a little more control over the connection settings, run the Client Connection Wizard. You don't have as many options as you do when running the similar wizard for the PC client, but you can specify a connection name, provide your username and password for automatic logon, and choose whether to run an application or display the entire Desktop. Click the Finish button, and the wizard will put a shortcut to that connection on your H/PC's Desktop.

Adjusting Client Connection Settings

Everything's ready to go on the client side, but you may still have some work to do to get the server side configured. The following are optional—but useful—settings that allow you to define how long a session may last, whether someone can take remote control of a user's terminal session, how the RDP protocol is configured, and client path and profile information. The location of these settings depends on whether you've set up the member accounts on the terminal server itself (as a member server) or are editing the main user database on a Win2K domain controller. If the former, the settings will be in the Local Users And Groups section of the Computer Management tool in the Administrative Tools folder. If the latter, the settings will be in the Active Directory Users and Computers tool in the Administrative Tools folder.

In this example, I'll use the Active Directory Users and Groups tool, shown in Figure 14.12. The settings for user accounts in the Local Users and Groups option are the same as the ones in the user accounts stored in the Active Directory, the only difference being that the Active Directory account properties have tabs related to user contact information.

FIGURE 14.12

Edit account properties from the Users *folder in Active Directory Users and Computers.*

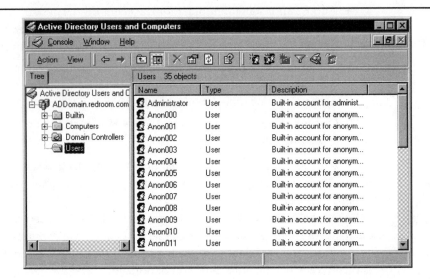

Open the Users folder, find the user you want, then right-click it and choose the Properties item. This properties sheet controls all user settings, so I'll concentrate here on the settings that apply to Terminal Services.

NOTE Unfortunately, you have to configure all user settings—for Terminal Services and in general—individually, rather than configuring group settings. This is definitely suboptimal, but that's the way it is.

Remote Control

The ability to take remote control of a user's session comes in very handy when troubleshooting time comes. Rather than trying to talk someone through a series of commands ("Okay, find the Programs folder. Got it? Now look for the icon that says 'Microsoft Word'..."), you can take over the session, manipulating it from your session while displaying it also for the user. The person whose session you're controlling will be able to see exactly how to complete the task and will have it done for them.

The settings for the kind of remote control that you can take are defined from the Remote Control tab of each user's properties sheet, shown in Figure 14.13.

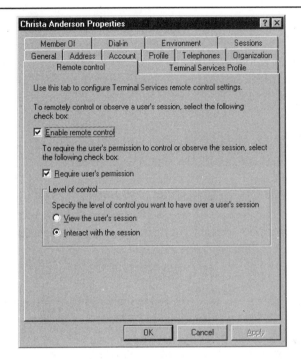

First, you must specify whether remote control is even permitted for the session (by default, you can take control of any session, no matter what rights the owner of the session has). Specify also whether the user whose session is being shadowed must permit the action before the remote control can begin. If you choose this option, the person who originated the session will see a message box telling them that such and such person of such and such domain is attempting to control their session, offering the chance to accept or refuse the control.

NOTE If a user refuses the remote control connection, you can't control the session even from an account with Administrator privileges.

The final option on this tab determines what kind of control you can have over this user's session. For troubleshooting purposes, you'll find it most useful to be able to interact with the session, so you can actually show the user how to do something (or just do it for them). Choosing this option means that both the original user and the person with remote control over the session can send mouse clicks and keystrokes to the terminal server for interpretation. Graphical output is displayed on both the original session and the remote control view of the session.

If you're choosing the option to view the user's session, the person remotely controlling the session isn't really controlling it, but is only able to watch and see what the original user is doing. The person who set up remote control can't use the mouse or keyboard with the remotely controlled session. This could potentially be a troubleshooting tool if you're trying to find out exactly what someone's doing wrong and help them correct it, while making sure that you can't interfere. Most often, however, I find the option to take control of the session more useful than the ability to watch.

Session Time-outs

The status of a client session isn't a binary proposition. Rather than connected/not connected, the state of a client session may be active, disconnected, or reset. An active session is what it sounds like: a session that's actively in use. In a disconnected session, the client has shut off the client interface to the session, but the session—and all its applications—is still running on the server. When a client resets a session with the Logoff command, the session ends and all applications in the session are shut down.

Although the distinction may not sound significant at first, the difference between these two session types is important. When clients disconnect from their sessions, all their data is still loaded into memory and their applications are running, exactly as they left them. This means that a client can disconnect while going to lunch, and thus secure the session without having to start over. The only catch to a disconnected session is that it still uses up CPU cycles and some memory, since the session thread still gets its crack at the CPU and because all the user data is still active. However, as the data stops being accessed, Win2K will swap it out to the paging file on the hard disk and replace it in physical memory with more recent data; when the client reconnects to the session and tries to use the data, the data will be paged back in. The still-running client session also won't impact available network bandwidth much because the terminal server will detect that the session is idle and stop sending video updates to the client machine.

If a user attempts to reconnect to the terminal server with more than one disconnected session running, a dialog box will display the disconnected sessions, their resolution, and the time that they've been disconnected. The user can then pick the session to reconnect. If the user doesn't pick a session in a minute or so, the highlighted session will be reestablished. The other session will remain on the terminal server, still in its inactive state.

Win2K gives you the option of controlling how long a session may stay active, how long it may stay disconnected without being terminated, how long active but idle sessions may stay active before they're disconnected—and even whether a particular user may connect to the server at all. These settings are controlled from the Sessions tab you see in Figure 14.14.

FIGURE 14.14

Configuring session
connection settings

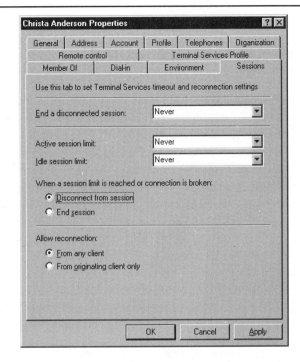

You can control how long the setting may remain active before being disconnected or terminated. If you want to prevent people from forgetting to log off from their terminal session at the end of the day or at lunch, use this setting.

As I already discussed, a disconnected session is still using up terminal server resources. This is by design, so that users can reconnect to a session and have all their applications and data still loaded, but if a session is permanently abandoned, there's no point in leaving it up. Choose a time-out period that reflects the amount of time you're willing to give a user to get back and use their connection before their applications are all closed.

You can determine also how long a session can be idle before being disconnected or terminated. This isn't quite the same setting as the first one, which limits connection time whether or not the session is still getting input. Rather, this setting limits the amount of time that a session can be idle before being shut down. I think this setting is a little more useful in most cases, given that the session must be unused for a certain period before it is shut down.

The default for all three settings is Never, meaning that there's no restriction on how long a session may be running, disconnected, or idle. The maximum time-out period is 2 days.

TIP If you want to gather some statistics about how long people are staying logged in, or how long disconnected sessions are remaining idle on the server, you can get this information from the Terminal Services Manager.

The settings on the bottom of the tab determine how disconnected and reestablished connections should be handled. You may have noticed that two of the time-out options gave you the choice of disconnecting or terminating the session at the end of the time-out session, but no option for specifying which it should be—disconnection or resetting the connection. The answer depends on whether you pick Disconnect (the default) or End (which resets the connection) for broken or timed-out connections. The other option controls how users may reconnect to disconnected sessions. By default, they can reconnect to their client session from any client machine, but you can specify that users may only reestablish the connection from the same machine they started from. If this option is selected and they try to reconnect from a different client machine, then they'll start a new session and their current session will still be running on the terminal server. If a user has more than one disconnected session running on the same terminal server, when they reconnect they'll have a choice of which session they want to use. The session(s) not chosen will continue to run on the terminal server.

Setting Client Path Information

Win2K spreads per-user files all over the place. Unless you specify otherwise, user home directories are in subfolders of the terminal server's Profiles menu and are identified by user name. Their temporary directories are subfolders of the terminal server's temporary directory, and identified by session ID. To keep all per-user information in a single place, you may want to specify a new home directory. This will give you a fighting chance of applying per-user system quotas and keeping all files in one place for easier recovery.

Profile Paths and Home Directories

Although a default home directory is automatically created for each user in the user's profile, this can cause the user's profile to grow tremendously, slowing the logon process and increasing system resource use. To prevent this from happening, set the path location for the Terminal Services profile from each user's properties sheet, as shown in Figure 14.15.

Notice the implication: you don't have to use the same user profile or home directory for local and remote sessions. The profiles can be the same, but don't have to be. Just type the path for the user's profile (being sure to specify the server in case the user logs in to a different server) and specify the location of the home directory for terminal service use.

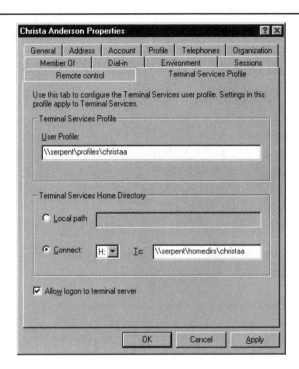

The checkbox on the bottom of this tab controls whether the person is permitted to log onto the terminal server at all. By default, anyone with an account on the domain or server may do so.

Define the Session Environment

The Environment tab in the properties sheet sets the Terminal Services environment for the user, replacing any related settings (such as an application to run at logon) that might already appear in a user's client logon settings. If you want to automatically run an application at logon, type its path in the Program File Name box (sadly, there's no browse function). The working directory goes in the Start In box. Notice that supplying the name of an application does not limit the terminal server session to only running that application and then ending when the application is terminated. All this does is run the application when the session starts—the main Desktop still remains available.

The settings in the Client Devices section at the bottom of this tab don't all apply to Win2K clients. The first one, Connect Client Drives at Logon, applies only to ICA

clients and is related to the Citrix client's ability to redirect client drives for use in terminal server sessions (and it normally confuses users as to whether they're saving files
to their local drives or to the terminal server, so I wouldn't use it if I were you). The
printing options, however, do apply to RDP clients. Checking Connect Client Printers
at Logon specifies that any printers mapped from the terminal server session should
be reconnected. Default to Main Client Printer specifies that the client should use its
own default printer, not the one defined for the terminal server.

Set the Location of Temporary Directories

Rather than using the default location for user temporary files, you can specify a new
one in the user's home directory. Unlike the other settings we've discussed, this one is
not set from the user properties sheet. Instead, you'll use the `flattemp` command and
edit user system settings.

First, log on as the user for whom you're making the change and open the System
applet in the Control Panel. Turn to the Advanced tab, and click the Environment
Variables button to open the dialog box in Figure 14.16.

 TIP Rather than logging on as the person whose environment you're editing, you can
remotely control a terminal server session that that person is running. This allows you to
edit their settings as though you were that person.

Editing the location of
temporary files

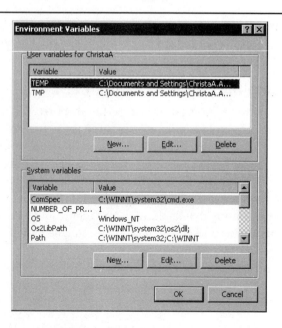

Double-click the values of TEMP and TMP and type the new location in the dialog box that appears. When you've done this for every user, you're ready for the next step. From the command line, run `flattemp /enable`. This will tell Win2K to point all users either to a single temporary directory or to one specified for them in the System applet. To reverse this, run `flattemp /disable` to point all users back to the default location for their temporary files.

WARNING   If user home directories are located on a network share instead of on the terminal server, then you'll be vulnerable to application errors if an application attempts to write to the temporary directory when there's a network error. This won't hurt the disk volume, but the application will respond as it would if the disk had died, and you may lose data. You can avoid this problem by keeping terminal server home directories on the terminal server.

Configuring Terminal Services for All Connections

You can configure general settings for all terminal services connections from the Terminal Services Configuration tool in the Administrative Tools folder (see Figure 14.17). If you're running Terminal Services alone, you'll have only the RDP connection in this folder; if you have other multiuser Windows components added (like MetaFrame's ICA protocol, or direct video support), they'll be in the folder as well.

FIGURE 14.17

Configure display protocol settings from this tool

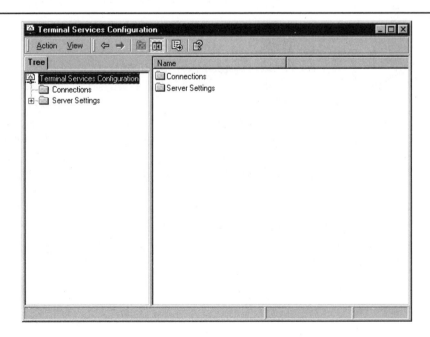

What can you do here? The Server Settings folder contains settings that apply to all connections made to the server. The Connections folder shows all installed display protocols (if you're running Win2K only, then RDP will be the only object in this folder).

 NOTE Win2K only supports one RDP connection per network adapter. If your terminal server has more than one NIC installed, you can configure the RDP protocol for each adapter separately.

The *Server Settings* Folder

The Server Settings folder (see Figure 14.18) contains options that control the creation and deletion of per-session temporary files and the types of access permitted to the terminal server. The options here are identical whether the server is set up to be an ordinary server with remote administration capabilities or an application server.

FIGURE 14.18

Server settings folder for a terminal server in remote administration mode

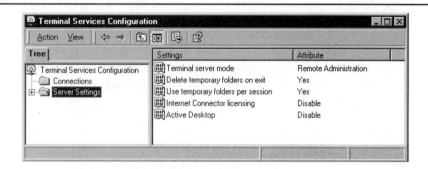

As discussed earlier in the section "Installing (or Removing) Support for Terminal Services," the terminal server mode indicates what kind of access is permitted to the terminal server. The server may be set up as an application server or as an ordinary server that can be remotely administered. Application servers permit as many users as you have licenses for to run terminal sessions on the server. Remote administration mode is for administrative work only.

Deleting the temporary folders on exit means that when a user logs off a terminal server session, the temporary folder they used—and all the .tmp files in it—is deleted. This setting, set to Yes by default, keeps the terminal server from getting cluttered with .tmp files, but ensures that those files are only deleted when they're no longer needed. Using temporary folders per session means that a separate TMP folder will be created for each session started, with those new folders (identified by session ID) being placed by default in subfolders to the main Win2K Temporary Files directory.

The Internet Connector licensing option affects *all* terminal server sessions, not just those that come through the Internet, so only enable this option for terminal servers accepting only Internet connections. Enable this option only if you're using Terminal Services to provide Windows applications to non-employees, because regular employees must use a TS CAL even if accessing the terminal server via the Internet. Unless you're running a server for an application service provider, you've little need to support ICLs.

The second-to-last option lets you turn off Active Directory on the terminal server sessions. Unless you really need it for some reason, I'd turn it off and save the resources. Finally, you can choose the type of permissions you want to apply to this terminal server: TSE 4 file access is compatible with all applications (but may leave some system folders vulnerable to changes from users) or Win2K file access that may not work with all applications (because it denies permissions to some system folders) but does not allow users to tamper with those files.

The *Connections* Folder

Use the Connections folder to configure protocol-wide settings. First, you can disable RDP so that no one can connect to the server, something you might want to do if you know you're going to be taking the server down for maintenance and don't want to have to bother with kicking people off. To do so, just right-click the protocol and choose Disable Connection from the All Tasks part of the pop-up menu. The command to reenable the connection is in the same All Tasks section.

For more detailed control of RDP, choose the Properties option from the pop-up menu. Most settings in the RDP-Tcp dialog box work the same way as their counterparts in the per-user connection settings, which normally take precedence. For a more uniform set of protocol configurations, you may edit the settings here and check the boxes that tell the protocol properties not to inherit their settings according to the user. The two settings that aren't configurable on a per-user basis control security, and are found on the General and Permissions tabs.

General Tab

The General tab shown in Figure 14.19 controls the degree of encryption used with RDP.

By default, the protocol is set for Medium encryption, meaning that all communications between client and server are encrypted with the standard 40-bit algorithm (56-bit if the client is running Win2K Professional). Low encryption only protects communications from the client to the server—not the other way around—and High encryption protects communications in both directions with 128-bit encryption.

TIP The greater the level of encryption, the worse the session performance will be, due to the encryption/decryption overhead at both ends of the connection. Only use Medium or High encryption if you're concerned about the signal being intercepted.

You don't have to worry about the check box at the bottom of the General tab unless you've installed a third-party authentication package on the server. In that case, checking this box tells Win2K to use its native authentication scheme to validate terminal session user logons, rather than using the third-party package.

Configuring RDP access security

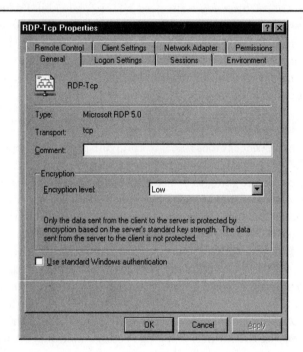

Permissions

Those familiar with the NT/Win2K argot will remember that you secure a Win2K network by defining user rights for what people can *do* on the network and setting permissions for the resources that people can *use*. Terminal Services security is controlled with permissions, on a per-group or per-user basis.

To set or edit the permissions assigned to terminal server sessions, turn to the Permissions tab. You'll see a dialog box like the one in Figure 14.20. From here, you can edit the basic permission sets of the groups for whom some kind of access to terminal server functions has been defined.

TIP If you turn to the Permissions tab and see a list of security IDs instead of user or group names, and the cursor changes to an hourglass when over the dialog box, don't panic. The terminal server is retrieving the names from the domain controller and will show the user and group names after a few seconds. If this doesn't happen—if the SIDs never resolve to user and group names—then there's something wrong with either the domain controller or the connection between the two servers.

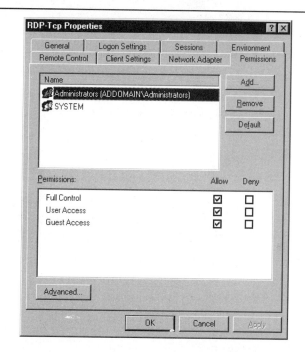

Not sure how to interpret the check boxes? If a permission is checked, then it's explicitly enabled or disabled, depending on which box is checked. If a permission is clear on both sides, then it's implicitly enabled. You can explicitly enable or disable the permission by checking the appropriate box.

Fine-Tuning Access to Terminal Server Functions The first page only shows the default groups and the basic permissions they've been assigned. For more control over the permission process, click the Advanced button to open the dialog box shown in Figure 14.21.

From here, you can see the state of the defined permissions. A key icon symbolizes a granted permission; a padlock symbolizes a denied one. (When you first open this dialog box, you should only see keys—no permissions are explicitly denied by default.) The comment below the list of users and groups notes whether the high-lighted permission applies to the basic membership of that group only or to sub-groups within that group.

FIGURE 14.21

Setting advanced permissions

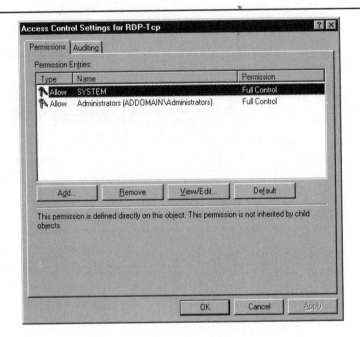

You can adjust these permissions either by adding new users or groups to the list (getting them from the domain controller) or by editing the permissions of the groups already there. To define permissions for a new user or group, click the Add button. The print server will retrieve a list of users and groups from the domain displayed in the Look In box. Choose a user or group from the list and click it. You'll open a dialog box like the one in Figure 14.22.

 TIP If the user or group you want isn't displayed in the list, type it into the box. If you've already created an account for this user or group, you'll be able to edit its permissions.

By default, new users and groups have limited permissions. If you add a new user—even a domain administrator—using the Add button on the Permissions tab, then the new user will only have Logon permission (Guest access) if you don't specify otherwise. You will need to specify the access you'd like to grant or deny to the groups and users you're adding to the list.

The permissions listed here have the characteristics outlined in Table 14.3. I'll talk more about how to use these functions in the later section "Managing Terminal Sessions."

FIGURE 14.22

Defining the permissions for a new user

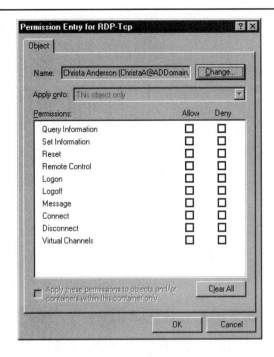

TABLE 14.3 TERMINAL SERVICES PERMISSIONS	
Access Type	**Effect**
Query Information	Allows users to gather information about people using the terminal server, processes running on the server, sessions, and so forth
Set Information	Allows users to set the level of control other users have over the session
Reset	Allows users to reset other connections, ending them and logging the other user off the computer
Remote Control	Allows users to take control of or view other user sessions
Logon	Allows users to connect to the terminal server
Logoff	Allows users to disconnect from the terminal server
Message	Allows users to send messages to other terminal server clients
Connect	Allows users to connect to other terminal servers
Disconnect	Allows users to disconnect from other terminal servers
Virtual Channels	Enables virtual channels for that group

When making your changes, remember how permissions work in Win2K:

- If a person or group is a member of more than one group, then the least restrictive set of permissions applies. For example, if Sue is a member of Everyone, who can print documents but may not manage them, but also a member of Power Users, who can manage documents, then Sue can manage documents.

- The only exception to the rule is when an option is explicitly denied. Being denied access overrides any other permissions that a person may have as a member of another group.

Changing permissions for an existing user or group works in much the same way: select a name, click the View/Edit button, and you'll see the same set of options to explicitly grant or deny permissions.

 TIP If you want to cancel all permission changes for a user or group and start over, click the Cancel button. If you want to remove every granted or denied permission associated with a user or group, click Clear All.

Terminal Services Licensing

Licensing single-user computers is complicated enough. Bring terminal servers into the equation, and the complication increases. Do you have to pay for only the operating system? Only the client sessions that are active at any given time? Only some client sessions? What about applications—an application is only loaded on one machine, right? And who's in charge of keeping track of all these licenses, anyway?

Licensing is never fun and it's not glamorous, but it's part of the cost of doing business. Read on to make some sense of the Terminal Services licensing environment.

The Win2K Licensing Model

First, let's take a look at how the licensing model works in Win2K. In TSE, licensing was handled by a license manager service that came with TSE. You told the license manager how many terminal services licenses you had, and it kept track of how they were used. This is no longer true in Win2K. Instead, you have a license server, which may or may not be the terminal server. A new player is also involved. No longer can you just tell the license server how many TS licenses you have—now you have to get official licenses from Microsoft.

As shown in Figure 14.23, several players cooperate to make Terminal Services licensing work in Win2K:

- The terminal servers
- The license servers
- The Microsoft clearinghouse that enables the license servers and the access licenses

FIGURE 14.23

The Win2K Terminal Services licensing model

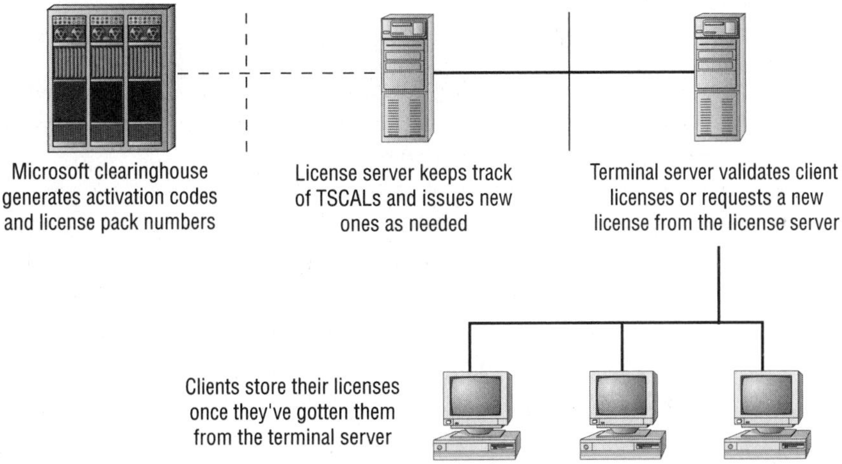

Microsoft clearinghouse generates activation codes and license pack numbers

License server keeps track of TSCALs and issues new ones as needed

Terminal server validates client licenses or requests a new license from the license server

Clients store their licenses once they've gotten them from the terminal server

The first time a client tries to log onto the terminal server, the terminal server will either take the license the client proffers (I'll answer the question of just how a client would have such a license in a minute), or, if the client doesn't have one, the terminal server will find the license server by discovery (broadcasts in workgroups and NT 4 domains or by polling the domain controllers in Win2K domains) and request a license from the license server. If the license server has a license to issue, it will give it to the terminal server, who will issue it to the client machine (not the user, the client machine) that's attempting to make the terminal connection. The client can then present its license to the terminal server and log on. If the license server does not have an available license—even a temporary license—then the client cannot log on. If the terminal server can't connect to the license server for some reason, then the terminal server will accept preexisting licenses but clients without valid temporary or permanent licenses will not be able to log onto the terminal server.

When a client disconnects from the terminal server, it retains its license—the license does not go back to a pool. Therefore, if I log into the terminal server once from my office desk and once from my home office, I'll use up two separate licenses.

The license server puts people planning to run Win2K and NT 4 in a mixed domain in a difficult position because the license service must be running on a domain controller. (Those who worked with RC2 may recall that this was not true then, but it is with the RTM version of Win2K.) If you attempt to install the licensing service on a member server, it won't run. In other words, the primary domain controller for your network may not be an NT 4 server, because Win2K computers cannot be subordinate domain controllers to an NT 4 domain controller. It's a good idea to make two domain controllers terminal license servers so that clients can always get licenses if they need them.

Understanding Session Licensing

Access to the server running Terminal Services is licensed on a per-seat basis, not per user—computers are licensed, not people. When Microsoft first released Windows NT, Terminal Server Edition, it made a terrible marketing decision. Any client connecting to the terminal had to have a valid NT Workstation license. At $400 a pop, NTW licenses aren't cheap, so a lot of people took a look at TSE and said, "Nice, but not worth the money." In an effort to win those people back, in February 1999 Microsoft revamped their licensing structure, giving NT Workstation clients a built-in license to access the terminal server, but requiring you to purchase terminal server licenses (which cost approximately $150/seat instead of $400) for computers running any other operating system.

In Win2K, the licensing structure includes four license types:

- Terminal Server Client Access Licenses
- Terminal Services Internet Connector Licenses
- Built-in licenses
- Temporary licenses

 NOTE Not all Terminal Services functions use licenses. When you're running Win2K's Terminal Services capabilities in Remote Administration mode (an option when you're installing Terminal Services), you don't need TSCALs because Remote Administration mode comes with two administrator's licenses.

Terminal Server Client Access Licenses

Terminal Server Client Access Licenses (TSCALs) are for named user accounts in the domain and issued on a per-seat basis. Anyone in a company who's using the terminal server must have a TSCAL, regardless of whether they're connecting to the terminal server via Microsoft's RDP display protocol or Citrix's ICA display protocol (which they would if you'd installed MetaFrame for Windows 2000). To access a Win2K server at all, of course, a client also needs a 2000 Client Access License (2000 CAL). TSCALs are sold for the retail trade in 5-packs and 20-packs; a 5-pack costs $749 retail and an upgrade from a TSE 5-pack costs $349. (For those not mathematically minded, that comes to just under $150/head retail, which is about what TSE TSCALs cost.)

The way that you buy TSCALs determines how you pay for them and how much flexibility you have in the purchase. Most people who buy small volumes of Microsoft products will buy their TSCALs as part of a 5-CAL or 20-CAL Microsoft License Pak (MLP). Physically, an MLP is a thin cardboard envelope that contains the End User License Agreement (EULA) denoting the number of CALs purchased. The MLP for TSCALs in Win2K also includes a license code, a 25-character alphanumeric code that indicates what the license is for and how many TSCALs it purchases (so that you can't fudge the entries and say that you bought 20 TSCALs when you really only bought 5). You can only install an MLP once. Small to medium customers will get their licenses through a program called Microsoft Open License, which allows you to purchase a user-specified quantity of licenses, after which Microsoft issues you an Open License Authorization and license numbers for the licenses, which you can install as many times as you need to. Select and Enterprise Agreements for large customers work like open licenses, except that the customer provides their Enrollment Agreement number instead of the Open License numbers.

Internet Connector Licenses

The Windows 2000 Terminal Services Internet Connector License (TSICL) allows a maximum of 200 concurrent users to connect anonymously to a terminal server via the Internet. That's right—you can't use a TSICL to dial into the network from home but will instead need a TSCAL for your home computer. The TSICLs are solely for the purpose of demonstrating Web-enabled applications to Internet users. Not only that, but according to Microsoft, you can't install the TSICL pack on a Win2K terminal server that's for employees. The server will only allow client access to terminal services through the Internet—anyone who logs onto that server will use one of the TSICLs and will connect as an anonymous user. A 200-pack ICL for Win2K costs $9,999, and these ICL packs are only available to Microsoft Select volume customers.

Frankly, the TSICLs aren't good for much, since you can't legally use them to give employees home access to terminal services. Although it might sound as though the TSICLs are useful for application service providers (ASPs, which are companies that lease applications to people via a dial-up connection), they're really not. Microsoft is still figuring out how the licensing for ASPs will work. Ultimately terminal services for ASPs may be available in the form of an additional product (Win2K for ASPs) or as an add-on product to Win2K—they don't know yet which way they'll go. As of October 1999, Microsoft was working with about 50 ASPs to see how client licensing should work. At this point, they're sticking to the same model used with TSCALs, so that ASPs are charged each month for the number of user accounts they're supporting. The Citrix model for ASPs, in contrast, charges ASPs per month based on the number of concurrent users they've averaged for that month.

Built-In and Temporary Licenses

The two remaining license types are simpler. Win2K Professional comes with a TSCAL; all other operating systems (including NT Workstation) must purchase a TSCAL. You can't move a built-in license from one computer to another. Finally, the license server issues temporary licenses when a terminal server requests a license and the license server has none to give (perhaps because you haven't installed a license pack yet). The license server then tracks the issuance and expiration of the temporary licenses.

Byzantine enough for you? Table 14.4 is a cheat sheet.

TABLE 14.4: TERMINAL SERVICES PERMANENT CLIENT ACCESS LICENSE TYPES		
Situation	**Terminal Services License Type Required**	**Cost**
Users connecting from Win2K Professional desktops	Built-in license	N/A
Users connecting from any desktop not using Win2K Professional	Terminal Server Client Access License (TSCAL)	A 5-pack of TSCALs costs $749 retail and an upgrade from a TSE 5-pack costs $349
Anonymous users connecting to the terminal server via the Internet	Terminal Services Internet Connector License (TSICL)	Costs $9,999 for 200 simultaneous anonymous connections

The Terminal Services Licensing Tool

To help you keep track of the licenses used, Win2K includes the Terminal Services Licensing tool, found in the Administrative Tools program group of any Win2K Server with the Terminal Services Licensing service running on it.

 TIP Terminal Services Licensing is one of the services you can install during Setup, like support for Terminal Services itself. To add it after installing Win2K Server, open the Add/Remove Programs applet in the Control Panel and click the Add Windows Components icon. Follow the Windows Components Wizard and just pick the component from the list of available options.

When you first start the licensing tool, it will browse for license servers on the network and then report back with the ones it found, as shown in Figure 14.24.

FIGURE 14.24

Use the Terminal
Services Licensing
tool to manage
license usage.

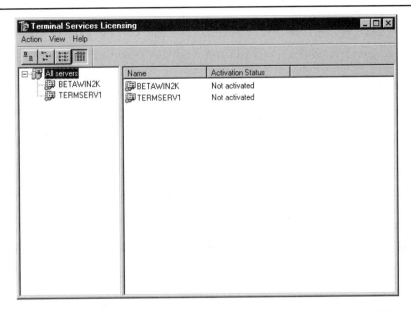

Unfortunately, Win2K took a cue from Citrix and set up the same kind of licensing. You can't just plug in the terminal server, tell the license server how many licenses you've bought, and let people log in. Although the temporary licenses will function for a limited time (90 days), to fully enable the terminal server licenses you'll need to activate the server and download the license key.

Until Win2K, only Citrix products (MetaFrame and WinFrame) required activation. Activation is essentially a way of making sure that you've really paid for the licenses you're using. (According to Citrix, it also helps technical support keep track of you for better customer support, but I have a sneaking suspicion that the "let's make sure people are paying for what they use" issue is a little more important—not that it wouldn't be important to me, of course.) When you activate a license, you're providing your product number to Microsoft. Microsoft then runs an encryption algorithm on it and sends you back the results as your activation code. You then give Microsoft back the activation code, they run another encrypting algorithm on it, and they send you a license code that corresponds to that activation code. This is an extra step, and that's annoying, but the procedure itself really isn't too arduous. Besides, Microsoft tells me that activation of TSCALs is a sort of pilot to see how activation goes. If the trial is a success, then you'll see activation required for other Microsoft products as well. Better get acquainted with how it works.

When you first open the Terminal Services Licensing tool, it looks like Figure 14.24. As you can see, the licensing server is present but not yet activated, so it can only issue temporary licenses that expire after 90 days. To make the license server ready to monitor license usage and to issue TSCALs, you'll need to activate the server and install the license pack assigned to that server. To do so, follow these steps:

1. Right-click the server and choose Activate Server from the context menu. Click through the opening screen.

2. Choose a method of contacting Microsoft to get a license. You have four options for contacting Microsoft to give them your product number. The Internet, the default option, gives you a direct connection to Microsoft but requires that the license server have an Internet connection. Other options include the Web (whether from the license server or another computer with an Internet connection), the telephone, or fax. For this example, I'll choose the Web (see Figure 14.25) and click Next.

FIGURE 14.25

Choose a way of contacting the Microsoft clearinghouse to get an activation code and valid license packs.

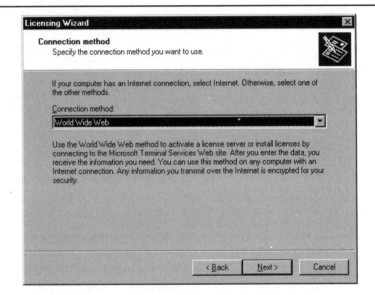

NOTE If you choose to contact the licensing people via telephone or fax, the next screen of the wizard will display a list of countries to choose from so that you've got a shot at making a toll-free call. The United States is not the default choice, which is international-minded of Microsoft but inconvenient to those of us not used to having to browse all the way to *U*.

3. Now I need to take the product ID displayed in the screen (see Figure 14.26) and go to https://activate.microsoft.com. On this Web page, you'll have a choice of activating a license server or installing license packs. Choose to activate the server and choose Next.

FIGURE 14.26

Take the product ID
here and send it to
Microsoft to generate
an activation code.

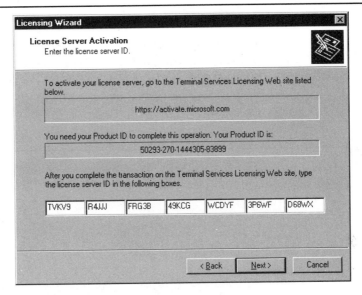

4. On the next screen of the Web wizard, fill in the required product ID number, personal information, and purchase method (Select or Enterprise, Microsoft Open License, or Other to install via a retail licensing code). Click Next, review the information on the screen, and then click Next again to submit it. The Web site will spit out your activation code. Give it to the wizard to activate the server, which will then appear in the licensing tool with a status of Activated (green, and with a little picture of a certificate instead of the red X that unactivated servers get).

 WARNING Be very sure that you have entered the product ID correctly, or the activation code won't work on your server. The Microsoft licensing clearinghouse generates that activation code by performing an algorithm on your product ID.

5. Back on the Web site, you can quit now and enter the activation code you just got into the activation wizard, or, while still in the Web wizard, you can get client licenses based on the code displayed. You'll need client licenses, so you might as well continue. Click Yes to move to the next screen of the Web licensing tool, where you'll need to fill in the codes of all the license packs you have (the MLP number, or your Open License or Enrollment Agreement number, depending on what kind of customer you are). Again, confirm the information that you've entered and click Next to submit it.

6. The Web site will spit out a valid license pack number that will work with the server you activated, and which you can plug into the license server. Notice that it will only work with this server, and, if the license pack number is for a retail purchase, you can only install it once. To install the license pack number, return to the Terminal Services Licensing tool, right-click the activated server, and choose Install Licenses from the context menu. When prompted, fill in the license pack number as shown in Figure 14.27.

FIGURE 14.27

Installing the client access licenses

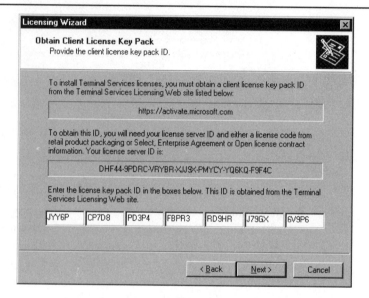

Once you install the license pack, the license server is ready to go.

All that said, here's a warning: you've got 90 days to activate a TSCAL license server. Use those 90 days to make sure that you're running the licensing service on the computer that you want to take the job. The client licenses you create will only work on the server you've activated, and the activation code is based on the product ID.

Application Licensing

Application licensing in a terminal server environment is simpler than you might think: whatever licensing that is applied to a product in a single-user environment applies to the terminal server environment. For example, Microsoft Office 97 is licensed on a per-seat basis. If you install Microsoft Office onto the terminal server, then every computer that will ever run a Microsoft Office application will need to have an Office license, even if the application only runs once a year. However, because Office is licensed on a per-seat basis, if you already have a licensed copy of MS Office installed on a PC client running terminal services, that client may use Office in the terminal session (perhaps when dialing into the terminal server from home) without purchasing an additional Office license, because that computer is already licensed to run the application suite. Be sure to get familiar with the licensing a given application requires so you can see how it will work in the multiuser environment.

Configuring Applications for a Multiuser Environment

After going through all that to license your sessions and applications under Terminal Services, they'd *better* work...

Not all applications work well in a thin client environment. Some use up too many CPU cycles or too much memory, some can't tell the difference between a user and a computer, some store information in locations inappropriate to a multiuser operating system. Sometimes you're stuck with these problems, and if you really need to run those applications, you'll need to do it from the client desktop. However, some problems are fixable, if you take a little time.

 NOTE   If you're running the terminal server session from a PC, you can run applications that don't work well in a multiuser environment from the local computer instead of the terminal server.

Choosing Applications

First, which applications should you be trying to run at all? An application suitable for a terminal server environment fits the following profile:

- Undemanding of CPU cycles and memory
- Modular in video output for better caching
- Stores user data in per-user spaces, not in per-machine spaces
- Identifies users by username, not computer name
- Stores global data in global locations, not local ones

 WARNING   Poorly designed applications that can limp along in a single-user environment will bring a terminal server to a screeching halt. For example, the effect of memory leaks in an application is exponentially increased because multiple instances of the application—all leaking—may be running.

The good news is that their compute-bound and bitmap-dependent natures make video games run horribly in a terminal server environment, so you don't have to worry about people bribing the network administrator to install Baldur's Gate on the server. The bad news is that other modern applications don't meet these criteria, not just games. If nothing else, the extra bells and whistles that many newer applications include make them flunk the first test—that of not using too many resources.

However, you can often tweak an application to make it work better in a multiuser environment than it would if left to its own fell devices. Installing applications in a multiuser environment takes a little more care than does installing them for a single-user environment, but that's part of the price of thin client networking.

Make Your Applications Play Well With Others

Even if an application doesn't need any massaging to make it work right when shared among multiple people, you can't necessarily install it exactly the same way you would if installing it for a single person's use.

To work properly in a multiuser environment, applications should edit the HKCU branch of the Registry to add user-specific information, rather than HKLM. Otherwise, those settings apply to the machine, not to the user. This means that not only are per-user settings available to everyone using that particular machine, but the settings will only be available at that machine—if the user logs into another machine, the settings won't be available. If you've only got one terminal server in your network, it won't matter for this reason if application settings are machine-specific, but a single terminal server will generally only serve a couple of dozen people, tops, and maybe fewer than that if client demands are high. Even if you do only have one terminal server, you've still got the problem of trying to keep user-specific information limited to the people who set it up. For example, say that Web browser bookmarks are stored in a machine-specific area. In a terminal server environment, that means everyone will have the same bookmarks—and will overwrite each other's settings at will.

Point made: user-specific settings should go into HKCU, not HKLM. However, you can't *install* applications into HKCU. HKCU applies only to the current user, not all users, and the identity of the current user will change depending on who's logged in—the contents of HKCU are different for each terminal server session.

To get around this dilemma we need some user-specific settings, but we need to keep them someplace all users can get to, at least at first. Win2K manages this by providing a global installation mode that exploits the machine-wide settings of HKLM.

Installing Applications for Multiple Users

Each Terminal Services session has two operating modes: Execute and Install. The names are descriptive of what the modes are for: Execute mode is for running applications or installing for single users, and Install mode is for installing applications to be available to multiple users. The mechanics of installing an application depend on which mode you're in when running the application's Setup program.

If you install an application while in Execute mode, it installs and edits the Registry however it would if you installed it for use on a single-user computer. When a session is in Install mode, all Registry entries created during that session are shadowed under HKLM\Software\Microsoft\Windows NT\CurrentVersion\Terminal Server\Install. Any edits that an application makes to HKCU or HKLM are copied to HKLM\Software\ Microsoft\Windows NT\CurrentVersion\Terminal Server\Install\Machine.

When it comes to Win32 applications, you don't have to know all this. What you *do* have to know is that when the session is in Execute mode, if an application attempts to read an HKCU Registry entry that doesn't exist, Terminal Services will look in HKLM\Software\Microsoft\Windows NT\CurrentVersion\Terminal Server\ Install for the missing key. If the key is there, Terminal Services will copy it and its subkeys to the appropriate location under HKCU, and copy any .ini files or user-specific .dlls to the user's home directory. For users without home directories, the files go to their personal folder within *%systemroot%*\Profiles. In short, Win2K makes the basic settings for each application machine-specific, then copies these base settings into the user Registry entries so that the user can customize the application. Notice that this doesn't mean that the application keeps returning to its pristine state every time the user runs it—the keys are only copied from their Install mode location to their user location if the keys don't already exist under HKCU. Although some applications (such as Microsoft's TechNet) allow you to bypass Add/Remove Programs by starting the Setup program without running SETUP.EXE, if you run an installation program without using Add/Remove Programs, the installation will fail.

 NOTE Unfortunately, there's no way to spoof a user's identity to install an application for an individual while logged in with another account (if you logged in as Administrator and wanted to install an application for a particular user, for example). Nor can you specify a subset of users who should have access to a particular application. If you want only a couple of people to have access to an application that will be stored on the terminal server, they'll need to install the application from their sessions, or you'll need to take remote control of their sessions and install the application for them.

If you attempt to install an application from its Setup program without using the Add/Remove Programs applet, the installation will fail on a terminal server, and Win2K will nag you to run the Add/Remove programs applet to put Win2K into Install mode. You cannot install an application for a single user if you've set up the server to be an application server.

When the application's Setup program finishes running, you'll go back to the wizard, which will prompt you to click the Next button. Finally, you'll see a dire-looking dialog box (see Figure 14.28) telling you to click the Finish or Cancel buttons when the installation process is complete, but warning you in capital letters not to do so until the installation is complete. Clicking Finish or Cancel returns the session to Execute mode.

FIGURE 14.28

Don't click the Finish button until the application is completely installed, or the settings won't all get copied.

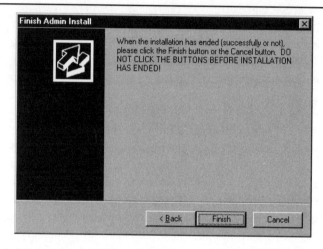

Install mode's usefulness isn't limited to the installation process. Using application compatibility scripts or hand tuning, you can use Install mode to configure an application with general settings to apply to all users, as in the following examples.

You can put a session into Install mode with either the change user command-line utility (if installing applications with Run or with the installation program that comes with the application), or with a setting in the Add/Remove programs applet in the Control Panel.

change user has three options:

- /execute, the default, in which applications install in single-user mode

- /install, used to put the session into Install mode so that applications will be available to all users

- /query, which reports the mode that the session is in, like this:

  Application EXECUTE mode is enabled.

So, before running a setup program, open a command prompt and type **change user/install**. This will cause Win2K to shadow new Registry entries as I described earlier, so that they'll be copied to each user's personal Registry settings as the user runs the application for the first time.

Just bear in mind that *any* changes you make to an application while in Install mode will be copied to that Registry key and therefore apply to all users using the application for the first time.

Using Application Compatibility Scripts

Given that just about all of the applications the terminal server users will be running were originally designed for a single-user environment, many applications require a little manipulation to get them optimized for a multiuser system. Win2K Server includes some application compatibility scripts for some commonly used applications. You can find the scripts for the applications in Table 14.5 in *%systemroot%*
`Application Compatibility Scripts\Install`.

TABLE 14.5: COMPATIBILITY SCRIPTS INCLUDED WITH WIN2K

Application	Script
Corel Office 7	`Coffice7.cmd`
Eudora Pro 4.0	`Eudora4.cmd`
Executive Software International Diskeeper 2.0	`Diskpr20.cmd`
Lotus Smart Suite 9	`Ssuite9.cmd`
Lotus Smart Suite 97	`Ssuite97.cmd`
Microsoft Access 2.0	`Office43.cmd`
Microsoft Access 7.0	`Office95.cmd`
Microsoft Access 97	`Office97.cmd`
Microsoft Dr. Watson	`Drwatson.cmd`
Microsoft Excel 5.0	`Office43.cmd`
Microsoft Excel 7.0	`Office95.cmd`
Microsoft Excel 97	`Office97.cmd`
Microsoft Excel 97 (standalone installation)	`Msexcl97.cmd`
Microsoft Exchange 4.0	`Winmsg.cmd`
Microsoft Exchange 5.0 and later	`Winmsg.cmd`
Microsoft ODBC	`Odbc.cmd`
Microsoft Office 4.3	`Office43.cmd`
Microsoft Office 95	`Office95.cmd`
Microsoft Office 97	`Office97.cmd`
Microsoft Office 2000	`Requires Transform file`
Microsoft Outlook 97	`Outlk98.cmd`
Microsoft Outlook 98	`Outlk98.cmd`
Microsoft Outlook Express	`Outlk98.cmd`
Microsoft PowerPoint 4.0	`Office43.cmd`
Microsoft PowerPoint 7.0	`Office95.cmd`
Microsoft PowerPoint 97	`Office97.cmd`
Microsoft Project 95	`Msproj95.cmd`
Microsoft Project 98	`Msproj98.cmd`
Microsoft Schedule+ 7.0	`Office95.cmd`
Microsoft SNA Client 4.0	`Sna40cli.cmd`

Continued ▶

TABLE 14.5 CONTINUED: COMPATIBILITY SCRIPTS INCLUDED WITH WIN2K

Application	Script
Microsoft SNA Server 3.0	Mssna30.cmd
Microsoft SNA Server 4.0	Sna40srv.cmd
Microsoft Visual Studio 6.0	Msvs6.cmd
Microsoft Word 6.0	Office43.cmd
Microsoft Word 7.0	Office95.cmd
Microsoft Word 97	Office97.cmd
Microsoft Word 97 (standalone installation)	Msword97.cmd
Netscape Communicator 4.0x	Netcom40.cmd
Netscape Communicator 4.5x	Netcom40.cmd
Netscape Communicator 4.6x	Netcom40.cmd
Netscape Navigator 3.x	Netnav30.cmd
Peachtree Complete Accounting 6.0	Pchtree6.cmd
Powersoft PowerBuilder 6.0	Pwrbldr6.cmd
Visio 5.0	Visio5.cmd

These scripts are designed to customize the application's setup to be appropriate for terminal server users, first setting up the command environment, then making sure that the session is in Install mode, checking the Registry for evidence of the application to be configured, and finally editing the Registry as needed. The contents of the scripts vary based on the application, but generally speaking, they do things like turn off CPU-intensive features (such as the FindFast utility that comes with Microsoft Office), add multiuser support to the application, or set user-specific application directories for applications that need them.

To use the scripts, just run them right after you install the application they customize, before anyone has had a chance to use the application themselves. For example, when you run the script for Office 97, Notepad will open and display the RootDrv2.cmd file, prompting you to pick a drive letter for the customized installation to use. Provide a drive letter, save the file, and close Notepad, and the script will run. Log off and log back on, and the new settings will be applied.

 TIP To make sure that no one tries to use the application before you've run the compatibility script, disable the RDP connection while finalizing the application setup.

The release notes on the Win2K CD detail the customization requirements for each application and inform you of any limitations that exist on these applications in a multiuser environment. Rather than reproduce the entirety of this very complete documentation, let's take a simple example to show you why this kind of customization is necessary and how the script works.

You've probably encountered the Dr. Watson program a time or two in the past. If an application crashes, Dr. Watson runs and saves the debugging information to a file that you can send to the application manufacturer. The default location for this file is the system root directory, which normal users do not have permission to access and to which you don't *want* to *give* those users access. If an application crashes, Dr. Watson will not be able to write the debug files to its usual location and will prompt the user for a new file location.

If you want to keep things simple—and don't want to have to wonder where the debugging files are being written—then run the Dr. Watson application compatibility script. This will edit the application's settings to save the debugging files to the user's home directory, as specified in `RootDrv2.cmd`.

You're not limited to using the default settings included in these scripts. To edit one of them, right-click the script's icon and choose Edit from the context menu to open the file in Notepad. Before changing anything, I'd recommend that you inspect the readme file on the Win2K installation disk, so you know what you're doing.

What if your application doesn't have a script made for it? The `Templates` folder in the `Install` directory includes `.key` files (you can open these in Notepad as well) that show you where each Registry entry for application settings is located and what the values should be. Based on this information and using an existing `.cmd` file for a template, you can use the Windows scripting language to create a new script. Alternatively, you can manually edit the user settings from the application interface while the session is in Install mode, as described below.

Hand-Tuning Applications

If you don't need to edit many per-application settings, it might be simpler to make the changes from the user interface while in Install mode, rather than trying to create a new compatibility script. You can also manually edit applications that *have* compatibility scripts but don't include some settings that you need to configure, like turning off the animated Help feature in Microsoft Office.

Turn Off CPU and Bandwidth-Stressing Features   Terminal servers are designed to squeeze every last bit of juice out of system resources so that nothing is wasted. Therefore, they're often stressed—they're *supposed* to be stressed. Given that, don't waste CPU cycles on producing effects that don't necessarily add any real content to the end product, and don't waste network bandwidth on sending those useless effects to the client. In Office 97, for example, turn off sparkle text and the Office Assistant. In other applications, look for pretty effects that don't do anything constructive and see whether you can disable them.

Provide Path Information   Many applications have settings for file locations—places to save files to, places to open files from, template locations, and so forth. However, those locations will often be different for different users. To make sure that file locations for each user are correct, enter a drive letter—and then map that drive letter to different locations for each user. For example, the Save As location for all Word users could be H:, but H: would direct each user to their private home directory.

Using the Registry to Tune Applications

Of course, if an application doesn't have a setting in its interface, you can't use Install mode to tune that setting. However, all is not necessarily lost. You can edit some application settings directly within the Registry, in HKLM\Software\Microsoft\ Windows NT\CurrentVersion\Terminal Server\Compatibility\Applications. Obligatory warning follows:

 WARNING   Be careful when editing the Registry. Neither registry editor has an Undo feature, and neither will tell you if you edit a value to a meaningless entry. Back up the Registry before you edit it, and remember that a mistyped entry in the wrong place can wipe out needed information, or render Win2K unbootable.

More specifically, keep the following in mind:

- When editing value data, notice whether the values are shown in hex, decimal, or binary. When you're editing string values, you can choose to display them in any of those formats. Just be sure that you're entering the data in the chosen format. 15 decimal is F hex, but 15 hex is 21 decimal. You can guess how mixing up hex and decimal could get very ugly, very quickly.

- If you're replacing a key (and, if you try out these hacks, you will be), be very sure that the key that's selected is the one you want to replace. Restoring a key deletes all the present information in the key and replaces it with what's in the restored key. For example, say that you want to replace the contents of the MSOFFICE key that's a subkey of Applications. If you have Applications selected when you restore the saved .reg file, you will wipe out every subkey of Applications and replace it with the information that should have gone into MSOFFICE.

- Never run a .reg file unless you know exactly what it contains and what it will do. Executing a .reg file imports the contents of that file into the Registry—permanently. There is no Undo feature.

Now that you're thoroughly intimidated, read on to see how to make your applications play well with others and call you by your name.

Bad! Bad Application! Go to Sleep! Reducing Demands of Windows Applications

Even if you turn off CPU-hogging effects, some applications are just more cycle-hungry than others. In a terminal server environment, this is a Bad Thing. Not only do CPU-sucking applications themselves underperform in a multiuser environment because they're contending with other applications, but they hurt other applications' performance by denying them cycles. You can edit the Registry to make Win2K keep a closer eye on Windows application management, denying CPU cycles to applications that use too many, known internally as Bad Applications. Doing so will give more cycles to the other applications that the CPU-sucker was starving, but will also make the errant application less responsive itself.

To make the edit, open REGEDT32 and turn to the key HKLM\Software\Microsoft\ Windows NT\CurrentVersion\Terminal Server\Compatibility\Applications. As you can see in Figure 14.29, within the Applications key, you'll see a long list of keys for installed applications.

 NOTE Use REGEDT32, not REGEDIT for this process. You'll need tools found only in REGEDIT32.

FIGURE 14.29

The contents of the Applications subkey

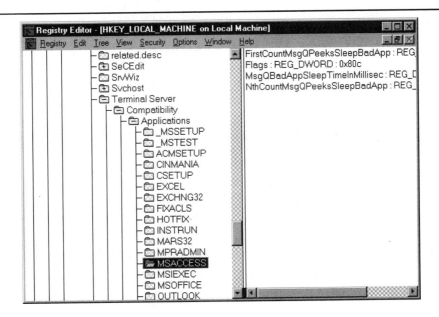

First, check to see whether the application you want to configure is already listed; if it is, then a key with the name of the application will be present. If the key exists, then open it. If the key doesn't exist, or doesn't include the values you need to edit, then you'll need to get the values elsewhere. Find the SETUP key, designed for Win32 applications.

 NOTE SETUP1 is almost identical to SETUP. The only difference is in its Flags value, which is set for both Win16 and Win32 applications.

Open SETUP and look at the values within it, which I've described in Table 14.6.

TABLE 14.6: BAD APPLICATION REGISTRY VALUES

Value Name	Description	Default Value
FirstCountMsgQPeeksSleepBadApp	Number of times that the application will query the message queue before Win2K decides that the application is a Bad Application. The lower this value, the sooner Win2K will decide that the application is Bad and the more quickly the other two values will apply.	0xf (15 decimal)
MsgQBadAppSleepTimeInMillisec	The number of milliseconds that a suspended application will be denied CPU cycles. The higher this value is, the longer the application will sleep.	0
NthCountMsgQPeeksSleepBadApp	The number of times that a Bad Application can query the message queue before Win2K will put it to sleep again. The lower this number, the more often the misbehaving application will go to sleep.	0x5 (5 decimal)
Flags	Describes the type of application to which these settings apply. Your options are: 0x4 for Win16 applications; 0x8 for Win32 applications; or 0xc for both types.	0x8 (Win32 only)

Assuming that you're starting from scratch, you're going to save the SETUP key, import the key to a new (or existing) key for the application, then edit these settings:

1. First, highlight SETUP, choose Save Key from the Registry menu, and as shown in Figure 14.30, save the key to the default directory with some name and a .reg extension.

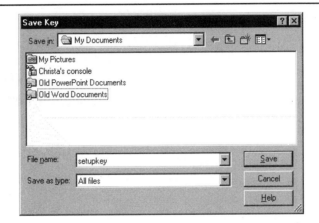

2. Now, highlight the Applications key and choose Add Key from the Edit menu. In the dialog box shown in Figure 14.31, name the new key the filename of the application you're configuring, minus the extension—for example, wordstar.exe's key would be named wordstar. Leave the Class field blank, and click OK. The new key will appear below Applications.

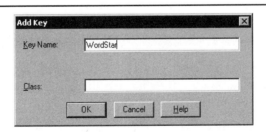

3. Now, with your new key highlighted, pick Restore from the Registry menu and choose the .reg file you created earlier. The Registry Editor will warn you that you're about to replace the contents of the selected key with the contents of the file you're importing. Once you're sure that you're replacing the right key, click Yes.

Finally, double-click value data entries to make your edits in the dialog box shown in Figure 14.32, bearing in mind the information I've given you about what those edits will do. Make sure that you've set the flags properly according to whether the application you're editing is a 16-bit or 32-bit application, and don't forget to notice whether you're making changes in hex or decimal (or binary, if you're a true glutton for punishment).

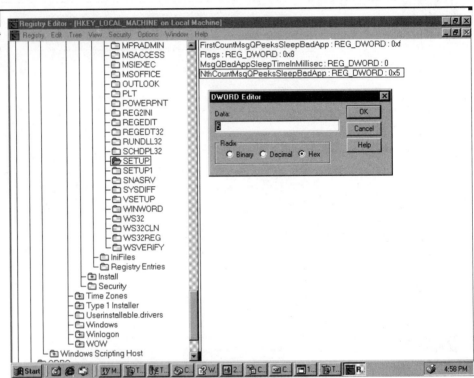

FIGURE 14.32

Edit string values to set the Bad Application parameters you want.

The settings will take effect when you next open the application. Because you edited a key in HKLM, the changes will apply to all instances of the application running on this terminal server.

The Hack that Was...   Windows Terminal Server, and terminal sessions running on early betas of Win2K Server, had a little problem when it came to running Win-Chat, the graphical chat application that comes with Windows. Because WinChat referenced computers, not users, you couldn't use it from a terminal server session to talk to someone running another terminal session. Try to connect to someone, and you'd see a list of computers to choose from, as you see in Figure 14.33. Chat sessions with yourself get dull, so that made WinChat pretty well useless.

The intrepid user of Terminal Services is not foiled by such petty machinations, however. There's a cool hack that you could use to make the application reference usernames instead of computer names. In HKLM\Software\Microsoft\Windows NT\ CurrentVersion\Terminal Server\Compatibility\Applications, where we just edited the Bad Application settings, there's a value for Flags, which in the previous section was 8 or c, signifying that the settings applied to either a Win32 application or to both Win16 and Win32 applications.

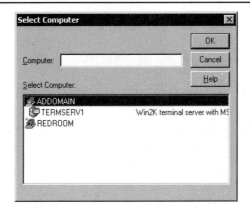

FIGURE 14.33

WinChat only provides a list of computers to connect to, not a list of users.

 TIP To apply more than one flag to an application, add together the value of all the flags you want to use and make that the value of the Flags entry.

There are several other compatibility flags you can apply to Flags with varying results. One flag tells Win2k to make the application return the version number; another tells it to make the application use the system root directory instead of the user's system directory. For our purposes here, the important value is 0x10 (that is, 10 hex), which tells an application to look for users by their usernames, not their computer names. So, you could edit the value of Flags for the WINCHAT key to 18, telling Win2K, "Not only is this a Win32 application, but it should reference usernames, not computer names." No reboot necessary; just restart WinChat. It wouldn't display usernames—that would have been handy, but no dice—but if you plug a username into the browse function, it would find that user and place the call.

You're probably thinking that I'm going to tell you that Microsoft fixed this problem in Win2K. In a way, you would be correct: you will no longer have problems running WinChat in a terminal server session and only being able to reference computers. This is because Microsoft has evidently decided that there was no point in having a messaging application that "didn't work" from terminal server sessions available to those sessions. Now, if you attempt to run WinChat from a Win2K Server terminal session, you get an error message telling you that that application cannot be used from a terminal server remote session. When I asked Microsoft why they did this, the answer was that they were more interested in pushing NetMeeting than WinChat.

Well, that's *one* way to cut down on support calls, I suppose. The good news is that this hack will still work if you have any other applications that reference computer names instead of usernames. You just can't use it any longer to fix WinChat.

Managing Terminal Sessions

Thus far, you've configured client settings and set up applications. Everyone's happily typing away in their session. But what if they're not so happy? Win2K includes terminal services management capabilities that allow you to keep tabs on what's happening on the terminal server. These capabilities work both from the GUI and from the command line.

Introduction to Command-Line Tools

Like the rest of Win2K, Terminal Services has some excellent GUI tools that make it easy to quickly get used to working with the service. That GUI can't do everything, however, and what it can do it can't always do *quickly*. Thus, the Win2K command-line tools that allow you to manage terminal sessions come in handy when it's time to make batch files—or just to do something quickly without taking the time to hunt down the right tool or part of the Microsoft Management Console. Experienced WinFrame hands may find some of these tools similar in function to command-line utilities found in WinFrame, although the tools are typically wrapped into a single tool (such as query) and the WinFrame tools made switches to the main Microsoft tool.

There are far too many options to go into complete detail about every one of the command-line tools listed in Table 14.7, but the following sections should help you get an idea of how you can manipulate Terminal Services from the command line and the GUI administration tool.

 TIP   To see a complete list of all options for a command, type its name and /? at the command line.

TABLE 14.7: SUPPORTED WIN2K TERMINAL SERVICES UTILITIES

Command	Function
change logon	Temporarily disables logons to a terminal server.
change port	Changes or displays COM port mappings for MS-DOS program compatibility. For example, you could use this utility to map one port to another one, so that data sent to the first would actually go to the second.
change user	Flips between Execute mode and Install mode.
cprofile	Removes unnecessary files from a user profile. You can only run this tool on profiles not currently being used.
dbgtrace	Enables or disables debug tracing.
flattemp	Enables or disables redirected temporary directories, which you can use to send .tmp files to a location other than the default.
logoff	Ends a client session specified by session name or session ID, either on the local terminal server or on one specified.
msg	Sends a message to one or more clients.
query process	Displays information about processes.
query session	Displays information about a terminal server session.
query termserver	Lists the available application terminal servers on the network.
query user	Displays information about users logged on to the system.
register	Registers applications to execute in a system or user global context on the computer.
reset	Resets (ends) the specified terminal session.
shadow	Monitors another user's session. Cannot be executed from the console, and cannot shadow the console.
tscon	Connects to another existing terminal server session.
tsdiscon	Disconnects from a terminal server session.
tskill	Terminates a process, identified by name or by process ID.
tsprof	Copies the user configuration and changes the profile path.
tsshutdn	Shuts down a terminal server.

Those who used TSE will notice that many of the command names have changed. The utilities still provide the same functions as the commands in TSE, but you'll have to learn new names for most of them.

Terminal Services Manager

To help you keep track of who's using the terminal server, what processes they're running, and the status of their connections, Win2K includes the Terminal Services Manager, found in the Administrative Tools program group and shown in Figure 14.34.

FIGURE 14.34

The Terminal Services Manager tool

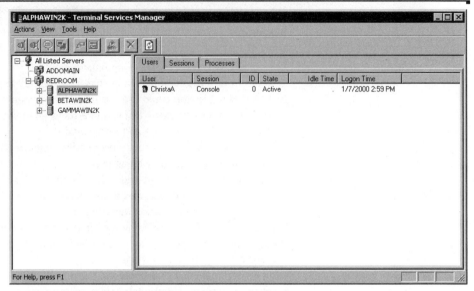

The pane on the left shows all domains in the network, and all terminal servers within those domains. (You can use this tool to manage any terminal server that's listed; you don't need to be physically at that console.) The contents of the right pane depend on what's selected: if it's the domain or the entire network, then all current connections to that server (active or disconnected) and the name of the server hosting them are displayed; if it's a terminal server, then all current connections to that server are displayed; if it's a username, then all the processes running in that user's context, or information about the user session, are displayed. Notice also that the right-hand pane is tabbed, with the contents of the tabs depending on whether you've got a domain, server, or user selected on the left. Broadly speaking, you use the administration tool to get information about:

- Users: what their session IDs are, what applications they're running, what server they're using
- Sessions: what the ID of that session is, what's running in that session, what the status of the session is, how long the client has been logged in, and information about the computer the client is logged in from (IP address, RDP version, and so forth)
- Processes: the process IDs and the executable files (*images*) these processes are associated with

It's not hard to figure out what information you're looking at—a short period of poking around will teach you where everything is. More important is the question of what you can do with this tool. In the following example, I'll show you how to use the management tools to see what's running on the server, send messages to people on the server, terminate remote processes, and close user sessions. For this example, I'll refer to a bogus game called TSQUAKE, a Terminal Services–compliant version of Quake.

 NOTE In NT and Win2K, an executable file is internally known as an *image*. This is because, technically speaking, an application isn't the piece getting CPU cycles, but a collection of commands called *threads* that get CPU time to do whatever they need to do. The threads have an executing environment called the *process* that tells them where to store and retrieve their data. You don't really have to worry about that here except to understand what these processes and images the administration tool refers to are.

 NOTE Technically speaking, a process is an environment for the parts of an application that run, not an executable component itself. The .exe is the executable image of this process, the part that includes the code that needs CPU cycles. For the sake of consistency with the interface, I'll refer to programs running on the terminal server as processes.

Gathering Information

Who's playing TSQUAKE again?

To find out, you'll need to know who's logged into the server or servers and what processes are running in their sessions. You can use both the Terminal Services Manager and the command line to get this information.

From the GUI, select the terminal server or domain for which you want information. In the right-hand pane, three tabs will become visible: one listing users currently logged into the terminal server; one showing the current active and disconnected sessions; one showing the processes currently running on the terminal server.

Flip to the Processes tab associated with the domain (see Figure 14.35) to see a complete list of all processes running in the domain, the server they're running on, the session they're in and the name of the user who owns that session. This screen will also show the process ID (PID), which will come in handy when it comes time to terminate processes.

You can get more than just process information from this screen. Select a terminal server in the left-hand pane. From the tabs that appear on the right, you can find the information described in Table 14.8.

FIGURE 14.35

Viewing processes running on a terminal server

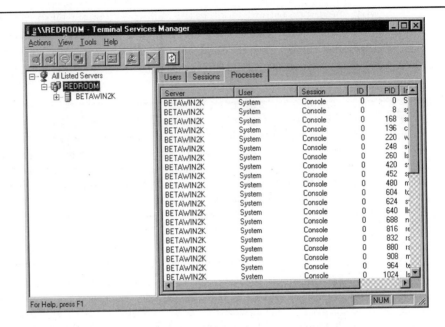

TABLE 14.8: FINDING INFORMATION IN THE TERMINAL SERVICES MANAGER

Data Type	Tab
Client computer name or IP address	Sessions
Image names for processes	Processes
Process IDs	Processes
Protocol used for each session	Sessions
Session idle time	Users
Session IDs associated with processes	Processes
Session status	Users, Sessions
User logon time	Users, Sessions
Username associated with processes	Processes
User session IDs	Users, Sessions

Everything you need to find out which user and which PID is associated with which session, and how busy that session is, is here. If you use the command-line query utility, you can get much the same information that you can from the Terminal Services Manager tool, but you have to do it a piece at a time. From the command line, there's no way to retrieve a list of all processes running in a domain or across all domains, so first you'll have to isolate the terminal server. For example, to see a complete list of all terminal servers in the current domain, type:

query termserv

Win2K will return a complete list of all terminal servers in the domain, like this:

```
Known Microsoft Terminal Servers
————————————————
WIN2KBETA3*
TERMSERVA
TERMSERVB
```

Need the list from another domain? Add the domain name you're retrieving the list from to the command, like this:

query termserv /domain:*domainname*

You'll get the same output, customized for the domain you specified.

Once you've got the name of the server you need to check out, look for TSQUAKE by querying for processes, like this:

query process

Win2K will return a list of all processes running in the current session, as shown below:

USERNAME	SESSIONNAME	ID	PID	IMAGE
>administrator	console	0	1152	explorer.exe
>administrator	console	0	1348	osa.exe
>administrator	console	0	1360	findfast.exe
>administrator	console	0	532	infoview.exe
>administrator	console	0	2052	depends.exe
>administrator	console	0	2172	cmd.exe
>administrator	console	0	764	taskmgr.exe
>administrator	console	0	1256	tsadmin.exe
>administrator	console	0	1636	mmc.exe
>administrator	console	0	1500	winword.exe
>administrator	console	0	2092	regedit.exe
>administrator	console	0	1776	query.exe
>administrator	console	0	1652	qprocess.exe

To query the process list for a different user, add that person's username to the command, like this:

query process gertrude

 TIP You can also list processes associated with a particular session name or session ID, although for most purposes I find it easier to reference usernames.

Okay, but what you really want is a list of everyone who's goofing off and using up CPU cycles. Although you can't get a list of all processes running in a single domain or across domains, you can retrieve a list of all users with a particular process running in their sessions, like this:

```
C:\>query process winword.exe
    USERNAME          SESSIONNAME        ID    PID   IMAGE
   >administrator     console             0    1500  winword.exe
    christa           rdp-tcp#1           1    1400  winword.exe
```

Use *this* command to track down those TSQUAKE users.

Sending Messages

Once you've got your list of people running TSQUAKE, you can let them know that they're caught. From both the GUI and the command line, you can send messages to a single person, to multiple people, and even across domains.

From the left-hand pane of the Terminal Services Manager tool, select the terminal server the people are using. In the right, select the people to whom you want to send a message (Ctrl-click to select multiple user names). From the Actions menu, choose Send Message to open the dialog box shown in Figure 14.36. Click OK, and the message will instantly pop up on the screen of everyone you included on the recipient list.

FIGURE 14.36

Sending a message to users

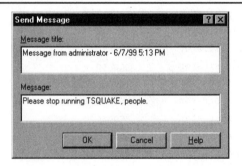

You can also send messages from the command line with the msg utility. This works much like msg did in single-user Windows, with one exception: messages sent to a username will be sent to all instances of that name, not just one. This is so that a person running multiple sessions will be sure to get their message.

msg has lots of options. Its basic syntax looks like this:

msg {*identifier*}[/SERVER:*servername*] [/TIME:*seconds*] [/v] [/w] [message]

The identifier can be a user name, a session ID, a session name, or a filename containing an ASCII list of all users the message should go to. The /TIME parameter doesn't delay the message; rather, it's a time-out period that cooperates with the /w switch that waits for user response before giving control of the command prompt back to the message's sender.

NOTE Like the other command-line utilities, `msg` runs on the server you're connected to unless you specify otherwise.

To send a message to a single user, run `msg` like this:

`msg gertrude Gertrude, please close TSQUAKE. You're wasting CPU power.`

If you want some kind of record that Gertrude saw the message—or at least clicked OK—use the /v (for "verbose") switch as follows:

`msg gertrude /v Gertrude, I mean it. Close the game.`

You'll see output like the following:

```
Sending message to session RDP-Tcp#1, display time 60
Timeout on message to session RDP-Tcp#1 before user response
```

To send a message to everyone logged into that terminal server, use an asterisk, like so:

`msg * Hey, everyone—Gertrude's got enough free time to play TSQUAKE. Anyone got anything for her to do?`

Alternatively, send a message to a preset group by typing all recipient names into a Notepad file and saving it, then referencing the file like this:

`msg @users Hey, everyone—Gertrude's got enough free time to play TSQUAKE. Anyone got anything for her to do?`

The only catch to sending messages to multiple users is that if you add the /w option, `msg` works sequentially. That is, it will send the message to the first person in the list (going in order of session ID) and wait for either a response or a time-out before sending the message to the second person in the list.

Terminating Applications

Gertrude and the other TSQUAKE players aren't paying attention to your pleas. Time to get tough and terminate the application. Every instance of TSQUAKE that you close will exit immediately, with no warning to the user and no chance to save data.

 NOTE Before we get into this, let me distinguish between terminating and resetting. Both options close applications with no warning, but single processes are terminated and entire sessions are reset.

To kill a single application from the GUI, select the server or domain in the left-hand pane and turn to the Processes tab in the right. All running processes will appear here, identified by the name of the server they're running on, who's got them open, the PIDs of the processes, and other relevant information. As elsewhere, you can Ctrl-click to select multiple processes. When every process to be terminated is selected, right-click and choose End Process from the context menu (it's the only option). The selected applications will close instantly.

You can also terminate applications from the command line. Just be careful. This procedure is open to error and you will not make people happy if you accidentally close the wrong process and lose all their data.

The command to kill terminal server applications is `tskill`, related to the `kill` command that appeared for the first time in NT 3.5's Resource Kit and which stops an application by killing its process. Like the Terminate menu command, `tskill` will stop an application as soon as it's executed, with no time allowed for saving data or other tasks. It's very intrusive, so you should only use it when there's simply no other way of getting an application to stop.

The syntax of `tskill` is as follows:

`tskill processid | processname [/SERVER:servername] [/ID:sessionid | /a] [/v]`

Notice that you can reference a process either by its name or its process ID. The former is easier, and necessary if you're using the /a switch to close all instances of an application on the terminal server. The latter is necessary if you're only trying to close specific instances of the application, perhaps leaving untouched the instance of TSQUAKE that your boss has open.

So, to kill all instances of TSQUAKE that are running on the currently selected server, you'd type:

`tskill tsquake.exe /a`

To kill only selected instances, get the PID by running `query process` or `query user` and plug it in, like this:

`tskill 1875`

Sadly, you can't list several PIDs at once to kill, so if you need to pick and choose processes without killing all instances, you'll need to terminate instances of a process one at a time.

 TIP Although you need to supply the executable extension with `query process`, the command won't work if you supply the extension with `tskill`. So, it's `query process tsquake.exe`, but `tskill tsquake`.

Taking Control of User Sessions

Sometimes, the best plan isn't to just shut down applications from the terminal server. Instead, you can take control of a user session, see what they're doing (as opposed to listing processes, which just tells you what processes are active in the context of a given session). This can be especially helpful for troubleshooting purposes, such as if Gertrude says that she didn't mean to run TSQUAKE, but couldn't figure out how to shut it down once she had it running. Taking remote control of the session gives you the same degree of control that you'd have if logged on as that user.

You can remotely control a user's session in one of two ways: from the Terminal Services Manager or from the command line.

TIP You can only take remote control of a terminal server session from another terminal server session, not from the console. The remote control option in the Terminal Services Manager and the shadow command-line utility won't work from the console.

To use the GUI, start a terminal server session, logging on with an account with Administrator privileges. From within the session, start the Terminal Services Manager. Select a terminal server in the left-hand pane and switch to the Users tab so that user sessions are showing. Find the session you want to shadow, and choose Remote Control from the Actions menu. A dialog box like the one shown in Figure 14.37 will prompt you for the hotkey combination you want to use to end remote control of your own session (so that you can get back to the original session).

FIGURE 14.37

Choose a hotkey combination to toggle back to your original session.

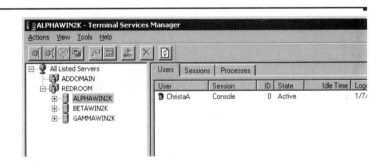

If the user session is configured to require user permission for control, then a dialog box will appear on the screen, letting the user know that someone has requested permission to control their session. If they permit the control, then you're in charge of their session without further ado. If they don't permit the control, then you'll see an error message telling you that you couldn't get permission to control the session.

NOTE The degree of control you have over a user's session that you're remotely controlling depends on the settings in the user's account settings.

The command-line utility for taking remote control of a user session is called shadow, after the WinFrame and MetaFrame name for remote control. Its syntax is as follows:

```
shadow {sessionname | sessionid} [/SERVER:servername] [/v]
```

To use it, start a terminal services session with administrative privileges. Open the command prompt and run query user *username* or query session *username* to find the session ID or session name of the user whose session you want to shadow. You can't shadow based on username, so you'll need this information even if you know the account name of the person whose session you're shadowing.

If shadowing a session on the same terminal server that you're logged into, the command syntax for shadowing session ID 1 is as follows:

shadow 1

If that session requires user permission to be remotely controlled, then you'll see the following message while your session waits for permission to take over the remote one:

```
Your session may appear frozen while the remote control approval is being
negotiated.
Please wait...
```

Once you've got permission, you're in, just as you would be when using the GUI remote control option.

The only tricky part to shadowing from the command prompt is that you had best do it at least once from the GUI before trying the command-line utility. The shadow command does not prompt you for a hotkey combination to end remote control and return to your session. It will use the one defined for the GUI, so if you know what that hotkey combination is, you can use it. Just make sure you know how to return to your own session from the remote control.

Ending—or Preventing—User Sessions

That's it—Gertrude's kicked off the server until she can learn to stop using it incorrectly.

If you want to stop an entire terminal session, not just a single process within it, you can either disconnect or reset the connection. Disconnecting, you recall, cuts the user off from the session (although there's normally nothing to keep a user from reconnecting), but leaves all applications running and data in memory. When the user reconnects to a session they were disconnected from, then they're right back where they left off. A reset connection, in contrast, closes all applications the person had open. Disconnected sessions still use some system resources, albeit not much because their data will eventually be paged to disk and they won't have new user input to process. Reset sessions use no resources.

To disconnect or reset a session from the Terminal Services Manager tool, select it in the left-hand pane and choose Reset or Disconnect from the Action menu. You'll see a dialog box warning you that the session will be disconnected or reset; click OK, and the selected session or sessions will be ended.

You can also end user sessions from the command line with the `tsdiscon` and `reset` session commands. The syntax for `tsdiscon` is as follows:

```
tsdiscon [sessionid | sessionname] [/SERVER:servername] [/v]
```

Once again, you can choose to identify sessions to close by session name or session ID. To find out both, run `query session` to get output like the following:

SESSIONNAME	USERNAME	ID	STATE	TYPE	DEVICE
>console	Administrator	0	active	wdcon	
rdp-tcp	65537	listen	rdpwd		
rdp-tcp#2	Christa	2	active	rdpwd	
		1	idle		
		3	idle		

Find the session name or ID you want, and plug it into the `tsdiscon` command like this: **tsdiscon 2**. Once you've pressed the Enter key, the user of the selected session sees a message, "Terminal Server has ended the connection," and is given a Close button to push.

 TIP I find it easiest to reference session IDs. You always have to use a number—you can't choose to disconnect a session attached to a particular username—so you might as well choose the shortest identifier you can get away with.

The syntax for resetting a session is similar to that used for disconnecting it:

```
reset session {sessionname | sessionid} [/SERVER:servername] [/v]
```

Once again, the user will see a dialog box telling them that Terminal Server ended the connection and prompting them to close.

What if you'd like to keep people off the terminal server altogether, perhaps while you're installing new applications on it? If no one's yet connected, you can disable the RDP protocol from the Terminal Services Configuration tool located in the Administrative Tools program group. Open the tool so that it looks like the window in Figure 14.38 and right-click the RDP protocol. From the pop-up menu that appears, choose All Tasks/Disable Connection.

 WARNING If you disable the connection from the Terminal Services Configuration tool, you'll reset any existing sessions.

FIGURE 14.38

Resetting the RDP protocol

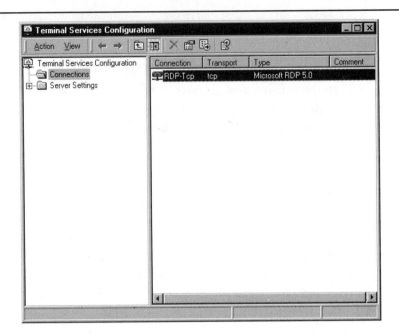

If you've reset all connections in preparation for shutting down the server, you can also shut down the server without going to the console. tsshutdn's syntax is as follows:

```
tsshutdn [wait_time] [/SERVER:servername] [/REBOOT] [/POWERDOWN]
         [/DELAY:logoffdelay] [/v]
```

Most of these options are what they appear to be. wait_time specifies the amount of time (in seconds) until the server is shut down, and servername specifies a server if you don't want to shut down the one you're currently logged into. /REBOOT reboots the server and /POWERDOWN shuts it down if the server has Advanced Power Management drivers (if not, the server shuts down all server processes and displays the Click to Restart message).

So, for example, you could combine tsshutdn and msg to tell everyone that the server's going to be rebooted in five minutes. First, send the following message:

Msg * The server will go down in 5 minutes for maintenance. Please log off.

Second, run the tshutdn command with the following parameters:

tshutdn 300 /reboot

Say, however, that you don't want to shut down the server. You just want to keep any new sessions from starting. To disable the protocol for new sessions without disturbing the ones already in place, you'll need to use the change logon command utility. Its syntax is as follows:

change logon {/QUERY | /ENABLE | /DISABLE}

```
/QUERY    Query current terminal session login mode.
/ENABLE   Enable user login from terminal sessions.
/DISABLE  Disable user login from terminal sessions.
```

Typing change logon /disable prevents any further connections from being made until you reenable the protocol. Anyone who tries to connect will see an error message telling them that remote logins are currently disabled. Disabling RDP does not, obviously, affect the console session as it's not dependent on RDP.

This isn't all there is to know about Terminal Services. Chapter 20 will discuss some capacity planning issues unique to terminal servers and give you some hints about how you can set up a terminal server to best support user needs. User profiles and system policies, also important to Terminal Services, are discussed in Chapter 8.

Even apart from those chapters, however, Terminal Services is a big topic worthy of a book in itself. In these pages, I've given you a look at what Terminal Services are and how they're implemented in Win2K, shown you some of the application tweaking you'll need to do to configure applications for a multiuser environment, and given you some management guidance. This isn't everything you could possibly learn about Terminal Services, but it's a start.

CHAPTER **15**

How Running a Big Windows 2000 Network Is Different

The goal of this chapter is to take the Windows 2000 concepts you've learned about so far and expand them beyond one server or workstation to the enterprise. That is, now that you've read about the Active Directory, group policies, sites, and SYSVOL replication, how do the things you know about Windows 2000 change as you start to scale up these services? Indeed, Windows 2000 in general, and the Active Directory in particular, was designed with large enterprises in mind. Given the dizzying array of new infrastructure services, this chapter will cover some of the things you'll need to think about as you scale Windows 2000 in your own environment.

Active Directory Design Issues

As you start to think about how you will deploy Windows 2000 and the Active Directory, your first tasks will be around planning the AD namespace. That is, how many Win2K domains will you have, how many trees, and how many forests? What will be your criteria for adding new domains, trees, and forests? I can't stress enough how important it is to thoroughly plan how you intend to get from your current environment—be it NT 4, NDS, or something else entirely—to an infrastructure based on Windows 2000. This entails not only thinking about the end goal (e.g., I want to consolidate to one domain in the end), but also thinking about how you'll get there, how long it will take, and how you'll accommodate exceptions to your design.

Enterprise Forests

To start with, what are some of the issues you're likely to face as you build a large AD infrastructure? We'll start at the top—with the *forest root*. When you build that first Win2K DC into the first Win2K domain, you're asked if this is the first DC in the domain tree and the first tree in the forest. If you answer yes to both of these questions, you're innocently making some important decisions about the future of your Active Directory.

No matter how many domain trees you add into your forest, this first domain, the forest root, will play a special role in your AD infrastructure. Figure 15.1 shows an example of a forest of two domain trees. Mycompany.com was the first domain in the forest, and so it becomes the forest root. This role remains the same regardless of the fact that the subco.com domain tree is also part of the forest.

As of the current product, you can't remove or rename the forest root within the Active Directory. Because of its special role, it must remain as is for the life of your forest. Given this, consider using the forest root domain as an "infrastructure container" for your organization. That is, use this domain to house your infrastructure elements only. Build child domains underneath it to keep your business objects like users, computer, printers, and so on. In the root domain, only keep a handful of enterprise-wide administrators who are authorized to make changes to infrastructure elements such as sites and schema and to add other domain trees.

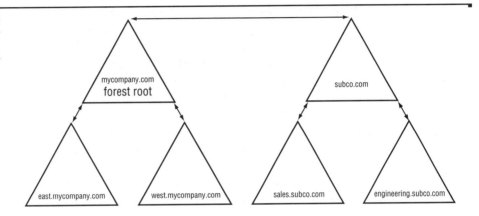

FIGURE 15.1

Viewing the forest root in a multidomain Active Directory forest

Modifying the Schema, Merging Forests: Limited Flexibility

Another consideration as you grow your AD environment is the schema. As you know, the schema is the structure and relationship of your AD classes and attributes. A default schema ships with Windows 2000, but you can extend it to meet your own needs. Using the Schema AD MMC snap-in, or via the Active Directory Services Interface (ADSI)—a set of APIs for programmatically accessing the Active Directory and other directory services—you're free to add your own classes and attributes to your Active Directory. This idea works well if you have total control of your AD environment, but it presents a problems as your organization expands and contracts. This is because you can currently only have one schema per forest. What this means is that, when you define your forest, the schema in place on that first domain is replicated to all other domains in the tree and all subsequent trees that are made part of the forest.

Now let's take the scenario where either your organization buys a new company or an existing division within your organization has built its own AD infrastructure. In either case, an existing but separate forest would exist, since the acquired company would have been required to build their own forest root when they installed their first AD domain. Furthermore, each of these distinct forests may have had schema changes made to it, making it incompatible with yours. In the current release of

Windows 2000, there are no tools available to merge AD forests, or schemas. What this means is that you have two choices. The first option is that you can create explicit nontransitive trust relationships between domains in one forest to allow access to domains in the other (a la NT 4 trusts). In this case, you would maintain multiple forests within your enterprise.

There are advantages and disadvantages to this, but one that should not be underestimated is the fact that there is no good solution for administration of multiple forests. In a single-forest environment, there are two universal groups which have management scope over the entire forest by default—Enterprise Admins and Schema Admins. These two groups only exist in the forest root domain. The Enterprise Admins group is automatically made a member of the local Administrators group in each subsequent child domain in the forest and in each domain tree (if your forest includes multiple domain trees). In a multiple-forest environment, there is no common administrative control. Enterprise Admins from one forest have no control over another forest unless explicitly created via trust relationships.

Another option for dealing with multiple forests is that you can decide which forest will remain and use Microsoft-provided, or third-party, migration tools to migrate objects from one forest to the other. In the latter case, you would treat the "foreign" forests as if they were downlevel NT 4 domains to be migrated to Win2K domains. Of course, all schema changes made in the foreign forests would be lost as you migrate those objects to your enterprise forest.

Sites

Sites are boundaries of replication for the three naming contexts described in "Replication Issues" later in this chapter. Within a site, replication of these naming contexts is automatic and occurs every five minutes by default. Sites can be created to link groups of subnets that represent a set of high-bandwidth connections. Sites also cross domain boundaries—you can have two DCs from different domains in the same site. Sites have several roles above that of just controlling replication. For example, you can create group policy objects on sites, allowing you to associate desktop management with a particular network subnet. As your Win2K network grows, maintenance of sites grows. Sites are built manually by you, the administrator. Note that sites can only be defined within the forest root domain. Even though you can load the MMC AD Sites and Services snap-in focused on a child domain controller, you won't be able to define sites there unless you're a member of the Enterprise Admins group or a member of the root domain's Domain Administrators Group. This prevents administrators in child domains from randomly defining sites that could impact your replication topology.

Associated with sites are subnet objects. You must manually define each logical IP subnet within your Active Directory infrastructure and associate those subnets with the appropriate site object. To further complicate matters, you'll need to associate sites that you define to a given site link. Site links let you group sites of equal "cost" from a network perspective. The process of both manually defining sites and site links and manually associating subnets to them can be onerous in a large AD infrastructure. To exacerbate the challenge, each site link (see Figure 15.2) and each NTDS connection object between servers in a single site give you the ability to control the replication schedule.

FIGURE 15.2

Viewing the replication schedule options on a site link

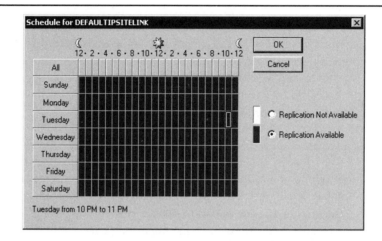

As you grow your AD infrastructure to hundreds of sites and dozens of site links, the task of maintaining this mass of schedules can quickly become overwhelming. Today, the only tool you have at your disposal to manage sites is the MMC snap-in for AD Sites and Services. It's clear that Microsoft will have to provide a better interface over time for managing sites in large Win2K infrastructures.

Organizational Units

The point I want to make about organizational units in a large Win2K infrastructure is this: Keep it simple! The fact that OUs exist in the AD and provide a convenient point for delegating administrative control can lead to overuse. Microsoft recommends no more than 10 levels deep of OUs, but frankly, it would be difficult to manage the complexity of such a deep hierarchy. Given the inheritance model within the AD, if you had to manage 10 levels of nested OUs—each with associated security, delegated administration, and group policy objects—you would quickly tear your hair out! The best approach as you grow your AD infrastructure is to start with as flat an OU structure as possible. This means fewer layers. You can always move objects around within a domain later as you find better groupings for users.

Think about the following trade-off: In many cases you can either group objects by OU or by security group. For example, you could bound a set of users in the finance department either by creating a Finance OU or by creating a Finance security group within a larger OU. The path you take depends upon your goal. By bounding a group of users within an OU, you make it easier to segregate those users for purposes of delegating administration and applying group policies. However, you may find yourself creating extra work if those users get the same group policy as four or five other OUs with similar needs. In that case, you have to either create extra group policy objects or link existing GPOs from another OU to your new one.

By classifying users via security group within a larger, more generic OU structure, you may find it harder to cleanly pick those users out of the crowd when it comes to managing their special needs.

In the end, you will likely choose some combination of OUs and security groups to manage and segregate your users to provide the proper amount of administrative and configuration control.

GPOs

The group policy object is a powerful feature in Win2K, but it's also one that has the highest likelihood of causing you management nightmares as you scale up your infrastructure. This is due in part to the fact that you can define GPOs at so many different levels and in part to the fact that Microsoft provides little if any troubleshooting tools to determine what's going on during GPO processing. To review, GPOs can be defined at the local machine, site, domain, and OU levels, they are inherited from level to level, and their effects can be filtered via security groups. Additionally, GPOs are only processed by machine or user objects. You can define multiple GPOs at each level of the hierarchy. You can have some GPOs forcibly override others, or conversely, you can prevent overriding of a GPO. Finally, each GPO contains several different *nodes* of functionality, each providing sometimes unrelated control of your users and computers. All of this makes for a potentially complex environment for controlling and managing users and computers via GPOs. So what can you do to keep a handle on GPOs as you benefit from their significant capabilities?

The answer to that is the same as the answer to managing many aspects of your AD infrastructure—keep it simple. Just because you can define multiple GPOs at multiple levels of your AD hierarchy doesn't mean you should. As an example, each GPO contains multiple nodes of functionality—for example, Software Installation, Security, Logon/Logoff Scripts, Folder Redirection, Administrative Templates, and so on. It makes logical sense to group some of these nodes in one GPO. For example, you might define a "security" GPO that only employs the user and computer security options. In this way, you can easily delegate administration of that GPO to your security folks and be assured that they won't accidentally modify a software installation setting that unpublishes Microsoft Word for the whole enterprise.

Similarly, in addition to defining single- or limited-function GPOs, consider limiting the number of GPOs defined at the site, domain, and OU levels. Define domain-level GPOs only for policies that must have an impact on the whole domain, such as security. Leave software installation or administrative template policy to OUs. The benefits to this strategy will become apparent as you begin to think about Resultant Set of Policy (RSOP). RSOP is basically the effective policy on a given user or computer within a given container in your AD infrastructure. It means, for user x on computer y, "Tell me what my effective policy is when I log on." Microsoft will provide little or no help in this area out of the box. However, some third-party ISVs like Full Armor software (www.fullarmor.com) plan to provide RSOP tools to help you manage your GPO deployment. Consider obtaining these tools if you plan to deploy GPOs in any significant way in Win2K.

Another consideration is the time it takes to process GPOs at user logon or machine start-up. The more GPOs a user or computer has to process, the more delay there will be in start-up or logon. This is especially noticeable at user logon time, since GPOs normally process prior to the user's shell loading. You can modify this behavior via an administrative template policy, but in many cases, you won't want to. Given this behavior, it's important to do what you can to minimize the processing time of GPOs. Microsoft has attempted to streamline the processing of GPOs in a couple of ways. First, they give you the option of disabling either the computer or user configuration settings in a particular GPO. If you've defined a GPO that only sets policy on one or the other, it's a good idea to check the box in the Group Policy property page to disable processing for that part of the GPO. This reduces the time it takes to process the GPO significantly. Additionally, GPO version will be tracked at each processing. If no changes have occurred from one logon or machine start-up to the next, then the GPO will not be processed. There's an administrative template available to override this behavior, but it will add to the processing time significantly.

Modifying GPOs

One more point to consider when deploying GPOs: Because GPOs are yet another object in the Active Directory, they are subject to the same multimaster replication processes as other AD objects. Therefore, it is possible to have two people editing the same GPO at the same time. The results, of course, could be disastrous if two people make changes that cancel each other out on replication. To prevent this scenario, the Group Policy snap-in by default will always focus on the DC which currently has the PDC role within a given AD domain to edit GPOs. You can see this by selecting the View menu option while highlighting a GPO from the Group Policy MMC snap-in.

You will see an option called DC Options. Figure 15.3 shows an example of the choices you have for focusing the Group Policy snap-in, with the default choice shown here.

Leaving this option at the default will ensure that GPO changes are always made at the same server and reduce the chance that two people will be editing a GPO on two different DCs.

FIGURE 15.3

Viewing the options for focusing group policy object editing

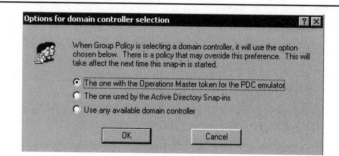

Replication Issues

Replication of various parts of the Win2K infrastructure has a big impact on reliability and availability as you scale your environment. Replication of the Active Directory, the global catalog, SYSVOL data, and Dfs can all have an impact on performance, availability, and the user experience. In this section, I'll discuss some of the main challenges you'll encounter when deploying these various services.

First, however, I want to review the concept of *naming contexts*. Win2K has three naming contexts that are replicated in a well-known way—domain, schema, and configuration. You can think of naming contexts as replication paths or loops through your Win2K environment. The domain naming context is the replication path that only traverses domain controllers within a single domain. It is responsible for replicating changes to the Active Directory database for a given domain. The schema naming context is responsible for replicating schema changes across the entire forest, and the configuration naming context holds information related to replication topology and is also replicated across the entire forest.

When you define sites and site links, you're basically defining the replication topology for these three naming contexts. In addition, Win2K itself, through the Knowledge Consistency Checker (KCC) process, will define *DS connection objects* between specific DCs within your forest to fill in the details of who replicates to whom and how often. This replication topology can become very complex. Using tools such as repadmin.exe from the Win2K Resource Kit for diagnosing replication problems and ReplMon (also from the Resource Kit) for monitoring and manually triggering replication across DCs will go a long way toward making replication management in Win2K something less than a black art.

SYSVOL

SYSVOL, as you know, is the successor to the NETLOGON share from NT 4. In Win2K, as in NT 4, the SYSVOL share is replicated to all DCs in a domain. Under SYSVOL resides most of the data associated with GPOs, as well as any legacy NETLOGON information for your downlevel NT 4 and Win 9x devices. SYSVOL uses the new NT File Replication Service (FRS) to replicate content between all DCs in a domain. FRS replicates, by default, on the same schedule as the Active Directory and respects site boundaries just as AD replication does. You can change FRS's replication schedule. From the AD Users and Computers snap-in, choose the View/Advanced Features option and drill down into the System\File Replication Service feature. From there, if you highlight the Domain System Volume (SYSVOL share), right-click, choose Properties from the context menu, and then choose the Change Schedule button, you can adjust when SYSVOL replication can take place during the day. This means that, given the normal site replication schedule, you can block out hours during the day where SYSVOL replication will not happen. You should use this option sparingly, since your SYSVOL and Active Directory could easily get out of sync if you modify one and not the other. Remember that intersite replication will take longer than intrasite replication, so for example, if you've added a new logon script to a GPO that is focused on a particular DC, then it may take a while for that script to replicate to all associated SYSVOL shares on all DCs within the domain.

Dfs

Dfs, or Distributed File System, presents a separate but important set of challenges from SYSVOL. Let's review some of the capabilities of Dfs in Win2K to see how you might get in trouble deploying it in a large infrastructure.

Dfs gives you the ability to define fault-tolerant root shares within a given domain. Note that you can only define one FT root per server. FT roots are referred to by the domain name rather than a server name. For example, I could map a drive to the share `\\us.mycompany.com\dfsroot`. Underneath a particular Dfs root are any number of DFS links. DFS links appear as logical subdirectories to the Dfs root but physically point to any number of shares located on other servers (Win2K, NT 4, and even NetWare and Unix file systems) in your environment. Each DFS link can have a replica associated with it as well. For example, under my fictitious dfsroot share, I might have a DFS link called apps where I keep all of my application setup packages.

Under each DFS link, I can add replica members. These represent shares on other servers where the same content is available. For example, my DFS link called apps may have two replica members—shares called apps on \\servera and \\serverb. Replica members are normally used when you have some read-only content, like application binaries, that you wish to make available from more than one server. In this example, suppose servera exists in Site X and serverb exists in Site Y. Clients in Site X connecting to the Dfs share \\mycompany.com\dfsroot\apps would be redirected to \\servera\apps, and clients in Site Y would be redirected to \\serverb\apps. Thus Dfs provides some level of server affinity based on site topology.

Another feature of Dfs is to provide the file replication to all of those replica members. Dfs replication actually uses the NT File Replication Service but creates its own replication topology, which you have no control over. By default, Dfs creates a star topology between all replica members that you designate. There is also no easy way to tell when Dfs replicas have "converged" (all content changes have been replicated to all replicas). For large networks with many different replica members located across varying WAN links, you're likely to find Dfs replication inadequate. The replication available in Dfs is really meant for smaller networks where read-only content is replicated across a few servers. In fact, if you choose to use the automatic replication available in Dfs, you are limited to 256 replica members per child node. However, if, when you create DFS links, you choose the manual replication option, you can safely support up to 1,000 replica members. Note that by choosing manual replication, you are saying to Dfs that you plan to provide your own mechanisms for replicating content to each replica member—outside of the Dfs infrastructure.

You may even be tempted to use Dfs replication to replicate data that is not read-only, such as users' home folders. The current incarnation of Dfs is not really suited to this kind of approach. This is principally because you really have no control over when Dfs will "converge" replicas. As a result, if a user manages to make changes to his home folder on two different replica members before those changes have propagated, you could get into a situation where changes are getting lost. With Dfs, your best approach is to simply use the fault-tolerant feature as a way of abstracting physical location from logical share names. Let Dfs create a distributed file tree that is sensitive to site topology. If you must use Dfs replication, stick to read-only content, or purchase some other near-real-time replication software to do the actual content replication.

How GPO Replication Is Different and Special

I want to mention the special case of GPOs and how they replicate within your Win2K infrastructure. This behavior can become a major issue in larger environments with many GPOs deployed across sites with varying WAN link speeds. To review, group policy objects are actually composed of two elements. The Group Policy Container (GPC) is an object within the Active Directory that stores the reference to a particular GPO. The GPC is replicated just as other AD objects are, in a multimaster fashion, on a per-property basis. The other element of a GPO is the Group Policy Template (GPT). The GPT is really the guts of the GPO. It's the physical files that make up a GPO. Things like shutdown and start-up scripts, logon and logoff scripts, administrative templates and the resulting `registry.pol` file, and security templates are kept in the GPT, which is replicated within the SYSVOL share.

Given the fact that these two elements are distinct entities with potentially different replication behavior, there exists the possibility that a GPC will replicate before its associated GPT does. What this means is that a user or computer could start processing a GPO before all of it has been replicated around the infrastructure. To prevent this from happening, it's a good idea to disable a particular GPO prior to editing it, make the changes, give them time to propagate, and then enable it again. To disable a particular GPO, load the AD Users and Computers MMC snap-in (or the AD Sites and Services snap-in if it's a site-based GPO). Focus on the container (site, domain, or OU) where the GPO resides, right-click, and choose Properties from the context menu. Select the Group Policy tab, highlight the GPO of interest, and choose the Options button. From there, you can disable or enable the GPO.

Deploying Infrastructure Services

When you're ready to start deploying a large-scale Win2K infrastructure, there are a number of services that you need to provide to enable proper functioning of the Active Directory and your Win2K clients. Domain Name System (DNS) and the global catalog are two such infrastructure services that are critical to the proper functioning of your Win2K environment. In this section, I'll discuss some of the challenges of deploying these services in a robust way and make some recommendations to ensure that they remain highly available.

DNS

As you know, the use of Domain Name System (DNS) is all-important in Windows 2000. It replaces WINS as the name service of choice for Win2K devices. It also serves a crucial role in the registration of special service (SRV) records related to locating Active Directory domain controllers and services such as authentication, Lightweight Directory Access Protocol (LDAP), and the global catalog. Therefore, when designing your Active Directory deployment, you'll need to put quite a bit of thought into how you'll make DNS services highly available across your network.

Remember that you can create three kinds of zones in Windows 2000. The first type, standard primary, works just like NT 4 or Unix-based DNS servers, where the zone files are kept in a text file and replication between servers is single-master based. That is, for a given zone, the server that is primary for that zone originates all changes, and those changes are replicated to standard secondary zones in a process called a zone transfer. This replication is one-way and only can originate from the primary. In this configuration, you could potentially have a Win2K DNS server serving as the primary for a zone that replicates to both Win2K- and Unix-based secondary DNS servers.

The second type of zone is the standard secondary, to which I've already referred. Creating this type of zone indicates that you've already defined a primary somewhere and you wish to add another replica server to it.

The third type of zone is one that is integrated into the Active Directory. An AD-integrated zone is just as it sounds. The zone file and all its records are actually stored in the Active Directory. More importantly, they are replicated from domain controller to domain controller using the same multimaster replication schedule as other directory objects. This means that the whole idea of one-way zone transfers goes away. It also means that, if you have an AD-integrated zone, you'll need to run the actual DNS service on a domain controller so it can find those zone files. There's no support for running DNS on a standard member server if you integrate your zones with the AD. So, when it comes time to add a new DNS server to your network, you simply install the DNS service on a DC, point your clients to it, and you're in business. AD-integrated zones also support the concept of incremental zone transfers. When an older-style DNS implementation needs to update secondary zones, it copies the whole of the primary zone to the secondaries regardless of whether one or one hundred records have changed since the last update. Incremental zone transfers allow a DNS implementation to only update those records that have changed since the last update. Win2K DNS supports incremental zone transfers for both AD-integrated and non-AD-integrated zones.

Earlier in this chapter, I talked about how the AD uses three naming contexts to scope replication of data. The domain naming context replicates AD object data, and its scope is only within a single domain. If you choose to use AD-integrated zones for DNS data, then this DNS zone information is replicated using the domain naming context. As such, AD-integrated DNS data does not replicate across domain boundaries. What this means for your DNS design is that, if you plan to have multiple domains and want to use AD-integrated zones, you'll need to either run all of your DNS servers within a single domain or have separate zones for each part of your DNS namespace—each within its own domain.

As an example, suppose you have an AD domain tree composed of mycompany.com as the root domain and usa.mycompany.com as a child domain. You may choose one of two options. In the first option, DCs in mycompany.com could host the AD-integrated zones for both mycompany.com and usa.mycompany .com. In the second option, DCs in mycompany.com could host only the zone for mycompany.com. DCs in usa.mycompany.com could then host the usa.mycompany .com zone exclusively and forward requests to servers in the root for mycompany.com. The advantage of the first scenario is that, if you place all of your DNS servers within the root domain, you can effectively isolate administration of them to DNS administrators within the root, preventing administrators in child domains from easily tampering with them.

Placing DNS Servers

When it comes time to decide where to place DNS servers—be they DCs running AD-integrated zones or just member servers with standard primary or secondary zone files—you should think about this service the way you think about placing WINS servers in NT 4 today. To that end, you want your DNS servers to be highly available but not overly deployed. Remember that in Win2K, as in NT 4, client DNS resolvers cache name resolution requests to either WINS or DNS. This caching behavior reduces the frequency that a client needs to talk with a DNS server and therefore reduces concerns about name resolution traffic on the network. As such, you don't need to necessarily keep DNS servers physically close to your client segments.

This is helpful if you choose to deploy AD-integrated DNS servers in a multidomain environment where all of your DNS servers reside in the root domain but your workstations reside in some child domain. For example, if you have a number of branch offices with workstations and servers residing in the child domain, you might consider deploying a DC from the child domain in the branch office to provide local authentication. However, if your DNS servers were located on DCs in the root domain only and your plan was to deploy a DNS server in every branch office, then you would face the requirement of deploying two DCs per branch office to achieve your result—possible, but perhaps not practical or cost effective. In that case, it probably makes more sense to keep only a few centrally located and managed DNS servers. The ultimate decision comes down to how often your clients need name resolution services, what kind of bandwidth is available between server and client, and how tolerant your client applications are of name resolution problems.

A final point to take into consideration when placing DNS servers is that clients will be unable to authenticate to your AD domain if they're not able to locate a global catalog server. This behavior can be modified to disable the requirement that a GC be available to logon. However, if you disable the GC requirement, membership in universal groups will not be available. This means that a user who is a member of universal group that has rights to a resource will not be able to get to that resource if the Global Catalog is unavailable. The ability to locate a GC server is in part related to how and where you place your GC servers, but it also depends upon the availability of a special record within DNS. SRV resource records that point to GC servers are only stored in the DNS zone for your forest root domain under _msdcs.gc.

Global Catalog Servers

If you remember, the global catalog (GC) contains a special view of your AD infrastructure. The GC is a service that runs on select DCs within your AD forest. It contains an instance of every object within a forest—and a small subset of those objects' attributes—and is used as a quick index for searching for objects within the directory. Because the GC replicates across the entire forest rather than just within domain boundaries, it also contains any universal groups that you have defined for the forest and the members of those groups as well. This is a feature unique to universal groups and the GC. Local and domain groups are enumerated in the GC, but their membership is not stored there. It's important to keep this in mind as you build universal groups. The larger the number of universal groups you define, and the more members they contain, the larger the amount of data that will have to be replicated to all GC servers.

Remember that GC replication occurs in addition to any AD replication that goes on between DCs. This means that the amount of GC data replicating around your network becomes a function of the amount of data within the GC as well as how many servers you've designated as GC servers.

GC Server Placement

So, we've established that the GC plays a critical role in the proper operation of your AD infrastructure for a number of reasons. First, you must have a GC server available to your Win2K clients in order for them to be able to authenticate to the domain. Next, the GC holds important information about the objects in your forest and allows clients to query that information without having to go directly to the domain and server where those objects are stored. Given these roles, it's important to think about GC server placement as you roll out your infrastructure. Just as with DNS, GC servers should be highly available but not overly deployed. Too many GC servers means too much data replicating around your network. The extreme case is where every DC in your forest is also a GC server. This is generally unnecessary.

However, you might consider the method clients use to locate GC servers via DNS as a way of driving GC placement decisions on your network. That is, a client will first look for a GC server within its own site. This helps keep GC as well as authentication traffic local to the site. So, start by placing a GC server in each site—if you have a DC in a particular site, make it a GC server as well.

You can define a DC as a global catalog server from the Sites and Services MMC snap-in. Select the site where your server resides, open the Servers folder, and select the server you wish to make a GC server. Under the server, right-click the NTDS Settings container, choose Properties, and check the box to enable the GC service (see Figure 15.4).

If you have more than one DC in a site and it's a large site, you might want to create a second GC server to share the load amongst clients within that site. Remember also that GCs span domains. You don't necessarily need a GC running on the DC in every domain. The goal is to have at least one GC in every site that has a DC.

FIGURE 15.4

Viewing the dialog within the Sites and Services snap-in for enabling the GC service

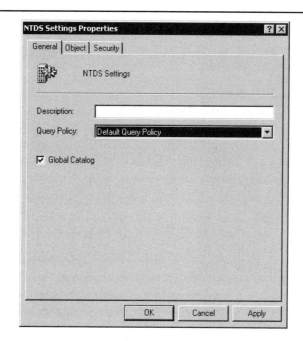

Operations Masters

When Win2K (nee NT 5) was first announced, much ado was made about the fact that the primary domain controller (PDC) of NT 4 days went away—that changes could be made from any domain controller in your AD domain. This is only partly true in the Win2K infrastructure. The PDC role has actually been replaced and augmented in Win2K with five distinct roles, termed *Operations Masters* (previously called FSMO, or Floating Single Master Operation). These Operations Master roles each must reside on single server(s) within your enterprise forest and must be manually moved or changed in the event that a server holding that role becomes unavailable. The roles are as follows:

Domain Naming   The Domain Naming role resides on a single server throughout the forest and is responsible for ensuring unique domain names. Defined in the Domains and Trusts MMC snap-in.

Schema   The Schema role resides on a single server throughout the forest. Given the invasive nature of schema changes, it makes sense that only one server at a time be allowed to make the change and this is the role of the schema master. Defined in the AD Schema MMC snap-in.

PDC   The Primary Domain Controller role resides on a single server *per domain*. It is intended to provide downlevel (NT 4) Backup Domain Controllers that reside in a Win2K domain with a PDC for backward compatibility. It's also used by the Group Policy snap-in as the default location for making changes to group policies.

RID Pool   The Relative Identifier Pool role resides on a single server *per domain*. A RID is a sequential number assigned to any new object that is created in an AD domain. Since AD uses multimaster replication, there needs to be a way of ensuring that each DC that can create new objects does not overlap RID assignments from other DCs. The RID Pool role ensures this by allocating and tracking a pool of RIDs for each DC.

Infrastructure   The Infrastructure role resides on a single server *per domain* and has responsibility for maintaining interdomain consistency between AD objects—specifically for those objects that cross domain boundaries, such as sites, GC, and replication topology.

By default, each of the three domain-specific roles will reside on the first DC you build in your first domain (or child domain). In fact, all five roles will exist on the first DC you build in a new forest. For redundancy, you should plan to move at least the PDC role to a server that is separate from the other two domain roles. This ensures that failure in one will not result in failure of some critical function dependent upon these roles (e.g., the ability to create new users from NT 4). Additionally, it's probably a good idea, once you have some more DCs in your environment, to move the other roles to servers that are highly reliable and well controlled. You don't have to put each of the five roles on a separate server, but neither should you have them all on a single server. Microsoft also recommends having the PDC and Infrastructure roles on separate DCs.

Domain Migration Strategies and Downlevel Coexistence

There are many issues to consider as you plan for migration of your existing NT infrastructure to Win2K. Indeed, a whole book could be written on the topic. In this section, I'll discuss some of the options you have for migration and some of the caveats as you begin to migrate to Win2K.

Migration Options

Microsoft really only provides one option out of the box for you to move your existing NT 4 domains to Win2K. That option is in-place upgrade. That is, starting with the PDC in one of your master domains, begin to upgrade DCs, servers, and workstations one by one until you're finished, then move on to the next domain. As you migrate domains into Win2K, you can use tools like Movetree and SIDWalker to consolidate domains—moving objects from many converted domains into fewer domains at your own speed. As you can imagine, this won't work for everyone. As a result, you have a couple of different options, provided by third-party vendors and Microsoft, to migrate users and computers more slowly.

The first class of tools, from vendors like Entevo (www.entevo.com), FastLane Technologies (www.fastlanetech.com), and Mission Critical Software (www.missioncritical.com), lets you take groups of users or computers defined in your NT 4 domains and re-create them in Win2K domains. The re-created accounts and groups will have, of course, lost their associated Security IDs (SIDs). To get around that issue, these tools also ferret out file, printer, and other resources that were owned by the old user accounts and append an Access Control Entry (ACE) to the Access Control List (ACL) on each of those resources pointing to the new account. This approach not only provides a more controlled migration to Win2K, but also provides a back-out strategy, since the old accounts are usually left in place until you choose to remove them.

Another available method for migrating domains is the ability to clone a *security principal*—either a user or group. In this scenario, a user or group SID from an NT 4 account is actually placed in the SID History property of the associated new Win2K group or user account, thereby providing access to resources by that Win2K user or group account without having to re-ACL those resources up front. There will be tools from Microsoft (in the Resource Kit) as well as the third-party vendors mentioned earlier that will utilize this cloning capability.

Downlevel Coexistence

If you have a decent-sized NT 4 infrastructure today, it's likely you'll be in a mixed NT 4/Win2K environment for some time. This is generally well supported in Win2K, but there are a couple of things to keep in mind in this kind of environment. If you remember, a Win2K domain can exist in two different modes—Mixed and Native. In Mixed mode, NT 4 backup domain controllers can still be added to your environment alongside Win2K DCs. In Mixed mode, some features within Win2K are disabled, including the use of universal security groups and group nesting.

Once you switch a domain to Native mode, these advanced features are enabled, but you can no longer add NT 4 BDCs to the domain (of course, you can still have NT 4 workstations and member servers in a Native mode domain).

Another facet of living in a mixed environment is the challenge of management across both versions. For the most part, you can use Win2K MMC snap-ins to manage NT 4 services such as WINS, DNS, DHCP, IIS, and others. However, the AD Users and Computers snap-in does not provide User Manager or Server Manager functionality over NT 4 domains. In that case, you'll still need to use these downlevel tools on your NT 4 or Win2K administrative workstations to manage NT 4 domains. As of this writing, however, Microsoft has yet to provide Win2K-friendly versions of these tools.

In this chapter, we looked at some of the issues related to designing your Win2K infrastructure for a large enterprise, including the limitations of multiple forests and the schema. We examined how AD elements such as sites, OUs, and GPOs must be thought about differently as you scale them up—with a eye toward simplicity. We looked at some of the benefits and limitations of replication of objects like the SYSVOL share, Dfs, and GPOs and how to not get in trouble using these services. We looked at considerations for placing infrastructure services such as DNS, global catalog servers, and Operations Masters. Finally, we examined some of the options for migrating from NT 4 infrastructure to Win2K, focusing on some of the options other than in-place upgrade that you'll be able to choose from when you're ready to migrate.

CHAPTER 16

Integrating NetWare with Windows 2000 Server

L ess than a decade ago, one company—Novell—owned a majority of the network operating system market. NetWare, in its various versions, reportedly enjoyed market share rates that reached into the 70 percent range. Chances were good that if you had a network in your office, Novell was the platform it was running on.

As is true with much of life, nothing lasts forever. When Microsoft came along with Windows NT, they began to—quite frankly—eat Novell's lunch in the NOS market. However, even though Microsoft was making inroads into organizations with NT, often those organizations weren't in a position to simply toss their existing Novell equipment out the window. Due to this fact, cross-platform integration became a key issue with both operating systems. As a result of this, Microsoft has included a wide variety of options for integrating Windows 2000 Server and NetWare.

Integration versus Migration

When integrating NetWare and Windows 2000 networks, there will be a key decision involved very early in the design process: *migrate* or *integrate*? But no matter whether you decide to migrate to Windows 2000 and get rid of NetWare completely or integrate both networks together so that users can reach resources on both systems, Microsoft has included the tools you'll need to get the job done.

Integration

As is the case in many environments, legacy applications and systems have a tendency to just stick around. Although the year 2000 bug has forced many organizations to replace outdated systems with newer ones, many legacy systems and applications still exist in the networking world, and will be sticking around for a while longer. Novell NetWare servers often fall into this category of "legacy systems."

Even if you have NetWare servers that you need to connect to that aren't necessarily considered legacy systems, Microsoft has a complete set of tools to allow for a high level of integration between Microsoft and Novell networks. These tools include the following:

IPX/SPX (NWLink) protocol support   Although newer releases of NetWare support the TCP/IP protocol natively, earlier versions only supported one protocol stack—IPX (Internetwork Packet Exchange) and SPX (Sequenced Packet Exchange). To successfully communicate with older NetWare servers, you will need to use this protocol (it is not necessarily installed in Windows 2000 by default).

Gateway (and Client) Service for NetWare A wonderful little utility that allows a Windows 2000 server to attach to a NetWare server, access file and print resources on the server, and share them to its own clients as if they were hosted directly on the Windows 2000 box itself. The Gateway Service for Net-Ware (GSNW for short) is primarily useful for keeping only one client stack loaded on your workstations—the Microsoft networking client.

File and Print Services for NetWare networks An optional tool (it doesn't come with Windows 2000 Server) that you can use if you would prefer to have your Windows 2000 server share its resources with NetWare clients. File and Print Services for NetWare (FPNW for short) will let your Windows 2000 Server act as if it were a NetWare server. Workstations with nothing other than a Net-Ware client loaded on them will be able to access resources on a Windows 2000 server running FPNW.

Migration

For some organizations, retiring NetWare systems and completely migrating to Windows 2000 is the way to go. For these instances, Microsoft has included the Directory Services Migration Tool to make that job easier.

The Directory Services Migration Tool (DSMT for short) is a great utility that will let you connect to an NDS- or a bindery-based NetWare network and import all the users, files, and security settings from the target system. The DSMT will let you do these migrations across the wire, so that you don't have to worry about accidentally destroying data on your Novell systems. You can import all of the information from the target server(s); model, rearrange, and manipulate it as necessary; and then apply the information to your Windows 2000 server.

Running the DSMT is dependent on having the Gateway (and Client) Service for NetWare installed on your server, and optionally the NWLink protocol for IPX support (if IPX-only servers will be migrated). Since migration will depend on these items, let's get started with installing the basic components you'll need—IPX (NWLink) and GSNW.

Getting Started

Before starting a process to migrate from or integrate with an existing NetWare network, there are a few things you will need to have in place no matter what you are doing. First, you will need a compatible set of protocols so that your two networks can talk to each other. Secondly, you will need the Gateway Service for NetWare components installed on any servers that need to talk to Novell systems.

Adding Protocol Support

Protocol support should be relatively straightforward, since NetWare generally only speaks two languages—IP and IPX. NetWare's native tongue is IPX, so you will find it to be the primary protocol in most NetWare 3.*x* and early 4.*x* networks. Servers running IntraNetWare and later versions of NetWare could be running IPX, IP, or both protocols. In any case, load the appropriate protocols on your system so that your servers can speak with each other. Also, if you plan on running File and Print Services for NetWare, you will need to make sure that your Windows 2000 server has the same protocol loaded that your NetWare clients will be using.

If you will be installing NWLink on your Windows 2000 server in order to use IPX when communicating with NetWare systems, you may need to know the frame type used by your NetWare servers and an appropriate network address to use, if any. To add the NWLink IPX/SPX/NetBIOS protocol to your server, start by choosing Start/Settings/Control Panel and launching the Network and Dial-Up Connections icon. This will bring you to a listing of any and all network connections installed on your system—either local area or dial-up. Find the appropriate icon for the local area network connection that you will use to connect to your NetWare servers, and then edit the properties by right-clicking the icon and selecting Properties. The network properties for your LAN adapter should look similar to Figure 16.1.

FIGURE 16.1

Editing local area connection properties

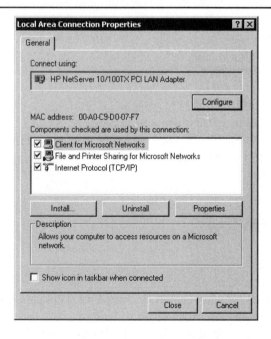

As you can see from the dialog box shown in Figure 16.1, this is a local area network connection that only has TCP/IP installed on it. To add support for NWLink IPX/SPX/NetBIOS compatible transport, click the Install button and in the dialog box that comes up, select Protocol. Clicking the Add button will take you to a listing of protocols that you can select from, shown in Figure 16.2.

FIGURE 16.2

Choosing a protocol to add

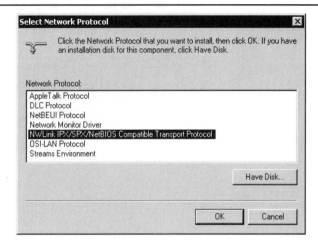

Select NWLink IPX/SPX/NetBIOS Compatible Transport Protocol from the list of supported protocols, and then click OK. Windows 2000 will add support for this protocol to the local area network adapter.

In many instances, the defaults Windows 2000 Server will apply to the NWLink protocol will be acceptable. However, if your situation requires fine-tuning this protocol for your network environment, edit the parameters for this protocol by highlighting it on the Local Area Connection properties page and then clicking the Properties button. This will take you to a dialog box similar to the one shown in Figure 16.3.

Through this dialog box, you can enter internal IPX network information and framing types to use. If you intend to have this Windows 2000 server offer services to NetWare clients (file, print, routing, etc.), enter an internal IPX network number in the field at the top of the dialog box. Make sure to use a network number that is *not* in use by any other NetWare servers on your network. Secondly, if you would like to manually configure the framing type for Windows 2000 Server to use for IPX packets, choose the Manual Frame Type Detection radio button and then press the Add button. NetWare servers running version 3.11 and earlier typically use an Ethernet 802.3 framing type, and all newer NetWare servers usually default to Ethernet 802.2 framing. Enter the appropriate framing information and IPX network numbers in the fields provided and then press OK.

If you will be using TCP/IP to communicate with your NetWare servers, you will need to know an appropriate IP address, subnet mask, and default gateway to use for communicating with your systems. Your TCP/IP configuration on your Windows 2000 server will need to reflect those settings in order to communicate properly.

FIGURE 16.3

Editing NWLink properties

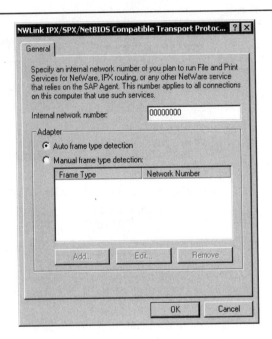

NOTE   TCP/IP should be installed on your system as an operating system default, but if it has been removed from your system for whatever reason, please see Chapter 17 for further details on installing TCP/IP.

Adding Client Support

The next step in accessing NetWare networks is to add the necessary client support to your system. The steps for this are quite similar to adding IPX protocol support. Start from the properties page for your local area network adapter; press the Install button and select Client from the dialog box that comes up. This will bring you to a list of additional client software similar to the one shown in Figure 16.4.

FIGURE 16.4

Adding client software

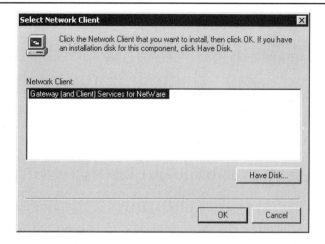

Select Gateway (and Client) Services for NetWare and then press OK to continue. Windows 2000 will require a reboot, and then the next time you log in you will be taken to a configuration dialog box like the one shown in Figure 16.5.

FIGURE 16.5

Configuring the NetWare client

Depending on the NetWare systems you are trying to connect to, the way you configure the Select NetWare Logon dialog box will change accordingly. This dialog box will determine which server you will log into by default, or where in an NDS tree you will log in. If you plan on connecting to NetWare resources on NDS-aware servers, select the radio button for setting a Default Tree and Context and enter the appropriate tree and context information for the user account you intend to use for this system. If you will be connecting to bindery-based NetWare servers (or NDS-aware servers running bindery emulation), select the radio button for setting a Preferred Server and enter the name of the server in the data-entry field.

Lastly, if you want your Windows 2000 server to execute any NetWare login scripts during the logon process, check the Run Login Script check box. Press OK when you are finished and the Gateway (and Client) Service for NetWare should now be installed and selected for your local area network adapter.

Verifying Client Connectivity

Once you have added the necessary client support for accessing NetWare resources, you should be able to test your configuration by opening up a command prompt and typing in the command **net view /network:nw**. If your connectivity is configured correctly, you will see a listing of NetWare servers on your network.

Try to connect to one of your NetWare servers via the Windows 2000 Explorer interface. Double-click My Network Places and then select the Entire Network option; you should have icons available to explore either the Microsoft Windows networks or NetWare networks.

Double-clicking NetWare or Compatible Networks will bring you to a window like the one shown in Figure 16.6, where you should be able to see all of your NDS trees and servers.

FIGURE 16.6

Browsing NetWare directories and servers

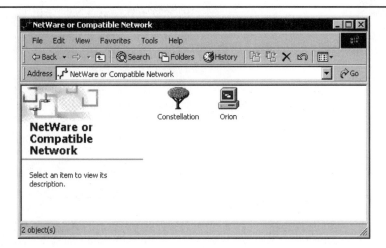

As you can see in Figure 16.6, my test network has an NDS tree called Constellation and a server called Orion. Clicking on NDS tree resources or server resources should take you further through your NetWare network. If you are having difficulty connecting to resources at this point, stop here and take the time to troubleshoot the problem before continuing, since most everything else relies on these services. Make sure that you check for proper usernames, context, passwords, etc.

Integrating NetWare and Windows 2000 Server

Now that you (presumably) have the appropriate protocol and client loaded to talk to NetWare servers, you are ready to begin integrating these two platforms together. Before beginning, however, it is important to ask yourself who will be accessing resources on which system.

Will workstations configured for Microsoft networking need to access resources on NetWare servers? If so, you have two main options for integrating these two platforms. The first option is to load a separate client stack for each platform on all of your workstations (not a desirable option in most circumstances), so that each workstation can talk directly with each server. This adds memory overhead to your client workstations, not to mention the amount of time it takes to visit every desktop to configure an additional client stack. It also potentially requires that users remember two separate logins—one for the Microsoft network, and one for the Novell network.

The second—and preferable—option for letting Microsoft networking workstations access NetWare resources is to let your Windows 2000 server act as a sort of "NetWare proxy" by configuring the gateway portion of GSNW. Your Windows 2000 server can then accept requests for NetWare-based data on behalf of the workstations, retrieve the data from the target servers, and then pass it directly back to the user. As far as the end user is concerned, they are simply accessing another shared resource on a Windows 2000 server—NetWare resources will look identical to Windows 2000 resources.

If you have NetWare clients that will need to access resources on a Windows 2000 server, your options are similar. The first option is again to load a separate client stack for each platform on all of your workstations so that each workstation can talk directly with each server. Just like before, this requires a significant amount of memory overhead on your client workstations, and usually a visit to every desktop to configure the client—not a desirable option in most circumstances.

Instead, you can have properly configured NetWare clients access resources directly on Windows 2000 servers by configuring File and Print Services for NetWare on your server. To NetWare clients on your network, your Windows 2000 server will appear to be just another NetWare server available on the network. Users will be able to connect to your server through their NetWare client stacks and access resources as necessary.

Configuring Gateway Services for NetWare

Assuming you installed the Gateway (and Client) Service for NetWare back in the "Getting Started" section, you already have part of the solution installed to provide gateway services to NetWare resources. By default, when you installed the Gateway (and Client) Service for NetWare, it walked you through the configuration for the *client* portion of the software—selecting a preferred server or tree/default context to use. The *gateway* portion of this feature is available through the Control Panel.

But before we begin configuring gateway services, there are a few things you'll need to have in place to make GSNW work as a gateway. They are as follows:

- An account defined on your NetWare server or in your NDS tree that can log into the server(s) your Windows 2000 server will need to connect to. Appropriate permissions should be applied to this account for controlling what resources can be accessed.

- A group defined on your NetWare server or in your NDS tree called NTGATEWAY. The account mentioned in the previous bullet point must be made a member of this group.

- Resource(s) (directories and/or print queues) on your NetWare server that have had permissions granted for the user account specified above.

Once you have these items completed, begin enabling gateway services by going to the GSNW controls page located in Start/Settings/Control Panel/GSNW. This should take you to a screen similar to the one you used when you were first installing and configuring the Gateway (and Client) Service for NetWare. Click the Gateway button on this screen to enter the Configure Gateway dialog box, shown in Figure 16.7. From this dialog box, you will end up defining two things for the Gateway Service for NetWare: the account that GSNW should use when accessing the Novell server for resources, and the file resources that it should share with the rest of the Microsoft network.

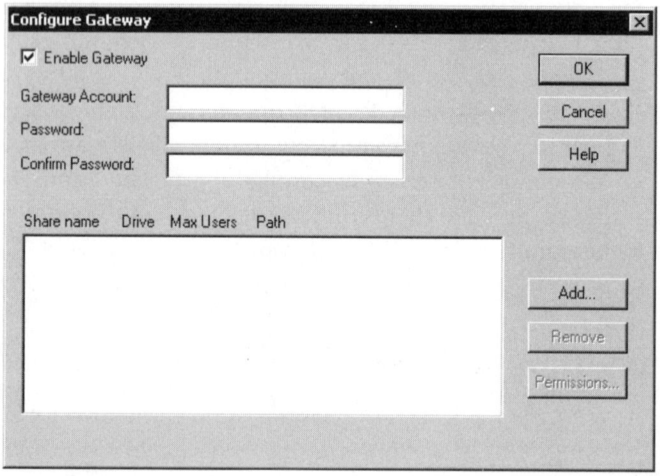

FIGURE 16.7

Configuring gateway shares in GSNW

NOTE All access to NetWare resources through GSNW will take place under the same username and context as far as NetWare is concerned. For example, you could have 30 users all accessing resources on a NetWare server, but as far as NetWare is concerned, you will only have one connection—the Windows 2000 server. This is both good and bad. The advantage is that you can squeeze your way around some Novell license restrictions if necessary. The bad news is that you can't control security permissions on an individual level; everyone accessing resources through GSNW will do so with the exact same security context, that of the gateway account.

In the Configure Gateway dialog box, the first thing to do is check the Enable Gateway box to allow gateway services on your system. After that, you must define a NetWare (bindery or NDS) account that GSNW will use when logging into the NetWare server to access resources. This account must have adequate permissions assigned to the volumes and directories that you want to grant access to, and it must also be made a member of a NetWare group called NTGATEWAY. Personally, I always like to use an account name that makes sense to me when I see it in a Novell monitor list. I'd also recommend setting the password to never expire for this specific user; otherwise, your gateway might stop functioning on a regular basis.

Defining File Shares

Once you have defined an appropriate gateway account for your system, you can begin to share file resources from your NetWare server through the Configure Gateway dialog box by pressing the Add button to add shares to your system. You will see a small dialog box, like the one in Figure 16.8, in which you will enter all of the necessary details for this connection.

FIGURE 16.8

*Defining a new
GSNW share*

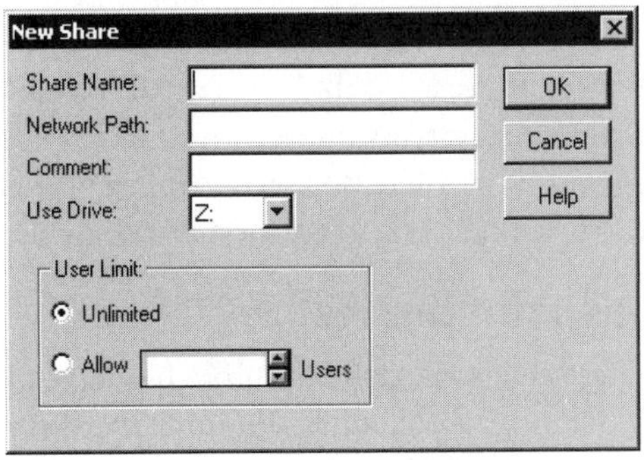

New Share	
Share Name:	OK
Network Path:	Cancel
Comment:	Help
Use Drive: Z:	
User Limit	
● Unlimited	
○ Allow ___ Users	

If you're familiar with sharing resources on a Windows 2000 server, this dialog box should look familiar. Enter the following information in the appropriate fields:

Share Name   This is the name that Microsoft networking users will see when they list the shares available on a particular server.

Network Path   This is the location of the NetWare resources that you'd like Windows 2000 Server to share. You can enter the name as a standard UNC path in the format of \\servername\volume; for example, a UNC path of \\orion\sys would share the SYS: volume of the NetWare server ORION.

Comment   If you would like to include any plain-English comments for this share (such as "These resources located on NetWare"), enter them here. Any subroutines in Windows that display share comments will display the text entered here.

Use Drive   Even though you are providing a gateway service for a NetWare resource, your system will want to connect to it via a network drive letter. In a sense, you are mapping a drive, and then sharing a mapped drive (something that normally isn't allowed). Enter the drive letter that Windows 2000 Server should use for this connection.

User Limit   If you would like to restrict the number of users connected to any given NetWare resource, enter a user restriction here or leave it set to Unlimited.

 NOTE   In addition to defining the account for the gateway to use, the account you are *logged in with* when configuring GSNW must also have rights to the Novell server(s) you are creating gateway connections for. If this is not the case, you will see an error message indicating so when you try to create a share.

Once you have entered the necessary information, pressing OK will create a drive mapping on your system and a share name for users to connect to. To test this, try accessing your Windows 2000 server from a properly configured workstation, and check if you can see your NetWare share in the list of resources for the server.

Defining Print Shares

Print shares can also be defined through GSNW, although the interface is slightly different. To share a NetWare-based printer with Microsoft networking clients, you will actually need to begin by going through the normal "add a printer" routine for Windows 2000.

Launch the Add Printer Wizard by selecting Start/Settings/Printers and then clicking the Add Printer icon. Proceed through the normal routines to add a network printer to your Windows 2000 server (for details on setting up a network printer, please see Chapter 11). At the second step of the wizard, select the radio button option to type in a printer name or browse for a printer, as shown in Figure 16.9.

FIGURE 16.9

Entering a URL for a network printer

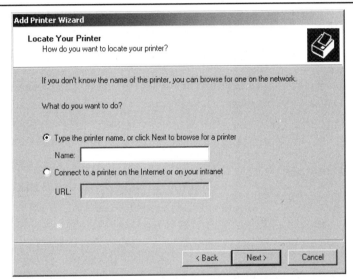

At this point, you can directly enter the URL for your NetWare print queue, or leave the field blank to browse to the print queue you want to create a gateway to. Either way, enter the appropriate NetWare print queue name in this field and then press Next to proceed to the final step of the wizard, where you can enter an appropriate print driver for Microsoft networking clients to use when accessing this resource.

 NOTE When adding a printer to your Windows 2000 server as a gateway item, the account you are logged into Windows 2000 with when you make the connection *as well as* the gateway services account must *both* have appropriate access rights to the print queue.

When you are finished, you should have a printer configured on your Windows 2000 server that is actually a print queue on a NetWare server. The final step necessary to make this printer available to Microsoft networking clients is to share the printer and assign it appropriate permissions. Sharing printers is covered in detail in Chapter 11, so if you are unfamiliar with this process, please check there for detailed information.

Setting Security on Print and File Shares

Once you have configured the necessary items for providing gateway services for file and print shares, you may find that you want to control who can access these resources based on their Windows account. This is controlled through setting share permissions for the resources you've created a gateway for, and works in much the same way as setting share permissions for any other resource on your system.

Share permissions are typically an "all-or-nothing" type of setting for your system. For example, with share permissions, you will either grant access to all of a printer or a set of directories, or none at all. For printers, this is a rather straightforward process and makes sense. However, for file shares you might want to control who can access certain subdirectories on the Novell volume you are sharing. Unfortunately, this can't be done when setting share permissions for a gateway resource. If a user is granted the appropriate share permissions to use the gateway resource, he or she can access all of the items available on that resource (as configured by the permissions assigned in NetWare to the gateway account used). Therefore, in setting share permissions on file resources, it really is an all-or-nothing scenario—either the user can access all of the shared resources on the NetWare server, or they can't access any.

Now, as far as read or write permissions are concerned, you can set those options via share permissions for a NetWare resource. Therefore, even though all users accessing the NetWare resources will all see the same directories and files, you can control who has read-only access and who has read-write access. Again, you can't assign these rights on a specific directory or file level, only to the entire resource you've shared. To apply share permissions to a NetWare resource, go back to the GSNW configuration page (Start/Settings/Control Panel/GSNW). Press the Gateway button, and you will see the dialog box you have previously used to define a shared NetWare resource. Highlight the share you want to modify the permissions for and then press the Permissions button to go to the Access through Share Permissions dialog box, shown in Figure 16.10.

FIGURE 16.10

*Modifying share
permissions*

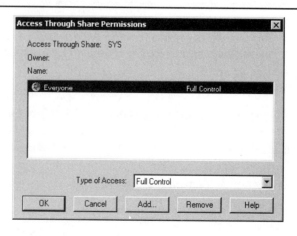

This permissions dialog box functions exactly the same as a share permissions dialog box would if you were sharing local resources from the Windows 2000 server. You can define read-only access or read-write access as necessary by modifying the permissions assigned to each user and group. For more detailed information on modifying share permissions, please see Chapter 9.

File and Print Services for NetWare

So far, in terms of integration, we've talked primarily about how to let Microsoft networking clients access resources on NetWare servers. But what if you run into a situation where the opposite is true? What if you have some NetWare client workstations that—for one reason or another—have to stay configured as NetWare clients, but they need to access file and print resources on a Windows 2000 server?

The answer to this question is through a software package known as File and Print Services for NetWare (FPNW), a Windows 2000 Server add-on package available from Microsoft that will allow your server to *appear* as a Novell server to Novell networking clients.

By mimicking the broadcasts, protocols, and conventions that a NetWare server typically uses, your Windows 2000 server can act and behave just like a NetWare server (with the exception that you can't run NLMs on a Windows 2000 server) as far as your desktop clients are concerned. NetWare clients can attach to your server, perform a standard NetWare login, and then access resources that appear to be on a standard NetWare SYS: volume. Everything appears as normal as far as the users are concerned.

Underneath it all, Windows 2000 Server is actually being quite creative by adopting several NetWare characteristics, such as listening for GetNearestServer broadcast packets, providing a SYS: volume (which is typically the C:\SYSVOL directory on the Windows 2000 server) to access resources, etc., etc. If you have a need to get NetWare clients on your Windows 2000 server, but can't (or don't want to) upgrade them to a Microsoft client stack, FPNW is definitely a product worth looking into.

Migrating from NetWare and NDS to Windows 2000 and Active Directory

In the highly competitive world of computer software, making it easy for users to convert from a competitor's software package to your own is a key strategy in gaining market share. As software continues to improve, users tend to look for the latest and greatest features and capabilities, and getting those features sometimes means converting to a completely different product.

The network operating system market is no different, and I'm sure that Microsoft would like nothing better than to see Novell close up shop tomorrow (although they'd never publicly admit it). In the earlier versions of NT, Microsoft included a tool called NWConvert along with the NT operating system in an effort to make that dream a reality. NWConvert was a good tool for converting bindery-based NetWare servers to NT servers. NWConvert would copy the files, users, groups, and account restrictions over from a NetWare server, across the wire, to a NT server.

NWConvert was a useful tool, but it was limited by the fact that it could only work on bindery-based NetWare servers. NDS is being implemented more and more, which conversely has made NWConvert less and less useful. Never one to stay too far behind the times, Microsoft has rebuilt this utility (actually, Computer Associates wrote it) for Windows 2000 Server. Now, the utility is referred to as the Directory Services Migration Tool (DSMT) and is a full-blown, two-stage, project-based migration tool capable of migrating entire NDS trees or sections of trees to Active Directory–enabled Windows 2000 networks.

Although server migration is certainly no small subject, hopefully the information that follows will give you a good overview of the DSMT, what it can do, and how to use it.

 NOTE DMST was originally part of the Windows 2000 build. As this book was going to press, we learned that Microsoft officially decided to remove DMST from Windows 2000, and offer it instead as part of their Microsoft Directory Synchronization Services (MSDSS). Since the capability still exists in the MSDSS add-on package (albeit under a different name), we left the content in the book so you can see how this capability looks and decide if it would be useful for you when you're migrating to Windows 2000.

DSMT Overview and Conventions

The DSMT has a number of unique characteristics that make it a great tool to use when migrating data and users off of NDS- or bindery-based networks. Some of the reasons why it's such a good tool include:

- It's a non-destructive, across-the-wire tool. Information is read across the network from NetWare servers and the NDS tree and stored on the Windows 2000 server. Nothing needs to be loaded on the NetWare server for this tool to work, and nothing is ever written back to the NetWare environment.

- It's a two-stage tool. Since large migrations can often be a process that must be managed carefully, you can control the pace of your migration by reading the necessary information in from the NetWare server or NDS tree. Once you have read the data, it is stored on your Windows 2000 server, where you can analyze it, manipulate it if necessary, and then write the data out to the Active Directory and your Windows 2000 server.

- It's a project-based tool. It isn't necessary to handle an entire NDS tree or an entire Novell server at once during a migration. You can work on migrating portions of each of these resources and work at your own pace. You can define different "projects" for different portions of your migration as necessary.

Throughout the discussion of the DSMT, there are several naming conventions that will be commonly used. They are:

Project A DSMT container that holds one or many "views."

View A set of object data—users, groups, organizational units, etc. Some of the view data may be imported from NetWare, some of it may have been created by hand, and some of it might have been imported from other locations. The view is the central repository for all information (with the exception of files) that you would eventually like to export to the Active Directory.

Discover The process of importing object data (users, groups, etc.) from either a NetWare server or another location.

Configure The process of exporting object data (users, groups, etc.) from a view to the Active Directory.

Installing and Configuring the DSMT

Depending on how you chose to configure Windows 2000 Server during installation, the DSMT may or may not be installed on your system. Let's work under the assumption that the DSMT is not installed on your computer and walk through the steps to install and configure it.

To add the DSMT to a server that doesn't have it, start by choosing Start/Settings/Control Panel and double-clicking the Add/Remove Programs icon. This will launch the Add/Remove Programs dialog box, which should have Add/Remove Windows Components listed as one of the options on the left-hand side. Click the Add/Remove Windows Components option and the Windows Components Wizard will launch, allowing you to add components to or remove components from your Windows 2000 server. You'll find the DSMT available as one of the options under the Networking Services component, as shown in Figure 16.11. Either install all of the networking services by checking that box, or install the DSMT individually by pressing the Details button and selecting Directory Service Migration Tool.

FIGURE 16.11

Installing the DSMT

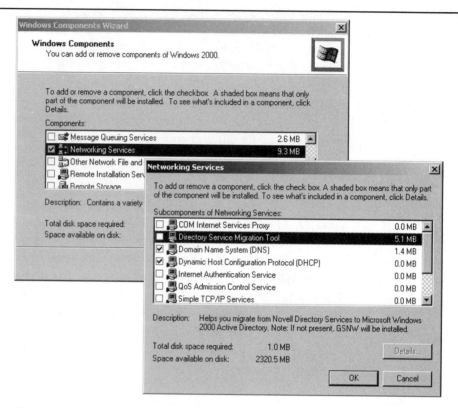

After you have successfully installed the DSMT onto your system, the program should be added to your Administrative Tools group by default. Launch the DSMT from the Start menu to begin working on your migration.

DSMT General Options

After successfully installing the DSMT, one of the first things you will probably want to do is configure the tool for your specific environment. From the scope pane of the DSMT MMC, right-click the Directory Service Migration Tool item and then select the Options command. This should take you to the first page of options you can set for the DSMT, shown in Figure 16.12.

There are very few options on the General tab. The first is to choose a location for the DSMT to store project data (users, files, etc.) that it is working on migrating. The second option is the check box at the very bottom of the dialog box, which allows you to select whether or not the DSMT should display objects from the NDS environment that don't have an exact match in the AD. Leaving this box checked will instruct the DSMT to only display NDS objects that have a corresponding counterpart in AD—anything that doesn't translate directly from NDS to AD will be ignored.

FIGURE 16.12

Setting General options for the DSMT

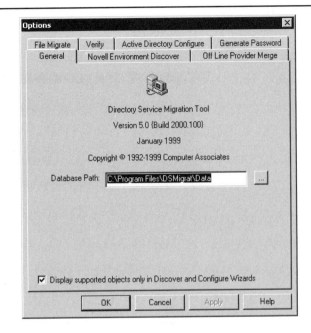

Novell Environment Discover Options

When discovering items from Novell servers, there are a few options you might want to set. These parameters are defined in the Novell Environment Discover options tab, shown in Figure 16.13.

If you intend to import data from bindery-based systems, there will be no O= or organization attribute (one of the highest attributes in an NDS tree) defining the overall organization. Binderies are flat by nature, simply containing user accounts and other details, so you can assign a default Organization attribute to apply when discovering data from a bindery-based Novell server by entering the name to use in the Default Bindery Organization Name field.

You can also restrict the number of objects to import during a discover operation by entering an appropriate value in the Maximum Number of Objects in a View field. This is particularly useful if you have a very large NDS structure with thousands of objects, but you don't want to import them all just yet—maybe you are testing a migration plan and want to see how it works. Entering a value here will limit the number of objects imported in a discover operation.

Verify Options

While discovering data from an NDS environment, the DSMT can take steps to verify the integrity of the data it is receiving. These verifications are in the form of field-length checks and counters that can be applied to the NDS structure. The Verify options tab is shown in Figure 16.14.

FIGURE 16.13

Setting Novell Environment Discover options

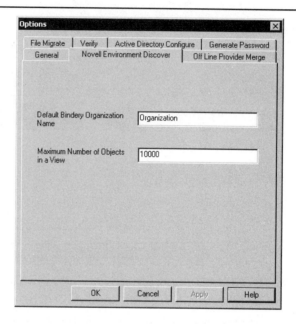

FIGURE 16.14

Setting Verify options

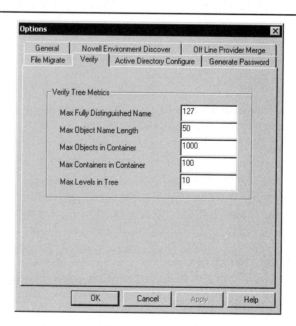

As you can see, most of these options are for setting field lengths and controlling counters during the discovery process. Here's a brief description of each of these fields:

Max Fully Distinguished Name   Controls the maximum length for the long name of an NDS object. An NDS long name includes the names of all organizational units and the organization, in addition to the object name.

Max Object Name Length   Specifies how long an individual object name (such as a username or an OU) can be.

Max Objects in Container   Implements controls on how many individual objects (such as users) can be in any one container (such as an O or OU).

Max Containers in Container   Implements controls on how many container objects (such as OUs) can be in any one container (such as an O or OU).

Max Levels in Tree   This setting controls how many levels deep into an NDS tree the discover process will go.

For most circumstances, the default values for these options should be acceptable.

Active Directory Configure Options

When it comes time to configure objects to Active Directory (to write the objects you've imported out to AD), the DSMT can handle multi-valued options in a number of ways, based on the options you choose in Figure 16.15.

Setting Active Directory Configure options

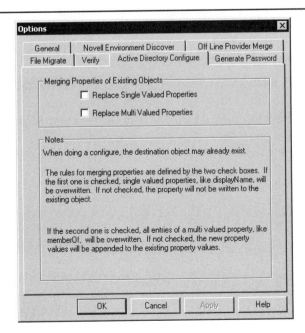

These parameters only apply in circumstances where an NDS object may already exist in your target Active Directory. For example, if you had an identical organizational unit (OU in NDS parlance) defined in a Novell environment as well as in your Active Directory environment, that would be an object that exists in both your discovered environment (NDS) and the environment you want to configure (AD). Let's look at an example.

Let's say—for whatever reason—you have a user account named Cheryl in your NDS *and* your AD structure. Now, the account for Cheryl has a number of "properties" associated with it. Properties are things like the user's first name, last name, what groups he/she is a member of, etc. Now, if the DSMT runs into a situation where the same object that came from the NDS environment needs to be written to the AD environment, it can do one of two things:

Replace Single-Valued Properties   If this option is checked, any single-valued properties (that is, username, password, or anything else with only one value associated with it) within AD will be overwritten with the same single-valued properties from the NDS environment. For example, let's suppose that Cheryl's first name was misspelled (as Cheryll) in NDS, but was correct in AD (as Cheryl); the misspelled version of her name will overwrite the existing, correct version. Leaving this option blank will tell DSMT not to overwrite single-valued properties when configuring objects to Active Directory.

Replace Multi-Valued Properties   This option functions the same as the option for replacing single-valued properties, except it's for object properties that are multi-valued. Examples of multi-valued object properties include the listing of groups that a user account is a member of.

Generate Password Options

Since the DSMT can't "read" user passwords from a NetWare server or an NDS structure, you will need to choose an option for how you want to handle passwords for user objects that are migrated. The Generate Password property page, shown in Figure 16.16, will let you control what DSMT ends up doing.

As you can see from this property page, there are four main things that the DSMT can do when it comes to the passwords for NDS users. The first option is to "Assign NO password to each user," in effect leaving the password for the newly configured AD user blank. The next option—"Assign a unique randomly generated password to each user"—will create a unique 12-character password for each user. The third option is to "Set each password to the user's logon name," a rather straightforward option. And finally, you can select the "Assign each user the same custom password" option.

Once you have selected the appropriate option for creating passwords for AD users, you can control whether or not the AD users can and should change those passwords through the three checkboxes at the bottom of the property page. These options behave exactly the same as their counterparts in defining a normal Active Directory user, so we won't discuss them in detail here.

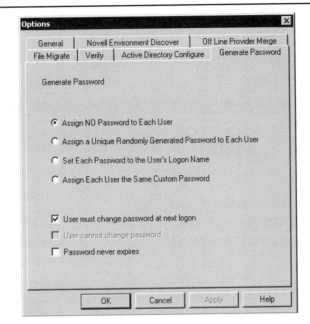

FIGURE 16.16

Setting Generate Password options

Importing Bindery/NDS Data

Once you have configured the DSMT the way you want it, the next step for migrating data from a NetWare/NDS environment is to define a project for importing some (or all) of your NetWare/NDS data into the DSMT. The process of importing data is referred to as *discovering*, and once you have discovered data from your NetWare/NDS environment, that data is stored in the DSMT in the database location defined in the General options. Once you have a working copy of the data, you can view it, manipulate it, and generally tweak it any way you'd like before you finally end up exporting it to Active Directory.

To begin, you will need to define a new project. Start the creation of a new project by highlighting the Directory Services Migration Tool in the scope pane of the DSMT MMC and then selecting New/Project from the Action pull-down menu. The DSMT will prompt you for a project name to use and a brief description about the project. Enter an appropriate name and then press OK to continue.

Once you have a project defined, the next step is to create a "view"—basically, a set of imported data—of your NetWare resources. Start the process to create a view by highlighting your project in the scope pane of the DSMT MMC and then selecting New/View from NetWare from the Action pull-down menu. This will start the Discover Wizard that will walk you through the discovery process.

The first step of the Discover Wizard will simply ask you for a name to use for this view—personally, I like to use meaningful names for the type of data within the view. For example, if I am migrating an entire NDS organizational unit, I will name the view after the OU. Choose a meaningful name, and then press Next to move on to the next step of the wizard, shown in Figure 16.17.

FIGURE 16.17

Specifying a context to discover

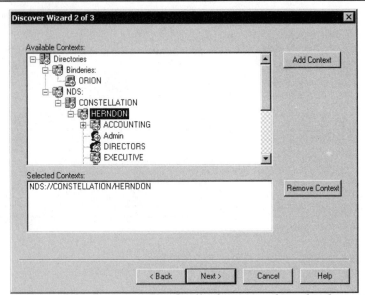

The second step of the Discover Wizard will ask you to select a bindery server or NDS context (or group of contexts) to import into the DSMT. As you can see from Figure 16.17, I have chosen to import all the data for the entire HERNDON organization within the NDS tree called CONSTELLATION. If I wanted to do a part of the tree at a time, I could have just as easily selected individual organizational units instead, such as ACCOUNTING, DIRECTORS, EXECUTIVE, etc.

In any case, navigate through your NDS structure, or your list of bindery servers, to select the context(s) or binderies that you want to discover. Press the Add Context button for each item that you want to discover, and you will then see that item listed in the Selected Contexts area of the wizard.

Click Next to proceed to the final step of the wizard (which is simply a confirmation page). When you click the Finish button on the last step of the wizard, the DSMT will start working its magic and importing all of your NDS or bindery data into this view. Once that has successfully been completed, you should see your organization, organizational units, and objects (users, groups, etc.) listed below your newly defined view in the scope pane of the DSMT MMC. As you can see from the example shown in Figure 16.18, all of the containers and objects have been successfully imported from my NDS environment to the DSMT.

FIGURE 16.18

View of the DSMT MMC after importing NDS objects

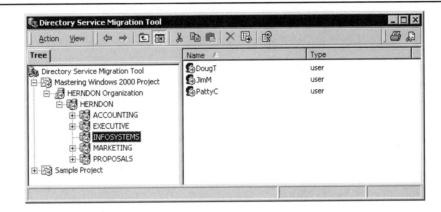

Manipulating NDS Data in the DSMT

Once you have successfully imported your bindery or NDS data from your NetWare environment, there are a number of things that you can do to manipulate or "tweak" the data as necessary before writing the data to your Active Directory environment.

Modifying Objects Individually

One of the first things that you can do is actually edit the properties of any of the objects the DSMT imported by double-clicking them. For example, double-clicking the user named Admin brings up the object properties in a dialog box like the one shown in Figure 16.19.

Now, we won't be going through the options listed here, because these are all fields and parameters pulled from the NDS or bindery user account imported by the DSMT. As you can see from the figure, there are multiple screens of properties for this object, all of which can be manipulated by hand while the data is still in the DSMT. The same is true for editing groups, organizational units, or any other object types the DSMT has picked up.

Also, if you would like to change the organization of individual objects—for example, move certain users and groups from one organizational unit to another—you can do this manually as well by simply dragging and dropping objects wherever you want them to be. This is a great way to correct any errors that existed in your NDS structure before writing it to the Active Directory.

FIGURE 16.19

Modifying object
(user) properties in
the DSMT

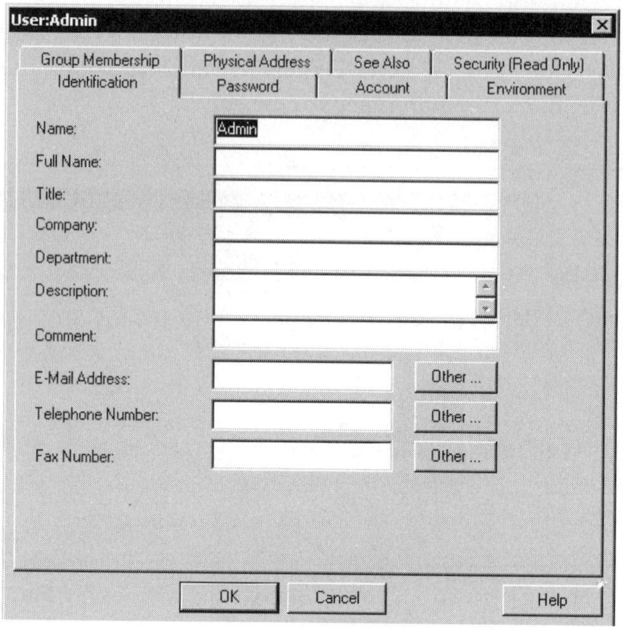

Changing Passwords (for User Objects)

Perhaps you forgot to configure the password options for the DSMT before running the discovery process. Or maybe you've changed your mind and want to change every user object password to blank instead of the random password option you chose earlier. If so, in the DSMT MMC, highlight either the view you want to work with or any level below the view (organization, organizational unit, etc.) and then select the All Tasks/Generate User Password option from the Action pull-down menu.

This should bring up a dialog box exactly like the one shown back in Figure 16.16, in which you can choose the password options you want to apply. Once you select an option and press Finish, the new passwords will be applied immediately. If you chose to generate user passwords on an organizational unit level, only the users listed within that specific OU will have their passwords changed. Again, remember: this information is being changed in the DSMT database only, not in your live NDS structure.

Finding and Replacing Text in Object Names

Let's say that you want to globally find and replace specific text strings in object names that you've imported from NDS. For example, maybe user accounts on your system were always appended with a 01, but now you want to remove that convention. You could, of course, go through each user account by hand and change each name, but who wants to go through all that? Technology is here to make our jobs easier. So instead, in the DSMT MMC, highlight either the view you want to work with or any level below the view (organization, organizational unit, etc.) and then select the All Tasks/Find and Replace Object Names option from the Action pull-down menu. This will bring you to the dialog box shown in Figure 16.20.

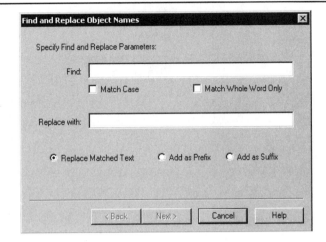

Through this dialog box, you can command the DSMT to perform a search-and-replace operation on the objects in your view (or organization, or organizational unit, depending on where you started this utility from). Enter the string that you want the DSMT to find in the Find field, the text you want it replaced with in the Replace With field, and then press Next to begin the replacement operation.

Now, just like a good word processor would do, the DSMT won't simply go through and change everything it finds that matches without checking with you first. After you define your find-and-replace strings and press Next, the DSMT will go through all the targeted objects and find the matches and ask you to select the ones you want to perform the replace operation on. Select the appropriate objects and then press Finish; your changes will be written to the DSMT copy of the data.

Writing Objects to Active Directory

Once you are certain that you have your data in the DSMT just the way you want it, one of the final steps necessary is to write the data to the Active Directory. To begin this process, in the scope pane of the DSMT MMC, highlight your organization or organizational units that you want to write to AD. From the Action pull-down menu, select the All Tasks/Configure objects to Active Directory option, which will bring you to the wizard shown in Figure 16.21.

FIGURE 16.21

*Selecting a target
AD location*

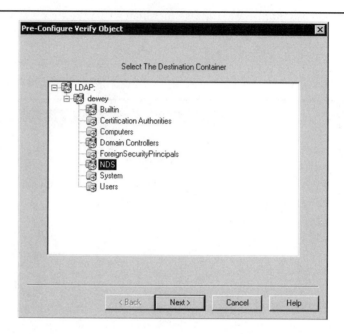

In the first screen of the wizard, you can select a target location within Active Directory to export your data to. You can export the data to any site or to any organizational unit within the site. Just to make sure that you don't overwrite any existing Active Directory objects that might have the exact same name, I would recommend creating a separate organizational unit object within your Active Directory to copy your objects into. In the example shown in Figure 16.21, I've called this organizational unit NDS, but you could call it Bindery or the specific NetWare server name if you prefer. This way, you can be sure that you are copying your objects from the DSMT to a location where they won't overwrite anything else. Once you have made the transition to AD and are certain that everything is working fine, then you can move your objects around within the Active Directory tree to their correct locations.

NOTE Creating a separate OU to copy your NDS records to will require you to copy each organizational unit that you've imported from NDS to AD, instead of copying the entire organization. Since it is logically impossible for an "organization" to exist below an "organizational unit"—even if it came from NDS—the DSMT will not let you do it.

In any case, select the appropriate location to copy your objects into, then press Next. The wizard will begin copying your DSMT information into the Active Directory, checking for conflicts with any existing data. When the trial copy is completed, you will see a dialog box similar to the one shown in Figure 16.22.

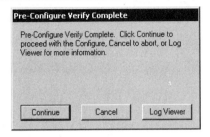

This dialog box is the last chance you'll have to change your mind before the DMST writes its data to the Active Directory. I would recommend pressing the Log Viewer button to check to see if serious error messages have been written to the log. For example, if you try to export a username from the DSMT with the same name as a user that already exists in the Active Directory, there will be a log message indicating this error. Investigate any errors that could cause problems for your Active Directory and resolve them before writing the final data to the directory. Once you are sure that the data you will write to the Active Directory is clean, click the Continue button and the NDS and/or bindery objects will be written out to your Active Directory.

Once this task has completed, you should be able to open up the Active Directory Users and Computers MMC (from Start/Programs/Administrative Tools) and see your bindery/NDS users listed there.

Migrating File Resources

Now, migrating user accounts is a good thing, but what about the files? After all, user accounts don't do much good if there aren't any files around for the user to access, right? Well, fortunately there are two file migration options available to you through the DSMT: copying just the files from one server to another, or copying the files and their associated NetWare permissions.

Depending on which option you choose, the location where you start this operation is slightly different. The functionality is primarily the same, so we'll just discuss copying files and their associated permissions; copying just the files would simply be a subset of that operation.

To copy the files and permissions from a NetWare server to your Windows 2000 server, select your view (note, not the project or the organization, but your "view") from the scope pane of the DSMT MMC. From the Action pull-down menu, choose All Tasks/File System Migrate, which will begin the File Migrate Wizard.

The first two steps of the wizard will ask you separately if you want to migrate the security and then the files (since each can be migrated independently). Presumably, you will want to migrate both, so select Yes for each option and then click Next. This should bring you to the step of the File Migrate Wizard where you can select a source and destination for file transfer. This step of the wizard is shown in Figure 16.23.

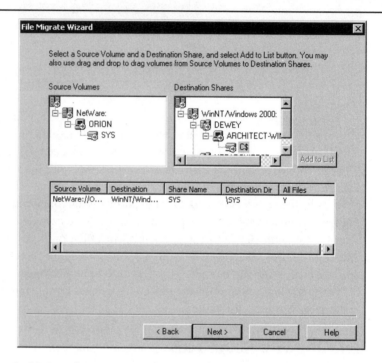

Through this interface, you can choose which NetWare volume you want to migrate files from (you must do the entire volume, as you can't select specific directories), and which Windows 2000 Server destination share you will store the files on. You do not have to store the files on the same server that you are running the DSMT on, so choose a hard drive on a server that has enough storage space available and highlight the share for that drive letter. Make sure both source and destination have been selected and then press the Add to List button to set these copy locations. Click Next to continue to the next step of the wizard.

By default, the DSMT will copy the NetWare volume to a directory on the server you've selected and give that directory the same name as the NetWare volume. The DSMT will automatically start sharing the newly created directory under the same name as well. If you wish to change the share name or target directory, the next step of the wizard will allow you to adjust the options of the file copy source and destination you've entered. If you feel like changing the target directory or share name, highlight the copy pair you wish to edit and press the Edit button. This should take you to a dialog box where you can modify the directory and share name options. Press Next to continue to the next step of the File Migrate Wizard, shown in Figure 16.24.

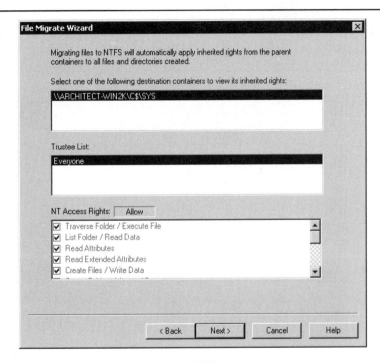

Assuming you are migrating files to an NTFS partition on your target server, you can control what rights are inherited by files and directories copied to your system. Since NTFS will want to automatically apply inherited rights from the parent directory (presumably the root) to all the subdirectories and files that it will create in this copy, you can view those rights through this window. If you want to change the rights that will be inherited by the files and directories that you copy over, you will need to modify the permissions assigned to your target location (again, presumably the root)—you can't change them through this interface.

After you have verified that the rights that will be inherited look okay, press Next to finish the wizard. You will proceed through one last verification dialog box, and after that the file copy operation will begin. When the copy operation is complete, you can check the log file that has been created to verify that your data has been copied without any errors.

CHAPTER 17

Understanding and Using TCP/IP in Windows 2000 Server

When NT first appeared, TCP/IP was the mildly scary, obscure, complex protocol used by just a few—those "oddballs" in research, education, and government who were attached to that large but still-private club called "the Internet." Most of us chose either NetBEUI in small networks for its simplicity or IPX for its partial interoperability with Novell NetWare.

Since the early '90s, however, IPX has been dethroned as the corporate protocol of choice and TCP/IP has replaced it. Furthermore, most of the basic pieces of Windows 2000 that separate it from earlier implementations of NT—a directory structure integrated with the Domain Name System, a workstation installation tool (Remote Installation Services), and other components first introduced in Windows 2000—simply must have TCP/IP to run. In a very large sense, TCP/IP is *the* mandatory protocol for Windows 2000.

TCP/IP is a big subject, so the book takes three chapters to cover it. In this first chapter, I'll explain what TCP/IP is and how its networks—both the worldwide Internet and your firm's intranet—work. In this first chapter, you'll see how to build a basic intranet and you'll understand some of the vexing-but-necessary parts of putting one together—in particular, you'll learn about IP addresses, subnet masks, and IP routing. I'd like to be able to tell you, "You needn't worry about any of that—just run the Intranet Creation Wizard," or some other mythical tool, but sadly such tools are just that—mythical. But things like subnet masks sound scarier than they actually are, which is why I'm going to take you through the ugly details.

In the next chapter, we'll look at three very basic and essential TCP-related technologies that allow you to create an infrastructure for your network—the Dynamic Host Configuration Protocol (DHCP), the Domain Name System (DNS), and the Windows Internet Name Service (WINS).

Then, in Chapter 19, you'll see how to set up the server service that is perhaps the most popular type of server on TCP/IP-based networks—a Web server, with the built-in Internet Information Server (IIS) shipped with Windows 2000.

A Brief History of TCP/IP

Let's start off by asking, "What *is* TCP/IP?" TCP/IP is a collection of software created over the years, much of it with the help of large infusions of government research money. Originally, TCP/IP was intended for the Department of Defense (DoD). You see, DoD tends to buy a *lot* of equipment, and much of that equipment is incompatible with other equipment. For example, back in the late '70s when the work that led to TCP/IP was first begun, it was nearly impossible to get an IBM mainframe to talk to a Burroughs mainframe. That was because the two computers were designed with entirely different *protocols*—something like Figure 17.1.

FIGURE 17.1

Compatible hardware, incompatible protocols

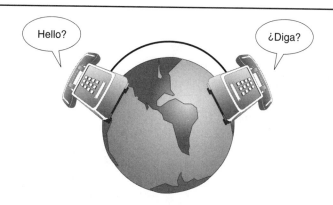

FIGURE 17.1

Compatible hardware, incompatible protocols

To get some idea of what the DoD was facing, imagine picking up the phone in the U.S. and calling someone in Spain. You have a perfectly good hardware connection, as the Spanish phone system is compatible with the American phone system. But despite the *hardware* compatibility, you face a *software* incompatibility. The person on the other end of the phone is expecting a different protocol, a different language. It's not that one language is better or worse than the other, but the English speaker cannot understand the Spanish speaker, and vice versa. Rather than force the Spanish speaker to learn English or the English speaker to learn Spanish, we can teach them both a universal language such as Esperanto, the universal language designed in 1888. If Esperanto were used in my telephone example, neither speaker would use it at home, but they would use it to communicate with each other.

That was how TCP/IP began—as a simple *alternative* communications language. As time went on, however, TCP/IP evolved into a mature, well-understood, robust set of protocols, and many sites adopted it as their *main* communication language.

Origins of TCP/IP: From the ARPAnet to the Internet

The original DoD network wouldn't just hook up military sites, although that was an important goal of the first defense Internetwork. Much of the basic research in the U.S. was funded by an arm of the Defense Department called the Advanced Research Projects Agency, or ARPA. ARPA gave, and still gives, a lot of money to university researchers to study all kinds of things. ARPA thought it would be useful for these researchers to be able to communicate with one another, as well as with the Pentagon. Figures 17.2 and 17.3 demonstrate networking both before and after ARPAnet implementation.

FIGURE 17.2

Researchers before
ARPAnet

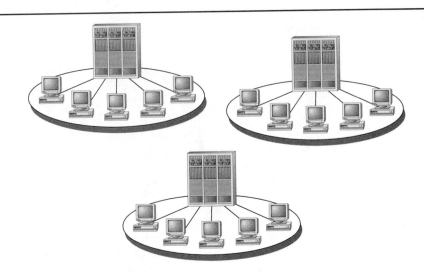

FIGURE 17.3

Researchers after
ARPAnet

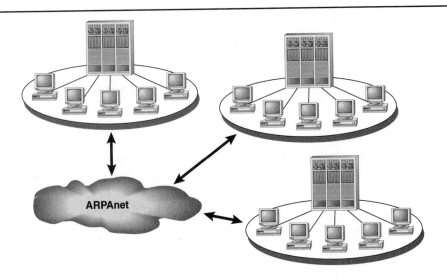

The new network, dubbed ARPAnet, was designed and put in place by a private contractor called Bolt, Barenek and Newman. For the first time, it linked university professors both to themselves and to their military and civilian project leaders around the country. Because ARPAnet was a network that linked separate private university networks and the separate military networks, it was a "network of networks."

ARPAnet ran atop a protocol called the Network Control Protocol (NCP). NCP was later refined into two components, the Internet Protocol (IP) and the Transmission Control Protocol (TCP). The change from NCP to TCP/IP is the technical difference between ARPAnet and the Internet. On 1 January 1983, ARPAnet packet-switching devices stopped accepting NCP packets and only passed TCP/IP packets, so in a sense, 1 January 1983 is the "official" birthday of the Internet.

ARPAnet became the Internet after a few evolutions. (Well, that's a "few evolutions" unless you happen to believe that Al Gore invented it in his spare time while a senator.) Probably the first major development step occurred in 1974, when Vinton Cerf and Robert Kahn proposed the protocols that would become TCP and IP. (I say "probably" because the Internet didn't grow through a centralized effort, but rather through the largely disconnected efforts of a number of researchers, university professors, and graduate students, most of whom are still alive—and almost *all* of whom have a different perspective on what the "defining" aspects of Internet development were.) Over its more than 20-year history, the Internet and its predecessors have gone through several stages of growth and adjustment. Ten years ago, the Internet could only claim a few thousand users. Nowadays, hundreds of millions of people are on the Internet. The Internet appears to double in size about every year. It can't do that indefinitely, but it's certainly a time of change for this huge network of networks.

Internet growth is fueled not by an esoteric interest in seeing how large a network the world can build, but rather by just a few applications that require the Internet to run. Perhaps most important is Internet e-mail, followed closely by the World Wide Web, and then the File Transfer Protocol (FTP)...but more on those later in Chapter 18.

Originally, the Internet protocols were intended to support connections between mainframe-based networks, which were basically the only ones that existed through most of the 1970s. But the 1980s saw the growth of Unix workstations, microcomputers, and minicomputers. The Berkeley version of Unix was built largely with government money, and the government said, "Put the TCP/IP protocol in that thing." There was some resistance at first, but adding IP as a built-in part of Berkeley Unix has helped both Unix and the Internet grow. The IP protocol was used on many of the Unix-based Ethernet networks that appeared in the 1980s and still exist to this day. As a matter of fact, you probably have to learn at least a smidgen of Unix-like commands to get around the Internet—but don't let that put you off. In this chapter, I'll teach you all the Unix you need and show you how much of the old Unix stuff can be fulfilled by Windows 2000. You will find, however, that most ISPs are still driven by Unix.

In the mid-1980s, the National Science Foundation created five supercomputing centers and put them on the Internet. This served two purposes: It made supercomputers available to NSF grantees around the country, and it provided a major "backbone" for the Internet. The National Science Foundation portion of the network, called NSFnet, was for a long time the largest part of the Internet. It is now being superseded by the National Research and Education Network (NREN). For many years, commercial users were pretty much kept off the Internet, as most of the funding was governmental; you had to be invited to join the Net. But those restrictions have been relaxed and now the majority of Internet traffic is routed over commercially run lines rather than government-run lines.

In fact, commercial and private users dominate the Internet these days, so much so that the government and educational institutions are now working on a faster "Internet 2."

It's customary to refer to the Internet as the Information Superhighway. I can understand why people say that; after all, it's a long-haul trucking service for data. But I think of it more as "Information Main Street." The Internet is growing because businesses are using it to get things done and to sell their wares. Much of this book was shipped back and forth on the Internet as it was being written. Heck, that sounds more like Main Street than a highway.

Nowadays, nearly every firm has at least some presence on the Internet; not having a Web page is almost like not having a phone. Remember when fax machines became popular in the early 1980s? Overnight people stopped saying, "Do you have a fax?" and just started saying, "What's your fax number?" It's getting so that if you don't have an Internet address, you're just not a person. For example, my Internet mail address is `help@minasi.com`.

Goals of TCP/IP's Design

But let's delve into some of the techie aspects of the Internet's main protocols. When DoD started building this set of network protocols, they had a few design goals. Understanding those design goals helps in understanding why it's worth making the effort to use TCP/IP in the first place. Its intended characteristics include:

- Good failure recovery
- Ability to plug in new networks without disrupting services
- Ability to handle high error rates
- Independence from a particular vendor or type of network
- Very little data overhead

I'm sure no one had any idea how central those design goals would be to the amazing success of TCP/IP both in private intranets and in *the* Internet. Let's take a look at those design goals in more detail.

Good Failure Recovery

Remember, this was to be a *defense* network, so it had to work even if portions of the network hardware suddenly and without warning went offline. That's kind of a nice way of saying the network had to work even if big pieces got nuked.

Can Plug In New Subnetworks "on-the-Fly"

This second goal is related to the first one. It says that it should be possible to bring entire new networks into an intranet—and here, again, *intranet* can mean your company's private intranet or *the* Internet—without interrupting existing network service.

Can Handle High Error Rates

The next goal was that an intranet should be able to tolerate high or unpredictable error rates and yet still provide a 100-percent reliable end-to-end service. If you're transferring data from Washington, DC, to Portland, Oregon, and the links that you're currently using through Oklahoma get destroyed by a tornado, then any data lost in the storm will be resent and rerouted via some other lines.

Host Independence

As I mentioned before, the new network architecture should work with any kind of network and not be dedicated or tied to any one vendor.

This is essential in the '90s. The days of "We're just an IBM shop" or "We only buy Novell stuff" are gone for many and going fast for others. (Let's hope that it doesn't give way to "We only buy Microsoft software.") Companies must be able to live in a multivendor world.

Very Little Data Overhead

The last goal was for the network protocols to have as little overhead as possible. To understand this, let's compare TCP/IP to other protocols. While no one knows what protocol will end up being *the* world protocol 20 years from now—if any protocol *ever* gets that much acceptance—one of TCP/IP's rivals is a set of protocols built by the International Standards Organization, or ISO. ISO has some standards that are very similar to the kinds of things that TCP/IP does, standards named X.25 and TP4. But every protocol packages its data with an extra set of bytes, kind of like an envelope. The vast majority of data packets using the IP protocol (and I promise, I *will* explain soon how it is that TCP and IP are actually two very different protocols) have a simple, fixed-size 20-byte header. The maximum size that the header can be is 60 bytes if all possible options are enabled. The fixed 20 bytes always appears as the first 20 bytes of the packet. In contrast, X.25 uses dozens of possible headers, with no appreciable fixed portion to it. But why should *you* be concerned about overhead bytes? Really for one reason only: Performance. Simpler protocols mean faster transmission and packet switching. We'll take up packet switching a little later.

But enough about the Internet for now. Let's stop and define something that I've been talking about—namely, just what *are* TCP and IP?

Originally, TCP/IP was just a set of protocols that could hook up dissimilar computers and transfer information between them. But it grew into a large number of protocols that have become collectively known as the *TCP/IP suite*.

The Internet Protocol (IP)

The most basic part of the Internet is the Internet Protocol, or IP. If you want to send data over an intranet, then that data must be packaged in an IP packet. That packet is then *routed* from one part of the intranet to another.

A Simple Internet

IP is supposed to allow messages to travel from one part of a network to another. How does it do this?

An intranet is made of at least two *sub*nets. The notion of a subnet is built upon the fact that most popular LAN architectures (Ethernet, Token Ring, and ARCNet) are based on something very much like a radio broadcast. Everyone on the same Ethernet segment hears all of the traffic on their segment, just as each device on a given ring in a Token Ring network must examine every message that goes through the network. The trick that makes an Ethernet or a Token Ring work is that, while each station *hears* everything, each station knows how to ignore all messages save for the ones intended for it.

You may have never realized it, but that means that in a single Ethernet segment or a single Token Ring ring, there is *no routing*. If you've ever sat through one of those seemingly unending explanations of the ISO seven-layer network model, then you know that in network discussions, much is made of the *network layer*, which in ISO terms is merely the routing layer. And yet a simple Ethernet or Token Ring never has to route. There are no routing decisions to make; everything is heard by everybody. (Your network adapter filters out any traffic not destined for you, in case you're wondering.)

But now suppose you have *two* separate Ethernets connected to each other, as you see in Figure 17.4.

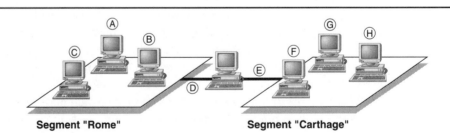

FIGURE 17.4

Multisegment intranet

Segment "Rome"   Segment "Carthage"

In Figure 17.4, you see two Ethernet segments, named Rome and Carthage. (I was getting tired of the "shipping" and "finance" examples that everyone uses.) There are three computers that reside solely in Rome that I've labeled A, B, and C. Three more computers reside in Carthage, labeled F, G, and H.

Subnets and Routers: "Should I Shout, or Should I Route?"

Much of intranet architecture is built around the observation that PCs A, B, and C can communicate directly with each other, and PCs F, G, and H can communicate directly with each other, but A, B, and C *cannot* communicate with F, G, and H without some help from the machine containing Ethernet cards D and E. That D/E machine will function as a *router*, a machine that allows communication between different network segments. A, B, C, and D could be described as being in each other's "broadcast range," as could E, F, G, and H. What I've just called a broadcast range is called more correctly in intranet terminology a *subnet*, which is a collection of machines that can communicate with each other without the need for routing.

For example, F and H can communicate directly without having to ask the router (E, in their case) to forward the message, and so they're on the same subnet. A and C can communicate directly without having to ask the router (D, in their case) to forward the message, and so they're on the same subnet. But if B wanted to talk to G, it would have to first send the message to D, asking, "D, please get this to G," so they're not on the same subnet.

Now, this whole trick of somehow knowing that F and H are on the same subnet and so do not need to enlist the aid of a router—F can just "shout" the message and H will hear it—or knowing that A and F are on different subnets and so A would need the help of D to get to F or that F would require E's assistance to get to A is IP's main job. Essentially, IP's job is to figure out "should I shout, or should I route?" and then, if routing's the way to go, IP's got to figure out which router to use, assuming there's a choice of routers.

IP Addresses and Ethernet Addresses

Before continuing, let's briefly discuss the labels A, B, C, and so on and how those labels actually are manifested in an intranet. Each computer on this net is attached to the net via an Ethernet board, and each Ethernet board on an intranet has two addresses: An *IP address* and an *Ethernet address*. (There are, of course, other ways to get onto an intranet than via Ethernet, but let's stay with the Ethernet example as it's the most common one on TCP/IP intranets.)

Ethernet Addresses

Each Ethernet board's Ethernet address is a unique 48-bit identification code. If it sounds unlikely that every Ethernet board in the world has its own unique address, then consider that 48 bits offers 280,000,000,000,000 possibilities. Ethernet itself only uses about one quarter of those possibilities (2 bits are set aside for administrative functions), but that's still a lot of possible addresses. In any case, the important thing to get here is that a board's Ethernet address is predetermined and hard-coded into the board. Ethernet addresses, which are also called Media Access Control (MAC) addresses (it's got nothing to do with Macintoshes) are expressed in 12 hex digits. (*MAC address* is synonymous with *Token Ring address* or *Ethernet address*.) For example, the Ethernet card on the computer I'm working at now has MAC (Ethernet) address 0020AFF8E771, or as it's sometimes written, 00-20-AF-F8-E7-71. The addresses are centrally administered, and Ethernet chip vendors must purchase blocks of addresses. In the example of my workstation, you know that it's got a 3Com Ethernet card because the Ethernet (MAC) address is 00-20-AF; that prefix is owned by 3Com.

 NOTE You can see an NT machine's MAC address in a number of ways. You can type **net config workstation** or **net config server** (it's the string of hex in parentheses). Or you can run the System Information snap-in (\program files\Common Files\Microsoft Shared\MSInfo\Msinfo32.msc), then open up the System Information folder, then the Components folder inside that, then the Network folder inside *that*, and finally the Adapter folder inside the Network folder. One of the reported pieces of information will be the MAC Address.

IP Addresses and Quad Format

In contrast to the 48 bits in a MAC address, an IP address is a 32-bit value. IP addresses are numbers set at a workstation (or server) by a network administrator—they're not a hard-coded hardware kind of address like the Ethernet address. That means that there are four billion distinct Internet addresses.

It's nice that there's room for lots of machines, but having to remember—or having to tell someone else—a 32-bit address is no fun. Imagine having to say to a network support person, "Just set up the machines on the subnet to use a default router address of 10101110100-10101001010101000010111." Hmmm...doesn't sound like much fun—we need a more human-friendly way to express 32-bit numbers. That's where *dotted quad* notation comes from.

For simplicity's sake, IP addresses are usually represented as *w.x.y.z*, where *w*, *x*, *y*, and *z* are all decimal values from 0 to 255. For example, the IP address of the machine that I'm currently writing this at is 199.34.57.53. Each of the four numbers is called a *quad*; as they're connected by dots, it's called *dotted quad* notation.

Each of the numbers in the dotted quad corresponds to 8 bits of an Internet address. (*IP address* and *Internet address* are synonymous.) As the value for 8 bits can range from 0 to 255, each value in a dotted quad can be from 0 to 255. For example, to convert an IP address of 11001010000011111010101000000001 into dotted quad format, it would first be broken up into 8-bit groups:

11001010 00001111 10101010 00000001

And each of those 8-bit numbers would be converted to its decimal equivalent. (If you're not comfortable with binary-to-decimal conversion, don't worry about it: Just load the NT Calculator, click View, then Scientific, and then press the F8 key to put the Calculator in binary mode. Enter the binary number, press F6, and the number will be converted to decimal for you.) Our number converts as follows:

11001010   00001111   10101010   00000001
   202   15   170   1

which results in a dotted quad address of 202.15.170.1.

So, to recap: Each of these computers has at least one Ethernet card in it, and that Ethernet card has a predefined address. The network administrator of this network has gone around and installed IP software on these PCs and, in the process, has assigned IP addresses to each of them. (Note, by the way, that the phrase "has assigned IP addresses to each of them" may not be true if you are using the Dynamic Host Configuration Protocol, or DHCP. For the first part of this chapter, however, I'm going to assume that you're not using DHCP and that someone must hand-assign an IP address to each Ethernet card.)

Let me redraw our intranet, adding totally arbitrary IP addresses and Ethernet addresses, as shown in Figure 17.5.

FIGURE 17.5

Two-subnet intranet with Ethernet and IP addresses

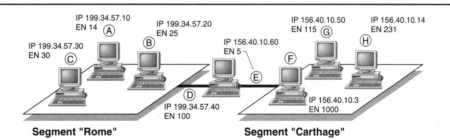

IP Routers

Now let's return to the computer in the middle. It is part of *both* segments. How do I get one computer to be part of two networks? By putting two Ethernet cards in the computer in the middle. (A computer with more than one network card in it is called a *multihomed* computer.) One of the Ethernet cards is on the Rome subnet, and the other is on the Carthage subnet. (By the way, each computer on an intranet is called a *host* in TCP-ese.)

Now, each Ethernet card must get a separate IP address, so as a result, the computer in the middle has *two* IP addresses, D and E. If a message is transmitted in Rome, adapter D hears it and E doesn't. Then, if a message is transmitted in Carthage, adapter E hears it but D doesn't.

How would we build an intranet from these two subnets? How could station A, for example, send a message to station G? Obviously, the only way that message will get from A to G is if the message is received on the Ethernet adapter with address D and then resent out over the Ethernet adapter with address E. Once E resends the message, G will hear it, as it is on the same network as E.

In order for this to work, the machine containing boards D and E must be smart enough to perform this function whereby it resends data between D and E when necessary. Such a machine is, by definition, an *IP router*. It is possible with Windows 2000 to use a Win2K computer—any Win2K computer, not just a Windows 2000 Server computer—to act as an IP router, as you'll learn later.

Under IP, the sending station (A, in this case) examines the address of the destination (G, in this case) and realizes that it does not know how to get to G. (I'll explain exactly *how* it comes to that realization in a minute.) Now, if A has to send something to an address that it doesn't understand, then it uses a kind of "catchall" address called the *default router* or, for historical reasons, the *default gateway* address. A's network administrator has already configured A's default router as D, so A sends the message to D. Once D gets the message, it then sees that the message is not destined for itself, but rather for G, and so it resends the message from board E.

Routing in More Detail

Now let's look a little closer at how that message gets from A to G. Each computer, as you've already seen, has one *or more* IP addresses. It's important to understand that there is no relationship whatsoever between an Ethernet card's address and the IP address associated with it: The Ethernet MAC address is hardwired into the card by the card's manufacturer, and the IP addresses are assigned by a network administrator.

But now examine the IP addresses and you'll see a pattern to them. Rome's addresses all look like 199.34.57.*x*, where *x* is some number, and Carthage's addresses all look like 156.40.10.*x*, where, again, *x* can be any number. The Ethernet addresses follow no rhyme or reason and are grouped by the board's manufacturer. That similarity of IP addresses within Rome and Carthage will be important in understanding routing.

Now, let's reexamine how the message gets from A to G:

1. The IP software in A first says, "How do I get this message to G—can I just broadcast it, or must it be routed?" The way that it makes that decision is by finding out whether or not G is on the same *subnet* as A is. A subnet is simply a broadcast area. Host A then, is asking, "Is G part of Rome, like me?"

2. Station A determines that it is on a different subnet from station G by examining their addresses. A knows that it has address 199.34.57.10 and that it must send its message to 156.40.10.50. A has a simple rule for this: If the destination address looks like 199.34.57.*x*, where, again, *x* can be any value, then the destination is in the same subnet and so requires no routing. On the other hand, 156.40.10.50 is clearly *not* in the same subnet.

If, alternatively, G *had* been on the same subnet, then A would have "shouted" the IP packet straight to G, referring specifically to its IP and Ethernet address.

3. So station A can't directly send its IP packets to G. A then looks for another way. When A's network administrator set up A's IP software, she told A the IP address of A's *default router*. The default router is basically the address that says, "If you don't know where to send something, send it to me and I'll try to get it there." A's default router is D. So now A has a sort of sub-goal of getting a message to nearby D, with IP address 199.34.57.40. We're almost ready to hand this over to the Ethernet card—*except* that Ethernet cards don't understand IP addresses; they understand MAC addresses.

TCP/IP's got an answer for this: ARP, the Address Resolution Protocol. A just sends a broadcast to the local segment, saying, "If there's a machine out there that goes by the IP address 199.34.57.40, please send me back your MAC address." D hears the request and responds that its MAC address is 100.

A then sends an Ethernet frame from itself to D. The Ethernet frame contains this information:

- Source Ethernet address: 14
- Destination Ethernet address: 100
- Source IP address: 199.34.57.10
- Destination IP address: 156.40.10.50

4. Ethernet card D receives the frame and hands it to the IP software running in its PC. The PC sees that the IP destination address is not *its* IP address, so the PC knows that it must route this IP packet. Examining the subnet, the PC sees that the destination lies on the subnet that Ethernet adapter E is on, so it ARPs to get G's MAC address; G responds, "My MAC address is 115," and then E sends out a frame, with this information:

- Source Ethernet address: 5
- Destination Ethernet address: 115
- Source IP address: 199.34.57.10 (note this is A's address, not E's)
- Destination IP address: 156.40.10.50

5. G then gets the packet. By looking at the Ethernet and IP addresses, G can see that it got this frame from E, but the original message really came from another machine, the 199.34.57.10 machine.

That's a simple example of how IP routes, but its algorithms are powerful enough to serve as the backbone for a network as large as the Internet.

TIP There are different kinds of routing algorithms in TCP/IP. Windows 2000 supports the Routing Information Protocol (RIP) version 2, Open Shortest Path First (OSPF), and IGMP version 2. For other routing approaches, or for very high-capacity routing needs, you need either third-party software or a dedicated hardware router to build large, complex intranets with Windows 2000. But Windows 2000 can handle a considerably larger set of routing tasks than did its predecessors.

A, B, and C Networks, CIDR Blocks, and Subnetting

Before leaving IP routing, let's take a more specific look at networks, subnets, and IP addresses.

The whole idea behind the 32-bit IP addresses is to make it relatively simple to segment the task of managing the Internet or, for that matter, *any* intranet.

To become part of the Internet, you'll need a block of IP addresses and a name (like acme.com) or a set of names. Find a local Internet Service Provider (ISP) for the block of addresses. ISPs may also handle registering names for you, but it's just as easy to register a name yourself with Network Solutions; surf over to www.internic.net to find out how.

But how do the *ISPs* get their IP addresses? Originally, an organization named the Internet Assigned Numbers Authority (IANA) handed out addresses. In 1993, however, an Internet document RFC 1466 (the rules describing how things work in the Internet are called Requests for Comment, or RFCs) explained that it made more sense to distribute the job as the Internet became bigger. The IANA, which is now in the process of becoming the Internet Corporation for Assigned Names and Numbers (ICANN), divides its number-assigning authority among three Regional Internet Registries (RIRs, inevitably): RIPE ((Réseaux IP Européens) handles Europe, the Middle East, Africa, and the better part of Asia; APNIC (Asia Pacific Network Information Center) handles the rest of Asia and the South Pacific; and ARIN (American Registry for Internet Numbers) handles the Americas. Rather than say "The IANA/ICANN, RIPE, ARIN, APNIC, or one of their suborganizations," however, I'll just say "IANA" when referring to the IP-allocating groups.

A, B, and C Class Networks

The IANA or an ISP assigns a company a block of IP addresses according to the company's size. That block of addresses is called a *network*. (As you'll soon see, a subnet is just a subdivision of a that set of assigned addresses, hence "sub" net.) Big companies get A class networks (there are none left; they've all been given out), medium-sized companies get B class networks (we're out of those, too), and others get C class networks (they're still available). Although there are three network classes, there are five kinds of IP addresses, as you'll see in Figure 17.6.

Internet network classes and reserved addresses

0XXXXXXX AAAAAAAA	LLLLLLLL	LLLLLLLL	LLLLLLLL

Class A addresses: Values 0-126

01111111			

Reserved loopback address: Value 127

10XXXXXX AAAAAAAA	AAAAAAAA	LLLLLLLL	LLLLLLLL

Class B addresses: Values 128-191

110XXXXX AAAAAAAA	AAAAAAAA	AAAAAAAA	LLLLLLLL

Class C addresses: Values 192-223

1110XXXX			

Reserved multicast addresses: Values 224-239

1110XXXX			

Reserved experimental addresses: Values 240-255

A=Assigned by NIC
L=Locally administered

Because it seemed, in the early days of the Internet, that four billion addresses left plenty of space for growth, the original designers were a bit sloppy. They defined three classes of networks of the Internet: Large networks, medium-sized networks, and small networks. The creators of the Internet used 8-bit sections of the 32-bit addresses to delineate the difference between different classes of networks:

A class networks   A large network would have its first 8 bits set by the NIC, and the network's internal administrators could set the remaining 24 bits. The leftmost 8 bits could have values from 0 to 126, allowing for 127 class A networks. Companies like IBM get these, and there are only 127 of these addresses. As only 8 bits have been taken, 24 remain; that means that class A networks can contain up to 2 to the 24th power, or about 16 million, hosts. Examples of A class nets include General Electric (3.x.x.x), BBN (4), IBM (9), Xerox (13), Hewlett-Packard (15), Columbia University (15), Apple (17), DEC (16), MIT (18), Ford (19), Eli Lilly (40), DuPont (52), Merck (54), Boeing (55), the U.S. Postal Service (56), various defense groups—remember who built this—and some unexpected ones: Networld+Interop, which has the 45.x.x.x network set aside for its use (not bad, an A network for two week-long conferences a year!), the U.K. Department of Social Security, and Norsk Informasjonsteknologi.

B class networks   Medium-sized networks have the leftmost *16* bits preassigned to them, leaving 16 bits for local use. Class B addresses always have the values 128 through 191 in their first quad, then a value from 0 to 255 in their second quad. There are then 16,384 possible class B networks. Each of them can have up to 65,536 hosts. Microsoft and Exxon are examples of companies with B class networks. (So Apple and IBM have A class networks and Microsoft's only got a B class. What do you want to bet that this kind of thing keeps Bill up late nights?)

C class networks   Small networks have the leftmost *24* bits preassigned to them, leaving only 8 bits for local administration (which is bad, as it means that class C networks can't have more than 254 hosts), but as the NIC has 24 bits to work with, it can easily give out class C network addresses (which is good). Class C addresses start off with a value from 192 to 223. As the second and third quads can be any value from 0 to 255, that means that there can potentially be 2,097,152 class C networks. (That's what my network, minasi.com, is.) The last C network, when it's assigned, will be 223.255.255.*x*; remember that the owner of that network will be able to control only *x*.

Reserved addresses   A number of addresses are reserved for multicast purposes and for experimental purposes, so they can't be assigned for networks. In particular, address 224.0.0.0 is set aside for *multicasts*, network transmissions to groups of computers.

More and more people have two kinds of IP addresses: Addresses used in their company's *internal* Internet (or "intranet," as we say nowadays) and a range of "official" Internet addresses obtained from an ISP or directly from a part of the IANA.

There is a class of routers called Network Address Translation (NAT) routers which can perform a small bit of magic and let you use private, non-IANA–assigned IP addresses on your company's intranet and still be able to communicate with the Internet.

Most NAT routers require that you use a particular set of IP addresses in your intranet. Specified in RFC 1918, this range of addresses is:

- 10.0.0.0–10.255.255.255
- 172.16.0.0–172.31.255.255
- 192.168.0.0–192.168.255.255

So, for example, suppose your firm had obtained a C class address range from the IANA or an ISP: 256 addresses. Although you have thousands of computers, the fact that there are only 256 addresses is no problem as the NAT router can handle communications with the Internet.

And it's a good idea to use those addresses even *if* your firm isn't currently connected to the Internet; this way, you're ready if you ever *do* hook up.

You Can't Use *All* of the Numbers

There are some special rules to IP addresses, however. There's a whole bunch of numbers that you can never give to any machine. They're the default route address, the loopback address, the network number, the broadcast address, and the default router address.

The Default Route Address

As you'll see later, the address 0.0.0.0 is another way of saying "the entire Internet." But as 0.x.x.x is in the A class range of addresses, all of 0.x.x.x must be set aside—all 16 million addresses.

The Loopback Address

The address 127.0.0.1 is reserved as a loopback. If you send a message to 127.0.0.1, then it should be returned to you unless there's something wrong on the IP software itself; messages to the loopback don't go out on the network, but instead stay within a particular machine's IP software. And so no network has an address 127.xxxxxxxx.xxxxxxxx.xxxxxxxx, an unfortunate waste of 16 million addresses.

The Network Number

Sometimes you need to refer to an entire subnet with a single number. Thus far, I've said things like "My C network is 199.34.57.*x*, and I can make *x* range from 0 to 255." I was being a bit lazy; I didn't want to write "199.34.57.0 through 199.34.57.255," so I said "199.34.57.*x*."

It's not proper IP-ese to refer to a range of network addresses that way. And it's necessary to have an official way to refer to a range of addresses.

For example, to tell a router, "To get this message to the subnet that ranges from 100.100.100.0 through 100.100.100.255, first route to the router at 99.98.97.103," you've got to have some way to designate the range of addresses 100.100.100.0–100.100.100.255. We could have just used two addresses with a hyphen between them, but that's a bit cumbersome. Instead, the address that ends in all binary 0s is reserved as the *network number*, the TCP/IP name for the range of addresses in a subnet. In my 100.100.100.*x* example, the shorthand way to refer to 100.100.100.0 through 100.100.100.255 is "100.100.100.0."

Notice that this means you would never use the address 100.100.100.0—you never give that IP address to a machine under TCP/IP.

For example, to tell that router, "To get this message to the subnet that ranges from 100.100.100.0 through 100.100.100.255, first route to the router at 99.98.97.103," you would type something like **route add 100.100.100.0 99.98.97.103**. (Actually, you'd type a bit more information, and I'll get to that in the upcoming section on using your NT machine as a router, but this example gives you the idea.)

IP Broadcast Address

There's another reserved address, as well—the TCP/IP broadcast address. It looks like the address of one machine, but it isn't; it's the address you'd use to broadcast to each machine on a subnet. That address is all binary 1s.

For example, on a simple C class subnet, the broadcast address would be $x.y.z.255$. When would you need to know this? Some IP software needs this when you configure it; most routers require the broadcast address (as well as the network number). So if I just use my C class network 199.34.57.0 (see how convenient that .0 thing is?) as a single subnet, then the broadcast address for my network would be 199.34.57.255.

Default Router Address

Every subnet has at least one router; after all, if it didn't have a router, then the subnet couldn't talk to any other networks, and it wouldn't be an intranet.

By convention, the first address after the network number is the default gateway (router) address. For example, on a simple C class network, the address of the router should be $x.y.z.1$. This is not, by the way, a hard-and-fast rule like the network number and the IP broadcast address—it is, instead, a convention.

Suppose you have just been made the proud owner of a C class net, 222.210.34.0. You can put 253 computers on your network, as you must not use 222.210.34.0, which describes the entire network; 222.210.34.255, which will be your broadcast address; and 222.210.34.1, which will be used either by you or your Internet Service Provider for a router address between your network and the rest of the Internet.

Now, once you get a range of addresses from the IANA or an ISP, then you are said to have an *IP domain*. (*Domain* in Internet lingo has nothing to do with domain in the Win2K security sense.) For example, my IP domain (which is named minasi.com, but we'll cover names in a minute) uses addresses in the 206.246.253.x network, and I can have as many Win2K domains in there as I like. However, from the point of view of the outside Internet, all of my Win2K domains are just one Internet domain: minasi.com.

Subnet Masks

If you had a trivially small intranet, one with just one subnet, then all the devices in your network can simply transmit directly to each other and no routing is required. On the other hand, you may have a domain so large that using broadcasting to communicate within it would be unworkable, requiring you to subnet your domain further. Consider IBM's situation, with an A class network that can theoretically support 16 million hosts. Managing *that* network cries out for routers. For this reason, it may be necessary for your IP software on your PC to route data over a router even if it's staying within your company. Let's ask again, and in more detail this time, "How does a machine know whether to route or not?"

That's where subnets are important. Subnets make it possible, as you've seen, for a host (a PC) to determine whether it can just lob a message straight over to another host or if it must go through routers. You can tell a host's IP software how to distinguish whether or not another host is in the same subnet through the *subnet mask*.

Recall that all of the IP addresses in Rome looked like 199.34.57.*x*, where *x* was a number between 1 and 255. You could then say that all comembers of the Rome subnet are defined as the hosts whose first three quads match. Now, on some subnets, it might be possible that the only requirement for membership in the same subnet would be that the first *two* quads be the same—a company that decided for some reason to make its entire B class network a single subnet would be one example of that. (Yes, they *do* exist: I've seen firms that make a single subnet out of a Class B network, with the help of some bizarre smart bridges. And no, I don't recommend it.)

When a computer is trying to figure out whether the IP address that it owns is on the same subnet as the place that it's trying to communicate with, then a subnet mask answers the question, "Which bits must match for us to be on the same subnet?"

IP does that with a *mask*, a combination of 1s and 0s like so:

11111111 11111111 11111111 00000000

Here's how a host would use this mask. The host with IP address 199.34.57.10 (station A in Figure 17.5) wants to know if it is on the same subnet as the host with IP address 199.34.57.20 (station B in Figure 17.5). 199.34.57.10, expressed in binary, is 11000111 00100010 00111001 00001010. The IP address for B is, in binary, 11000111 00100010 00111001 00010100. The IP software in A then compares its own IP address to B's IP address. Look at them right next to each other:

11000111 00100010 00111001 00001010 *A's address*
11000111 00100010 00111001 00010100 *B's address*

The leftmost 27 bits match, as does the rightmost bit. Does that mean they're in the same subnet? Again, for the two addresses to be in the same subnet, certain bits must match—the ones with 1s in the subnet mask. Let's stack up the subnet mask, A's address, and B's address to make this clearer:

11111111 11111111 11111111 00000000 *the subnet mask*
11000111 00100010 00111001 00001010 *A's address*
11000111 00100010 00111001 00010100 *B's address*

Look down from each of the 1s on the subnet mask, and you see that A and B match at each of those positions. Under the 0s in the subnet mask, A and B match up sometimes but not all the time. In fact, it doesn't matter whether or not A and B match in the positions under the 0s in the subnet mask—the fact that there are 0s there means that whether or not they match is irrelevant.

Another way to think of the subnet mask is this. The IANA and friends give you a range of addresses and you allocate them as you see fit. Of the 32 bits in your IP addresses, some are under your control and some are under the IANA & Co's control. In general, however, the bits that the IANA controls are to the left, and the ones that *you* control are to the right. For example, the IANA controls the leftmost 8 bits for an A class network, the 16 leftmost bits for a B class network, and the leftmost 24 bits for a C class network.

How do you know what value to use for a subnet mask? Well, if you have a class C number and all of your workstations are on a single subnet, then you have a case like the one we just saw: A subnet mask of 11111111 11111111 11111111 00000000, which, in dotted quad terminology, is 255.255.255.0. Remember that, by definition, the fact that I have a C network means that the IANA has "nailed down" the leftmost or top three quads (24 bits), leaving me only the rightmost quad (8 bits). Since all of my addresses must match in the leftmost 24 bits and I can do anything I like with the bottom 8 bits, my subnet mask must be 111111111 1111111 11111111 00000000, or 255.255.255.0. Again, with subnet masks, the 1s are always on the left and the 0s on the right—you'll never see a subnet mask like "11111111 11110000 00001111 11111000" or "00000000 11111111 11111111 11111111."

Getting back to my C network, however, that 11111111 11111111 11111111 00000000 mask assumes that I'll use my entire C network as one big subnet. Instead, I might decide to break one C class network into two subnets. I could decide that all the numbers from 1 to 127—00000001 to 01111111—are subnet 1 and the numbers from 128 to 255—10000000 to 11111111—are subnet 2. In that case, the values inside my subnets will only vary in the last 7 bits rather than (as in the previous example) varying in the last *8* bits. The subnet mask would be, then, 11111111 11111111 11111111 10000000, or 255.255.255.128.

The first subnet is a range of addresses from *x.y.z.*0 through *x.y.z.*127, where *x.y.z* are the quads that the NIC assigned me. The second subnet is the range from *x.y.z.*128 through *x.y.z.*255.

Now let's find the network number, default router address, and broadcast address. The network number is the first number in each range, so the first subnet's network number is *x.y.z.*0 and the second's is *x.y.z.*128. The default router address is just the second address in the range, which is *x.y.z.*1 and *x.y.z.*129 for the two subnets. The broadcast address is then the *last* address in both cases, *x.y.z.*127 and *x.y.z.*255 respectively.

Subnetting a Class C Network

If you're going to break down your subnets smaller than C class, then having to figure out the subnet mask, network number, broadcast address, and router address can get kind of confusing. Table 17.1 summarizes how you can break a C class network down into one, two, four, or eight smaller subnets with the attendant subnet masks, network numbers, broadcast addresses, and router addresses. I've assumed that you are starting from a C class address, so you'll only be working with the fourth quad. The first three quads I have simply designated *x.y.z*.

TABLE 17.1: BREAKING A C CLASS NETWORK INTO SUBNETS					
Number of Desired Subnets	**Subnet Mask**	**Network Number**	**Router Address**	**Broadcast Address**	**Remaining Number of IP Addresses**
1	255.255.255.0	*x.y.z.*0	*x.y.z.*1	*x.y.z.*255	253
2	255.255.255.128	*x.y.z.*0	*x.y.z.*1	*x.y.z.*127	125
	255.255.255.	*x.y.z.*128	*x.y.z.*129	*x.y.z.*255	125
4	255.255.255.192	*x.y.z.*0	*x.y.z.*1	*x.y.z.*63	61
	255.255.255.	*x.y.z.*64	*x.y.z.*65	*x.y.z.*127	61
	255.255.255.	*x.y.z.*128	*x.y.z.*129	*x.y.z.*191	61
	255.255.255.	*x.y.z.*192	*x.y.z.*193	*x.y.z.*255	61
8	255.255.255.224	*x.y.z.*0	*x.y.z.*1	*x.y.z.*31	29
	255.255.255.	*x.y.z.*32	*x.y.z.*33	*x.y.z.*63	29
	255.255.255.	*x.y.z.*64	*x.y.z.*65	*x.y.z.*95	29
	255.255.255.	*x.y.z.*96	*x.y.z.*97	*x.y.z.*127	29
	255.255.255.	*x.y.z.*128	*x.y.z.*129	*x.y.z.*159	29
	255.255.255.	*x.y.z.*160	*x.y.z.*161	*x.y.z.*191	29
	255.255.255.	*x.y.z.*192	*x.y.z.*193	*x.y.z.*223	29
	255.255.255.	*x.y.z.*224	*x.y.z.*225	*x.y.z.*255	29

For example, suppose you want to chop up a C class network, 200.211.192.*x*, into two subnets. As you see in the table, you'd use a subnet mask of 255.255.255.128 for each subnet. The first subnet would have network number 200.211.192.0, router address 200.211.192.1, and broadcast address 200.211.192.127. You could assign IP addresses 200.211.192.2 through 200.211.192.126, 125 different IP addresses. (Notice that heavily subnetting a network results in the loss of a greater and greater percentage of addresses to the network number, broadcast address, and router address.) The second subnet would have network number 200.211.192.128, router address 200.211.192.129, and broadcast address 200.211.192.255.

In case you're wondering, it is entirely possible to subnet further, into 16 subnets of 13 hosts apiece (remember that you always lose three numbers for the network number, router address, and broadcast address) or 32 subnets of 5 hosts apiece, but at that point, you're losing an awful lot of addresses to IP overhead.

I should note that in some cases, subnetting won't work the way I've said it does. Suppose I chop up my C network using the 255.255.255.192 subnet mask. I've said that this gives me four subnets: 199.34.57.0, 199.34.57.64, 199.34.57.128, and 199.34.57.192. You can set up the network like that, and in every case I've ever encountered, things will work fine. But there may be cases where you'll run into trouble, so it's fair to warn you that RFC 950, the RFC that defines how to subnet an IP network, says this:

> In certain contexts, it is useful to have fixed addresses with functional significance rather than as identifiers of specific hosts. When such usage is called for, the address zero is to be interpreted as meaning "this," as in "this network." The address of all ones are to be interpreted as meaning "all," as in "all hosts." For example, the address 128.9.255.255 could be interpreted as meaning "all hosts on the network 128.9." Or, the address 0.0.0.37 could be interpreted as meaning "host 37 on this network." It is useful to preserve and extend the interpretation of these special addresses in subnetted networks. This means the values of all zeros and all ones in the subnet field should not be assigned to actual (physical) subnets. In the example above, the 6-bit wide subnet field may have any value except 0 and 63.

What this means in English is this: RFC 950 says to use neither the first subnet nor the last subnet. Thus, if you're going to be completely RFC compliant (which is never a bad idea), you would *not* be able to use subnets 199.34.57.0 and 199.34.57.192. And my earlier example of dividing 199.34.57.0 into two subnets by using subnet mask 255.255.255.128 would not work at all.

Should you care? If you're using modern routers or NT machines for routers, you won't run into trouble using all possible subnets. But if you've got some routers that are sticklers for the rules, you might cause trouble by using those other subnets. It's kind of a shame, as the 255.255.255.192 subnet for a C network yields four 62-address subnets, and staying strictly RFC compliant means you only get *two* 62-address subnets.

Oh, and one more reason to understand RFC 950's restrictions: If you take any exams, such as the Microsoft or Cisco certification exams about TCP/IP, the RFC 950 answer will be right—the practical answer will be "wrong," even if it *would* work in the real world.

Classless Internetwork Domain Routing (CIDR)

Now that we've gotten past some of the fine points of subnet masks, let me elaborate on what you see if you ever go to the IANA or an ISP looking for a domain of your own.

The shortage of IP addresses has led the IANA to curtail giving out A, B, or C class addresses. Many small companies need an Internet domain, but giving them a C network is overkill, as a C network contains 256 addresses and many small firms only have a dozen or so computers that they want on the Internet. Large companies may also want a similarly small presence on the Internet: For reasons of security, they may not want to put all of the PCs (or other computers) on the Internet but rather on an internal network not attached to the Internet. These companies *do* need a presence on the Internet, however—for their e-mail servers, FTP servers, Web servers, and the like— so they need a dozen or so addresses. But, again, giving them an entire 256-address C network is awfully wasteful. But, until 1994, it was the smallest block that an ISP could hand out.

Similarly, some companies need a few hundred addresses—more than 256, but not very many more. Such a firm is too big for a C network but a bit small for the 65,536 addresses of a B network. More flexibility here would be useful.

For that reason, the IANA now gives out addresses without the old A, B, or C class restrictions. This newer method that the IANA uses is called Classless Internet Domain Routing, or CIDR, pronounced "cider." CIDR networks are described as "slash x" networks, where the x is a number representing the number of bits in the IP address range that the InterNIC controls.

If you had an A class network, then the IANA controlled the top 8 bits and you controlled the bottom 24. If you decided somehow to take your A class network and make it one big subnet, then what would be your subnet mask? Since all of your A network would be one subnet, you'd only have to look at the top quad to see if the source and destination addresses were on the same subnet. For example, if you had network 4.0.0.0, then addresses 4.55.22.81 and 4.99.63.88 would be on the same subnet. (Please note that I can't actually imagine anyone doing this with an A class net; I'm just trying to make CIDR clearer.) Your subnet mask would be, then, 11111111 00000000 00000000 00000000, or 255.0.0.0. Reading from the left, you have eight 1s in the subnet mask before the 0s start. In CIDR terminology, you wouldn't have an *A class* network; rather, you would have a *slash 8* network. It would be written "4.0.0.0/8" instead of "4.0.0.0 subnet mask 255.0.0.0."

With a B class, the IANA controlled the top 16 bits, and you controlled the bottom 16. If you decided to take that B class network and make it a one-subnet network, then your subnet mask would be 11111111 11111111 00000000 00000000, or 255.255.0.0. Reading from the left, the subnet mask would have 16 1s. In CIDR terms, a B network is a *slash 16* network. So if your firm had a B network like 164.109.0.0 subnet mask 255.255.0.0, in slash format that would be 164.109.0.0/16.

With a C class, the IANA controlled the top 24 bits, and you controlled the bottom 8. By now, you've seen that the subnet mask for a C network if you treated it as one subnet is 11111111 11111111 11111111 00000000. Reading from the left, the subnet mask would have 24 1s. In CIDR terms, a C network is a *slash 24* network. Thus, one of my C networks (206.246.253.0, mask 255.255.255.0) can be written "206.246.253/24." Grasping this /24 nomenclature is important because you'll see it on some routers. My Ascend router never asks for subnet masks—just slashes.

Where the new flexibility of CIDR comes in is that the InterNIC can in theory now not only define the A-, B-, and C-type networks, it can offer networks with subnet masks in between the A, B, and C networks. For example, suppose I wanted a network for 50 PCs. Before, the InterNIC would have to give me a C network, with 256 addresses. But now they can offer me a network with subnet mask 11111111 11111111 11111111 11000000 (255.255.255.192), giving me only 6 bits to play with. Two to the sixth power is 64, so I'd have 64 addresses to do with as I liked. This would be a *slash 26* (/26) network.

In summary, Table 17.2 shows how large each possible network type would be.

TABLE 17.2: CIDR NETWORK TYPES

InterNIC Network Type	"Subnet Mask" for Entire Network	Approximate Number of IP Addresses
slash 0	0.0.0.0	4 billion
slash 1	128.0.0.0	2 billion
slash 2	192.0.0.0	1 billion
slash 3	224.0.0.0	500 million
slash 4	240.0.0.0	25 million
slash 5	248.0.0.0	128 million
slash 6	252.0.0.0	64 million
slash 7	254.0.0.0	32 million
slash 8	255.0.0.0	16 million
slash 9	255.128.0.0	8 million
slash 10	255.192.0.0	4 million
slash 11	255.224.0.0	2 million
slash 12	255.240.0.0	1 million
slash 13	255.248.0.0	524,288
slash 14	255.252.0.0	262,144
slash 15	255.254.0.0	131,072
slash 16	255.255.0.0	65,536
slash 17	255.255.128.0	32,768
slash 18	255.255.192.0	16,384
slash 19	255.255.224.0	8192
slash 20	255.255.240.0	4096
slash 21	255.255.248.0	2048
slash 22	255.255.252.0	1024
slash 23	255.255.254.0	512
slash 24	255.255.255.0	256
slash 25	255.255.255.128	128
slash 26	255.255.255.192	64
slash 27	255.255.255.224	32
slash 28	255.255.255.240	16
slash 29	255.255.255.248	8
slash 30	255.255.255.252	4
slash 31	255.255.255.254	2
slash 32	255.255.255.255	1

I hope it's obvious that I included all of those networks just for the sake of completeness, as some of them simply aren't available, like the slash 0, and some just don't make sense, like the slash 31—it only gives you two addresses, which would be immediately required for network number and broadcast address, leaving none behind for you to actually use. The smallest network that the American subgroup of the IANA, ARIN, will allocate a network is a slash 20, a 4,094-address network.

CIDR is a fact of life if you're trying to get a network nowadays. With the information in this section, you'll more easily be able to understand what an ISP is talking about when it says it can get you a slash 26 network.

What IP *Doesn't* Do: Error Checking

Whether you're on *an* intranet or *the* Internet, it looks like your data gets bounced around quite a bit. How can you prevent it from becoming damaged? Let's look briefly at that, and that'll segue to a short talk on TCP.

An IP packet contains a bit of data called a *checksum header*, which checks whether the header information was damaged on the way from sender to receiver.

Many data communications protocols use checksums that operate like this: I send you some data. You use the checksum to make sure the data wasn't damaged in transit, perhaps by line noise. Once you're satisfied that the data was not damaged, you send me a message that says, "OK—I got it." If the checksum indicates that it did *not* get to you undamaged, then you send me a message that says, "That data was damaged—please resend it," and I resend it. Such messages are called ACKs and NAKs— positive or negative acknowledgments of data. Protocols that use this check-and-acknowledge approach are said to provide *reliable* service.

But IP does not provide reliable service. If an IP receiver gets a damaged packet, it just discards the packet and says nothing to the receiver. Surprised? I won't keep you in suspense: It's TCP that provides the reliability. The IP header checksum is used to see if a header is valid; if it isn't, then the datagram is discarded.

This underscores IP's job. IP is not built to provide end-to-end guaranteed transmission of data. IP exists mainly for one reason: Routing. We'll revisit routing a bit later, when I describe the specifics of how to accomplish IP routing on a Win2K machine.

But whose job *is* end-to-end integrity, if not IP's? The answer: Its buddy's, TCP.

TCP (Transmission Control Protocol)

I said earlier that IP handled routing and really didn't concern itself that much with whether the message got to its final destination or not. If there are seven IP hops from one point to the next, then each hop is an independent action—there's no coordination, no notion of whether a particular hop is hop number three out of seven. Each IP hop is totally unaware of the others. How, then, could we use IP to provide reliable service?

IP packets are like messages in a bottle. Drop the bottle in the ocean, and you have no guarantee that the message got to whomever you want to receive it. But suppose you hired a "message-in-the-bottle end-to-end manager." Such a person (let's call her Gloria) would take your message, put it in a bottle, and toss it in the ocean. That person would also have a partner on the other side of the ocean (let's call him Gaston), and when Gaston received a message in a bottle from Gloria, Gaston would then pen a short message saying "Gloria, I got your message," put *that* message in a bottle, and drop that bottle into the ocean.

If Gloria didn't get an acknowledgment from Gaston within, say, three months, then she'd drop *another* bottle into the ocean with the original message in it. In data communications terms, we'd say that Gloria "timed out" on the transmission path and was *resending*.

Yeah, I know, this is a somewhat goofy analogy, but understand the main point: We hired Gloria and Gaston to ensure that our inherently unreliable message-in-a-bottle network became reliable. Gloria will keep sending and resending until she gets a response from Gaston. Notice that she doesn't create a whole new transmission medium, like radio or telephone; she merely adds a layer of her own watchfulness to the existing transmission protocol.

Now think of IP as the message in the bottle. TCP, the Transmission Control Protocol, is just the Gloria/Gaston team. TCP provides reliable end-to-end service.

By the way, TCP provides some other services, most noticeably something called *sockets*, which I will discuss in a moment. As TCP has value besides its reliability feature, TCP also has a "cousin" protocol that acts very much like it but does *not* guarantee end-to-end integrity. That protocol is called UDP, or the User Datagram Protocol.

That's basically the idea behind TCP. Its main job is the orderly transmission of data from one intranet host to another. Its main features include:

- Handshake
- Packet sequencing
- Flow control
- Error handling

Whereas IP has no manners—it just shoves data at a computer whether that computer is ready for it or not—TCP makes sure that each side is properly introduced before attempting to transfer. TCP sets up the connection.

Sequencing

As IP does not use a virtual circuit, different data packets may end up arriving at different times and, in fact, in a different order. Imagine a simple intranet transferring four segments of data across a network with multiple possible pathways. The first segment takes the high road, so to speak, and is delayed. The second, third, and fourth do not and so get to the destination more quickly. TCP's job on the receiving side is to then reassemble things in order.

Flow Control

Along with sequencing is flow control. What if 50 segments of data had been sent and they all arrived out of order? The receiver would have to hold them all in memory before sorting them out and writing them to disk. Part of what TCP worries about is *pacing* the data—not sending it to the receiver until the receiver is ready for it.

Error Detection/Correction

And finally, TCP handles error detection and correction, as I've already said. Beyond that, TCP is very efficient in the way that it does error handling. Some protocols acknowledge each and every block, generating a large overhead of blocks. TCP, in contrast, does not do that. It tells the other side, "I am capable of accepting and buffering some number of blocks. Don't expect an acknowledgment until I've gotten that number of blocks. And if a block is received incorrectly, I will not acknowledge it, so if I don't acknowledge as quickly as you expect me to, then just go ahead and resend the block."

Sockets and the Winsock Interface

Just about anything that you want to do with the Internet or your company's intranet involves two programs talking to each other. When you browse someone's Web site, you have a program (your Web browser, a *client* program) communicating with their Web server (obviously, a *server* program). Using the File Transfer Protocol, or FTP, which I'll discuss later in this chapter, requires that one machine be running a program called an *FTP server* and that another computer be running an *FTP client*. Internet mail requires that a mail client program talk to a mail server program—and those are just a few examples.

Connecting a program in one machine to another program in another machine is kind of like placing a telephone call. The sender must know the phone number of the receiver, and the receiver must be around his or her phone, waiting to pick it up. In the TCP world, a phone number is called a *socket*. A socket is composed of three parts: the IP address of the receiver, which we've already discussed, the receiving program's *port number*, which we *haven't* yet discussed, and whether it's a TCP port or a UDP port—each protocol has its own set.

Suppose the PC on your desk running Windows 2000 wants to get a file from the FTP site which is really the PC on *my* desk running Windows 2000. Obviously, for this to happen, we've got to know each other's IP addresses. But that's not all; after all, in my PC I have a whole bunch of programs running (my network connection, my word processor, my operating system, my personal organizer, the FTP server, and so on). So if TCP says, "Hey, Mark's machine, I want to talk to you," then my machine would reply, "Which *one* of us—the word processor, the e-mail program, or what?" So the TCP/IP world assigns a 16-bit number to each program that wants to send or receive TCP information, a number called the *port* of that program. The most popular Internet applications have had particular port numbers assigned to them, and those port numbers are known as *well-known ports*. Some well-known port numbers include FTP (TCP ports 20 and 21), the common mail protocol SMTP (TCP port 25), Web servers (TCP port 80), Network News Transfer Protocol (NNTP, TCP port 119), and the Post Office Protocol version 3 (POP3, TCP port 110).

How Sockets Work

So, for instance, suppose I've written a TCP/IP-based *chat* program that allows me to type messages to you and receive typed messages from you. This fictitious chat program might get port number 1500. Anyone running chat, then, would install it on port 1500. Then, to chat with my computer which is at an imaginary IP address of 123.124.55.67, your chat program would essentially "place a phone call"—that is, set up a TCP session—with port 1500 at address 123.124.55.67, sometimes written 123.124.55.67:1500. The combination of port 1500 with IP address 123.124.55.67 is a *socket address*.

In order for your computer to chat with my computer, my computer must be *ready* to chat. So I have to run my chat program. It would probably say something like, "Do you want to chat with anyone, or do you just want to wait to be called?" I tell it that I just want to wait to be called, so it sits quietly in my PC's memory, but first it tells the PC, "If anyone calls for me, wake me up—I'm willing to take calls at port 1500." That's called a *passive open* on TCP.

Then, when your computer wants to chat with my computer, it sends an *active open* request to my computer, saying, "Want to talk?" It also says, "I can accept up to *x* bytes of data in my buffers." My computer responds by saying, "Sure, I'll talk, and I can accept up to *y* bytes of data in my buffers."

The two computers then blast data back and forth, being careful not to overflow the other computer's buffers. When a buffer's worth of information is sent by your computer, then your computer doesn't send my computer any more data until my computer acknowledges that it received the data.

Once the chat is over, both sides politely say "good-bye" and hang up. My computer can choose to continue to wait for incoming calls, as before.

Winsock Sockets

The value of sockets is that they provide a uniform way to write programs that exploit the underlying Internet communications structure. If, for example, I want to write a networked version of the game Battleship, then I might want to be able to quickly turn out versions for Windows, OS/2, the Mac, and Unix machines. But maybe I don't know much about communications, and don't *want* to know much. (I'm probably supposed to note here that Battleship is a registered trademark of Milton Bradley or someone like that; consider it done.) I could just sit down with my C compiler and bang out a Battleship that runs on Unix machines. Just a few code changes, and *presto*! I have my PC version.

But the PC market requires some customization, and so a particular version of the sockets interface, called Winsock, was born. It's essentially the sockets interface but modified a bit to work better in a PC environment.

The benefit of Winsock is that all vendors of TCP/IP software support an identical Winsock programming interface (well, identical in theory, anyway) and so TCP/IP-based programs should run as well atop FTP software's TCP/IP stack as it would atop the TCP/IP stack that ships with NT. That's why you can plop your Netscape Web browser on just about any PC with TCP/IP and it should work without any trouble.

Internet Host Names

Thus far, I've referred to a lot of numbers; hooking up to my Web server, then, seems to require that you point your Web browser to IP address 206.246.253.200, TCP port number 80, which is written "206.246.253.200:80" in socket terminology.

Of course, you don't actually do that. When you send e-mail to your friends, you don't send it to 199.45.23.17; you send it to something like robbie@somefirm.com. What's IP got to do with it?

IP addresses are useful because they're precise and because they're easy to subnet. But they're tough to remember, and people generally prefer more English-sounding names. So TCP/IP allows us to group one or more TCP/IP networks into groups called *domains*, groups that will share a common name like microsoft.com, senate.gov, army.mil, or mit.edu.

Machines within a domain will have names that include the domain name; for example, within my mmco.com domain I have machines named micron133.mmco.com, narn.mmco.com, minbar.mmco.com, zhahadum.mmco.com, and serverted.mmco.com. Those specific machine names are called *host names*.

How does TCP/IP connect the English names—the *host* names—to the IP addresses? And how can I sit at my PC in mmco.com and get the information I need to be able to find another host called archie.au when archie's all the way on the other side of the world in Australia?

Simple—with HOSTS, DNS, and in the next chapter and if you have pre-Windows 2000 machines on your network, WINS. The process of converting a name to its corresponding IP address is called *name resolution*. Again, how does it work? Read on.

Simple Naming Systems (HOSTS)

When you set up your subnet, you don't want to explicitly use IP addresses every time you want to run some TCP/IP utility and hook up with another computer in your subnet. So, instead, you create a file called HOSTS that looks like this:

```
199.34.57.50   keydata.mmco.com
199.34.57.129  serverted.mmco.com
```

This is just a simple ASCII text file. Each host goes on one line, and the line starts off with the host's IP address. Enter at least one space and the host's English name. Do this for each host. You can even give multiple names in the HOSTS file:

```
199.34.57.50   keydata.mmco.com markspc
199.34.57.129  serverted.mmco.com serverpc bigsv
```

You can even add comments, with the octothorp (#):

```
199.34.57.50   keydata.mmco.com markspc #The Big Dog's machine
199.34.57.129  serverted.mmco.com serverpc bigsv
```

Ah, but now comes the really rotten part.

You have to put one of these HOSTS files on *every single workstation*. That means that every single time you change anyone's HOSTS file, you have to go around and change *everybody's* HOSTS file. Every workstation must contain a copy of this file, which is basically a telephone directory of every machine in your subnet. It's a pain, yes, but it's simple. If you're thinking, "Why can't I just put a central HOSTS file on a server and do all my administration with *that* file?"—what you're really asking for is a *name server*, and I'll show you two of them, the Domain Name System (DNS) and the Windows Internet Name Service (WINS), in this chapter.

You must place the HOSTS file in \WINNT\SYSTEM32\DRIVERS\ETC on an NT or Windows 2000 system, in the Windows directory on a Windows for Workgroups or Windows 95/98 machine, and wherever the network software is installed in other kinds of machines (DOS or OS/2).

HOSTS is reread every time your system does a name resolution; you needn't reboot to see a change in HOSTS take effect.

Domain Name System (DNS)

HOSTS is a pain, but it's a necessary pain if you want to communicate within your subnet. How does IP find a name outside of your subnet or outside of your domain?

Suppose someone at exxon.com wanted to send a file to a machine at minasi.com. Surely the exxon.com HOSTS files don't contain the IP address of my company, and vice versa?

Well, back when the Internet was small, HOSTS was sufficient—the exxon.com and minasi.com machine *would* have found each other in HOSTS back in 1980. The few dozen people on the early Internet just all used the same small HOSTS file. With the Internet's machine population in the hundreds of millions, however, that's just not practical; we needed something better.

The Internet community came up with an answer in 1984: Distribute the responsibility for names. That's done by the Domain Name System, or DNS. There is a central naming clearinghouse for *the* Internet called the InterNIC Registration Services. (Obviously, if you're only running a private intranet, then *you* perform the function of name manager.)

Instead of trying to keep track of the name and IP address of every single machine in the Internet, the InterNIC requires that every Internet domain have at least two machines running which contain a database of that domain's machines. These machines are called *DNS servers*.

The InterNIC then needs only to know the IP address of the domain's DNS servers, and when a request for a name resolution comes to the InterNIC's servers, the InterNIC servers just refer the questioner to the domain in question's local DNS machines.

Thus, if you wanted to visit my Web site at `www.minasi.com`, you'd start up your Web browser and point it at `http://www.minasi.com`. Before your browser could show you anything, however, it would need to *find* the machine named `www.minasi.com`. So it would fire off a DNS query, "What's the IP address of `www.minasi.com`?" to its local DNS server. The local DNS server probably wouldn't know, and so it would ask the InterNIC's DNS servers. The InterNIC's servers would know that the IP address for minasi.com's DNS server is 206.246.253.111 and would tell your local DNS server that it could find `www.minasi.com`'s IP address by asking the question of the 206.246.253.111 machine. So your local DNS server would then re-ask the question, this time of my local DNS server, and would then get the answer 206.246.253.200. And most DNS servers remember past queries for a few hours or perhaps a day, so if you revisited my Web site the same day, when your Web browser asked your local DNS server for the IP address of `www.minasi.com`, your local DNS server would respond, "206.246.253.200," without hesitation.

You've no doubt noticed that many Internet domains end with *.com*, but there are other endings as well. The InterNIC started off with six initial naming domains: EDU was for educational institutions, NET was for network providers, COM for commercial users, MIL was for military users (remember who built this?), ORG was for organizations, and GOV was for civilian government. For example, there is a domain on the Internet called whitehouse.gov; you can send Internet mail to the President that way, at `president@whitehouse.gov`. There are more root domains these days, like .fi for sites in Finland, .uk for sites in the United Kingdom, and so on.

What kind of computer do you need to run a DNS server? Just about any kind—there's DNS server software for IBM mainframes, DEC Vaxes, Unix and Linux, and of course, Windows 2000—in fact, a DNS server module not only ships with Windows 2000, you can't even run an Active Directory without a DNS server. You'll see how to set up a DNS server in the next chapter.

E-Mail Names: A Note

If you've previously messed around with e-mail under TCP/IP, then you may be wondering something about these addresses. After all, you don't send mail to minasi.com, you'd send it to a name like `help@minasi.com`. `help@minasi.com` is an e-mail address. The way it works is this: A group of users in a TCP/IP domain decide to implement mail.

In order to receive mail, a machine must be up and running, ready to accept mail from the outside world (that is, some other subnet or domain). Now, mail can arrive at any time of day, so this machine must be up and running all of the time. That seems to indicate that it would be a dumb idea to get mail delivered straight to your desktop. So, instead, TCP mail dedicates a machine to the mail router task of receiving mail from the outside world, holding that mail until you want to read it, taking mail that you wish to send somewhere else, and routing that mail to some other mail router. The name of the most common TCP/IP mail router program is *sendmail*. The name of the protocol used most commonly for routing e-mail on the Internet, by the way, is the *Simple Mail Transfer Protocol*, or SMTP. Once e-mail is sitting on your local mail server, you then retrieve it via another mail protocol, the Post Office Protocol (POP3).

Unfortunately, Microsoft did not include an SMTP router or POP3 program in either the workstation or the server version of NT, so either you have to connect up to an existing mail router in order to get Internet mail or you have to buy a third-party mail product to work under NT or Windows 2000.

You can see how mail works in Figure 17.7.

FIGURE 17.7

The interrelationship of host names, e-mail names, and the Internet

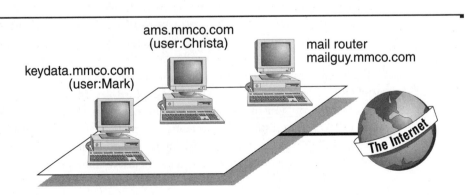

ams.mmco.com
(user:Christa)

mail router
mailguy.mmco.com

keydata.mmco.com
(user:Mark)

The Internet

In this small domain, we've got two users: Mark and Christa. Mark works on keydata .mmco.com, and Christa works on ams.mmco.com. Now, suppose Christa wants to send some mail to her friend Corky, executive director of Surfers of America; Corky's address is corky@surferdudes.org. She fires up a program on her workstation, which is called a *mail client*. The mail client allows her to create and send new messages as well as receive incoming messages. She sends the message and closes her mail client. Notice that her mail client software doesn't do routing—it just lets her create, send, and receive messages.

The mail client has been configured to send messages to an SMTP server, which is running in this subnet on mailguy.mmco.com. mailguy is kind of the post office (in Internet lingo, a *mail router*) for this group of users. The SMTP server on mailguy.mmco.com stores the message, and it then sends the message off to the machine with the DNS name surferdudes.org, trusting IP to route the message correctly to surferdudes. Hmmm... there's no one machine named surferdudes.org; where should the mail go? As you'll learn in the next chapter, a DNS administrator can advertise that e-mail should go to a particular machine. Thus, surferdudes.org might have a machine named po.surferdudes .org; when mailguy.mmco.com tries to send the mail to corky, mailguy first asks DNS, "What machine is supposed to get mail for surferdudes?" and DNS replies, "po.surferdudes.org."

Additionally, the SMTP server knows the names Christa and Mark. It is the workstation that is the interface to the outside world *vis-à-vis* mail. Note, by the way, that *DNS* has no idea who Mark or Christa is; DNS is concerned with *host* names, not *e-mail* names. It's DNS that worries about how to find mailguy.mmco.com.

A bit later, Corky gets the message and sends a reply to Christa. The reply does *not* go to Christa's machine ams.mmco.com; instead, it goes to mailguy.mmco.com because Corky sent mail to christa@mmco.com. The mail system sends the messages to mmco.com, but what machine has the address mmco.com? Simple: DNS directs it to send mail for mmco.com to mailguy.mmco.com.

Eventually, Christa starts up the mail client program once again. The mail program uses POP3 to send a query to the local mail router mailguy.mmco.com, saying, "Any new mail for Christa?" There *is* mail, and Christa reads it.

Getting onto an Intranet

So far, I've talked quite a bit about how an intranet works and what kinds of things there are that you can do with an intranet. But I haven't told you enough yet to actually get *on* an Internet, whether it's your company's private intranet or *the* Internet.

- You can connect to a multiuser system and appear to the Internet as a dumb terminal.

- You can connect to an Internet provider via a serial port and either a protocol called the Serial Line Interface Protocol (SLIP) or one called the Point-to-Point Protocol (PPP) and appear to the Internet as a host.

- You can be part of a local area network that is an Internet subnet and then load TCP/IP software on your system and appear to the Internet as a host.

Each of these options has pros and cons, as you'll see. The general rule is that in order to access an intranet, all you basically have to do is to connect up to a computer that is already on an intranet.

The essence of an intranet is in *packet switching*, a kind of network game of hot potato whereby computers act communally to transfer each other's data around. Packet switching is what makes it possible to add subnetworks on-the-fly.

Dumb Terminal Connection

This was once a common way to attach to the Internet. You'd dial up to a multiuser system of some kind—usually a Unix box of some stripe—and do simple terminal emulation. You'd then have a character-based session with typed commands only—no mouse, no graphics. Very macho, but not as much fun as surfing with a graphical Web browser. On the other hand, the distant multiuser machine did all the heavy lifting, computing-wise.

Unfortunately, this terminal access approach was kind of limited. Suppose, for example, that I live in Virginia (which is true) and I connect to the Internet via a host in Maine (which is not true). From the Internet's point of view, I'm not in an office in Virginia; instead, I'm wherever the host that I'm connected to is. I work in Virginia, but if I were dialing a host in Maine, then from the Internet's point of view I'd be in Maine. Any requests that I make for file transfers, for example, wouldn't go to Virginia—they'd go to my host in Maine.

Now, that can be a bit of a hassle. Say I'm at my Virginia location logged on to the Internet via the Maine host. I get onto Microsoft's FTP site—I'll cover FTP in Chapter 18, but basically FTP is just a means to provide a library of files to the outside world—and I grab a few files, perhaps an updated video driver. The FTP program says, "I got the file," but the file is now on the host in Maine. That means that I'm only half done, as I now have to run some other kind of file transfer program to move the file from the host in Maine to my computer in Virginia.

SLIP/PPP Serial Connection

If you've got one of those $10/month or $20/month Internet accounts, then you fit in this category.

A somewhat better way to connect to a TCP/IP-based network—that is, an intranet or the Internet—is by a direct serial connection to an existing intranet host. If you use

PCs, then you may know of a program called LapLink that allows two PCs to share each other's hard disks via their RS232 serial ports; SLIP/PPP are similar ideas. An intranet may have a similar type of connection called a SLIP or PPP connection. The connection needn't be a serial port, but it often is. SLIP is the *Serial Line Interface Protocol*, an older protocol that I sometimes think of as the *simple* line interface protocol. There's really nothing to SLIP—no error checking, no security, no flow control. It's the simplest protocol imaginable: Just send the data, then send a special byte that means, "This is the end of the data." PPP, in contrast, was designed to retain the low overhead of SLIP and yet to include some extra information required so that more intelligent parts of an intranet—items like routers—could use it effectively. The *Point to Point Protocol* works by establishing an explicit link between one side and another, then uses a simple error-checking system called a *checksum* to monitor noise on the line.

Which protocol should you use? The basic rule that I use is that SLIP doesn't provide error checking but uses less overhead, and PPP provides error checking and uses more overhead. Therefore, when I'm using error-correcting modems, I use SLIP. On noisy lines and without error-correcting modems, I use PPP.

You may use PPP even if you *don't* have an account with an ISP. Windows 2000 supports PPP via Routing and Remote Access Service (RRAS), so if you dial into your company's servers, you do that with PPP. Windows 2000 only supports SLIP on the client side: You can dial into a SLIP server with Dial-Up Networking, but RRAS won't let you set up a Windows 2000 system as a SLIP server.

LAN Connection

The most common way to connect to an intranet is simply by being a LAN workstation on a local area network that is an intranet subnetwork. Again, this needn't be *the* Internet—almost any LAN can use the TCP/IP protocol suite.

This is the connection that most Windows 2000 servers will use to provide TCP/IP services. Microsoft's main reason for implementing TCP/IP on NT is to provide an alternative to NetBEUI, as NetBEUI is quick and applicable to small networks but inappropriate for large corporate networks. In contrast, TCP/IP has always been good for intranetworking, but one suffered tremendously in speed. That's not true anymore, however; for example, a quick test of TCP/IP versus NetBEUI on one of my workstations showed network read rates of 1250K/sec for NetBEUI and 833K/sec for TCP/IP and write rates of 312K/sec for NetBEUI and 250K/sec for TCP/IP. Again, TCP's slower, but not by a lot. And NetBEUI doesn't go over routers.

Terminal Connections versus Other Connections

Before moving on to the next topic, I'd like to return to the difference between a terminal connection and a SLIP, PPP, or LAN connection. In Figure 17.8, you see three PCs on an Ethernet attached to two minicomputers, which in turn serve four dumb terminals.

FIGURE 17.8

*When Internet connec-
tions involve IP
numbers and when
they don't*

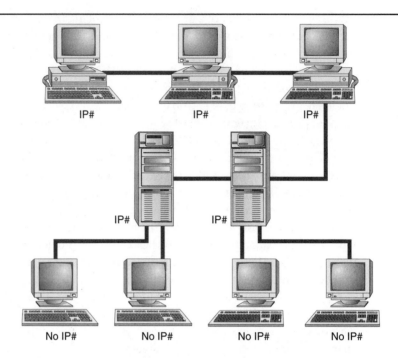

The minicomputer-to-minicomputer link might be SLIP or PPP, or then again they might be LANed together. Notice that only the *computers* in this scenario have intranetwork protocol (IP) addresses. Whenever you send mail to one of the people on the PCs at the top of the picture, it goes to that person's PC. If you were to scrutinize the IP addresses—and most of the time, you will not—you'd see that everyone had the same IP address. In contrast, the people at the *bottom* of the picture get their mail sent to one of the minicomputers, and so in this example, each pair of terminals shares an IP address. If Shelly and George in your office access your company's intranet through terminals connected to the same computer, then a close look at mail from them would show that they have the same IP address. But, if you think about it, you already knew that; if you send mail to george@mailbox.acme.com and to shelly@mailbox.acme.com, then the machine name to which the mail goes is the same; it's just the usernames that vary.

So, in summary: If you want to get onto *the* Internet from a remote location, then your best bet is to sign up with a service that will bill you monthly for connect charges, like Delphi. To attach to a private intranet, you need to dial up to a multiuser computer on that intranet, or you need a SLIP or PPP connection, or you have to be on a workstation on a LAN that's part of that intranet. You then need to talk to your local network guru about getting the software installed on your system that will allow your computer to speak TCP/IP so that it can be part of your intranet.

NOTE There *is* one case where Figure 17.8 isn't complete. If one of the terminals pictured is not simply a dumb ASCII terminal attached to a minicomputer but is instead a Windows Terminal—still a dumb terminal, but one built to work specifically with Windows 2000 Terminal Services, Windows Terminal Server 4, or Citrix Metaframe—then that terminal will have its own IP address.

So Where Do I Get My IP Addresses?

You can't get anywhere in the next section without some IP addresses. How does what you've read so far in this chapter relate to where you should go to get IP addresses?

- If you're part of a large corporation, there is almost certainly a group who manages (or doles out, in other words) the IP addresses; if so, go to them for the IP addresses you'll need.

- If you're just playing around with this, then you can use any addresses you like, provided you're not connected to the Internet. But it's a good idea to use one of the RFC 1918 ranges in any case—it's a good habit.

- If you're with a small firm and it's your job to get the firm on the Internet, then you've got two tasks. First, you've got to figure out how you'll be connected. Do you need constant, 24/7 connection to the Internet? You will if you intend to run your own Web or mail servers on your site, and in that case, you'll probably need to get a Frame Relay connection to your ISP. On the other hand, does your firm just need periodic access to the Internet? Then you may be perfectly happy with the cheaper alternative of some kind of shared dial-on-demand system, either using analog modems or ISDN. Second, how many IP addresses do you need? If you put in a NAT router, by purchasing one from Cisco or some other router vendor, or if you use a Windows 2000 machine as a NAT router (you'll read later how to do that), then you'll only need one dedicated IP address from your ISP. On the other hand, if you want all of your firm's computers to have their own routable IP addresses, then you should expect to have to pay your ISP a bit more for them than you would for just one IP address—but having all routable IP addresses keeps things simpler, in my experience.

- If you're a home user with an existing Internet connection, such as a dial-up modem, an ISDN dial connection, cable modem, or DSL, and you want to share that connection with other machines on a home network, then just use Internet Connection Sharing, which you'll read about later in this chapter.

The Basics of Setting Up TCP/IP on Windows 2000 with Static IP Addresses

Enough talking about TCP/IP internetworking; let's do it, and do it with Windows 2000.

Traditionally, one of the burdens of an IP administrator has been that she must assign separate IP numbers to each machine, a bit of a bookkeeping hassle. You can adopt this "static" IP address approach, and in fact you will *have* to assign static IP addresses to at least a few of your systems. In actual fact, however, you'll find that assigning a static IP address to every single IP-using computer in your enterprise soon palls, and you'll assign IP addresses to most systems automatically with the Dynamic Host Configuration Protocol, covered in the next chapter.

No network can completely avoid static IP addresses, however, so we'll start out with this older method of putting an IP address on a Windows 2000 computer. In the next chapter, we'll take up dynamic IP addressing with DHCP.

Here's the most basic set of TCP/IP configuration tasks, and the first ones we'll tackle:

1. Load the TCP/IP protocol on the Windows 2000 system.

2. Set the IP address and subnet, default gateway, and DNS server.

3. Prepare the HOSTS file, if you're going to use one.

4. Test the connection with Ping.

Let's take a look at those steps, one by one.

Installing TCP/IP Software on a Windows 2000 Machine

Before you can configure TCP/IP on a Windows 2000 system, you've got to have TCP/IP loaded. Now, the chances are very good that you already have TCP/IP loaded because it is the default protocol—if you installed Windows 2000 and chose Typical Settings in the Network Setup part, then you've already got TCP/IP on your system, so skip ahead to the next section, "Configuring TCP/IP with a Static IP Address."

If not, however, it's simple to install it. Open up the Control Panel (Start/Settings/Control Panel) and then open up the Network and Dial-Up Connections applet that you'll find in Control Panel. You'll see something like Figure 17.9.

This window describes each NIC in your system and also lists every item in your Dial-Up Networking directory—so if you've got your system set up to be able to dial an ISP or perhaps a distant Windows 2000 network, then you'll see a line for each of those DUN directory entries—as well as an icon which can start a wizard that will add new DUN directory entries. This computer hasn't got a modem and therefore has never dialed up anywhere, so there are just the two entries. If this machine had two NICs, then you'd see two Local Area Connection entries.

FIGURE 17.9

Network and Dial-Up

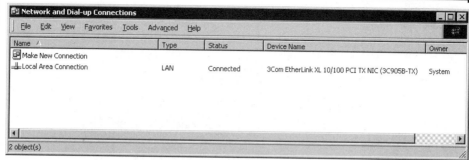

I want to install TCP/IP on the NIC, so right-click that and choose Properties, and you'll see a dialog box like Figure 17.10.

FIGURE 17.10

Properties for the NIC

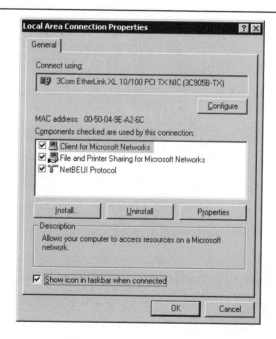

I set up this example machine with just the NetBEUI protocol, as you see in the dialog box. To add TCP/IP, click the Install button and you'll get a choice of things to install, as you see in Figure 17.11.

Click Protocol and Add and you get a list of protocols that you can add. Select Internet Protocol (TCP/IP), as you see in Figure 17.12.

Click OK, and the machine will run the disks for a while as it installs TCP/IP with the default settings, which will automatically configure TCP/IP on this system with DHCP. We're going to change that in the next section, but you've now got TCP/IP on your system.

FIGURE 17.11

Choosing to install an adapter, protocol, or service

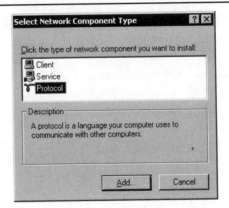

FIGURE 17.12

Choosing to add TCP/IP protocol

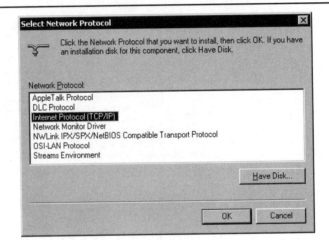

Configuring TCP/IP with a Static IP Address

Now let's apply an IP address to the TCP/IP software on this system. If you're not already there, get to the Local Area Network Connection property page—right-click My Network Places, choose Properties, then right-click Local Area Connection in the dialog box that follows, and choose Properties on the resulting context menu. (You can also get to it from the Control Panel, as described in the preceding section.) It'll look something like Figure 17.13.

FIGURE 17.13

LAN Connection
property page

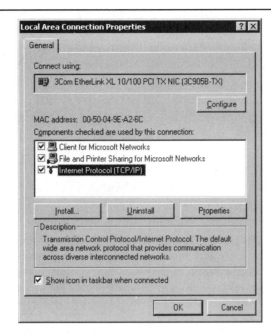

Click Internet Protocol (TCP/IP) and then the Properties button. You'll see a dialog box that looks like Figure 17.14, or anyway it will once we're through with it.

FIGURE 17.14

IP Properties after
modification

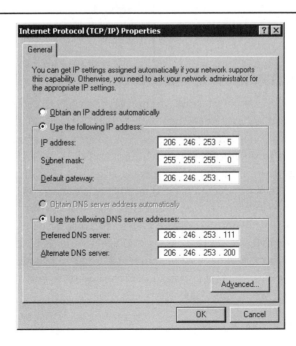

When you first see this dialog box, the Obtain an IP Address Automatically and Obtain DNS Server Address Automatically radio buttons will be selected. You should click the Use the Following IP Address and Use the Following DNS Server Addresses radio buttons. As mentioned earlier, you'll need to know four things to configure this screen—your IP address, the subnet mask, the IP address of your default gateway, and the IP addresses of one or more DNS server. In the case of the computer I'm configuring here, the IP address is 206.246.253.5, the subnet mask is 255.255.255.0, the default gateway is 206.246.253.1, and I've got two DNS servers, at 206.246.253.111 and 206.246.253.200. You might not use any DNS servers (although I can't imagine why); in that case, be sure to set up a HOSTS file and remember that it goes in the machine's \winnt\system32\drivers\etc directory.

WARNING Do not—and I repeat, do not—simply type in numbers to make your dialog box match mine. I can pretty much guarantee that if you type in IP addresses from my network at your location, it's not going to work. Again, you must get IP addresses from either your local network folks, an arm of the IANA, or an ISP.

Click OK to clear the IP and LAN property pages, and you'll have your IP address configured. But does it work? Read on.

Testing Your IP Configuration

There are two basic tools you'll use to verify that TCP/IP's working on your system: IPCONFIG and Ping.

IPCONFIG

First, check your IP configuration by opening up a command prompt and typing **ipconfig /all;** you'll then see a screen like Figure 17.15.

IPCONFIG/ALL should be your first step when checking a TCP/IP installation or when troubleshooting one. This particular IPCONFIG output starts out with some general information about this machine and then displays specific information about the Ethernet adapter. It's laid out like this because, in some cases, you may have two or more NICs in a system, and each NIC will have an IP address. Additionally, you may have a modem on your system and may be connected to the Internet via a dial-up connection. In that case, you'd again have more than one IP address—your Ethernet card would have an IP address (the one you just assigned it if you were following along with the text above), and your modem would have an IP address that your ISP gave it when you dialed up.

FIGURE 17.15

IPCONFIG /ALL output

```
Command Prompt                                                        _ □ X

C:\>ipconfig /all

Windows 2000 IP Configuration

        Host Name . . . . . . . . . . . . : ca
        Primary DNS Suffix . . . . . . . : win2ktest.com
        Node Type . . . . . . . . . . . . : Hybrid
        IP Routing Enabled. . . . . . . . : No
        WINS Proxy Enabled. . . . . . . . : No
        DNS Suffix Search List. . . . . . : win2ktest.com

Ethernet adapter Local Area Connection:

        Connection-specific DNS Suffix  . :
        Description . . . . . . . . . . . : 3Com EtherLink XL 10/100 PCI TX NIC (3C905B-TX)
        Physical Address. . . . . . . . . : 00-50-04-9E-A2-6C
        DHCP Enabled. . . . . . . . . . . : No
        IP Address. . . . . . . . . . . . : 206.246.253.5
        Subnet Mask . . . . . . . . . . . : 255.255.255.0
        Default Gateway . . . . . . . . . : 206.246.253.1
        DNS Servers . . . . . . . . . . . : 206.246.253.111
                                            206.246.253.200
```

Anyway, looking at the IPCONFIG output, A is the machine's name—I was just using one-letter names the day that I was setting this machine up.

 WARNING In general, you should avoid underscores in your computer names. Microsoft's old-style NetBIOS-based networking doesn't mind it, but the Internet document on legal Internet names, RFC 952 (October 1985), doesn't permit underscores. According to RFC 952 in its "assumptions" section, each piece of an Internet name can be no more than 24 characters long—that is, each piece between the periods—and the only legal characters are a–z, 0–9, and the hyphen/minus sign. In fact, the earliest 32-bit Microsoft TCP/IP software, the code that shipped with Windows for Workgroups 3.11, would simply refuse to work on a machine with an underscore in its name. That's not true anymore, and in fact, Active Directory uses a fair number of underscored names, but that's acceptable, as AD communications will mainly just go on amongst computers running Microsoft software. But avoid underscores in workstation names as it may potentially cause trouble when trying to use resources on the Internet that may be running on computers that aren't running Microsoft software.

Node Type answers the question, "How does the system convert an old-style NetBIOS name like \\SNOOPY into an IP address?" That's a long and complicated story, and we'll take it up in the next chapter. IP Routing Enabled asks whether or not this computer is acting as an IP router. As you saw in the example in the beginning of the chapter with machines A through H, you've got to have two IP connections to do that, so this clearly isn't a potential router—but I'll show you before the end of the chapter how to make a Windows 2000 machine into an IP router. I'll explain WINS Proxy Enabled in the next chapter.

Looking at the specific information under Ethernet Adapter Local Area Connection, the first entry is Adapter Domain Name. This refers not to a Windows 2000 domain but to an Internet domain name, like minasi.com, microsoft.com, or whitehouse .gov. Back in the NT 4 and earlier days, NT's TCP/IP software would only let you put a machine in just one Internet domain. That wasn't a big deal for most of us, but some people wanted their systems to be able to seem to be members of several domains, to have a sort of multiple citizenship in two or more domains. Such a machine might have a NIC in it which was connected to acme.com's network, and it might have another NIC in it connected to apex.com's network. If the machine's name were tadpole, then it might want to be able to be recognized both as tadpole.acme.com and tadpole.apex.com.

Now, when configuring tadpole under NT 4, you would have had to choose whether tadpole was in acme.com or apex.com—you couldn't choose both as you had to choose domain membership for the whole machine. Under Windows 2000, however, you can say that one NIC is a member of acme.com, and that the other is a member of apex.com. In my particular case, I really have no need to do that, which is why Adapter Domain Name is empty. In fact, I haven't set the Internet domain name for the adapter *or* the entire machine as I'm going to get to that a bit later in this chapter.

Next are the IP addresses of the two DNS servers, an English-like description of the NIC, and the NIC's MAC address. DHCP Enabled indicates whether I punched in the IP address directly or let DHCP set the IP address for me. As I set the IP address myself, the value is "no." If it were "yes," then—as you'll see in the next chapter—IPCONFIG would furnish more DHCP-specific information. Finally, IPCONFIG reports the IP address, subnet mask, and default gateway.

Ping

So all of the settings are correct—but can you reach out to the outside world? TCP/IP has a very handy little tool for finding out whether or not your TCP/IP software is up and running and whether or not you have a connection to another point—*Ping*.

Ping is a program that lets you send a short message to another TCP/IP node, asking, "Are you there?" If it is there, then it says yes to the ping, and Ping relays this information back to you. You can see an example of Ping in Figure 17.16.

FIGURE 17.16

A sample Ping output

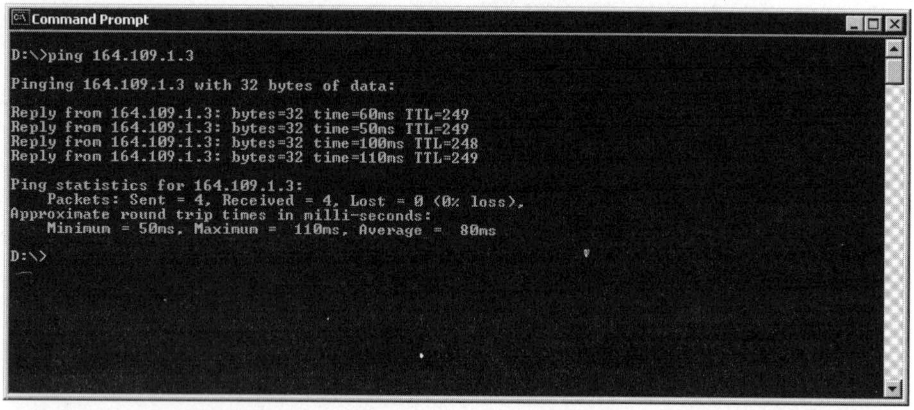

In the figure, I pinged the IP address of a server I know of on the Internet. The ping was successful, which is all that matters, and it's a very telling test as the address that I pinged is across the Internet from my system—the fact that I got a response from 164.109.1.3 means that not only is my TCP/IP software working across my segment and across my enterprise, but across the Internet as well.

But when *you're* testing your Internet software, don't use that IP address as there's no sense in flooding the Digital Express guys, the folks who own that machine. Instead, go ahead and ping my router—206.246.253.1. (I used to use www.microsoft.com as my Ping example, but now they've got their system rigged so that it won't respond to pings. I guess they couldn't figure out a way to charge for them.)

Use the approach outlined in the sidebar "How Do I Make Sure That TCP/IP Is Set Up Properly?" to get the most out of Ping.

How Do I Make Sure That TCP/IP Is Set Up Properly?

With these Ping tests, you're demonstrating two things: First, that your IP software can get a packet from your computer to the outside world (in other words, that your IP connectivity is functioning), and second, that your connection to a DNS server for name resolution is working.

First, test IP connectivity by pinging specific IP addresses.

In most cases, your connection will work the first time. Start out with an overall "does it work?" test by pinging some distant location on the Internet. As mentioned in the text, you're welcome to ping my router, 206.246.253.1. If that responds correctly, then you've demonstrated that your IP software can get out to the Internet and back.

If it doesn't work, then try pinging something not so far—your default gateway. (Actually, the next thing to do is to look around back and make sure the network cable is still in place. There's nothing more embarrassing than calling in outside network support only to find that your LAN cable fell out of the back of your computer.) If you can successfully ping the default gateway but not my router, then either your firm's external Internet routers have failed or perhaps your default gateway is configured incorrectly. Another tool you might try is tracert, a souped-up Ping that shows you each of the hops that the IP packet had to use to get from your machine to the destination. It's a command-line command: Just type **tracert** followed by an IP address or DNS name. You can see a sample output in the following figure.

Continued ▐▶

CONTINUED

```
Command Prompt                                                    _ □ X
C:\>tracert 164.109.1.3

Tracing route to ns.digex.net [164.109.1.3]
over a maximum of 30 hops:

  1   <10 ms   <10 ms    10 ms  206.246.253.1
  2    40 ms    51 ms    50 ms  209.96.135.97
  3    41 ms    50 ms    40 ms  hme22.core1.NewportNews.visi.net [206.246.195.62]
  4   381 ms   460 ms   451 ms  atm51.maeeast.WashDC.visi.net [206.246.247.186]
  5     *       61 ms   240 ms  mae-east2.digex.net [192.41.177.192]
  6    60 ms    50 ms   190 ms  iad1-core4-pos3-0.atlas.digex.net [165.117.52.194]
  7    70 ms    60 ms    90 ms  dca1-cpe1-pos11-0-0.atlas.digex.net [165.117.52.229]
  8    60 ms    70 ms    81 ms  ns.digex.net [164.109.1.3]

Trace complete.

C:\>
```

If you can't get to the default gateway, then try pinging another computer on your subnet. If you can get to another machine on your subnet but not the gateway, then perhaps you've got the wrong IP address for the gateway or perhaps the gateway is malfunctioning.

If you can't get to another system on your subnet—and I'm assuming that you've already walked over and checked that the other machine is up and running—then it may be that the IP software on your computer isn't running. Verify that by typing **ping 127.0.0.1**.

127.0.0.1 is the "loopback" address. IP software is designed to *always* report success on a ping to 127.0.0.1, if the IP software is functioning. Recheck that you've installed the TCP/IP software and rebooted after installing.

Once you're certain that IP works, try out DNS. Try pinging a distant location, but this time, don't do it by IP address, do it by name—try pinging www.whitehouse.gov, www.internic .net, or www.minasi.com. If the ping works, great; if not, check that you've got the right address punched in for your DNS server and then check the DNS server.

Configuration II: Setting Domain Names

Thus far, my computer's name is just plain CA, which is a mite shorter than most Internet names; one might expect a name more like a.minasi.com or the like, a name that looks like *specific machine name.organization name.root*, where *root* is a suffix like *com, gov, edu, org, net*, or some country identifier.

I intend for my computer CA to be part of an Internet domain named win2ktest.com, so its complete Internet name, or FQDN (Fully Qualified Domain Name), will be ca.win2ktest.com. What that really means, in essence, is that if someone pings ca.win2ktest.com, I want the machine to respond. If I decide to run Web server software on it later, then I want people to be able to see whatever content is on it by pointing their Web browsers to `http://ca.win2ktest.com` rather than having to use `http://206.246.253.5`. (I know this probably seems obvious to many of you, but stay with me, there's a point coming.)

I would have guessed that unless I found some way to tell CA that its full name was actually ca.win2ktest.com, it wouldn't know to respond when someone pinged it by its full name. But, as it turns out, that's wrong.

If you're sitting at your computer and you type **ping ca.win2ktest.com**, then your computer asks your local DNS server what ca.win2ktest.com's IP address is. *Then* your computer just pings that IP address, and ca.win2ktest.com never even knows *what* name your computer originally called it by. If one of the people running IBM's DNS servers were to decide on a whim to insert an entry into IBM's DNS database that said "iguana.ibm.com has IP address 206.246.253.5," then anyone anywhere pinging iguana.ibm.com would end up pinging my computer.

The point is, then, that in order to have my computer named CA recognized as ca.win2ktest.com, I've got to be concerned more with informing win2ktest.com's DNS server of CA's IP address than I should be concerned about telling *CA* that it's in win2ktest.com. So how do I ensure that win2ktest.com's DNS server finds out about CA? As it turns out, there are three ways to do this. (And even though handling DNS servers is a topic I won't get into until next chapter, it's worth covering this here.)

Add a Static DNS Entry

The first way to make the DNS server for the Internet domain win2ktest.com know that there's a machine named ca.win2ktest.com whose IP address is 206.246.253.5 is for an administrator to simply sit down at the DNS server and *tell* it. Depending on what kind of machine the DNS server is running on, the admin will either edit a file or run some kind of management tool. (Again, you'll see how to do that with Windows 2000's DNS server in the next chapter.)

Join the Windows 2000 Domain of the Same Name

The second way to tell the DNS server for the Internet domain win2ktest.com to include CA.win2ktest.com in its list of known hosts is for CA to join the win2ktest.com *Windows 2000* domain. This is a positive side effect of Windows 2000's unifying of Windows 2000 domain names and Internet (DNS) domain names. If the server named CA joins a *Windows 2000* domain named win2ktest.com, then by default the DNS server for the *Internet* domain named win2ktest.com adds a record in that Internet domain for ca.win2ktest.com. Doing that is fairly easy as long as you have a domain administrator account on win2ktest.com.

While logged onto CA with an account with local administrative powers, right-click the My Computer icon and choose Properties. You'll see a property page with several tabs, one of which is labeled Network Identification. Click that tab and you'll see a screen something like Figure 17.17.

FIGURE 17.17

Network Identification tab

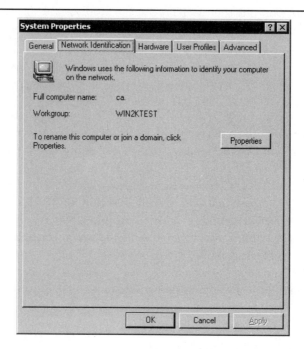

As you can see, this machine is not currently a member of a domain. (It doesn't matter that the workgroup is called win2ktest; workgroups are unrelated to domains insofar as we're concerned here.) Note that the full computer name is simply CA, not CA with anything after it. I'll join CA to the win2ktest.com domain, and we'll see that change. I click Properties and see something like Figure 17.18.

Note that I've already filled it in, changing the Workgroup radio button to the Domain radio button and filling in the domain name win2ktest.com. When I click OK, though, the dialog stops and asks me to demonstrate that I'm an administrator with the ability to create new domain accounts in the win2ktest.com domain, as you see in Figure 17.19.

FIGURE 17.18

Change Domain dialog

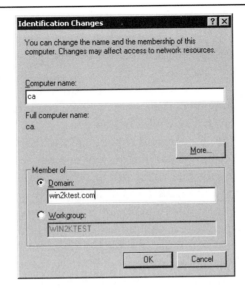

FIGURE 17.19

Checking domain
administration
credentials

I fill in an administrator name and password and click OK. The system runs the
hard disk for a while and finally I get the message "Welcome to the win2ktest.com
domain." And—no surprise—I've got to reboot to make it take effect. (Interestingly,
the screen in Figure 17.17, when it returns, reflects the name change I've just done,
with a yellow "caution" triangle indicating that the changes don't take effect until
after I reboot.)

After the reboot, two things happen: First, another look at the Network Identification
tab shows that the machine's full computer name is now ca.win2ktest.com. Second,
a peek in the DNS database for win2ktest.com shows that there's now an entry for
ca.win2ktest.com with IP address 206.246.253.5. But how does the DNS server know?
Because all Windows 2000 domains are partially built around a DNS server, and in particular a DNS server that accepts RFC 2136–compliant dynamic updates. When CA
booted up, it saw that it was a member of win2ktest.com and so it located the win2ktest
.com DNS server and added its name to the win2ktest.com names database.

Directly Entering the Domain Name into Network Identification

But wait—this may not always make sense. Pepsi owns Taco Bell, Pizza Hut, and Kentucky Fried Chicken. From an internal corporate point of view, it may be (I don't know, as I've never worked for any of the four entities) that everyone working for any of the four think of themselves as "Pepsi employees," and Pepsi may be headquartered in one large complex in New Bern, NC, birthplace of Pepsi-Cola. So from an internal management and IT point of view, they're one organization.

But to the outside world, the four entities seem to behave like separate firms, particularly on the Internet: A visit to `www.kfc.com`, `www.pepsi.com`, `www.tacobell.com`, and `www.pizzahut.com` gave no clue that they were all owned by the same firm. It just might be, then, that Pepsi doesn't want to be forced to make its DNS names jive with its Windows 2000 domain names. And they aren't, with Windows 2000. You just have to do a little fiddling in the Network Identification tab.

Now that CA's a member of the win2ktest.com Windows 2000 domain, let's say for the sake of example that we wanted it to be part of the minasi.com Internet (DNS) domain.

I start renaming CA DNS-wise by returning to Network Identification: Right-click My Computer, choose Properties, click the Network Identification tab. As before, click Properties. This time, however, click the More button and you'll see a dialog box like Figure 17.20.

FIGURE 17.20

NetBIOS Computer and Domain Names dialog

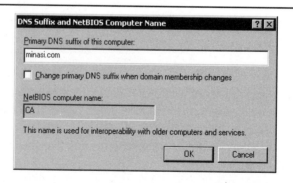

Notice the check box that says Change Primary DNS Suffix When Domain Membership Changes —*that's* the only thing connecting Internet domain names with Windows 2000 domain names! To let this computer be part of the minasi.com Internet domain but still be part of the Windows 2000 win2ktest.com domain, I just uncheck the box, and in Primary DNS Suffix of This Computer, I just fill in minasi.com. Of course, after such a momentous change, a reboot is required!

Before leaving this topic, I should point out that there is one more side effect to associating a machine with a domain—the domain search order. Bring up TCP/IP properties—again, right-click the Local Area Network Connection icon and choose Properties, then click Internet Protocol (TCP/IP) and then click the Properties button— and then click the Advanced button, and you'll get a property page with four tabs, one labeled DNS. Click the DNS tab and you'll see a screen like Figure 17.21.

FIGURE 17.21

*DNS advanced
property page*

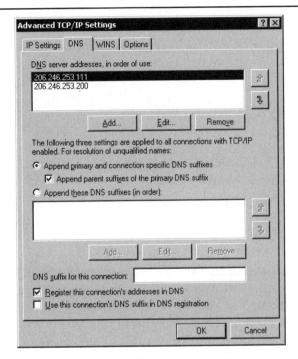

The top field in the screen, DNS Addresses, in Order of Use, is a bit mislabeled; it really means "these are the DNS servers that IP will use to resolve DNS names." The section in the middle of the dialog is the part that I'm mainly interested in here, the part that starts at the radio button labeled Append Primary and Connection Specific DNS Suffixes through the radio button labeled Append These DNS Suffixes (in Order).

To understand domain search order, consider the following question. Suppose you're part of the research division of American Rocketry, Ltd., working in their Tidewater regional offices in southeast Virginia. American Rocketry might have divided up their DNS domain, americanrocket.com, into three divisions: Research, management, and manufacturing, each with its own child domains: research.americanrocket.com, mgmt.americanrocket.com, and manufacturing.americanrocket.com. Furthermore, the folks running the research.americanrocket.com DNS server might have decided to divide up the DNS management job further with two child domains as there are two research facilities—one in the Tidewater area and one at the Bonneville Salt Flats in Utah—so they've created child domains tidewater.research.americanrocket.com and bonneville.research.americanrocket.com. If you work in Tidewater as a researcher and your computer's name is surveyor, then the complete DNS name of your computer is surveyor.tidewater.research.americanrocket.com. If there's a Web server down the hall that holds all of the content that you use in your intranet named memoryalpha, then to get to it you've got to start up your Web browser and point it at `http://memoryalpha` `.tidewater.research.americanrocket.com`—which could get a bit tedious.

The value of domain search order is this: Your system will be configured with a computer name of surveyor and a domain name of tidewater.research.american-rocket.com. Now that Windows 2000 knows your domain name, you can refer to another system in the tidewater.research.americanrocket.com by its computer name rather than having to type in the FQDN; you could point the Web browser to `http://memoryalpha` and the browser would find the Web server without any trouble. Just type in a computer name without any periods in it, and your system will know to add your domain name to the end before querying DNS.

By default, Windows 2000 does just that—it adds your domain name to the end before querying DNS, and that's how NT 4 operated as well. But as Windows 2000 offers you the ability to put different NICs in different Internet domains, you may have a system with multiple-domain citizenship; that's what Append Primary and Connection Specific DNS Suffixes refers to.

But what if you're working for a firm like my mythical Pepsi example, where a workstation might be in tacobell.com, pizzahut.com, pepsi.com, or kfc.com? Then you might want to have your system try a whole *bunch* of DNS queries before giving up. That's why you have the option later on in the dialog box to enter domain names to search.

Before leaving this dialog box, note Register This Connection's Addresses in DNS. Remember that the DNS servers associated with an Active Directory enterprise can accept dynamic, RFC 2136 DNS updates so that a workstation or server can insert itself into the DNS name database rather than requiring an administrator to sit down and enter that machine's IP address and name by hand. Windows 2000 machines automatically seek out their local DNS server and try to add themselves to that DNS server's list of names and IP addresses. If, for some reason, you do *not* want your work-station to do that, then you can just uncheck the box.

Handling Old Names: Configuring Your Workstation for WINS

While in that advanced property page for TCP/IP, click the WINS tab and you'll see something like Figure 17.22.

FIGURE 17.22

WINS client
configuration tab

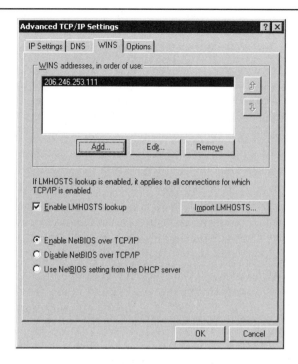

Now, if you're *really* lucky, then you'll never have to look at this screen. But I doubt that you're that lucky.

I'll cover WINS in detail in the next chapter, but for now all you need to understand is that you have one or two Windows 2000 (or possibly NT) servers acting as name resolvers or WINS servers. This dialog box lets you fill in the names of a primary and secondary WINS server.

In brief, here's what WINS is all about. As you've read, most of the Internet in general as well as Windows 2000 uses something called *DNS* to convert network names to network addresses (or, in network lingo, to "resolve network names,"), but now I'm saying that we'll *also* use something else, called *WINS*, to do what sounds like the same thing. What's going on? In truth, you shouldn't really have to set up WINS at all; NT and Microsoft enterprise networking in general should use DNS for all of its name resolution, but it didn't in Windows for Workgroups, Windows 9*x*, NT 3.*x*, and NT 4. It wasn't until Windows 2000 shipped that Microsoft networking started relying on Winsock and DNS. The reason is that Microsoft wanted NT's networking modules to work like the already-existing LAN Manager system, and LAN Manager used a naming system based on its NetBIOS application program interface. A computer's NetBIOS name is the computer name that you gave it when you installed it. When you type **net view \\ajax**, something must resolve \\ajax into an IP address—a NetBIOS-to-IP resolution. WINS does that. In contrast, the rest of the Internet would see a machine called ajax as having a longer name, like ajax.acme.com. If there were a Web server on ajax, then someone outside the company would have to point her Web browser to `http://ajax.acme.com`, and some piece of software would have to resolve ajax.acme .com into an IP address. That piece of software is the socket or Winsock interface, and in either case, it will rely upon not WINS but *DNS* to resolve the name. In a few words, then, programs written to employ NetBIOS will use WINS for name resolution, and programs written to employ Winsock use DNS for name resolution.

I can probably guess what you're thinking now, and, yes, DNS and WINS should be integrated, and they eventually were, but not until Windows 2000 arrived. Why would you continue to have WINS servers if you've got Windows 2000? Because it's pretty likely that you've still got some Windows for Workgroups, Windows 95 or 98, and/or NT 4 servers and workstations still floating around. All of the time that they were working on Windows 2000, Microsoft kept promising us that WINS would no longer be necessary once Windows 2000 came out, but there was some fine print, namely "...so long as you throw away all of your old machines or put Windows 2000 Professional or Server on them." Most of us can't afford to do that, so we'll be living with WINS servers for the time being—which means that your Windows 2000 systems must know where those WINS servers are, hence this dialog box.

In Figure 17.22, I told this computer that there's a WINS server at 206.246.253.111 by clicking Add, filling in the IP address, and clicking OK. You could only tell pre–Windows 2000 systems about two WINS servers, but for some reason Windows 2000 allows you to list as many WINS servers as you like in this dialog box.

Even at its best, WINS couldn't do the whole name resolution job. Some tough name resolution problems could only be solved with a HOSTS-like file called LMHOSTS. The Enable LMHOSTS Lookup check box lets you use an LMHOSTS file if you've got one installed on your system. I'll explain LMHOSTS in detail in the next chapter.

The Enable NetBIOS over TCP/IP versus Disable NetBIOS over TCP/IP radio buttons embody a deceptively momentous choice, so it's odd that the choice is tucked away in this obscure property page. Another way of phrasing the WINS-versus-DNS dichotomy is to say that all of the Microsoft operating systems prior to Windows 2000 built all of their networking tools atop a programming interface called NetBIOS, and Windows 2000 breaks with that tradition by instead using another programming interface called Winsock. An all–Windows 2000 network would be perfectly happy running only network programs—Web servers, e-mail, file servers—that used Winsock. But if those servers want to communicate with older Windows and NT systems, then they must use older networking programs that are compatible with these old systems, and those older networking programs are built atop NetBIOS.

That means that if your Windows 2000 system is acting as a file or print server for any older machines, it needs to keep NetBIOS around. If it's running any applications built for pre–Windows 2000 versions of NT, it'll probably need NetBIOS. Put simply, you can't shut off NetBIOS until you're free of both old client machines and old network applications. But one day you'll be able to axe NetBIOS, and when you can, you should as it'll reduce network chatter and free up server memory and CPU power.

Adding IP Addresses to a Single NIC

If you're still in the Advanced TCP/IP Settings page, click the IP Settings tab, and you'll see something like Figure 17.23.

FIGURE 17.23

IP Settings advanced property tab

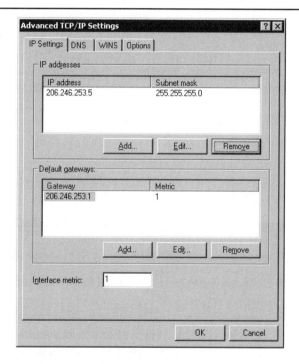

This NIC already has the 206.246.253.5 IP address that I gave it earlier. But notice the Add button. This lets you attach different IP addresses to the NIC to assign more than one IP address to a single NIC.

Why would you want to do that? Normally, you wouldn't. But there *is* one case wherein it would be very useful—when you're hosting multiple Web sites on a single Web server.

For example, suppose I've got two Internet domains, minasi.com and win2kexperts .com. I intend to put up a Web site for minasi.com (www.minasi.com) and another for win2kexperts.com (www.win2kexperts.com). But I want them to be very different Web sites; perhaps the minasi.com site is a personal site and the win2kexperts site is a business site. Even though www.minasi.com and www.win2kexperts.com are both hosted on a machine at 206.246.253.100, I don't ever want anyone visiting the business site to see pictures of my last vacation, and I don't think my friends care much about my professional resume.

I separate the two by creating two *virtual sites*. There are two basic ways to give a single Web server "multiple personalities." You'll read more about how to do that with Internet Information Server in Chapter 19, and in that chapter you'll learn *one* way to create multiple virtual sites. That method doesn't work with old browsers—Netscape 1.*x*, Internet Explorer 1.*x* and 2.*x*, Spyglass—but only with *really* old browsers, so what you'll read in Chapter 19 may well be all you need. But if you ever need the slightly more expensive (and when I say "expensive" here, I mean that you'll have to use an IP address for each virtual site) method that works with *any* browser, then here's briefly how to do it—and it's a great example of why you'd put multiple IP addresses on a single NIC:

1. I assign an extra IP address to the Web server so that it now has two addresses— let's say they're 206.246.253.100 and 206.246.253.101.

2. I then set up DNS so that `www.minasi.com` points to the first address, 206.246.253.100, and `www.win2kexperts.com` points to the second address, 206.246.253.101.

3. I've already got the minasi.com Web site running, so I'll need a place to put the win2kexperts.com content. I just create a folder on the Web server called w2kx and put the HTML, images, and so on for win2kexperts.com there.

4. I next tell the Web server to create a "new site." It then basically needs to know two things: Where to find the content (`c:\w2kx`) and which IP address to associate with the site. I've got to tell it to "start" the site, and I'm in business.

The important thing here is to understand that every one of these sites, each of these "personalities" of your Web server, burns up an IP address, and as you see, you use the IP Settings property tab to add those extra IP addresses to your Web server's NIC.

Whew! Getting IP running on that system was a bit of work. Good thing we can do most of our machines automatically with DHCP—but even that requires configuring, which is why we went through all of this detail. Now that I've got IP on a system, I can return to some of the more techie infrastructure issues—like IP routing.

Setting Up Routing on Windows 2000, NT, and Windows Machines

Up to now, I've assumed that all of your TCP/IP-using machines had a single default gateway that acted as "router to the world" for your machines. That's not always true, as real-life intranets often have multiple routers that lead a machine to different networks. I've also assumed that your Windows 2000 network is connected to the Internet, or to your enterprise intranet, via some third-party (Compatible Systems, Bay

Networks, Cisco Systems, or whomever) router. That's also not always true, as NT machines can act as IP routers.

Routing problems aren't just *server* problems; they're often workstation problems, as well. So, in this section, I'll take on two topics:

- How to set up routing tables on your workstations and servers
- How to use your Windows 2000 servers as IP routers

An Example Multirouter Internet

Suppose you had a workstation on a network with two gateways, as shown in Figure 17.24.

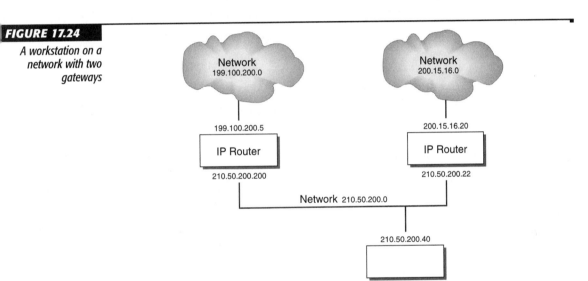

FIGURE 17.24

*A workstation on a
network with two
gateways*

As is the case for most of these diagrams, a multinetwork picture can be cryptic, so here's an explanation of what you are looking at.

First, there are three separate Ethernet segments, three separate subnets. They are all C class networks, just to keep things clean. Two of the networks are only represented by clouds; thus, the cloud on the left containing 199.100.200.0 is just shorthand for an Ethernet with up to 254 computers hanging off it, with addresses ranging from 199.100.200.1 through 199.100.200.254. Notice that I said 254, not 253, because *there is no default gateway for these subnets*. As there are only three subnets, this is an intranet, not part of the Internet. One side effect of not being on the Net is that you can use the .1 address for regular old machines. I left the Internet out of this first example because I found that it confused me when I was first trying to get this routing stuff down. I'll add it later, I promise.

There is also another cloud, to the right, representing a network whose addresses range from 200.15.16.1 through 200.15.16.254—network number 200.15.16.0.

In between is a third subnet with address 210.50.200.0. You see a rectangle representing a PC in the middle which has only one Ethernet card in it, and its IP address is 210.50.200.40. The rectangles on the right and left sides of the picture are routers, computers with two Ethernet cards in them and thus two IP addresses apiece. Each has an address on the 210.50.200.0 network, and each has an address either on the 200.15.16.0 network or on the 199.100.200.0 network.

Adding Entries to Routing Tables: Route Add

Having said that, let's now figure out how to tell the machine at 210.50.200.40 how to route anywhere on this network. These are some of the facts it needs to know:

- To get a message to the 199.100.200.0 network, send it to the machine at 210.50.200.200.

- To get a message to the 200.15.16.0 network, send it to the machine at 210.50.200.22.

- To get a message to the 210.50.200.0 network, just use your own Ethernet card; send it out on the segment, and it'll be heard.

You tell a workstation how to send packets with the *ROUTE ADD* command. Simplified, it looks like this:

```
route add destination mask netmask gatewayaddress
```

Here, *destination* is the address or set of addresses that you want to be able to get to. *Netmask* defines how *many* addresses are there—is it a C network with 250+ addresses, something subnetted smaller, or perhaps a "supernet" of several C networks? *Gatewayaddress* is just the IP address of the machine that will route your packets to their destination.

The ROUTE ADD command for the 199.100.200.0 network would look like this:

```
route add 199.100.200.0 mask 255.255.255.0 210.50.200.200
```

This means, "Send a message anywhere on the 199.100.200.0 network, send it to the machine at 210.50.200.200, and it'll take care of it."

Just a reminder on subnetting, for clarity's sake: Suppose the network on the upper left wasn't a full C network, but rather a subnetted part of it. Suppose it was just the range of addresses from 199.100.200.64 through 199.100.200.127. The network number would be, as always, the first address (199.100.200.64), and the subnet mask would be 255.255.255.192. The ROUTE ADD command would then look like

```
route add 199.100.200.64 mask 255.255.255.192 210.50.200.200
```

Anyway, back to the example in the picture. Add a command for the right-hand-side network; it looks like

```
route add 200.15.16.0 mask 255.255.255.0 210.50.200.22
```

That much will get a Windows 2000, NT, or Windows system up and running.

Understanding the Default Routes

Even if you don't ever type a ROUTE ADD command at a Windows workstation, you'll find that there are routing statements that are automatically generated. Let's look at them. First, we'd need an explicit routing command to tell the 210.50.200.40 machine to get to its own subnet:

```
route add 210.50.200.0 mask 255.255.255.0 210.50.200.40
```

Or, in other words, "To get to your local subnet, route to yourself."

Then, recall that the entire 127.*x.y.z* range of network addresses is the loopback. Implement that like so:

```
route add 127.0.0.0 mask 255.0.0.0 127.0.0.1
```

This says, "Take any address from 127.0.0.0 through 127.255.255.255 and route it to 127.0.0.1." The IP software has already had 127.0.0.1 defined for it, so it knows what to do with that. Notice the mask, 255.0.0.0, is a simple class A network mask.

Some Internet software uses intranet multicast groups, so the multicast address must be defined. It is 224.0.0.0. It looks like the loopback route command:

```
route add 224.0.0.0 mask 255.0.0.0 210.50.200.40
```

The system knows to multicast by "shouting," which means communicating over its local subnet.

Viewing the Routing Table

Let's find out exactly what routing information this computer has. How? Well, on Windows 2000, Windows NT, Workgroups, and 95/98 workstations, there are two commands that will show you what the workstation knows about how to route IP packets. Type either **netstat -rn** or **route print** at a command line—the output is identical, so use either command—and you see something like Figure 17.25.

Notice that the output of ROUTE PRINT is similar to the way you format data in ROUTE ADD. Each line shows a network address, which is the desired destination, the netmask, which indicates how many addresses exist at the desired destination, and the gateway, which is the IP address that the workstation should send its packets to in order to reach the destination. But note two more columns: Interface and Metric.

FIGURE 17.25

Sample ROUTE PRINT output

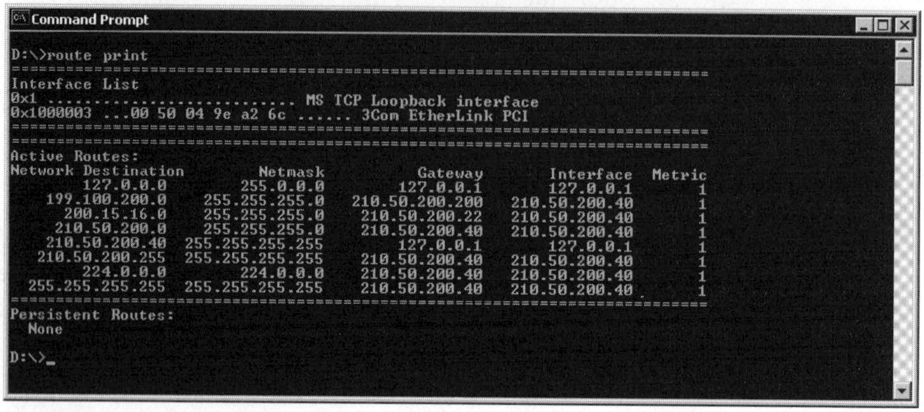

```
Command Prompt                                                        _ □ X

D:\>route print
================================================================================
Interface List
0x1 ............................ MS TCP Loopback interface
0x1000003 ...00 50 04 9e a2 6c ...... 3Com EtherLink PCI
================================================================================
================================================================================
Active Routes:
Network Destination        Netmask          Gateway       Interface  Metric
        127.0.0.0        255.0.0.0        127.0.0.1        127.0.0.1    1
    199.100.200.0    255.255.255.0   210.50.200.200    210.50.200.40    1
      200.15.16.0    255.255.255.0     210.50.200.22    210.50.200.40    1
     210.50.200.0    255.255.255.0     210.50.200.40    210.50.200.40    1
    210.50.200.40  255.255.255.255        127.0.0.1        127.0.0.1    1
   210.50.200.255  255.255.255.255    210.50.200.40    210.50.200.40    1
        224.0.0.0        224.0.0.0    210.50.200.40    210.50.200.40    1
  255.255.255.255  255.255.255.255    210.50.200.40    210.50.200.40    1
================================================================================
Persistent Routes:
  None

D:\>_
```

The Interface Column

Interface asks itself, "Which of my local IP addresses—the ones physically located inside me, like my loopback and all the IP addresses attached to all of my network cards—should I use to get to that gateway?" On this computer, it's a moot point because it only has one network card in it.

What might this look like on a multihomed machine, like the router on the left-hand side? It has two IP addresses, 199.100.200.5 and 210.50.200.200. A fragment of its ROUTE PRINT output might then look like this:

Network Destination	Netmask	Gateway	Interface	Metric
199.100.200.0	255.255.255.0	199.100.200.5	199.100.200.5	1
210.50.200.0	255.255.255.0	210.50.200.200	210.50.200.200	1

There are two networks that the router machine can get to (obviously, or it wouldn't be much use as a router), and each one has a gateway address, which happens to be the local IP address that the router maintains on each network. But now notice the Interface column: Rather than staying at the same IP address all the way through, this tells the computer, "I've already told you which gateway to direct this traffic to; now I'll tell you which of your local IP addresses to employ in order to get to that gateway in the first place."

The Metric Column

The metric column (what, no English option?) tells IP how many routers it will have to pass through in order to get to its destination. A metric value of 1 means "your destination is on the same subnet." A metric value of 2 would mean "you have to go through one router to get to your destination," and so on. Since the .40 workstation must go through a router to get to either the 199.100.200.0 or the 200.15.16.0 network, both of those networks get a metric of 2.

TIP Just think of it this way: Metric = the number of routers you must travel through *plus* 1.

Ah, but how did the computer know that it would take a router jump to get to those networks? Well, you see, *I* told it.

I have to confess here that I left off a parameter on the ROUTE ADD command, simply to make the explanation palatable. As I knew that the metric was 2 for both routes, I just added the parameter metric 2 to the end of both ROUTE ADD statements. The revised, complete commands look like

```
route add 200.15.16.0 mask 255.255.255.0 210.50.200.22 metric 2
route add 199.100.200.0 mask 255.255.255.0 210.50.200.200 metric 2
```

You'll learn a bit later that a protocol called *RIP* will make this process automatic, but for now I want to stick to this manually constructed set of routing tables. (Using hand-constructed routing tables is called *static routing*; the automatic methods like RIP are called *dynamic routing*, and I'll get to them later.)

ROUTE PRINT Output Explained

Now that you can decipher each column in the ROUTE PRINT output, I'll finish up explaining the output.

The first line is the loopback information, as you've seen before. It's automatically generated on every NT/Workgroups/9x machine running the Microsoft TCP/IP stack. The second and third lines are the manually entered routes that tell your machine how to address the 200.15.16.0 and 199.100.200.0 networks. The fourth line is another automatically generated line, and it explains how to address the 210.50.200.0 subnet, which is the local one. The fifth line refers to 210.50.200.40 itself. The mask, 255.255.255.255, means that these aren't routing instructions to get to an entire network, but rather routing instructions to get to a particular computer. It basically says, "If you need to get data to 210.50.200.40, send it to the loopback address." The result: If you ping 210.50.200.40, then no actual communication happens over the network. The sixth line defines how to do a local subnet broadcast. Again, it doesn't point to an entire network, but rather to the particular subnet broadcast address. The seventh line serves Internet multicasting, as you saw before. And the final address is for something called the *limited broadcast address*, a kind of generic subnet broadcast address.

Adding the Default Gateway

Suppose you wanted to set up my 210.50.200.40 machine. How would you do it? More specifically, you'd ask me, "Which is the default gateway?"

Well, in the TCP/IP configuration screen that you've seen before, you'd obviously be able to supply the information that the IP address should be 210.50.200.40 and the subnet mask should be 255.255.255.0. But what should you use to fill in the Default Gateway field? I mean, there are *two* gateways, 210.50.100.22 and 210.50.100.200. Which should you use?

The answer? *Neither.* A *default gateway* is just another entry in the routing table, but it's not specific like the ones you've met so far; it's a catchall entry. This network doesn't get to the Internet, and it can only see two other subnets, each with their own routers (gateways), so I left the Default Gateway field blank. And there's an advantage to that.

"Destination Host Unreachable"

If I were to try to ping some address not on the three subnets, like 25.44.92.4, then I wouldn't get the message that the ping had timed out, or experienced an error, or anything of the sort; rather, I'd get a "destination host unreachable" message. That's important: "Destination host unreachable" doesn't necessarily mean that you can't get to the destination host, but it *does* mean that your workstation doesn't know *how* to get to that host—it lacks any routing information about how to get there at all. Do a ROUTE PRINT and you'll probably be able to see what's keeping you from getting to your destination.

Building a Default Gateway by Hand

When *would* a default gateway make sense in our network? Well, let's add an Internet connection to the network, as shown in Figure 17.26.

FIGURE 17.26

Network with an Internet connection

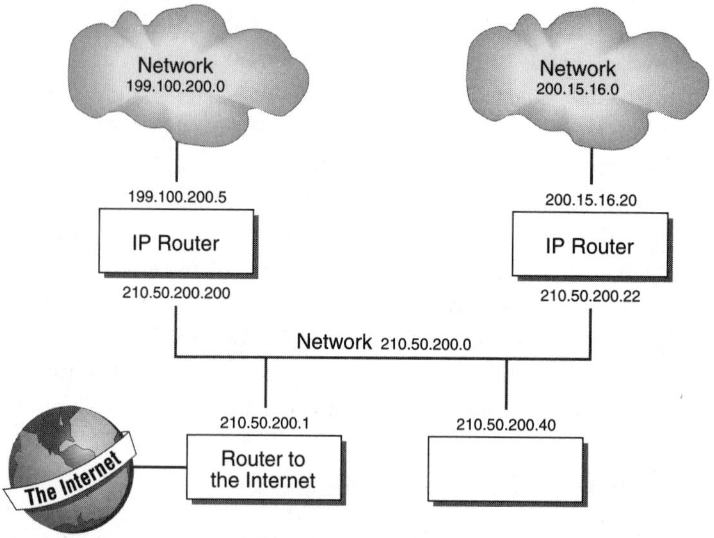

Now we need another ROUTE ADD command—but what should it look like? I mean, what's the generic IP address of the whole Internet?

Believe it or not, there *is* such an address: 0.0.0.0. Think of it as "the network number to end all network numbers." Remember, any given network's number is just the first address of the network. And what's the first address of the Internet? 0.0.0.0. And the network mask? Well, since it doesn't matter *what* address bits match which other address bits—after all, no matter what your address is, you're still on the particular "subnet" which is the entire Internet—the subnet mask is also 0.0.0.0. So the command looks like

```
route add 0.0.0.0 mask 0.0.0.0 210.50.200.1
```

Handling Conflicts in Routing Information

However, it appears that there are some conflicts here. Look at some of the instructions that you've given the IP software about how to route:

- There's a rule about handling the specific address 210.50.200.40: Just keep the message local at 127.0.0.1, no routing.

- There's a rule about how to handle the range from 210.50.200.0 through 210.50.200.255: Shout it out on the subnet, no routing.

- There's a rule about how to handle the range from 199.100.200.0 through 199.100.200.255: Send it to 210.50.200.200.

- There's a rule about how to handle the range from 200.15.16.0 through 200.15.16.255: Send it to 210.50.200.22.

- There's a rule about how to handle *all* Internet addresses: Send the messages to 210.50.200.1.

Here's what I mean about a conflict: Suppose you want to send an IP packet to 200.15.16.33. You have one rule that says, "Send it to 210.50.200.22" and another that says, "Send it to 210.50.200.1." Which rule does the software on your workstation (or server) follow?

Answer: When in doubt, first look for the route with the smallest metric. If there is more than one candidate, then take the *most specific* one—in other words, choose the one with the most specific subnet mask.

In this case, there are two entries in the routing table that point to the destination, 200.15.16.33. I haven't shown you their metrics, but both of them require hopping over one router, so each route has metric 2. As their metrics are tied, you look next to the subnet mask. As the 210.50.200.1 route has a very generic subnet mask (0.0.0.0), your machine would ignore it in comparison to the more specific 210.50.200.22's subnet mask of 255.255.255.0.

Suppose workstation 210.50.200.40 wanted to get a message to another machine on the subnet; let's say that its address is 210.50.200.162. Again, there's a routing conflict, as one route entry just says to send it to 210.50.200.40—in other words, don't route, shout! There's another routing entry—the 0.0.0.0 one again—that says it can also get the IP packet to 210.50.200.162, as it claims it can get any packet *anywhere*.

Which to choose? Well, if constructed correctly, an excerpt of the routing table will look something like this:

Destination	Netmask	Gateway	Interface	Metric
0.0.0.0	0.0.0.0	210.50.200.1	210.50.200.40	2
210.50.200.0	255.255.255.0	210.50.200.40	210.50.200.40	1

The first entry is the default gateway. It's got metric 2 because you've got to hop over at least one router to get to the Internet. (In actual fact, it's probably not a bad idea to set this value a bit higher, just to be sure internal IP packets *never* try to get sent over the Internet.) The second entry basically says, "To send data to your local subnet, just say it out loud on your Ethernet card"—again, don't route, shout. As the Internet metric is higher, your machine will know not to try to send a local message by sending it to the default gateway.

One more thing: You wouldn't, of course, want to have to type in those ROUTE ADD commands every time you start up your computer. So you'd use a variation on the ROUTE ADD command. Just type **route -p add…**. When you add the **-p** that entry becomes permanent in your system's routing table.

All Routers Must Know All Subnets

I've talked about how I'd set up my sample network from the point of view of a workstation. It would work, but you can see that it's a real pain to punch in all of those ROUTE ADD statements for each workstation. The answer is to make the routers smarter; *then* you can just pick one router to be the default gateway for the .40 workstation, and the workstation needn't worry about anything. So let's take a minute and see how each of the three routers in this system would be set up.

The first router is the one on the left, which routes between 199.100.200.0 and 210.50.200.0. It must know three things:

- It can get to 199.100.200.0 through its 199.100.200.5 interface.
- It can get to 210.50.200.0 through its 210.50.200.200 interface.
- It can get to the Internet through 210.50.200.1, which it gets to through its 210.50.200.200 interface.

In fact, you would not have to type in routing commands telling it how to get to 199.100.200.0 or 210.50.200.0; assuming it's an NT machine, the NT routing software figures that out automatically. But you can tell it to get to the Internet by setting a default gateway:

```
route add 0.0.0.0 mask 0.0.0.0 210.50.200.1 metric 2
```

The routing software is then smart enough to realize that it should get to 210.50.200.1 via its 210.50.200.200 interface.

The second router, the one on the right, routes between 200.15.16.0 and 210.50.200.0. It can get to both of those networks directly, and, as with the first router, we don't have to tell it about them. But to get to the Internet, it must route packets to 210.50.200.1, and so, like the first router, it should have a default gateway of 210.50.200.1.

Now let's tackle the third router, the machine at 210.50.200.1, which is the Internet gateway. It must know that it should use the Internet as its default gateway. For example, on my Compatible Systems routers, there is a magic address WAN which just means the modem connection to the Internet. I essentially tell it, "Route add 0.0.0.0 mask 0.0.0.0 WAN," and packets travel to and from the Internet over the modem. The router must then be told of each of the three subnets, like so:

```
route add 210.50.200.0 mask 255.255.255.0 210.50.200.1 metric 1
route add 199.100.200.0 mask 255.255.255.0 210.50.200.200 metric 2
route add 200.15.16.0 mask 255.255.255.0 210.50.200.22 metric 2
```

Using RIP to Simplify Workstation Management

Thus far, I've shown you how to tell your workstations how to exploit routers on the network. In most cases, you won't need to build such large, complex routing tables by hand, and in almost no case will you *want* to build those tables.

Ideally, you shouldn't have to type in static tables; instead, your workstations could just suck up routing information automatically from the nearby routers, using some kind of browser-type protocol. You *can* do such a thing with the *Routing Information Protocol*, or RIP.

RIP is an incredibly simple protocol. Routers running RIP broadcast their routing tables about twice a minute. Any workstation running RIP software hears the routing tables and incorporates them into its *own* routing tables. Result: You put a new router on the system, and you needn't punch in any static routes.

RIP version 2 ships as part of Windows 2000. The Microsoft implementation supports both IP and IPX. Routes detected by RIP show up in ROUTE PRINT statements just as if they were static routes.

An Alternative Dynamic Routing Protocol: OSPF

While RIP has been around for some time, it's an awfully chatty protocol. Twice a minute, each RIP router broadcasts its entire routing table for all to hear. A more intelligent and bandwidth-parsimonious but more complex to set up dynamic routing protocol is available in the form of the Open Shortest Path First (OSPF) protocol. You have to feed the routers a bit more information about the layout of your sites, but once you do, OSPF quickly generates the shortest routes for your packets.

Using an NT Machine as a LAN/LAN Router

In the process of expanding your company's intranet, you need routers. For a network of any size, the best bet is probably to buy dedicated routers, boxes from companies like Cisco Systems, Bay Networks, or Compatible Systems.

Dedicated routers are fast and come with some impressive management tools: Neat GUI programs that let you control and monitor your network from your workstation. But routers have one disadvantage: They're expensive. I haven't seen an Ethernet-to-Ethernet IP router available for less than $3,000. Again, don't misunderstand me: These routers are probably worth what they cost in terms of the ease that they bring to network management and the speed with which they route data. But you might have more than one subnet on a given site, and you might *not* have the three grand, so you're looking for an alternative.

How about a software alternative? Any Windows NT 4 workstation or server can act as a simple IP router—all you need is a multihomed PC (one with two or more network cards installed in it) and Windows NT 4. Just open up the Control Panel, open the Network applet, then the Protocols tab, and the TCP/IP protocol. Click the Routing tab, and you see an option called Enable IP Routing. That's how you turn on NT's routing capability.

Making a Windows 2000 system a router is a bit more complex. Let's see how to set up this router. Let's return to that cross-Mediterranean rivalry and set up a LAN-to-LAN router for Carthage and Rome. Imagine you have an intranet that looks like Figure 17.27.

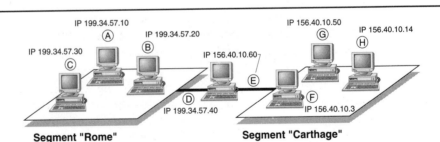

FIGURE 17.27

A sample intranet

IP 199.34.57.10 (A)
IP 199.34.57.20 (B)
IP 199.34.57.30 (C)
IP 199.34.57.40 (D)

IP 156.40.10.50 (G)
IP 156.40.10.14 (H)
IP 156.40.10.60 (E)
IP 156.40.10.3 (F)

Segment "Rome"   **Segment "Carthage"**

We're going to use the machine that's on both Rome and Carthage as the router. (Actually, there's no choice here, as it's the *only* machine in both TCP/IP subnets, and any router between two subnets must be a member of both subnets.) First I'll look at how to set up the machine with adapters D and E as a router, then I'll take a slightly more complex example:

1. The machine between Rome and Carthage—let's call it MEDITERRANEAN—needs two Ethernet cards. Install two network cards (let's use Ethernet for this example) in a Windows 2000 system machine. Microsoft *intended* for you to only be able to use Windows 2000 Server, but you can use Professional as well

with a Registry hack, so long as you're only doing static routing—I haven't been able to figure out how to make Professional do RIP or OSPF routing.

2. Configure the Ethernet card on the Rome subnet with IP address 199.34.57.40 and the Ethernet card on the Carthage subnet with IP address 156.40.10.60. Here's how: Once you've got a second NIC installed in the MEDITERRANEAN system, open up Network and Dial-Up Connections and it'll look like Figure 17.28.

FIGURE 17.28

Network and Dial-Up Connections with two NICs

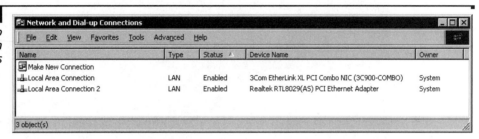

3. Right-click either one of the two connection objects and choose Properties, and you'll then see the screen that lets you modify the TCP/IP properties for that NIC, including its static IP address. Once I've set the IP addresses properly, an IPCONFIG/ALL looks like Figure 17.29.

Note that this IPCONFIG output is larger than the previous ones, mainly because it's got to report on two NICs. There's no DNS server specified and no domain name specified because (1) it simplified the IPCONFIG output and (2) routers usually needn't have DNS names for their interfaces. Note also that IP Routing Enabled is No. That's important—just because a Windows 2000 system has NICs attached to different subnets doesn't automatically mean that the system will act as a router.

4. Next, turn on routing. You can turn on simple static routing for either a Windows 2000 Server or Professional machine by looking in the key HKEY_LOCAL_ MACHINE\System\CurrentControlSet\Services\TCP/IP\Parameters for the value named IPEnableRouter, which will be set to 0. Change the value to 1, reboot the system, and it'll do static routing between the subnets that it's directly connected to.

FIGURE 17.29

*IPCONFIG/ALL before
enabling routing*

FIGURE 17.29

*IPCONFIG/ALL before
enabling routing*

```
Command Prompt

E:\>ipconfig /all

Windows 2000 IP Configuration

        Host Name . . . . . . . . . . . . : MEDITERRANEAN
        Primary DNS Suffix  . . . . . . . :
        Node Type . . . . . . . . . . . . : Hybrid
        IP Routing Enabled. . . . . . . . : No
        WINS Proxy Enabled. . . . . . . . : No

Ethernet adapter Local Area Connection:

        Connection-specific DNS Suffix  . :
        Description . . . . . . . . . . . : 3Com EtherLink XL PCI Combo NIC (3C900-COMBO)
        Physical Address. . . . . . . . . : 00-60-08-9C-A4-2E
        DHCP Enabled. . . . . . . . . . . : No
        IP Address. . . . . . . . . . . . : 199.34.57.40
        Subnet Mask . . . . . . . . . . . : 255.255.255.0
        Default Gateway . . . . . . . . . :
        DNS Servers . . . . . . . . . . . :

Ethernet adapter Local Area Connection 2:

        Connection-specific DNS Suffix  . :
        Description . . . . . . . . . . . : Realtek RTL8029(AS) PCI Ethernet Adapter
        Physical Address. . . . . . . . . : 00-C0-DF-E4-65-AC
        DHCP Enabled. . . . . . . . . . . : No
        IP Address. . . . . . . . . . . . : 156.40.10.60
        Subnet Mask . . . . . . . . . . . : 255.255.255.0
        Default Gateway . . . . . . . . . :
        DNS Servers . . . . . . . . . . . :

E:\>_
```

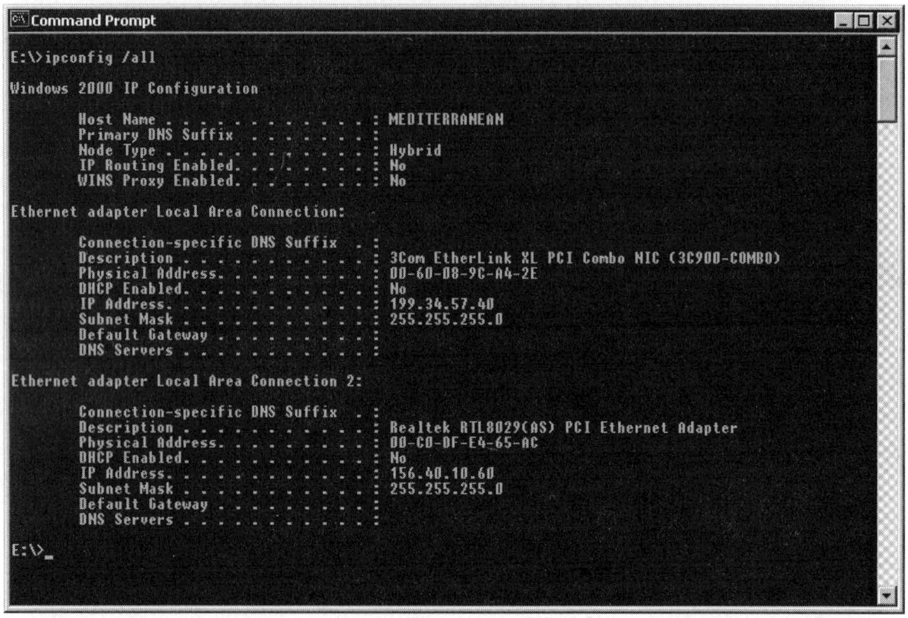

I suggested the Registry hack because it's the only way that I've found to make a Professional machine an IP router—which is odd, because under NT 4 Workstation there was a check box in the Control Panel to enable IP routing. Maybe it was an oversight, or perhaps Microsoft wants to sell you a copy of Server if you want to do IP routing?

In any case, if the routing machine is running Windows 2000 *Server*, then no Registry fooling-around is needed. Instead, click Start/Programs/Administrative Tools/ Routing and Remote Access, which will show you an MMC console like Figure 17.30.

Click the plus sign next to MEDITERRANEAN. You'll see a red arrow pointing down, indicating that routing hasn't been turned on yet. To turn routing on, right-click MEDITERRANEAN in the left-hand pane and choose Configure and Enable Routing and Remote Access. That, not surprisingly, starts off a wizard, the Routing and Remote Access Configuration Wizard. Click Next and you'll then see a screen like Figure 17.31.

Setting up a router can be a bit challenging, so Microsoft decided fairly late in the Windows 2000 development process to try to build four "precooked" router setups and then offer them in combination with a fourth option that allowed you to build the router as you like. Take that fifth option, Manually Configured Server, and click Next and then Finish to complete the wizard. Windows 2000 will beep and ask you if you want to start the Routing and Remote Access Service; click Yes. You'll then see a screen like Figure 17.32.

FIGURE 17.30

*Opening RRAS
Administrator screen*

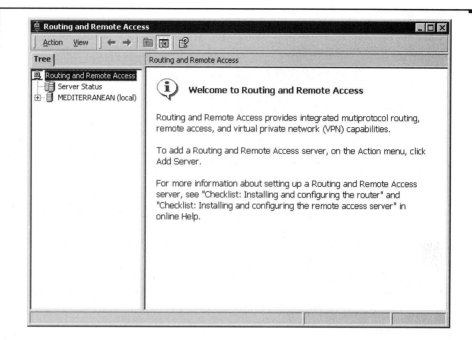

FIGURE 17.31

*Initial RRAS setup
wizard screen*

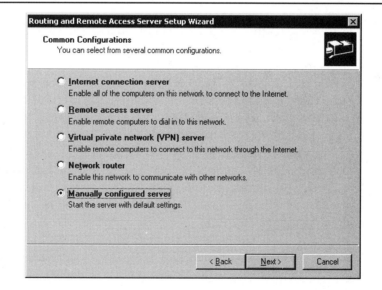

FIGURE 17.32

*RRAS management
console with routing
enabled*

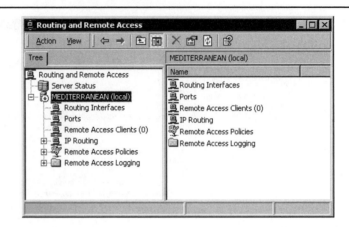

With Windows 2000, Microsoft combined what were two separate functions under earlier versions of NT—IP routing and remote access. (Actually, they combined them with an optional add-in called Routing and Remote Access, or by its beta name, Steelhead, but not many people used it. I was amused when at a briefing a Microsoft developer surprised the audience by referring to Steelhead as "merely a 'technology demonstration,'" presumably rather than something they were serious about. It was, after all, a bit late to have told us that!)

As we chose "manual setup," Windows 2000 turned on some things that we don't want—in particular, Windows 2000 turned on dial-up connections, which don't make sense on this server, as it lacks a modem. We can fix that by right-clicking MEDITERRANEAN and choosing Properties, which shows a dialog box like the one in Figure 17.33

You can see that this router is set up as a remote access server; uncheck Remote Access Server and then click the radio button labeled Local Area Network (LAN) Routing Only, then click OK to make those changes take effect. You'll be asked if it's all right to restart the router software; click OK to let it.

There's nothing more to do. As MEDITERRANEAN's routing is turned on and because it's directly connected to both the 199 and the 156 network, it will automatically route packets between the networks. Of course, the machines on both networks must know to use one of MEDITERRANEAN's NICs, either via a ROUTE ADD statement or by referring to MEDITERRANEAN's local NIC as their default gateway. By the way, if you set up a machine like this one, to do NIC-to-NIC routing but not any remote access, and then change your mind, just go back to the RRAS snap-in and right-click on the server and choose Disable Routing and Remote Access. Once RRAS is disabled on a server, you can just right-click the server and once again choose Configure and Enable Routing and Remote Access; the wizard will again run, and you can change any of your RRAS configuration choices then.

FIGURE 17.33

Reconfiguring the router

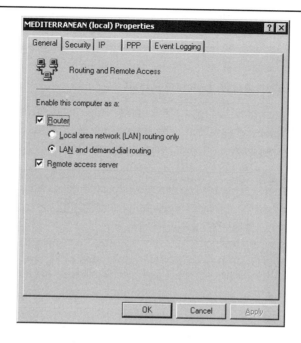

One more point before moving on. You've already learned how to use ROUTE ADD from the command line to add a static route. RRAS lets you do that from the GUI as well. In the left-hand panel, you see an object labeled IP Routing. Open it and you'll see two other objects, one labeled General and the other labeled Static Routes. Right-click Static Routes and choose New Static Route..., and you'll see a dialog box like Figure 17.34.

FIGURE 17.34

Dialog box for adding a new static route

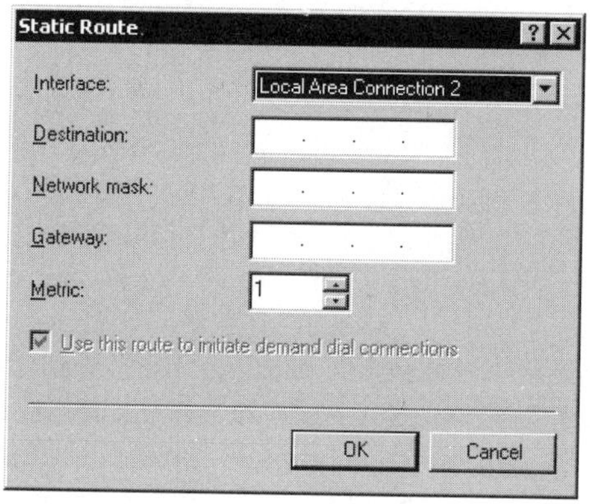

Okay, so it's not a very useful dialog box—I could probably type the ROUTE ADD command more quickly than I could open this dialog and punch in its values—but at least it's not another three-screen wizard that only asks one question, right?

More Complex Static Routing

By now, you've set up an IP router to move traffic from one subnet to another. It will *not*, however, route traffic between three or more subnets. Why not? Well, the default router software isn't very smart. Look at Figure 17.35, and you'll see what I mean.

FIGURE 17.35

Internet with three subnets

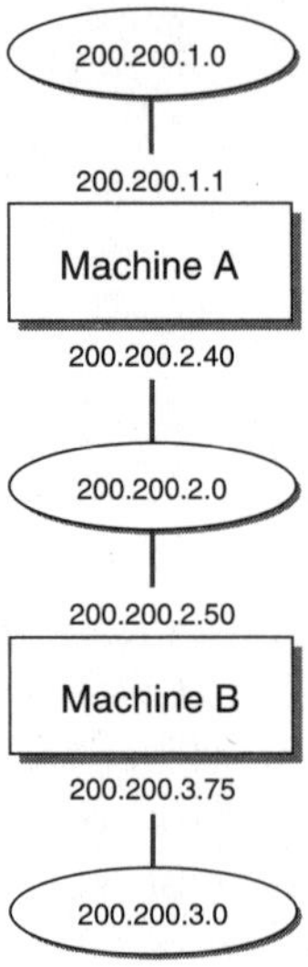

Here, you see an intranet with just three subnets: 200.200.1.0, 200.200.2.0, and 200.200.3.0. For ease of discussion, let's call network 200.200.1.0 "network 1," 200.200.2.0 "network 2," and 200.200.3.0 "network 3." The network 1 to network 2 router, machine A, has addresses 200.200.1.1 and 200.200.2.40, and the network 2 to network 3 router, machine B, has addresses 200.200.3.75 and 200.200.2.50.

Once you turn on IP routing in machine A, it's smart enough to be able to route packets from network 1 to network 2 and packets from network 2 to network 1. But if it receives a packet from network 1 intended for network 3, it has no idea what to do about it.

Machine B has the same problem, basically. It knows how to go from network 2 to network 3 and from network 3 to network 2, but it has no idea how to find network 1.

How do you solve this problem? Either with static routes or with RIP. The best answer is probably to put the RIP router on both machine A and machine B, and they will end up discovering each other's routes through the RIP broadcasts. But how would you tell machine A how to find network 3 and how would you tell machine B to find network 1? With static ROUTE ADD commands.

On machine A, tell it about network 3 like so:

```
route add 200.200.3.0 mask 255.255.255.0 200.200.2.50
```

(Or, if you're feeling GUI, use RRAS.) You're saying to this machine, "In order to find network 200.200.3.0, use the IP address 200.200.2.50; it's attached to a machine that can get the packets to that network." For the sake of completeness, you might add the "metric 2" parameter to the end.

On machine B, tell it about network 1 in a similar way:

```
route add 200.200.1.0 mask 255.255.255.0 200.200.2.40
```

Remember that in both cases the "mask" information says, "I'm giving you information about a subnet, but the mask says how useful the information is." And if you want the router to *remember* these routes through reboots, don't forget the –p option to make the route permanent.

Using a Windows 2000 Server as an Internet Gateway/Router

Consider this. Your company has purchased a full-time PPP account from some Internet provider. You have your LAN running TCP/IP with IANA-approved IP numbers. All you need is a machine that will route your local traffic over the Internet when you want to FTP, use e-mail, or whatever.

From a hardware point of view, it's pretty easy: You just need a PC containing both an Ethernet card and a serial port, with a dial-up PPP connection. That machine is essentially doing the job of TCP/IP routing. How do you do that in Windows 2000?

The Overview

There are a number of "what ifs" that you have to consider if you want to use your NT machine as a LAN-to-WAN Internet gateway.

Consider a Dedicated Router as an Alternative

The first piece of advice is: Don't, if you can avoid it. In my company, I use the Compatible Systems mr900i, a terrific box that I picked up for $850. It's very easy to manage, comes with a very nice Windows-based router management program, does RIP, is much cheaper than buying a Pentium and a copy of NT, and is as fast as the wind. I'd recommend it as the way to go if you want to hook up your net to *the* Net. On other networks, I've used the Ascend "pipeline" router, another quite good product in the $1000 to $2000 range, which includes an optional security package to turn the router into a firewall-like device. In another network, I've used the Cisco 1602, at a cost of about $2000 if I recall right. I liked the Compatible box best of the three, as they had both the best tech support and, again, a Windows-based router management program—the others could only be controlled by a cryptic command-line interface or a complex text-based menu structure.

Whatever you choose (if you choose not to go the way of a Windows 2000–based router), there are many good options that are far more stable software-wise than something as complex as an off-the-shelf PC acting as a server. And that's not a slam at Windows 2000, just a recognition that anything with a greater number of "moving parts," so to speak, is more likely to break—there's no floppy drive, hard disk, video card, or dozens of drivers written by dozens of different companies running in a dedicated router, unlike a Windows 2000 box.

WAN Connection Options

But there are times that I don't have access to a dedicated router, and perhaps I'd like to use my Windows 2000 machine as my Internet router. So let's see how to accomplish that. Take a look at Figure 17.36.

FIGURE 17.36

LAN/WAN router overview diagram

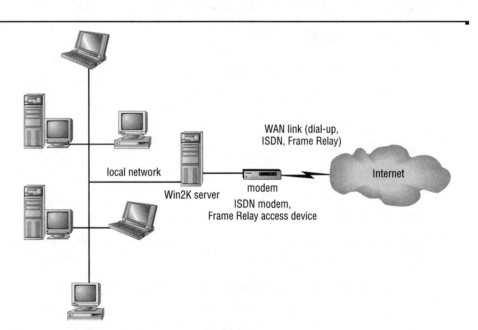

To the left in Figure 17.36, you see your company's local area network connected to the Windows 2000 machine that will act as the gateway server. There's nothing special there, it's just a regular network. I'll assume for the purposes of this explanation that you've obtained IANA-approved IP addresses for each of the machines in your network.

To the right is the connection between your gateway and the Internet. It could be a number of different possible types of connections, but the most likely are modem, ISDN, or Frame Relay.

WARNING In general, cable modem and DSL would *not* be possible connections for a configuration such as I've described here, where you obtain a number of IP addresses from an ISP and put them on your local machines and then use a gateway to connect to the Internet. While there's no *technical* reason why that's so, I don't know of any cable modem or DSL provider who offers more than one IP address to a customer; every one that I've asked just looks at me helplessly. Restricting cable modem and DSL customers to just one IP address is unfortunate, as cable or DSL would make for a low-cost, high-speed way to connect a lot of PCs to the Internet. But, then, perhaps that's the point: If you've got a lot of machines to connect, then I guess the provider wants to charge more. However, there *is* a way for one computer to share a cable modem or DSL (or any other type) connection with all of the PCs on its local network, a tool called Internet Connection Sharing. The difference is that you must use Network Address Translation (NAT) routing, where all of your local machines get nonroutable IP addresses. You'll read about Internet Connection Sharing a little later in this chapter.

Modem and ISDN connections are dial-up connections, not continuous connections. If you intend to host any Internet servers on your local network, such as if you want to run your own DNS, Web, FTP, or e-mail servers, then your network needs a "persistent" connection; it must be connected to the Internet 24 hours a day, 365.24219878 days a year (to be *nearly* exact, that is).

Dial-up is a pain for building consistent connections because it's hard to keep up and connected. Years ago, when I had my company connected to the Internet on a shoestring budget, I connected our network to our ISP with a 14.4Kbps modem. I used a "flat-rate" phone account, one that cost $25 a month with no charges for local calls. The call to the ISP was local, so I figured I'd just dial up and not hang up. Essentially, I figured, $25 a month bought me a moderately noisy 14.4K dedicated line to the Internet—good deal, right?

It was a constant pain, and let me try to convince you not to try it for your routed Internet connection. First of all, the phone company computers go around and periodically disconnect any dial-up connection that's been up and running too long. Second, most ISPs think *fault tolerant* refers to their belief that customers will tolerate the ISP's faulty infrastructure, so many ISPs end up rebooting their systems periodically, which kicks anyone off the modems and drops the dial-up connection.

Back in 1992, when I had the 14.4 connection running, I had to establish the dial-up connection myself, and when the connection would drop periodically, I'd have to reestablish it with a few commands at the router. You'll see that RRAS has a feature called *on-demand dialing*, which is supposed to sense whenever anyone on the local network needs to get to the Internet, and when the Windows 2000 router senses that need, it dials up the Internet. It *sounds* as if this might be the way to ensure that a dial-up connection dials up and stays up: Why not just run a simple batch file that does a ping to somewhere out on the Internet and use the Scheduler service to automatically run the batch file every 20 minutes or so? Seems like a great idea, but in my experience the demand dialer has trouble figuring out whether or not the modem is currently connected. I've had RRAS tell me that a demand-dial connection was up and running when I could clearly see that the "carrier detect" light on the modem was off.

ISDN offers some of the same problems with the extra fact that you usually get charged by the minute for ISDN connections, which can run up the meter fairly quickly.

The answer for many may be a dedicated connection called a *Frame Relay* connection. You're charged a flat monthly rate for it, depending on things like how far away you are from the ISP and how fast the connection is. In my experience, a fairly low-speed, 56Kbps Frame Relay runs around $150-$200 per month. That's just the telco charges for the frame, however; the ISP will levy additional charges to rent you the IP addresses, route your packets, and whatever other services they offer. Instead of a modem to connect your server to the Frame Relay, you get a Frame Relay access device, or FRAD, which is either an external box that looks something like a modem and connects to your server with a serial port or a board that plugs into a slot inside the server. In any case, a Frame Relay connection ends up looking to Windows 2000 like a Dial-Up Networking connection, and whoever sells you the FRAD will include a "modem driver" for the FRAD so that Windows 2000 will understand how to use the FRAD. (Be *very sure* that a Windows 2000 driver exists before buying a FRAD. Make sure they know how to make it work with Windows 2000.)

Collect the Pieces and Get Started

Before beginning, make sure you have the following information close to hand:

- Addressing information from the ISP: Your range of IP addresses, subnet mask, and router IPs.
- DNS server addresses from your ISP.
- If you are dialing into the ISP, correct phone numbers.
- Account name and password for the ISP.
- Verify that your system will be able to log in "hands off" with either a protocol called CHAP (Challenge-Handshake Authentication Protocol) or PAP (Password Authentication Protocol). While it's unlikely, there are some ISPs that actually still require you to pop up a dumb terminal screen and punch in an account name and password. RRAS can't handle that kind of login as far as I can see (even with a prebuilt script), so double-check that you can PAP or CHAP in.

Once you've collected that information, get started by doing the following:

- Get network cards in all of the local machines and in the server.
- Install the TCP/IP protocol on them and assign the ISP-assigned IP addresses to the local machines (DHCP's the easiest way).
- Attach the WAN connection device—modem, ISDN, FRAD, or whatever—on the gateway.

Test the ISP Connection

In an minute, we'll show RRAS how to connect your LAN to the Internet via a WAN. But before doing that, we'll figure out how to connect to the ISP in the first place.

No two connections work the same way. Some ISPs automatically assign IP addresses as you connect, and some require you to preconfigure your system with a particular IP address. If you're dialing up with a modem, you may have a choice of phone numbers and a bit of experimentation may reveal that one of them gets a high-speed connection more consistently. ISDN is always a challenge to get working and Frame Relay can be pretty easy once you've done it a few times. Essentially what I'm suggesting is that you do a "dry run" of hooking up to the outside world. Plan to do it on a Tuesday morning, when your ISP's help desk is fully staffed and has recovered from answering all of the questions from the wave of frustrated people who couldn't connect all weekend (when there's no one or only a small staff at the help disk) and so angrily called on Monday.

Of course, you'll be using your system as a Dial-Up Networking client computer. If you need help on setting up a dial-out to the Internet, read Chapter 22, which discusses both DUN and its server-side partner, Remote Access Service (RAS).

Configure RRAS on the Gateway

Next, start up RRAS on the gateway—Start/Programs/Administrative Tools/Routing and Remote Access. As before, right-click on the icon representing the gateway and choose Configure and Enable Routing and Remote Access. That'll start a wizard as you see in Figure 17.37.

FIGURE 17.37

*Starting the
RRAS Wizard*

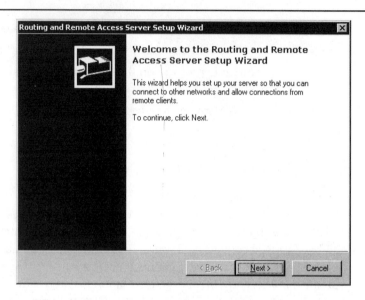

Click Next, and you'll see several options for routing, as you see in Figure 17.38.

FIGURE 17.38

Routing options

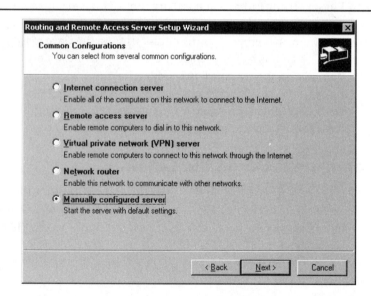

Again, take the Manually Configured Server option and click Next; you'll then see
something like Figure 17.39.

FIGURE 17.39

*Completing the
RRAS Wizard*

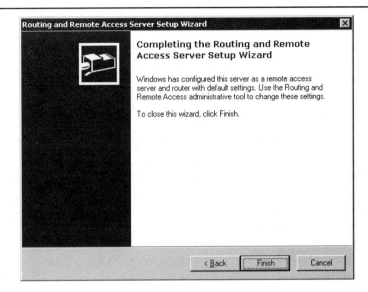

Click Finish and you'll be asked if it's all right to start the service. Click Yes and the service will start. You'll then see a RRAS screen that looks like Figure 17.40.

FIGURE 17.40

*RRAS management
console*

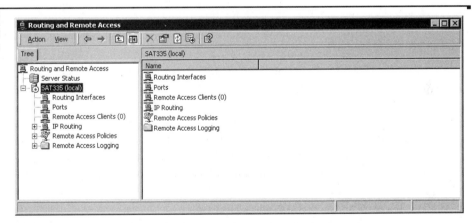

Now, by default this machine will accept dial-ins, for unless you *want* dial-ins, let's disable them for security reasons. Right-click the server name and choose Properties and you'll see a screen like Figure 17.41.

FIGURE 17.41

RRAS properties

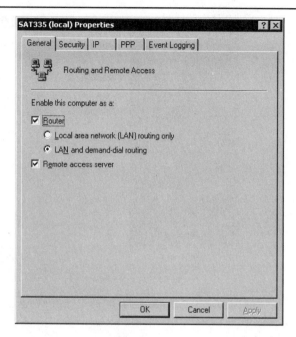

Uncheck Remote Access Server, then click OK. You'll be asked if it's all right to restart the routing service; click Yes to indicate that it's fine. You'll be back at the RRAS screen. Click the Routing Interfaces object in the left-hand pane and you'll see something like Figure 17.42.

I should note that at this point the folks who are doing a full-time connection, like Frame Relay, are done. You may have to do something to tell RRAS that you have "dialed" that connection—sorry I'm being vague, but this varies from vendor to vendor and that's why you want to be very sure that they've got good Windows 2000 support before buying their FRAD—but other than that, you've now got a connection out to the Internet, a connection to your local network, and routing is enabled.

For those with modems and ISDN, however, we're not done, so we'll move on to Figure 17.42.

Now right-click the Routing Interfaces object and choose New/Demand-Dial Interface, which kicks off yet another wizard, the Demand Dial Interface Wizard. I'll spare you the first screen, but if you click Next from the opening screen, you'll see a screen like Figure 17.43.

FIGURE 17.42

RRAS screen with
server opened

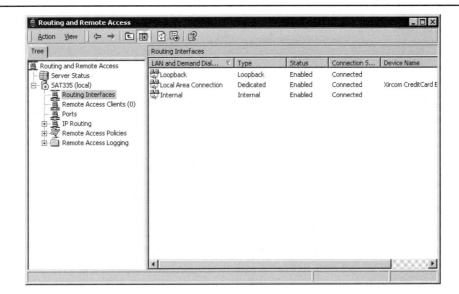

FIGURE 17.43

Naming the direct-dial
interface

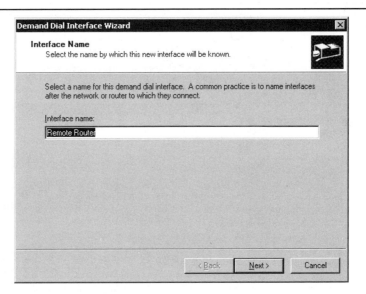

Give the connection a name and click Next, and the wizard will show you something like Figure 17.44.

As RRAS handles virtual private network (VPN, covered in detail in Chapter 22) connections as well as more common dial-up type connections, the wizard next asks you which type of connection you're creating. Choose the modem/ISDN option and click Next and you'll see the next panel, as in Figure 17.45.

FIGURE 17.44

VPN or direct-dial?

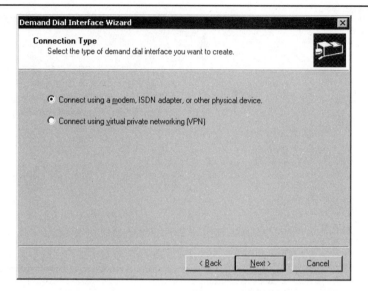

FIGURE 17.45

Which device to use?

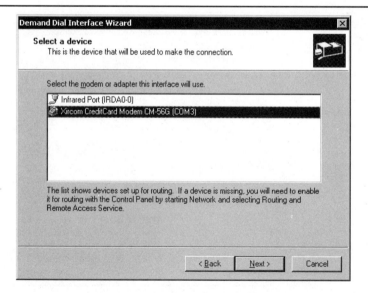

You'll only see this screen if you have multiple potentially possible devices for WAN connection. Now, in my world, infrared isn't much of a WAN link, but I guess it's just a matter of taste. Click the modem, ISDN box, or whatever you're going to use to dial out, and click Next, and you'll see something like Figure 17.46.

FIGURE 17.46

What number to dial?

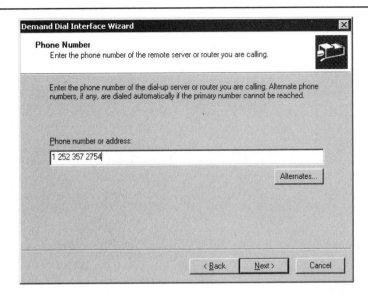

Enter the number that the modem should dial and click Next to see Figure 17.47.

FIGURE 17.47

Configuring the routing connection

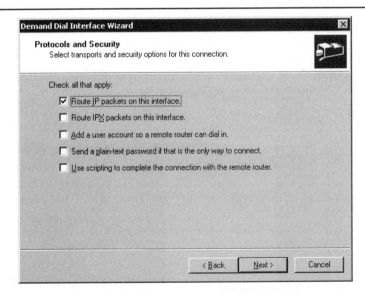

I've clicked only Route IP Packets on This Interface, and then clicked Next to see Figure 17.48.

FIGURE 17.48

User ID for dial-in

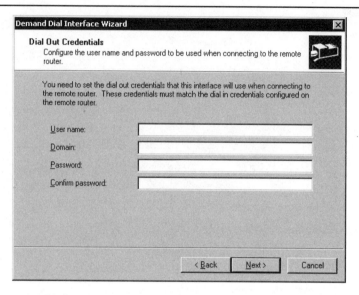

Here, Domain is only relevant if you're dialing into a Windows 2000 or NT 4 RAS/RRAS server. For dial-up to a standard ISP, just leave Domain blank. Fill in the user account name and password, then click Next (one *would* think that they could have consolidated a few of these wizard screens, hmmm?), click Finish and then click the Routing Interfaces object, and you'll see a screen like Figure 17.49.

FIGURE 17.49

Routing Interfaces listed

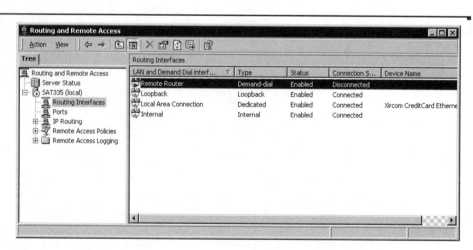

Notice that RemoteRouter is one of the listed interfaces. Right-click it and choose Properties, and you'll see a property page for the interface. Click Options and you'll see something like Figure 17.50.

FIGURE 17.50

Making the interface persistent

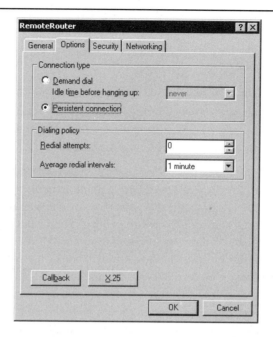

By default, the modem only dials up when the gateway senses that one of the local systems needs to access the Internet. I suspect that you'll find that a somewhat unsatisfactory option because of the relatively large amount of time that the gateway will require to dial up and establish the Internet connection. For example, suppose I sit at one of the local machines and type "ping www.whitehouse.gov"; it will probably take so long for the gateway to complete the Internet dial-in that the ping will have long ago timed out. A better answer, I believe, is to just click the Persistent radio button. That way, RRAS tries to establish the dial-up connection and keep it up.

Lower-Cost LAN-to-WAN Routing with Internet Connection Sharing

The preceding section explained how to connect a set of machines on a LAN connection using the traditional method—get a connection device of some kind, get a bunch of IP addresses from an ISP, and so on. But that can be an expensive proposition. Newer routing technologies make it possible for you to connect as many computers as you like to the Internet through a gateway machine. What's new about that? Well, as with the example we just saw, all of those computers are connected to the gateway with a local area network, and the gateway is connected to the Internet somehow. What's *different* is this:

- The only machine on the network with a "regulation," IANA- or ISP-issued IP address is the gateway.
- The other machines have nonroutable addresses.
- All of the "heavy lifting," routing-wise, is being done by the gateway computer. In fact, the ISP has no idea whatsoever that all of those other computers are accessing the Internet via the gateway.

This functionality, generically called Network Address Translation, or NAT, routing, was until recently fairly expensive to implement, requiring special routers. But Windows 2000 comes with the software to turn a Windows 2000 server into a NAT router. Even more amazing, Microsoft included this capability in Windows 2000 *Professional* as well—and even in the revised version of Windows 98, the "second edition"! Called Internet Connection Sharing, this will work on any kind of Internet connection, whether it's a modem, ISDN, cable modem, DSL, or whatever.

 NOTE Just to be on the safe side, check your "use agreement" with your ISP. Some ISPs specifically forbid any kind of sharing.

In the remaining part of this chapter, I'll walk you through setting up ICS with a Windows 2000 machine. My example uses a dial-up modem, but it'll work essentially the same for anything. But note that you can only do this if Windows 2000 supports your modem—I'm told that several kinds of cable modems only run under Windows 95, and though I've not seen that myself, clearly a situation like that would preclude sharing that cable modem with Windows 2000.

Get Connected to Your ISP

The first step is just to get connected to your ISP. Right-click My Network Places and choose Properties, and you'll see a screen like Figure 17.51.

Double-click the Make New Connection icon, and you'll get the inevitable welcome screen from a wizard that will help set up the connection to the ISP. Click Next to get past it, and you'll see Figure 17.52.

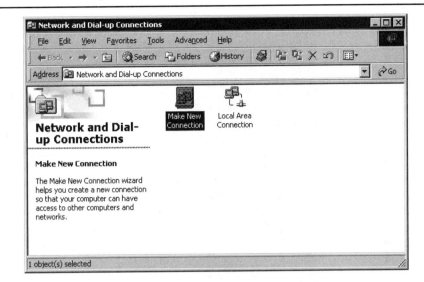

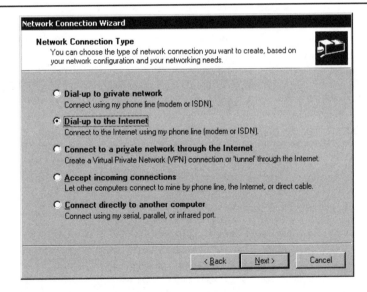

Tell the wizard that this is just a modem dial-up to the Internet by clicking the radio button labeled Dial-Up to the Internet and click Next. For some reason, this kicks off the Internet Connection Wizard (the wizardry is getting a trifle thick for my taste) and you'll see Figure 17.53.

FIGURE 17.53

Introducing the Internet Connection Wizard

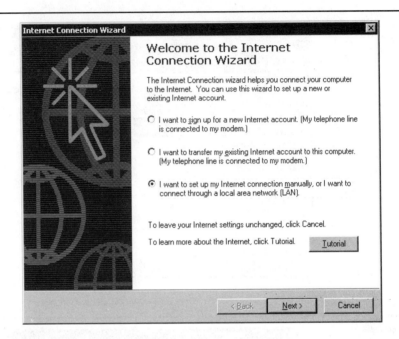

Pick the last option, and click Next. You'll see something like Figure 17.54.

FIGURE 17.54

Dial or direct connect?

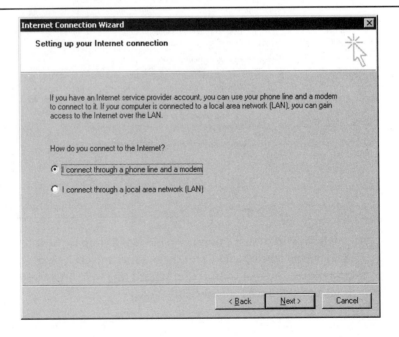

As you're dialing in, select Connect Using My Phone Line. (Again, though, didn't you already answer that question back in Figure 17.50? Maybe Microsoft needs to run the "hearing test wizard.") Click Next and you'll fill in the phone line, as you see in Figure 17.55.

FIGURE 17.55

Phone number to call

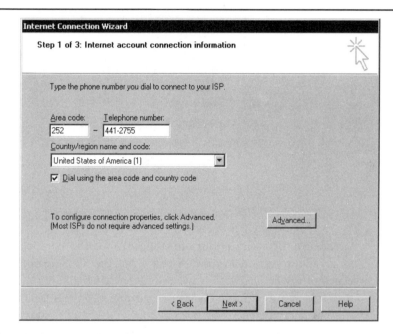

Although that's a fairly self-explanatory item, I included 17.55 to point out that there's an Advanced button on the screen. I had to use it to set up my ISP's connection and you may also, so let's take a look at what it does. Click Advanced and you'll se a property page with two tabs, one labeled Connection (which you'll probably never have to worry about) and another labeled Addresses (which you may have to worry about). You see the Addresses tab in Figure 17.56.

While it's possible for an ISP to automatically configure your system when you dial in, giving your system an IP address and telling it where to find the DNS servers, not all do. In my experience, most of them can do the IP address, as nearly everyone dials in with PPP nowadays—I say "nowadays" because as recently as 1995 many ISPs still only supported the simpler SLIP protocol—and PPP does the IP address assignment to the client (that is, your dialing-in PC) with no trouble. But many ISPs still require you to punch in the addresses of their DNS servers—here's where you do it. There's room to fill in up to two DNS servers; then click OK to return to the screen where you fill in the phone number, and click Next. In the next screen, you can enter your user account name and password; click Next, and you can give the dial-up entry a descriptive name—I used Coastal Net ISP—then click Next.

FIGURE 17.56

Setting the DNS server addresses

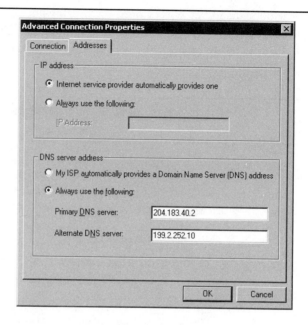

After that, the wizard wants to set up an e-mail account, asking "Do you want to set up an Internet mail account now?" Click the No radio button and then Next. You can at this point click Finish and the system will dial up to the Internet, but don't do that yet—uncheck the box labeled "To connect to the Internet immediately, select this box and then click Finish," and *then* click Finish. Network and Dial-Up Connections will look something like Figure 17.57.

FIGURE 17.57

Dial-up object created

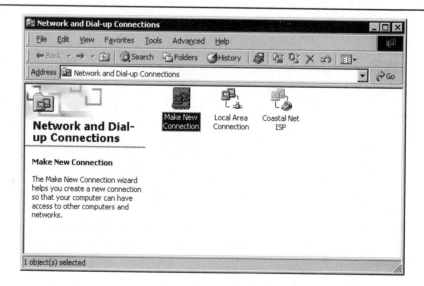

For some reason, you have to *first* create the dial-up object, *then* modify its properties to share its connection. So right-click the new object and choose Properties, and you'll see a property sheet with several tabs, one of which is labeled Sharing; click that tab, and you'll see a screen like Figure 17.58.

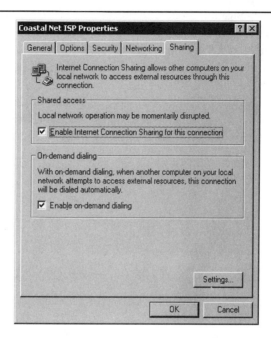

Check Enable Internet Connection Sharing for This Connection, and the On-Demand Dialing section will change from grayed to enabled. If the connection is not a full-time connection, then check Enable On-Demand Dialing. That will tell your gateway to dial out whenever anyone on the network needs to get on the Net. Again, call setup time may mean a long wait at first, so tell people to do something like a "ping" to some outside IP address and wait a minute or so, to give the connection enough time to get set up, and *then* to start up the Web browser, e-mail program, or whatever.

When you click OK to clear the property page, you'll get a confirmation message saying something like this:

> When Shared Access is enabled, your LAN adapter will be set to use IP address 192.168.0.1. Your computer may lose connectivity with other computers on your network. If these other computers have static IP addresses, you should set them to obtain their IP addresses automatically. Are you sure you want to enable Shared Access?

The "192.168.0.1" address is part of the nonroutable IP addresses. Your computer then becomes a DHCP server, believe it or not, and if you set the computers on the local network to get their addresses from DHCP and reboot them, they'll all be able to communicate with each other *and* with the gateway, and the gateway will get their packets to and from the Internet without trouble.

So is ICS just for home, or is it for businesses as well? Well, it's pretty powerful and some small to medium firms may give it a whirl for their Internet connectivity. But it lacks management tools and there's no way to find out, for example, how many addresses the server has given out or to modify the 192.168.0.*x* address range. But that hole in ICS may not be of sufficient importance to see ICS quickly move out of the home and into the office.

Well, by now, you're on an intranet in the traditional way. Microsoft adds two possible options to this setup: The *Dynamic Host Configuration Protocol (DHCP)* and the *Windows Internet Name Service (WINS)*. We'll meet these two, as well as the essential third (DNS) and a few other services, in the next chapter.

CHAPTER 18

Building a Windows 2000 TCP/IP Infrastructure: DHCP, WINS, DNS, Sites, and More

Whether you're hooking up a two-computer intranet in your house to share an Internet connection or weaving a world-spanning internet, you've got to solve two basic problems. First, every system on the network needs a unique IP address and requires configuration—it needs to know the address of its default router, what its domain name is, where the nearest DNS server is, and the like. And second, it needs help finding its way around the network: How do I send mail to Jane over at Acme Industries? How do I connect to the server that will let me buy books or shoes online? Or, more mundanely, how do I find a server that will log me on?

TCP/IP-based Windows 2000 systems use three technologies to accomplish IP configuration and name management: The Dynamic Host Configuration Protocol (DHCP), the Domain Name System (DNS), and the Windows Internet Name Service (WINS). Of the three, WINS is something of a relic, a technology that in *theory* you can forgo altogether, but in practice you can only do it if your network is both purely Windows 2000–based (all machines run Windows 2000) and if your network-aware applications are built for Windows 2000 rather than NT 4 or earlier operating systems. A TCP/IP-based network can make good use of the File Transfer Protocol (FTP) and telnet for network support, and this chapter talks about how to use them. Finally, all firms need e-mail, but for some reason Windows 2000 doesn't ship with an e-mail server. There's no need to spend money for a mail server, however; in this chapter, you'll learn where to find a no-cost Windows 2000–based Internet mail server and how to set it up.

DHCP: Automatic TCP/IP Configuration

In Chapter 17, you learned how to set up IP on a Windows 2000 system. Ah, but now ask yourself, "Do I really want to walk around to 3,000 workstations and do this by hand?" Auuugghhhh! Oops, sorry, what I really meant was, "Of course not." Who wants to have to remember which IP address you gave to *that* machine so that you don't put the address on *this* machine? Or how'd you like to get a phone call every time some visiting dignitary needs an IP address for his laptop? No thanks. DHCP will greatly simplify the task, so let's see how to set it up.

 WARNING By the way, this discussion assumes that you've already read the preceding chapter; don't think that if you decided from the start to go with DHCP that you could jump in here without reading the preceding chapter.

Simplifying TCP/IP Administration: BOOTP

"I have a little list…it never can be missed…." Well, okay, that's not exactly what Poobah sings in *Mikado*, but it fits here. You see, back when I first put TCP/IP on my company's computers, in 1993, I had to keep this list of PCs and IP addresses in a notebook. It was basically a kind of master directory of which IP addresses had been used so far.

Obviously, I had to consult it whenever I put TCP/IP on each new computer. Obvious, sure, but what's unfortunate is that I never seemed to have the notebook with me when I needed it. So I started keeping this list of computers and IP addresses on one of my servers, in a kind of common HOSTS file. It served two purposes: First, it told me what IP addresses were already used, and second, it gave me a HOSTS file to copy to the local computer's hard disk.

But, I recall thinking, this is silly. Keeping track of IP addresses and the machines using them is a rote, mechanical job—you know, the kind of job that computers are good at.

Unknown to me, the Internet world apparently had a similar feeling and so invented a TCP/IP protocol called BOOTP, which became DHCP, as you will see. With BOOTP, a network administrator would first collect a list of MAC addresses for each LAN card. I've already mentioned the 48-bit identifiers on each network card, which are good examples of MAC addresses.

Next, the administrator would assign an IP address to each MAC address. A server on the company's intranet would then hold this table of MAC address/IP address pairs. Then, when a BOOTP-enabled workstation would start up for the day, it would broadcast a request for an IP address. The BOOTP server would recognize the MAC address from the broadcaster and would supply the IP address to the workstation.

This was a great improvement over the static IP addressing system that I've described so far. The administrator didn't have to physically travel to each workstation to give it its own IP address; she needed only to modify a file on the BOOTP server when a new machine arrived or if it was necessary to change IP addresses for a particular set of machines.

Another great benefit of BOOTP is that it provides protection from the "helpful user." Suppose you have user Tom, who sits next to user Dick. Dick's machine isn't accessing the network correctly, so helpful user Tom says, "Well, *I'm* getting on the net fine, so let's just copy all of this confusing network stuff from my machine to yours." The result was that both machines ended up with identical configurations—including identical IP addresses, so now neither Tom *nor* Dick can access the network without errors! In contrast, if Tom's machine is only set up to go get its IP address from its local BOOTP server, then setting up Dick's machine identically will cause no harm, as it will just tell Dick's machine to get *its* address from the BOOTP server. Dick will get a different address (provided that the network administrator has typed in an IP address for Dick's MAC address), and all will be well.

DHCP: BOOTP Plus

BOOTP's ability to hand out IP addresses from a central location is terrific, but it's not dynamic. The network administrator must know beforehand what all of the MAC addresses of the Ethernet cards on her network are. This isn't *impossible* information to obtain, but it's a bit of a pain (usually typing **ipconfig /all** from a command line yields the data). Furthermore, there's no provision for handing out temporary IP addresses, like an IP address for a laptop used by a visiting executive. (I suppose you could keep a store of PCMCIA Ethernet cards whose MAC addresses had been preinstalled into the BOOTP database, but even so, it's getting to be some real work.)

DHCP improves upon BOOTP in that you just give it a range of IP addresses that it's allowed to hand out and it just gives them out first come, first served to whatever computers request them. If, on the other hand, you want DHCP to maintain full BOOTP-like behavior, then you can; it's possible with DHCP to preassign IP addresses to particular MAC addresses (it's called *DHCP reservation*), as with BOOTP.

With DHCP, you only have to hard-wire the IP addresses of a few machines, like your BOOTP/DHCP server and your default gateway.

 WARNING Both DHCP and BOOTP use UDP ports 67 and 68, so you won't be able to install both a BOOTP server and a DHCP server on the same computer. Now, Microsoft does not supply a BOOTP server; this note would mostly be only relevant if you tried to install a third-party BOOTP server. But Windows 2000/NT also allows you to make a computer a *BOOTP Forwarding Agent*. If you enable that software on a DHCP server, the server stops giving out IP addresses.

Let's see how to get a DHCP server up on your network so the IP addresses will start getting handed out, and then we'll take a look at how DHCP works.

Say No to Static IP: Use DHCP Everywhere!

In a minute, I'll get into the nitty-gritty of setting up DHCP servers and handing out IP addresses. But before I do, let's take up a big, overall network configuration question: Which machines should have static IP addresses, and which machines should get their addresses from DHCP servers?

In general, the answer is that the only machines that should have static IP addresses should be your WINS servers, DNS servers, and DHCP servers. In actual fact, you'll probably put the WINS, DNS, and DHCP server functions on the same machines.

"But wait!" I hear you cry, "Are you suggesting that I let my domain controllers, mail servers, Web servers, and the like all have floating, random IP addresses assigned by DHCP willy-nilly?" No, not at all. Recall that you can assign a particular IP address to a particular MAC address using a DHCP reservation. My suggestion, then, is that you sit down and figure out which machines need fixed IP addresses, get the MAC addresses of the NICs in those machines, and then create reservations in DHCP for those machines. (You'll see how a bit later.)

Installing and Configuring DHCP Servers

DHCP servers are the machines that provide IP addresses to machines that request access to the LAN. DHCP only works if the TCP/IP software on the workstations is *built* to work with DHCP—if the TCP/IP software includes a *DHCP client*. Microsoft offers TCP/IP software with DHCP clients for Windows for Workgroups and DOS. NT 3.5, 3.51, and 4 workstations as well as Windows 95 and 98 workstations are already DHCP aware. Of course, Windows 2000 Professional machines also include DHCP clients.

Installing the DHCP Service

To get ready for DHCP configuration:

- Have an IP address ready for your DHCP server—this is one computer on your network that *must* have a hardwired ("static") IP address.
- Know which IP addresses are free to assign. You use these available IP addresses to create a pool of IP addresses.

You install the software to make your server a DHCP server in the same way that you install most other network services, from the Add/Remove Windows Components applet of the Control Panel. Step-by-step, it looks like this:

1. Open the Control Panel (Start/Settings/Control Panel).
2. Open Add/Remove Programs.
3. Click Add/Remove Windows Components and wait a bit while the Windows Components Wizard starts up. (Why we needed a wizard when a dialog box would do, particularly when a dialog box would appear 15 seconds more quickly than the wizard, is a mystery. But, then, I guess that all of the wizards I've ever read about were mysterious.)
4. Click Next to bring up the list of Windows components.
5. Click Networking Services and then the Details button.
6. Click the check box next to Dynamic Host Configuration Protocol (DHCP).
7. Click OK to return to Windows Components.
8. Click Next to install the service. The system will say that it is "Configuring Components" for a while, probably a few minutes. A couple of rounds of Free-Cell, and the screen labeled Completing the Windows Components Wizard appears.
9. Click Finish to end the Wizard.
10. Click Close to close Add/Remove Windows Components.

And best of all, you needn't reboot afterward. You control DHCP with the DHCP snap-in, which you'll find in Administrative Tools: Start/Programs/Administrative Tools/DHCP. Start it up, and the opening screen looks like most MMC snap-ins, with the left and right panes. This particular one lists your server, with a plus sign next to it. Click the plus sign and you'll see a screen like Figure 18.1.

FIGURE 18.1

DHCP manager opening screen

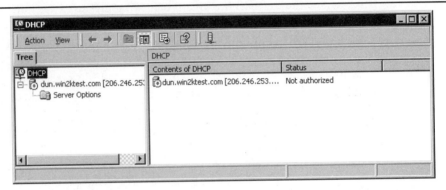

Notice that this snap-in lists the server in the left-hand pane. That's because you can control as many DHCP servers as you like from this program. All you need do to add a DHCP server to the list of servers that you control is to just click Action, followed by Add Server.

Authorizing DHCP Servers

It's sort of small, so you may not be able to see it in the screen shot, but to the left of "DUN [206.246.253.111]" is a small arrow that points downward—in color, it's red. That arrow represents a very nice touch on Microsoft's part.

You see, under NT 4, 3.51, and 3.5, anyone with an NT Server installation CD could set up NT Server on a computer and make herself an administrator of that server. With administrative powers, she could then set up a DHCP server. Now, the job of a DHCP server, recall, is to hand out IP addresses to computers who want to be part of the network. The problem arises when the administrator of this new server decides just for fun to offer a bunch of meaningless IP addresses, a range of addresses that your firm doesn't actually own. The result? Well, the next time that a machine in the company needs an IP address, it asks any server within earshot for an IP address. The server with the meaningless addresses responds, as do the valid servers—but the server with the bogus addresses is likely to respond more quickly than the valid servers (it doesn't have anything else to do) and so many client PCs will end up with IP addresses from the server with the bogus addresses. Those addresses won't route and so those people won't be able to get anything done on the network.

Why would someone set up a server with bogus addresses? Usually it's not for a malicious reason. Rather, it's more common that someone's just trying to learn DHCP and so sets up a server to play around with, not realizing "test" DHCP servers are indistinguishable from "real" DHCP servers to the client machines. Such a DHCP server is called a *rogue* DHCP server.

Windows 2000 solved the problem of rogue DHCP servers by disabling new DHCP servers until a domain administrator "authorizes" them in the Active Directory. With Windows 2000, anyone can set up a DHCP server, but the server won't start handing out addresses until authorized. This isn't foolproof, as only machines who are members of Active Directory–based domains seek to be authorized. Someone who wanted to maliciously set up a rogue DHCP server could simply install a copy of Windows 2000 Server and not join it to the domain, *then* set up a DHCP server—but, again, that's not the most common problem.

You authorize a server with the DHCP snap-in, and again, you've got to be logged in as a domain administrator to do this. From the DHCP snap-in, click the server and then click Action/Authorize, and you'll see a dialog box like the one in Figure 18.2.

FIGURE 18.2

List of authorized DHCP servers

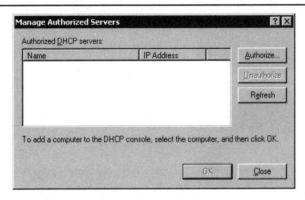

You can see that there are no servers authorized yet, so let's authorize this one. Click Authorize and you'll see the dialog box in Figure 18.3.

FIGURE 18.3

Authorizing a new DHCP server

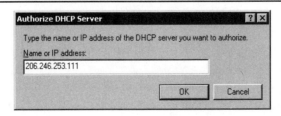

I've filled in the IP address of this server. Click OK, and you'll be asked to confirm that you do indeed want to add this server. Click the Yes button, and you'll return to the list of authorized servers. Click Close to close that dialog and you'll see the DHCP snap-in looking as in Figure 18.1, save that the red down-pointing arrow is now green and points up.

NOTE You may have to click the server and then press F5 to refresh the display in order to see the green arrow.

Now you can offer IP addresses with this server.

Creating a Range of Addresses: DHCP "Scopes"

That DHCP snap-in's really not much to look at, is it? Well, it won't be, as there are no scopes set up yet. Scopes? What's a scope?

Creating the Scope

In order for DHCP to give out IP addresses, it must know the range of IP addresses that it can give out. Microsoft calls a range of IP addresses, and the descriptive information associated with them, a *scope*. To create a scope, right-click the server's icon and choose New Scope, which starts the New Scope Wizard. Click Next from its opening screen and you see a screen like the one in Figure 18.4.

FIGURE 18.4

Naming the scope

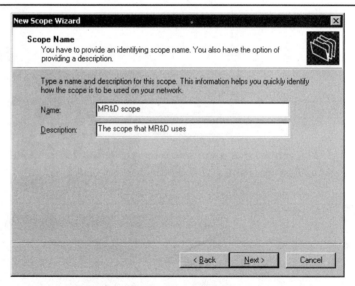

In this screen, you simply identify the scope, giving it a name and a comment. In my experience, I've never really figured out why there's a name *and* a comment, as the name has no real use; it could well *be* a comment, in effect. Fill in appropriate values for your network, and click Next to see a screen like Figure 18.5.

FIGURE 18.5

Defining the IP address range

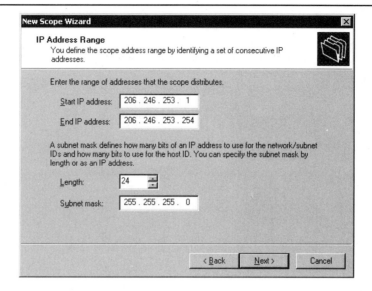

Specify IP Address Range

A scope is simply a range of IP addresses—a pool from which they can be drawn. In the example in Figure 18.5, I've created a scope that ranges from 206.246.253.1 through 206.246.253.254—in other words, I'm going to use DHCP to manage the entirety of my C class network.

NOTE   I don't want to get too sidetracked on the issue of scopes just now (we'll cover multiscope considerations later), but let me mention why you'd have more than one scope on a DHCP server. You can assign a scope to each subnet serviced by your DHCP servers—and, yes, it *is* possible for one DHCP server to handle multiple subnets. In contrast, however, a DHCP server won't let you create more than one scope *in the same subnet*. I will, however show you how to get more than one server to act as a DHCP server (for the sake of fault tolerance) in a minute.

I put DHCP in charge of giving out *all* of my Internet addresses, but clearly that makes no sense, as I must have at least *one* static IP address around—the one on my DHCP server. So I need to tell the DHCP server not to give *that* one away, but how to do it? Click Next twice—the wizard seems to need two clicks on the Next button here—to see the next screen, where I'll tell the server what addresses to avoid, as in Figure 18.6.

FIGURE 18.6

Excluding address ranges

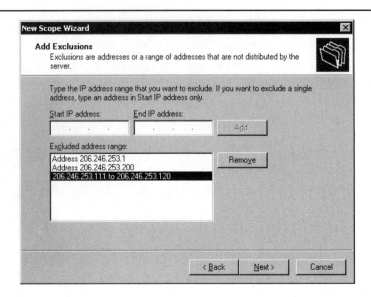

As you see, I've excluded several addresses: The .1 address is a dedicated LAN/WAN router, the .200 machine has a static address, and while working on this book I temporarily set aside the .111 through .120 addresses for static IP. Notice that you can specify one address by itself; you don't *have* to specify starting and ending addresses in a one-address range.

Specifying More Ranges: Superscopes

As you read in Chapter 17, in general there's a one-to-one relationship between physical network segments and subnets. IP was designed to let systems that could directly "shout" at each other do that, communicating directly rather than burdening routers.

Sometimes, however, you'll see two separate subnets on a single segment. That's often because a single network can't accommodate all of the segment's machines. For example, if you started your enterprise with 180 hosts and acquired a slash 24 network, you'd have enough addresses for 254 devices, presuming that you didn't subnet. But what about when your firm grows to need 300 machines? You might go out to your ISP and get another slash 24, another 254 addresses.

Now you've got two networks. You *could* break your network up into two segments and apply one set of network addresses to each segment. But you might not want to: Suppose your one segment can support all of your machines and you can't see the point in messing around with more routers—what then?

You create a superscope. The idea with a superscope is that it contains more than one range of IP addresses—more than one scope—but applies them to a single segment. You can do it simply—just define two separate scopes on a DHCP server, then right-click the server, choose New Superscope and you'll have the superscope. You can then add scopes to the superscope as you like.

But what about the mechanics of a superscope? When you put a new machine on this subnet and it broadcasts to find a DHCP server and get an IP address, will it get an IP address from the first scope or the second? The answer is that it doesn't matter. If you're just shoehorning two IP subnets onto the same physical segment simply because you're out of IP addresses on an existing subnet, then it doesn't matter whether a workstation gets an IP address from the first range of IP addresses or the second range of IP addresses, as all of the enterprise's routers know how to find either range.

Once in a while, however, you have two ranges of IP addresses on the same physical network for a reason—perhaps one range is composed of IANA- or ISP-assigned IP addresses and the other is composed of nonroutable addresses. You probably have good reasons, then, to put some computers on the routable addresses and some on the nonroutable addresses. But how to get DHCP to help there? After all, both the routable and nonroutable ranges are in the same shouting radius, so to speak. When a workstation asks DHCP for an address, how would DHCP know whether to give that workstation a routable or nonroutable address?

The answer is that DHCP can't—there's no magic here. There would have to be some kind of setting on the client that the client could use to give DHCP a clue about what network it wanted to be a member of, the routable or nonroutable. What you must do in a situation like that is decide which machines go in the routable network and which go in the nonroutable network and then enter their MAC addresses by hand into DHCP with *reservations* (which we'll cover later), much as network administrators must when using BOOTP instead of DHCP.

Set Lease Duration

Returning to the wizard, click Next and you see a screen like Figure 18.7.

As you'll read in a few pages, when I explain the internals of DHCP, the DHCP server doesn't give the client PC an IP address to use forever. The client PC only gets the IP address for a specific period of time called a *lease*, and by the time the lease period's up, the client must either lease it or another address from a DHCP server, or the client must stop using IP altogether, immediately. But how long should that lease be? While that was something of an issue when DHCP first appeared in NT 3.5, it doesn't matter all that much what you set it for now, so long as you set it for longer than a few days; the default of eight days is probably good. We'll talk more about lease durations when we discuss DHCP internals later. Click Next to move to Figure 18.8.

FIGURE 18.7

Set lease duration

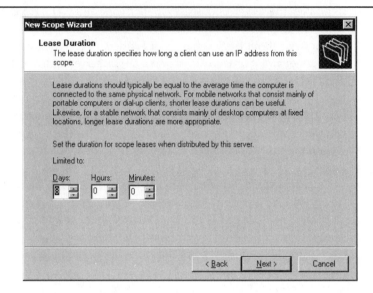

FIGURE 18.7

Set lease duration

FIGURE 18.8

Configure DHCP options

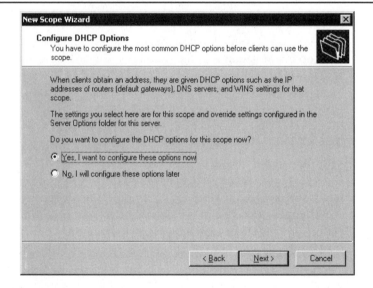

Setting Client Options

Remember all of those options in the Advanced tab for TCP/IP Properties when you configured static IP addresses in the preceding chapter? Well, you needn't travel around to the workstations and set them, as DHCP lets you configure those things right from the server. DHCP can provide default values for a whole host of TCP/IP parameters, including these basic items:

- Default gateway
- Domain name
- DNS server
- WINS server

Notice I said "default." You can override any of these options at the workstation. For example, if you said that by default everyone's DNS server was 10.0.100.1 but wanted one particular PC to instead use the DNS server at 10.200.200.10, then you could just walk over to the PC and use the Advanced button in the TCP/IP property page (see Chapter 17 if you don't recall how to find that) to enter a DNS name. Even though the DHCP server would offer a DNS server address of 10.0.100.1 to the PC, the PC's DHCP client software would see that the PC had been configured to use 10.200.200.10 instead and would use that address rather than 10.0.100.1. Any other DHCP-supplied options, however, wouldn't be ignored. The general rule is, then, that anything configured on the client overrides anything that DHCP suggests.

Click Next to see the first client option, as you see in Figure 18.9.

FIGURE 18.9

Set default gateway

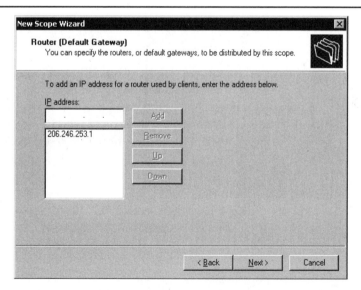

You may recall that in the last chapter I said that when configuring TCP/IP on a Windows 2000 machine, the "big four" characteristics, so to speak, are IP address, subnet mask, IP address of the default gateway, and address or addresses of local DNS server(s). By its very nature, any DHCP lease gives the first two; this is the third.

While you *can* enter any number of gateways, there's no point in entering more than one, as I've never found a situation wherein Microsoft's IP could use a second, third, or fourth possible gateway upon discovering that the first gateway's down. I've only specified one gateway, as you see in Figure 18.9. Click Next to see the next option screen, as in Figure 18.10.

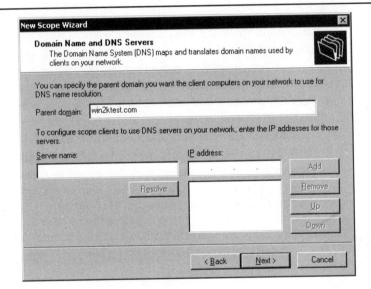

FIGURE 18.10

Set domain name

In this wizard screen, you tell the DHCP server that whenever it leases a client PC an IP address from this scope, it should also set that client PC's DNS domain name to some value—win2ktest.com, in this case—and to tell the client PC that it can find DNS servers at some address. I've chosen *not* to specify DNS servers, however, because *all* of the scopes in my enterprise share two DNS servers, and I don't want to have to reenter these DNS servers for every scope. As you'll see in a few pages, I can instead just tell this server, "Give this particular DNS server to *all* scopes." Click Next to see the next screen, as in Figure 18.11.

Most of us will still have the necessary evil of WINS servers; here's where you tell the client where to find your enterprise's WINS servers.

FIGURE 18.11

Set WINS server(s)

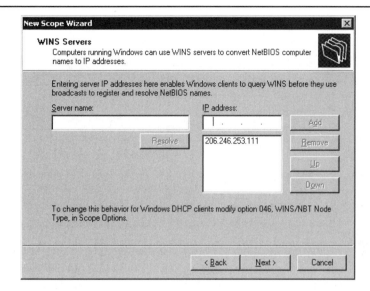

FIGURE 18.11

Set WINS server(s)

Activate the Scope

Click Next and you can get the scope started, as you see in Figure 18.12.

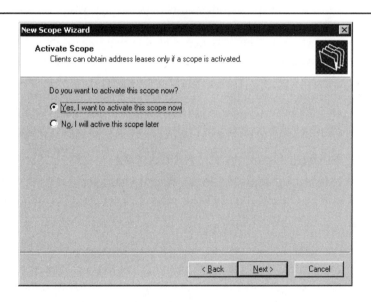

FIGURE 18.12

Activate the scope?

That's all for the basic scope options, so the wizard's done. On the way out, it asks if you're ready for this server to start handing out leases on IP addresses. Click Yes and Next, and the wizard will finish, starting the scope in the process. The DHCP snap-in then looks like Figure 18.13.

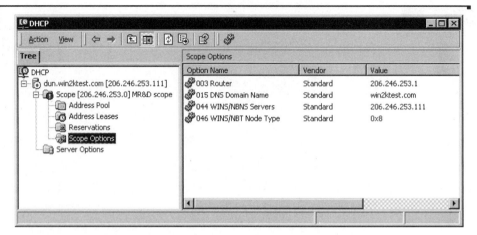

Taking a minute and looking at the hierarchy shown in Figure 18.13 underscores a few things about how DHCP works. The snap-in allows you to control any number of DHCP servers from a central location, although you see only one in this example screen, the machine at 206.246.253.111. Each server can have a number of subnets that it serves, with one range of IP addresses for each subnet. The ranges are called scopes, and again this example machine only shows one scope, but could host many—I've seen one large corporate DHCP server that hosts 1,200 scopes! Within the scope there are several pieces of information: The range of addresses (Address Pool), the list of addresses that this server has given out (Address Leases), addresses that we've preassigned to particular systems (Reservations, which we'll cover a bit later), and particular TCP/IP settings that the DHCP server should give to any clients (Scope Options). Notice that the options include something that we didn't set—WINS/NBT Node Type. That's DHCP-ese for the fact that the client PC will be set up to use a WINS server, that the client will be set up as something called a *hybrid node*, which I'll cover later in this chapter in the WINS section.

Setting Options for All Scopes

Notice the folder lower in the interface labeled Server Options. They're useful when you're putting more than one scope on a server. It could be that if you've got three different subnets and a couple hundred machines, you've only got two DNS servers, and those machines serve your entire enterprise. When configuring those scopes, it would be a pain to have to retype in those DNS servers—the same two DNS servers—for all three scopes. Server Options solves that problem by allowing you to set options for *all* of a given server's scopes in one operation. Just right-click the Server Options folder and choose Configure Options to see a dialog box like the one in Figure 18.14.

FIGURE 18.14

Server Options dialog

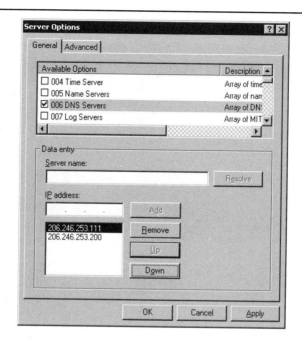

Here I've clicked DNS, and you can see that it allows me to enter DNS server addresses, as the wizard did. A bit of scrolling down shows that there are a *lot* of potential DHCP options. But, despite the fact that there seem to be bushels of sadly unused parameters mutely begging to be used, *don't*. Even though they exist, the Microsoft DHCP *client*—the part of Windows, DOS, Windows 95/98, NT, and Windows 2000 that knows how to get IP addresses from a DHCP server—does not know how to use any options save the ones I just mentioned. Microsoft included the other things just to remain compatible with BOOTP.

Advanced Server Configuration

Before leaving configuration, let's take a look at some overall server configuration items—in particular, logging and DNS client registration. In the DHCP snap-in, right-click the server and choose Properties. You'll see a page with three tabs. The first is named General, as you see in Figure 18.15.

FIGURE 18.15

*General server
configuration page*

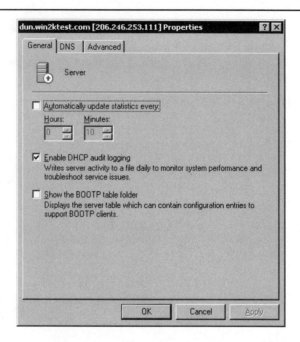

The main thing to notice here is the "logging" option. It's a default option, so don't worry about having to check it. But where is the log kept? Well, for one thing, there are seven logs, one for each day of the week—that makes finding a record for an action on a particular day easier. The logs are in simple ASCII format, so you can examine them with Notepad, although it would be nicer if the DHCP snap-in would go get them *for* you. They're in \winnt\system32\dhcp in files whose names include the day of the week. Part of one log looks like the following:

```
63,07/03/99,00:44:30,Restarting rogue detection,,,
51,07/03/99,00:45:30,Authorization succeeded,,win2ktest.com,
11,07/03/99,00:47:09,Renew,206.246.253.135,
PC400.win2ktest.com,00105A27D97A
10,07/03/99,00:48:00,Assign,206.246.253.2,
PC400.win2ktest.com,5241532000105A27D97A000000000000
10,07/03/99,00:48:00,Assign,206.246.253.3,
PC400.win2ktest.com,5241532000105A27D97A000001000000
63,07/03/99,01:51:51,Restarting rogue detection,,,
51,07/03/99,01:52:52,Authorization succeeded,,win2ktest.com,
```

Rogue detection is a process whereby the DHCP server seeks to find unauthorized DHCP servers. To entrap these dastards, the DHCP server craftily pretends that it is just a PC looking for an IP address. It gets offers from other DHCP servers, and the DHCP server then checks their IP addresses against the list of authorized DHCP servers in the Active Directory. If it finds a scoundrel, then it reports that in the Event Viewer.

On the third line, you see that the machine at 206.246.253.135 has "renewed" its IP address—that is to say, it has said to the DHCP server, "You once gave me this IP address and the lease is running out. May I extend the lease?" The two "assign" statements give the .2 and .3 addresses to PC400 to then hand out—you see, PC400 is a RAS server and needs IP addresses to give away to dial-in clients. RAS has given those two addresses for PC400 to use.

The Advanced property page has another interesting tab, the DNS tab. Click it, and you'll see a screen like the one in Figure 18.16.

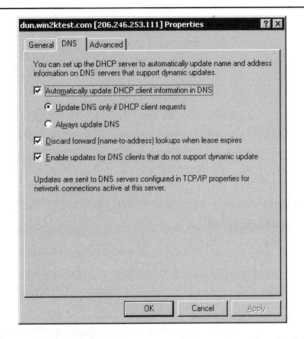

FIGURE 18.16

Configuring the dynamic DNS client from DHCP

While DNS is a topic for later in this chapter, let me jump ahead a bit and explain briefly how it works. DNS is a database of machines and names: My local DNS server is the machine that knows that there's a machine named dun.win2ktest.com that has an IP address of 206.246.253.111. But how does it *know* that? With DNS under NT 4, I'd have to start up a program called the DNS Manager and hand-enter the information. But under Windows 2000, dun.win2ktest.com is smart enough to talk to its local DNS server and say, "Listen, I don't know if you knew this, but I'm a machine on the network, my name's dun.win2ktest.com, and my IP address is 206.246.253.111." Additionally, the DNS server—which is running Windows 2000—is smart enough to *hear* this information; older DNS servers wouldn't be expecting machines to register themselves with their local DNS server, and the local DNS server wouldn't have a clue about what to do with the information anyway. But post-1998 DNS servers have a feature called *dynamic* DNS, which enables them to accept this name/address (*name registration*) information from other machines rather than having to have a human type the information in.

There are two important points to notice in the preceding paragraph. First, the DNS server's got to be smart enough to listen to and act upon the name registrations when they come from the clients. Second, the clients have to be smart enough to *issue* name registration information! If my workstation's running NT 4 rather than Windows 2000, then it's not been programmed to offer name/address information to its DNS server because the whole dynamic DNS technology didn't even exist in 1996 when Microsoft wrote NT 4! From the point of view of the state-of-the-art DNS server running on the Windows 2000 server, then, the old Windows 9*x*, Windows for Workgroups, and NT clients are just plain dumb. Or, more exactly, from the point of view of the DNS server, those clients *don't even exist*. There's no way that the DNS server could figure out that they are there.

That's what the dialog box in Figure 18.16 accomplishes. The Windows 2000 DHCP server will notice when it's handing out an IP address to a machine that doesn't know about dynamic DNS; while the DHCP server cannot modify the code running on the older client, it can fill in for the older client's lack of knowledge, and register the client's name/address with DNS for it. Notice the option labeled Enable Updates for DNS Clients That Do Not Support Dynamic Update; that's the feature I've been discussing here. Make sure that box is checked.

Monitoring DHCP

Once you've got a DHCP server set up and running, you may want to find out how many leases remain, who's got those leases, and the like. Open up the Address Leases folder and you'll see something like Figure 18.17.

FIGURE 18.17

Assigned leases

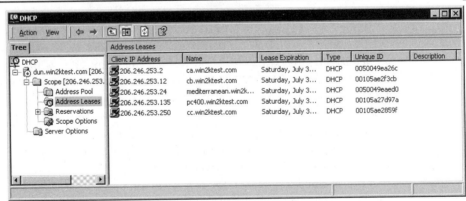

This folder displays all of the leases that DHCP has currently outstanding, who's got them—that is, the machine's name—as well as the machine's MAC address.

But how many addresses are left? Right-click any scope and choose Display Statistics and you'll see a message box like Figure 18.18.

FIGURE 18.18

Lease statistics

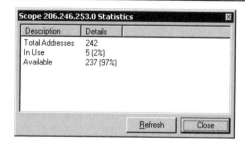

With just a few clicks, you can bring up this message box and find out whether your network's hunger for IP addresses is being met.

DHCP on the Client Side

Now that you've set up DHCP on a server, how do you tell clients to use that DHCP? Simple. Any Microsoft operating system from Windows for Workgroups to Windows 9*x* to NT 3.*x* to NT 4.*x* to Windows 2000 all have DHCP configuration as an installation option, although some of those clients refer to it as "automatic" configuration rather than DHCP configuration. (By the way, the Microsoft Client software for DOS and Windows supports DHCP as well.)

Once a system has gotten an IP address, you can find out what that address is by going to that system, opening up a command line, and typing **ipconfig /all**. On a Windows 95 workstation, click Start and Run, and then type **WINIPCFG** and press Enter. Windows 98 supports both IPCONFIG *and* WINIPCFG. Windows NT only supports IPCONFIG. IPCONFIG's useful for other DHCP client–fiddling, as well. You can force a DHCP client to abandon its DHCP-supplied IP address and look for a different one by typing first **IPCONFIG /RELEASE** and then **IPCONFIG /RENEW**.

DHCP in Detail

That's setting up DHCP. But how does it work, and unfortunately, how does it sometimes *not* work?

DHCP supplies IP addresses based on the idea of *client leases*. When a machine (a DHCP client) needs an IP address, it asks a DHCP server for that address. (*How* it does that is important, and I'll get to it in a minute.) A DHCP server then gives an IP address to the client, *but only for a temporary period of time*—hence the term *IP lease*. You might have noticed that you can set the term of an IP lease from DHCP; just right-click any scope and choose Properties, and it's one of the settings in the resultant window.

The client then knows how long it's got the lease. Even if you reboot or reset your computer, it'll remember what lease is active for it and how much longer it's got to go on the lease.

 TIP On a Windows 3.x machine, lease information is kept in DHCP.BIN in the Windows directory. On a Windows 95 machine, it's in HKEY_LOCAL_MACHINE\System\CurrentControlSet\ Services\VxD\DHCP\Dhcp-infoxx, where xx is two digits. And if you wish to enable or disable the error messages from the DHCP client on a Windows 95 machine, it's the value PopupFlag in the key HKEY_LOCAL_MACHINE\System\CurrentControlSet\Services\ VxD\DHCP; use "00 00 00 00" for false, or "01 00 00 00" for true. Alternatively, opening a command line and typing **IPCONFIG/Release** will erase this information. To find the place in the Registry holding DHCP lease information on an NT machine, run REGEDIT and search for "DHCPIPAddress" in HKEY_LOCAL_MACHINE\System\CurrentControlSet. The key or keys that turn up are the location of the DHCP lease info. On a Windows 2000 system, it's probably hkey_local_machine\system\currentcontrolset\services\ TCPIP\parameters\Interfaces; within there you'll find GUIDs (Global Unique IDs, the things that look like {CE52A8C0-B126-11D2-A5D2-BFFEA72FC}) for each adapter and potential RAS connection. There's a DHCPIPAddress value in each adapter that gets its addresses from DHCP.

So, if your PC had a four-day lease on some address and you rebooted two days into its lease, then the PC wouldn't just blindly ask for an IP address; instead, it would go back to the DHCP server that it got its IP address from and request the particular IP address that it had before. If the DHCP server were still up, then it would acknowledge the request, letting the workstation use the IP address. If, on the other hand, the DHCP server has had its lease information wiped out through some disaster, then it will either give the IP address to the machine (if no one else is using the address), or it will send a *negative acknowledgment*, or *NACK*, to the machine, and the DHCP server will make a note of that NACK in the Event Log. Your workstation should then be smart enough to start searching around for a new DHCP server. In my experience, sometimes it isn't.

Like BOOTP, DHCP remembers which IP addresses go with what machine by matching up an IP address with a MAC (Media Access Control, that is, Ethernet address).

Normally a DHCP server can send new lease information to a client only at lease renewal intervals. But DHCP clients also "check in" at reboot, so rebooting a workstation will allow DHCP to reset any lease changes such as subnet masks and DNS services.

Getting an IP Address from DHCP: The Nuts and Bolts

A DHCP client gets an IP address from a DHCP server in four steps:

1. A *DHCPDISCOVER* broadcasts a request to all DHCP servers in earshot, requesting an IP address.

2. The servers respond with *DHCPOFFER* of IP addresses and lease times.

3. The client chooses the offer that sounds most appealing and broadcasts back a *DHCPREQUEST* to confirm the IP address.

4. The server handing out the IP address finishes the procedure by returning with a *DHCPACK*, an acknowledgment of the request.

Initial DHCP Request: DHCPOFFER

First, a DHCP client sends out a message called a DHCPDISCOVER saying, in effect, "Are there any DHCP servers out there? If so, I want an IP address." This message is shown in Figure 18.19.

DHCP
client

DHCP
server

Enet addr: 00CC00000000
IP addr: 0.0.0.0

Enet addr: 00BB00000000
IP addr: 210.22.31.100

"Is there a DHCP server around?"

IP address used: 255.255.255.255 (broadcast)
Ethernet address used: FFFFFFFFFFFF (broadcast)
Transaction ID: 14321

You might ask, "How can a machine communicate if it doesn't have an address?" Through a different protocol than TCP—UDP, or the *User Datagram Protocol*. It's not a NetBIOS or NetBEUI creature; it's all TCP/IP-suite stuff.

Now, to follow all of these DHCP messages, there are a couple of things to watch. First of all, I'm showing you both the Ethernet addresses (Token Ring addresses for those of you using Token Ring) and the IP addresses because you see that they tell somewhat different stories. Also, there is a *transaction ID* attached to each DHCP packet that's quite useful. The transaction ID makes it possible for a client to know when it receives a response from a server exactly *what* the response is responding to.

In this case, notice that the IP address the message is sent to is 255.255.255.255. That's the generic address for "anybody on this subnet." Now, 210.22.31.255 would also work, assuming that this is a C class network that hasn't been subnetted, but 255.255.255.255 pretty much always means "anyone who can hear me." If you set up your routers to forward broadcasts, then 255.255.255.255 will be propagated all over the network; 210.22.31.255 would not. Notice also the destination Ethernet address, FFFFFFFFFFFF. That's the Ethernet way of saying, "Everybody—a broadcast."

DHCP Offers Addresses from Near and Far

Any DHCP servers within earshot—that is, any that receive the UDP datagram—respond to the client with an offer, a proposed IP address, like the one shown in Figure 18.20. Again, this is an offer, not the final IP address.

FIGURE 18.20

DHCP step 2: DHCPOFFER

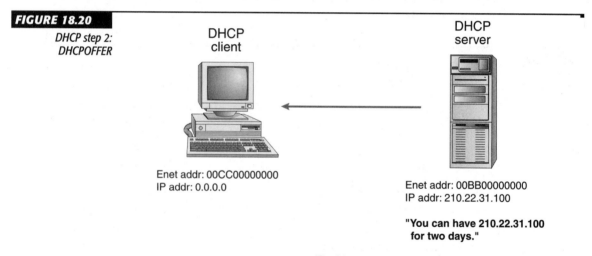

DHCP
client

DHCP
server

Enet addr: 00CC00000000
IP addr: 0.0.0.0

Enet addr: 00BB00000000
IP addr: 210.22.31.100

**"You can have 210.22.31.100
for two days."**

IP address used: 255.255.255.255 (broadcast)
Ethernet address used: 00CC00000000 (directed)
Transaction ID: 14321

This offering part of the DHCP process is essential because, as I just hinted, it's possible for more than one DHCP server to hear the original client request. If every DHCP server just thrust an IP address at the hapless client, then it would end up with multiple IP addresses, addresses wasted in the sense that the DHCP servers would consider them all taken, and so they couldn't give those addresses out to other machines.

Side Note: Leapfrogging Routers

Before going further, let's consider a side issue that may be nagging at the back of your mind. As a DHCP client uses *broadcasts* to find a DHCP server, where do routers fit into this? The original UDP message, "Are there any DHCP servers out there?" is a broadcast, recall. Most routers, as you know, do not forward broadcasts—which reduces network traffic congestion and is a positive side effect of routers. But if DHCP requests don't go over routers, then that would imply that you have to have a DHCP server on every subnet—a rather expensive proposition.

The BOOTP standard got around this by defining an RFC 1542, a specification whereby routers following RFC 1542 would recognize BOOTP broadcasts and would forward them to other subnets. The feature must be implemented in your routers' software, and it's commonly known as *BOOTP forwarding*. Even if you live in a one-subnet world, by the way, that's worth remembering, as it's invariably a question on the Microsoft certification exams: "What do you need for client A to communicate with DHCP server B on a different subnet?" Answer: The router between A and B either must be "RFC 1542–compliant" or "must support BOOTP forwarding."

Okay, so where do you *get* an RFC 1542–compliant router? Well, most of the IP router manufacturers, like Compatible Systems, Cisco, and Bay Networks, support 1542. New routers probably already support it; older routers may require a software upgrade. Another approach is to use a Windows 2000 or NT system as a router, as Windows 2000 and NT routing software includes 1542 compliance. But what if you've got dumb routers, or router administrators that refuse to turn on the BOOTP forwarding? Then you can designate an NT or Windows 2000 machine as a *DHCP Relay Agent*.

A DHCP Relay Agent is just a computer that spends a bit of its CPU power listening for DHCP client broadcasts. The DHCP Relay Agent knows that there's no DHCP server on the subnet (because you told it), but the DHCP Relay Agent knows where there *is* a DHCP server on another subnet (because you told it). The DHCP Relay Agent then takes the DHCP client broadcast and converts it into a directed, point-to-point communication straight to the DHCP server. Directed IP communications can cross routers, of course, and so the message gets to the DHCP server.

What do you need to make a DHCP Relay Agent? Well, with NT 4, you could use any NT machine—workstation or server. For some annoying reason, Windows 2000 only includes software to make a DHCP Relay Agent with Server.

To make an NT machine into a DHCP Relay Agent, just open up the Control Panel, then the Network applet. Click the Protocols tab and double-click the TCP/IP protocol. In the resulting dialog box, you'll see a tab labeled DHCP Relay. Click it, and you'll see a dialog box like the one shown in Figure 18.21.

To make this work, just click the Add button and fill in the IP address of a DHCP server or servers. The dialog box is simple, but there are two things that confuse people about making a computer into a DHCP Relay Agent, so let me note them in the following tip and warning.

FIGURE 18.21

Configuring an NT 4
computer to be a
DHCP Relay Agent

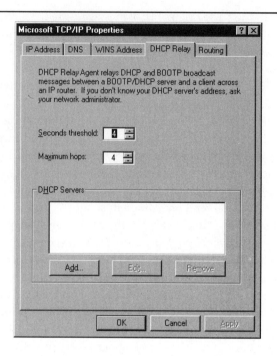

 TIP   The NT DHCP Relay Agent runs on a computer on the subnet, *not* a computer acting as a router on a subnet. However, the Windows 2000 DHCP Relay Agent can run on a router PC or a non-router. You should only have one DHCP Relay Agent on each subnet.

 WARNING   Under no circumstances should you make a DHCP server into a DHCP Relay Agent. The net effect will be for the DHCP server to essentially "forget" that it's a DHCP server and instead to just forward every request that it hears to some other DHCP server. This prompts me to wonder why the silly DHCP Relay Agent function isn't grayed out altogether on a DHCP server—certainly the Obtain an IP Address from a DHCP Server option is.

To make a Windows 2000 system—remember, server only—into a DHCP Relay Agent, you've got to use Routing and Remote Access Service. Basically any RRAS configuration will do; you needn't enable WAN routing or dial-in. Look back to Chapter 17 to see how to configure an RRAS system—again, click Start/Programs/Administrative Tools/Routing and Remote Access, then right-click the server's name and choose Configure and

Enable Routing and Remote Access to start the wizard, then choose Manually Config-ured Server, and finish the wizard. You'll see a screen like the one in Figure 18.22.

FIGURE 18.22

RRAS main screen

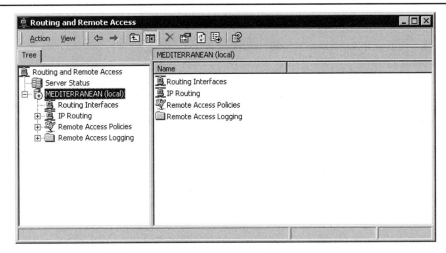

Open the IP Routing object (click the plus sign) and one of the objects that you'll see will be DHCP Relay Agent. Choose it and the RRAS management console will look something like Figure 18.23.

FIGURE 18.23

RRAS console with DHCP Relay Agent highlighted

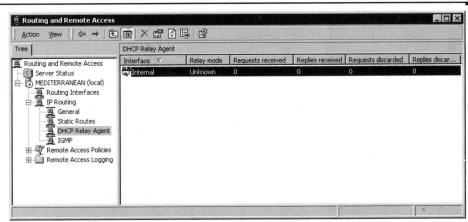

Double-click the Internal object and you'll get a dialog that lets you configure hop counts, in the unlikely event that you'll need to do that.

You've got to configure the agent, so right-click it and choose Properties and you'll see a dialog like the one in Figure 18.24.

You configure the agent by telling it where to find DHCP servers. Enter the IP address of the DHCP server and click Add to add a server to the list. Finally, you've got to enable the agent to listen on the local network for DHCP requests to forward. Right-click DHCP Relay Agent and choose New Interface. Choose Local Area Connection and the Agent will then be active on the network.

FIGURE 18.24

Relay Agent configuration screen

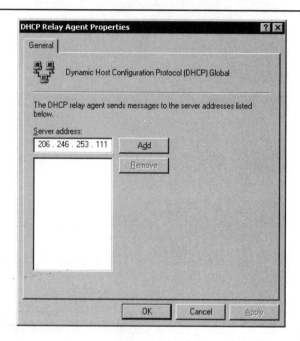

Discussion of Relay Agents and 1542-compliant routers leads me to yet another question. What if a DHCP server from another subnet gave an IP address to our client? Wouldn't that put the client in the wrong subnet? If a DHCP server serves a bunch of different subnets, how does it know which subnet an incoming request came from? DHCP solves that problem with BOOTP forwarding.

Assuming that you have routers that implement BOOTP forwarding, then a client's original DHCP request gets out to all of them. But how do we keep a DHCP server in an imaginary subnet 200.1.2.*x* from giving an address in 200.1.2.*x* to a PC sitting in another imaginary subnet, 200.1.1.*x*? Simple. When the router forwards the BOOTP request, it attaches a little note to it that says, "This came from 200.1.1.*x*." The DHCP server then sees that information, and so it only responds if it has a scope within 200.1.1.*x*.

Anyway, notice that although to the higher-layer protocol (UDP) this is a broadcast, the lower-layer Ethernet protocol behaves as though it is not, and the Ethernet address embedded in the message is the address of the client, not the FFFFFFFFFFFF broadcast address. Notice also that the transaction ID on the response matches the transaction ID on the original request. End of side trip, let's return to watching that client get its address from DHCP....

Picking from the Offers

The DHCP client then looks through the offers that it has and picks the one that's best for it. If there are multiple offers that look equally good, it picks the one that arrived first. Then it sends another UDP datagram, another broadcast, shown in Figure 18.25.

It's a broadcast because this message serves two purposes. First, the broadcast *will* get back to the original offering server if the first broadcast got to that server, which it obviously did. Second, this broadcast is a way of saying to any *other* DHCP servers who made offers, "Sorry, folks, but I'm taking this other offer."

DHCP step 3:
DHCPREQUEST

DHCP
client

DHCP
server

Enet addr: 00CC00000000
IP addr: 0.0.0.0

Enet addr: 00BB00000000
IP addr: 210.22.31.100

**"Can I have the 210.22.31.100 IP address,
and thanks for the other offers, but no thanks."**

IP address used: 255.255.255.255 (broadcast)
Ethernet address used: FFFFFFFFFFFF (broadcast)
Transaction ID: 18923

Notice that both the Ethernet and the IP addresses are broadcasts, and there is a new transaction ID.

The Lease Is Signed

Finally, the DHCP server responds with the shiny brand-new IP address, which will look something like Figure 18.26.

It also tells the client its new subnet mask, lease period, and whatever else you specified (gateway, WINS server, DNS server, and the like). Again, notice it's a UDP broadcast, but the Ethernet address is directed, and the transaction ID matches the previous request's ID.

You can find out what your IP configuration looks like after DHCP by typing **IPCONFIG /ALL**. It may run off the screen, so you may need to add |**more** to the line. This works on DOS, Windows for Workgroups, and NT machines. You can see a sample run of IPCONFIG /ALL in Figure 18.27. Windows 95 machines have a graphical version of IPCONFIG called Winipcfg.

FIGURE 18.26

DHCP step 4:
DHCPACK

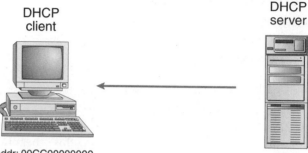

DHCP
client

DHCP
server

Enet addr: 00CC00000000
IP addr: 0.0.0.0

Enet addr: 00BB00000000
IP addr: 210.22.31.100

**"Sure; also take this subnet
mask, DNS server address,
WINS server, node type,
and domain name."**

IP address used: 255.255.255.255 (broadcast)
Ethernet address used: 00CC00000000 (directed)
Transaction ID: 18923

FIGURE 18.27

Run of IPCONFIG

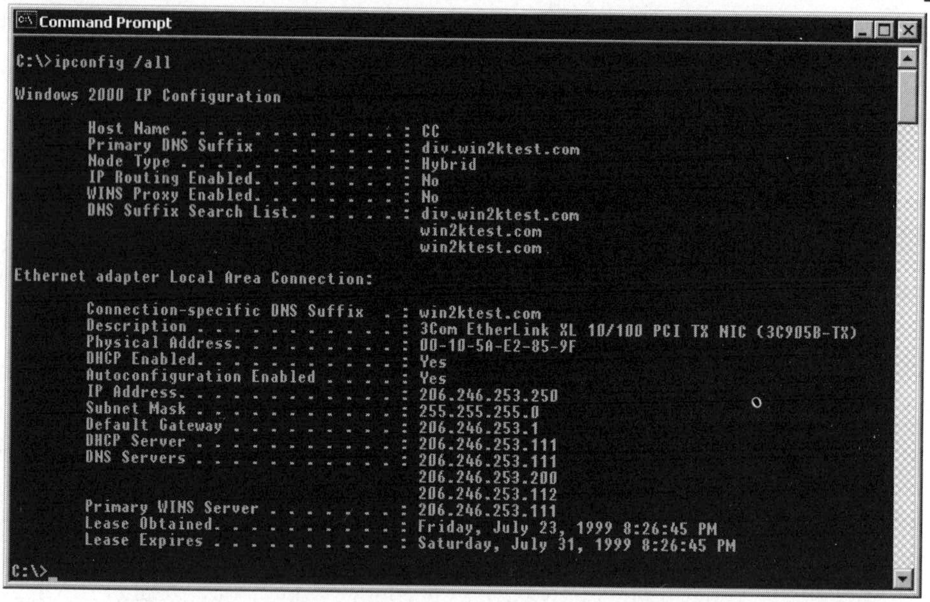

```
Command Prompt                                                          _ □ ×

C:\>ipconfig /all

Windows 2000 IP Configuration

        Host Name . . . . . . . . . . . . : CC
        Primary DNS Suffix  . . . . . . . : div.win2ktest.com
        Node Type . . . . . . . . . . . . : Hybrid
        IP Routing Enabled. . . . . . . . : No
        WINS Proxy Enabled. . . . . . . . : No
        DNS Suffix Search List. . . . . . : div.win2ktest.com
                                            win2ktest.com
                                            win2ktest.com

Ethernet adapter Local Area Connection:

        Connection-specific DNS Suffix  . : win2ktest.com
        Description . . . . . . . . . . . : 3Com EtherLink XL 10/100 PCI TX NIC (3C905B-TX)
        Physical Address. . . . . . . . . : 00-10-5A-E2-85-9F
        DHCP Enabled. . . . . . . . . . . : Yes
        Autoconfiguration Enabled . . . . : Yes
        IP Address. . . . . . . . . . . . : 206.246.253.250
        Subnet Mask . . . . . . . . . . . : 255.255.255.0
        Default Gateway . . . . . . . . . : 206.246.253.1
        DHCP Server . . . . . . . . . . . : 206.246.253.111
        DNS Servers . . . . . . . . . . . : 206.246.253.111
                                            206.246.253.200
                                            206.246.253.112
        Primary WINS Server . . . . . . . : 206.246.253.111
        Lease Obtained. . . . . . . . . . : Friday, July 23, 1999 8:26:45 PM
        Lease Expires . . . . . . . . . . : Saturday, July 31, 1999 8:26:45 PM

C:\>
```

Lost Our Lease! Must Sell!

What happens when the lease runs out? Well, when that happens, you're supposed to stop using the IP address. But that's not likely to happen.

When the lease is half over, the DHCP client begins renegotiating the IP lease by sending a DHCP request to the server that originally gave it its IP address. The IP and Ethernet addresses are both specific to the server.

The DHCP server then responds with a DHCPACK. The benefit of this is that the DHCPACK contains all of the information that the original DHCPACK had—domain name, DNS server, and so on. That means you can change the DNS server, WINS server, subnet mask, and the like, and the new information will be updated at the clients periodically, but no more than 50 percent of the lease time.

Now, if the DHCPACK doesn't appear, then the DHCP client keeps resending the DHCP request out every two minutes until the IP lease is 87.5 percent expired. (Don't you wonder where they get these numbers from?) At that point, the client just goes back to the drawing board, broadcasting DHCPDISCOVER messages until someone responds. If the lease expires without a new one, the client will stop using the IP address, effectively disabling the TCP/IP protocol on that workstation.

But if you've messed with the DHCP servers, then the renewal process seems to get bogged down a bit. It's a good idea in that case to force a workstation to restart the whole DHCP process by typing **ipconfig /renew**; that will often clear up a DHCP problem.

Even with an infinite lease, however, a DHCP client checks back with its server whenever it boots. Therefore, you can often change from infinite to fixed leases by just changing the lease value at the server. Then stop and restart the DHCP service.

Forcing a Particular IP Address on a Client: DHCP Reservations

Sometimes, BOOTP doesn't seem like a bad idea. There are times that you'd like to be able to say, *this* computer gets *that* IP address. Fortunately, it's easy to accomplish that with DHCP reservations.

Look at the DHCP snap-in and you'll see a folder labeled `Reservations`. Right-click that folder and choose New Reservation. You'll see a dialog box like the one in Figure 18.28.

FIGURE 18.28

*Reserving an IP
address*

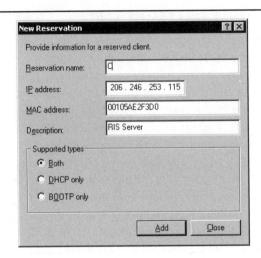

Here, you see that I'm assigning the .115 address to a machine with a particular MAC address.

So far, it sounds like DHCP pretty much hasn't changed since NT 4, and in large measure that's true. But it has added superscopes and support for dynamic DNS even on systems that don't understand dynamic DNS. And there's one more neat difference. Once you've created a reservation, open the `Reservations` folder and you'll see an object representing that reservation. Right-click it and you'll see Configure Options; click that and you'll see that you can set things like DNS server, domain name, WINS server, and the like for one specific reservation! Now, that's a pretty neat new feature.

Designing Multi-DHCP Networks

Clearly the function of the DHCP server is one that shouldn't rest solely on the shoulders of one server (well, okay, servers don't have shoulders, but you know what I mean). So, how can you put two or more DHCP servers online to accomplish some fault tolerance?

Microsoft seems, however, a bit confused about how to go about providing multiple DHCP servers for a given subnet and has offered different advice at different times.

In one document, "Windows NT 3.5 Family Upgrade Course,"† they said several things. First, "There is NO mechanism in DHCP that allows two or more DHCP Servers to coordinate the assignment of IP addresses from overlapping IP address pools."

No argument there. If you had two different DHCP servers on the same subnet, and they both thought that they could give out addresses 202.11.39.10 through 202.11.39.40, then there would be nothing keeping the first server from giving address 202.11.39.29 to one machine while simultaneously the other server was giving out that same 202.11.39.29 address to another machine. (It's almost as if help-ful Tom has returned!)

Then, they go on (pages 147 and 148) to demonstrate two different machines run-ning DHCP server, and each machine has a different scope. Both scopes are, however, taken from a single subnet.

In contrast, the NT Resource Kit† (version 3.5, but 3.51 has no updates on the mat-ter) takes issue with the idea of more than one scope referring to a subnet like so: "Each subnet can have only one scope with a single continuous range of IP addresses...."

What this boils down to is this: I don't know what the official Microsoft approach to DHCP fault tolerance *is*. I *do*, however, know what works, and what has worked for me. Like many people, I came up with an approach like the one in the NT training guide. I just run DHCP on multiple machines and create multiple scopes that refer to the same subnet. I make absolutely sure that the ranges of addresses in the scopes do not overlap at all, and everything seems to work fine.

Name Resolution in Perspective: Introduction to WINS (Even for Windows 2000) and DNS

Consider the two following commands, both issued to the same server:

```
ping server01.bigfirm.com
```

and

```
net use * \\server01\mainshr
```

In the Ping command, the server is referred to as server01.bigfirm.com. In the NET USE command, that same server is called server01. The difference is important for these reasons:

- Ping relies upon a traditionally Internet-oriented programming interface called *Winsock,* and any program running Ping generally needs access to something called a *DNS server* in order to execute the Ping command.

- NET USE relies upon a traditionally Microsoft networking–oriented program-ming interface called *NetBIOS,* and any program running NET USE generally needs access to something called a *WINS server* in order to execute the NET USE command.

Let's do a bit of background work in order to understand Winsock, DNS, NetBIOS, and WINS.

Two Different Lineages, Two Different Names

The Ping command is clearly a TCP/IP/Internet kind of command. You can't run it unless you're running TCP/IP, and as a matter of fact, it's a valid command on a Unix, VMS, Macintosh, or MVS machine so long as that machine is running a TCP/IP protocol stack.

In contrast, NET USE is a Microsoft networking command. You can do a NET USE on an NT network no matter what protocol you're running, but the command usually wouldn't be valid on a Unix, VMS, Macintosh, or whatever kind of machine; in general, Microsoft networking is pretty much built to work on PCs. (Yes, I know, NT is in theory architecture independent, so you could find an Alpha machine using NET USE commands, but on the whole, NT is an Intel *x86* operating system at this writing—and I haven't seen announcements of an NT/390 for the IBM mainframe world, NT VAX for the Digital world, or NT SPARC for the Sun world.)

Application Program Interface = Modularity

The difference is in the network application programming interface (API) that the application is built atop. API? What's that?

Well, years ago, most PC software had no understanding of networks at all. But that's not true anymore; there are many "network-aware" programs around. For example, the software that lets a Windows 2000 system be a file server is network aware; what good would a file server be without a network? Other network-aware server software includes Web servers like Internet Information Server or e-mail servers like Exchange.

Desktop machines—*clients*—use network-aware software as well. The program that lets you browse file servers with My Network Places on Windows 2000 systems, browse Network Neighborhood on Windows 9*x* and NT 4 systems, or do command-line commands like NET VIEW (which lets you view the servers in a workgroup or the shares on a server) or NET USE is generically called a "client for Microsoft networking" and is network aware. So also is a Web browser (the client software for a Web server) or an e-mail client.

But the programmers who build network-aware applications like file server clients or Web browsers aren't generally the programmers who write the rest of the networking software—the NIC drivers, the protocols, and so on. Different pieces of network software are usually designed to fit together in a modular fashion. But the only way that the folks who write the Web browsers can remain compatible with the folks who write the TCP/IP code is if the application developers and the protocol developers agree on an interface, a kind of "software connector" between the two pieces of software. More and more, designers build software to be modular specifically so that the Web browser people don't have to coordinate closely with the TCP/IP protocol–writing people.

The interface between a protocol and the applications that rely on it is called the application programming interface, or API. Think of an API as being something like the controls you use when driving a car. Your car's steering wheel, accelerator, and other controls form the interface that you see, and you learn to use them in order to operate the car. You might have no idea while you're driving what's under your car's hood—you just push down the accelerator and the car goes faster. If someone snuck into my garage tonight and replaced the internal combustion engine in my Honda with a magic engine that didn't use gas, I would have no idea, nor would I care until I eventually noticed that the gas gauge seemed to be broken. As a driver, I really don't have to know anything at all about engines—all I've got to know is that the pedal on the right makes the car go faster. So long as the magic engine makes the car go vroom-vroom when I push down the right pedal, I'm happy.

The "automobile API" consists of a few "primitive" commands: Brake the car, accelerate the car, shift the car's transmission, and so on. There is no command "back the car out of the driveway," and yet I can still back a car out of a driveway by just assembling a number of the primitive commands into the actual action of backing a car out of a driveway. The best part about this generic automobile API is that once you learn how to drive one car, you can instantly use another. In other words, you are an "application designed for the car driver controls API."

In contrast, consider how private pilots learn to fly. They have two pedals on the floor of their plane, but the left pedal turns them left and the right pedal turns them right. Someone trained as a private pilot would be an "application designed for the private plane API." Taking someone who can fly a plane and plunking him down in a car without any other training wouldn't work too well. In the same way, if an application is built for *one* network API, then it won't work on another. But if you built a car whose controls acted like an airplane's, airplane pilots could drive the car without any trouble.

NetBIOS and Winsock

I'm stretching a point a bit here, but we could say that cars and planes are just different ways of solving the same problem—transportation. In the same way, various network vendors over the years have tackled the same problem and come up with different solutions. In particular, Microsoft has, since 1985, built their network applications atop a network API of their own creation called the Network Basic Input-Output System, or NetBIOS. The Internet world, on the other hand, has used a different network API called *sockets*. In the PC world, we've got a special version of sockets called *Winsock*.

Recall that the value of an API is that it separates your network applications from your network vendor—you needn't buy your network operating system from the same people that you bought your network fax software from. For example, if you buy a network fax application that was designed for a network API named NetBIOS, you should be able to run that network fax application on any network at all, so long as the network supports the NetBIOS API. Similarly, at one time there were several vendors selling a version of TCP/IP for Windows for Workgroups back in 1992–1994. If the Winsock implementations on each of those TCP/IP versions were built right, then you should have been able to run the exact same copy of Eudora Light (a free Internet e-mail program) or Netscape Navigator on any of them.

Can your network live with just Winsock or NetBIOS programming interfaces? Probably not. You want to run the NetBIOS-based programs because anything written for Microsoft networks prior to Windows 2000 was written to run on NetBIOS. And you want to run Winsock-based programs because so many Internet-type applications exist—Web and e-mail stand out, but there are many more—and they're built to work with Winsock.

 NOTE In fact, one of the major changes in NT wrought by Windows 2000 was that all of Windows 2000's networking will work fine on Winsock and doesn't need NetBIOS at all. But any Windows 9x, Workgroups, or NT system needing to access data on Windows 2000 servers will do so via NetBIOS. Similarly, any pre–Windows 2000 applications running on a Windows 2000 system can only run atop NetBIOS, even if all of the systems in the network are Windows 2000 systems. The result is that virtually all Windows 2000 systems need a complete NetBIOS infrastructure.

Name Resolution Defined

Something that both NetBIOS and Winsock have in common is that they both want to support easy-to-work-with machine names. Yes, every machine on the Internet and on most Windows 2000 networks (I say "most" because there's probably a few people left not using IP) has a unique IP address, but no one wants to use that to identify servers: Opening My Network Places should show servers with names like \\PERSONNEL rather than 220.10.99.32, and Amazon wants to be able to tell you to shop for books at www.amazon.com rather than 208.216.182.15. So we need some kind of database server around that can translate www.amazon.com to 208.216.182.15 and \\PERSONNEL to 220.10.99.32. This problem of converting a name into an IP address is called *name resolution*. For NetBIOS and Winsock, it's the same problem, but with two different solutions. NetBIOS looks for its name resolution from a Windows Internet Name Service (WINS) server; Winsock looks for its name resolution from a Domain Name System (DNS) server.

NetBIOS versus Winsock still not clear? Then consider one more analogy. Think of the APIs as communications devices. Telephones and the mail service are communications devices, also, so I'll use them in an analogy. Ping's job is to communicate with some other PC, and NET USE also wants to communicate with some PC. But Ping uses Winsock (the telephone) and NET USE uses NetBIOS (the mail). If you use the telephone to call a friend, then that friend's "name" as far as the phone is concerned may be something like (707) 555-2121. As far as the mail is concerned, however, the friend's "name" might be Paul Jones, 124 Main Street, Anytown, VA, 32102. Both are perfectly valid "names" for your friend Paul, but they're different because different communications systems need different name types. In the same way, server01.bigfirm.com and \\server01 are both perfectly valid but different names for the same server.

Handling Legacy and NetBIOS Names: The Windows Internet Name Service

Anyway, for those of you NT 4 vets hoping that WINS would bite the dust in Windows 2000, sorry, looks like we've still got to support it. So let's see how to support this "legacy name resolving system." (*Legacy* is computer industry-ese for "crappy old stuff that we hate and that's why we upgraded in the first place but we can't seem to get rid of all of it and so now we have to support both the new incomprehensible stuff *and* the crappy old stuff." But *legacy* sure makes it sound better, at least to me.)

NetBIOS atop TCP/IP (NBT)

The NetBIOS API is implemented on the NetBEUI, IPX/SPX, and TCP/IP protocols that Microsoft distributes. That makes Microsoft's TCP/IP a bit different from the TCP/IP you find on Unix (for example), because the Unix TCP/IP almost certainly won't have a NetBIOS API on it; it'll probably only have the TCP/IP sockets API on it. (Recall that as with all PC implementations of TCP/IP, Microsoft's TCP/IP form of sockets is called the Winsock API.)

NetBIOS on the Microsoft implementation of TCP/IP is essential, again to make older operating systems and applications happy. And NetBIOS over TCP (which is usually abbreviated NBT or NetBT) needs a name resolver.

Now, basic old NetBIOS converted names to network addresses by just broadcasting—"Hey, I'm looking for \\AJAX, if you're out there, \\AJAX, tell me your IP address!"—but clearly that's not going to be the answer in a routed environment; all of those "name resolution shouts" will stop dead at the routers. If \\AJAX is across a router from us, our software will never find \\AJAX.

NetBIOS name resolution over TCP/IP is, then, not a simple nut to crack. Many people realized this, and so there are two Internet RFCs (Requests for Comment) on this topic, RFC 1001 and 1002, published in 1986.

B Nodes, P Nodes, and M Nodes

The RFCs attacked the problem by offering options.

- The first option was sort of simplistic: Just do broadcasts. A computer that used broadcasts to resolve NetBIOS names to IP addresses is referred to in the RFCs as a *B node*. To find out who server01 is, then, a PC running B node software would just shout out, "Hey! Anybody here named server01? "

Simple, yes, but fatally flawed: Remember what happens to broadcasts when they hit routers? As routers don't rebroadcast the messages to other subnets, this kind of name resolution would only be satisfactory on single-subnet networks.

- The second option was to create a name server of some kind and to use that. Then, when a computer needed to resolve a name of another computer, all it needed to do was send a point-to-point message to the computer running the name server software. As point-to-point messages *do* get retransmitted over routers, this second approach would work fine even on networks with routers. A computer using a name server to resolve NetBIOS names into IP addresses is said to be a *P node*.

Again, a good idea, but it runs afoul of all of the problems that DNS had. *What* name server should be used? Will it be dynamic? The name server for NetBIOS name resolution is, by the way, referred to as a NetBIOS Name Server, or NBNS.

- The most complex approach to NetBIOS name resolution over TCP/IP as described in the RFCs is the *M node*, or *mixed* node. It uses a combination of broadcasts and point-to-point communications to an NBNS.

Microsoft Follows the RFCs, Almost

When Microsoft started out with TCP/IP, they implemented a kind of M node software. It was "point-to-point" in that you could look up addresses in the HOSTS file, or a file called LMHOSTS, and if you had a DNS server, then you could always reference that; other than those options, Microsoft TCP/IP was mainly B node-ish, which limited you to single-subnet networks. (Or required that you repeat broadcasts over the network, clogging up your network.) Clearly, some kind of NBNS was needed, and the simpler it was to work with, the better. As the RFCs were silent on the particulars of an NBNS, vendors had license to go out and invent something proprietary and so they did—several of them, in fact, with the result that you'd expect: None of them talk to each other.

That's where WINS comes in.

WINS is simply Microsoft's proprietary NBNS service. What makes it stand out from the rest of the pack is Microsoft's importance in the industry. They've got the clout to create a proprietary system and make it accepted widely enough so that it becomes a *de facto* standard.

Microsoft's NetBIOS-over-TCP client software not only implements B, P, and M nodes, it also includes a fourth, non-RFC node type. Microsoft calls it an H, or Hybrid, node.

But wait a minute; isn't *M node* a hybrid? Yes. Both M nodes and H nodes (and note well that at this writing, M nodes are RFCed and H nodes aren't) use both B node and P node, but the implementation is different:

- In M node, do a name resolution by first broadcasting (B node) and then, if that fails, communicate directly with the NBNS (P node).
- In H node, try the NBNS first. If it can't help you, then try a broadcast.

M Node versus H Node

"Hmmm…" you may be saying, "Why would anyone want to first broadcast, *then* look up the answer in the name server? Why clutter up the network cable with useless broadcasts when we could instead go right to the source and reduce network chatter?"

The answer is that it's a matter of economics. Recall that the RFCs on NetBIOS over TCP were written back in the mid '80s, when a typical PC had perhaps an 8MHz clock rate and a 5MHz internal bus. An Ethernet full of XTs would have had a lot of trouble loading the network enough for anyone to even notice. The bottleneck in networks in those days was the CPU or disk speed of the network server. But if the network includes routers—and if it doesn't, then broadcasting is all you need—then consider what the routers are connected to: Wide area network links, probably expensive 9600, 14,400, or 19,200bps leased lines. In a network like this, the LAN was a seemingly infinite resource, and wasting it with tons of broadcasts was of no consequence. In contrast, creating more traffic over the WAN by having every machine ask for NetBIOS names (presuming the NetBIOS Name Server was across the WAN link) could greatly reduce the effectiveness of that expensive WAN. Besides, the reasoning went, the vast majority of the time a PC only wanted to talk to another PC on the same LAN, so broadcasts would suffice for name resolution most of the time. The result? M nodes.

The economic picture in 1994, when Microsoft was inventing WINS, was another story entirely: LANs were clogged and WAN links were far cheaper—so H nodes made more sense.

You can force any DHCP client to be a B, P, M, or H node. One of the options that you can configure via DHCP is the WINS/NBNS Node Type. You give it a numeric value to set the client's NetBIOS name resolution technique. A value of 1 creates a B node, 2 is used for a P node, 4 for an M node, and 8 for an H node, the recommended node type.

Understanding the NBT Names on Your System

A major part of the NetBIOS architecture is its lavish use of names. A workstation attaches up to 16 names to itself. Names in NetBIOS are either group names, which can be shared—workgroups and domains are two examples—or normal names, which can't be shared, like a machine name. As you'll soon see that WINS keeps track of all of these names, you may be curious about what all of them *are*—so let's take a minute and look more closely into your system's NetBIOS names.

You can see the names attached to your workstation by opening a command line from a Windows for Workgroups, Windows 95, NT, or Windows 2000 machine and typing **nbtstat -n**. You get an output like this:

```
Node IpAddress: [199.34.57.53] Scope Id: []


      NetBIOS Local Name Table


  Name        Type      Status
  ---------------------------------------------
  MICRON133  <00> UNIQUE   Registered
  ORION      <00> GROUP    Registered
  MICRON133  <03> UNIQUE   Registered
  MICRON133  <20> UNIQUE   Registered
  ORION      <1E> GROUP    Registered
  MARK       <03> UNIQUE   Registered
```

In this example, the ORION group names are my workgroup and domain. MICRON133 is my machine's name, and MARK is my name—notice that NetBIOS registers not only the machine name, but the person's name as well. You can see the list of registered names on any computer in your network by typing **nbtstat -A <ip address>**, where the -A *must* be a capital letter.

But why is there more than one MICRON133? Because each different part of the Microsoft network client software requires names of its own, so they take your machine name and append a pair of hex digits to it. That's what the <00>, <20>, and the like are—suffixes controlled by particular programs. For example, if some other user on the network wanted to connect to a share named STUFF on this computer, she could type **net use * \\micron133\stuff**, and the redirector software on her computer would then do a NetBIOS name resolution on the name MICRON133<00>, as the <00> suffix is used by the redirector. Table 18.1 summarizes suffixes and the programs that use them.

TABLE 18.1: EXAMPLES OF MACHINE NAMES	
Unique Names	**Where Used**
<*computername*>[00h]	Workstation service. This is the "basic" name that every player in a Microsoft network would have, no matter how little power it has in the network.
<*computername*>[03h]	Messenger service.
<*computername*>[06h]	RAS Server service.
<*computername*>[1Fh]	NetDDE service; will only appear if NetDDE is active or if you're running a NetDDE application. (You can see this by starting up Network Hearts, for example.)
<*computername*>[20h]	Server service; name will only appear on machines with file/printer sharing enabled.
<*computername*>[21h]	RAS Client service.
<*computername*>[BEh]	Network Monitor agent.
<*computername*>[BFh]	Network Monitor utility.
<*username*>[03h]	Messenger service; any computer running the Messenger service (which is just about any MS networking client) would have this so that NET SEND commands to a user could be received.
<*domain name*>[1Bh]	Primary domain controller.
<*domain name*>[1Dh]	Master Browser.
Group Names	**Where Used**
<*domain name*>[00h] or <*workgroup name*>[00]	Domain name; indicates that the computer is a member of the domain and/or workgroup. If a client is a member of a workgroup whose name is different from a domain, then no domain name will be registered on the client.
<*domain name*>[1Ch]	PDCs and BDCs would share this; if a machine has this name registered, then it is a domain controller.
<*domain name*>[1Eh] or <*workgroup name*>[1Eh]	Used in browser elections, indicates that this computer would agree to be a browser. Will only show up on servers. (Potential browser.)
MSBrowse	Domain Master Browser.

No matter what kind of computer you have on a Microsoft enterprise network, it will have at least one name registered—the *<computer name>*[00] name. Most computers also register *<workgroup>*[00], which proclaims them as a member of a workgroup. Those are the only two names you would see if you had a DOS workstation running the old LAN Manager network client without the Messenger service or a Windows for Workgroups 3.1 (not 3.11) workstation that had file and printer sharing disabled.

Most modern client software would also have the Messenger service enabled and so would have the *<computer name>*[03] and *<username>*[03] names registered, as well.

Adding file and/or printer sharing capabilities to a computer would add the *<computer name>*[20] name. Servers all agree to be candidates for browse master by default, so unless you configure a machine to *not* be a candidate for browse mastering, then the *<workgroup name>*[1E] name will appear on any machine offering file or printer sharing. If the machine happens to be the browse master, it'll have *<workgroup name>*[1D] as well. Workstations use the [1D] name to initially get a list of browse servers when they first start up: They broadcast a message looking to see if the [1D] machine exists, and if it does, then the [1D] machine presents the workstation with a list of potential browsers.

Browse masters get the network name [01][02]__MSBROWSE__[02][01] as well—it's a group name, and only the *master* browsers are members. Master browsers use that name to discover that each other exists.

Name Resolution before WINS: LMHOSTS

Clients written prior to WINS, or clients without a specified WINS server, try to resolve a NetBIOS name to an IP address with a number of methods. The tools they'll use, if they exist, are:

- A HOSTS file, if present
- Broadcasts
- An LMHOSTS file, if present
- A DNS server, if present

You met HOSTS before—it's just a simple ASCII file. Each line contains an IP address, at least one space, and a name. LMHOSTS works in a similar way to HOSTS. And yes, you'd do well to understand LMHOSTS, as it solves many name resolution problems with pre–Windows 2000 servers and perhaps even Windows 2000 servers in an enterprise with both Windows 2000– and NT 4–based domains.

Introducing LMHOSTS

Recall that HOSTS is an ASCII file that lists IP addresses and Internet names, like the following:

```
100.100.210.13 ducky.mallard.com
```

```
211.39.82.15 jabberwock.carroll.com
```

Microsoft reasoned that if a simple ASCII file could supplement or replace DNS to resolve Winsock names, why not create an ASCII file to hold NetBIOS names? The result is the LMHOSTS file. LMHOSTS consists of pairs of IP addresses and names, like HOSTS, but the names are 15-character *NetBIOS* names, not Internet-type names:

```
100.100.210.13 ducky
211.39.82.15 jabberwock
```

I assumed in the above example that the NetBIOS name is identical to the leftmost part of the Internet name, although that's not necessary, as you may recall from the earlier discussion in this chapter about setting up TCP/IP on a system.

Representing Hex Suffixes in LMHOSTS

But how to handle the nonprinting characters in a NetBIOS name, the <1B> used by the primary domain controller, the <1C> used by all domain controllers? Recall that the hex suffixes are always the 16th character in a NetBIOS name, so write out a suffixed NetBIOS name like so:

- Enclose the name in quotes.

- Add enough spaces to the end of the name so that you've got 15 characters in the name.

- After the spaces, add **\0x** followed by the hex code.

For example, suppose I had a domain named CLOUDS and a domain controller named \\CUMULONIMBUS at address 210.10.20.3. I'm creating an LMHOSTS file that I can put on systems around the network so that they can find \\CUMULONIM-BUS and recognize it as the primary domain controller for CLOUDS. The LMHOSTS file would look like this:

```
210.10.20.3 cumulonimbus
210.10.20.3 "clouds          \0x1B"
```

This indicates that the machine at IP address 210.10.20.3 has two names (or at *least* two names). As CLOUDS is a six-letter word, I added nine spaces to the end of it.

A Special Suffix for Domain Controllers: #DOM

In most cases, the only hex suffix you'll care about is <1C>, the suffix indicating a domain controller. You can create an entry for it as above, with a \0x1C suffix, or you can use a special metacommand that Microsoft included in LMHOSTS: #DOM.

To indicate that a given entry is a domain controller, enter a normal LMHOSTS entry for it, but add to the end of the line **#DOM:** and the name of the domain controller. In the CUMULONIMBUS example above, you could register CUMULONIM-BUS's name and the fact that it was a domain controller for CLOUDS like so:

```
210.10.20.3 cumulonimbus #DOM:clouds
```

But \x01C and #DOM behave a bit differently, in my experience. If you enter a \x01C entry in an LMHOSTS, then NT will use it and only it, ignoring WINS or any other information—so if you're going to use an \0x1C entry, make sure it's right! Furthermore, if you try to tell NT about more than one domain controller in a given domain using the \0x1C suffix, it will only pay attention to the *last* one mentioned in the LMHOSTS file.

"Listen to Me!": The #PRE Command

This is a bit out of order, as I haven't taken up WINS in detail yet, but as long as I'm discussing LMHOSTS, it kind of fits. As you'll learn later, a normal H node type of client will first send a name resolution question to a WINS server before consulting its local LMHOSTS file, if one exists. Only if the WINS server returns a failure, saying, "I'm sorry, I can't resolve that name," does the client look in its LMHOSTS file. But sometimes you want to tell a PC, "I have a particular entry here in LMHOSTS that is more important than anything that WINS tells you. If you need to look up this particular NetBIOS name, use the LMHOSTS entry rather than looking at WINS." For those entries, you can use the #PRE metacommand. In the case of CUMULONIMBUS, the line above would look like:

```
cumulonimbus  #DOM:clouds  #PRE
```

#PRE's job is this: If WINS and LMHOSTS offer conflicting answers to the question, "What's the IP address of CUMULONIMBUS," then in general the client listens to WINS rather than LMHOSTS—in other words, by default WINS, uh, wins. But #PRE gives an LMHOSTS entry precedence over anything that WINS has to say.

Centralized LMHOSTS: #INCLUDE, #ALTERNATE

LMHOSTS is powerful, but could include a fair amount of running around, because for a user's PC to benefit from LMHOSTS, *the LMHOSTS file must be on the user's PC.* Yuck. That means you'd have to go out Amongst The Users, a happy time for some but a...ummm...mixed blessing for others. Every time you changed LMHOSTS, you'd have to walk around replacing the old LMHOSTS file with a new one on every single machine—ugh, double yuck. Is there a better way?

Sure. You can put a small LMHOSTS file on a user's machine with just one simple command: "Go to this server to read the 'main' LMHOSTS file." Even better, you can specify as many backups for this server as you like. You do it with the #INCLUDE and #ALTERNATE metacommands. Here's a sample LMHOSTS:

```
#BEGIN_ALTERNATE
#INCLUDE \\shadows\stuff\lmhosts
#INCLUDE \\vorlons\stuff\lmhosts
#INCLUDE \\centauri\stuff2\lmhosts
#END_ALTERNATE
```

You can use #INCLUDE without the #ALTERNATEs, but it seems to me that if you're going to go to all the trouble of having a central LMHOSTS, you might as well add some fault tolerance, right? And I would hope that it would go without saying that \\SHADOWS, \\VORLONS, and \\CENTAURI would either have to be on the same subnet as the client PC, or you should add a few lines above the #BEGIN ALTERNATE to tell the PC where to find those three servers.

#INCLUDE also takes local filenames:

```
#INCLUDE D:\MORENAME
```

LMHOSTS is a pretty powerful tool, and it still makes sense in today's NetBIOS-using networks because, as you'll see, WINS is not without its flaws.

How WINS Works

You've seen that the world before WINS was a rather grim place, where everyone shouts and many questions (well, resolution requests) go unanswered. Now let's look at what happens with WINS.

WINS Needs NT or Windows 2000 Server

To make WINS work, you must set up an NT Server or Windows 2000 Server machine (it won't run on anything else, including NT Workstation) to act as the WINS server. The WINS server then acts as the NBNS server, keeping track of who's on the network and handing out name resolution information as needed.

WINS Holds Name Registrations

Basically, when a WINS client (the shorthand term for "any PC running some kind of Microsoft enterprise TCP/IP network client software designed to use WINS for NBT name resolution") first boots up, it goes to the WINS server and introduces itself, or in WINS-speak, it does a name registration. (In fact, as you recall, most machines have several NetBIOS names, so clients register each of those names with WINS.) The client knows the IP address of the WINS server either because you hard-coded it right into the TCP/IP settings for the workstation or because the workstation got a WINS address from DHCP when it obtained an IP lease.

You may recall that the client actually gets *two* IP addresses, one for a "primary" and one for a "secondary" WINS server. The client tries to get the attention of the primary and register itself on that machine. But if the machine designated as a primary WINS server doesn't respond within a certain amount of time, the client next tries to register with the secondary WINS server. If the secondary will talk to the client and the primary won't, the client registers with the secondary. You can tell that this has happened by doing an IPCONFIG /ALL at the client. Among other things, this reports the address of the primary WINS server. If that address is the *secondary's* address, then you know that the primary was too busy to talk—and that turns out to be an important diagnostic clue, as you'll see later when I discuss how to design multiserver WINS systems.

In the process of registering its name with a WINS server, the workstation gets the benefit of ensuring that it has a unique name. If the WINS server sees that there's another computer out there with the same name, it will tell the workstation, "You can't use that name." The name registration request and the acknowledgment are both directed IP messages, so they'll cross routers. And when a workstation shuts down, it sends a "name release" request to the WINS server telling it that the workstation will no longer need the NetBIOS name, enabling the WINS server to register it for some other machine.

WINS Client Failure Modes

But what if something goes wrong? What if you try to register a name that some other workstation already has, or what if a workstation finds that the WINS server is unavailable?

Duplicate names are simple—instead of sending a "success" response to the workstation, the WINS server sends a "fail" message in response to the workstation's name request. In response, the workstation does not consider the name registered and doesn't include it in its NetBIOS name table; an nbstat -n will not show the name.

But if a workstation can't find the WINS server when it boots up, then the workstation simply stops acting as a hybrid NBT node and reverts to its old ways as a Microsoft modified B node, meaning that it depends largely on broadcasts but will also consult LMHOSTS (and perhaps HOSTS, if configured to do so) if they're present.

It's My Name, but for How Long?

Like DHCP, WINS only registers names for a fixed period of time called the *renewal interval*. By default, it's 6 days (144 hours), and there will probably never be a reason for you to change that. Forty minutes seems to be the shortest time that WINS will accept.

In much the same way that DHCP clients attempt to renew their leases early, WINS clients send "name *refresh* requests" to the WINS server before their names expire— *long* before. According to Microsoft documentation, a WINS client attempts a name refresh very early after it gets its names registered—after one-eighth of the renewal interval. (My tests show that it's actually *three*-eighths, but that's not terribly important.) The WINS server will usually reset the length of time left before the name must be renewed again (this time is sometimes called the *Time To Live*, or TTL). Once the client has renewed its name *once*, however, it doesn't renew it again and again every one-eighth of its TTL; instead, it only renews its names every one-half of the TTL. (My tests agree with that.)

Installing WINS

Installing WINS is much like installing all the other software that we've installed elsewhere in this chapter and in the book.

When you're planning how many WINS servers you need and where to put them, bear in mind that you need not put a WINS server on each subnet (which is one of the great features of WINS). It *is* a good idea to have a second machine running as a secondary WINS server, however, just for fault tolerance's sake. Remember that if a workstation comes up and can't find a WINS server, it reverts to broadcasting, which will limit its name resolution capabilities to just its local subnet and will cause it to do a lot of shouting, which adds traffic to the subnet. Why would a WINS client not find a WINS server if there's a working WINS server?

Well, normally the client would find the server just fine, but in some small percentage of the cases, the WINS server might be too busy to respond to the client in a timely fashion, causing the client to just give up on the server. That will probably only happen very rarely, unless you're overloading the WINS server. Unfortunately, a very common way to overload a WINS server is to put the WINS server function on the same machine that's also acting as a domain controller. Think about it: When is a WINS server busiest? First thing in the morning, when everyone's booting up and registering names. When's a domain controller busiest? First thing in the morning, when everyone's logging in. That leads to a tip.

 WARNING If possible, don't put the WINS server function on a domain controller.

That's where a secondary is useful. If you have a backup domain controller, then put a WINS server on that machine as well. The WINS software actually does not use a lot of CPU time, so it probably won't affect your server's performance unless you have thousands of users all hammering on one WINS server. If *that's* the case, I'd dedicate a computer solely to WINS-ing.

To get a WINS server set up, follow these directions:

1. Open the Control Panel (Start/Settings/Control Panel).

2. Open Add/Remove Programs.

3. Click Add/Remove Windows Components and wait a bit while the irritating Windows Components Wizard starts up.

4. Click Next to bring up the list of Windows components.

5. Click Networking Services and then the Details button.

6. Click the check box next to Windows Internet Name Service.

7. Click OK to return to Windows Components.

8. Click Next to install the service. The system will say that it is "Configuring Components" for a while, probably a few minutes. A bit later, the screen labeled Completing the Windows Components Wizard appears.

9. Click Finish to end the wizard.

10. Click Close to close Add/Remove Windows Components.

No reboots needed anymore—thanks, Microsoft—and you'll see in Start/Programs/ Administrative Tools that you've got a new snap-in to control WINS. Start it up, click the plus sign next to the server, and it will look like Figure 18.29.

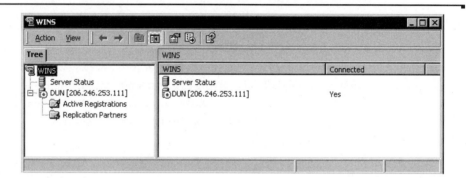

No need to authorize WINS servers, in case you're wondering. The first thing you should do on your WINS server is inform it of the machines on your subnet that are not WINS clients but use NetBIOS on TCP/IP. There won't be many of them, but they may exist; for example, you may have some old pre-1995 Microsoft Windows machines around. Machines with hard-coded IP addresses don't need to be entered, so long as they use WINS: If they know the address of a primary or secondary WINS server, they will register their names with that server. If you *do* have an old system requiring a static mapping, right-click Active Registrations and choose New Static Mapping. You then see a dialog box like the one shown in Figure 18.30.

Alternatively, if you have an existing LMHOSTS file, you can click Action at the top menu, then Import Hosts, and the program will take that information to build a static-mapping database.

FIGURE 18.30

The Static
Mappings table

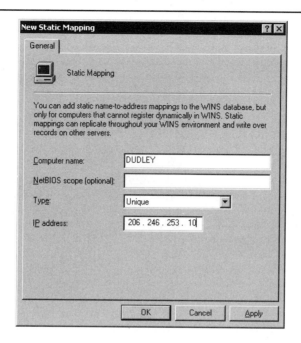

Configuring a WINS Server

Right-click the server in the left-hand pane of the WINS snap-in, and choose Properties. You'll see a property page like the one in Figure 18.31.

WINS will regularly back up its database—a good disaster recovery step—if you fill in a directory name in Default Backup Path. You can even use a UNC, like \\ajax\ central\wins or the like. A check box allows you to tell WINS to also do a backup specifically when the server is shut down.

Click the Database Verification tab, and you'll see a page like Figure 18.32.

This is a real improvement in WINS over NT 4's WINS service. WINS has always had trouble as a distributed database: Name records get transmitted around the network and databases get corrupted. The corruption spreads and before you know it, you're erasing your WINS databases and starting all over. The option at the top of the screen tells your WINS server to periodically check its records against those of any other server in your enterprise. It's a good idea. If you enable it, I'd let it check every 24 hours, as is the default, and to check against the *owner* rather than a random server. *Owner* in WINS terminology means "the WINS server that generated the original name record." Thus, it could be in a multi-WINS server world that I registered my PC's name with WINS Server 1, which then told WINS Server 2 about me. (This happens automatically, recall—you needn't do anything to get your system registered with WINS except to specify a WINS server in your TCP/IP settings.) WINS Server 2 might run into some kind of trouble and corrupt the record about my machine. But checking with WINS Server 1 would point out the problem, and WINS Server 2 would be set straight.

FIGURE 18.31

Server configuration property page

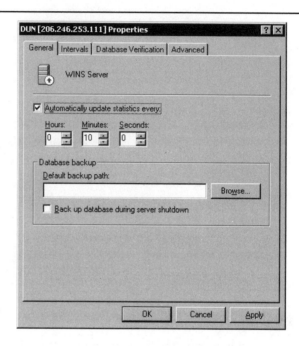

FIGURE 18.32

Configuring WINS Verification

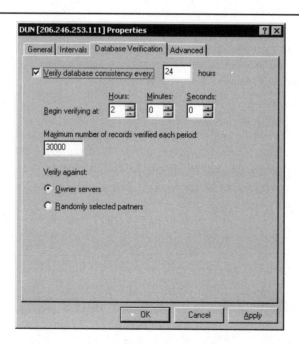

Click the Advanced tab and you'll see a page like the one in Figure 18.33.

FIGURE 18.33

Advanced WINS server configuration

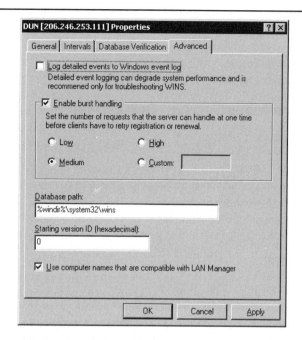

The first interesting thing here is logging. You can leave logging enabled, but think twice about Log Detailed Events. Basically, if you enable this, then (1) WINS adds a lot of chatter to the Event Viewer, and (2) WINS gets *really* slow. It's not a bad idea if you're trying to get some insight into what WINS does on a small network, but I've had it freeze a WINS server right up on me.

Enable Burst Handling is a workaround to handle an old WINS problem. WINS is busiest first thing in the morning, when everyone's logging on and trying to register their system names. Before registering a name, however, WINS must check its database to ensure that there's no duplication, that no one's trying to register a computer name that already exists. But that takes time…so WINS cheats.

The chances are good that early morning (busy time) registrations are simply reregistrations, so WINS goes into burst mode, meaning that it pretty much agrees to every registration request. It then says, "Come back and reregister in a few minutes," which gives it a chance to *really* check a registration when things are slower. It only shifts into burst mode when it's got a lot of outstanding registration requests in its queue. How many? That's what the radio buttons are for—to set how soon WINS goes into burst mode. The default is probably fine, but if you're getting a lot of refused registrations—where WINS simply doesn't respond—then set the threshold to low.

Designing a Multi-WINS Network

Thus far, I've discussed a situation wherein you've got one WINS server and a bunch of clients. I've *also* mentioned the notion of a secondary WINS server, suggesting that at least one additional WINS server would be in order. How should you set up this second WINS server? And how about the third, fourth, and so on? And while we're at it, how many WINS servers should you have?

From Many Servers, One Database

The theory with multiple WINS servers is that you might have one in Europe, one in Africa, and one in North America. Europeans do their registrations with the European server, Africans with the African server, and Americans with the North American server. Then, on a regular basis, the three WINS servers get together and create a master worldwide list of WINS records, a kind of sort/merge amalgamating three different databases. But how to do it? We certainly don't want to have to transmit—*replicate* is the WINS term—the entire African name-server database over WAN links to Europe and America, particularly since the database probably hasn't changed all that much since yesterday.

As a result, WINS time-stamps and sequence-numbers name records so that it can take up less WAN bandwidth. That's great in theory, but in practice it means that WINS servers that are being asked to *do* all that sorting and merging will be pretty occupied CPU-wise, which will of course mean that they're falling down on the job as name resolvers. It also means that it might be a good idea to designate a relatively small number of servers—say, perhaps *one*—to essentially do nothing but the sort/merges.

Minimize the Number of WINS Servers

People assume that as with domain controllers, it's a great idea to have a local WINS server, and lots of them. But it's not, and in fact you should strive to keep the WINS servers to an absolute minimum

A local WINS server would be great because it could quickly perform NetBIOS name resolutions for nearby machines. And in fact it would be great if you could install a WINS server in every location that only did name resolutions—but remember that every WINS server does *two* things: Name resolutions and name registrations. This, in my opinion, is the crux of why multiple WINS networks can be a pain. If you could simply say, "Go to local machine X for name resolutions, but for those infrequent occasions when you need to do a name *registration*, go across the WAN to the central WINS server named Y," then WINS would be more trouble free. Sure, a morning logon would get a bit slower, as the registration would happen over the WAN, but you'd not get the corrupted WINS databases that are sadly so common in big WINS installations.

People want a local WINS server for name resolution, but in actual fact they're not getting much for it. If your WINS server were across the WAN from you, how much time would a name resolution take? Well, an entire name resolution request and response is only 214 bytes. Let's see, at 56Kbps that would be...hmmm, three-hundredths of a second. Here's a case where the wide area network will *not* be the bottleneck! WINS may have its drawbacks, but one thing that it was designed to do, and designed well, is to respond to name resolution requests quickly. Even a 66MHz 486 running NT 4's WINS server can handle 750 resolution requests per minute—so when it comes to WINS servers, remember: Less is more.

Adding the Second WINS Server

Of course, having said that, a *second* WINS server isn't a bad idea.

When setting up a Microsoft TCP/IP client, you're prompted for both a primary and a secondary WINS server address. When your PC boots up, the PC goes to the primary WINS server and tries to register the PC's NetBIOS name with that WINS server. If it's successful, it never even tries to contact the secondary WINS server unless a subsequent name resolution attempt fails.

What that implies is important. Suppose you've been a good network administrator and created a backup WINS server, and then you've pointed all of your workstation's "Secondary WINS Server" fields to that backup. The primary goes down. Where are you?

Nowhere very interesting, actually. You see, that secondary WINS server doesn't know much, as no one has ever registered with it. If a WINS client successfully registers with its primary server, it does not try to register with the secondary server.

If the primary goes down and everyone starts asking the secondary to resolve names, the secondary will end up just saying, "Sorry, I can't answer that question." So you've got to convince the primary to replicate to the secondary. Fortunately, there's an easy way—*push/pull partners*.

Keeping the Second Server Up-to-Date

In general, you've got to configure two WINS servers to be push/pull partners, but it's possible to have them discover each other with a setting in the WINS snap-in. Right-click the Replication Partners folder, choose Properties and click the Advanced tab, and you'll see a screen like Figure 18.34.

Here, I've checked the box Enable Automatic Partner Configuration, which will cause the WINS server to periodically broadcast (well, actually it will *multicast*) to find other WINS servers and from there to automatically replicate. This will, however, usually only work for WINS servers on the same subnet, as most routers don't pass IP multicasts. On a big network, this is a bad idea, but for a small network it'll save the administrator a bit of time and trouble.

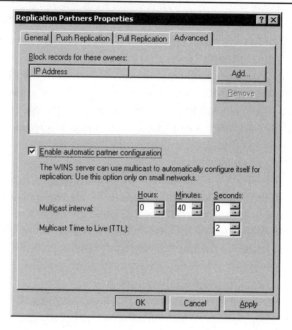

Alternatively, you've got to introduce the replication partners. WINS database replications transfer data from a *push* partner to a *pull* partner. Those terms *push* and *pull* aren't *bad* terms description-wise, but they need a bit of illumination. Suppose for the purposes of the example that you've got two machines named Primary and Secondary. Suppose also that Primary is the machine that gets the latest information, as it is the *primary* WINS server, and that all we really want to do with Secondary (the name of the machine that is the secondary WINS server) is have it act as a kind of backup to Primary's information. Thus, Secondary never really has any information to offer Primary. In that case, we'd have to set up Primary to *push* its database changes to Secondary.

You can tell a WINS server to create a push, pull, or push/pull relationship with another WINS server by right-clicking the folder labeled Replication Partners and choosing New Replication Partner. You're prompted for the IP address of the WINS server that you want to establish a replication relationship with.

In a push/pull relationship, data gets from Primary to Secondary in one of two ways. First, Secondary (the pull partner) can request that Primary (the push partner) update Secondary, telling Secondary only what has changed in the database. Alternatively, Primary can say to Secondary, "There's been a fair amount of changes since the last time I updated you. *You really should request an update.*" I italicized the last sentence to underscore that it's really the pull partner that does most of the work in initiating the database replication updates. All the push partner really "pushes" is a suggestion that the pull partner get to work and start requesting updates.

Having said that, could I just tell Secondary to be a pull partner with Primary, without telling Primary to be a push partner for Secondary? Wouldn't it be sufficient to just tell Secondary, "Initiate a replication conversation with Primary every eight hours"? It would seem so, as there wouldn't any longer be a need for Primary to do any pushing—but there's a catch. If Secondary starts pulling from Primary, Primary will refuse to respond to Secondary's pull request unless Primary has been configured as a push partner with Secondary, because WINS servers are configured by default to refuse replication requests from all machines but partners, remember?

 TIP WINS services are totally independent of Windows 2000 domain security, as is DHCP. A WINS server can serve workstations throughout your network. In fact, if your network is connected to the Internet and doesn't have a firewall, you could actually *publish* your WINS server address, and other networks across the Internet could share browsing capabilities! (Whether or not you'd *want* to do that is another issue.)

Controlling Replication

So now we see that the right thing to do is to make Secondary a pull partner with Primary and make Primary a push partner with Secondary. What triggers the replication? What kicks off the process of WINS database replication? To see, right-click any server listed in the `Replication Partners` folder, choose Properties, and click the Advanced tab. You'll see a screen like the one in Figure 18.35.

FIGURE 18.35

Configuring WINS replication

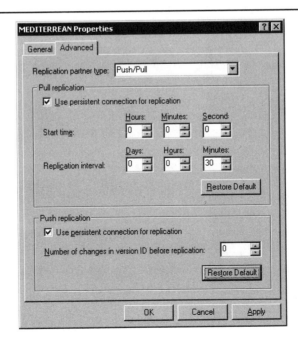

Well, recall that either the push partner or the pull partner can start the conversation. In the case of the former, you configure a push partner to tap its partner on the shoulder and suggest a replication session based on the number of database changes. You can tell Primary, "Notify Secondary whenever 50 changes have occurred to the WINS database on Primary," or whatever number you like, so long as you like numbers above 19; 20 is the minimum number of changes that NT will allow you to use to trigger replication. (You can alternatively trigger replication from the WINS snap-in.) The default, zero, essentially turns off push triggers.

A pull partner, in contrast, can't possibly know how many changes have occurred and so needs another way to know when to request updates. So pull partners request updates based on time—you configure a pull partner to contact its partner every so many minutes, hours, or days.

 TIP The bottom line, however, is that most of us will just set up our WINS replication relationships to the defaults, particularly if we set up our WINS enterprise as a hub-and-spoke design, as you're about to read. You *might* want to set your partners to replicate less often in a large enterprise.

Replication Design

Now that Microsoft has had four years' experience supporting big clients using WINS, some Microsofties have recommended to me a push/pull partner architecture something like a hub-and-spoke design. You see it pictured in Figure 18.36.

FIGURE 18.36

Suggested primary/secondary WINS server configuration

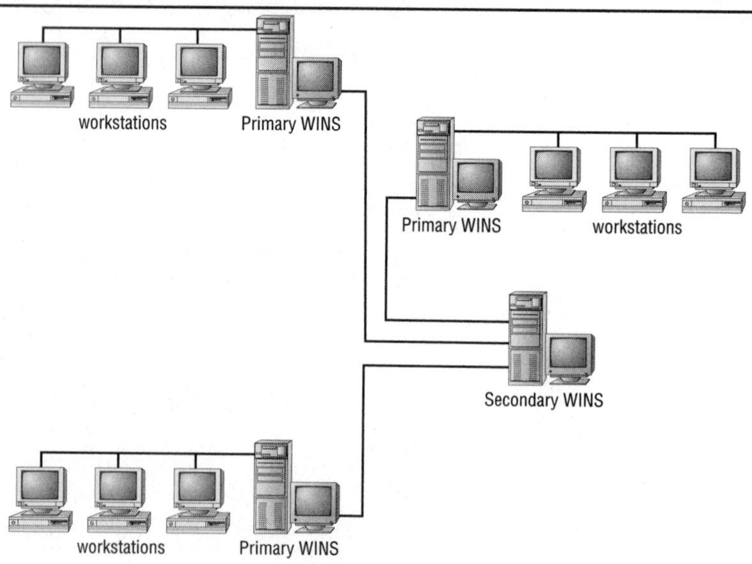

workstations Primary WINS

Primary WINS workstations

Secondary WINS

workstations Primary WINS

The goal of this design is to keep WINS servers responsive while still handling replication. In the picture, you see three different networks, each served by a WINS server labeled Primary WINS. In each network, each workstation points to the local WINS server as its primary server and the central machine labeled Secondary WINS as its secondary. In other words, then, every machine in the enterprise designates that one central machine as their secondary WINS server and a closer machine as their primary WINS server.

The main job of the central WINS server is to gather the three primary WINS servers' databases, aggregate them into one enterprise-wide WINS database, and replicate that database out to the local primaries. Each primary WINS server, then, designates the central WINS server as its sole push/pull partner.

Many firms implement a mesh-type structure, where every WINS server designates every other WINS server as a push/pull partner. The result is a nightmare of corrupted WINS databases and lost records. To add another WINS server, just make sure that it has some kind of connectivity to the central WINS server and make it a push/pull partner of that machine. If you end up with too many WINS servers for one central machine, just put hubs and spokes on the ends of the hubs and spokes, building a hierarchy.

 WARNING No matter what kind of WINS replication architecture you create, ensure that there are no loops in your replication. For example, if WINS server A replicated to B, which replicated to C, which replicated to A, then records can be replicated and rereplicated, causing WINS problems.

Notes on Avoiding WINS Problems

Sources inside Microsoft tell me that WINS generates more support calls than any other of NT's "core" network technologies. That won't be surprising to anyone who's ever tried to track down a WINS problem. Here are a few tips to save you some time and help you avoid having to pay Microsoft more money to keep the product that you bought from them working.

WINS Servers Should Point to Themselves as a Primary WINS Server Only

When you're configuring the TCP/IP stack on a WINS server, do not fill in a value for a secondary WINS server, and in the Primary field, fill in the server's own value. This avoids a situation wherein the WINS server is busy but needs to reregister its own address. As it is busy, however, it cannot—believe it or not—respond quickly enough to *itself*. As a result, the WINS client software on the WINS server seeks out another

WINS server, and so WINS server A's name registrations end up on WINS server B. The result is WINS instability, as the WINS server software is built assuming that each WINS server's name is registered on its own database.

Be Careful Replicating to "Test" WINS Servers

Don't set up a "test" WINS server, register a few names on it, have a "production" WINS server pull the names from the test server, and then shut off the test WINS server for good. WINS will refuse to delete names that it got from another server, no matter how old and expired they are, until it can do a final double-check with the WINS server that it got the names from originally; shut off the test and never turn it back on, and those records will never go away without a bit of operator intervention!

To remove all of the records created by a defunct WINS server, go to one of its replication partners and start WINS Manager. Right-click the `Active Registrations` folder, then choose All Tasks/Delete Owner. That allows WINS to finally purge the old owner's records.

Don't Make a Multihomed PC a WINS Server

A PC with more than one NIC can hear communications from several subnets. That's gotten WINS in trouble when a WINS server is multihomed, as WINS sometimes gets confused about where a name registration came in from. Several service packs have claimed to fix it, but each service pack brings more trouble reports. My suggestion: Don't make a multihomed machine a WINS server.

By the way, the same advice goes for PDCs. Multihomed PCs shouldn't be PDCs. The reason is that the PDC ends up being the master browser in a domain, and again, having workgroup announcements coming in from several different network segments causes problems for the browser software.

Don't Make a DC a WINS Server

As explained earlier, both the domain controller and WINS functions are at their busiest at the same time. Mixing DC and WINS responsibilities on a single machine will make a mediocre DC and a mediocre WINS server. (Of course, on a small network this isn't the case; if you have 25 users, feel free to make one machine your domain controller, WINS, DHCP, DNS, and file server—but be sure you know how to do disaster recovery on it!)

Deleting and Purging WINS Records

You'll eventually look at your WINS name database and realize that there are a bunch of old, useless records that you'd like to get rid of. Some of those records may be, as mentioned earlier, garbage left over from an old, now-defunct WINS server. Those are easy to get rid of—just choose the Delete Owner function, as described earlier.

For other records, though, the approach is a bit different.

Consider how a record gets created and propagated around an enterprise. A machine named TRAY (what server doesn't have a tray?) registers itself with WINS Server 1. That generates a record in WINS Server 1's database. WINS Server 1 is said to be the "owner" of that record.

Now suppose WINS Server 1 replicates TRAY's name record (or more likely, records) to WINS Server 2. WINS Server 2 now contains copies of those records, but it also knows that WINS Server 1, not itself, originated—"owns"—those records. Working at WINS Server 2, an administrator deletes the TRAY record. (In `Active Registrations`, right-click a record and choose Delete.) But the record still exists on WINS Server 1, and in time WINS Server 1 will rereplicate that record to WINS Server 2, so TRAY's record will reappear.

The alternative to deleting is *tombstoning*. When you tombstone a record, you don't remove it from the database; rather, it marks it as being in a *tombstone state*.

The purpose of the tombstone is this: WINS Server 2 has already written TRAY off, but it knows that the rest of the enterprise doesn't know that TRAY is history. So the next time WINS Server 1 replicates a TRAY record to WINS Server 2, WINS Server 2 may be tempted to insert a new record in its database for a machine named TRAY— but then it sees the tombstone record with TRAY's name and so can say, "Ah, I should just ignore that record; I have more up-to-date information than WINS Server 1 does." When WINS Server 2 next replicates to WINS Server 1, it'll tell WINS Server 1 that TRAY is tombstoned, and so WINS Server 1 will tombstone TRAY in its database as well. Eventually TRAY will be marked as tombstoned in the entire WINS enterprise.

By the way, tombstoned entries don't get purged from a WINS database until WINS runs a *scavenging operation*. That happens every three days by default, or you can initiate a scavenging operation from the WINS Manager by right-clicking a server, then choosing Scavenge Database.

 TIP If for some reason you stop the WINS service more often than every three days, your WINS database will never be scavenged. If that's the case, manually initiate scavenging from the WINS Manager.

A badly designed WINS replication structure may need a bit of tombstoning help, and here Windows 2000's graphical WINS Manager is of assistance. When you click Delete Mapping, you get an option—delete or tombstone? You'd use tombstone *always* if you want to delete a record on server X but you're working from server Y. You'd typically delete rather than tombstone if you're sitting right at the server that owns the record that you're about to delete. And if you found that you'd been trying to get rid of a record but it keeps coming back, you'd tombstone it.

WINS Proxy Agents

Using an NBNS (NetBIOS Naming Server) like WINS can greatly cut down on the broadcasts on your network, reducing traffic and improving throughput. But, as you've seen, this requires that the clients understand WINS; the older network client software just shouts away as a B node.

WINS can help those older non-WINS-aware clients with a *WINS proxy agent*. A WINS proxy agent is a regular old network workstation that listens for older B node systems helplessly broadcasting, trying to reach NetBIOS names that (unknown to the B node computers) are on another subnet.

To see how this would work, let's take a look at a very simple two-subnet intranet, as shown in Figure 18.37.

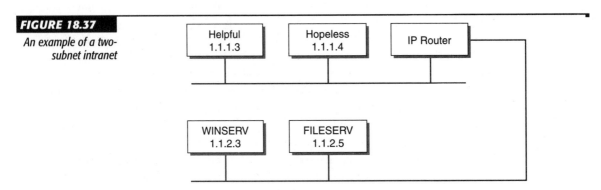

FIGURE 18.37

An example of a two-subnet intranet

Here, you see two C class subnets, 1.1.1.0 and 1.1.2.0. There's a router between them. On 1.1.1.0, there are two workstations. One is a WINS-aware client named HELPFUL, which is also running a WINS proxy agent. The other is an old B node client named HOPELESS, which is not WINS-aware. On 1.1.2.0, there are a couple of servers, a machine acting as a WINS server and a regular old file server.

When HOPELESS first comes up, it'll do a broadcast of its names to ensure that no one else has them. The machine that it really should be talking to, of course, is WINSERV, but WINSERV can't hear it. HELPFUL, however, hears the B node broadcasts coming from HOPELESS and sends a directed message to WINSERV, telling it that there's a workstation named HOPELESS trying to register some names.

WINSERV looks up those names to ensure that they don't already exist. If they *do* exist, then WINSERV sends a message back to HELPFUL, saying, "Don't let that guy register those names!" HELPFUL then sends a message to HOPELESS, saying, "I'm sorry, but *I* already use the name HOPELESS." That keeps HOPELESS from registering a name that exists on another subnet.

Assuming that HOPELESS names do *not* currently exist in the WINSERV database, however, WINSERV does *not* register the names; putting a WINS proxy agent on 1.1.1.0 doesn't mean that the non-WINS clients will have their names registered with

WINS. That means that it's okay to have the same NetBIOS name on two different computers, so long as they are both B node clients and are on different subnets.

Suppose then that HOPELESS does a "Net Use d: \\fileserv\files"—in that case, the name \\fileserv must be resolved. Assuming that HOPELESS does not have a HOSTS or LMHOSTS file, HOPELESS will start broadcasting, saying, "Is there anyone here named FILESERV? And if so, what's your IP address?" HELPFUL will intercede by sending a directed IP message to WINSERV, saying, "Is there a name registered as FILESERV, and what is its IP address?"

WINSERV will respond with the IP address of FILESERV, and HELPFUL will then send a directed message back to HOPELESS, saying, "Sure, I'm FILESERV, and you can find me at 1.1.2.5." Now HOPELESS can complete its request.

 TIP Make sure there is only *one* WINS proxy agent per subnet! Otherwise, two PCs will respond to HOPELESS, causing—how do the manuals put it? Ah yes—"unpredictable results."

DNS: Name Central in Windows 2000

Windows 2000 turned names in Microsoft networking on its head. From 1985's MS-Net through the versions of LAN Manager through Windows for Workgroups, Windows 9*x*, and NT 3.*x* and 4.*x*, NetBIOS reigned supreme and anyone running a TCP/IP-based network needed WINS to support NetBIOS names, as you've just read. DNS, where it existed, was something of an afterthought.

With Windows 2000, all of that changes. The heart of naming in Windows 2000 is DNS. As you've already read, in a network of *only* Windows 2000 systems and applications, WINS would be completely unnecessary. Whether you've got old systems in your Windows 2000–based network or not, however, DNS is all-important: Active Directory simply cannot run without it.

DNS is, for those just joining us, a name resolution system invented in 1984 for the Internet. It enables you to point your Web browser to a "friendly name" like www.continental.com when you want to look up Continental Airlines' flight schedule rather than having to know that Continental's Web server is at IP address 208.229.128.54. It makes e-mail work smoother through its MX records (which you'll read about later) and has proven itself to be an easily expanded way of maintaining names in the largest network in the world. DNS's ability to grow—its *scalability*—is a real plus for Active Directory, as Microsoft hopes that AD will be the basis of some very large networks.

How DNS Works: Dimensions of the Problem

Building a database system that can answer questions like "what's the IP address of www.continental.com?" sounds awfully easy. As you read in the last chapter, prior to the mid-'80s, the ARPAnet muddled along with just simple ASCII files—HOSTS files—for the entire Net. Why not stay with that?

Well, first of all, there was the "how do we keep it up-to-date?" problem. Assume there's about 200 million machines on the Internet—and don't take that as gospel; it's just an order-of-magnitude guess—and that each line in the HOSTS file was an average of 40 characters long. The HOSTS file would, then, be 8,000 megabytes—8 gigabytes—in size. That would be impractical to have to update and then to redistribute over the Internet.

What About a Central Database?

Well, granted, 8 gigs is a lot to shoot over the Net constantly. But the reality of the matter is that most of us won't need to resolve more than a million names into IP addresses *over the course of our entire lives*. So, instead of worrying about giving everyone a copy of HOSTS, why not have a central machine or cluster of machines and let anyone who wants to make queries of those systems?

When seen as a simple flat-file database, HOSTS isn't really that monstrous. Assuming that the database was sorted in some way, a mythical central HOSTS database machine could locate any record in it by examining no more than 28 of the 200 million records, using an elementary search algorithm called a *binary search.*

Of course, *getting* to that central machine might take a bit of doing: If it were processing DNS name resolution requests from the whole world, then it would probably be very busy indeed! So perhaps we could set up a few dozen or hundred DNS servers around the world...hmmm, but then we'd be back to the problem of getting those updated HOSTS files to them without choking the Net.

But centralizing a worldwide HOSTS database would have still *another* problem, a very large one. Say I'm the network administrator at acme.com and I add a new workstation called roadrunner.acme.com at 200.40.29.10. I want the rest of the Internet to be able to resolve this name—perhaps it's a Web server with information about some of our new products for desert pest eradication—and so I need to get that name/IP pair into the worldwide HOSTS file. Clearly I have to send a message of some type to the folks who run the central HOSTS file with that information and they then enter that information in the file, when they get time. But consider how many updates they'd get every day—a staggering number! They'd need tremendous processing power just to keep up with the incoming updates.

DNS Overview I: Local Control, Worldwide Access

Trying to centralize Internet names is a wasteful effort when you consider a few things:

- First, people don't visit every single site on the Internet with equal frequency. So it's not really essential to have a machine somewhere that holds the name and IP address of every single Internet-connected computer in the world.

- Second, when people go someplace once, they tend to go there again. So whatever technique we'll use to resolve names ought to have a bit of memory so that the second time I go there in the same day, I should find the IP address close at hand rather than a complete replay of the name resolution query process.

- Third, and most important, the majority of the name resolutions that I do during the day are for hosts in my own company—accessing a local file server, getting my mail, logging on. It doesn't make sense to make my PC go to Tasmania to find a server that can tell me the IP address of the computer next to me. (That is, of course, unless I *live* in Tasmania.)

The answer that the Internet world hit upon—the Domain Name System—works well within the needs of the Internet community. It works roughly like this:

- **Each organization runs and maintains its own DNS server, which describes the machines in its own part of the Internet.** If I point my Web browser to www.ibm.com, then ultimately some machine has to tell me that www.ibm.com is the name of a machine with IP address 204.146.18.33. Now, the machine that resolved www.ibm.com to IP address 204.146.18.33 is one of IBM's DNS servers—it's a computer owned and operated by IBM, not the InterNIC. The InterNIC doesn't have anything at all to do with running IBM's DNS servers: If IBM's DNS servers go down, it's IBM's problem and no one else's.

- **A central group, the InterNIC, keeps track of domain names and corresponding DNS servers.** There's a huge database running on some Oracle servers in Herndon, Virginia that, simplified, really only keeps track of the names of registered domains and the names and addresses of the DNS servers of those registered domains. The InterNIC can't tell me what the IP address of www.ibm.com is, but they *can* tell me that IBM advertises six DNS servers that *can* answer that question, and the InterNIC can tell me the IP addresses of those six IBM DNS servers. And there's no magic about how the InterNIC knows the IP addresses of any given domain's DNS servers, because the InterNIC is the group that registers domain names—and the InterNIC simply refuses to register a new domain name until you tell it the names and IP addresses of at least *two* machines that you'll run some kind of DNS server on and keep your domain's machine names and IP addresses on.

- **DNS server software is smart enough to query *other* DNS servers to get a name resolved**. If I point my Web browser at my Web server, www.minasi.com, then the browser has to ask one of my local DNS servers to resolve that name into an IP address. It's an easy question, as the DNS servers for minasi.com will instantly know that www.minasi.com is at IP address 206.246.253.200. And notice that my local DNS servers do two very different jobs. First, they respond to systems from *outside* minasi.com that are trying to resolve names inside minasi.com. Second, they handle name resolution queries from *my* computers about Internet addresses, both inside my domain and anywhere else in the Internet. For example, if I want to surf over to www.midwinter.com/lurk/lurker.html to get the latest scoop on some Babylon 5 information, then my Web browser will ask my local DNS server what the IP address of www.midwinter.com is. My DNS server will have no clue whatsoever. *But* my DNS server will be smart enough to open hailing frequencies to one of the InterNIC's servers in Herndon and ask it, "Who are the DNS servers for midwinter.com?" Herndon will respond that either 199.165.129.201 or 192.65.216.6 can answer name resolution queries for midwinter.com. My DNS server then talks to one of *those* machines, asking it for the IP address of their www.midwinter.com machine. The distant DNS servers respond that the IP address is 199.165.129.193. My DNS server will then hand that information to my Web browser, and in no time I'm reading pages from the server.

NOTE Two definitions are in order here. This process of working one's way from DNS server to DNS server in order to find an IP address is called *recursion*. Second, the DNS servers who hold the name/IP address pairs for a given domain are said to be *authoritative* for that domain.

- **DNS server software is smart enough to remember names that it has resolved recently**. If I return to midwinter.com later in the day, my DNS server won't have to go through all of that rigmarole again, as it caches recently resolved names. How recently? That's a function of the other domain's DNS server. If midwinter.com's DNS server said that its responses were cacheable for a week, then my DNS server would remember www.midwinter.com's IP address for a week.

Those, then, are the basics of DNS: A top-level set of root servers that know little more than the IP addresses of millions of lower-level DNS servers for each of the Internet's domains, and the millions of lower-level DNS servers that hold the databases of names and IP addresses of machines in those domains.

DNS Overview II: Fault Tolerance with Secondary DNS Servers

Why does the InterNIC require two DNS servers before it'll register you? Simple: For fault tolerance. You'll see how to do this a bit later in the chapter, but briefly here's how DNS servers cover their backs.

Each domain has one and only one primary DNS server, the server that's authoritative for the domain. And when you set up a DNS server for a particular domain, you must tell the DNS server whether it is the primary DNS server for that domain. The alternative to being the *one* primary is to be any of a number of secondary DNS servers. On a regular basis, the secondary servers in a domain contact the primary DNS server and copy its database to theirs. Put simply, the secondary DNS servers are just machines that hold a backup copy of the primary DNS server's database. They can also satisfy DNS name resolution queries when the primary is too busy or is down. Changes to the domain's database can't be made to the secondaries, only to the primary.

When the primary DNS server will be down for some time, you can promote any secondary to be the primary DNS server for a domain. In general, however, that's something that an administrator's got to initiate—secondary DNS servers will not promote themselves.

DNS Overview III: Zones, Domains, and Delegation

I've been talking about DNS servers associated with—"authoritative for"—particular domains. But truthfully, that's not very precise terminology, as strictly speaking, DNS servers don't hold name information for domains, they hold them for *zones*. What, then, is a zone? It's a DNS-specific term that basically means "the range of Internet addresses that this DNS server will be concerned about." To see how this works, consider Acme Industries (acme.com), a firm familiar to any Warner Bros. cartoon fan.

When Acme got their Internet connection, they set up a primary DNS server at their corporate headquarters in Chicago and gave DNS names to their machines. There are machines with names like jills-pc.acme.com, bigserver.acme.com, www.acme.com, and so on.

As time went on, however, Acme began to feel the bite of competition from their hated and long-time rival, Apex Limited (apex.com). So they moved their "gadgets" group—the guys who brought us Acme Instant Hole, Acme Rocket Sled, or Acme Spring-Powered Shoes—to Mexico in the hopes of lower prices. Meanwhile, Acme bought a munitions firm in Belgium and decided to close their other big domestic division, the "explosives" group, and sell the Belgian explosives instead.

At this point, Acme's got three loci of operation: The suits in Chicago, the gadgeteers in Mexico, and the demolitions folks in Belgium. The question for Acme's network engineers is "how do we arrange our DNS?" They decide to create two child domains, explosives.acme.com and gadgets.acme.com. While some machines will stay in the top acme.com domain—the web server, www.acme.com, is an obvious choice—many machines will either be *machinename*.explosives.com or *machinename*.gadgets.com. Why split up the domain into child domains? Any of a number of reasons, but one obvious one might be just simplicity—you can look at a machine's name and immediately figure out which department it belongs to.

 NOTE Please note I'm talking here about DNS domains, not Windows 2000 domains. Windows 2000 allows Acme to divide up its DNS names into subdomains as much as it likes, while still being able to keep all of its machines and users in as many or as few domains as it likes.

Acme has two basic options for setting up their DNS, shown in Figures 18.38 and 18.39.

FIGURE 18.38

Acme with one DNS zone

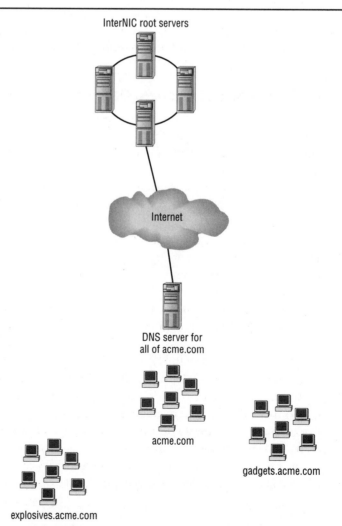

FIGURE 18.39

Acme with three DNS zones

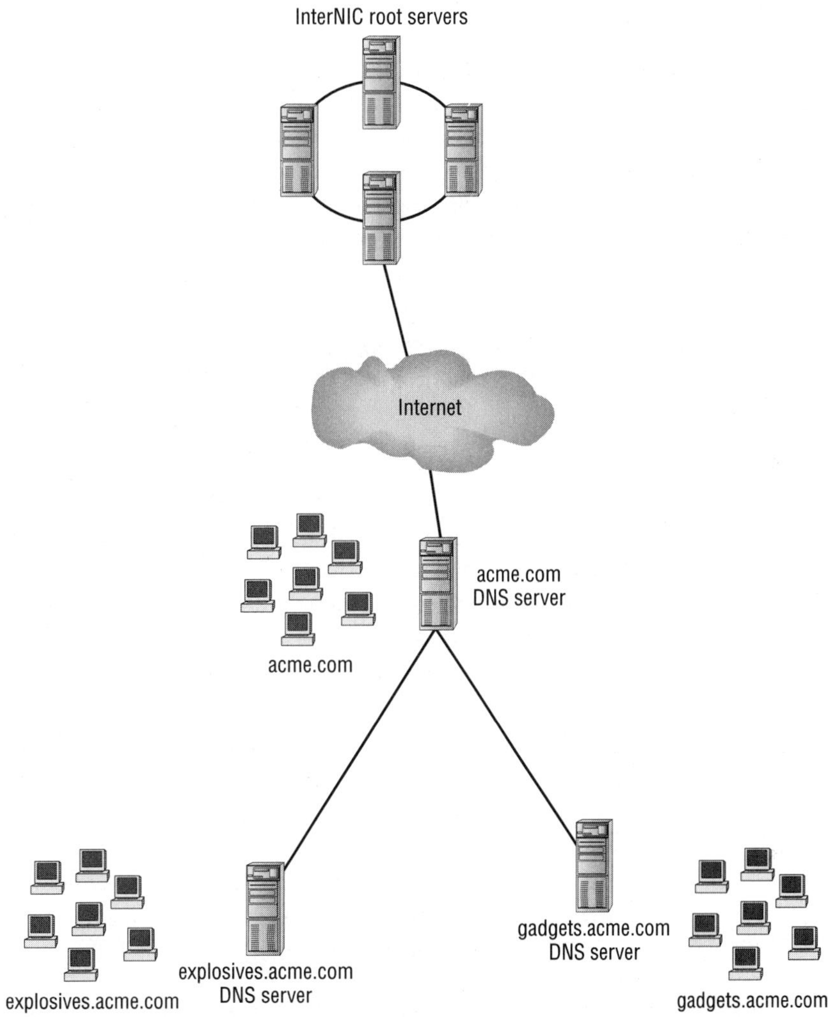

In the first figure, Acme keeps things as they've been: There is one server that is the primary authority for all of Acme's machines. It's a perfectly fine answer, but not everyone may like it.

This is not, understand, a *wrong* answer; it's just one of several possible answers, and some may not like it. The folks in Belgium must rely on some network operators in Chicago to keep their machines properly listed in the DNS database, and it may be that every time Belgium needs some new machines and IP addresses stuffed into the database, it's morning in Belgium and the middle of the night in Chicago, so the Belgians get to wait. And, as they're the explosives guys, that might weigh heavily on the minds of the suits in Chicago when the Belgians ask for their own DNS server. Mexico could experience the same kinds of long-distance administration problems as the ones that Belgium faces. That could lead to the setup shown in Figure 18.39.

In Figure 18.39, Explosives has their own DNS server, and Gadgets has one of their own as well. The acme.com DNS server in Chicago has a pretty sparse database—basically, it just names a few machines in Chicago and then contains a few records that say, "While I *am* the acme.com DNS server, don't ask me about anything with a name like something-dot-explosives.acme.com or something-dot-gadgets.com; rather, go ask these other machines." In DNS terms, we'd say that the acme.com server has *delegated* name resolution for gadgets.acme.com to some DNS server in Mexico and delegated name resolution for explosives.acme.com to some other DNS server in Belgium.

NOTE The InterNIC, by the way, knows nothing of this, nor does it care. Remember, that's the beauty of the whole DNS approach, delegating name server authority to local machines.

Delegating authority for a subset of Acme names will have the effect of making a name resolution query from an outside server take a bit more time: Instead of answering most name queries, the acme.com DNS servers will usually refer the questioner to either the explosives.acme.com or gadgets.acme.com DNS servers. The big point, however, and the one that makes the Belgians happy, is that when they add a new machine to their network and so need to add a new DNS name record, they needn't wait for Chicago. In fact, Chicago *can't* add a new Belgian record, as the authoritative DNS server for Explosives is, again, in Belgium.

Now, acme.com is still just one domain, but its DNS responsibilities—techies would say "DNS *namespace* duties"—have been spread out. What, then, to call these subsets of domains for which Acme's new DNS servers are authoritative? The term is *DNS zone* or *zone*. In Figure 18.38, Acme implemented their DNS as one zone. In Figure 18.39, Acme has three zones: Its top-level acme.com zone, the explosives.acme.com zone, and the gadgets.acme.com zone.

DNS Overview IV: Forward and Reverse Lookup Zones

Thus far, I've described DNS's main task as converting host names like kiwi.fruit.com to IP addresses like 205.22.42.19. But DNS can do the reverse as well; you can ask a DNS server, "What host name is associated with IP address 205.22.42.19?"

The process of converting a host name to an IP address is called a *forward name resolution*. The process of converting an IP address to a corresponding host name is called *reverse name resolution*.

DNS maintains information about a given domain like fruit.com in files called *zone files*. Fruit.com, then, has a zone file that DNS can use to look up kiwi.fruit.com's IP address. But where does DNS go to look up the host name associated with IP address 205.22.42.19?

Well, recall that the Internet authorities hand out blocks of addresses. There's a DNS zone called a *reverse lookup zone* for each Internet network. So, assuming that fruit.com's working with a C class network 205.22.42.0, it's someone's job to keep a reverse lookup zone for 205.22.42.0.

The *name* of the reverse lookup zone is odd, though. To construct it, take the dotted quads that the Internet authorities gave you—drop the ones that you control—and reverse them, then add ".in-addr.arpa" to the end of the name. Thus, whoever is responsible for 205.22.42.0 would create a reverse lookup zone 42.22.205.in-addr.arpa. A few other examples:

- 164.109.0.0/16, a B network, would drop the two zeroed quads and reverse the remaining two to yield a reverse zone name of 109.164.in-addr.arpa. Notice there were only two dotted numbers, as it's a B network and the owner controls the bottom two quads.

- 4.0.0.0/8, an A network, would have reverse zone 4.in-addr.arpa. In the case of an A network, only the top quad is set, so there's only one number in the reverse zone.

- 200.120.50.0/24, a C network, would drop the zeroed quad and reverse the numbers to get a reverse zone name of 50.120.200.in-addr.arpa.

Common DNS Record Types

But DNS databases contain more than just names and IP addresses. DNS databases contain several kinds of database records. Take a look at Figure 18.40 and you'll see a listing of some DNS records at the minasi.com domain. Don't worry that you haven't seen the DNS snap-in before; I'm just providing this figure to show a few examples as I introduce each record type.

FIGURE 18.40

Sample DNS records for a domain

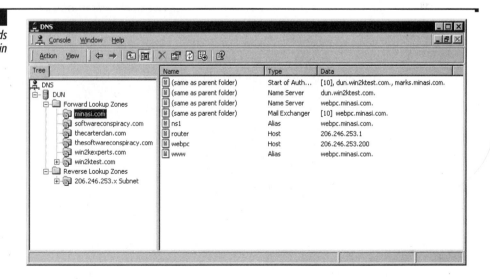

A Records (Hosts)

The simple record that says that dun.win2ktest.com is at IP address 206.246.253.200, the record that relates names to IP addresses, is called an *A record* or host record. (It's called an A record because DNS's internal database, a set of ASCII files called *zone files*, uses an A to indicate that a record is a host record. You'll learn about zone files later.) As you saw in Figure 18.40, A or host records are usually the most numerous—there's one for a machine named webpc at 206.246.253.200 and one for a machine named router. The router entry, by the way, does indeed point to the network's router. Giving the router a name isn't necessary; it just makes pinging it easier.

NOTE   I know that I'm calling them A records even though the graphical UI doesn't call them that. But I'm doing it because, again, zone files use the A designation—webpc's record in a zone file might look like "webpc A 206.246.253.200"—and I believe that you'll agree by the end of the chapter that you can get a lot done with zone files, from both an administration and troubleshooting standpoint. So throughout this section, I'll be presenting the records both as Windows 2000 refers to them and as zone files refer to them.

Cheap "Clusters": Building Fault Tolerance with Multiple A Records and Round-Robin DNS

This isn't a record type, but as long as I'm talking about A records, let me explain a great (and free!) way to handle a lot of Web traffic.

Suppose I've got a Web server at IP address 206.246.253.100. I've named it www.minasi.com because, well, that's what people expect the Web server at minasi.com to be named. But now let's suppose that several thousand people all decide at the same time to hit my Web site to find out how to hire me to speak at their next engagement. (Hey, it could happen.) At that point, my poor Web server's overloaded, lots of people get some kind of "server is too busy to respond to you" message, and I lose lots of potential business. That would be bad. Really bad.

Alternatively, I could set up three more machines with IIS on them, at IP addresses 206.246.253.101 through 206.246.253.103. *Then*—and here's the clever part—I just enter host name records, A records, for each of them and name *all* of them www.minasi.com. My DNS snap-in might then look like the Figure 18.41.

FIGURE 18.41

Preparing for round-robin DNS on www.minasi.com

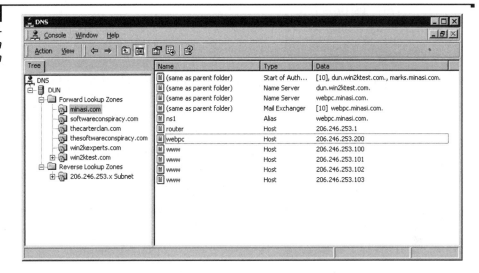

Now that I've got all four machines each named www.minasi.com, suppose someone points her browser to www.minasi.com. My DNS server is then asked by *her* DNS server to resolve the name www.minasi.com. So my DNS server looks at the four addresses that have "www.minasi.com" and responds with the first IP address, 206.246.253.100. Then, seconds later, someone else's DNS server asks my DNS server what IP address goes with www.minasi.com. My DNS server then responds with the next www.minasi.com address, 206.246.253.101. The third person who asks for the IP address gets 206.246.253.102, the fourth gets 206.246.253.103, and upon the fifth request, DNS cycles back to 206.246.253.100.

This process, called *round-robin DNS*, spreads out the load on a machine. If I had these four Web servers set up, they each would get roughly one-fourth of the incoming Web requests. In that way, I could build a "scalable" Web site. Now, understand that this *isn't* a replacement for Windows 2000 Advanced Server and multisystem clusters. DNS has no idea what's going on with the various Web servers, and if one of them goes down, DNS knows nothing of the problem and just keeps giving out the bad server's IP address to every fourth inquirer. But it's a free way of doing load balancing and worth a try before spending tens of thousands of dollars on cluster systems.

NOTE   Note that while I used an example of four consecutive IP addresses, you need not use consecutive addresses for your round-robin groups.

SOA Records (Start Of Authority)

Every domain has a *Start of Authority* record, abbreviated in zone files as an *SOA* record. It's the record that names the primary DNS server for the domain, provides an e-mail address for an administrator for the domain, and specifies how long it's okay to cache its data. It also alerts the outside world when any of the domain's records have changed through a serial number. In Figure 18.40, the [10] in the SOA record is the domain's serial number and indicates that since the domain was set up, there have been 10 changes—new records, deleted records, modified records. Secondary DNS servers can use this to see whether or not data on the primary server has changed, requiring them to go get updates from the primary DNS server.

Name Server/NS Records (DNS Servers)

Name Server records (called *NS* records in a zone file) define the name servers in the domain. The two NS records name the two DNS servers currently supporting the domain.

 NOTE By the way, a single machine running DNS server software can act as a DNS server for as many zones as you like, within the limits of CPU power and memory space. You need not dedicate one server to one zone. Actually, you saw that in Figure 18.40; notice that this DNS server acts as a name server for several domains.

Notice that both records look like "(same as parent folder) Name Server *server-name*." There's a couple of interesting points to be made here. First, notice that the servers' IP addresses aren't listed anywhere here. That's because they are both servers on another domain—to find their IP addresses, you'd search DNS for their A records in win2ktest.com.

Second, notice the "(same as parent folder)"; what that means is that these are name servers for this domain. But you can also use the NS records to delegate authority to a subdomain, a zone. An NS record for an imaginary zone westcoast.minasi.com might look like (in zone file terms):

```
westcoast    NS  surfers.earthlink.net
```

That record would say, "To resolve names for *somename*.westcoast.minasi.com, go to surfers.earthlink.net." Knowing how to create NS records that point to DNS servers for subdomain zones will come in handy later when we're seeing how to cope with non–Windows 2000 DNS servers.

CNAME Records (Aliases)

Many times, you'll need a host to respond to more than one name. For example, webpc.minasi.com does a number of different things, including serving as the Web server. I'd like the 206.246.253.200 machine to respond to webpc.minasi.com as well as to ns1.minasi.com and www.minasi.com. I do that with a *CNAME* record (the GUI tool calls them Aliases). A CNAME record says something like, "If you need a machine to respond to 'www' in this domain, then point to the machine at webpc.minasi.com." Notice how a CNAME record looks:

```
www Alias webpc.minasi.com.
```

Notice that the left-hand portion only says "www," not "www.minasi.com." If you create a CNAME within a given domain, the CNAME must be for a name that ends with the domain's name, hence "www" rather than "www.minasi.com." In contrast, the machine that it's being equated to, webpc.minasi.com, need not be in the domain, and so its full name is entered in the DNS record.

CNAME, by the way, stands for *canonical name*. I don't know why they didn't use ALIAS from the very beginning—it's got the same number of letters—but for whatever reason, we call these CNAME records in the DNS business.

MX Records (Mail Exchange)

If I send mail to `bill@acme.com`, then I've told my e-mail program that I want the mail to go to someone named Bill and that Bill has an account on some server in the acme.com domain. What I *haven't* told my e-mail program is where exactly to send the e-mail for Bill, what his mail server's name is. If it's not immediately obvious why this is important, consider: If you know that my domain is named minasi.com, how do you know where to find my Web or FTP server? There's an *informal* convention in the world that I'd call my Web server www.minasi.com and my FTP server ftp.minasi .com, but nothing *requiring* that. You can't simply tell your Web server, "Go check out the minasi.com Web site." But you *can* tell an e-mail program, "Send this mail to minasi.com." That's because DNS includes something called a Mail Exchange or MX record, which answers the question, "Which machine is the mail server for minasi.com?" This particular one says that mail for `someone@minasi.com` should go to the machine named webpc.minasi.com.

Notice that the MX record has a "preference" number in brackets, [10]. That lets you specify more than one MX record for a given domain. If I wanted to be sure that some server could pick up mail even if webpc.minasi.com was down, I could set up e-mail software on an "emergency backup" machine. But I wouldn't want anyone delivering mail there while webpc.minasi.com was functioning, so I'd use the preference number to control that. With the preference number, you indicate to DNS which mail server you prefer—lower numbers are preferred over higher numbers. I could, then, create the emergency mail server and give it a preference number higher than 10. It would then be ignored for mail unless webpc.minasi.com was down.

Pointer (PTR) Records (Reverse Host Records)

Those are the common record types you'll find in a forward lookup zone. Look in a reverse lookup zone, however, and you'll find one more type—a pointer record. Look at Figure 18.42 for an example.

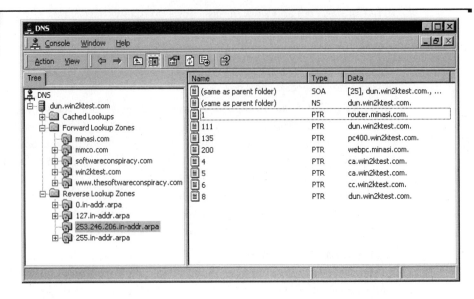

A pointer record works just like a host record—an A record—except that where you use an A record to look up the IP address associated with a given host name, a pointer record lets you look up a host name associated with a particular IP address. As you'll see later, you probably won't have to worry too much about these, as Windows 2000's DNS snap-in will, upon request, create pointer records automatically whenever it creates a host record.

DNS Improvements in Windows 2000

Thus far, all you've seen is a GUI-ized version of a standard DNS server. But Windows 2000 offers a few things beyond that—two new features in particular, in fact.

RFC 2136 Dynamic DNS

In the old days, DNS was a bit of a pain to administer. Most DNS servers required that you sit down and type in the names and IP addresses of any machines that you wanted the outside world to be able to resolve. And that's actually "sit down and type in the names"—DHCP didn't talk to DNS, so anyone wanting to inform the DNS server of all of the systems which had acquired IP addresses through DHCP had to first dump out the list of DHCP leases (there's a Resource Kit tool, DHCPCMD, that made it possible) and then key in each of the machine names and IP addresses by hand. Introduced in April of 1997, RFC 2136 simplified that by defining a method for building DNS servers whose name databases could be updated in an automated fashion—dynamic updates.

Windows 2000's DNS servers rely upon dynamic update to allow Active Directory to maintain much of its information in DNS.

RFC 2052 SRV Records

As you read a page or two back in the section on MX records, DNS has been of great help over the years to computers trying to find mail servers.

This notion of using DNS to identify servers was extended by RFC 2052, introduced in October of 1996. The SRV record lets you identify any type of server. As Windows 2000 domain controllers use LDAP to communicate, Active Directory identifies domain controllers as LDAP servers in DNS; machines can then discover domain controllers not by broadcasting, as they did in NT 4, but by simply looking them up in DNS. Active Directory also uses DNS to identify global catalog servers. As Windows 2000 evolves, it's likely that more and more functions—server types—will identify themselves through DNS SRV records.

DNS Server Roles: Caching DNS Servers

Thus far, I've been talking about setting up DNS servers to store the name records of an organization. But you may want to set up a DNS server even if you're never in charge of administering a single zone.

The reason for this is simple: *DNS caches data.* Suppose you've got a small branch office in Louisville, a branch with 40 PCs in it. They all need DNS services, but the "official" company DNS servers are in corporate headquarters in Memphis. You set up a local NT server to be a DNS server and set up all of the 40 PCs to refer DNS queries to that server. Here's why it makes sense: Presumably everyone in the building tends to go to the same places—the corporate intranet, AltaVista, CNN, or whatever. The first person in the morning who looks something up on Microsoft's Web site causes that local DNS server to ask Microsoft what IP address (or addresses, in the case of Microsoft) their Web server resides at. Now, that request generates WAN traffic and might be a bit slow. But for the rest of the day, anyone needing to get to Microsoft's Web site will find that the first part of surfing microsoft.com—the actual name resolution—happens quite quickly, as their *local* DNS server already knows where Microsoft is.

Such a server is called a *caching* DNS server. To set such a thing up, just do the following:

1. Install the Microsoft DNS service.

2. Reboot the server.

3. Point all of the local machines to that server.

That's it—there's nothing else to do.

Setting Up a Small Domain with DNS Manager: An Example

There is a lot to know about running a DNS server. But many small domains will be able to get away with just a few basics, so I'll start the "how-to" part of the DNS story with a look at how to set up a DNS server under Windows 2000 for a small imaginary domain.

Introducing Bowsers.com

Suppose for the sake of argument that I'd like to set up a domain named bowsers.com, pictured in Figure 18.43. It's C class network number 210.10.20.0.

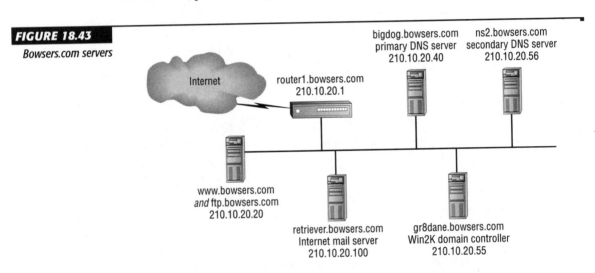

FIGURE 18.43

Bowsers.com servers

There are just a few machines that are important enough that they must have entries in DNS:

- As I've mentioned before, it's convenient to name the router at 210.10.20.1.
- The mail server for bowsers.com is a machine named retriever.bowsers.com, at 210.10.20.100.
- The Web server for bowsers.com is a machine named www.bowsers.com, at 210.10.20.20.
- That same 210.10.20.20 machine is also the FTP server, and we want it to respond to the name ftp.bowsers.com.

- There is a machine that acts both as a major file server for the organization and as the primary DNS server; it's named bigdog.bowsers.com, at 210.10.20.40.

- The Windows 2000 domain controller runs on gr8dane.bowsers.com, and it has IP address 210.10.20.55.

- There's another DNS server at ns2.bowsers.com with address 210.10.20.56.

Installing the DNS Service

I'll start off at the bigdog.bowsers.com machine, where I'll set up the DNS server service. Name servers must be running a DNS server service of some kind, and although they needn't use Microsoft's DNS server program, it's free, so I'll use that one. In case you want to follow along and build a small DNS zone of your own—you needn't in order to understand this—then start off with a machine named bigdog and a static IP address of 200.10.20.40. (Clearly, you shouldn't be connected to the Internet when doing this.) I then changed its DNS name to bigdog.bowsers.com in the Network Identification tab. (Right-click My Computer, choose Properties, then the Network Identification tab.)

The steps to installing DNS are exactly the same as for installing any of the other network services—DHCP or WINS—but here's what you do:

1. Open the Control Panel (Start/Settings/Control Panel).

2. Open Add/Remove Programs.

3. Click Add/Remove Windows Components and wait a bit while the irritating Windows Components Wizard starts up.

4. Click Next to bring up the list of Windows components.

5. Click Networking Services and then the Details button.

6. Click the check box next to Domain Name System (DNS).

7. Click OK to return to Windows Components.

8. Click Next to install the service. The system will say that it is "Configuring Components" for a while, probably a few minutes. A bit later, the screen labeled Completing the Windows Components Wizard appears.

9. Click Finish to end the wizard.

10. Click Close to close Add/Remove Windows Components.

You needn't reboot. Click Start/Programs/Administrative Tools/DNS and you'll see the DNS snap-in. You'll see an icon representing your server in the left-hand pane; click the plus sign next to it and you'll see a screen like Figure 18.44.

FIGURE 18.44

*Initial DNS
snap-in screen*

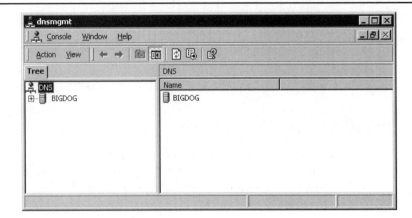

Creating the Bowsers.com Zone

Click the plus sign next to BIGDOG, you'll see a container named Forward Lookup Zones and another named Reverse Lookup Zones. I'll create the bowsers.com zone— a forward lookup zone—by right-clicking the Forward Lookup Zones container (you may have to click the plus sign next to Forward Lookup Zones first) and choosing New Zone, which invokes a wizard, as you see in Figure 18.45.

FIGURE 18.45

*New Zone Wizard
opening screen*

It'd be really nice if Windows 2000 came with an "Expert Mode setting" that would let us bypass these wizards, but there isn't one. Perhaps in Windows 2002 Server. In any case, click Next to see Figure 18.46.

FIGURE 18.46

Choosing a zone type

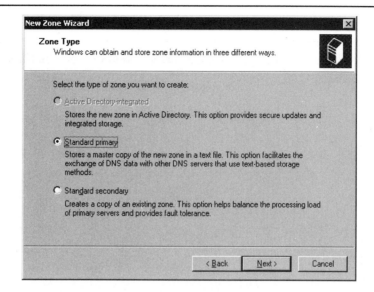

Here, you tell the wizard whether to create a primary or secondary zone. Choose Standard Primary. The first option, an "integrated Active Directory primary zone," is grayed out because this is a stand-alone server. If, however, I were to build a Windows 2000 domain named bowsers.com, then this DNS server would automatically convert this zone to an AD integrated zone. Click Next, and you'll see Figure 18.47.

FIGURE 18.47

Name the zone.

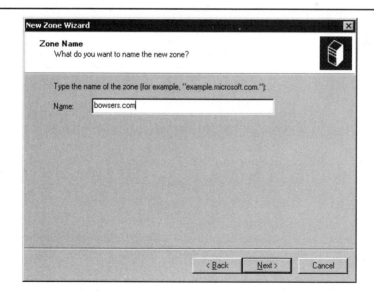

Here, I tell it the name, bowsers.com, and click Next to see Figure 18.48.

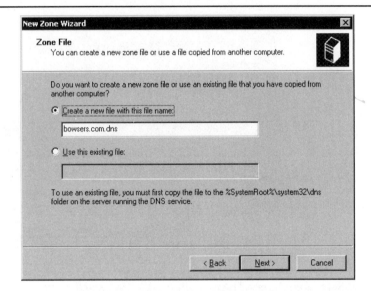

In this figure, you see a really nice feature of this server software. It suggests a name for the zone file that it's about to create, which is not a big deal. What's really nice, however, is that you can choose any filename—and, more important, you can point the server at an already-existing zone file. *That* means that disaster recovery on DNS servers is a snap:Just install the DNS service on a new system, set its IP address to equal the IP address of the DNS server that it's replacing, copy the zone files from the old server (or its backups) to the new server, and then just re-create the zones with a few clicks of the wizard. You then point the wizard at the already-existing files—meaning that you needn't re-create any DNS records—and in a few minutes you've completely rebuilt your DNS server.

Click Next, and you'll get a confirmation screen like the one in Figure 18.49.

Click Finish, and you've got your zone.

FIGURE 18.49

*Wizard confirmation
screen*

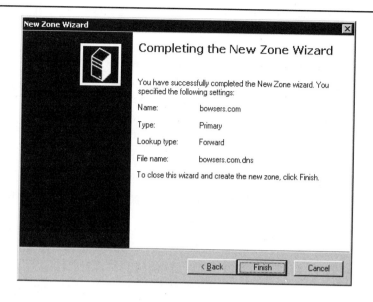

Creating the Reverse Lookup Zone

Next, let's get the reverse lookup zone created so that when I create host records in the forward zone, there's a reverse zone to create pointer records in.

Before I do that, however, I should point out that you may not ever have to *create* a reverse lookup zone. Some ISPs insist on managing the reverse zones, so the ISP that bowsers.com got its C network from might say "You've got DNS responsibility for bowsers.com, and you've got the addresses in 210.10.20.0, but we'll keep track of its reverse lookup zone for those IP addresses." Try to get them to allow you to run the reverse lookup zone, if you can, because I've found that Windows 2000 works much better when you control them both, or at least when you're very careful to have records in the reverse zone *at least* for your DNS servers. As you'll learn a bit later, there's a useful tool that you can use for diagnosing DNS troubles called NSLOOKUP.

More specifically, here's the problem. In the example that I'm working through now, the DNS server for bowsers.com is bigdog.bowsers.com at 210.10.20.40. But remember that your TCP/IP configuration doesn't ask you to tell it the name of your DNS server—it wants the IP address of your DNS server, and that seems to lead to the potential trouble.

What I've seen is that if I start up NSLOOKUP, then it knows only the IP address of the DNS server that it's supposed to be using. NSLOOKUP's first act is to contact your DNS server and say to it, "I have your IP address, but what's your host name?" In other words, NSLOOKUP does a reverse lookup on the DNS server's IP address—so somewhere, some reverse lookup zone had better know about the DNS server!

For example, if I started up NSLOOKUP on a system that looked to 210.10.20.40 as its DNS server, then NSLOOKUP would ask bigdog.bowsers.com the host name of the machine with IP address 210.10.20.40. If whoever's running the 20.10.210.in-addr .arpa zone hasn't added a pointer record for 210.10.20.40, then NSLOOKUP for some reason acts like it can't find a DNS server

In any case, to create the reverse lookup zone, right-click the container labeled Reverse Lookup Zones and choose New Zone, which will kick off the same wizard that you just saw. The first two panels are identical—choose to create a primary zone again—and you'll see the third panel, which looks different, and looks like Figure 18.50.

FIGURE 18.50

Defining the reverse lookup zone

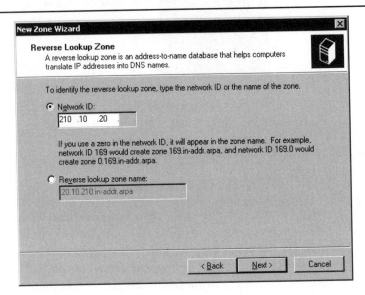

Here, the wizard makes life easy for you—you just type in the network number of your block of IP addresses and it flips the numbers around, and when you click Next, the wizard adds the ".in-addr.arpa" suffix, as you see in Figure 18.51.

Again, you can either create a new zone here, or revivify a dead zone by pointing the wizard at an old zone file. Click Next and Finish, and you've got two zones, as you see in Figure 18.52.

FIGURE 18.51

*Choosing a zone
file name*

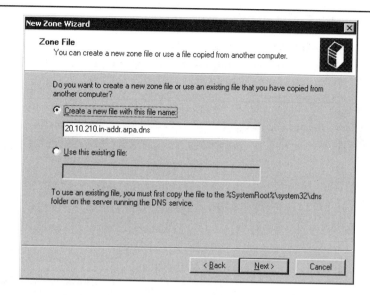

FIGURE 18.52

*DNS snap-in with
forward and
reverse zones*

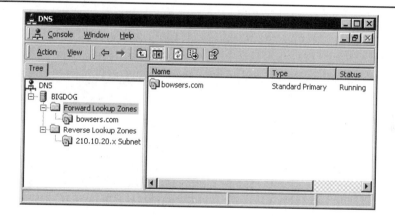

 NOTE   Note that there isn't always a one-to-one relationship between forward and reverse lookup zones. For example, on my network, which is just one C network, I host the mmco.com, minasi.com, win2ktest.com, win2kbugs.com, win2kexperts.com, softwarecon-spiracy.com, and thesoftwareconspiracy.com domains. All machines in those seven domains have IP addresses somewhere in my 206.246.253.0/24 network range. Thus, I've got seven forward lookup zones but only one reverse lookup zone.

Cleaning Up after the Wizard

The wizard makes a few assumptions about your zones that you might not agree with, so it's worthwhile taking a closer look at its work. I right-click the bowsers.com container and choose Properties, which brings up a five-page property sheet. The first tab is labeled General, as you see in Figure 18.53.

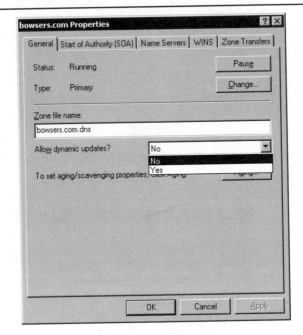

This tab points to the zone file, which is how you'd tell DNS to go work with a backup file if the original zone file were somehow corrupted. Notice that there's a button to pause this zone, meaning to tell the DNS server to stop responding to resolution requests for this zone, and a button that'll let you change the server's status from primary for the zone to being one of potentially many secondaries for the zone. This is an important button because *this* is the way that you promote a secondary DNS server to become the primary for the zone.

The setting you'll probably want to fool with, however, is the one labeled Allow Dynamic Updates. Recall that RFC 2136 updates are one of Windows 2000's most significant new DNS abilities. By default, the wizard disables that feature (oh, good call, Wiz!), which will cause you *big* problems if you want this DNS server to serve a Windows 2000 domain. DNS servers for Windows 2000 domains *must* be able to accept dynamic updates, or you simply can't set up a Windows 2000 domain. So click the Allow Dynamic Updates drop-down and change the setting from No to Yes.

Next stop is the Start of Authority tab. It looks like Figure 18.54.

FIGURE 18.54

Start of Authority tab

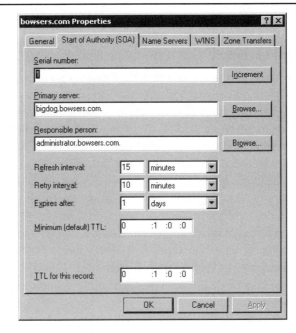

What Microsoft's done here is just to GUI-ify the fields that you find in a standard SOA record. And while putting graphical interfaces on many tools often seems hardly worth the effort, it's much appreciated here. Let's take a look at each of these fields.

First is the serial number. It indicates how many changes have been made to the zone since it was created. Here you see a serial number of 1 because I haven't done anything to it yet. In general, leave this alone and let the server increment it automatically as needed.

Primary Server identifies the DNS server authoritative for this domain. As you know, I'm using bigdog.bowsers.com, which is of course a member of this DNS domain. But don't expect that to always be the case—it's very common for small domains to pay their ISP to maintain the DNS servers for those domains. In that case, the primary DNS for bowsers.com might be in another domain altogether.

Responsible Person names the e-mail address of someone to whom to address problems and questions. It's an e-mail address, but it's formatted strangely—administrator .bowsers.com is the way that an SOA record stores the address administrator@bowsers .com. In any case, it's wrong, as I'm the person setting this up, so I'd replace administrator.bowsers.com with help.minasi.com, as my e-mail address is help@minasi.com.

The next three numbers instruct secondary servers how to get information from the primary server. Refresh Interval here tells all secondary servers to query this primary server at least once every 15 minutes (which is the Windows 2000 default, but truthfully seems a bit short—I'd set it to an hour minimum). If they try to connect and can't, however, the Retry Interval instructs the secondaries to try to communicate with the primary every 10 minutes. The Expires After tells the secondaries that if they are unable to communicate with the primary DNS server for an entire day, they should assume that the information that they have is too far out-of-date, and to discard it. In other words, when a secondary cannot access the primary for more than one day, then the secondary basically just stops answering name resolution queries.

The final two entries direct other DNS servers how long to cache name resolution data. TTL stands for Time To Live and is expressed as days:hours:minutes:seconds.

Minimum (Default) TTL advises other DNS servers how long to cache information received from this server. It's 60 minutes by default, so any DNS server that does a name resolution on bowsers.com and then needs the same name resolved 59 minutes later need not requery one of the bowsers.com DNS servers. Sixty minutes is the Microsoft default, and personally I think it's a bit short—I'd set it somewhere between four hours and a day. The field is called Minimum TTL because every single record in a DNS zone file can have its own separate TTL. The vast majority of the time, however, you won't assign a specific TTL to a specific DNS record, so this default TTL sets the value for the records that are silent on TTL.

The final field, TTL for This Record, allows you to set a different TTL just for this SOA record.

The next tab is the Name Servers property page, as you see in Figure 18.55.

FIGURE 18.55

Name Servers property page

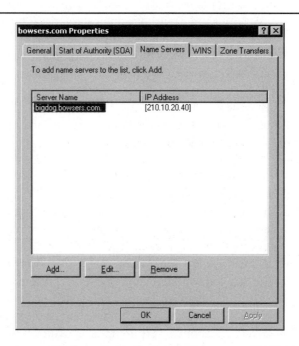

This is where you specify the names of other name servers. We'll use this later to add ns2.bowsers.com to our list of name servers. The next page is the WINS page, and while it was an interesting feature under NT 4, I can't recommend it now, so click the Zone Transfers tab to look at that page, as you see in Figure 18.56.

FIGURE 18.56

Zone Transfers property page

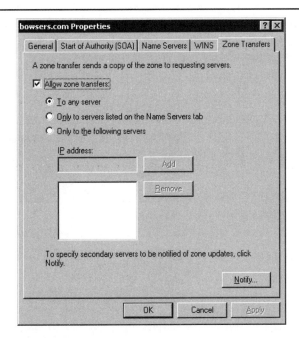

In order for a secondary DNS server to operate, it's got to copy the information in the primary DNS server's zone files to its own zone files—to ensure that its database of names and IP addresses is up-to-date. Copying zone information from one server to another is called *zone transfers*.

By default, this DNS server will transfer the contents of its zone files to any server that asks. But knowing the names of your system's machines can help bad guys compromise security on your network, so Windows 2000 gives you the option to disallow transfers altogether, to name a set of acceptable DNS servers to limit transfers to, or to just transfer to the other name servers listed on the Name Servers page—a quite logical option. If you've got a group of people in your organization who set network security policy, then check with them before leaving zone transfers open to just anyone.

I'm done working with bowser.com's configuration, so I click OK to close the property page. Then I need to do the same thing to 20.10.210.in-addr.arpa's zone—fix the responsible party and allow dynamic updates, at the very least, and possibly modify the time intervals in the SOA record.

Creating Host Records

Thanks to dynamic DNS, you no longer have to type in the name of every single host in your enterprise. But you'll want to enter a few of them immediately, just so that your DNS server will know what machines you're talking about when you name a second name server, a mail server, or give a second name to a given machine—so let's see how to add a new A type host name record.

Right-click the bowsers.com folder and choose New Host and you'll see a dialog like Figure 18.57.

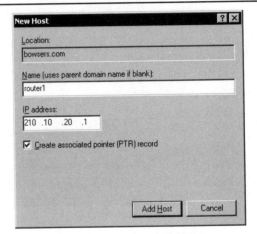

In that figure, I've filled in the information about bowsers.com's LAN/WAN router, at 210.10.20.1. I've also checked Create Associated Pointer (PTR) Record, which will create a pointer record in the reverse lookup zone. I click OK and then create the other hosts, so that my DNS snap-in looks like Figure 18.58.

Again, there will be plenty more systems on this network, but they're workstations that need only host records—and dynamic DNS (with DHCP's help) creates those host records automatically.

FIGURE 18.58

Host names all entered

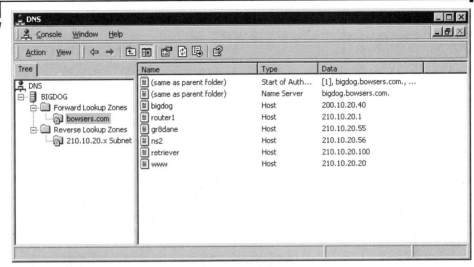

Identifying the Second Name Server

Next, I'll tell the network that there's another DNS server around. I can't click New Name Server or anything like that. Again, I've got to right-click the bowsers.com container and choose Properties, then click the Name Servers page. It has an Add button on it, and when I choose it and fill in ns2's information, it looks like Figure 18.59.

FIGURE 18.59

Defining NS2 as a DNS server for the domain

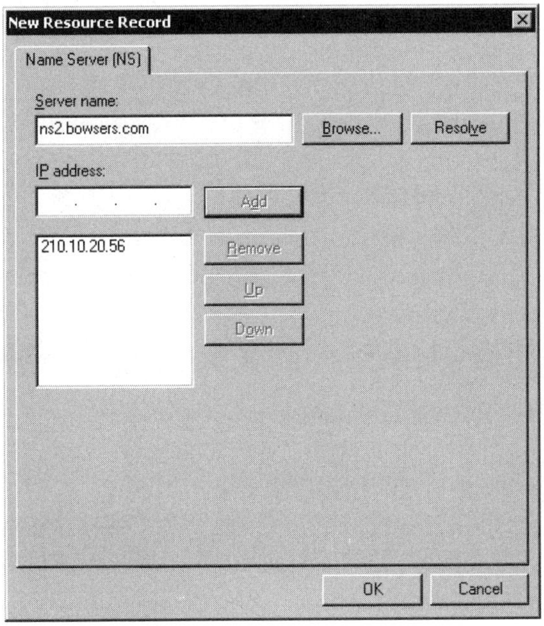

Here, I've filled in its name and IP address, although just the IP address is sufficient.

Creating the MX Record

We run our SMTP/POP3 server on retriever.bowsers.com at 210.10.20.100, but the outside world doesn't know that—mail to someone@bowsers.com will never get to us. I'll fix that by adding an MX record for retriever. Right-click the bowsers.com container and choose New Mail Exchanger and a dialog like Figure 18.60 appears.

Notice that this dialog wants to see retriever's full DNS name, retriever.bowsers.com. That's because a machine on an entirely different domain might be the desired mail server. By default the DNS server suggests a mail preference value of 10, and since there's only one mail server on this domain, it doesn't matter what value we set here—there's no other server to "prefer."

FIGURE 18.60

Making retriever the designated mail server

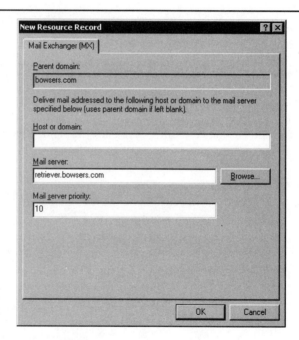

Giving the Web Server a Second Name

The last initial configuration job to get out of the way is the FTP server. We've got a machine that acts both as a Web server and as an FTP server. Its current name is www.bowsers.com, so people will clearly have no problem finding our Web server. But people assume that an FTP server will have the name ftp, so it'd be nice if the machine also answered to ftp.bowsers.com. We add this second name with the

CNAME or Alias function; right-click bowsers.com and choose New Alias and you'll see a dialog like the one in Figure 18.61.

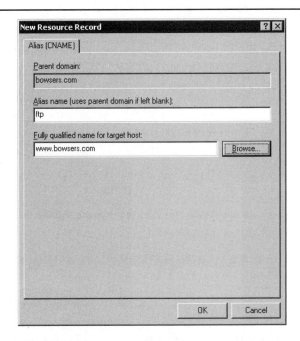

As the alias is to be an alias relevant to this domain, you don't fill in the domain name—ftp is sufficient. (In fact, you *can't* enter ftp.bowsers.com in that field and have it work properly.) The alias could, however, refer to a machine outside of the domain—perhaps www.pooches.com holds the FTP libraries for both bowsers.com *and* pooches.com—and so you fill in the second field with a complete DNS name.

At this point, bowsers.com looks like Figure 18.62 in the snap-in.

The reverse lookup zone doesn't know about NS2, so it's worthwhile opening its property page and adding NS2 to its list of name servers. And of course, my work's not done yet—retriever had better be ready to accept mail, the Web and FTP server programs on www need to be running, and the secondary zones on ns2 need setting up—but the basics are out of the way.

FIGURE 18.62

Bowsers.com state after configuration

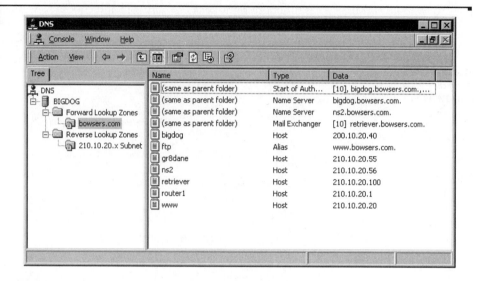

Creating a Secondary DNS Server for Bowsers.com

We've got one DNS server set up; now let's set up a secondary for a bit of backup, safety, and fault tolerance. Recall that we've planned for a secondary DNS server named ns2.bowsers.com at 210.10.20.56. I install Windows 2000 Server on that system, give it the IP address 210.10.20.56, and start up the DNS snap-in.

Notice so far that I've not done anything to make this server a "secondary" DNS server, and in fact there *is* no such thing as a secondary DNS server—there are only secondary zones hosted on a particular DNS server. Recall that a DNS server can host many zones. When you set up any given zone on a DNS server, you identify whether that DNS server's role will be primary or secondary *for that zone*. In fact, it's quite common to see DNS servers that are primary for some zones but at the same time serving as secondary, "backup" servers in other zones.

To make ns2.bowsers.com a secondary DNS server for bowsers.com, I start the process of creating a new zone as before—in the snap-in, I right-click the Forward Lookup Zones container and choose New Zone and the wizard appears. Clicking past the first screen, I see the screen that asks what type of zone this will be, as you see in Figure 18.63.

FIGURE 18.63

Opting for a secondary zone

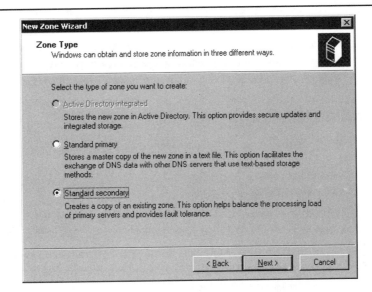

By clicking the Standard Secondary radio button, I warn the wizard to ask me different things. When I click Next, it asks me, as it has before when creating primary zones, for the name of the zone and what to call the zone files. But the next screen asks something new, as you see in Figure 18.64.

FIGURE 18.64

Identifying the primary DNS server

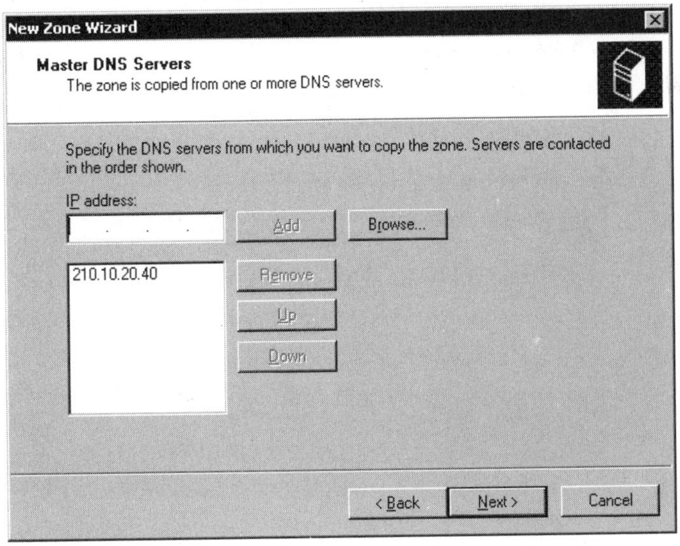

As this is to be a secondary server, serving mainly to back up information from another server, the secondary server must know where to find the original information. I enter the IP address of bigdog.bowsers.com and click Add and Next, then Finish, and the secondary is created. In a moment or two, you'll see a zone in Forward Lookup Zones named bowsers.com; open it, and you'll see all of the bowsers.com records.

Testing the Configuration

Well, by now, your DNS server should be up. But how to check it? With a diagnostic tool called NSLOOKUP. It's a command-line utility, one of those old cryptic Unix utilities. If DNS is a server, think of NSLOOKUP as a simple diagnostic client. It'll talk to any DNS server and let you make simple queries, queries that mimic an outside computer trying to resolve a name. When you type **nslookup**, it responds with a > prompt. I'll work from bigdog for this example. These are the commands I'll use:

- First, I type NSLOOKUP to start the program. The system will respond with the IP address of the DNS server that it's currently using to resolve names. Notice it's 210.10.20.40, bigdog.

- Then *ls -d BOWSERS.COM* says, "List everything you know about BOWSERS.COM." That will show me what bigdog knows.

- Now that I've seen that bigdog answers queries about the domain correctly, let's try out the backup, ns2.bowsers.com. The command server 210.10.20.56 or server ns2.bowsers.com tells NSLOOKUP to direct its name queries to that server from this point on.

- Let's try a different type of query. *set type=any* and *bowsers.com* says to show a summary of information about bowsers.com.

- *exit* exits NSLOOKUP.

You can see the session in Figure 18.65.

FIGURE 18.65

Running NSLOOKUP to test the DNS server

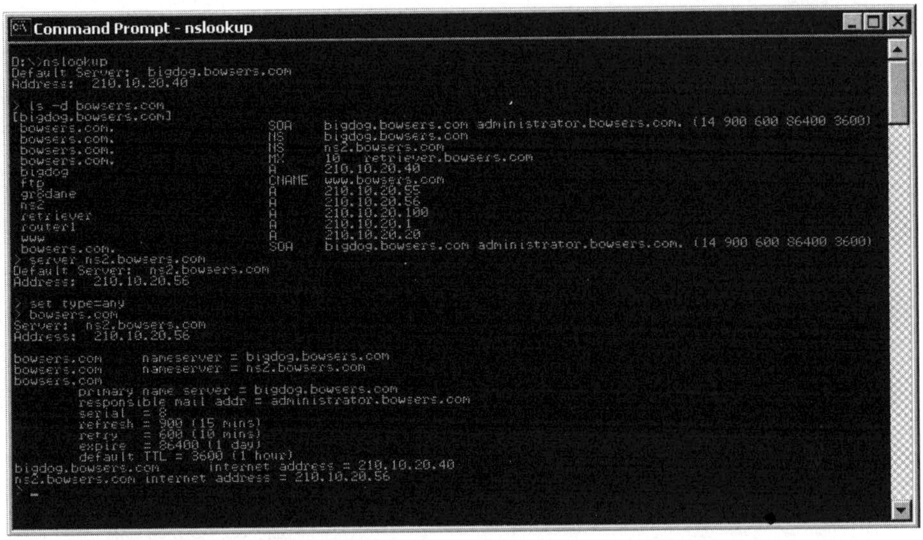

Creating Subdomains in DNS

Now bowsers.com is running well. But suppose we wanted to delegate control of some of bowsers to another group within the organization, as you see in Figure 18.66.

In that figure, I've added three systems—ns1.hounds.bowsers.com (210.10.20.110), blood.hounds.bowsers.com (210.10.20.115)—it is, of course, the system that runs the search engine—and beagle.hounds.bowsers.com (210.10.20.15). Notice that all of the names have gotten longer—they're all *something*.hounds.bowsers.com—and that means that we'll need another DNS server. For whatever reason, the bowsers.com IT management decided to let some other folks administer their own DNS, and so wants to give them a new subdomain, hounds.bowsers.com. There are three parts to setting up a new subdomain that someone else's DNS server keeps track of:

- Tell the upper-level domain that there will be a lower-level domain under another system's control.

- Tell the upper-level domain's DNS server where to find a DNS server for the new lower-level domain.

- Set up the new lower-level domain's DNS server.

FIGURE 18.66

*Expanded
bowsers.com DNS
structure*

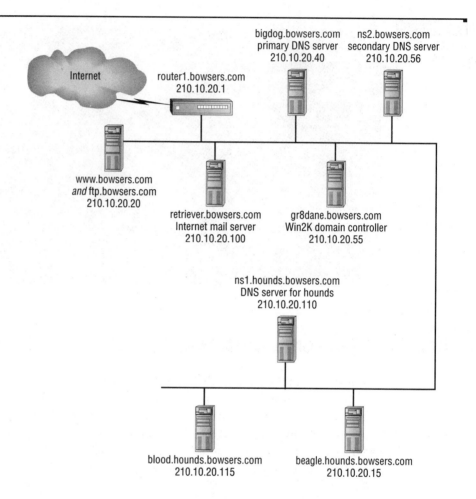

In DNS-ese, we'd call this *delegating control of a zone*. Briefly, do it this way:

1. Right-click the upper-level domain in the DNS snap-in and choose New Domain.

2. In the resulting dialog box, fill in the name of the new subdomain; in the case of hounds.bowsers.com, fill in **hounds**.

3. Create a host record for the new DNS server for the subdomain.

4. Right-click the upper-level domain again and choose New Delegation, then follow the Zone Delegation Wizard's prompts.

5. Go to the new DNS server for the new subdomain and set up the new subdomain in the exact same way that you've already created other DNS domains.

Here's a look at a step-by-step example of how to do it in bowsers.com.

Prepare the Upper-Level Domain's DNS Server

Returning to the DNS snap-in for bigdog.bowsers.com, the primary DNS server for bowsers.com, I expand the server to show Forward Lookup Zones, then expand that container to show the bowsers.com container. I right-click that container and choose New Domain. I get a dialog box like Figure 18.67.

FIGURE 18.67

Creating a container for hounds.bowsers.com records

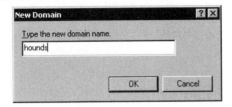

Once I've filled it in with the new name—notice I don't fill in hounds.bowsers .com, but hounds—I click OK. The DNS snap-in immediately shows the change, as you see in Figure 18.68.

FIGURE 18.68

DNS snap-in showing new subdomain hounds

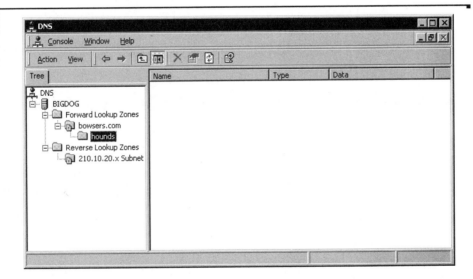

If you don't see the new folder icon below your existing higher-level domain, try pressing F5 to refresh the display.

Create a Host Name Record for the New DNS Server

My next goal is to tell bowsers.com that this new subdomain will be someone else's problem—namely, ns1.hounds.bowsers.com's problem, at 210.10.20.110. But one of the quirks of the way that DNS—and this is DNS in general, not just Microsoft's DNS—delegates is that it will not simply accept a command that says, "Let 210.10.20.110 do all of the name resolutions for the subdomain hounds.bowsers.com"; rather, that new DNS server's got to have a fully qualified domain name, which means it needs an A record before we can go any further. (Much of the Internet DNS literature about setting up delegation refers to this A record as a "glue record" because it glues the upper-level and lower-level domains together, in essence.)

Now, of course, there's an easy way out here: The DNS server for hounds.bowsers.com doesn't *have* to be a machine in the hounds.bowsers.com domain. We could just put the ns1 machine into the upper-level bowsers.com domain, and in fact that's what some domains do. But many network managers prefer to have machines inside a given domain named ns1.*domain-name* and ns2.*domain-name* as the local DNS servers. It's nice to have a regular convention so that it's easy to find a DNS server. It's a matter of taste; in any case, I've got ns1 diagrammed as a member of the hounds.bowsers.com domain, so let's put it there.

I can't create an A record for ns1.hounds.bowsers.com up in the upper-level bowsers.com container—the GUI won't let me. Instead, I right-click the hounds container and choose New Host and create an A record with a host name of NS1 there. As it's in the hounds folder, its fully qualified domain name is then the desired ns1.hounds.bowsers.com. (I create this A record in precisely the same way that I showed how to create a host record a few pages back, so I'm not running through a screen shot.)

Tell the Upper-Level Domain to Delegate Control to the Lower-Level Domain's DNS Server

Next, we'll tell bowsers.com that it needn't worry about name resolution for anything whose name ends with hounds.bowsers.com. I right-click the bowsers.com folder and choose New Delegation, which starts up a wizard. Click Next past its title screen and you'll see a screen like Figure 18.69.

FIGURE 18.69

Naming the sub-domain to delegate to

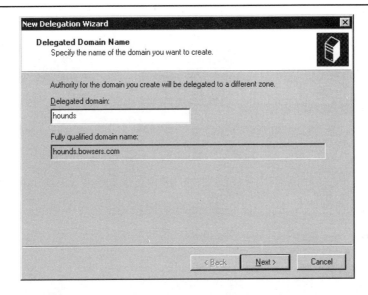

Here, I fill in the name of the subdomain. Again, it's just the new part of the domain name, hounds rather than hounds.bowsers.com. I then click Next and see something like Figure 18.70.

FIGURE 18.70

What DNS server to delegate to

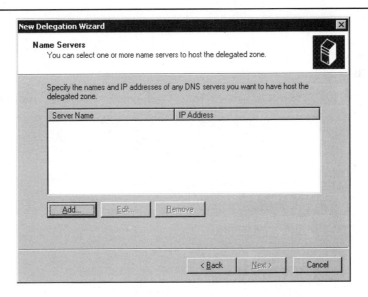

This panel wants to know the name and IP address of the DNS server (or servers) for the new subdomain. I can enter a name/IP address pair by clicking Add, which shows me the dialog in Figure 18.71.

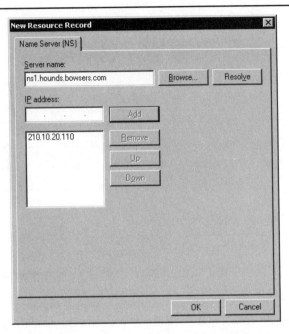

As I explained before, you've got to fill in *both* IP address and name to satisfy this
dialog box. As I've already got a host record for ns1.hounds.bowsers.com, however, I
can alternatively click the Browse button and look for it. Click OK, and I return to the
wizard. I then click Next, and the final screen is a confirmation. Click Finish, and the
delegation is done. The snap-in now looks like Figure 18.72.

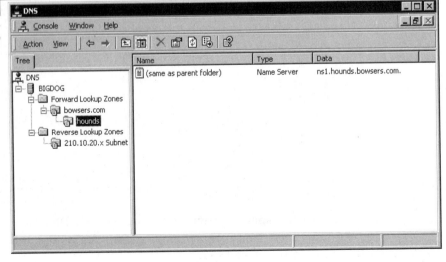

It doesn't look very different on a black and white page, but that hounds folder has gone from a light yellow color to gray, indicating that it's a delegated domain. You may not see the color change on your system immediately—you may have to click `bowsers.com` and/or hounds and press F5 to see it. At this point, the work's done on this server; time to go work at ns1.hounds.bowsers.com.

Creating the Lower-Level Domain, hounds.bowsers.com

Working from ns1.hounds.bowsers.com, run its DNS snap-in, right-click its `Forward Lookup Zones` and choose New Zone. From this point on, it ought to look familiar. You create a subdomain with exactly the same wizard that you used to create the domain.

In fact, if you think about it, that makes perfect sense. If you get a domain name from the InterNIC like bowsers.com, then the InterNIC has already gone to *its* domain named simply com and delegated control of a subdomain of com—that is, bowsers.com. We don't think about that much because it's not anything we worry about normally. But the second part of the process, creating the zone, we *do* think about, as that's usually our job as network engineer types.

Private Roots versus Internet Connectivity

Now that you've seen how to build zones and delegate, I can deliver one last piece of DNS overview—a clearer look at the DNS *namespace*. The main reason that you'd care about all of this would be if you must build your own private root.

You've read that DNS servers are smart enough to work their way up to the top of the DNS server hierarchy, and that at the top of that hierarchy is a bunch of servers run by the InterNIC. That's usually true, but not always. Your DNS servers might *not* be attached to any machine in the outside world. You might have your own little private intranet not attached to the Internet for reasons of security or cost. In that case, however, you've still got to have a DNS server hierarchy. The difference is that *you* build all of it. In that case, your DNS hierarchy is said to have a *private root*.

Presuming that you end up having to build a private root, let me add a bit of detail to how the Internet DNS naming hierarchy works so that you can understand what you've got to get done in your private name hierarchy. Take a look at Figure 18.73.

Now, I know that there's a good chance that you've seen a diagram like this before, but stay with me and let me try to bring out the less-obvious pieces. Most of us are used to the idea that we've got a domain like acme.com and can put machines in it (mypc.acme.com) or subdivide the domain (hispc.gadgets.acme.com), but let's step back a minute and consider the domain named com.

FIGURE 18.73

DNS name hierarchy

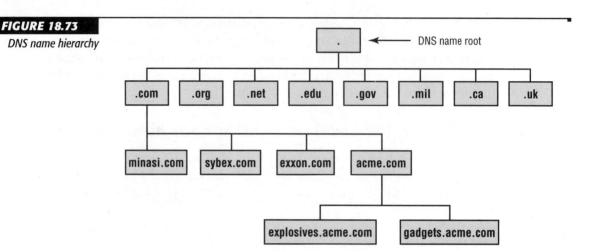

Yes, there *is* a domain named com. The InterNIC owns it. Somewhere, there's a zone file for com with an SOA record, an NS record, and an A record, at least. And, as you know, the InterNIC subdivides that domain into other subdomains with names like microsoft.com, exxon.com, acme.com, and so on. When I bought the minasi .com name from the InterNIC, I essentially paid them to delegate that name to two of my name servers. There's also a domain simply named gov, another named net, org, de (Germany's domain), edu, and so on. I suppose it would be completely possible to create a domain simply named minasi—not minasi.com, but minasi—if I could persuade the InterNIC to sell it to me.

But now let's step back yet another level and ask, "Is com a subdomain of some other domain?" The answer is yes—com is a subdomain of a domain named . (yes, that's a period). It's where all DNS names begin. And saying that doesn't make any sense at all until I tell you this: *All fully qualified domain names* should *end in a period*. Strictly speaking, the PC that I'm working on at the moment's name is pc400.win2ktest .com. with the period at the end. In practice, TCP/IP-aware software doesn't require that you add the period. But if you visualize every fully qualified domain name as ending with a period, then it's possible to see how a DNS name corresponds to the DNS hierarchy:

- PC400 is a host in a domain called win2ktest.
- Win2ktest is a subdomain of the domain named com.
- Com is a subdomain of a the domain named . (and sometimes just called the *root*).

Somewhere in northern Virginia, there's a zone file for the . domain, with an SOA record, an NS record naming the server that's authoritative for the . zone, and an A record telling the IP address of a primary or secondary name for the . domain. The InterNIC keeps 13 different servers acting as root servers at this writing.

If you want your own DNS hierarchy instead of using the public DNS system, you can easily accomplish that with Windows 2000's DNS server. All there is to building a private root is really to just create a zone for . and populate it with the proper information—but you'll see how to do that a little later on in this chapter. Oh, and I forgot the other reason for building a private root: it makes for a great joke at the company. You set up the private root DNS server, choose some victim, and point his machine at your DNS server, where you've got bogus domains built for cnn.com, microsoft.com, and so on. (Just kidding—it would be a fair bit of work just for a few sadistic yucks.)

How to Bypass the GUI and Fix DNS Problems Directly: Understanding the DNS Boot, Cache, and Zone Files

Thus far, we've worked with the Windows 2000 DNS server via its GUI interface and wizards. They're fine for many tasks, but in my experience they're a bit "fragile"—the DNS tree is built from a chain of data, and if any of those links aren't in place, then the GUI may refuse to run at all.

Starting up the DNS snap-in and having it refuse to work is pretty scary—"Do I have to reinstall *all* of Windows 2000 to fix this?" most of us would wonder—but there's a way to work with and fix many DNS problems by just modifying a few ASCII files. You'll find that one of the best DNS troubleshooting tools is Notepad, believe it or not.

There's another reason for understanding these DNS ASCII files. Other DNS server implementations, such as NT 4's DNS server and most Unix implementations of DNS servers, are driven by almost the same ASCII files and file formats as Microsoft's Windows 2000 DNS server. Learning how to do a bit of under-the-hood work with Windows 2000's DNS server, then, equips you to work with other DNS server implementations as well.

DNS Boot Order

First let's take a look at what files DNS reads to get started and in what order it reads them. There are just a few files that control a DNS server's behavior: One named BOOT, another named CACHE.DNS, and one zone file for each of the zones for which the DNS server is responsible:

- BOOT has two main jobs. First, it tells a DNS server whether the server is a root name server or not. Second, it tells the DNS server what domains it acts as the primary DNS server for and which domains it acts as the secondary DNS server for. Non-Microsoft DNS server implementations have always kept this "boot" information in a file called BOOT, but for some reason Windows 2000 DNS servers store the information in either the Active Directory, the server's Registry, or a normal BOOT file. By default Windows 2000 DNS servers store the BOOT information in the Active Directory, but for purposes of failure recovery and troubleshooting, I prefer to use the traditional method of saving the information in a separate file named BOOT. I'll show you how to change your DNS servers so that they use a BOOT file instead of Active Directory or the Registry as well, a little later.

- CACHE.DNS is a file listing the names and IP addresses of your DNS hierarchy's top-level root name server or servers. For people attached to the Internet, CACHE.DNS contains the addresses of the 13 InterNIC root servers. For someone in a private DNS system, CACHE.DNS would contain the addresses of the private DNS's name servers. Microsoft's Windows 2000 DNS server software uses a file named CACHE.DNS to store its root server information (rather than Active Directory or the Registry), so in this way the DNS server software that Microsoft ships with Windows 2000 Server behaves precisely like other DNS servers.

 NOTE Not *every* machine has a CACHE.DNS: A DNS hierarchy's root name servers do not have CACHE.DNS files.

- A DNS server will have a zone file for each zone for which it is a primary or secondary server. A zone file contains all of the zone's data—who its name servers are, its SOA record, its host name records, MX records, CNAME records, and the like. As with CACHE.DNS, Microsoft's Windows 2000 DNS server software behaves like other DNS servers and maintains zone information in simple ASCII files, formatted in the same way as other DNS servers.

The BOOT File

BOOT files connect a DNS server to the hierarchy of DNS servers and tell the DNS server which zones it is authoritative for. By default, however, the DNS server software that comes with Windows 2000 doesn't use BOOT files—so let's change that.

The first way to change how a Windows 2000 DNS server stores BOOT information is through the GUI:

1. Open the DNS snap-in.

2. Locate the icon depicting your DNS server.

3. Right-click the server's icon and choose Properties. A property page will appear with tabs labeled Interfaces, Forwarders, Advanced, Root Hints, Logging, Security, and Monitoring. Click Advanced.

4. You'll see a single-selection drop-down list box labeled Load Zone Data on Startup; choose Boot from File.

5. Click OK.

6. Close the DNS snap-in.

If that sounds like too much clicking, then open up your Registry Editor of choice, navigate to `HKEY_LOCAL_MACHINE\System\CurrentControlSet\Services\DNS\Parameters`. Look for the key `BootMethod`; if it's not there, then create it—it's of type `REG_DWORD`. Set its value to 1. (If the value is 2, the BOOT information is stored in the Registry and if the value is 3, it's stored in Active Directory.)

Windows 2000's DNS server stores all of its configuration files—BOOT, `CACHE.DNS`, and any zone files—in `\winnt\system32\dns`.

There are only three kinds of records that you'll see in a BOOT file: *Primary* tells a DNS server that it's a primary DNS server for a zone, *secondary* tells the DNS server that it's a secondary DNS server for a zone, and *cache* tells the DNS server where to find the list of root servers.

Primary Record

BOOT files often contain a line like the following:

```
primary    minasi.com    minasi.com.dns
```

This record tells this DNS server that it is the primary DNS server for the minasi.com zone, that it is authoritative for the zone. It also identifies the file that contains minasi.com's zone information—`minasi.com.dns`. You don't *have* to name a zone's file with a name of zone name + .dns, but it's customary.

In the primary record, the word *primary* is followed by at least one space, then the name of the zone, then at least one space, and finally the zone file name.

When a DNS server is the primary root server, it has this line in its BOOT file:

```
primary    .    root.dns
```

As you recall, the name of the root of the DNS namespace is .; the zone file's name is often `root.dns`, but it could be anything. All you're doing in this line is telling the DNS server where to find the file that contains the root zone information.

Secondary Record

You might see this line in a BOOT file:

```
secondary win2ktest.com 210.10.30.11 win2ktest.com.dns
```

This tells this server that it is a secondary DNS server for the win2ktest.com zone. The format of the record is very similar to the primary record, save for an extra bit of information—the IP address of the *primary* DNS server for that zone.

A secondary root server would have a line in its BOOT file that looked like this:

```
secondary  . 124.99.21.3  rootfile.dns
```

That line would tell the server that it was a secondary DNS root server, that the primary root server was at IP address 124.99.21.3, and that the server could find the root zone file information in a file called `rootfile.dns`.

Cache Record

Primary and secondary records tell a DNS server, "You are authoritative in some manner for some given zone." Cache records say, "In case you need to find a name server for a particular zone quickly and don't feel like searching around, here's the name of a file that contains a list of name servers for that zone." Such a list is sometimes called a *hints* file.

I suppose you *could* put all kinds of hints files on your DNS—perhaps you access Microsoft's Web site so much that you can't *stand* the idea of having to wait while your DNS servers work their way around the Net to get the address of Microsoft's DNS servers—but I've never seen it. So far as I've ever seen, the only destination worth storing hints about was the root of the DNS hierarchy, the root of the namespace. You point your DNS server at any hints files with the cache record. It looks like:

```
cache  zone-name
➥ name-of-file-containing-list-of-DNS-servers-for-that-zone
```

As I said, the place you're most likely to store hints about is the root domain, the one named ., and by convention the name of the file that you store the root hints in is called `cache.dns`. The most common cache record that you'll see in BOOT files is, then:

```
cache  . cache.dns
```

But if you *did* want to keep that file that listed all of Microsoft's DNS servers, then you might call that file `microsoft.cache`, and you'd tell your DNS server about it by adding this line to the BOOT file:

```
cache microsoft.com microsoft.cache
```

BOOT Examples: DNS Disaster Recovery

Okay, ready for the secret of disaster recovery under DNS? It's so easy you won't believe it. Let's assume that you have the `cache.dns` and zone files for a dead DNS server, but the server stored its BOOT information in the Active Directory, as is the default—so you've got cache and zones, but no BOOT file to start the process off! How do you take those files and get DNS back up and running in no time?

Well, step one is to install the DNS service on a new server. Step two is to get it to boot from the BOOT files rather than from something in the Registry or Active Directory. Step three is to stop the DNS service so you can restore the `cache.dns` and zone files. Step four is to rebuild a BOOT file—so let's use a few examples to review what a BOOT file would look like.

In one simple example, suppose we're rebuilding a DNS server which was the primary DNS server for apex.com. The zone file for apex.com is the default, `apex.com .dns`. The server wasn't a root server. The BOOT file then looks like this:

```
primary        apex.com     apex.com.dns
cache          .            cache.dns
```

Now let's try one where the server was primary for apex.com (zone file name `apex.com.dns`), acme.com (zone file name `acme.com.dns`), and secondary for reliable .com (zone file name `reliable.com.dns`). The primary DNS server for reliable.com has IP address 201.10.22.9. This server's not a root server. The BOOT file then looks like this:

```
primary   apex.com  apex.com.dns
primary acme.com acme.com.dns
secondary reliable.com 201.10.22.9 reliable.com.dns
cache    .    cache.dns
```

For the final example, suppose we've got a server just like the last one, but it's the root server. The root domain needs a zone file and we've decided to follow tradition and call it root.dns. The BOOT file would then look like:

```
primary   apex.com  apex.com.dns
primary acme.com acme.com.dns
secondary reliable.com 201.10.22.9 reliable.com.dns
primary    .    root.dns
```

Notice that the "cache" record goes, replaced by a primary record for the root.

The *CACHE.DNS* File

If you're connected to the Internet and your DNS servers are part of the worldwide DNS namespace, then you'll probably never have to look at this file. But if you're working with a private root, then you *will* have to modify the file—so let's take a look at one. With the comments (the lines starting with semicolons) removed, the one on my DNS servers looks like this:

```
@                      NSa.root-servers.net.
a.root-servers.net     A198.41.0.4
@                      NSb.root-servers.net.
b.root-servers.net     A128.9.0.107
@                      NSc.root-servers.net.
c.root-servers.net     A192.33.4.12
@                      NSd.root-servers.net.
d.root-servers.net     A128.8.10.90
@                      NSe.root-servers.net.
e.root-servers.net     A192.203.230.10
```

```
@                           NSf.root-servers.net.
f.root-servers.net          A192.5.5.241
@                           NSg.root-servers.net.
g.root-servers.net          A192.112.36.4
@                           NSh.root-servers.net.
h.root-servers.net          A128.63.2.53
@                           NSi.root-servers.net.
i.root-servers.net          A192.36.148.17
@                           NSj.root-servers.net.
j.root-servers.net          A198.41.0.10
@                           NSk.root-servers.net.
k.root-servers.net          A193.0.14.129
@                           NS1.root-servers.net.
1.root-servers.net          A198.32.64.12
@                           NSm.root-servers.net.
m.root-servers.net          A202.12.27.33
```

As you can see, it is 13 pairs of records. Each pair starts off with an @ sign, then *NS*, then a DNS name. The following line starts off with the DNS name, then a capital *A*, then an IP address. There is at least one space between each of the line's parts. The people at Microsoft formatted the file so that the *A*s and *NS*s line up nicely, but that's not necessary.

The records with *NS* in them are *name server* records. Their job is to identify a name server—a DNS server—for any given zone. You read them right-to-left: "A.root-servers.net is a name server for the zone named @." Sounds, good, but what domain is @? @ is just a shorthand way of saying, "Look, you already know what zone we're talking about, so don't make me write it out all over again, okay?" As we're talking about the root—recall, the cache record in BOOT identified this as a file of hints about the root—the @ signs are just a short way of writing .; and yes, I know—typing . is as easy, if not easier, than typing @—but it's one of those matters of convention that everyone seems to follow. Blame it on the Unix guys. As you'll see later when we examine zone files where the zone names are longer than one character, however, that @ can be quite useful. In any case, we read that first NS record as saying, "a.root-servers.net is a name server for the root domain."

The A records are called *host* records because they identify host names. An A record's job is simple: It links a DNS name and an IP address. Read these left-to-right; the first one would be read, "The machine named a.root-servers.net is at IP address 198.41.0.4."

Now the reason for the pairs of records is a bit clearer: The NS record says, "You can find a root name server at a.root-servers.net," but to find the server we ultimately need the IP address more than we need the name, and so the A record answers the question, "Okay, so now I know that a.root-servers.net is the machine I want, what's its IP address?" And there are 13 pairs of records because the InterNIC runs 13 root servers.

In contrast, what would this look like if you were running a private namespace, a private DNS hierarchy? For example, suppose you had only two root DNS servers, one named root1.acme.com at 100.100.20.17 and another called root2.acme.com at 100.100.20.18. For the purposes of hints, we don't care which is primary and which is secondary. Your `cache.dns` file would then look like this:

```
@                ns   root1.acme.com
root1.acme.com   a    100.100.20.17
@                ns   root2.acme.com
root2.acme.com   a    100.100.20.18
```

Like the other DNS files, cache/"hints" files go in `\winnt\system32\dns` and, as they are ASCII, can be easily edited with Notepad.

Zone Files

DNS servers have only one BOOT file, and most have only one CACHE.DNS file (some, like root servers, have none), but many DNS servers have more than one zone file, as many DNS servers act as primary or secondary servers for more than one zone.

Zone files are longer and more varied than BOOT or hint files, but they're understandable with a little explanation. As a matter of fact, you already know of the kinds of zone file records that we'll see:

- The A records relate host names to IP addresses.
- The NS records identify name servers for particular zones.
- The MX records identify mail servers for particular machines or zones.
- The SOA record describes the characteristics of the zone and who to contact if there's a problem with the zone.
- The CNAME record lets you add an extra recognized name to an IP address.
- A PTR record is the reverse of an A record; given an IP address, it tells you the host name associated with it.

Most records have three pieces of information on them: The object being described, the record type, and the descriptive information. For example, consider a record like:

`banana A 200.10.18.4`

This would mean "the host named banana in this domain has IP address 200.10.18.4." Notice that the leftmost part of the text says banana rather than banana-dot-whatever the domain's name is. Within zone files, descriptive labels in general are assumed to be only host names, and zone names are appended automatically. If you *don't* want that to happen, put a period at the end of the name, as in banana. A 200.10.18.4—that would assign the IP address to a host whose fully qualified domain name was simply banana, with no .com or the like after it.

```
www cname spider.acme.com
```

This means to take *www* and add it to the domain name, and use that name to refer to a machine named spider.acme.com.

Let's look at an example of a zone from the GUI point of view and then what the corresponding zone file looks like. Take a look at Figure 18.74 to see the GUI perspective.

FIGURE 18.74

minasi.com zone displayed in DNS snap-in

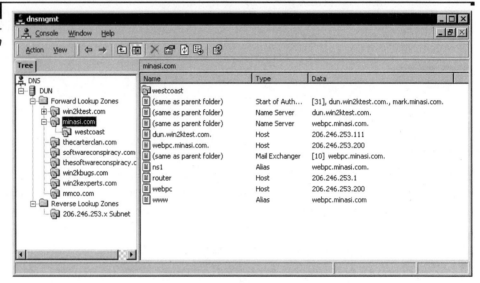

Notice that there is a delegated domain—that the folder labeled westcoast is gray—followed by an MX record, two name server records, an SOA record, two host records, and two aliases.

Now here's that same information as represented in the zone. Remember that on each line, anything to the right of a semicolon is a comment and can be ignored. The comments here were generated automatically by the DNS snap-in:

```
;
;   Database file minasi.com.dns for minasi.com zone.
;      Zone version:  36
;

@         IN  SOA dun.win2ktest.com.  mark.minasi.com. (
                  36              ; serial number
                  900             ; refresh
                  600             ; retry
                  86400           ; expire
```

```
                            3600        ) ; minimum TTL

;
;   Zone NS records
;

@                           NSdun.win2ktest.com.
@                           NSwebpc.minasi.com.


;
;   Zone records
;

@                           MX10webpc.minasi.com.
ns1                         CNAMEwebpc.minasi.com.
router                      A206.246.253.1
webpc                       A206.246.253.200


;
;   Delegated sub-zone:  westcoast.minasi.com.
;
westcoast                   NSns1.westcoast.minasi.com.
ns1.westcoast               A206.246.253.115
ns1.westcoast               A206.246.253.115
;   End delegation

www                         CNAMEwebpc.minasi.com.
```

SOA Record in Zone File Format

The first record is the SOA record. Notice how it starts: @ IN SOA dun.win2ktest.com....
The @ means "this is the Start Of Authority record for whatever zone this file describes."
As we know that this is the zone file for minasi.com, that means that this is the SOA
record for minasi.com. The *IN* is a holdover from the early days of DNS—it stands for
Internet and refers to the fact that at one point it appeared that there would be other
namespaces that DNS would worry about. Strictly speaking, every one of these records
needs the "IN" part, but it appears that the Windows 2000 DNS server doesn't need it.
You might have to edit zone records to insert an *IN* before the record type—for example, all of the *A*s might have to become *IN As*—if you wanted to put a Windows 2000
DNS zone file on an older DNS server.

Following the @ IN SOA is dun.win2ktest.com. That's the DNS name of the authoritative DNS server for this zone. Following that is the e-mail address of the technical

contact for the domain, the e-mail address of the person to mail to if there's a problem with the domain. Then there are the five numbers that the SOA record uses to describe the domain data, as explained earlier.

NS and A Records in Zone File Format

Next are two NS records, as follows:

```
@                          NSdun.win2ktest.com.
@                          NSwebpc.minasi.com.
```

This should look familiar—we just saw something like it in the hints file. @ ns dun.win2ktest.com means "dun.win2ktest.com is a name server for this domain." Note that there's no A record, as dun.win2ktest.com is in another zone. Webpc's got an A record, later on.

Dynamic A Records: Adding TTLs to Records

Because I built this domain solely for demonstration purposes, I entered all of the host records by hand. But remember that one of the great things about Windows 2000's DNS server is the RFC 2136 dynamic update support, which means in English that in general you won't have to hand-enter A records for the workstations—they'll register themselves with the DNS server, and that server will create A records for them automatically. But if you take a look at one of the resulting records, you'll see an extra number, as in the following example two records:

```
wallypc  1200  A  206.246.253.50
metrion   900  A  206.246.253.118
```

Notice the 1200 and 900 values. That's an example of an extra feature available in nearly every kind of DNS record—a *Time To Live* parameter. You may recall that the SOA record included Time To Live (TTL) information for the zone as a whole. That was the amount of time that an external DNS server could cache information about the zone. So, for example, if someone from ford.com looks at my Web site, the Ford DNS server ends up learning my domain's SOA and NS records, as well as the A record for the Web server. The ford.com DNS server caches that information in case someone else at Ford wants to surf my site. But the SOA record at my site tells the Ford DNS server not to cache that information for longer than a day—so if someone at Ford wants to surf my site tomorrow, the Ford DNS server will have to requery my DNS server for up-to-date information. That "expire this information in one day" rule applies to any information from my site—the SOA, NS, or A records.

I guess that Microsoft figured that records inserted through the dynamic update process might change more often than once a day, however, and so they add a smaller TTL value to particular records. The wallypc record says, "There's a machine named wallypc.minasi.com at IP address 206.246.253.50—but don't assume that'll be true for more than the next 20 minutes (1,200 seconds), so if you need to talk to wallypc again after 20 minutes, come back to the DNS server and reconfirm wallypc's IP address; don't continue to cache the name resolution information."

Interestingly enough, a look at a large active zone file showed that some of the records had time-out values of 1,200, or 20 minutes, and some had time-out values of 900 seconds, 15 minutes. The difference? The pre–Windows 2000 systems that had their name and address registered by DHCP got 900-second TTLs. The Windows 2000 systems that registered themselves got 1,200-second TTLs.

In any case, any time that you look at a record in a DNS zone file and see a seemingly out-of-place number, it's a TTL value in seconds.

MX Records in Zone File Format

The next block of records includes an MX record. Notice how it's laid out; again, starting with an @ to indicate that it refers to the entire domain, then the record type *MX*, then the preference value, and finally the name of the mail server.

CNAME Records in Zone File Format

Next, a CNAME equates ns1.minasi.com—recall, the statement needn't say ns1.minasi .com because, in general, items to the left without periods get the zone name suffixed automatically—to a machine named webpc.minasi.com. The following two records tell us that router.minasi.com is the name for the machine at 206.246.253.1 and that webpc.minasi.com is the name for the machine at 206.246.253.200.

After that, there's again a set of NS and A records. But notice that the NS record doesn't start with @, it starts with westcoast. This statement says, "A machine named ns1.westcoast.minasi.com is a DNS server for a zone named westcoast.minasi.com." Once again, westcoast becomes westcoast.minasi.com because it is the leftmost item on the line. The following line tells the IP address of ns1.westcoast.minasi.com, and again, notice that the name used on the record isn't ns1.westcoast.minasi.com; it's simply ns1.westcoast, as the rest is implied. Notice also that there are two of them, the result no doubt of a minor glitch in the DNS service.

Finally, there's another CNAME equating www.minasi.com with webpc.minasi.com.

Application: Building a Private Root

Okay, now you're a zone file maven. Let's put that knowledge to work. First project: create a private root. Suppose you've got two DNS servers (we could do more, but it would get monotonous), one named ns1.apex.com at 10.10.10.10 and the other named ns2.apex.com at 10.10.10.20. We'll configure it so that ns1.apex.com will be the DNS name hierarchy root, the top of the namespace. Then we'll configure ns2.apex.com in the same way that we'll configure *all* DNS servers that aren't root servers. Just to keep this clear, we're not going to set up any zones yet, not even apex.com—just the root structure.

Setting Up the Root Server

First, be sure that the machine at ns1.apex.com thinks that its name is ns1.apex.com. As there's not a DNS server around to tell it that, you'll have to enter it in the Network Identification page: Right-click My Computer, choose Properties, then click the Network Identification page. Click the Advanced button, then the More button. Uncheck Change DNS Domain Name When Domain Membership Changes, and in the field labeled DNS Domain Name of This Computer, enter **apex.com** and click OK until you're back at the Desktop. You'll have to reboot. This renaming step isn't absolutely necessary, but the DNS server's GUI interface will make a bit more sense this way.

Also, as this is a DNS server, make sure that it looks to itself for DNS services; in the IP Properties screen, the address in Preferred DNS Server should be its own IP address.

Next, make the DNS server boot from the BOOT file, either from the snap-in or with a Registry Editor. Then stop the DNS server service on ns1.apex.com so that you can monkey with the DNS files.

The root server's BOOT file will have one line:

```
primary    .    root.dns
```

By now, you know that this just says that this server is the primary DNS server for a zone that happens to be called .; furthermore, the zone's zone file is named root.dns. Looking in root.dns, we see a pretty straightforward zone file:

```
@    IN SOA ns1.apex.com. joe.apex.com (1 900 600 86400 3600)
@    NS  ns1.apex.com.
ns1.apex.com  A     10.10.10.10
```

The first line is the SOA record, as always. I copied the numbers from Windows 2000's defaults. The second says, "A machine named ns1.apex.com is the name server for this zone (which is the root)." The third supplies an IP address for ns1.apex.com. And remember that both BOOT and root.dns go in \winnt\system32\dns.

Notice that I had to spell out ns1.apex.com; that's because the zone we're working from here is the root zone, not the apex.com zone.

Start up the DNS server service again and your root's up and running.

Wait, NSLOOKUP Is Complaining!

At this point, you may be tempted to try to run NSLOOKUP to see if you can resolve names. You'll get an error message along the lines of "can't find server" or the like. You didn't do anything wrong, don't worry.

Remember, the first thing that NSLOOKUP does is a reverse lookup on the DNS server's IP address. Recall that IP Properties stores the IP address of a DNS server, not its name. So if NSLOOKUP can't get its reverse lookup request fulfilled, it can't report the name of the server.

The answer is simple. Just be sure to set up a reverse lookup zone if you control your in-addr.arpa zone, or ask your ISP to enter the records for your DNS servers if they control the reverse lookup zone. Once you set up the reverse lookup zone, put in PTR records for all of your DNS servers. Then NSLOOKUP will be happy. And to put NSLOOKUP though its paces, **set type=any**, then press Enter, and then **apex.com** and Enter and you should see the SOA information as well as the name server information.

Setting Up the Other DNS Servers

Next, let's see how to set up the other DNS servers. As before, first change their `Boot-Method` value to tell the DNS server to use the BOOT file, and then stop the service while you modify the files. Ensure that the DNS server points to itself in the Preferred DNS Server field of IP Properties.

The BOOT file will just contain a cache record to help ns2 find the DNS root server. The BOOT file is one line:

```
cache  .  cache.dns
```

But don't use the `cache.dns` file that automatically ships with Windows 2000; that points to InterNIC root servers that you can't get to. Instead, it'll point to your one root server, and its contents then look like:

```
@              ns   ns1.apex.com
ns1.apex.com   a    10.10.10.10
```

Start the DNS service and your DNS enterprise—both servers—now recognizes ns1 as the root. For the third and later servers, just repeat the steps you just did for this second DNS server.

Application: Disaster Recovery Summary

As you've seen, you can rebuild a DNS server easily with these ingredients:

- The BOOT file
- The `cache.dns` file
- The zone files

In a pinch, it's not hard to build BOOT, `cache.dns`, or zone files from scratch. Given the files, get DNS running on a new computer, stop the DNS service, put the files in place, and start the service again. You need not even reboot.

Application: Grafting an Active Directory Domain into an Enterprise with Old DNS Servers

Suppose you bring Windows 2000 into your firm, acme.com. At a meeting of the IT planning staff, you sell the CIO on the whole idea of Active Directory as a directory service. Everyone loves the idea (or at least no one has attacked you with a sharp object)…until you enthusiastically say something like,

"And Microsoft was even smart enough to use DNS as its naming infrastructure!"

All of a sudden, the Unix guys, who have been scowling in the corner, say in unison, "Whaaaaaat????" They're not dumb. They know what this means. You see, if your firm is like many, your internal DNS servers are probably running on Unix boxes rather than something else. The program that the Unix box is running, Bind, is well understood and fairly stable. The Unix folks know that if Active Directory uses DNS as its naming system, then that almost certainly means that Windows 2000 comes with a DNS server—and while they were able for years to safely shoot down any ideas about using NT 4's DNS server, Windows 2000's DNS server is pretty well integrated with Active Directory. No, you don't *have* to use Windows 2000's DNS server to make Active Directory work, but the Unix guys see the writing on the wall. No way they're polluting their Bind system with some less-reliable DNS server from Redmond, they say. Active Directory? "I say it's spinach," they say, "and I say I don't like it."

You've got several answers to this objection. First of all, you may be able to make them happy and keep using Bind. Any DNS server that supports RFC 2136 dynamic updates and RFC 2052 SRV records and that allows you to put underscores—which are not exactly kosher, RFC-wise—into host names will support Active Directory. You needn't use Microsoft's DNS server. I'm told that some versions of Bind meet those three criteria.

But perhaps your enterprise is on an earlier version of Bind or some other DNS server and doesn't want to upgrade. What to do? Simple—get them to delegate a subdomain to your DNS servers. That way, if acme.com doesn't want to have all of its DNS servers assimilated into the Microsoft DNS Collective, then they needn't be. The Unix servers can continue to handle the acme.com top-level domain. You just ask for a subdomain like win2k.acme.com or something and you then put all of the Windows 2000 machines in the subdomain. The DNS server that keeps track of them can then be a Windows 2000 server without affecting the rest of acme.com.

Why is this an application of understanding zone files? Because someone may decide to make it *your* job to add the records to the Bind servers that delegate the win2k.acme.com zone to your Windows 2000 server. And this way, you'll be able to just sit right down and make the necessary modifications. Although, now that I mention it, there's this *Vi* editor thing you should know about….

Name Resolution in More Detail

Now that you know how to configure DNS and WINS, you may be faced with a troubleshooting problem in reference to name resolution. Perhaps you try to FTP to a site inside your organization, but you can't hook up. Even though you know that `ftp.goodstuff.acme.com` is at one IP address, your FTP client keeps trying to attach somewhere else. You've checked your DNS server, of course, and its information is right. Where else to look?

Review: Winsock versus NBT

Remember first that there are two kinds of name resolution in Microsoft TCP/IP networking, Winsock name resolution and NetBIOS name resolution. A NET VIEW *somename* needs NetBIOS over TCP name resolution, or NBT name resolution. In contrast, as FTP is, like Ping, an Internet application, it uses Winsock name resolution. So, to troubleshoot a name resolution problem, you have to follow what your client software does, step-by-step.

DNS/Winsock Name Resolution

I type "ping lemon," and get the response "unknown host lemon." But I suspect there's a LEMON out there, and I'm not talking about a computer from a certain Texas computer company. How did Windows 2000 decide that it couldn't find LEMON? It certainly takes long enough to decide that it can't find lemon, after all—usually on the order of 20 to 30 seconds on a 400 MHz system. *Something* must be going on.

When faced with a question like this, I turned to the Microsoft documentation for help, but there wasn't much detail. So I ran a network monitor and issued Ping commands to computers that didn't exist, to see the sequence of actions that the network client software tried in order to resolve a name. The HOSTS and LMHOSTS files do not, of course, show up in a network trace, so I inserted information into those files that didn't exist on the DNS or WINS servers and then tried pinging again, to demonstrate where the HOSTS and LMHOSTS files sit in the name resolution hierarchy. (And if you think about it, LMHOSTS and WINS should have nothing at all to do with a Winsock resolution. Perhaps in a non-Microsoft world, but not in Windows 2000.) Pinging for a nonexistent "apple," I found that the name resolution order proceeds as shown in Figure 18.75.

FIGURE 18.75

The name resolution order

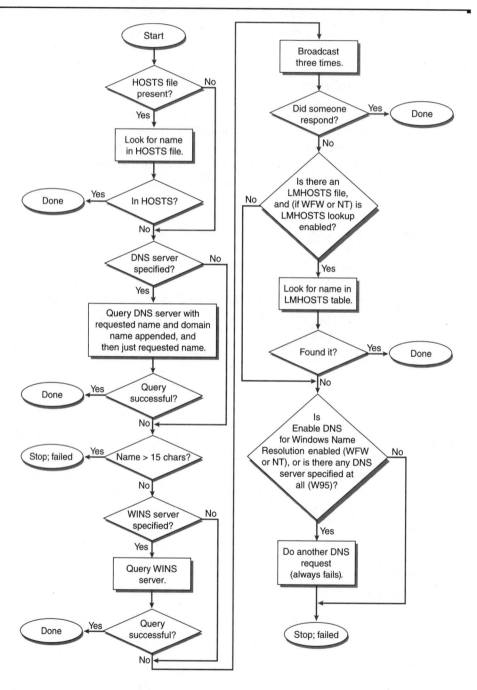

Step-by-step, it looks like this:

- First, consult the HOSTS file, if it exists. If you find the name you're looking for, stop.

- Next, if there's a specified DNS server or servers, then query them. First, query apple. NT machines then query apple.mmco.com, tacking on the domain name; Windows 95 workstations don't do the second query.

This happens whether or not the box Enable DNS for Windows Name Resolution (found in the Advanced Microsoft TCP/IP Configuration dialog boxes of NT 3.51 and Windows for Workgroups—there's no corresponding option in Windows 2000) is checked. If DNS has the name, then stop.

- After that, the client looks to see if the name has 16 or more characters, or if it's got a period in its name. If it does, then the process stops, a failed name resolution attempt.

- Next, if there's a specified WINS server or servers, then query the WINS server(s). The name WINS looks for is apple <00>, the name that *would* be registered by the Workstation service, if the apple machine existed.

- If that fails, then do three broadcasts looking for a machine with NetBIOS name apple <00>, requesting that it identify itself and send back its IP address. Again, this would succeed with a workstation running some NetBIOS-over-TCP/IP client, even a relatively old one, as it would have registered the apple <00> name already, if only on its own name table. Unfortunately, this only works if the machine is on the same subnet.

- If the name still hasn't been resolved, read the LMHOSTS file. (Under NT 3.51 and Windows for Workgroups, do not do this if the box labeled Enable LMHOSTS Lookup is unchecked; skip this step.) As with the earlier steps, stop if you find a match; if not, keep going.

- If you're running an NT or Windows for Workgroups machine with the box Enable DNS for Windows Name Resolution checked (the option seems not to exist in Windows 2000), then you've instructed your system to do a DNS lookup every time a WINS lookup fails. If that box is checked, then a second and last DNS lookup will happen. If, on the other hand, you *don't* have the Enable DNS box checked, then there's nothing left to do.

Look at that sequence: HOSTS, DNS, WINS, broadcast, LMHOSTS, and DNS again. This surprised me for a couple of reasons. First, it seems that every unsuccessful name resolution results in broadcasts, the *bête noire* of those of us trying to keep the network traffic to a minimum. My guess is that the broadcasts aren't part of an according-to-Hoyle IP stack, but Microsoft just threw them in for good measure and the WINS query as well. Then, if you've checked Enable DNS for Windows Name Resolution, the client software performs a DNS lookup as a matter of course after any failed WINS lookup; unfortunately, that leads to a redundant DNS lookup here. In short, if your Windows 95 workstation knows of a DNS server, it will use that DNS server when doing both DNS and NetBIOS name resolutions.

The broadcasts are a pain, but they *would* be of benefit when you tried to execute a TCP/IP command on a computer in your network but wanted to use the shorter NetBIOS name rather than the longer DNS name, such as apple instead of apple.mmco.com.

Getting back to an earlier question, what happened on that workstation that could not access the FTP site? There was an old HOSTS file sitting in the `Windows` directory that pointed to a different IP address, an older IP address for the FTP server. HOSTS is read before anything else, so the accurate information on the DNS or WINS servers never got a chance to be read. So be very careful about putting things in HOSTS if they could soon become out-of-date!

There is an explicit Enable DNS for Windows Name Resolution check box in Windows for Workgroups and NT 3.51 clients, but how do you control whether or not DNS gets into the act on a Windows 95 client? You can't, at least not entirely; where Workgroups and NT 3.51 separate the options about whether to specify a DNS server and whether or not to use that DNS server as a helper when resolving NetBIOS names (that's what Enable DNS for Windows Name Resolution means), Windows 95 seems not to do that.

Controlling WINS versus DNS Order in Winsock

Now, what I just showed you is the order of events by default in NT, Windows 9*x*, or Windows 2000 clients. But if you feel like messing around with the way that Winsock resolves names, you can. As usual, let me take this moment to remind you that it's not a great idea to mess with the Registry unless you know what you're doing.

Look in the Registry under HKEY_LOCAL_MACHINE\System\CurrentControlSet\ Services\TCPIP\ServiceProvider and you see HostsPriority, DNSPriority, and NBTPriority value entries. They are followed by hexadecimal values. The lower the value, the earlier that HOSTS, DNS (and LMHOSTS), and WINS (and broadcasts) get done. For example, by default DNS's priority is 7D0 and WINS's is 7D1, so DNS goes before WINS. But change DNS's priority to 7D2, and WINS does its lookup and broadcast *before* the client interrogates the DNS server.

Again, I'm not sure *why* you'd want to do this, but I include it for the sake of completeness and for the enjoyment of those who delight in undocumented features.

Name Resolution Sequence under NetBIOS

Having looked at the steps that the system goes through to resolve a DNS name, what happens when the system attempts to resolve a NetBIOS name? Again, it's an involved process, but in general the factors that affect how NBT resolves names are:

- Is the workstation an NT 3.51 or Windows 95 workstation?
- Is LMHOSTS enabled?
- Is DNS enabled to assist in Windows (NetBIOS) name resolution?
- Is the network client software WINS aware?

Summarized, the name resolution sequence appears in Figure 18.76.

FIGURE 18.76

Name resolution sequence under NetBIOS

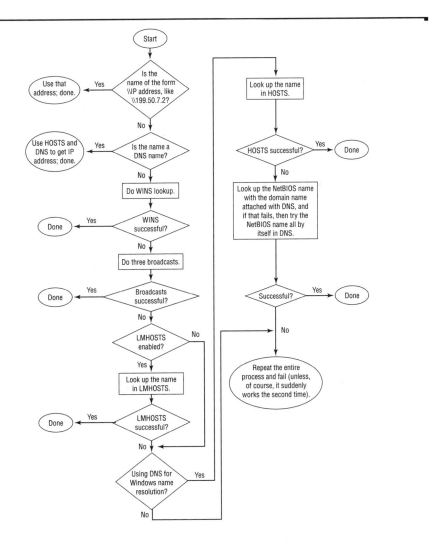

The same components that went into Winsock name resolutions contribute to NBT resolutions, but in a slightly different order. The NBT name resolver uses the following steps; if any succeed, then it stops looking:

- If the client is a Windows 98, NT 4, or Windows 2000 system, then the very first thing to check is whether or not the name to the right of the \\ is either an IP address or a recognizable DNS name—that is, that it has a period in its name. If the name is just an IP address, as in a command like net use * \\199.33.29.15\Stuff, then forget the name resolution and just go to that IP address. If it's a DNS name, like net use * \\myserver.region8.acme.com\files, then resolve the name using the normal Winsock approach. (Just look back a page or two for an explanation of that approach.)

- If the name wasn't IP or DNS—or the client was too old to be able to respond to that—then the next part is the WINS client, if the client software is WINS aware. If WINS is disabled under Windows 95, or if there is no WINS server specified in Workgroups or NT 3.51, then the client skips this step.

- If WINS isn't being used, then the client does three broadcasts. For example, NET VIEW \\APPLE causes three broadcasts looking for a workstation with the name apple registered rather than apple.mmco.com or the like.

- Next, if LMHOSTS is enabled—and it appears that LMHOSTS is *always* enabled on Windows 95/98 clients but must be enabled with the Enable LMHOSTS check box for NT 3.51 and Workgroups—then the client looks up the name in LMHOSTS. Surprised? When doing NBT name resolutions, LMHOSTS gets consulted *before* HOSTS, a reversal over Winsock name resolutions. Recall that LMHOSTS only contains 15-character NetBIOS names, not longer DNS-like names.

- If you've checked Enable DNS for Windows Name Resolution in Workgroups or NT 3.51, or if you have specified a DNS server in Windows 95/98, then the workstation's client software will look at HOSTS, and if HOSTS can't help, it will interrogate the DNS server (or servers, as you can specify up to four DNS servers).

The NT/Workgroups clients and the 95/98 clients use DNS differently. The NT/Workgroups clients do a DNS query for the name with the domain name appended to it and then a DNS query of just the name. For example, if your domain is acme.com and you're doing a net view \\myserver, then an NT workstation will ask DNS first to resolve the name myserver.acme.com—it automatically adds the domain name for the first resolution. Then, if the DNS server can't resolve the name with the domain name attached, the client will request that the DNS server just resolve myserver.

In contrast, the Windows 95/98 client software only asks the DNS server to resolve the name with the domain name appended; in my example, a Windows 95/98 workstation would ask DNS to resolve myserver.acme.com but would not ask about myserver.

- The last part is *really* strange. If the client software is the NT client (not the Workgroups or Win95/98 clients), and if it's been unsuccessful so far, then it goes back and does it all over again, I suppose in the hope that it'll work the second time.

You've seen how Winsock and NBT resolve names; now you're ready to look at the "battle of the network names...."

What if DNS and WINS Conflict?

Here's a question that I get in class sometimes. I present it here mainly as a review of what you've read so far.

WINS will generally have accurate name information for your local domain, at least among the WINS-aware machines, as it gets its naming information from the horse's mouth, so to speak; you can't *use* a WINS name server unless you *contribute* a bit of information—that is, address information about yourself. DNS, in contrast, gets its information from people typing data into ASCII files, so the data could be wrong. That leads students to the following question.

What if you have a Microsoft networking client that is not only WINS aware but also uses a DNS server: In that case, which name service does the workstation query first? Suppose you have a machine named ollie.acme.com whose IP address is 207.88.52.99. Not only does WINS know of ollie, DNS does too—but suppose DNS incorrectly thinks that ollie's IP address is 207.88.52.100. Type **ping ollie.acme.com**, and what will happen? Will the system look to the .99 address, or the .100 address?

If you've been dutifully following along through this chapter, then you may see how to answer this question. First, ask yourself, "Is this a Winsock or an NBT name resolution request?" As the application is Ping, the answer is Winsock. Go to the Winsock name resolution flowchart and you see that the DNS server gets first crack at answering the name resolution request.

There's a lot more to network name resolution on NT networks than I guessed when I first looked into this, as you can see, but now you're equipped with all the information that you need to tackle a mystery along the lines of "machine X says it can't see machine Y."

Identifying Subnets with Site Manager

Once you've built your TCP/IP infrastructure, you've got to tell Active Directory about it. There are a number of reasons for that, but the most important is that Active Directory is smarter than the old SAM-based NT 4 domain system in the way that it uses bandwidth. When replicating from domain controller to domain controller, it needs to know whether it's communicating via a high-speed link, and thus can be voluble without worrying about choking the link, or if perhaps it's talking to its domain controller sibling over a 56K link and then will take the time to compress the data a bit, becoming a trifle more terse and bandwidth friendly.

But the domain controller can't know the answer to that question unless you help it. A DC knows that it can communicate at high speed with another DC if they're both in the same *site*. But how does it know that?

How Sites Work

The answer is this: They look to find themselves in the Servers container of one of the Sites containers of Active Directory. There is a separate container for each *site*, where a site is defined as "a collection of subnets that communicate with each other at very high data rates." You define sites and then place domain controllers in sites.

Workstations and servers, however, don't get that help. They've got to choose domain controllers to log them and their users in, and clearly they want to be logged in by a nearby domain controller. They determine who's nearby by examining what subnet *they're* in, then the subnet that each domain controller's in to figure out which DC is nearest. They need to know which subnets are close to one another—in other words, which subnets are in the same sites.

"But," you might wonder, "how did Active Directory figure out what sites it had, what subnets it had, and which subnets go into what sites?" *That's* the part that requires a little administrative elbow grease, so let's see how to apply that elbow grease. Our tool of choice will be a snap-in called Active Directory Sites and Services, located in Administrative Tools. Open it up and you'll see a screen like Figure 18.77.

FIGURE 18.77

Initial Active Directory Sites and Services screen

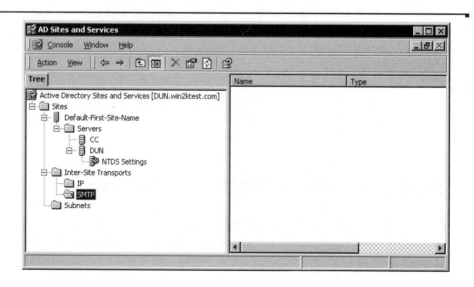

Notice that there's only one site, one called Default-First-Site-Name. When you create an Active Directory forest, AD just creates a site by that name and assumes that everything's in it. Open up Default-First-Site-Name, and you'll see that your domain controllers are in there. The idea with setting up AD's site topology is that you must:

- Define each subnet.
- Define each site.
- Assign each subnet to a site.

From there, the domain controllers figure out by themselves which site they belong to.

Defining a Site

Suppose I set up another site, across town from my first site. Active Directory's got to know about that site. Right-click the Sites folder and choose New Site, and you see a screen like Figure 18.78.

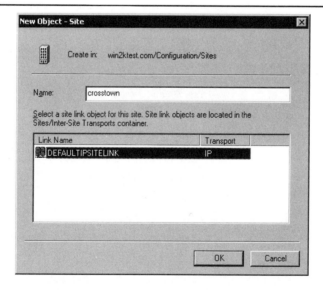

I just fill in a name for the new site (Crosstown) and click OK. When I do, I get a message box like Figure 18.79.

FIGURE 18.79

Checklist for hooking up the new site

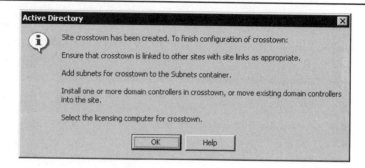

Defining a Subnet and Placing It in a Site

Next, we'll describe the subnets in our enterprise. Suppose the original site is at 206.246.253.0 and the crosstown site is at 200.200.200.0. I need to tell Site Manager about these subnets. You see me creating a new subnet in Figure 18.80.

FIGURE 18.80

Creating a new subnet

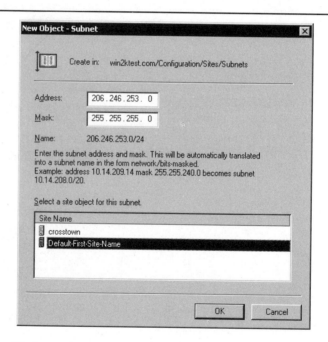

Notice that AD then asks me to associate the subnet with a particular site. I'll define another subnet for the crosstown site, 200.200.200.0, as well, and now Active Directory Sites and Services will look like Figure 18.81.

FIGURE 18.81

Sites and Services after defining sites and subnet

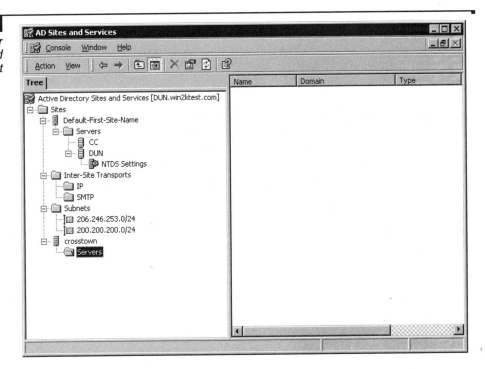

Placing a Server in a Site

A look at Figure 18.81 shows that I opened up the first site to show a container inside it called Servers, and then inside that I've got a server named CC. If CC were actually in Crosstown, then I could tell AD that by moving the server to Crosstown; I just right-click CC and choose Move and I'll see a dialog like Figure 18.82.

FIGURE 18.82

Moving a server

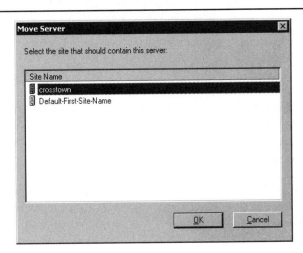

It's a little bit of work, but arranging your servers in Sites and Services Manager pays off if you've got an enterprise that spans WAN links.

Let's move on from this very Windows 2000–specific treatment of TCP/IP infrastructure to three more common Internet tools—Telnet, FTP, and Internet mail.

Using Telnet for Remote Login

Back in the late mid-Triassic period of computing, around 1973, you wouldn't sit at a computer, you'd sit at a terminal that was connected in some way to a computer. If a computer at the National Institutes of Health contained some database that I wanted to do analysis on, I'd put a modem on my terminal, get an account at NIH, find out the phone numbers of their dial-in modems, and then I'd dial one of those numbers. Once the modem was done squawking and I was connected at the princely speed of 300bps, I'd interact with NIH. But I'd interact solely with characters, 25 lines of 80 columns of characters.

From the '60s on, the government has maintained a lot of mainframes with some very useful data on them. Before the growth of the Internet, anyone doing research could get an account and dial into those mainframes to use the government's data— but the long distance bills could bankrupt you.

Early Telnet Uses

But then the Internet appeared.

For early Internet—ARPAnet, actually—programmers built a set of programs, a server program and a terminal program, that would let a mainframe accept incoming connections over the Internet much like modem dial-ins and that would let someone sitting at a Unix terminal somewhere attach to that mainframe as if dialing in. The early (mid-Cretaceous, actually) programmers called the pair of programs *Telnet*.

For years, Telnet was a great way for groups to offer information over the Internet. Some people adapted programs used to host dial-in PC-based bulletin board systems to Telnet. Others put data of general interest on Telnet—for example, the University of Michigan once had census data available over Telnet, and a travel agency let you book tickets on Telnet. Network Solutions, the people who run DNS, had a search engine built into Telnet that would let you look up a domain name to see if it was taken. Most of those are gone now, replaced with Web sites.

Modern Uses for Telnet

But Telnet's still quite useful for network administrators, so it's great that Windows 2000 includes a Telnet server that will support up to two simultaneous connections. Think of Telnet on Windows 2000 as being sort of a low-bandwidth form of Windows

Terminal Server. You can't run any graphical applications over it; you just get a C:\> style command line, but you can get an awful lot done with just that.

Before you can telnet into your machine, though, you've got to start up the server part of Telnet. That part's easy, but you've got to then configure it to accept regular Telnet connections.

Setting Up the Telnet Server

Telnet is built as a service under Windows 2000. You can start it by just opening up a command line and typing **net start tlntsvr** and pressing Enter. Alternatively, you can tell your system to always have the Telnet server available by setting up the Telnet service to start automatically.

Here's what you need to do to set up the Telnet service to start automatically:

1. Right-click the My Computer icon and select Manage.

2. Under Computer Management, you'll see Services and Applications; open it up by clicking the plus sign next to it.

3. Inside Services and Applications, you'll see Services; click that and the list of services in the system will appear in the right-hand pane of the window.

4. The service you're looking for is named just Telnet; right-click it and choose Properties.

5. You'll see a single-selection drop-down list box labeled Startup; choose Automatic, then click OK to close the window. Close the Computer Management window

While Telnet's often a potential security risk because it passes passwords in cleartext over the network, Microsoft has reduced that risk by modifying the way the Telnet server behaves. Instead of using cleartext passwords, it uses an NT-style authentication approach called NTLM. It requires not only a modified Telnet server but a modified Telnet client as well—but Windows 2000 comes with a client like that.

Assuming that you're already logged onto the domain, you can just start a session from a command line by typing **telnet** *servername*, where *servername* is the name of the server that you want to establish the Telnet session on.

On the other hand, you *may* decide that you'd like remote administrators to be able to log in with any kind of Telnet client rather than just the Windows 2000 client. You can do that, but again, be warned that allowing standard Telnet clients to attach requires allowing cleartext passwords—check with your security group before doing this. Here's how to tell a server's Telnet server software to accept standard Telnet logins:

1. First tell the Telnet server to accept usernames and passwords for login security. To do that, open up a command line and type **tlntadmn** and press Enter.

2. Choose 3 and Enter; this will let you modify a Registry setting.

3. Then choose 7 and Enter to modify the NTLM option; this controls how logins occur. The default value of 2 requires a special Telnet client that I was unable to find—you'll want to change the value to 1 so that regular Telnet clients can access this server.

4. Tlntadmn will show you the current NTLM value and will confirm that you do indeed want to change it; confirm that you do by entering **y** and Enter.

5. Enter a new value of **1** and press Enter.

6. Again you'll be asked to confirm that you want to make this change; do so by entering **y** and Enter.

7. Enter **0** and Enter to exit the Registry section.

8. Enter **S** and Enter to stop the service.

9. Enter **4** and Enter to start the service.

10. Enter **0** and Enter to stop the tlntadmn program.

11. Telnet's now ready to go. From any machine with a Telnet client, you can just open a command line and type **telnet *machine_name***, where *machine_name* is either the DNS name or IP address of your server.

Using FTP for File Transfer

If you have a PC or Macintosh on your desk, think for a moment about how you use that computer in a network situation. You may have a computer elsewhere in your building that acts as a *file server*, a computer that holds the files shared in your facility or your department. How do you ask that server to transfer a file from itself to your computer? You may say, "I don't do that"—but you *do*. Whenever you attach to a shared network resource, you are asking that system to provide your computer with shared files. Now, how you actually *ask* for them is very simple: You just connect to a server, which looks like an extra folder on your desktop if you're a Mac user or an extra drive letter, like X: or E:, if you are a PC user. The intranet world has a facility like that, a facility that lets you attach distant computers to your computer as if that distant computer were a local drive: It is called NFS, the Network File System. But NFS is relatively recent in the TCP/IP world. It's much more common to attach to a host, browse the files that it contains, and selectively transfer them to your local host. You do that with FTP, the *File Transfer Protocol*.

There are three essentials of FTP: How to start it up, how to navigate around the directories of the FTP server, and how to actually get a file from an FTP server. After that, we'll look at a special kind of FTP called *anonymous FTP*. So let's get started by looking at how the files on an FTP server are organized.

FTP Organization

The first time that you get on an FTP server, you'll probably want to get right off. FTP, like much of the TCP/IP world, was built from the perspective that software's got to be *functional* and not necessarily pretty or, to use an overused phrase, user-friendly. If you're a PC user, the Unix file structure will be somewhat familiar, as the DOS file structure was stolen—uhh, I mean, *borrowed*—from Unix. Mac users will need to find an FTP client, of which there are many.

Now, I just referred to the Unix file structure. That's because FTP servers *usually* use Unix. But some don't, so you may come across FTP servers that don't seem to make any sense. For the purposes of this discussion, I'll assume that the FTP servers here are Unix, but again, be aware that you may run into non-Unix FTP servers. The occasional FTP server runs on a DEC VAX, and so probably runs the VMS operating system; some others may run on an IBM mainframe, and so may be running either MVS or VM. Very rarely, an FTP server may run under DOS, OS/2, NT, or some other PC operating system. But let's get back to our look at a Unix FTP server.

FTP uses a tree-structured directory represented in the Unix fashion. The top of the directory is called `ourfiles`, and it has two directories below it—*sub*directories— called `ourfiles/bin` and `ourfiles/text`, as shown in Figure 18.83. In the Unix world, `.bin` refers to executable files, files we might call program files in other operating systems, or more specifically, EXE or COM files in the PC world or load modules in the IBM mainframe world. The `text` directory contains two directories below *it*; one's called `contracts` and one's called `announcements`.

FIGURE 18.83

An example of how files on an FTP server are organized

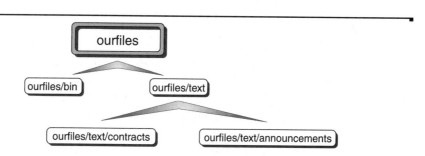

A couple of notes here. PC users may think that things look a bit familiar, but there *are* a couple of differences. First, notice the subdirectory named `announcements`. That name is more than eight characters long—that's quite acceptable, even though it *isn't* *acceptable* in the PC world. Unix accepts filenames of hundreds of characters. Second, notice that there are not *backslashes* between the different levels, but instead *forward* slashes; that's also a Unix feature. Now, what complicates matters for users of non-Unix systems is that FTP pretty much assumes that *your* system uses the Unix file system as well. That means that you have to be comfortable with traversing *two* directory structures—the one on the remote FTP server, and the one on your local hard disk.

FTP Client Types

How FTP looks to you from this point on depends on what kind of client software you use to access an FTP server. With Windows 2000, you've got three choices: The standard command-line interface, Internet Explorer, or My Network Places. First, let's look at the command-line interface.

File Navigation with Command-Line FTP Clients

You get an FTP command line—I'll demonstrate it in a minute—that expects you to tell it where to get files *from, and* where to send files *to*, using these two commands:

- remote—cd
- local—lcd

That's because there's a tree structure on both the remote system—the one that you're getting the files from—and the local system. Let's look at a few examples to nail down exactly how all this cd-ing works.

Moving in FTP

When I enter an FTP site, I start out at the top of the directory structure. This top is called the *root* of the directory. In my example, the root is called ourfiles. To move down one level, to ourfiles/text, I could type **cd files**. That says to FTP, "Move down one level relative to the current location." Alternatively, you could skip the relative reference and say absolutely, "Go to ourfiles/text"—the way that you do that is by typing **cd /ourfiles/text**. The fact that the entry *starts* with a slash tells cd that your command is not a relative one, but an absolute one.

Now let's try moving back up a level. At any point, you can back up one level either by typing the command **cdup** or by typing **cd ..** . The two periods (..) mean one level upward to both DOS and Unix. Or you can do an absolute reference, as in **cd /ourfiles**.

Now suppose I'm all the way at the bottom of this structure. It's a simple three-level directory, and you often see directory structures that are a good bit more complex than this one. To move back up from ourfiles/text/announcements to ourfiles/text, you can do as before and either type **cdup** or **cd ..** . Or you could do an absolute reference, as in **cd /ourfiles/text**. To go back *two* levels, you can either issue two separate **cdup** or **cd ..** commands or use an absolute reference, as in **cd /ourfiles**. To type two **cdup** or **cd ..** commands, you type the command, then press Enter, then type the second command. Do not try to issue two commands on the same line.

An FTP Example of Navigation: Get a Scandal

There's a really neat project run by a group of volunteers called The Gutenberg Project. They take text whose copyright has expired and type it into text files. They then put these text files on both FTP and Web sites for anyone to download and read.

For example, one of my favorite of Arthur Conan Doyle's Sherlock Holmes stories is "A Scandal in Bohemia," which Gutenberg has at `ftp://sailor.gutenberg.org/pub/gutenberg/etext99/advsh10.txt`. (Their general Web home page is at `www.sailor.gutenberg.org`.) Let's go fetch the scandal.

First, I'll FTP to `ftp.gutenberg.org`. I type **ftp ftp.gutenberg.org**, and then I get a Name? prompt. This site doesn't know me, so I can't log on with a local name and password. That's where the idea of *anonymous* FTP becomes useful. You see, you can often log on to an FTP site and download data that's been put there specifically for public use. Anonymous FTP is just the same as regular FTP except that you log in with the name anonymous. It responds that a guest login is okay but wants my e-mail address for a password. I put in my e-mail address, and I'm in. Now, it might be that there are places on this server that I *cannot* get to because I signed on as anonymous, but that doesn't matter—Sherlock is in the public area. Next, I can do a dir command and see what's on this directory:

```
ftp> dir
200 PORT command successful.
150 Opening ASCII mode data connection for /bin/ls.
total 26
dr-xr-xr-x   8 0         0           512 Mar  2 13:49 .
dr-xr-xr-x   8 0         0           512 Mar  2 13:49 ..
-rw-rw-r--   1 1010      2000       1956 Feb 27  1997 README
dr-xr-xr-x   3 0         1           512 Feb 22  1997 bin
dr-xr-xr-x   2 0         2           512 Feb  3  1997 dev
dr-xr-xr-x   2 0         0           512 Feb 18  1997 etc
lrwxrwxrwx   1 0         1             4 Mar  2 13:49 ftp1 -> ftp1
drwxr-xr-x   2 1010      10000       512 Feb  5  1997 messages
drwxrwxr-x   4 0         2000        512 Nov  2  1998 pub
-rw-r--r--   1 0         1            81 Oct 30  1998 tmp.txt
dr-xr-xr-x   4 0         0           512 Feb 22  1997 usr
-rw-rw-r--   1 1010      14          913 Feb 26  1997 welcome.msg
226 Transfer complete.
ftp: 744 bytes received in 0.19Seconds 3.90Kbytes/sec.
ftp>
```

It's not a very pretty sight, but let's see what we can see. Notice all the *r*s, *x*s, *w*s, and *d*s to the left of each entry? That represents the privilege levels of access to this file. One of the important things is whether or not the leftmost letter is *d*—if it is, then that's not a file, it's a directory. Notice that entry pub; that's commonly where generally available files are stored—*pub* is short for *public*.

Typing **cd pub** takes me a level down. Another DIR shows a directory named gutenberg—a likely candidate—and I could keep searching around, but I found from Gutenberg's Web site that the file I'm looking for was at ftp://sailor.gutenberg .org/pub/gutenberg/etext99/advsh10.txt. I can navigate there by typing **cd gutenberg/etext99**.

Notice that there are no spaces except between the cd and the directory name, and notice also that, in general, you must be careful about capitalization—if the directory's name is Literature with a capital *L*, then trying to change to a directory whose name is literature with a lowercase *l* will probably fail. Why *probably*? It's another Unix thing; the Unix file system is case sensitive. In contrast, if you found yourself talking to an NT-based TCP/IP host, then case would be irrelevant. How do you know what your host runs? Well, it is sometimes announced in the sign-on message, but not always. The best bet is to always assume that case is important.

Anyway, once I get to the directory, I can do a dir command to see if advsh10.txt is there. Dir advsh10.txt confirms that the file is there.

Before we get the file, there's one more thing that I should point out. Years ago, most files that were transferred were simple plain text ASCII files. Nowadays, many files are *not* ASCII—even data files created by spreadsheets and word processors contain data other than simple text. Such files are, as you probably know, called *binary* files. FTP must be alerted that it will transfer binary files. You do that by typing **binary** at the ftp> prompt. FTP responds by saying, "Type set to I." That is FTP's inimitable way of saying that it's now ready to do a binary file transfer, or as FTP calls it, an *image* file transfer.

Transferring a File

Now let's get the file...as it's a text file, I just type **get advsh10.txt**, press Enter, and wait. Once the transfer's done, I get some throughput statistics.

Now, when we get the file, it'll take some time to transfer. There's no nice bar graphic or anything like that to clue us about how far the transfer has proceeded. There *is* a command, however, that will give you *some* idea about how the transfer is progressing—*hash*. Type **hash**, and from that point on, the system will print an octothorp (#) for each 2K of file transferred. For example, say I'm on a Gutenberg system and I want to download the Bible, bible10.zip. (Is it sacrilegious to compress the Bible? Interesting theological question.) The file is about 1600K in size, so I'll see 800 octothorps.

Each line shows me 80 characters, so each line of # characters means 160K of file were transferred. It'll take 10 lines of # characters (*10 lines!*) before the file is completely transferred.

Remember that Gutenberg location. If you're ever stuck for something to read, they've literally got hundreds of books online. Even better, as they are just simple ASCII, there are programs that will transfer the files to a small computer such as a PalmPilot or a Windows CE palmtop—the easily portable, electronic book's almost here!

Downloading to the Screen

Before leaving the command-line FTP client, there's one more tip that I'd like to share with you—how to download directly to your computer screen.

Sometimes you'll come across a short file, like the READMEs that are so common around the computer world. Such a file may describe what's in an FTP directory. You'd like to examine it but the whole idea of first downloading it and then bringing up the file in Notepad seems a lot of work. In that case, download it instead to the screen.

You do that by typing **get *filename* -**.

Of course, this depends on the system that you're working with, but it may only be possible to do this "get" if your FTP session is set for ASCII transfers rather than binary transfers. You can change that by just typing **ascii** at the command line. You see the response "Type set to A."

Graphical FTP Clients

In one example of how the world keeps getting better, you can often avoid command-line FTP. In many cases, all you need do is to point your browser to an FTP site by typing **ftp://*address***, like **ftp://ftp.3com.com**, in the Address field.

 TIP You need the *ftp://* prefix on the address on some browsers because when you just type in an address, like ignatz.mouse.com, then the browser assumes that you want it to connect to a Web server rather than an FTP, Telnet, or other server, and so it interprets the address as http://ignatz.mouse.com. What's the difference between ftp://ignatz.mouse .com and http://ignatz.mouse.com? It's a matter of addresses. It's possible to have many kinds of servers running on the same system. They're distinguished by their port numbers: just as your dentist's office might be in 210 Main Street *and* your dermatologist's office might also be at 210 Main Street, they probably don't *share* an office—the dentist's full address isn't 210 Main Street, it's more like suite 118, 210 Main Street, and perhaps the dermatologist is at suite 305, 210 Main Street. Different ports on a server are like different rooms in a building. Web servers are by default at port 80—but http:// is easier to remember than "connect me to port 80." FTP works on another port, actually two ports—20 and 21—Telnet uses 23, and so on.

In any case, most Web browsers can double as a graphical FTP client. You can navigate a directory structure by just clicking a directory to enter it or pressing the Backspace key to back up a level. The trouble with most Web browsers as FTP clients, however, is that they only work when you're logging onto the FTP site as anonymous; they don't give you a chance to specify a user ID and password. Thus, if the site requires an account to access it, your browser is just booted off the site.

Windows 2000 adds a new feature called FTP folders that solves that problem, however. Just open up My Network Places and double-click Add Network Place. You'll be prompted to type either a UNC, like \\someserver\somevolume, or a URL, like http://www.someplace.com or ftp://ftp.someplace.com. What's particularly nice about this is that the wizard creating the new Network Place entry asks you if you need to specify a user ID and password to access the new Network Place. The FTP site then shows up in My Network Places as if it were a local set of folders, combining the simplicity of a GUI front end for FTP with the flexibility of being able to control how you log on.

That's about all that we'll say here about FTP. There is lots and lots more that FTP can do, but I've given you the basics that you can use to get started and get some work done in the TCP/IP world. If this all looks ugly, user-unfriendly, and hard to remember, then, well, it *is*, at least to someone used to a Macintosh or Windows. But there's no reason why a graphical FTP program couldn't exist, and indeed some are appearing. FTP is two things—the FTP protocol, which is the set of rules that the computers on an intranet use to communicate, and the program *called* FTP that you start up in order to do file transfers. The FTP *protocol* doesn't change and probably won't change. But the FTP *program*, which is usually known as the FTP *client*, can be as easy to use as its designer can make it. So go on out, learn to spell *anonymous*, and have some fun on those FTP sites! To set up your own FTP site (as well as your own Web site), read about the Internet Information Server (IIS) in Chapter 19. Right now we're going to look at electronic mail.

A Free E-Mail Server for Windows 2000

Computers all by themselves are of little value for anything more than acting as a glorified calculator. Hooking up computers via networks has been the thing that's really made computers useful, and of course networks are a big part of communications. But networks are of no value unless people use them—and people won't use them without a reason. This brings me to electronic mail. E-mail is often the "gateway" application for people, the application that is the first network application that they'll use; for some people, it's the *only* application that they'll ever use. And e-mail is probably the most important thing running on the Internet.

Most offices have some kind of internal e-mail, such as Microsoft Exchange, Lotus cc:Mail, or the like. But connecting that e-mail to the outside world—that is, the Internet—is an expensive proposition; when we bought our cc:Mail/Internet gateway at TechTeach International, it had a list price of $4,000. That's a shame, as the protocols for Internet mail are well documented and there's lots of free code around to support them. In this section, I'll tell you about my favorite, a piece of software from the European Microsoft Windows Academic Centre (EMWACS).

Internet E-Mail Protocols

There are two main Internet e-mail protocols that most of us care about: The Simple Mail Transfer Protocol (SMTP) and the Post Office Protocol (POP3).

SMTP is the "mail" Internet e-mail protocol. SMTP grew up at a time when most users on the Internet were running Unix machines, each with its own IP address. Each Unix machine ran two mail programs. The first was a program that could package up a mail message and send it to its destination; the most common one was one named *sendmail*. The second program was a so-called *daemon*, a program that always runs in the background, kind of like a DOS Terminate and Stay Resident (TSR) program. The daemon would constantly listen for incoming mail in the form of TCP/IP packets sent from another system running sendmail.

The SMTP/sendmail approach worked fine as long as every system on the Internet could run some kind of mail daemon, *and* so long as every system was up and running 24 hours a day, seven days a week. But primitive PC operating systems don't handle daemons well, and most people don't leave their workstations up and running all of the time, even if they *are* running an operating system that handles daemons well. Additionally, while many systems may run all of the time and while they may have an operating system that likes daemons just fine, they aren't connected to the Internet all of the time.

In any case, it'd be nice to enhance SMTP with some kind of mail storage system, allowing one computer to act as a kind of "post office." Suppose you've got 500 people on your network with varying operating systems and uptimes. So you set up one computer that *is* up 24 hours a day, seven days a week. This computer runs the mail daemon, the program that listens. You tell that computer, "Accept mail for everyone in the company, and hold onto it." That's the computer I'll call a *post office*. Then, when a user wants her mail, she just connects to that post office and pulls down her mail. In the Internet world, we let a client computer like the one on her desktop communicate with a post office computer with a protocol called POP3, the Post Office Protocol. Such a program is a small application referred to as a *POP3 client*. Actually, every POP3 client that I know of might be better referred to as a *POP3 Message Receiver/SMTP Message Sender*. The program only uses POP3 to get your mail; when you create a new message, it just sends it to a computer running the SMTP receiver service (the daemon), which then hands it to the SMTP delivery service (sendmail or one of sendmail's cousins).

In order for *your* office to send and receive Internet mail, you'll need a computer to act as a post office. The computer uses SMTP to talk to other post offices, and those post offices may choose to communicate with you at any hour of the day, so the computer must be attached to the Internet 24 hours a day, seven days a week. So that your users can retrieve their mail, they'll need programs that act as POP3 clients. Finally, that post office computer will need to run a POP3 *server* so that it can respond to mail requests.

EMWACS's Internet Mail Service (IMS) software can take you a good way toward that goal. It consists of three services that'll run on any Windows 2000 Server machine:

- The SMTP receiver service, the listening "daemon" program. The program that does this is called SMTPRS.EXE. When another post office gets mail for you, it will communicate with SMTPRS.EXE. Similarly, if you create a new mail message and tell your mail client to mail it out, the mail client will send the message to SMTPRS.EXE.

- The SMTP delivery service, which sends messages to other post offices. The delivery service is called SMTPDS.EXE. SMTPDS only has to listen to SMTPRS. When the receiver service gets a new piece of mail, it gives it to SMTPDS, the delivery service. If the mail is destined for another post office, SMTPDS establishes a connection with that other post office and shoots the mail over there. If the mail is destined for *this* post office, then SMTPDS just drops the mail into the proper user's mailbox.

- The POP3 server. Called POP3S.EXE, this program responds to requests from POP3 client programs, delivering mail to those clients when requested.

Where can you find a POP3 client? Right in Windows 2000, NT, or Windows 95—the program attached to the Inbox tool can act as a POP3 client. I'll show you how to set that up later, but first let's get the server software set up. Or, if you find the Microsoft tool not to your liking, surf on over to http://www.eudora.com/eudoralight, where you'll find Eudora Light, an excellent mail client written by the Qualcomm people. They write terrific software, and even better, they have a 32-bit version of their Eudora mail client that they give away absolutely free.

Setting Up Your Mail Server: IMS Limitations

Before you install IMS, you should be aware of some of its limitations. There are a few things you must do to a Windows 2000 machine before it can serve well as a post office. Because you might find some of the constraints unduly confining, let's take a look at them before you go further.

The Mail Server Must Have a Static IP Address

Each service must be able to find the IP address of the computer that it is running on. You can check this by typing the name of each service followed by the -ipaddress parameter; for example, once you have IMS installed on a Windows 2000 machine, you can type **smtprs -ipaddress**, and you should see the IP address and DNS name of that machine.

In my experience, the IMS components can't find a machine's IP address if that machine gets its IP address from DHCP; just being in a DNS table doesn't seem to do the trick. So you've got to run IMS on a machine with a static IP address.

DNS Must Be Able to Find the Mail Server

This ought to be kind of obvious, but I thought I'd mention it anyway. If you send mail to bob@fin.shark.com, and DNS can't find fin.shark.com, then the mail isn't going very far. The IMS services actually try to resolve the name of the computer they're sitting on when they first start. If the IMS services *can't* resolve the name, then they will refuse to run.

The Mail Server Only Serves Users in Its Users Group

If the mail server receives mail for a user it doesn't recognize, it just refuses the mail. How, then, does it distinguish the users that it recognizes? They must be in the mail server's Users group. If the mail server has joined a domain, then that domain's Domain Users group will be sitting in the server's local Users group.

The POP3S Server Doesn't Accept Blank Passwords

There may be a way to do this, but I haven't figured it out. If you try to get your mail, then of course you'll be asked for your username and password. If your password is empty, then POP3S will refuse your connection, and you won't be able to retrieve your mail.

The Software Doesn't Have Performance Monitor Counters

Unlike a lot of Windows 2000 software, the EMWACS mail software won't install Performance Monitor counters. Yes, yes, I know, I'm getting a bit nitpicky about a piece of *free* software, but it'd be nice to use the power of Perfmon with IMS.

How the IMS Software Works

You install the three services on a Windows 2000 server. Once they're up and running, anyone can send mail to *somename@servername*, where *somename* is a valid Windows 2000 user on that server and *servername* is the Internet host name of the server. So, for example, if my local server were named altair.mmco.com and my username were markm, you could send mail to markm@altair.mmco.com. Of course, you could also allow that server to accept any mail for all of mmco.com by just putting an MX record for mmco.com pointing to altair.mmco.com.

Downloading the EMWACS Software

As I write this, the EMWACS folks have progressed to version 0.8x of their mail software and stopped. The 0.8 version works fine for me, but if you want a more-developed version, then, well, you'll have to pay for it—see the section later about Rockliffe's MailSite, the program that IMS grew up to be.

At this writing, you'll find the free version, IMS 0.8, at `http://emwac.ed.ac.uk/ html/internet_toolchest/ims/ims.htm`. Just point your Web browser to that location and you'll see instructions on how to download the software. They also have documentation on the product in HTML format—be sure to get that, because it'll have more detailed installation instructions than you can read here.

Unzipping the EMWACS Software

As I'm using an Intel-based server for my mail system, the file I downloaded was named `IMSi386.ZIP`. Since it's a zipped file, you'll need PKUNZIP or a similar program to decompress the files.

Create a directory that you'll unzip the files into. (I called mine `C:\EMWACS`.) Copy the `IMSi386.ZIP` file there, open up a command line, and type **PKUNZIP -d IMSi386**; that will unzip the file and create any necessary directories. Do the same with the ZIP file containing the documentation; that will create a directory called `HTML`, which will contain the documentation.

Then copy these files to the `\WINNT\SYSTEM32` directory:

- `SMTPRS.EXE` (the receiver daemon)
- `SMTPDS.EXE` (the sendmail delivery agent)
- `POP3S.EXE` (the POP3 server)
- `IMS.CPL` (the Control Panel applet to control the mail server)
- `IMSCMN.DLL` (a DLL to support the programs)

You can put most of them in different directories, but I find it easiest to just stick them in the SYSTEM32 directory. The `IMS.CPL` file *must* go in `\WINNT\SYSTEM32`.

Installing the Services

Next, register the services with Windows 2000. Open up a command line, change the drive and directory to the `\winnt\SYSTEM32` directory, and type the name of each service followed by **-install**:

```
smtprs -install
smtpds -install
pop3s -install
```

Each module should acknowledge that it has installed correctly. Next, tell Windows 2000 to automatically start these services whenever your start the computer. Go to the Control Panel and open the Services applet. You'll see three new services:

- IMS POP3 Server
- IMS SMTP Delivery Agent
- IMS SMTP Receiver

One at a time, click each service, and then click the Startup button. Choose Automatic, and the service will start when the computer does. Do this for each of the three services. Because they haven't been started yet, be sure to also click the Start button for each service.

Set Users to Log On as Batch Jobs

IMS requires that any user who tries to access his mailbox be able to log on to the server running IMS as a *batch job*. Odd as it sounds, it's necessary. Of course, Windows 2000 hasn't made it easy; here are the steps you'll need to follow:

1. While sitting at the machine running IMS, start the Group Policy snap-in: Click Start/Run, fill in **gpedit.msc**, and press Enter.
2. You'll see `Local Computer Policy` and `Local User Policy`. Open the folder labeled `Local Computer Policy`.
3. Within `Local Computer Policy`, open the folder named `Windows Settings`.
4. Within `Windows Settings`, open `Security Settings`.
5. Within `Security Settings`, open `Local Policies`.
6. Within `Local Policies`, open `User Rights Assignment`.
7. Inside that folder, you will see a number of rights. Find and double-click Log On as a Batch Job.
8. In the dialog box that appears, click Add.
9. You'll see another dialog with a list of user groups. Find the group named simply Users and double-click it to add it to the list of groups with the Log On as a Batch Job right.
10. Click OK twice to clear the two dialog boxes.
11. Close `GPEDIT.MSC`.

Adding the local Users group will work fine if the Domain Users group from your domain is a member of the local Users group—which it should be, by default.

If users aren't able to log on as batch jobs, they'll be denied login to the Windows 2000 mail server from their client software (Inbox, Eudora, or whatever). And, once again, don't forget that the mail server will *refuse* to receive mail from users who aren't in its local Users directory. So, suppose you want to set up a mail server M1 in domain RED, but you want it to accept mail for people in domain BLUE as well. First, make sure that RED trusts BLUE. Then go to Local Users and Groups on server M1 and make sure that the group M1\Users contains both RED\Domain Users and BLUE\ Domain Users.

Configuring the Services

Next, you'll see an applet labeled EMWAC IMS in the Control Panel. Double-click that, and you'll see a screen like in Figure 18.84.

FIGURE 18.84

Configuring directories for IMS mail

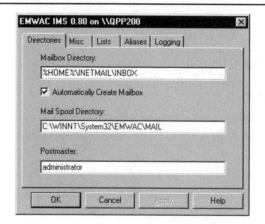

First, tell IMS where to put the mailboxes. Each user gets her own subdirectory in which IMS keeps her mail. If you check the Automatically Create Mailbox check box, then IMS will, as the label suggests, create a user's mailbox automatically. That way, IMS only creates a directory when necessary.

IMS lets you specify a couple of ways to organize user mailboxes—with the %home% and %username% variables. If you use %home% in the mailbox name, IMS will substitute the user's home directory, the one specified in the Profiles button on the User Manager. If you use %username% in the mailbox name, then IMS will substitute the user's Windows 2000 username.

For example, suppose I've got users named Sue and John as accounts on a Windows 2000 server. Their home directories are on the server at D:\Users\username. I could put their mailboxes in a directory E:\MAIL by telling IMS to set Mailbox Directory to E:\MAIL\%username%. As mail came in for Sue and John, IMS would end up creating directories E:\MAIL\JOHN and E:\MAIL\SUE. Mail messages would then accumulate in each directory as each user received mail. Note two things: First, E:\MAIL need not be shared, and second, neither John nor Sue need have File and Directory permissions on E:\MAIL or on either subdirectory.

Does that sound like it violates Windows 2000 security? It doesn't. You see, neither John nor Sue ever tries to access E:\MAIL; rather, John and Sue run programs—POP3 mail clients—that communicate in client-server fashion with the POP3S service, which in turn provides them with their mail messages. Now, it *is* a fact that POP3S must have access to that mailbox directory or nothing will happen.

If you set up the mailbox directories as I've just suggested, then they are very secure from user tampering. If, on the other hand, you don't care whether users can directly access their mailboxes, then use the %home% variable. For example, if you were to tell IMS to put mail in %home%\mail, John's mail would sit in D:\USERS\JOHN\MAIL, and Sue's would sit in D:\USERS\SUE\MAIL. In general, I avoid the %home% variable because, first, it confuses the mail server if a user does not have a home directory, and second, it puts the mail directories under direct user control, which isn't always the best idea.

The Mail Spool Directory is just a temporary holding directory for the mail server, and I just use the default. Postmaster is the e-mail name of the person who gets the error messages. (It's a good idea, by the way, to log into the mail server with the postmaster's name.)

Next, click the Misc tab and you'll see the screen in Figure 18.85.

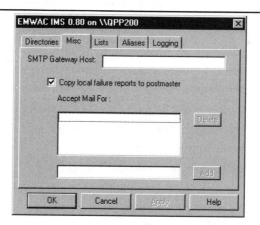

You can use this tab to tell the mail system to accept mail for other Internet domains; however, you *can't* use this to tell it to accept mail for other Windows 2000 domains—remember, you do that by putting global groups from other domains into the mail server's local Users group. The only thing I'd do here is to check Copy Local Failure Reports to Postmaster. That way, you can keep track of systemic problems. Finally, click the Logging tab and enable logging for each of the three services.

Once you've got IMS configured as you like it, close the Control Panel applet and start and stop each service so your configuration changes take effect. Or, if you don't want to wait around for the services to stop and start, write a batch file to do it:

```
net stop "IMS POP3 Server"
net start "IMS POP3 Server"
net stop "IMS SMTP Delivery Agent"
net start "IMS SMTP Delivery Agent"
net stop "IMS SMTP Receiver"
net start "IMS SMTP Receiver"
```

By now, you should be ready to set up your mail client.

Setting Up Your E-Mail Client

A server's no good without clients. In the case of a mail server, the accompanying clients are of course called e-mail clients.

To connect to your mail server, you'll need an Internet mail client of some kind. Examples include Outlook (which can act as an Exchange client, an Internet mail client, or both), Outlook Express, Eudora (the free version or the professional version; it's a great program, and you can find it at www.eudora.com), Pegasus (free, www.pegasus.usa.com), or the mail client built into Netscape Navigator. Technically, they are all *POP3/SMTP clients*. Some support a third protocol, IMAP4, but that doesn't matter to us, as IMS doesn't support IMAP4, just POP3 and SMTP.

To tell your e-mail client to look to your IMS server for mail, you've got to configure it to look for your mail account. Exactly how you do that varies from client software to client software, but in every case the e-mail software will probably need to know a few things:

Do you use POP3 or IMAP4?   POP3; again, IMS doesn't support IMAP4.

The name of your SMTP server   Fill in the name of your IMS server; it acts as your SMTP server.

The name of your POP3 server   Here you should also fill in the name of your IMS server as it acts in the roles of both SMTP and POP3 servers.

Your e-mail address   Your e-mail address is *name@servername*, where *name* is your Windows 2000 user account name. For example, if your IMS server is on domain FLOWERS and you log on to the FLOWERS domain as JaneD, then your e-mail address is janed. The *servername* will either be the fully qualified domain name of the machine running IMS, such as violets.flowers.com, or just the name of the domain, if you've directed people to the server with an MX record—if an MX record for flowers.com in DNS says that mail for flowers.com should go to violets.flowers.com, then your e-mail address is janed@flowers.com. Without an

MX record, e-mail addresses must specify the particular server, so in that case the address would be `janed@violets.flowers.com`.

Your account name and password   Fill in the Windows 2000 username and password. Even if IMS is running on a machine that's not a domain controller, you needn't include the domain prefix—in my experience, I can enter a username like mark rather than orion\mark.

From there, any other configuration options will be matters of taste—how often to check for mail and the like. Once your client's set up, send yourself a piece of mail and your mail server will be officially operational!

MailSite: "EMWACS Pro"

As you've read, I've been a fan of the free Internet Mail Service (IMS) software for NT and Windows 2000 from EMWACS for a long time. EMWACS mail doesn't do everything that I'd like; in particular, I wish that it did IMAP4, a protocol that lets you check your mail by only retrieving the *headers* of the mail messages rather than the entire message. That's important because I travel a lot, and it's usually just my luck to dial into the mail server at home at 31Kbps (the actual speed of most of my "56Kbps" sessions) only to find that some idiot has put me on his "joke distribution list" and today's yuk includes a five-megabyte bitmap. (Imagine how much laughing I do after waiting 20 minutes for this laff riot to download.) Additionally, many clients like EMWACS when I show it to them but are leery of installing software that's not supported; they're looking for something commercial, with support.

I was pleased, then, to hear that Rockliffe Systems (`www.rockliffe.com/`) has taken the EMWACS IMS software, extended it tremendously, and is selling it as a product called *MailSite*. The core is still EMWACS, but there's a lot more, including my much desired IMAP4. (I know, you're asking yourself, "Why doesn't he just use Exchange?" I know Exchange, I've taken and passed the Microsoft certification exam on it, have run it on client systems and even on my network for a while, but for some reason I just don't *like* it. All I really need is POP3/SMTP/IMAP4, and Exchange seems a bit of overkill. Basically, what I'm saying is that there's nothing *wrong* with Exchange—I just don't like it.)

You can go to their Web site and download MailSite and try it out for 30 days, as is the case with much software nowadays. (The program files are over 5MB in size, so pick a time of Internet quiet for the download.) The good news is that they've added a lot of nice GUI administrative support to IMS, as well as removed the need for any user-rights fiddling. The system's quite fast and of course does IMAP4 as well as all the mailing list stuff you could want. And if you're a current EMWACS IMS administrator, you won't have any trouble—it took me less than five minutes to install the software and get it running. The bad news is the price, about $700. Is it worth it? As always, it depends. If you're managing multiple mail servers, MailSite offers remote mail server administration, a big plus. The MailSite folks seemed helpful when I called their tech support line and asked a few dumb questions. And if your shop is a mixed Windows 2000/NT/Unix shop and you don't really want to be assimilated into the Exchange collective, then MailSite's something to check out. (*I'm* certainly enjoying it, although having to bring down the mail server every 30 days so I can go get another 30-day trial license is cumbersome…just kidding.)

E-Mail Security Concerns

As the Internet grows, more and more gateways will be built to other e-mail systems. You can't get everywhere, but in time, you'll be able to reach anyone from the Internet. Now, that's a good thing, but as e-mail becomes more important, it's also essential to keep your mind on the fact that e-mail is *not secure*. Your mail packets get bounced all around the Internet, as you know—but think about what that means. Suppose you send a message to someone on the Internet, and my computer is part of the Internet—a piece, as it happens, that sits between you and the person to whom you're sending mail. Mail can sit in intermediate computers like mine, *on the hard disk*, for seconds, minutes, or hours at a time. It's a simple matter to use any number of utility programs to peek into the mail queue on the mail that's "just passing through." *Never* say anything on mail that you wouldn't want as public knowledge. Even if someone doesn't peek at your mail, that someone probably backs up his or her disk regularly, meaning that the message may sit on magnetic media for years in some archive. I sometimes imagine that in the middle of the 21st century, we'll see "the unpublished letters of Douglas Adams"—e-mail notes that someone stumbled across while picking through some 70-year-old backups; you know, it'll be the latter-day equivalent of going through some dead celebrity's trash. Anyway, the bottom line is this: Don't write anything that you wouldn't want your boss, your spouse, your parents, or your kids to read.

Windows 2000 Internet Security: Some Thoughts

Now that you know how to put your NT/Windows 2000–based network on the Internet, *should* you? Some companies have and they've been quite dismayed to find "open season" declared on their network as computer-wielding slime of all kinds invaded their systems and their data.

Putting your local LAN on the Internet *can* leave you open to attacks from criminals, because the Internet wasn't really designed with security in mind. But remember that you're running NT/Windows 2000, one of the more security-conscious networks.

I'm not a security expert, so please don't take this section as guaranteed advice on how to secure your network from outside attack. But follow along with me and let's see if a little common sense can help you shore up your computers and data. A good book on the subject of NT/Windows 2000 security vis-à-vis the Internet is Mark Joseph Edwards's *Internet Security with Windows NT* (29th Street Press, 1996). Mark's Web site, `www.ntshop.net`, is the best place to go on the Net for information about new NT/Windows 2000 security threats.

First, where do the security holes exist in an NT/Windows 2000 network? Again, not speaking as a security expert, here are the main problems that I see, whether on an Internet or not.

Internal Users Can Easily Get a List of User IDs

Earlier in this book, you learned how to configure a set of home directories. First, you create a share called USERS on an NTFS volume, giving the Everyone group or, better, the Domain Users group, Full Control. Then you set the top-level directory permissions to Read and Execute and assign Domain Users no file permissions at all. Users need Read and Execute to navigate from the top-level directory to their individual home directories. Then you set the file and directory permissions for each directory to Full Control for each particular user.

The problem is that there's no way to keep a user from moving up to the top-level directory and seeing the names of all of the users' home directories. Result: Now he's got a list of all of the users' IDs, making hacking a bit easier.

Additionally, any user on an NT workstation or Windows 2000 Professional machine can type **net user/domain** and get a list of users in the workstation's domain. Again, these are mainly things you're concerned about for internal users, but inside hacking is probably more prevalent than outside hacking.

Internal Users Can Easily Crash Shared Volumes

If you haven't enabled disk quotas, any user with Write access to a volume can, either accidentally or purposefully, write as much data to a shared volume as the volume can hold. The result is that now there's no space left for other users. Worse yet, if that's the volume that held the pagefile, then the pagefile can't grow in size, which might crash Windows 2000 altogether.

Microsoft File and Print Services Will Operate across the Internet

There's no surprise here—heck, it's a feature, and I don't mean that facetiously. But it's also a security hole if you don't look closely into it.

First of all, what is it that you want to secure? I'll assume it is your data. Because you don't want an outside intruder to be able to destroy data on your servers or lock you out of your own network, let's consider this question: How could someone get access to your data?

For the moment, I'll assume you are not running any Internet services like FTP, Gopher, or Web servers; I'll get to them in a minute, but let's consider a network consisting of standard file servers.

Attacks could come in the following forms:

- Someone with Read access to your files could steal company information.
- Someone with Write access to your files could modify or delete them.
- Someone with Write access could use your file servers to store her own personal data, data she might not want to keep on her own computers—perhaps because the data is unlawful to have, like someone else's credit card numbers.
- Someone with Write access could cripple your servers by filling up their free space with nonsense files, crashing the servers.
- Presumably someone could crash your mail servers by sending thousands of automatically generated pieces of mail to the servers. Enough mail messages will fill the hard disks of those servers as well.
- Access to your print servers could, again, let intruders fill up the print servers' hard disks with spooled files, as well as causing your printers to run out of paper.

There are, however, several types of actions you can take to detect and/or deter an outside attack.

Detecting Outside Attacks

Windows 2000 comes with some built-in tools to make detecting attacks easier:

- Audit failed logons.
- Use the Performance Monitor to alert you when logon failures exceed some reasonable value.
- Periodically log network activity levels. If all of a sudden your network gets really busy at 3 A.M. for no good reason, then look closely into exactly *what's* going on at 3 A.M.

Deterring Attacks

The main steps to take to deter attacks include the following:

- Don't use obvious passwords.
- Don't enable the Guest accounts on Internet-connected machines.
- Rename the built-in Administrator account.
- Don't let the built-in Administrator account access the servers over the network.

- Lock out users after a certain number of failed attempts.
- Make passwords expire after a certain length of time.
- Install a firewall to filter out UDP ports 136 and 137.
- Put the Web, FTP, and Gopher servers on a separate machine in its own domain, with no trust links to other domains.
- Don't put any services on your DNS servers except DNS.

It seems to me that only by directly accessing your file servers through the normal NET USE interface, via an NFS interface, or through an FTP service would someone be able to read or write data on your computers over the Internet. I'll assume that you're not going to run NFS, that you'll put the FTP server where compromising it won't matter, and that you'll focus on the file server interface.

In a nutshell, here's the scenario that you should worry about. Suppose I know that you've got a server named S01 whose IP address is 253.12.12.9 and that it has a share on it named SECRET. I just create an LMHOSTS file with one line in it, like so:

```
253.12.12.9 S01
```

Now I can type **net use X: \\s01\secret**, and my Internet-connected PC sends a request to 253.12.12.9 for access to the share. Assuming the Guest account isn't enabled on S01, then S01 will first ask my PC, "Who are you?" I'll see that as a request for a username and password. When I respond with a valid username and password from the server's domain, I'm in. Actually, this is how I access my network's resources from across the Internet when I'm on a client site—two seconds' work with an LMHOSTS file, a NET USE, and I'm accessing my home directory from thousands of miles away.

To do that, I needed to know:

- A valid username on my network
- The password for that account
- The IP address of a server on the domain
- The name of a share on the domain

All right, suppose I want to hack some company with the name bigfirm.com. Where do I start? Step one is to find out what its range of IP addresses is. That's easy. Just telnet to internic.net and type **whois bigfirm.com**, and you'll get the network number and responsible person for that network. (You can alternatively run a Web-based search page with your Web browser; point it to www.internic.net.) You'll also get the IP address of their DNS name servers. The other way to find this information would be to type:

```
nslookup
set type=all
bigfirm.com
```

Bigfirm will dump the names and addresses of their DNS servers and their mail servers. Because there has to be a secondary DNS server to make the InterNIC happy, there will be at least two name servers. Now, bigfirm is probably thinking—the way most of us do—"It doesn't take much CPU power to run a DNS server. Let's put some shared directories there, too."

As Joe Slimeball Hacker, I'm thinking, "Cool—fresh meat."

You see, you've got no choice but to publish two of your IP addresses, the addresses of your DNS server and its backup. *So don't put anything else on it.* Once, I would suggest to firms that they just run DNS on old, slow machines. That's not an option any more, as we now need dynamic DNS, which means you're running Windows 2000 on a system and DNS on that system. It's a shame to make a server solely a DNS server, but it might not be a bad idea from a security point of view.

Now suppose you're smart and there's nothing else on the DNS servers. So I've got to fish a bit, but that's not hard, as whois told me your range of IP addresses. I'm a slimeball, but I'm a *thorough* slimeball (after all, I don't have a life, so I've got lots of time), and I'm willing to try all of your IP addresses to find out which ones have servers. There are even, believe it or not, freeware programs for Windows, NT, and Windows 2000 that will scan a range of IP addresses looking for machines attached to those addresses.

Alternatively, it's a simple matter to create an LMHOSTS file that includes a NetBIOS name for every possible IP address; for example, if I know that you have C class network 200.200.200.0, then I can create an LMHOSTS file with NetBIOS named N1, which equals 200.200.200.1, N2 equals 200.200.200.2, and so on. Then I need only do a net view *servername* for each name from N1 through N254. The IP addresses that have a computer attached to them running the server service will be the ones that challenge me for a name and password. The ones that *don't* won't respond at all.

What can you do? Not terribly much, except to be sure that the default Administrator accounts on those systems aren't blank—no sense in making things too easy. And it sure offers some incentive for getting rid of your old machines and applications and getting your enterprise off NetBIOS, doesn't it?

Next, I'm looking for a user account name or two. How can I get this? I don't think you can do a NET USER remotely without contacting the domain controller, which means you'll have to have a domain ID and password to get NET USER to work from the outside—whew, that's one less thing to worry about!

But there *is* a way to find at least some usernames. When a user logs on to a Windows 9x, NT, or Windows 2000 machine, the machine registers not only its own machine name on the network, but the user's name as well. It does that so alerts with that name on them can get to the proper user. For example, suppose you've asked the Performance Monitor to alert you in your username of JILL02 if a server gets low on free space. How does the network know where you are?

It's quite simple. When you log on, the Messenger Service—assuming that it's running—registers your username as one of the NetBIOS names attached to your workstation. Assuming you are logged on to a server whose IP address is 200.200.200.200, anyone doing an nbtstat -A 200.200.200.200 would not only see the computer's name, they'd see your name as well.

So, supposing that someone named *paulad* was logged in at the 200.200.200.200 machine (that's physically logged in, not connected over the network), a look at the nbtstat output would show me that there's a user named *paulad* who's logged on.

So now I've got a username, and probably the username of an administrative account since paulad is logged on to a server; good news for Joe Hacker. What can you do about that? Disable the Messenger Service, and the name never gets registered. And, by the way, speaking of nbtstat, if you run an nbtstat -A and the name MSBROWSE shows up, you've found a browse master. There's a good chance that a browse master is a domain controller, right? So maybe it's a good idea to set `MaintainServerList=No` for the domain controllers; you make that change in HKEY_LOCAL_MACHINE\System\CurrentControlSet\ Services\Browser\Parameters. Just let the other servers handle the browse master part; you'll remove a clue that a hacker could use. Unfortunately, however, all domain controllers have other names registered to them that pretty much identify them as domain controllers.

Now that I've got a username, I need a password. Now *that's* a problem. Even if I could physically attach my computer to your network, I wouldn't get a password with a network sniffer—NT uses a challenge/response approach to password verification. When you try to log on to an NT domain, the domain controller sends your workstation a random number that your workstation then applies to your password using some kind of *hashing* function, a mathematical function that produces a number when supplied with two inputs. The result is what gets sent over the network, not the password. (As I said earlier, there is one exception to this rule; when you change your password, the new password *does* go over the network to the server, but that's pretty rare.)

Where do I get the password? I can do one of two things. First, taking what I know about the user, I can try to guess a password. Second, I can run a program that tries to log on repeatedly, using as passwords every word in the dictionary—this is sometimes known as a *dictionary hack*.

The defense against this should be obvious. First, don't use easy-to-guess passwords. Use more than one word with a character between it, like *fungus#polygon*. Second, don't make it easy for people to try a lot of random passwords: Lock them out after five bad tries.

That leads me to a caution about the Administrator account. If you don't have the Resource Kit, *you can't lock it out*. Windows NT 4 Resource Kit now contains a utility for locking out the Administrator account. It is called `Passprop.exe`. When enabled, the Administrator account can only be used to log on at the domain controllers, not remotely or over the network. As I write this, no one I've talked to knows if there will be a passprop for Windows 2000.

If you don't have the new Resource Kit, then no matter how many times you try a faulty password, the Administrator account doesn't lock. So if you don't do something about it, all the slimeballs on the Internet can spend all of their free time trying to figure out your Administrator password. What can you do about that?

There are two possibilities. First, rename the account. Don't leave it as *Administrator.* Second, limit its powers. You cannot delete the Administrator account, nor can you disable it. But you can remove its right to access the server over the network. By removing this right, you force someone with the Administrator password to physically sit down at the server in order to control that server. Unfortunately, that won't be easy, because the ability to log on to a server locally is granted to the Administrators group, and the Administrator account is a member of that group. You aren't allowed to remove the Administrator account from the Administrators group, so all you can do, I suppose, is to remove the entire Administrators group's right. Then just grant the individual administrative accounts the Log On over the Network right. (You'll also have to remove the Everyone group and add user accounts back in one at a time—unfortunately, the Administrator is built into the Domain Users group and can't be removed.)

Now, these measures—disabling Guest, renaming Administrator, removing Administrator's right to log on over the network, locking out repeated penetration attempts, setting Performance Monitor to alert you to excessive failed logon attempts, using well-chosen passwords—may be sufficient, and you've no doubt noticed that they're all options that don't cost a dime. But if you want greater security, then look into a firewall. The firewall doesn't have to do much, but it's got one really important job: To filter out two ports on UDP.

UDP is the sister protocol to TCP; just as there is a TCP/IP, there is also a UDP/IP. TCP is connection oriented, whereas UDP is not connection oriented; it just drops messages on the network like messages in a bottle, hoping that they'll get where they would like to go. Whenever you execute a Microsoft networking command, such as net use or NET VIEW, you are running an application that sends commands to a server using UDP and UDP port numbers 136 and 137. *Ports* are software interfaces that are used to identify particular servers; for example, when you send mail from your desktop, you usually use TCP port number 25, and when you receive mail from your desktop, you usually do it on TCP port 110. Web browsers listen on TCP port 80, in another example.

Firewalls are powerful and sometimes complex devices. Once you install them, they have a million setup options and you're likely to wonder if you've caught all the ones you need. Running NetBIOS over IP services happens on UDP ports 136 and 137;

tell your firewall to filter those and it's impossible for someone to access normal file server services.

Application Security Holes

One way that Internet hackers have gotten into Internet domains is through bugs in common Unix Internet programs. Those things happen in NT, as well, which leads me to this final piece of advice: put the Internet services, such as FTP, Web servers, finger servers, and the like, on a machine all by themselves. Make sure the machine is in a domain all by itself without any trust relationships.

Is this because I know of any security holes in NT implementations of common Internet programs? No, this advice is just common sense—put simply, I don't know that they *can't* be compromised, so I counsel caution.

Many security consultants seem to be approaching Internet security in the same way that they handled virus consulting 10 years ago: They're shouting, "The sky is falling!" and spinning frightening worst-case scenarios in the hopes of drawing droves of frantic customers to them. In the end, however, just a few common-sense steps protected most of us from viruses. With a bit of knowledge, we can also move out of the "bogeyman" stage of Internet security and into the "rational planning" stage.

In this chapter, we've moved from the basics of TCP/IP to building the infrastructure needed to support basic business needs over TCP. Next, we'll take up one of the most commonly used TCP/IP applications: Web servers, as well as the related news and FTP servers.

CHAPTER **19**

Internet Information Services in Windows 2000 Server

Unless you've been living in a cave somewhere for the past five years, you're undoubtedly aware that the Internet is becoming a major part of the way that the world works. Notice I said *world*, not just *companies*. With each passing day, the Internet is having more and more of an impact on the daily lives of countless people. The amount of information available to anyone, anywhere, at any time is simply mind-boggling, and this trend is only going to continue to grow in the future.

Not one to miss out on such a significant part of people's lives, Microsoft is doing everything that they can to be a part of this revolution. While some of their tactics might be questionable—such as tying their Internet Explorer browser directly in with their most recent operating systems—other approaches are quite beneficial. The most significant benefit is the inclusion of the latest version of Internet Information Server with the base Windows 2000 Server operating system.

Internet Information Server is a full-featured platform capable of servicing HTTP (Web), FTP (file transfers), NNTP (news), and SMTP (e-mail) tasks for an organization. Due to its integration with the Windows 2000 operating system, it is relatively easy to set up, configure, and manage. IIS is capable of scaling to meet even the most demanding of environments—Microsoft runs their own Web site on IIS, and their site receives millions of hits per day.

Currently, Internet Information Server is enjoying second-place title as the most widely implemented Web server around, according to Web server statistics available at Netcraft (`www.netcraft.com/survey/`). According to the May 1999 statistics, Internet Information Server (in its various versions) accounted for 22.89 percent of 5,414,325 Web sites that were queried. So what was the first-place Web server? A package known as Apache, an open-source version of the original NCSA HTTPd Web server. In the same survey, Apache accounted for 57.22 percent of the servers sampled, and was increasing in market share.

Since Microsoft doesn't typically enjoy being second place to anyone, this could mean good things for administrators if Microsoft continues to add more features and functionality into IIS. Even if Microsoft doesn't add anything new, IIS is a robust platform that can meet the Internet needs of most organizations right out of the box. Let's start our discussion by taking a closer look at each of the services that IIS can provide.

A Closer Look: What IIS Can (and Can't) Do

Internet Information Server is really an overall umbrella for a suite of TCP/IP-based services all running on the same system. Although some of the services rely on shared components between them, overall they are functionally independent from one another. Just like an electrician who has different tools for different jobs, IIS has different Internet capabilities to help meet different needs. With the release of Windows 2000, Microsoft has reached version 5 for Internet Information Server. The following sections will briefly discuss some of the standard functionality included with IIS 5.

World Wide Web (HTTP) Server

If you're reading this book, and this chapter specifically, I'll assume that the World Wide Web is nothing new to you. Internet Information Server includes an HTTP server so that you can publish data that you want to the World Wide Web quickly and easily. IIS's Web service is easily configurable and reliable, it and supports security and encryption to protect sensitive data.

You can use IIS's Web service to host a Web site for your own domain or multiple domains, an intranet, and the Internet, and even allow users to pass through your IIS Web server to access HTML documents on machines *within* your organization. In addition, FrontPage server extensions are supported in IIS 5, allowing clients to easily publish and manage Web sites through FrontPage, Microsoft's what-you-see-is-what-you-get (WYSIWYG) Web site creation tool.

File Transfer (FTP) Server

Although the use of File Transfer Protocol is not the only way to send a file from one location to another, it is by far the most widely supported as far as the Internet is concerned. FTP was one of the original means of copying files from one location to another on the Internet, long before the days of graphical browsers, HTTP, and Web sites. Since the protocol has been around for so long, support is available on almost any platform, including midrange and mainframe systems that might not typically support HTTP.

In IIS 5, the FTP service includes support for resuming broken file transfers. This capability allows client workstations to restart an aborted file transfer at the point where it ended. This helps save on network bandwidth since clients don't have to re-request an entire file—they can simply resume where their transfer left off.

Network News (NNTP) Server

Sometimes referred to as *Usenet*, Network News Transport Protocol (NNTP) is something that I hope to see start taking off in the near future, simply due to the great functionality it provides. By using Internet standards (RFC 977), the NNTP service can be used as a means of maintaining a threaded conversation database on an IIS server, just like in Usenet groups on the Internet. Users with properly configured newsreader programs can navigate through and participate in these conversation databases.

Although services like Deja (www.deja.com) have recently made Usenet better known, it is still isn't as widely used as something like HTTP. That's unfortunate, since NNTP represents such a great cross-platform protocol for managing threaded conversation databases. Hopefully the inclusion of NNTP in with IIS 4 (and now IIS 5) will increase the use of this capability.

Simple Mail Transfer (SMTP) Server

At first glance, having a mail service included in IIS might seem like Microsoft is cannibalizing their own e-mail platform—Exchange. Unfortunately, if you are hoping that you might use this feature as an e-mail platform for your organization, you will be a bit disappointed. Microsoft has included an SMTP service in with IIS primarily for support of the other services within IIS—namely HTTP and NNTP. In other words, the SMTP server that comes with IIS is *not* sufficient to act as an e-mail server. If you want a Windows 2000–based mail server, you'll have to either look at a commercial product or use the free EMWACS SMTP/POP3 server available at HTTP://emwac.ed.ac.uk/html/internet_toolchest/ims/ims.htm.

For example, some of the FrontPage server extensions require having a mail capability available on a Web server. If a visitor to a FrontPage Web site hosted on your IIS server fills out a form, and the results of that form are to be e-mailed to a specific e-mail address, the SMTP service is the process that will handle that. The SMTP service is missing an important component—a POP3 or IMAP service—that would be necessary for IIS to act as a full-blown mail server for an organization. POP3 or IMAP is the means by which clients retrieve their specific messages from their mailbox on a mail server.

Since SMTP is simply a *transfer* protocol, there is no real structure given to the storage of messages once they have been received by your system. All e-mails sent to your SMTP server will simply be dropped in a directory, in a plain-text format. Although you *could* manually go through each message and determine who to send it to, I'm sure you can see that most people wouldn't want to do that. Even receiving a minimal amount of e-mail, on a daily basis, could make that a full-time job in itself.

However, having the SMTP service available is great if you have outgoing mail needs for your server, even beyond the support for FrontPage and NNTP. By using a properly formatted text file and copying it into the outgoing e-mail directory, you can easily have Windows 2000 send mail to any address on the Internet as long as it can connect to the target server. For example, maybe you have a nightly job that creates a summary report you would like e-mailed to customers or suppliers each day. Through some creative use of batch files and scheduling, this could easily be done with the SMTP service included in Windows 2000 Server.

Installing Internet Information Services

By default, Windows 2000 Server should have installed Internet Information Services on your system automatically. However, you may want to check to make sure that all the services that you need (HTTP, NNTP, SMTP, FTP) have been installed. If for some reason they weren't installed, or if they have been removed since the initial installation, adding them to the server again is relatively easy. The only requirement necessary to install Internet Information Services is that the TCP/IP protocol be installed on the system.

To install Internet Information Services, go into the Control Panel and launch Add/Remove Programs, then click the Add/Remove Windows Components button. This will launch the Windows Components Wizard, from which you can add or remove any parts of the Windows 2000 operating system. In the list of components, check the option for Internet Information Services (IIS), as shown in Figure 19.1.

FIGURE 19.1

Installing Internet Information Services (IIS)

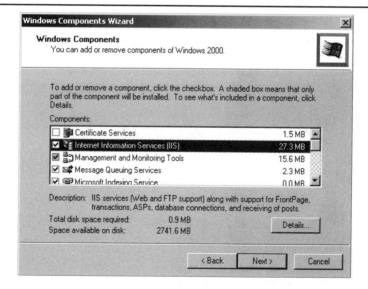

By default, selecting this option will install all of the components of IIS on your Windows 2000 Server—including support for HTTP, FTP, NNTP, and SMTP. If you would prefer to only install certain services (WWW, for example), press the Details button and uncheck the options you don't want to install. If this server will be connected to the public Internet, it might be a good security precaution to uninstall services you don't plan on using. Even though you can always disable the services once they're installed, the best security of all is to not have anything on the system that you don't need.

Click OK when you've selected the options you want to install, and Windows 2000 Server will begin installing the necessary components.

Default Configuration

If you chose to install all the IIS services (either as part of your initial setup of Windows 2000 Server or after the fact), you should end up with a default configuration similar to the following:

- Default (empty) Web site with FrontPage extensions, responding on TCP/IP port 80 on all configured IP addresses

- Administrative Web site, responding on a random TCP/IP port number on all configured IP addresses, with access restricted to the *localhost* (127.0.0.1) IP address only

- Default FTP server, responding on TCP/IP port 21 on all configured IP addresses

- Default NNTP virtual server, responding on TCP/IP port 119 on all configured IP addresses

- Default SMTP virtual server, responding on TCP/IP port 25 on all configured IP addresses

Looking at these services through the Internet Services Manager MMC, you should see a screen similar to the one in Figure 19.2.

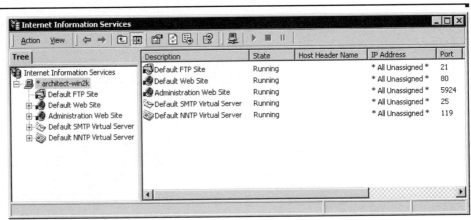

FIGURE 19.2

Internet Services Manager MMC with default IIS settings

If you will be connecting this server to the Internet, and you know in advance that there are certain services you won't be using, I would recommend stopping them through the MMC interface. This will prevent anyone from using these services without your being aware of it (for example, someone using your SMTP server—if it's configured incorrectly—as a mail relay for "spam" e-mail) and protect you against any security breaches that might be found at a later date. Since some of these default sites can't be deleted, the best option is simply to disable them if you don't plan on using them. However, the documentation for IIS is dependent, in its default configuration, on the default Web service being available, so keep that in mind when shutting down services on your system.

Global IIS Configuration

From the main view of the Internet Information Services MMC, you can set parameters for your system that will apply on a global (server) level by editing the server properties, or you can set parameters that will apply on an individual site level by editing the site properties as needed. Unfortunately, this can be a bit confusing due to the fact that there are individual site properties that can override global server properties. In any case, to set global defaults and parameters for your system, right-click your IIS server in the scope pane of the IIS MMC and then select Properties to edit the property sheet for your server. You should see a property page similar to the one in Figure 19.3.

FIGURE 19.3

Editing global IIS server properties

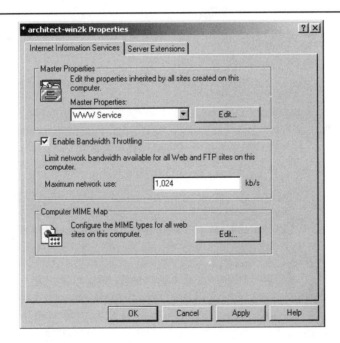

From this page, there are a number of settings you can modify for your system, including global defaults for the IIS service and default settings for the server extensions installed on the system. For example, if you know that all Web sites on your server are going to use `index.html` as their default start page instead of the Microsoft standard `default.html`, you could set that option in the master properties for the Web service. By selecting the WWW or FTP service from the Master Properties pull-down box (located under the Internet Information Services tab) and pressing the Edit button, you can define any of a number of settings for sites hosted on your system. The settings you can define here are defined in the "Setting Up A Web Site and Configuring Web Services" section later in this chapter.

If you already have sites running and configured on your system and change the global parameters for your server, Windows 2000 will also give you the option to apply these changes to the individual Web/FTP sites on that system. For example, in Figure 19.4, I have set a limit for each Web site on my server to use no more than 5 percent of the CPU on the system. Windows 2000 is indicating that this conflicts with settings for one of the Web sites on the system.

FIGURE 19.4

Setting global properties that override individual site properties

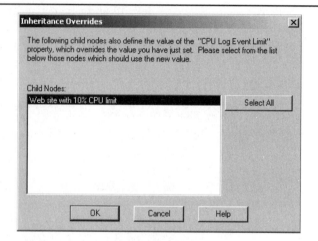

An existing Web site already has a CPU limit of 10 percent in place, so Windows 2000 is asking me if I would like to apply the new global default to the individual Web site in question. By selecting the site(s) to change and then clicking OK, Windows 2000 will apply the global defaults to the individual site(s). If you plan on hosting a number of Web sites on your server, this is a great way to make across-the-board changes to your system.

In addition to setting global defaults for Web and FTP sites, you can also use a feature called bandwidth throttling to control how much bandwidth IIS uses on your network. This option is a great feature for a number of reasons. First, if you have other Internet-based services on your network that require a set amount of bandwidth, setting this parameter will ensure that IIS doesn't consume all of your available bandwidth. This is good for making sure that there is enough bandwidth left on your Internet connection for e-mail, etc.

For example, let's say that you have a T1 connected to your organization's network, but you don't want the IIS process to ever consume more than one-quarter of the bandwidth on this connection. By using the figures in Table 19.1, you can see that a full T1 (1,544,000 bits per second) represents approximately 193KBps, so to limit IIS to one-quarter of your T1, you would enter a value of 48 here.

TABLE 19.1: COMMON BANDWIDTH CONVERSIONS

Connection Type	Bandwidth, in Bits/Sec	Bandwidth, in Kilobytes/Sec
56K	56,000	7
64K	64,000	8
128K	128,000	16
256K	256,000	32
512K	512,000	64
T!	1,544,000	193
10Base-T	10,000,000	1,250
T3	44,736,000	5,592
100Base-T	100,000,000	12,500

Bandwidth throttling is also a great feature for testing how well a Web site will perform over a slow link. Want to see how a Web site is going to look and perform for someone dialing in over a 56K connection? Try setting the bandwidth throt.. e down to 7 or 6KBps. It is also useful in benchmarking and scaling systems.

One important note to make about bandwidth throttling, however, is that *bandwidth throttle settings on individual Web sites will override global server settings*. To me, this seems a bit backwards, but it is the way that Microsoft chose to implement this capability. So why not just use the individual site settings and ignore the global settings? The main reason is because there is no way to set bandwidth throttle settings for the other services in IIS.

The last option you can set for your global IIS site is the MIME (Multipurpose Internet Mail Extensions) mappings that the IIS Web service will send to client browsers when a file is requested. For most implementations of IIS, the defaults in this area should be fine. However, if you need to add, remove, or change any mappings on your system, press the Edit button and then make changes as necessary.

Under the Server Extensions tab, you can control a number of settings for Web sites on your system, including global security settings. The options available when setting global server extension settings are shown in Figure 19.5.

FIGURE 19.5

*Configuring server
extensions*

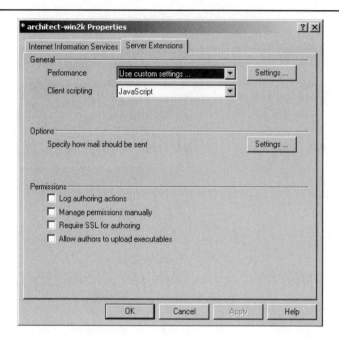

Once again, many of these same features are editable for each individual Web site, but there might be instances where you want to define a global default to be used for all sites. However, be careful when making changes to global server extension settings. Unlike other global IIS settings that will give you a warning when conflicting values are encountered, extension settings will be immediately applied to all sites on your IIS server with no regard to any existing values in place. Unless you have a specific need to define global settings, I would recommend leaving the options in this dialog box at their defaults and changing the server extension settings for each individual site as needed. Definitions for the settings available can be found later in the "Modifying Web Site Properties" section.

Once you have the global settings configured correctly on your server, it's time to start publishing content. In the next two sections, we will discuss setting up Web and FTP sites on your system and the configuration items associated with each. For the purposes of our discussions throughout the remainder of this chapter, we'll assume that you are configuring new sites or virtual servers in each case.

Setting Up a Web Site and Configuring Web Services

When you are ready to start building a Web site, the steps you must follow are quite easy. First, you will need to have the following information available:

- What IP address you want this Web server to live on (or if it should respond on all available IP addresses).

- What TCP/IP port number this Web server should listen to on the previously specified IP address(es). Typically, this is port 80.

- What TCP/IP port number this Web server should listen to for secure communications on the previously specified IP address(es). Typically, this is port 443.

- What "host header name" your Web site will respond to if you will be configuring multiple Web sites on a single IP address. Host header names are common Web site names, such as www.microsoft.com.

- What directory on your system will house your Web site content (HTML, scripts, etc.).

Creating a New Web Site

Begin creating your Web site by selecting your IIS server in the Internet Services Manager MMC and then choosing New/Web Site from the Action pull-down menu. This will launch the Web Site Creation Wizard, which will walk you through the process to create a Web site. The first question the wizard will ask is for a descriptive name for your site. Enter an appropriate name, and then click Next to proceed to the next step in the wizard, shown in Figure 19.6.

FIGURE 19.6

Web Site Creation Wizard, IP Address and Port Settings section

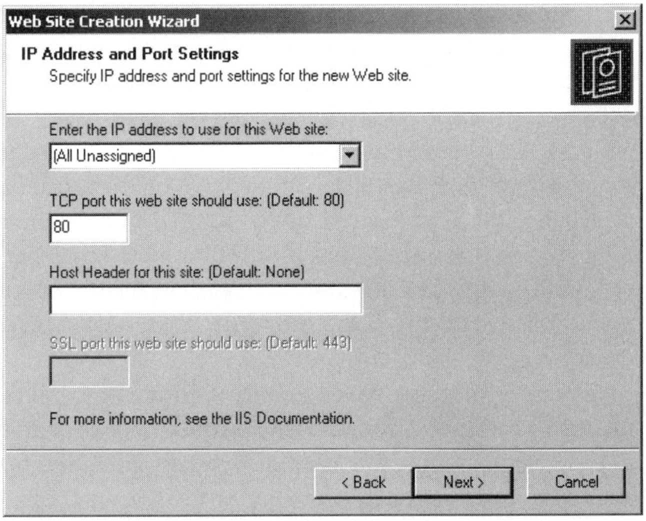

In the second step of the Web Site Creation Wizard, you will need to enter information about how your Web site can be reached. Namely, this is defined by three items: the IP address used, the port used, and any host header strings sent to your server. IIS will use any and/or all of these items to determine which Web site on your system to direct users to. If you are only hosting one Web site, the defaults should be acceptable. However, if you will be hosting multiple Web sites (for example, a private, internal Web site and a public, external Web site), the correct configuration here is important.

The first piece of information the Web Site Creation Wizard wants to know about is which IP address to use for this Web site. This is primarily for servers with more than one network adapter or with multiple IP addresses assigned to a single network adapter. For systems with more than one network adapter, you can host a different site on each adapter by choosing the appropriate IP address in this field. If you have a network adapter with multiple IP addresses assigned to it (see Chapter 17), you can assign a different Web site to each address. Although the latter configuration is primarily seen in larger Web-hosting type arrangements, it can still be useful. If you'd prefer to have IIS simply display the same site to any IP address configured on the server, leave the default All Unassigned value in place; otherwise, select the appropriate IP address from the pull-down list.

TIP If you are going to have an internal, private Web site published on your internal network adapter and an external, public Web site published on your external Internet network adapter, make sure that the IP address for your internal adapter is not reachable from the outside world. You can test this by trying to ping—from the public Internet—your internal IP address, or by trying to connect to it via a browser.

The second thing the Web Site Creation Wizard needs to know is which port to use for your Web site. By default, port 80 is the standard port assigned to the HTTP protocol. If you will be hosting a public Web site, accessible to anyone, leave the selection at port 80. Browsers will try to connect to Web sites on this port when a user types in a URL. However, if you have custom needs or want to secure your Web site a bit, you can change this port to any number from 1 to 65535. In order to connect to your Web server with a customized port, users will need to know the port number and append it to the URL string as follows: `http://www.netarchitect.com:9000`. This would direct a user's browser to attempt to open up an HTTP session on port 9000 instead of the default port 80.

Unique IP addresses have typically been the way that multiple Web sites have been hosted on the same physical box. However, since IP addresses are becoming more and more of a commodity, there is a means of assigning multiple Web sites to the same IP address and port number—through the use of something called host header names. A host header name is a means of including the host name a browser is requesting (e.g., `www.microsoft.com`) into the HTTP header transmitted to the HTTP server. For example, when a client browser begins to open a Web site, it will (by default) look up the IP address for the host name in the URL, and open a TCP connection on port number 80. Once that connection is established, it will transmit its request for a page to the server, and include the host header name information in with the request. IIS will look at the host header name information, compare the name to those in its list of servers, and then respond accordingly by returning the correct pages for the corresponding site. This is a quick and easy way to host multiple sites on a single server, but clients must be using at least Microsoft Internet Explorer 3 or Netscape Navigator 2 for this to work correctly. Anyone using an older browser than that will be directed to the default Web site instead.

The last option in this phase of the wizard is to define an SSL (Secure Sockets Layer) port number to use for this Web site. SSL is the means by which Web servers and browsers can maintain secure communications between each other. You have probably used SSL if you have ever purchased anything over the Internet. Since SSL requires having an appropriate certificate installed on your IIS system (more on this later), this option will be grayed out if you don't have one installed. By default, port 443 is the correct number to use for secure communications.

NOTE SSL and host header names don't mix. If you are planning on using SSL, you can only assign one host header name to your site, since the domain name is encoded in the certificate. If you need to host multiple SSL sites on the same box, use multiple IP addresses.

Hosting Multiple Virtual Web Sites

In previous versions of Windows NT, hosting multiple Web sites (sometimes referred to as "virtual sites") on the same physical system was often a tricky operation, sometimes requiring modifications to the system Registry. Fortunately, this process has been made much easier in Windows 2000. For example, let's say you wanted to host two different Web sites on your server—one for www.microsoft.com and one for www.sybex.com. The steps that you would follow to make this happen are:

1. Create DNS records for each of your Web sites, each pointing to the same IP address or to unique IP addresses (for more information on creating DNS records, please see Chapter 18).

2. Choose how you want to determine which site on your server visitors are trying to reach, via *one* of the following options:

   • Host header records: The easiest of all three choices, host header records allow you to specifically enter the site name—for example, www.microsoft.com—in your definition of a Web site. Modern browsers (IE 3 or Netscape 2 or later) will transmit the name of the site to the server, and the server will return the pages for the appropriate sites. Enter the appropriate host header names in the host header field shown back in Figure 19.6.

Continued

CONTINUED

- **Multiple IP addresses:** Whether you have multiple NIC cards installed in your server or you have programmed multiple IP addresses for a single NIC card, assigning a unique IP address to each unique Web site is one of the more common ways to host multiple Web sites on the same system. In the IP address field in Figure 19.6, enter an appropriate, unique IP address for each site that matches the DNS records you defined in step 1.

- **Unique port numbers:** Although less common than the other two methods of hosting multiple sites, using a unique TCP port number for each site can also allow you to host multiple sites on the same system. This is more commonly seen with sites that don't need to be publicly accessible, since browsers will use port 80 by default. You can enter a custom port number in the TCP port field shown in Figure 19.6; however, client browsers will have to append the port number to their URL to be able to access the site (e.g., http://www.microsoft.com:200 for accessing port 200).

3. Using the Web Site Creation Wizard, create two virtual Web servers on your system, one for the www.microsoft.com site and one for the www.sybex.com site. Define each site with a unique host header name, IP address, or TCP port—depending on how you want to control virtual sites on your system.

4. Place the necessary Web content for each site in the directory defined for the site.

Here's an example of how you'd put a site named www.joeslabs.com and another named www.janesmarket.com on a single server—say, on a machine named spider.acme.com at 210.10.20.40:

1. Create a folder for the Joeslabs content on the spider.acme.com machine; for example's sake, let's say that you put it on E:\joeslabs. Put the files relevant to the Joeslabs site—default.htm, the JPEGs, any other HTML or script files—in E:\joeslabs.

2. Similarly, create a folder for the www.janesmarket.com content, perhaps on E:\janesmarket. Put the Janesmarket content in E:\janesmarket.

3. Ensure that DNS points to 210.10.20.40 for both www.janesmarket.com and www.joeslabs.com. In each zone, you'd probably just create a CNAME record pointing to spider.acme.com.

4. Install IIS on spider.acme.com.

5. Create the Joeslabs site: From the Internet Services Manager, right-click the icon representing spider.acme.com and choose New/Web Site, which starts up the Web Site Creation Wizard. Click Next to get past the opening screen, then type in some descriptive text for the Joeslabs Web site; "Joeslabs Web site" will do fine, although the actual text is pretty irrelevant, it's mainly to remind you as the Web administrator which of your sites does what. Then click Next to get to the IP Address and Port Settings page.

Continued ▶

CONTINUED

6. In the IP Address and Port Settings page (see Figure 19.6), you'll see the three alternative methods that you can use to distinguish this site from others running on this server: you can use a different IP address, a different port, or a different host header record. Of the three, the third option—different host header record—is by far the easiest and least costly. (Who wants to burn up an IP address for each Web site? Well, *you'd* have to, if you were still using IIS 4!) In the field labeled "Host Header for this site: (Default: None)," fill in the URL that you want people to use when referring to this site—www.joeslabs.com.

7. Click Next and then fill in the "home directory" for this site, which means point the server to the folder with the content. Fill in E:\joeslabs and click Next.

8. Set the access permissions on this directory. In most cases, you can just take the defaults, and only allow users to read files and run scripts. Click Next and then Finish, and www.joeslabs.com is done.

Once you have all the information entered correctly, press Next to move on to the next step of the wizard, shown in Figure 19.7.

Specifying anonymous access and the path to files for a site

The next step of the wizard is where you will define the location for your files for this Web site, and whether to allow anonymous access to the site. The path is pretty much straightforward: enter the local path that IIS should use for files when someone connects to this site. Or, if you intend on hosting your content on another machine

within your organization, you can enter a UNC path in the form of *servername*\
sharename. If you choose the latter option, the wizard will prompt you for an appropriate username and password combination to use when retrieving content from the
target system.

If you will be making this a publicly accessible Web site, leave the "Allow anonymous access to this Web site" box checked. This will allow any user to connect to the
Web site without providing any form of authentication. However, if you want this to
be a private, secured site, uncheck the box to remove anonymous access. Specific
security settings that you can apply are discussed in the "Modifying Web Site Properties" section later in this chapter. Click Next to move on to the final step in the wizard, shown in Figure 19.8.

FIGURE 19.8

*Setting Web site access
permissions*

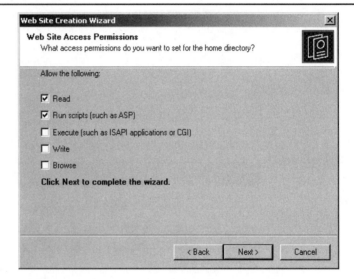

The last step in the Web Site Creation Wizard is to define access permissions to be
used for this site. The permissions applied here will start at the root of the site and
automatically be applied to any subdirectories below this site. Of course, you can
always change the site settings later, or implement custom settings for any subdirectories below the site. Briefly, each of these access settings controls the following:

Read   Allows users to read files from your Web server. In most instances, you
will want this option set for the root of a new site. The primary reason for disabling this option is for directories that contain CGI (Common Gateway Interface) or ISAPI (Internet Server Application Program Interface) applications,
which will usually be set on a subdirectory level.

Run scripts (such as ASP)   If you need to allow the execution of Active
Server Pages (ASP) scripts on your site, enable this option.

Execute (such as ISAPI applications or CGI)   If you need to allow the execution of ISAPI or CGI applications on your site, enable this option. When you enable this option, it is inclusive of the Run scripts option as well.

Write   If client browsers either will need to upload files on your Web server or will be writing data to a file (maybe filling out a registration form, or something like that), you will need to have write permissions enabled. Personally, I prefer to only enable write permissions in subdirectories of a Web site, not the main directory itself.

Browse   If a user does not send a request for a specific file on your Web server (for example, `default.html`) and there is no default document defined on your system, IIS will return an HTML representation of the files and subdirectories in the root of your site. Except in special circumstances, this option should probably be left disabled.

Once you have defined the necessary security for your site, click Next to finish the wizard and your Web site will be created. If you have HTML content to publish, you can start by putting the necessary files in the directory you defined for this site. By default, all new Web sites (unless you changed the global server properties for this option) will use `default.htm` or `default.asp` as their default home page, so make sure that the `.htm` or `.asp` file you want presented to users when they first visit your site is named appropriately. By using a client workstation with a browser, you should be able to test your site to make sure that it is operating correctly.

Modifying Web Site Properties

Once you are sure that your site is functioning correctly, you might find a need to fine-tune some of the parameters of the site. To change any of the settings for your site, return to the Internet Services Manager MMC and select your site in the scope pane. From the Action pull-down menu, select Properties to edit the property pages for this site.

Web Site Properties

The first page in the Web site properties will look similar to the one shown in Figure 19.9. From this page, you can edit a number of general parameters for your Web site:

Web Site Identification   Here, you can change the friendly name, IP address, TCP port number, or SSL port number assigned to your Web site. Obviously, changing any of the latter options will change the way clients access your site, so plan your changes accordingly. If you want to change the host header record for your Web site, click on the Advanced button to get to the advanced identification properties for this site, and press the Add button. You should see a screen similar to the one shown in Figure 19.10.

FIGURE 19.9

Web site properties for an IIS Web site

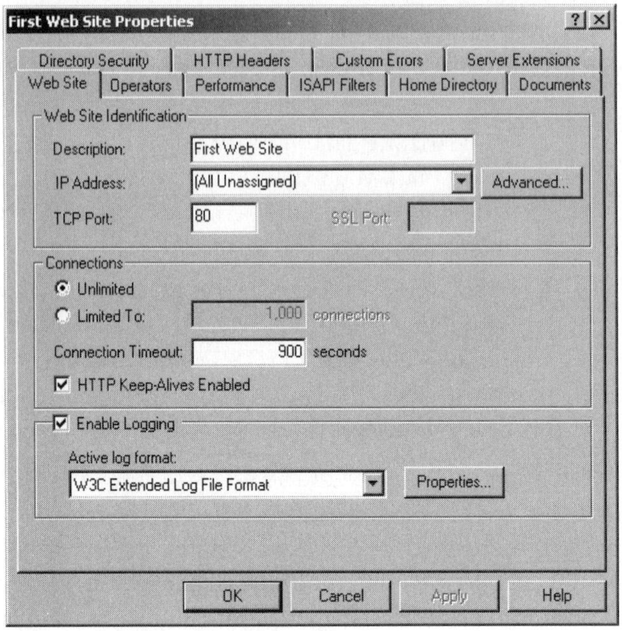

FIGURE 19.10

Advanced Web site identification properties

From this dialog box, you can change the host header name for this Web site either by adding a new identity (IP address, port, host header name) or by modifying the existing record.

Connections   Returning back to the property sheet shown in Figure 19.9, the next group of options you can modify is how IIS will manage incoming connections. You can limit the number of connections to your system or allow an unlimited amount, enter a timeout value for IIS to close out idle connections, and enable HTTP keep-alives. Enabling HTTP keep-alives allows client browsers to maintain an open connection in between individual requests to a Web server. Since Web pages are often made up of several elements (text, graphics, etc.) that must be opened individually, this option increases performance on servers. Disabling this option could cause browsers to open a separate connection for each Web page element.

Enable Logging   You can enable or disable logging for this Web site by checking or unchecking the Enable Logging box. Since log files take up space on your system, you might consider disabling this option for an internal Web site. If you enable logging, you have a number of format options to choose from in the Active Log Format pull-down box, including W3C Extended Log File Format, ODBC Logging, NCSA Common Log File Format, and Microsoft IIS Log File Format. Depending on which option you choose, there are properties that you can edit for that format by pressing the Properties button. For example, choosing the ODBC Logging option and clicking Properties will take you to a dialog box where you can define the ODBC data source name, table, etc. The W3C Extended Log File Format properties will allow you to define how often new logs are created, where they are stored, and which data items to log.

Operators Properties

Moving to the next tab in the Web site properties pages will take you to the Operators page, pictured in Figure 19.11.

FIGURE 19.11

*Operators properties
for an IIS Web site*

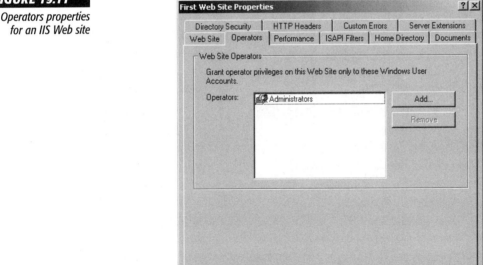

From this page, you can define Windows 2000 accounts that have operator privileges for this specific Web site. A user will need to be authenticated as a Windows 2000 user, not as an anonymous user, to be able to use their operator privileges. By clicking

Add, you can grant operator privileges to any users that need them. Operator privileges will grant users the rights defined below:

Web site operators can:

Modify Web server access permissions and logging

Modify default Web documents and Web site footers

Modify page content expiration, HTTP headers, and/or content ratings

Web site operators cannot:

Modify the identification (IP address, port, host header) of a Web site

Modify the anonymous user account and password

Modify bandwidth throttles

Create virtual directories or modify existing virtual directory paths

Select or deselect application isolations

Performance Properties

The next options you can configure for your Web site are performance related and can be found under the Performance properties page shown in Figure 19.12.

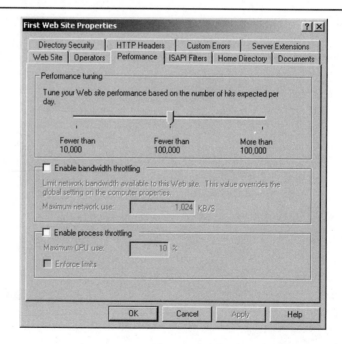

Depending on the size of your Web site and the amount of traffic you expect you will be handling, you can modify several parameters to adjust the behavior of your site:

Performance Tuning   Depending on the number of hits you expect to receive in a day, you can adjust the Performance Tuning slider to one of three positions: Fewer Than 10,000, Fewer Than 100,000, or More Than 100,000. Setting this option to be slightly higher than the hits you expect to receive will yield the best performance (don't set it too high—that can actually decrease performance).

Enable Bandwidth Throttling   Just as I discussed back in the global server options for IIS, you can control the amount of bandwidth that the overall server or an individual site can consume. Any settings defined here will override the global server settings. Refer back to table 19.1 for a listing of common bandwidth sizes and their translations into kilobytes/second.

Enable Process Throttling   If you will be executing applications on your server through IIS, you can limit the amount of CPU time a process can control. This can prevent an errant application from consuming all available resources on your system. Enter a percentage value for the maximum CPU use this Web site is allowed. If you would like to just receive an event log notification if this limit is exceeded, leave the Enforce Limits check box blank. Otherwise, check the box to enforce this limit, and CPU processing time will be restricted to the value you've set for this specific Web site.

ISAPI Filters

The next property page—ISAPI Filters (shown in Figure 19.13)—lets you set options for which ISAPI filters are installed for a specific Web site and the order they execute in.

ISAPI filters are programs that respond to events that occur on the server during the processing of an HTTP request. The list of ISAPI filters displayed for a Web site is a combination of ISAPI filters globally defined for the server, plus ISAPI filters specifically designed for the individual Web site. If two or more filters are registered for the same event, filters with a higher priority are executed first. Filters can be added, removed, modified, or disabled from this list by using the Add, Remove, Edit and Disable buttons on the right side of this property page. To change the order of execution for filters, adjust them with the up and down arrows on the left side of this property page.

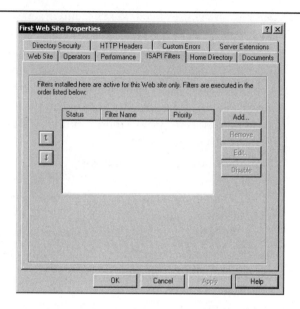

Home Directory Properties

The next tab in the Web site properties pages is the Home Directory page, shown in Figure 19.14.

This group of settings lets you control where IIS will look for Web content, and what security permissions to use while handling it.

By selecting the appropriate radio button on the top of this property page, you can control where IIS will go to look for the content for this site, or if it will send users to another Web site. Based on the selection you make, the lower portion of this property page will change accordingly. If you select the option for a directory located on this computer, you will need to enter the local path in the lower portion of the property page.

If you select the option for a share located on another computer, the Local Path field will change to a Network Directory field, where you will need to enter the correct *\\servername\sharename* UNC path. When you choose to use a share located on another computer for your files, you might need to enter login credentials for the IIS service to use when it is accessing the other system. The IIS service will actually log into the other system, retrieve the files, and present them to the user just as if the files were local. This is a great way to distribute an entire Web site throughout an organization. If individual departments are responsible for maintaining different sections of a site, you can use this feature to direct requests for their content to their servers, instead of requiring all your departments to publish their data to one system.

Lastly, if you choose to redirect users to another URL, IIS will create an HTML redirection page pointing users to the URL you specify. The Local Path field will change to a Redirect To field, where you can enter a full URL to send users to. Redirecting users to a URL can be configured through three different options: redirect users to an exact URL, redirect users to a lower subdirectory, or permanently redirect users to an exact URL. Redirecting users to an exact URL is pretty straightforward; users are sent to the exact URL you enter, just as if you typed it into their browser for them. Redirecting users to a lower subdirectory will let you create an alternate directory in your Web site structure. The last option, for permanently redirecting users to a URL, is very similar to the first option, with the exception that a permanent redirection will send a "301 Permanent Redirect" message to the browser, instead of the usual "302 Temporary Redirect." The net result of this is that some browsers will modify any bookmarks or favorites on file if they receive a permanent redirection.

If you chose either of the first two options for your content location—a directory on your IIS computer or a share on another server—a number of security settings will be displayed at the bottom of the property page. These settings can be used to control what can and can't be done on your site:

Script Source Access   This option is only available when read or write access is enabled. This option allows access to source code, including scripts in ASP applications.

Read   Allows users to read files from your Web server. In most instances, you will want this option set for the root of a new site. The primary reason for disabling this option is for directories that contain CGI or ISAPI applications, which will usually be set on a subdirectory level.

Write   If client browsers will either need to upload files on your Web server or will be writing data to a file (filling out a registration form, etc.), you will need to have write permissions enabled. Personally, I prefer to enable write permissions in subdirectories of a Web site and not the main directory itself.

Directory Browsing   If a user does not send a request for a specific file on your Web server (for example, default.html), and there is no default document defined on your system (see the next section), IIS will return an HTML representation of the files and subdirectories in the root of your site. Except in special circumstances, this option should probably be left disabled.

Log Visits   Depending on whether or not you want logging information stored about visitors to your site, check or uncheck this box. Logs will be stored in the format defined in the Web Site properties page covered earlier in this chapter.

Index This Resource   To speed searching for text data, select Index This Resource, which will cause the Microsoft Indexing Service to index all the content of this site.

Application Name   If your site is going to be the starting point for an application, this is where to enter the name of the application.

Execute Permissions   This pull-down box will let you define whether or not to allow the execution of scripts, the execution of scripts and executable files (.exe and .dll), or nothing at all.

Application Protection   To prevent errant applications from taking out other processes on your system, you can control the level of protection for each application. Low protection will allow applications to execute in the same memory space as the IIS process itself; medium protection will pool applications for this site together; and high protection will isolate each application from any others.

Documents Properties

Continuing with our Web site configuration, the next settings tab in the Web site property pages is the Documents tab, shown in Figure 19.15.

When users attempt to connect to your Web server without specifying a specific document to retrieve, IIS will look through the list of default documents (if enabled) to return to the user. By default, the IIS installation process will add default.htm and default.asp to this setting for the global server properties, which are then inherited by each Web site. If for some reason you would prefer to use another name—perhaps index.html—you can add the name to the list of default documents by pressing the Add button. IIS will look through this list, in order, and return the first matching document it finds. If you would prefer to adjust the order, use the arrows to the left of the document list to place the documents you want to look for first at the top of the list.

FIGURE 19.15

*Documents properties
for an IIS Web site*

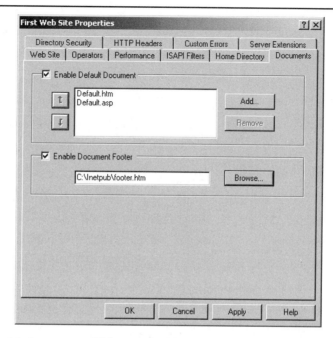

If you want to have every Web page within your site sent out with a common footer (for example, copyright and disclaimer information) you can have IIS do this by selecting the Enable Document Footer option. The document footer is an HTML file that IIS will merge in at the bottom of each page it displays. The footer file should *not* be a complete HTML file in and of itself (with <HTML> </HTML> tags, for example). Instead, it should just contain the basic HTML code you want displayed, for example:

```
<h2>This is a footer</h2>
```

This is all that would be necessary for a footer file to display the text shown as a heading type 2.

Directory Security Properties

The next section of the Web site property pages—Directory Security—allows you to control who accesses your Web site based on authentication, client IP addresses, or ACL settings on files, and gives you the ability to secure communications when clients connect to this Web site. The Directory Security property page is shown in Figure 19.16.

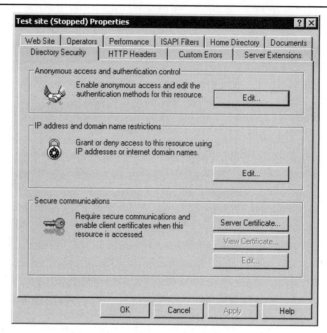

The first method for securing a Web site is to define an authentication method to validate users. Since browsers—by default—will try to access a site anonymously, one option available is to remove anonymous access from your site. Click the Edit button in the Anonymous Access and Authentication Control box to edit the authentication properties of your system. The Authentication Methods dialog box is shown in Figure 19.17.

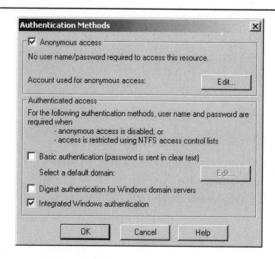

By default, Windows 2000 will allow anonymous access for Web sites and directories, unless you have overridden this option in the global server settings. There are two primary means of securing your Web site—or certain areas of your Web site. The first is to remove the check mark from the Anonymous Access box. This will effectively make your entire site a secured site, and require an authentication before a user is allowed to connect at all, even to the default home page. If you choose this option, then the Authenticated Access area in the lower half of the figure becomes important in determining just *how* clients will authenticate themselves. If you remove anonymous access from your site, you must have *some* authentication option selected, or else you will effectively disable all access to your site.

The options under Authenticated Access control what level of authentication users must negotiate to get connected to your protected site. The details of each type are as follows:

Basic authentication   This is the most basic level of authentication (and therefore, the most widely supported) for validating a user accessing a Web resource. Practically all Web browsers, including Microsoft's and Netscape's, support this type of authentication. Using this authentication method, usernames and passwords are transmitted in clear text and checked against the accounts in the domain of the IIS server (if you would like to use another accounts domain for validation, press the Edit button next to Select a Default Domain). If you expect to be running a public Web site, accessed by users on various platforms and browsers, this is probably the best option for requiring authentication on your site; however, it is the least secure of all the authentication types.

Digest authentication   A feature new to Windows 2000 Server and IIS 5, digest authentication securely transmits a hash value over the Internet instead of a password, thus keeping system passwords confidential. There are a few requirements for using this type of authentication, however. Namely, client workstations must be using Internet Explorer version 5 or later, and user passwords in the Active Directory must also be stored as clear text. This is the most secure of all the authentication types.

Windows authentication   A new name for the Windows NT challenge/response authentication option in previous versions of IIS, Windows authentication requires users to use Internet Explorer for their Web browser. Password hashes are transmitted over the Internet, instead of the actual passwords, so this is a more secure means of authentication. User accounts are again checked against the accounts in the domain of the IIS server. Any version of Internet Explorer after version 2 can support this method of authentication. Windows authentication, like anonymous authentication, is selected by default. This is a good option for secure authentication for Internet Explorer users that haven't migrated to IE 5 or greater yet.

The second method for securing areas of your Web site is to leave anonymous authentication enabled, but to apply security settings to the specific files and directories you want to protect. This will only work on NTFS volumes (you can't define permissions on FAT volumes), and it will allow you to make some areas in your Web site open to the public, while leaving other areas protected.

The method by which this works is really quite simple. When anonymous authentication is enabled, IIS will use the anonymous user account first to try to read a file and pass it back to the user requesting it. For publicly accessible Web content, without any permission settings restricting access, the IIS process should be able to access that content via the anonymous user. However, if IIS fails in accessing that file due to a security restriction, it will look to the authentication options defined previously to determine if it should request an authentication from the user. If an authentication option is set, IIS will prompt the user for a username and password combination, and then IIS will use those credentials when accessing the file. Therefore, if you want to restrict access to specific files or directories to certain users, you must add them to the permissions applied to those files or directories, and exclude access for the anonymous user account. (For more information on placing security rights on files in NTFS, see Chapter 9.)

Another means of securing a Web site is to restrict who can access the site based on an IP address, a range of IP addresses, or a domain name. This requires knowing in advance who should be connecting to your site, and from where, but it is particularly useful when setting up Web sites designed to interface with clients or suppliers. By clicking the Edit button in the IP Address and Domain Name Restrictions area in Figure 19.16, you will see a screen similar to the one in Figure 19.18, in which you can enter any restrictions you'd like.

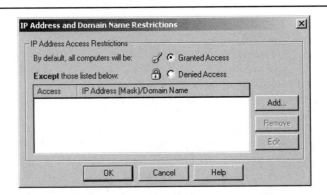

FIGURE 19.18

The IP Address and Domain Name Restrictions dialog box

Select the radio button option to either grant access or deny access to everyone, and then enter the exception list by selecting Add. Individual IP address restrictions are useful for home or traveling users connecting to a Web site, and groups of computers can be defined by entering a network address and subnet mask. Domain name restrictions are useful as a last resort when you don't know the IP addresses of client systems that will be accessing your Web server. Since IIS only knows who is connected to it by an IP number, the server must do a reverse-DNS lookup, which means that the server will have to do quite a bit of processing just to determine if it's okay to let the user in. Unless your situation requires using domain names, it's probably worthwhile to find out the exact IP address ranges to allow into your site and configure them accordingly.

 NOTE Many hosts out on the Internet don't actually have reverse-DNS records assigned to them, and some hosts have incorrect reverse-DNS records assigned to them. Therefore, if you were to put in a restriction based on a host/domain name, it might not work quite as well as you want it to.

IP address restrictions can be combined along with authentication restrictions, allowing for some very secure Web site access. For example, if you have users who frequently work from home—on a computer with a fixed IP address—you could secure your site (or a portion of it) by allowing connections only from specific IP addresses *and* require a secure user authentication before allowing access.

The last option for securing a Web site is to require encrypted communications between the client browser and the server, preventing anyone from intercepting data as it travels across the Internet. This is done with SSL (Secure Sockets Layer) encryption, discussed later in this chapter in the "Communicating Securely with SSL" section.

HTTP Header Properties

The next group of settings you can control for your IIS Web site are what headers the IIS service should include with HTTP pages it transmits. These parameters are adjusted under the HTTP Headers tab, pictured in Figure 19.19.

HTTP headers let you control a number of things that your Web server will transmit to Web browsers along with the HTML pages on your site. The primary things most administrators would want to control are content expiration, content ratings, and MIME file types. However, custom headers can be added as necessary for new HTML standards that haven't been implemented in IIS as of yet.

By checking the Enable Content Expiration box, you can effectively control how browsers will handle their cached pages when communicating with your site. If a user has visited your site before, the pages may still be in the cache of their machine; however, you may only want pages to be valid for a day or two, depending on the type of material being presented. By selecting an expiration option (to expire immediately, expire after a certain number of days, or expire on a set date) you can force browsers to request a new page from your server after the expiration interval has been reached.

FIGURE 19.19

*HTTP header proper-
ties for an IIS Web site*

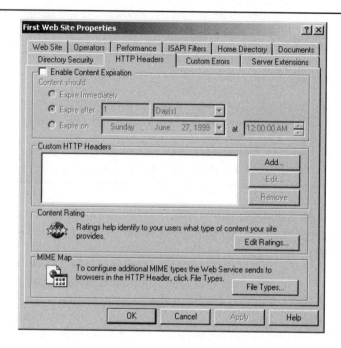

If your Web site will be hosting material that contains content some people might find objectionable, you can enable content ratings for your site or for areas of your site as needed. In the Content Rating area, click the Edit Ratings button to go to the Content Ratings property page. From there, you can learn about the Platform for Internet Content Selection (PICS) system that was developed by the Recreational Software Advisory Council (RSAC) and is used to determine a "rating" for a Web site's content. There is also a questionnaire that you can walk through to determine an appropriate rating for your Web site. Once you have a set of ratings you want to apply to your site, click on the Ratings tab in the Content Ratings property page to begin entering those ratings (see Figure 19.20).

As you can see from the screen, there are four primary categories for rating a Web site—violence, sex, nudity, and language. For each of these categories, there are five levels—0 through 4—that dictate how strongly offensive the content of your site is in each category. For example, level 0 for language is defined as "inoffensive slang," while level 5 is defined as "explicit or crude language." The settings you apply here will have a direct correlation to the content settings available in Internet Explorer or Netscape Navigator, and will effectively block visitors from reaching your site if your content ratings exceed their browser settings. Set your ratings accordingly and enter an e-mail address and an expiration date for your content settings. Once the content ratings are set, IIS will transmit them out with every page on the corresponding Web site or subdirectories of the site.

FIGURE 19.20

Implementing content
ratings

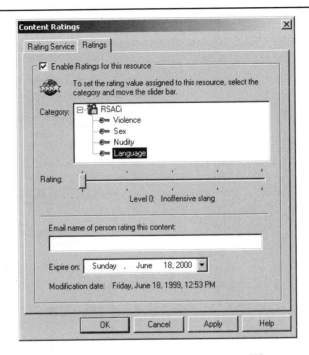

If you have a need to add or remove MIME types on your IIS server, go back to the HTTP Headers tab and click the File Types button in the MIME Map area. Through the File Types dialog box that will come up, you can add additional MIME file types to your system by clicking the New Type button and entering the appropriate associated extension and content type as prompted. The content type should be in the format of *mime type/file name extension*. To remove a MIME file type, highlight the file type in the list of registered file types and then press the Remove button.

If there are custom HTTP headers you would like transmitted to browsers along with each page, you can enter them in the Custom HTTP Headers box by pressing the Add button. One thing custom headers are useful for is for HTML standards that have been developed but have not made their way into IIS as of yet.

Custom Errors Properties

When building your Web server and Web sites, there may be occasions when you want to control how and what is displayed to users who receive an error. For example, you might want to have a custom HTML page displayed when a user reaches a 404 error (page not found). To customize the error messages on your site, click the Custom Errors tab on the Web site properties pages. The page for custom errors is shown in Figure 19.21.

FIGURE 19.21

*Custom error proper-
ties for an IIS Web site*

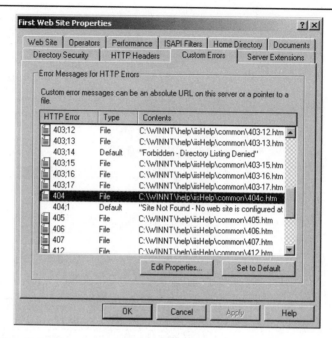

Through this dialog box, you can choose from having a default error message, file,
or URL displayed for any type of HTTP 1.1 error. The HTTP error types (along with their
subtypes) are listed in the left-hand column, the types of response are in the middle column, and the details of those responses are in the right-hand column. In a default
installation of IIS, there will be some messages that will contain default responses (just
one line of text), and other errors that will be defined by HTML files. Windows 2000
stores its default IIS error message files in the %systemroot%\help\iisHelp\common
directory, which you can use as templates to define your own error messages.

To change an error message on your system, find the HTTP error number you want
to change in the list (along with the subtype if necessary) and edit the properties of
that error message. From the Error Mapping Properties dialog box, you can change
the message type and the location of the file or URL to display (if you've chosen that
type of response).

FrontPage Server Extensions

The final tab in the Web site properties pages is for managing server extensions in a
site. If you've created a new site, you probably won't see anything under this tab until
you add server extensions to your site (they aren't installed by default).

Installing FrontPage Server Extensions   To add server extensions to a site, highlight the site in the scope pane of the MMC, and select the Configure Server Extensions option from the All Tasks item in the Action pull-down menu. Or right-click
your site and select the same option, as shown in Figure 19.22.

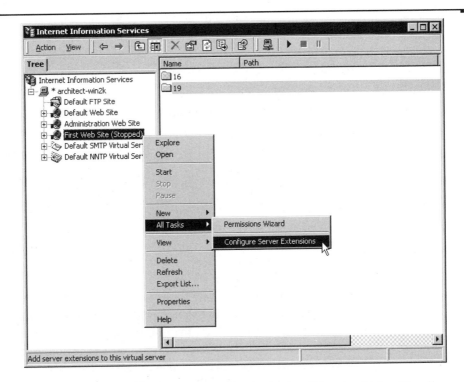

FIGURE 19.22

Adding server extensions to a site

This will launch the Server Extensions Configuration Wizard, which will walk you though the necessary configurations for adding server extensions to this site. The first step of the Server Extensions Configuration Wizard is shown in Figure 19.23.

FIGURE 19.23

Defining groups in the Server Extensions Configuration Wizard

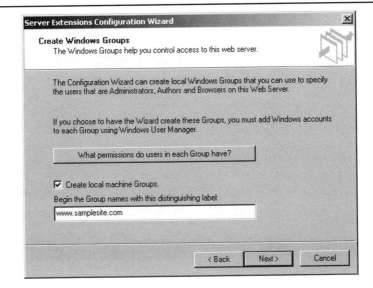

This first step in the wizard is to create special local machine groups on your system specific to the Web site you are configuring. Three groups will be created on your system, as follows:

Browsers   Users defined as browsers can browse content on this server, but can't modify any content.

Authors   Users defined as authors can both browse and modify content on this server.

Administrators   Users defined as administrators can browse and modify content on this server, in addition to being able to create new Webs, change Web settings, and control who has authoring access.

If you will be hosting multiple sites on your system, enter a distinguishing label in the "Begin the Group names with this distinguishing label" field. For example, the Browsers group created using the example shown in Figure 19.23 will end up being named `www.samplesite.com Browsers` in the directory. Click Next to proceed to the next step of the wizard, shown in Figure 19.24.

The second step of the Server Extensions Configuration Wizard allows you to define which group or user account should be the ultimate administrator for this Web server. This group has authority over the Administrators group defined in the previous step of the wizard. By default, the wizard will select the Administrators group; however, you may want to change this to another group or user on your system depending on your environment. Choose an appropriate user or group here and then click Next to move on to the last step of the wizard, shown in Figure 19.25.

FIGURE 19.24

Defining access control in the Server Extensions Configuration Wizard

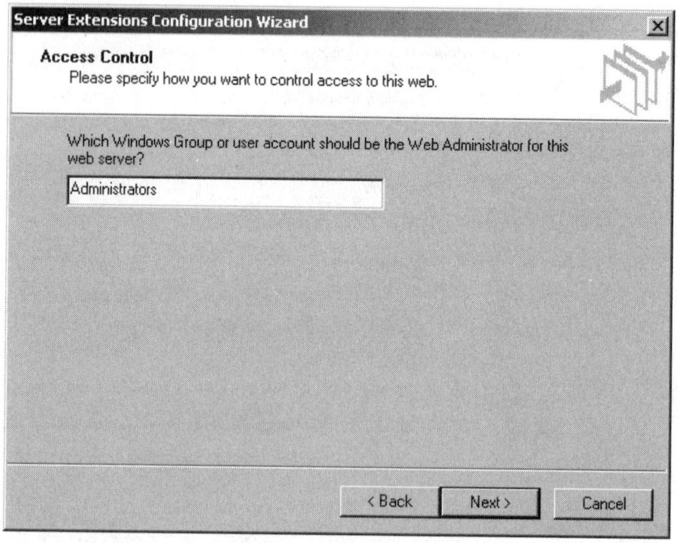

FIGURE 19.25

Defining e-mail
properties in the
Server Extensions
Configuration Wizard

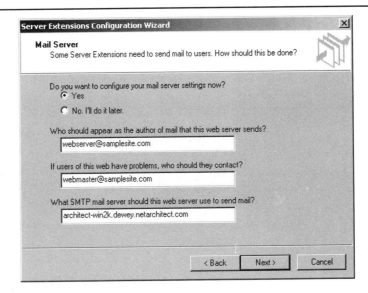

As we discussed earlier in this chapter, some FrontPage server extensions are designed to send e-mail to users. For example, a form on a Web site that collects registration information for a conference or seminar might use FrontPage extensions to have the results of the form e-mailed to a specific address. In order for those extensions to send mail, they must know how to send mail and what server to use to send it. You can configure these options during the wizard or later in the server extensions properties for this Web site. If you don't want FrontPage extensions to send e-mail out from your Web site, leaving these options unconfigured will prevent them from doing so.

If you decide to configure the mail properties, the information required is rather straightforward. In the "Who should appear as the author of mail that this Web server sends?" field, enter an e-mail address that will appear in the From: field of all outgoing messages. If you feel that you might want to collect replies from users, enter a valid e-mail address in this field, otherwise I'd recommend using an e-mail address that doesn't exist. In the "If users of this Web have problems, who should they contact?" field, enter the e-mail address of the Webmaster for this site. Lastly, you will need to enter the host name of an SMTP server that the FrontPage extensions can use in the "What SMTP mail server should this Web server use to send mail" field. You can either enter the name of another system here, or if you've configured the SMTP services in IIS, you can use the full name of your Web server itself (don't use the Web site name unless that is the actual name of your IIS system).

Once you have entered all of this information, click Next to finish the wizard, and the FrontPage extensions will be added to your Web. Your Web server, which might have only had a few files in it before, will now have all of the necessary subdirectories installed to support FrontPage clients.

Configuring FrontPage Server Extensions   When you have installed FrontPage extensions on a site, the Server Extensions properties page for your Web site will finally become active and allow you to modify the properties for the site. The Server Extensions properties page is shown in Figure 19.26.

FIGURE 19.26

Server extensions properties for an IIS Web site

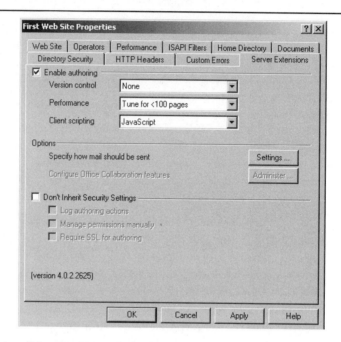

By adjusting the properties on this page, you can control the behavior of the Front-Page server extensions for this site as follows:

Enable Authoring   If you are editing the properties of a root Web, this option will be available. It will allow you to control whether users can author content on the site via FrontPage or not. The Enable Authoring option must be selected to adjust the Version Control, Performance, or Client Scripting settings.

Version Control   To keep track of who's editing Web content on your site, keep tabs on changes, and prevent one author's changes from overwriting another's, you can enable the built-in version control capabilities by selecting Use Built-In from the pull-down box.

Performance   Based on the number of pages you have on your Web site, you can adjust how the server extensions will allocate cache memory for your system. Since cached pages in memory can be returned to users quicker than pages retrieved from disk, you can increase your performance by selecting the appropriate setting here. However, since cache takes additional memory away from other system processes, don't set this value higher than necessary for the number of pages on your site—either less than 100, 100 to 1000, or greater than 1000. If you have more than 1000 pages on your site, select the Use Custom Settings performance option to fine-tune the cache parameters by hand.

Client Scripting   When the FrontPage server extensions automatically generate Web pages for users, they can handle scripts one of two ways—either creating VBScript or JScript. Choose the option that is appropriate for your environment and the users who will be connecting to your Web site.

Specify How Mail Should Be Sent   If you decide to change the mail configuration parameters that you previously specified in the Server Extensions Configuration Wizard—or if you skipped that part of the wizard—press the Settings button for this option to change these options. From there, you can change the Web server's email address (the From: address your mail server will use when sending mail), the contact (usually "Webmaster") address for your site, which SMTP server to use, and the mail encoding and character set to use. The last two options are not configurable through the Server Extensions Configuration Wizard, so if you need to apply custom settings to those parameters, this is the dialog in which to do it.

Don't Inherit Security Settings   Each FrontPage root Web on your IIS server will automatically inherit the global server extension security settings of the Web server by default, as discussed earlier in this chapter. If you need to override those settings for a specific site, select this option and you will be able to manage each item individually for this site. Enabling this option will enable the Log Authoring Actions, Manage Permissions Manually, and Require SSL for Authoring items described below.

Log Authoring Actions   When an author takes action on the system (modifying content, for example), this option will log details of that transaction into the log file, `Author.log`, stored in the `_vti_log` directory of the Web site. The log will contain the name of the author performing the action, the name of the Web the action was performed on, the remote host name, and any operation-specific data.

Manage Permissions Manually   Selecting this option will disable the normal security-changing behaviors of the FrontPage server extension administrative tools (i.e., the MMC interface). When this option is selected, any options within the FrontPage server extension properties that would normally change the security of your site (when modified) will not implement any changes.

Require SSL for Authoring   If you want to require that authors encrypt information as it is transmitted to your Web site, or if you are using basic authentication and want to make sure passwords aren't transmitted over the Internet in clear text, select this option.

Virtual Directories

As Web sites begin to grow, often there is a need to organize levels of content into subdirectories off of the main root of the site. Just like a hard drive on a computer, in time there are often too many files to manage in one directory, so subdirectories become necessary. There are two main ways to do this for a Web site. The first is to actually create a subdirectory in the site's content directory and place content into that directory. For example, let's say you have a site that is stored in C:\Inetpub\wwwroot and is accessed by a URL of www.companyname.com. If you decide you want to move all of your graphics files to a separate subdirectory, you could create a subdirectory called C:\Inetpub\wwwroot\images and then move all of your graphical content into that directory. To access files in that directory, client browsers would access the URL www.companyname.com/images.

However, what if you want to have content available as a subdirectory in your site, but you can't move the content to a normal subdirectory within your site's structure? This is where the concept of Virtual Roots comes into play. Virtual roots are a means of defining a subdirectory off of the root of your site (or even a lower level of your site) and then creating an *alias*, or a pointer to a directory somewhere else on your system or on another computer on your network. By using virtual roots, you are not forced to move all your Web content to one system and then place it in an orderly structure for visiting users. Instead, you can have content stored anywhere on your machine or on any system within your network, and users can access it through a simple directory structure.

For example, consider the diagram shown in Figure 19.27. This is representative of how I actually use virtual roots on one of my Web servers, to bring all my content into one logical structure.

As you can see from the diagram, the root of the Web site content and the two subdirectories are easily accessible from the client browser through the main URL and simple names that exist right off of the root of the URL. These three different directories are actually stored on different machines and different physical hard drives, yet to the browsing user they all seem to be in one logical structure.

I use this layout primarily for two reasons: for protected content and for data for which it is easier to create a virtual root than to move it to my IIS server. All of the publicly accessible content for my Web site is stored on a FAT volume on the same server that is running IIS. Since this content is stored in FAT (and my IIS server allows anonymous connections), anyone can get to this content without any restrictions. However, there is some content on that system that I wanted to have protected by username, so that only certain users could access the content. That data has to be stored on an NTFS volume and in a protected directory (namely, the D:\ipmonitor directory). By creating a virtual root alias and pointing it to that directory, it appears as though it is right off of the root of my Web server, even though it is stored on a separate physical drive.

FIGURE 19.27

Sample use of virtual roots

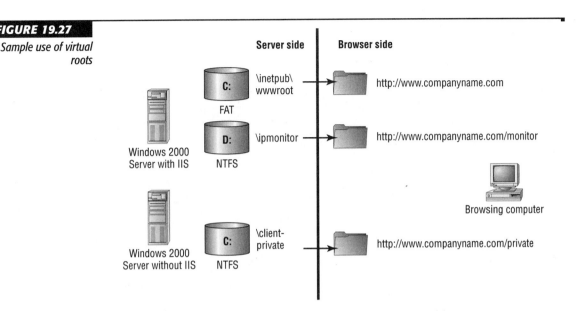

The same is true for client documents and files, which are stored on a completely separate system on my network that isn't running IIS. While I could have loaded IIS on that server and connected it to the Internet, it was easier to simply create a virtual root for that data instead. Now when clients access that directory, the data they receive actually comes from another server inside of my network.

As you can see, virtual roots can be very flexible and make structuring your Web site much easier. Like everything else in Windows 2000, Microsoft has created a wizard for defining virtual roots.

Defining a Virtual Directory

To launch the Virtual Directory Creation Wizard, return to the Internet Information Services MMC and highlight the Web site you want to work with in the scope pane of the window. Select New/Virtual Directory from the Action pull-down menu, and the wizard will start walking you through the configuration process. The first step of the wizard is shown in Figure 19.28.

The first thing you will need to specify for your virtual directory is the alias that refers to it. The alias is the directory name that client browsers will need to use to access the directory. For example, if a user were accessing the URL http://www.companyname.com/documents on your Web server, documents would be the alias. The alias does not need to match the name of the directory where the files are actually coming from, so you can use whatever name works best in this field. Press Next to proceed to the next step of the wizard, shown in Figure 19.29.

FIGURE 19.28

*Defining an alias for a
virtual directory*

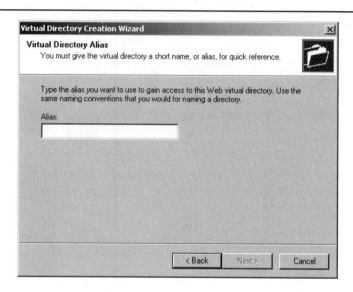

FIGURE 19.28

*Defining an alias for a
virtual directory*

If you want to define a virtual directory that points to another directory on the same computer, enter the path name here (such as D:\documents). IIS will define the virtual directory as pointing to another directory on the same server. However, if you want this virtual directory to point to data located on a share on another server, enter the UNC path to that system here. When you click Next, the Virtual Directory Creation Wizard will take you to another dialog box, shown in Figure 19.30, for entering user credentials.

FIGURE 19.29

*Defining a content
directory for a virtual
directory*

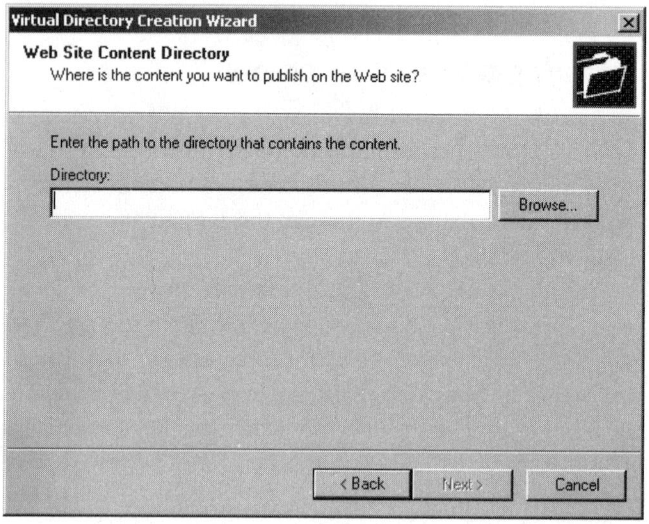

FIGURE 19.30

Entering a username and password to access shared content via a virtual directory

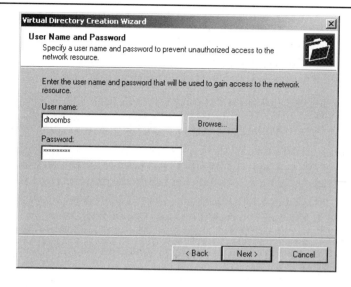

When IIS needs to contact another server for Web content, it will need to do so with a specific username and password combination. Enter an appropriate set of credentials here, one that would have appropriate access rights to the content you are trying to reach. Click Next to move to the last step of the wizard—defining access permissions—shown in Figure 19.31.

FIGURE 19.31

Defining access permissions for a virtual directory

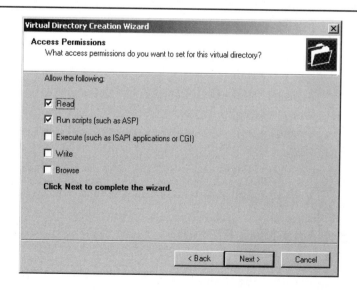

This step in the wizard is identical to the one mentioned earlier in this chapter and shown in Figure 19.8. All the definitions and permissions function the same for a virtual directory as they do for a standard directory, so return to that section for a further definition of these items.

Once you have entered all of the required information, you should have a new virtual directory item listed below your Web site. You can test this to make sure that the virtual directory responds accordingly by launching a browser and then navigating to your virtual directory. If everything has gone according to plan, IIS should return content from the appropriate location.

You can modify properties for a virtual directory in exactly the same manner that you would for a Web site—by editing the property pages for the directory itself. You can edit the following property pages for a virtual directory: Virtual Directory (equivalent to Home Directory for a site), Documents, Directory Security, HTTP Headers, and Custom Errors. These pages are functionally identical to the pages defined earlier in this section for modifying the properties for an entire site.

Setting Up an FTP Site and Configuring FTP Services

Although many file transfers on the Internet today take place via HTTP, FTP is still an important protocol to support if you will be running a public Web site, simply due to its broad range of client support. FTP client software has been developed for almost every computing platform imaginable—including mainframe and midrange systems. Clients who might not be able to retrieve files from your system via HTTP will most likely be able to do so via FTP.

To set up FTP services on Internet Information Server, have the following information ready in advance:

- What IP address you want this FTP server to listen on (or if it should respond on all available IP addresses).

- What TCP/IP port number this FTP server should listen to on the previously specified IP address(es). Typically, this is port 21.

- Whether to allow read access to your FTP site, write access, or both.

- What directory on your system will house your FTP files.

Creating a New FTP Site

As with most everything in Windows 2000 Server, the creation of a new FTP site begins with a wizard—in this case, the FTP Site Creation Wizard. To start the wizard, select your IIS server in the scope pane of the Internet Services Manager MMC. Select the New/FTP Site command from the Action pull-down menu, and the wizard will walk you through the necessary configuration process.

The first step in the wizard, shown in Figure 19.32, will prompt you for a friendly name to use when referencing your FTP site.

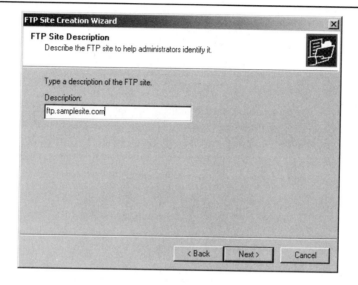

Choose a meaningful name for your site, and click Next to proceed to the next step of the wizard, shown in Figure 19.33.

For users to be able to reach your FTP server, you need to assign an IP address and TCP port number for the service to listen to for incoming connections. By default, the wizard will want to assign your FTP server to listen to TCP port 21 on all available IP addresses on the system. If you have multiple IP addresses assigned to your server (for example, for an internal interface and an external interface), you might want to select the specific address for your system in the IP Address pull-down box. Or if you will be making your FTP site available to the Internet, but don't want to have it readily accessible on the default port of 21, you can assign it to any other port number from 1 to 65535.

 TIP Changing the port number for your FTP site is often a good idea if you will only be using it to publish or receive files for a few selected clients, suppliers, etc. One of my own clients recently had their FTP server discovered (presumably by scanning for devices responding to TCP port 21) and used by hackers as a repository for pirated software.

If the defaults are acceptable, click Next to move on to the next step of the FTP Site Creation Wizard, shown in Figure 19.34.

FIGURE 19.34

Setting the FTP site home directory in the FTP Site Creation Wizard

FTP Site Creation Wizard

FTP Site Home Directory
The home directory is the root of your FTP content subdirectories.

Enter the path to your home directory.

Path:

C:\Inetpub\sample-ftp   Browse...

< Back   Next >   Cancel

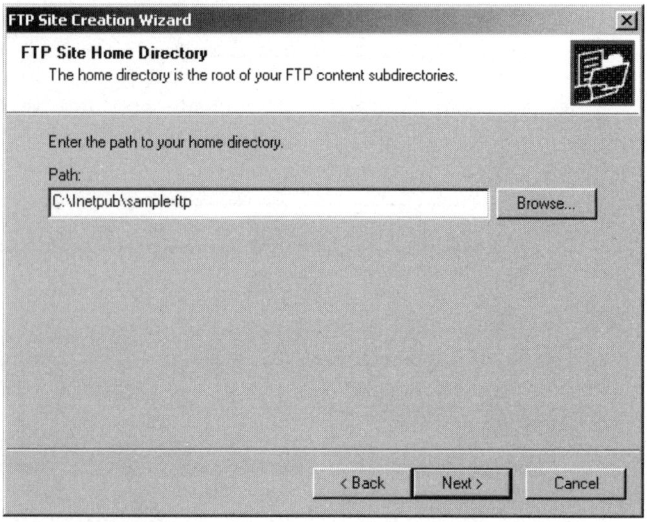

When FTP clients initially connect to your server, they will be placed in the home directory of your system and won't be able to proceed any higher on your system than the home directory. For them, the home directory that you specify will be their "root" directory. Their root directory can either be a directory on your IIS server or a share on another system on the same network. From the root directory, you can create subdirectories below your home directory in order to organize the files available for download or the files you expect to be receiving. Enter the appropriate directory name or UNC path here and press Next to proceed. If you entered a UNC path for your root directory, the next step of the wizard will prompt you for a username and password for IIS to use when accessing that share. Otherwise, if you entered a local path, the next step is the final step of the wizard, shown in Figure 19.35.

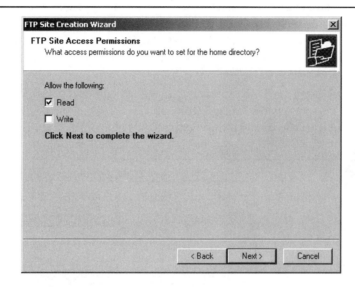

Once you have defined how your site is reachable and what directory on your system should service the site, the last thing IIS needs to know is whether or not to allow read access, write access, or both read and write access to your site. The choices here are rather self-explanatory: if you're using your FTP server simply to provide downloadable files for users or clients, then read access only would be your best choice; if you want to receive files, then select write access; if necessary, you can also select both. Click Next to finish your site, and the FTP Site Creation Wizard will build your site and start it up for you immediately.

Once your site is created, all you need to do is place the content in the home directory that you would like visitors to be able to access. This might be anywhere from a few files to a few thousand files. If you have more than a handful of files, you will probably want to organize them into some logical directory structure to make things easy to find. Whatever the case may be, make the files on your system easy to find and your users will be appreciative.

Also, it is common for FTP sites with more than just a handful of files to put index.txt and/or readme.txt files in directories throughout the site, in order to help users understand what type of content is available in each directory. After all, nobody likes trying to guess what directory names or 8.3 filenames actually mean.

Modifying FTP Site Properties

Although the FTP Site Creation Wizard does an excellent job of configuring a functional FTP site for you, there are some additional parameters that you might want to adjust for your system. For example, you might want to have a logon message displayed to users connecting to your system, or you may want to limit the number of simultaneous users on your system. In any case, to adjust the parameters for your FTP site after the wizard has created it, you will use the FTP site property pages.

FTP Site Properties

To reach the FTP site property pages, highlight your new FTP site in the scope pane of the Internet Services Manager MMC and then select Properties from the Action pull-down menu. This should bring you to a dialog box similar to the one shown in Figure 19.36.

FIGURE 19.36

*Editing FTP site
properties*

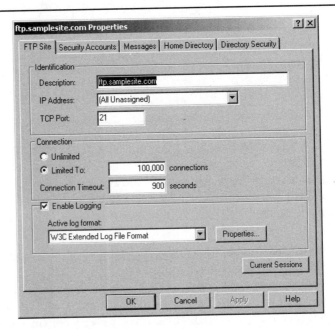

From this page of FTP site properties, you can change a number of parameters about your site, defined as follows:

Identification   This group of controls allows you to change the "friendly name" for your site, the IP address your site listens to, and the TCP port number that it listens to. By default, the IP address for your site to listen to (unless you chose something else in the wizard) will be set to All Unassigned, causing your new site to listen for FTP users on any IP address that isn't already in use by another site on your system. To host multiple FTP sites on your system, assign each site a separate address in this field or adjust the port number.

You can change this port number as a means of securing your site (people won't know to look for an FTP server on port 28,324, for example) or so that you can host multiple FTP sites on the same IP address. You can enter a value from 1–65535 in the TCP Port field. However, once you change the port number, users will need to know which port number to use, since FTP client software will typically default to port 21.

Connection   Depending on the capacity and bandwidth available for your system, you may want to limit the number of simultaneous connections to your server in order to maintain adequate performance. If you are planning on running a large site and handling lots of traffic, the Unlimited option might be the best choice. If you choose to limit the connections, users who attempt to log in after the connection limit has been reached will receive a message (which you enter into the Message Properties page, described later in this section).

A "connection"—as far as IIS is concerned—is not necessarily defined as all activity from a single user. For example, a user connecting to your FTP site through a browser could launch multiple simultaneous downloads from your site. Each download session in that case would be considered a "connection." Therefore, limiting your server to five connections doesn't necessarily guarantee that five users will be able to access your site at any time; one user could take up all five connection spots.

TIP   If you plan on allowing write access to your FTP site, and you know that you'll never have more than a few users connected to your FTP server at a time, you might consider limiting your system to one or two connections. If someone on the Internet were to find your server and start using it as a repository for pirated files or pornography, they'll probably start advertising its accessibility. Limiting connections is a way to at least minimize potential abuse of your system.

To make sure that users don't stay connected to your server indefinitely, enter a time-out value in seconds in the Connection Timeout field. If for some reason an FTP session fails to close its connection appropriately, this will ensure that phantom open connections won't eventually fill up your server.

Enable Logging   One of the best ways to keep track of what's happening on your system is to log the activity. Checking the Enable Logging option (enabled by default) will allow you to log activity on your site in a number of formats: Microsoft IIS Log Format, W3C Extended Log File Format, or via ODBC Logging. Depending on which logging option you choose, clicking the Properties button will yield a specific set of parameters you can adjust for each type of log.

Current Sessions   Although this technically isn't a parameter to be adjusted, there may be times when you need to monitor who is connected to your FTP server and disconnect some or all of the users connected to your site. Clicking the Current Sessions button will take you to the FTP User Sessions dialog box shown in Figure 19.37.

All users connected to your FTP server will be listed in this dialog box, along with their associated IP address and the amount of time they've been connected. Users who are connected to your system anonymously—logging in via the username "anonymous" (more on this subject in the next section)—will have a question mark located in the user icon and will be listed by the e-mail address they supplied to the password prompt from the FTP server. Users who have logged in as an actual Windows 2000 user account will have a normal user icon next to the Active Directory username they're logged in as. To disconnect any users from your system, highlight their record and press the Disconnect button. To disconnect all users from your system (for example, if you're preparing to shut the system down for maintenance) click the Disconnect All button.

FIGURE 19.37

Monitoring current FTP user sessions

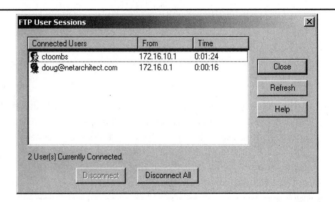

Security Account Properties

On an FTP server, there are generally two types of connection that users typically make: anonymous logins or user logins. Anonymous logins are overwhelmingly common on the Internet, and it is how most publicly accessible FTP servers run.

In an anonymous login, users connect to an FTP server with the username "anonymous" and an e-mail address for a password. No checking is done on this password; it is simply recorded for informational purposes. By configuring a server in this manner, any user can gain access and get files as necessary. If you plan on running a publicly accessible FTP site, it is customary to allow anonymous logins.

The opposite of an anonymous login is a user login, which requires a valid Active Directory username and password combination before logging in. User logins allow you to control user access to a greater level—you can assign security to directories on an FTP server, restricting access to certain directories based on username.

NOTE   FTP passwords are transmitted over the Internet in clear text. If you have users that will be logging into your FTP server with their Active Directory user accounts, their passwords will be in plain view of anyone who might intercept their traffic.

Once you have decided what type of logins you want to allow, you can enforce these settings via the Security Accounts properties page, shown in Figure 19.38.

The upper half of this property page controls what type of logins to allow on your server. If you don't want to allow any anonymous connections at all, uncheck the Allow Anonymous Connections box; this will disable the remaining options on the top half of the property page. Otherwise, when anonymous users connect to your system, they will end up inheriting the security rights of the account defined in the Username field.

FIGURE 19.38

Editing security accounts properties

 NOTE   Disabling anonymous logins will force everyone to connect to your FTP server via a username and a password. Since FTP sessions are transmitted over the Internet in clear text, this could potentially expose user passwords defined on your system to anyone who might be looking for them.

Checking the Allow Only Anonymous Connections check box will effectively restrict any users from accessing your FTP server via a normal user login. This is particularly useful in case any user or administrative passwords within your organization are dis-covered—FTP can not be used as a mean to gain access via those accounts if this option is checked.

Lastly, if you choose to change the account or password for your FTP site, leaving the Allow IIS to Control Password box checked will cause IIS to change the Active Directory password of the specified user as well as store the new password to use for FTP access.

If you need to grant administrative privileges to users for managing any FTP sites on your system, add those usernames to the list of operators by pressing the Add but-ton and then selecting users from the directory. Users that you want to make FTP site operators must *also* be members of the Administrators group.

 TIP By default, most Web browsers will attempt to do an anonymous login when con-necting to an FTP site. To override this behavior, you can place the username and pass-word the browser should use in the URL string. The correct URL format for a user login via a browser is `ftp://username:password@sitename.com`.

Message Properties

Although the FTP client interface is often cold and impersonal, you can add your own messages to your FTP server. Whether you need to inform users about new files that were recently added, tell them what site they are connected to, display a legal warn-ing message, or just send a friendly message, you can do this through the Messages page, shown in Figure 19.39.

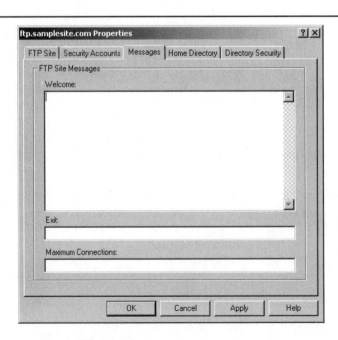

The messages properties are rather self-explanatory. The Welcome message is displayed to users when they first connect to your FTP site, and, if they are using a browser to access your server, on each subdirectory screen below the root. If your server has reached the maximum number of allowable connections (set in the FTP site properties discussed earlier in this section), then the Maximum Connections message will be sent to the user and their session will immediately be disconnected.

Speaking of disconnection, if a user (using something *other than* a browser for FTP access) disconnects properly from your FTP server, they will see the message you have defined in the Exit field. Browsers don't typically display exit messages, so if you have something important to pass along to users, it's better to put it in the welcome message than the exit message.

Home Directory Properties

If you read through the previous section on setting up Web sites, the property page for Home Directory (shown in Figure 19.40) should look somewhat familiar to you. Although some of the settings and options are different for FTP sites, the general concept is the same.

FIGURE 19.40

Editing home directory properties

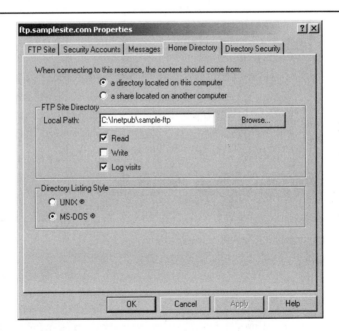

This group of settings lets you control where IIS will look for FTP files and what security permissions to use for this location:

Content location   By selecting the appropriate radio button on the top of this property page, you can control where IIS will go to look for the content for this site, or if it will send users to another Web site. Based on the selection you make, the path information box below the radio button options will change. If you select the option for a directory located on this computer, you will need to enter the local path in the lower portion of the property page.

If you select the option for a share located on another computer, the Local Path field will change to a Network Directory field, where you will need to enter the correct *servername**sharename* UNC path. When you choose to use a share located on another computer for your files, you might need to enter login credentials for the IIS service to use when it is accessing the other system. The IIS service will actually log into the other system, retrieve the files, and present them to the user just as if the files were local. This allows you to build a distributed FTP site throughout your organization, even though all the files are presented to the user just as if they were all on one machine.

Security settings   Regardless of the location you choose for your content, you can control whether users are allowed read and/or write access to your files as needed. The FTP service will apply these settings for how it handles the directory overall, and these settings can be complemented by additional security permissions applied to files and directories on files stored on an NTFS partition.

Log visits   Depending on whether or not you want logging information stored about visitors to your site, check or uncheck this box. Logs will be stored in the format defined in the FTP site properties dialog box, covered earlier in this section.

Directory listing style   This setting will control how IIS will return directory-listing information to users in response to the dir command from an FTP client—in either an MS-DOS-style listing or a Unix-style listing. This setting has no bearing on how IIS will return information in response to the ls command from an FTP client.

Directory Security Properties

The last section of the FTP site property pages—Directory Security—allows you to control who accesses your Web site based on client IP addresses. The Directory Security property page is shown in Figure 19.41.

Through this page, you can secure your FTP site somewhat by restricting who can access the site based on an IP address or a range of IP addresses. This requires knowing in advance who should be connecting to your site, and from where, but it is particularly useful when setting up FTP sites designed to interface with business partners. Select the appropriate radio button to allow access from all IP addresses by default (Granted Access) or to restrict access from all IP addresses by default (Denied Access). Create exceptions to this rule by pressing the Add button and adding an IP address or a range of IP addresses (by using a network mask). IIS will enforce these restrictions with all visitors to your site.

FIGURE 19.41

*Editing directory
security properties*

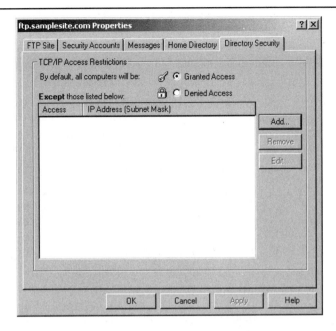

As with IP address restrictions for Web sites, you can set up some highly secure FTP sites by restricting access based on IP address, and then requiring authentication (i.e., denying anonymous connections) to access your site.

Virtual FTP Directories

If your FTP site begins to grow over time, you might find that you will need to add additional resources to your system as subdirectories off of the main root of the site. Just like a hard drive on a computer, in time there are often too many files to manage in one directory, so subdirectories become necessary. There are two main ways to do this for an FTP site. The first is to actually create a subdirectory in the site's content directory and place content into that directory. For example, let's say you have a site that is stored in C:\Inetpub\ftproot and is accessed on an FTP server at ftp.companyname.com. If you decide you want to move all of your executable files to a separate subdirectory, you could create a subdirectory called C:\Inetpub\FTProot\bin and then move all of your executable content into that directory. To access files in that directory, FTP clients would access the ftp.companyname.com/bin directory.

However, what if you want to have content available as a subdirectory in your site, but you can't move the content to a normal subdirectory within your site's structure? This is where the concept of virtual directories comes into play. Virtual directories are a means of defining a subdirectory off of the root of your site (or even a lower level of your site) and then creating an *alias*, or a pointer to a directory somewhere else on your system or on another computer on your network. By using virtual directories, you are not forced to move all your FTP content to one system and then place it in an orderly structure for visiting users. Instead, you can have content stored anywhere on your machine or on any system within your network, and users can access it through a simple directory structure.

Virtual directories can also be used to grant different security permissions to the same set of files, based on which directory the user is in. For example, you might have an alias called "source" which points to a directory called C:\source on your local system. The alias is defined only with read access. You could add a second alias to your system, called "source-RW" for example, which could point to the exact same directory on your system but allow full read/write access.

Defining a Virtual Directory

To launch the Virtual Directory Creation Wizard, return to the Internet Information Services MMC and highlight the FTP site you want to work with in the scope pane of the window. Select New/Virtual Directory from the Action pull-down menu and the wizard will start walking you through the configuration process. The first step of the wizard is shown in Figure 19.42.

FIGURE 19.42

Defining an alias for a virtual directory

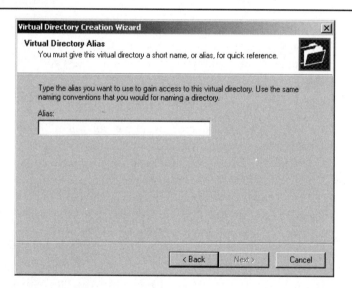

The first thing you will need to specify for your virtual directory is the alias that refers to it. The alias is the directory name that FTP clients will use to access the directory. For example, if you want to have a directory called "patches" available off the root of your site when users first connect, then "patches" would need to be the alias. The alias does not need to match the name of the directory from where the files are actually coming, so you can use whatever name works best in this field. Click Next to proceed to the next step of the wizard, shown in Figure 19.43.

If you want to define a virtual directory that points to another directory on the same computer, enter the path name here (such as D:\patches). IIS will define the virtual directory as pointing to another directory on the same server. However, if you want this virtual directory to point to data located on a share on another server, enter the UNC path to that system here. When you click Next, the Virtual Directory Creation Wizard will take you to another dialog box for entering user credentials, shown in Figure 19.44. Otherwise, you will skip ahead to the dialog box shown in Figure 19.45.

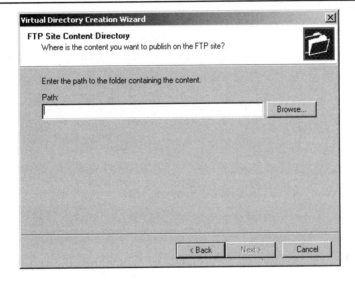

FIGURE 19.43

Defining a content directory for a virtual directory

FIGURE 19.44

Entering a username and password to access shared content via a virtual directory

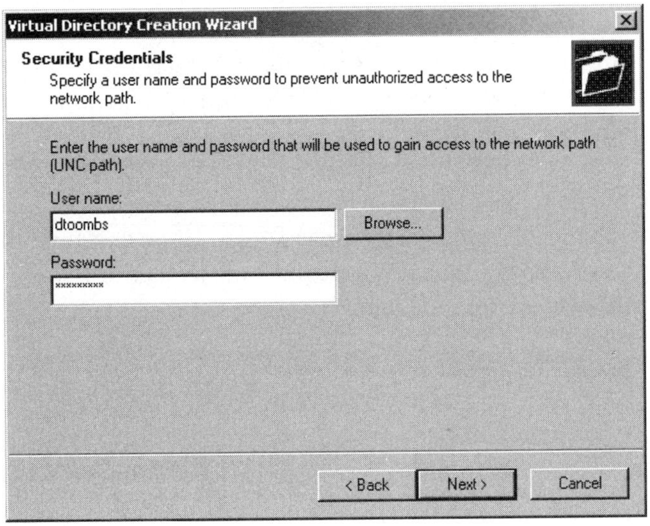

When IIS needs to contact another server for FTP files, it will have to do so with a specific username and password combination. Enter an appropriate set of credentials here, one that would have appropriate access rights to the content you are trying to reach. Click Next to move to the last step of the wizard—defining access permissions—shown in Figure 19.45.

FIGURE 19.45

Defining access permissions for a virtual directory

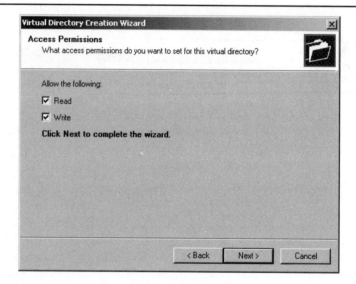

This step in the wizard is identical to the one in the FTP Site Creation Wizard mentioned earlier and shown in Figure 19.35. Define whether you want to allow read or write access to your system, or both, and check the appropriate boxes.

Once you have entered all of the required information, you should have a new virtual directory item listed below your FTP site. You can test this to make sure that the virtual directory responds appropriately by launching an FTP client and then navigating to your virtual directory. If everything has gone according to plan, IIS should return content from the appropriate location.

You can modify properties for a virtual directory in exactly the same manner that you do for an FTP site—by editing the property pages for the directory itself. You can edit the following property pages for a virtual directory: Virtual Directory and Directory Security. These pages are functionally identical to the pages, defined earlier in this section, for modifying the properties for an entire FTP site.

Setting Up an NNTP News Server and Configuring NNTP Services

Newsgroups are one of the Internet's older technologies, but they're not as well known as some of the Internet's more visible counterparts—namely Web browsing and e-mail. Newsgroups are a way of collecting and threading messages posted by users together to form a sort of "conversation" database between the participants of a newsgroup.

These conversation databases can be used to discuss almost anything you can think of—questions about company benefits, organizational news releases, politics, society, technology, etc. This concept was once referred to as *collaboration* or *groupware*, in which companies within an organization could collaborate and share ideas electronically on a set of "bulletin boards" focusing on a specific topic. While some organizations have been able to implement this and make their organizations more productive, this capability still hasn't caught on as much as it should have.

The Internet is filled with literally tens of thousands of these groups, covering every imaginable topic under the sun. You name it, and there has probably been a newsgroup defined somewhere to discuss it. Thanks to IIS 5, you can easily set up and administer your own NNTP server for internal users to read, post, and reply to messages related to topics important for your organization. To get started with setting up a newsgroup server, you'll need to know the following:

- What IP address you want this NNTP server to listen on (or if it should respond on all available IP addresses).
- What TCP/IP port number this NNTP server should listen to on the previously specified IP address(es). Typically, this is port 119.
- Whether to allow anonymous access to your site or to require user authentication.
- What directories your system will use to store and manage your NNTP database files.

Creating a New NNTP Server

Even though IIS installs and configures a default newsgroup server when you set it up, you might need to have another server on your system. For example, you might need to have a public newsgroup server available to anyone on the Internet, and then a private newsgroup server available to internal staff. To start installing your server, begin by making sure that you have all of the bullet items listed above ready, and then select your IIS server in the Internet Services Manager MMC. Selecting the New/NNTP Virtual Server option from the Action pull-down menu will launch the New NNTP Virtual Server Wizard. The first step of the New NNTP Virtual Server Wizard is shown in Figure 19.46.

FIGURE 19.46

Defining a friendly name for an NNTP virtual server

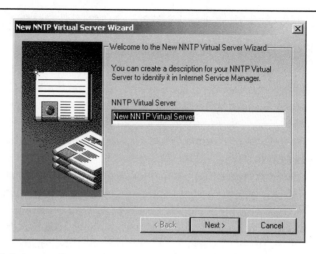

This step of the wizard wants you to specify a friendly name to use when referencing your new NNTP virtual server. This name is simply for administration purposes; your users won't see it, so choose a name that's appropriate and then click Next to proceed to the next step of the wizard, shown in Figure 19.47.

In order to access your NNTP server, users will need to establish a TCP/IP connection to your server on a specific IP address and TCP port number. By default, NNTP servers typically communicate on port number 119. Unless you have special circumstances, you will probably want to use this as the default port number for your system.

If you are going to be running only one newsgroup server on your system, these settings might be just fine, depending on the content on your newsgroups and the configuration of your system. For example, if you were going to run an internal confidential database for the discussion of sales and marketing strategies, you probably wouldn't want to make that database available on a publicly accessible IP address. Users from the outside world could potentially connect to your system and read all of your confidential information stored in the newsgroup, so make sure you correctly determine which IP address(es) to use for your site.

Newsgroup readers—by default—will look on port 119 for a newsgroup server, so enter **119** here in the port field. If you would prefer to change the TCP port that your server responds on (necessary if you only have one IP address and you want to run multiple newsgroup servers), you can do so here. Keep in mind that all the clients connecting to this system will probably have to manually change their configurations accordingly.

Click Next when you've completed the IP configuration, and you'll move to the next step of the wizard, shown in Figure 19.48.

FIGURE 19.47

Defining IP addresses and TCP ports for an NNTP virtual server

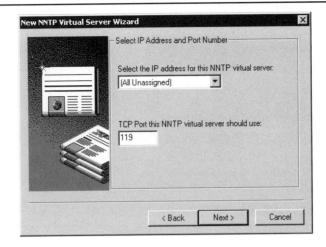

FIGURE 19.48

Defining directories and anonymous access control for an NNTP virtual server

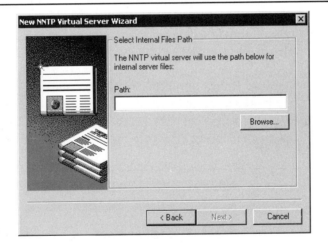

IIS requires two separate directories on your system to maintain an NNTP virtual server: one in which to store internal files for its own processing, and one to store the actual newsgroup content. In this first screen, you need to supply the directory that IIS should use for its own internal files. When you've entered this, click Next to continue to the next step, shown in Figure 19.49.

FIGURE 19.49

Defining a storage area for NNTP content files

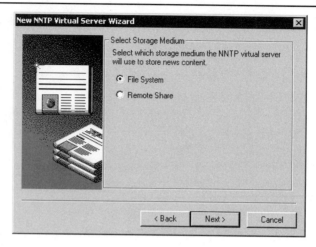

In this step of the wizard, you will be defining a "storage medium" for IIS to use when storing news content. This storage medium can be either on the IIS server itself or on another server. If you will be storing the news content directly on your IIS server, select the radio button for File System and then press Next to proceed to the next step of the New NNTP Virtual Server Wizard, shown in Figure 19.50.

If you decide to store news content on another system, select the radio button for Remote Share. Doing so will change the next step of the wizard to prompt you for a share name and username/password combination to use to access the news content stored on another system. For the sake of brevity, we'll assume you chose the File System option and proceed directly to the next step of the wizard.

FIGURE 19.50

Defining a path to store newsgroup messages

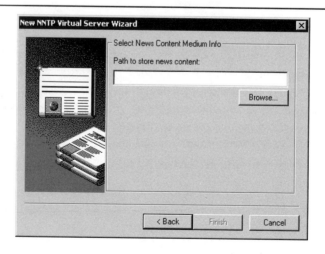

NOTE IIS will require approximately 548 bytes of storage in its internal working directory for each newsgroup message that will be stored on your system, in addition to the space required for the articles themselves.

Click Finish after this step, and you will have a functional NNTP virtual server running on your IIS server.

Modifying NNTP Virtual Server Properties

Since the New NNTP Virtual Server Wizard only has a few steps to it, there are a number of settings and parameters that you will probably need to set for your site. For example, you might want define newsgroup names, control security, limit the size of postings, etc. To adjust the parameters for your NNTP site after the wizard has created it, you will use the NNTP virtual server property pages.

General Properties

To reach the NNTP virtual server property pages, highlight your new NNTP virtual server in the scope pane of the Internet Services Manager MMC and then select Properties from the Action pull-down menu. This should bring you to a dialog box similar to the one shown in Figure 19.51.

Through this page, you can change the following items to fit your needs:

Name To modify the friendly name for your site, enter the information here. This information is only used for administrative purposes in the MMC interface; users will not end up seeing it.

IP Address Enter the IP address for your site to use here. If you intend to have multiple IP addresses servicing the same site or you want to change the ports this site uses, click the Advanced button.

Advanced...TCP Port and SSL Port By default, NNTP sites typically use TCP port number 119 for standard connections and port 563 for secure connections. Changing these values will usually require changing the configuration of newsreader software on client computers as well.

Connection... Depending on the capacity of your server and the other jobs it's responsible for, you might want to limit the number of connections you allow into your NNTP server. By default, IIS sets this value at 1,000, with a time-out value of 10 minutes (600 seconds), if you choose to enable it.

Enable Logging   If you are running an anonymous NNTP server, you might want to enable logging for your system in case you ever need to trace where a specific posting came from.

Path Header   Path headers refer to a string that is used for the "path" line in each newsgroup posting. Path lines are used to determine how a newsgroup posting will reach its destination. For more information on path lines and having newsgroup servers pass messages to each other, see RFC 1036.

Configuring general settings for an NNTP virtual server

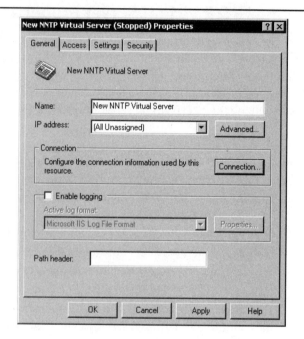

NNTP Settings

For settings specific to newsgroups and postings themselves, go to the Settings property page, shown in Figure 19.52.

FIGURE 19.52

*Configuring NNTP
Settings for an
NNTP virtual server*

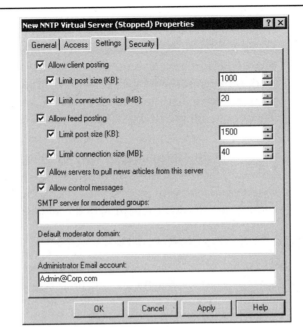

From this page, you can edit the following options:

Allow Client Posting   To disallow client posting on this system, uncheck this box. Obviously, on most systems, you will want to leave this checked.

Limit Post Size   For publicly accessible NNTP servers, you might find a need to limit the size of any one message that can be sent to your system. Otherwise, individuals might overload your system by loading huge binary files to your system, quickly filling up all the available disk space on your server. Enter a reasonable limit here, or leave the default of 1 megabyte (1000 kilobytes).

Limit Connection Size   Much like the Limit Post Size setting mentioned above, another way that individuals could potentially overload your system is by flooding it with numerous smaller messages that fit within the Limit Post Size restriction. In order to compensate for this, you can set a maximum limit, in megabytes, that an NNTP user can post during a single session to your server.

Allow Servers to Pull News Articles from This Server   If other downstream newsgroup servers will connect to your site and download a feed of messages, leave this box checked.

Allow Control Messages   Control messages are specially formatted newsgroup messages designed to control the configuration of an NNTP server; for example, to create a new newsgroup across a collection of NNTP servers, a control message can be sent out instructing all servers to create the new group. Or a control message might instruct all other participating news servers to cancel (delete) a specific message from all systems.

SMTP Server for Moderated Groups   Moderated groups (discussed a bit later in this section) are newsgroups that have their postings approved by a moderator before they are publicly posted. This is done via e-mail, so the NNTP process needs to have an accessible SMTP server to use for sending messages. If you will be configuring the SMTP service on your IIS server (discussed later in this chapter), you can use your own system as the SMTP server.

Default Moderator Domain   When moderation e-mail messages are sent from your IIS system, they will be sent with a To: address of *newsgroup name@default moderator domain* unless a specific moderator is specified for a group. Enter the domain portion of the address to use in this field.

Security Account Properties

In order to define operator permissions for specific user accounts on your NNTP server, click the Security tab to get to the Security property page (shown in Figure 19.53). Here, you can define operators capable of accessing and making configuration changes to a virtual NNTP server.

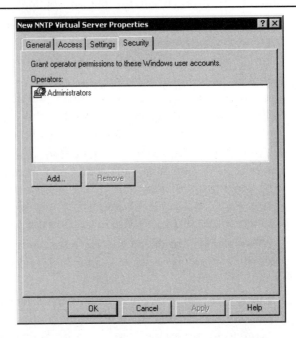

Add the Windows user accounts that should have operator privileges to this window by pressing the Add button and selecting the appropriate accounts.

Access Properties

Through the Access property page, you can make changes to how your NNTP server is to be accessed. For example, you can allow for "anonymous" access (this is typically enabled by default), which means that any user that can successfully connect to the IP address of your NT server can access the newsgroups contained on it. Or you can require authenticated access. You can also define SSL encryption certificates (discussed later in this chapter) to use when communicating with your server, and grant or deny connections based on IP addresses. The Access property page is shown in Figure 19.54.

FIGURE 19.54

Editing access properties

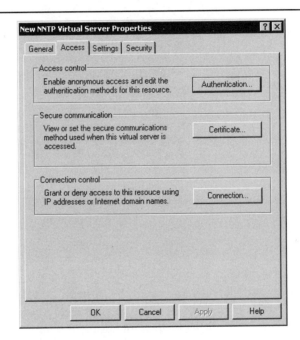

Access Control   Clicking theAuthentication button in the Access Control area will take you to another dialog box, shown in Figure 19.55, for editing what type of authentication users should use when connecting to your system.

By default, IIS will select all three authentication options for you—Allow Anonymous, Basic Authentication, and Windows Security Package. Anonymous access is rather straightforward; no username or password is required to connect, and all requests for content will be directed through the anonymous account defined on the Security Accounts property page.

Basic authentication utilizes an authentication protocol built into NNTP called AUTHINFO. This protocol negotiates a username and password authentication over the Internet in clear text. This authentication method will have the widest means of support, but at the risk of transmitting passwords from your system in plain view of anyone who might be looking for them.

"Windows security package" authentication is another way of saying Windows challenge/response authentication. This typically limits client support to Windows platforms only, but it provides for a secure means of authenticating users without passing clear-text passwords over the internet.

FIGURE 19.55

Editing authentication methods

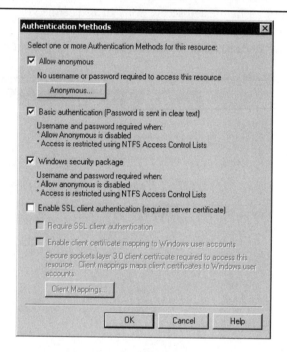

If you would prefer to encrypt the authentication process between the client and your NNTP server, you can select the Enable SSL Client Authentication check box. This will allow your server to authenticate the client connecting to it in order to set up a secure, encrypted SSL tunnel. However, the client connecting to your server must have an SSL certificate installed for this to work. If you've enabled SSL client authentication, you can require this type of authentication for all users by checking the Require SSL Client Authentication check box. Based on the certificates that your users have installed, you can have those certificates map directly to a Windows user account by checking the Enable Client Certificate Mapping to Windows User Accounts box and then entering appropriate mappings by clicking the Client Mappings button. Doing this will basically tell IIS, "If someone hands you this certificate, assume that it is Windows user XYZ." The end user does not need to actually provide a username and password; simply having the certificate is enough identification.

Connection Control   Another means of securing your NNTP server is to restrict who can access the site based on IP address, a range of IP addresses, or a domain name. This requires knowing in advance who should be connecting to your site, and from where. By clicking the Edit button in the IP Address and Domain Name Restrictions area, you will see a screen similar to the one back in Figure 19.18, in which you can enter any restrictions you'd like.

Secure Communication   If you would like to protect your NNTP data as it travels from your server to the client (and vice versa), you can set up SSL communications properties through the Secure Communications area. This requires having an SSL certificate installed on your system, and is discussed in greater detail in the "Communicating Securely with SSL" section later in this chapter.

Directory Properties

Since all newsgroup content must be stored in files, you will need to define where those files are to be stored. Initially, you did that in the wizard when you provided the system with directories to use for the NNTP content. However, since the wizard assumes several "defaults" for you, you might want to edit the directory properties yourself.

To edit the directory properties, go back to the Internet Information Services MMC and expand the NNTP server item that you created. Select the item for Virtual Directories in the scope pane, and you should see the directories you originally specified in the results pane. Highlight the appropriate directory to modify, and then either select Action/Properties from the pull-down menu or right-click the directory and select Properties. An example is shown in Figure 19.56.

FIGURE 19.56

Editing directory properties

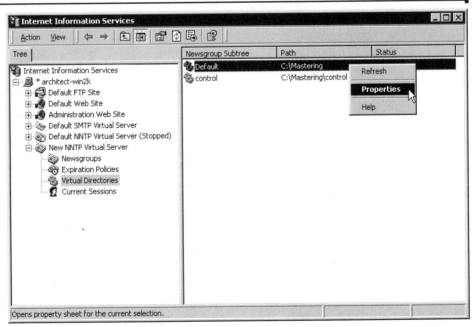

Once you have selected a directory to edit, you should set a property page similar to the one shown in Figure 19.57.

FIGURE 19.57

*Directory
property page*

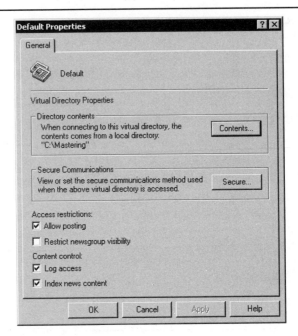

You can store content in a directory on the IIS server itself or on a share on another server by pressing the Contents button in the Directory Contents portion of this property page. If you decide to use a network share for storing your content, you will need to define an account that IIS uses to connect to the share.

Based on the newsgroups stored in this directory, you can control some specific parameters:

Allow Posting   To disallow posting to newsgroups—that is, to the newsgroups stored in this directory—uncheck this box.

Restrict Newsgroup Visibility   If you will be using access controls on your system to define who can access which newsgroups, you can control what newsgroups those users will even see by selecting this option. Choosing this option can add a significant amount of processing overhead to your system if you have a large number of groups, so you might want to leave this option disabled.

Log Access   This setting works in conjunction with the Enable Logging check box on the General property page for the NNTP site. If you want to log access to your system, you must have both check boxes checked. This allows you to log access to some directories as needed, without necessarily logging all access to all directories.

Index News Content Checking this box will instruct the Microsoft Indexing Service to index the content of this site, allowing users to search for text in postings.

Lastly, the Secure Communications section of this property page is used to require SSL communication sessions for newsgroups stored in this directory. SSL is discussed in greater detail later in this chapter in the "Communicating Securely with SSL" section.

Defining Groups

Messages on an NNTP server are typically stored in different hierarchical groups based on their content. Levels of hierarchy are delineated by a dot between each word. For example, on the Internet, common newsgroup names such as `rec.pets.dogs` (for dog lovers) are part of the overall recreation hierarchy (`rec`), then the pets hierarchy. This type of organization gives users an easy way to find the information they are looking for. Additional groups could include `rec.pets.cats` and `rec.pets.ferrets`, thus keeping the messages for each topic isolated from other messages.

Within your organization, you can also use a similar structure for newsgroups. For example, you might choose to define groups along divisional, departmental, and then topical lines. For example, a group called `accounting.payroll.withholding` could be used to handle discussion messages and questions from employees regarding their withholding from their paychecks, whereas `sales.advertising.radio` could be used to discuss the effectiveness of radio advertisements and to brainstorm for new topics.

For each level of hierarchy in the name of the newsgroup, IIS will create a separate directory in the content directory defined for your site (discussed earlier in this chapter). For example, if you create a group called `accounting.payroll.withholding`, IIS will create three subdirectories in your content directory. The first subdirectory will be called `accounting`. Within the `accounting` subdirectory, there will be another subdirectory called `payroll`, and within the `payroll` directory, there will be another subdirectory called `withholding`. If these directories are created on an NTFS volume, you can control which users can access which groups (assuming you've required authenticated access) by applying appropriate permissions to each directory. Therefore, you can restrict confidential information to only the individuals who should receive it and leave everything else open to the public.

As you can see, there are many possible uses for newsgroups. Since the default configuration of a newsgroup server doesn't typically include any groups (other than control groups, if needed), you will most likely want to add some groups to your system.

You define newsgroups from the main Internet Information Services MMC screen by expanding your NNTP server item in the scope pane, and then highlighting the Newsgroups option below it. Once you have the Newsgroups item highlighted, you can select the New/Newsgroup option either from the Action pull-down menu or by right-clicking the Newsgroups option, as shown in Figure 19.58.

FIGURE 19.58

Setting up new
newsgroups

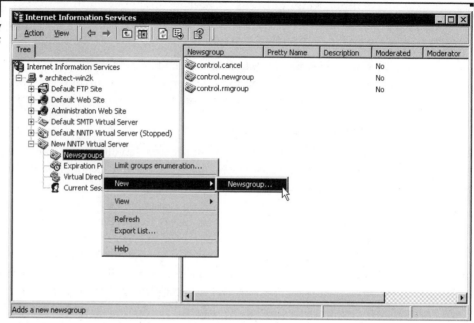

Selecting New/Newsgroup launches the New Newsgroup Wizard, which will walk
you through the process to define a new newsgroup. The first step of the wizard,
shown in Figure 19.59, will prompt you for an appropriate name for your newsgroup.
As previously discussed, enter the name for your desired newsgroup here and then
press Next to proceed to the next step of the wizard, shown in Figure 19.60.

FIGURE 19.59

Defining a new
newsgroup name

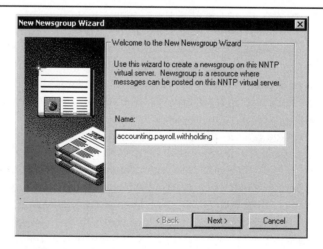

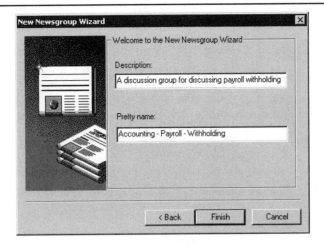

To enter descriptive information about this group above and beyond the information that the name of the group gives, use the Description field. You can also enter a "pretty name" for this newsgroup that will be returned to NNTP clients that issue a LIST PRETTYNAMES command.

Once you have entered this information, click the Finish button and your new newsgroup will be created. However, as is true with most of the wizards in Windows 2000, a few assumptions are made for this group and automatically saved as defaults. If you would like to change the properties of the group you've just created, highlight it in the results pane of the MMC and then select the Properties option either from the Action pull-down menu or by right-clicking the group. That should bring you to a group properties page similar to the one shown in Figure 19.61.

In this screen, you can edit the properties you just defined for this group, plus enable some additional options, as defined below:

Read Only If only the moderator should be allowed to post to this group, check this box. No other users will be allowed to make postings to this group.

Moderated The default setting for new newsgroups is to leave them unmoderated—meaning that all postings are publicly available immediately; there is no "checking" process that occurs. If you prefer to have a moderator manage the messages on your system, click the Moderated option. Enter an appropriate e-mail address for the moderator in the Moderator field, or press the Set Default button if you prefer to use the moderator defined in the NNTP settings (discussed earlier in this section). Newsgroup messages will be e-mailed to the operator for approval before being published.

FIGURE 19.61

*Editing group
properties*

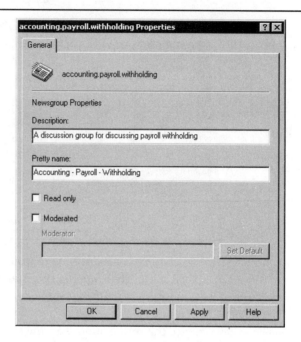

Defining NNTP Server Expiration Policies

In a perfect world, disk space would be amazingly dirt cheap, and installing terabytes worth of storage would simply be a Plug-and-Play operation. This would allow you to keep all news articles posted on your server forever and ever (amen).

Welcome to reality. If you're running an NNTP server that will be handling a fair amount of traffic, it will eventually consume all available disk space on your system, unless you expire old articles. To add an expiration policy to your system, select your NNTP server in the scope pane of the Internet Services Manager MMC and expand it. Select Expiration Policies, then select New/Expiration Policy from the Action pull-down menu.

This will start you through a wizard in which you define which newsgroups to expire and when. The first step of the wizard will prompt you for a friendly name for your expiration policy. Enter whatever you feel is appropriate in this box and then press Next to move on to the next step of the wizard, shown in Figure 19.62.

If you want to have IIS simply expire all newsgroup articles on your system after a set number of hours or days, select the radio button for All Newsgroups on This Virtual Server. Otherwise, if you want to have custom expiration policies for certain groups (for example, you might want some groups to never expire), select the button for Only Selected Newsgroups on this Virtual Server. If you choose the second option, when you click Next, you will be taken to a dialog box to enter the groups you want the policy to apply to. Enter the appropriate groups and then click Next to proceed to the last step of the wizard, shown in Figure 19.63.

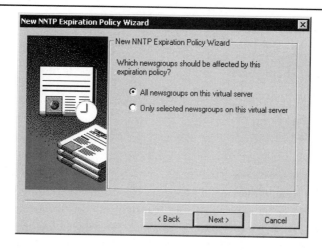

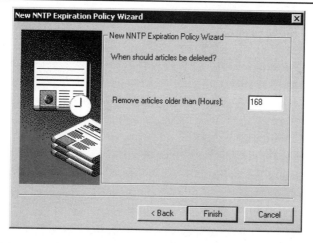

This step of the wizard is quite straightforward: enter the number of hours that IIS should wait before purging a newsgroup article. The default you will find here is 168 hours—or 7 days. If you have a low-traffic site and want to keep articles around longer, then increase this value accordingly.

Press Finish when you are done, and you should see your new expiration policy appear in the MMC as a sub-item under your NNTP server. To go back and make changes to the policy, simply edit the properties for the policy item.

Virtual NNTP Server Directories

Virtual NNTP server directories have a bit of a different function than virtual directories defined for Web and FTP sites. On Web and FTP sites, users can navigate through different directories on your system, but on a newsgroup server the only thing users can navigate to are newsgroups. So what's an NNTP virtual directory designed to do?

NNTP virtual directories are designed primarily as a means to spread newsgroup content out across systems. Content is spread across systems based on hierarchy names. For example, you might have the content for the entire accounting.* hierarchy stored on one server and have the content for the sales.* hierarchy stored on another server.

The primary benefits of doing this are increased speed and performance (you don't have one server doing all the work), and if you suddenly run out of disk space on one system, you can start spreading the content around. To create an NNTP virtual directory, begin by selecting your NNTP virtual server in the scope pane of the Internet Services Manager MMC and highlighting the Virtual Directories option below it. Select the New/Virtual Directory option from the Action pull-down menu to launch the New Virtual Directory Wizard, shown in Figure 19.64.

FIGURE 19.64

Defining a subtree for an NNTP server virtual directory

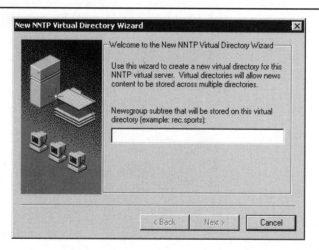

To carve off an entire section of your hierarchy structure and store it in a virtual directory, enter the left-most portion of the group name you want to store. For example, if you entered rec.pets in this field, you would end up storing the groups rec.pets.dogs, rec.pets.cats, and rec.pets.ferrets in this virtual directory, but rec.games.chess would still be stored in the primary directory defined for this NNTP server. Enter the appropriate hierarchy name and then press Next to proceed to the next step of the wizard.

The next step of the wizard will ask you for a "storage medium" for this content—this is exactly the same as what you saw back in Figure 19.49. The wizard will also prompt you for either a directory or a remote share and username/password combination based on your answer. The location you provide the wizard with is where all of the content for the hierarchy you specified will be stored. By clicking Finish, you will have created a virtual directory on your server for your NNTP content.

Setting Up an SMTP Server and Configuring SMTP Services

As you've seen throughout this chapter so far, there will probably come a time when your IIS server will need to send e-mail to someone. Whether it is for support of Front-Page extensions or to forward a newsgroup posting to a moderator for approval, your server will need to communicate via SMTP with another host for the transfer of e-mail.

Microsoft has included a basic SMTP server along with IIS 5 for exactly this reason—so that services on your server can send e-mail out to other hosts as needed.

To set up a new SMTP server on IIS, you will need to know the following information in advance:

- What IP address you want this SMTP server to listen to for inbound connections (or if it should respond on all available IP addresses).
- What TCP/IP port number this SMTP server should listen to on the previously specified IP address(es). Typically, this is port 25.
- A "default domain" name to use for the sending of messages.
- What directory on your system to use for incoming and outgoing e-mail files.

Creating a New SMTP Server

Once again, Microsoft has included a wizard to make the creation of a new SMTP server relatively straightforward.

To begin the creation of a new SMTP server, start by selecting your IIS server in the scope pane of the Internet Services Manager MMC, then select the New/SMTP Virtual Server option from the Action pull-down menu. This should bring you to the first step of the New SMTP Virtual Server Wizard, shown in Figure 19.65.

FIGURE 19.65

Defining a friendly name for an SMTP virtual server

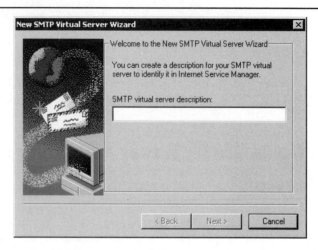

This step of the wizard wants you to specify a friendly name to use when referencing your new SMTP virtual server. This name is simply for administration purposes; your users won't see it, so choose a name that's appropriate and then click Next to proceed to the next step of the wizard, shown in Figure 19.66.

In order to access your SMTP server, other SMTP servers will need to establish a TCP/IP connection to your system on a specific IP address and TCP port number. By default, the New SMTP Virtual Server Wizard will want to have your site listen on all available IP addresses for incoming connections. If you are going to be running only one SMTP server on your system, these settings should be fine. However, if you intend on running multiple SMTP servers on your system (for example, if you plan on hosting several virtual domains on your IIS server), you might want to specify a specific IP address for this server to use.

FIGURE 19.66

Defining IP addresses for an SMTP virtual server

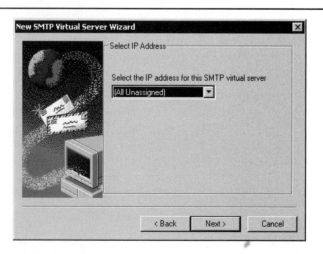

Click Next when you've completed the IP configuration, and you'll move to the next step of the wizard, shown in Figure 19.67.

FIGURE 19.67

*Defining a directory for
an SMTP virtual server*

Since IIS will need a location to store incoming and outgoing e-mail messages, you must create a directory on your server to store this information. Unlike other services within IIS, in this service, you cannot define a share on another computer as the target location for your files. Instead, you must define a local path to be used for storing your SMTP content. Enter the appropriate directory to use, then click Next to proceed to the final step of the wizard, shown in Figure 19.68.

FIGURE 19.68

*Defining a
default domain*

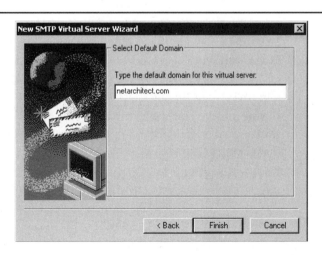

The last step of the wizard will ask you to enter the default domain that this virtual server should service, such as netarchitect.com (you don't need to use the @ sign). Enter the appropriate domain to use, click the Finish button, and your new SMTP virtual server should be created. If you receive an error message at this point, check back in the Internet Services Manager MMC to see if the default SMTP server installed with IIS is running on the same IP address and TCP port of the system you've just defined. If it is, stop that system and then start your server again.

Modifying SMTP Virtual Server Properties

Since the New SMTP Virtual Server Wizard only asks you for a few configuration items, there are a number of settings that you will probably want to adjust for your system. To adjust the parameters for your SMTP virtual server after the wizard has created it, you will use the SMTP virtual server property pages.

General Properties

To reach the SMTP virtual server property pages, highlight your new SMTP virtual server in the scope pane of the Internet Services Manager MMC and then select Properties from the Action pull-down menu. This will bring you to a dialog box similar to the one shown in Figure 19.69.

From this page, you can edit a number of options for your server, including the following:

Name To modify the friendly name for your SMTP server, enter the information here. This information is only used for administrative purposes in the MMC interface; users will not end up seeing it.

IP Address Enter the IP address for your SMTP server to use here. You can assign your server to a specific IP addresses or have it respond on any free IP addresses on the system by selecting the All Unassigned option. To edit the TCP port number for this SMTP server, click the Advanced button.

Connection By clicking the Connection button in this area, you can control the concurrent connection limits and time-out values for SMTP sessions going in and out of your server.

Enable Logging To keep track of what e-mails your server has sent and received, turn on logging by checking the Enable Logging box. Logging choices include W3C Extended Log Format, IIS Log File Format, NCSA Common Log File Format, and ODBC Logging.

FIGURE 19.69

Configuring general settings for an SMTP virtual server

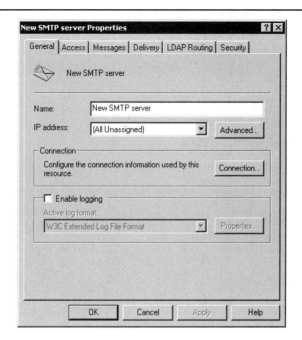

Security Properties

To delegate administrative controls for this server to specific users, click the Security tab to get to the Operators property page, shown in Figure 19.70.

This dialog box is really quite self-explanatory. Simply press Add to add Windows server accounts or groups to the list of administrators for this SMTP server. Users listed here will be able to change parameters for this *specific* SMTP server via the Internet Services Manager MMC.

FIGURE 19.70

Configuring operators for an SMTP virtual server

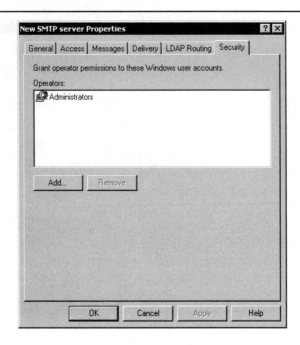

Messages Properties

Because the SMTP protocol can be used to move unknown amounts of data from one system to another, to protect yourself, you set a number of parameters regarding the delivery of messages on your system. Abuse via SMTP—such as someone e-mailing you a 1 gigabyte file and consuming too much disk space or the unauthorized relaying of messages—happens sometimes, so to properly protect your system you can fine-tune the message properties by selecting the Messages tab, shown in Figure 19.71.

There are a few properties you can change here that handle how both inbound and outbound messages are controlled. They are as follows:

Limit Message Size To (Kilobytes)   To limit how large a message a mail client can send to your server, enter an appropriate value in this field. This limit will be applied after a message has been received in its entirety. The minimum for this value is 1KB.

Limit Session Size To (Kilobytes)   Instead of waiting around to receive the end of a message that has already exceeded the maximum message size, you can enter a value in this field; when a session reaches this point, IIS will close off the connection. The minimum value for this field must be equal to or greater than the previously defined maximum message size value.

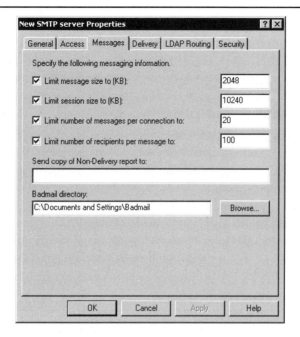

Limit Number of Outbound Messages per Connection To During a connection to an SMTP server, a client may send a number of messages to the system for delivery. Unfortunately, some SMTP servers are unknowingly used for the unauthorized relay of junk e-mail (often referred to as *spamming*), delivering hundreds of thousands of messages. By forcing a client to establish a new connection every x number of messages, an SMTP server becomes less desirable to a spammer for use as a relay point, so hopefully the spammer will move on. I would recommend leaving the default value in this field.

Limit Number of Recipients per Message To Although this setting would seem to limit the number of people you can send a single message to, it is really included for compliance with RFC 821, which defines SMTP. RFC 821 states that the maximum number of recipients per e-mail message is 100. But what if you have a message destined for 150 recipients? The message will be sent in one session to the first 100 recipients, and then a second session will be opened for the remaining 50 recipients.

Send Copy of Non-delivery Report To Non-delivery of a message, for whatever reason (invalid e-mail address, etc.), will typically cause the SMTP server to generate a non-delivery report (NDR) e-mail message for the sender. If you would like to have a copy of the NDRs also e-mailed to a specific mailbox, enter the appropriate e-mail address here.

Badmail Directory When the SMTP service sends a non-delivery report (as mentioned above), it will go through the typical delivery routine for an e-mail message. However, under certain circumstances, the non-delivery report might be undeliverable. In such cases, the SMTP service will automatically place the message in this directory and consider the message permanently undeliverable. It's a good idea to check this directory every now and then to see if anything is piling up in there.

Access Properties

Although most SMTP communications across the Internet occur anonymously, you can require authenticated access to your system if you desire. If you choose to require authenticated access to your SMTP server, the Access properties page is where you will make these changes. You can also control what IP addresses and domain names can attach to your system, define secure communications, and set relay restrictions here. The Access properties page is shown in Figure 19.72.

From this dialog box, you can control authentication, secure communications, address restrictions, and relay restrictions on your SMTP server by clicking the appropriate button.

FIGURE 19.72

Configuring Access properties for an SMTP server

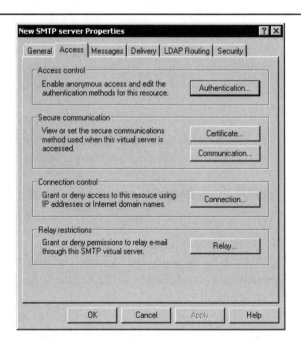

Access Control   By default, SMTP connections are anonymous in nature: no authentication is required from a client accessing your SMTP server in order to send messages through it. If you want to change this behavior, click the Authentication button in this box to go to the Authentication Methods dialog box, shown in Figure 19.73.

Anonymous Access By default, all three authentication options are initially selected. If you don't want clients to be able to send messages anonymously through your SMTP server, uncheck this first option.

Basic Authentication If you chose to disable anonymous access, this is the first option that you can choose for client authentication. Basic authentication works via AUTH and USER/PASS commands sent between systems in clear text. User accounts are verified against the accounts database local to the IIS machine. If a valid account is found, message processing can proceed. Otherwise, the SMTP session is never completed. Although this isn't necessarily a secure means of authentication, it will have a wider base of support than the next authentication option.

Windows Security Package Another name for the Microsoft challenge/response authentication, this option requires that both the SMTP server and SMTP client be running a Windows platform. User accounts are verified against the accounts database local to the IIS machine. If a valid account is found, message processing can proceed. Otherwise, the SMTP session is never completed.

FIGURE 19.73

Configuring authentication properties for an SMTP server

Connection Control If you prefer to control who accesses your SMTP server via IP addresses or domain names instead of authentications, click the Connection button in this area to edit the connection properties, shown in Figure 19.74.

FIGURE 19.74

Configuring IP address and domain name restrictions for an SMTP server

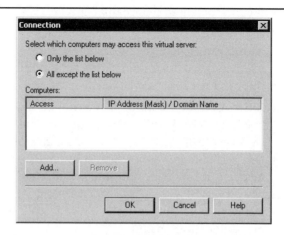

Select the radio button option to either allow only the addresses and domain names you specify or allow everyone except the addresses and domains you specify. Enter the exception list by clicking Add. From the dialog box that follows, you can either grant or deny access to a single computer (via an IP address), a group of computers (via an IP address and a subnet mask), or an entire domain (via a domain name). IP addresses are usually the best option if you know which addresses to allow or deny. Since IIS only knows who is connected to it by an IP number, the server must do a reverse-DNS lookup if you select the domain name option, which adds quite a bit of processing for the server to do just to determine if it's okay to let the user in. Unless your situation requires using domain names, it's probably worthwhile to find out the exact IP address ranges to allow into your site and configure them accordingly.

 NOTE Many hosts out on the Internet don't actually have reverse-DNS records assigned to them, and some hosts have incorrect reverse-DNS records assigned to them. Therefore, even if you were to put in a restriction based on a host/domain name, it might not work quite as well as you want it to.

Relay Restrictions   Since an SMTP server will typically deliver any message sent to it, abuse can become a problem if someone decides to park tens of thousands of messages on your system for delivery. Spammers will often find misconfigured third-party SMTP servers to relay their junk mail, park a few thousand messages onto the system, and then move on to another server. This behavior is known as *relaying* a message, and it is an inherent part of the SMTP protocol—a protocol that was designed when the Internet was a more trusting, friendly place.

To defeat this behavior, many SMTP servers (including Microsoft Exchange) now include powerful relay controls that will allow you to determine whether or not the SMTP server should receive any messages for domains other than the ones that it hosts. For example, if your system lives in a domain called mycompany.com, then your SMTP server will—by default—only accept incoming messages destined to e-mail addresses ending in @mycompany.com. Any other messages will be denied, unless you specifically allow relaying by pressing the Relay button in the Relay Restrictions area and adjusting the properties page shown in Figure 19.75.

As you can see, the format of this dialog box is similar to that for allowing and denying IP address restrictions to the SMTP service as a whole. By default, all hosts are denied relay access, unless you enter specific hosts in the list box. You can either grant or deny access to a single computer (via an IP address), a group of computers (via an IP address and a subnet mask), or an entire domain (via a domain name). IP addresses are usually the best option if you know which addresses to allow or deny.

If you have enabled authentication options on your system, you can check the "Allow all computers which successfully authenticate to relay" box at the bottom of this dialog box, giving anyone with an appropriate user authentication the rights to relay.

FIGURE 19.75

Configuring relay controls on an SMTP server

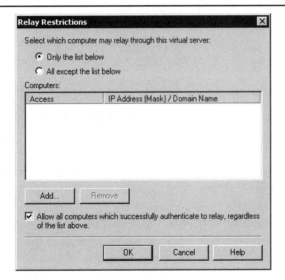

Delivery Properties

Click the Delivery tab to define parameters about how messages are delivered into and out of your SMTP server. This will bring you to a property page like the one shown in Figure 19.76.

This page is divided up into a number of options, both inbound and outbound, for controlling the delivery of messages.

Outbound   When an SMTP server receives a message, it will attempt to deliver it almost immediately. For a number of reasons, it is possible that the SMTP server will fail to deliver the message—the receiving host might be too busy, the receiving host might be down, orInternet connectivity might not be available. For whatever reason, the SMTP service will continue to try to deliver the message for the intervals specified in this section.

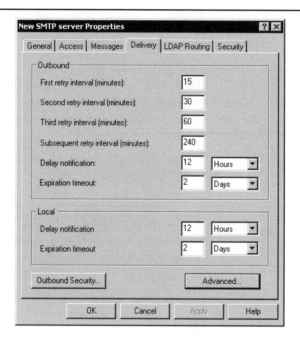

If the SMTP server fails at delivering the message after the first attempt, it will try again three times at the minute values specified in the First Retry Interval, Second Retry Interval, and Third Retry Interval fields. After the third retry value, if the message still hasn't been delivered, the SMTP service will attempt to deliver the message at the interval defined in the Subsequent Retry Interval field.

Eventually, if the message has failed enough times, the SMTP service will send a notification e-mail message to the user listed in the From: field of the e-mail message, letting him or her know that the message is still "in the queue" but hasn't been delivered to it's destination yet. This interval is defined in the Delay Notification field. If the message eventually hits the value defined in the Expiration Timeout field, the message will be aborted and sent back to the user who sent it, along with a notification of the failure. These same values can be set for local delivery as well at the bottom portion of this screen.

Outbound Security   As we saw earlier in this chapter, inbound authentication controls can be set for the IIS SMTP service. If the SMTP server that your system will be communicating with requires a similar means of authorization, you will end up defining these options in the Outbound Security settings area. Click the Outbound Security button to edit the Outbound Security property page, shown in Figure 19.77.

FIGURE 19.77

Configuring outbound
authentication for an
SMTP server

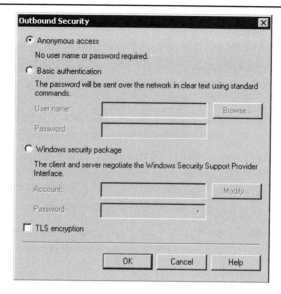

For more detailed information on the types of outbound authentication available, the section titled "Access Control" contains working definitions of anonymous access, basic authentication, and windows security package. Whatever authentication your receiving systems will require, select a radio button to enable that type of security and supply the appropriate account information. For a basic authentication, click the Browse button to select a username and password to use. For windows security package authentication, click the Modify button to define a Windows account username, domain name, and password to use.

Advanced Delivery Options   The following options are advanced parameters for controlling the outbound delivery of messages. Clicking the Advanced button on the Delivery page will take you to a screen similar to the one in figure 19.78.

Maximum Hop Count   When an SMTP server receives a message, it may be sent through a number of other severs before reaching its final destination (a mailbox). However, a pair of misconfigured SMTP servers might bounce a message back and forth between themselves indefinitely (known as ping-ponging), with the message getting larger at each step of the way and never reaching its destination. To prevent this, the SMTP service can perform a "hop count" on a message—basically, counting the number of Received headers present in a message—and reject the message if there are too many hops in the message path. By default, this is set to 15, which should be acceptable for most circumstances.

Masquerade Domain   To override the domain name in an outgoing message with a specific domain name, enter the domain name here. The domain name entered in this field—if any—will replace the existing domain name listing in the From: field of the outgoing message.

Fully Qualified Domain Name Enter the fully qualified domain name (FQDN) of your SMTP server in this field. A fully qualified domain name typically has at least three segments to it: host.domain.tld (tld is for top-level domain).

Smart Host If you would prefer to have another SMTP server handle all of the outgoing messages for this SMTP service, enter a domain name or host address of that host here. If you enter an IP address, Microsoft suggests entering it in brackets [ ] so that the SMTP service will immediately know that it should try to connect to the smart host via IP address and skip name resolution.

Attempt Direct Delivery before Sending to Smart Host If you have defined a smart host in the previous field, you can tell SMTP that it should try to deliver messages on its own first. If it cannot deliver the messages on its own, it will immediately send them on to the smart host for delivery.

Perform Reverse DNS Lookup on Incoming Messages When incoming messages are received by SMTP, IIS can perform a reverse-DNS lookup on the IP address noted in the header of the message and insert the fully qualified domain name of the IP address into the Received header. If the reverse-DNS lookup fails, no FQDN is put into the Received header. Reverse-DNS lookups can slow down message processing, so depending on the volume of messages that you're receiving, you might want to leave this option unchecked unless necessary.

FIGURE 19.78

Configuring advanced delivery properties

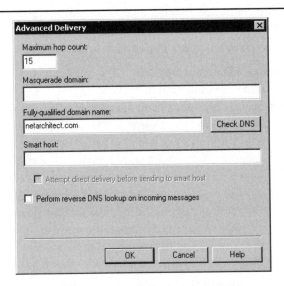

Adding Additional Domains

By default, your SMTP server will only process messages destined for the domain you specified during the New SMTP Virtual Server Wizard. All other domain names will be considered by IIS to be "non-local," and therefore need to be relayed.

However, if you want to host multiple domain names on your system for e-mail or allow relaying for specific domains, you can do so by adding additional domain names through the Internet Services Manager MMC. Select your SMTP virtual server from the scope pane of the MMC and expand it. Below the SMTP server, you should see an item for Domains. Select that item, and you will see your currently defined domain in the results pane on the right-hand side of the MMC. With the Domains option highlighted, select New/Domain from the Action pull-down menu, or simply right-click Domains and choose New/Domain, as shown in Figure 19.79.

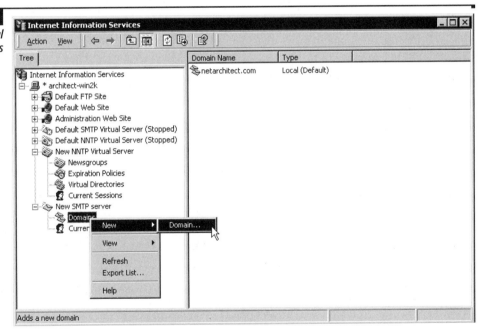

FIGURE 19.79

Configuring additional SMTP domains

Selecting the New/Domain option brings you to a two-step wizard, the first step of which is shown in Figure 19.80.

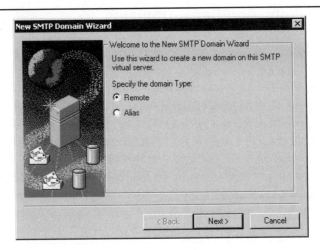

FIGURE 19.80

*Adding a domain to an
SMTP server*

The first step of the wizard wants to know whether to add a local ("alias") or remote domain. This will define whether the SMTP service should immediately store the message in the Drop directory once it receives it (local/alias), or if it should try to pass it on to another mail system (remote). Make the appropriate selection and then click Next to proceed to the last step of the wizard, entering the actual domain name. Once you enter a new domain for your system, the SMTP server will begin receiving/accepting traffic for e-mail addresses within that domain.

Maintaining Your SMTP Server

After you've gone through all of these configuration items, you should have a fully-functional SMTP server on your system servicing the domain you defined in the New SMTP Virtual Server Wizard. As with any process on your system, it will require a bit of maintaining and fine-tuning from time to time.

SMTP Directories

If you look at the directory you defined during the setup of your site, you should see four subdirectories, titled Badmail, Drop, Pickup, and Queue.

These are the directories that the SMTP service will use when processing incoming or outgoing messages. Incoming messages to your system will end up in the Drop directory, so it is worth looking in there every once in a while to see if mail has been sent to your system. Incoming e-mail messages will be stored in .eml files and will look somewhat like this:

```
x-sender: dtoombs@usa.net
x-receiver: doug@netarchitect.com
Received: from architect1.netarchitect.com ([172.16.10.1]) by ARCHITECT-
WIN2K.dewey.netarchitect.com with Microsoft SMTPSVC(5.0.1993.0993.0);
    Wed, 30 Jun 1999 23:10:42 -0400
```

```
From: dtoombs@usa.net
Bcc:
Return-Path: dtoombs@usa.net
Message-ID: <ARCHITECT-WIN2K3DEj00000001@ARCHITECT-
WIN2K.dewey.netarchitect.com>
X-OriginalArrivalTime: 01 Jul 1999 03:10:44.0718 (UTC)
FILETIME=[4F00A0E0:01BEC36F]
Date: 30 Jun 1999 23:10:44 -0400

This is a test message - sent from dtoombs@usa.net,
to doug@netarchitect.com,
received by the Microsoft IIS 5.0 SMTP service.
```

Outgoing messages from your system will be placed in the Pickup directory, either by the FrontPage extensions or the NNTP service as needed. However, you can also use the Pickup directory for your own administrative uses by placing properly formatted messages in there for delivery. For example, if you have a service process that generates a status report every night (perhaps a backup log) and want to have it automatically e-mailed, you can simply have a process create a properly formatted text file and place it in the Pickup directory. The SMTP service will see the file there and attempt to deliver it. A properly formatted outgoing SMTP message would look similar to the following:

```
x-sender: doug@netarchitect.com
x-receiver: mark@minasi.com
From: doug@netarchitect.com
To: mark@minasi.com
Subject: Hello from Doug

Hello Mark. Hope that everything is going well with you.
```

If you intend to use the Pickup directory for your own messages, I'd recommend that you compose your text file in another directory first before placing it in the Pickup directory. If you begin to compose a message directly in the Pickup directory, the SMTP service will attempt to pick it up while you are working on it.

If the SMTP service runs into a message that it can't deliver to its intended recipient, and for which a non-delivery notification can't be returned to the sender, it will drop the message in the Badmail directory and leave it there. Every now and then it is probably worthwhile to check the Badmail directory and see if any messages have piled up.

Lastly, the Queue directory is where the SMTP service holds messages that it has pulled out of the Pickup directory. It will try sending a message immediately upon taking the message out of the Pickup directory, but if for some reason it can't deliver the message, it will hold it in the Queue directory until such time that it can be successfully delivered.

Communicating Securely with SSL

We all know that the Web is a great place to find information, but I have a feeling that we've only seen the tip of the iceberg as far as the Internet is concerned. The force that is truly driving the Internet into the next millennium is commerce. The Internet lends itself to transactional chores very well, just due to its nature and makeup. However, most commerce transactions contain some form of proprietary or confidential data, whether it's bank account numbers or corporate plans for a new product launch. All sorts of information that is confidential in nature is being transmitted across the Internet, and that trend will continue in the future.

To meet the challenge of securing confidential data, Netscape developed a protocol called Secure Sockets Layer (SSL) to be used in conjunction with HTTP as a means of providing secure communication channels between clients and servers. Through the use of *certificates*—encryption keys handed out by a trusted third-party organization—Web servers and Web browsers will negotiate an encrypted connection between themselves, preventing any data from being intercepted during transmission.

Some reasons to implement SSL are obvious—for example, if you intend to accept credit card numbers on your Web site from clients who are ordering products. Obviously, your clients might be concerned about their confidential information (their credit card number) crossing the Internet in the clear, so you can encrypt the ordering process to ensure that even if someone does intercept the transmission, it will be useless in its native form. However, some reasons for implementing SSL are less obvious but equally as important—for example, confidential information such as brokerage statements, corporate financial statements, tax returns, medical records, etc. All are equally private as far as most individuals are concerned, and will become transmitted over the Internet more and more frequently as time goes on.

Fortunately, Microsoft has made the process of obtaining a security certificate easy in IIS 5 through the inclusion of the IIS Certificate Wizard, an administrative wizard that will create a *certificate request* for your system. You will, in turn, submit that request to a certificate authority—commonly referred to as a CA—which is the trusted third party. The CA will then send you a certificate that the wizard will help you install on your server. Before getting this process started, you will need to have the following ready:

- A functional IIS server. Although this seems obvious, there's more to it than simply having an IIS server that runs. Since certificates are highly specialized encryption keys—they even have the name of your server embedded in them—it's best to have your site working exactly how you want it *first*, and then add the security certificate and turn on encryption as one of the last items to do.

- Organizational details. Details that a CA will require from your organization include name, organizational unit, country, state, locality, and a name, e-mail address, and phone number for the contact individual requesting the certificate.

- Server details. Certificates are based on the server that they were requested for, and will have that server name (either an internal NetBIOS-style name or a fully qualified domain name) embedded within the key. Therefore, once you enable encryption, it's important that you don't change the name of your server—otherwise you will need to request a new certificate.

Requesting a Certificate

To begin the process of requesting a certificate, start the Internet Services Manager MMC and select your Web site in the scope pane. Then, select the Properties option from the Action pull-down menu. This will get you into the property pages for this Web site, as discussed earlier in this chapter. Click the Directory Security tab to get to the security property pages, shown earlier in Figure 19.16. Click the Server Certificate button to launch the IIS Certificate Wizard. The first screen of the wizard (after the welcome screen) is shown in Figure 19.81.

FIGURE 19.81

Starting the IIS Certificate Wizard

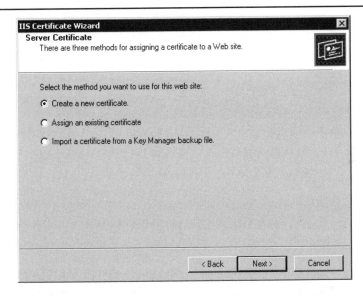

Assuming that you are requesting a new certificate for your site, select the Create a New Certificate option. Clicking Next will take you through roughly eight steps required to collect the necessary information about your organization: organization name, organizational unit, server name, contact information, etc. Enter the information requested at each step and click Next to move through the wizard. One of the final steps of the wizard will ask you where you want to store your request (assuming you selected the "Prepare the request now, but send it later" option in the second step of the wizard); the default is `c:\certreq.txt`. If this name is acceptable, click Next to proceed to the final step of the wizard.

After you have entered all of the necessary organizational and server information for your certificate request, the wizard should show you the information it has collected in a step similar to the one shown in Figure 19.82.

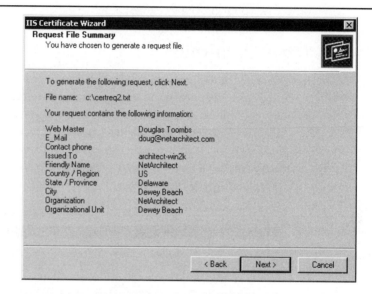

Assuming your information is correct, click Next, and the wizard will create the appropriate certificate request and place it in the file you specified. This file is simply a text file containing all of the information you entered through the wizard, encoded in a certificate request. A sample certificate request is shown here:

```
---BEGIN NEW CERTIFICATE REQUEST---
HIICMzOCMhACNQDwDzAYDBAGN1DECxHPRXIjSGA0NWD0BXEpTjHrmtrwDAYDVQQL
EDVEZWdEeYErMEMjACUHChMMTmV0QXJjaGl0ZWN0MRQwEgYDVQQHEwtEZXd1eSBC
ZWFjaDERMA8GA1UECBMIRGVsYXdhcmUxCzAJBgNVBAYTA1VTMFwwDQYJKoZIhvcN
AQEBBQADSwAwSAJBANDWZ6269T1vwQ22oFxUBUf+dRVpmLFHiak9v+kyp580/ZRz
QdTQc01nWvxZGHWXINwDEU5cUatk0cX3ImfBxv0CAwEAAaCCATcwNQYKKwYBBAGC
NwIBDjEnMCUwDgYDVR0PAQH/BAQDAgM4MBMGA1UdJQQMMAoGCCsGAQUFBwMBMIH9
BgorBgEEAYI3DQICMYHuMIHrAgEBH1oATQBpAGMAcgBvAHMAbwBmAHQAIABSAFMA
QQAgAFMAQwBoAGEAbgBuAGUAbAAgAEMAcgB5AHAAdABvAGcAcgBhAHAAaABpAGMA
IABQAHIAbwB2AGkAZAB1AHIDgYkAmg0YS5nRhWq1rh47DAbamYuDeux8a+ueRdAC
GKnL06A+a0Rwy/qdQZfPWLo11aNa/L15umsktG5agP092QtK9WH/72gfWAjmL3og
E4UHAnrIiy1WI8WdA6pvSIGB/fXDpi21GaeWUeA71su7E27apemVifiXUzVUR/kU
2NgmKrkZZZZZZZZZZZDANBgkqhkiG9w0BAQUFAANBAGGPA0RMoqXYzK4mriO+W0hJ
yK6EjShHF2awrGrZepW1iorpun5XGVWI1+UVC811bm/bxu4WacvQCXd1++IVBaB4
---END NEW CERTIFICATE REQUEST---
```

Once you have your request file, you need to submit that file to a CA so that they can issue a certificate to you. For my testing purposes, I chose to use VeriSign over at www.verisign.com. In any case, choose a CA that you would like to use and then submit your request file through whatever mechanism they provide.

Depending on the CA you are working with, and the level of trust you want for your certificate, your request might take anywhere from a few minutes to a few days or weeks to process. Once your request has been approved, you will receive a certificate for installation on your server (a sample certificate basically looks exactly like the encryption key in the certificate request). To install the certificate, return to the Directory Security tab in the properties of your Web site (you need to install your certificate to the same site you requested it from) and press the Server Certificate button again.

This time when you launch the IIS Certificate Wizard, it will realize that you have previously requested a certificate for this Web server and it will ask you if you would like to import that certificate now, as Figure 19.83 shows.

FIGURE 19.83

Importing a certificate with the IIS Certificate Wizard

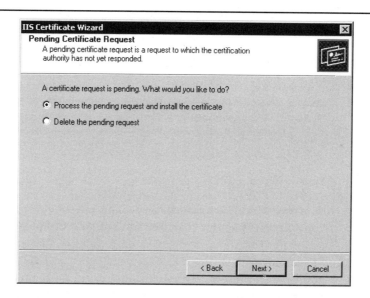

Import the certificate by entering the path to the certificate in the next step of the wizard. If everything goes as it should, you should see a summary of your certificate, similar to the one shown in Figure 19.84.

If this certificate is acceptable, click Next, and the certificate will be installed into your Web server.

FIGURE 19.84

*Summary of an
imported certificate*

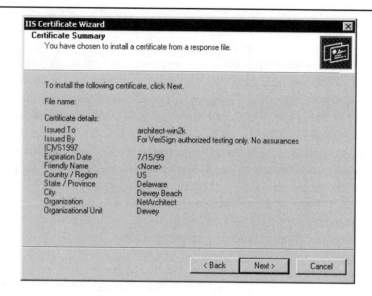

```
IIS Certificate Wizard                                              [X]
  Certificate Summary
     You have chosen to install a certificate from a response file.


     To install the following certificate, click Next.

     File name:

     Certificate details:
     Issued To             architect-win2k
     Issued By             For VeriSign authorized testing only. No assurances
     (C)VS1997
     Expiration Date       7/15/99
     Friendly Name         <None>
     Country / Region      US
     State / Province      Delaware
     City                  Dewey Beach
     Organization          NetArchitect
     Organizational Unit   Dewey



                              < Back      Next >       Cancel
```

NOTE It's worthwhile mentioning that you can only install one certificate per Web site, but you can install the same certificate into multiple Web sites as long as they are referenced by the same name.

Securing a Site or Directory

Once your certificate is installed, the Edit button should light up in the Directory Security property page for your Web site. You can require SSL security for your entire site or in directories (real or virtual) within your site. In either case, the settings are mostly the same.

To enable encryption on a specific directory or site, go to the Directory Security property page for that directory or site. Click the Edit button to enable security, and you will go to a Secure Communications property page similar to the one shown in Figure 19.85.

In this page, the most important setting to enable is Require Secure Channel (SSL). This will enforce secure communications for anyone trying to reach this resource (directory or site). Anyone attempting to access this resource over a standard HTTP connection will be instructed that they cannot reach the content unsecured and that they must use HTTPS to access the desired content. If you have a domestic-only build of Windows 2000 Server, you will also have the option to enable strong (128-bit) encryption, instead of relying on standard 40-bit encryption (sometimes referred to as *weak*).

FIGURE 19.85

*Implementing secure
communications*

As clients access your system, you can also accept or require client certificates as a means of authenticating who can access your system. If you want to require that only users with certificates access your system, select the Require Client Certificates radio button, and any users who do not have a client certificate installed in their system will not be able to access the secure content of your site.

Since it is possible for clients to provide certificates to your server (in addition to your server presenting a certificate to your clients), you can use this as a means of authenticating users and knowing exactly who is accessing your Web site. By checking the Enable Client Certificate Mapping check box, and then clicking the Edit button, you can "map" specific certificates to specific Windows user accounts. In effect, you are telling your IIS server, "If you receive *this* particular certificate, then assume that this is user John Doe accessing the Web server." If IIS knows who the exact user is, it can take advantage of permissions placed on files and directories for controlling who can access what content.

CHAPTER **20**

Tuning and Monitoring Your Win2K Network

Even without any tuning, Win2K works pretty well so long as you throw enough hardware at it. The goal isn't always just having enough resources, though—it's putting those resources in the right places. To help you tune your servers' hardware and run services in the way that they'll do most good, Win2K includes some performance monitoring tools.

The trick to using performance monitoring tools is *asking the right questions*. These tools are not omnipotent gods, but more like slightly dim-witted genies. Like such genies, performance monitoring tools are very literal-minded little cusses. They can give you the answers if you ask, but only if you ask correctly, and if you ask the wrong questions, you'll drown in a sea of irrelevant data. (Somewhat less metaphorically, you'll also slow down your servers and clog your network's bandwidth with unimportant queries.) Thus, in this chapter I'll talk about the genies—er, performance monitoring tools—that come with Win2K and about figuring out which questions to ask the oracle. Once done with that, I'll talk about the tuning you can do based on the information you gathered. To round off, I'll talk about how you can tune network browsing to make your network more responsive to the people using it.

Roundup of Tuning Support Tools and What to Do with Them

Before I get into a description of how to use these tools, here's a quick tour of the rogues' gallery:

- System Monitor
- Performance Logs and Alerts
- Event Viewer

 NOTE Win2K also has a Network Monitor tool that's a crippled version of the one included with Microsoft System Management Server. The one included in Win2K is pretty useless for most things, however, because it can only monitor data traveling between the monitored computer and the rest of the network.

System Monitor

The System Monitor is Win2K's replacement for the Performance Monitor. Strictly speaking, it's not really a replacement but more of a reorganization. When you open the System Monitor, you'll see that it has two components, a Performance Monitor–like tool called the System Monitor and the Performance Logs and Alerts, which is a related logging function.

TIP To open the System Monitor quickly, type **perfmon** (the executable name of the Performance Monitor) into Run. Win2K will start the System Monitor with the Performance Monitor screen active. Typing **sysmon** into Run does nothing, by the way.

With the System Monitor, you can:

- Provide a simple, visual view of your servers' vital signs (one that looks great on a PowerPoint presentation of why you need more hardware, incidentally)
- Log network data over time and export that data to a file you can import into a spreadsheet

Performance Logs and Alerts

The other half of the Performance tools is the Performance Logs and Alerts, which takes care of the logging functions of NT 4's Performance Monitor. With it, you can:

- Log minimum, maximum, average, and current values of critical system values
- Send alerts to the event log or run a program when counters exceed user-set tolerances or important events occur

Event Viewer

The Event Viewer (located in the Administrative Tools program group) maintains several separate eventlogs on the server:

- System log
- Security log
- Application log
- DNS server log
- File Replication Service log
- Directory Service log

NOTE The Event Viewer for member servers in the domain only displays the application log, system log, and security log.

The System log records the starting and stopping of services and any system-related events. The Security log records any audited events that relate to security issues, such as users accessing files or changing the Security Accounts Database. The Application log records application-specific events that aren't far-reaching enough to make it into the System log. The DNS server log records events associated with resolving Domain Name System (DNS) names from IP addresses. The File Replication Service log lists events relating to the File Replication Service, and the Directory Service log records events related to domain controllers keeping up with the security database.

Observing Performance Patterns with the System Monitor

If you can't measure it, you can't tune it.

As noted earlier, the Performance Monitor is the graphical display tool in the System Monitor. When you switch to this tool, you see an opening screen like the one in Figure 20.1.

FIGURE 20.1

Performance Monitor tool

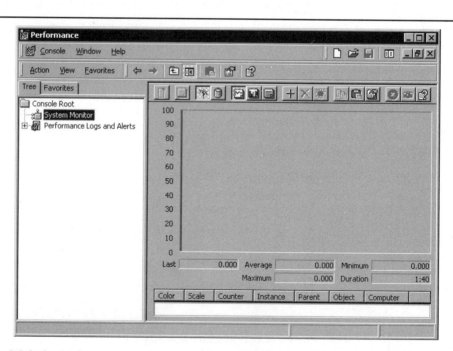

With the Performance Monitor, you can log minima, maxima, and averages of critical system values and get a simple, visual view of your network's "vital signs." However, as you can see, the Performance Monitor tool doesn't do anything until told to. Read on for more information about how to build charts and analyze their contents.

Creating and Viewing Charts

When you first start Performance Monitor, all you see is a blank screen; you have to select the objects, instances, and counters that you want to monitor. Objects, instances, and counters are defined as follows:

Object   Is any Win2K system component that possesses a set of measurable properties. An object can be a physical part of the system (such as the memory or the processor), a logical component (such as a disk volume), or a software element (such as a process or a thread).

Instance   Shows how many occurrences of an object are available in the system.

Counter   Represents one measurable characteristic of an object. For example, the Processor object has several counters, including the percentage of processor time in use and the percentage of time the processor spends in Privileged and in User modes.

To look at all the system areas you can monitor, right-click on the blank area of the System Monitor and choose Add Counters from the context menu to open the Add Counters dialog box. The first item, Processor, includes information on several counters listed in the Counter box; for example, the variable that reports how many interrupts per second the system processes is called the Interrupts/sec counter.

Win2K contains hundreds of counters to track system data, such as the number of network packets transmitted per second or the number of pages swapped in and out of memory per second. You can use them to create charts and reports that help you assess and tune system performance.

To add a counter to the chart, click the button in the toolbar that has a plus sign on it. This will open the dialog box shown in Figure 20.2.

FIGURE 20.2

Add counters to the Performance Monitor

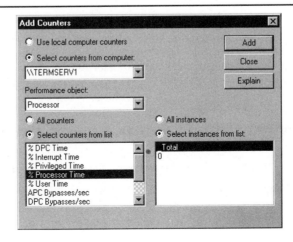

The mechanics of adding counters is a simple matter. Choose a performance object, then pick one of its performance counters. If there's more than one instance of the object (for example, if the server has more than one processor), then you'll have the choice of monitoring counters for all objects of that class or only a specific one. Click the Add button, and that counter will be added to the chart and will show up in the Performance Monitor, as in Figure 20.3.

FIGURE 20.3

Performance Monitor output

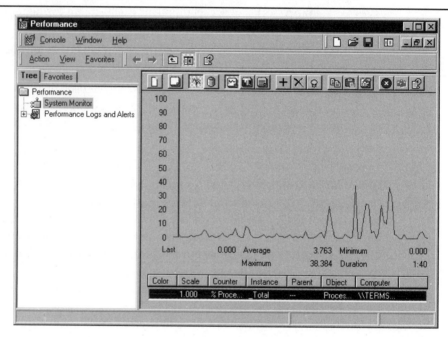

This is nice, but what are you looking at, and how do you know which counters to monitor of the dozens available?

NOTE There *is* an Explain button you can click to show more information about the currently highlighted counter. However, the information that's displayed isn't always all that useful—especially the counters new to Win2K—and not always strictly accurate. Use the information in the Explain text box as a starting point for further research if you need exact details about what a counter's monitoring, not as a final word.

But First... What Counters Should I Chart?

Now that you have a new weapon—the System Monitor—you need something to point it to. A quick perusal of the System Monitor shows that there are *lots* of things to monitor, and I mean *lots* of things. Watching them all would take more time than you have and logging it would require staggering amounts of disk space.

What I want to do next is to (1) introduce you to the art of tuning, (2) point out the most likely causes of problems for file servers and applications servers, and (3) recommend a few counters that you can monitor to keep an eye on your network with minimum trouble.

Let me set the following scenario: you have a network up and running. But with time, the network seems to be slowing down. People are complaining. The Powers That Be start applying pressure on you to find out what's wrong and to find it out *now*.

What can you do? Well, the obvious thing to do is to throw money at it, right? Go buy more memory, an extra processor if it's an SMP (Symmetric Multiprocessor) server; get a faster network card; get a faster disk.

Doing those things *may* get you a faster server. But it's also a good way to throw money down a rat hole. If your server is spending all its time waiting for the disk drive, then getting a faster CPU may indeed speed up the server—but only by a tiny percentage. If the problem is a slow disk, your money's better spent (logically) on a faster disk controller than on a faster CPU.

In a few words, you tune a troubled server by locating and removing its bottlenecks. The four big sources of performance bottlenecks are the:

- Disk subsystem

- Network card and software

- CPU

- Memory, which includes both the RAM and the disk

"Remove the bottlenecks" isn't, strictly speaking, a meaningful phrase; it's kind of like saying, "Measure the top of the sky." That's because bottlenecks never go away; they just move. For example, suppose your goal is to get to work as fast as possible, and you're a law-abiding citizen. It's a 40-minute drive right now. The 30 MPH speed limits on local roads are, you feel, keeping you from getting to work as quickly as you'd like. So you convince the local, state, and federal authorities to remove all the speed limits. The result: you now get to work in 26 minutes. But after a while you notice another limit: the other drivers. They get in your way, forcing you to slow down. So you decide to go to work at 2 A.M., when virtually no one's on the road. That's better: you're down to 18 minutes now. Ah, but that's when you realize that the *real* problem is your Ford Escort, with its maximum speed of 85 MPH. So you pick up a Porsche, reducing your commute to 14 minutes—*when* you make it in to work, that is; at 120 MPH, it's easy to wrap that Porsche around a lamppost. The final bottleneck, then, is a combination of the road (too many twists and turns) and you (reaction time's too slow).

Notice in my example, however, that removing each bottleneck saved less and less time with each improvement. You often find that in networking, too. There is no way to remove all bottlenecks, but you can probably easily get rid of the *big* ones to get the most out of the time you devoted to tuning.

Win2K servers tend to either act as file servers or application servers. That's important information for tuning, because they tend to bottleneck in different places. File servers tend to respond well to increased memory, as well as to speedups in disk and network boards. Application servers (including terminal servers) tend to respond well to speedups in CPU and memory speed.

Resolving Memory Bottlenecks The biggest performance drain on a Win2K system is memory. Windows applications are memory-hungry, and Win2K itself is memory-hungry—NT gets greedier with each passing generation. If you install Win2K Server with the bare minimum of memory and then actually try to use it as a server, you're not going to be happy with the result.

Background: A (Very Basic) Primer on Virtual Memory When you're monitoring memory, you're actually monitoring both physical memory and hard disk access. The reason has to do with how Windows operating systems eke the most use possible out of physical memory—some of the apparent contents of that physical memory are actually on disk, in what's called *virtual memory*.

Virtual memory is a result of what Dorothy Parker would have said if she were a network administrator: you can never be too rich, too thin, or have too much RAM installed. No matter how much you have, it seems, physical memory can't keep up with the data storage needs of Win2K and any applications it's running. Therefore, Windows operating systems (and other operating systems) support virtual memory, a kind of memory simulation that allows the server to support more applications and data in memory than it actually has physical memory to support. The largest Win2K servers I've seen have 1GB of RAM installed, but Windows operating systems support up to 4GB of virtual memory space: 2GB to be shared among all system-level processes, and 2GB for the exclusive use of each user process running on the server. The Win2K memory manager is responsible for organizing each process's access to virtual memory so that processes don't write on each other's data in *physical* memory.

 NOTE One of the reasons Win2K needs so much memory is because it uses a *big* chunk (like, 25% or so) of this memory for caching recently used file data. Servers that aren't file servers don't need to do this. In the section later in this chapter on "Basic Tuning Stuff," I'll explain how to make Win2K stop thinking of itself as a file server and start giving you back some memory.

Virtual memory works like this: when an application is loaded into memory, it stores its data in physical memory to store data it needs to run and present user files. As more and more applications (and the operating system) are using this storage space, things start getting crowded. To allow applications to keep their important data in physical memory where they can get to it instantly, the Win2K memory manager shuffles less important data to a file on disk called the *paging file*.

How does the memory manager decide what's important? Good question. The answer depends on the operating platform. On multi-processor *x*86 systems, the memory manager uses the first-in-first-out (FIFO) algorithm, which basically means the data that's been in memory longest gets shuffled to the paging file first, regardless of how recently it's been used. On single-processor *x*86 systems, the memory manager uses a different priority scheme: the least recently used (LRU) algorithm, which analyzes how recently data's been used. The data that hasn't been used for a while goes to the paging file first. This scheme is a bit more logical, as it evaluates how recently you've used data instead of just assuming that anything old is less necessary. It's just a bit more complicated.

But what if a process needs the paged data back? Processes can't use data that's stored on disk. In that case, the process sends a request to the memory manager: "Hey, fella—I need that data that was stored at address C00000 (for example)." The memory manager makes soothing noises, then quickly executes a *page fault* to bring the data that *was* stored at virtual address C00000 back into physical memory so the process can get to that data. To the process, it looks as though the data was in memory all the time, but it really wasn't. And there will have been a slight delay in getting the data to the process—faulting data back into physical memory takes longer than retrieving it from physical memory because disks are slower than RAM. You measure access times (the time required to read or write data) on RAM in nanoseconds, or billionths of a second, and on disk in microseconds, or thousandths of a second. So, although you can't escape paging, it's to your advantage to minimize the amount of time your server spends doing it.

What kind of data is stored in memory? Several kinds, actually:

- Each application (and the operating system) has a *working set* that is the sum of all the data that application is currently working with. Working sets can be trimmed—made smaller—if there's a shortage of physical memory, but the smaller an application's working set, the slower the application will run, because it's going to have to keep requesting data back from the paging file, and paging data back into memory takes time.

 NOTE If you're using Terminal Services, then there will also be a per-session working set.

- *Page table entries* (PTEs) are structures the memory manager needs to map each user process's virtual address space. The memory manager needs this map to see how each process is using its view of the 2GB of user virtual memory addresses and keep processes from overwriting each other's memory.

- Some operating system data must remain in memory all the time and cannot be paged to disk. The range of virtual memory addresses called the *non-paged pool* stores this data. The *paged pool* stores operating system data that can be paged to disk.

- The *system cache* is the data used by the entire operating system that Win2K keeps in RAM for quick access. The System Monitor Help describes the system cache as though it were synonymous with the disk cache, but it's not—the disk cache of recently used on-disk data and disk data structure is one part of the entire system cache.

The Win2K memory manager allocates memory to the operating system and to user processes by first *reserving* it for the process that needs it (defining a range of virtual memory addresses for later use) and then *committing* it (ensuring that a place in the paging file is available to store data the process wants to put in those virtual memory addresses). Processes can reserve all the memory they want, but when it comes time to commit that memory, some on-disk storage *must* be available to back it. Win2K has to assume that all user data will move to the paging file at some time.

When a process is done with memory, it's supposed to give it back to the system to be marked as available for other processes—*free* it. Some processes do the opposite, taking more and more memory even though they're not using it, or just not giving back memory that they're not using anymore, and not giving it back until you reboot the machine. This is a result of buggy programming and is called a *memory leak*. Memory leaks are frustrating because they starve other processes without giving you any gain at all. Give them enough time, and memory leaks will shut down your server.

Important Memory Performance Counters   That's not everything there is to know about virtual memory, but it's enough to make people avoid you at parties and to give you an idea of why you're interested in monitoring the following counters (see Table 20.1). You can use this information to help you read other memory counters, too.

TABLE 20.1: IMPORTANT MEMORY COUNTERS

Counter	Description	What This Tells You
Memory: Available Bytes	Records the memory currently available on the server.	A low value may indicate that your server is low on memory or that one of the programs is experiencing memory leaks (especially if the number keeps decreasing). You should always have 4MB or more available. If you don't, then check for memory leaks or add more memory.

Continued

TABLE 20.1 CONTINUED: IMPORTANT MEMORY COUNTERS

Counter	Description	What This Tells You
Memory: Commit Limit	Records the amount of memory that can be committed without extending the paging file. You can always grow the paging file up to the limit of available space on the volume.	Extending the paging file is an expensive procedure (requires CPU time) so it's a good idea to do this as little as possible. Make the paging file as large as you think you'll need—at least 2.5x the size of RAM you have installed.
Memory: Committed Bytes	Records the amount of memory committed to processes running on the server.	Records the amount of used RAM that requires space in the paging file in case the data must be paged to disk. Therefore, this is memory in use and unavailable to other processes, not just reserved in case a process needs it.
Memory: Pages Input/sec	Records the rate at which pages of data are written to RAM from the paging file to resolve page faults.	As this value describes hard page faults (the Page Faults counter includes soft page faults, which pull data from another area of memory and don't incur much of a hit), it's a good measure of how often you're having to waste time pulling data back from disk.
Memory: Pages Output/sec	Records the rate at which pages of data are written to the paging file to free RAM.	If the server seems to be running more slowly than it used to, monitor this counter. A high rate may indicate that the server doesn't have enough RAM to support all the data that the running applications need to keep handy.
Memory: Pages/sec	Records the current rate at which pages (4KB chunks of data on an x86 system, 8KB on an Alpha system) are read from disk back into physical memory to satisfy a page fault, or written to disk to free RAM.	A value of more than 20 pages per second implies a lot of paging and suggests that your server needs more memory.

Continued ▸

TABLE 20.1 CONTINUED: IMPORTANT MEMORY COUNTERS

Counter	Description	What This Tells You
Paging File: % Usage	Records the percentage of the paging file currently in use.	If this value approaches 100%, then you need to enlarge the paging file or add more RAM. Although Win2K will make the paging file larger if need be, it's better if you do this manually so that Win2K doesn't need to use up CPU cycles to grow the paging file as needed.
Paging File: Usage Peak	Records the peak size of the paging file.	If this value is close to the maximum size of the paging file, you need to either enlarge the paging file or add more RAM. A high value implies that the paging file isn't big enough to hold all the data it must.
Physical Disk: %Disk Time	Records the percentage of time the disk spends servicing read or write requests.	Monitor this value for the physical disk that the paging file(s) are located on. If this amount seems to be increasing, check paging file usage and consider adding more memory.
Physical Disk: Avg Disk Queue Length	Records the average number of read and write requests waiting for the disk during the selected interval.	If this number is increasing at the same time the number of Memory: Page Reads/sec is increasing, that indicates that a lot of paging is going on. Monitor this value for the physical disk that the paging file(s) are located on.
Physical Disk: Avg Disk sec/Transfer	Records the length of time it takes the disk to transfer data to or from disk.	Monitor this value for the physical disk that the paging file(s) are located on to find out how responsive those disks are. This information may encourage you to move the paging file to a faster disk.

Continued ▶

TABLE 20.1 CONTINUED: IMPORTANT MEMORY COUNTERS		
Counter	**Description**	**What This Tells You**
Process: Private Bytes	Records the virtual memory committed to that process.	This counter shows you how much memory a process (for all practical purposes, an application) is using. Especially if you're monitoring a terminal server, consider moving demanding applications to the client side or a different server to prevent other processes from being starved for memory.
Process: Working Set	Records the amount of RAM that that process is using to store data. The larger the working set, the more memory the process is consuming.	If a process's working set increases over time when you're not doing anything with it (like over a weekend), the process may be experiencing a memory leak.

NOTE Notice that not all the counters you'll be monitoring for memory usage are in the Memory process object.

Memory's complicated. Examining other potential server bottlenecks is, thankfully, a bit simpler.

Resolving CPU Bottlenecks Two counters can help you watch the overall CPU climate: Processor/% Processor Time and Processor/Interrupts/second.

Critical CPU Counters If Processor: % Processor Time rises above 75% on average, then that CPU is working pretty hard. Also, you might keep an eye on interrupts/second. If this value exceeds 3500 on a Pentium system, then more than likely something's going wrong, either a buggy program or a board spewing out spurious interrupts.

Handling Excessive Interrupts One common cause of excessive interrupts is badly designed device drivers. Are you running any beta device drivers? I've seen beta video drivers that spew out thousands of interrupts per second. You can test this by running the standard VGA driver and comparing the interrupts before and after.

Another source of excessive interrupts is timer-driver programs. Some years ago, one network manager I know was seeing 4000 interrupts/second on a fairly quiet 486-based file server. After some playing around with the system, he realized that he was opening Schedule+ in his Startup group. He shut it down, and his interrupts/second dropped to a normal rate.

I'd like to tell you that there's a System Monitor counter that lets you track interrupts/second on a program-by-program basis, but there isn't because much of this is just trial and error. Now and then, I see a board that sends out a blizzard of interrupts if it's failing or, sometimes, when it's just cold. You might see this when you turn a workstation on Monday morning and it acts strangely for half an hour, then settles down.

Move Programs Around   As I've recommended with other bottlenecks, one way to stop straining a resource is to stop asking so much of it. If you're running SQL Server 6.5 on a Pentium 233MHz with 64MB of RAM, there's not much I can do to help you, except tell you to move SQL Server elsewhere.

Buying More Silicon   The ultimate (and least desirable) answer is to buy more horsepower. But don't just throw away your money. Remember that there are two ways to make your system faster with CPUs: either buy a faster CPU or add another CPU to an existing multiprocessor computer. (If you don't have them yet, think seriously about buying SMP systems for your big servers.)

You'll find that a second processor does not increase performance by 100%, unfortunately. And for some programs a second processor offers no improvement at all. That's because not all Win2K programs are designed to be multithreaded and so don't take advantage of extra processors. You can pinpoint single-threaded applications by watching Process: % Processor Time, and log activity on all the processors. If you have a dual-processor system, and one processor is working hard (up over 50% utilization) and the other processor isn't doing anything at all, that pretty much proves that the application is single-threaded.

By the way, don't run one of those graphics-intensive screen savers on a server. Something like 3Dpipes can suck up tons of CPU cycles. Microsoft says that changes in the NT architecture after NT 3.x (namely, moving many of the graphical components of the Win32 subsystem from user mode to the kernel so the commands to execute graphics instructions can be processed quicker) have removed the problem under version 4 and later. However, my experiments don't support this in Win2K. Figure 20.4 shows some output from a remote Performance Monitor session (that is, I'm monitoring the server from across the network to make sure that Performance Monitor doesn't impact the system) viewing an idle Win2K server with a 350MHz CPU. The Processor: % Processor Time counter I've selected shows the percentage of time the processor is doing something, rather than running the "Idle thread" (the cybernetic equivalent of busywork) that Win2K provides the CPU with when no other threads need CPU time.

FIGURE 20.4

Use Performance Monitor to see how various applications eat up CPU cycles.

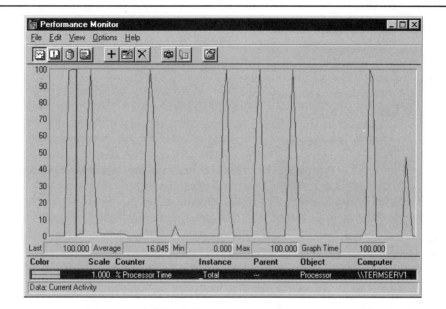

 NOTE Actually, I can tell that the graphic subsystem uses the CPU time here by monitoring another counter: Processor: % Privileged Time. The graphics subsystem works in privileged mode. The high percentage of time the CPU spends in privileged mode when running the screen saver clinches the deal, given the location of the graphic subsystem.

As you can see, this produces periodic spikes of nearly 100% utilization. As soon as I shut off the screen saver, the CPU time drops to almost nothing. Now, if *that* doesn't convince you to keep those screen savers to the bare minimum…

Resolving Disk Bottlenecks   The hard disks on your servers represent another potential sticking point for server production. For file servers, the bottleneck is obvious: the whole point of a file server is to grab data and pass it to the network for distribution. For application servers, the disk problem is more related to paging, because of the memory burden that applications incur. If you're running SQL Server or Exchange or supporting terminal server sessions, it's easy to run up against the amount of memory installed in the server—and when that happens, the server goes after your disk drive to support virtual memory.

There're a lot of counters for physical disks, but most of them don't tell you much in diagnostic terms except to help you see whether the disks are living up to their specifications. A couple that *do* are in Table 20.2.

TABLE 20.2: IMPORTANT DISK COUNTERS		
Counter	**Description**	**What This Counter Tells You**
Physical Disk: % Disk Time	Reports the percentage of time the physical disk is busy.	If it's busy more than 90% of the time, then it's too busy—you'll improve performance if you get another disk or do less with that one.
Physical Disk: Current Disk Queue Length	Reports the current number of data transfer operations waiting for the specified physical disk (or all disks, if you choose) to handle them.	This value should be as small as possible. If it's averaging more than 2, your disk waits are slowing you up.

 NOTE To use disk counters in NT, you had to enable them with the `diskperf -y` command. (These counters slowed down 386 computers, but this hasn't been an issue since 486 machines became available.) You don't have to do this in Win2K, and `diskperf` is no longer supported.

Resolving Network Bottlenecks Your network's apparent speed (not what it's rated at, but how responsive it is) is a function of how much traffic there is on the network and how quickly the server can process user requests.

First, how busy is the network? You'll need to monitor the transport protocols you're running on the server. Recall that TCP/IP has several different parts—it's a suite of protocols, not a single one like NetBEUI—and the parts do different things. So, for example, a lot of IP datagrams tell you that your network card is getting a lot of regular (that is, data-related) traffic. A suddenly large number of ICMP datagrams could signify problems—or demonstrate that someone is pinging the heck out of your server. Look for differences in traffic levels, both on the protocol level and for the entire network card (you can monitor both). Are you getting transmission errors for inbound or outbound network traffic? How busy is the local network segment?

Second, how busy is the server? Is it seeing logon errors? How quickly are people logging on at different times of day? How many files are open on the server? If it's a terminal server session, how many users is it supporting? If it's an FTP server, then how many connections are you having to maintain? Is the server experiencing non-paged pool failures, failing to allocate memory to components that need non-paged memory because there's too little RAM installed on the system?

 NOTE You can only get accurate network segment data if you have the Network Monitor for SMS installed. The Network Monitor that comes with Win2K only monitors data going to and from the monitored server. Therefore, you can get pretty much the same information from Network Interface that you can from Network Segment.

Lots of questions. I'd suggest that you poke around the performance objects a bit to look for specific counters you want to monitor for your server, but Table 20.3 includes some of the more common counters you should watch.

 TIP If your server is an Internet server of some kind (email, FTP, Web, etc.), be sure to monitor the counters appropriate to its function.

TABLE 20.3: IMPORTANT NETWORK-RELATED COUNTERS

Counter	Description	What This Counter Tells You
Server: Bytes total/sec	Reports the rate at which the server is sending and receiving network data.	The total of bytes going in and out of the server per second gives you a pretty good indication of how busy the server is. If you do something to change the server load, like adding another server of that kind or added load balancing to the network, you can monitor this value to see whether the change actually did any good.
Server: Files open	Reports the current number of files open at the moment of reporting. This is a current total, not a total of all the files that have been opened during a given time.	This counter is a good indicator of the traffic load a file server is experiencing. Sadly, there's no way to monitor file openings on a per-user or per-file basis.

Continued ▶

TABLE 20.3 CONTINUED: IMPORTANT NETWORK-RELATED COUNTERS

Counter	Description	What This Counter Tells You
Server: Pool Nonpaged Failures	Reports the number of errors the server is reporting as it tries to allocate non-paged pool.	Lots of errors means that the server is running low of RAM and you'll need to add more.
Server: Server Sessions	Reports how many people currently have connections to the server.	This counter may not tell you how busy the server is, but it can tell you how popular it is—especially if it's popular at an hour when no one should be accessing the server at all.
Network Interface: Bytes Total/sec	Reports the rate at which the network card is sending and receiving network data.	If this rate is significantly lower than what you'd expect, given the speed of your network and network card, it's time to do a little investigating to see whether something's wrong with the card.

Be sure to also monitor the protocols you've got installed for error conditions or heavy traffic at odd times.

Finally, if you're interested in using Performance Monitor like the Event Viewer, log the Server object's errors. This can give you reports on failed logon attempts, file access attempts, and other attempted access that can indicate someone's trying to break into the network.

Remote Performance Monitoring

There's one big problem with running the performance monitor on a server: the performance monitor *itself* consumes resources. To keep an eye on servers on the network, consider monitoring them remotely. You'll use a little network bandwidth but fewer resources on the monitored machine—and you'll get a more accurate reading because you're not stressing the server by running the monitor on it.

 NOTE   The only time when it's to your benefit to run Performance Monitor locally is when you're monitoring counters related to network traffic. Monitoring remotely will increase network traffic and skew the results.

Setting up remote performance monitoring is quite simple. When you're adding a counter to the monitor, you have a choice between adding the counter for the local machine or another one (see Figure 20.5). You can monitor any generation of NT computer, so if you've got a mixed environment it doesn't matter. You can also use Win2K Professional computers to do the monitoring, so you don't have to tie up a server for this task.

FIGURE 20.5

Adding a performance counter

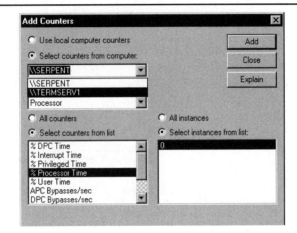

Make sure you've selected Select Counters from Computer, and type in the name of the computer you want to monitor with two preceding backslashes, like this: **\\Serpent**. (At least as of RC2, there's no Browse feature, so you have to know the name of the server you want to monitor. Annoyingly, Performance Monitor doesn't consistently "remember" the names of remote servers that it's monitored previously. Sometimes it does, and sometimes it develops amnesia.)

 WARNING Type server names carefully. If you mistype, it takes the System Monitor a very long time to discover that the server you've specified does not exist on the network.

When you're done choosing the counter you want to monitor, add it as you normally would and close the dialog box. The remote computer's counter will be added to the list and identified by the computer name (see Figure 20.6).

One of the cool things about doing remote performance monitoring is that it lets you compare server stress easily. Try this: select the same performance counter on two servers, like Processor: % Interrupt Time, which will show you what percentage of time the processor spends handling interrupt requests from hardware.

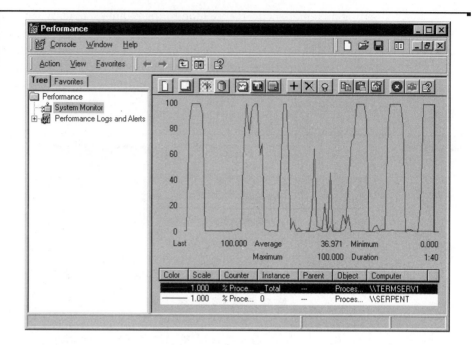

 WARNING Do *not* try to run the Performance Monitor from a terminal server session, even if you've only installed the administrative terminal services and don't intend to support application users. The constant graphical updates made in Performance Monitor do not update smoothly on the client side. Besides, you're still running the monitor on the server and consuming resources—you're just *watching* from a different computer.

Saving Chart Data

When you've identified the counters you want to monitor, you can save that information and reuse it later. You can reuse the counters to monitor again (because what you need to monitor once, you almost certainly will need to monitor again) or make them into an .HTM file that you can display in a browser.

To save chart settings, right-click somewhere on the Performance Monitor's display of current counters. You'll see a pop-up menu from which you can add counters, edit Performance Monitor properties, or save the data. Choose Save As... to save the data, and you'll be prompted for the name of the .HTM file. (This data will always be saved as a hypertext document.) The default folder is your personal My Documents folder, but you can browse for the right folder as you would with any Save As... operation. Type a name for the file, and it's saved.

If you open the file, it will open in your browser as shown in Figure 20.7.

FIGURE 20.7

*Saved Performance
Monitor chart*

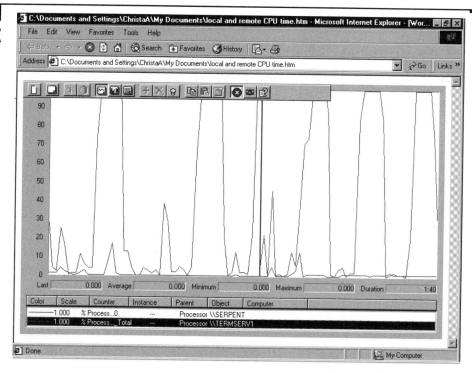

So long as the Performance Monitor is still running, you can dynamically update the output in this .HTM chart. To do it steadily, click the Freeze Display button (the red button with the white X on it) in the browser to deselect it. You'll see a warning that all current data will be cleared from the display; click OK and the display will clear and the browser fill with the updated Performance Monitor data. To manually update the data (perhaps if you're making a presentation and don't want people to be distracted watching the updates to the output), then keep the Freeze Display button activated and click the Update Data button (the camera between the Freeze Display and Help buttons).

What about reusing this data in a later Performance Monitor session? I'll talk more about how to use this data in the section "Logging Performance Data."

Logging Performance Data

The NT4 Performance Monitor included some logging support integrated with Perf-Mon itself. In Win2K, you've got the Performance Logs and Alerts section of the System Monitor to do that kind of work for you. Using a combination of comma-delimited and tab-delimited files and .HTM documents, you can pass information between the Performance Monitor and the Logs and Alerts—or even on to another application such as Excel.

Understanding Log Types

The System Monitor supports three types of logs: counter logs, trace logs, and alert logs. Counter logs record data from local or remote computers about hardware usage and system service activity. Trace logs are event-driven, recording monitored data such as disk I/O or page faults. When a traced event occurs, it's recorded in the log. Alert logs take trace logs one step further. They monitor counters and wait for them to exceed user-defined tolerances. When this happens, the event is logged. You can also set up an alert log to *do* something when the event happens, like sending a message or running an application.

 NOTE You can either set up perpetual logging or log only for a preset period of time, so you aren't overwhelmed with data.

Creating Logs

To create a log, turn to the Performance Logs and Alerts section of the System Monitor. Open the folder for the type of log you want, so that its contents (or lack thereof) are displayed in the right-hand details window. Right-click empty space in the Details window and choose an option for creating a new log from the pop-up menu that appears.

What happens from here depends on the type of log you're creating.

Counter Logs

If you're starting from scratch, choose the New Log Settings… option. Provide a unique descriptive name for the log in the box provided. Click OK, and you'll see the General tab of the log property sheet as shown in Figure 20.8.

You aren't yet monitoring anything. To begin, click the Add button, and you'll open the same Select Counters dialog box you used to add counters to a Performance Monitor chart (see Figure 20.9). Make sure you've selected the computer that you want to log (as with charting, logging takes up resources, so consider running logs remotely).

Click the Add button to add counters—you can add more than one from this window; just keep pushing the Add button—and click the Close button when you're done. The counters you selected will now be added to the Counters list on the General tab.

FIGURE 20.8

When you create a new log, it will contain no counters to monitor.

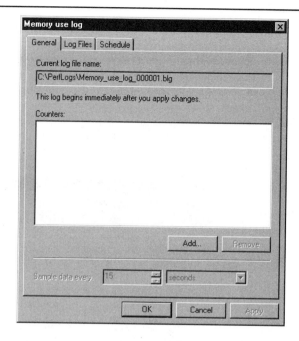

FIGURE 20.9

Adding counters to log

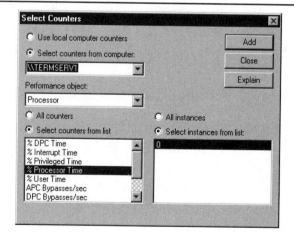

Back in the General tab, you can edit the sampling interval from its default of 15 seconds. The Sample Data Every box will accept an integer between 1 and 10,000, and the drop-down list of time units supports seconds, minutes, hours, or days. Pick an interval based on the duration of your expected logging time—the longer the period you're logging for, the wider you'll probably want the interval to be so you can see trends.

NOTE You can reuse performance monitor counters that you've previously saved as an .HTM file. If you plan to do so, start the creation process by choosing New Log Settings From... in the New menu. You'll be prompted to provide the name of the saved file. After that, the process will work exactly as it does for creating a new counter log file from scratch. The General tab will display the counters used in the saved Performance Monitor file.

Turn to the Log Files tab (see Figure 20.10) to edit file settings for the log.

FIGURE 20.10

Edit file settings to control file type, size, and name.

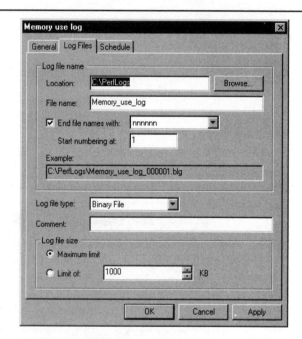

Most of these options are fairly self-explanatory, but let's take a quick tour:

- By default, logs are stored in a \Perflogs folder on your Win2K server's boot partition. Unless you regularly back up this location, you might want to put the logs somewhere else for safekeeping.

- The name of the log is the filename. It must conform to the naming convention of the file system where you're storing the log.

- The auto filename suffix is an extension to the log filename that allows you to identify logs by their name, if you maintain more than one with the same file-name. The *nnnnnn* naming means that the files will be numbered in order (the first serial number determines the first number that will be used). Other options identify the file by the date it was created, whether by year, or month, day, and hour, or some other mechanism. Open the drop-down list to find the naming convention that works best for you.

- The log file comment will appear next to the list of log names in the folder, so add a comment if the log file requires further description.

- Unless you specify otherwise, the file is a binary file, but you can also save the data as a binary circular file, comma-delimited file (.CSV), or tab-delimited file (.TSV). CSVs and TSVs can both be opened in analysis applications such as Microsoft Excel. The only limitation to CSV and TSV logs is that they must log all at once—they can't accommodate logs that start and stop. Binary and binary circular files (both of which have .BLG extensions) are for recording data intermittently, when data collection may stop and then resume while the log is recording data. The binary files create sequential lists of all events, while the binary circular files record data continuously to the same log file so that previously written records are overwritten when new data is available.

- Choose whether to limit the log file size. If you're planning to log for only a certain period of time (specified on the Schedule tab), then you may not want to limit the log's size, so you don't lose any of the data you choose to save. However, if you don't plan to choose an automatic ending time, it might not be a bad idea to limit the log size so you don't get more data than you can usefully examine.

When you've edited all the file settings, turn to the Schedule tab (see Figure 20.11) to finish creating the counter log file.

FIGURE 20.11

Editing scheduling settings for the log file

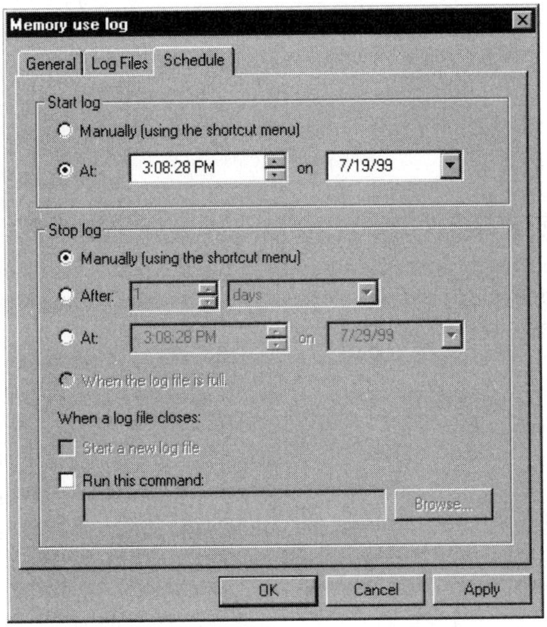

Normally, the log is set to start as soon as you finish (that is, it's set to start automatically at the time you started creating the log, which means it will begin logging as soon as you finish setting up options). You may not want to begin auditing the server as soon as you create the file if you're trying to gather information about server information under circumstances that you know will apply at a specific time. To manually start the log, choose that option here. Alternatively, you can specify a specific date and time the log should start.

Unless you specify otherwise, the log will keep collecting data until you shut it off manually. To schedule a stopping time or logging duration, click the After button and specify the time or period for which you want to log. In this same dialog box, you can also tell the System Monitor to restart the log when the preset period is ended (as you might do if you wanted to compare data from several different times of day) and name an application to run when the log is completed.

Click OK, and the new log will appear in the Details side of the Counter logs folder. Its icon will be red until the log starts collecting data, either at the time you specified on the Schedule tab or when you right-click the log object and choose Start from the pop-up menu.

Trace Logs

To create a new trace log, select that object in the left-hand pane and right-click in the right. As with counter logs, you can choose to either start from a saved Performance Monitor chart (New Log Settings From...) or create a new log from scratch (New Log Settings). Type a unique name for the trace log when prompted, and click OK. When you do so, you'll see the General tab in Figure 20.12.

Normally, only the system counters are available on this tab. (To enable them, click the Events Logged by System Provider radio button.) To make others available, click the Nonsystem Providers radio button and click the Add button. Choose the counter provider from the list and click OK to add it to the General list.

 TIP File I/O and page faults are not normally included in the trace log because of the very high values they're likely to register—a *lot* of I/O and page faults happen on a server operating normally. Microsoft recommends limiting the log to two hours if you want to include that data in the log.

The Log Files tab of the trace log creator works the same way the one for counter logs does, and so does the scheduler. The trace log creator includes one tab not in the counter log creator: Advanced (see Figure 20.13). Edit the settings here to make the buffers smaller or larger or to clear them periodically to make way for new data.

FIGURE 20.12

Choose counters for
the trace log.

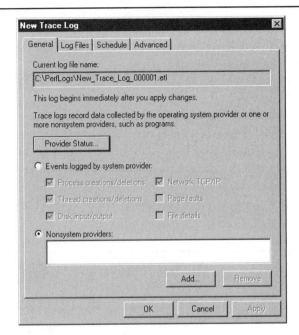

FIGURE 20.13

You can edit the size of
the buffers reserved
for a trace log.

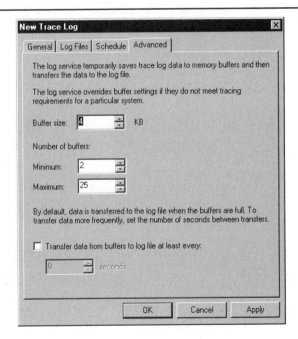

When you've edited all the trace log settings, click OK to return to the System Monitor. The log file will appear in the list. Its icon will be red until the log is running, then it'll turn green when it starts automatically or when you start it by right-clicking it and choosing Start.

Alert Logs

The initial stages of creating an alert log are much like those of creating a trace or counter log. Open the Alert Logs folder so that its contents are displayed on the right side of the System Monitor tool. Right-click anywhere in the blank area on the right side of the display and choose New Alert Settings... to define new counters to log or New Alert Settings From... to open a saved Performance Monitor file and use its counters. Choose a name for the new alert, then click OK to open the alert log's property sheet (see Figure 20.14).

General tab of the alert log's property sheet

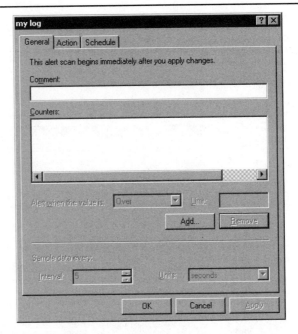

Assuming you're creating this log from new data, you'll need to add counters to the log as you did for a counter log. Click the Add button to open the dialog box in Figure 20.15, and choose the computer and performance counters you want to monitor. When you're done making selections (remember, you can add as many counters as you like by clicking the Add button), click Close to return to the General tab. The counters will show up in the list.

Below the list of added counters, you'll need to specify tolerances for each counter you choose. When the counter exceeds those tolerances, the alert log will add an entry to the file. For example, say that you added Physical Disk: Avg Disk Queue Length to the log. That monitors the number of read and write requests waiting for processing to the specified physical disk. If more than four requests are waiting, then that implies that the disk is too busy to handle all the demands placed on it and you need to do something about that. Therefore, you'd set the tolerances for this counter to be over 4, as shown in Figure 20.16.

FIGURE 20.15

Adding counters to a log

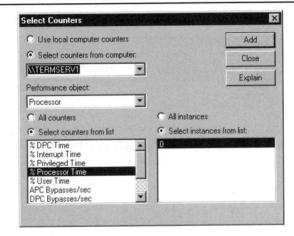

FIGURE 20.16

Adjust alert tolerances

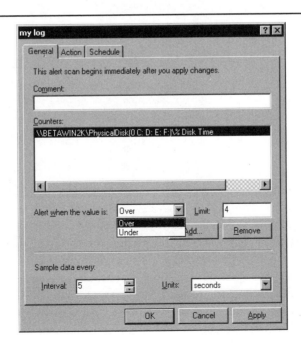

Notice that the default sampling interval for alerts (5 seconds) is much shorter than the one for counters. This is because of the different nature of the log—it's assumed that you're a little more concerned about the contents of this one. Use the drop-down lists to edit the sampling intervals if you need to.

 TIP Tune alert logs carefully. The shorter interval and extra processing required to manage alerts will impact a server.

The scheduling tab for alert logs works just like the one you used to configure counter and trace logs, but the Action tab (see Figure 20.17) is something new. From this tab, you'll need to tell the System Monitor what you want it to do when it generates an alert.

FIGURE 20.17

Edit alert settings

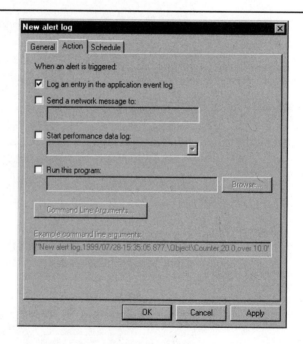

Normally, System Monitor just adds an entry to the Event Viewer's application event log. If the alert isn't something that you need to know about right away, then you can leave it at that. More important alerts, however, like those generated by network errors or a severe shortage of memory, may require immediate action. From the Alert menu, you can tell System Monitor to send you (or someone else) a message when writing an entry in the alert log, or even to have it run a specific application that you can use to resolve the problem. Use this tab to send arguments to the application.

Once again, when you're done editing the alert log's properties, click OK to add it to the `Alert Logs` folder. When it's running, its icon will be green.

Viewing Log Data

The method of viewing log output depends on the file type you've saved the log in. Excel and other spreadsheet applications can read tab-delimited and comma-delimited files without translating, so you can open those files without preparation. The output may require some massaging to make a good presentation, but it will be there.

Alert logs don't go into a regular file but directly to the Event Viewer's Application log (see Figure 20.18). When the counters exceed the tolerances you've set up, Win2K will add an Information record to the Application event log.

FIGURE 20.18

Output of an alert log

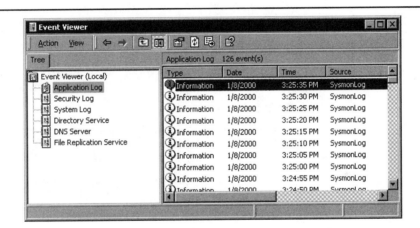

Whattheheckhappened? Troubleshooting with the Event Viewer

Win2K defines an event as any significant occurrence in the system or in an application that users should be aware of and have the chance to log. Critical events—those that can impact server availability—deserve immediate notifications, which is why you'll see "low on virtual memory" announcements on your monitor without asking for them. Less critical but still important events are recorded in the Event Viewer, a tool in the Administrative Tools program group.

To make Win2K record, retrieve, and store logs of events, you must activate and configure event logging. You can edit just about any kind of event on a server: file and directory access, services starting (or failing to start), unexpected conditions on the server, or, as discussed earlier, alert logs based on System Monitor data.

Understanding Log Types

Win2K maintains six types of logs. Three you may recall from NT4 and earlier: system, security, and application. System events (see Figure 20.19), the only ones logged by default, are generated by Win2K system components or related services and drivers. Security events (see Figure 20.20) record changes to any security settings or any audited access such as attempts to open files or folders. You can monitor both successful and failed security events. Application logs (see Figure 20.21) contain events generated by applications or by alert logs.

FIGURE 20.19

System log

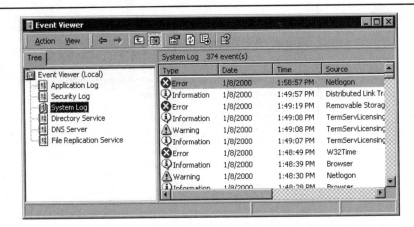

FIGURE 20.20

Security log

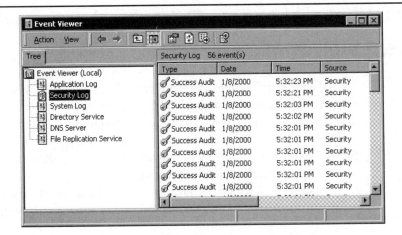

FIGURE 20.21

Application log

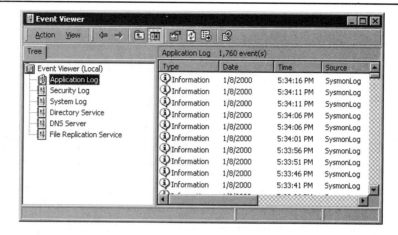

Three other logs—Directory Service, DNS Server, and File Replication Service—are new to Win2K. They're for keeping track of AD-related events. The Directory Service log entries record information regarding the NT Directory Service, problems connecting to the global catalog, and any issues regarding Active Directory in your network. The DNS Server entries record any events related to running the Directory Name Service in your Active Directory. Finally, the File Replication event log records any notable events that took place while the domain controller attempted to update other domain controllers.

To view any log, open the Event Viewer. From the left-hand pane showing the log types, click the type you want to view. The display in the right-hand pane will change to show the log's contents.

Viewing Remote Event Log Data

You can connect to any NT or Win2K computer with an account in your domain (or in another, trusted domain). To do so, right-click the main Event Viewer folder in the left-hand pane of the tool. From the pop-up menu that appears, choose Connect to Another Computer. You'll see a dialog box that looks like the one in Figure 20.22.

Enter the name of the computer you want to monitor (for example, SERPENT). Alternatively, you can browse for the computer you want to monitor. The other computer can be running Win2K or Windows NT or can be a LAN Manager 2.*x* server.

TIP The domain controller will not appear in the list, but you can monitor it by typing its name.

FIGURE 20.22

Choose a computer to manage.

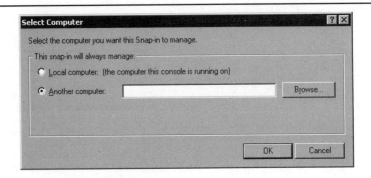

Click Finish, click Close, and then click OK.

If the new computer requires a low-speed connection, right-click the log you want to view, and then click Properties. On the Action menu, click Properties, and then click Low Speed Connection (on the General tab).

Alternatively, you can right-click the root of the Event Viewer being logged to open its pop-up menu. Click the Connect to Another Computer option and type the name of the computer you want to manage. If you're not sure of its name, click the Browse button to find the computer you want (see Figure 20.23).

FIGURE 20.23

Find a computer to manage.

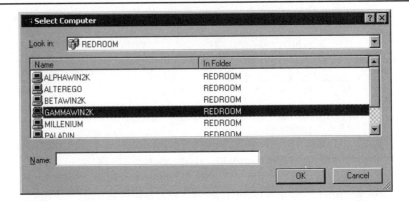

NOTE You can only monitor NT or Win2K computers that have a computer account in the selected domain and are currently connected to the network. All computer accounts will be listed, even if a particular computer is offline at the moment.

When you've chosen a computer, click OK back in the Select Computer dialog box. The Event Viewer information displayed will now be the remote computer's.

Reading Log Entries

There're five categories of log entries, each identifiable by an icon:

- Information events describe the successful completion of a task, such as the beginning of a service.
- Warning events aren't necessarily bad but describe unexpected behavior that might point to future problems if not corrected.
- Error events describe fatal errors that mean a task failed. Error events may lead to data loss; they always mean that the server wasn't able to do something you asked it to do.
- Success events describe an audited security event that Win2K completed as requested.

 TIP Some third-party services log successful starting as a success event instead of an information event.

- Failed events describe an audited security event that Win2K could not complete as requested.

Each entry also includes the following information pertinent to the event:

- Date and time logged
- Object logging the event (such as the service that failed to start)
- Computer name of the server where the event was generated and, if applicable, the name of the person responsible for generating the event
- If applicable, the category of event. This number won't tell you much—it's for the internal use of whatever server component logged the event.
- Event number describing the event type to Win2K

Double-click any event in any log to open its property sheet (see Figure 20.24) and see more information about the event. The explanation is sometimes more than a little cryptic or is incomplete, but sometimes—and this gets easier with practice—you can glean useful information from the explanations of the events.

Troubleshooting with the Event Viewer takes a little practice. For best results, you'll need to know what your system looks like when it's running normally so you can more easily identify the events that indicate something is broken. Reading the Event Viewer on a regular basis also lets you find out about problems you may not have known you had, like misconfigured services, undetected because no one's using them much, or a drive running low on disk space.

FIGURE 20.24

Event details for a
System log entry

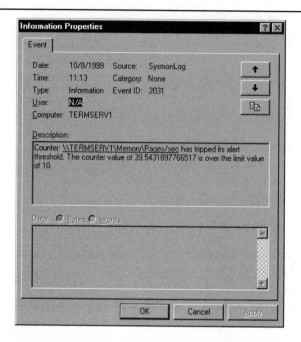

The following dialog shows:

Information Properties

Event

Date: 10/8/1999   Source: SysmonLog
Time: 11:13   Category: None
Type: Information   Event ID: 2031
User: N/A
Computer: TERMSERV1

Description:
Counter: \\TERMSERV1\Memory\Pages/sec has tripped its alert threshold. The counter value of 39.5431897766517 is over the limit value of 10.

Data: ● Bytes ○ Words

OK   Cancel   Apply

TIP The Win2K Resource Kit includes a Windows 2000 Event Log Database that purports to list every message that could be included in any Event Viewer log. It's not especially helpful because it doesn't include any more information than is already in the Event Viewer entries, but it's a good look at all the thousands (yes, I mean thousands) of event types you might encounter. You'll need Access installed to view this database. To run it, open the Resource Kit management console (if you've installed the Resource Kit, you can get to this from the Programs program group) and view the tools in alphabetical order.

Managing and Archiving Log Contents

That's what you're looking at. *Managing* all that data can be a task unto itself.

Discarding Old Data

The Event Viewer logs will keep filling up according to their settings. After a while (and, if you're recording something that happens a lot, "a while" may not be long), they get full. Unless you specify otherwise, an event log cannot get any bigger than 512KB.

To keep the data fresh, the Event Viewer normally overwrites events more than seven days old with the newer information on the principle that data more than a week old isn't helpful anymore. To edit this, open the property sheet for a log by right-clicking its icon and choosing Properties. Turn to the General tab shown in Figure 20.25.

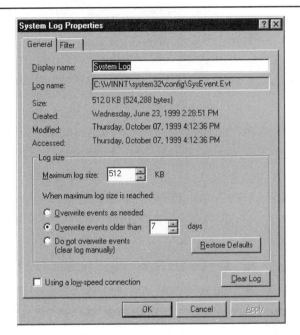

FIGURE 20.25

Edit the settings governing how data is discarded when the log is full.

 WARNING If you click the Clear All Events button on this tab, you'll delete all the entries in that log. Save logs before clearing them if you think you might need the data again.

Filtering Data

Normally, the Event Viewer will display all records that it's collected, with the most recent entries at the top of the log. You can simplify the view of all this data by applying filters to the logged data. Filters don't affect what information is logged, only how it's displayed.

To filter a log's events, right-click the log's icon in the left-hand pane and choose Filter from the View menu. You'll see the Filter tab shown in Figure 20.26. Choose the filtering options you want, described in Table 20.4. Only event logs with the options you specify (you can apply as many as you like) will appear in the event log once you've applied the filter.

FIGURE 20.26

Filter data to display only pertinent information.

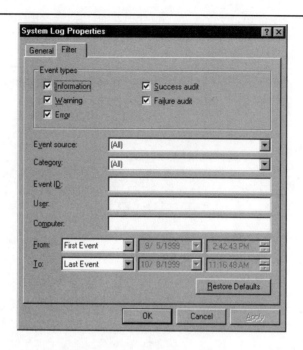

TABLE 20.4: FILTERING OPTIONS FOR EVENT LOGGING

Option	Description
Category	Includes all events within a given category. This filter is most useful for security events, as most system events do not belong to any category and the application categories are numbered, with no keys.
Computer	Includes all events on that particular computer. As the computer in question is the one you're monitoring and you can only display one computer's event log at a time, it's not clear to me why this filter is part of the Event Viewer.
Error	Includes all error events, those which mean that Win2K was unable to complete a requested task for some reason.
Event ID	Includes all events with that event ID. You can only specify one event ID at a time—you can't, for example, filter the event log to display both event ID 7000 and event ID 4002.
Event Source	Displays events stemming from a user-specified source (a driver, system component, or service).
Failure Audit	Displays failed security events such as opening a file or changing a security setting. The events this will include depend on the security and auditing settings for the domain or computer.

Continued ▶

TABLE 20.4 CONTINUED: FILTERING OPTIONS FOR EVENT LOGGING	
Option	**Description**
Information	Displays information events. Information events typically mean that everything worked as planned, but you can use information events to reassure yourself that yes, that service started as planned, so it couldn't be a problem there.
Success Audit	Displays successful security events such as opening a file or changing a security setting. The events this will include depend on the security and auditing settings for the domain or computer.
User	Displays events that are associated with a particular user, generally the user working at the console when the event was generated. Not all events have a user associated with them—this is mostly a System Log thing.
View From and To	Use these boxes to specify a range of events to display. Unless you tell it otherwise, the event log will display all events in the log from the oldest to the newest, but you can provide starting and finishing dates and times.
Warning	Includes warning events, which tell you that something didn't go as expected (or, for alert logs, that a counter exceeded the tolerance you set up) but that the problem isn't immediately critical.

Filters work like Boolean AND statements, not OR statements. That is, if you specify event ID 7000 and check the Error box, then the log will only display entries that are errors associated with event ID 7000, not all errors and all entries with event ID 7000.

 TIP Want to view all data of a certain type but aren't sure how to filter the event log? Click the column heading that corresponds to the type of data you want to view, and the log will sort its entries based on that type. For example, if you want to see all the entries associated with the Browser service, click the header for the Source column. All entries related to the Browser service will be grouped together.

Saving and Retrieving Log Data

Like I said, logs get full. You may want the data in them for future reference, however, so you don't necessarily want to just clear all log file entries. To save a log file, right-click the log's icon in the left-hand pane of the Event Viewer. From the context menu, choose Save Log File As.... A Save dialog box will open. Type the name of the log, click Save, and you're done. You can now clear the file to begin logging afresh.

To open a saved log, right-click the Event Viewer icon in the left-hand pane and choose Open Log File. You'll see a dialog box like the one in Figure 20.27. Browse for the .EVT file containing the saved log, choose a log type and a display name, and click OK.

When you've loaded the saved event log, it will appear alongside the other event logs as shown in Figure 20.28.

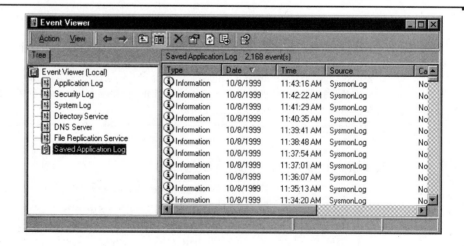

Basic Tuning Stuff

You've now got the information, but what can you do with it? Open the Control Panel, and we'll see.

Optimizing Server Processing Power

Windows NT Server 4 and NT Workstation had several obvious differences, but one of the major differences wasn't obvious. The core files required to run NT Server and NT Workstation were and are the same, but at boot time the OS looks in the Registry key `HKLM\System\CurrentControlSet\Control\ProductOptions`. Run REGEDT32 and look in that key on a Win2K system, and, among other information, you'll see a value for Product Type. That value was (and is—this hasn't changed) WinNT for Windows NT Workstation/Win2K Professional computers, LanmanNT for domain controllers, and ServerNT for server computers.

Why does this value matter? Based on the value of this key, NTLDR makes some decisions about how to configure the system, including runtime policy decisions such as how operating system components and user processes contend for memory and even how the processes contend for CPU time.

The most obvious result of this is that NT Server gave a little more time to the application in the foreground than the ones in the background. But NT Workstation gave a *lot* more time to the application in the foreground, on the premise that the application you're directly interacting with is the one you want to be most responsive. If you ran, say, Microsoft Word from an NT Server machine, it would run rather less well than if you ran the application from an NT Workstation computer. This is because even when you were typing into Word, NT Server would be a little distracted, checking with any other running processes to make sure they were happy and getting enough CPU time. NT Server is meant to be a *server*, not a workstation.

 NOTE You could edit the Performance settings in the System applet of the Control Panel, but I'm talking about the way the operating systems were set to run under normal conditions.

Ah, but what about terminal services? It's a server, but a server of a very special kind, since it's providing computing resources to a bunch of client machines. For that reason, terminal services should give more time to foreground applications than to background applications and services, as the foreground applications are the most important to the overall performance of the server.

Windows NT, Terminal Server Edition (TSE), was designed to always run foreground applications more efficiently, because if you installed TSE it was assumed you were using the server for terminal services—otherwise, you would have saved yourself some money and stuck with single-user NT. Win2K, on the other hand, comes with terminal services but doesn't have to run them—the multi-user capability is a service instead of a core part of the operating system and, as such, can be installed and uninstalled.

If Terminal Services is running and you've set up Win2K to be an application server when you installed the services, then the operating system is normally optimized for running foreground applications. (You've got another option of installing terminal services only for remote administration of the server, in which case the server is optimized for fulfilling server functions.)

If you're using terminal services for its usual function of supporting clients running applications from the terminal server, then this is fine. If you're using terminal services for remotely administering a server for the moment, however, you may want to give equal time to all server applications. To do so while still running terminal services, open the System applet in the Control Panel. Turn to the Advanced tab, and click the Performance Options button to open the dialog box you see in Figure 20.29.

In the Application Response section, make sure the Background option is selected. This tells Win2K to give all running applications equal access to CPU cycles. This may make your foreground applications a little more jerky, but other applications will respond to user requests more smoothly.

FIGURE 20.29

Edit performance options.

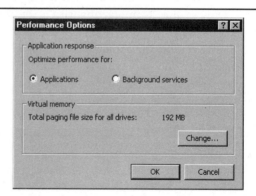

Editing Virtual Memory Settings

While we're in the Performance dialog box of the System applet, take a look at the virtual memory sections (see Figure 20.30).

The default location for the paging file is `%systemroot%\pagefile.sys`. This isn't always the best place for it, however. First, if you run out of room on the system partition, the system paging file may not be able to grow as big as it needs to, which in turn will mean that your server is starved for virtual memory. Page files aren't small, running in the hundreds of megabytes on a typical server. Second, the faster the disk that the paging file's stored on, the faster the data can be paged back into physical memory after a page fault. If you add a new and faster disk to your system, it may well be to your advantage to move the paging file there.

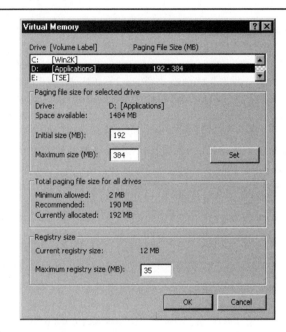

IGURE 20.30

Virtual memory settings for Win2K

To move the paging file from its original location, open the dialog box shown here and select the local drive where you want the paging file to go. Type in a minimum and maximum size for the paging file in the boxes provided. Also, select the drive where the paging file *was* and zero it out.

TIP It's not a good idea to force the paging file to grow. Although it will get bigger as needed, the process of making the file get bigger is resource-intensive. You'll get better performance if you make the minimum size of the paging file something resembling its necessary size.

When you finish, the size of the new paging file should be shown in the Paging File Size column next to the right drive, and that space in the original drive should be blank. Click the Set button to establish the paging file.

NOTE For what should be obvious reasons, you can't put the paging file on a network-accessible drive. (In case it's not obvious, you don't want the memory manager putting important data on a disk that might not be available when the memory manager needs that data *back*.) And although removable drives such as Jaz drives will show up in the list of local drives that you could put a paging file on, they're displayed with a free space of 0MB, so you can't put the drives there.

You'll need to restart the server, but once you do, the paging file will be moved to the new location.

What if you zero out the original page file but forget to specify the location of a new one? You'll be prompted to reboot the computer as usual for changing the size of the paging file. However, when you reboot, Win2K will display a nastygram telling you that the computer either has no paging file or it's too small. It will create a temporary paging file called `temppf.sys`, storing it in the `%systemroot%\system32` folder. You must follow the instructions here (and also provided on the nastygram) for creating a new paging file on the appropriate disk. Your server will work until you do this, but it will have no virtual memory. The new paging file will grow slowly as needed, causing you to run low on virtual memory from time to time. Conveniently, you cannot delete a paging file from Explorer, as it's a file in use.

Tuning the System Cache

Win2K's default memory settings reflect NT's legacy as a file-sharing NOS. By default, it's set up with a large *system cache*, which is a range of virtual memory addresses reserved for caching recently used data related to file sharing, whether from hard disks, CD-ROM, or network-accessible drives. The cache includes any data related to file reads and writes, including file contents, read and write activity to a file, or the metadata that describes a drive's structure and organization. The system cache has a range of virtual memory addresses dedicated to it, with the exact size of the range depending on the amount of physical memory installed in the server. Just as the size of the paging file increases as you install more physical memory, the system cache does, too, up to an initial limit of 512MB on an *x86* system.

NOTE You can see how much physical memory your server's system cache is using by monitoring the value of Memory: System Cache Resident Bytes. Although the System Monitor has a counter called Memory: Cache Bytes, this counter doesn't actually reflect just the System Cache working set. It reflects the entire system working set, including paged pool, and any driver code and NTOSKRNL data that can be paged to disk.

Up to 512MB of virtual memory addresses is a lot. If a server's supporting file sharing, then it needs this big reserved virtual memory space. However, caching all that data may cause a lot of disk thrashing as the data goes in and out of physical memory. If a particular server isn't doing file sharing, you can save yourself some physical memory by changing the memory usage parameters for network use. To do so, open Network and Dial-Up Connections. Right-click Local Area Connection and open its property sheet. Select File and Printer Sharing For Microsoft Networks, and open that service's property sheet as shown in Figure 20.31.

The default setting is Maximize Data Throughput for File Sharing. If you're not using the server to share files, change this setting to Maximize Data Throughput for Network Applications, or to Balance. (Minimize Memory Used setting is only a good idea for servers serving a very few users, like under 10.) This should reduce the amount of paging to disk that your server's doing.

FIGURE 20.31

Server Optimization options

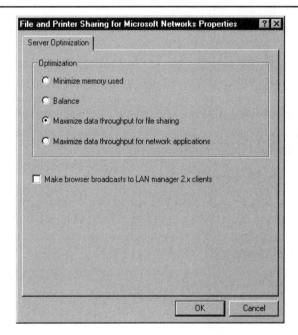

Server Tuning

There's actually quite a bit you can do to make servers more responsive. Doing so requires tuning the server *and* keeping unnecessary junk off the network.

Simplify Protocols

One of the best pieces of network-tuning advice I can give you is to remove unnecessary protocols and services. Protocols and services steal memory and CPU time. Multiple protocols require multiple browse lists, which in turn steal CPU time from the machine that is the master browser, and Win2K Server machines are often elected as master browsers. One of the most common reasons a Win2K system fails to recognize a workstation, leading to a "no domain controller was available to…" error message, is that the server simply has too many protocols to listen to. Try to pick *one* protocol and work with that one.

If you're using the TCP/IP stack, you find that it sometimes receives short shrift from the network because the more frenetic IPX and NetBEUI protocols grab more processor attention. (Must be an age thing—they're younger and therefore more hyper.) As a result, the TCP/IP stack may end up dropping more messages than it would if the other protocols didn't exist; one other symptom is an incomplete browse list. If you can, remove extraneous protocols. If possible, just trim down to TCP/IP.

One Remedy: Segment the Network

If the network utilization is getting excessively high, you have to reduce the network traffic on that network segment. You can do that either by removing network applications—put the company Web server on a segment of its own, for instance—or by breaking up existing segments. Instead of three segments of 100 PCs, break it up into six segments of 50 PCs apiece.

But then you have to be sure to get good, fast routers to connect the network segments. Win2K servers can do the job fairly well on low-volume networks, but look to dedicated routers from companies like Compatible Systems or Cisco Systems for more heavy-traffic network segments.

Raise Server Priority

By default, the file server actually has a lower priority than the print server, causing printing to slow down the server. Printing priority is set by default to 2, and file server priority is set to 1; larger numbers are better. You can change the priority by modifying the Registry. Open the Registry Editor on the file server and turn to HKLM\System\CurrentControlSet\Services\lanmanserver\parameters. Add a value entry Thread-Priority of type DWORD, and set it to 2.

Ensure That Win2K Can Continue to Autotune

Win2K's file server module includes almost two dozen tuning and control parameters. Most of them control exactly how much memory Win2K devotes to different parts of the server module. For example, what's the maximum number of sessions the server will have to keep track of at any moment in time? Win2K must know that so it can pre-allocate some RAM as working space, a place in memory to track each session. That's set by an "autotuning" parameter every time you start up a server. Similarly, what's the maximum amount of memory the server service can use at any time, both in pageable (able to be swapped out to disk) and non-pageable flavors? More autotuned parameters.

Could you choose to control these parameters yourself? If you wanted to, you certainly could, but I wouldn't recommend it. But doing some basic administrative tasks could well inadvertently make it impossible for Win2K to tune its own parameters.

Elsewhere in this book, you'll see commands that start with NET CONFIG SERVER; for example, as you'll read in the upcoming section on the Browser, typing **net config server /hidden:yes** puts a server in "Romulan cloaking device" mode, wherein the server never appears in My Network Places. Alternatively, you might want to add a comment to the My Network Places display of your server by typing **net config server /srvcomment:*whatever comment you like***. In either case, using the NET CONFIG SERVER command (lower- or uppercase doesn't matter, by the way, save for whatever case you desire within the message itself) has a nasty side effect.

For some reason, when you set *one* parameter with NET CONFIG SERVER, Win2K writes out the current values of *all* the autotuning parameters. (These parameters are in HKLM\System\CurrentControlSet\Services\lanmanserver\parameters.) The nasty side effect is this: when Win2K starts up the Server service, the Server service looks in the Registry to see if these autotunable parameters are present. If they are, NT does *not* attempt to re-tune them. Actually, this is true even if you never touched NET CONFIG. Edit a server's comment from the Server tool in Administrative tools on an NT 4 Server, and the entries will be in Parameters *then*, too.

Why would you care? This matters mainly if you have changed the amount of RAM in your system. Add more RAM and reboot, and NT will adjust all the auto-tunable parameters. But if they've been inadvertently cast in concrete by the simple act of hiding or naming a server, that autotuning doesn't happen.

How, then, to restore autotuning? Look in HKLM\System\CurrentControlSet\Services\lanmanserver\parameters; you'll see a whole bunch of entries *if* you've done a NET CONFIG SERVER at some point. (If you've never configured the server at all, there will still be a couple for *NullSessionPipes* and *NullSesssionShares*, but that's all.) Then start deleting those value entries. Don't get *too* nuts—if you've made your server a time source, don't delete TimeSource, or if you've hidden the server, don't delete Hidden, Srvcomment, ThreadPriority, or any other entry you have entered in the past for some reason. In particular, you'll probably need to remove entries named *anndelta, enableforcedlogoff, enablesoftcompat, maxnonpagedmemoryusage, maxpagedmemoryusage, maxrawbuflen, maxworkitems, opensearch, sessconns, sessopens, sessusers, sessvcs, userpath, users, Leave NullSessionPipes, NullSessionShares, Size* (does it matter?), *LMAnnounce*, and *EnableSharedNetDrives*. (And please don't ask me what they do; the documentation on most of them is pretty spotty. If you want, search the Knowledge Base for any of the keywords and you probably will either get nothing or a fairly useless definition. One of the odder parameters has to be anndelta, a holdover from LAN Man; the Knowledge Base says, "This parameter is ignored." Great, guys, so why bother?)

Using the Most Current Drivers

One of the simplest things you can do to make your server happy is make sure it's always got the most recent certified drivers. (Sometimes, manufacturers release drivers on a beta basis, but I'd be cautious about using those on a production machine.) New drivers may provide better performance or add features—or fix problems caused by other drivers, like the runaway network card diagnostic service that gave me a deep and lasting appreciation for the powers of the Recovery Console (covered in Chapter 21). Buggy device drivers can also produce a blizzard of interrupts, which will slow down the CPU as it attempts to respond to all these requests for processing even if there's nothing to process.

 TIP To detect excessive interrupts in a video board, try comparing values of Processor: % Interrupt Time or Processor: Interrupts/sec with the video in normal mode and in VGA mode. If you see many more interrupts while the video's in normal mode, try replacing the video driver.

To update a driver in your system, open the System applet in the Control Panel and turn to the Hardware tab. Click the Device Manager button to open the Device Manager shown in Figure 20.32.

FIGURE 20.32

Check hardware settings and update drivers from the Device Manager.

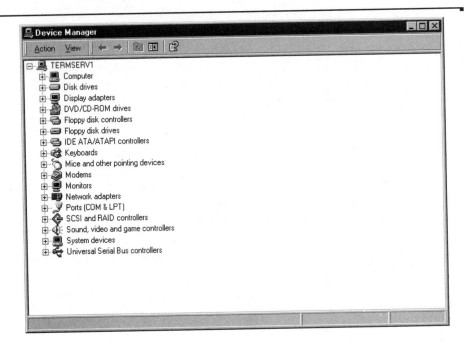

Find the category of device you want to update, then choose the particular device and double-click it to open its property sheet. (For this example, I'll update the driver on my network card.) You want the Driver tab, shown in Figure 20.33.

FIGURE 20.33

Turn to the Driver tab to view driver information and update files.

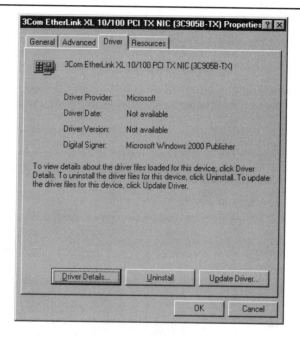

First, see what the current driver version is by clicking the Driver Details button to open the dialog box shown in Figure 20.34.

FIGURE 20.34

View driver information to check its version and creation date.

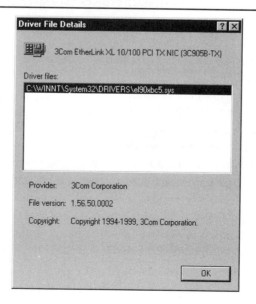

Adding Drivers Manually

Armed with this information, I can go to the 3Com site (www.3com.com, if you're interested) and search for new drivers. Typically, there's a Downloads section on any manufacturer's Web site. Go there and look for drivers for your class of device. You'll need to know the model number of the device, so make sure you've got that information on hand. Find the driver you want. If the version on the Web site is newer than the one installed on your server, download to a floppy disk or the network.

Armed with the location of the new driver, click the Update Driver button in the Drivers tab of the property sheet for the device. This will start the Update Device Driver Wizard. After the obligatory "Welcome to Wizard X" screen, you'll see the screen shown in Figure 20.35.

FIGURE 20.35

Choose whether you want Win2K to search for the driver for your device or you want to find it yourself.

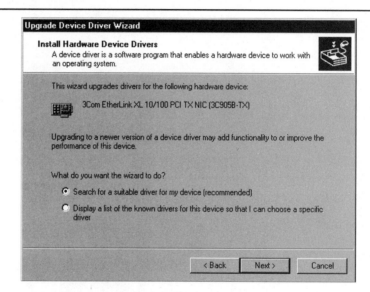

If you tell the wizard to search your drivers, check the boxes of the locations where it should look, making sure to check the Specify Location box if you plan to update the drivers from the network.

If you tell the wizard that you want to find the driver yourself, it will search your hard disk and report back with a list of all compatible drivers located on the disk. As this list doesn't report version numbers or dates (see Figure 20.36), it's not very useful (if it only returns one driver, then it's found the one you're already using). I'd suggest letting the wizard search for appropriate drivers from CD-ROM and floppy disk.

Your server will grind away for a minute as the wizard searches for .INF files that match your device. When it reports back, it will tell you it found a driver already installed (if the device was already working, it did) but also give you the option of choosing another driver to use. If you check the box asking to see the other drivers and click Next, you'll see a list showing the drivers found and reporting only which one is currently installed.

FIGURE 20.36

The wizard will return a list of currently available drivers.

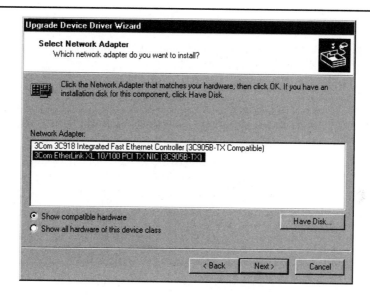

Check the driver you want to use and click Next. The wizard will install the new driver.

You Knew It Was Coming... Hardware and Other Performance Recommendations

Finally, there's the obvious way to resolve performance problems: throw more hardware at them. By using the System Monitor, you should have a pretty good idea what hardware in your system is contributing to the bottlenecks. Get more memory, if your server needs it (many, many Win2K problems can be resolved by adding more memory to a server because the OS uses so much storage). Use *fast* memory—this is the place to install that 100MHz SDRAM even if no other machines on the network get it. Make sure, too, that you're using a 100MHz motherboard so that memory can communicate with the CPU as quickly as it's capable of.

More CPU power can also help. Servers, especially terminal servers which are apt to be compute-bound, will benefit from having the fastest processors (or more than one fast processor) that you can afford.

Disks... Servers should use SCSI, because SCSI devices can multitask. Even if you've got multiple EIDE drives on the server, data transfer involving one EIDE device means that data transfer with the others is on hold. Using multiple SCSI disks means that RAID works more efficiently—data transfer from a striped or mirrored disk array is faster than to and from individual disks, because of the multiple read/write interfaces. Consider putting a page file on each physical disk in the server, so you can read and write to more than one part of the paging file at the same time.

 NOTE For more information about disk striping and mirroring, turn to Chapter 7, "Managing Windows 2000 Storage."

Even if you can find ISA network cards for your server, don't use them. PCI cards will communicate with the CPU much more efficiently than ISA and have a higher data transfer rate. If the network cards support IRQ10, use it instead of IRQ5 (which most network cards use). IRQ10 has a higher priority. And while you're thinking about networks, consider segmenting yours to isolate heavy traffic areas and keep them from impacting the rest of the network.

Finally, if you're still running into hardware problems, think about limiting what you're asking the server to do. Don't run services or transfer protocols you don't need, as they'll consume memory that you could use elsewhere. If you're not running terminal server sessions, you don't need to install the service. If all the server's devices are SCSI, you don't need ATDISK, the IDE interface.

Configuring Network Browsing

One last bit to tuning Win2K performance is tuning browsing. Win2K is inherently the front end to the network. The faster that people can find the resources they want on the network, the happier they'll be.

I've always liked Mark's explanation of why network browsing is important in today's networks:

"Years ago, I used an IBM PC Network program. To use network resources, you had to hook up to a drive on a server by saying to the PC Network program, 'Attach me to drive E: on the machine named AVOCADO.' Nice and simple, but it begged the question: How did you know that the server was named AVOCADO and that it had shared a drive called E:? The answer is, *you had to know the name of the resource before you could connect to that resource.* There was no 'scan the network to find out what's available' feature to the network. (An IBM guy once explained to me that this was a 'security feature.' Now why didn't *I* think of that?)"

Mark wanted a "net scan" command, something that would shout to the other systems on the network, "Hey! Whaddaya got?" As it turns out, that's not very simple. The whole process of offering services on a network is part of what's known generically as *name services* or *directory services*, and they're not easy to offer. Chapter 2 covers

Active Directory, but, unless you're prepared to go Win2K all the way, there's more to the problem of resource publication than Active Directory setup.

Solving the Directory Service Problem

How would *you* tell a workstation about every service available on the network? There's a couple ways to do this.

Static Service Lists

The simplest approach would be to put a file with some kind of services database on the network, kind of like one of the Yellow Pages sites on the Web. For example, you might have an ASCII file stored on each PC that says, "There is a file server on machine BIGPC with a shared disk called BIGDISK, and the computer named PSRV has a shared printer named HP4L." This approach has the advantage of being very fast and very simple to understand. If a new resource becomes available, you just add it to the service list file.

Anyone who's ever used the aforementioned Yellow Pages sites on the Web probably already knows the disadvantage of such a system: it's static. If there're any changes to the system, some poor fool (that would be *you*, the network administrator) has to go around to all the workstations and update the file. Two hundred workstations = two hundred updates. Even worse, static service lists don't take into account services that are temporarily unavailable due to a downed server or some such problem.

Although this method sounds too primitive to use, NetWare 3.*x* uses a variant of it. Each workstation identifies itself to the desired server via information stored in a file called NET.CFG. That's a hard-wired server name, which means that changing a server's name in this network would mean editing everyone's NET.CFG file. This is presumably the reason you don't often edit server names in NetWare 3.*x* world—and why Novell handles resource publishing differently in NetWare 4.*x* and later.

Periodic Advertising

Another approach to resource publishing is an occasional broadcast. Every 30-60 seconds (depending on how the network administrator sets it up), each resource on a NetWare 3.11 network shouts to the rest of the network, "I'm here!" Novell calls this the Service Advertising Protocol (SAP) and it's a good idea, working well in many cases.

It's not the perfect answer, however. In a network with only one or two servers (a server is any computer on a network that's sharing a resource, recall) it might be okay, but imagine the traffic on a network with a fair number of servers! Periodic advertising works well on small-to-medium LANs with few servers, but, on larger networks, the sheer volume of broadcasts flooding the network makes the system unworkable.

There's another reason why periodic advertising doesn't work well on an enterprise network: routers. Most networks of any size are divided into *segments*, with the segments connected with *routers* that can identify the segment traffic goes to. (For more details on how segments and routers work, turn to Chapter 17, on TCP/IP.) In general, routers move messages from one segment to another and are smart enough to avoid retransmitting messages unnecessarily. This is a Good Thing, because it means that routers cut down on network congestion.

Trouble is, routers generally do not retransmit broadcast messages, which means those SAP broadcasts don't get sent to other segments. I say "generally" because you can, in fact, configure most routers to forward broadcast traffic if you want to, but you most often *won't* want to because that defeats the congestion-reducing characteristic of browsers. In short, unless you set up your routers to forward all broadcasts, SAP announcements will remain on their local segment, effectively dividing your network into workgroups that don't talk to each other.

Larger networks, therefore, need some other method of publishing resources.

Name Servers

Yet another approach, and the one used by most enterprise networks, is to assign the task of keeping track of network services to a *name server*. Servers identify themselves to the name servers, which publish a list of those servers and the resources each of those servers offers. Each segment gets its own name server, but the name servers communicate to keep each other updated with currently available resources on the network. Because name servers talk to each other in one-on-one directed communication, they can communicate across routers—no broadcasts.

A name server isn't usually dedicated to that single task; often, it's another kind of server as well, such as a file server. It's a name server because a network administrator (that would be you again) set it up to become one. Setting up name servers and getting them organized is a bit of work, but that's about the only downside.

Sound like a good plan? Microsoft will be happy to hear that you think so—name serving is the basis of the Active Directory (just as it was the basis of the NetWare Directory Services that Novell included starting with NetWare 4). Chapter 2 talks about the Active Directory in detail.

There's one catch to Active Directory, though: legacy clients. Pre-Win2K machines are not AD-aware. To make Windows 9*x* clients AD-aware, you can apply the DSCLIENT patch in the `Clients` folder on the Win2K Server installation CD. However, this patch does not work for NT 4 workstations and will not run on them.

I rather like Microsoft's advice (taken from the "Active Directory Technical Summary" in the January 2000 TechNet) about how to deal with this problem:

"To migrate Windows NT Workstation-based clients [to connect to the Active Directory client], upgrade them to Windows 2000 Professional."

Assuming you didn't necessarily want to upgrade all your NT Workstation clients, or can't do so (hardware that supported NT 4 may well not support Win2K Professional), you're stuck with a mixed-mode domain, which means you'll need to use Microsoft's earlier answer to the question of how to let network clients find network resources: browsing.

Browse Services

Browse services are actually a bit like name servers but have one major difference: rather than your having to set them up, the name servers set themselves up automatically. The Microsoft name for these automatic name servers is *browse services*. The servers that publish resources on the network are called either browse masters or master browsers—both names are correct. Master browsers are different from name servers in that no one computer is fixed as the resource publisher. When a client computer logs onto the network, it finds a master browser by broadcasting a request for a master browser and saying, "Are there any master browsers out there?" The first master browser (a network may have several master browsers, as you'll see) to hear the cry responds to the request and says, "Direct all your name service requests to me."

When a server starts up, it does the same thing, broadcasting "Are there any master browsers out there?" When the server finds one, it tells the master browser, "I am Server AARDVARK with the following shared resources. Please add me to your list of servers." The list of servers a master browser maintains and publishes is called a *browse list*. Browse lists are the entries in Network Neighborhood on Windows 9x and NT 4 clients (see Figure 20.37), the contents of the My Network Places Me folder in Windows 2K (see Figure 20.38), or the output you get if you type **net view** from the command prompt (see Figure 20.39).

FIGURE 20.37

Sample browse list from NT 4 or Windows 9x client

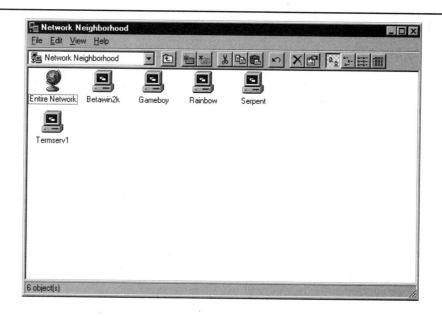

FIGURE 20.38

Sample browse list from Win2K client

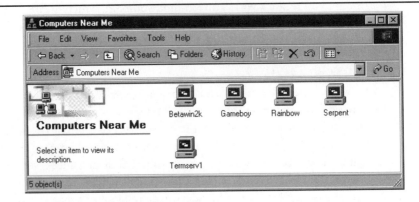

FIGURE 20.39

Sample browse list from net view *on DOS or Windows client*

At the top of a Network Neighborhood or Computers Near Me browse list, all you see are the servers in the network—you can see what resources each server is sharing by double-clicking the server's icon. To get a complete list of shares from a server with the net view command, you'd pick a server (say, SERPENT) and type **net view \\serpent**.

Browse lists for an entire network consisting of dozens of hundreds of servers could get pretty large, so you'll subdivide your network based (usually) on your company's administrative structure. If you're not using Win2K domain security, your network will be subdivided into workgroups, which are essentially groups of computers that share a browse list. If you're using Win2K domain security, your network will be subdivided into domains. If your network has multiple domains or workgroups, you'll browse each one individually.

How Browsing Works

Let's look in a little more detail at how browsing works. It can take up to 60 minutes for a browser to notice that a resource has disappeared, and in the meantime, the browser will blithely report that the resource is still available. The reason has to do with how the browser service and service advertising work.

When a server joins the network, it announces its presence then and at intervals of 1, 2, 4, 8, and 12 minutes. Thereafter, it re-announces itself every 12 minutes. A server must re-announce itself regularly to keep on the master browser's list; if a master browser does not hear from a server for three periods of 12 minutes, the master browser removes the server from its browse list.

If the network uses TCP/IP and is segmented, it's got a domain master browser responsible for updating each segment's master browser every 12 minutes. A master browser can take up to 36 minutes to realize, "Oops—that server seems to be gone from the network." If the timing is just wrong, then it might be another 12 minutes before the master browser gets around to updating its browse list with the master browser. We're up to 48 minutes. Again, if the timing's wrong, it might be as long as another 12 minutes before the domain master browser updates the browse lists on the other master browsers.

Because a server joining the network announces itself and its shared resources to the master browser when it joins, new services are advertised from the master browser almost immediately, although they may take up to 12 minutes to get to the backup browsers if the timing is off.

Choosing a Master Browser

Who are these master browsers that your servers and clients are announcing themselves to? A network set up for browsing may contain any or all of the following kinds of servers:

- Non-browser servers, which do not maintain browse lists, but announce themselves periodically to the master browser.
- Potential browsers, which are not master browsers but can become a Browser server if necessary.
- Backup browsers, which maintain a browse list of servers and domains they retrieve from the master browser and share this browse list with clients.
- Master browsers, which receive server and domain announcements, send browse lists to backup browsers, respond to clients requesting browse server lists, promote potential browsers to backup browsers when needed, and tell the master browsers of other domains their domain name and master browser.
- Preferred master browsers, which are backup browsers with one extra distinction: they're given preference in browser elections. This does not mean these browsers will *always* become master browsers if there's an election, but they have more oomph in elections than those machines for which this value is FALSE.
- Domain master browsers, which are domains' primary domain controllers given a special bias in browser elections so they'll become domain master browsers.

You only have to worry about domain master browsers if you're running a subnetted TCP/IP network, which, these days, means you almost certainly have to worry about domain master browsers.

- Each workgroup or domain elects one master browser per transport protocol used and will maintain one backup browser for each 15 computers—the master browser decides who the backup browsers are from the potential browsers available and updates them at intervals from its own list. Why one master browser for each transport protocol? If two computers aren't using the same transport protocol, they can't communicate—they can't even see each other. To make sure everyone on the network can see resources, you must maintain a separate master browser for each protocol, even though the browse lists will be merged so computers supporting multiple protocols don't have multiple browse lists.

Domain Democracy: How Elections Work

How does someone get to be a master browser? It's done with a process called an *election.* The first time a server (in the loose Microsoft sense of "a computer sharing resources with the network") joins the network, it calls out for the master browser, so that it can advertise itself, servers being the self-promoting little things that they are. If no master browser responds, the server announces, "Anarchy! We must have an election to see who will be the master browser!"

Elections are also held when any of the following events take place:

- A master browser is powered down gracefully.

- A server powers up only to discover that the existing master browser is of lower status than the server. (I'll get to the ranking system among servers in a minute.) For example, if a Win2K Professional workstation joins the network and discovers that the master browser is, of all things, a Windows 95 machine, the Win2K workstation will experience a fit of elitism and call for elections.

- A computer with a YES value for the Registry entry MaintainServerList (more on this in a moment) joins the network.

When there's an election, the master browser is chosen with a scoring system that works like this:

- NT Servers beat NT Workstations, which beat everything else.

- If there's a tie, then if one of the candidates is a primary domain controller, it will win.

- If neither of the candidates is a primary domain controller, then the election goes to the machine using WINS—not as a server but just a client.

- If both machines are using WINS, the election goes to the current master browser.

- If there is no current master browser, the election goes to a preferred master browser.

- If there's still a tie (more than one preferred master browser or none), the election goes to a backup browser.

- If there's more than one backup browser, the current backup browser wins the election.

- If there's still a tie, the election goes to the computer that's been up and running longest.

- If there's *still* a tie, then the election goes to the computer with the name closest to the beginning of the alphabet. For example, machine AARDVARK will beat machine ZEBRA.

Rigging Elections

It's a lot of work coming up with someone to maintain a browse list for the domain. You can simplify the election process and cut down on the number of elections by doing some backstairs finagling.

Not everyone who wants to be a master browser is a good candidate. Workstations, for one, make bad master browsers because they're apt to get turned off, or rebooted, on a regular basis. Every time the master browser goes down, it's election time.

To prevent Windows 9x computers from participating in elections, you'll need to edit a Registry value. The easiest way to do this is to open the Control Panel and run the Network applet. Turn to the Configuration tab and find the entry for File and Printer Sharing for Microsoft Networks in the list of installed network components. (If you don't find this entry, then the computer is not set up for file and print sharing and won't maintain a browse list anyway.) Click the Properties button to open the dialog box shown in Figure 20.40.

The default setting for MaintainServerList in Windows 95 and Browse Master in Windows 98 is Auto, which means "Make me a master browser if needed." If you make this value Enabled, then you're saying, "If there's a tie during an election, make me master browser" *and* "When I start up, always force an election." Instead, make the value Disabled, which makes the workstation say, "If nominated, I will not run; if elected, I will not stand" (or words to that effect). You can accomplish the same thing by editing the Windows 9x workstation's Registry so that the value of HKLM\System\ CurrentControlSet\Services\VxD\VnetSetup\MaintainServerList is 0. 1 corresponds to an Enabled value, 2 to an Auto value.

 TIP To prevent NT Workstations and Win2K Professionals from becoming master browsers, set the value of HKLM\System\CurrentControlSet\Services\Browser\ Parameters\MaintainServerList to No, instead of the default value of Yes.

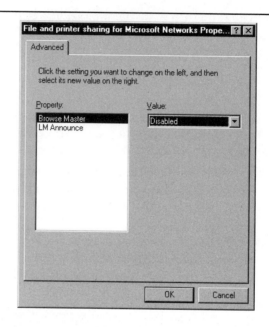

Master Browsers on a TCP/IP Network

On a TCP/IP network, the browse setup gets a little more complicated because of routers.

Each segment of the network elects a master browser, as I've already described. To keep all the segments updated, one of those master browsers becomes the domain master browser. The DMB asks each segment's master browser (SMB, for lack of a better term) for an updated copy of its browse list. The DMB then replicates this updated list to the SMBs so they have a complete list of all network resources.

You can tweak a Registry value to give a master browser an edge in becoming the DMB. In `HKLM\System\CurrentControlSet\Services\Browser\Parameters`, find the value IsDomainMaster and set it to True. (The other possible value is False, and that's the default.)

Stupid Browser Tricks

Finally, here's a couple of things you can do to optimize browsing for your network.

Keep Shared Resources off the Browse List

Just because you're sharing a resource with the list doesn't mean you necessarily want that resource to show up in everyone's browse list. To share a resource but hide it, add a dollar sign to its share name, like this: MYDRIVE$. To keep an entire *server* off the browse list, go to that server, and from the command prompt type **net config server /hidden:yes**. (Yes, you're typing "server", not the name of the server you want to hide.) Go to a client on the network and refresh the browse list, and that server will be gone from the browse list.

 TIP You can still use the connect to the server and any shares it's got if you know the UNC names for those shares, like \\serpent\freelnce.

Adjust the Browse Refresh Time

As I said earlier, the default refresh time for backup browsers and master browsers is 12 minutes. You can edit the refresh rate for servers in the domain, if you don't mind editing the refresh rate for *all* servers in the domain. Go to HKLM\System\ CurrentControlSet\Services\lanmanserver\parameters and add a new value called Announce (if it's not already there) with a DWORD value. Unspecified, the default value is 240 seconds—4 minutes. You can set this value higher or lower to decrease or increase the update interval. It's a compromise either way. If you set a shorter value, you'll increase network traffic as the browser updates its entry with the master browser. If you set a greater value, you'll cut down on network traffic but make the browse lists less up-to-date.

That's a look at some ways you can tune Win2K to make it perform better, both on a server level and at a network level. Proper tuning is mostly a matter of looking for the big four: disks, memory, CPU cycles, and network responsiveness. Get all those right, and your user base will be happy.

CHAPTER 21

Preparing for and Recovering from Server Failures

Coincidence, gremlins, or incentive from The Powers That Be to do my homework?

The day I planned to start working on this chapter, one Win2K server on my network stopped booting. I'd been out of town for a few days and so shut all the computers on the network down (power in Virginia is notoriously chancy during the summer months). Came back, booted up the server, and it worked fine. Added support for an additional transport protocol, and rebooted as required. This time, the system couldn't find a bootable device.

Uh-oh.

Why did this happen? Dead hard disk? Something disconnected? NetBEUI ate my hard disk? (Geez—when Microsoft makes TCP/IP the default transport protocol, they're not kidding around, are they?) The initial question, however, wasn't "What happened?" but "How badly is this going to screw me up?" Regardless of the reason why the machine didn't boot, the fact remains that it didn't. Had this been a production server instead of a test machine, I would have been in a world of hurt. Or could have been, if I weren't prepared for this kind of eventuality.

There's nothing quite like that sinking feeling when a server dies. You can't always prevent this from happening; sometimes, you're just stuck with the whims of the malignant forces in the universe. What you *can* do is either fix the problem or recover from it. That—and how to prevent problems when you can—is what I'm going to talk about in the course of this chapter. In the following pages, I'll cover:

- Some basics of preventing preventable disasters
- How to use the Windows Backup tools to create manual and automatic backups
- How to use the System Information tool to debug hardware problems
- What's going on when your computer boots
- The use of the recovery tools found in Windows 2000
- Disaster recovery tips

I'll explain the tools that Win2K provides to help you recover from disaster in a bit. Now, let's look at how to use common sense to avoid some disasters in the first place.

Preventing Stupid Accidents

The really clever and crafty infiltration or crashing of your network might merit a little appreciation (once you recover from it and keep it from happening again). It's the *preventable* infiltrations or server crashes that lead to gray hair. To keep your servers running and secure, you need to:

- Physically secure your network. If the bad guys (and the careless good guys) or Mother Nature can't get to your network hardware, it's a lot harder for them to damage it.

- Protect your network's user and system data with a good backup strategy.

- Prepare for the worst with a point-by-point disaster recovery plan that anyone in your organization can follow. Don't be dependent on one person knowing how to return the network to working order.

- Understand how your server works so you can troubleshoot problems and perhaps prevent more problems in the future.

When something goes wrong with your system, think *noninvasive*. Step 1 is *not* popping the top on the server. Three of your most valuable troubleshooting implements are the Windows 2000 installation CD, the Emergency Repair Disk you can use to fix your Win2K installation, and your notebook, in which you record every change you make to the network and record resolutions to problems. (The brain is Tool 3A. Sometimes it shuts off in times of stress, so you rely on the notebook.) When the time comes for troubleshooting, that notebook will be an invaluable diagnostic tool, and a cheat sheet for, "I know I've seen this before. How did I fix it last time?"

A basic concern in any computer security system is the need for physical security, a blanket term for the many ways in which you can protect your server and network from physical harm: stupid accidents, environmental—er—"incidents," and theft. Entire books have been devoted to the question of how to physically secure a network, so I'm not going to cover everything here. What follows is an outline of the kinds of protection you should be looking for, both physical and logical.

 NOTE Protecting your network is a never-ending process; every safeguard has a counter. You can't protect yourself from every possible disaster, so come up with a balance between how much it would cost you to recover from a disaster, how likely it is that you'll be hit by that particular disaster, and how much the protection costs. If protecting your data costs more than the data is worth, then it's time to relax a little.

Power-Protect Servers

Always use a UPS and power conditioner to power-protect servers and network hardware such as hubs and routers. This will protect the backbone of your network from power surges and dirty power. Power protection also will help prevent data loss and will let you shut down the servers in an orderly fashion (or shut down the servers automatically). I've had very good luck with the American Power Conversion Smart UPS series.

> **WARNING** Don't ground only the server room, ground the entire office. Grounding only the server room is equivalent to putting a giant "KICK ME" sign on your servers, as they'll be the easiest path to ground.

What about client-side power protection? At one time, UPSs were so expensive that it wasn't cost-effective to protect each client station. These days, you can get a low-end UPS for about $100, so think about the investment to give user machines power protection and a little bit of time to save documents and shut down. Power strips with surge protectors don't do the trick. Because of their high tolerance for voltage—they'll pass jolts that will damage a PC—power strips are a convenient way of plugging several devices into one outlet, but not a power-protection mechanism.

> **TIP** Don't plug a printer into a UPS designed for a computer only. First, it won't hurt the printer to lose power suddenly. Second, laser printers can draw around 15 amps when they're running. A *kitchen* (you know, that place in your house with a refrigerator, stove, garbage disposal, and other power hogs) only draws about 10 amps.

Speaking of client power protection, one advantage to running terminal services instead of a traditional desktop environment is that you don't have to worry about protecting a Windows terminal—at least not for reasons of protecting data. When a terminal services client computer loses power, the client's session is disconnected, not terminated. That is, all client applications and data remain active and in memory on the terminal server so long as the server is running. When the session is restored, it will be exactly as it was when it was disconnected. In other words, a power outage will cause no data loss as long as the terminal server is protected. For more information about terminal services in Win2K, turn to Chapter 14.

For extreme quick-and-dirty power protection for network client machines, tie five knots in each computer's power cord, as close to the wall as you can. If lightning strikes the wiring, the concentration of current within the loop of the knot will kill the cord and thus break the lightning's path to the client machine. I know that this one is hard to believe, but it really works. As Mark tells it:

> During the summer of 1990, a massive electrical storm hit Washington, D.C. [where Mark lived at the time]. I had tied knots in all of the computers in the house beforehand, but hadn't thought to do this to the television. During the storm, one of my neighbor's houses took a direct

lightning hit and a huge power surge hit my house's wiring. The cords of all the computers were warmed up a bit, but the power surge never touched the computers themselves. The television was another matter. The surge traveled straight through the cord to the TV's innards and rendered the television DOA. I couldn't have asked for a better test, although at the time I wasn't in a mood to appreciate the benefits of having had a control group.

Keep the Servers Pure

Reduce the likelihood of Bad Things happening to your servers by keeping them away from potential problems. Look for evidence of old leaks in the ceiling, and keep equipment away from them. Make sure that the server room is climate-controlled. The air conditioning used for the rest of the office might not be sufficient in an enclosed room, given all the heat that computers emit. And don't position any computer in direct sunlight.

Finally, avoid introducing new contaminants around the servers. Although it may be impossible to keep people from eating or drinking near their workstations, you can—and should—keep food out of the server room. The proliferation of nonsmoking offices makes the next suggestion almost unnecessary, but if your office permits smoking, don't smoke or let other people smoke around the servers or workstations. Smoke particles inside a hard disk can chew up its surface.

Limit Access to Servers

Most people using the network don't have a valid reason to do anything to a Win2K server (except a terminal server, of course, and then they're only using it remotely). One way to keep people away from your servers is to lock said servers in a separate room. If people can't get near the servers, they can't:

- Reboot or shut down the server

- Steal data-containing hard disks from the server

- Reinstall Win2K and thus have the chance to create a new Administrator account

User permissions that prevent a person from shutting down a server from the console don't prevent that same person from shutting down a server with the Big Switch. Therefore, if locking up the servers isn't an option, you can physically disable the Reset button and/or the A: drive so that people can't just shut down the server unless they have Win2K permissions to do so.

NOTE An OS-dependent protection utility such as `floplock` (in the NT 4 Resource Kit) doesn't prevent people from using the floppy drives from another operating system or from booting from a floppy. If you want to disable the floppy drives for all operating systems, edit the BIOS to remove support for floppy drives (this setting is typically in the Standard BIOS setup) and password-protect the machine for booting.

Use Passwords Effectively

Win2K's security is built on user authentication. When you log on to a Win2K domain, your username and password are compared with the information stored in the Security Accounts Manager on the domain controller. Once you're authenticated on the network, you're assigned a security token that contains a list of your rights and permissions based on your user identity and group membership. Whenever you try to do something—read a file, install an application, whatever—the Win2K security manager compares your rights and permissions with what you want to do, and permits or denies access based on the results of that comparison.

The only thing that keeps people from impersonating each other, therefore, is the password on their accounts. Once someone has an account's password, they can use that account and all the rights and permissions associated with it. Passwords are the biggest port of entry into your Win2K network.

Why Passwords Are Vulnerable

Previous editions of *Mastering Windows NT Server* included some tips on creating hard-to-crack passwords. The widespread availability of password-cracking programs such as L0phtCrack renders most of these tips semi-obsolete for stopping anyone who *really* wants to break in and who can get physical access to the server, because they give anyone with access to the network an extremely powerful tool for cracking passwords. L0phtCrack, for example, can retrieve password hashes from the Registry, from the Repair directory in your Win2K installation, or even from the network. Once the tool has the password file, it extracts the password hashes (encrypted passwords) and performs a series of three attacks to decrypt the hash:

Dictionary attack In a dictionary attack, L0phtCrack tests all the words in a dictionary or word file (the tool itself comes with a word file of 25,000 words) until it finds a match.

Hybrid attack If the dictionary attack doesn't produce results, the next step is to see whether the user took a known word and added numbers or other characters to it, so as to foil a dictionary attack.

Brute force attack The final stage is a brute force attack, in which the password hash is compared against every key combination possible. Brute force attacks take much longer (sometimes days—depends on how fast the computer doing the cracking is) than either of the other two attacks, but they can eventually crack just about any password using characters found only on a standard keyboard.

Just about any password is vulnerable to a brute force attack if given enough time. "Enough time" may mean a couple of days even on a fast computer, but if the cracker has the password hashes, then the delay won't stop the cracker unless people change their passwords during the cracking process.

 NOTE The longer and more complicated a password is, the longer it will take to crack it. Win2K is better protected in this respect than NT 4 was. Although NT 4 could technically support much longer passwords, the password-entry box in User Manager for Domains only had room for 14-character passwords. Win2K's password text box supports 56-character passwords, which will plainly take much longer to crack. Then again, can *you* accurately type 56 characters of mixed-case letters and numbers when you're typing blind? I can't, and I bet most of the users on your network can't either.

All that said, passwords are far from useless. You'll notice that using a tool such as L0phtCrack requires physical access to the Win2K server or to the network. The answer? *Keep untrusted people off the network.* Protect the Administrators account, only giving Administrator rights to the most trusted people. If your network is connected to the Internet, close TCP/IP ports that you don't need, and audit failed attempts to connect to the gateway from the Internet. For the people on the inside who *do* have access to the network, institute a zero-tolerance policy for password-cracking tools for anyone without a really good reason to have them.

Keeping Out the Idle Curious

Your network's security is threatened not only by the actively malicious, but also by the idle curious. Password-choosing schemes are best for keeping out those people who aren't interested enough to get serious about breaking into someone's account, but will go poking through Joe Blow's files in his private home directory if Joe makes it easy for them. To keep these people out of other people's accounts, follow the guidelines for choosing passwords below. They won't foil L0phtCrack, but they'll foil someone guessing passwords.

Impose password policies. Passwords must be of a minimum length, changed regularly (but not too regularly, to avoid people reusing passwords too often), and shouldn't be reused often. Set policies to require passwords to include numerals and other non-letter characters, and take advantage of the fact that Win2K passwords are CasEsenSitiVe (hint, hint).

Don't let people use easy-to-guess passwords. No personal names, spouse's names, dog's names, or other easy associations. Ideally, passwords should not reflect that person's job, either. A few years ago, a friend of mine doing network security for one department of the Pentagon told me that he'd had to institute this rule after discovering that the analysts in his division had all chosen passwords based on the names of battleships—words directly related to their division's mission.

Don't write down passwords. The most difficult password in the world will do no good if it's on a sticky note on the base of the monitor or under the keyboard. This is the dilemma inherent to all password protection. If you make passwords easy to remember, they're often easy to guess. Make them too hard to remember or require too many of them, and users will start writing them down.

Delete or disable unused accounts. An unused account is an account that isn't getting its password changed regularly and doesn't have someone using it who might notice something strange going on. If you'll need an account later, but not now, disable it so as to retain its security ID while making it impossible to use at the moment. If you'll never need an account again (perhaps for someone who has left the company), delete it.

 NOTE If you delete an account and then re-create it, the account will have a new security ID even if it has the same username and password as the original account. You'll have to re-create all user rights and permissions from scratch.

On a final note, those who use badges for company identification (a group that seems ever larger) can consider using biometric devices for user authentication. Digitizing user-specific data onto a card that the user must keep with them at all times eliminates the problem of written-down or guessed passwords. So long as people keep hold of the card with the digitized password, their account is pretty safe.

Backup Programs and Approaches

Backups are your first line of defense against server failures and your last recourse when all else fails. When it comes right down to it, the data on your servers is the important part. The box is replaceable, and you can reinstall the operating system if you need to. What you can't replace is the data on the drive. And if you lose that data and can't get it back, your company's life is probably over.

To help you protect your company's most important asset, Win2K comes with a new version of the Windows Backup tool, complete with more features, support for a wide array of media (unlike previous versions, which you couldn't even run if you didn't have a tape drive), and an integrated scheduler.

Basic Backup Procedures

Experienced users of NT 4 may recall that the backup utility was in the Administrative Tools folder. In Win2K, you'll find it in the System Tools section of the Accessories folder. Open the Backup application, and you'll see the tool shown in Figure 21.1.

TIP I find terminal sessions convenient for performing many administration tasks, but do not run backup operations from a remote computer. There're too many animations and too many screen updates required for this to work well.

FIGURE 21.1

The opening screen of Windows Backup

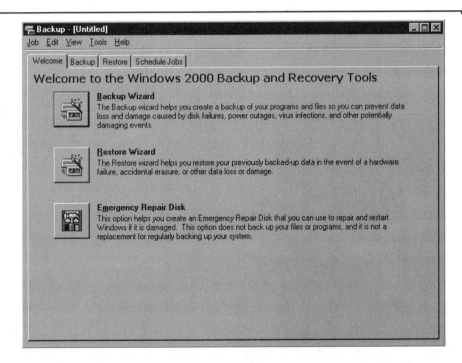

From here, you can back up data, restore data, or create a repair disk. Let's start with backing up. If you click the Backup Wizard button, you'll start a wizard designed to help you create a backup set. After the opening screen, you'll see the screen shown in Figure 21.2, asking you what data you want to back up.

FIGURE 21.2

*Choose a range of files
to back up.*

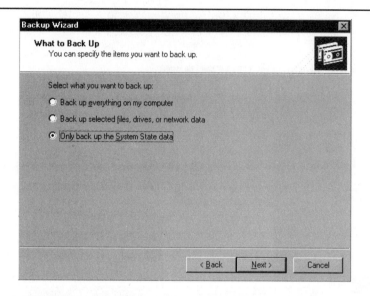

The third option allows you to only back up the System State data. The System State data, if you're wondering, is Registry information, system boot files, and the COM+ Class Registration database—system configuration information that you'll need to restore your server if you have to reinstall. On Win2K Certificate Servers, this data will also include the Certificate Services database, and on domain controllers, it will include a copy of the Active Directory and the SYSVOL directory, which is that server's copy of the public files shared among all domain controllers in the domain.

Backing up everything on the computer backs up all local drives (but no network drives even if they're mapped to local drive letters), and backing up selected files, drives, or network data lets you choose exactly what data you want to protect. Choose the option you want and click Next. For this example, I've chosen to back up the System State data.

Next, Backup looks for a place to put these files (see Figure 21.3). The default backup location is your floppy drive. (Given that backing up the System State data alone will take upwards of 200MB, this isn't a very practical default option, but you can browse for a new location anywhere on the local server or on a network-accessible volume.)

Once you've told Windows Backup where to put the backup file, click Next to display the final screen that displays your backup options (see Figure 21.4). If you click the Finish button, you'll start the backup.

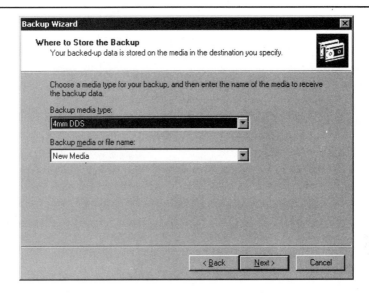

FIGURE 21.3

Specify a backup destination.

FIGURE 21.4

The final screen of the wizard displays the current backup settings.

That's a very basic backup, using all the default options. If you want a little more control over how the backup is performed (that is, the options for How and When), click the Advanced button before clicking Finish to start the second part of the wizard and decide on the options listed in Table 21.1.

TABLE 21.1: ADVANCED BACKUP OPTIONS

Option	Default Setting	What It Means
What type of backup should be performed?	Normal	You can choose from normal, copy, incremental, differential, or daily backups. These backup types are described later, under "Choosing a Backup Type."
Verify data?	No	Verifying a backup compares the data on the backup media with the source media, to make sure that the data was copied correctly. Verifying a backup takes some additional time, but I'd do it anyway—it's a good way of getting a written record that the data was written as expected.
Use hardware compression?	No	This option is only available if you're backing up to tape. If you choose it, then the tape will have a higher capacity than it would have had otherwise.
Append or replace existing backup sets?	Append	If the backup media already contains a backup, you have the option of either replacing that backup or adding the present backup to the catalog. The option you choose depends on which is more important to you: keeping the backup media uncluttered so you can easily find the backup set for restoration, or maintaining multiple backup sets. I'd suggest replacing full backups (although you should always archive at least one full backup in case something happens to the current one) and appending incremental and differential backups.
Restrict access?	No	If you've chosen to replace any backup sets already on the media, you can choose whether to restrict access to those sets to members of the Administrators group and the person creating the backups.
What is the name of the backup and the media?	Time and date backup was created	Provide a name for the backup set. If you're using new media, or replacing the data on existing media, you can choose a new name for the tape or file.
When should the backup run?	Now	You can choose to run the backup now or pick a time at which it should run. If you're backing up a server, then you'll almost certainly want to schedule it for later, when people aren't using the data.
Back up migrated remote storage data?	No	Backs up rarely used files that have been automatically moved to remote storage.

The only Advanced backup option that might cause you any trouble is the scheduling tool, which I'll cover later in the section "Scheduling Automated Backups." When you've finished choosing options, you'll see the Finish screen again, showing the updated options (see Figure 21.5).

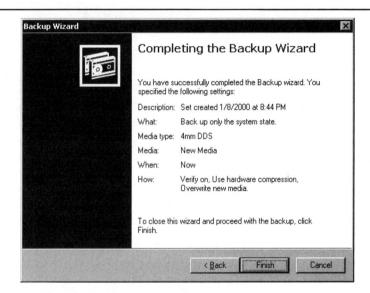

Advanced Backup Options

Above I've described the simple version of running a backup, the best version for those who want to make sure that *all* files are backed up. Those with more experience in backups will be glad to know that there are more options you can use to fine-tune your backups, including choosing files and folders to protect, choosing types of backups to perform, and scheduling automatic backups of local or network-accessible media.

Choosing Files to Back Up

Most often, you won't want to back up every file on your server. You don't have to. The Backup tool includes an Explorer-like interface from which you can pick and choose files, folders, and drives to back up.

This part works much like earlier versions of Backup. In Windows Backup, turn to the Backup tab (see Figure 21.6). You select objects for backup by checking the box next to them. You can't select every object—only those that have a clear box. Gray boxes don't represent partially selected options, as you might expect, given the meaning of gray boxes in other parts of Win2K. In this case, the gray box means that the object cannot be selected and you must drill down into it to find the selectable objects. Notice that My Documents is in the top tier of selectable objects, which makes for a handy way to back up all your documents if you keep personal files in that folder.

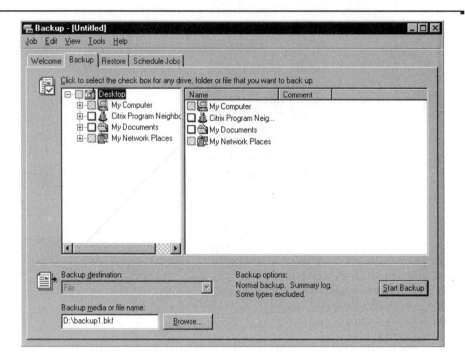

Backing Up the Local Computer Let's start with objects stored on the local server. I'm not going to bother backing up the system drives because I can restore them easily if I've got the System State data saved, but I've got another drive that I use for some data storage. To get to it, I double-click My Computer to expose the locally mapped drives (see Figure 21.7).

This is a list of the assigned drive letters of all partitions. The drives listed here are *logical* drives, not physical drives. If you have any reason to do so, you can change their arrangement by clicking on the headings of the Name, Total Size, or Free Space columns to organize the drives by one of those criteria. Notice that this list includes all drives on the server, not just fixed or local drives. Windows Backup for NT 4 didn't recognize any drives for backup but fixed media and network drives, so to back up removable drives you had to go through the hassle of sharing the drive with the network from Explorer and then connecting to it from the server doing the backup. This limitation no longer exists in Win2K.

FIGURE 21.7

Contents of My Computer

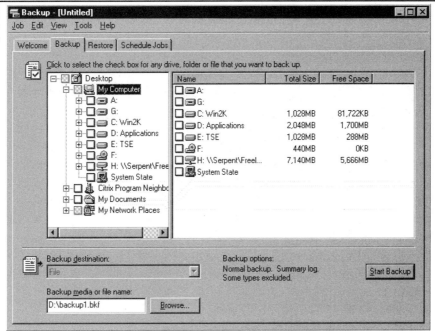

Perhaps I *think* that the Applications drive (drive D:) is the one with the data I want to protect, but I'm not sure. I can find out for sure by double-clicking the drive to see its folders. If I wanted to, I could drill down yet further within those folders to expose the subfolders, all the way down to file level. In this case, I'm going to drill down one level to see the NCD folder. I want to keep the contents of the NCD folder safe—because this is a cool add-on to Terminal Services that requires some configuring, and I want to make sure that I've got all the files backed up so I don't have to reconfigure them. So I check the box next to the NCD folder. If I open the NCD folder, I'll see that all the files and folders within the NCD folder are now selected.

I can deselect any object within this folder and prevent it from being backed up (see Figure 21.8). If I do so, then the check mark in the NCD folder's box will be gray, instead of the blue it is if all its contents are selected. Similarly, the box next to the logical drive that the NCD folder is stored on will have a gray check mark indicating that part of its contents are selected for backup, but not all.

You can choose as many different files and folders on as many different drives as you like to be part of a backup set. They don't have to be juxtaposed or arranged in any kind of logical form, but will retain their location on the final backup media. That is, if you choose to back up both E:NCD\files\config and C:\My Documents\ Myfile.doc, then Myfile.doc will still have its placement information so that the backup media know that the file goes in My Documents, not in the NCD folder.

FIGURE 21.8

Contents of the NCD
folder to be backed up

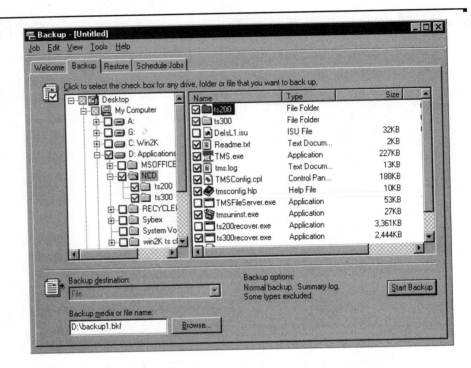

 TIP   Having trouble selecting objects to back up? When the cursor changes to a check mark, you're in the box.

Although this drilling-down technique looks like it should work on the System State data, it doesn't. When you open My Computer to see all the local drives, you'll see another entry in the list—the System State data. If you double-click this object to view its contents, you'll see contents like those in Figure 21.9. Notice that these objects have gray boxes, so you can't select them. When using Windows Backup, you can back up all the system data or none of it, but you can't pick and choose.

 TIP   Well, you can't pick and choose *easily*, but you can pick and choose. If you back up the contents of the %*systemroot*%\system32\config folder, you'll back up all the Registry files.

FIGURE 21.9

*Contents of the
System State
folder*

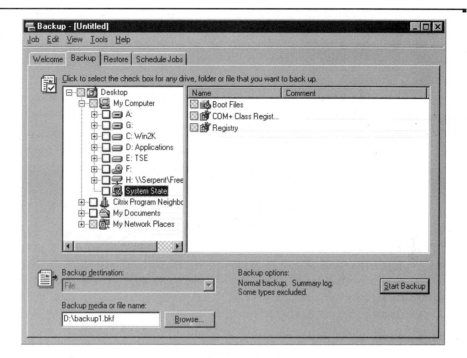

Backing Up Network-Accessible Files   You can back up the contents of any
folder shared with the network from any computer on your network. Doing so is
much like backing up local files and folders, except that you have to first find the
computer you're looking for and then drill down as needed to the drive you want to
select. There is no domain-wide list of shared folders on the domain—you have to
know which server contains the data you want to protect.

To get to the network server, double-click My Network Places to reach Entire Network. Entire Network will have an entry for Microsoft Windows Network. Double-
click *that* and you'll get a list of all domains on the network.

Finally, within the domain you'll see a list of all computers with accounts on the
domain. Select the one you want and start drilling into its shared drives to back up files
as you would for a local computer. The only difference between backing up a network-
accessible computer and a local one is that you can't back up the System State information for a network computer.

Advanced Backup Settings

In Windows Backup, there are a number of advanced options you can set. In either
the Backup tab or the Restore tab, choose Tools/Options to go a tabbed dialog box
that contains all backup and restore options.

Choosing a Backup Type The default backup type for Windows Backup is Normal, which is a not-very-descriptive way of saying that Windows Backup performs full backups (copies all files and resets the archive bit on all copied files) unless told otherwise. If you turn to the Backup Type tab shown in Figure 21.10, you can choose one of the options described in Table 21.2.

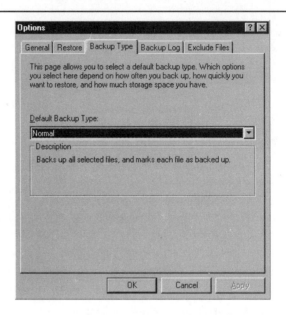

TABLE 21.2: BACKUP TYPES SUPPORTED IN WINDOWS 2000

Backup Type	Description
Normal	Copies all selected files and then resets the archive bit
Incremental	Copies all selected files with the archive bit set and resets the bit
Differential	Copies all selected files with the archive bit set but does not reset the bit
Daily	Copies all selected files that were edited the day the backup was performed
Copy	Copies all selected files but does not reset the archive bit

 NOTE The *archive bit* is a hidden file attribute applied to a file when it's created or edited. It's used to tell a backup or copy utility, "Hey, this file has changed." Resetting the archive bit removes the archive bit from a file; setting the bit adds it.

You can use these backup types in combination to back up files completely and efficiently. The longest interval you'll want to have between backups is probably a day—lose more than a day's worth of work, and you're in big trouble. (Losing a day's worth of work is bad enough, which is why companies with really critical data use RAID to protect their data, as is discussed in Chapter 7.) However, running a normal backup every day takes up a lot of time and space, so most people probably won't want to do that. Instead, you can run a normal backup at regular intervals, perhaps once a week. To keep a daily record of changed files, you can run a differential or incremental backup each day. Running a daily differential backup gives you a daily copy of all the files that have changed since the last full backup. Either differential or incremental backups work well as a supplement to a regular normal backup. I find differential backups easier to perform and restore, since restoring a server becomes a matter of restoring the most recent normal backup and the last differential one. Restoring incremental backups is a slower process, as you must restore each incremental backup made since the last full backup individually. However, incremental backups give you records of which files changed on each day the backup was performed, and they take less time to perform than differential backups.

Daily backups aren't really a method of preserving data, but more a way of quickly finding files that you're currently using and transferring them to other media. You might find it useful to run a daily backup on a user's files to copy the ones he needs to a laptop for a business trip. Copying files is only useful if you want to make a complete copy of all selected files without resetting the archive bit. A copy action like that is a way of copying files to a new location.

Choosing a Logging Type   Backup logs are a useful troubleshooting tool. If something goes wrong with the backup, then you can inspect a text-based log to see *what* went wrong. In fact, it's a good idea to at least scan the backup logs produced after each backup to make sure that the procedure went as expected.

How much information do you log? Normally, Windows Backup logs only errors and important events, but if you turn to the Backup Log tab of the Options dialog box (see Figure 21.11), you can choose not to log (bad idea, as that disables a troubleshooting tool) or to log *everything* (also a bad idea for anything other than a daily or perhaps incremental backup, as it will make your logs so big that it will be hard to find errors). Unless you need a complete record for some reason, the summary log option (the default) is probably your best bet.

Which Files Do You Want to Back Up?   Even if you're running a full backup, you don't necessarily want to save *everything*. For example, do you really need to preserve the contents of the paging file? Probably not. For this reason, Windows Backup does not normally back up any files that don't contain real data—a user cache, a page file, temporary Internet files for the person running the backup, and the like. You can edit this list in the Exclude Files tab of the Options dialog box (see Figure 21.12).

FIGURE 21.11

Choose a logging option.

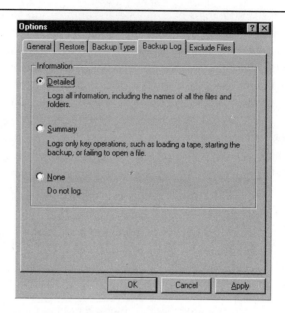

FIGURE 21.12

Change the files to exclude, or edit the settings for excluded files.

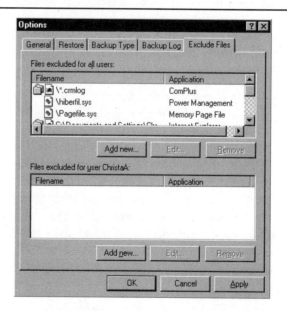

The Add New and Remove buttons on this tab are pretty self-explanatory. Unless you have real reason to remove one of the already excluded files from the list, I'd suggest that you leave them alone, as the files listed are not really anything you need to back up.

To add files to exclude from the backup, click the Add New button to display the dialog box shown in Figure 21.13. The list in the upper half of the dialog box contains all the file types recognized by the server. You have to know the extension for the type of file you want to exclude from the backup, but many of the extensions are labeled so you can be sure that you've got the right one. (If an extension isn't labeled and you don't recognize it as an application file extension, files of that type are probably part of the operating system and can be reinstalled. Just be sure to check before you exclude the files from the backup.) In the Registered File Type list, click the file type that you don't want to back up, Ctrl-clicking to select more than one option at a time. When you click OK, you'll see your selection(s) added to the list of excluded file types. For example, if you don't want to back up any application files (on the principle that you can reinstall the applications if necessary), then you'd find .exe in the list, highlight it, and click OK.

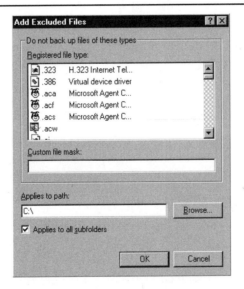

The Custom File Mask text box is for extensions that aren't registered file types (ones you've created yourself for certain files), or for filtering files by name. The syntax for this file mask depends on whether you're filtering by filename or extension. If you want to eliminate all files *named* abc.* from the backup, then type **abc** in the box—no asterisks necessary. To eliminate all files with the *extension* .abc, then type **.abc** (note the period) in the box.

 NOTE You must enter each custom file mask separately. If you enter two at once—say, for .abc files and .def files—then you're telling Windows Backup to skip all files with the extension .abc. def. Using semicolons or other punctuation to separate the entries doesn't work.

By default, your file mask will apply to the entire C: drive. To edit this to apply to a different drive or only a specific folder, type in a new path or click the Browse button to open a file tree (see Figure 21.14) from which you can choose the path you want the mask to apply to.

When you click OK to exit the Add Excluded Files dialog box, the path information will be listed with the file types to be excluded on the Exclude Files tab.

The file types you've excluded will apply to all users. If you'd like to exclude file types only for the person currently logged in (there's no way to specify another user or a group) then click the Add New button at the bottom half of the Exclude Files tab. You'll enter the same Add Excluded Files box that you saw previously, and it works the same way. The only difference is that the files you exclude will only apply to the ones you own. For example, if I chose to exclude .doc files for myself, then everyone else's .doc files would be backed up, but mine (the ones I created and own) would not.

 TIP The per-user masking depends on current file ownership, so if a file was created by Joe but Jane took ownership of it, the file would still be backed up if Joe added it to his personal file mask, but not if Jane did. It doesn't matter whether Joe, Jane, or Fred is running the backup: so long as Jane owns that file, then it's excluded from the backup.

Notice that the exclude tool really only excludes files—you can't use it to include only files with certain extensions in the backup. Sadly, there doesn't seem to be any way to specify that only certain files should be backed up. Even the command-line utility NTBACKUP (which I'll discuss a little later in the "Scheduling Automated Backups" section) doesn't accept wildcards.

General Backup Options   The General tab of the Options dialog box contains the options explained in Table 21.3. These options control the settings that really don't fit anywhere else in the categories of options.

TABLE 21.3:   GENERAL OPTIONS FOR BACKUP AND RESTORE OPERATIONS

Option	What It Means	Default Setting
Compute selection information before backup and restore operations.	This is a confusingly worded way of saying that Windows Backup will count the files and folders to be backed up or restored before actually performing the operation. I'd leave this enabled; it doesn't add much to the time required to run the operation, and this information can save you from backing up or restoring the wrong volume or backing up to media too small to hold it.	Enabled
Use the catalogs on the media to speed up building restore catalogs on disk.	This is the fastest way for Windows Backup to create a list of all the files and folders in the backup. You should only disable this option if you're restoring data from several tapes and don't have the one with the catalog (the first tape) or if the catalog is damaged. With this option disabled, Windows Backup will scan the entire backup set and attempt to build its own catalog. Since reading tapes is a slow process, this could take a long time for a large backup set—perhaps hours.	Enabled
Verify data after the backup completes.	This compares the data on the disk with the data on the backup media after the backup has been completed and records any differences. Although verifying adds some time to a backup, I'd recommend doing it. It's a good way to be sure that files were written correctly.	Disabled
Back up the contents of mounted drives.	Normally, mounted drives (logical drives mapped to a path on another logical drive—read Chapter 7 to learn more about them) can be backed up like other media. If you check this box, the data won't be backed up—just the path information.	Enabled
Show alert message when I start Backup and Removable Storage Management is not running.	If the Removable Storage Management service isn't running, you can start it from the Services object in the System Tools folder of Local Computer Management.	Enabled

Continued ▶

TABLE 21.3 CONTINUED: GENERAL OPTIONS FOR BACKUP AND RESTORE OPERATIONS

Option	What It Means	Default Setting
Show alert message when I start Backup and there is compatible Import Media available.	If this box is checked and you add new remote storage media, Backup will display a message on start-up saying that it's found more media for the Import pool (to which files can be archived).	Enabled
Show alert message when new media is inserted into Removable Storage.	If this box is checked, Backup will display a dialog box when it detects new media.	Enabled
Always move new import media to the Backup media pool.	If this box is checked, Backup will assume that any new media it detects should be added to the Backup media pool, and thus be available for backups.	Disabled

 NOTE Removable Storage Management is used with tape drives and other archiving media. If you normally back up to a file on any kind of disk (including a removable disk like a Jaz drive) instead of tape, you don't have to worry about the Removable Storage Management settings.

Saving Backup Options

You can define settings for a backup job and save them to be used later or reused at your discretion. To do so, make sure that you've chosen the files to back up. Then, in the Windows Backup utility, choose Job/Save Selections. You'll see a Save Selections dialog box prompting you to save the backup script (normally saved in *%systemroot%*\ `Documents and Settings\`*%username%*`\Local Settings\Application Data\` `Microsoft\Windows NT\NT Backup\data`).

If you load a saved backup script when you have files and folders selected for backup, Backup will ask whether you want to use the currently selected folders or clear them. Clear them to load the backup script, and you'll be ready to run the backup job.

Scheduling Automated Backups

To be safe, you should back up data servers at least once a day. Trouble is, the best time to back up is late at night when everyone's off the network. With NT 4, you could use the AT command or WinAT utility to schedule backups created from the command line; with Windows 2000, you have the choice of two backup-scheduling methods, one using the GUI, and one using the AT command for running scripted backups created with an updated command-line version of NTBACKUP.EXE.

There are a few ways you can schedule jobs from Windows Backup:

- In the Backup Wizard, one of the Advanced options asks whether you want to run the backup you've created now or schedule it for later. If you choose to schedule it for later, you'll be taken to the Schedule Job dialog box, which I'll discuss in a minute.

- In Windows Backup, when you create a backup job from the Backup tab and click the Start Backup button, you'll see a dialog box, like the one in Figure 21.15, that prompts you for the name of the backup and allows you to start the backup now or schedule it for later. If you click the Schedule button, you'll be taken to the Schedule Job dialog box.

FIGURE 21.15

When creating a backup job, you have the option of running it immediately or running it at a later time.

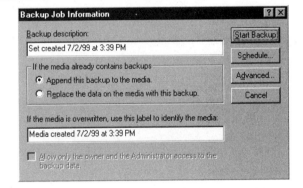

FIGURE 21.15

When creating a backup job, you have the option of running it immediately or running it at a later time.

 TIP Save backup jobs before starting them. If you're scheduling a job to run later, you'll need to do this anyway, and if you think you'll ever want to run a backup job with the same parameters again, you'll save yourself some time by saving the job now.

- In Windows Backup, if you're creating a new backup job, you can turn to the Schedule Jobs tab, where you'll see a month calendar like the one shown in Figure 21.16. To create and schedule a backup job from the Schedule Jobs tab, click the Add Job button in the lower right corner of the screen to start a Backup Wizard very similar to the one described earlier under "Basic Backup Procedures"—the only difference between the two wizards is that this one includes the Advanced options in the main wizard, rather than through the Advanced button on the wizard's final screen. One of the options you'll be presented with is the choice of running the backup now or later, with the default time for "later" being midnight of the day you set up the backup job (see Figure 21.17). To schedule a job, select Later and click the Set Schedule button to open the scheduler.

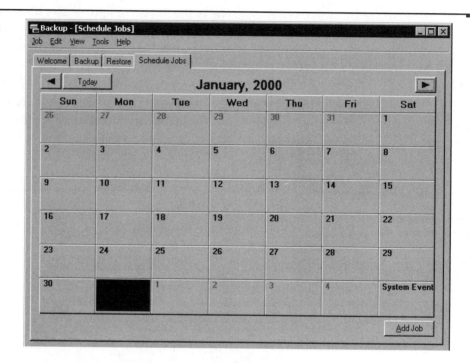

The Scheduler   No matter how you get to it, the Schedule tab of the Schedule Job dialog box looks like Figure 21.18. The basic options are pretty straightforward. Choose the interval at which you want the backup job to run (once, daily, weekly, monthly, at system start-up, at logon, or when the computer is idle) and the starting time and date. If you select the Show Multiple Schedules check box at the bottom of the screen, a new drop-down list will appear at the top of this dialog box, showing the varying intervals and starting times that you've chosen for this job.

FIGURE 21.18

Choose a time and frequency for the backup job.

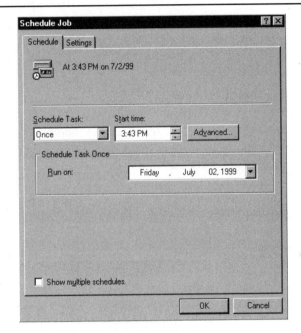

    TIP   If you want to run a backup job biweekly (once every two weeks), show multiple schedules and create two monthly backup jobs that start on different days.

The Advanced button takes you to the Advanced Schedule Options (see Figure 21.19), which apply only if you want to repeat the backup job, apart from any interval that you set in the main scheduling screen. Most often, you won't need to touch these options. You don't need to use them for scheduling jobs at regular intervals; this set of options would be more useful for a shorter task and one that might actually need to be run every 10 minutes or so. (Frequent backups are a Good Thing, but let's not get carried away.)

FIGURE 21.19

*Advanced backup
scheduling options*

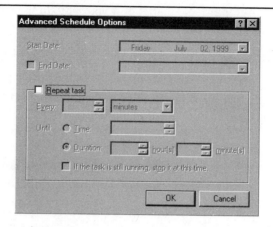

More likely, you'll use the Settings tab back in the main Schedule Job dialog box
(see Figure 21.20). From here, you can specify how long the job should run (a backup
job that lasts more than 72 hours seems suboptimal) and whether the job should be
deleted from the list of tasks when it's done unless it's supposed to run again. The Idle
Time settings could be useful, as only permitting a backup to run when the server is
idle is a good way of making sure that all data files are closed (or at least unused). The
only catch to this setting is that you won't be able to back up if the server is used for
anything, like being a Web server, that's likely to keep it busy at odd hours.

FIGURE 21.20

*Configure job settings
for the scheduled
backup.*

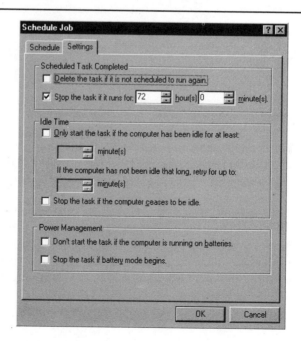

TIP Windows Backup doesn't back up open files. If you're backing up local files only, you can make sure that all files are closed during a backup. Apply the **net stop** and **net start** commands; this will stop the Server service before the backup begins, but then restart it after the backup is completed. I'll discuss the syntax in the next section on scheduling backups from the command line.

The final options in the Settings tab, on battery use, aren't likely to apply to a server. They're there to help you conserve battery power by not running nonessential tasks when your power supply is limited. Accessing the hard disk takes a lot of power, so backups are an especially draining task when the power is low.

When you've finished adding jobs to the scheduler, they'll appear on the Schedule Jobs tab's calendar, as shown in Figure 21.21.

FIGURE 21.21

Scheduled jobs appear in the calendar.

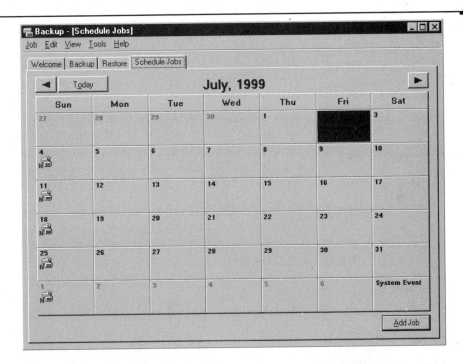

You're not stuck with the options for a scheduled job once it's created. To edit the settings for a scheduled job, just click its icon in the calendar to open the Scheduled Job Options dialog box shown in Figure 21.22.

FIGURE 21.22

You can edit all job settings even after the job is added to the task list.

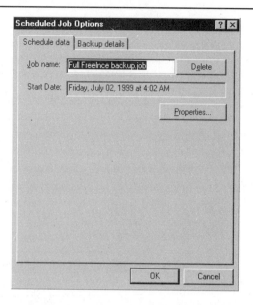

Click the Properties button to edit the timing and settings for the backup job. The Schedule and Settings tabs that appear are the same ones you saw when scheduling the job. The Task tab that also appears, however, is new. Here, you can use the command-line switches to edit the job settings, specify a new user in whose context the job should run, and create some identifying information for the job. You must know the command-line switches to NTBACKUP (discussed in the next section) to edit the settings from the Task tab.

Backing Up from the Command Prompt In previous versions of NT, you had to know how to use NTBACKUP because you couldn't schedule backups otherwise. The only way to run an automatic backup was to create a command-line job and schedule it via the AT command or the graphical WinAT utility in the Resource Kit. Since the Windows 2000 version of Windows Backup supports scheduling, this isn't true any longer, but you'll need to know the command-line switches to edit the task settings of a previously scheduled job. The syntax for NTBACKUP has not become any simpler in Win2K—quite the opposite.

TIP If you're just learning NTBACKUP's syntax, you can examine the command-line syntax on the Task tab of the Scheduled Job Options properties sheet. All the options that you selected with the GUI will appear here as command-line switches. You'll need to pare down some of the parameters because they'll show full path information, but the basic structure will be correct.

To run automatic backups from the command prompt, you can use the command-line utility AT to define a time and conditions under which NTBACKUP should run.

NTBACKUP's syntax has become more complicated in Win2K, not less. Some of the capabilities that existed in earlier versions of the command-line backup utility now have a new syntax, and some options are new. Even if you're an old hand at backing up from the command line, you'll need to relearn how to use the switches. Let's take this one step at a time (see Table 21.4).

TABLE 21.4:   NTBACKUP COMMAND-LINE OPTIONS

Argument	Function
backup	Tells NTBACKUP that you're running a backup operation. You must include this argument.
systemstate	Specifies that all System State data should be backed up and sets the backup type to normal or copy. You can only use this switch if you're backing up drives on the local computer; for security reasons, you cannot back up system configuration information on any other computer. In other words, if you're going to back up the registries of other computers, you can't do all your backing up over the network from a single backup server.
bks file name	This is the name of the selection information file in which the backup will be stored. More than one backup can go in the same .bks file, if you choose to append backups. You must create this file from the GUI before referencing it from the command line.
/j "job name"	Tells NTBACKUP the name of the backup job.
/p "pool name"	Tells NTBACKUP which media pool (a logical grouping of removable media, like a tape library) to copy the backup files to. Most often, this will be the backup media pool. You won't use this option with /g or /t, as those switches specify that a certain tape should be used, with /f, which specifies the name of a file to back up to, or with /a, since you must append backup files to a specific tap and, not an entire media pool.
/g "guid name"	Specifies the name of the tape that will be overwritten or appended with this backup job. Don't use this switch with /p, as that specifies that NTBACKUP will use a media pool instead of a particular tape.
/t "tape name"	Specifies the tape name of the tape that will be overwritten or appended with this backup job. Don't use this switch with /p, as this specifies that NTBACKUP will use a media pool instead of a particular tape.

Continued ▶

TABLE 21.4 CONTINUED: NTBACKUP COMMAND-LINE OPTIONS

Argument	Function
/n "new tape name"	Specifies the new tape name of the tape that will be overwritten or appended with this backup job. Use this switch to name a tape. Don't use this switch with /p, as this specifies that NTBACKUP will use a media pool instead of a particular tape. You also can't use this switch with /a, because you can't append data onto a tape that is new or that you're renaming.
/f "file name"	Specifies the path and name of the file in which the backup will be copied. As this switch directs the backup to a file, not a tape or media pool, you can't use it with any of the switches specific to removable media: /p, /t, or /n.
/d "description"	Specifies the description of the backup set, like "Full backup of SERPENT on 6/20/99."
/ds "server name"	Backs up the directory service on the specified Microsoft Exchange server.
/is "server name"	Backs up the information store on the specified Microsoft Exchange server.
/a	Appends the backup set to any data on the media. If backing up to a tape, you must use this switch with either /g or /t to specify the tape you want to append to. You can't use this switch with /p, as you must append to a specific tape, not an entire media pool.
/v:yes or no	Specifies whether the backup procedure should be verified or not. Verifying the data (making sure the data in the backup matches the source) takes a little time, but reassures you that the data was written correctly.
/r:yes or no	Specifies whether the tape should be available only to its owner/ creator and members of the Administrators group.
/l:f or s or n	Tells NTBACKUP what kind of log file to create: full (logging every copied file), summary (logging only important events and errors), or none (in which case the backup won't be logged).
/m backuptype	Tells NTBACKUP what kind of backup to run: normal, copy, incremental, differential, or daily.
/rs:yes or no	Tells NTBACKUP whether or not to back up the removable storage database that records the location of archived files. If you're using removable storage, you should back up this database regularly to make sure that you can retrieve archived files.
/hc:on or off	Tells NTBACKUP whether to use hardware compression (available only if you're backing up to a tape drive, and then only if that tape drive supports it—most do). Go ahead and use hardware compression if it's available, as it will allow you to get more use out of your tapes.

NOTE If you don't specify options for the switches /v /r /l /m /rs /hc, then the settings already in the GUI version of Windows Backup will control. For example, verification is disabled by default, so if you don't enable it from the command line and don't change it from the GUI, your backups won't be verified.

Let's start with a simple example. To back up all the files in H:\Sybex to the file system1.bkf, you would type:

```
ntbackup backup h:\sybex\ /f d:\system1.bkf
```

To perform a differential backup of the same folder, verify the backup, and name the backup job "Differential backup of Sybex folder," you'd type:

```
ntbackup h:\sybex\" /m differential /f d:\system1.bkf /j
➡ "Differential backup of Sybex folder"
```

Once you've created a backup job, you can use the command-line AT command to schedule the backup. The AT command schedules commands and programs to run on a computer at a specified time and date. The AT command's syntax looks like this:

```
AT [\\computername] [ [id] [/DELETE] | /DELETE [/YES]]
AT [\\computername] time [/INTERACTIVE]
    [ /EVERY:date[,...] | /NEXT:date[,...]] "command"
```

 TIP AT is dependent on the Task Scheduler service. You can see a list of all currently running services by typing **net start**.

As you can see from Table 21.5, AT isn't quite as complicated as NTBACKUP.

TABLE 21.5: AT SYNTAX

Argument	Function
\\computername	Specifies a computer that the job should run on. If you don't specify another computer, then the job will run on the same computer that AT's running on.
id	This is the job ID assigned to a task when you've scheduled it with AT. Use the job ID to reference the task.
/delete	Deletes the task with that job ID (or all jobs, if you don't specify a particular ID) from the jobs list. If you delete a backup, it won't be run.
/yes	If you omit this switch, AT will ask you whether you're sure you want to delete the task in question from the jobs list. If you're sure and don't want to be prompted, use this switch.

Continued ▶

TABLE 21.5 CONTINUED: AT SYNTAX

Argument	Function
/time	Specifies the time when the task should run. AT uses a 24-hour clock, so add 12 to the hours after noon. 3:00 P.M. becomes 15:00, 7:30 A.M. becomes 19:30, and so forth.
/interactive	Tells the job to interact with the desktop of the user logged on at the time the task is running. Normally, you won't want to use this option if you're automating a backup. The whole point of this exercise is to run the backup when no one's around to supervise it.
/every:date[,…]	Runs the task on the specified days of the week or month. If you don't specify a date with this switch, then the task is scheduled for the current day (which means that you could potentially schedule a job to run before the time when you created it, meaning the job will never run). Dates use numbers; days of the week may be abbreviated thus: Su M T W Th F S.
/next:date[,…]	Runs the task on the next occurrence of the specified day. If you don't specify a date, then it will assume that you mean the current day of the month. Dates use numbers; days of the week may be abbreviated thus: Su M T W Th F S.
command	This is the Win2K command or batch program to be run as specified.

NOTE If you don't specify a date at all, AT will add 1 to the current date and run the task on the next date that matches. So, if you create a job on June 28 but don't specify a date for the task, AT will schedule it for June 29. AT is smart enough to know how many days are in a month, so if you create a job on the 30th, it will schedule the job for the 1st or the 31st, depending on what month it is.

You can use AT with the full syntax of the NTBACKUP command, but I find it simpler to save the NTBACKUP settings you want as a batch file and then reference the batch file. First, it means less typing when it comes to scheduling the job. Second, unless you're backing up a network-accessible drive, you're going to want to stop and start the network before and after the backup to make sure that all files are backed up—again, NTBACKUP won't back up open files. A sample batch file might look like this:

```
net stop server

ntbackup h:\sybex\" /m differential /f d:\system1.bkf /j
➥ "Differential backup of Sybex folder"

net start server
```

Save this batch with a `.bat` extension in a text editor such as Notepad, naming it, say, `differential.bat`. You'll be able to reference it with AT like this:

at 5:47 /every:M,T,W,Th,F,S differential

Every day but Sunday, the file `differential.bat` will run. (Sunday is the day I do full backups.) It will stop the Server service, run the backup with the settings you specify, then start the Server service when it's done.

If you want to be sure that a job is added to the list properly, type **at** at the command prompt to view the contents of the job list:

```
Status ID    Day                    Time       Command Line
         -----------------------------------------------------------
         1    Each Su                5:47 AM    full
         2    Each M T W Th F S      5:47 AM    differential
```

If I wanted to delete task 2 from the job list, I'd use AT like this:

```
AT 2 /delete
```

Viewing Backup Logs

Unless you specify otherwise, every time you back up, a backup log is created. To see the contents of these logs, you can click the Report button in the dialog box that tells you that the backup is complete. Alternatively, to pick any log to view, choose Report from the Tools menu in Windows Backup. You'll see a list of backups, as shown in Figure 21.23.

FIGURE 21.23

Choose a backup log to view.

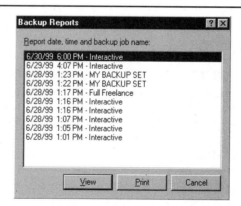

In the Backup Reports dialog box, find the report you want based on its job name or time and date stamp, and click the View button. The log will open in Notepad and provide output something like what's below:

```
Backup Status
Operation: Backup
```

```
Active backup destination: File
Media name: "Media created 6/28/99 at 1:07 PM"

Backup of "H: \\Serpent\Freelnce"
Backup set #5 on media #1
Backup description: "Set created 6/28/99 at 1:23 PM"
Backup Type: Normal

Backup started on 6/28/99 at 1:23 PM.
Warning: The file \Sybex\Win2K Server\2447c21.doc in use - skipped.
Backup completed on 6/28/99 at 1:29 PM.
Directories: 10
Files: 307
Skipped: 1
Bytes: 294,829,336
Time:   6 minutes and   26 seconds
```

Notice that in this log you can see what folders and directories were backed up, how long it took to run the backup, and whether any errors occurred (like that file that didn't get backed up because it was open).

Restoring Data

Backups don't do you a lot of good unless you can put them back on the server where they came from. To restore files, open Windows Backup again. You can either run the Restore Wizard or turn to the Restore tab.

WARNING Windows 2000's version of NTFS uses some file attributes not found in FAT or the Windows NT version of NTFS. If you restore files backed up from a Win2K NTFS volume to a FAT or NT NTFS volume, you will lose any data dependent on those attributes. This means that all file permissions, disk quota information, remote storage information, encryption, mounted drive information, and other data dependent on NTFS 5 attributes will be kaput.

Basic Restoration Techniques

To restore files from the Restore Wizard, go to the Welcome tab of Windows Backup and click the Restore Wizard icon. You'll see the usual Welcome screen. Click through it, and you'll be prompted to pick the media you want to restore from (see Figure 21.24). The options available here will depend on what kind of media you've backed up to. If

you've backed up to a file, you'll need to click the Import File button to import the
.bkf file holding your backups.

FIGURE 21.24

*Available media for
restoration*

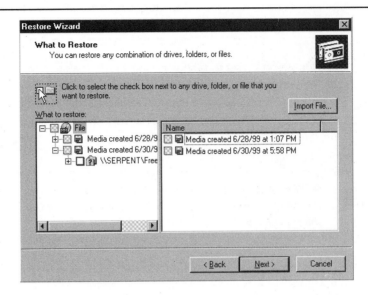

The backup sets on the media will be listed as folders, as shown in Figure 21.25.
They'll be described according to volume backed up, size, type of backup, and
description.

FIGURE 21.25

*Each backup set on
the media will appear
separately.*

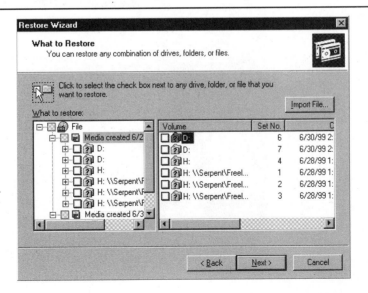

NOTE If a backup operation was aborted for any reason—by Windows Backup or by the user—you will not be able to restore it. Such backups will still appear in the catalog, but will have a question mark where their size should be. One more reason to ensure you can restore backups *before* you need them.

Double-click a set to catalog it, and you'll be able to browse its contents. Check the boxes next to the files and folders in the backup set that you want to restore. As with selecting files for backup, a checked folder with all contents selected will have a blue check mark; if you've only selected certain files within the folder, its check mark will be gray.

 NOTE If there are any errors within the folders of a backup set, the folder will have a red exclamation point on it and the corrupted file will have another exclamation point. You will not be able to restore any damaged files.

When you finish picking files to restore, the wizard will display a screen, like the one in Figure 21.26, that displays the current restore options. Back up to edit any file or media settings, or click the Advanced button to specify a new restoration location or change the file restoration options for preexisting files and remote storage information.

FIGURE 21.26

Final restoration options

WARNING The Advanced options that you choose will apply to all future restoration operations until you change them again. For example, if you edit the options so that the files on the hard disk are always replaced with the files from the backup, that option will remain in place until you manually change it to another one.

Where Should Files Be Restored?

Unless you tell it otherwise, Windows Backup restores files to their original location. But what if you're restoring data to a new drive that has a drive letter that's different from the original? Or you want to put the contents of a daily backup on a Zip disk? From the first screen of the advanced section of the Backup Wizard, you can choose from three location options:

- Original location
- Alternate location (files and folders will be restored, folder structure intact, to the location you specify)
- Single folder (files will all be put within a single folder in the folder you specify, and the original folder structure will be lost)

If you tell Windows Backup to restore the files to an alternate location or to a single folder, then the wizard will display a text box where you type (or browse for) the restore path. You can only restore data to an alternate location, not system configuration information such as the Registry. Any system configuration files must go back to their original locations.

TIP To edit this option without running the Restore Wizard, turn to the Restore tab of Windows Backup. In the lower left-hand corner of this tab, there's a drop-down list of the restoration location options.

What If a File with That Name Already Exists?

The second screen in the advanced section of the Backup Wizard tells Windows Backup what to do if a file with the same name as the file being restored already exists on the volume. Normally, Windows Backup will not replace the file on the existing media, on the principle that if you've already got the file, you shouldn't need to replace it. However, sometimes you'll want the file from the backup, not the one on the hard disk. A Word document with a macro virus may be present on the hard disk, but you don't want the infected file. To cope with some of the situations in which you might want to replace the file already on the hard disk, Windows Backup supports three replacement options:

- Do not replace the file on the disk (the default).

- Replace the file on the disk if it's older than the file on the backup.
- Always replace the file on the disk with the one on the backup.

Sadly, Windows Backup does not have an option to prompt you if it discovers a duplicate file on the media that you're restoring data to. That would have been handy for those times when you're restoring corrupted files but don't necessarily want to replace *every* file that already exists on disk.

 TIP To edit this option without running the Restore Wizard, choose Options from the Tools menu in Windows Backup. Turn to the Restore tab and choose the file replacement you want to use.

What Other Data Should Be Restored? The next screen in the advanced section of the Restore Wizard asks what non-data information you want to replace (see Figure 21.27).

FIGURE 21.27

The non-data information that you can restore depends on the file system the original data was stored in. FAT volumes only let you restore the Removable Storage Management database.

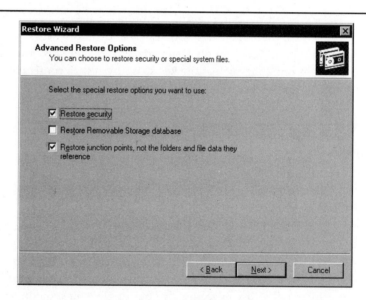

If you're restoring data backed up from a Win2K NTFS drive to a Win2K NTFS drive, you'll have the option to restore the security settings (permissions) to the files, which were backed up when you backed up the file. By default, Windows Backup will do so.

What happens if you tell Windows Backup to not restore the settings? Depends on whether the file already exists on disk:

- If the file exists in the location that you backed it up to, then the security settings attached to the file on disk will be applied, even if you're replacing the file.
- If the file does *not* exist on disk (if you're replacing a deleted file, for example) and you choose to not restore security settings, then the restored file will give the administrator of the local server and the system account full control—and wipe out any previous settings.

 NOTE Notice that the way security settings are restored means that if you elect not to restore security settings to a file that Everyone had access to, you'll need to explicitly grant that permission again.

Other non-data information to restore includes the Removable Storage Management database and junction points. Although this option will always be available, you only need to worry about restoring the Removable Storage Management database if you're using removable storage. Basically it's a catalog of where all the files archived to removable storage are. This database, stored in %*systemroot%*\system32\ntmsdata, will be replaced if you choose to restore the data, so only choose this option if you're sure that the backed-up database is accurate, or you won't be able to find files.

You'll only be asked about junction points if you have mounted drives—logical drives mapped to a path on another volume—on your server. *Junction points* are physical locations on a mounted NTFS volume that point to another area of the disk or to another disk. They're used when you choose to mount a new volume to an empty folder on an NTFS volume instead of assigning that folder a drive letter. Normally, Windows Backup will restore both the junction points and the files and folders to which they point. If you check the box that tells it to only restore the points, not the data, you may lose access to the data.

When you've picked all the Advanced settings, click the Finish button on the last page of the wizard (see Figure 21.28). If restoring from a backup file, Windows Backup will prompt you for the name of the file, then complete the restoration. During the process of restoring the files to disk, Windows Backup will display a Restore Progress dialog box.

Viewing Restore Logs

When a restore operation is over, the Restore Progress dialog box will remain open. Click the Report button to open the restore report in Notepad. Alternatively, you can choose Report from the Tools menu and pick the report you want from the list of available reports. The restoration report will be appended to the backup report originally created for that job, so if you don't see the information you're looking for right away, page down for it.

Restoring Configuration Settings

You can only restore System State data to drives on the server this data was originally backed up from, but otherwise the process of restoring configuration data is much the same as restoring any other data—when prompted to do so, pick the System State folder from the backup set and start the restoration.

However, there are a couple of catches. First, if you restore System State data to its original location (that is, you don't specify an alternate location for it), then Windows Backup will replace the System State data currently on your computer with the System State data you are restoring. However, if you restore the System State data to an alternate location, only the Registry files, SYSVOL directory files, and system boot files are restored to the alternate location. You can't restore the Active Directory directory services database, Certificate Services database, or COM+ Class Registration database to an alternate location.

NOTE In order to restore the System State data on a domain controller, you must first start your computer in Directory Services Restore Mode, available from the Advanced Start menu when you boot Windows 2000. This will allow you to restore the SYSVOL directory and the Active Directory.

Performing an Authoritative Restore

If you're backing up a Win2K domain controller, the System State data includes Active Directory data. You can restore that data. However, if you have more than one domain controller in your domain (and I'm betting that you do) and the Active Directory is replicated to any of these other domain controllers, you need to get that information replicated onto the other domain controllers.

To do this properly, you must perform what's called an *authoritative restore*. Normally, Backup doesn't operate in authoritative mode. Any data that you restore—including Active Directory objects—will retain its original update sequence number used by the AD replication system to detect and spread AD changes among the domain controllers in your domain. Because of this, any data restored in non-authoritative form (would that be in "peon mode"?) looks like old data and won't get propagated to the other domain controllers. Not only that, but the Active Directory replication system will *replace* that restored data with the "newer" data from the other domain controllers, if any exists.

Authoritative restore solves this problem. After you've restored the System State data but before you've restarted the server, run the NTDSUTIL utility in the Windows 2000 Resource Kit. At the prompt, type **Authoritative Restore**. This will give the System State data you just restored the highest update sequence number in the Active Directory replication system, so *that* data will be replicated throughout the domain.

Troubleshooting Hardware with the System Information Tool

If you want current nuts-and-bolts information about the hardware in your servers, you can dig out those .pdf files you printed from the Web sites and read all your handwritten notes about configuration changes that you made.

For those less than thrilled about this idea, Windows 2000 has the System Information tool (see Figure 21.29), located in the System Tools section of the Computer Management (Local) MMC add-in. Using this tool, you can view the following on either the local computer or any Win2K computer running the Windows Management

Instrumentation Service (listed among the other system services in the Services and Applications object in the Computer Management add-in):

- A system summary showing you the basic hardware and software configuration of the server
- Hardware resources used on the server
- Configuration information for the hardware
- Information about all parts of the server software environment

FIGURE 21.29

The System Information tool

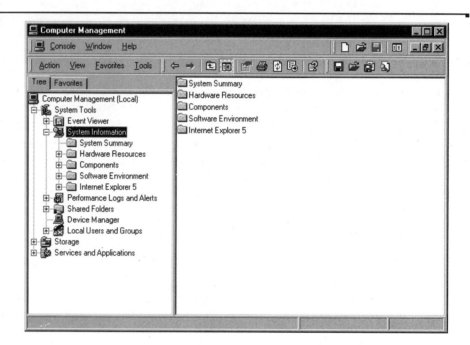

 TIP Typing **winmsd** from Run will start the System Information tool. For those who don't remember, MSD was the original Microsoft Diagnostics tool, which became WinMSD in Windows.

The System Information tool is a neat piece of work. Unlike WinMSD, it can actually *tell* you something about your server's hardware. It's not 100 percent accurate—as I wandered through it, I found a couple of minor pieces of misinformation, like saying that my compressed drive was not compressed—but it's close. And it provides a lot more information than WinMSD ever did and in a reasonably organized manner. Read on to learn how to use this tool to monitor your Win2K server.

System Summary

The system summary information is just that—a snapshot of your system like the one shown in Figure 21.30. The information here is roughly that which used to be on the Version tab of NT 4's WinMSD, with the addition of BIOS version and some memory information. You can't change the data here, just see what the situation is. About the only information you need pay especial attention to is the available memory. You can get memory information in *many* places around Win2K (the Task Manager is another tool that you can use for this), but here it is in black and white: how much physical and virtual memory you have and have remaining.

FIGURE 21.30

System summary information for a Win2K server

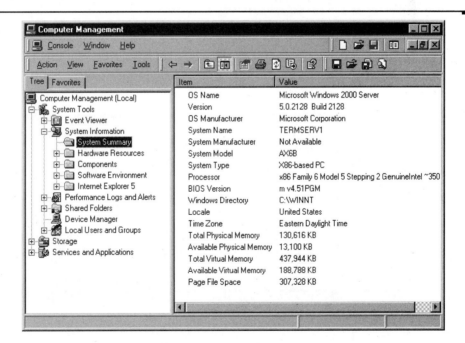

Hardware Resources

The Hardware Resources folder (see Figure 21.31) lists all the resources that might be used by the hardware in your services and shows what hardware actually *is* using those resources, as described in Table 21.6.

FIGURE 21.31

The Hardware Resources *folder with the contents of one folder showing*

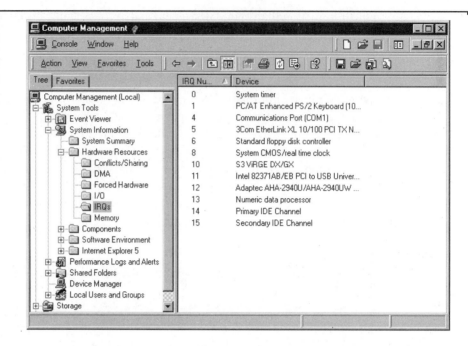

Why is this information important? Basically, everything in Table 21.6 represents either a channel for devices to pass information to the CPU for processing or a storage place for such data while it's waiting for CPU time. Each channel has to have its own hotline to the CPU so that when the CPU responds to a call for processing (an *interrupt*) it knows whose data it's crunching and can pass back the results accordingly. Some devices can share some kinds of channels; IRQs, for example, can be shared by some modern hardware. But storage areas cannot be shared, and not all channels can be shared. If you suspect that two or more devices are using the same resources and can't share, then you can use this tool to find out.

TABLE 21.6: RESOURCES USED BY SERVER HARDWARE

Resource Type	Description
Conflicts/Sharing	This folder lists the components either sharing an IRQ or in conflict over one. Components sharing an IRQ should be working fine (or if they're not, the IRQ in common shouldn't be the problem). If multiple devices are in conflict over an IRQ, however, then one or all won't work.

Continued

Resource Type	Description
TABLE 21.6 CONTINUED: RESOURCES USED BY SERVER HARDWARE	
DMA	Direct Memory Access (DMA) channels are rarely required; most often these days, they're used by audio devices. Basically, the DMA chips on the motherboard can move data from a device to RAM without the CPU having to be involved in the process. Any device that can use DMA needs its own DMA channel as its dedicated path for data moving.
Forced Hardware	Lists older devices not supporting Plug and Play that require specific IRQs.
I/O	This folder shows what devices are using what parts of virtual memory for storage. The information here is similar to what's in the Memory folder, but is taken from the perspective of the memory, not the devices using it.
IRQs	Interrupt request lines, or IRQs, represent each device's hotline to the CPU. IRQs are like DMA channels in that they're specific to a given device, but are unlike them in that they don't take care of the process of shoving data to the CPU—the CPU must still be involved. Some devices can share IRQs.
Memory	This folder shows the I/O buffer areas that each device is using to store data waiting for processing. Essentially, these buffer areas are mailboxes that the CPU can use both to pick up data waiting for it and drop off instructions for the device to which that I/O area belongs. Each device must have its own I/O area so that the CPU will drop off the appropriate instructions to each device. It's going to cause no end of confusion if the CPU asks the network card to play a sound.

Components

The Hardware Resources folder looks at the types of resources available and shows you what devices are using them. The Components folder's approach is opposite—you look at the devices installed and see what resources they're using. But not only resources. The properties sheets for the installed devices provide just about all information relevant to a piece of hardware, including resources used, driver versions, and the type of device it is. This folder is shown in Figure 21.32.

FIGURE 21.32

The contents of the Components folder

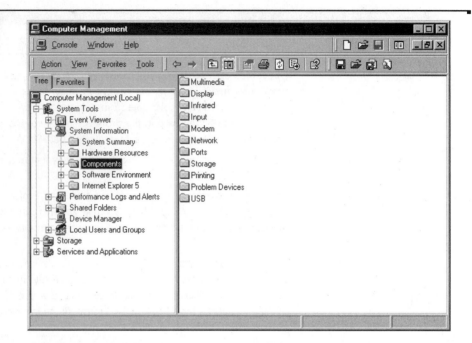

 NOTE The Components folder is a list of all *possible* devices, not actual devices. For example, even if your server doesn't have a modem installed, it will still have a Modem folder.

The exact data within a given object in the Components folder depends heavily on what the device it represents does. For example, the data for the display reports information such as the color density, refresh rate and resolution, video adapter's name, and other display-related information. The network's folder has three subfolders: one for the adapter, one for protocols used, and one for Winsock version information. Storage media show their size, media type, compression data, and so forth. There's even a section for problem devices, listing any devices that Win2K can tell aren't working as expected. For instance, at one time I had a SCSI removable drive attached to this server. After I removed the drive, Win2K still expected to find it, so it's now listed in the Problem Devices folder.

Software Environment

The information in the Software Environment folder (see Figure 21.33) describes all of the software running on the system, who's using it, and what files and services are loaded. It includes the components listed in Table 21.7.

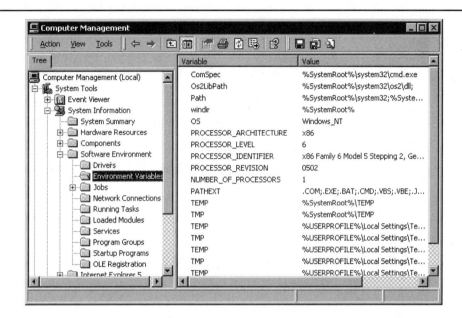

FIGURE 21.33

The Software Environment *folder with one folder open*

TABLE 21.7: SYSTEM PARTS DESCRIBED IN THE SOFTWARE ENVIRONMENT **FOLDER**

System Part	Description
Drivers	This folder lists all the drivers installed on the system, and for each driver gives a brief (and more or less explanatory) description, its type (kernel driver or file system driver), its state (whether stopped or running), and its status as OK.
Environment Variables	This folder lists all the environment variables for the server, including the CPU identification, location of all temporary files, path information for system files, and OS version.
Jobs	This folder contains a folder for each kind of job that might be running on the system (for example, print jobs). The folder will list all currently running jobs of that type.

Continued ▶

TABLE 21.7 CONTINUED: SYSTEM PARTS DESCRIBED IN THE SOFTWARE ENVIRONMENT FOLDER

System Part	Description
Network Connections	This folder lists all current network connections and the drive letters they're mapped to (if applicable).
Running Tasks	This sounds like it should be the job list, but it's not. Instead, it's a list of all the executable files run by the services running on the server. File path, version, file size, and file date are all listed here. If you want to know what version of a given .exe you've got, this is where to look.
Loaded Modules	This folder is like the Running Tasks folder, except that it lists all dynamic link libraries in memory. Version, size, file date, manufacturer, and path information are all displayed. If you want to know what version of a given .dll you've got, this is where to look.
Services	This folder lists all the (non-boot or system) services available on the server by name. The state of each service, its start mode (manual, automatic, or disabled), and its type are all shown.
Program Groups	This folder lists all the groups available from the Start menu. The view shows the users for whom the groups are customized (this information is stored as part of each user's profile, so you may have several different listings of the same program group, each associated with a different user). Terminal server profile associations will be displayed here.
Startup Programs	This folder lists all the programs configured to run at system start-up.
OLE Registration	This folder shows all the object linking and embedding associations used to open data files in the right kind of application.

Internet Explorer 5

The contents of the final folder, Internet Explorer 5, seem to reflect Gates's passionate insistence that Internet Explorer is indeed part of the core operating system. As you can see in Figure 21.34 and Table 21.8, all the settings for IE are listed here, although (as with the other settings in the System Summary folder) you can't change any of them.

FIGURE 21.34

Contents of the
Internet
Explorer 5 *folder*

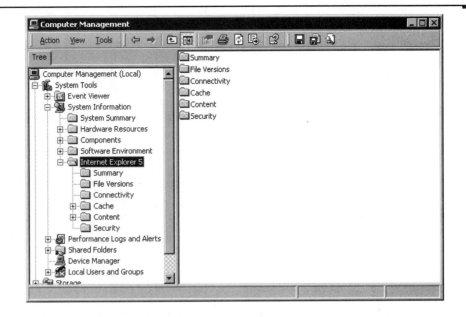

TABLE 21.8: SYSTEM CONFIGURATION SETTINGS IN THE INTERNET EXPLORER 5 FOLDER

System Part	Description
Summary	This folder lists basic version and path information about IE. The most useful information here indicates the degree of encryption IE is set up to use, which printers are set up to work with IE, whether the Content Advisor (ratings software) is on, and whether the Internet Explorer Administration Kit is installed.
File Versions	This folder lists all the files installed that support IE, including their version number, date, size, path, and the company supplying them. If a file is expected but not present, it's still listed, but its version is recorded as "file missing."
Connectivity	This folder lists the connection settings for the browser. Most of what's here applies to proxy server settings, but also listed is whether or not the dialer is set up to kick in when you start IE.

Continued ▶

TABLE 21.8 CONTINUED: SYSTEM CONFIGURATION SETTINGS IN THE INTERNET EXPLORER 5 FOLDER	
System Part	**Description**
Cache	This folder lists the objects in the IE cache (stored when you view online content so that when you need the images again they can be loaded from the cache).
Content	This folder lists the content controls in place on your IE setup. Again, it's indicated whether or not the Content Advisor is enabled. Any certificates in place (your own or someone else's) are also listed here.
Security	This folder lists the security settings you have in place for different site classes: trusted, local intranet, Internet, and restricted.

Saving System Configuration Information

All this information is great, but sometimes it won't help you get the answers you need to resolve problems with the server. That doesn't mean that it can't get someone *else* the answers they need to fix problems. The System Information tool lets you save and load configuration information. Using this capability, you can save your server's configuration to a text file or system information file. You can then e-mail that file to a tech support person with Windows 2000 installed (or not, but if not they'll have to read the text file) who can then load the file and view your computer's information as if they were connected to the server.

 TIP To save only part of the system information, select the part you want to save before starting the save procedure. For example, to save only information related to the network card's configuration, make sure that folder is selected in the left-hand pane.

Saving and Opening System Information Files

To save information as a file, open the Action menu in the System Information tool and choose Save as System Information File. In the dialog box that appears, type a name for the file and click Save. The server will chug away for a minute or two as it inventories your system, and then store the file in your My Documents folder unless you specify otherwise. The file isn't too big—mine is 198KB—so you can fit it onto a floppy if necessary. The file will have an .nfo extension.

You can't open an .nfo file from the System Information tool. Instead, you'll need to open an instance of the Microsoft Management Console. Add the System Information snap-in to the console, telling the MMC that you want information about the local computer.

Back in the console, your snap-in should now appear in the left-hand pane. In the console tree, select System Information. From the Actions menu, choose All Tasks, and then choose Open System Information File from the menu that appears. Find the .nfo file you want, and click Open. The saved file will now appear in your console window.

 NOTE You can also open the .nfo file from NT's WinMSD.

I'm not sure that the saving-as/loading process is completely foolproof. Without doing an exhaustive comparison of the two files, I found discrepancies between the original system information and the contents of a system information file loaded into the MMC—for example, the server's USB information was unknown in the imported file but visible from the System Information tool. If you give a copy of this file to someone for troubleshooting help, I'd suggest that you be prepared to answer questions based on your reading of the original information.

Saving System Information as Text

Saving system information as a text file works much the same way as saving it as an .nfo file. In the System Information tool, choose Save as Text File from the Action menu. Again, the default location is the My Documents folder. When you click the Save button, the server will inventory itself to make sure that the most current settings are saved, then put them into a .txt file that you can read with an editor such as Notepad. It's a long file; this is a partial dump of the information I collected from one server:

Directory	C:\WINNT
User Name	REDROOM\ChristaA
Time Zone	Eastern Standard Time
Daylight Savings Time	Eastern Daylight Time
Total Physical Memory	130612 kbytes
Available Physical Memory	14572 kbytes
Total Virtual Memory	2097024 kbytes
Available Virtual Memory	1988656 kbytes
Page File Space	311252 kbytes
Page File	C:\pagefile.sys

Needless to say, I'd rather analyze the data from a system information file than from a 94KB ASCII file, but the fact that you can save the information as text means that you *can* give someone your system configuration for analysis without them having a copy of Win2K or NT handy.

 NOTE You can also print out a copy of the system configuration information, but be warned—a full copy will make several dozen pages. This server's file made 41 printed pages.

Understanding the Boot Process

Windows 2000 includes several tools that can help you recover from problems related to the operating system, but these tools are no good if you can't get to the Advanced Options menu available at boot time for troubleshooting (discussed later) or get the Setup menu to recognize that your server does, in fact, have a hard disk. In this section, I'll describe the steps the server follows to boot, including the outward manifestations of those steps so you can figure out which step went wrong.

Prequel: The Hardware Must Work

Before you can even attack the problem of "What's wrong with Win2K?" you must make sure that it's not a problem of "What's wrong with the server?" You will not be able to boot the server if either of the following are true:

- The boot drive, the boot drive's disk controller, or the cable connecting the two is malfunctioning or incorrectly set up.
- The CPU or the motherboard is dead.

Other hardware can give you problems, but these are the two that will really stop you in your tracks. To isolate the problem, watch and see where the problem appears:

- A computer that does not boot *at all*, does not make noise, does not do anything at all, is experiencing a dead power supply or a dead power cord.
- A computer that will start its fan working but doesn't do anything beyond that probably has a problem with its motherboard.
- A computer that will count up memory but isn't displaying anything on the monitor (you can hear it, but you can't see it) and beeps at you probably has a problem with the video card.

- A computer that will boot and find the CD and floppy but doesn't find the hard disk controller probably has a problem with the hard disk controller.

- A computer that will boot and identify the hard disk controller but doesn't find a bootable hard disk probably has a hard disk problem. If you're still not positive and you have a spare system around, swap in an easy part of the computer, like the hard disk controller, if you're not sure whether the problem lies in the disk or the controller.

 TIP Keep an eye on the fans in your servers. Those fans are vital to keeping delicate components cool. A cooked computer is a dead computer, sooner or later. A company called PC Power and Cooling (www.pcpowercooling.com) makes a temperature sensor, the 110 Alert, that fits inside a PC and squawks when the internal temperature rises above 110 degrees.

Finally—is the server plugged in? Is its UPS turned on? I know, I know... but check.

Step 1: Load NTLDR

The first part of Windows 2000 that loads is NTLDR, a small program in the root directory of the boot partition of the server's hard disk. It's doing the following:

1. Shifting your processor into 386 mode

2. Starting a very simple file system that allows Win2K to boot from the hard disk

3. Reading the contents of BOOT.INI to display a menu of other possible boot options

4. Accepting your choice of which OS to load

Assuming that you choose to load Windows 2000 Server, NTLDR passes control to NTDETECT.COM, a program that detects the hardware on your server.

Step 2: Run NTDETECT

NTDETECT.COM is in charge of figuring out what hardware is present on your server. It's is looking for the following:

- Your PC's machine ID type
- The bus type
- The video board type
- The keyboard and mouse type
- The serial and parallel ports present on the computer

- The floppy drives present on the computer

Once NTDETECT has run without problems, it builds the Hardware key of the Registry, listed in HKEY_LOCAL_MACHINE. That part of the Registry is built each time you reboot your computer, so it will always reflect the current hardware configuration.

 TIP If you can't get past the NTDETECT stage of system start-up, there's likely some hardware conflict on your server.

Step 3: Load NTOSKRNL

Next, the Win2K kernel (NTOSKRNL) loads with the Hardware Abstraction Layer (HAL.DLL), some assembly-language code that acts as an interface between the server's hardware and the operating system and allows Win2K to be hardware-independent. The kernel loads in four phases:

- The kernel load phase
- The kernel initialization phase
- The services load phase
- The Windows subsystem load phase

 NOTE NTOSKRNL and HAL.DLL are stored in the System32 directory of your Win2K installation. Both must be present on the hard disk for Win2K to load.

Kernel Load Phase

Once HAL.DLL and NTOSKRNL are loaded into memory, Win2K loads the system settings, storing them in HKLM\System\CurrentControlSet\Services. Win2K reads the system information to determine which drivers it must load and in what order.

Which Services Are Loading?

Curious about which services are loading during this stage? Run the Registry Editor and turn to `HKLM\System\CurrrentControlSet\Services`. In this key are keys for all the services currently installed on the server. Open one of these keys and look at the start value for that service.

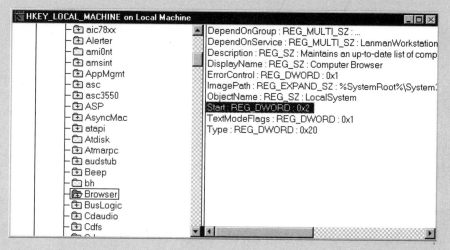

Possible values include:

- 0, which tells Win2K to load the service during the kernel load phase.
- 1, which tells Win2K to load the service during the kernel initialization phase.
- 2, which tells Win2K to start the service during the services load phase.

A value of 3 indicates that the service is enabled but requires a manual start, and a value of 4 indicates that the service is disabled.

Kernel Initialization Phase

After the kernel load phase, the Win2K kernel initializes. Once Win2K has initialized the kernel's internal variables, the kernel scans the current control set for drivers with a start value of 1 and starts them. Win2K builds a new current control set, but does not yet save it. AUTOCHK.EXE, a CHKDSK-like utility, runs to make sure that the file system is intact. This is also the stage where the Win2K pagefile is set up.

Services Load Phase

Next, Win2K loads the Services Manager (SMSS.EXE) and the Win32 subsystem. All services with a start value of 2 start, and Win2K writes the current control set to the System key.

Windows Subsystem Start Phase

Finally, the Windows subsystem (the main part of Win2K, the one that you'll most often interact with) initializes. The Win32 subsystem starts WINLOGON.EXE, which handles interactive user logons and logoffs. WinLogon listens for the *secure attention sequence* (Ctrl+Alt+Delete on all unmodified Win2K machines), which, in effect, tells WinLogon, "Hey! Someone's trying to log on! Listen for their username and password!" WinLogon captures the name and password and passes them to the local security authority (LSASS.EXE), which compares the username and password to the information stored in the Security Accounts Manager. If they match and the user has logon rights, another process called USERINIT.EXE runs the shell referenced in the shell value of HKLM\Software\Microsoft\Windows NT\CurrentVersion\WinLogon (normally EXPLORER.EXE, which loads the usual Win2K Desktop).

What *you* see of all this is the logon screen prompting you to press Ctrl+Alt+Delete to log on.

Fixing Minor Problems with the Advanced Options Menu

So that's the boot process—but what do you do if it doesn't happen quite that way?

No matter how careful you are, mistakes sometimes happen or something just goes wrong. In such a case, you'll need to fix your installation, hopefully without reinstalling the operating system. Installing Windows 2000 isn't too dreadful a prospect, but doing so takes time, especially if you must then reconfigure the server to restore all the settings you need. I'd prefer to spend my time doing something a little more useful.

Here's an apparently easy one: you configured the video display to a refresh rate that your monitor can't support, and you can no longer see anything. It's hard to restore the right settings when you can't see what you're doing, but the initial boot menu no longer displays a VGA setting that loads vanilla video drivers. How do you repair this kind of problem without reinstalling the operating system?

If you've made some change to your operating system that makes it unusable, all is not lost—so long as the system will boot at all and can recognize the hard disk that the operating system is installed on. The Advanced Options menu gives you several methods for fixing or debugging a broken Win2K installation. You get to this menu by pressing F8 when the boot menu appears. Do so, and you'll see a text menu like the following:

```
Windows 2000 Advanced Options Menu
Please Select an Option
Safe Mode
Safe Mode with Networking
Safe Mode with Command Prompt

Enable Boot Logging
Enable VGA Mode
Last Known Good Configuration
Directory Services Restore Mode (Windows 2000 domain controllers Only)
Debugging Mode
Boot Normally
Return to OS Choices Menu
```

NOTE   Previous versions of NT used to display the message "Press the Space Bar to display the Last Known Good Menu during the boot process." This option no longer exists. If you don't open the Last Known Good menu from the Advanced Options menu, you can't open it.

Using Safe Mode Options

The various forms of Safe Mode—with networking, without networking, with command prompt—load a minimal version of Windows 2000 with only the drivers needed to support that minimal version. These tools can be handy when something is preventing your system from booting and you suspect an errant driver. Whichever mode you choose, during boot, Win2K will display a list of all the drivers and services as they're loading. When you log off, the machine will restart as usual.

Safe Mode

Safe Mode starts Win2K with only the drivers and services required to boot the computer. No network drivers are loaded, and network-dependent services are changed to start option 3 (meaning that they're set for manual starting), but can't be started even from the Services section of the MMC or with `net start`. Use this version of Safe Mode to fix problems related to network services.

Safe Mode with Networking

Safe Mode with Networking is what it sounds like—a pared-down version of Win2K that includes network support. Use this version when you need network support and you're sure that the network drivers are not causing any problems.

Safe Mode with Command Prompt

If you're expecting Safe Mode with Command Prompt to be a strictly command-line version of Win2K, you're mistaken. When you boot to this option, you'll see a list of the files that Win2K is loading, and then the graphical interface will appear, running in 640 × 480. However, rather than loading the Desktop, Win2K will use the command prompt for its shell.

Safe Mode with Command Prompt is a network-disabled version of Win2K that replaces the EXPLORER.EXE shell normally used with CMD.EXE. You can do anything on the local computer that you can do in the usual shell—you can even run GUI applications, if you don't mind them running with a maximum resolution of 800 × 600 (640 × 480 by default, but you can edit the Display options from the Control Panel) and 16 colors. But everything you do you must start from the command prompt or from the Task Manager (still available if you press Ctrl+Alt+Delete). Use Safe Mode with Command Prompt to run a stand-alone version of Win2K when something is wrong with Explorer that keeps Win2K from starting. You can run Explorer from this mode and gain access to the graphical Desktop, if you like, but you're not dependent on it as you are in the other versions of Safe Mode. If you don't open Explorer, you can shut down the server with the shutdown command.

 TIP To get a complete list of all the commands supported from the command prompt, type **help | more**. (You can just type **help**, but there's more commands than will fit on a single screen.) To get help with the syntax of a specific command, type *commandname* /?.

The Last Known Good Configuration

Ever edited your system, rebooted, and then exclaimed, "I shouldn't have done that!" In some cases, the Last Known Good menu can help you reverse history so that you (effectively) didn't do whatever that was. So long as the change you made produced no system-critical errors involving drivers or system files, and you successfully booted and logged onto the server once before you ran into the problem, you can load the Last Known Good Configuration and choose from three different system start-up options: using the current configuration, using the last known good configuration—loaded the last time the server successfully booted and you started a session from the console—or restarting the computer.

Understanding How Last Known Good Works

The Last Known Good Configuration option works because of the way Win2K maintains configuration information. Every time you boot the computer and log on, the configuration information for the local machine is stored in HKLM\System\CurrentControlSet. Win2K also stores a backup copy of this information and assigns it a number for organization purposes. This backup is used should the default set of configuration information—the current set—become corrupted and unusable.

NT 4 typically stored four copies of the configuration information: \ControlSet001, \ControlSet002, \CurrentControlSet, and \Clone. The CurrentControlSet wasn't really a control set, but was a pointer to one of the numbered control sets, perhaps 001. Control set 002 might have been the Last Known Good configuration, the one stored after the previous boot. The clone was a copy of the CurrentControlSet pointer.

Win2K organizes its current and backup configuration sets a little differently. As you can see from Figure 21.35, Win2K stores several copies of the configuration information, numbering them consecutively. Win2K only maintains a current control set, which is a pointer to one of the numbered sets, no clone. Another numbered set is maintained as a Last Known Good configuration, to be used if the default configuration set becomes unusable.

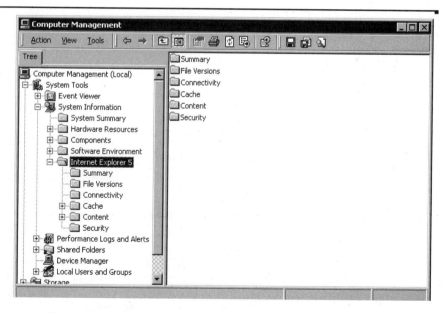

You can't tell which configuration set your server is currently using from the numbers. To find this information out, look in the \Select key in HKLM\System (see Figure 21.36). There are four values here: Current, Default, Failed, and LastKnownGood. If you restart the machine and boot normally (that is, without using the Advanced Options menu), then the Default control set will be used. The value of Failed is the configuration set that had been the default when you chose to start the machine from the Last Known Good Configuration menu. Because you told Win2K to not start with that configuration set, it's now marked as Failed even if nothing is actually wrong with it.

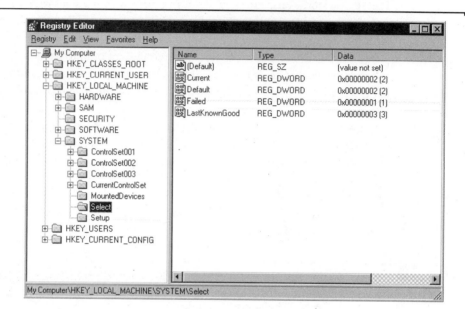

Repairing a Server with the Last Known Good Configuration

That's just background so that you know what's happening; you don't have to tweak the Registry to make the Last Known Good option work.

To use this option, restart the computer and follow these steps:

1. When the system has finished recognizing its hardware and displays the boot menu, press F8 to open the Advanced Options menu.

2. Choose Last Known Good from the boot menu and press Enter. The boot menu will now reappear with the words Last Known Good Configuration at the bottom of the screen in blue letters. This is to remind you that, by loading that option, you're choosing to reverse all non-security-related changes made to the Registry during the last session.

3. If you *do* choose to use the Last Known Good configuration, Win2K will display the Last Known Good/Hardware Profiles menu. All hardware profiles created previously will be listed here. If you haven't created any new hardware profiles, then your current configuration will be listed, called Profile 1.

4. Choose the profile you want, and press Enter to boot the computer.

Win2K will start with the settings you started your last session with. After you log on, you'll see an information message telling you that Win2K couldn't start with the current configuration and is starting with a previously saved configuration.

The Last Known Good option can't always help you. It applies only so long as you have never logged on with the new configuration, but *have* logged on, and can boot the computer now. That means that it won't work if any of the following apply:

- You have never logged on successfully (that is, if you're just installing Win2K).

- You edited the server's configuration, rebooted, and logged on successfully, and now want to restore your system to the way it was before the change.

- The change that you want to reverse is not related to control set information. You can't remove changes to user profiles or system policies with the Last Known Good menu, for example. Passwords are also unaffected by the Last Known Good option, so you can't use this option to recover from a forgotten Administrator's password.

- The system boots, someone logs on, and the system hangs.

- The system won't boot at all and is unable to get to the boot menu.

Enable VGA Mode

Those familiar with NT Server will remember that in previous versions of the operating system the boot menu had two entries for each instance of NT installed on the computer: one with whatever graphics settings you'd chosen, and one designed to run in vanilla VGA mode. There was a good reason for this. In NT 3.1, there was no VGA mode, and if you set up the wrong driver and logged on (making the Last Known Good option useless) then you had to go through a complicated sequence of keystrokes to navigate blindly to the Display applet in the Control Panel and fix things.

The VGA option is no longer in the main menu, however. To get to it, you must press F8 at boot time and choose Enable VGA Mode from the Advanced Options menu. Use this option if you've installed a bad video driver and need to correct the problem. Unlike the Last Known Good menu, this option will work at any time, not just before you've successfully logged on.

Enable Boot Logging

Enabling boot logging from the Advanced Options menu starts Win2K as usual, except that it creates a file called NTBTLOG.TXT and stores it in the top of your system root directory. The output looks like what's in Figure 21.37.

FIGURE 21.37

Sample output from
a boot log

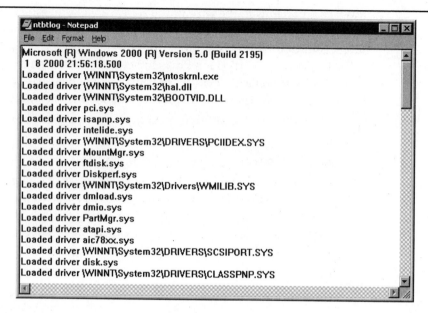

```
ntbtlog - Notepad                                          _ □ X
File  Edit  Format  Help
Microsoft (R) Windows 2000 (R) Version 5.0 (Build 2195)
 1  8 2000 21:56:18.500
Loaded driver \WINNT\System32\ntoskrnl.exe
Loaded driver \WINNT\System32\hal.dll
Loaded driver \WINNT\System32\BOOTVID.DLL
Loaded driver pci.sys
Loaded driver isapnp.sys
Loaded driver intelide.sys
Loaded driver \WINNT\System32\DRIVERS\PCIIDEX.SYS
Loaded driver MountMgr.sys
Loaded driver ftdisk.sys
Loaded driver Diskperf.sys
Loaded driver \WINNT\System32\Drivers\WMILIB.SYS
Loaded driver dmload.sys
Loaded driver dmio.sys
Loaded driver PartMgr.sys
Loaded driver atapi.sys
Loaded driver aic78xx.sys
Loaded driver \WINNT\System32\DRIVERS\SCSIPORT.SYS
Loaded driver disk.sys
Loaded driver \WINNT\System32\DRIVERS\CLASSPNP.SYS
```

If you're running into problems, then you can check out this log to see what drivers did—and did not—load. It's normal for some drivers to not load; they're available, but if you haven't got anything running that requires them, Win2K won't start them, so as to save memory. But if your network, for example, isn't working, you can scan the list of drivers to make sure that NDIS.SYS is present.

TIP   At a time when the server is working normally, enable boot logging and save the output under another name, noting the date and any new changes to the server. (You can do this pretty easily—all file systems in Win2K support long filenames.) If something does go wrong with the machine, you can compare the healthy boot record with the sick one to find the discrepancy.

Directory Services Restore Mode

Choosing this mode is the second step for restoring a domain controller. Ordinarily, you can restore the Active Directory from Windows Backup and then log back on again normally. When you log on after restoring the Active Directory data, the AD should recheck its indices and perform an integrity check.

The Directory Services Restore Mode is for those times when you want to be doubly sure that the AD data is back and re-indexed. When you choose this option, it will kick you back to the main boot menu, showing in blue text at the bottom of the screen that you're in Directory Services Restore Mode. The system will boot in Safe Mode with Networking, run CHKDSK on all the volumes, then present the logon screen for you to log on as the administrator of the local domain.

As soon as you log on while in Directory Services Restore Mode, run REGEDT32 and look for a subkey called `Restore in Progress` within HKLM\System\CurrentControlSet\Service\NTDS. The presence of this key (created by NTBACKUP) tells the Active Directory to check all its indices the next time you boot the system normally.

Debugging Mode

This final option in the Advanced Options menu, Debugging Mode, sends debugging information to a computer connected to a Windows 2000 computer you're booting via the serial port. The basic gist of this is that it's a way to monitor the progress of a server's boot from another server.

Preparing for Recovery

If the situation is too dire for any of the Advanced Options menu options to help you, all is not lost. Before it's time to reinstall, it's time to drag out one of Windows 2000's recovery tools: the Emergency Repair Disk or the Recovery Console, both of which are available through the Repair option in Setup.

Installing the Recovery Console

How do you get to the recovery tools? You can install the Recovery Console from the Windows 2000 installation CD. Open the Run tool in the Start menu and type **d:\i386\winnt32 /cmdcons** where d: is the drive letter of your installation CD. The first time you do this, Win2K will display the message box shown in Figure 21.38.

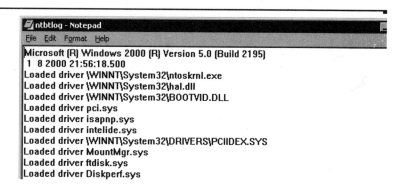

```
ntbtlog - Notepad
File  Edit  Format  Help
Microsoft (R) Windows 2000 (R) Version 5.0 (Build 2195)
 1  8 2000 21:56:18.500
Loaded driver \WINNT\System32\ntoskrnl.exe
Loaded driver \WINNT\System32\hal.dll
Loaded driver \WINNT\System32\BOOTVID.DLL
Loaded driver pci.sys
Loaded driver isapnp.sys
Loaded driver intelide.sys
Loaded driver \WINNT\System32\DRIVERS\PCIIDEX.SYS
Loaded driver MountMgr.sys
Loaded driver ftdisk.sys
Loaded driver Diskperf.sys
```

Windows 2000 Setup will copy some files from the installation CD, then prompt you to restart the computer. The Recovery Console will be in the Startup menu (the text menu you see when you start up the computer) when you reboot, listed as Microsoft Windows 2000 Command Console. To start it, just choose that option before the 30-second timeout to whatever your default start-up option is.

Creating the Emergency Repair Disk

Every time you successfully edit your system's configuration, you should back the configuration up against the time when you unsuccessfully edit the settings. This backup disk is called the Emergency Repair Disk.

 TIP Re-create the Emergency Repair Disk *after* you have successfully booted with the new configuration information. This way, you'll know that the configuration you're backing up works.

Previous versions of NT had a utility called RDISK that you could use to create a repair disk after installation. If you're looking for RDISK in Win2K, you won't find it. Yes, Win2K still offers the same Emergency Repair Disk (ERD) functionality, but you now use a utility in the Backup program to make it, and it is *not* the same disk. Strictly speaking, the ERD is no longer a repair disk, but a boot disk to run the repair tools on the CD.

To create the ERD, follow these steps:

1. Run the Backup utility found in Accessories/System Tools. On the initial screen of the utility, you'll find buttons for three wizards: Backup Wizard, Restore Wizard, and Emergency Repair Disk. Click the Emergency Repair Disk button.

2. When prompted, put a blank, formatted disk in the A: drive and click OK. You'll have the option of copying the Registry files to the Repair directory. I strongly recommend that you do so.

 NOTE The updated files will be in %*systemroot%*\Repair\RegBack.

Win2K will copy AUTOEXEC.NT, CONFIG.NT, and SETUP.LOG to the disk. The two .NT files are not bootable—this isn't a boot disk. Rather, they're the files that Win2K needs to boot the files necessary for running 16-bit applications such as the Repair utility. AUTOEXEC.NT installs support for the CD-ROM (which you'll need to repair Win2K), the network redirector, and DPMI Memory. CONFIG.NT loads DOS into the Upper Memory Block (UMB), out of conventional memory, and loads HIMEM.SYS, needed to read memory above 640KB.

Know Thy ERD

It's important that you realize that the ERD you get with Windows 2000 is different from the NT 4 ERD. The Win2K ERD does not include Registry data—probably a reflection of the fact that people with complex systems could easily have a Security key file too big to fit on a disk. You can see the contents of the two ERD types below (the Win2K ERD is on top):

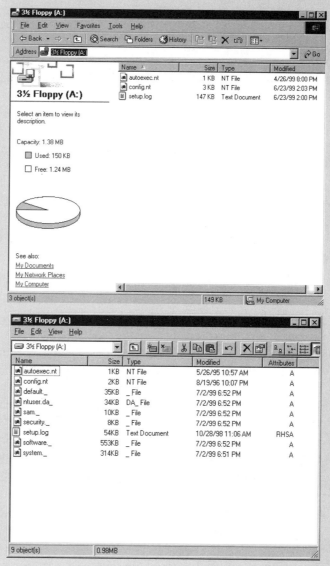

Continued

CONTINUED

You can replace parts of the system Registry from the Recovery Console, if you update the information in the RegBack folder on a regular basis. (The original files are in the \Config folder; the backups in \Repair\RegBack.) Just don't expect to have that information anywhere if you don't back it up when creating the ERD.

Curious about what you *do* with the ERD? Turn to the next section.

Repairing–or Recovering–a Damaged Installation

The Last Known Good menu and the Safe Mode boot options aren't always enough to get a wounded installation back on its feet again. You've still got some options before reinstalling, though. As I discussed in the previous section, Windows 2000 offers two repair tools: the Recovery Console and the Emergency Repair Disk. Both work on volumes formatted with either FAT or NTFS—one of the cool things about Win2K, since this means that you can now format a system partition with NTFS but still have access to troubleshooting tools.

Understanding Repair Options

The two repair options aren't identical. The Emergency Repair Disk is a simple procedure for those times when you don't know precisely what the problem is, but you want to fix it and get on with your life. There's little finesse involved: you start installing Win2K; when asked whether you're doing a real installation or a repair, you choose to repair; and then you plug in the ERD and let Setup repair files that are different from the ones originally installed. (There's a little more to it than that, but that's the basic story. I'll go through the procedure a bit later in "Using the Emergency Repair Disk.") So long as you haven't replaced any drivers or DLLs in your system folders with new ones, you can safely choose to restore all system files to their originals, and you'll still get your Win2K installation back as you left it—just fixed.

The Recovery Console is a little more complicated. Rather than a means of restoring damaged files, it's a command-line utility from which you can perform a variety of tasks:

- Copy system files from a floppy disk or CD to a hard disk (although not from a hard disk to a floppy disk)

- Start and stop services

- Read and write data in the system directory on the local hard disk

- Format disks
- Repartition disks

Use the Recovery Console when you know precisely what's wrong and what you want to accomplish. If you don't know what's wrong, this is not an easy way of finding out.

In short, if your Win2K installation is dead and you're not sure why, then use the Emergency Repair Disk to see whether restoring the original installation files will fix the problem. If you know what the problem is—like, for example, a bad or missing .sys file or a runaway service—then you can use the Recovery Console to copy the missing file to its new location without changing any other files.

If you didn't set up the Recovery Console before Win2K became unbootable (or you want to run the ERD repair utility), then you'll need to run Setup from the installation CD. After Setup has copied all the files it needs to access the hardware it needs to run Setup, it will ask you whether you want to install Win2K, repair it, or exit Setup. Choose R to open the Windows 2000 Repair Options menu, from which you can either repair an installation with the Recovery Console (press C) or with the Emergency Repair Disk (press R).

Using the Recovery Console

When you choose to run the Recovery Console, it will scan the disk and find any installations of Windows NT/2000 on the disk. Pick the one you want to repair. Type the number of the option you want, and supply the password for the admin account. You're in.

 TIP You can repair Windows NT Server 4 installations with the Recovery Console. Start the Repair Console as you normally would. When it returns the list of found NT installations, pick the NT 4 one. That said, *don't* run out and try this on all your NT 4 servers using older hardware, as I've seen Win2K Setup blow up a computer that couldn't handle it, to the point that I had to reinstall the original OS. This is only a good idea on that new loaded-to-the-gills Intel-only server you bought no earlier than January 1999.

If the term "console" led you to expect some kind of GUI, you'll be surprised to see a simple command-line interface. Although it looks like an ordinary command prompt, the Recovery Console is not the command prompt that you can open from the Accessories folder. First, it supports only a few commands and only locally—this is not a network tool. Second, those commands are specialized for this interface and only perform a limited set of functions. The wildcard options in the copy command don't work in the console, you can only copy files from removable media to the system partition (but not the other way around—you can't use the console to back up files to other media) and although you can move to other logical drives on the hard disk, you can't read files on any partition other than the system partition—or even perform a dir function on them. If you try, you'll get an Access Denied error. The Recovery Console is not a command-line version of Win2K, cool as that would be.

 NOTE I'd expected that the Recovery Console would include a command-line version of REGEDIT, like Windows 9x does. Sadly, it does not.

You can't back up files. You can't read the contents of any directory not in the system root. You can't use wildcards. You can't edit security information. What *can* you do with the Recovery Console?

Mostly, you can fix your system partition to make it usable again. As you can see in Table 21.9, the Recovery Console is a set of commands that you can use to manipulate the files and structure of the system partition. As you can see, there are a lot of functions with duplicate commands that use the same syntax; unless I specify otherwise, there's no difference between the two commands.

TABLE 21.9: SUPPORTED RECOVERY CONSOLE COMMANDS

Command Name	Function
attrib	Changes the attributes of a selected file or folder.
batch	Runs the commands specified in a text file so that you can complete many tasks in a single step.
cd or chdir	Displays the name of the current directory, or changes directories. Typing **CD..** closes the current directory and moves you up one in the tree.
chkdsk	Runs CheckDisk.
cls	Wipes the screen of any previous output, so you can see better.
copy or extract	Copies files from removable media to the system folders on the hard disk. Does not accept wildcards.
del or delete	Deletes one or more files (does not accept wildcards).
dir	Lists the contents of the current or selected directory.
disable	Disables the named service or driver.
enable	Enables the named service or driver.
diskpart	Replaces the FDISK tool you're probably familiar with. Creates or deletes disk partitions.
fixboot	Writes a new partition boot sector on the system partition.
fixmbr	Writes a new Master Boot Record (MBR) for the partition boot sector.

Continued ▶

TABLE 21.9 CONTINUED: SUPPORTED RECOVERY CONSOLE COMMANDS

Command Name	Function
format	Formats the selected disk.
listsvc	Lists all the services running on the Win2K installation.
logon	If you have multiple Win2K (or NT) installations on the local hard disk, you can use this command to pick the installation you want to repair.
map	Displays the drive letter mappings currently in place. Handy for getting the information you need to use DISKPART.
md or mkdir	Creates a directory.
more, type	Displays the contents of the chosen text file.
rd or rmdir	Deletes a directory.
rename or ren	Renames a single file.
systemroot	Makes the current directory the system root of the drive you're logged into.
extract	Extracts a compressed installation file (one with a .cab extension) to the local fixed disk. Only works if you're running the Recovery Console from the installation disk.

 WARNING If you thought the Registry Editor was potentially dangerous, the Recovery Console is just as bad or worse. You can really screw up your system here, to the point that the only thing to do is reinstall and reload your backups. There's no Undo feature, not all the commands ask for confirmation, and there's no Read Only setting like the one in REGEDT32. If you're not used to working from the command line, review what you want to do and the tools you need to do it before you open the console.

Some of the commands shown in Table 21.9 will look familiar to old DOS hands, but many of them work a little differently from the way they did under DOS, using a slightly different syntax or only working under specific circumstances. Let's take a look at how you can use these commands to get things back up and running.

Enabling and Disabling Services

Why would you need to enable or disable services from the command line? Therein lies a tale...

Earlier this year, I bought a new PC. Installed everything, ran the installation program for the 3Com network card in the server. Life was good.

Until I rebooted the computer.

You see, a diagnostic program was part of the setup for the NIC—an unavoidable part that you could not choose to not install. (Trust me: I tried, on several computers with the same set of hardware.) Whenever I started up NT, this diagnostic program would scan the system and display a message that a newer version of my NIC's driver was available—did I want to use the new driver? Click OK or Cancel, and the message box would close for a second and then reopen, with the same message. Add to this that the searching and displaying was using up 100 percent of CPU time for a 350MHz Pentium II doing *nothing else but running the diagnostic*. Running the Task Manager (when I could get a spare cycle here or there to open it) didn't help, because the program wouldn't shut down even when I killed the process.

> **NOTE**   Worried about this happening to you? Although I've run into several people who've had the same problem with one version of the driver for the 3Com 3C905X Ethernet 10BaseT card, this issue seems to be fixed in the driver published in April 1999. Other than this glitch, I've been very happy with these NICs.

Okay, I figured—the problem is a runaway service, so if I can shut down the service I will resolve the problem. But shutting down the service is hard when you're clicking OK in a repeatedly reappearing dialog box and then frantically grabbing CPU cycles to open the Control Panel and then Services before the dialog box opens and the CPU usage starts running at 100 percent again.

In this case, I was finally able to get to the Services applet, find the service (named 3Com Diagnostics, or some such, so identifying the problem child wasn't hard), and then stop and disable it. Problem solved. But it took a lot of time and mouse-clicking to get to that point. A tool that would enable me to boot to the command prompt and disable that service without having to work around the CPU-eating message box would have been nice. And that's where the services-related tools in the Recovery Console come in.

The first step to fixing a problem like this is running the listsvc utility. There's no arguments to this—just type **listsvc** from the command prompt, and Windows 2000 will display a list of all the services and drivers currently installed for that installation of Win2K, a short description of what they are, and their start type (boot, automatic, manual, system, or disabled). Seeing all the services will probably take a few pages of screen, but the services are listed alphabetically, so you can find the one you want fairly easily. Write down its name.

> **TIP**   The names of services and drivers are not case sensitive.

Once you've found the suspected problem child, it's time for the disable command. The syntax is simple: **disable** *servicename*. Win2K will then notify you that it found the Registry entry for this service (or tell you that it can't find an entry for this service, in which case you need to check your spelling and try again). It will also display the current start type and new start type for the service. Write down the current start type for the service in case you want to start it again.

To make the change take effect, type **exit** to leave the Recovery Console and restart the computer. See if disabling that service fixed the problem. If it did, then you're home free. (Not sure how you'd know? Depends on what the problem was. In the case of the runaway 3Com diagnostics, the fix was pretty immediate. As soon as I turned off the service, the problem disappeared.) If it didn't, then you can return to the console, enable that service, and try something else.

You don't have to disable a service to keep it from running when Win2K starts, however. Instead, you could change its start type from automatic to manual. To do so, or to reenable a service you disabled, you'll need to use the enable command. Like disable, enable's syntax is simple: **enable** *servicename*. If run on a disabled service, using this syntax will enable the service and restore it to whatever its start type was when it was disabled.

To change a service's start type without disabling it, add the new start type to the end of the enable command, like this:

```
enable servicename start_type
```

where start_type is one of the options in Table 21.10.

TABLE 21.10: START TYPES	
Start Type	**Meaning**
Service_boot_start	Boot
Service_system_start	System
Service_demand_start	Manual
Service_auto_start	Automatic

So, for example, instead of disabling the 3Com diagnostic service, I could have changed its start type from automatic to manual. That way, I could have started it at any time during the Win2K session, but it wouldn't start automatically.

Replacing Damaged Files

Perhaps the problem isn't a runaway driver or service, but a corrupted part of the operating system, as in error messages that say Bad or Missing NTOSKRNL.EXE. In such a case, you may need to replace all or part of your operating system (although, if we're talking about more than a few files here or you aren't sure what's broken, you might consider hauling out the Emergency Repair Disk). The tools most likely to apply to this scenario are the ones to create and delete directories, rename files, change attributes, and copy or extract files from other media.

Creating directories is simple. The command syntax is as follows:

```
md [drive:]path
mkdir [drive:]path
```

where *drive:* is the drive letter of the drive on which you want to create the folder, if it's not the current one, and *path* is the name of the directory you want to create. Just make sure that, if you don't spell out the location of the new directory, you're currently in the place where the new directory should be created.

The syntax for the rmdir and rd commands (for deleting directories) is the same as that for md. The only part of directory deletion that you have to watch is that you can't delete directories unless they're empty, with no subdirectories. If you try, you'll get an error message telling you that the directory is not empty, and there's no switch to make rd act like deltree (an old DOS command that would delete subdirectories).

Before you delete a directory, run the dir command to check out its contents and make sure that you really do want to remove it. Conveniently, dir displays all files, hidden or not, and shows their attributes.

Rather than deleting entire directories, however, you're more likely to need to replace individual files. That's where copy and extract come in. The copy command is what it sounds like: a method of copying a file from one location to another, with the caveat I've mentioned before that you can only copy *to* the system directory, not copy files from the system directory to removable media such as a Jaz drive. The syntax for copying files is simple:

```
copy source [destination]
```

where *source* is the name of the original file and *destination* is the directory where you're pasting the original (along with a new name, if you need it). If you don't specify a directory, the file will be copied to the directory from which you're running the command. The extract utility works the same way as copy and uses the same syntax, with one exception: you can only use extract if you started the Recovery Console from the Repair option in Setup. Neither copying utility supports wildcards (so you can't copy the entire contents of a directory very easily), but copy automatically decompresses compressed installation files for you. Both utilities will alert you if a file with the name of the one you're pasting already exists in that location.

If you're not sure that you want to replace an existing file, try renaming it and then copying the new file to the relevant location. The syntax for `rename` is as follows:

```
rename [drive:][path] filename1 filename2
```

`rename` works only on single files, and the renamed file must be in the same place as the original. That is, you can't use this command to move files. To do that, you'd need to use copy.

Fixing Boot Sectors and Boot Records

Your computer uses a couple of pieces of information to navigate your hard disk. Those two pieces are the boot sector and the Master Boot Record (MBR). Most of the time, these pieces are pretty safe, but some things (like some viruses) can target and infect them, or they can be lost. In such a case, you'll need a way to restore them.

First, a little background. The partition boot sector contains the information that the file system uses to access the volume. The Master Boot Record (discussed below) examines the information in the boot sector to load the boot loader.

The Windows 2000 boot sector contains the following information:

- A jump instruction
- The name and version of the operating system files (such as Windows 2000)
- A data structure called the BIOS Parameter Block, which describes the physical characteristics of the partition
- A data structure called the BIOS Extended Parameter Block, which describes the location of the Master File Table for NTFS volumes
- The bootstrap code

Most of the information in the boot sector describes the physical characteristics of the disk (for example, the number of sectors per track and clusters per sector), in addition to the location of the File Allocation Table (for FAT volumes) or the Master File Table (for NTFS volumes). The layout and exact information included in the boot sector depends on the disk format used.

Given that a disk may have more than one partition, how does the hard disk know where to find the different partitions? The first sector on every hard disk (whether the hard disk has an operating system on it or not) contains that disk's Master Boot Record (MBR). The MBR contains the partition table for that disk and a small amount of code used to read the partition table and find the system partition for that hard disk. Once it finds that partition, the MBR loads a copy of that partition's boot sector into memory. If the disk is not bootable (has no system partition) then the code never gets used and the boot sector is not loaded.

In short, a hard disk needs a functioning MBR to boot. The MBR is in the same place on every hard disk, so it's potentially an easy virus target.

Okay—all that said, to write a new boot sector to a drive, type **fixboot**. This will write a new boot sector to the current boot drive. To create a new MBR, type **fixmbr**.

Deleting, Creating, and Formatting Partitions

The Recovery Console includes tools not only for fixing Windows 2000, but for completely wiping things out and starting over. With these tools you can repartition and reformat your hard disk. *Partitioning* is setting up logical drives on the disk; *formatting* is placing a file system on those drives so you can store data on them.

 WARNING You probably already know this, but just in case you've forgotten, repartitioning and formatting are *destructive*. Any data on the hard disk you've reformatted or repartitioned is history. Keep your backups.

Before you start formatting or repartitioning, you might want to take a look at what you've already got in place. The Recovery Console's map command can help you do that. Type **map** at the command prompt, and you'll see output like the following:

?		0MB	Device\HardDisk0\Partition0
C:	FAT16	1028MB	Device\HardDisk0\Partition1
?		3310MB	Device\HardDisk0\Partition0
E:	NTFS	1028MB	Device\HardDisk0\Partition2
H:	NTFS	1028MB	Device\HardDisk0\Partition3
G:		1028mb	Device\HardDisk0\Partition4
?		227MB	Device\HardDisk0\Partition0
A:			Device\Floppy0
D:			Device\CDROM0

You can see from this that logical drive G: on the hard disk hasn't been formatted, because it's not showing any file system. To format it, you would use the following syntax:

```
format g:  [/q] [/fs:filesystem]
```

Here, /q tells format to do a quick format (not checking for bad sectors), and the /fs switch is for specifying the file system to use. You don't have to specify a file system (your options are NTFS, FAT32, and FAT), but if you don't, Win2K will format it to NTFS. When you run this command, Win2K will tell you that all data on that drive will be lost and ask you to confirm that the format should proceed. Do so, and a few seconds later you will have a newly formatted drive.

TIP You can convert a FAT partition to NTFS, but you cannot convert an NTFS partition to FAT.

You can format the G: drive safely, or at least without affecting any other logical drives. What you can't do, even before formatting, is repartition to make the G: drive bigger, perhaps giving it some of that space that isn't used on the disk. To do that, you need to boot the Disk Administrator and make G: part of a volume and then extend that volume—anyway, it's all in Chapter 7. If you do want to repartition the disk to reorganize its structure, run diskpart.

When you're done with the Recovery Console, type **exit** and press Enter. The computer will reboot.

Using the Emergency Repair Disk

You have two options for the Emergency Repair Disk: Manual Repair, in which you can choose from a list of repair options (not another one!) or Fast Repair, which repairs your installation for you. I'm not a trusting type, so I'll choose M for Manual to be sure that I get the options I want.

 NOTE If you choose Fast Repair, then the repair utility will perform all the tasks proffered by the Manual Repair utility.

By default, the repair utility will inspect the start-up environment, verify the Windows 2000 system files to make sure none are missing, and inspect the boot sector. Choose the options you want, and press Enter to continue.

Now, you'll need that ERD. Make sure it's in the floppy drive and press Enter. If you don't have an ERD, you may still be able to repair the installation by pressing L to let Setup try to find the Win2K installation for you. Setup will look around to find a Win2K installation, and then ask you whether the installation found at such and such a location is the one you want to repair. If it is, press Enter.

Setup will read from Setup.log on the ERD and then start doing the operations you selected. If it comes across any files in your existing installation that don't match the ones logged in Setup.log, which is a record of all files installed originally, it will tell you and then offer you a choice of skipping the file, repairing it (that is, replacing it with the one that Windows 2000 Server would install), or choosing to repair all files that differ from the original. There is no "skip all" function, so you'll have to make a decision for each file if you're pretty sure that you want to keep some of the files logged in Setup.log. It's inspecting the entire Win2K directory, so this may take a while.

There's really no way to know which file represents the problem, unfortunately. All this process does is note which files are different from what Setup would have installed. If you've run Win2K for any length of time and made any modifications, quite a few files may be different. However, replacing these files won't restore Win2K to a just-installed condition because your Registry files are not replaced.

When it's done, the computer will reboot and (hopefully) run Windows 2000.

 NOTE Your security information—policies, accounts, passwords—will be as you left it. The ERD does not record or replace security information.

Troubleshooting Login Failures: "No Domain Controller Found..."

One of the most confusing and common Windows 20000 mysteries is the one that occurs when you sit down at a computer and try to log in to your domain, only to be told that no domain controller could be found to validate your login.

It can happen from any client type, whether DOS, Mac, Windows 9*x*, NT, or Windows 2000 Professional, and the same things tend to make it happen. But be ready for some bad news: you can't always fix it.

When you tell your workstation to try to log you in to a domain, your workstation must first find one of the machines that contains a copy of the database of domain users in passwords—in other words, a domain controller, whether primary or backup. All domain controllers announce themselves to the world by registering a NetBIOS name of *domainname*<1C>; for example, if a domain named URSAMAJOR had a domain controller named MIZAR, then MIZAR would register not only its personal NetBIOS name MIZAR<00> but also URSAMAJOR<1C>.

 NOTE <1C> is just an easily written way of saying "the hexadecimal value 1C." As all NetBIOS names are 16 characters in length and URSAMAJOR is only nine characters long, the full NetBIOS name would look like URSAMAJOR followed by seven blanks, nine bytes of value hexadecimal 20—hex 20 is the ASCII code for blank—finally ending with a hex 1C. It's just easier to write URSAMAJOR<1C>, which is why I represent it that way here.

The URSAMAJOR<1C> name is different from the MIZAR<00> name, however, as only one machine has the MIZAR<00> name, but many machines can claim the

URSAMAJOR<1C> name; it's a "group" name, and each and every other domain controller in URSAMAJOR registers the name.

But how does your workstation find one of these domain controllers? Step 1 is a broadcast, a simple shout, "Is there a machine named URSAMAJOR<1C> here?" This is the first step no matter what protocol you're using. (There is *one* way to keep this broadcast from happening—only one—and I'll cover it in a minute.) The idea is that it's always best to find a local domain controller, if one exists, and a broadcast will find that. If you're using NetBEUI, IPX, or TCP/IP in broadcast-only mode, that's as far as the workstation goes to find a domain controller. If there's not one within "earshot," so to speak, then the logon will fail.

If you're using TCP/IP with LMHOSTS, then the client will look in its LMHOSTS file for an entry with a #DOM command, like so:

```
200.116.73.18 MIZAR #DOM:URSAMAJOR #PRE
```

Sometimes that won't work, however, due to quirks in the TCP client software. An alternative form of the LMHOSTS line sometimes works better:

```
200.116.73.18 "MIZAR       \0x1C" #PRE
```

In this formulation, you directly enter the hex 1C rather than relying on the #DOM metacommand. It leads to some interesting behavior. First, entering one of these 0x1C entries *completely short-circuits the domain controller discovery process*. The machine doesn't broadcast, it doesn't talk to WINS, and it doesn't even do all that much looking around in LMHOSTS, either. In fact, if you enter several domain controller names, all using the 0x1C formulation, the NT machine will only look at the *last* one. Furthermore, if the domain controller named in LMHOSTS isn't up and available, then the NT machine simply cannot log on, because again it doesn't even think to look in WINS or to broadcast.

Using the 0x1C formulation, then, can be quite powerful because it guarantees that a Win2K server or workstation can find a domain controller, but it has two drawbacks: it's labor intensive, as you'll have to put an LMHOSTS file on every Win2K machine, and it's not at all fault tolerant, as you end up creating a life-and-death relationship between a particular Win2K machine and its assigned domain controller.

A TCP/IP-using system that has been pointed to a WINS server will look in the WINS server's database of machine names for a machine with the URSAMAJOR<1C> name. WINS maintains a list of up to 25 domain controllers, and it sends that list to the workstation. The workstation then sends messages to all of those domain controllers, asking them if they'll log it on. The first one to respond to your workstation is the one that the workstation uses to log on.

Assuming that the workstation has located a domain controller, it then asks the domain controller to verify the requested user's credentials. The domain controller does that, and all is well. That's basically all there is to a login.

Check the Basics

So what can go wrong? There are a few basic, obvious things that can mess up a login, and, while it may seem that I'm insulting you by asking you to check them, I can only say that I've done every one of these at least once:

- Check that the domain name is spelled correctly. It's not possible to misspell a domain name on a Win2K or NT workstation, as you couldn't join a domain in the first place if you'd misspelled it, but it's quite easy to do so on a DOS, Windows 9*x*, or Mac system.
- Check that there's network connectivity. It may just be that the Ethernet hub had its power cord kicked out, or that the network cable fell off the back of the card.
- Check that you typed your name and password correctly.

If You're Dialing In

Many login failures occur because you're dialing into a Win2K network. How you attack them depends on whether you're running NT/Win2K or Windows 9*x*.

If you're running Windows 2000 Professional, then the usual reason that your system can't find a domain controller is that it's not hooked up to a WINS server or an LMHOSTS file. I strongly recommend that when you set up a Dial-Up Networking phone book entry to dial in to a RAS server, you pre-specify the address of your WINS server or servers right in the phone book entry. (You'll see more about this in the next chapter.) Consider building a simple LMHOSTS file with entries pointing to the domain controllers in your organization.

If you're trying to get Windows 95 or 98 to dial in to a Windows 2000 domain and for some reason can't always make it work, don't feel bad—Dial-Up Networking for Windows 9*x* has some problems. Fortunately, there is a solution—patch files from Microsoft. Microsoft rearranges their Web site too often for me to tell you exactly where to find it, but there is a file called MSDUN13.EXE that completely updates the Windows 95 Dial-Up Networking code; there's a similar one for Windows 98, I'm told.

If You're Local

Local systems can also benefit from a double-check that you've got a proper WINS server nearby or an LMHOSTS file. In some cases, it makes sense to have LMHOSTS even *if* you've got WINS servers—here's why.

Suppose you have a geographically scattered domain with many domain controllers, many systems whose names are registered as URSAMAJOR<1C>—WINS should know of all of them, shouldn't it? Sadly, it doesn't: WINS only remembers the last 25 domain controllers that it has heard of. If a domain controller local to you has fallen off the edge, then WINS won't tell you about it, with the result that you'll end up trying to log in over a presumably slower WAN link. Even if WINS knows of all of your domain controllers, however, how will it know which one is geographically closest to you? It doesn't.

How, then, to ensure that you find a local domain controller? Two thoughts.

First, there's always LMHOSTS. Sorry if I sound like a broken record, but it's a very useful tool.

Second, you might modify the order in which NetBIOS name resolution takes place. By default, when your system goes looking for URSAMAJOR<1C>, it first looks in its name cache in RAM. If it can't find the domain controller there, it looks to WINS. If WINS doesn't have the answer, then the PC broadcasts to find the answer, and so on.

All logins start with a single broadcast. But perhaps your local DC is busy and doesn't respond quickly enough. Can you bias things a bit more in its favor? Yes, by modifying how NetBIOS names are resolved over TCP/IP. If you tell NetBIOS to always first broadcast, *then* ask WINS, you'll be more likely to find local domain controllers if they are within shouting distance. The downside will be, of course, that every single time your workstation tries to resolve *any* name, it will broadcast first, so be aware of that. But if this sounds like a good answer to you, then change the NetBIOS node type (it's in DHCP) from hex 0x8, a "hybrid node," to hex 0x4, a "mixed node."

Tell the Workstation to Be More Patient

Sometimes you do everything and you still can't find a domain controller, particularly if you're logging in from an NT machine. Here's why: you may recall that NT and Win2K machines also log in to the domain, just as users do. If you try to log in the very first second that the login screen appears, your system may simply be too busy to get the login done quickly—and it times out.

The fix? Well, there are a couple of possibilities. The first one's not pretty, but it'll work: when you turn your workstation on, wait a bit and let the hard disk settle down before trying to log on.

That's about the best you can do on a Windows 9x or 3.x workstation. But if your workstations are Win2K or NT, we can do a bit better.

The problem is that the Netlogon service is the part of an NT workstation that goes out and finds a domain controller. But it's impatient and only waits about 15 seconds for a response. How to tell it to be more patient? Why, with a Registry entry, of course. Remember, you're trying to make the *client* more patient, not the server, so this Registry change goes on your workstations, although it could benefit the servers as well: recall that trust relationships can be broken if domain-controller-to-domain-controller logins across trusts don't happen quickly enough.

Anyway, the modification goes in HKLM\System\CurrentControlSet\Services\ Netlogon\Parameters. If it's not already there, add a REG_DWORD entry named ExpectedDialupDelay. Set it to the number of seconds that you'd like your workstation to wait before deciding to give up on finding a domain controller. Minimum acceptable value is 0, maximum 600.

 TIP If you've got a particularly busy network, or some very overloaded domain controllers, you might consider adding this to all of your workstations via a system policy.

Troubleshooting Start-Up Mysteries: How *Do* I Get Rid of That Program?

Here's a short problem-and-solution, but I promise you it'll be useful one day:

You install some piece of software, and the install crashes, so you decide to just forget it and throw the software away. But the next time you boot the system, you see an error message because NT's trying to start the software but can't find it, or perhaps it *does* load some piece of it, leading to more error messages. What's causing the program to run?

The obvious place to look is in Start/Programs/Startup; any icons in there will run automatically when you log on. However, the contents of the Startup folder don't necessarily show everything—they show the files that have been told to put their icons in the Startup folder. Many people do not know that Win2K has a file named WIN.INI that contains a run= and a load= command, both of which can start programs. But the *really* sneaky one is a Registry key: HKLM\Software\Microsoft\Windows\ CurrentVersion\Run. In it, you'll see value entries of type REG_SZ where the value entry is some descriptive name and the data is a program's filename and any start-up options. If you've got a mysteriously starting program, chances are good it's in that Registry key. Delete the entry, and the program should stop starting up.

Planning for Disaster Recovery

Sometimes using the Last Known Good configuration or the Recovery Console doesn't fix your problems. Hard disk failures or natural disasters require a bit more in the way of hard-core disaster recovery.

What does *disaster recovery* mean? Essentially, it's exactly what it sounds like: a way of recovering from disaster—at best, turning a potential disaster into a minor inconvenience. Disaster can mean anything: theft, flood, an earthquake, a virus, or anything else that keeps you from being able to access your data. After all, it's not really the server that's important. While a server may be expensive, it is replaceable. Your data, on the other hand, is either difficult or impossible to recover. Could you reproduce your client mailing list from memory? What about the corporate accounts?

Creating a Disaster Recovery Plan

The most important part of a disaster recovery plan lies in identifying what "disaster" means to you and your company. Obviously, permanently losing all of your company's data would be a disaster, but what else would? How about your installation becoming inaccessible for a week or longer? When planning for disaster, think about all the conditions that could render your data or your workplace unreachable and plan accordingly.

Implementing Disaster Recovery

Okay, it's 2:00 P.M. on Thursday, and you get a report that the network has died. What do you do?

Write Things Down

Immediately write down everything that everyone tells you: what happened, when it happened, who gave you the information, and anything else that happened at the same time that might possibly be related. Do not trust it to memory. First, you're apt to be a bit stressed at this point. Second, if it happened once, it could happen again—and if you write down the results of your interviews, you may not have to start from scratch.

Check the Event Logs

If you can get to them, look at the security and event logs on the server to see if you can tell what happened right before the server crashed. If you're using directory replication to maintain a physically identical file server (also known as a *hot start* server because it's ready to go whenever you need it), the log information may be on the replicated server, even if you can't get to the original.

Ascertain the Cause of the Failure and Fix It

"Easy for you to say," I hear someone muttering. It can be done, however. Once you know what events happened, it becomes easier to find out what they happened to.

Find Out If It's a Software Problem

Is it a software problem? If it is, have you changed the configuration? If you've changed something, rebooted, and been unable to boot, it's time to use the Last Known Good configuration discussed earlier. If you can boot but the operating system won't function properly, use the Emergency Repair Disk to restore the hardware configuration.

If you have another server with a Windows 2000 Server installation identical to the server that failed, switch servers and see if the backup server works before you reinstall the operating system. If the hot start server doesn't work, you could be facing a network problem.

Find Out If It's a Hardware Problem

Is it a hardware problem? If you have a hot start server around the office, put it in place of the failed server and see if you can bring the network back up. If so, the problem lies with the dead server, and you can fix or replace it while you have the other one in place. If not, check the network's cabling.

If one drive from a stripe set or mirror set has died, the system should still be fine (if the drive that died is not the one with the system partition on it), but you should still fix the set anyway. Striping and mirroring gives you access to your data while the missing data is being regenerated, but if something else happens to the set before you regenerate the missing data, you're sunk, because the set can only deal with one error at a time.

If necessary, reload the backups.

Make a Recovery "Coloring Book"

No matter how much you know about reformatting SCSI drives or rebuilding boot sectors byte by byte, I guarantee you that the fastest way to recover from a disaster will often turn out to be a three-step process: replace the bad hard disk and attendant hardware, install a fresh copy of NT Server on the new hard disk, and restore the data on the disk.

That sounds simple, but it's amazing how complex it can be in the heat of battle. Let's see, I'm reinstalling Windows 2000 Server, but what was the name of the domain? What IP address does the domain controller get? What's the WINS server address? Which services went on this server? What was the administrator's password set to?

At my shop, we decided to sit down and write a step-by-step, click-by-click instruction manual. It tells a future network administrator which buttons to click and what text to type in the unlikely event that he's ever got to take a brand-new machine and rebuild our domain controller on it.

Just for an example, we have a primary domain controller on one of our domains that (as the logon traffic is relatively light) is also our DHCP, WINS, and DNS server. So, suppose the machine goes up in smoke, leaving us nothing but backup tapes—

how do we rebuild that machine? We sat down and wrote out exactly what to do in order to:

- Install Windows 2000 Server on a new machine
- Restore the SAM and SECURITY databases
- Install DHCP on the machine
- Restore the old DHCP database to the machine
- Install WINS on the machine
- Restore the WINS database
- Install the DNS server on the machine
- Restore our DNS zones and records
- Restore the user data

Assume that the person who'll be doing this knows nothing more than how to click a mouse and shove CDs into drives, someone with oatmeal for brains. Sound insulting? It's not; I like to think of myself as of at least basic intelligence, but under pressure I sometimes just don't think as well as I need to. If you're good under pressure, then great—but making the disaster recovery guide an easy read is also a big help to your coworkers.

Don't underestimate how long this will take: putting the whole document together took two research assistants a couple of weeks, and it ended up being a 100+-page Word document! (Part of the reason why it was so large is that it made lavish use of screen shots wherever possible, and yours should, too. Just click on the window you want to include in your document, press Alt+Prtsc, choose Edit/Paste Special in Word, choose Bitmap, and uncheck Float over Text.)

NOTE Once you finish the document, be careful where you keep it. The document will contain the keys to your network: usernames of domain administrator accounts, the passwords of those accounts, and the like.

Making Sure the Plan Works

The first casualty of war isn't always the truth—it's often the battle plan itself.

The most crucial part of any disaster recovery plan lies in making sure that it works down to the last detail. Don't just check the hardware; check everything. When a server crashes, backups do no good at all if they are locked in a cabinet to which only the business manager has the keys and the business manager is on vacation in Tahiti.

In the interest of having your plan actually work, make sure you know the answers to the following questions.

Who Has the Keys?

Who has the keys to the backups and/or the file server case? The example mentioned above of the business manager having the only set of keys is not an acceptable situation, for reasons that should be painfully obvious. At any given time, someone *must* have access to the backups.

You could set up a rotating schedule of duty, wherein one person who has the keys is always on call, and the keys are passed on to the next person when a shift is up. However, that solution is not foolproof. If there's an emergency, the person on call could forget to hand the keys off to the next person, or the person on call could be rendered inaccessible through a dead beeper battery or downed telephone line. Better to trust two people with the keys to the backups and server, so that if the person on call can't be reached, you have a backup key person.

Is Special Software Required for the Backups?

Must any special software be loaded for the backups to work? I nearly gave myself heart failure when, after repartitioning a hard disk and reinstalling the operating system, I attempted to restore the backups that I'd made before wiping out all the data on the file server's hard disk. The backups wouldn't work. After much frustration, I figured out that Service Pack 2 had been installed on the server. I reinstalled the service pack from my copy on another computer, and the backups worked. I just wish I had figured that out several hours earlier...

Do the Backups Work, and Can You Restore Them?

Do the backups work, and do you know how to restore them? Verifying backups takes a little longer than just backing them up, but if you verify, you know that what's on the tape matches what's on the drive. So, as far as restoring goes, practice restoring files *before* you have a problem. Learning to do it right is a lot easier if you don't have to learn under pressure, and if you restore files periodically, you know that the files backed up okay.

Have Users Backed Up Their Own Work?

In the interest of preventing your operation from coming to a complete halt while you're fixing the downed network, it might not be a bad idea to have people store a copy of whatever they're working on, and the application needed to run it, on their workstation. People who only work on one or two things at a time could still work while you're getting the server back online.

Disasters shouldn't happen, but they sometimes do. With the proper preventive planning beforehand, they can become entertaining war stories, rather than sources of battle fatigue.

Calling in the Marines: Disaster Recovery Services

Disaster recovery isn't always fully successful. Perhaps your backups don't work or are destroyed themselves. One more option remains before you have to tell everyone that everything they were working on for the past month is irretrievably gone: data recovery centers. Data recovery centers are staffed by people who are expert at getting data off media (most often hard disks, but not always) that can't be accessed by normal means.

Not all data recovery centers are the same. Some data recovery centers (in fact, the first data recovery centers) are staffed with people who are really, really good at getting dead hard disks back up and running. Using their skill, they can resuscitate the dead drive, copy its contents to other media, and then return the data—on the new media—to you.

Other data recovery services can retrieve data not recoverable with ordinary methods. These services operate at a binary level, reading the data from the dead media (sometimes even opening the hard disk, if the problem is serious enough) and then copying the data to your preferred media. Turnaround time is typically no more than a day or two, plus the shipping time.

The cost of data recovery depends on:

- The method of recovery used (the places that just fix hard disks tend to be cheaper, but can't always recover the data)
- The turnaround time requested
- The amount of data recovered

Consider storing irreplaceable data on a different physical drive from data you can easily replace. A data recovery service can't selectively restore data. That is, if the data files and the system files are stored on a single physical disk, you can't save yourself a little money by asking the center only to recover the data files, even if the data is on two different logical partitions.

Until recently, you had to send the hard disk to the data recovery center to have its data retrieved, and this meant not having the data for at least a couple of days. Remote data recovery services can fix some software-related problems without requiring you to ship the drive anywhere or even take it out of the computer case. Using a direct dial-up connection, the data recovery center may be able to fix the problem across the telephone line. As of mid-1999, the only data recovery center I've found that offers this capability is OnTrack (www.ontrack.com).

CHAPTER **22**

Installing and Managing Remote Access Service in Windows 2000 Server

FEATURING:

I t seems like it was only a few years ago that the concept of remote computing or dial-up connectivity was relatively unknown. As far as most of the world was concerned, there was no such thing as the Internet, the idea of telecommuting hadn't been born yet, and e-mail didn't exist. Remote connectivity and dial-up modems were vague, mysterious technologies as far as the average person was concerned. Once considered the tools of businesses and technically oriented individuals to simply get "data" from one location to another, these concepts have now become part of everyday life.

Technology has changed the world in some remarkable ways, but the most amazing way is how "connected" people are these days (or, at least, can be if they *want* to). Home computers are becoming more and more common, and the average home consumer can buy a dial-up modem just as easily as a toaster or CD player. Employees are being equipped with everything from laptops to palmtops and being sent out on the road, with the expectation that they should be just as connected on the road as they are when they're in the office. For better or for worse, this onslaught of technology has brought with it a demand for "easy connectivity—anytime, anywhere."

These demands have put a heavy burden on the backs of system administrators. Not only does the typical administrator have to handle day-to-day support issues *within* the office, but with so much work happening outside the office it seems to have made an already difficult job seem impossible at times. Unfortunately, there isn't a magical solution for everyone yet (I doubt there ever will be), but Microsoft's Remote Access Service has been designed and improved over the years to help administrators deal with some of these demands.

Originally developed in the early days of Windows NT, RAS was initially bundled as part of the base operating system. I've always felt the reason for this (at least partially) was to give NT a competitive advantage against other network operating systems out on the market—namely Novell. When remote computing was first starting to take off, Novell was the primary player in the NOS market and they had developed add-on products like NetWare Connect to support dial-up connections to NetWare networks. Products like NetWare Connect worked well and gave users the connectivity they needed, but these products had to be purchased separately and the license costs often increased in direct proportion to the number of simultaneous dial-in connections that needed to be supported.

While I can't be absolutely certain this is the reason Microsoft chose to bundle RAS in with the operating system for free, it certainly seems like a reasonable assumption. As many recent court cases have highlighted, "bundling" is a popular Microsoft tactic to gain market share. Personally, I know of at least a few organizations that started deploying NT in its early days simply because of the number of things that were included for free with the operating system—things they would have had to pay extra for with any other network operating system. Whatever the reasons were, NT began to take off, and RAS capabilities grew with each new version of the operating system.

Microsoft has improved RAS with each new version of Windows NT to the point where it has grown into a full-featured remote access platform capable of handling even the most demanding environments. By the time Windows NT 4 was released, RAS was a solid, reliable part of the NT operating system. The Internet was a few years along in its transition from the government and education environment into the commercial world, and it was becoming more common for people to try to leverage their investments in Internet connectivity to meet their remote access needs. With the release of NT 4, Microsoft included support for Point-to-Point Tunneling Protocol as a means of encapsulating RAS packets and sending them over the Internet instead of a modem. The phrase "virtual private networking" started becoming a buzzword in the vocabulary of network administrators, and Microsoft improved on the virtual private networking capabilities of NT 4 by later releasing a routing update called Routing and Remote Access Service (RRAS).

With the final advent of Windows 2000, Microsoft has put together the most comprehensive set of remote access capabilities to date, consolidating all the previous technologies and capabilities in an easy-to-use interface. But with *so* many options available, at times it can be hard to know which is your best choice. In the pages that follow, we'll discuss what some of your options are, some common scenarios you will probably run into, and the solutions for those problems.

Common Applications for Remote Access Service

For the purposes of this text, we'll assume that Remote Access Service is divided into two distinct functions: accepting inbound calls and placing outbound calls. With the advent of Windows NT 4, Microsoft now commonly refers to the latter as Dial-Up Networking (DUN for short), and receiving inbound calls has pretty much always been referred to as Remote Access Service (or RAS). Even though RAS and DUN share some of the same setup and installation routines, when you see a reference to DUN, you can assume it is for an outbound call.

With that clarification taken care of, let's take a look at some of the tasks you can accomplish with the Remote Access Service in Windows 2000 Server.

Connecting to the Internet

One of the more commonly used capabilities of Dial-Up Networking is to allow your computer to dial into an ISP—usually via Point-to-Point Protocol (PPP)—and communicate with distant servers and hosts across the Internet. Although this might commonly be used for simple browsing and file transfers on a server, it is becoming common for e-mail and proxy servers to function entirely over dial-up connections to the Internet.

Windows 2000 Server includes a number of functional improvements over previous versions of Windows NT when it comes to dial-up networking. Features such as demand dialing, re-establishing failed links, and repetitively dialing non-responsive numbers make Windows 2000 dial-up networking a robust platform for establishing Internet connections and keeping them online.

Accepting Incoming Calls from Remote Clients

Traveling workers, telecommuters, and late-night workaholics all share one thing in common—they all eventually need access to corporate resources from remote locations. Remote Access Service can serve as a platform to get these users connected into your internal networks and servers.

Whether you need to allow access to your NT network, Novell servers, Unix hosts, or any other internal devices, RAS can act as a universal gateway for all your inbound communication needs. By accepting inbound connections from a number of different devices (analog, ISDN, X.25, VPN) and routing the traffic to your internal network, RAS can provide seamless networking for your users. Workstations dialed into a network over RAS will work exactly the same as they would if they were connected directly to the network (albeit a bit slower—more on this subject later).

Connecting to a Private Network

In addition to connecting a Windows 2000 Server to the Internet, there are often times when it's necessary to connect one network to another—perhaps to transfer data to suppliers or clients. In any case, Windows 2000 Server can be connected to another private network just as easily as to the Internet and take advantage of the same link reliability features.

Acting as an Internet Gateway

In response to popular demand, Microsoft has added the capability for a Windows 2000 Server to share an Internet connection among clients connected to an internal network. By the addition of Network Address Translation (NAT) capabilities in Windows 2000 Server, Windows can now act as a sort of proxy for getting internal clients connected to the Internet.

 NOTE It is worthwhile to note that this "proxy" service for getting internal clients connected to the Internet over a shared connection is completely different from the Microsoft Proxy BackOffice application.

Although this service will primarily be of use to small and home offices, it is a dramatic (and welcome) addition to the suite of services contained in RAS.

Accepting Virtual Private Networking Connections from Remote Clients

Along with the advent of the Internet in the corporate world, the concept of virtual private networking has emerged and become one of the hottest areas in networking. Virtual private networking, loosely defined, is a means of running a secure, private network over an insecure public network. Or, in plain English, you can have clients get connected (securely) to your office network by simply having an Internet connection and a valid (public) IP address and then establishing a VPN session to your RAS server. The VPN session is secure and encrypted, so your private data is protected as it passes over the public network (i.e., the Internet).

Microsoft has leveraged their investments in RAS in the development of virtual private networking in Windows 2000. By incorporating Point-to-Point Tunneling Protocol and Layer 2 Tunneling Protocol within the operating system, you can effectively set up "virtual" modems that work over IP networks, instead of analog or digital circuits. The methodology and terms used to implement these virtual modems are the same that are used for regular modems, so learning how to implement virtual private networking is made easier.

Dialing Up a Remote Network and Routing Traffic

With the addition of the Routing and Remote Access Service update to Windows NT 4, Microsoft made it easier for a Windows NT Server to act as a dial-up router, connecting to remote networks as needed and routing traffic. This type of connection between locations is commonly referred to as wide area networking or WAN connectivity.

With no more hardware than a dial-up modem at each site, internal clients and workstations can access resources on remote networks through this capability. By simply programming your internal workstations and devices to use your Windows 2000 Server as a "gateway," RAS can accept client traffic destined for a remote network, establish a connection to that network, and then pass the traffic across the connection as necessary. Since most office-to-office connectivity has traditionally been handled via costly dedicated circuits, having this ability is a tremendous benefit.

Already, this capability is helping organizations act in a completely "virtual" capacity—appearing to have a centralized network of resources that are actually individual servers spread across a number of sites, joined by demand-dialed dial-up connections.

Bandwidth Planning and Considerations

Before we begin discussing what types of hardware and software you need to start using RAS, it's important to make sure you have an understanding of when RAS would and wouldn't be a good solution. The two most important factors in determining this are speed and reliability.

No discussion of remote access would be complete without defining the two different types of communication that are often referred to when you hear the phrase "remote access." These are sometimes referred to as *remote-node* and *remote-control* technologies. They may sound similar, and as far as end users are concerned they're basically the same, but these two methods of remote access are in fact very different. Unfortunately, many administrators are often left with implementing vague management directives such as "make sure that our employees can work while they're on the road," which are an amazing oversimplification of remote access's complexities. It's important to understand the capabilities and limitations of each type of access so you can make the best decision for your needs.

Remote Node

RAS is a remote node method of communication and a very flexible and versatile means of getting users or networks connected to one another. Overall, I prefer remote node communication solutions over remote control for most applications, but having an understanding of how remote node works will help you understand when is the best time to use it.

One of the simplest ways to conceptually visualize remote node communication is to view the phone line connecting a client to a network as a *very* long network cable. Like any normal network cable in your office, this one is plugged into two locations. It starts at the user's workstation or laptop, goes through the phone company, and then ends at a modem in your office. Visualize that entire connection as a network cable. That modem, in turn, is connected to a RAS server (or another similar device), and the RAS server is—presumably—connected to your network. The RAS server accepts the incoming data from that dial-in user and then simply "passes" their data onto a local network segment. The same is true for outgoing data. The RAS server will see any outgoing data destined for that user on the network and transmit it over the phone line. As far as end-user functionality goes, your network should work exactly the same way in the office as it does dialing in, albeit much slower.

Since typical office network connections these days are running at speeds of upwards of 10,000,000 to 100,000,000 bits per second, throughput can be amazingly fast. So fast, that it is easy to overlook the amount of data that is actually traveling across your network. Considering the fact that the best analog modems available today are only reaching speeds of 56,000 bits per second, throughput can be a problem with remote-node solutions. Basic math indicates that there's only about 1/20th of the bandwidth available over a 56k modem in comparison to a 10-megabit Ethernet connection. That simple fact has a direct impact on the speed and performance of applications being used on the network. For example, a 2.5-megabyte Word document might open up in just a few seconds on a 10-megabit Ethernet connection in an office, but on a 56k modem connection, that document could take upwards of a few minutes to open up.

Calculating Modem Transmission Times

Use the following formula to calculate modem transmission times:

$$\frac{\text{File size in "bytes"} * 8}{\text{Speed of connection in "bits" (i.e., 56k = 56,000)}} = \text{Transmission time in seconds}$$

Case in Point: Choosing the Right Remote Access Solution

If you implement a RAS solution without having some of these facts in your arsenal, you could end up with a solution that is effectively useless. Consider, for example, the case of one of my clients—let's call them the XYZ Corporation. The XYZ Corporation was in the process of moving into a new building but had to leave their accounting software and data on the file server in their old building due to a number of licensing and political issues. The accounting software was an old FoxPro file-based program that had served them well for many years, but it was eventually being replaced when they moved.

Their initial desire was to just have users dial in to the network in the old building and work on the accounting application as they did before. However, since the accounting application was "file-based" as opposed to being "client-server" (more on that later), the amount of data going back and forth between their workstations and servers was simply too great to make a remote-node solution work for their application. Simple analysis of their traffic indicated that their primary users of the accounting software were easily transferring 20 to 40 megabytes worth of data across their network in *as little as an hour*. If you've ever downloaded a large application from the Internet over a modem, you know how long it takes to move that much data—you probably start your download overnight and check it again the next morning.

Remembering our calculations from earlier, only about 1/20th of the bandwidth was available to XYZ Corporation over a dial-up remote-node connection. Quite simply, they were not going to be able to move that much data over a modem and maintain usable response times—a remote-node solution was *not* going to work for this client with this specific application.

The key factor that worked against XYZ Corporation was the fact that their critical application was file-based instead of being client-server. I can't emphasize enough how important it is to understand the mechanisms that computers typically use to move data around, so let's walk through some example applications of each of these types, see how they work, and see why some don't work well with remote-node solutions while others do.

File-Based Apps vs. Client-Server Apps

Consider, if you will, a simple Microsoft Access database of names and phone numbers that you have stored on your computer. For discussion purposes, we'll assume that you have not "indexed" this database (a process which makes searching databases faster) and are trying to look up the phone number for an individual with the last name of Toombs. To find this name and number, you'd start by launching your Microsoft Access application, opening your phone number database, and then doing a search on the last name. Once you submit your search, your CPU would talk to your hard drive controller, tell it to open up the database on your hard drive, and retrieve the first record in the database. When the first record comes back, it turns out that it's for somebody named Anderson. The CPU realizes that Anderson doesn't equal Toombs, so it dumps the first record from its memory and then requests the second one. The second record is for Daily. Daily doesn't equal Toombs either, so once again the CPU would dump that record from memory and read the third one. And so on, and so on, until it finally got to the record for Toombs. Once it successfully finds Toombs, it displays the record on the screen.

The important factor to take note of is the repetitive process the CPU had to go through to get the data it needed. It had to keep communicating with the hard drive controller to get the next record, and then receive the response (the actual data) and check it. Given how speedy today's computers are, this all happens in the blink of an eye. But as you can see, there's a lot of communication that has to go on to make that simple operation work.

That communication, however, is all taking place between the internal components of your systems—from the CPU, across the data bus, through the hard drive controller, to the hard drive, and back again. Since these devices are directly connected to each other, they're very fast. However, suppose you move that phone number database off your hard drive and onto a file server so everyone in your office can access it. If you do the same search as before, each time Microsoft Access has to get a new record to check, the CPU will send a request to the network controller instead of the hard drive controller. The network controller will transmit the request to the server for the record and wait for the response from the file server. Once again, the CPU has to request this information over and over again from the network until it finally finds the record for Toombs. Since a hard drive on a network file-server probably isn't going to respond as fast as the hard drive in your computer, response time suffers.

To put some rough numbers to it, when the database was stored on the computer's internal hard drive you might have had a maximum of 20 megabits worth of bandwidth between the components inside your computer (hard drive, controller, bus, and CPU). Let's assume the last-name search took 1 second to complete. Once you move the database on your file server, your maximum bandwidth might have stepped down to only 10 megabits, assuming you're on a 10-megabit network. In theory, a search that took 1 second before could now take 2 seconds. That's still not too bad, and these are rough numbers (don't hold me to them), but they do illustrate the point we're about to make.

The 1-second query operation became a 2-second query operation when the phone number database was moved off the local hard drive and onto the network file server. Part of the reason for that is the fact that the bandwidth between our CPU and the actual data was cut in half, from 20 megabits to 10. Since the CPU had to keep requesting each record in the file, the bandwidth available between the CPU and the data source plays a key role. Now, what if someone was dialing in to the network and trying to perform the same query? If you recall the 1/20th figure discussed earlier in regards to 56k modems, you can probably see where this is heading. Cutting the bandwidth down from 10 megabits to 56 kilobytes could potentially increase our search time twentyfold. It's entirely possible that our simple query could take upwards of 40 seconds over the 56k dial-up connection.

Now, I'll be the first to admit that I'm oversimplifying things here considerably to make a point. In reality, our example query probably wouldn't take 40 seconds over a dial-up connection, but the response time would be noticeably sluggish. Even if it only took 10 to 15 seconds to retrieve the data, slowdowns like that eventually produce productivity problems. The key to all this is the fact that bandwidth is a huge factor in remote computing if you have any applications that are file-based. So what's the solution? Try to stick with applications that are client-server based.

In keeping with our name-lookup scenario above, let's assume that the data is stored in a SQL Server database instead of a standard Microsoft Access file. Using Microsoft Access (the *client* in client-server) as a "front-end" on your workstation, you can submit the same query for the last name Toombs as before. However, instead of requesting each record individually this time and checking them one by one, Access will transmit a request to the SQL Server software (the *server* in client-server) for a specific record. Access will transmit a specific request such as "get me the record(s) with a last name of Toombs." Small requests like those transmit very quickly, even over a slow connection (like a 56k modem). At that point, the responsibility of retrieving the correct data has shifted from the copy of Microsoft Access running on your CPU and is now in the hands of the SQL Server. Since the SQL Server presumably has high-speed access to the drives that store the data (most likely its own drives), it can find the answer in a few microseconds and then return an appropriate response back to Access.

The key thing to look for in determining whether an application is client-server or not is to see if there are two separate parts to the application. One part will run on your client workstations, and a second part will run on the server that stores your data (or at least on a server nearby with a high-speed connection on it). If there are two parts to your application, it is probably a client-server application and you shouldn't run into too many difficulties with remote-node users using it. However, if there aren't two parts to your application—if the only part is the client software that just uses directories and files on your file servers—you might run into performance problems using remote-node solutions.

Opening up Word documents and Excel spreadsheets is—in effect—a file-based application, so it's worthwhile to look at your average document size to see how quickly it might transmit over a slow connection. Refer to the transmission times formula earlier in this section and figure out how long some sample documents would take to transmit over a modem. If most of your documents are simple and text-based, you probably won't run into too many performance issues. However, if your users typically work with large, multi-megabyte documents on your server, you might need to consider other options.

Remote Control

If remote-node communications can be viewed as using a phone line as a long network cable, then remote-control communications should be viewed as using a phone line as a long keyboard, mouse, and video cable. Remote-control solutions, by definition, allow you to remotely take control of a workstation on your network over a dial-up connection. Software on a workstation would typically have some sort of remote-control software running on it (such as pcAnywhere) and a modem attached to it. This is sometimes referred to as the host PC, since it is typically waiting to host an incoming caller. Then, presumably from another location, another workstation with compatible remote-control software would call into the host PC.

Once the two PCs have negotiated a connection, the host would begin sending its screen data to the calling computer, in effect letting the person at that calling station see everything that is on the remote screen. The calling workstation would then pass any keystrokes or mouse movements to the host PC, which would perform those actions just as if the user were sitting at the host PC doing them him- or herself. In effect, the remote-control software is tapping into the keyboard, mouse, and video input/output of the host PC and making it available to a remote PC over a phone line.

Traditionally, remote-control solutions have been a bit more expensive to develop and scale due to the increased hardware requirements on each side. Whereas one RAS server with an adequate amount of modems would theoretically be able to handle 256 simultaneous inbound modem connections, having that many simultaneous connections using certain remote-control products could require 256 computers—one to receive each of the connections. That can be rather cost prohibitive in most cases, not to mention being difficult to manage. However, it is worth mentioning because in some cases it might be the only remote access solution that would work in your environment.

It is also worth mentioning that Microsoft is including some remote-control functionality in Windows 2000 with the bundling of Terminal Server with the base operating system (hmmm…there's that "bundling" concept again). If you are in a position where a remote-node solution won't meet your needs, you might want to take a look at it and see if Terminal Server will work for you. Terminal Server can be a worthy option since it doesn't require a separate computer to handle each inbound connection; instead, it requires one huge computer, and everybody runs a Windows session on that device (note: there are some other third party products which function in a similar manner).

 NOTE For more detailed information on Terminal Server, see Chapter 14, "Supporting Clients with Windows Terminal Services."

Since you've gotten this far, I'm assuming that you feel RAS is the right solution for you and you're ready to start working with it and implementing it on your network. If that's the case, keep reading. Let's talk a bit about what type of hardware and circuits you're going to need to have in place to make this all work.

RAS Hardware Requirements

One of the first things to determine in remote networking is where you plan on connecting to and how fast you want to connect. Often, one or both of those criteria will help you determine what your available communications options are. In most instances, that will leave you with one of the following options:

Connection Type	Typical Maximum Speed	Typical Maximum Distance
Analog modem	Asymmetrical: 53kbps down, 33.6 up	Unlimited, usually domestic
ISDN	BRI—128kbps, PRI—1.544mbps	Unlimited, usually domestic
X.25	2400bps—64 kbps	Global
Serial cable	Serial port max—230kbps in most cases	"Physically near (less than 50 feet)" according to Microsoft

Connection Type	Typical Maximum Speed	Typical Maximum Distance
InfraRed	Varies	Very close, line-of-sight
Parallel cable	Up to 500kbps	Very close
Frame Relay	1.544mbps	Global

Of course, it should go without saying that any devices you are considering purchasing for use with RAS should be checked against Microsoft's Hardware Compatibility List (HCL) to make sure they are compatible with Windows 2000. By checking for HCL compatibility, you can be sure your choice of hardware has been specifically tested for compatibility with Windows 2000 and has met the standards Microsoft has deemed necessary to be considered "compatible."

Also, if you're purchasing modems from a manufacturer that has a number of different models to choose from, pick your product carefully. While some modems might cost more than others due to features like voice or fax capability, if you're looking at two different models from the same manufacturer with the same capabilities, I'd suggest buying the more expensive of the two. The reason for this is quite simple: lower-cost modems are often designed by manufacturers primarily for light-duty home use applications. These are usually the modems you will see on the shelves in retail computer outlets. They are marketed to consumers and designed with tolerances and specifications targeted at the average consumer's needs. This doesn't take into consideration the more demanding needs of using modems for routing links, mail servers, etc.

Case in Point: Choosing the Right Modems

Here's a real-life case in point from one of my clients. ABC Software Company was having a number of problems with users calling into their RAS server. They had purchased modems built by one of the top manufacturers (if I told you the name, 90 percent of you would recognize it), but they had purchased the consumer-grade modems off their local computer store's shelf for roughly $100 each. Well, ABC Software Company seemed to always be running into odd, unpredictable problems with their remote access users. These users were unhappy and constantly calling with support issues since their connections would randomly get dropped, they'd have trouble negotiating connections, sometimes the modems wouldn't answer at all, etc. Again, these modems on their RAS server were built by one of the top manufacturers, but they weren't the right tools for the job.

We decided to remove all the $100 modems and replace them with the $200 commercial-grade modems from the same manufacturer. The modems were the same speed and had roughly the same features, but as soon as we changed to the new modems all the odd problems with their dial-in users disappeared. Just like that. The moral of the story: Saving money is good, but not if it ends up costing you more in the long run.

With that out of the way, let's take a closer look at your hardware and circuit options, and then we'll jump into configuring RAS on your Windows 2000 Server.

Analog Modems

Analog modems are the most commonly used connection device on RAS servers these days, so a good portion of our examples and configurations throughout this chapter will be using them.

A primer on how modems operate is in order for those of you who are unfamiliar with the technology. Modems are devices that accept binary signals (ones and zeroes) from whatever device they are connected to, convert those binary signals into audible tones, and then transmit those tones over a phone line at a prescribed speed. (This process is described as "modulation" and is the derivative of the "mo" part of the word "modem.")

On the other side of the telephone line, another modem receives these audible tones and converts them back into the binary ones and zeroes they represent. Once they have been converted back ("demodulated"), they are passed through to the device the modem is connected to as binary data. As you probably guessed, this "demodulation" process represents the "dem" in the word "modem."

Therefore, to complete a remote access or dial-up networking connection via a modem, you will need the following:

- Modem on the transmitting computer
- Modem on the receiving computer (this may be out of your control, for example, if you are dialing into an ISP)
- Telephone connection between the two modems

In today's world, analog modems can transmit *and* receive data over traditional phone lines at speeds anywhere from 300 to 33,600 bits per second (sometimes referred to as the baud of the modem). As we mentioned earlier, the modems on either end of the connection convert the stream of bits to analog signals and transmit them over the phone line at a pre-negotiated speed. But what about those "56k" modems?

When 56k Isn't Quite 56k

A lot of hype and marketing has gone into the 56k modems that are currently available on the market. The modem manufacturers would love for you to believe that these modems are running at the full 56,000 bits per second, in both directions, but unfortunately that isn't quite the case. If you're planning on implementing a remote access solution for your organization, it's important to understand exactly how these modems work, what speeds you can hope to get from them, and what you can and can't expect from them.

First, you should realize that 56k modems *cannot* send and receive data at that speed in both directions. At the time of this writing, the maximum bidirectional speed anyone has been able to get out of typical analog connections is 33,600 bits per second. Much of that has to do with analog connections and the signal loss that is inherent as the analog data travels from one location to another. However, modem manufacturers are clever and found a way to work around that limitation by removing half the analog signaling from the equation. By using a special server-side modem at one of the locations and a digital connection directly into the phone company's central office, data can be sent all the way from the server-side modem to the phone company with zero signal loss. Once the signal is within the phone company's systems, it usually travels through their system completely digital as well. The net result of this is that speeds of up to 56,000 bits per second are possible but only in one direction—the direction going from the server-side modem to the phone company. Communication in the other direction—from the location with the analog modem toward the phone company—is still limited by the inherent signal loss and peaks out at 33,600 bits per second.

Companies like Internet Service Providers have been the primary beneficiaries of 56k technology, and 56k modems are a great tool for getting a bit more speed when connecting to the Internet. However, it's important to realize that *you cannot purchase two identical 56k modems, plug them into regular analog lines, and expect to get a connection any higher than 33,600 bits per second between them.* Without having a server-side modem at one of your locations and a digital line from that modem to the phone company, you will be bound by the existing 33,600 limitations.

It's also worth mentioning that even when dialing into a location with a server-side modem that supports 56k, under current FCC regulations in the United States, if you're using an analog line you will *never* get a 56,000 connection. The FCC has placed limits on the amount of voltage *any* device can transmit over a phone line, which currently restricts all modems to a maximum capability of 53,000 bits per second. However, most analyses and studies of 56k modems have revealed that reasonable speeds to expect for your connections are anywhere from 42,000 to 48,000 for data coming from the server-side modem (or "downlink speed") and, of course, 33,600 for data going to the server-side modem (or "uplink speed"). The amount of speed you get will depend on the quality of the equipment at your local phone company, the condition of the lines in your area, and your physical distance from the phone company's central office. One of my own computers was never able to get speeds higher than 42,000–44,000bps when dialing into a local ISP until I recently moved. Nothing else changed with my computer except the location it was in, but when I dialed in from my new home I was consistently connecting at 48,000 bits per second.

ISDN

A number of years ago, a 56k analog modem would be more than enough bandwidth for most remote data needs. However, as computers have grown in size and complexity, so have the files and data that computers typically need to move around. Downloading multi-megabyte items from the Internet, such as Windows 2000 Service Packs, could literally take hours over a standard dial-up connection. Fortunately, Integrated Services Digital Network (ISDN) is an option to get more bandwidth without having to get a dedicated circuit in place.

ISDN typically comes in two different flavors, ISDN Basic Rate Interface (BRI) or ISDN Primary Rate Interface (PRI). The main difference between the two is speed (and therefore, price). BRI can support data speeds of up to 128kbps over standard copper telephone lines, and PRI supports data speeds of up to 1.544mbps over T1 cable. Since ISDN BRI can run over the same copper wires that most people have wired in their homes, it's more commonly implemented.

ISDN BRI consists of three separate data channels on one connection. Two of the channels are 64kbps bearer channels, commonly referred to as B channels. These two channels, when combined, make up the 128kbps that ISDN can use to move data from one location to another. The third channel (commonly referred to as the D channel) is a special 16kbps out-of-band channel used for signaling between your equipment and the phone company. Although all three channels add up to 144kbps, most ISDN implementations will either use one or both B channels, so we'll refer to ISDN as being able to support 64kbps or 128kbps.

To use ISDN for remote access, you will need the following:

- An ISDN modem at each location and, optionally, an NT1 network termination device (most ISDN modems come with these built in today)
- A digital ISDN connection at each location

Direct Options (Null Modem, Parallel, and Infrared)

Given the affordability and broad universal support for network cards these days, using a null modem or parallel cable to connect two computers has really become more of a niche than a mainstream use of RAS. However, there may be occasions when it is the only option—maybe you have a specialty device that can't support a network card and can only communicate with the outside world via a serial or parallel port. If that's the case, a null modem cable, parallel cable, or Infrared connection between your systems can be used for a connection.

Null modem cables are typically available at any computer store or through mail-order catalogs. However, according to Microsoft, standard off-the-shelf null modem cables might not be wired correctly for use with RAS. If you have the option, have your cabling vendor build a custom cable according to the pin configurations listed in

Table 22.1. By connecting the null modem cable to the serial ports on each of your devices, you can connect your two computers together as needed. However, you will be limited to your serial port's speed and distance limitations of roughly 50 feet.

TABLE 22.1: MICROSOFT-SPECIFIED NULL MODEM CABLING REQUIREMENTS FOR RAS.							
9-pin to 9-pin		**9-pin to 25-pin**		**25-pin to 25-pin**		**Mac RS422/423 to 25-pin**	
Host system	**Calling system**	**25-pin**	**9-pin**	**Host system**	**Calling system**	**Mac**	**Win 2000**
3	2	2	2	2	3	1	6, 8
2	3	3	3	3	2	2	20
7	8	4	8	4	5	3	3
8	7	5	7	5	4	4, 8	7
6, 1	4	6, 8	4	6, 8	20	5	2
5	5	7	5	7	7	6	—
4	6, 1	20	6, 1	20	6, 8	7	—

Source: Microsoft Corporation

Parallel connections can be made between two computers using the standard or enhanced (ECP) parallel ports of each device. By connecting devices together in this fashion, it is reasonable to expect throughput speeds of up to 500–600kbps, but the distance between devices is again very limited. Microsoft lists a specific vendor, Parallel Technologies, in their help files included with Windows 2000 as a source for compatible parallel cables to use.

 NOTE To contact Parallel Technologies about their DirectParallel line of products, call (800) 789-4784 or visit them on the Web at www.1pt.com.

Infrared connections are new in Windows 2000 Server and will probably serve as a useful option for small offices. Since the connection distance is limited by the strength of the infrared signal *and* a direct line-of-sight requirement, it will be an easy method of connecting (no cables!) but limited in usefulness.

X.25

X.25 is a protocol that coordinates communication between multiple machines, routing information through a packet-switched public data network. Instead of establishing direct connections from one device to another, all devices in an X.25 network simply connect to a "cloud" and pass their data to the cloud. It is up to the company that maintains and manages the cloud to ensure that the data reaches the correct destination point. X.25 is a relatively outdated technology, which is why throughput speeds top out at 56k to 64k.

So, why use X.25? Well, even though it is an extremely slow transport medium, it is also an exceptionally reliable one. There is an extensive amount of error checking and correction that occurs as a part of the X.25 protocol, which makes it a worthwhile consideration in areas with poor telecommunication services. X.25 is available globally and in some cases may be the only reasonable option for connectivity in certain countries.

Frame Relay

Frame Relay is quickly becoming a preferred option to X.25 connections, as it functions on roughly the same principle—each system passing data into a data cloud—but at much higher speeds. Frame Relay can support connections ranging from 56kbps all the way up to 1.544mbps. Since Frame Relay only requires a single connection from each site into the cloud, it is an excellent choice for global connectivity, since dedicated wide area network links across continents could end up being prohibitively expensive to implement.

RAS Installation and Setup

Now that we've laid the groundwork for understanding how remote access works, it's time to start working through some of the sample applications discussed earlier. Although we have gone to great lengths to accurately walk through each possible configuration, these configurations were documented with Windows 2000 Server Beta 3 and might be slightly different by the time the final product ships.

Installing Devices for Remote Access

Since a modem is one of the most widely used tools for remote access services, we'll start by quickly walking through installing your modem on a Windows 2000 Server, making sure that the correct drivers are installed, ports are selected, etc.

To begin adding modems to your system, start by clicking the Start button on the Windows desktop. Choose the Settings/Control Panel option, and then double-click the Phone and Modem options icon. If this is your first time using this option, you will be probably be prompted for information about your area code, what type of dialing the system should use (tone or pulse), etc. After you've entered some of that preliminary information, you will be taken to the Phone & Modem Options applet. Click the Modems tab. More than likely, you won't have any modems listed. Click the Add button to launch the modem installation wizard, as seen in Figure 22.1.

FIGURE 22.1

Install New Modem wizard

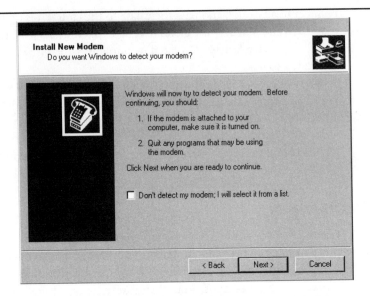

Depending on your preferences, you can either have Windows 2000 attempt to detect your modem automatically or you can select it manually from a list. If your modem is a bit older (as in, it was on the market before Windows 2000), you are probably safe letting Windows 2000 attempt to find the correct driver for your modem. Leave the Don't Detect My Modem; I Will Select It from a List box unchecked and click Next to begin the detection process.

If your modem is newer than the release of Windows 2000, or if you prefer to configure these options yourself (*I* prefer setting all these things myself), check the Don't Detect My Modem; I Will Select It from a List box and click Next. You'll be taken to the Install New Modem screen as shown in Figure 22.2.

From here, you can choose from a myriad of different modem drivers. Find the driver that matches your modem, select it, and then click Next to install it. If for some reason an appropriate driver isn't listed for your modem, you can always use one of the standard modem drivers listed in the Standard Modem Types selection under Manufacturers. The standard modem drivers are reasonably good and are reliable in most circumstances. There are even standard modem drivers for 56k modems supporting the v.90, x2, and k56Flex standards. If your modem manufacturer included a driver disk along with the purchase of your modem, click the Have Disk button and insert your driver diskette in the appropriate drive. You will need to tell Windows to look in that location by giving it the appropriate path to check for the driver (usually A:\; consult your modem manufacturer's documentation for further information).

FIGURE 22.2

Install New Modem
selection screen

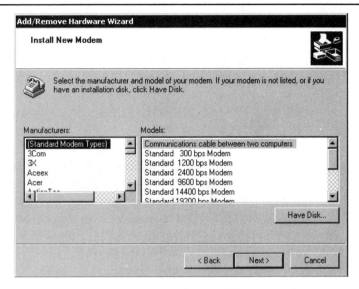

If you are installing your driver by hand, you will need to tell Windows what communications port this modem is connected to, as shown in Figure 22.3.

FIGURE 22.3

Selecting
communications ports

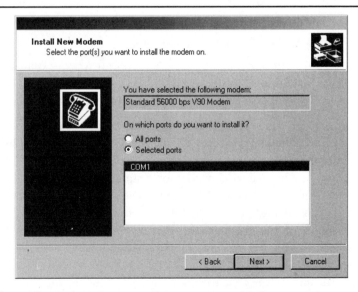

If you have identical modems on all your communications ports, you can select the All Ports radio button. Otherwise, you should select the port your modem is currently attached to. If you have multiple modems on many ports (but not "all ports"), hold down the Ctrl button while selecting each port. When you have selected the correct ports, click Next to complete the installation. You should receive a confirmation dialog box indicating that your modem has been successfully installed.

Now that you have a modem installed, it's time to take it for a test drive. One of the easiest things to do in Windows 2000 is define a dial-up connection to the Internet, so we'll start there first.

Connecting to the Internet

It's no secret that Windows 2000 was designed with the Internet in mind. Given that fact, Microsoft has made it easy to get your computer connected to the Internet. If you are running a Windows 2000 Server as a proxy server so your internal clients can surf the Web or if you're running it as an e-mail server, dial-up connections to the Internet are an option worth looking into. Due to some readily available "fine tuning" parameters you can set for dial-up connections, you can create a rather reliable link to the Internet with just a modem. Let's get started...

The first thing you'll need to do before connecting to the Internet is set up an account with an Internet Service Provider (ISP). We won't go through the specifics of how to do that here, but once you have an account you will need a minimum of three things handy to create your dial-up connection to the Internet:

- A local access phone number to dial (whether analog or ISDN)

- A username and password combination

- Optionally, an IP address to assign to your dial-up connection, and DNS addresses to use (most ISPs won't require you to program this information in, but in case yours does, be sure to have this handy in advance)

When you're ready to build your connection to the Internet, hit the Start button on your desktop and select the Settings option. Within the Settings option, you should see a choice for Network and Dial-up Connections. Choose that option, and you should get a window that looks similar to the screen in Figure 22.4.

From here, double-click the Make New Connection icon to start the Network Connection Wizard, which will present you with a list of connection types you can establish. Select the Dial-up to the Internet option and then click Next.

Selecting the Dial-up to the Internet option will then launch the Internet Connection Wizard, which will walk you through the process of setting up an ISP account. The initial step of the wizard will ask you whether you want to define a new ISP account, transfer an existing ISP account, or configure your settings manually. For the purposes of being thorough, we'll walk through the manual setup option.

After selecting the I Want to Set Up My Internet Connection Manually option, you will be asked whether you want to set up your Internet connection over a modem or a LAN. If you have in-house Internet connectivity that is already running, then a LAN would be the option you would want to choose. However, since we're discussing modems, we'll walk through the modem configuration.

FIGURE 22.4

Network and Dial-up Connections window

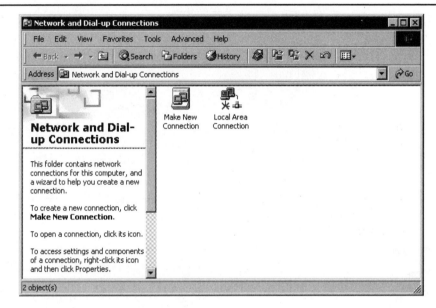

After you select the Connect through a Phone Line and a Modem option and click Next, you will be taken through a three-step process to collect the information we discussed earlier, starting with the phone number as shown in Figure 22.5.

Enter the area code and phone number of your ISP's local access number in the fields provided. Select your appropriate country code, and leave the field Dial Using the Area Code and Country Code checked unless you want to override Windows 2000's ability to check the area code of the number you're dialing against its current location and adjust the dialing string accordingly.

As we mentioned before, if you need to manually assign an IP address for your server or DNS server addresses to use, this is the screen from which to do it. Click the Advanced button and you'll see a dialog box for setting the advanced connection properties of this dial-up connection. Click the Addresses tab, and you will see a screen like the one in Figure 22.6.

FIGURE 22.5

*Internet Connection
Wizard screen*

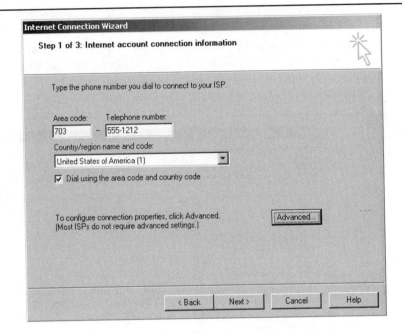

FIGURE 22.6

*Advanced connection
properties*

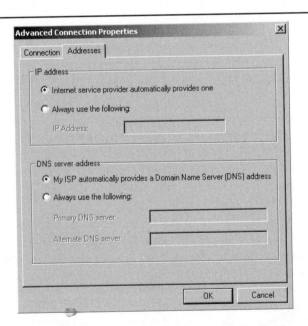

Even though most ISPs will assign you an address automatically, if your ISP requires you to manually assign yourself an IP address, click the Always Use the Following radio button in the top half of the window and enter the appropriate address in the IP Address field. Some ISPs may still require you to enter DNS server information (DNS is how

Windows 2000 translates names like www.microsoft.com into IP addresses). If so, click the Always Use the Following radio button in the bottom half of the window, and enter your primary and secondary DNS server IP addresses exactly as your ISP provided them to you. Once you're finished with any advanced settings, click the Next button to proceed to step two of the Internet Connection Wizard, as shown in Figure 22.7.

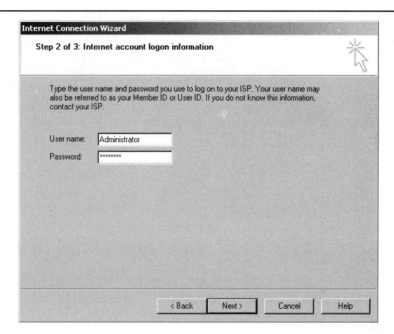

FIGURE 22.7

Defining user credentials in the ICW

Step two of the Internet Connection Wizard is rather straightforward. Here you will enter the user credentials (username and password) your ISP has provided you for use with your account. This information will be stored along with all the other information for this dial-up networking entry so Windows 2000 doesn't have to prompt you for it every time you want to make a connection. If you don't feel comfortable having this information stored on your machine, leave the password field blank. You will receive a warning dialog box asking if you want to proceed with a blank password. Answer Yes, we will correct this later in the text.

When you've entered your user credentials, click Next to complete the last step of the Internet Connection Wizard: assigning a "friendly name" to this connection. You can choose whatever you want here. Later, you will reference this connection by the name you give it. Enter a descriptive connection name, and then click Next.

If you have an Internet mail client installed on your system (namely Outlook Express), the Internet Connection Wizard will ask if you would like to configure your mail settings at this point. For the purposes of this chapter, we'll skip those settings for the time being—you can always set them later. The last thing you should see is a dialog box indicating that you have finished defining your connection.

Once you've completed defining your Internet connection, it should be shown as a grayed-out icon in the Network and Dial-up Connections window, as shown in Figure 22.8.

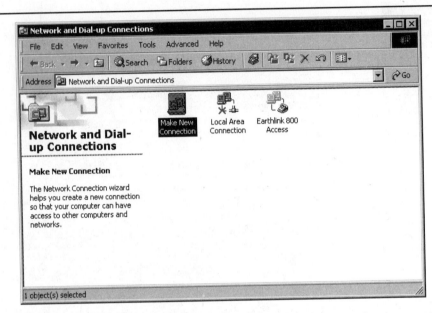

At this point, you could double-click your new ISP connection and get connected to the Internet if you provided a password in step two of the Internet Connection Wizard. If that's the case, launch the icon and verify that it is working correctly. Once you're successfully connected, you should be able to connect to hosts on the Internet.

Optional Internet Connection Settings

After you've verified that your Internet connection is working properly, there are some optional settings you might find useful for controlling the behavior of this dial-up connection. Such items include:

- Programming a list of alternate numbers for Windows 2000 to attempt dialing
- Disconnecting idle connections (good for per-minute connections such as ISDN)
- Automatic redialing of busy or non-responsive numbers
- Automatic re-establishing of connections that have dropped

All these features are useful enough by themselves. However, if you're running a Windows 2000 Server that *depends* on having an Internet connection available, you'll find these extra features useful. It takes much less administration when a server can take care of establishing and re-establishing its own Internet connections without any human intervention.

To get to these options, open the Network and Dial-up Connections window again and right-click your ISP dial-up entry. Select the Properties option, and you should get to the dialog box shown in Figure 22.9.

FIGURE 22.9

Editing general properties of dial-up entries

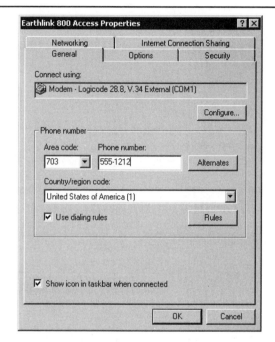

If your ISP has several local phone numbers available for you to use, you can program Windows 2000 to cycle through the entire list until it gets a connection. Click the Alternates button next to the phone number, and you should see a screen like the one in Figure 22.10.

From the Alternate Phone Numbers dialog, you can enter as many numbers as you would like Windows 2000 to use to attempt to establish this connection. Click the Add button to add a new number to the list, and then use the arrow buttons on the right-hand side of the dialog box to adjust the order of which number should be dialed first.

As an additional option, Windows 2000 can remember which number was successful last time you connected and try that one first if you check the Move Successful Number to Top of List option. This will make sure that if for some reason one of your ISP's local access numbers goes offline for an indefinite period of time, it won't stay in the top of the list and Windows 2000 won't keep trying to dial that number first.

FIGURE 22.10

*Entering alternate
dial-up numbers*

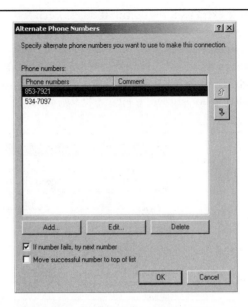

When you're finished entering alternate numbers, click the OK button to return to the main properties dialog box for this dial-up connection. To reach the rest of the editable items for this connection, click the Options tab. This should bring you to a screen similar to Figure 22.11.

FIGURE 22.11

*Editing options for
dial-up entries*

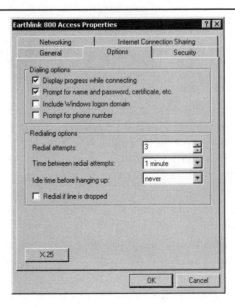

This dialog box has a number of options available, the most useful of which regard dialing, idle timeouts, and re-establishing broken connections. Let's go through these one by one and show how they can be used.

Prompt for name and password, certificate, etc. When you first created this dial-up networking entry using the Internet Connection Wizard, one of the steps you should have gone through (step two) was for entering a username and password to use for this connection. If you decided not to enter your password directly into the settings for this dial-up networking entry, you will want to check this option. Otherwise, Windows 2000 will simply try to use a blank password when establishing this connection. Checking this option will cause Windows 2000 to prompt you for a username and password to use instead of the existing username and password stored with this dial-up networking entry.

Redial attempts and Time between redial attempts If your local ISP has a problem with busy signals, you will appreciate these options. By choosing the number of times to attempt to redial and the time to wait between attempts, you can program Windows 2000 to keep dialing up your ISP until a number becomes available. Personally, I've found this setting to be extremely useful in times of inclement weather when everyone is stuck in their homes and clogging my ISP's lines.

Idle time before hanging up If the same phone company that serves my area serves yours, then you are accustomed to paying for your ISDN access by the minute. These per-minute charges can add up to a rather substantial phone bill if your ISDN connection stays up all day. If your server only really needs to have a connection during business hours (for example, for proxy server clients browsing the Internet), set an appropriate idle timeout value here in minutes. Once the specified number of minutes has passed without any activity, Windows 2000 will drop the connection.

Redial if line is dropped It's simply a fact of life—dial-up connections "drop" sometimes. It just happens, but it can cause considerable headaches if people are depending on this connection being up and you happen to be away when it goes down. Checking this option causes Windows 2000 to automatically redial and re-establish your connection if it drops. Assuming something hasn't failed on the ISP side of your connection, your link should come back up automatically within about a minute.

For this feature to work, you must have the Remote Access Auto Connection Manager service running. This service doesn't automatically start on Windows 2000 Server by default, so you will need to enable it manually. To do this, enter the Computer Management administrative tool by selecting Start/Programs/Administrative Tools/ Computer Management or by right-clicking My Computer and selecting the Manage option. This will bring you into the Microsoft Management Console (MMC) for managing computers on your network. In the left-hand pane of the MMC, you should see an option for Services under the Services and Applications group (you might need to expand Services and Applications to see it). Click the Services icon in the left-hand pane, and you should see a listing of all the services running on your Windows 2000 Server in the result pane. The MMC screen should look like Figure 22.12.

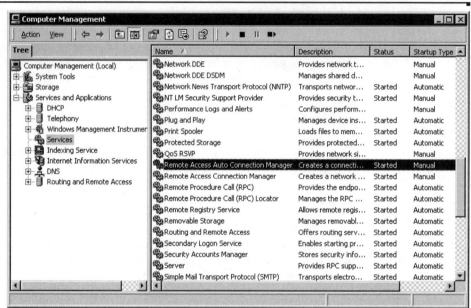

Find the Remote Access Auto Connection Manger service in the listing on the right, and double-click it to edit the properties. From here, you can start the service manually, and configure it to start up automatically every time your Windows 2000 Server boots up. The property sheet for this service should look like Figure 22.13.

To start this service manually, click the Start button in the dialog box. If everything goes OK, the status of this service should change to Started. Now, to make sure that this service starts every time your Windows 2000 Server boots, select Automatic from the Startup Type pull-down box. Click OK to save your changes and then exit the Computer Management MMC.

To test the redial functionality, try establishing a connection with this ISP dial-up entry and then pull the phone plug out of your modem. Wait a few seconds so that you're sure the carrier has dropped (if you have an icon in your taskbar indicating you're connected, it should disappear) and then plug the phone line back in. Within a minute, Windows 2000 should attempt to re-establish this connection for you without any intervention whatsoever.

FIGURE 22.13

Service properties for RAS Auto Connection Manager

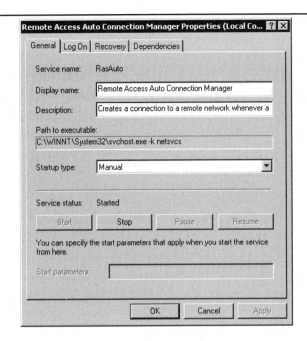

FIGURE 22.13

Service properties for RAS Auto Connection Manager

Accepting Incoming Calls from Remote Users

In today's business world there are a number of buzzwords which tend to make an administrator's job a bit more challenging. Phrases like telecommuting, mobile computing, and sales force automation are all centered around one common principle—getting corporate data into the hands of people who need it, exactly when they need it, wherever they are located. In terms of systems administration, this typically means accepting inbound connections from remote clients. If you have yet to face this administrative challenge, rest assured that in the near future you most likely will. The tendency toward remote computing simply shows no signs of slowing down anytime soon.

Whatever your dial-in needs are, Windows 2000 can act as a universal gateway to get remote clients into your network. Thanks to built-in support for Point-to-Point Protocol (PPP), an RFC-defined dial-up standard, Windows 2000 can receive calls from almost any type of device. PCs, Macintosh systems, Unix hosts, and even Personal Digital Assistants (PDAs) such as the 3Com PalmPilot can all establish PPP connections to remote networks. Windows 2000 can accept traffic from any of these devices and route it to the devices on your internal network, whether they're NT servers, Novell servers, Unix hosts, etc.

To start accepting incoming calls from remote clients, you will need the following:

- Windows 2000 Server with remote access software configured to accept incoming calls

- Connection device of some sort (modem, ISDN, X.25, etc.) connected to the Windows 2000 Server to accept calls from the remote clients

- Client computer capable of establishing a PPP session (Windows 95, 98, and NT 4; Windows 2000 Professional; Macintosh; 3Com PalmPilot; etc.)

- Connection device of some sort (modem, ISDN, X.25, etc.) connected to the remote client and capable of establishing a connection to the corresponding device on the Windows 2000 Server

- Circuit (phone line, ISDN line, etc.) between the two devices

- User account on your Windows 2000 Server (or within your Active Directory) with dial-in rights granted to it

For the sake of brevity, we'll assume that you've gone through the detailed steps earlier in this chapter to add your modems (ISDN devices or whatever you might be using) to your Windows 2000 Server and they are functioning properly. With that out of the way, let's get started on accepting incoming calls from remote clients.

To be sure we're all working from the same baseline, we'll assume that you do not have the Routing and Remote Access Service installed on your computer. If you do have it installed, going through this procedure will stop your existing services and re-install them with the answers provided to the configuration wizard.

Remote Access Server Installation and Setup

Start the installation for Routing and Remote Access Service by clicking Start/Programs/ Administrative Tools/Routing and Remote Access. You will see a Microsoft Management Console (MMC) window appear, and you should see your server listed somewhere in the left-hand pane of the MMC window. Right-click your server, and select the Configure and Enable Routing and Remote Access option.

This will begin the RRAS installation process. This process is aided by a wizard that will help you configure the necessary services to allow remote clients to dial in. After a welcome dialog box (to which you will answer yes), the first dialog box you will see should look similar to the screen shown in Figure 22.14.

The first step of the configuration wizard is to determine what role your Windows 2000 Server will play. If you are simply looking to accept connections from dial-in clients, click the Remote Access Server radio button, and then click Next to move onto the next step of the wizard.

FIGURE 22.14

RRAS configuration
wizard: role of server

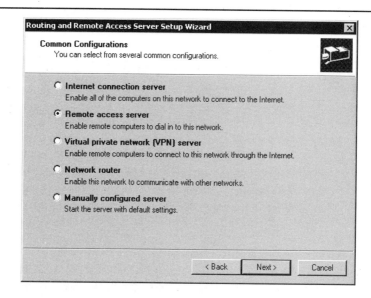

FIGURE 22.14

RRAS configuration
wizard: role of server

Figure 22.15 shows the next step of the configuration wizard, which allows you to verify that the protocols installed on your server are correct for the type of remote access you are trying to provide to your dial-in clients. The only correct answer to this dialog box is to answer Yes, All of the Required Protocols Are on This List; answering No, I Need to Add Protocols will cause the wizard to stop at this step and abort the configuration process. Therefore, it is recommended that you select Yes and continue to the next step of the wizard, shown in Figure 22.16.

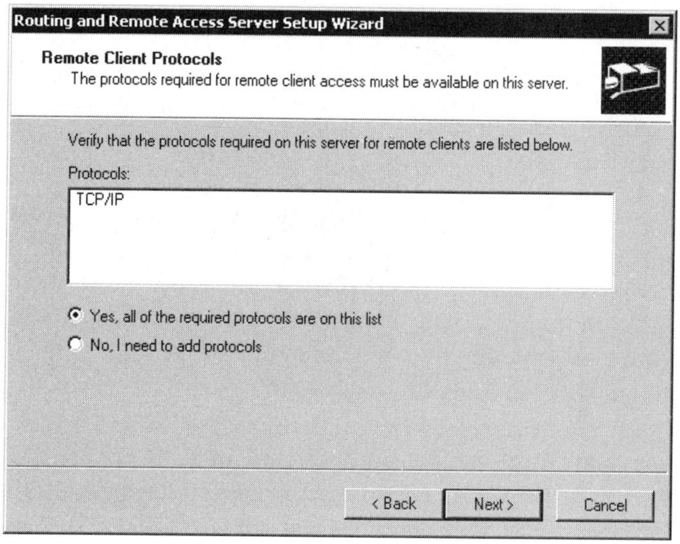

FIGURE 22.15

RRAS configuration
wizard: configuring
protocols

FIGURE 22.16

RRAS configuration wizard: IP address assignment

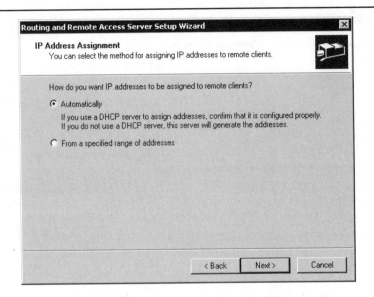

NOTE You cannot, at this step of the wizard, specify only to use certain protocols. Although the dialog box might lead you to believe you can "select" which protocols to use, in reality the RRAS configuration wizard will automatically assume that you want to allow connections on all protocols. To remove protocols from your RRAS server, you will need to go back and manually re-configure it after the wizard is through.

The next step of the wizard—assuming you have TCP/IP installed on your server—will ask you how to handle assignment of IP addresses to remote dial-in clients. Since every device on the network must have its own IP address, your dial-in workstations need a way to get addresses as well. By default, RRAS will want to assign addresses to your dial-in users automatically from a DHCP server. If you have a DHCP server running, you will probably want to accept the default Automatically option. Whether DHCP and RAS are running on the same server or on separate systems, the RAS service will attempt to obtain a DHCP-assigned address from the internal network and then pass it along to the remote client to use. The key with this option is to make sure you have a working DHCP server somewhere on your network and that it has enough IP addresses that can be used for dial-in connections.

NOTE For further reading on setting up a DHCP server, please see Chapter 18, "Building a Windows 2000 TCP/IP Infrastructure: DHCP, WINS, DNS, Sites, and More."

Under some special circumstances, you might want to control which IP addresses RAS hands out to dial-in clients. For example, if you have developed login scripts or other automation routines that are dependent on IP addresses, having a preset range might be useful. Or, you might have security policies in place on your networks that only allow certain IP addresses to connect to certain devices. Either way, if you need to make sure RAS clients always fall within a certain range of IP addresses, select the From a Specified Range of Addresses option and then click Next to proceed to Address Range Assignment, shown in Figure 22.17.

FIGURE 22.17

RRAS configuration wizard: address range assignment

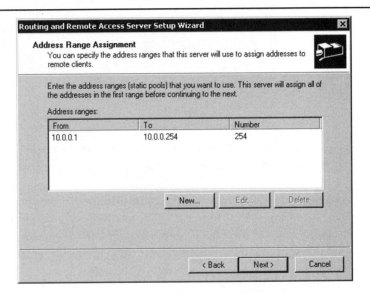

Through address range assignment, you can enter a series of IP address ranges for RRAS to use when clients dial in to your network. You can make these ranges as small or as large as you would like—just so long as you know that they are usable addresses within your network. To add a range (or ranges) to your system, click the New button and enter a start and end range of IP addresses to use. The New Address Range dialog box will automatically calculate how many addresses are in the range you provided. In the example shown in Figure 22.17, I have already entered a range of 10.0.0.1 to 10.0.0.254 for this RRAS server to use. When you have finished entering your addresses, click Next to proceed with the next step in the wizard, shown in Figure 22.18.

Although the next step of the wizard might look like it's simply asking if you have a RADIUS server available on your network, it's actually asking far more than that. This step of the wizard is asking how you would like to handle dial-in authentications. In earlier beta copies of Windows 2000, previous versions of this step of the wizard provided far more configuration flexibility at this point in the process. Unfortunately, your choices are now limited to two simple options.

FIGURE 22.18

*RRAS configuration
wizard: RADIUS
services*

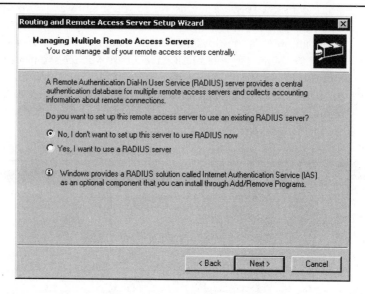

If you are currently using RADIUS services on your network (Remote Authentication Dial-In User Service) for authentication and logging of other dial-in access, you can set up your RRAS server to use the existing RADIUS server instead of using its own authentication and logging mechanisms. To specify your own RADIUS information, select the Yes, I Want to Use a RADIUS Server option and then click Next. Since RADIUS is outside the scope of this chapter, we'll assume that you will stick to using Windows 2000's own authentication and logging mechanisms. Therefore, you can leave the default No, I Don't Want to Set Up This Server to Use RADIUS Now option and then click Next to continue.

Since the option for RADIUS selection is the final step of the wizard, your server should be configured after you click Finish on the final panel of the wizard.

 NOTE   One of the more impressive things about Windows 2000 that was easy to overlook was the fact that the entire process for adding RAS services was completed without rebooting the server *at all.* My commendations go to Microsoft on finally getting their operating system working so that it doesn't require a reboot after every minor change.

Granting Dial-In Permissions to User(s)

Once you've successfully installed the Routing and Remote Access Service, the next thing to do is grant dial-in permissions to a user account in your Active Directory tree. (We'll assume you already have an account created for this purpose.)

NOTE If you need to add a new account for this exercise, please see Chapter 8, "Managing and Creating User Accounts."

To grant dial-in permissions to selected users, choose the Active Directory Users and Computers MMC by clicking Start/Programs/Administrative Tools/Active Directory Users and Computers. Navigate through the Active Directory tree to the user you want to grant dial-in permissions to, and right-click the corresponding record. By selecting the option to edit the properties for this user, you'll be taken to a dialog box to edit options for this user. Click the Dial-In tab, and you should be left with a screen similar to the one in Figure 22.19.

FIGURE 22.19

Granting dial-in permissions via user properties

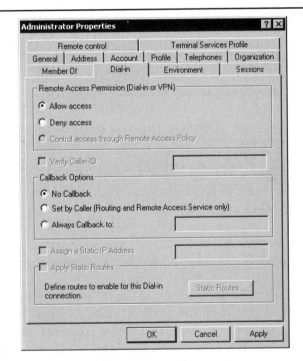

By default, the user account you've selected will probably have the Deny Access option selected at the top of the dialog box. Click Allow Access to grant dial-in permissions to this user. You also have the option to edit some user-specific settings through this dialog box.

For example, if you'd like to implement an additional measure of security by making sure a certain user's remote access session always comes from a specific phone number, you have a few options available. First, if your modem and phone line supports Caller-ID service, you can simply select the Verify Caller-ID option box and enter the phone number this user must call in on. However, if you are using hardware that doesn't support Caller-ID or that service is unavailable in your area, you can achieve the same type of security by having your RAS server call the user back at a certain phone number. Selecting one of the Callback options available in the middle of the screen activates this feature.

If you have home users who dial in either via long-distance or local–long-distance, callback options might also save you some money when it comes to your remote access costs. If the telephone service you have in your office has a better per-minute rate than the rates your users typically have in their homes, you can save money on your remote access connections by having your RAS server call users back at the cheaper rates.

In addition to callback options, you can also specify a fixed IP address for this specific user to receive. This is a new feature in Windows 2000 and can be exceptionally useful when setting up internal access policies based on IP address (firewall rules, etc.).

Now, take a moment and relax. Your server is set up to receive calls. You should be able to test this by calling the number associated with your RAS server from a standard phone and getting a carrier tone. If you don't hear a carrier tone, double-check your work and make sure everything is connected properly. If for some reason you still don't get a carrier tone when you call in, try rebooting the server (oddly enough, this happened to me once, and rebooting it corrected the problem).

Changing RAS Server Configurations after Installation

Wizards are both a blessing and a curse for the Windows operating system. Although they make complex tasks easier, they also tend to assume a number of answers for you with no chance to change those assumptions. The RRAS configuration wizard is guilty of this practice, as it will make a number of assumptions for you as you configure your system. You may want to check these configurations to make sure they are exactly the way you want them to be.

If you need to change any of your configuration at a later time, you can easily do so by right-clicking your server in the Routing and Remote Access MMC and then selecting Properties. Through the RRAS properties dialog boxes, you can add or remove support for certain protocols for dial-up connections, increase authentication security, and fine-tune the PPP controls for establishing connections to client systems. We'll walk through each of these areas, starting with the controls for security shown in Figure 22.20.

Through this screen you can control a number of behaviors for the security and encryption used with your dial-up connections. Although there are pros and cons for using each (with the pros usually being increased security and the cons being limited client support), we'll discuss each option briefly so you can make your own judgements as to which is best to use.

FIGURE 22.20

*Editing security proper-
ties for RAS service*

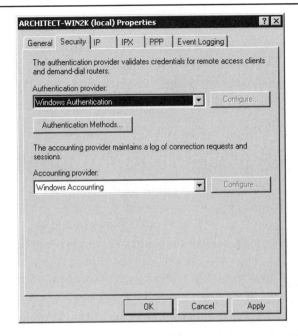

By default, the authentication provider that should be automatically configured is Windows Authentication. If you have an external RADIUS server, you can change Windows to use the RADIUS server instead by selecting the RADIUS option from the pull-down box and then clicking the Configure button to define the RADIUS servers to use. Since RADIUS servers are out of the scope of this chapter, we'll simply stick to Windows Authentication methods.

By clicking the Authentication Methods button below the Authentication Provider pull-down box, you will be taken to a screen similar to the one shown in Figure 22.21.

FIGURE 22.21

*Editing authentication
types for RAS service*

As you can see, there are a number of authentication options to choose from, as defined below:

Extensible Authentication Protocol (EAP)   Since security and authentication is a constantly changing field, embedding authentication schemes into an operating system is impractical at times. To solve this problem, Microsoft has included support for Extensible Authentication Protocol, which is simply a means of "plugging in" new authentication schemes as needed. Currently, Windows 2000 Server only supports MD-5 Challenge and Transport Level Security (TLS, primarily used for smartcard support), but this option will allow for future authentication protocols to be plugged into the operating system easily.

Microsoft Encrypted Authentication (v1 and v2), MS-CHAP
Microsoft's derivative of CHAP, or Challenge-Handshake Authentication Protocol (see below). Using MS-CHAP allows you to encrypt an entire dial-up session, not just the original authentication, which is especially important when it comes to setting up virtual private networking sessions. MS-CHAP v2 support is included in Windows 2000 for all types of connections and in Windows NT 4 and Windows 95/98 (with the Dial-Up Networking 1.3 upgrade) for VPN connections.

Encrypted Authentication (CHAP)   Defined in RFC (Request for Comments) 1334, and later revised in RFC 1994, the Challenge-Handshake Authentication Protocol is a means of encrypting authentication sessions between a client and server. Since this protocol is defined by an RFC, it enjoys a broad base of support among many operating systems and other devices.

Shiva Encrypted Authentication (SPAP)   SPAP, short for Shiva Password Authentication Protocol, is an encrypted password authentication method used by Shiva LAN Rover clients and servers. Windows 2000 Server can act as a server when Shiva LAN Rover clients are dialing in by providing the correct authentication sequence for them.

Unencrypted (clear text) Password (PAP)   Password Authentication Protocol (PAP) is one of the last two options listed, and it is also one of the least secure. It is no more secure than a simple conversation from your server saying "What is your name and password?" to the client, the client responding with "My name is Doug and my password is 'let-me-in'." There is no encryption of authentication credentials whatsoever.

Unauthenticated Access   At first glance, this option wouldn't seem to make much sense—leaving a wide-open access point to your network with no authentication required whatsoever. However, when paired with Caller-ID verification, this option can make a simple and secure method for getting clients connected to your network.

If a dial-in user provides a username only, that username will be checked against the Active Directory. If there is a Caller-ID verification set for that user, the Caller-ID information will be checked and the connection will be accepted or rejected based on whether the information matches. If the user does not send a username at all, the Guest account will be used by default. Therefore, if you intend to use this option, you might want to disable the Guest account on your system (a good security practice to get in the habit of anyway).

Within the properties for the RAS service, you have the ability to fine-tune each protocol accepted by the RAS server and passed on to the internal network. By clicking the appropriate tabs (shown in Figure 22.22) for IP, IPX, NetBEUI, and AppleTalk, you can edit the following options for each protocol:

Allow <*Protocol*> -Based Remote Access and Demand Dial Connections (IP, IPX, NetBEUI, and AppleTalk)   To enable or disable support for individual protocols, check the boxes for each protocol to allow and un-check the boxes for each protocol to reject. If you used the automatic wizard to install Remote Access Service, you might find that Windows 2000 Server enabled support for all the protocols on your system by default. However, good security practices dictate only opening up support for the protocols you need, so it's probably a good idea to remove any protocols you aren't using.

Entire Network Access for Remote Clients (IP, IPX, NetBEUI, and AppleTalk)   One way to increase the security of your dial-in system is to only allow dial-in users to access the dial-in server itself. For example, if traveling workers only need to access a set of word processing documents or spreadsheets, these could be kept on the remote access server. By unchecking the Entire Network Access for Remote Clients box, clients will only be able to access the RAS server itself.

Additionally, this is a useful option for protecting certain types of servers. For example, perhaps you only want your dial-up users to access your Windows 2000 or NT network which runs solely on TCP/IP. However, you might have Novell NetWare servers on your network running IPX that you don't want to allow access to. By removing access to the entire network for the IPX protocol, you can allow dial-in access to some systems and not others.

Dynamic Host Configuration Protocol—or—Use Static Address Pool (IP Only)   As was previously discussed in the configuration of Remote Access Service, here you can select whether your RAS server will use a DHCP server to hand out IP addresses to dial-in clients or if it will manually assign addresses from a static pool. If you choose to assign addresses from a static pool, you will need to provide the correct TCP/IP network address range and subnet mask to use.

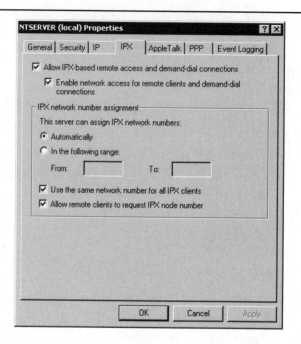

 NOTE For more information on calculating address ranges and subnet masks, see Chapter 17, "Understanding and Using TCP/IP in Windows 2000 Server."

IPX Network Number Assignment—Automatic or in the Following Range (IPX only) Since IPX network numbers typically consist of two parts—a network address and a node number—you can configure what addresses RAS will assign to clients through this screen. If you have NetWare servers on your network, you may find it useful to assign a specific network number to your dial-in clients. For example, you might modify the login script on your NetWare servers to behave one way for internal clients and differently for dial-in clients, based on the IPX network number of the workstation.

Use the Same Network Number to All IPX Clients (IPX only) If this option is checked, the RAS server will automatically assign the same network number to all IPX clients—either an automatic network number or one defined by allocating numbers. This will reduce the number of RIP announcement packets the RAS server will need to broadcast.

Allow Remote Clients to Request IPX Node Number (IPX only)
If your dial-in clients are capable of asking for a specific node number, check

this option and your RAS server and dial-in client will negotiate a node address accordingly.

If you need to fine-tune the parameters for your RAS server to use when establishing PPP sessions with clients, click the PPP tab to edit the properties of these items, as shown in Figure 22.23. The default settings will be acceptable in most instances, but if needed you can enable or disable the following options.

Multilink Connections   Multilink Point-to-Point Protocol (MPPP for short) was defined in RFC 1717 as a means of joining (often referred to as "bonding") two or more PPP sessions together to increase bandwidth. Effectively, you could double or triple your bandwidth between a client and a server if you had two or three modems at each location, two or three phone numbers, etc. This option must be selected if you want to be able to choose the next option.

Dynamic Bandwidth Control (BAP/BACP)   Defined in RFC 2125, Bandwidth Allocation Protocol (BAP), and Bandwidth Allocation Control Protocol (BACP) are similar in nature to Multilink protocol in that they are both used to bond connections together for increased bandwidth. However, while Multilink protocol is a "fixed" solution that will automatically join all the channels it can together, BAP/BACP will only initiate additional connections as needed due to high bandwidth utilization. This is an excellent option if you have connections that are subject to per-minute charges and don't need to have them online all the time.

LCP Extensions   Enabling Link Control Protocol (LCP) extensions is a necessary part of supporting callback security on a RAS server. If you are planning on having your system be able to call users back at a specified number, you must have this option enabled.

Software Compression   Never missing an opportunity to define a protocol for something and create another standard, Microsoft has developed the Microsoft Point-to-Point Compression Protocol (MPPC) to compress data as it travels across a remote access link. MPPC is defined in RFC 2118.

In addition to configuring protocol and authentication types to use, you may also want to configure what ports on your system are used to accept incoming RRAS calls. For example, you may have some modems that are to be used strictly for dial-in, and others strictly for dial-out. Unfortunately, the RRAS configuration wizard will simply assume you want to use *all* your modems for dial-in purposes.

To alter the configuration of ports on your system, return to the Routing and Remote Access MMC and expand your server in the left-hand pane of the window. Below your server, you should see an option for Ports. Highlight that option, and then select Properties from the Action pull-down menu (or by right-clicking the item). That should take you to a window similar to the one shown in Figure 22.24.

FIGURE 22.23

Editing PPP properties for RAS service

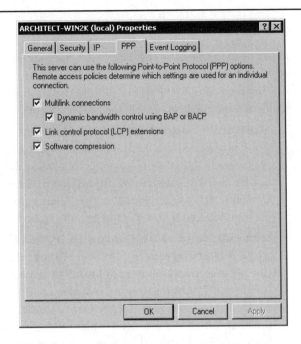

FIGURE 22.24

Configuring RRAS ports via the Routing and Remote Access MMC

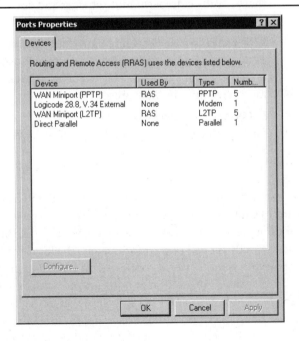

As you can see on this screen, all the interfaces that can support RRAS clients are listed for you to choose from. Highlight the interface(s) that you'd like to accept incoming calls from, and then click the Configure button. This will open the individual property sheet for this device. Check the box labeled Remote Access Connections (Inbound Only) and—if you can—enter the phone number for the line connected to that device in the Phone Number of This Device field. The phone number will allow you to support Bandwidth Allocation Protocol (BAP) for devices to initiate additional connections to your server (although since this requires multiple modems and lines at each location, it might not be an option you need). Repeat this procedure for all the ports on your server.

NOTE It is important to note that *all* types of ports are automatically configured for your RRAS server—including the VPN ports for PPTP and L2TP. If this server is accessible over the Internet, these ports will be "openings" that outsiders can use to try to authenticate to your network. I recommend that you change the Maximum ports value for L2TP to zero and for PPTP to one (the minimum value allowed in RC2), unless you specifically intend to implement virtual private networking (discussed later in this chapter).

Client Configurations

Now that you have a RAS server that's running smoothly, it's time to enable some clients and get connected into the network. While we can't cover every possible platform under the sun when it comes to remote access, we'll look at a few of the more common options, namely Windows NT 4 Workstation and Windows 9*x*. Windows 2000 Professional Dial-Up Networking will follow a routine very similar to the Windows 2000 Server Dial-Up Networking steps, outlined in detail in the next section.

All these client configurations assume that you have Dial-Up Networking already installed on your system and correctly configured. Assistance on installing Dial-Up Networking on other platforms is outside the scope of this book.

TIP I frequently get calls from clients who have configured one of their users' home computers to dial into the corporate network but are having trouble browsing the Network Neighborhood and seeing any resources. In most cases, this is due to the workgroup and domain settings on the home system not matching the settings for workstations in the office. Make sure you use the same settings in both locations.

Windows NT 4 Workstation

From the Windows NT 4 desktop, double-click My Computer and then Dial-Up Networking to bring up the main Dial-Up Networking program. If this is the first time you are using Dial-Up Networking, you might get a message about your phonebook being empty—this is OK because it is simply Windows telling you it doesn't know how to dial anyone yet. If you get that message, click OK to continue, and that should leave you at the main Dial-Up Networking screen as shown in Figure 22.25.

FIGURE 22.25

*Dial-Up Networking in
Windows NT 4
Workstation*

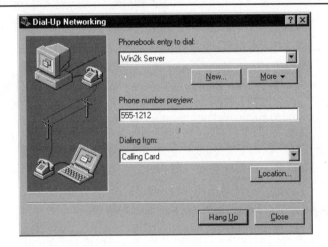

To add a new entry for your Windows 2000 Server, click the New button to start defining a new phonebook entry. The initial screen will let you enter information such as a friendly name to use for this phonebook entry, the number to dial, which modem to use, etc. Enter the appropriate information as needed and then click the Server tab to enter information about the server you are calling into. Your phonebook entry screen should look similar to Figure 22.26.

By default, Windows NT 4 Workstation will assume you are going to be dialing into a PPP-compatible server, so it will use that selection as a default for the dial-up server type pull-down box. Also, NT Workstation will assume you want to use software compression and PPP LCP extensions (as seen by the check boxes in the bottom of the window). These are also acceptable defaults for most dial-up connections and can be left checked in most cases. These settings directly correspond to the PPP settings defined on the configured RAS server.

FIGURE 22.26

Selecting server options for a new phonebook entry, Windows NT 4 Workstation

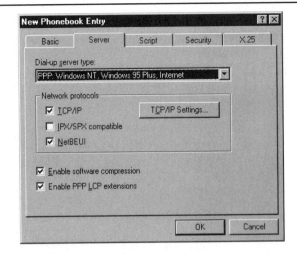

By far, the most important settings in this dialog are the network protocol settings. In general, these settings should correspond directly to the protocols configured when installing the RAS server service, as seen back in Figure 22.15. The client workstation obviously cannot connect on certain protocols if they are not installed on your server, so make sure you are using the same protocols in each location. If you plan on using TCP/IP (which I expect most readers will), click the TCP/IP Settings button to define protocol-specific parameters if necessary. The TCP/IP Settings screen should look like the one in Figure 22.27.

For most installations, the default TCP/IP settings should work fine, but if your situation is a bit more specific, you can enter values for the IP address the client should use and which DNS servers and WINS servers to use for name resolution. If you don't enter any settings for the DNS and WINS servers to use, the dial-up networking client will inherit the same values the RAS server uses itself. This is an important point, because if you are using DHCP to assign addresses, you might assume that any DHCP scope options you have added to your address space would be automatically passed along to your RAS clients. However, even if your RAS server is consulting your DHCP server for addresses to use, it will not pass DHCP scope options along to RAS clients. Settings for DNS servers and WINS servers to use will come directly from the same settings programmed into your RAS server. So, if you're using DHCP on your network, make sure you hard-code an IP address for your RAS server and program in the correct name server addresses.

FIGURE 22.27

TCP/IP settings on Windows NT 4 Workstation Dial-Up Networking

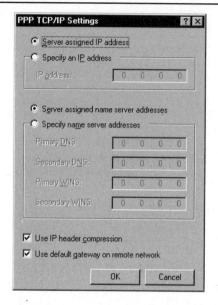

Once you have set your server and protocol settings as necessary, click the security tab to define the appropriate authentication options for your dial-in client. The security settings are shown in Figure 22.28. Just as the correct configuration for the server settings on the dial-up client depends on how your RAS server was configured, the security settings on the client will depend on how the security is configured on the RAS server as well.

FIGURE 22.28

Security settings on Windows NT 4 Workstation Dial-Up Networking

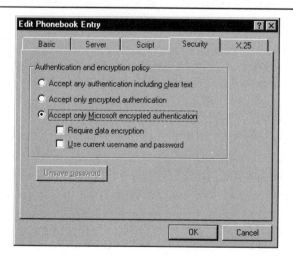

By default, Windows NT 4 Workstation selects the option to Accept Any Authentication Including Clear Text. If the RAS server is configured to only allow MS-CHAP authentication, then the Dial-Up Networking client will submit an MS-CHAP authentication and should be validated without any difficulty. If you run into problems logging in, make sure your authentication settings between your server and your client match on at least some level.

When you have completed making the necessary settings for this dial-up networking entry, click OK and then press Dial to dial into your Windows 2000 Server. You will be prompted for a valid username, password, and domain name to log in with. Use the username(s) you granted dial-in permission to on your servers, click OK, and if everything goes according to plan your Windows NT 4 Workstation should be connected!

Windows 9x

From the Windows 9x desktop, double-click My Computer and then Dial-Up Networking to bring up the Dial-Up Networking program. If this is the first time you are using Dial-Up Networking, you might be asked to enter information about your local area code, whether to use touch tone or pulse dialing, and any prefixes you need to dial. Simply fill in the information and click OK to continue. This should bring you to the Make New Connection window as shown in Figure 22.29.

FIGURE 22.29

Windows 9x Make New Connection

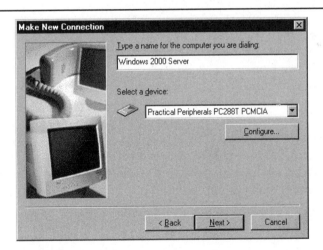

At the first step of the Make New Connection dialog box, you can enter a friendly name for this Dial-Up Networking connection and select which modem you'd like to use. Enter this information and then click Next to continue to the next step, shown in Figure 22.30.

FIGURE 22.30

*Windows 9x Make
New Connection,
step two*

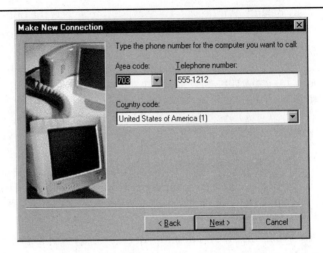

In the second (and final) step, enter the area code and phone number of your RAS server and then click Next to complete the creation of this Dial-Up Networking entry. By default, Windows 9x will assume a number of things about this Dial-Up Networking entry, including which protocols and security settings you'd like to use. For example, Windows 9x will select all the protocols installed on your system and try to use them over this Dial-Up Networking connection.

If you'd prefer to configure these options yourself instead of having Windows 9x assume what you want, go back to the main Dial-Up Networking window (the one with the Make New Connection icon) and you should see an icon for your Dial-Up Networking session. Right-click the icon, and select Properties to edit the configuration. You will see the property sheet for this Dial-Up Networking connection, as shown in Figure 22.31.

From here, you can (and should) change the security and protocol settings to match those of your RAS server. For example, if you only run TCP/IP on your corporate network, you don't necessarily need to have NetBEUI and IPX selected in your Dial-Up Networking session. Configure the settings accordingly, and then launch your session to verify that it works.

FIGURE 22.31

*Editing Windows 9x
Dial-Up Networking
Entry Properties*

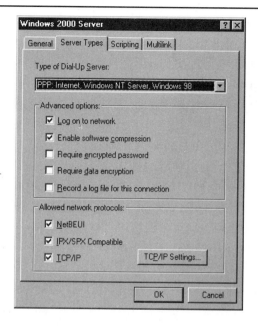

Managing Connected Users

If you need to keep tabs on users connected to your network, the Routing and Remote Access MMC can give you an overview of all remote access connections currently connected to your server. Whether connections are coming into your systems from VPN connections, serial connections, analog modems, or ISDN lines, you can get an overview of all your remote connections from one convenient console.

To manage connected users, start by launching the Routing and Remote Access MMC by selecting Start/Programs/Administrative Tools/Routing and Remote Access. By expanding the details for your RAS server in the left-hand pane, you should see a sub-item for Remote Access Clients listed below your system, along with a number next to it in parentheses. This number indicates the number of dial-in users currently connected to your system. This screen should look similar to the one in Figure 22.32.

From this screen, you can get an overview of how long users have been connected to your network, who is currently connected, which ports are in use, etc. By double-clicking any of the listed connections on your system, you can get advanced details about that individual connection, such as what IP/IPX addresses were assigned to the system, how much data has been transferred, etc. You can disconnect an individual connection from the same property sheet by clicking the Hang Up button, or you can disconnect a user by right-clicking that user's connection in the main list of connected users. In addition to being able to disconnect a user from the main listing of connected users, you can also send a message to an individual user or to all connected users by right-clicking a connection and selecting either Send Message or Send to All, respectively.

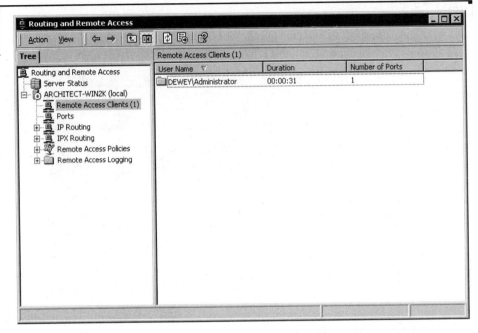

Connecting to a Private Network

Much like connecting to the Internet, there will be times when you might need to connect your Windows 2000 Server to another private network. Maybe one of your servers needs to collect data from a client's systems or transmit product orders to a supplier. The private network might be another Windows 2000 network, a Windows NT network, a Novell network, or a network that contains a combination of servers and other systems. In any case, dial-up networking can get your Windows 2000 Server connected with a minimal amount of effort.

Before getting started, there are a few things you will need to have to complete making a connection to another network. Namely, you will need to have the following information available in advance:

- Access phone number to dial
- Username and password combination
- Protocols that will be used on the remote network
- Authentication the remote network will require

To get started, we'll once again be working through the Network Connection Wizard by clicking Start/Settings/Network and Dial-Up Connections and then choosing the Make New Connection icon. When the wizard starts, you should see the screen shown in Figure 22.33.

FIGURE 22.33

Network Connection Wizard: connect to private network

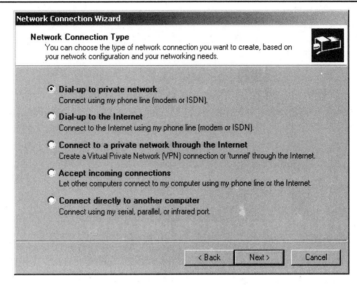

From this point, select the first option, Dial-Up to Private Network, and click Next to continue to the next step of the wizard, as seen in Figure 22.34.

FIGURE 22.34

Network Connection Wizard: enter phone number

Enter the phone number as prompted, and then click Next to get to the last step of the wizard, pictured in Figure 22.35.

FIGURE 22.35

*Network Connection
Wizard: share
connection*

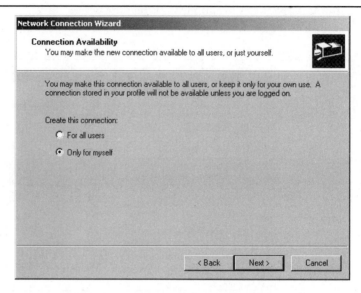

The last step of the Network Connection Wizard will ask if you would like to make this dial-up connection available to all users or to keep it just for use by the machine itself. For the purposes of simply connecting a Windows 2000 Server to another network, select the Only for Myself option here. The other option, For All Users, would end up sharing this connection for other users on the network, a topic discussed in the next section ("Acting as an Internet Gateway"). Click Next when you are finished, and you will have successfully created a Dial-Up Networking entry.

However, Windows 2000 will have assumed several things about your dial-up networking entry that might not work for your specific situation. To double-check everything, edit the properties for this dial-up connection by right-clicking the icon for it in the Network and Dial-Up Connections window. Pressing the Networking tab on the property page should bring you to a property sheet similar to the one shown in Figure 22.36.

Windows 2000 will assume you want to use a number of defaults when you try to connect to this remote network. For example, it will assume you want to use *all* the protocols loaded on your system for this connection, it will assume it can use unsecured passwords, etc. Some of these options might not make sense in specific situations. For example, if you are connecting to an IPX-only network, it doesn't make much sense to try and negotiate a TCP/IP connection. Even though Windows 2000 will realize that it can't establish the TCP/IP connection, why even try?

To fine-tune this connection, remove or add specific protocols as needed by checking the boxes next to the protocols listed under the Networking tab of the Dial-Up Networking entry property sheet. If you are connecting to a remote TCP/IP network and the device you are dialing into does not provide you with an IP address or DNS server addresses automatically, you can program these in by highlighting the TCP/IP protocol and then clicking the Properties button. This will bring you to the specific TCP/IP settings to use for this connection, as shown in Figure 22.37.

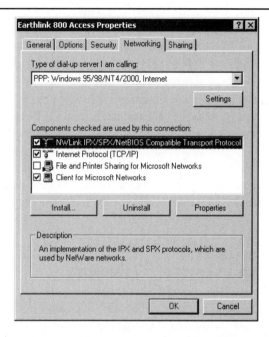

FIGURE 22.36

Dial-Up Networking entry properties

FIGURE 22.37

Editing TCP/IP properties for Dial-Up Networking entries

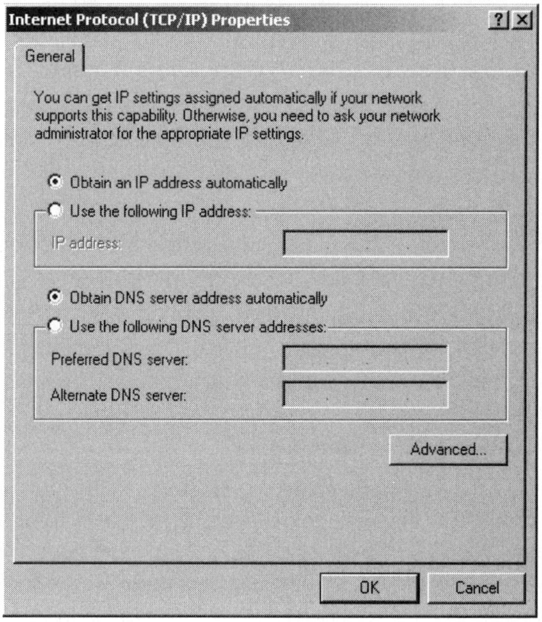

On this screen you can enter the necessary information for your TCP/IP connection. If you are accessing a remote network that uses WINS servers but does not provide those addresses to you, enter them in the advanced TCP/IP settings area by clicking the Advanced button and then clicking the WINS tab.

Once you have your protocols configured correctly, click OK to get back to the main property page for this dial-up connection. If you need to edit any other properties, such as the type of security or authentication to use, click the appropriate tabs and make those settings as necessary.

If you think this looks similar to the steps to connect to the Internet described earlier in this chapter, you are correct. Basically, all the mechanisms are the same in Dial-Up Networking, but different wizards will take a different approach to the settings that are applied by default. Therefore, some of the same advanced options discussed in the "Connecting to the Internet" section (re-establishing failed links, redialing non-responsive numbers, etc.) are available for regular dial-up connections to private networks. As a matter of fact, you can even use the Dial-Up to a Private Network wizard to define a connection to the Internet. Which brings us to our next topic....

Acting as an Internet Gateway

One of the hottest little "niche" applications people always seemed to want to do with Windows NT 4 Server was to share an Internet connection with everyone else inside their organization. After all, NT servers were usually set up to share other resources (files, printers, etc.)—so it made sense that NT Server should have been able to share an Internet connection, right? Not exactly. With enough tweaking and some strict rules to follow, you *could* actually have NT Server dial an Internet connection and route traffic for internal hosts out to the Internet. However, the setup would be difficult and cumbersome, and it requires having valid (InterNIC-assigned) IP addresses available for everyone within the organization. Simply sharing a $10/month unlimited access Internet account is not an option.

Now, Microsoft has included a variety of capabilities in Windows 2000 Server which make this task relatively easy. With the correct information about what type of connectivity you need to the outside world, Windows 2000 Server can act as an Internet gateway for your internal clients, leveraging an existing Internet connection among all the workstations in your organization.

 NOTE The Internet gateway capabilities of Windows 2000 Server worked so well that in the course of writing this chapter I was actually using my Windows 2000 Server (Beta 3) as an Internet gateway for my laptop and other test machines.

Although Microsoft has included some great tools for sharing connections on your network, it is important to note a number of subtle hints Microsoft has included in their documentation for this feature of Windows 2000 Server. First and foremost, Microsoft often makes several references to small or home office networks, implying that this capability really isn't designed for use in medium-to-large environments. I would have to agree with them on this point; if you have a reasonable number of workstations on your network, you will probably be far better off going with a product such as Microsoft Proxy Server and a dedicated Internet connection.

The second point Microsoft makes repeatedly throughout their documentation is that "you should not use this feature in an existing network with other Windows 2000 Server domain controllers, DNS servers, gateways, DHCP servers, or systems configured for static IP" (source: Microsoft Windows 2000 on-line help). Since this configuration requires a very specific IP configuration to work correctly, implementing this on a network that doesn't conform to that configuration could cause lots of difficulty. I would agree with Microsoft on this point as well.

Although acting as an Internet Router isn't one of the options normally available through the Make a New Connection wizard used throughout this chapter, fortunately one of the other options will configure most everything necessary. By using the steps detailed in the last section, "Connecting to a Private Network," and connecting to the Internet as the "Private" network, you can make Windows 2000 act as an Internet gateway, routing traffic from your internal clients out to the Internet and back again.

Configuring Windows 2000 Server to Act as an Internet Gateway

Start with the same steps listed in the section "Connecting to a Private Network" and go all the way up to Figure 22.34, using a local access number for your ISP as the number of the private network to dial.

This time, when the Network Connection Wizard asks if you would like to make this connection available to all users (pictured in Figure 22.35), select For All Users instead of Only for Myself. This will enable the sharing properties for this connection. Click Next, and you should end up with a screen like the one in Figure 22.38.

On this screen, you will have two options for how this shared connection should be handled. The first option is simply to enable sharing for this connection; leave this option checked. The second option tells Windows 2000 Server when it should establish the connection. If this box is unchecked, the only way to establish the connection to the Internet will be manually. However, users typically expect connections to be available whenever they want them, so enabling the on-demand dialing option will allow Windows 2000 Server to automatically establish this connection as needed, with no outside intervention. If you are going to be implementing a shared Internet connection, you probably want to select this option. When you check the box for on-demand dialing and click Next, you will probably receive a warning dialog box similar to the one in Figure 22.39.

FIGURE 22.38

Defining sharing options

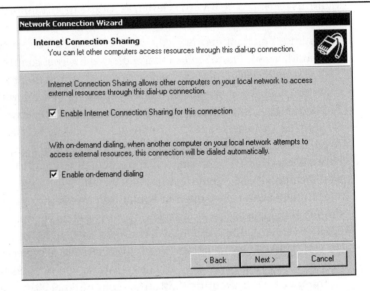

FIGURE 22.39

Static IP address change warning

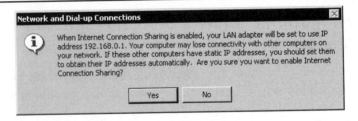

This dialog box lets you know that Windows 2000 Server will need to make a number of changes to its IP configuration for this functionality to work, including specifying a fixed IP address to use for the server's internal network connection. If anyone is connected to your server at this point, make sure they are disconnected before continuing, otherwise they may lose their connections to the system. Click Yes to continue, and Windows 2000 Server will make the appropriate IP changes to support sharing an Internet connection.

The last step of the wizard should ask you to assign a friendly name to this connection. Go ahead and assign a meaningful name to this connection and then click Finish. Once you have completed the wizard, you should see an icon for your shared connection in the Network and Dial-up Connections dialog box. Launch the connection to verify that everything is working correctly. When you are prompted for your

ISP username and password, enter your credentials and then check the Save Password box below the field for the domain. This will save your username and password for this connection so that when it is demand-dialed it will have what it needs. Once you have established that your ISP connection works correctly in and of itself, it's time to define a few rules as to what you want to allow across your Internet connection.

Defining Application and Service Configurations

By default, Windows 2000 Server will not automatically route any traffic from your client workstations to the Internet. You must define specific rules as to what type of traffic (i.e., what TCP/IP protocols) can go across your shared connection. To do this, begin by editing the properties for your shared Internet access connection by right-clicking the Dial-Up Networking icon in the Network and Dial-Up Connections window and then selecting Properties. Click the Sharing tab, and you should see settings for enabling shared access for this connection and on-demand dialing. At the bottom of the window is a button labeled Settings. By clicking the button, you can define settings for which applications and services can go across your shared Internet Connection. The Internet Connection Sharing Settings dialog box is pictured in Figure 22.40.

FIGURE 22.40

Configuring shared access settings

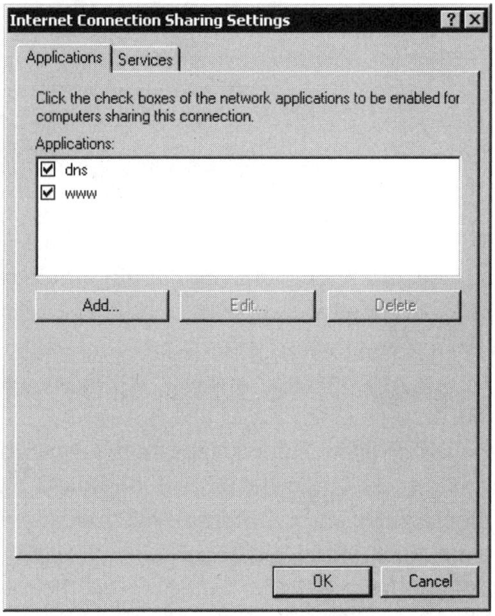

As a point of clarification, "applications" typically refer to connections that come from your internal network (for Web browsing, e-mail, etc.) and are destined out to the Internet. However, sharing an Internet connection can also allow you to accept traffic from external hosts targeted at systems within your network. For example, maybe you have a small Web server running in your organization that you would like people to be able to access. Using a shared Internet connection not only lets your users share access to the Internet, but it can be programmed to allow the Internet access to your internal shared resources as well.

This is one of the reasons why it's important to define rules as to what is allowed in and out of your shared Internet connection. Let's start by adding a few rules to allow Web browsing across the shared Internet connection. From the Settings screen, make sure you are looking at the Applications tab. More than likely you won't have any applications listed on your system (unlike the example in Figure 22.40). Press Add to add an application (in effect, a TCP/IP protocol) to your system. The dialog box to add a Shared Access Application is shown in Figure 22.41.

FIGURE 22.41

Adding a shared access application

To allow shared access for a TCP/IP application, Windows 2000 Server needs to know how that application functions. Specifically, Windows 2000 Server needs to know which ports the application uses and whether the application uses TCP or UDP connections. One of the first applications you will probably want to add will be support for DNS—the means by which clients and browsers can translate names like www.microsoft.com into IP addresses.

To add DNS support, enter a name for the application (I've used "dns" in Figure 22.40) and the port on the remote server that Windows 2000 will be communicating with. For DNS, this port is 53, and the protocol to use for the request (with my ISP) is TCP, so I've selected the TCP radio button below the port. DNS responses from the target system will generally come back in on the same port that the client made the request from, which can be any number from 1024–65535. Therefore, I've put 1024-65535 in the TCP field for the incoming response to allow the DNS server to respond with the appropriate information.

As you can see, knowing how ports work is a key component of using shared Internet access. Some applications even get complicated by sending responses on UDP *and* TCP ports. For information on some commonly used Internet application ports and for the information necessary to configure your own applications as needed, see Table 22.2. Once you have configured an application for DNS, add applications as needed for the applications on your internal network.

TABLE 22.2: TCP/IP WELL-KNOWN PORTS AND SERVICES

Protocol Type	Destination Port/Protocol	Response Port(s)/Protocol(s)
FTP	21/TCP	1024-65535/TCP
Telnet	23/TCP	1024-65535/TCP
SMTP	25/TCP	1024-65535/TCP
Gopher	70/TCP	1024-65535/TCP
HTTP	80/TCP	1024-65535/TCP
POP3	110/TCP	1024-65535/TCP
NNTP	119/TCP	1024-65535/TCP

If you need to have outside clients access services on a computer on your internal network, you will need to add definitions to the services tab of the Shared Access Settings dialog box. Unless you want people from the outside world connecting to your internal systems, I would recommend leaving this blank. But if you have a Web server or FTP server that you need to have people connect to, this is the area to do it. Clicking the Services tab will take you to a screen almost identical to the one for Applications with several services listed on it. Clicking a service will allow you to define an internal host that Windows 2000 should direct that type of traffic to. Or you can click the Add button to add a service, and you will see a dialog box like the one shown in Figure 22.42.

FIGURE 22.42

Adding a shared access service

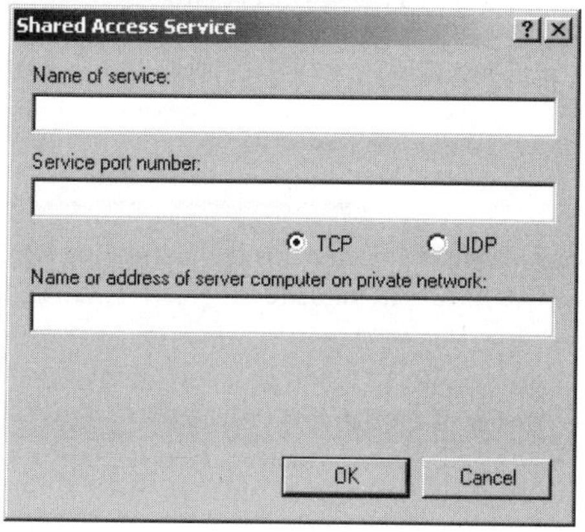

Services work a bit differently from applications because external hosts won't connect *directly* to the IP address assigned to your internal workstation that has the destination service (especially since in most cases the internal IP addresses won't be routable addresses on the Internet). Instead, external systems will connect to your Windows 2000 Server on a specific port, and based on what port they connect to, Windows 2000 will redirect the request to one of your internal systems. Therefore, the definitions for services vary a bit.

Start defining your service by giving it a name, for example, http, ftp, etc. In the field for service port number, put the port you will expect incoming connections to come to. Again, you can use Table 22.2 to determine which ports to use. If you wanted to allow incoming http traffic, for example, you would put 80 in the field for service port. Finally, in the last field for adding a service, tell Windows 2000 which of your internal computers to redirect the request to by entering either the name or IP address of the correct internal network computer. If you are using DHCP to assign addresses to your internal computers, I would recommend referencing the system by name in this dialog box.

Once you have completed this definition, hit OK and then make sure this service is checked in the Shared Access Services definition for settings. Now, if you have a connection that is demand-dialed, it's important to note that this won't typically work for incoming connections. That is, your ISP won't know that it should dial *your* server up whenever someone on the Internet tries to access one of your systems. Therefore, if you are going to accept incoming service connections I'd recommend having your Internet connection online at all times.

Once you have defined the appropriate application and service settings, it's time to configure your clients to direct their Internet traffic to your Windows 2000 Server for routing.

Configuring Clients

Once your server is ready, you will need to tell your clients to route their Internet traffic to your Windows 2000 Server. When the Windows 2000 Server receives these packets, it will realize that they are destined for the Internet and route them as necessary (initiating your demand-dialed connection if needed). You can either program each workstation manually or let DHCP do it for you by defining the correct scope and options to use.

 NOTE For more information on configuring DHCP scopes, see Chapter 18, "Building a Windows 2000 TCP/IP Infrastructure: DHCP, WINS, DNS, Sites, and More."

The following information will work in your DHCP scope for getting your clients connected to the Internet (other slight variations would work as well; this is merely an example):

- Address range: 192.168.0.2 to 192.168.0.254
- Address mask: 255.255.255.0

- Default gateway: 192.168.0.1

- DNS servers to use: enter your ISP's DNS server addresses

To enter these settings manually on a Windows 2000 Professional, NT 4, or 9*x* client, edit the TCP/IP properties of your computer to change the IP address to something in the range listed above. The mask should be 255.255.255.0 as listed above, and the default gateway should be 192.168.0.1, the IP address your Windows 2000 Server will give itself once you enable shared access. In Windows NT 4 Workstation, this would look similar to the dialog box shown in Figure 22.43.

FIGURE 22.43

TCP/IP settings for shared access on Windows NT 4 Workstation.

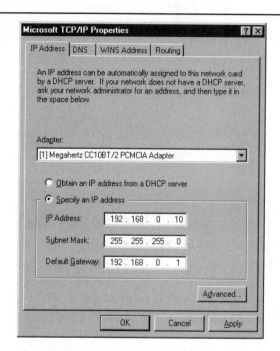

The last setting to make is the DNS server setting. Since your workstation will need to look somewhere to translate host names into IP address, you will need to put the DNS server IP addresses for your ISP into your connection settings. In NT 4 Workstation, clicking the DNS tab and adding new DNS servers to your system does this. If you don't know the IP addresses of your ISP's DNS servers, I would recommend contacting them to ask them directly or see if they list the appropriate settings somewhere on their Web site.

Once you have the correct DNS and TCP/IP settings programmed in, reboot your workstation and log back into the network. Once your computer is up and running, you should be able to allow access across your shared Internet connection for the protocols you defined on your server (DNS, Web, etc.). You should see your Windows 2000 Server automatically initiate the connection as needed whenever one of your client systems tries to access the Internet.

Accepting Virtual Private Networking Connections from Remote Clients

Virtual private networking is one of the hottest subjects in networking today. With the widespread presence of the Internet, it only makes sense that corporations and organizations would want to try to leverage existing investments in Internet connections for their corporate networks. But as exciting as virtual private networking can be, it can also be a rather complex subject. Since it is basically a means of layering one logical network over another, the complexities of making a network connection are, in effect, doubled.

VPN Overview

Loosely defined, a VPN allows you to run a secure, private network over an unsecured public network. You can use virtual private networking to get clients connected to your network over the Internet and do it securely, even though the Internet is inherently an unsecured network.

One of the better analogies I've found for explaining the concepts of a virtual private network is to refer to them as "pipes." To conceptualize VPNs, think of two pipes, one large and one small. Now, imagine that the small pipe actually runs *inside* of the large one. It starts and ends at the same places the large pipe does, and it can carry materials on its own, completely independent of whatever is happening in the large pipe. As a matter of fact, the only thing the small pipe is dependent on the large pipe for is the determination of the start and end points. Beyond that, the small pipe can operate independently of the large pipe in terms of direction of travel, materials it carries, etc.

To add another layer to this analogy, let's assume that the large pipe is made out of a transparent material, and the small pipe is made out of metal. If anyone were to take a look at the pipe-within-a-pipe, they would easily be able to see whatever was moving through the outside (large) pipe. However, whatever was traveling through the inside pipe would remain a mystery.

If this is starting to make sense, you should be thinking to yourself that the large pipe represents the unsecured network (i.e., the Internet) and the small pipe represents the virtual private network. VPN is a way of tunneling data packets through a connection that already exists but that can't be used on its own for privacy reasons. Obviously, the Internet is a perfect example of a network that often can't be used on its own for privacy reasons.

So, what benefit does this have for the overworked network administrator? Well, for starters, it could reduce or eliminate your need to maintain a pool of modems at your site for remote dial-in users. Remote users don't need to call directly into your network to get connected; they can simply call into a local ISP and get a valid Internet (unsecured) connection. Assuming you have a VPN/RAS server running on your network (and it's connected to the Internet), once the remote user has connected to their ISP, the client just has to establish the VPN (secured) session with the RAS server. The cost of maintaining modems and phone lines is removed and off-loaded to the ISP. As long as your RAS server is connected to the Internet, you can support multiple incoming calls all over that one connection. Also, in keeping with this example, since the VPN session is being established over the Internet, there is no need for any long distance calls. If your remote user is hundreds of miles away, the cost to connect to your network is the same as if they were local, since the only call they would need to make would be to their ISP. This is a great way to support a geographically dispersed user base.

Microsoft has gone a long way toward making virtual private networking easy to implement in Windows 2000. However, if there is one piece of advice I could give everyone trying to implement virtual private networking, it is this—get a good, solid RAS server working and accepting incoming connections *first*. Use standard connections (analog modems, ISDN, etc.) on your RAS server first to make sure everything is functioning correctly. Once you are sure RAS is working correctly for standard connections, only then is it advisable to try implementing VPN connections. Since virtual private networking adds another layer of functionality "on top of" RAS, it is crucial to have a stable foundation to begin with. RAS can be peculiar in its behavior at times, so it is important to have all your configurations working correctly (DHCP address assignment, browsing, etc.). If only I had a nickel for every time I heard someone say "this VPN thing is messed up," only to find out that if they dial into their network over a modem connection, they experience the exact same problems...

A Brief History of VPN: PPTP, L2F, and L2TP

When virtual private networking was first being developed back in the mid-1990s, two of the largest companies in the computer/networking industry tried to run with implementations of VPNs in the hopes that they would enjoy widespread implementation and therefore become an "industry standard." The two companies were Microsoft and Cisco, and each had their respective VPN technologies. Microsoft was approaching the VPN market from the operating systems point of view and had developed Point-to-Point Tunneling Protocol (PPTP) as a means to securely transmit data across unsecure networks. At the same time, Cisco was taking the lead in VPN from a strictly networking point of view with a protocol called Layer 2 Forwarding, or L2F.

Now, when either of these companies decides to develop an industry standard, they can usually get away with it if one doesn't already exist. No single standard had obtained a large enough share of the VPN market to be considered an industry standard, so the playing field was literally wide open. However, the sheer muscle and momentum that either one of these companies can put behind an initiative wasn't necessarily enough to displace the other. Each protocol had its strengths and weaknesses, and Microsoft and Cisco's offerings enjoyed moderate successes.

Now, I'm speculating a bit here, but I think that since neither industry giant was going to successfully displace the other in the VPN market, they decided it would be better to cooperate than compete. In any case, Microsoft and Cisco made the decision to collaborate on virtual private networking by merging their protocols, PPTP and L2F, into one hybrid protocol. The final product of that collaboration is Layer 2 Tunneling Protocol, or L2TP for short.

Windows 2000 Server includes L2TP support for establishing virtual private networking connections but also includes support for PPTP for backwards compatibility with other operating systems. At the time this book was being written, L2TP was only supported in Windows 2000 (Server and Professional) and *might* be available for Windows 98 sometime in the future. However, according to the white papers I've read recently, Microsoft isn't committing to L2TP support for Windows 98 just yet. Therefore, the only option today for supporting legacy clients (NT 4, Windows 9*x*) across a virtual private network is to include support for PPTP.

OK, enough said. Let's assume you've got a good solid RAS server running and get on to the fun stuff.

Implementing VPN via PPTP and L2TP

If you went through the section "Accepting Incoming Calls from Remote Users," congratulations—you have 80 percent of what you need to support VPN connections in place already. When you install Remote Access Service, Windows 2000 Server should have added support for five PPTP connections and five L2TP connections by default. If you didn't go through the section to accept incoming calls from remote users, stop reading now and go back to complete the steps listed there. For the remainder of this section, we'll assume you have a functional RAS server in place.

We'll start by verifying that support for PPTP and L2TP is in place through the Routing and Remote Access MMC. Start the RRAS MMC by selecting Start/Programs/Administrative Tools/Routing and Remote Access. In the left-hand portion of the MMC window, you should see the name of your RAS server listed; expand the information for that server by double-clicking it. Right-click the listing for ports, and then select Properties (shown in the following figure) to edit the ports. The ports property sheet should look similar to the one in Figure 22.44.

FIGURE 22.44

Ports Properties

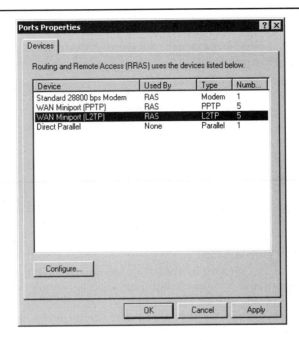

In the Ports Properties screen, you will see all the ports that Windows 2000 has recognized and can use for Remote Access Service. Each device has a usage listed, a device name, a type, and a number of ports associated with it. By default, RAS should have PPTP and L2TP devices installed on your system and probably has five ports associated with each.

Depending on which type of connections you will be allowing and how many you want to allow, you can edit your protocols and circuits accordingly from here. For example, if you are only going to have Windows 2000 clients connecting to your network over virtual circuits, you can stick with just supporting L2TP. However, if you need to support legacy clients accessing your network via virtual circuits, PPTP is your only choice. In any case, to edit the port properties for either type, double-click the item to edit or just highlight it and click the Configure button. This will take you into the port configuration screen shown in Figure 22.45 (the screen looks the same whether you are configuring PPTP, L2TP, or modem ports).

To configure your server to accept VPN connections, make sure the Remote Access (Inbound Only) option is checked in the Configure Ports dialog box. For the Phone Number of This Device field, enter the public Internet IP address of your server (assuming the Internet is the public, unsecured network you will be using). This is the IP address that clients will eventually connect to across the Internet for establishing VPN circuits.

FIGURE 22.45

*Configuring RAS ports
(PPTP shown)*

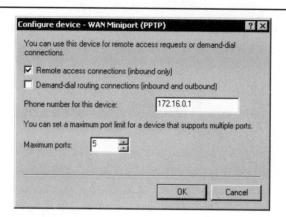

Depending on how many simultaneous virtual private networking connections you plan on supporting, adjust the Maximum Ports value accordingly and then click OK.

 TIP I strongly recommend that you use a fixed IP address and Internet connection for your server. Yes, you *can* use a dial-up connection from your RAS server to the Internet, and you can even make dynamic IP addresses work for this. But with dynamic IP addresses, your server's IP address will change every time it has to re-establish its link, quickly becoming a management nightmare.

Depending on how many simultaneous virtual private networking connections you plan on supporting, adjust the Maximum Ports value accordingly and then click OK.

 TIP I would recommend disabling any and all VPN connections that you *don't* plan on using. For example, if you are only going to support L2TP connections from Windows 2000 clients, disable PPTP by unchecking the Remote Access (Inbound Only) option on the property sheet for PPTP. This will prevent anyone from trying to establish a connection to your server via PPTP without your knowing about it.

Client Configuration

To get a client workstation connected to a Windows 2000 Server running VPN protocols, you will need to have one of the following:

- Windows NT 4, Workstation, or Server (PPTP only)
- Windows 95 with the Dial-Up Networking 1.2 upgrade or better (PPTP only)
- Windows 98 (PPTP only now; L2TP *might* be included later)
- Windows 2000 Professional (PPTP or L2TP)

Since older operating systems such as Windows 95 and Windows NT 4 don't install PPTP by default, the first thing to do is add PPTP support to the client system. PPTP is a standard protocol, just like NetBEUI or NWLink, so the procedures for adding this new protocol are roughly the same.

Windows NT 4 Workstation   Assuming you already have Dial-Up Networking set up and installed on your NT 4 Workstation, the first step to adding VPN support is to add the Point-to-Point Tunneling Protocol in the Control Panel/Network applet. Start by clicking Start/Settings/Control Panel/Network, and then click the Protocols tab. Clicking the Add button from the Protocols property page will bring you to the protocol properties dialog box, as shown in Figure 22.46.

FIGURE 22.46

Protocols property page in NT 4 Workstation

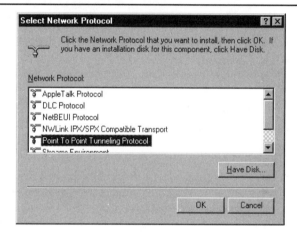

Once you have selected the Point-to-Point Tunneling Protocol and clicked OK, NT 4 Workstation will ask you how many simultaneous virtual circuits you'd like to support in the dialog box in Figure 22.47.

FIGURE 22.47

Configuring the number of virtual circuits to support

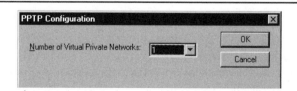

However many circuits you choose here will determine how many virtual ports Windows NT 4 will add to its configuration. Each virtual port will be called VPNx, with "x" referring to the specific port number. In effect, they function similarly to modems running on COM ports (COMx), so think of these VPN devices as virtual modems. If you will only be connecting to one virtual private network at a time, choose 1 and click OK.

Once you have completed selecting the number of virtual circuits to support, NT 4 Workstation will invoke RAS setup to allow you to add your new virtual modem(s) to the RAS configuration, as shown in Figure 22.48.

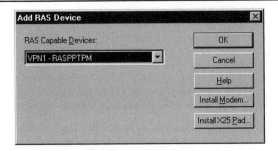

Click the Add button in Remote Access Setup and you should see your VPN device in the Add RAS Device window. If you see a modem or some other device there, try pulling down the list and then selecting your VPN device. Once you have your VPN device selected, click OK and it will be added to your RAS configuration.

Once you are back to the Remote Access Setup screen, highlight your VPN device and click the Configure button. This device should be configured for Dial-Out Only as shown in Figure 22.49.

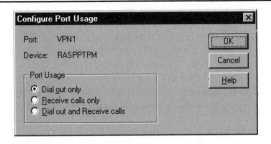

Once everything is set correctly, click OK and RAS will start the installation routine. This will most likely require a reboot of your computer, so go ahead and restart it and get back into Windows. To use your VPN device, the last step you need to perform is creating a Dial-Up Networking entry.

Double-click My Computer and then Dial-Up Networking to begin creating a new Dial-Up Networking entry. Creating a VPN Dial-Up Networking entry is almost identical to creating a regular Dial-Up Networking entry for a phone line, except that you will use an IP address instead of a phone number to dial and the VPNx device instead of a modem. This is shown in Figure 22.50.

FIGURE 22.50

FIGURE 22.50

Creating a VPN Dial-
Up Networking entry
in Windows NT 4
Workstation

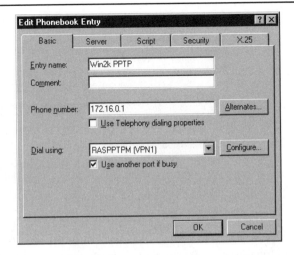

As you can see, this Dial-Up Networking entry will call a VPN server at IP address 172.16.0.1, the same IP address used in the configuration of the RAS/VPN server earlier in this chapter. As long as the VPN device is selected in the Dial Using pull-down box, everything should be set for this connection.

The first step to actually making this connection is to make sure you have an actual, valid Internet IP address before doing so. If you need to use Dial-Up Networking to connect to an ISP for this, do that first. Once you have a valid IP address available, launch your VPN Dial-Up Networking Connection to get connected to your remote system. Once you provide a set of valid user credentials, you should end up getting connected at 10,000,000 baud (10 megabits, equivalent to the speed of a 10Base-T network).

Windows 9x   Windows 9x takes a unique approach to implementing virtual private networking through the use of a Microsoft VPN adapter. Instead of adding support for PPTP or other protocols (like in other Microsoft operating systems), all you need to do is add the VPN adapter to your system to get connected.

NOTE   To add VPN support for Windows 95, you must have the Dial-Up Networking upgrade v1.2 or later installed on your system. VPN support is included in Windows 98 right out of the box.

Start by editing the network properties of Windows 9x by selecting Start/Settings/Control Panel/Network. When the network property sheet comes up, click the Add button, and then select Adapter as the component type you'd like to install. Your screen should look like Figure 22.51.

FIGURE 22.51

*Adding the Microsoft
VPN Adapter to
Windows 9x*

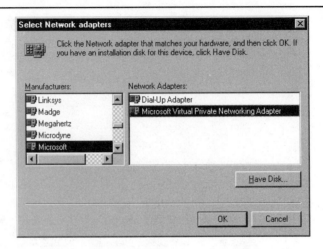

In the list of adapters supplied, scroll down to Microsoft for the manufacturer, then select the Microsoft Virtual Private Networking Adapter listed on the right-hand side of the screen. Click OK and Windows 9x will add the VPN adapter to its system. Of course, this will require a reboot for the changes to take effect.

Once your system has rebooted, the next step to getting connected is creating a Dial-Up Networking entry to connect to your VPN server. From the Windows 9x desktop, double-click My Computer, then Dial-Up Networking, and then Make New Connection to launch the Make New Connection wizard, shown in Figure 22.52.

FIGURE 22.52

*Windows 9x Make
New Connection
wizard*

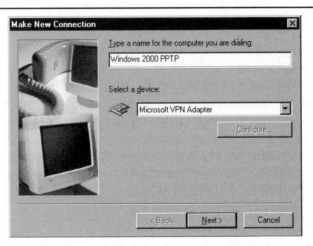

From the Select a Device pull-down box, choose the Microsoft VPN Adapter if it isn't already selected. Click Next to move to the next step of the wizard shown in Figure 22.53.

FIGURE 22.53

Entering the IP address
of a VPN server in
Windows 9x

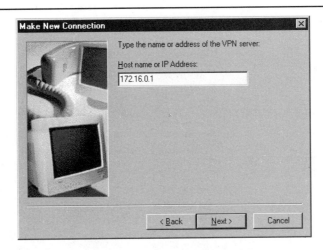

Enter the IP address or DNS name of your VPN server in the box as needed. In the example in Figure 22.53, we have used an IP address of 172.16.0.1, the same IP address used in the configuration of the RAS/VPN server earlier in this chapter. After entering the hostname or address, clicking on Next will complete the wizard and place a VPN Dial-Up Networking entry on your system.

To make the VPN connection, you must make sure you have an actual, valid Internet IP address before doing so. If you need to use Dial-Up Networking to connect to an ISP for this, do that first. Once you have a valid IP address available, launch your VPN Dial-Up Networking Connection to get connected to your remote system. Once you provide a set of valid user credentials, you should end up getting connected at 10,000,000 baud (10 megabits, equivalent to the speed of a 10Base-T network).

Windows 2000   Windows 2000 adds a few nice features to the client side of establishing VPN connections, namely the ability to automatically associate one DUN entry with another. For example, if you need to dial an ISP before you can connect with your virtual private network, Windows 2000 can join these two functions. The end result is that when you (or your users) need to connect to the virtual private network, doing so only requires launching one Dial-Up Networking session.

Like most of the remote access functionality in Windows 2000, to define a VPN connection, you will begin with Start/Settings/Network and Dial-Up Connections, and then the Make New Connection wizard. From the first screen of the wizard, select the option to Connect to a Private Network through the Internet as shown in Figure 22.54.

FIGURE 22.54

Creating a VPN
connection on
Windows 2000

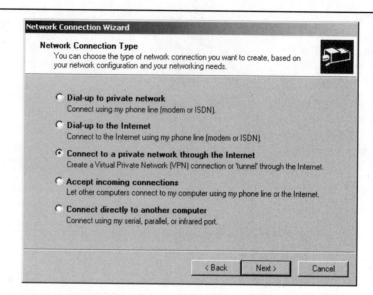

Click Next to continue, and Windows 2000 will then ask if you need to establish a public network (Internet) connection first before establishing the virtual private networking connection, as shown in Figure 22.55.

FIGURE 22.55

Creating a public connection before a VPN connection

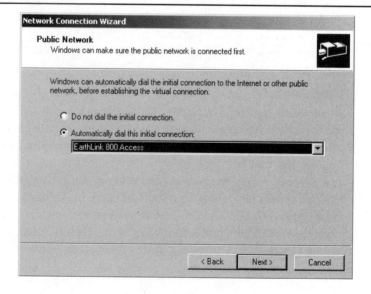

If the Windows 2000 device you will be connecting already has a valid, public Internet IP address, answer Do Not Dial the Initial Connection to this question. Otherwise, if you need to obtain an IP address first from an ISP, select Automatically Dial This Initial Connection and choose the connection that will get you connected to the Internet. Doing so will cause your VPN Dial-Up Networking connection to initiate an ISP connection first. Click Next to continue on to entering the IP address or host name of the target server, as shown in Figure 22.56.

FIGURE 22.56

Entering the IP address of the VPN server

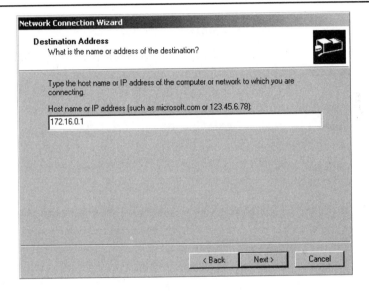

Much like many of the other client platforms we've already discussed, you will need to enter the IP address of your target system or a DNS-resolvable host name. As you can see, this Dial-Up Networking entry will call a VPN server at IP address 172.16.0.1, the same IP address used in the configuration of the RAS/VPN server earlier in this chapter. Click Next to continue, and the final step of the wizard will ask you whether you want to make this VPN connection available to all users or just yourself. For the purposes of this section, we'll assume that you just want to use the VPN connection for yourself, so click the Only for Myself radio button and click Next to finish creating the Dial-Up Networking entry.

When it comes time to actually establish this connection, if you selected the option to have Windows 2000 dial an initial connection, you will see a dialog box like the one in Figure 22.57 asking you if the public network connection should be initiated first.

FIGURE 22.57

Windows 2000 asking
if an initial public
network connection
should be
established first

VPN Performance Considerations

Our section on virtual private networking wouldn't be complete without taking a bit of time to discuss performance issues to consider. Although virtual private networking is a neat technology, unfortunately there are some times when it just might not make sense to use it. Careful planning and consideration should help you determine if it is a solution that can add value to your organization.

In the right set of circumstances, virtual private networking can provide fast, reliable, and secure connections to remote networks across the Internet (or another unsecured network). However, in the wrong set of circumstances, virtual private networking can make an already slow dial-up connection seem even slower.

So what are the right circumstances? In my professional opinion, the right circumstances are when you have high-speed connectivity on your RAS server at the very least and preferably when you have high-speed connectivity on both your RAS server and your DUN client. On occasions when I have been able to implement VPN circuits at locations with a T1 or better available at both the server and client ends, performance has been wonderful and the connections reliable. However, due to the protocol overhead involved with PPTP and L2TP and the inherent latency of the Internet, if you are planning on implementing a VPN with dial-up modems on each side of your connection, I would urge you to think twice.

"But wait," you might be thinking, "I want to implement a VPN to reduce costs, not increase them." Well, I wish I could say that Microsoft's VPN implementations were going to give you the performance you might expect over modem connections, but they just won't. Simply due to the additional complexities of encrypting the data, bundling the payload data inside a TCP/IP packet, and the latency of communications across the Internet, you can expect a decrease in your performance ranging anywhere from 10 to 50 percent. Now, without getting into all the technical details, it is worthwhile to note that this isn't entirely Microsoft's fault; after all, they can't be blamed for the fact that the Internet can be inherently slow at times (or can they?). However, even with the worst-case scenario of a 50 percent reduction in performance, if there is a T1 on each side of the virtual private network, the effective speeds of the network are still roughly in the 760kbps range. However, if you're using a 56k modem on each side of the virtual private network, which probably won't connect much faster than 48kbps, you can easily see how a 50 percent performance penalty can make a connection go from "slow" to "unusable."

Simply put, if you are using a modem on your RAS server and a modem on your DUN client, you will get your best possible speeds by having one dial directly into the other. By doing so, there is no protocol overhead getting in the way, nor is there the need for your data to travel across dozens of routers as it works its way to its destination. By creating a direct connection, data packets go directly from the DUN client to the target network.

However, everything in life is a trade-off, and it will be up to you to decide if this will work adequately enough for your needs. After all, what is adequate to one person might be great to another and unacceptable to yet another. In either case, expect a performance penalty when implementing virtual private networking and plan your bandwidth accordingly.

Dialing Up a Remote Network and Routing Traffic

With the release of the Routing and Remote Access Service update to Windows NT 4 Server, Microsoft was able to improve on the routing capabilities that already existed in Windows NT. Although Windows NT 4 shipped with routing capabilities right out of the box, they were limited and cumbersome, to say the least.

Now Microsoft has included all the capabilities of the Routing and Remote Access Service update in Windows 2000 Server, making this operating system a platform capable of solving a number of common routing scenarios right out of the box. When you need to get data from one location to another, Windows 2000 Server might be an adequate solution for your needs.

Let's take an example of routing traffic from a central office to a remote office over an analog connection. Many organizations are often faced with a connectivity dilemma when opening remote offices, especially if there are only a small number of computers at the remote site. Installing dedicated links between locations can be cost-prohibitive depending on the number of people at the remote site, but having a group of individuals completely isolated from the organizational network usually isn't an acceptable alternative either. Windows 2000 Server is a perfect solution for this scenario, as it can establish demand-dialed links between locations whenever traffic needs to pass from one site to another. By using simple modems and ordinary phone lines, Windows 2000 can be a low-cost alternative to installing dedicated WAN links. To get started, let's walk through the details of a sample scenario.

Sample Network

Our sample network consists of the following:

- Number of sites: Two—Virginia and Delaware
- TCP/IP subnet for Virginia: 10.16.0.*x* with a subnet mask of 255.255.255.0
- TCP/IP subnet for Delaware: 172.16.0.*x* with a subnet mask of 255.255.255.0
- Windows 2000 RRAS Server in Virginia: ARCHITECT4 with an IP address of 10.16.0.4
- Windows 2000 RRAS Server in Delaware: ARCHITECT-WIN2K with an IP address of 172.16.0.1
- Phone number for analog line connected to Virginia Windows 2000 RRAS Server: (703) 555-9779
- Phone number for analog line connected to Delaware Windows 2000 RRAS Server: (302) 555-0386
- User account created in the Virginia Active Directory and granted dial-in permissions: DELAWARE-ROUTER, password: delaware
- User account created in the Delaware Active Directory and granted dial-in permissions: VIRGINIA-ROUTER, password: virginia

In effect, our network looks similar to the diagram shown in Figure 22.58.

FIGURE 22.58

Diagram of sample network

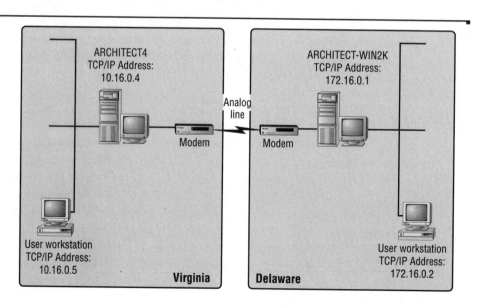

Setting Up the First Server

To start building a demand-dialed analog connection between these two locations, you will need to have your Windows 2000 Server able to function as a router. If you've worked through any of the configurations previously discussed in this chapter, your system is probably configured to simply act as a Remote Access Server. Changing roles for the server is as simple as editing the properties for the Remote Access Service.

 NOTE For the purposes of walking through the first server configuration, I will be configuring the necessary components on our Delaware router first, using the details defined above.

To change roles for your server, open up the Routing and Remote Access MMC by selecting Start/Programs/Administrative Tools/Routing and Remote Access. Edit the properties for Remote Access Service on your server by right-clicking your server name and then selecting Properties. You should see a dialog box similar to the one pictured in Figure 22.59.

FIGURE 22.59

Editing RAS server properties to add routing capabilities

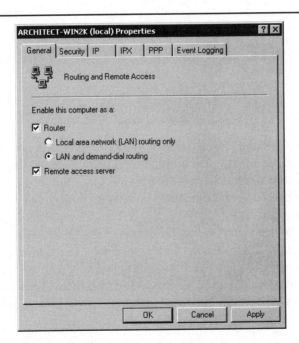

To add routing services to your system, check the box labeled Router and then select one of the two radio buttons below that option. If you will only be using LAN-based interfaces (Ethernet adapters, etc.) as your routing devices on your system, you can leave the Local Area Network (LAN) Routing Only option selected. However, if you intend to use dial-up connections (as we will in this example), demand-dialed links, or VPN connections, select the LAN and Demand-Dial Routing option. Click OK to apply the changes, and Windows 2000 Server should stop and restart the Routing and Remote Access Service to implement the changes.

When you return to the Routing and Remote Access MMC, the next step will be to enable routing support for one of the ports on your system. In the Routing and Remote Access MMC, right-click the option for Ports and select Properties to get to the Ports Properties sheet. Once you have the Ports Properties sheet available, double-click the device you intend to use as your demand-dialed connection (if the device you want to use isn't listed, go back to the section on adding RAS devices earlier in this chapter). The configuration page for that device should look similar to the dialog box in Figure 22.60.

FIGURE 22.60

Editing properties for the demand-dialed port

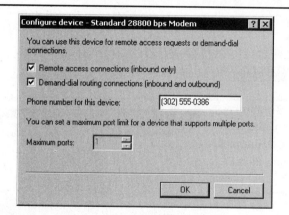

Configure this device by checking the Demand-Dial Routing Connections option and clicking OK. If you would eventually like to use Bandwidth Allocation Protocol with this configuration—to increase bandwidth by adding mode dial-up connections as needed—enter the phone number for your connection and click OK to accept the changes.

When you return to the Routing and Remote Access MMC, you might have noticed a new item for Routing Interfaces in the results pane of the window when you look at your Windows 2000 Server, as shown in Figure 22.61. This option was added when routing services were added to the server, and it is where you will begin to add your demand-dialed interface.

FIGURE 22.61

Adding a demand-
dialed interface to the
RRAS MMC via Routing
Interfaces

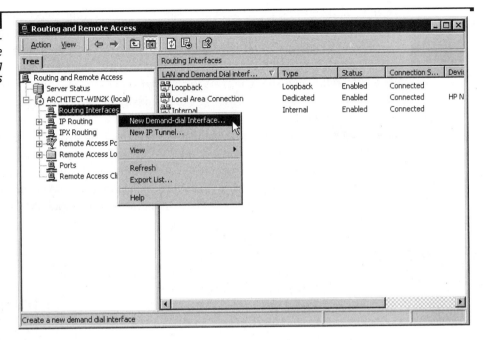

FIGURE 22.61

Adding a demand-dialed interface to the RRAS MMC via Routing Interfaces

To start creating a demand-dialed interface, right-click the Routing Interfaces selection, and then choose the option to add a new demand-dial interface. This will launch the Demand Dial Interface Wizard, which will walk you through steps to create your demand-dialed interface. The first step of the wizard is shown in Figure 22.62.

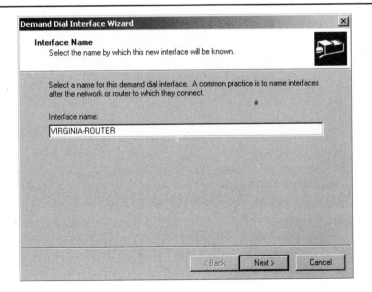

FIGURE 22.62

Defining a name for a demand-dialed interface

In most cases of assigning a friendly name to a RAS or other type of connection, any name will do. However, in creating demand-dialed routing connections, the name assigned to a demand-dialed interface is important. The name assigned to a demand-dialed connection *must* match the name of the user account entered into the Active Directory at the *same* site. The same must be true on both sides of the wide area network. To quote Microsoft directly: "The username in the authentication credentials sent by the calling router must exactly match the name of a demand-dial interface on the answering router." If the username does not match a demand-dial interface name, the answering router will assume that the incoming call is a RAS *user*, not a remote router. Therefore, whatever name is entered here must also be used as a username on the same system's Active Directory. Since we're walking through setting up our Delaware remote office in our example, I've decided to call this interface VIRGINIA-ROUTER. When you have entered the appropriate name, click Next to continue to the next stage of the wizard, shown in Figure 22.63.

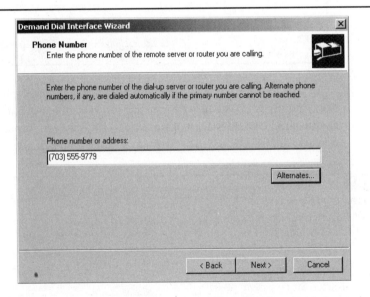

The next step of the wizard should be relatively self-explanatory. The wizard needs to know what phone number Windows 2000 Server should dial when it is attempting to establish the demand-dialed interface. Enter the number exactly as your system should dial it, including any prefixes, area codes, etc. If you have a list of alternate numbers that Windows 2000 Server can use to establish this demand-dialed connection, click the Alternates button and enter the information there. When you click next to move to the next step in the Demand Dial Wizard, you should see a dialog box similar to the one pictured in Figure 22.64.

FIGURE 22.64

Selecting protocols to
route, credentials to
use, and connection
options for a demand-
dialed interface

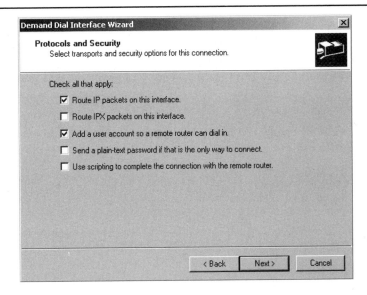

Depending on the network you are connecting to, here you can select which protocols Windows 2000 Server should route. In addition to selecting the appropriate
protocols for the remote network, you can also choose to have Windows 2000 create a
user account so that the remote network's router can dial into your system. Lastly,
you can choose custom connection options such as sending a plain-text password if
that is the only way the remote router will let you connect, or any advanced scripting
options you might need. Depending on the options you select from this screen, the
remainder of the Demand Dial Wizard will vary, but for the purposes of our example
we'll assume you've selected IP and decided to create a user account for a remote
router as seen in this figure. Click Next to continue to the next step of the wizard,
shown in Figure 22.65.

As previously stated, the friendly or descriptive name you use for a demand-dialed
connection needs to be the same as the credentials for that connection, otherwise the
answering router will assume the incoming caller is simply a RAS connection, not a
router. Since we are defining a demand-dialed interface to call into the VIRGINIA-
ROUTER device, if that device were to call the Delaware system we're configuring, it
would identify itself as VIRGINIA-ROUTER. Therefore, the username field is grayed
out by default, preventing you from changing it. This is an important point, because
if you decide to change the user accounts used by RRAS at a later date, but don't
change the interface names accordingly, you could end up with a broken routing system. Enter a password for this account to use, and make a note of it. Click Next to
continue to the next screen in the wizard, as seen in Figure 22.66.

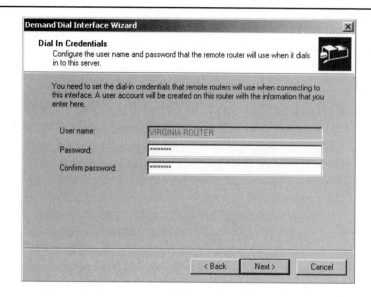

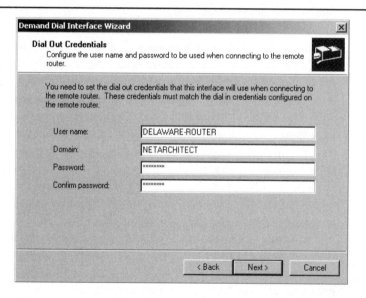

As the last step of the wizard in our sample scenario, you will need to define the user credentials your Windows 2000 Server will use when calling into a remote network. The username used here must match the name of a demand-dialed interface on the remote system exactly or else the remote system will simply assume your Windows 2000 Server is a standard RAS user. Enter the appropriate domain, username, and password combination for your configuration and then click Next to complete the wizard.

Although the wizard has completed, there is still one step remaining on your first system: defining a static route entry for the remote IP network. In effect, you will need to tell your Windows 2000 Server "whenever you need to contact these IP addresses, use this demand-dialed interface to get there." By entering a static routing entry for the remote network's IP address range and then defining the demand-dialed interface as the connection to use, Windows 2000 will know to route any packets for that network by dialing into the remote router.

To add a static route, select the IP Routing option in the left-hand pane of the Routing and Remote Access MMC. It is an option listed under your server, so you might need to expand the view of your system. Expand the IP Routing selection by clicking the plus sign next to it, and then right-click the Static Routes option. Highlighting Static Routes and then selecting the Action pull-down menu should make a New Static Route option appear. Select this option and you should end up with a dialog box similar to the one in Figure 22.67.

FIGURE 22.67

Defining a static route to a remote network

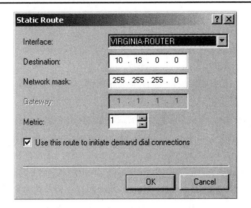

Here you can define the necessary parameters for the remote network, starting with the interface Windows 2000 Server should use to get the packets to their destination. For the purposes of demand-dialed routing, you should make sure you have your demand-dialed interface listed in the interface section. Next, define the IP network address range by entering a destination network address and network mask in the field. Windows 2000 Server will use this information to determine if packets—when it receives them—match the IP address range of the remote network. If the packets match the range defined, Windows 2000 will route them. Lastly, you can leave the metric at 1, and make sure the Use This Route to Initiate Demand Dial Connections option is selected. Once you have all this information entered, click OK and you should see your static route appear in the results pane of the Routing and Remote Access MMC.

At this point, you have completed exactly half the work required to have your systems routing data over analog links. The other half of the job is to go through the exact same steps on the other system by configuring a demand-dial interface in the same manner just described.

Once you have both systems configured correctly, you should be able to test your connection to see if it works by doing a Ping from one system to another.

 NOTE For more information about Ping, see Chapter 17, "Understanding and Using TCP/IP in Windows 2000 Server."

Start at one of your Windows 2000 Servers configured with a demand-dialed interface, go to a command prompt, and ping one of the IP addresses on the distant network. You should see your demand-dialed connection come online and start passing traffic. However, it is important to realize that for the type of communication you are attempting, your call setup times might take too long. For example, the Ping command typically sends four ICMP echo requests, and then waits 1.5 seconds after each one for a response. All total, a test of four Pings should take no longer than six seconds. However, if you are using analog connections, your call setup times are most likely going to be in the range of 20–30 seconds. Therefore, your connection won't come online in time to satisfy the request. For testing purposes, I would recommend using an indefinite Ping by using the –t option on the command line, such as ping –t 172.16.0.1.

To solve problems like these and others, there are some fine-tuning controls you can use for your demand-dialed connection. For example, if you are using analog lines to connect sites and the analog lines aren't billed per-minute, it might make sense to have your demand-dialed connection online all the time. This is called making a "persistent" connection. From the Routing and Remote Access MMC, click the selection for Routing Interfaces in the left-hand pane of the window. In the results pane, you should see your demand-dialed interface listed. Right-click the demand-dialed interface and select Properties to edit the property sheet for this connection. You should see a four-tabbed dialog box similar to the one in Figure 22.68 (shown with the Options tab selected).

There are a number of settings you can control through this dialog box, but some of the most useful are listed under the Options tab shown in Figure 22.68. For example, if you are using an ISDN connection to reach your distant network and your ISDN is billed per minute, you can enter an idle timeout value in the Connection Type area of the window so your connections don't stay on any longer than necessary. Or, if the opposite is true, and you aren't billed per minute for your connections, you can select the persistent connection option to have the link stay online all the time. If for some reason the link fails, Windows 2000 Server will bring it right back online again. Set the options you would like to use, and then click OK to accept them.

FIGURE 22.68

Editing router interface properties

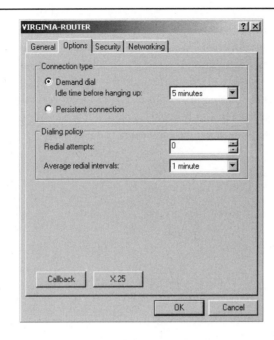

When you right-click the demand-dial routing interface in the Routing and Remote Access MMC, there are also some other options you could set in addition to editing the properties of the item itself. One of the more useful items is setting the hours in which this connection can be established. If you would like to restrict the times when your demand-dialed connections can be brought online, select the Dialing Hours option when you right-click the routing interface. You should end up with an hourly grid dialog box like the one pictured in Figure 22.69 in which you can select the hours to allow and disallow connections.

FIGURE 22.69

Defining dialing hours for demand-dialed connections

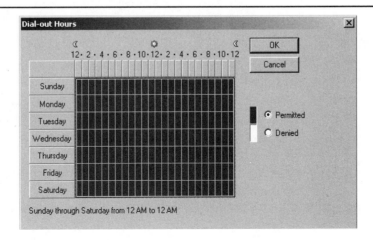

Once you have completed everything, you should have a functional wide area network running between locations and passing data as necessary. Through the use of this functionality, I have seen organizations that have set up completely "virtual" wide area networks consisting of multiple sites that all look as if they're operating as one large network, but in reality they are each small sites connected to a master network over analog links. Although Windows 2000 isn't designed to displace high-end routers in complex routing scenarios, it is a good solution for a lot of networking problems—some of which you may face.

APPENDIX

Performance Objects in Windows 2000

Win2K supports the performance objects described briefly in the following table. (I haven't included every counter in all cases, but by referring to this table you should be able to find the performance object you need to monitor the information you want.) Because the performance objects are related to the services you're running on a server and the protocols in use, your servers may include some performance counters not shown here or may not include all the objects in this list. This is a reasonably representative sample, taken from a Win2K server running IIS and Terminal Services, having Network Monitor installed, and using TCP/IP and NetBEUI to communicate with the network. Whatever services and protocols you have installed on a server, you'll always see the objects related to disk, memory, processor, and network usage (with the exception of the Network Usage object, which will only appear if you've installed the Network Monitor). I've included a little extra background for process objects relating to functions new to Win2K or that may be unfamiliar to you. For more information on unfamiliar services or features, check the index and read in more detail elsewhere in the book.

PERFORMANCE OBJECTS IN WINDOWS 2000		
Object	**Description**	**More Information**
ACS/RSVP Services	The ACS counters record how much network bandwidth the service is using, counting network sockets, API sockets, and the size of API notifications. The Reservation Services Virtual Protocol (RSVP) enables multimedia applications to get the amount of network space they need, based on administrator-defined policies and the amount of bandwidth available. RSVP-specific counters include timers relating to how much bandwidth an application has, the number of interfaces RSVP is aware of, and the number of message buffers it has.	Admission Control Service (ACS) allows network administrators to control the amount of network bandwidth allocated to a specific application, such as streaming video.

Continued ▶

PERFORMANCE OBJECTS IN WINDOWS 2000 CONTINUED

Object	Description	More Information
Active Server Pages	Monitors errors, status of client requests, the number of pending client requests, the number and duration of client sessions with the Web server, the amount of time the cache is hit (showing how efficient the Web server is in reusing data to service client requests), and the status of all ASP transactions.	Records information relating to client requests for Active Server pages from a Web server.
Browser	Counters include the rate at which servers in the domain announce themselves to the network, the number of election packets received by the server, and the number of browse requests the server has satisfied.	Records browser activity on the network.
Cache	Records cache activity, including the number of times data can be read from the system cache without having to page it back into memory, the amount of cached information flushed (written) to disk, and the asynchronous reads that write a copy of the requested data to an applications buffer.	The disk cache is the part of RAM that's reserved for file-related data, including both recently used files and the header information that points the file system driver to their location on the disk.
Distributed Transaction Coordinator	The DTC counters record the status of these transactions, including the response time required, the number of committed transactions, the number of transactions aborted by the DTC or by the network administrator, and the number of transactions MTS performs per second.	The Distributed Transaction Coordinator (DTC) is the transaction processing component of the Microsoft Transaction Server (MTS). DTC makes sure that all MTS transactions are executed only if all systems involved in the transaction carry it out.

Continued ▮▶

PERFORMANCE OBJECTS IN WINDOWS 2000 CONTINUED

Object	Description	More Information
FTP Service	Records the number of FTP clients, the number of current connections, bytes sent and received from the FTP server, files sent and received, the maximum number of connections during a session, total logon attempts (successful and unsuccessful), and other information related to providing FTP services.	The File Transfer Protocol is used for file exchange over a TCP/IP network.
IAS Accounting Clients	Monitors information relating to accounting packets sent and received by clients, including the rate at which packets are sent and received, how many are dropped or malformed, and the total number of processed packets.	The Internet Authentication Service (IAS) provides a central point for authenticating, authorizing, accounting, and auditing dialup or virtual private network (VPN) users connecting to RADIUS-compatible remote access servers.
IAS Accounting Server	Records information relating to IAS accounting packets sent and received by servers, including the rate at which packets are sent and received, how many are dropped or malformed, and the total number of processed packets.	
IAS Authentication Clients	Records information relating to IAS authentication packets received by clients, including the rate at which packets are sent and received, how many are dropped or malformed, and the total number of processed packets.	

Continued

PERFORMANCE OBJECTS IN WINDOWS 2000 CONTINUED

Object	Description	More Information
IAS Authentication Server	Records information relating to IAS authentication packets received by servers, including the rate at which packets are sent and received, how many are dropped or malformed, and the total number of processed packets.	
ICMP	The ICMP counters record the number of diagnostic messages that the server has received. This object also includes ICMP packets with errors (received and refused).	The Internet Connection Management Protocol (ICMP) is part of the TCP/IP suite of networking protocols. It's used for maintaining route tables and reporting transmission problems (the ping command uses the ICMP protocol). Most of the time you won't need to monitor any counters associated with this object unless you're trying to detect an excessive level of ping requests slowing down the server.
IMDB Service	The IMDB counters record the percentage of the cache currently in use, the number of tables and groups in the cache, and the current number of client connections to the cache.	The In-Memory Database (IMDB) provides database applications fast access to data. It does this by keeping the data in RAM instead of making the application wait for the file system to retrieve data from disk. This is like the file cache but for database information only.
Internet Information Services Global	Records activity related to serving Internet (WWW and FTP) client requests. Counters for this object record the caching and retrieval of binary large objects (BLOBs) used for handling the large strings of data associated with video and image files, and also of file handles and URLs.	This counter applies to *all* Internet-related requests, not just FTP or HTTP.

Continued ▶

PERFORMANCE OBJECTS IN WINDOWS 2000 CONTINUED

Object	Description	More Information
IP	The IP counters record events associated with the sending and receiving of IP datagrams, including the rate at which they're sent, received, and processed; the discard rate for outbound and inbound packets; and the discard rate. These counters also include fragmentation rates (necessary when a large packet goes onto a network that can't handle packets that big).	The Internet Protocol addresses and routes packets between hosts, using unacknowledged packets called *datagrams*. Monitoring IP traffic tells you how much data is going in and out of the network and whether it's being successfully transmitted.
Job Object	The counters associated with job objects are very similar to the ones associated with processes, monitoring total CPU time used by the job absolutely or within a specified period, the time spent in user time and kernel time, and the page fault rate for all processes in the job. The object also includes counters describing how many processes are or have been associated with a job object.	Until some new applications are written, you don't really have to worry about monitoring job objects. A job object is a nameable, securable, shareable object that controls certain attributes of the processes associated with it. Such attributes include the default working set allowed by each process within the job, its total CPU time limit, the per-process CPU time limit, the maximum number of processes associated with the job object, the priority class for the processes, and the processor affinity, if any (that's the preferred processor to use in a multi-processor computer). The main function of a job is to allow Win2K to deal with certain processes as groups, rather than separately. Most processes will not be associated with job objects, as this functionality is new to Win2K and currently few applications are written to support them.

Continued ▶

PERFORMANCE OBJECTS IN WINDOWS 2000 CONTINUED

Object	Description	More Information
Job Object Details	The counters work the same way as the Process Details counters except on a per-job basis.	
Memory	These counters include values for the number of page faults, data read from and written to the paging file, the amount of memory that can be committed (promised to a process, but not yet used) without extending the paging file, the amount of system code currently in physical memory, and any other data that Win2K maintains to help you keep tabs on memory usage.	The Memory object contains many performance counters related to the way Win2K uses physical and virtual memory for user and system processes.
NBT Connection	Counts the total number of bytes sent via NBT connection to another computer or all computers, the number of bytes received, or both.	NetBIOS over TCP/IP (NBT) resolves IP addresses for NetBIOS applications. (Note that this is different from DNS or WINS name resolution—this applies to NetBIOS applications on a TCP/IP network only.)
Network Interface	This object records performance counters applying to the physical network card in the computer (or to the loopback connection, if you prefer). Records bytes and packets received and set, current bandwidth available, and the number of errors experienced.	The Network interface is the physical network card.
Network Segment	Counters for this object can monitor the types of traffic on the segment (multicast or broadcast), display how much of the local network bandwidth is available, and show the total bytes and frames received on the segment each second.	Monitors traffic on the local network segment if you have SMS's Network Monitor installed.

Continued ▶

PERFORMANCE OBJECTS IN WINDOWS 2000 CONTINUED

Object	Description	More Information
Objects	Records the number of each type of Win2K object (processes, threads, events, mutexes, sections, semaphores) currently on the server.	Objects are Win2K's representation of system resources or computer parts. Processes represent (roughly) executable programs, threads are the executable parts of processes, sections are areas of memory that processes use for storing data, semaphores are devices threads use to gain exclusive access to data they share with other threads, and mutexes make sure that only one thread is executing a given section of code. Sections may be shared among processes, so you may have fewer sections than processes.
Paging File	Records the current or peak usage of the paging file (or of each paging file, if you have more than one).	The paging file is the area on logical hard disks where data being used is stored when RAM is too full to hold all current data.
Physical Disk	These counters can monitor the percentage of time a disk spends reading or writing data, the average size of a data transfer, the average size of the queues of data waiting to be processed, and the rate at which the disk processes read and write requests.	Records data reads and writes to each physical disk on the server. The logical disks located on each physical disk are identified, so you can tell which disk you want to monitor.
Process	These counters include data transfer required, the percentage of time a process spends executing in kernel or user mode, the amount of time the process has been running, memory use by the process, the number of threads in a given process, and the process's priority.	Monitors the resource usage by a single process running on the server or all processes. The ratio of processes to executable programs is roughly 1:1, and processes exist for all the parts of the operating system.

Continued ▶

PERFORMANCE OBJECTS IN WINDOWS 2000 CONTINUED

Object	Description	More Information
Processor	Monitors the percentage of time the CPU spends doing various tasks, such as handling interrupts or running user programs. Also monitors the rate at which the CPU does these tasks, measured as so many tasks per second.	The processor is the final authority in handling all processes within the computer. Monitor processor activity to make sure your CPU can keep up with the demands placed on it.
Redirector	Redirector performance counters can record the rate at which bytes/packets are sent and received on the network, the number of connections the server has to various redirector types, the number of commands currently queued for processing, and the number of network errors generated each second.	The redirector is the part of the operating system that sends client requests to the network if required and accepts incoming requests for processing.
Server	Records the status of client sessions with the server, including how many sessions there are, the rate of logons, and how many have ended due to timeouts or other errors. Server performance counters can also monitor the amount of virtual and physical memory the server is using and the rate at which the server is sending and receiving bytes.	
Server Work Queues	The server work queue describes the amount of work that's waiting for the server to get to it. Counters can record the active and available threads and the rate at which the server is transmitting bytes of data or performing read and write operations.	

Continued ❚▶

PERFORMANCE OBJECTS IN WINDOWS 2000 CONTINUED

Object	Description	More Information
SMTP Server	Records information related to mail-handling operations, including the number of connections, the number of tries it takes to successfully send a message, the total number of bytes received over time, the number of undeliverable messages generated (according to the reasons they were undeliverable), successful and unsuccessful directory service lookups, the rate and number of DNS lookups, and the rate at which the SMTP server is sending and receiving messages and other data.	The Simple Mail Transfer Protocol (SMTP) is used for transferring mail over a TCP/IP network. Any data in this object is mail-related.
System	Records information related to the size of the Registry relative to its quota, the rate at which data is passed to the file system, the rate at which the file system handles this data, the current number of processes active on the system, the number of threads waiting for processor time, and the number of seconds since the last reboot (which makes me wonder how optimistic Microsoft is about Win2K's stability, if they're counting in seconds).	The System performance object is a server-wide look at how the components of the server are doing their jobs.
TCP	Records data relating to TCP connection status and the rate at which segments (TCP packets) are sent and received.	TCP is the protocol working with IP to make sure data gets where it's supposed to go. For speed reasons, IP doesn't make explicit connections or check to see whether data got through as planned.

Continued ▶

PERFORMANCE OBJECTS IN WINDOWS 2000 CONTINUED

Object	Description	More Information
Telephony	Records data relating to telephone calls serviced by the computer, including the number of existing and used lines, the rate of incoming and outgoing calls, and the number of telephone devices connected to the server.	
Terminal Services	This number will include the console and the two connections created by default for the first two users, even if no one is currently connected to them.	Records the number of active and inactive (disconnected) terminal sessions.
Terminal Services Session	Records performance data for the selected terminal session, including memory usage, cache hits, thread counts, compression data related to the display protocol, transmission errors, and the percentage of time the CPU spends processing user and kernel data for that session.	Monitor these counters to see which sessions are taking up the most resources. You might use the data you collect from these counters to identify demanding users and make them use a special terminal server so they don't impact other users.
Thread	Records thread-related information for all threads running on the system or a selected one. Counters can display the amount of time a thread has been running, its priority, the virtual addresses it's referencing, the percentage of time it's spending executing in kernel or user mode, and its state (waiting, running, ready, terminated, etc.).	Threads are the executable parts of a process, and the parts that actually get scheduled CPU time.
UDP	These counters record the rate at which UDP datagrams are sent or received by the server.	UDP is a transport-layer connectionless protocol used for very small messages and with broadcast capabilities. You will probably never need to monitor this object—user data's sent with IP, not UDP, and ping use ICMP packets.

INDEX

Note to the Reader: Page numbers in **bold** indicate the principal discussion of a topic or the definition of a term. Page numbers in *italic* indicate illustrations.

G

H

S

W

X

Y

Z

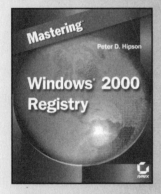
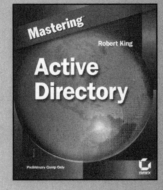

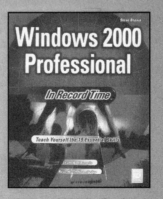

This Book Will Help You Get Your Job Done

You'll find that while *some* of Windows 2000 is simply improved versions of familiar tools, much of it is very different. Anyone saddled with the job of managing a Windows 2000 network, or even more challenging, anyone asked to *design* a Windows 2000–based network, needs to learn a lot of new overall concepts *and* specific task-oriented skills. *Mastering Windows 2000 Server* is designed to help in both areas.

Here are just a few examples of the essential information you'll find inside *Mastering Windows 2000 Server*.

Active Directory

- The book includes two introductions to AD:
    - One tailored for people who are already experts in NT 4.
    - Another tailored for NT newcomers.
- Read complete explanations of AD components and structural tools.
- Learn firsthand with step-by-step walk-through examples of all of AD's significant capabilities.

Change and Configuration Management Tools

- Remote Installation Services lets you pre-build complete workstation images and deliver them to new computers with just one floppy; the book contains complete instructions on how to use RIS.
- Learn how to use the Group Policy snap-in, which allows an administrator to control hundreds or thousands of user desktops from a central location.
- Windows 2000 lets you easily place applications on users' desktops from a central location with the Microsoft Installer; inside, you can read how to use the Installer and how to create your own Installer packages so that you can deploy *any* application in your enterprise.
- Windows 2000 finally lets you control how much disk space each user consumes, through disk quotas. But there are some severe limitations and potential pitfalls with those quotas, and you'll learn here how to work with them.

Offering Network Services

- Dfs (Distributed File System) frees your users from having to know a lot of server names and share names. With Dfs—explained in this book—you can make all of your enterprise's shares look like one integrated library of data.